ENCYCLOPEDIA OF WORLD BIOGRAPHY

2

ENCYCLOPEDIA OF WORLD BIOGRAPHY

SECOND EDITION

Bardeen
Briand

2

GALE

DETROIT • NEW YORK • TORONTO • LONDON

Staff

Senior Editor: Paula K. Byers
Project Editor: Suzanne M. Bourgoin
Managing Editor: Neil E. Walker

Editorial Staff: Luann Brennan, Frank V. Castronova, Laura S. Hightower, Karen E. Lemerand, Stacy A. McConnell, Jennifer Mossman, Maria L. Munoz, Katherine H. Nemeh, Terrie M. Rooney, Geri Speace

Permissions Manager: Susan M. Tosky
Permissions Specialist: Maria L. Franklin
Permissions Associate: Michele M. Lonoconus
Image Cataloger: Mary K. Grimes

Production Director: Mary Beth Trimper
Production Manager: Evi Seoud
Production Associate: Shanna Heilveil
Product Design Manager: Cynthia Baldwin
Senior Art Director: Mary Claire Krzewinski

Research Manager: Victoria B. Cariappa
Research Specialists: Michele P. LaMeau, Andrew Guy Malonis, Barbara McNeil, Gary J. Oudersluys
Research Associates: Julia C. Daniel, Tamara C. Nott, Norma Sawaya, Cheryl L. Warnock
Research Assistant: Talitha A. Jean

Graphic Services Supervisor: Barbara Yarrow
Image Database Supervisor: Randy Bassett
Imaging Specialist: Mike Lugosz

Manager of Data Entry Services: Eleanor M. Allison
Data Entry Coordinator: Kenneth D. Benson

Manager of Technology Support Services: Theresa A. Rocklin
Programmers/Analysts: Mira Bossowska, Jeffrey Muhr, Christopher Ward

Copyright © 1998
Gale Research
835 Penobscot Bldg.
Detroit, MI 48226-4094

ISBN 0-7876-2221-4 (Set)
ISBN 0-7876-2542-6 (Volume 2)

Library of Congress Cataloging-in-Publication data is available.

Printed in the United States of America
10 9 8 7 6 5 4 3

ENCYCLOPEDIA OF WORLD BIOGRAPHY

2

B

John Bardeen

John Bardeen (1908-1991) was the first person to win the Nobel Prize twice in the same discipline. The first award was made for his part in the discovery of the transistor, and the second for his part in developing the theory of superconductivity.

John Bardeen was born in Madison, Wisconsin, on May 23, 1908. He was the son of Althea Harmer and D. Charles R. Bardeen, who was professor of anatomy and dean of the medical school at the University of Wisconsin. John Bardeen graduated from Madison Central High School in 1923 and earned bachelor and masters degrees in electrical engineering from the University of Wisconsin in 1928 and 1929 respectively.

Early Work and Doctoral Studies

In 1929 and 1930 Bardeen worked as a research assistant in electrical engineering, investigating geophysical and other sorts of problems with professor Leo J. Peters. In 1930 Peters and Bardeen took positions with Gulf Research and Development Corporation in Pittsburgh, where they worked on some early applications of geophysics to petroleum prospecting.

Bardeen resigned from Gulf in 1933 to resume his formal studies. He earned his doctorate at Princeton University in 1936, with a mathematical thesis on the work function of metals. His advisor at Princeton was Eugene Wigner. Between 1935 and 1938 Bardeen was a member of the Society of Fellows at Harvard University, where he investigated further problems in the physics of metals with Percy

Bridgman and J. H. Van Vleck. (It is worth noting that Van Vleck, who had first taught quantum mechanics to Bardeen in 1928 and 1929 at the University of Wisconsin, also gave Walter H. Brattain [one of the other inventors of the transistor] his first course in quantum mechanics when Brattain was a graduate student at the University of Minnesota.)

First Efforts at Theory of Superconductivity

From 1938 to 1941 Bardeen was an assistant professor of physics at the University of Minnesota. During this time he made his first efforts at devising a theory of superconductivity.

In a superconducting medium, electrical resistance drops to zero below the critical temperature, and currents once begun flow indefinitely. (The phenomenon was first observed in 1911 by Kammerligh Onnes for the element mercury, for which the critical temperature is 4.2 K.-Kelvin). In 1933 it was discovered that a fundamental property of superconductors is that they exclude magnetic fields from their interiors. Fritz and Heinz London were able to describe this property of superconductors in terms of macroscopic electrodynamic potentials, and in the same year Fritz London suggested that superconductivity was a quantum effect manifested on the macroscopic scale. It was more than 20 years, however, before a microscopic quantum theory of superconductivity was developed.

Bardeen's first attempt at a theory of superconductivity was based on the idea of a gap in the energy levels available to electrons. Electrons in superconducting states would be unable to absorb energy quanta unless the quanta were large enough to carry them over the energy gap into states representing normal conductivity, and they would consequently be trapped in superconducting states. Bardeen sug-

gested that the energy gap would arise from interactions of the electrons in a conductor with static displacements of the crystal lattice, but his theory was unsuccessful.

In 1941 Bardeen left the University of Minnesota for a position with the Naval Ordnance Research Laboratory that lasted the duration of World War II. His concerns during the war were with underwater ordnance and minesweeping.

Nobel Prize in Physics

Bardeen was hired in the fall of 1945 by Bell Telephone Laboratories. Here he became a member of William Shockley's semiconductor research division, playing a major part in the invention of the point-contact transistor. It was Bardeen who determined why Shockley's first design for a semiconductor amplifier would not work; the energy states of a semiconductor favored the formation of a layer of charge on its surface, and this charge screened the interior from the influence of an electric field that was required by Shockley's design. Walter H. Brattain, another member of Shockley's group, investigated the properties of the surface states, and from his experiments grew a practical semiconductor amplifier, the transistor. The transistor was first demonstrated on December 16, 1947, and Bardeen, Brattain, and Shockley were awarded the Nobel Prize in Physics in 1956 for their discovery.

Bardeen's interest in superconductivity was reawakened in 1950 by the discovery of the isotope effect; it was found that the critical temperature for a superconductor depended on the square root of its atomic mass. Bardeen concluded that the interaction of electrons with ions in a crystal lattice must play an important part in superconductivity, but he was still unable to explain the phenomenon. The Ginzburg-Landau equations, which gave a phenomenological description of the ordering of conduction electrons in a superconductor but did not explain the causes of that ordering, also appeared in 1950.

More Research on Superconductivity

Bardeen left Bell Laboratories in the fall of 1951 for a professorship at the University of Illinois. In 1955 he renewed his research on the phenomenon of superconductivity, this time with the aid of his graduate student J. R. Schrieffer and of Leon N. Cooper. In 1956 Cooper discovered that an attractive potential between pairs of electrons could give rise to a gap in the energy levels available to electrons, and hence to a condensation of electrons in superconducting states. The attraction between electrons is not direct, in fact, but arises from a dynamic interaction of pairs of electrons with the crystal lattice. An electron may produce a vibration of an ion in the lattice, and this vibration will be experienced by a second electron as an attraction towards the first electron. Bardeen, Cooper, and Schrieffer discovered that the pairing of the electrons is such that (for a state in which no current flows in the superconductor) an electron with a given momentum and spin will be paired with an electron having the opposite momentum and spin. The two electrons are not close together, and in order for the pairing to occur all pairs of electrons must have the same net momentum. Hence the superconducting state is stable against perturbations since one Cooper pair cannot be destroyed without destroying all of them. As well as the vanishing resistance of a super-conductor, the theory of Bardeen, Cooper, and Schrieffer justified the equations of Ginzburg and Landau and London's description of the magnetic properties of a superconductor.

Although a magnetic field is excluded from the interior of a superconductor, it is possible for a magnetic field to destroy superconductivity; the cost in energy to exclude magnetic flux from the superconductor may be greater than the energy gained in the transition to the superconducting state, and the superconductor reverts to its normal condition. For type I superconductors, the fields necessary to destroy superconductivity are quite small. In some type II superconductors fairly strong magnetic fields can be tolerated, and alloys designed to have type II superconducting properties can be used to make practical superconducting electromagnets.

For their successful model of superconductivity, Bardeen, Cooper, and Schrieffer were awarded the Nobel Prize in physics in 1972. Subsequent refinements of their work have produced ever better agreement of theory and experiment.

Honors and Awards

Among many other honors, John Bardeen was elected to the National Academy of Sciences in 1954. He married Jane Maxwell in 1938, and they had three children. After 1975 he served as emeritus professor at the University of

Illinois. He died in Boston on January 30, 1991, as the result of heart failure following surgery that had revealed the presence of lung cancer.

In 1994, The Minerals, Metals and Materials Society established the John Bardeen Award which recognizes individuals who have made outstanding contributions and shown leadership in the field of electronic materials.

Further Reading

Bardeen, Shockley, and Brattain recount their experiences in developing the transistor in their Nobel addresses: John Bardeen, ''Semiconductor research leading to the point contact transistor,'' *Nobel Lectures: Physics, 1942-1962* (Amsterdam, 1964); William Shockley, ''Transistor technology evokes new physics,'' *ibid.* ; and Walter H. Brattain, ''Surface properties of semiconductors,'' *ibid* . (Appended to each of these addresses is a short biography of the author.) Developments in the understanding of superconductivity through 1972 are discussed in their Nobel addresses by Schrieffer, Cooper, and Bardeen: J. R. Schrieffer, ''Macroscopic quantum phenomena from pairing in superconductors,'' *Science,* 180 (1973); Leon N. Cooper, ''Microscopic quantum interference in the theory of superconductivity,'' *Science,* 181 (1973); and John Bardeen, ''Electron-phonon interactions and superconductivity,'' *ibid.* Bardeen can be found on the World Wide Web on the Minerals, Metals and Materials Society's page, http://www.tms.org/Society/Honors/1997/Bardeen97.html. and at http://www.invent.org/book/book -text/5.html. □

Daniel Barenboim

Daniel Barenboim (born 1942) was an Israeli pianist and conductor. After receiving an international musical education, he established himself as one of the most highly regarded young conductors and performers in the world.

Daniel Barenboim was born in Buenos Aires on November 15, 1942. His Jewish Ukrainian parents were both music teachers who, on the advice of violinist Adolf Busch, allowed their prodigy son to début as a pianist at the age of seven in Buenos Aires. Two years later the family moved to Europe where Barenboim played at the Salzburg Mozarteum and studied conducting with Igor Markevich. The following year, 1952, the family settled in Israel, although Barenboim returned to Europe to study piano with Edwin Fischer. At this time, he met the conductor Wilhelm Furtwängler, who influenced Barenboim's conducting. He studied at the *Accademia di Santa Cecilia* in Rome where, as one of the youngest graduates ever, he received a diploma in 1956. During this period he also took composition lessons from Nadia Boulanger in Paris.

He made his début in England in 1955 and played a Mozart concerto at the Festival Hall for the bicentennial of that composer's birth. For his American début in 1957 he played Prokofiev's First Piano Concerto, with Leopold Stokowski conducting. The following year he played again

in New York and gave concerts throughout the world as well.

Barenboim began conducting in Israel in 1962 and then appeared on the podium in Australia. In 1964, he made the first of his appearances with the English Chamber Orchestra, an ensemble he both conducted and performed with as a pianist regularly. He also toured with the English Chamber Orchestra in Latin America and the Far East. He conducted the London Symphony Orchestra in 1968 in New York and appeared with the Berlin Philharmonic Orchestra in 1969 and with the New York Philharmonic Orchestra in 1970. After 1970, he appeared regularly with the New York Philharmonic Orchestra, the Chicago Symphony Orchestra, and other major orchestras in the United States. He also frequently appeared with the London Philharmonic Orchestra and with the *Orchestra de Paris,* of which he was named conductor in 1975. He directed London's South Bank Summer Music festival for two seasons in 1968 and 1970. He conducted Mozart's *Don Giovanni* at the Edinburgh Festival in 1973, followed by *Le Nozze di Figaro* in 1975.

He appeared as conductor with many leading performers, including Artur Rubinstein, Clifford Curzon, and Isaac Stern. Further, he accompanied vocalists Fischer-Dieskau and Janet Baker in performances of *Lieder* and played chamber music with violinists Pinchas Zukerman and Itzhak Perlman and with the English cellist Jacqueline du Pré, to whom he was married in 1967. He gave the première of Alexander Goehr's Piano Concerto in 1972.

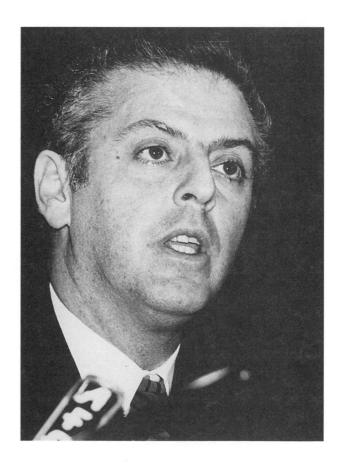

Barenboim established himself as an important interpreter of the Classical and Romantic repertories. He overcame initial opposition to his apparent flamboyance, manifest in the flexible tempo in his conducting of Mozart and Beethoven and his lavish attention to detail, which it was sometimes thought compromised the integrity of the score. His emotionalism was tempered and his judgment subsequently confirmed, however, and his intuitive powers as an interpreter were highly regarded. He branched out as a conductor to include the music of Bach, Bruckner, Tchaikovsky, Elgar, and the French composers in his programs.

His repertory as a pianist was comparatively narrow but also masterful. He recorded all the Mozart piano concertos, and his version of the complete Beethoven piano sonatas was especially well-received. He also recorded the Beethoven piano concertos and violin and piano sonatas. He performed the piano music of Chopin and Brahms as well.

In the late 1980s Barenboim was appointed as the Artistic Director of the Opera de la Bastille in Paris. He was not to last long in this position as the president of the Paris Opera Association forced Barenboim to resign his post because Barenboim refused to reduce his substantial salary.

After leaving the Opera de la Bastille, Barenboim was chosen to succeed Sir Georg Solti as the conductor of the Chicago Symphony Orchestra thanks to Solti pressing for Barenboim to take over the position.

Further Reading

An article on Barenboim appeared in *The New Grove Dictionary of Music and Musicians* (1980) and in *Baker's Biographical Dictionary* (1978). Irving Kolodin wrote an article on the conductor-performer, "Barenboim's Maturing Art," for the *Saturday Review* (September, 1980). "Daniel Barenboim, piano," by H. Goldsmith, may be found in *HiFi/MusAm* (March, 1981). Additional reading includes *Musiker im Gesprach—Daniel Barenboim/Maurizio Pollini*, by J. Meyer-Josten (Frankfurt-am-Main, no date) which was reviewed in *Musikerziehung* (February, 1981).

Additional information on Barenboim can be found in "Playing With Ire" in *Chicago* (September, 1995) and "Daniel Barenboim: Banished From the Bastille, He'll Take Command in Chicago" in *Ovation* (July, 1989). □

Willem Barents

The Dutch navigator Willem Barents (died 1597) was his country's renowned Arctic explorer, having discovered Spitsbergen and the Barents Sea.

Willem Barents was born on the island of Terschelling off the Friesland coast of the Netherlands. He became the pupil of Petrus Plancius (Peter Platevoet), a theologian-cartographer whose sermons are often said to have been lessons in geography and astronomy.

Barents took part in two unsuccessful Arctic voyages before his memorable discovery. In 1592 Jan Huyghen van Linschoten of Enkhuizen returned from a voyage to Goa with a Portuguese fleet and wrote a widely read *Itinerary*. This stimulated Dutch interest in the Orient, though at the time it seemed dangerous to contest the Portuguese monopoly of the route around the Cape of Good Hope. In 1595 Amsterdam merchants, undiscouraged by the English failure to find a Northeast Passage 40 years earlier, decided to resume the search. They prepared two ships, placing one under Jacob van Heemskerck and the other under Jan Corneliszoon Rijp. Barents, who as pilot sailed with Heemskerck, became the acknowledged leader of the expedition.

The ships left Vlieland, a small port near Amsterdam, on May 18, 1596, and about three weeks later discovered Bear Island, south of the then-unknown Spitsbergen; they so named the island because of an encounter with a polar bear whose hide did not prove vulnerable to Dutch blunderbusses. Pressing northward, the Dutch ships came on June 17 to Spitsbergen, uninhabited islands. During the rest of June the Dutch explored the western coast of the main island, thinking it a part of Greenland.

After a return to Bear Island, the ships separated, Rijp to resume exploration of Spitsbergen, and Barents and Heemskerck to cross the Barents Sea to Novaya Zemlya, previously discovered but not explored to its northern limit. Barents and Heemskerck rounded the northernmost point, naming it Hook of Desire, and sailed eastward, at first believing, from the open water encountered, that they had discovered the Northeast Passage. By November, however, the ice had grown thick and it finally imprisoned the ship. Barents and Heemskerck were 81°N at their highest latitude, beyond any point previously reached. Still close to Novaya Zemlya, realizing that they must build a solid shelter ashore in order to survive, they made one of logs and driftwood and moved into this "Safe House" in October. They lived there until June 1597, suffering but at first in good spirits, calling themselves "burghers of Novaya Zemlya." At Epiphany they had a cheerful party on their remaining liquor and crowned one man "king" of Novaya Zemlya.

Conditions then deteriorated; the firewood gave out, and the ship was crushed by ice. The men began to construct two small boats. Scurvy had been present for months, and one of the worst sufferers was Barents. He left with the rest as they slowly worked down Novaya Zemlya, but he grew so weak that he could take no part in manipulating the craft. Barents died at the end of June, soon after asking Gerrit de Veer, chronicler of the expedition, to lift him up for a final look at Novaya Zemlya. Heemskerck and the other survivors reached the Kola Peninsula and were rescued there by Rijp, who had returned to Holland and come back for trade.

In the 1870s European ships visited Safe House and found it partially caved in by snow. Objects left there by the Dutch explorers are in the Rijksmuseum in Amsterdam.

Further Reading

A translation of Gerrit de Veer, *The Three Voyages of William Barents to the Arctic Regions,* was published by the Hakluyt Society in 1876. Hendrik Willem van Loon, *The Golden Book of the Dutch Navigators* (1916; rev. ed. 1938), provides a racy but accurate account of Barent's voyages and many others. Edward Heawood, *A History of Geographical Discovery in the Seventeenth and Eighteenth Centuries* (1912), is also accurate. Some information on Plancius and his influence on Barents is contained in George Masselman's study of Dutch discovery and expansion, *The Cradle of Colonialism* (1963). □

Simeon Bar Kochba

Simeon Bar Kochba (died 135) led the last Jewish revolt against Roman rule in Palestine, 132-135.

Simeon Bar Kochba is surrounded by legend, and little is known of his life. From references in the Talmud, the Dead Sea Scrolls, and Roman sources, he emerges as a self-confident and decisive but temperamental man of great vigor and valor. Signatures on documents found in 1951 and later in caves near the Dead Sea indicate that Bar Kochba's true surname was Bar Kosba, the "son of Kosba" or the "man from Kosba." In the Talmud he is referred to as Bar Koziba, Aramaic for "son of a lie." This play on his name was probably coined by his critics or by those who were deceived in their belief that he was the Messiah.

The major cause of the uprising led by Bar Kochba was the great hostility of the Jews toward the Romans, who had ruled Palestine since 64 B.C. The earlier Jewish revolt (A.D. 66-70) had resulted in the destruction of Jerusalem and the Temple. Later Roman emperors failed to fulfill their promises to rebuild the Temple, and in 130 the emperor Hadrian ordered the rebuilding of Jerusalem as a Greco-Roman city with a shrine to Jupiter on the site of the Temple. Moreover, Hadrian's decree against bodily mutilation was interpreted as prohibiting circumcision, an important part of Jewish ritual.

When Bar Kochba raised the standard of revolt in 132, thousands of Jews from every part of Palestine, as well as from other lands, enlisted in his army; even the hostile Samaritans joined him. The Jewish patriots had been preparing for the rebellion for some years, gathering arms and fortifying numerous caves connected by subterranean passages. At first Bar Kochba met with considerable success. He took Jerusalem, erected an altar on the Temple Mount, and started to build a wall around the city. He assumed the title of *N'si Yisrael* (the Prince of Israel).

Hadrian sent Severus, his ablest general, to quell the rebellion. Severus hesitated to meet Bar Kochba in the field and instead besieged and captured one fortress after another, forcing the Jews to flee to the mountains and hide in caves. Their last stronghold was better, southwest of Jerusalem, where they held out for about a year; there Bar Kochba was killed in 135. The revolt had failed, and aside from the heavy Jewish military casualties thousands died of famine. Roman losses, too, were so heavy that Severus in his final report to the Roman Senate omitted the customary phrase, "I and the army are well." Bar Kochba, the hero, lived on in Jewish legend.

Further Reading

Accounts of Bar Kochba's rebellion may be found in the standard histories of the Jewish people. One of the best brief histories is Max L. Margolis and Alexander Marx, *A History of the Jewish People* (1927). A great multivolume history is Salo Wittmayer Baron, *A Social and Religious History of the Jews* (14 vols., 1952-1969). □

Ernst Barlach

The German sculptor Ernst Barlach (1870-1938), working predominately in wood, created important figurative carvings in that medium.

Ernst Barlach was born in Wedel, a small town near Hamburg, the son of a physician. He studied at the Hamburg School of Applied Arts (1888-1891) and the Academy of Art in Dresden (1891-1895). He briefly attended the Académie Julian while residing in Paris (1895-1896), but his stay in France did not leave any apparent mark on his sculpture.

Returning to Germany in 1897, Barlach periodically sketched for the journals *Jugend, Simplizissimus,* and *Die fliegende Blätter* and taught ceramics. One of his earliest known pieces, the *Cleopatra* of 1904, suggests the strong Art Nouveau interest of the time. Barlach's first mature work came as a result of a trip to southern Russia in 1906. He transformed his drawings of Russian peasants into small ceramic pieces, rounding out the generally rough features of the beggars, villagers, and shepherds. His work caught the eye of the Berlin art dealer and publisher Paul Cassirer in 1907. Two years later Barlach won the Villa Romana Prize and a subsequent year in Florence. Upon his return to Germany in 1910, and with Cassirer's continued support, he settled in the rural village of Güstrow, only occasionally traveling to Berlin.

Barlach began to carve in wood in 1907, and it became the principal material in which he worked throughout his life. He drew principally on the life of small German towns for his imagery, and his approach to the material recalls the simplicity and strength of expression found in Romanesque and Gothic sculpture of northern Europe. His works are only of single figures, and they depict man's loneliness, fear, and suffering. This pessimism, often emphasized by the gesture of the hands and the visionary gaze of the eyes, was spiritually akin to the mood of the German expressionist painters, but he was never affiliated with the expressionist movement. Like the graphic artist Kathe Köllwitz, he remained apart from any avant-garde movement or style.

Barlach's hatred of the suffering and chaos of war was forecast in his *Panic, Fright* (1912) and the *Abandoned Ones*

(1913). Like Daumier, Barlach depicted those who were left homeless by the conflagration. His themes remained constant, and he seldom altered his tendency to compose in a solid block form. His greatest works are his war memorials, and he is the sculptor who most successfully captured the terror of war in the 20th century. His best-known memorials are the *Hovering Angel* (1927) in Güstrow, the *Champion of the Spirit* (1928) in Mannheim, and the *Memorial for the Dead of World War I* (1928) in Magdeburg.

Barlach did not complete one ambitious commission, the facade figures for St. Catherine's Church in Lübeck (1930-1932), owing to the rise of the Nazis. Although he opposed the Nazis, he remained in Germany, where his work was condemned as degenerate; his Magdeburg and Güstrow memorials were removed. The continued persecution of the sculptor ultimately contributed to his death of heart failure in 1938.

Barlach's graphic work, both woodcuts and lithographs, reveals the same vital energy and bold composition found in his best sculpture. His work includes the *Modern Dance of Death* and illustrations for the writings of Goethe and Schiller. Barlach also illustrated some of his own plays.

Further Reading

The most important work on Barlach is the *catalogue raisonné* in German, Friedrich Schult, ed., *Das plastiche Werk* (1960). Schult also edited the catalogue raisonné of Barlach's graphic art, *Das graphische Werk* (1958). Two useful works in English are Alfred Werner, *Ernst Barlach* (1966), which provides a concise summary of and introduction to Barlach's sculpture, graphics, and dramatic pieces, and Carl Dietrich Carls, *Ernst Barlach* (1931; rev. ed. and trans. 1969), a good biographical study of the artist. □

Joel Barlow

American poet and diplomat Joel Barlow (1754-1812) is remembered as one of the Connecticut wits. He moved beyond New England to become one of the most cosmopolitan men of his generation.

Joel Barlow, born in Redding, Conn., on March 24, 1754, briefly attended Dartmouth and then went to Yale, from which he celebrated his graduation with the *Poem on the Prospect of Peace* (1778). As a collegian, he served briefly in the Connecticut militia in 1776. The nine years after his graduation were busily filled with schoolteaching, graduate study, further service in the Army as chaplain, newspaper editing and almanac making, a runaway marriage, preparing a revision on American principles of Isaac Watt's *Psalms* (1785), reading for the bar, and, with versifying friends, correcting overly democratic countrymen in the satirical *Anarchiad* (1786). His principal attention during these years, however, was directed toward completing and preparing for publication his long epic poem in heroic couplets, *The Vision of Columbus* (1787). This poem, dedicated to the king of France and sponsored by George Wash-

ington, brought Barlow something more than local fame as a forecaster in verse of what the new United States might become, both in commerce and in art.

In 1788 he went to Europe as agent for a company that wanted to sell western lands to French emigrants. That failing, he became a political journalist in France and England, to the dismay of his New England friends, because he was associated now with Thomas Paine, Horne Tooke, and Mary Wollstonecraft. In 1792 he published *Advice to the Privileged Orders,* in prose, and *The Conspiracy of Kings,* in verse, both antimonarchial tracts, and *A Letter to the National Assembly,* which brought him honorary citizenship in the new French Republic. The best-remembered of his writings of this period, however, is *The Hasty Pudding* (1796), written in homesick memory of a favorite New England dish.

Wealth came to Barlow suddenly and mysteriously, probably through shipping activities. As consul to Algiers (1795-1797), he arranged treaties with native rulers of Tripoli, Algiers, and Tunis. He was friend and adviser to young Robert Fulton and to Thomas Jefferson. In 1805 he returned to the United States, to expand and revise *The Vision of Columbus to The Columbiad* (1807)—a magnificently printed but woodenly written book. In 1811-1812 he was U.S. minister to France. He died in Poland on Dec. 24, 1812, en route as representative of President James Madison to a conference with Napoleon.

Further Reading

Selections from Barlow's writings are most readily found in V.L. Parrington, ed., *The Connecticut Wits* (1926). Biographical materials first gathered in Charles Burr Todd, *Life and Letters of Joel Barlow* (1886), and Theodore A. Zunder, *The Early Years of Joel Barlow* (1934), have been expanded in James L. Woodress, *A Yankee's Odyssey: The Life of Joel Barlow* (1958). See also John Dos Passos, *The Ground We Stand On* (1941), and Leon Howard, *The Connecticut Wits* (1943).

Additional Sources

Bernstein, Samuel, *Joel Barlow: a Connecticut Yankee in an age of revolution,* New York: Rutledge Books, 1985. □

Christiaan N. Barnard

The South African surgeon Christiaan N. Barnard (born 1922) performed the world's first human heart transplant operation in 1967 and the first double-heart transplant in 1974.

Christiaan N. Barnard was born on November 8, 1922, in Beaufort West, South Africa. He received his early education in Beaufort West and then went on to the University of Cape Town, where he received an M.D. in 1953. Barnard worked for a short time as a general practitioner before joining the Cape Town Medical School staff as a research fellow in surgery. With the hope of pursuing his research interests and gaining new surgical skills and experiences, he enrolled at the University of Minnesota Medical School (1955). After two years of study with Dr. Owen H. Wangensteen he received his Ph.D. from Minnesota and returned to his native country to embark upon a career as a cardiothoracic surgeon.

Before he left for America (1953-1955), Barnard had gained recognition for research in gastrointestinal pathology. He proved that the fatal birth defect known as congenital intestinal atresia (a gap in the small intestines) was due to the fetus receiving an inadequate supply of blood during pregnancy and that it could be remedied by a surgical procedure.

Upon his return to South Africa, he introduced open-heart surgery to that country, designed artificial valves for the human heart, and experimented with the transplantation of the hearts of dogs. All of this served as preparation for his 1967 human heart transplant.

Although Barnard was a pioneering cardiac surgeon, his innovations were founded upon a half-century of experimental heart surgery that preceded them. Of crucial importance was the first use of hypothermia (artificial lowering of the body temperature) in 1952 and the introduction in the following year of an effective heart-lung machine. These advances, combined with other techniques perfected in the 1960s, enabled a surgeon for the first time to operate upon a heart that was motionless and free of blood.

After a decade of heart surgery, Barnard felt ready to accept the challenge posed by the transplantation of the human heart. In 1967 he encountered Louis Washkansky, a 54-year-old patient who suffered from extensive coronary artery disease and who agreed to undergo a heart transplant operation. On December 2, 1967, the heart of a young woman killed in an accident was removed while Washkansky was prepared to receive it. The donor heart was kept alive in a heart-lung machine circulating Washkansky's blood until the patient's diseased organ could be removed and replaced with the healthy one.

In order to suppress the body's defense mechanism that would normally reject a foreign organism, Barnard and his team of cardiac specialists gave the patient large doses of drugs, which allowed the patient's body to accept the new organ. However, Washkansky's body was not able to defend itself against infection, and he died on December 21, 1967 of double pneumonia. Despite Washkansky's death, Barnard was rightly hailed around the world for his surgical feat. Within a year (January 1968) Barnard replaced the diseased heart of Philip Blaiberg, 58-year-old retired dentist. This time the accompanying drug dosage was lowered, and Blaiberg lived for 20 months with his new heart.

Barnard's innovations in cardiac surgery brought him honors from a host of foreign medical societies, governments, universities, and philanthropic institutions. As he travelled abroad to receive these awards, he was criticized for readily accepting the role of a celebrity. Nevertheless, after Barnard's successful operations, surgeons in Europe and the United States began performing heart transplants, improving upon the procedures first used in South Africa. The first human heart transplantation in America took place on December 6, 1967, by Dr. Adrian Kantrowitz. But the patient, an infant, lived only 6 hours.

Seven years after his initial heart transplant, Barnard made medical history once again when he performed a "twin-heart" operation (November 25, 1974). This time he removed only the diseased portion of the heart of 58-year-old Ivan Taylor and replaced it with the heart of a 10-year-old child. The donor heart acted as a booster and back-up for the patient's disease-ravished organ. Although Barnard was optimistic about this new operation, which he believed was less radical than a total implantation, the patient died within four months.

Rheumatoid arthritis, which had plagued Barnard since the 1960s, limited his surgical experimentation in later years. As a result, he turned to writing novels as well as books on health, medicine, and South Africa, while serving as a scientist consultant. He has also been presented many honorary doctorates, foreign orders, and awards, including the Dag Hammarskjold International Prize and Peace Prize, the Kennedy Foundation Award, and the Milan International Prize for Science. Barnard was also featured in a BBC program about transplant surgery, "Knife to the Heart: The Man With the Golden Hands," in early 1997.

Further Reading

Barnard's life can be studied in his autobiograpy, *One Life,* by Christiaan Barnard and Curtis B. Pepper (1969) and in two biographies: Peter Hawthorne, *The Transplanted Heart* (1968) and L. Edmond Leipold, *Dr. Christiaan Barnard, the man with the golden hands* (1971). On cardiac surgery see: R. G. Richardson, *The Scalpel and the Heart* (1970) and Stephen L. Johnson, *The History of Cardiac Surgery, 1896-1955* (1969). Other information on Barnard can be found in the *New York Times* (January 27, 1997); *Time* (October 7, 1996); and *People* (April 8, 1996). □

Edward Emerson Barnard

The American astronomer and astronomical photographer Edward Emerson Barnard (1857-1923) received the Lalande Medal from the French Academy of Sciences for his discovery of the fifth satellite of Jupiter.

Edward Barnard was born on Dec. 16, 1857, in Nashville, Tenn. His early education came mostly from his mother; he was employed at the age of nine in the studio of a Nashville photographer, where he remained for 16 years. His training in photographic processes and his knowledge of lenses were later of great value in his pioneer work in astronomical photography.

Barnard's interest in astronomy dated from 1876, when he read a stray copy of a popular book on astronomy and constructed his first telescope with a one-inch lens from a broken spyglass. Meeting Simon Newcomb the following

year persuaded him that to do work in astronomy he must be well grounded in mathematics, so he worked in his spare time to educate himself.

During the next few years Barnard continued to work in the photography studio, pursuing his astronomical studies in the evenings. His discovery of a number of unexpected comets led to a fellowship at Vanderbilt University, where he received a bachelor of science degree in 1887. He was then appointed junior astronomer at the recently established Lick Observatory, which had a new 36-inch telescope, then the largest in the world. There he discovered the fifth satellite of Jupiter, followed by the faint and distant sixth, seventh, eighth, and ninth. He also began his photography of the Milky Way, securing the first of the beautiful photographs of its intricate structure for which he became famous.

Barnard accepted a position at the Yerkes Observatory in 1895, and in 1897 he began observing with the great 40-inch photographic telescope (still the largest refractor in the world) that had been secured through the efforts of President William Harper of the University of Chicago and Edward Everett Hale, the greatest astronomical entrepreneur of the period. Barnard next began the micrometric triangulation of some of the globular clusters, which he continued for nearly 25 years, hoping to detect motions of the individual stars.

The observatory's acquisition in 1904 of the 10-inch Bruce photographic telescope gave added impetus to Barnard's photography of comets and his mapping of the Milky Way. In all, Barnard collected 1400 negatives of

comets and nearly 4000 plates of the Milky Way and other star fields. His published papers number more than 900.

Barnard was married in 1881 to Rhoda Calvert of Yorkshire, England. He died in Wisconsin on Feb. 6, 1923, surviving his wife by two years.

Further Reading

The only account of Barnard's life, written with a firsthand knowledge of his work, is Edwin Brant Frost's biographical memoir in *Memoirs of the National Academy of Sciences,* vol. 21 (1926). Robert S. Richardson, *The Star Lovers* (1967), includes a chapter on Barnard. See also Frank Schlesinger's article, "Historical Notes on Astro-Photography of Precision," in Harlow Shapley, ed., *Source Book in Astronomy, 1900-1950* (1960); Otto Struve and Velta Zebergs, *Astronomy of the 20th Century* (1962); and Willie Ley, *Watchers of the Skies: An Informal History of Astronomy from Babylon to the Space Age* (1963). □

Frederick Augustus Porter Barnard

Frederick Augustus Porter Barnard (1809-1889) was an American educator and scientist who, as president of Columbia College, worked to develop the institution into a modern university.

Frederick Barnard was born in Sheffield, Mass., on May 5, 1809. He attended Yale from 1824 to 1828, graduating second in his class. After two years of teaching at the Hartford, Conn., grammar school, he returned to Yale as a tutor. His growing deafness led to his acceptance in 1831 of a position at a Hartford school for deaf-mutes, and a year later he moved to the New York Institution for the Deaf and Dumb. In 1837 he was appointed professor of mathematics and natural philosophy at the University of Alabama, where he remained for 17 years, the last six as professor of chemistry. In 1854 he moved to the University of Mississippi as professor of mathematics and two years later became head of that institution.

Barnard's scientific activities and the many papers he published in his fields led to his election as president of the American Association for the Advancement of Science in 1860. Since the Civil War prevented further meetings until 1866, he remained president for the longest term in the history of the association.

The Civil War ended instruction at the University of Mississippi. Although a slaveholder, Barnard was a strong unionist. He refused a request from Jefferson Davis to aid the South in exploiting its natural resources and moved to Washington, D. C., where he worked on war maps for the Coast Survey. In 1863 he published a *Letter to the President of the United States by a Refugee* , denouncing slavery, the Southern "conspiracy," and Northern Copperheads; this letter was widely noticed in newspapers and periodicals.

Shortly afterward he was elected president of Columbia College in New York City. He took office in 1864, and throughout his 24-year term he strove to develop the college into a modern university. He revived a feeble school of mines that would become a leader in its field. He pushed for the elective system for undergraduates, introducing many new, advanced courses. Upon the foundations of a strong college he hoped to erect a graduate school of distinction. He worked to strengthen the schools of law and medicine and hoped to start a school of education offering comparable professional training. Lack of resources prevented the full realization of his ambitions in his lifetime.

An early advocate of higher education for women, Barnard pushed hard, though unsuccessfully, to engage Columbia in this task. When, six months after his death, Columbia opened a college for women, it was named in his honor.

Barnard continued to publish scientific papers until the year before his death. In 1888, at the age of 80, he asked to be relieved of his duties. He died on April 27, 1889.

Further Reading

John Fulton, *Memoirs of Frederick A. P. Barnard* (1896), written with the assistance of Barnard's wife, contains many useful excerpts from his writings. William F. Russell, ed., *The Rise of a University,* vol. 1: *The Later Days of Old Columbia College* (1937), is composed of selections from Barnard's annual reports as president of Columbia; arranged in topical order, the reports clearly present his ideas and attitudes. A description of what it was like to serve on the Columbia faculty under

Barnard is in John W. Burgess, *Reminiscences of an American Scholar: The Beginnings of Columbia University* (1934).

Additional Sources

Chute, William Joseph, *Damn Yankee!: The first career of Frederick A. P. Barnard, educator, scientist, idealist,* Port Washington, N.Y.: Kennikat Press, 1978. □

Henry Barnard

American educator Henry Barnard (1811-1900) was influential in improving public schools and in promoting an educational literature in the United States.

H
enry Barnard was born in Hartford, Conn., on Jan. 24, 1811. He graduated from Yale in 1830, taught briefly in Pennsylvania, and returned to Yale to study law. He was admitted to the bar in 1833-1834. Barnard's tours of the South and West and, in 1835, of Europe nourished growing interests in education and in politics that were finally combined when he was elected to the Connecticut Legislature in 1837. He secured passage of a bill creating a board of commissioners to supervise the state's faltering common schools, was appointed to the board, and in 1838 became its executive secretary.

Barnard, who found the schools poorly maintained and attended, wanted public education "good enough for the best and cheap enough for the poorest." He believed that thorough moral training in the common schools was the surest safeguard of the community's happiness. An intensive campaign featuring public meetings and teachers' institutes, the creation of the *Connecticut Common School Journal,* which he edited, and a series of annual reports describing school conditions and suggesting remedies yielded legislation reorganizing the schools. But in 1842 a hostile assembly disbanded the board as "a useless expense."

Barnard accepted a similar position in Rhode Island, where, employing techniques developed in Connecticut, he energetically canvassed the state to express his belief that social unity and stability could be achieved through education. The result, in 1845, was an act creating the state's first school system.

In poor health, Barnard resigned in 1849 to return to Connecticut as head of the state normal school, a post which also included superintendency of the state's common schools. He tirelessly sought to keep educational issues before the people. His annual reports covered a vast array of educational topics and exerted a wide influence. Barnard's report for 1853 was later published as a history of Connecticut education; in 1854 he wrote an authoritative book on school architecture. Trips to Europe in 1852 and 1854 disclosed that his fame had become international. But, again in uncertain health, he resigned in 1855 to develop a new project, the *American Journal of Education.*

For 25 years the *Journal* provided a unique professional literature, disseminating all types of educational information at precisely the time that the nation was striving to establish public schooling on a secure footing. Carefully edited and frequently published by Barnard at his own expense, the *Journal* came to overshadow his other achievements. From 1858 to 1860 he served as chancellor of the University of Wisconsin and in 1866-1867 as president of St. John's College in Maryland. As the nation's outstanding educator, he was appointed the first U.S. commissioner of education in 1867, resigning three years later. He continued to edit the *Journal,* eventually producing thirty-two 800-page volumes, until his retirement in 1880. He died in Hartford on July 5, 1900.

Further Reading

John S. Brubacher, ed., *Henry Barnard on Education* (1931), contains selections from Barnard's *Journal.* Bernard C. Steiner, *Life of Henry Barnard* (1919), although old, is complete and thoroughly documented. Richard Emmons Thursfield, *Henry Barnard's American Journal of Education* (1945), analyzes the content and impact of the *Journal.*

Additional Sources

Downs, Robert Bingham, *Henry Barnard,* Boston: Twayne Publishers, 1977.

MacMullen, Edith Nye, *In the cause of true education: Henry Barnard & nineteenth-century school reform,* New Haven: Yale University Press, 1991. □

Djuna Barnes

Djuna Barnes (1892–1982) was a major literary figure in Paris of the 1920s and 1930s, who retired into reclusiveness and produced only a small body of work.

A major figure on the Paris literary scene of the 1920s and 1930s, Djuna Barnes was best known for her experimental novel *Nightwood,* one of the most influential works of modernist fiction. Described by Elizabeth Hardwick of the *Times Literary Supplement* as "a writer of wild and original gifts," Barnes was acclaimed by such writers as "Graham Greene, Samuel Beckett, Janet Flanner, Laurence Durrell, Kenneth Burke, Sir Herbert Read, and Dylan Thomas," Andrew Field pointed out in the *New York Times Book Review.* Field noted, too, that "a list just as long could be made of important writers who borrowed heavily from her." Barnes was at various times a poet, journalist, playwright, theatrical columnist, and novelist. But her prolific career was brought to a voluntary end in the 1930s when Barnes virtually gave up writing and retreated into nearly half a century of silence. She lived like a recluse, "a form of Trappist," Louis F. Kannenstine quoted her as saying in the *Dictionary of Literary Biography,* refusing to grant interviews or to approve the reprinting of most of her early writings. Because of this silence, Barnes's work is still not as widely celebrated as is that of many of her contemporaries.

Born in 1892 in Cornwall-on-Hudson, New York, Barnes began writing at an early age to support her mother and three brothers. She contributed frequently to New York City newspapers and to such magazines as *Smart Set* and *Vanity Fair.* In 1915, her first collection, *The Book of Repulsive Women: 8 Rhythms and 5 Drawings,* appeared as a chapbook. With the production in 1919 of three one-act plays by Eugene O'Neill's Provincetown Players, Barnes first gained serious recognition for her work. Her contributions to modernist publications of the day established her reputation among the avant-garde community. In 1920, Barnes left New York for Paris, where she was to live for the next twenty years and write the "relatively small body of work" upon which her "literary reputation must ultimately rest," as Kannenstine stated. This small body of work consists of four volumes: *A Book, Ladies Almanack, Ryder,* and *Nightwood.*

A Book, a collection of Barnes's plays, short stories, poems, and drawings, appeared in 1923. The plays produced by the Provincetown Players are collected here, as well as early stories set in Paris and inspired by the people Barnes knew there. The poet Raymond Radiguet, who died at the age of twenty, is the inspiration for one story. Two Dutch sisters, friends of Barnes and fixtures of Paris cafe society, inspire two other stories. All of these characters "are restless, estranged from society and themselves," Kannenstine wrote. Later editions of *A Book* were published as *A Night among the Horses* and *Spillway. Horses* adds several short stories to the original collection, while *Spillway* consists only of the short stories from the original collection.

In *Ladies Almanack,* published in 1928, Barnes based her characters on prominent lesbian writers of 1920s Paris, particularly those in author Natalie Barney's circle of friends. Written in Elizabethan prose, the book depicts a lesbian society in which one woman is sainted. Barnes described the book as "a slight satiric wigging," as Hardwick quoted her. The satire, however, is gentle and amiable. "The primary intention of *Ladies Almanack,*" Kannenstine believed, "is to confront the anomaly of sexual identity." The book was privately printed and distributed in Paris.

Barnes's first novel, *Ryder,* was also published in 1928. As in *Ladies Almanack,* there is an element of satire in the book. Barnes parodies "biblical language, Chaucer, heroic couplets, mystical literature, the epistolary novel, mock-epic tales, and other forms," Donald J. Greiner explained in the *Dictionary of Literary Biography. Ryder* is ostensibly a family chronicle revolving around Wendell Ryder, his wife, mother, and mistress. Ryder brings misery to all the women in his life because of his conviction that he has a mission to love women. Told in nonchronological chapters, many of which could stand on their own, *Ryder* is a "kaleidoscope of moods and styles," Joseph Frank wrote in *Sewanee Review.* Many of the qualities for which Barnes is known are first displayed in *Ryder.* "Of the fantastical quality of her imagination; of the gift for imagery, . . .; of the epigrammatic incisiveness of her phrasing and her penchant, akin to the Elizabethans, for dealing with the more scabrous manifestations of human fallibility—of all these there is evidence in *Ryder,*" Frank stated. Greiner believed that the publication of *Ryder* moved Barnes into the ranks of important literary innovators. "With *Ryder*," he noted, "she joined [James] Joyce, [T. S.] Eliot, and [Ezra] Pound in breaking through the conservative restrictions on poetry and fiction by looking over her shoulder at past literary models while stepping toward the future with experiments in technique and structure that would influence writing for the next fifty years."

Although *Ryder* was considered a bold experiment, it is *Nightwood,* Barnes's second novel, that most critics believed to be her most successful and important work. It is, Stephen Koch wrote in the *Washington Post Book World,* "a recognized masterpiece of modernism." *Nightwood* combines comedy and horror in a fiction without narrative structure or conventionally developed characters. "It would be more appropriate," Kannenstine believed, "to speak of *Nightwood*'s situation than its plot." *Nightwood,* Frank explained, "lacks a narrative structure in the ordinary sense." It is, however, organized according to nonliterary models. Various critics have demonstrated that *Nightwood* borrows its structure from poetry, music, drama, psychology, or the visual arts, but Kannenstine maintained that no one explanation of its structure was correct. Instead, "all are correct: all of these function simultaneously," he declared. "The novel is essentially transgeneric." It also incorporates a broad spectrum of literary styles, including that of the Elizabethans and Jacobeans, the writers of the Old Testament, and the Surrealists, while "parodying the venerable traditions of plot, character, setting, and theme, and maintaining extreme authorial detachment," as Greiner wrote in the *Dictionary of Literary Biography.*

The book traces the love affairs of the young woman Robin Vote in 1920s Paris. She first marries Felix Volkbien, but leaves him for the journalist Nora Flood. She then leaves Nora for Jenny Petherbridge. Brokenhearted, Nora turns to Dr. Matthew O'Connor, but he is unable to relieve her suffering and eventually breaks down. "The plot relates little more than the theft of one person's lover by another," Sharon Spencer observed in *Space, Time and Structure in the Modern Novel.* "Yet, through the heightened intensity of its language, and through the adroit structuring of its disjunct elements, *Nightwood* leaves the reader with a coherent and powerful impression of spiritual agony." This agony is commented on by Stanley Edgar Hyman in *Standards: A Chronicle of Books for Our Time.* Hyman compared *Nightwood* to Nathanael West's *Miss Lonelyhearts,* another tragic novel of the 1930s. "In the years since the 30s," Hyman wrote, "we have had nothing to equal those two great cries of pain, in their combination of emotional power and formal artistry." "For all its power," Koch said of *Nightwood,* "this is the bleakest modernism of all, a modernism like a wailing wall."

Although *Nightwood* has a tragic and even nightmarish side, it is also a humorous novel. Elizabeth Pochoda, commenting in *Twentieth Century Literature,* called *Nightwood* "a tremendously funny book in a desperately surgical sort of way." The novel's humor lies in its wit and its use of paradox and hoax, Pochoda argued, and all actions in the novel "are reduced to their initial hoax. Only then is sympathy allowable. The apparently touching love story of Robin

and Nora is also a kind of hoaxing, and we are not permitted to weep with Nora over her loss. Once the bloodthirsty nature of such love is uncovered we are allowed the sympathy appropriate to such an inevitable delusion." Greiner, writing in *Critique: Studies in Modern Fiction,* saw the paradoxical combination of humor and sadness as fundamental to all black humor. Barnes's "sense of humor is evident from the beginning," Greiner wrote, "and her use of funny elements with a depressing theme reflects the perplexing mixture so vital to black humor." *Nightwood,* Greiner concluded, "remains the most successful early example of the American black humor novel."

While interweaving humor and horror, *Nightwood* explores the theme of "man's separation from his primitive, yet more fundamental animal nature," Greiner observed in the *Dictionary of Literary Biography.* This separation between human and animal is expressed by Dr. O'Connor who, at one point in the novel, states that man "was born damned and innocent from the start, and wretchedly—as he must—on these two themes—whistles his tune." As Pochoda saw it, the reduction of all actions in *Nightwood* to "their initial hoax" eventually reveals the futility of language to communicate truth. Beginning with a historical allusion, the novel "turns its back on history, on faith in coherent expression, and finally on words themselves," Pochoda stated. "The novel bows down before its own impotence to express truths." In the last scene of the novel, Robin is transformed into a dog. This scene of devolution into beast is written, in contrast to the exuberance of the rest of the book, in a plain and unenergetic style to show the ultimate failure of language to overcome the animal within man. "The novel," Pochoda noted, "ends in wordlessness and failure, with the impasse of life intact and its contradictions nicely exposed."

Writing in the *International Fiction Review,* Robert L. Nadeau had a Freudian explanation for the devolution in *Nightwood.* He argued that the novel "does not depict human interaction on the level of conscious, waking existence. It is rather a dream world in which the embattled forces of the human personality take the form of characters representing aspects of that personality at different levels of its functioning." The transformation of Robin into an animal takes place, Nadeau wrote, "after she divests herself of the demands of the superego, or that whole complex of forms and values known as "civilization,'.... She is an animal—pure and simple."

In his biography *Djuna: The Life and Times of Djuna Barnes,* Field showed that much of *Nightwood* is autobiographical. He identified the main characters as friends of Barnes in Paris and found that Barnes herself was the character Nora. Robin was identified as Thelma Wood, a woman with whom Barnes had a love affair. But how much of the novel is taken from life is unclear. Field's account, Koch maintained, "is sometimes impossibly evasive, especially on matters sexual." Hardwick saw the biography as being "under considerable strain" because Barnes "was noted for her silence."

Shortly after publishing *Nightwood,* Barnes ceased writing and, in 1940, she returned to New York City. For the rest of her life she lived in a small apartment in Greenwich Village and published only one play and two poems. Her withdrawal from the literary world caused her reputation to pale. And Barnes's refusal to allow much of her earlier work for magazines to be reprinted kept the scope of her achievement unknown. In her book *Shakespeare and Company,* Sylvia Beach admitted that Barnes "was not one to cry her wares."

Despite her reserve, Barnes maintained a secure place in American letters because of *Nightwood,* which has been in print since it first appeared in 1936. *Nightwood,* Greiner wrote in the *Dictionary of Literary Biography,* "stands high in the list of significant twentieth-century American novels." Nadeau described it as "a truly great piece of American fiction," while Dylan Thomas, according to Field in the *New York Times Book Review,* called *Nightwood* "one of the three great prose books ever written by a woman." Hardwick believed that to Barnes's name "there is always to be attached the splendor of *Nightwood,* a lasting achievement of her great gifts and eccentricities." Barnes was, Koch maintained, a "strange and impossible genius." Since the 1970s, some of Barnes's earlier writings have been found and reprinted in book form and a bibliography of her work has been assembled by Douglas Messerli. Greiner believed that "Djuna Barnes's work will eventually receive the attention it deserves."

Further Reading

Baldwin, Kenneth H. and David K. Kirby, editors, *Individual and Community: Variations on a Theme in American Fiction,* Duke University Press, 1975.

Beach, Sylvia, *Shakespeare and Company,* Harcourt, 1959.

Broe, Mary Lynn, editor, *Silence and Power: A Re-evaluation of Barnes,* Southern Illinois University Press, 1986.

Cohn, Ruby, *Dialogue in American Drama,* Indiana University Press, 1971.

Contemporary Literary Criticism, Gale, Volume 3, 1975, Volume 4, 1975, Volume 8, 1978, Volume 9, 1979, Volume 29, 1984.

Cook, Albert, *The Meaning of Fiction,* Wayne State University Press, 1960.

Dictionary of Literary Biography, Gale, Volume 4: *American Writers in Paris, 1920-1939,* 1980, volume 9: *American Novelists, 1910-1945,* 1981.

Field, Andrew, *Djuna: The Life and Times of Djuna Barnes,* Putnam, 1983 (published in England as *The Formidable Miss Barnes: The Life of Djuna Barnes,* Secker & Warburg, 1983).

Fowlie, Wallace, *Love in Literature: Studies in Symbolic Expression,* Indiana University Press, 1965.

Frank, Joseph, *The Widening Gyre: Crisis and Mastery in Modern Literature,* Rutgers University Press, 1963.

Friedman, Melvin, *Stream of Consciousness: A Study in Literary Method,* Yale University Press, 1955.

Gildzen, Alex, editor, *A Festschrift for Djuna Barnes on Her 80th Birthday,* Kent State University Libraries, 1972.

Hyman, Stanley Edgar, *Standards: A Chronicle of Books for Our Time,* Horizon Press, 1966.

Kannenstine, Louis F., *The Art of Djuna Barnes: Duality and Damnation,* New York University Press, 1977.

Messerli, Douglas, *Djuna Barnes: A Bibliography,* David Lewis, 1975.

Muir, Edwin, *The Present Age from 1914,* Cresset Press, 1939.

Nemerov, Howard, *Reflexions on Poetry & Poetics,* Rutgers University Press, 1972.

Nin, Anais, *The Novel of the Future,* Macmillan, 1968.

Scott, James B., *Djuna Barnes,* Twayne, 1976.

Spencer, Sharon, *Space, Time and Structure in the Modern Novel,* New York University Press, 1971.

Taylor, William E., editor, *Modern American Drama: Essays in Criticism,* Everett/Edwards, 1968.

Atlantic, May, 1962.

Berkeley Daily Gazette, March 31, 1961.

Chapel Hill Weekly, September 9, 1962.

Chicago Sunday Tribune, April 8, 1962.

Critique: Studies in Modern Fiction, spring, 1964, August, 1975.

Hollins Critic, June, 1981.

International Fiction Review, July, 1975.

Journal of Aesthetics, September, 1957.

Massachusetts Review, summer, 1962.

Modern Fiction Studies, winter, 1973-74.

Nation, January 2, 1924, April 3, 1937.

New Statesman, October 17, 1936, February 8, 1958.

New York Herald Tribune Book Review, October 14, 1923, March 7, 1937, April 29, 1962.

New York Times, April 20, 1958, June 28, 1980.

New York Times Book Review, April 29, 1962, January 9, 1983, December 1, 1985.

Northwest Review, summer, 1958.

Renascence, fall, 1962.

San Francisco Chronicle, April 13, 1958.

Saturday Review, November 17, 1928.

Sewanee Review, summer, 1945, summer, l968.

Southern Review, Number 2, 1966-67, January, 1969.

Time, April 20, 1962.

Times Literary Supplement, April 4, 1958, September 12, 1980, January 21, 1983, October 7, 1983, March 20, 1987.

Twentieth Century Literature, May, 1976 *Virginia Quarterly Review,* autumn, 1958.

Washington Post Book World, February 1, 1981, June 12, 1983.

Chicago Tribune, June 21, 1982.

Newsweek, July 5, 1982.

New York Times, June 20, 1982.

Publishers Weekly, July 2, 1982.

Times (London), June 21, 1982.

Washington Post, June 21, 1982. □

Phineas Taylor Barnum

Phineas Taylor Barnum (1810-1891), America's greatest showman of the 19th century, instructed and amused a nation with his museum and later his circus.

Speaking of his youth, P. T. Barnum said, "I was always ready to concoct fun, or lay plans for moneymaking, but hard work was decidedly not in my line." Indeed, he succeeded in making a great deal of money by working hard at having fun. His love of a joke came to him naturally. When he was born in Bethel, Conn., in 1810, his grandfather deeded him a parcel of land known as Ivy Island. The growing boy was constantly reminded of his property. When he was 10 years old, he went to visit his estate and discovered it to be "a worthless piece of barren land."

Early Occupations and Joice Heth

When Phineas was 15, his father died, leaving his widow and five children penniless. Phineas immediately became clerk in a country store, where he learned the fine art of Yankee trading. During the next 10 years he was a shop owner, director of lotteries, and newspaper publisher. When he was 19 he eloped with a local seamstress, Charity Hallett (who would remain his wife for 44 years and give him four daughters). At 22, as publisher of the *Herald of Freedom,* he was jailed for libelously accusing a deacon of usury; upon his release 60 days later, Barnum was met by a band and "a coach drawn by six horses" for a parade back to town.

The embryo showman was developing, but it was not until 1835, when he encountered Joice Heth, that the Prince of Humbugs was born. Joice Heth was a disabled African American woman who, her sponsors claimed, was 160 years old and had been the infant George Washington's nurse. Seeing her possibilities as a human curiosity, Barnum purchased the right to exhibit her, along with the documents validating her age, and set her upon her couch in Niblo's Garden in New York City. She was extremely popular, but when interest began to flag, a newspaper item appeared suggesting that Joice was not human at all but an "automaton" made of whalebone, indian rubber, and springs. The exhibition hall was full once more, for Barnum always knew how to use the news as well as the advertising sections of newspapers. Finally, upon her death in 1836, when an autopsy proved that Joice had been no more than

80 years old, Barnum was as surprised and indignant as anyone else. He had learned, however, that "the public appears disposed to be amused even when they are conscious of being deceived."

American Museum

For the next four years Barnum was an itinerant showman in the West and South. By 1840 he was back in New York, poor, weary of travel, and without prospects. When he heard that the struggling Scudder's American Museum (with its collection of curiosities) was for sale, Barnum determined to buy it. "With what?" asked a friend. "Brass," Barnum replied, "for silver and gold I have none." He mortgaged himself to the building's owner, proposing for collateral good references, a determination to succeed, and a "valuable and sentimental" piece of property known as Ivy Island. By the end of 1842 the museum was his, and a year later he was out of debt.

Barnum's American Museum was to become the most famous showplace of the century. Here, in constantly changing and elaborately advertised parade, the public could see educated dogs and fleas, automatons, jugglers, ventriloquists, living statuary, albinos, obese men, bearded women, a great variety of singing and dancing acts, models of Paris and Jerusalem, dioramas of the Creation and the Deluge, glassblowing, knitting machines, African Americans performing a war dance, conjoined twins, flower and bird shows, whales, mermaids, virtuous melodramas such as *The Drunkard,* a menagerie of rare animals, and an aquarium—"all for twenty-five cents, children half price."

His showman's delight in seeking out the splendid and the curious knew no bounds. "The one end aimed at," he said, "was to make people think, and talk, and wonder, and . . . go to the Museum." His Great Model of Niagara Falls with Real Water was actually 18 inches high; the Feejee Mermaid was really a monkey's head and torso fused to a fish's tail; the Woolly Horse of the Frozen Rockies had in truth been foaled in Indiana. Only half in jest did Barnum seek to buy Shakespeare's birthplace, hire the Zulu leader who had recently ambushed a British force, and tow an iceberg into New York harbor. Altogether, the museum showed over 600,000 exhibits during its existence.

Tom Thumb and Jenny Lind

General Tom Thumb was Barnum's greatest attraction. Charles S. Stratton, a native of Bridgeport, Conn., was 25 inches tall and weighed 15 pounds when he entered Barnum's employ in 1842. When he died in 1883, at the age of 45, he had made millions of dollars and delighted international audiences. In the first of Barnum's many European junkets the General entertained Queen Victoria, King Louis Philippe, and other royalty with his songs, dances, and impersonations in miniature. Of the 82 million tickets Barnum sold during his lifetime for various attractions, Tom Thumb sold over 20 million.

In 1850 Barnum turned impresario, introducing the most renowned singer of her time, Jenny Lind, to the American public. The immensely profitable tour of this gracious "Swedish Nightingale" was prepared with ingenious public relations but conducted with dignity and generosity by Barnum. Its success initiated the vogue of European concert artists visiting the United States.

Fires and Bankruptcy

Barnum's irrepressibility helped him overcome numerous professional misfortunes. Five times he was almost ruined by fire, but each time he recouped. In 1857 his famous house, Iranistan, fashioned after George IV's Pavilion at Brighton, burned to the ground. The original museum burned in 1865, and new museums burned in 1868 and again in 1872. Finally, in 1887, the great circus in its winter quarters, with most of its menagerie, was lost. But the showman's greatest financial catastrophe had nothing to do with show business. For years he had cherished the dream of building a city out of the farmland of East Bridgeport—a benevolent endeavor, he thought. In order to attract business, he signed some notes guaranteeing the debts of the Jerome Clock Company. As a result, he lost all he owned. Thus, in 1855, at the age of 46, the great Barnum was bankrupt. But he worked his way back, in part from successful lectures on "The Art of Money Getting," and by 1860 he was free of debt once more.

Throughout his life Barnum was a political liberal, serving in the Connecticut Legislature in the late 1860s, where he diligently fought the railroad interests, and as mayor of Bridgeport in 1875-1876. A year after the death of his first wife, Charity, in 1873, Barnum married Nancy Fish, an English woman 40 years his junior.

"The Greatest Show on Earth"

In April 1874 Barnum opened his Roman Hippodrome in New York; this was to grow into the great circus. He did not invent the circus, an ancient form of entertainment, but along with his enterprising young partner, James A. Bailey, whose circus merged with Barnum's in 1881, he made it a three-ring extravaganza the likes of which had never been seen before. Barnum's last great coup was his 1881 purchase from the London Zoo of the largest elephant in captivity, Jumbo. Violent objections by the English only made Jumbo and the circus that much more appealing. The variety and splendor of the show delighted the American audiences that Barnum had trained, over the years, to be delighted. In 1882 the circus opened its season in Madison Square Garden, where it was to become an American institution; and everywhere the "big top" traveled, a "Barnum Day" was declared. Circling the arena in an open carriage as leader of the parade always brought roars of approval (and great satisfaction) to the aging genius.

By 1891 Barnum's body began to fail, though not his spirit. His child's delight in the joke, the curious, and the splendid had set an entire nation to wondering and laughing and buying. A few weeks before his death, Barnum gave permission to the *Evening Sun* to print his obituary, so that he might have a chance to read it. On April 7 he asked about the box office receipts for the day; a few hours later, he was dead.

Further Reading

Barnum's autobiography, *Struggles and Triumphs of P.T. Barnum* (1871; rev. ed. 1967), was frequently revised by Barnum until 1888. It is detailed, though somewhat self-righteous and therefore less appealing than Waldo Brown, ed., *Barnum's Own Story: The Autobiography of P. T. Barnum . . .* (1927; rev. ed. 1961). This work combines Barnum's first autobiographical venture of 1855, which offended some readers for its frank confession of humbugs, and the more staid book of 1871. Irving Wallace, *The Fabulous Showman: The Life and Times of P. T. Barnum* (1959), is one of the most interesting treatments, providing not only a history of Barnum's career but sketches of his most famous associates and an analysis of Barnum's happy effect upon American society of the 19th century. For a history of the circus see Earl C. May, *The Circus from Rome to Ringling* (1932), and Fred Bradna, *Big Top: My Forty Years with the Greatest Show on Earth* (1952). □

Pío Baroja y Nessi

The Spanish novelist and essayist Pío Baroja y Nessi (1872-1956) ranks as one of the major writers of Spain's Generation of 1898. His many works consistently reveal harsh criticism of his country and a pessimistic view of life.

Pío Baroja was born on Dec. 28, 1872, in San Sebastián. In 1879 the family moved to Madrid, where at 15 he began to study medicine. He received his doctorate in medicine at the University of Madrid in 1893 and spent the next year as a country doctor in Cestona, a small Basque town. Disgusted by the hardships and petty intrigues of country life, Baroja renounced his medical post in 1895 and the following year joined his brother Ricardo in managing a bakery in Madrid. The shock of the Spanish-American War in 1898 provoked in him, as in many of his contemporaries, a poraries, a protest against Spain's social abuses and the corrosive influence of the Catholic Church. Toward the end of 1898 he began to contribute articles to the journal *Revista nueva* and made the first of many trips to Paris. Two years later Baroja published *Vidas sombrías* (Dark Lives), a collection of short stories, and his first novel, *La casa de Aizgorri* (The House of Aizgorri), a depressing tale about the ruin of an alcoholic family. This novel and *El mayorazgo de Labraz* (1903; Lord of Labraz) and *Zalacaín el aventurero* (1909; Zalacaín the Adventurer) form the first trilogy, *Tierra vasca* (Basque Country). Baroja grouped most of his novels into cycles or trilogies.

After the bakery failed in 1902, Baroja devoted himself entirely to writing, turning out two or more books almost every year until his death in 1956. He was extremely shy, and except for several trips abroad, he lived a secluded and sedentary life. Baroja wrote his best novels between 1902 and 1912; among them are *Camino de perfección* (1902; Road to Perfection), *La busca, Mala hierba,* and *Aurora roja* (1904; The Search, Weeds, and Red Dawn), *La feria de los discretos* (1905), *Paradox rey* (1906; king Paradox), and *El arbol de la ciencia* (1911; The Tree of Knowledge). He also

wrote about a dozen volumes of essays, of which the autobiographical *Juventud, egolatría* (1917; Youth, Egotism) is the best known.

Baroja's heroes are underworld characters—vagabonds, adventurers, prostitutes, anarchists—Whose cynicism and rebellious spirit embody the author's ideal of a life of action. Baroja believed that only action has any positive value in a hostile and absurd world. Personal failure is the dominant theme of a typical Baroja novel. Since the characters are committed only to a life of action, they lack a constructive purpose and are condemned to final ruin. The techniques he used to depict action in his novels include the sacrifice of structure to an almost haphazard flow of people, places, plots, and subplots, and the use of a style marked by short, choppy paragraphs.

Baroja enjoyed considerable fame within Spain and abroad, and many of his novels were translated into English. In 1935 he was admitted to the Spanish Royal Academy. His works influenced many younger writers, notably Ernest Hemingway, who visited Baroja in Madrid in 1956 to declare his debt to him. Baroja died on Oct. 30, 1956, at the age of 83.

Further Reading

The most comprehensive account of Baroja's life and work is in Spanish, Fernando Baeza, ed., *Baroja y su mundo* (2 vols., 1961). The best analysis of his novelistic technique is the chapter "Pío Baroja" in Katherine P. Reding, *The Generation of 1898 as Seen through Its Fictional Hero* (1936). Gerald Brenan, *The Literature of the Spanish People: From Roman*

Times to the Present Day (1951; rev. ed. 1953), contains useful information about Baroja. □

Salo Wittmayer Baron

Salo Wittmayer Baron (1895-1989), an Austrian-born American scholar and educator, was the foremost Jewish historian of the 20th century.

S alo Baron was born in Tarnow, Austria (now Poland), on May 26, 1895. From 1917 to 1923 he earned doctorates in philosophy, political science, and jurisprudence from the University of Vienna and a rabbinical degree from the Jewish Theological Seminary in Vienna. From 1919 to 1926 he lectured at the Juedisches Paedagogium (Jewish Teachers College) in Vienna.

Academic Appointments in the United States

In 1926 Baron traveled to the United States, where he was appointed professor of history and librarian at the Jewish Institute of Religion in New York City. In 1930 he became the first professor of Jewish history, literature, and institutions on the Miller Foundation at Columbia University, where he served with distinction until retiring in 1963. He was also the first director of Columbia's Center of Israel and Jewish Studies, established in 1950. After 1954 he was visiting professor at the Jewish Theological Seminary of America. In 1934 he had married Jeanette Meisel.

Baron was an active participant in communal and cultural activities as a member of a UNESCO Commission and of the U.S. Office of Education's Citizens Federal Commission on Education. As founder and president of the Jewish Cultural Reconstruction, Baron labored to restore libraries and reclaim Jewish cultural artifacts following World War II. He served as president of the American Academy for Jewish Research, the America Jewish Historical Society, and the Conference on Jewish Social Studies. He was a leading prosecution witness in the Adolf Eichmann trial in Jerusalem in 1961, providing testimony that established the historical context underlying Nazi activities.

Major Works

The prolific author of hundreds of books, articles, and reviews on topics of Jewish history, Baron is best known for his masterwork *A Social and Religious History of the Jews.* Originally published in three volumes in 1937, 18 volumes of a second greatly expanded and revised edition were issued between 1952 and 1983. Comprising a universal history of the Jewish people from ancient to modern times, taking social, religious, intellectual, economic, and political factors into account, as well as the interaction of Jewish with non-Jewish history, the work surpasses in scope and magnitude all previous attempts at a history of the Jewish race.

In addition to the mammoth *A Social and Religious History of the Jews,* the 19th volume of which Baron worked

on well into his 90s, his works include *The Jewish Community: Its History and Structure to the American Revolution* (3 vols., 1942), *Modern Nationalism and Religion* (1947),*History and Jewish Historians* (1964), *Ancient and Medieval Jewish History: Essays* (1972), and *The Contemporary Relevance of History: A Study in Approaches and Methods (1986).* He also edited a number of works, including *Judaism, Postbiblical and Talmudic Periods* (1954) and the two-volume *Jubilee Volume: The American Academy for Jewish Research,* a 1980 collaboration with Isaac Barzilay. From 1939 to 1989 Baron was a contributing editor of the quarterly *Jewish Social Studies.*

Legacy of Scholarship

As professor of Jewish history at Columbia University, Baron trained a generation of Jewish scholars who later occupied chairs in Jewish studies at leading universities throughout the world. His research as well as his concern for training others contributed greatly to the advancement of Jewish scholarship, especially in the United States. At the time of his death in November 1989, Baron was hailed as "undoubtedly the greatest Jewish historian of the 20th century," by historian Yosef Hayim Yerushaimi, himself the product of Baron's tutelage and the holder of the Salo Wittmayer Baron Chair of Jewish History, Culture and Society at Columbia University, a position established in 1980 to honor Baron's long association with the university.

Further Reading

For a comprehensive account of Baron's life and career, see Robert Liberles, *Salo Wittmayer Baron: Architect of Jewish History* (1995). Baron's obituary appeared in the *New York Times* (November 26, 1989). □

Luis Barragán

A Mexican architect and landscape architect, Luis Barragán (1902-1988) sought to reconcile traditional Mexican architecture with international modernism. Barragán has been termed a Surrealist, a Minimalist, and a Post-Modernist, yet his works are personal and evocative and often defy classification.

Luis Barragán was a 20th-century Mexican architect and landscape architect of vigorous and refined originality. He was born in 1902 in the state of Jalisco, where his family were builders by profession and also owned ranches. Growing up in Jalisco provided Barragán with a reserve of evocative regional images that would stay with him for the rest of his life and would appear with regularity in his designs.

Barragán was trained as an engineer and was entirely self-taught as an architect and landscape architect. This placed him outside the architectural mainstream and left him suspicious of architectural education, which, he felt, "estranged [architects] from their own emotional and intuitive capacities." Barragán once admitted that the only place he felt like a stranger was among architects. He worked for the most part in professional isolation, and a sense of this isolation comes through in his mature works, which are pervaded by a mood of quiet solitude.

Not surprisingly, then, it was not architects who were Barragán's greatest heroes, but practitioners of other creative professions: poets, philosophers, painters, sculptors. This is not to say that other architects did not have an impact on him. His Mexico City works of the 1930s owe a certain debt to Le Corbusier, whom he met on a European sojourn early in the decade. His emphasis on walls as planes in space also owes a debt to Mies van der Rohe. But Barragán was one of those rare creative personages who could borrow from diverse, and sometimes aesthetically contradictory, sources and bring the parts to a point of resolution that seemed to owe little to anyone. His unique goal was to reconcile international modernism with the Mexican regional styles he remembered from his youth.

Barragán was not a builder of skyscrapers; indeed, it is difficult to imagine what they would have looked like considering his abhorrence to the glassiness of modernism and his devotion to the Mexican vernacular. Many of his best known works consist of private residences and their gardens, with the relationship between the two being of prime importance. Barragán's conception of the garden, in which running water usually plays a significant role, has been described as "Persian" or "Islamic," with the garden con-

ceived of as the primary living space and the house itself as an adjacent area of retreat. An early visit to the Alhambra, with its compartmentalized and successive garden spaces, and the ideas of the French painter and landscape architect Ferdinand Bac, who ascribed a mystical, magical power to gardens, played seminal roles in Barragán's ideas about gardens and their relationship to houses.

Barragán's earliest Guadalajara works, such as the villa of G. R. Cristo of 1929, show quite literal references to Islamic architecture. The buildings of Morocco, which he learned of through books brought back from his first European journey in the early 1920s, were particularly influential.

In 1936 Barragán relocated to Mexico City, where his work underwent a transformation and became more in tune with the International Style. The new modernism had already been firmly established in the more cosmopolitan national capital, but it was not a style that was completely foreign to the newcomer from Guadalajara. Barragán had been in Paris in 1931-1932 and had attended lectures by Le Corbusier. Designs such as that in the Avenida Parque Mexico of 1936 have a markedly Corbusian feel, complete with ribbon windows, rooftop solaria, and machine-like interior fit and finish.

By the end of World War II Barragán's International Style phase had passed and he had returned to a more regional site-specific aesthetic. El Pedregal, for instance, is a housing development near Mexico City which Barragán laid out on a plateau of desiccated lava beds. Houses here were to be enveloped by lava rock walls in order to preserve the visual integrity of the site. Barragán's contributions include the master plan, demonstration gardens, entrances, and a fountain plaza.

Barragán's own house in the Tacubaya section of Mexico City was erected in 1947. In this work Barragán first successfully reconciled indigenous Mexican forms with the modernist aesthetic. The house looks inward to a courtyard, recalling provincial designs, while speaking in the rectilinear, austere language of the International Style.

Brilliant colors had become a Barragán trademark by the 1960s. His own previously stark-white house fell under the palette. New works as well, though Minimalist in form, were enlivened and humanized by the addition of color. The importance of color also comes through in Barragán's "equestrian trilogy," which consists of two housing developments and a private estate. The architect, an avid horseman himself, conceived of the subdivision of Las Arboledas, begun in 1958, with horseman in mind. In this design Barragán provided special paths for horses and gathering places for riders where water, rectilinear planes, and brilliant colors come together with nature to form a surreal, and yet serene, environment. The Los Clubes subdivision, begun in 1964, follows a similar formula. Here, in 1967-1968, Barragán erected San Cristobal, a private estate consisting of a stable, horse pool, swimming pool, and house. Color also plays an important role in this ensemble, with pink, red, and purple drawing attention to the Minimalist elements of the design and at the same time providing relief from their starkness.

Barragán has been placed in many categories over the years: Surrealist, Minimalist, Post-Modernist among them. His compositions often do suggest the paintings of de Chirico, and he does reduce the elements of his structures to the bare essentials. He has more recently been called a Post-Modernist due to his emphasis on the wall over the void (he disliked window walls because they lacked the "serene," protective quality of masonry), his use of sometimes quite brilliant color, and the site-specific, regionalist quality of his works.

In 1980 Barragán's long years of faithful, unassuming devotion to his art were given international recognition with the award of architecture's highest honor, the Pritzker Architectural Prize, the equivalent of a Nobel Prize for architecture. He died on November 22, 1988, at the age of 86, after a long bout with Parkinson's disease.

Further Reading

The Barragán bibliography is quite extensive and consists mainly of journal articles. There are two monographs on Barragán: *The Architecture of Luis Barragán* by Emilio Ambasz (1976) and *Luis Barragán* by Wiel Arets and Wim van den Bergh (Rotterdam: scheduled for 1990). The Ambasz book provides an illustrated listing of Barragán's work through 1976, as well as a lengthy bibliography of articles from both English and Spanish language journals. The entry on Barragán by C. Ray Smith in *Contemporary Architects* (1987) provides a chronological list of Barragán's works through 1984 as well as an updated bibliography. "Luis Barragán: The Influential Lyricist of Mexican Culture," an article by Mario Schjetnan G. in

Landscape Architecture (January 1982), provides a particularly insightful interview with Barragán in which he discusses his design philosophy. ☐

Vicomte de Barras

The French statesman and revolutionist Paul François Jean Nicolas, Vicomte de Barras (1755-1829), was a member of the Directory during the French Revolution.

Paul Barras (pronounced bå-rås) was born at Fox-Amphoux of an old noble family of Provence. He embarked upon a military career and took part in the Native American campaign in the years before the French Revolution. Returning to France shortly before 1789 with the rank of captain, he embraced the new revolutionary ideas. On July 14, 1789, he took part in the attack on the Bastille, and on October 5-6 he was involved in bringing Louis XVI back to Paris from Versailles.

In September 1792 Barras was elected to the National Convention, where he voted for the establishment of a republic and the death of the king. Barras spent much of his time on missions in the south, although he attended the convention, sitting with the Jacobins. At the siege of Toulon he met Napoleon Bonaparte who commanded the artillery. By the summer of 1794 Barras had joined the forces determined to overthrow Robespierre, and he helped to bring down the Jacobin regime on 9 Thermidor (July 27, 1794).

Barras's popularity and influence grew during the period of the Thermidorian Reaction. When the Directory was established in 1795, he became one of the five directors. Because of his military background the government called upon him to put down the royalist uprising of 13 Vendémiaire (Oct. 5, 1795). Remembering the young artillery officer from Toulon, who was in Paris at the time, Barras appointed Gen. Bonaparte to defend the Tuileries. The rebellion was crushed and the government strengthened, and Bonaparte, with Barras's help, was given command of the Army of Italy. This was Bonaparte's first real opportunity to display his military ability. Furthermore, Barras bestowed his former mistress, Josephine de Beauharnais, upon his protégé and was best man at their marriage in March 1796.

Barras's prestige reached its high point in 1797, when Bonaparte imposed peace upon Austria. During 1798-1799 the French people began to tire of the Directory, and when Bonaparte seized power on 18 Brumaire (Nov. 10, 1799), the government had little support outside of the Chamber of Five Hundred. Barras, opposed to Bonaparte's action, immediately resigned and went into retirement on his estate of Gros-Bois. His disapproval of the Consulate led to his exile to Brussels.

In 1805 Napoleon, then securely on the throne of France, allowed Barras to settle at Marseilles, where he remained until 1813. In the last months of the Empire he lived in Rome, but after Napoleon's abdication in April 1814, he returned to Paris. No more acceptable to the returning royalists than to the departed Bonapartists, Barras remained under surveillance and completely detached from politics. He died at Chaillot in 1829.

Further Reading

George Duruy, ed., *Memoirs of Barras* (trans., 4 vols., 1895-1896), remains the best available source on Barras in English. Georges Lefebvre, *The Directory* (trans. 1964), is somewhat sympathetic toward Barras. The principal biographies of Barras, however, remain untranslated. ☐

Raymond Barre

Raymond Barre (born 1924) served as prime minister of France from 1976 until 1981, heading the last of the Gaullist-Giscardian governments that dominated the first quarter-century of the Fifth Republic. He remained politically active, noted for his expertise as a professional economist and his commitment to reducing the state's role in directing the economy.

Raymond Barre was born in 1924 on the French island of Réunion in the Indian Ocean. After completing secondary school there, he went to Paris to study law and economics, earning degrees from the Institute for Political Studies in Paris and passing the *aggrégation* exam which allows individuals to teach in the university system.

Barre then pursued an academic career. At age 26 he joined the economics department of the University of Caen and subsequently taught at the Institute for Political Studies. He was appointed to the chair in political economy at the University of Paris in 1963.

Barre's early career was not restricted to academe. In the early years of the Fifth Republic (1958 to the present), he held a variety of advisory posts. For example, he served on the staff of the minister of industry from 1959 until 1962. In 1966, he was a consultant on wage and price policy for the Economic Planning Commission.

From 1967 until 1972, Barre served as vice president of the commission of the European Communities (Common Market) in charge of all economic and financial questions. He also helped develop French housing policy and served as a member of the board of directors of the Bank of France from 1973 until 1976.

Until then, Barre had never run for political office. His formal political career began in January 1976 when then Prime Minister Jacques Chirac appointed him minister of the economy and finance. That position did not last long. In August, President Giscard d'Estaing asked for and received Chirac's resignation and, in a surprising move, appointed Barre to succeed him as prime minister while retaining the Economics and Finance portfolio. Barre remained prime minister until Giscard's defeat in the 1981 presidential elections by François Mitterrand.

The years 1976-1981 were hard ones for the French economy. Like many other nations, France was still reeling from the slump that followed the 1973 oil embargo by the Organization of Petroleum Exporting Countries (OPEC). Although France actually was outperforming most of its competitors, Giscard and Barre thought the only longterm solution was to minimize state involvement and move toward a more classical market-driven economy. Therefore, they tried to loosen the general power the government had over investment, plant location, production, and other decisions. They refused to help out firms that were in danger of bankruptcy. The one area in which the Giscard-Barre team continued to strengthen state intervention was in aiding selected companies that could become "national champions," single strong firms in each industrial area that would be competitive in both the domestic and international markets.

Those policies did not stem the decline or produce a new spurt of economic growth. Many observers felt that Barre and his policies were responsible for France's economic slump which persisted after 1976. For others, including Barre himself, the problems were seen as a necessary start in restructuring the economy, the benefits of which would only become apparent late in the 1980s or 1990s. Largely as a result of this economic decline, Giscard lost the presidency and the Gaullist-Giscardian coalition lost its majority in the National Assembly when elections were held in 1981. Barre was reelected to the Assembly and became one of the leading opponents of President Mitterrand and his Socialist government's economic policies.

The French presidential elections in 1988 saw Barre running for the position as a candidate from the Gaullist party. Although he was defeated by the incumbent, Mitterand, Barre continued to keep active in politics after his unsuccessful presidential campaign by backing Lyon, France as the home of the Central Bank of the United Europe.

Further Reading

There are no biographies of Raymond Barre. On his role in the Giscard years, see J. R. Frears, *France in the Giscard Presidency* (London, 1981), and for the ideas he and Giscard tried to implement, see Valéry Giscard d'Estaing, *French Democracy* (1977).

Concerning Barre's activities after leaving the post of the Prime Minister see "Barre, Barre Black Sheep" in *Economist* (April 2, 1988), and "M. Rocard's Umbrella" in *Spectator* (July 30, 1988). □

Auguste Maurice Barrès

The French writer and politician Auguste Maurice Barrès (1862-1923) was the author of numerous novels, essays, and articles and was a member of the

Chamber of Deputies and of the Académie Française.

Maurice Barrès was born in Charmes near Nancy and passed a happy childhood in a well-to-do family. In 1882 Barrès went to Paris to study law, but he soon became involved in the literary life of the Latin Quarter and acquired a reputation as a rebel and dandy. He flaunted his egotism, while also expressing a profound desire for action, in his first trilogy, *Le Culte du moi* (*Sous l'oeil des barbares*, 1888, Under the Eye of the Barbarians; *Un Homme libre*, 1889, A Free Man; and *Le Jardin de Bérénice*, 1891, The Garden of Bérénice). The themes of exoticism and fascination with death and decay occur in these early works, as well as in some later ones, such as *Du Sang, du volupté et de la mort,* (1894, Of Blood, Pleasure, and Death), *Greco ou le secret de Tolède* (1911, Greco or the Secret of Toledo), and *Jardin sur l'Oronte* (1923, Garden on the Orontes).

Barrès made his political debut in 1889 as a successful Boulangist candidate for the Chamber of Deputies. Although presenting himself for election four more times after 1893, he did not reenter the Chamber until 1906, as deputy from the first arrondissement in Paris—a seat he held until his death.

In his second trilogy, *Le Roman de l'energie national* (*Les Déracinés*, 1897, The Uprooted; *L'Appel au soldat,* 1900, The Calling of the Soldier; and *Leurs Figures,* 1902, Their Faces), Barrès analyzes himself and his relation to Lorraine, the province of his birth. This examination leads his to believe that the individual, as well as the nation, is formed by the land and the dead. A rejection of the formative forces, and thus of identity, can only lead to disaster for both the individual and the collectivity. These novels serve as the literary expression of Barrès's espousal of nationalism as a political philosophy and as a guide to action.

Prior to 1906, Barrès, the leading anti-Dreyfusard intellectual, had been a vehement opponent of the parliamentary republic. After his reelection to the Chamber, he assumed a more moderate stance, viewing his proper role in politics as that of moral mentor.

Alsace-Lorraine was at the core of Barrès's political thought and literary activity. Before World War I he published two novels—*Au Service de l'Allemagne* (1905, In the Service of Germany) and *Colette Baudoche* (1909)— dealing with the dilemma facing people of French culture who chose to remain in the occupied territory. When the war broke out, he welcomed the conflict as the occasion for France's moral rejuvenation, and he devoted himself to propaganda sustaining morale on the home front. After 1918 he was one of the most prominent advocates of a strong Rhine policy and full implementation of the Treaty of Versailles. He died in December 1923 and was honored with a national funeral.

Further Reading

Very little of Barrès's work has been translated into English, and there is no full-length biography of him in English. A view of aspects of his work and life is in Flora Emma Ross, *Goethe in Modern France, with Special Reference to Maurice Barrès, Paul Bourget and André Gide* (1937). Michael Curtis, *Three against the Third Republic: Sorel, Barrès, and Maurras* (1959), has a detailed biographical and critical study of Barrès as an antirepublican intellectual. John Cruickshank, *French Literature and Its Background* (vol. 5, 1969), is useful for the literary background of Barrès's time. □

Sir James Matthew Barrie

The British dramatist and novelist Sir James Matthew Barrie (1860-1937) is best known for his play *Peter Pan*.

James M. Barrie was born in Kirriemuir, Angus, Scotland, on May 9, 1860, the son of a poor, hardworking weaver. Influenced by his mother's interest in literature and art, the ambitious Barrie studied at the University of Edinburgh and then wrote prolifically for a Nottingham newspaper for two years. Determined to earn his living as a writer, he moved to London.

After achieving literary success, Barrie married the actress Mary Ansell in 1894. Their childless union was perhaps marred by the influence of his mother, and they were divorced in 1910. During this period he had become attached to Sylvia Llewellyn Davies and her sons. The tragic death of Mrs. Davies in 1910 hardened the heretofore lighthearted writer. He was further grieved by the accidental deaths of Mrs. Davies's two sons, whose guardian he had been.

Barrie received many honors in his lifetime. He was made a baronet in 1913 and was granted the Order of Merit for his service during World War I. He died in London on June 19, 1937, and was buried at Kirriemuir.

His Works

Like his immortal Peter Pan, Barrie never wanted to face the pain and unhappiness of the adult world. Thus much of his writing is emotionally sentimental as well as thematically autobiographical. His first published fiction, *Auld Licht Idylls* (1888), is a collection of folktales set in ''Thrums,'' a town based on Kirriemuir. These stories and his novel *The Little Minister* (1891) found immediate acceptance.

His play *The Professor's Love Story* (1894) and the dramatization of *The Little Minister* (1897) proved so successful that Barrie decided to concentrate on writing for the theater. He did, however, continue to produce outstanding prose works, among them *Margaret Ogilvy* (1897), which was a biography of his mother. The character of the hardworking ''little mother'' evident in this work recurs in several of his plays and novels.

Barrie's reputation as a dramatist was firmly established with productions of *Quality Street* (1901) and *The Admirable Crichton* (1902); both works possess charm and easy grace. *Peter Pan,* his greatest success, was based on a story

created for Mrs. Davies's sons. The drama promptly became a classic following its initial performance in 1904. The character of Wendy in this play appears to be an amalgam of Barrie's mother and Mrs. Davies.

In his social comedies—*The Admirable Crichton* and *What Every Woman Knows* (1908)—Barrie satirizes a topsy-turvy society whose class structure is rigid and anti-quated. *The Twelve-Pound Look* (1910) criticizes feminine emancipation, and *Dear Brutus* (1917) advocates heavenly failure over worldly success. *Mary Rose* (1920), while light on the surface, has an underlying cynical vein.

Further Reading

The authorized biography of Barrie is Denis MacKail, *Barrie, the Story of J.M.B.* (1941). Also see Janet Dunbar, *J. M. Barrie: The Man behind the Image* (1970).

Additional Sources

Allen, David (David Rayvern), *Peter Pan & cricket,* London: Constable, 1988.

Birkin, Andrew., *J. M. Barrie & the lost boys: the love story that gave birth to Peter Pan,* New York: C. N. Potter: distributed by Crown Publishers, 1979.

Darlington, William Aubrey, *J. M. Barrie,* New York: Haskell House, 1974.

Darton, F. J. Harvey (Frederick Joseph Harvey), *J. M. Barrie,* New York: Haskell House, 1974.

Hammerton, John Alexander, Sir, *J. M. Barrie and his books; biographical and critical studies,* New York: Haskell House Publishers, 1974. □

René Barrientos Ortuño

René Barrientos Ortuñ (1919-1969), populist Bolivian president from 1966 to 1969, identified himself with the forgotten Indian masses, allied Bolivia closely with the United States, crushed Che Guevara's guerrillas, and was killed in a mysterious helicopter crash.

R ené Barrientos Ortuño was born at Tunary, a village near Bolivia's second city, Cochabamba, on May 30, 1919. His father was of Spanish ancestry and his mother was Indian, and she ensured that her son's first language was Quechua, which would later endear him to a huge Indian constituency. Following the death of his father when he was very young, he was sent to a Franciscan orphanage, striking out when he was 12 and putting himself through a private high school by working odd jobs. Upon graduation, he entered the military academy in La Paz.

Before he could graduate, however, he was bitten by the political bug and was expelled for activism. He supported the new, radical MNR (National Revolutionary Movement), which was to dominate much of Bolivia's later history.

Expelled or not, Barrientos ended up in the Army and was a lieutenant in 1952 when the MNR in a bloody revolt seized power under Victor Paz Estenssoro. In this period the MNR was thoroughly reformist, dedicated to changing the society as well as the economy and to upraising the forgotten and landless Indian masses through education, land reform, and nationalization of major foreign holdings. Despite the fact that one reform soon implemented was a drastic paring of the strength of the armed forces to a miniscule 5,000 officers and men, Barrientos—who was briefly sent to the United States for flight training—was an enthusiastic supporter of Paz and his movement. Blending his penchant for reformist politics with his love for the military life, Barrientos in the mid-1950s, before becoming chief of the small Air Force, ran the U.S. Army-financed "Civic Action" program in his native Cochabamba province.

Paz announced in 1964 that he would again run for the presidency (he had fulfilled his first term, been succeeded by Hernán Siles Zuazo, and then served a second time). His air force commander, now well-known both in and out of the military, used his influence to try and become his running mate. Paz, however, balked and instead demanded that Barrientos resign from the military for meddling in politics. Before he could resign, however, Barrientos was wounded (in one of five separate assassination attempts during his life). Returning from treatment at an American hospital in the Panama Canal Zone, Barrientos was given a hero's welcome by the Bolivian people, and Paz reluctantly accepted him as vice presidential candidate. The Paz/Barrientos team won handily.

In November 1964, some three months after inauguration, the vice president, claiming that Paz was preparing a

dictatorship, began a coup in Cochabamba supported by Gen. Alfredo Ovando Candia: Bolivia's 184th coup. Paz was easily ousted, and a junta ruled Bolivia, with Barrientos and Ovando as co-presidents from May 26, 1965, to January 1966.

Not content with a co-presidency, Barrientos spent much of 1965 roaming the interior, haranguing the peasants in their native tongue and building a massive rural power base. He pledged to "restore" the 1952 Revolution, enforce honesty and efficiency in the government, and seek much-needed development aid from the United States. By the end of the year he had created the FRB (Bolivian Revolutionary Front), a coalition of basically conservative peasant and business interests.

In January 1966 he resigned from the junta and campaigned actively throughout the country for the upcoming elections, which he won easily in July, his FRB capturing 62 percent of the votes. His presidency was strongly supported by peasant organizations (which he repaid by spending half of his time helicoptering around the interior to be with them), the business and middle classes, the military, and the U.S. embassy.

Barrientos' rule was characterized by moderate economic growth, a concerted drive to lessen the extensive powers of organized labor (bloody strike-breaking by the Army became common); significant increases in U.S. aid, including Green Beret and Central Intelligence Agency (CIA) training teams which trained and advised the elite new Ranger regiment which crushed the Ché Guevara guerrilla

movement in 1967; a growing centralization of political power at the expense of local and regional elites; and a quite successful courting of foreign investments. He made considerable progress in these areas, but his heavy-handed tactics (political arrests, exilings, martial law) alienated many. In negotiations with Chile (which had occupied the entire Bolivian seacoast in the 19th century War of the Pacific) to obtain a seaport he failed, disappointing more.

On April 27, 1969, again visiting his beloved interior, Barrientos was killed when the helicopter he was piloting hit a power line near Cochabamba. There is still considerable suspicion in Bolivia and elsewhere that the crash was not an accident but an assassination. Barrientos is still remembered fondly by many rural Bolivians as the president who cared.

Further Reading

There does not yet exist a biography of Barrientos, but a great deal of information on the man, his times, and his nation can be found in the following books: Dwight B. Heath, et al., *Land Reform and Social Revolution in Bolivia* (1969); James W. Wilkie, *The Bolivian Revolution and United States Aid Since* (1969); James M. Malloy and Richard S. Thorn, *Beyond the Revolution: Bolivia Since 1952* (1971); Christopher Mitchell, *The Legacy of Populism in Bolivia, from the MNR to Military Rule* (1977); and Herbert S. Klein, *Bolivia: The Evolution of a Multi-Ethnic Society* (1982). □

Justo Rufino Barrios

Justo Rufino Barrios (1835-1885) was a Guatemalan general and president whose sweeping innovations gave form to modern Guatemala and earned for him the sobriquet "the Reformer."

Justo Barrios was born on July 19, 1835, in the department of San Marcos in western Guatemala. His well-to-do parents had land holdings that extended into adjoining Mexico. He studied law in Guatemala City and became a notary, but in 1862 he returned home and engaged in farming until he joined the liberal revolution against conservative President Vicente Cerna.

The revolutionaries triumphed in June 1871, and their leader, Miguel Garcia Granados, became provisional president. Barrios, however, was the stronger personality. As military commander in the western departments, then as acting president, and finally as elected president after April 1873, he shaped the revolution and dominated Guatemala until his death.

Politically, Barrios ran an open dictatorship only slightly mitigated after 1879 by a charade of constitutionalism. He imposed internal peace and established central control over local affairs by means of appointed departmental governors (*jefes políticos*). As a lawgiver, he provided complete codes in many areas to replace the temporizing patchwork of legislation grafted on unrepealed Spanish laws accumulated since Guatemalan independence. In

1879 a compliant constituent assembly drafted a constitution accommodated to a strong executive, under which Barrios was overwhelmingly reelected in March 1880.

Barrios initiated far-reaching reforms of a pattern common to 19th-century liberals. He curtailed the powers of the Church by such measures as suppressing regular orders and nationalizing their properties, subjecting clerics to the civil courts, making civil marriage obligatory, and guaranteeing free exercise of all religions. Companion legislation provided for a public school system and made education laical, free, and compulsory. To encourage rapid economic growth of the country, he continued to promote coffee cultivation, offered land free or at moderate cost to prospective cultivators, and installed mechanisms to supply labor by Indians. To improve communications, he built roads and promoted railroad building, port development, and construction of telegraph, telephone, and cable lines. He stimulated immigration both for its direct effect and for the beneficial influence foreign settlers could exert on nationals.

Barrios also manipulated international affairs. He arranged a boundary settlement with Mexico that critics alleged served his own property interests better than the national welfare. Like other Central American strongmen, he intervened in neighboring states to overthrow hostile governments or to support those favorable to him. He proclaimed restoration of the Central American union, and when a previously compliant regime in El Salvador did not respond favorably, he declared war. On April 2, 1885, he was killed on the battle filed at Chalchuapa, El Salvador.

The Barrios regime set the pattern for "liberal" Guatemala until 1944. Barrios destroyed the traditional aristocracy but created another around the new entrepreneurs and other beneficiaries of his measures. He despised the Indian because of his cultural conservatism and his lack of sophistication; he believed him capable of no contribution to the new Guatemala other than as body given in labor or as an instrument of amalgamating the races.

Further Reading

The standard English source on Barrios is Paul Burgess, *Justo Rufino Barrios* (1926), an objective study by a Protestant missionary resident in Guatemala. Chester L. Jones, *Guatemala: Past and Present* (1940), contains a brief but excellent evaluation. □

John Barry

John Barry (1745-1803) was a U.S. naval officer during the American Revolution, distinguished by his gallant achievements. In the 1790s he was the senior officer in the American Navy.

John Barry, born in Ireland and always a staunch Roman Catholic, went to sea at an early age. In 1776 a Philadephia merchant selected him to be the master of a vessel trading with the West Indies. In that year Barry, already a veteran mariner, received a captain's commission in the Continental Navy. A myth persists that Barry was the first captain appointed to the first vessel purchased by Congress, but his initial ship was a hastily outfitted Philadelphia brigantine, the *Lexington*. He created quite an impression in his opening cruise by capturing a well-armed tender, giving safe convoy to several merchantmen, and eluding a British squadron. Barry's stature grew quickly, and he has been called the most popular officer in the Revolutionary Navy.

Barry's later commands were the *Effingham*, the *Raleigh* (which he had to run aground to avoid capture), and the *Alliance*. In the last years of the war he performed valuable service transporting supplies and dispatches between France and America. Unaware of the state of peace negotiations in Paris, he fought the last naval action of the Revolution more than a month after the conflict had officially ended. Barry remained in the service for two additional years, until the government sold the *Alliance*. The last captain to resign, he literally saw the Continental Navy come to an end.

Barry's retirement at his plantation home, Strawberry Hill, outside Philadelphia was not to be permanent. Congress, stung by the Barbary pirates' attacks on American shipping in the Mediterranean, resolved to create a new navy in 1794, and President Washington extended Barry a commission as senior captain in the service. After helping to supervise the naval construction program, he was made commander of the *United States,* the first of the new vessels to put to sea. The tall, white-haired Barry was accorded the

courtesy title of commodore, the second American naval officer ever to hold the title, and the first in 20 years. Between 1798 and 1801 Barry spent much of his time directing American naval operations in the West Indies, the period of the so-called Quasi-War with France. In semiretirement in 1802 the 57-year-old Barry was asked by President John Adams to assume command of the Mediterranean squadron, but ailing health compelled him to decline. He died the following year.

Further Reading

There is only one biography of Barry worthy of attention—an excellent study by a distinguished authority on the naval history of the Revolution, William B. Clark, *Gallant John Barry, 1745-1803: The Story of a Naval Hero of Two Wars* (1938). For early American naval history see Gardner W. Allen, *A Naval History of the American Revolution* (2 vols., 1913). □

Marion Shepilov Barry Jr.

Long-time mayor of Washington D.C., Marion Barry followed his third term in office with a conviction on cocaine possession charges, but Washingtonians had not seen the last of him. Released from prison in 1992, three years later, Barry assumed the office of mayor for the fourth time.

For over 20 years, politician Marion Barry has epitomized all that is good and all that is bad about big-city politics in America. The Southern-born civil rights activist fought to gain legitimacy for Washington, D.C.'s citizenry, wresting control of the capital city's governance from the U.S. Congress and taking important steps to cure the city's problems with crime and unemployment. As he moved from business organizer to school board member to mayor, however, Barry was increasingly implicated in the corruption and graft that seemed to pervade the city government. In 1990, after serving as mayor for 12 years, Barry was arrested and convicted on cocaine possession charges in an ugly and widely publicized scandal. Washingtonians had not seen the last of Barry, however, for in 1992 he was released from prison and elected to the city council by the capital's poorest ward, thus continuing one of the oddest political journeys in recent history.

Marion S. Barry was born on March 6, 1936, in tiny Itta Bena, Mississippi. When he was four, his sharecropper father died and his mother, Mattie B. Barry, moved to Memphis, Tennessee, where she worked as a domestic and married a butcher named David Cummings. Barry thrived in Memphis, earning high grades in school and becoming an Eagle scout. At the same time, he picked cotton, waited tables, and delivered papers to help his parents and seven younger sisters.

Barry's poor background made him an unlikely candidate for higher education, but his good grades led him to Memphis's all-black LeMoyne College, where he earned a bachelor's degree in chemistry in 1958. Barry received his

first taste of activism as a member of the college's chapter of the National Association for the Advancement of Colored People (NAACP). As chapter president, Barry led an effort to force a white college trustee to retract a disparaging remark he made about blacks while representing Memphis in a bus desegregation trial.

From LeMoyne, Barry went to Fisk University, a predominantly African American institution in Nashville where he earned his master's degree in chemistry. Barry helped form a NAACP chapter at Fisk, and in 1960, after participating in a workshop in nonviolence, organized the first lunch counter sit-ins in Nashville. Later that year, Barry and others interested in nonviolent protest met with the Reverend Martin Luther King, Jr., at Shaw College in Raleigh, North Carolina. There they established the Student Nonviolent Coordinating Committee (SNCC; often pronounced "snick"), which became an important organizing force in the civil rights movement. Barry was named SNCC's first national chairman.

Through the early 1960s, Barry tried to balance education and activism as he shuttled between SNCC headquarters in Atlanta and teaching appointments at the University of Kansas, the University of Tennessee, and Knoxville College. "He was totally political, totally committed to empowering the people, to getting people elected, not just getting them equality at the lunch counter," Lawrence T. Guyot, an SNCC veteran told the New York Times. In 1964, however, Barry gave up his doctoral work to labor full time for SNCC. He spent some time in New York City and then moved permanently to Washington, D.C., where he struck both friends and foes as a man with a mission. Gregarious, ebullient, and impatient, he soon became a leader of the capital's civil rights community. Washington's newspapers took one look at the six-foot-one-inch, 200-pound activist cloaked in African-style garb and dubbed him a "dashiki-clad militant."

Barry's early activities in Washington fell within the tradition of the protest movement. In January of 1966 he protested rising bus fairs with a successful one-day bus boycott. The following month, he formed the "Free D.C. Movement," which lobbied to free Washington from direct Congressional rule. "Free D.C." organized boycotts of merchants who wouldn't display its posters, thus forcing businesses to choose sides. Those who wanted customers in the predominantly black city chose "Free D.C." Barry's opponents labeled him an "extortionist and a caged panther," according to the New York Times, but the movement succeeded in gaining a form of home rule by 1973.

By 1967 Barry had begun to appreciate the resources of government. He split with the increasingly radical SNCC and, trading his dashiki for a business suit, persuaded U.S. secretary of Labor Willard Wirtz to appropriate $300,000 for "Youth Pride," a one-month project that would hire 1,100 African American youths to kill Washington's rats and clean its streets. Reaction to Youth Pride was mixed. Conservatives attacked the program as typical of "liberal" coddling of criminals and misfits, while the U.S. Attorney's Office investigated it for graft and corruption. But the jobs program was popular among inner-city constituents, gave

Barry an important means of distributing political favors, and made him a major player on the Washington, D.C. political scene. Barry quickly won other grants for the program and within months had expanded it to include Pride Economic Enterprises, a for-profit venture that ran several small businesses and a 55-unit apartment complex.

In 1970 Barry ran for and won a seat on the citizen's board of Washington's Pilot Police District Project, an organization that had been set up to create rapport between precinct officers and the African American community. The following year, he won a seat on the school board—D.C.'s main elected body before home rule—by claiming he could run the board better than his opponent, incumbent board president Anita F. Allen. Analysts thought that Barry's successful mediation of a dispute between teachers and the board helped him win the spot. Between 1972 and 1974, Barry served as school board president. In 1972 Barry also wed Mary Treadwell; their marriage lasted just four years.

In 1973 Congress approved limited home rule for D.C., opening the way for the first mayoral and city council elections in 100 years. On June 5, 1974, Barry announced he would run for city council president. That summer, after failing to win any major endorsements, he decided to run instead for an at-large seat, a post which he easily won. Shedding his business ties to become a full-time politician, Barry reached out to all minorities and crafted one of the country's strongest gay rights bills. In 1976 he won re-election with 78 percent of the vote. The next year, Barry's career almost reached a premature end. Radical Hanafi Muslims seized the District Building demanding cancellation of a movie on the life of Mohammed. In the chaos, they shot Barry in the chest, barely missing his heart. Barry recovered quickly, however, and was back to work a few weeks later.

On January 21, 1978, after three years in the city council, Barry announced his intention to run for mayor. Observers gave him little chance against fellow Democrats Sterling Tucker—city council president—and incumbent mayor Walter E. Washington. But Barry, who campaigned vigorously on promises to cut government waste, reduce infant mortality, and provide housing for the city's poor, made the three-way race work to his advantage, capturing the minority white vote while his opponents split the African American majority vote. Barry also received the support of the city's gay community and last minute endorsements from the Washington Post and the municipal unions. He won the primary with a 35 percent plurality and, on November 7, 1978, he took 66 percent of the vote against Republican Arthur A. Fletcher.

In the euphoria of his victory, the press mentioned Barry—the first former civil rights activist to become mayor of a large city—as a potential vice-presidential candidate or senator should the District of Columbia become a state. Barry himself concentrated on solidifying his political support. To show solidarity with the African American community, he provided housing projects and job programs, and moved to a working-class neighborhood in Ward 7. He courted labor and senior citizens by adding to the city's work force, and he cozied up to business by making favorable zoning and development decisions.

Barry also faced a number of problems during his first term. Teachers went on strike, a long snowstorm paralyzed the city, and a $409 million budget deficit forced cuts in jobs and services. To raise funds, Barry asked for federal aid and borrowed money in the bond market. Beyond the workings of the city government, elements of scandal began to tarnish Barry's reputation. In 1979, the *Washington Post* charged that Mary Treadwell, the mayor's former wife and a co-founder of Youth Pride Inc., had skimmed $600,000 in federal money from a Pride-run low-income housing project.

Despite these controversies, Barry won overwhelming victories in the 1982 primary and general election. During his second term, Washington regained its fiscal health, witnessed a renewal of its downtown, and saw a decline in unemployment and crime. The failures of the second term, however, seemed to have been caused by extreme examples of oversight. First, the city's housing stock declined noticeably, while the Barry administration failed to spend $8 million in federal grants. Moreover, Barry's administration was blamed for prison disturbances and arson at its Lorton Correctional Facility in July of 1986 that injured 22 inmates and guards and damaged 14 buildings. Barry blamed the riot on publicity given to a prison consultant's report which predicted that overcrowding would cause an uprising. The report, Barry told the *New York Times,* was a "self-fulfilling prophecy."

Such incidents pointed out the uncommonly high level of responsibility held by Washington, D.C.'s mayor. In most cities, responsibility for prisons would be shared by city, county, and state. In Washington, D.C., responsibility and power rest strictly in the mayor's hands. By the end of Barry's second term, evidence suggested that Barry was unable to manage that responsibility. Treadwell and Barry's chief aid, Ivanhoe Donaldson, were convicted of financial crimes. A female city worker with whom Barry had a "personal" relationship was convicted of selling cocaine. And Barry's third wife, Effie Slaughter, whom he had married in 1978, was forced to decline a sharply discounted mortgage when the transaction was made public.

Despite the controversy, Barry won a third term in 1986, gaining 71 percent of the primary vote and 61 percent of the vote in the general election, in which he was opposed by Carol Schwartz, a city councilwoman who made an issue of the fact that Barry's son, Christopher, went to private schools. Barry began his third term with a jubilant four-day celebration, but conditions in his administration soon deteriorated. A blizzard hit and the city failed to respond adequately. Then a fiscal crisis forced the mayor to eliminate 1,223 jobs and increase taxes on business and consumers. Barry blamed the city's fiscal crunch on Congress, noting that the federal government's real estate went untaxed except for what Congress decided to appropriate.

To make matters worse, the law seemed to be closing in on the mayor himself. On December 22, 1988, police officers about to make an undercover drug buy from Charles Lewis, a former Virgin Islands official and an acquaintance of Barry, were called back when they learned that the mayor was in Lewis's hotel room. The incident led to a grand jury investigation into possible interference by the mayor in the drug investigation. On January 19, 1989, Barry appeared before the grand jury and testified for three hours. Later, he told reporters he had done nothing wrong.

By April, Lewis had been convicted on four counts of cocaine possession in the Virgin Islands and faced multiple charges in Washington. On November 6, 1989, Lewis pleaded guilty to two conspiracy charges and named Barry as a person for whom he bought crack. Finally, on January 18, 1990, police arrested Barry in Washington's Vista Hotel, charging that he had smoked crack in the room of Rhasheeda Moore. Released on bond, Barry checked into Hanley-Hazelden Treatment Center in West Palm Beach, Florida, where, according to his spokesman, he spent seven weeks being treated for alcoholism.

By February 15, 1990, a grand jury returned nine counts against Barry based on the Moore incident, his visits to Lewis, and possible perjury before the grand jury. That May, the jury returned six new counts, five accusing him of cocaine possession, one of conspiracy. If convicted on all 14 counts the mayor could have faced 26 years in jail and fines of $1,850,000. Barry contended that the government's case was the work of overzealous prosecutors out to get a big-city mayor; Jay B. Stephens, the U.S. Attorney for the District of Columbia, told the *New York Times* that his office was "fairly enforcing the criminal laws without regard to the position or status of the offender."

On June 13, 1990, shortly before his trial was set to begin, Barry announced he would not run for a fourth term: "Now is a time for healing, for me personally and for you politically," the *New York Times* quoted him as saying. "This decision is not related to my legal situation. It is related to my recovery and to what I know is best for my wife and son who suffered for so long through this ordeal." Barry's drug trial lasted eight weeks, attracting publicity throughout the nation. Many local residents were saddened and angered by testimony that portrayed the mayor as a drug user, testimony which included a video-tape taken during the Moore incident. Others were outraged by what they considered a vendetta by white prosecutors against one of the country's most prominent African American politicians.

On August 10, 1990, the jury answered the prosecutor's 14 counts with a conviction on a single misdemeanor charge of cocaine usage. It acquitted him on another misdemeanor, and it failed to reach a verdict on the 12 remaining charges. That fall, while he made his appeals, Barry made what seemed a desperate bid for an at-large council seat on the city council. The *Washington Post* described his campaign "listless," "haggard," and "distracted." His candidacy flopped everywhere but Ward 8, where the city's poorest residents gave him a majority.

In October of 1990, Barry finally resigned as mayor of Washington, D.C. His lawyers were able to delay but not completely forestall U.S. District Judge Thomas Penfield Jackson's six month sentence—the longest allowed under federal guidelines. In sentencing Barry on September 27,

1991, Jackson accused Barry of giving an "aura of respectability" to the capital's violent drug culture, according to the *Los Angeles Times.*

In the spring of 1992, after serving his sentence, Barry returned to Washington politics. He rented a house in Ward 8 and ran for the city council, relying heavily on religious and African themes. Though opposed by almost every established politician, including the new mayor, Sharon Pratt Kelly, he campaigned vigorously and registered more than a thousand voters. On September 16, 1992, Barry took 70 percent of a record high turnout, defeating former ally Wilhelmina Rolark by a ratio of 3-to-1 in the primary. The following month, he won a two-year city council term in the general election, thus beginning a remarkable political rebirth.

Barry's unlikely return to public life continued into the mid 1990s. Late in 1993, Barry began to conduct polls, raise money, and line up potential support for a 1994 run for mayor. A January 1994 poll conducted by the *Washington Post* indicated that Barry was already more popular than mayor Sharon Pratt Kelly, whose administration was damaged by allegations of conflicts of interest in 1992. Personal healing accompanied political healing throughout January, when Barry married longtime friend Cora Lavonne Masters. The marriage, which was attended by Mayor Kelly, Jesse Jackson, poet Maya Angelou, and activist Betty Shabazz, focused on unity. Presenting himself as an example to Washington, D.C.'s largely poor population, Barry returned to politics with a successful campaign for a city council position in 1992.

In 1995 Barry assumed the office of mayor for the fourth time. The biggest challenges facing him were an estimated billion dollar debt and a possible take-over of the city's operations by the federal government. By spring Congress set up a financial control board when the city's schools, foster care programs, police force, and fire department began to show the effects of working under the huge deficit. But because Barry was able to establish a good relationship with Speaker of the House Newt Gingrich, according to the *New York Times Magazine,* "Republican hard-liners don't get to play social engineer" and massively reform the city. It is due to Barry's continued influence with the poorest members of his electorate that he was able to protect home rule of the district. However, Barry has "considerably less money to bring home to the District" with the reduced budget finally approved by Congress.

By May 1996 Barry was taking an indefinite personal leave. Friends attributed it to the long hours he has been working and the prostrate surgery he had undergone in December of the previous year. But rumors of Barry using drugs again; an investigation by the U.S. Attorney's Office into his dealings with real-estate investor, Yong Yun; allegations that Mrs. Barry misappropriated monies from the 1994 campaign; and the continued downsliding of city services made some wonder whether Barry's days in office were numbered. Indeed, *Newsweek* reporters Daniel Klaidman and Michael Isikoff wrote, "While Barry is unquestionably revered by thousands of lower-income residents, there are ample signs that many others are increasingly disenchanted

. . . Meanwhile, the mayor [continued to seek] 'spiritual rejuvenation,' . . . [while] insiders wondered whether the troubled reign of a shrewd political opportunist may finally be coming to a close." But Barry returned to work on May 13, 1996, after two weeks of personal introspection at retreats in Maryland and Missouri. Pronouncing himself spiritually renewed and mentally sharp, he denied rumors that his hiatus had been caused by drug or alcohol use or marriage problems. Although Barry appeared eager to resume his position as mayor, fiscal and racial troubles continued to plague Washington, D.C.

Concerned that racial divisions in the nation's capital had reached dangerous levels, Barry invited several religious, ethnic, business, and government to participate in a discussion of race relations on January 15, 1997 (the birthday of Martin Luther King Jr.). Despite the intentions of the hundreds who participated in Barry's "Day of Dialogue on Race Relations and Polarization," it was clear that little had changed in the city, one of the most racially divided in the U.S.

In an attempt to solve the fiscal problems of Washington, D.C., Barry unveiled his proposed budget for 1998, a $3.3 billion spending plan. Arguing that cities restructure debt all the time, Barry said that if the control board refused the plan, he would be forced to cut millions more from the Police Department, the Fire Department, and the public school system, even though the control board has made public safety and education its highest priority. Based on a 1995 law that created the control board, an agreement on the budget must be reached by the Mayor, the City Council, and the board before the budget is sent to Congress for approval.

Further Reading

Jet, January 10, 1994, pp. 35-36; February 20, 1995, p. 6.
The New York Times, May 14, 1996, p. A14; December 27, 1997, p. A18; January 15, 1997, p. A16; February 4, 1997, p. A14.
The New York Times Magazine, October 29, 1995, pp. 38-41, 44-45, 54-58, 76.
Newsweek, May 13, 1996, pp. 32-33. □

The Barrymores

The Barrymores were a famous American theatrical dynasty who, for three generations and well over a hundred years, provided America with important actors.

The fortunes and misfortunes of the remarkable Barrymore family started in America in 1827 with the debut of seven-year-old Louisa Lane, beginning a career that lasted 70 years. Acting with established stars of the day, she married an Irish comedian, John Drew. Best known for her comic roles, Louisa Drew also excelled as a theater manager. In 1861 she took over the Arch Street Theater in Philadelphia, becoming the second woman in America to assume theatrical management responsibilities.

The Louisa Lane-John Drew marriage produced three important actors: John, Jr., who eventually became one of the most important comic actors of his day (and incidentally provided a pattern and a measure of greatness for his niece and two nephews); Sidney, called Uncle Googan; and Georgiana, a spirited comic actor (who in 1876 married Maurice Barrymore and became the mother of the most celebrated Barrymores, Lionel, Ethel, and John).

Maurice Barrymore, born Herbert Blythe, was the son of an army officer stationed in India. Upon leaving Oxford University, he expressed an interest in acting; his horrified family suggested he change his name. He complied and also changed his country.

Because they were actors first and parents second, both Maurice and Georgiana Barrymore were on the road continually, and so the three children spent their early years in their grandmother's home. Maurice seems to have been an indulgent parent when home but almost forgot his children when away. Georgiana died of tuberculosis when her children were teenagers; thus their grandmother provided what stability they knew as children. Maurice had to be committed to a mental institution for the last two years of his life.

Ethel Barrymore

Ethel Barrymore (1879-1959)

Ethel Barrymore's early years were spent in a convent school; but by 1894 fortunes changed, particularly in theater management, and her grandmother, Louisa Drew, began touring again. Although Ethel would have preferred to become a concert pianist, she recognized that financial necessities required immediate returns. (In later life she said, "We became actors not because we wanted to but because it was the thing we could do best.") She joined her grandmother and Uncle Googan, making her professional debut in Montreal. For three years Ethel appeared in small roles, usually in productions headlined by more famous relatives.

In 1897, gaining recognition in London in the play *Secret Service,* she joined Sir Henry Irving in *The Bells* and *Peter the Great.* On returning to the United States, she appeared with her uncle John, and then in 1901 under Charles Frohman's management she had her own success in *Captain Jinks of the Horse Marines.* Other outstanding successes included *Alice-Sit-by-the-Fire* (1905), *Mid-channel* (1910), *The Constant Wife* (1920), and *The Corn Is Green* (1942).

Ethel Barrymore often played in vaudeville, using James Barrie's one-act play *The Twelve-Pound Look* as her vehicle. She also made films but, unlike her brothers, she never deserted the stage. Among the best films were *Rasputin and the Empress* (1932; the only production, stage or screen, in which the three Barrymores appeared together) and *None but the Lonely Heart* (1944).

In 1909 she married Russell Colt; they had three children. She carried on the family tradition by introducing her daughter, Ethel Colt, in the cast of the film *Scarlet Sister Mary.* In 1928 she was honored when a theater was named for her, and in 1952 she was awarded an honorary doctorate from New York University. Separated from her husband in 1920, she died in 1959 in Hollywood. She had found few roles worthy of her talent; nevertheless, she is recognized as one of America's greatest actors.

Lionel Barrymore (1878-1954)

The eldest of the Barrymore children, Lionel was the most reluctant to accept acting as a profession. From early youth he was interested in art, but at 15 he appeared in *The Rivals* with his grandmother. It was a near-disaster, but he continued in small roles, usually with a famous relative. His first public notice came as the organ grinder in John Drew's 1902 production with the improbable title *The Mummy and the Mockingbird.* He appeared with McKee Rankin and then married Rankin's actress daughter. In 1905 the newlyweds abandoned the stage; his interest in painting prompted Lionel to go to Paris to study at the Académie Julian. By 1909, convinced he had no career in art and lacking anything better to do, he returned to the stage.

Again great success was denied, though he continued in small parts on the stage and in the emerging silent-film field. In 1912 he joined D. W. Griffith in a one-reel film, opposite Mary Pickford, the script by Anita Loos. In 1917 he joined his brother, John, in *Peter Ibbetson.* His best role came the following year in *The Copperhead.* This performance placed him alongside the other greats of his family.

In 1925 Lionel left the stage for Hollywood. He made over 70 films, not counting the Dr. Kildare series. In 1931 he won an Oscar for his performance as the courtroom lawyer in *A Free Soul.* He directed seven films and is also remembered for his radio performances in Dickens's *A Christmas Carol.*

Throughout his life he continued painting as an avocation. Late in life he devoted time to serious musical composition, at which he had some success; one of his works was played by he New York Philharmonic. He was divorced in 1922 and remarried in 1923. He died in Van Nuys, Calif., in 1954.

John Barrymore (1882-1942)

Of the three Barrymore children, John was most haunted by the bright and dark spell of his father. That Maurice ended in an institution was one shadow; John was deeply attached to his grandmother, and her death when he was 15 was another. Perhaps those events can help define the maelstrom of his final years: the talent that mocked itself, the alcoholism, the emotional instability.

John also tried to avoid a stage career, though not as successfully as Lionel. John too attempted a career in art, working for a short time as a newspaper illustrator. But in 1904 he made his New York theatrical debut and for the next several years appeared in musical and light comedy.

In 1916 he turned to serious works. He was cast in Galsworthy's *Justice,* the role establishing his fame. Then came *The Jest, Peter Ibbetson, Redemption,* and, in 1920, Shakespeare's *Richard III,* directed by Arthur Hopkins. Although very successful, it closed after four weeks when John collapsed. In 1922 he returned to Shakespeare in what may have been America's best *Hamlet* of the 20th century, again directed by Hopkins. John always became bored playing long runs; this production lasted 101 performances, breaking by one Edwin Booth's record for the same play. The following season John took the production on tour for nine weeks and then in 1925 presented it at the Haymarket in London, repeating the New York success. When *Hamlet* closed in London he moved to Hollywood, returning to Broadway only once, in 1940, in a mediocre comedy and a parodying performance, *My Dear Children.*

John Barrymore was an important Hollywood personality; his exploits on and off stage helped build the reputation of that glamorous city. Among his better films were *Grand Hotel* (with Greta Garbo), *Romeo and Juliet, Bill of Divorcement, Topaz,* and *Twentieth Century.*

His personal life was stormy. He was married four times, each marriage beginning bright and ending very dark. He had three children. Alcohol became a habit; by 1936 he had difficulty remembering lines. The Hollywood years had earned him a quick fortune, but it was spent even faster. Then, his ability to remember lines gone, he turned to radio in a failing attempt to avoid bankruptcy. He died on May 29, 1942, in Hollywood.

Further Reading

Each of the three Barrymores wrote an autobiography, and each seems to expect the reader to look elsewhere for such factual information as dates and places: Ethel Barrymore, *Memories: An Autobiography* (1955); Lionel Barrymore, *We Barrymores* (1951); and John Barrymore, *Confessions of an Actor* (1926). Gene Fowler, *Good Night, Sweet Prince* (1944), is an intimate biography of John Barrymore with many references to Lionel Barrymore; it deals with its subject as honestly as can be expected from a close friend. A newer work is Hollis Alpert, *The Barrymores* (1964). Barbara Marinacci, *Leading Ladies* (1961), includes a section on Ethel Barrymore. □

Heinrich Barth

The German explorer Heinrich Barth (1821-1865) greatly expanded European knowledge of the western and central Sudan in Africa.

Heinrich Barth was born on Feb. 16, 1821, in Hamburg. He showed remarkable linguistic skill and learned English, French, Spanish, Italian, Arabic, and several African languages. In 1839 he entered the University of Berlin.

From 1845 to 1847 Barth visited most of the Mediterranean countries and then decided to pursue an academic career. Starting as an unsalaried university lecturer, he proved to be unpopular with his associates and a poor teacher and was forced to cancel his classes.

Meanwhile, James Richardson was assembling the English Mixed Scientific and Commercial Expedition to establish trans-Saharan communications with the banks of the Niger for commercial reasons, to help stop the slave trade, and to collect historical, geographical, and scientific information. Needing scientists, he accepted Barth, and they were joined by Dr. Adolf Overweg, also from Hamburg. They set out for the Sudan, crossing the Sahara Desert from Tripoli. Near Lake Chad, Barth and Overweg parted from Richardson because of disagreements. Richardson died in March 1851 and Overweg in September 1852, leaving Barth to complete the expedition.

Barth traveled in the central and western Sudan, and when his contacts with Britain were severed, he was presumed to be dead or lost. But Barth had become fascinated with African life and was carrying on a systematic study of the Sudan.

In the field of geography, Barth's maps and writings gave more complete information on the Sahara and Sudan than had previously been available. In history he discovered fragments of the *Tarikh es Sudan* (History of the Sudan) and the *Diwan* (History of the Kingdom of Bornu) and wrote about the decline of the Fulani empire. In unknown areas he carefully recorded local languages, histories, and trading patterns and described the social and administrative structure of African kingdoms.

Barth's trip to Timbuktu confirmed the reports of the French explorer René Caillié, and Barth's exploration on the upper Benue confirmed that the Benue empties into the Niger and that the Shari empties into Lake Chad. He did extensive work in linguistics, including the compiling of vocabularies for 40 African languages in the Lake Chad area. In 1855 he crossed the Sahara to Tripoli and returned to England in September.

Barth published a five-volume account (1857-1858) of his years in the Sudan, which was of immense value and interest to serious students of Africa but considered dull by most of the reading public. He died in Berlin on Nov. 25, 1865.

Further Reading

The basic reference on Barth is the journal he kept of his 5-year stay in the Sudan. The first American edition was published as *Travels and Discoveries in North and Central Africa* (3 vols., 1857-1859). A shorter version was edited by the British scholar A. H. M. Kirk-Greene as *Travels in Nigeria* (1962). William H. G. Kingston and Charles Rathbone Low, *Great African Travellers* (1904), is a detailed study of Barth's travels. For a good discussion of the motives and methods of explorers, including Barth, see Paul Herrmann, *The Great Age of Discovery* (1958). □

Karl Barth

The Swiss Protestant theologian Karl Barth (1886-1968), a giant in the history of Christian thought, initiated what became the dominant movement in Protestant theology up to the present day.

K arl Barth was born on May 10, 1886, in Basel, the eldest son of a Swiss Reformed minister. Raised in an atmosphere of evangelical piety and theological learning, Karl decided at the age of 16 to become a theologian. Between 1904 and 1908 he was educated at the universities of Bern, Berlin, Tübingen, and Marburg and studied under the leading Protestant religious scholars of the day. In 1908 Barth was ordained to the Swiss Reformed ministry. He then served as pastor of congregations in Geneva (1909-1911) and in the village of Safenwil (1911-1921). In 1913 Barth married Nelly Hoffman, and they had three sons and a daughter.

Early Theology (1919-1931)

Thoroughly educated in the liberal Protestant approaches to Christianity, early in his career Barth came to be troubled by liberalism's easy marriage between Christianity and overconfident modernity. The uncritical support of World War I by leading German intellectuals, including some of Barth's teachers, however, irrevocably exposed for him the bankruptcy of liberalism's religious anthropocentricity.

Faced with the task of preaching each week, Barth turned with fresh eyes to the Bible and discovered there what he was to call a "strange new world." In 1919 his explosive *Commentary on the Epistle to the Romans* catapulted the unknown pastor into international theological prominence. Strongly influenced by the recently discovered 19th-century religious thinker Kierkegaard, *Romans* stressed the "infinite qualitative difference" between God and man. According to the Bible's own testimony, said Barth, revelation is entirely the gracious self-disclosure of the utterly transcendent and otherwise hidden God in the person of Jesus Christ. This revelation is the crisis or judgment of all human activities, including religion. In this work Barth strongly opposed liberal theology's blurring of the divine-human distinction and the subordination of Christian faith and ethics to the passing standard of each historical period.

Romans brought Barth an invitation to become professor of reformed theology at the University of Göttingen in Germany, where he remained from 1921 to 1925. This post was followed by professorships at the universities of Münster (1925-1930) and Bonn (1930-1935). During this period Barth's understanding of the nature and method of Christian theological reflection developed into the mature position of his monumental *Church Dogmatics*. The first volume of the work appeared in 1932, and at Barth's death in 1968 it had grown to 13 volumes and was the most comprehensive exposition of theology since St. Thomas Aquinas's *Summa theologica*. Leading up to this main work were writings such as the sermons and lectures included in *The Word of God and the Word of Man* (1924) and *Theology and Church* (1928); and *Anselm: Fides quaerens intellectum* (1931), a study of the great 11th-century theologian whose method of "faith seeking understanding" had a decisive influence on the direction of Barth's developed theology.

In these early years the theological movement which Barth had begun, variously called "theology of the Word," "theology of crisis," "dialectical theology," "Neo-Reformation theology," and "neo-orthodoxy," attracted in varying degrees men who, with him, became the leading Protestant theologians of this century. Among them were Emil Brunner, Rudolf Bultmann, Dietrich Bonhoeffer, Paul Tillich, and Friedrich Gogarten.

Later Theology (1931-1968)

At Bonn, Barth assumed leadership of those Protestants in Germany who opposed the rising National Socialist or Nazi party. After Hitler came to power, Barth served as the chief drafter of the anti-Nazi Confessing Church's Barmen Declaration (1934), a confession of faith vigorously repudiating Nazi ideology on the basis of the gospel. The following year Barth was expelled from Germany. He returned to his native Basel and was a professor of theology at the university there until his retirement in 1962.

Barth's numerous writings after 1931, besides the successive volumes of *Church Dogmatics,* include *Credo* (1935), which comments on the Apostles' Creed; *The* *Knowledge of God and the Service of God* (1938), which is a good example of Barth's important recovery of the vital theological insights of the Protestant Reformation; *Dogmatics in Outline* (1947), which summarizes his theology; *Against the Stream* (1954), which includes some controversial essays on the cold war, describing communism in theological terms as far different from Nazism; and *Evangelical Theology: An Introduction* (1963), which contains the lectures he gave in the United States during his only visit, in 1962.

A lecture Barth delivered in 1956 entitled "The Humanity of God" (published in *The Humanity of God* [1960]) best describes the development which took place in his theology. He had begun, he said, with the "otherness" of God as the biblical theme which most needed attention; but the direction of his theological was toward a deepening concentration on Jesus Christ as the full revelation of God and therefore the sole object of theological thinking. In this light Barth had come to see more and more fully that the central theme of Scripture is the "togetherness" of the sovereign God and creaturely man in Christ—God's "humanity" in the Incarnation.

Barth's theological "revolution" was a dynamic, nonfundamentalistic recovery of the biblical message as the proclamation of the unique self-disclosure of God to man in Jesus Christ. He believed that Christian theology ought always to derive its entire thinking on God, man, sin, ethics, and society from what can actually be seen in Jesus as witnessed by the Old and New Testaments rather than from sources independent of this revelation. His voluminous writings explore the inexhaustibly fruitful implications of his total Christ-centeredness.

Thomas Oden said of him: "Barth looked like a casting agency's idea of a German professor, with his shock of wavy gray hair, high forehead and cheekbones, craggy eyebrows. His owlish eyes peered occasionally over his horn-rimmed glasses, which often sat at the tip of his nose. He was known for his geniality, modesty, patience and sympathy, and above all a pixyish sense of humor." Barth's chief avocation was a passionate love of Mozart's music. He died on Dec. 9, 1968.

Further Reading

Numerous studies of Barth's life and thought are available. Among the best in English are Thomas F. Torrance, *Karl Barth: An Introduction to His Early Theology, 1910-1931* (1962); George Casalis, *Portrait of Karl Barth* (trans. 1963); Herbert Hartwell, *The Theology of Karl Barth: An Introduction* (1964); and Thomas C. Oden, *The Promise of Barth: The Ethics of Freedom* (1969).

Additional Sources

Busch, Eberhard, *Karl Barth: his life from letters and autobiographical texts,* London: S.C.M. Press, 1976. □

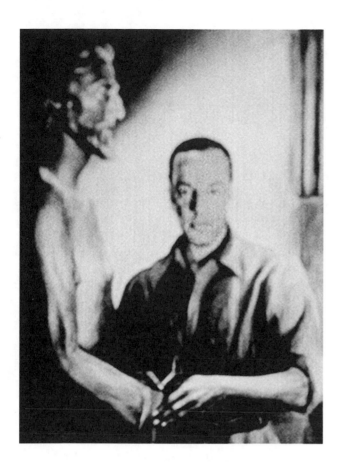

Richmond Barthé

Richmond Barthé (1901–1989) was a pioneer in American sculpture in the 1930s and 1940s in that he was one of the first African American artists to focus thematically on the lives of blacks, both in the United States and in Africa.

Trailblazing artist Richmond Barthé's sculpted works were seminal in that they focused on the lives of his fellow African Americans. He depicted African Americans at work in the fields of the South (*Woman with Scythe,* 1944), African Americans of distinction, and, in *Mother and Son* (1939), African Americans as victims of racial violence. He also sculpted images of African warriors and ceremonial participants.

Barthé was born on January 28, 1901, in Bay St. Louis, Mississippi, to Richmond Barthé, Sr., and Marie Clementine Robateau. His father died before Barthé was a year old, and his mother's sewing supported the family. She later re-married, to William Franklin, an old friend and Barthé's godfather. Franklin worked in various odd jobs, including as an ice man, delivering ice throughout the rural community. According to Barthé, he was artistically inclined from a very young age. In *A History of African American Artists,* he is quoted as saying, "When I was crawling on the floor, my mother gave me paper and pencil to play with. It kept me quiet and she did her errands. At six years old I started

painting. A lady my mother sewed for gave me a set of watercolors. By that time I could draw pretty well."

As a teenager, Barthé's artistic talent had attracted attention among several of his mother's clients, and among his stepfather's ice customers as well. Barthé used to help in the delivery during the summer. One of the customers, who knew of and admired Barthé's work, told the young boy that he would injure himself carrying such large chunks of ice all day long. She arranged for him to get a job with the Pond family in New Orleans, a very wealthy family with several homes and an interest in supporting the arts. Barthé stayed with the Ponds for several years, working as their houseboy while being encouraged to continue drawing and painting. Around this time, Barthé met Lyle Saxon, a writer working for the *New Orleans Times-Picayune,* and the two men became good friends. Saxon was very interested in Barthé's work and remained a champion of the artist after he became a well-known novelist.

Around 1923, a Catholic priest took an interest in Barthé's work and began looking for a local art school for him to attend. In the South, however, no school would admit a black, so the priest paid for Barthé to attend the prestigious Art Institute of Chicago. Here, Barthé rapidly developed as an artist, studying with several important teachers. Barthé's most influential teacher was Charles Schroeder. It was ultimately Schroeder who suggested that Barthé try sculpture. Schroeder did not intend to suggest that Barthé, who was mainly a painter then, shift his medium, but for him to incorporate three dimensions into his art. It turned out, however, that Barthé was a gifted sculptor, as was immediately apparent from the creation of his first busts in art school. An Art Institute show included three of his works. From that show, Barthé received his first commission as a sculptor. The Lake County Children's Home in Gary, Indiana, saw Barthé's work and hired him to do busts of Henry O. Tanner and Toussaint L'Ouverture for its home. Barthé, who had taken no classes in sculpting, thus began a career as a sculptor. His talents so impressed his teachers at the Institute that they advised him not to take any classes, fearing that formal training might ruin the creative spark in his work.

Having taken up sculpture, Barthé's began drawing the kind of critical attention artists dream about but rarely achieve at such a young age. In 1929, just out of art school, Barthé received an offer for a one-man show in New York, a tremendous honor. Barthé, however, was reluctant to accept, feeling he had not fully developed yet, not wanting to show in an important art center such as New York until he had refined his form more. Barthé declined the offer and spent a year studying at the Art Students League in New York. In 1930, after returning to Chicago, he had a large show at the Women's City Club. The show was a major success and it won him a Julius Rosenwald Fund fellowship.

In 1931, Barthé felt he was finally ready for a New York show and one was arranged at the Caz-Delbo Gallery, a prestigious showcase. Barthé's work at this show drew high praise and Barthé moved to the city when his Rosenwald fellowship was continued. In 1933, he exhibited at the Chicago World's Fair and, in 1934, Xavier University in

New Orleans awarded him an honorary master of arts degree. In 1934, Barthé had a show at the Whitney Museum of American Art in New York, the preeminent contemporary art museum in the country. After the show, the museum purchased three of Barthé's sculptures for its permanent collection. By this time, Barthé was selling so much work that for the first time he could abandon side jobs and devote himself entirely to art.

Later in 1934, he went to Europe where the cultural heritage he observed fascinated him and where he also made several important sales to private collectors. In 1939, Barthé held his second one-man show in New York. It was his largest exhibition to date, including 18 bronze works, and was held at the Arden Galleries. Again, critical response was enthusiastic and on the strength of the work exhibited at these shows, Barthé was awarded a Guggenheim fellowship in 1940 and in 1941. In 1943, *The Boxer* was purchased by the Metropolitan Museum of Art in New York, America's largest and most important museum.

After the Second World War, the world of art began to change drastically, focusing on abstraction or distorted representations of reality. Barthé was not interested in these trends and was increasingly forgotten by the artistic establishment. As a result, Barthé began devoting much of his time to making portrait busts for wealthy New York clients, especially people involved in the theater. During and after the war, Barthé made busts of John Gielgud and Maurice Evans. Later works were of Lawrence Olivier, Katharine Cornell, and Judith Anderson. In 1946, he was inducted into the National Institute of Arts and Letters. By the end of the 1940s, Barthé had grown tired of the art scene in New York (and depressed over his exclusion from it) and he bought a house in Jamaica on the advice of his doctor who told him that living in the city was hurting his health.

Over the next several years, Barthé became a tourist attraction on the island, while continuing to work. In 1953, he completed a forty-foot statue for the city of Port au Prince, Haiti, depicting Jean Jacques Dessalines, leader of the 1804 revolution. He also designed several Haitian coins that are still in use. At first, Barthé enjoyed the prestige of being an expatriate black artist living in seclusion on a small Caribbean island, but by 1969 he had grown restless and decided to move to Europe. He first went to Switzerland and then, in 1970, he moved to Florence. He stayed in Italy for the next seven years, then sold everything he owned and moved to California, where he rented an apartment from an admirer. Growing increasingly impoverished and old, and getting sick as well, Barthé became a charity case. The actor James Garner, who had only recently met him, was shocked that he should be living so poorly and began secretly paying his rent and medical expenses. Other artists and actors began to help Barthé too. The city of Pasadena renamed Barthé's street Barthé Drive. A fund-raising drive was also mounted to found the Barthé Historical Society and to fund thirty Barthé scholarships for artists.

Barthé's last known work was a bust of James Garner, made in appreciation for all of Garner's help late in Barthé's life. Barthé died on March 5, 1989.

Further Reading

Bearden, Romare, *A History of African American Artists, from 1792 to the present,* Pantheon Books, 1993.
Fine, Elsa Honig, "A Search for Identity," in *The Afro-American Artists,* Hacker Art Books, 1982.
New York Times, March 6, 1989. ☐

Sir Frederic Charles Bartlett

The British psychologist Sir Frederic Charles Bartlett (1886-1969) made his main contribution through the development of applied experimental psychology in Britain during and after World War II.

Frederic Bartlett was born on Oct. 22, 1886. He was educated privately and at St. John's College, Cambridge, of which he became a fellow. Strongly influenced by the physician, ethnologist, and psychologist W.H.R. Rivers, Bartlett showed early leanings toward anthropology; but circumstances, not the least of which was the outbreak of World War I, led him to a career in psychology. After the war Bartlett returned to Cambridge, succeeding C.S. Myers as director of the psychological laboratory in 1922 and becoming professor of experimental psychology in 1931, a post which he held until his retirement in 1952. He died at Cambridge on Sept. 30, 1969.

Bartlett's early interests lay in the experimental study of perception and memory. He distrusted the overanalytical approach of the German workers and endeavored to make the conditions of his experiments as lifelike as possible. In his book *Remembering: A Study in Experimental and Social Psychology* (1932), which had considerable influence, he brought together the results of a long series of experiments. Bartlett laid special stress upon the extent of reconstruction, and even invention, that takes place in recall and upon the part played by attitude, interest, and social convention in governing it. He later carried further the approach developed in *Remembering* to the study of other higher mental processes, in particular, thinking, and published a short book on the subject, *Thinking: An Experimental and Social Study* (1958).

Problems in Applied Psychology

On the outbreak of World War II, Bartlett turned over the resources of his laboratory almost entirely to applied work, and problems were brought to him in ever-increasing numbers by the armed services and by various government bodies. These problems were concerned with such matters as equipment design, training methods, fatigue, and personnel selection. To tackle them, Bartlett brought together a noteworthy group of young experimental psychologists under the leadership of K.J.W. Craik. Many of these were subsequently incorporated into the Medical Research Council's Applied Psychology Research Unit, of which Bartlett assumed direction after Craik's death. While mostly concerned with applied work, Bartlett was always alert to its potential scientific value and its importance for developing realistic theories of human behavior.

Outside experimental psychology, Bartlett retained his interest in anthropology, publishing the book *Psychology and Primitive Culture* (1923) and sponsoring the influential collective volume *The Study of Society: Methods and Problems* (1939). In his numerous papers on social issues, he invariably stressed the extent of common ground and the need to develop more disciplined research methods.

Bartlett played a leading part in the growth and development of psychology in Britain for more than 40 years. He was elected a fellow of the Royal Society in 1932, received seven honorary degrees, and was knighted in 1948.

Further Reading

Bartlett wrote a short account of his early life and of the history of the Cambridge Psychological Laboratory up to 1935 in Carl Murchison, ed., *A History of Psychology in Autobiography*, vol. 3 (1936). Muzafer Sherif, *Social Interaction: Process and Products* (1967), discusses social psychology and mentions Bartlett's contributions. □

Béla Bartók

Béla Bartók (1881-1945) was a Hungarian composer and pianist. His profound studies of folk songs not only revolutionized scholarship in this field but also furnished him with rich sources for his own creative work.

In the 19th century the wealth of Magyar folk music was virtually unknown to Hungarian composers. When Béla Bartók first transcribed a Hungarian folk tune in the field in 1904, he realized that this world of music was unknown to him. Subjecting it to systematic study, he soon gained a new basis for his musical esthetics. His mature work was founded on the assimilation of the essence of Hungarian folk music into his personal musical language. Appreciation of this accomplishment often lagged during his lifetime; in the quarter century after his death, however, Bartók's status as a major musical figure was firmly established.

Bartók was born in Nagyszentmiklós, Hungary (now Sânnicolaul-Mare, Romania), on March 25, 1881. His father was director of a government agricultural school; his mother, a teacher and pianist. She gave Béla his first piano lesson on his fifth birthday; his great gifts as pianist soon became evident, and at the age of 9 he began to compose. After he entered the Academy of Music at Budapest in 1899, his composing temporarily stopped. However, in 1902 the first Budapest performance of Richard Strauss's *Also sprach Zarathustra* inspired him to resume creative work. Bartók's first major composition was the symphonic poem *Kossuth* (1903). Three years later his first work based upon Hungarian peasant music was published: the *Twenty Hungarian Folksongs,* produced in collaboration with Zoltán Kodály (each composer set 10 songs).

In 1907 Bartók became professor of piano at the Academy of Music in Budapest. His tenure lasted nearly 30 years, being interrupted occasionally for folk-song research and concert tours. His first wife, Márta Ziegler, and second wife, Ditta Pásztory, were both his piano pupils. He never taught composition, fearing that to do so might endanger his own creative work.

Important Bartók works composed between 1907 and 1922 include the opera *Bluebeard's Castle* (1911), the First and Second String Quartets (1909, 1918), the ballet *The Wooden Prince* (1914-1916), the two Violin and Piano Sonatas (1921-1922), and the pantomime *The Miraculous Mandarin* (1918-1919).

After World War I Bartók intensified his career as a concert pianist. He gave the first performances of his first two Piano Concertos (1927, 1930-1931). In 1927 he made his first United States tour, performing a number of his own works to mixed critical reception. Significant compositions include the *Two Rhapsodies* for violin and piano (1928), the Fourth and Fifth String Quartets (1928, 1934), the *Cantata profana* (1930), and the earliest books of *Mikrokosmos,* which is a series of 153 progressive pieces for piano on which Bartók worked from 1926 to 1939.

Bartók's Views on Folk Music

Bartók's artistic intent at this point in his career is excellently summarized in his essay "The Influence of Peasant Music on Modern Music" (1931). He describes the various ways in which folk music can be transmuted into contemporary art music. In the simplest form the folk melody may be taken over unchanged or only slightly varied, with the addition of an accompaniment and perhaps some opening and closing phrases. The additional material may be merely ornamental in nature, or it may be of primary importance. The next logical step is for the composer to invent his own imitation of a folk melody, then to treat it exactly like the borrowed tune. To Bartók it made no difference whether the composer invented his own themes or borrowed material. He stated emphatically that the composer "has a right to use musical material from all sources. What he has judged suitable for his purpose has become through the very use his mental property.... The question of origins can only be interesting from the point of view of musical documentation."

The highest form of folk-influenced music, Bartók believed, is that in which the folk atmosphere has been completely assimilated. He described such music as follows: "Neither peasant music nor imitations of peasant melodies can be found in his [the composer's] music, but it is pervaded by the atmosphere of peasant music. In this case we may say he has completely absorbed the idiom of peasant music which has become his musical mother tongue." No better description could be given of the part played by folk music in Bartók's mature work.

Later Works

The political situation of Hungary became more and more unsettled in the mid-1930s. During this period Bartók produced important works: *Music for Strings, Percussion, and Celesta* (1936); *Sonata for Two Pianos and Percussion* (1937); *Contrasts* for violin, clarinet, and piano (1938); the Violin Concerto (1937-1938); and the Sixth String Quartet (1939). When Nazi Germany annexed Austria in 1938, he realized he would have to leave Hungary soon. After the death of his mother in 1939 his last tie was broken.

The following year Bartók and his wife settled in New York City. He was given a temporary appointment at Columbia University, transcribing the records of Serbo-Croatian folk songs in the Parry Collection, which lasted through 1942. Bartók's persistent ill health and resultant inability to perform publicly or to take another position left his financial situation precarious. Fortunately he received important commissions, and assistance from the American Society of Composers, Authors, and Publishers. The *Concerto for Orchestra* (1943) was commissioned by Serge Koussevitzky; the solo Violin Sonata (1944) by Yehudi Menuhin; and the Viola Concerto (1945) by William Primrose. The last-named work remained unfinished; it was completed by Tibor Serly, one of Bartók's pupils. Bartók worked on his Third Piano Concerto, which he composed for his wife, until a few days before his death. The last 17 measures were still incomplete when he died of leukemia on Sept. 26, 1945.

Bartók's works have steadily risen in popularity since his death. *The Concerto For Orchestra, Music for Strings, Percussion, and Celesta,* and *Sonata for Two Pianos and Percussion* have been widely performed and recorded; the six String Quartets belong to the classic repertory of 20th-century chamber music; and *Mikrokosmos* is considered standard piano-teaching material.

Further Reading

The standard biography of Bartók in English is Halsey Stevens, *The Life and Music of Béla Bartók* (1953; rev. ed. 1964). An excellent collection of essays from *Tempo* magazine, including selections from Bartók's writings, is *Béla Bartók: A Memorial Review* (1950). Agatha Fassett, *The Naked Face of Genius: Béla Bartók's American Years* (1958), gives a moving account of Bartók's last years. Bence Szabolcsi, *Béla Bartók, His Life in Pictures* (1956; trans. 1964), is a good pictorial biography. □

Bruce Barton

Bruce Barton (1886-1967), American business executive and Congressman, was the most famous advertising man of his day, thanks to his best-selling book *The Man Nobody Knows*.

Bruce Barton was born on August 5, 1886, in Robbins, Tennessee. Most of his youth, however, was spent in Oak Park, Illinois, where his father was pastor of the town's Congregational church. Young Barton showed an early interest in journalism. While still in high school he was both editor of the school paper and a reporter for the local weekly. He graduated from Amherst College in 1907, after having been voted Phi Beta Kappa, head of the student council, and "man most likely to succeed."

From 1907 to 1911 Barton was editor of two small magazines in Chicago, the *Home Herald* and *Housekeeper,* neither of which prospered. In 1912 he moved to New York City to become assistant sales manager in the publishing house of P. F. Collier and Son. It was there that Barton first revealed a talent for advertising. In 1913 he was assigned the task of writing the advertisements for the firm's *Harvard Classics* series of reprints. His eye-catching headlines and compelling texts helped sell over 400,000 copies. From 1914 to 1918 he tried his hand at journalism again, this time as editor of *Every Week* magazine. When that magazine failed he managed publicity for the United War Work Campaign, a fund drive for charitable organizations aiding the troops in World War I.

In 1919 Barton joined with fellow workers from the campaign to form the advertising agency that would later become known as Batten, Barton, Durstine, and Osborne. Barton was the chief copywriter and main creative force within the new agency. Barton could craft memorable lines for virtually any product or service—whether it be a correspondence school ("A wonderful two years' trip at full pay—but only men with imagination can take it") or electrical appliances ("Any woman who is doing any household task that a little electric motor can do is working for three cents an hour; human life is too precious to be sold at a price of three cents an hour").

United States Steel, seeking to improve its image after a damaging strike in 1919, was an early client. It was soon joined by such corporate giants as General Electric and General Motors. For General Mills, Barton created the character of "Betty Crocker," one of the most enduring symbols in American advertising.

Yet it was not his business skills that won Barton his widest fame. The average American knew him best as the author of countless magazine articles and newspaper columns on the themes of optimism and success. So popular was his message that his writings were collected in books with such titles as *More Power to You* (1919), *Better Days* (1924), and *On the Up and Up* (1929). But by far his greatest success as a writer was *The Man Nobody Knows,* published in 1925. In it Barton attempted to rectify what he considered the "sissified" image of Jesus presented in the Sunday schools. In Barton's retelling of the gospel story, Jesus was a go-getting young executive who "picked up twelve men from the bottom ranks of business and forged them into an organization that conquered the world." There were some who felt that Barton's portrayal of Jesus made religion seem too much a business, or business too much a religion. But the critics were a small minority. *The Man Nobody Knows* topped best-seller lists for two years. It was soon followed on the lists by *The Book Nobody Knows* (1926), Barton's reflections on the Bible.

When not directing his growing business or writing best-sellers, Barton was actively involved in politics. He was an early backer of his fellow Amherst alumnus, Calvin Coolidge, and from 1919 onwards he was a respected advisor to the national Republican party. In 1937 he ran for office himself, winning a seat in the U.S. Congress left vacant by the death of the incumbent.

During the two terms he represented his Manhattan district Barton emerged as one of the most effective opponents of President Franklin D. Roosevelt's New Deal. In 1940 he helped secure the Republican presidential nomination for dark-horse candidate Wendell Wilkie. Barton, meanwhile, attempted to unseat James Mead, the Democratic senator from New York. But in the end the master ad man fell victim to a clever slogan. President Roosevelt's sarcastic reference to his Congressional adversaries as "Martin, Barton, and Fish (linking Barton to Joseph Martin, the House minority leader, and Hamilton Fish, an isolationist congressman) became a catch phrase of that campaign year and helped ensure Barton's defeat.

Barton never again sought public office. After the election he returned to the active management of his advertising agency. In its early years the agency was primarily known for institutional advertising designed to enhance the public image of large corporations. But after World War II, and particularly after the hiring of Ben Duffy as president in 1946, the firm moved aggressively into the advertising of consumer goods. Companies such as Lever Brothers, Campbell Soup, and Revlon were added to the agency's growing list of clients. When Barton retired as chairman of the board in 1961, Batten, Barton, Durstine, and Osborne was the fourth-largest advertising firm in the United States.

During his retirement Barton maintained an office on Madison Avenue and continued to write for the popular press. Bruce Barton died in New York City on July 5, 1967. He had married the former Esther Randall in 1913. She died in 1951. The couple had three children.

Further Reading

For Bruce Barton's place in advertising history, see Stephen Fox, *The Mirror Makers: A History of American Advertising and Its Creators* (1984). Martin Mayer, *Madison Avenue, U.S.A.* (1958) provides an inside look at Batten, Barton, Durstine, and Osborne during Barton's later years. □

Clara Barton

The American humanitarian Clara Barton (1821-1912) was the founder of the American Red Cross. Her work made her a symbol of humanitarianism.

Clara Barton was born on Dec. 25, 1821, in North Oxford, Mass. She was the youngest child of Stephen Barton, a farmer and state legislator who had served in the Revolution under Gen. Anthony Wayne; she later recalled that his tales made war early familiar to her.

Well-spoken and well-read, at the age of 15 Clara Barton began teaching at nearby schools. In 1850 she went to teach at Bordentown, N.J., where state tradition required paid schooling and thus served few children. Barton offered to teach without salary if payment were waived. She later took pride in having established the first free school in New Jersey and having raised enrollment in Bordentown from 6 to 600. When town officials decided to appoint a male administrator over her, she resigned. At this time she suffered her first crisis of nervous illness, associated in part with uncertainty about her future.

In 1853 she obtained an appointment as copyist in the Patent Office in Washington, D.C., becoming the first woman in America to hold such a government post. She continued this work till April 1861, when the Civil War began and she determined to serve the Federal troops.

Civil War Activities

Although the U.S. Sanitary Commission was formed in June 1861 to aid soldiers, Barton had little association with it. (Casual reports later misnamed her as one of its founders.) Her own enterprise involved appeals for provisions to be carried into the war zones; she collected and stored them in Washington for personal distribution. In 1862 the U.S. surgeon general permitted her to travel to the front, and she implemented this order with directives from generals John Pope and James S. Wadsworth, who welcomed her work. Barton was present with Federal forces during the siege of Charleston, S.C., and also at engagements in the Wilderness and at Fredericksburg, Va., and elsewhere.

Barton's mission was not primarily that of a nurse. She became increasingly adept at obtaining and passing out

provisions, though her courage and humanity made her a vital presence everywhere. In 1864 she made her most influential connection, joining Gen. Benjamin F. Butler with the Army of the James. She later visited the notorious prison camp at Andersonville, Ga., to identify and mark Union graves.

In 1865 she conceived the project of locating missing soldiers and obtained a note of endorsement from President Lincoln. She set up the Bureau of Records in Washington and traced perhaps 20,000 names. She also lectured on her experiences until her voice failed in 1868.

Franco-Prussian War

Barton's health continued to trouble her; in 1869 she went to Geneva, Switzerland, for rest and a change. There, officials of the International Red Cross, organized in 1864, urged her to seek United States agreement to the Geneva Convention recognizing the work of the Red Cross; the powerful U.S. Sanitary Commission had been unable to obtain it. But before Barton could turn to the task, the Franco-Prussian War began.

She offered her services to the Grand Duchess of Baden in administering military hospitals. Her most original idea (developed further in later situations) was to put needy Strasbourg women to work sewing garments for pay. Later, with the French defeated and Paris held by the Commune, she entered the starving city to distribute food and clothing. She served elsewhere in France—in Lyons again instituting her work system. She was awarded the Iron Cross of Merit by the German emperor, William I, in 1873; this was one of many such honors.

American Red Cross

Clara Barton settled in Danville, N.Y., where for several years she was a semi-invalid. In 1877 she wrote a founder of the International Red Cross, offering to lead an American branch of the organization. Thus, at 56 she began a new career.

In 1881 Barton incorporated the American Red Cross, with herself as president. A year later her extraordinary efforts brought about United States ratification of the Geneva Convention. She herself attended conferences of the International Red Cross as the American representative. She was, however, far from bureaucratic in interests. Although wholly individualistic and unlike reformers who worked on programs for social change, she did a great social service as activist and propagandist.

In 1883 Barton served as superintendent of the Women's Reformatory Prison, Sherborn, Mass., thus deviating from a career marked by single-minded commitment to her major cause. As a Red Cross worker, she went to Michigan, which had been ravaged by fires in 1882, and to Charleston, S.C., which had suffered an earthquake. In 1884 she traveled the Ohio River, supplying flood victims. Five years later she went to Johnstown, Pa., to help it recover from a disastrous flood. In 1891 Barton traveled to Russia, which was enduring famine, and in 1896 to Turkey, following the Armenian massacres. Barton was in her late 70s when the Cuban insurrection required relief measures. She prepared to sail in aid of Cubans, but the outbreak of the Spanish-American War turned her ship into a welfare station for Americans as well. As late as 1900 she visited Galveston, Tex., personally to supervise relief for victims of a tidal wave. In 1900 Congress reincorporated the Red Cross, demanding an accounting of funds. By 1904 public pressures and dissension within the Red Cross itself had become too much for Barton, and on June 16 she resigned from the organization. (She even entertained unrealistic thoughts of beginning another one.) A figure of international renown, she retired instead to Glen Echo, Md., where she died on April 12, 1912.

Further Reading

Clara Barton was the subject of innumerable sketches and books, many merely eulogistic and even fanciful. She herself wrote *The Story of My Childhood* (1907), as well as enlightening accounts of her work, such as *The Red Cross in Peace and War* (1899). Most useful for general purposes is Ishbel Ross, *Angel of the Battlefield: The Life of Clara Barton* (1956). William E. Barton, *Life of Clara Barton, Founder of the American Red Cross* (2 vols., 1922), is adulatory but reproduces revealing letters. Percy H. Epler, *The Life of Clara Barton* (1915), details her life as it appeared to her contemporaries. ☐

Sir Edmund Barton

The Australian statesman and jurist Sir Edmund Barton (1849-1920) was a leading protagonist for federal union. As prime minister from the inauguration of the Commonwealth of Australia, he played a key role in the early phase of national administration.

Edmund Barton was born on Jan. 18, 1849, in Sydney and was educated there, graduating from the University of Sydney. He practiced law from 1871 and at the age of 30 was elected to the New South Wales Legislative Assembly. For 4 years from 1883 he was Speaker of the House. In 1889 and again from 1891 to 1893 he was attorney general.

For many years "inherent laziness" appeared to keep Barton from attaining the success his talents merited. But from the early 1890s he threw himself into the campaign to federate the Australian colonies. He was prominent in the Federal Convention which met in Sydney in 1891, helping to draft a bill to constitute the Commonwealth. When the aging Sir Henry Parkes retired, Barton accepted leadership of the federalists in New South Wales, and he kept the issue of colonial union alive in the face of strong opposition within the colonial legislature. Out of Parliament from 1894, he addressed hundreds of public meetings from which grew a movement to call the popularly elected Federal Convention of 1897. In the poll he gained three of every four votes cast in New South Wales and was subsequently made "leader of the convention" and chairman of its constitution-drafting committee. After the convention's recommendations were accepted by the various colonial electorates, Barton headed the delegation which sought approval of the measure by the British Cabinet.

With the Commonwealth Act in force, Barton was the only man acceptable to his colleagues as prime minister, and he was commissioned to form the first Australian Cabinet, which was sworn in on Jan. 1, 1901. In recognition for his services he was knighted in 1902.

Barton's administration quickly gained parliamentary approval for the Immigration Restriction Act, blocking admission of Asians by giving the immigration examiner the right to impose a dictation test in any European language he cared to choose. A separate act closed the door to South Sea Islanders and provided for repatriation of those already working on Queensland's sugar plantations.

He was soon plagued by what he described as "rancorous party strife," and having attained his objective of a united Australia, he decided in September 1903 to accept the second judgeship in the newly formed High Court of Australia. His distinguished career on the Court continued until his death from heart failure on Jan. 7, 1920.

Further Reading

A useful biography is John Reynolds, *Edmund Barton* (1948), which contains an appreciative foreword by Robert G. Menzies. Comments on events leading to federation are given in Alfred Deakin, *The Federal Story: The Inner History of the Federal Cause, 1880-1900*, edited by J. A. LaNauze (1944; 2d ed. 1963). Background is provided in John Quick and Robert Randolf Garran, *The Annotated Constitution of the Australian Commonwealth* (1901); H. G. Turner, *The First Decade of the*

Australian Commonwealth 1901-1910 (1911); Bernhard Ringrose Wise, *The Making of the Australian Commonwealth, 1889-1900* (1913); George Houstoun Reid, *My Reminiscences* (1917); Arther Norman Smith, *Thirty Years: The Commonwealth of Australia, 1901-31* (1933); Louise Overacker, *The Australian Party System* (1952); and John Quick, *Sir John Quick's Notebook,* edited by L. E. Freedman (1965). □

John Bartram

John Bartram (1699-1777) was the first native-born American botanist. He achieved considerable international fame as a collector of botanical specimens.

John Bartram was born on March 23, 1699, near Darby, Pa. He spent his youth farming, which may have sparked his interest in plants. His attempts to learn botany by purchasing books brought him to the attention of some Philadelphians, most notably James Logan, who encouraged him in the more systematic pursuit of that science. In 1728 Bartram purchased a plot of ground near Kingsessing, just below Philadelphia on the Schuylkill River, where he laid out a botanical garden and built a stone house. This garden, which survives in part to this day, was a mecca for visiting botanists throughout his lifetime and afterward.

Probably through Logan, who was William Penn's secretary, Bartram came into contact with a fellow Quaker, Peter Collinson, the London naturalist who acted as a patron to several American scientists. Their correspondence after 1733 provides many insights into the circumstances of the adoption of new plants in the respective countries. Collinson arranged for Bartram to collect specimens for him in America, providing partial support for the relatively poor American. The relationship between the two scientists was very close, and Collinson thought of Bartram as his pupil. Bartram's contact with Collinson brought him to the attention of Carl Linnaeus and other European naturalists, and Bartram established, through his collection of seeds and plant specimens, a substantial European reputation before he was well known in America.

Collecting New World Specimens

Bartram made several long-range collecting expeditions, some of them financed partly by European naturalists. He traveled 1100 miles across the Blue Ridge Mountains in 1738, explored the Catskill Mountains in 1755, and in 1760 traveled through the Carolinas. He was, however, forced to farm and to practice medicine locally in order to support his large family. Only in 1765, when Collinson got him an appointment as botanist to the king, was he assured of a steady income of any sort. Bartram was very honest and blunt, and he told Collinson that the £50 he was to receive for the post was not enough.

His European reputation brought Bartram to the notice of other American naturalists, particularly Cadwallader Colden of New York and Alexander Garden of South Carolina. Although some correspondence and cooperation oc-

curred between these American botanists, Garden and especially Colden (who had mastered the Linnaean system of classification) felt that Bartram lacked the systematic skills to go beyond simple collecting. Bartram seems to have been attracted to the field by a love of plants and living, growing things, rather than from any abstract sense of scientific accomplishment. He possessed excellent powers of observation but never became a systematic specialist in the modern sense of the word. His interests ranged also to geology, and he suggested a geological survey of the country to determine the potential usefulness of various parts of the North American continent. He also suggested a general western exploration expedition similar to that later accomplished by Lewis and Clark.

Bartram regretted his lack of opportunity to further his education and training in the sciences in the New World, and he became one of the founding spirits of what developed into the American Philosophical Society, America's first scientific society. Disagreement over the founding of this organization in 1743 may have contributed to Bartram's estrangement from his onetime sponsor James Logan. The Philosophical Society was not permanently founded at this time, and most of the support for Bartram's work continued to come from Europe, indicating that the Colonies were not yet strong enough to support a scientific establishment on their own.

Bartram was a person of very independent character, a complete individualist who, though he was willing to carry out projects for Peter Collinson, took little direction from others. Read out of a Quaker meeting for his unwillingness to acknowledge the divinity of Christ, he nevertheless carried his deep convictions to the point of freeing his slaves and rehiring them as paid servants. As for Native Americans, however, a frightening experience near Pittsburgh made him less tolerant. Thus, his humanitarianism, like his career, was individualistic rather than consistent.

His Significance

Bartram published journals of his travels, the most important of which was *Observations on the Inhabitants, Climate, Soil, etc . . . Made by John Bartram in His Travels from Pennsylvania to . . . Lake Ontario* (1751). The most significant part of his work was actual collecting of specimens for Collinson and others. In his celebrated garden he began some work with hybrid plants which, though not systematic, stimulated interest. The garden itself and Bartram's home became a focal point for botanical activity in the Colonies. His lack of knowledge of systematic classification seems, curiously, to have bothered his ambitious American friends more than it did the European scientists. Though some have suggested that he was in effect a "creation" of the gifted Londoner Collinson, at the time of his death, on Sept. 22, 1777, Bartram was regarded by Linnaeus as the greatest contemporary "natural botanist" in the world

Bartram married Mary Morris in 1723, by whom he had two sons. On her death in 1727, he married Ann Mendenhall, by whom he had five sons and four daughters.

Much of his energy was devoted to supporting this large family.

Further Reading

A selection of writings by John and William Bartram is available in Helen Gere Cruickshank, ed., *John and William Bartram's America: Selections from the Writings of the Philadelphia Naturalists* (1957). The standard biography of Bartram is Ernest Earnest, *John and William Bartram, Botanists and Explorers* (1940), replacing the older William Darlington, *Memorials of John Bartram and Humphrey Marshall: With Notices of Their Botanical Contemporaries* (1849). A popular account can be found in Josephine Herbst, *New Green World* (1954). General background is in Brooke Hindle, *The Pursuit of Science in Revolutionary America, 1735-1789* (1956).

Additional Sources

Berkeley, Edmund, *The life and travels of John Bartram from Lake Ontario to the River St. John,* Tallahassee: University Presses of Florida, 1982. ☐

William Bartram

The American naturalist William Bartram (1739-1823) published an account of his botanical expedition to the southeastern United States that was widely read in his country and Europe.

William Bartram was born on Feb. 9, 1739, near Philadelphia, Pa., in the house built by his father, John Bartram, the noted botanist. William displayed considerable talent for drawing in his youth but was not immediately interested in botanical work, instead engaging in trade for several years in Philadelphia and near Cape Fear, N.C. He began collecting botanial specimens in 1765-1766, while accompanying his father on a trip up the St. Johns River in Florida.

In 1768 Peter Collinson, a friend of the elder Bartram, showed some of the young man's drawings to George Edwards, the English naturalist, and to Dr. John Fothergill, a noted London physician. Fothergill extended his patronage to the young Bartram and in 1773-1777 sponsored his exploratory trip through the Southeast. Specimens were sent to Fothergill, but in 1778, on his return to Philadelphia, Bartram seems to have lost interest in continuing his work, refusing the offer of Benjamin Smith Barton to add to and publish his accounts.

On his father's death William began joint management of the gardens on the Schuylkill River with his brother John. By 1791 William had managed the Philadelphia publication, by subscription, of his account of his southeastern explorations, *Travels through North and South Carolina, Georgia, and E. and W. Florida,* his major contribution to science. It was immensely popular in Europe and went through many editions and translations, eventually providing inspiration to romantic poets such as Wordsworth and Coleridge (whose *Kubla Khan* and *Ancient Mariner*

were influenced by the work). He also furnished materials to Benjamin Smith Barton which found their way into Barton's publications *Elements of Botany* and *Essay toward a Materia Medica.*

Bartram was influential in starting the young Scot Alexander Wilson on his study of North American bird life. Chronic ill health forced him to decline the position of professor of botany at the University of Pennsylvania, offered in 1782, and the post of botanist on the Lewis and Clark expedition.

His botanical work is noted for its splendid imagery and eloquence. His standards of completeness and accuracy were high, and his list of native species of birds was excelled only by the later work of his protégé and friend Wilson. His dependability was not great, however, and his actual production of major works was limited to the *Travels.* Neither he nor his brother John rivaled the scope of their father, but William clearly inherited his father's scientific talent. The *Travels* was the first comprehensive treatment of the southeastern United States, including descriptions of flora and fauna, geologic formations, and Native American tribes. William never married. He died suddenly at his beloved gardens on July 22, 1823.

Further Reading

Bartrams's major work has been reprinted as *The Travels of William Bartram,* an edition by Mark Van Doren (1955). The standard biography is Nathan Bryllion Fagin, *William Bartram, Interpreter of the American Landscape* (1933). Ernest Earnest, *John and William Bartram, Botanists and Explorers*

(1940), is also useful. General background is in Brooke Hindle, *The Pursuit of Science in Revolutionary America, 1735-1789* (1956). □

Bernard Mannes Baruch

American statesman Bernard Mannes Baruch (1870-1965), a successful financier, served as chairman of the War Industries Board during World War I. After World War II he was U.S. representative to the United Nations Atomic Energy Commission.

On Aug. 19, 1870, Bernard Baruch was born in Camden, S.C. His father, Simon Baruch, had been a surgeon in the Confederate Army, while Bernard's mother came from an old South Carolina family. The Baruchs left South Carolina for New York City when Bernard was a small boy, and he received his education in the public schools. He graduated from the College of the City of New York in 1889 and soon joined the Wall Street brokers A.A. Houseman and Company. Beginning as a "runner," Baruch rose rapidly to partnership in the firm. He launched his own firm in 1903 and by 1910 had built a substantial and secure fortune.

Baruch married Annie Griffin of New York City in 1897. Three children were born to them. Baruch should have been a most contented man; his marriage was happy; his career prospered; he had time for sports and the theater. Yet there was another facet to Baruch that made him somewhat different from most Wall Street tycoons. His Jewish family placed more value on scholarship and service than on moneymaking and he was naturally drawn to a career of public service.

World War I

Woodrow Wilson first brought Baruch into Democratic politics during the presidential campaign of 1912, but it was not until 1916 that Baruch accepted a post in the intimate Wilson circle. Baruch was serving on the Advisory Commission of the Council of National Defense when war was declared in April 1917. In July he was named a member of the newly created War Industries Board. When the War Department fumbled its opportunity to control economic mobilization during the winter of 1917-1918, it became apparent to President Wilson that Baruch should become the chairman of the Board.

So many things were in flux in the War Department, in the operation of railroads, and in the control of fuel and food when Baruch became chairman that it is difficult to differentiate his work from that of others. Forces of reform converged from every direction. Although the United States did not complete its industrial organization and produce war material in quantity until the war's end, Baruch succeeded in coordinating American economic power for the first time in the nation's history. His work set precedents that were not overlooked by President Franklin Roosevelt when,

in the 1930s, he organized the country to fight the Great Depression.

As the Versailles Treaty failed and the economic nationalism of the 1920s intensified, Baruch grew pessimistic about world affairs. He fought for industrial preparedness in a period when politically it was considered almost treasonous. He remained active in Democratic party politics, supporting William G. McAdoo for the presidency in 1924 and Al Smith in 1928. Malicious and false charges that he had profited personally from World War I hurt him deeply. He was also subject to anti-Semitic attacks. Perhaps the greatest blows were struck by the elder Henry Ford, who, in his newspaper, the *Dearborn Independent,* accused Baruch of being a part of a Jewish conspiracy to control the world's economy.

World War II

Baruch never recovered from Ford's insulting charges, and he refused public positions during World War II partly because of the terrible hurts inflicted by the auto magnate. Baruch may have served without portfolio during World War II, but he was not without influence. It was the "Baruch Report" that set the stage for the solution of the 1942 rubber crisis, so critical to Allied victory. It was Baruch who recommended James F. Byrnes of South Carolina for director of the Office of War Mobilization. Baruch, the "park bench statesman," worked hard on plans for demobilization and postwar economic planning. He was on a mission to England as Roosevelt's personal emissary when he heard of the President's death.

United Nations

At 75 Baruch undertook his last public mission, as American representative to the United Nations Atomic Energy Commission. The Baruch Plan for international control of atomic energy faltered on the matter of inspection and became quickly embroiled in the politics of the cold war. A few scholars have seen the proposal as an attempt by the United States to retain a monopoly of atomic weapons, but at the time even some Soviet statesmen saw it as a valid first position for important negotiations.

Baruch resigned from the Commission in January 1947. He remained interested in politics and international affairs but shunned the national spotlight. He could look back on a life of action and commitment. The "Wolf of Wall Street" had found a political mentor in Woodrow Wilson. He had surmounted prejudices surrounding his origins, his work on Wall Street, and his religion, to become an adviser of presidents and ultimately an American elder statesman. He died in New York City on June 20, 1965.

Further Reading

The best biography of Baruch is Margaret L. Coit, *Mr. Baruch* (1957). Baruch's *My Own Story* (1957) and *The Public Years* (1960) are also informative. For Baruch and World War I see Grosvenor B. Clarkson, *Industrial America in the World War* (1923). For his part in the World War II see Donald M. Nelson, *Arsenal of Democracy: The Story of American War Production* (1946). Inis L. Claude, Jr., *Swords into Plowshares: The Problem and Progress of International Organization* (1956; 3d ed. 1964), discusses Baruch's work with the United Nations Atomic Energy Commission.

Additional Sources

Grant, James, *Bernard M. Baruch: the adventures of a Wall Street legend,* New York: Simon and Schuster, 1983. □

Mikhail Baryshnikov

Mikhail Baryshnikov (born 1948) was a ballet dancer who defected from the former Soviet Union to the United States. He explored both classical and modern ballet forms and was artistic director of the American Ballet Theater before resigning and establishing the White Oak Dance Project.

Mikhail Baryshnikov was born in Riga, Latvia, on January 27, 1948. His dance studies began in 1960. He trained for three years at the Riga State Choreographic School until his fifteenth birthday, when he traveled to Leningrad with an advanced student group. The son of Russian parents, Baryshnikov found a congenial home in Leningrad. Motivated to audition for ballet school there, Baryshnikov passed his entrance examination and was accepted into one of Russia's finest ballet training institutions (the Vagarova School). Here he studied with one of the great teachers of this century, Alexander Pushkin. He

joined the Kirov Ballet in 1967, entirely bypassing the usual years in the corps de ballet. He quickly became one of that legendary company's most brilliant soloists.

In a dramatic and adventurously romantic leap to the West, Baryshnikov defected from the former Soviet Union in June 1974. Still a member of the Kirov, he had been dancing in Toronto, Canada, with a touring troupe from Moscow's Bolshoi Ballet. Following the group's final Toronto performance, Baryshnikov leaped into a waiting car—rather than the chartered bus transporting the Russian dancers—and disappeared into the Canadian wilderness, soon to reappear to thunderous acclaim on American stages.

The successes of his early career had been marked by formal competitions and roles in modern and classical repertory. He won a gold medal at the Varna, Bulgaria, ballet competition in 1966, and in 1968 he won the gold medal at the First International Ballet Competition in Moscow. His professional debut, in the "peasant Pas de Deux" of "Giselle," would much later be echoed in the West in his New York City debut with American Ballet Theater in August 1974. His partner was Natalia Makarova, who had defected from the Kirov in 1970.

His Western admirers, critics and fans alike, immediately compared Baryshnikov with another of Pushkin's students, Rudolf Nureyev, who had fled the former Soviet Union and the haven of the Kirov Ballet in 1961. They found the 26-year-old Baryshnikov a restrained, less ostentatious proponent of the Russian ballet style than Nureyev. His technique was praised for its ease and purity, and his eleva-

tion and ballon (the ability to appear to pause, suspended in the air during leaps) were universally acclaimed. As Baryshnikov explored the various styles of American modern dance and contemporary ballet for which he had left the comparatively constrained environment of the Kirov, his abilities seemed limitless.

During his initial three years in the West, particularly as a principal dancer with American Ballet Theater from 1974 to 1978, Baryshnikov showed a voracious appetite for all the challenges that a welcoming dance world would present to him. He learned some 22 new roles, dancing the choreography of Antony Tudor, George Balanchine, John Neumeier, Roland Petit, John Butler, and Twyla Tharp, among others.

In a move that surprised many—because it presupposed a lower salary and less than the star-status billing—Baryshnikov joined the New York City Ballet in 1978. For 15 months he challenged himself with the unfamiliar style and rhythms of George Balanchine's choreography. The next phase of his career began in September 1980 when Baryshnikov became the artistic director of the American Ballet Theater.

Having successfully explored ballet in its classical form and in its contemporary styles, as well as the work of modern dance-makers, and finding himself at the head of one of the great American ballet companies, Baryshnikov continued his search for new avenues of expression in television and motion pictures. "The Turning Point," made in 1977, introduced him to audiences unfamiliar with his ballet work and earned him an Academy Award nomination; "White Nights" (1986) was his next screen effort.

Baryshnikov was named the artistic director of the American Ballet Theatre in 1980. During his tenure he was credited with adding numerous modern pieces to the repitore and with improving the company's fortunes both artistically and financially. In September 1989 Baryshnikov resigned as the creative director of the American Ballet Theatre due to a power struggle with the company's executive director and the board of trustees. He then co-founded the White Oak Dance Project and continued to perform.

Baryshnikov, in discussing his career, summarized his experiences in a comment he made to Gennady Smakov, author of "The Great Russian Dancers." The dancer said, "No matter what I try to do or explore, my Kirov training, my expertise, and my background call me to return to dancing after all, because that's my real vocation, and I have to serve it."

Further Reading

As is the case with most dancers, the most effective documentation of Mikhail Baryshnikov is the photograph. Most books focusing on him are in the category of photo albums attempting to illustrate his work through freeze-action shots.
Baryshnikov at Work, which is edited and introduced by Charles Engell France, features many photographs of the dancer by Martha Swope (1976). The same editor and photographer collaborated on *Baryshnikov in Color* (1980); this book also includes photographs of Baryshnikov by photographers other than Swope. Other books on this artist include: *Bravo, Baryshnikov* by Alan LeMond, with photos by Lois Greenfield

and others (1978); *Baryshnikov on Broadway,* with photos by Martha Swope and an introduction by Walter Terry (1980); *The Making of a Dance: Mikhail Baryshnikov and Carla Fracci in Medea/Choreography by John Butler,* photographed and edited by Thomas Victor, with an introduction by Clive Barnes (1976); and *Baryshnikov in Russia* by Nina Alovert (1985).
Baryshnikov's post American Ballet Theatre career is detailed in "After Baryshnikov, What?" in *Newsweek* (January 29, 1990); also in "White Oak Dance Project: Baryshnikov Hits a New Personal Best" in *Dance Magazine* (March, 1994) and in "Modern Dance Junkie" in *Village Voice* (March 25, 1997). □

Johann Bernhard Basedow

Johann Bernhard Basedow (1724-1790), a German educator, stated a program for total reform of the educational system. His work lent support to the philanthropists who felt that social and political reforms could best be made by first reforming the schools.

Johann Basedow was born in Hamburg on Sept. 11, 1724. He attended the universities of Leipzig and Kiel and upon graduation became a teacher, first as a private tutor in a wealthy home, then in several schools in Denmark and Germany. In each job he was a failure, but these failures inspired his zeal for educational reform.

The Philanthropinum

Influenced by men of the French Enlightenment, Basedow thought that knowledge properly applied could lead to the perfection of man and his institutions. He expressed these ideas in the books *Appeal to Friends of Mankind and to Men of Power concerning Schools and Studies and Their Influence on Public Welfare* (1768) and *The Method Book for Fathers and Mothers of Families and for Nations* (1770). Prince Leopold, ruler of Anhalt, was so impressed with the reform potential of Basedow's ideas that in 1771 he hired him to found an experimental school at Dessau. The Philanthropinum opened in 1774, the first school to completely break with tradition. It drew many interested visitors from far and wide, who either praised the school extravagantly, as did Kant, or criticized it bitterly. In 1774 Basedow also published the huge *Elementarwerk,* an encyclopedic collection of the material that was to be taught to children from birth to age 18.

Philosophy of the System

According to Basedow, the principal goal of education should be to prepare children for a happy, patriotic life of service to the community. As the school functions for the individual, it performs a service also for the state; since the state is but a community of individuals, it will experience good fortune only to the extent that each individual member does. The curriculum should contain only those things that

can be shown to be useful. Basedow scorned the stress in the traditional schools on developing verbal skills, especially in Latin. Things that can be touched, seen, heard, and manipulated—to show the child the extent to which he can control his environment—should be substituted for the traditional verbal exercises, which deal with mere symbols.

Teaching methods should include observations by the children of objects and activities of the real world. The teacher should not impose his will but should encourage self-direction on the part of the pupil into purposeful activity. Basedow advised that at play children learn most effectively. Pure intellectualization that ignores the individual psychological makeup of the learner is to be avoided. Games, manual work in the garden and in the shop, physical training, hiking—these were the activities appropriate to youth. The teacher should guide these activities by a nonauthoritarian and humane interaction with the pupils.

At Dessau, Basedow put his ideas to practice. To toughen the body and to foster the ability to withstand hardship, there were several fasting days each month. Competition was encouraged by a system of awards for merit in several activities.

Basedow was a very difficult man to work with. He was emotionally unstable, had disagreeable habits, and would not brook dissent. As a result, he was forced to leave the Philanthropinum 4 years after he had founded it. He spent the remaining 12 years of his life writing articles expanding on his three major works.

Further Reading

There are many books on Basedow in German. No full-length study of him in English exists, although there are numerous articles in educational journals. For background information see Friedrich Paulsen, *German Education Past and Present* (1912), and R. H. Samuel and R. Hinton Thomas, *Education and Society in Modern Germany* (1949). ☐

Matsuo Basho

Matsuo Basho (1644-1694) was one of the greatest Japanese poets. He elevated haiku to the level of serious poetry in numerous anthologies and travel diaries.

The name of Matsuo Basho is associated especially with the celebrated Genroku era (ca. 1680-1730), which saw the flourishing of many of Japan's greatest and most typical literary and artistic personalities. Although Basho was the contemporary of writers like the novelist and poet Ihara Saikaku and the dramatist Chikamatsu Monzaemon, he was far from being an exponent of the new middle-class culture of the city dwellers of that day. Rather, in his poetry and in his attitude toward life he seemed to harken back to a period some 300 years earlier. An innovator in poetry, spiritually and culturally he maintained a great tradition of the past.

The haiku, a 17-syllable verse form divided into successive phrases or lines of 5, 7, and 5 syllables, originated in the linked verse of the 14th century, becoming an independent form in the latter part of the 16th century. Arakida Moritake (1473-1549) was a distinguished *renga* (linked poem) poet who originated witty and humorous verses he called *haikai,* which later became synonymous with haiku. Nishiyama Soin (1605-1682), founder of the Danrin school, pursued Arakida's ideals. Basho was a member of this school at first, but breaking with it, he was responsible for elevating the haiku to a serious art, making it the verse form par excellence, which it has remained ever since.

Basho's poetical works, known as the *Seven Anthologies of the Basho School* (*Basho Schichibushy*), were published separately from 1684 to 1698, but they were not published together until 1774. Not all of the approximately 2,500 verses in the Basho anthologies are by Basho, although he is the principal contributor. Eleven other poets, his disciples, also contributed poems. These anthologies thus reflect composition performed by groups of poets with Basho as the arbiter of taste, injecting his comments on the poems of others, arranging his works in favorable contrast to theirs, and generally having the "last word." It was understood that he was the first poet of his group, and he expected a considerable amount of deference.

Early Life and Works

Basho was born in 1644 in Ueno, Iga Province, part of present-day Mie Prefecture. He was one of six children in a

family of samurai, descended it is said from the great Taira clan of the Middle Ages. As a youth, Basho entered feudal service but at the death of his master left it to spend much of his life in wandering about Japan in search of imagery. Thus he is known as a traveler as well as a poet, the author of some of the most beautiful travel diaries ever written in Japanese. Basho is thought to have gravitated toward Kyoto, where he studied the Japanese classics. Here, also, he became interested in the haiku of the Teitoku school, which was directed by Kitamura Kigin.

In 1672, at the age of 29, Basho set out for Edo (modern Tokyo), the seat of the Tokugawa shoguns and defacto capital of Japan. There he published a volume of verse in the style of the Teitoku school called *Kai-Oi*. In 1675 he composed a linked-verse sequence with Nishiyama Soin of the Danrin school, but for the next 4 years he was engaged in building waterworks in the city to earn a living. Thereafter, generous friends and admirers made it possible for him to continue a life devoted to poetic composition, wandering, and meditation, though he seems to have been largely unconcerned with money matters.

In 1680, thanks to the largesse of an admirer, Basho established himself in a small cottage at Fukagawa in Edo, thus beginning his life as a hermit of poetry. A year later one of his followers presented him with a banana plant, which was duly planted in Basho's garden. His hermitage became known as the Hermitage of the Banana Plant (Basho-an), and the poet, who had heretofore been known by the pen name Tosei, came increasingly to use the name Basho.

The hermitage burned down in 1682, causing Basho to retire to Kai Province. About this time it is believed that Basho began his study of Zen at the Chokei Temple in Fukagawa, and it has often been assumed erroneously that Basho was a Buddhist priest. He dressed and conducted himself in a clerical manner and must have been profoundly motivated by a mystical faith. Whatever experiences of tragedy or strong emotion that he suffered seem to have enlarged his perception of reality. His vision of the universe is implicit in all his best poems, and the word *zen* has often been applied to him and his work. His work and later life certainly could not be called worldly.

Travel Diaries

In 1683 the hermitage was rebuilt and Basho returned to Edo. But in the summer of 1684 Basho made a journey to his birthplace, which resulted in the travel diary *The Weatherbeaten Trip* (*Nozarashi Kiko*). That same year he published the haiku collection entitled *Winter Days* (*Fuyu no Hi*). It was in *Winter Days* that Basho enunciated his revolutionary style of haiku composition, a manner so different from the preceding haiku that the word *shofu* (haiku in the Basho manner) was coined to describe it.

Winter Days, published in Kyoto, was compiled under Basho's direction by his Nagoya disciple Yamamoto Kakei. Basho, wintering at Nagoya on his trip home to Iga, had summoned his disciples to compose a haiku sequence inspired by the season. Basho set the tone for the sequence by using the words ''wintry blasts'' in the first poem. The progress of the seasons was one of the main inspirations for the anthology, putting it in tune with the cosmic process. Nature, the understanding of its beauty and acceptance of its force, is used by Basho to express the beauty which he observes in the world. Basho enunciates the abstract beauty, *yugen,* which lies just behind the appearance of the world. The word *yugen* may be understood as the inner beauty of a work of art or nature which is rarely apparent to the vulgar. And the apprehension of this beauty gives the beholder a momentary intimation, an illumination, of the deeper significance of the universe about him. This view of the universe, while not original with Basho, was in his case undoubtedly inspired by some previous experience.

In 1686 *Spring Days* (*Haru no Hi*) was compiled in Nagoya by followers of Basho, revised by him, and published in Kyoto. There is an attitude of refined tranquility in these poems representing a deeper metaphysical state. The anthology contains one of the most famous of all Basho's haiku verse: ''An old pond/ a frog jumps in—/ splash!'' There has been much speculation on the significance of this verse, which has captured the fancy of many generations of lovers of Japanese poetry. But even the imagery alone can be appreciated by many different people at a variety of levels. Composition within the delicate confines of haiku versification definitely sets Basho off as one of the greatest mystical poets of Japan. The simplicity it exhibits is the result of the methodical rejection of much complication, not the simplicity with which one starts but rather that with which one ends.

In the autumn of 1688 Basho went to Sarashina, in present-day Nagano Prefecture, to view the moon, a hallowed autumn pastime in Japan. He recorded his impressions in *The Sarashina Trip* (*Sarashina Kiko*). Though one of his lesser travel diaries, it is a kind of prelude to his description of a journey to northern Japan a year later. It was at this time that Basho also wrote a short prose account of the moon as seen from Obasute Mountain in Sarashina. The legend of the mountain, where an old woman was abandoned to die alone, moved him also to compose a verse containing the image of an elderly woman accompanied only by the beautiful moon of Sarashina.

The Journey to Ou (*Oku no Hosomichi*) is perhaps the greatest of Basho's travel diaries. A mixture of haiku and *haibun,* a prose style typical of Basho, it contains some of his greatest verses. This work immortalizes the trip Basho made from Sendai to Shiogama on his way to the two northernmost provinces of Mutsu and Dewa (Ou). This diary reflects how the very thought of the hazardous journey, a considerable undertaking in those days, filled Basho with thoughts of death. He thinks of the Chinese T'ang poets Li Po and Tu Fu and the Japanese poets Saigyo and Sogi, all of whom had died on journeys.

Setting out early in the spring of 1689 from Edo with his disciple Kawai Sora, Basho traveled for 5 months in remote parts of the north, covering a distance of some 1,500 miles. The poet saw many notable places of pilgrimage, including the site of the hermitage where Butcho had practiced Zen meditation. The entire trip was to be devoted to sight with historical and literary associations, but Basho fell ill and again speculated on the possibility of his dying far from home. But he recovered and continued on to see the famous island of Matsushima, considered one of the three scenic wonders of Japan.

He proceeded to Hiraizumi to view ruins dating from the Heian Period. On the site of the battlefield where Yoshitsune had fallen, Basho composed a poem: "A wilderness of summer grass/ hides all that remains/ of warriors' dreams." In the province of Dewa he was fortunate enough to find shelter at the home of a well-to-do admirer and disciple. Passing on to a temple, Risshakuji, Basho was deeply inpired by the silence of the place situated amidst the rocks. It occasioned the verse which some consider his masterpiece: "Stillness!/ It penetrates the very rocks—/ the shrill-chirping of the cicadas."

Crossing over to the coast of the Sea of Japan, Basho continued southwest on his journey to Kanazawa, where he mourned at the grave of a young poet who had died the year before, awaiting Basho's arrival. He continued to Eiheiji, the temple founded by the great Zen priest Dogen. Eventually there was a reunion with several of his disciples, but Basho left them again to travel on to the Grand Shrine of Ise alone. Here the account of this journey ends. The work is particularly noteworthy for the excellence of its prose as well as its poetry and ranks high in the genre of travel writing in Japanese literature. Basho continued to polish this work until 1694; it was not published until 1702.

Mature Works

In 1690 Basho lived for a time in quiet retirement at the Genju-an (Unreal Dwelling) near Lake Biwa, north of Kyoto, and he wrote an account of this stay. Early in 1691 he stayed for a time in Saga with his disciple Mukai Kyorai.

As for his poetry, *Waste Land* (*Arano*) had been compiled by the disciple Kakei and published in 1689. It is the largest of the anthologies and contains a preface by Basho in which he characterizes his preceding anthologies as "flowery" and henceforth establishes a new standard of metaphysical and esthetic depth for haiku. *The Gourd* (*Hisago*) was compiled by the disciple Chinseki at Zeze in the province of Omi in 1690. It foreshadows in its excellence the mature and serious versifying which was to be the hallmark of the anthology *The Monkey's Raincoat* (*Sarumino*) in 1691. Compiled by Basho's disciples under his attentive supervision, *The Monkey's Raincoat* is composed of a judicious selection of haiku from the hands of many poets. It was while Basho was staying at the hermitage in Omi during the spring and summer of 1690 that the compilation was made. *The Monkey's Raincoat* contains some of Basho's own finest and essential haiku. This anthology, which may be compared with the finest anthologies in the history of Japanese literature, is arranged according to the four seasons. The title is taken from the opening verse by Basho, a poem of winter: "First cold Winter rain—/ even the monkey seems to want/ a tiny raincoat." Basho leads the contributors with the largest number of poems, followed by Boncho and Kyorai. But all the verses conform to Basho's tastes. The poems are linked by a subtle emotion rather than by a logical sequence, but they belong together.

In the late fall of 1691 Basho returned to Edo, where a new Banana Hermitage had been built near the site of the former one, complete with another banana plant in the garden. For the next 3 years Basho remained there receiving his disciples, discussing poetry, and helping in the compilation of another anthology, *The Sack of Charcoal* (*Sumidawara*) of 1694. The reason for the title, according to the preface, is that Basho, when asked if such a word could be used in haiku poetry, replied that it could. This anthology, together with its successor, *The Sequel to the Monkey's Raincoat* (*Zoku Sarumino*), exhibits the quality of *Karumi,* or lightness, an artistic spontaneity which is the fruit of a lifetime of poetic cultivation. It is a kind of sublimity reached by a truly great poet and cannot be imitated intellectually. *The Sequel to the Monkey's Raincoat* in 1698, appearing 4 years after Basho's death, is concerned with the seasons, traveling, and religion. It contains some of Basho's last and most mature poems.

In the spring of 1694 Basho set out for what was to be his last journey to his birthplace. At Osaka he was taken ill. Perceiving that he was near his end, Basho wrote a final poem on his own death: "Stricken while journeying/ my dreams still wander about/ but on withered fields."

Further Reading

Information on Basho and his works is available in Donald Keene, *Anthology of Japanese Literature: From the Earliest Era to the Mid-Nineteenth Century* (1955); Kenneth Yasuda, *The*

Japanese Haiku: Its Essential Nature, History and Possibilities in English (1957); Harold G. Henderson, ed. and trans., *An Introduction to Haiku: An Anthology of Poems from Basho to Shiki* (1958); Ryusaku Tsunoda, William Theodore de Bary, and Donald Keene, eds., *Sources of the Japanese Tradition* (1958; rev. ed., 2 vols., 1964), an anthology with commentary; R. H. Blyth, *A History of Haiku* (2 vols., 1963); Makoto Ueda, *Zeami, Basho, Yeats, Pound: A Study in Japanese and English Poetics* (1965); and Nobuyuki Yuasa's introduction to his translation of Basho's *The Narrow Road to the Deep North and Other Travel Sketches* (1966). □

Count Basie

(William) Count Basie (1904-1984) was an extremely popular figure in the jazz world for half a century. He was a fine pianist and leader of one of the greatest jazz bands in history.

The story of Count Basie is very much the story of the great jazz band that he led for close to 50 years (1935-1984), an orchestra with a distinctive sound, anchored by a subtle but propulsive beat, buoyed by crisp ensemble work, and graced with superb soloists (indeed, a catalogue of featured players would read like a Who's Who of jazz). But perhaps the most startling aspect of the band's achievement was its 50-year survival in a culture that has experienced so many changes in musical fashion, and especially its survival after the mid-1960s when jazz lost much of its audience to rock music and disco.

William Basie was born in Red Bank, New Jersey, on August 21, 1904. His mother was a music teacher, and at a young age he became her pupil. But it was in Harlem, New York City, that he learned the rudiments of ragtime and stride piano, principally from his sometime organ teacher, the great Fats Waller. Basie made his professional debut as an accompanist for vaudeville acts. While on a tour of the Keith vaudeville circuit he was stranded in Kansas City. Here, in 1928, after a short stint as house organist in a silent movie theater, he joined Walter Page's Blue Devils, and when that band broke up in 1929, he was hired by Bennie Moten's Band and played piano with them, with one interruption, for the next five years.

Moten's death in 1935 altered Basie's career dramatically. He took over the remnants of the band (they called themselves The Barons of Rhythm) and, with some financial and promotional support from impresario John Hammond, expanded the personnel and formed the first Count Basie Orchestra. Within a year or so the band had developed its own variation of the basic Kansas City swing style—a solidly pulsating rhythm underpinning the horn soloists, who were additionally supported by sectional riffing (i.e., the repetition of a musical figure by the non-soloing brass and reeds). This familiar pattern is evident in the band's theme song, "One O'Clock Jump," written by Basie himself in 1937, which has a subdued, expectant introduction by the rhythm section (piano, guitar, bass, and drums), then bursts into full orchestral support for a succession of stirring solos,

and concludes with a full ensemble riffing out-chorus. Like any great swing band, Basie's was exciting in *any* tempo, and in fact one of the glories of his early period was a lugubrious, down-tempo blues called "Blue and Sentimental," which featured two magnificent solos (one by Herschel Evans on tenor saxophone and the other by Lester Young on clarinet) with full ensemble backing.

A Huge Success

By 1937 Basie's band was, with the possible exception of Duke Ellington's, the most highly acclaimed African American band in America. In the racially segregated context of the pre-World War II music business, African American bands never achieved the notoriety nor made the money that the famous white bands did. But some (Ellington's, Earl Hines's, Jimmy Lunceford's, Erskine Hawkins's, Chick Webb's, and Basie's, among them) did achieve a solid commercial success. Basie's band regularly worked some of the better big city hotel ballrooms and shared with many of the other 1,400 big bands of the Swing Era the less appetizing one-nighters (a series of single night engagements in a variety of small cities and towns that were toured by bus).

Some of the band's arrangements were written by trombonist Eddie Durham, but many were "heads"—arrangements spontaneously worked out in rehearsal and then transcribed. The band's "book" (repertory) was tailored not only to a distinctive orchestral style but also to showcase the band's brilliant soloists. Sometimes the arrangement was the reworking of a standard tune—"I got

Rhythm," "Dinah," or "Lady, Be Good"—but more often a bandsman would come up with an original written expressly for the band and with a particular soloist or two in mind: two of Basie's earliest evergreens, "Jumpin' at the Woodside" and "Lester Leaps In" were conceived primarily as features for the remarkable tenor saxophonist Lester Young (nicknamed "Pres," short for "President") and were referred to as "flagwavers," up-tempo tunes designed to excite the audience.

Unquestionably the Swing Era band (1935-1945) was Basie's greatest: the superior arrangements (reflecting Basie's good taste) and the sterling performers (reflecting Basie's management astuteness) gave the band a permanent place in jazz history that even severe personnel setbacks couldn't diminish. Herschel Evans's death in 1939 was a blow, but he was replaced by another fine tenorist, Buddy Tate; a major defection was that of the nonpareil Lester Young ("Count, four weeks from tonight I will have been gone exactly fourteen days."), but his replacement was the superb Don Byas; the trumpet section had three giants— Buck Clayton, Harry "Sweets" Edison, and Bill Coleman— but only Edison survived the era as a Basie-ite.

Perhaps the band's resilience in the face of potentially damaging change can be explained by its model big band rhythm section, one that jelled to perfection—the spare, witty piano of Basie; the wonderful rhythm guitar of Freddie Green (who was with the band from 1937 to 1984); the rock-solid bass of Walter Page (Basie's former employer); and the exemplary drumming of Jo Jones. Nor was the band's excellence hurt by the presence of its two great blues and ballads singers, Jimmy Rushing and Helen Humes.

"April in Paris"

The loss of key personnel (some to the military service), the wartime ban on recordings, the 1943 musicians' strike, the economic infeasibility of one-nighters, and the bebop revolution of the mid-1940s all played a role in the death of the big band era. The number of 12 to 15 piece bands diminished drastically, and Basie was driven to some soul-searching: despite his international reputation and the band's still first-rate personnel, Basie decided in 1950 to disband and to form a medium-sized band (first an octet and later a septet), juggling combinations of all-star musicians, among them tenorists Georgie Auld, Gene Ammons, and Wardell Gray; trumpeters Harry Edison and Clark Terry; and clarinetist Buddy DeFranco. The groups' recordings (Jam Sessions #2 & #3) are, predictably, of the highest quality, but in 1951 Basie reverted to his first love—the big band— and it thrived, thanks largely to the enlistment of two Basie-oriented composer-arrangers, Neil Hefti and Ernie Wilkins; to the solo work of tenorists Frank Wess and Frank Foster and trumpeters Joe Newman and Thad Jones; and to the singing of Joe Williams. Another boost was provided in the late 1950s by jazz organist Wild Bill Davis's arrangement of "April in Paris" which, with its series of "one more time" false endings, came to be a trademark of the band for the next quarter of a century.

A stocky, handsome, mustachioed man with heavy-lidded eyes and a sly, infectious smile, Basie in his later years took to wearing a yachting cap both off and on the bandstand. His sobriquet, "Count," was a 1935 promotional gimmick, paralleling "Duke" (Ellington) and "Earl" (Hines's actual first name). He was a shrewd judge of talent and character and, ever the realist, was extremely forbearing in dealing with the behavioral caprices of his musicians. His realistic vision extended as readily to himself: a rhythm-centered pianist, he had the ability to pick out apt chord combinations with which to punctuate and underscore the solos of horn players, but he knew his limitations and therefore gave himself less solo space than other, less gifted, leaders permitted themselves. He was, however, probably better than he thought; on a mid-1970s outing on which he was co-featured with tenor saxophone giant Zoot Sims he acquitted himself nobly.

Among Basie's many recordings perhaps the most essential are The Best of Basie; The Greatest: Count Basie Plays . . . Joe Williams Sings Standards; and Joe Williams/Count Basie: Memories Ad-Lib. There are also excellent pairings of Basie and Ellington, with Frank Sinatra, with Tony Bennett, with Ella Fitzgerald, with Sarah Vaughan, and with Oscar Peterson.

In 1976 Basie suffered a heart attack, but returned to the bandstand half a year later. During his last years he had difficulty walking and so rode out on stage in a motorized wheelchair, his playing now largely reduced to his longtime musical signature, the three soft notes that punctuated his compositional endings. His home for many years was in Freeport, the Bahamas; he died of cancer at Doctors' Hospital in Hollywood, Florida, on April 26, 1984. His wife, Catherine, had died in 1983; they had one daughter. The band survived Basie's death, with ex-Basie-ite trumpeter Thad Jones directing until his death in 1986.

Further Reading

The best source for early Basie is Ross Russell's Jazz Style in Kansas City & The Southwest (1971). Two studies of the life of the band are Ray Horricks' Count Basie & His Orchestra and Stanley Dance's The World of Count Basie (1980), the latter a composite study of Basie and the band through bandsmen's memoirs. There is also a short biography, Count Basie (1985), by British jazz critic Alun Morgan. Good Morning Blues: The Autobiography of Count Basie as told to Albert Murray was published posthumously in 1985. □

Basil I

The Byzantine emperor Basil I (ca. 812-886), also known as Basil the Macedonian, ruled from 867 to 886. Despite his unsavory rise to power, he was a gifted statesman who gave the empire new vigor and began its most durable dynasty.

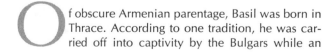

f obscure Armenian parentage, Basil was born in Thrace. According to one tradition, he was carried off into captivity by the Bulgars while an infant; escaping in his 20s, he sought his fortune in Constantinople and took service with a kinsman of the Caesar Bardas, uncle and guiding influence of Emperor Michael III. About 858 Basil attracted the attention of the Emperor through his great physical strength and his way with horses. He rapidly rose to high ranks, became Michael's boon companion, and in an arrangement of convenience married the Emperor's mistress.

Basil's influence grew, and his ambition was kindled. In May 866 Michael proclaimed Basil his co-emperor. Allegedly because of Michael's incapacity but apparently more out of fear of his whims, Basil murdered his benefactor on Sept. 24, 867, and seized the throne. He also deposed the great patriarch Photius, who was then embroiled in a struggle with the papacy which deeply split Church sentiments in the Byzantine Empire.

For all his ruthless opportunism and brutality, Basil displayed genuine ability and a lofty sense of his office. Though he replaced Photius, he abided by Photius's policies of Eastern Church independence from Rome and of the Byzantine orientation of the newly converted Bulgarian Church. He later reconciled himself with Photius and restored him in the patriarchate in 877. Active as builder and patron, Basil scored his greatest domestic achievement by initiating a reform of the legal system. This grand project was not completed by Basil, but it was taken up and realized by his son and successor, Leo VI. Basil's legal work opened a brilliant new phase in the Byzantine extension of the living Roman law.

Basil's reign was active militarily. In the 870s his forces broke the heretical sect of the Paulicians, whose strongholds had weakened the eastern frontiers. His armies also pushed successfully against the Arabs, beginning the great momentum that Byzantium would develop in territorial reconquest in the next century. Basil's fleet reestablished Byzantine authority in Dalmatia, and he was the first emperor in perhaps 2 centuries to reassert Byzantine interest in Italy. His dispatch of the general Nicephorus Phocas (the Elder) to Italy inaugurated a new era of Byzantine recovery in the peninsula's southern territories.

Determined to establish his family on the throne, Basil made his three eldest sons his co-emperors. But in 879 Constantine, the eldest and Basil's favorite, died, and Basil was left emotionally shattered and mentally unhinged. Increasingly manipulated by Photius and alienated from his heir, Leo, Basil died on Aug. 29, 886, reportedly of a hunting accident.

Further Reading

The only full-length study of Basil I is by Albert Vogt in French. Vogt wrote the account of Basil in *The Cambridge Medieval History*, vol. 4 (1923). See also George Ostrogorsky, *History of the Byzantine State* (1940; trans. 1956; rev. ed. 1969); *The Cambridge Medieval History*, vol. 4 (2d ed. 1966), pt. 1, edited by J. M. Hussey; and Romilly Jenkins, *Byzantium: The Imperial Centuries, A.D. 610-1071* (1966). □

Basil II

The Byzantine emperor Basil II (ca. 958-1025) ruled from 963 to 1025 and was called Bulgaroctonus (Bulgar-Slayer). He was the last and greatest of the emperors who brought Byzantium to its military zenith.

The elder son of Emperor Romanus II, Basil and his younger brother, Constantine, succeeded in title as children upon their father's death in 963. Their position was exploited by two successive military usurpers, Nicephorus Phocas (963-969) and John I Tzimisces (969-976). Upon John's death, while Constantine remained in the background, Basil attempted to rule but became dependent upon his great-uncle, the eunuch Basil the Chamberlain. A cunning politician of long experience, the chamberlain helped Basil face the challenges of two more would-be usurpers, the aristocrats Bardas Sclerus and Bardas Phocas. Amid these struggles the chamberlain's tutelage became intolerable, and Basil drove him from office.

The rebellions of the two Bardases eventually drove Basil to seek military help from Prince Vladimir of Kiev; this alliance led to Russia's subsequent conversion to Byzantine Christianity. The unit of Russian soldiers sent by Vladimir helped Basil stop Bardas Phocas in 989, and Bardas Sclerus capitulated shortly afterward. These long struggles to guarantee his throne left deep scars on Basil's personality. Easygoing and dissipated in his youth, he was turned by his ordeals into a dour, stern, self-denying ascetic. His experiences with ambitious warlords also bred in him a passionate hatred for the aristocrats and a determination to curb them.

With the aristocracy dominating the military high commands, Basil decided early to establish his own reputation as a soldier. An initial attempt at campaigning against Bulgaria, the deadly northern enemy of Byzantium, in 986 had proved an embarrassing failure. In 990, however, Basil resumed his efforts against Bulgaria, which would become the prime target of his mature military efforts. The 25 years of bitter war between King Samuel of Bulgaria and Basil that followed became both a personal duel and a fight to the death between the two enemy states.

With victories, devastation, and bold strategy, Basil wore Samuel down, segmented his territories, and crippled Bulgarian strength. The climax was reached in 1014, when the Byzantines captured the main Bulgarian army of some 14,000 men. Basil had these men blinded but left one in every hundred with one eye to serve as a guide. He sent them back to Samuel, who died from shock at the sight. Basil completed the annexation of Bulgaria and its incorporation into the empire with singular moderation and pragmatic wisdom.

The next years of the tireless Emperor's reign were spent in settling the empire's interests in eastern Asia Minor and the Caucasus. He began the dismemberment and annexation of independent Armenia. Then, still restless, Basil turned his attentions further westward. He planned an expedition to reconquer Sicily and expand Byzantine authority

in Italy; but before he could undertake this campaign, Basil suddenly took ill and died on Dec. 15, 1025. A bachelor, Basil left the throne to his younger brother, Constantine VIII, during whose reign (1025-1028) began the rapid erosion of the strength Basil had built up.

Further Reading

The chief scholarly study of Basil II is in French. Good general accounts in English are in George Ostrogorsky, *History of the Byzantine State* (1940; trans. 1956; rev. ed. 1969), and in Romilly Jenkins, *Byzantium: The Imperial Centuries, A.D. 610-1071* (1966), part of which is reproduced in J. M. Hussey, ed., *The Cambridge Medieval History,* vol. 4 (2d ed. 1966), pt. 1. □

St. Basil the Great

St. Basil the Great (329-379), Bishop of Caesarea in the Roman province of Cappadocia, was influential in the development of monasticism in the Eastern Orthodox Church and played a role in the Arian controversy.

One of 10 children, Basil came from a wealthy and noble Christian family of Cappadocia (now in Turkey); his younger brother Gregory, later known as Gregory of Nyssa, also became a bishop and a distinguished theologian. When he was 22, after studying in his native Caesarea and in Constantinople, Basil went to Athens for 5 years to further his liberal education. There he met Gregory of Nazianzus, a fellow student, with whom he formed a lifelong friendship. Basil, his brother Gregory, and Gregory of Nazianzus are often referred to as the "Cappadocian fathers."

Cenobitic Monasticism

After teaching rhetoric for a time in Caesarea, Basil decided to abandon the pleasures of secular life and to pursue instead the ideal of Christian perfection. He visited notable Christian ascetics in Egypt and the Near East and then returned, when he was about 30, to his family's estates on the Iris River to lead a life of monastic retirement and rigid discipline. Influencing others by his example, Basil was the inaugurator in Asia Minor of cenobitic monasticism, a system in which monks live in communities under a shared rule of life. Basil's writings on monasticism are the single most important body of regulative documents in Eastern Orthodox monasticism.

Bishop of Caesarea

Because of his leadership and learning, Basil was drawn away from monastic affairs into the wider life and conflicts of the Church. Between 359 and 370 two successive bishops of Caesarea summoned him to their service, the second of them ordaining him a priest. But Basil's strong convictions resulted in strained relations with his superiors, and he often left Caesarea to work among his monasteries.

In 370, however, he was made bishop of Caesarea, and until his death in 379 he was one of the most important figures of the Eastern Church.

The most pressing problem Basil faced was the still unresolved Arian controversy, which had severely troubled the Eastern Church over the preceding 50 years. While the Arians asserted that belief in the full deity of Christ was incompatible with monotheism, the chief problem for the various non-Arian groups had come to rest in the question of whether it was possible to preserve the distinctions among God the Father, Christ the Son, and the Holy Spirit, while continuing to assert the full deity of all three.

Basil was certain that Arianism was heretical, but he also believed that the Nicene party, adhering strictly to the language of the Council of Nicaea (325), had not yet presented a defensible theological formulation of the orthodox position. He took the decisive step of agreeing with the Nicene party that there is only one divine substance (Greek, *ousia*) shared by Father, Son, and Spirit, but of insisting at the same time that each of the three is an individual hypostasis within the triune deity.

As a Church leader, Basil showed notable courage in defying the Eastern emperor Valens, who was intent on forcing a creedal statement tolerant of Arianism on the Church and banishing anti-Arian bishops. In his prolonged attempts to bring order and understanding to the chaotic conflict of parties in the Eastern Church, Basil tried repeatedly but without success to win the aid of the Roman papacy in approving the growing coalition of non-Arian parties. Too much of a moderate to be acceptable to the staunchly Nicene position of the papacy, he paved the way nonetheless for the final victory of his cause at the Council of Constantinople in 381, a victory he did not live to see.

Further Reading

A full-length work on Basil is W.K. Lowther Clarke, *St. Basil the Great; A Study in Monasticism* (1913). G.L. Prestige, *St. Basil the Great and Apollinaris of Laodicea,* edited by Henry Chadwick (1956), contains a brief account of Basil's life and a discussion of his correspondence with Apollinaris. There is a brief appreciation of Basil in Hans von Campenhausen, *The Fathers of the Greek Church,* translated by Stanley Godman (1959). □

Daisy Mae Bates

Daisy Mae Bates (1861-1951) was a social worker among the Australian aborigines. One of the first Europeans to win their confidence, she compiled a unique collection of material about them.

Daisy Bates was born Daisy O'Dwyer Hunt at Ballychrine, Tipperary, Ireland. Following the death of her mother, she was raised in the family of Sir Francis Outram, a retired officer of the Indian Civil Service. In 1884 she emigrated to Australia for health reasons, and at Bathurst, New South Wales, she met and married John Bates. She returned to Britain in 1894 and took up journalism but in 1899 emigrated to Western Australia, partly in connection with a pastoral lease in which she was interested and partly on behalf of the *Times* to investigate charges of white cruelty to the aborigines.

Bates's reports suggested that the aborigines were incompetently and unwisely managed but refuted the idea that they were being treated cruelly. Having discharged her commission, Bates remained in Western Australia and for 35 years lived as a solitary European among the aborigines. Her work was officially recognized by the Western Australia government, which commissioned her to study particular tribes and made her the state's traveling Protector of Aborigines.

The death of her husband and the acquisition of property in the north of Western Australia did not distract her from the service to which she had now clearly resolved to devote her life and for which, in 1933, she was made a commander of the British Empire. The aborigines accepted her as their friend and referred to her as *Kabbarli,* or grandmother. She was admitted to some of their initiation ceremonies, from which their own women were excluded on pain of death, and made copious notes on all she observed, which formed the basis of a book she published in 1938. She was still working among the aborigines at the age of 80, but in 1945 ill health compelled her to retire to Adelaide. She died on April 18, 1951.

Bates not only studied the aborigines but also helped to feed them, nurse them, and settle disputes between them.

She took care to respect their tribal rules and customs and was critical of missionaries who attempted to undermine their beliefs and convert them to those of a totally alien world. She regarded the aborigines as a race doomed to eventual extinction but was concerned that the process should be as painless as possible. In this regard she concluded that what was needed was not "anthropological study of social laws" but "administration of British rule founded on our highest and best traditions."

Further Reading

There is little written about Daisy Bates. The best source of information is her own account of her life, *The Passing of the Aborigines: A Lifetime Spent among the Natives of Australia* (1938; 2d ed. 1966). Winifred Holmes, *Seven Adventurous Women* (1953), has a lengthy discussion of her.

Additional Sources

Bates, Daisy, *The long shadow of Little Rock: a memoir,* Fayetteville: University of Arkansas Press, 1987.
Blackburn, Julia, *Daisy Bates in the desert,* New York: Pantheon Books, 1994. □

Henry Walter Bates

Henry Walter Bates (1825-1892) was an English explorer and naturalist. His fame rests principally on his zoological work, especially his insect collection, and his discovery of the principle of mimicry.

Henry Bates was born in Leicester, the son of a manufacturer who intended him for a business career and apprenticed him to a hosiery maker. Bates had little formal education, but the Mechanics Institute in Leicester had a good library and offered evening courses. By attending the courses and reading, Bates learned Greek, Latin, French, draftsmanship, and composition. His growing interest in Zoology led him to spend his holidays roaming the countryside and collecting specimens.

In 1843 he met Alfred Russell Wallace, who later hit upon the idea of evolution and natural selection independently of Charles Darwin. The two young men decided to visit South America in the interest of science, but they were not able to leave until 1848 because of a lack of means. They arrived in Belém, Brazil, and spent 1 1/2 years exploring the Tocantins River. They next ascended the Amazon to Santarém and Óbidos, where they parted to explore separately. Bates went 370 miles farther up the Amazon to Ega, the first important town on the tributary Solimões, remaining there over a year before descending to Belém. For the next 8 years he made collecting trips along the Amazon and its tributaries. His farthest penetration was to Forte Boa (approximately 66°W), from which he wished to go to the Andes, but because of failing health he returned to England in 1859. He took over 14,000 specimens, mostly insects, of which about 8,000 had previously been unknown to science.

Bates reached England with health and financial circumstances both poor. He managed to publish his only book, *The Naturalist on the Amazons,* in 1863; Darwin contributed the preface. In 1864 Bates became assistant secretary of the Royal Geographical Society, a post he held until his death on Feb. 16, 1892. This relieved him of financial worries, enabled him to support his family, and gave him influence to use in behalf of many explorers, including some in the Africa he never visited. Besides his work for the society, Bates wrote papers for scientific journals and was considered a great authority, perhaps the greatest, on Coleoptera (beetles and weevils).

Bates was responsible for first formalizing the principle of mimicry, though it was further developed later. It is the principle of protective resemblance. Species of animals that are defenseless and edible develop resemblances to species that are injurious and unfit for food, thus gaining some immunity from attack. Animals may also come to resemble plants, though the phenomenon is most generally found among creatures structurally similar.

Further Reading

Barbara G. Beddall, ed., *Wallace and Bates in the Tropics: Introduction to the Theory of Natural Selection* (1969), offers excerpts from the writings of the two scientists. J. N. L. Baker, *A History of Geographical Discovery and Exploration* (1931; 2d ed. 1967), furnishes a concise account of Bates's travels in the Amazon region.

Additional Sources

Moon, Harold Philip, *Henry Walter Bates FRS, 1825-1892: explorer, scientist, and Darwinian,* Leicester: Leicestershire Museums, Art Galleries, and Records Service, 1976. □

Katharine Lee Bates

American poet and educator Katharine Lee Bates (1859-1929) was a leading force in the early development of Wellesley College in Massachusetts and a noted literary scholar. She captured her place in American history, however, when she penned the patriotic poem "America the Beautiful," which was first published in 1895. A musical setting of Bates's vision of the natural beauty and noble ideals of America later became a popular song that was unsuccessfully nominated to become the country's national anthem.

K atharine Lee Bates was an educator and writer who is best known for her poem, "America the Beautiful." After its publication in the *Boston Evening Transcript* in 1904, the poem gained nationwide popularity for its celebration of the spirit and natural beauty of the country. The musical setting of "America the Beautiful," created in the 1920s, was an unsuccessful contender to become the national anthem, but has remained one of the United States' most recognized and beloved songs.

Bates, the youngest of four children, was born August 12, 1859, in Falmouth, Massachusetts. Her father, William Bates, was a minister who had attended Middlebury College in Vermont and Andover Theological Seminary. Her mother, Cornelia Frances Lee Bates, was a schoolteacher who had been educated at Mount Holyoke College. The Bates had moved to the whaling town of Falmouth on Cape Cod in 1858, when William was offered the position of minister of the Congregational church there. Only a month after his youngest daughter was born, however, William Bates died of a spinal tumor. His death placed the family in economic straits. The pension provided to the Bates family was not sufficient to live on, so they all helped bring in extra money where they could. Bates's mother raised and sold vegetables and poultry and also worked as a seamstress. Her two brothers earned cash by picking cranberries, catching and selling herring and muskrat skins, and herding cows. Everyone in the household also did piece work taken in from a local tag manufacturer. Despite their impoverished situation and the necessity of long hours of work, Cornelia Bates strived to provide her children with an education.

Studied at Wellesley College

The family's fortune improved when they moved to Grantville, a town near Wellesley, Massachusetts, so that Cornelia could attend to an ailing sister. There, friends of the family secured a house for them and Bates was able to complete her schooling at Needham High School in the early 1870s. During her high school years, Bates discovered that a new college for women was being built in the nearby town of Wellesley. She set her sights on attending the new institution; after her family moved to Newtonville in 1874, she prepared for Wellesley by teaching and attending advanced courses at Newton High School. She was accepted to the college in 1876 and enrolled in Wellesley's second graduating class.

Bates thrived in the atmosphere of learning at Wellesley. In addition to the regular course work in her chosen fields of English and Greek, the college curriculum there included daily exercise such as boating and calisthenics as well as an hour of housework chores a day. Her favorite spot on the campus was the Browning Room, a quiet, comfortable room where she could peruse the papers of the poet Elizabeth Barrett Browning. She also enjoyed roaming the picturesque New England landscape around the college. Her solitary pursuits, however, did not keep her from being an active and admired part of the student body. She was elected by her fellow students to serve on the committee that drafted the class constitution and she was voted class president. During her student days at Wellesley, she decided to become an educator, an ambition she would fulfill in that very school. She also began to demonstrate her poetic abilities during this time, reading one of her poems at her graduation in her role as Class Day poet.

After her graduation in 1880, Bates began teaching at Natick High School. Only three years later, she became a member of the English department at Wellesley, where she would remain for the rest of her career. She left a permanent stamp on the style and quality of education at the college, earning the respect and affection of both fellow teachers and students for her innovative ideas. In 1890, her duties increased when she was named chair of the English department. Despite her teaching and administrative duties, Bates found time to compile an impressive number of publications during her career. Her more than forty books included not only volumes of her own poetry (some of which was published under the pseudonym James Lincoln), but also translations of Spanish and Icelandic works of literature, children's literature, critical versions of literary works, anthologies, and literary histories. Her work earned her a reputation as a noted scholar in literature.

Poem Inspired by Travels

Bates occasionally traveled throughout the country and to Europe to continue her studies and to give lectures. Her journeys to the western states in the year 1893 provided the inspiration for the poem that made Bates famous. It was during that summer that she visited the World's Columbian Exposition in Chicago and marveled at the impressive architecture of the exhibition halls celebrating the wonders of the age. Continuing on to a lecture engagement in Denver, Colorado, Bates was further moved by the beauty of the landscape she viewed on a trek to the top of Pike's Peak. In her journal, Bates recorded the feelings of awe and pride that these events had created in her in a poem now known as "America the Beautiful." The poem first appeared in a publication called *The Congregationalist* on July 4, 1895. The response to the work was very positive; after receiving a number of suggestions from readers, Bates wrote a revised version which was published in the *Boston Evening Transcript* in November of 1904. This new poem gained an even wider acclaim and soon was known throughout the country. As years passed, the patriotic poem continued to grow in popularity. In the 1920s, a contest to create a musical score for the poem was sponsored by the National Federation of Music Clubs. The resulting song captured the heart of Americans, and some felt that it should become the national anthem—an honor it did not receive. But the poem and its author had succeeded in becoming an established part of American cultural history.

Bates did not let her fame as the author of "America the Beautiful" distract her from her duties at Wellesley. She continued an active career as a scholar, teacher, and administrator until her retirement in 1925. Her family was an important part of her professional and personal life throughout these years: her sister Jane assisted with Bates' household chores and typing her manuscripts and her mother helped to translate Spanish literature and folktales for her books. Bates often entertained at her home, hosting gatherings for students and colleagues as well as noted literary guests such as the poets Robert Frost, Carl Sandburg and William Butler Yeats. She continued her own writing after her retirement, producing a number of articles and book reviews as well as a collection of poetry, *The Pilgrim Ship*, which was published in 1926. After a series of illnesses in her final years, Bates died of pneumonia on March 28, 1929, in Wellesley. While her literary studies and transla-

tions remain a respected body of work, it is her poem "America the Beautiful" that has become her most memorable contribution to American literature. The praises for the natural and spiritual resources of the United States contained in her verses captured a sense of national identity and pride that continues to resonate in the American imagination.

Further Reading

For more information see Burgess, Dorothy Whittemore Bates, *Dream and Deed: The Story of Katharine Lee Bates,* University of Oklahoma Press, 1952; Drury, Michael, "Why She Wrote America's Favorite Song," *Reader's Digest,* July 1993, pp. 90-93. □

William Bateson

William Bateson (1861-1926), an English biologist, was mainly concerned with evolutionary questions. His dissatisfaction with traditional Darwinian arguments about life's history led him to a career study of heredity and variation.

Under Darwin's influence, biologists of the last four decades of the 19th century turned their attention largely toward studies of the history of life. Using description and comparison of the structure and developmental characteristics of organisms as their primary tools they sought to delineate the basic life forms. Their second task was to determine variations from these forms and relationships among variations. Above all, they desired to reconstruct the lineage of all species. William Bateson directed his career toward a solution of the problems Charles Darwin could not answer.

Bateson was born on August 8, 1861. His father was a classics scholar and master of St. John's College, Cambridge. As a boy he showed mild interest in nature and demonstrated fair knowledge in natural history. His marks in science were encouraging, but few recognized his latent skill in this field. His father did not favor the pursuit of natural science. In this setting Bateson was described as "a vague and aimless boy."

When Bateson entered St. John's College in 1879 he experienced his first academic success and gained direction in science. In 1882 he won an honors examination, the Natural Science Tripos, and later gained a college scholarship. These successes led him to focus on biology. Adam Sedgwick and W. F. R. Weldon, renowned Cambridge scientists, contributed significantly to Bateson's knowledge and early understanding of biology.

The Iconoclast—Early Career

Bateson's first professional scientific work was done in the spirit of traditional biology. Study for the Natural Science Tripos introduced him to the acorn worm *Balanoglossus*. Little was known about the life history of

Balanoglossus, and Bateson wished to explore the possibility of its relation to the vertebrates. After two summers of study (1883 and 1884) under W. K. Brooks in America, Bateson published papers arguing for the position of *Balanoglossus* as a primitive chordate. Through this work he gained initial recognition as a biologist, and it led to his election as a Fellow of St. John's College (1885).

A seed of dissent was also found in Bateson's earliest professional work. While the *Balanoglossus* studies followed traditional biology in method and goal, Bateson weighted the evidence differently than did his forerunners and suggested a reorganization of the tree of phylogeny. Brooks had encouraged Bateson to view critically the conclusions about phylogeny reached through comparative studies in anatomy and embryology. Bateson came to regard these conclusions as speculative, not capable of being tested. Instead he gained an appreciation of experimental studies in heredity and variation.

In subsequent years Bateson became an outspoken critic of traditional biology. While he demanded high scientific standards for his own work and other's, his ideas were not popular, and he repeatedly failed to gain teaching appointments. His research during the early years of his career was meagerly funded through lectures and temporary fellowships, such as the Balfour Studentship, which he received in 1887.

Bateson's own program of research included rigorous experimentation and the extensive collection of facts. Through a survey of information acquired in this manner and the application of inductive reasoning, one could, Bateson believed, reach firm scientific conclusions. From 1886 to 1894 his work centered on the collection of information on variation in animals. His observation of discontinuity between species led him to believe that evolution does not take place through the selection of individuals possessing tiny, but advantageous, variations (Darwin's view). Instead, he believed that evolution, particularly the origin of a new species, takes place by great leaps in variation (hence the term discontinuous). This view was expressed in *Materials for the Study of Variation* (1894), a book that many regard as Bateson's best.

After ruling out the selective power of the environment as the driving factor in evolution, Bateson proposed that evolution can be understood through a study of inheritance which would, he expected, reveal the origin of variation—the phenomenon underlying evolutionary change. During the following years Bateson began an ambitious program of breeding experiments. He wished to know exactly the nature of the transmission of characteristics from parent to offspring. This understood, he could investigate errors in transmission—in short, he could study variation.

Bateson and the Discovery of Mendel

Through his work on heredity and variation, Bateson became peculiarly well suited to recognize the significance of Gregor Mendel's work. First published in 1866 and then forgotten, this work on the inheritance of characters in garden peas was discovered by Hugo De Vries in 1900. Bateson soon also read the republished paper and immediately advanced the view to students and colleagues. To his dismay, however, his former teacher and a bastion of scientific opinion in England, W. F. R. Weldon, reviewed Mendel's work and denied it any significance. Fearing that Mendel's view would be lost for a second time, Bateson formulated a vigorous defense that initiated a bitter controversy but ensured that Mendel would not easily be forgotten.

For Bateson, Mendel's view provided an answer to some vexing biological questions. First, it accorded well with a view supporting discontinuity of variation and, Bateson believed, solved the controversy about whether variation was continuous or discontinuous. Second, it proposed a hereditary unity underlying particular characters—a unity that is retained regardless of combination with other characters and maintained as a hereditary factor even if not manifested in visible character. Thus it answered the question of how a variation could remain distinct when the variable organism bred back into a large population of the normal type. Mendel's view also provided an experimental and quantitative method by which discrete characters could be followed through generations—a rigor that appealed to Bateson. It was, in fact, a principle that organized and explained all Bateson's preconceptions about the nature of organisms and evolution.

Mendelism also provided Bateson with hope for a union between his scientific conceptions and the mainstream of biological opinion. During the ten years following his discovery of Mendel, Bateson became the foremost proselytizer for the Mendelian view. In this task he met considerable success. Genetics, a term that Bateson himself applied to the study of heredity and variation, became a prodigious and respectable pursuit. Bateson subsequently gained serious and highly qualified students, among whom were R. C. Punnett, E. R. Saunders, and L. Doncaster. These students aided him in his most commonly remembered scientific achievements—the demonstration of Mendelian phenomena in animals, a determination of the distribution of hereditary factors that had initially been thought to be anomolous to the Mendelian view, and the discovery of the tendency for factors to be inherited in groups (the phenomenon later called linkage).

These achievements led to numerous honors and improvements in Bateson's academic position. In 1907 he was invited to give a series of lectures at Yale—the Silliman Lectures, published in 1913 as *Problems in Genetics.* In 1910 Bateson became director of the John Innes Horticultural Institution at Merton. There he continued his research and writing, but he slowly slipped from his leading role in biology.

The Conservative Period

Genetics acquired a distinctly materialistic bent in the second decade of the 20th century. Researchers at Columbia University under T. H. Morgan moved the field with their chromosome theory of inheritance. They proposed that the factors of inheritance—genes—were material units arranged serially on the chromosomes. Recognizing that they lacked the sophistication to investigate the manner by which these proposed material factors were translated into visible characters, these researchers limited their investigation to the transmission of characters from one generation to the next. Studies of the frequencies at which factors were inherited together led to a positioning of factors on chromosomes. In essence, a genetic map was created.

Results from Columbia were impressive and convinced most biologists of the accuracy of the chromosome theory. Bateson was, however, philosophically oriented against a materialistic position. He believed that substance alone possessed no capacity to reproduce and manifest itself in a visible character. On the contrary, forces—waves, for example—by causing similar arrangements of substance could be the hereditary factors. This, applied to development, could explain the repetition of body parts or, applied to inheritance, could explain why offspring were similar to parents. Even variation was regarded by Bateson not as a change in substance, but as a change in arrangement brought on by a change in force or motion during development. Thus, for Bateson, inheritance and development were intimately bound. This union was ignored by Morgan and his colleagues. While they made great strides in characterizing inheritance, their refusal to deal with development indicated, Bateson believed, the weakness of their theory.

Few biologists shared Bateson's suspicion of materialism. That evidence for the chromosome theory was circumstantial did not bother them as it bothered Bateson. While Bateson called for a demonstration that material units on chromosomes gave rise to inheritable characters, they were satisfied that linkage groups correlated well with chromosome number—this correlation was the strongest evidence the Columbia group could initially produce for the chromosome theory. It was a popular theory, however, and it became more popular as the evidence mounted in its favor. Oriented against this trend, Bateson once again found himself critic of prevailing biological thought.

Despite failing health, Bateson continued his research at the John Innes Horticultural Institution until his death in 1926. In addition, he continued his lifelong avocation, the collection of art. His election as a trustee of the British Museum was related to the knowledge gained through this avocation. This final honor pleased him greatly and topped his impressive list, which included the Darwin Medal (1904), election as president of the British Association for the Advancement of Science (1914), and the Royal Medal (1920).

Further Reading

The most comprehensive biography of Bateson is the memoir by his wife, Beatrice Bateson. It includes samples of his letters and is found in the book *William Bateson, F. R. S. Naturalist* (1928, 1985), which also contains numerous papers and addresses by Bateson. Other biographical sources are William Coleman's article in the *Dictionary of Scientific Biography* and "William Bateson" by his student R. C. Punnett (*Edinburgh Review*, 1926). Lindley Darden gives a perceptive analysis of Bateson's adoption of the Mendelian view in "William Bateson and the Promise of Mendelism," *Journal of the History of Biology* (1977), and A. G. Cock writes about Bateson's breeding experiments, discusses Bateson's conflicts with the conservative factions of English biology, and characterizes Bateson's approach to scientific investigation in "William Bateson, Mendelism and Biometry," *Journal of the History of Biology* (1973). "Bateson and Chromosomes: Conservative Thought in Science," *Centaurus* (1970) is a lengthy article by William Coleman on the factors which contributed to Bateson's rejection of chromosome theory. For a general study of biology during this period, see Garland Allen, *Life Science in the Twentieth Century* (1975). □

Fulgencio Batista y Zaldívar

Fulgencio Batista y Zaldívar (1901–1973) was a Cuban political and military leader. Army general in the 1930s, "strong man" and elected president in the 1940s, and dictator in the 1950s, he dominated Cuban politics for more than 2 decades.

Fulgencio Batista was born in Banes, Oriente Province, on January 16, 1901, the son of a poor railroad laborer. After attending a Quaker missionary school, he worked in a variety of menial jobs. At age 20 he joined the Cuban army.

The military afforded Batista an opportunity for rapid upward mobility. Ambitious and energetic, he studied at night and graduated from the National School of Journalism. In 1928 he was advanced to sergeant and assigned as stenographer to Camp Columbia in Havana. At the time, Cuba was going through a period of considerable turmoil. The growing economic depression added to public misery, and the overthrow of Gerardo Machado's dictatorship in 1933 released a wave of uncontrolled anger and anxiety. Unhappy with a proposed pay reduction and an order restricting their promotions, the lower echelons of the army began to conspire. On September 4, 1933, Batista, together with anti-Machado students, assumed leadership of the movement, demoted army officers, and overthrew Carlos Manuel de Céspedes's provisional government. Batista and the students appointed a short-lived five-man junta to rule Cuba, and on September 10 they named a University of Havana professor of physiology, Ramón Grau San Martin, provisional president. Batista soon became a colonel and chief of staff of the army.

Grau's nationalistic and revolutionary regime was opposed by the United States, which refused to recognize it, and by different groups within Cuba which conspired against it. On January 14, 1934, the unique alliance between students and the military collapsed, and Batista forced Grau to resign, thus frustrating the revolutionary process that had begun with Machado's overthrow.

Batista emerged as the arbiter of Cuba's politics. He ruled through puppet presidents until 1940, when he was elected president. Desiring to win popular support, he sponsored an impressive body of welfare legislation. Public administration, health, education, and public works improved. He established rural hospitals and minimum-wage laws, increased salaries for public and private em-

In a rigged election in November 1954, Batista was "re-elected" for a 4-year term. This time he neglected social and economic problems, and corruption and graft reached unprecedented proportions. Political parties and groups called for new elections but with little success. Fidel Castro began guerrilla operations, with the assistance of his Argentine compatriot, Ernesto "Che" Guevera, in Oriente Province. Soon other groups, like the Civic Resistance movement, organized into an urban underground and began terrorist warfare in Cuba's cities. An attack on the presidential palace in 1957 by the students and followers of deposed President Prio nearly succeeded in killing Batista. On December 9, 1958, U.S. financier William D. Pawley met with Batista on behalf of the State Department, offering sanctuary for Batista and his family in Florida. To his regret, Batista refused the generous American offer, and finally, defections in the army precipitated the crumbling of the regime on December 31, 1958. With rebel forces numbering over 50,000, Batista escaped to the Dominican Republic, and though a new president took office in Cuba, Castro soon arrived in Havana to take power. Later Batista moved from the Dominican Republic to the Portuguese Madeira Islands, where he wrote several books, among them *Cuba Betrayed* and *The Growth and Decline of the Cuban Republic,* which are apologies for his divisive role in Cuban politics. Batista never returned to Cuba, and died of a heart attack in Marbella, Spain on August 6, 1973.

Further Reading

The best-known work on Batista is Edmund A. Chester, *A Sergeant Named Batista* (1954), which, although eulogistic, contains valuable information on his life and policies. See also Robert Smith, ed., *Background to Revolution: The Development of Modern Cuba* (1966), and Hugh Thomas, *Cuba: The Pursuit of Freedom* (1971). Another good source is *Cuba: A Short History* (1993), edited by Leslie Bethell. □

ployees, and started a program of rural schools under army control. He legalized the Cuban Communist party and in 1943 established diplomatic relations with the Soviet Union. The army received higher pay, pensions, better food, and modern medical care, thus ensuring its loyalty. On December 9, 1941, following the attack on Pearl Harbor, Batista brought Cuba into World War II on the Allied side. Air and naval bases were made available to the United States, which purchased most of Cuba's sugar production and provided generous loans and grants.

In 1944 Batista allowed the election of his old-time rival, Grau San Martin. After an extensive tour of Central and South America, Batista settled at Daytona Beach, Florida, where he wrote *Sombras de America* (1946), in which he surveyed his life and policies. In 1948, while still in Florida, he was elected to the Cuban Senate from Santa Clara Province. He returned to Cuba that year, organized his own party, and announced his presidential candidacy for the June 1952 elections.

Batista, however, prevented the election from taking place. Aware perhaps that he had little chance to win, he and a group of army officers overthrew the constitutionally elected regime of President Carlos Prio Socarrás on March 10, 1952. Batista suspended the 1940 constitution and Congress, canceled the elections, and dissolved all political parties. Opposition soon developed, led primarily by university students. On July 26, 1953, young revolutionaries led by Fidel Castro unsuccessfully attacked the Moncada military barracks in Oriente Province.

José Batlle y Ordóñez

José Batlle y Ordóñez (1856-1929) was a Uruguayan statesman and newspaperman. The dominant political figure in his country's history, he was twice president of Uruguay and made it the most stable and democratic country in Latin America.

José Batlle was born in Montevideo on May 21, 1856, to a politically active family affiliated with the Colorado party. His father, Lorenzo, a general in the army, was president of the republic (1868-1872); he was ousted by an uprising, however, and the family lived in modest circumstances after that time.

Batlle was deeply committed to socially progressive goals from early youth. After completing preparatory school in Montevideo, he entered the National University in 1873. He led a student group working for social reform, but the coming of Uruguay's first true military dictator in 1876 discouraged him. In 1879, without having obtained a degree, Batlle went to Paris in a self–imposed partial exile; he returned after 17 months, impoverished and frustrated by inaction.

In February 1881 Batlle began work as a journalist and political critic for *La Nación* of Montevideo. In 1886 he participated in a military uprising against the current dictator and was jailed briefly. Three months later, in July, he founded *El Día*, which remained his personal and partisan journal until his death. When the dictator Máximo Santos went into exile in November, Batlle undertook the goal of reorganizing the Colorado party and of cleansing it of its record of supporting oligarchic and dictatorial governments.

In 1887 Batlle briefly was *jefe político* (presidentially appointed governor) of Minas Department. He was sharply critical of the party's leadership, however, and resigned to run for the Chamber of Deputies. In what he felt was a rigged election, he was defeated. In 1890 he was elected a Colorado deputy for Salto Department but continued his strong criticism of national and party leadership. After a short civil war in 1897, he was elected a senator for Montevideo Department in 1898, despite the antagonism of senior Colorado leaders. Batlle was elected president of the Senate in a bitter fight that split his party, then in 1902 was elected president of the republic for the term 1903-1907. He remained the real chief of the country until his death.

Batlle's first presidential term was partially taken up by the country's last great civil war, in 1903-1904. As during many earlier clashes, conservative, rural, and oligarchic Blancos (the opposition party) fought Colorados. Peace in 1904 was facilitated by a division of influence between the great Blanco ranches of the interior and the Colorado-led urban groups. Batlle introduced reforms that were disappointingly mild in relation to his partisan language. The bases were laid for broad change, however.

Batlle was not allowed to succeed himself and spent the interim term (1907-1911) required by the constitution in Europe. He returned to the presidency in 1911. The state became deeply committed to progressive and democratic socialism, anticlericalism, broad government ownership of basic enterprises, extended rights for urban labor, greatly extended rights of popular democratic participation in politics, and broad programs for social improvement and distribution of goods and services. Batlle respected his bargain with the landowners, and reforms did not affect the interior.

Batlle influenced the country to adopt a unique political experiment, the plural executive, in 1918. This National Council of Administration had nine nationally elected members who shared some powers formerly given the single president. The office of president was retained, however. The plan was very inefficient and failed under the stress of the world depression of 1933. Batlle's goal had not been efficiency, however, but to preclude power to any one strong man. He was very successful in this goal.

Batlle remained politically active and held a seat in the Council for one term. He died in Montevideo on Oct. 20, 1929.

Batlle's 30 years of party dominance permitted him to implant his values in the country. He was modestly successful in training successors. Unlike any Latin American politician before or after, he held nearly all power, yet used it not for personal gain but to create a consensus in favor of modernizing and liberalizing middle-class goals. His political system survived, and although bitter economic and political crises began in the middle 1950s, the norms of his system endured to preclude military seizure of power, political dictatorship, or successful extremist attacks on the constitution by harshly persistent, radical Castroites.

Further Reading

The major works on Batlle are in Spanish. In English see Milton I. Vanger, *José Batlle y Ordóñez of Uruguay: The Creator of His Times, 1902-1907* (1963). General works on Uruguayan politics include Simon G. Hanson, *Utopia in Uruguay* (1938); Russell H. Fitzgibbon, *Uruguay: Portrait of a Democracy* (1954); Philip B. Taylor, *Government and Politics of Uruguay* (1962); and George Pendle, *Uruguay* (3d ed. 1965). □

Kathleen Battle

American soprano Kathleen Battle (born 1948) divided her career between the opera and concert singing. Her light, sweet voice and charming stage presence were especially suited to operatic ingénue roles.

Lyric coloratura soprano Kathleen Battle was born on August 13, 1948, in Portsmouth, Ohio. The youngest of seven children whose father was a steel worker, she attended public schools in a segregated school system. She remained relatively unexposed to opera until her teens and, no doubt aware of the limited opportunities afforded to African Americans, steered a practical course for herself, studying typing and shorthand in high school. Although she took the advice of a high school music teacher to study music at the University of Cincinnati College Conservatory, she opted not for the performance curriculum but for an education degree, which would enable her to teach. Her voice teacher during her college years was Franklin Bens.

Having received a bachelor's degree in 1970 and a master's in 1971, Battle taught grades four through six for the next two years in the Cincinnati public school system. Meanwhile, she continued to take voice lessons and also to study German and acting while taking singing jobs in and around Cincinnati.

In 1972 she auditioned successfully for Thomas Shippers, then the director of both the Cincinnati Symphony Orchestra and the Spoleto Festival. He arranged for her professional debut that year in a performance of the Brahms *Requiem* in Spoleto. Her American debut followed as a repeat performance of the piece with the Cincinnati Orchestra later that year.

The following year Battle came to the attention of James Levine while singing at the Cincinnati May Festival. He immediately engaged her in his guest-conducting tour around the United States. Included in this tour was the Ravinia Festival, to which she returned for several summers as an artist in residence. She moved to New York in 1975 after an engagement in a Broadway production of Scott Joplin's *Treemonisha*.

She made her professional operatic debut as Rosina in Rossini's *Barber of Seville* with the Michigan Opera Theater, and her New York debut followed in 1976 with the City Opera as Susanna in Mozart's *The Marriage of Figaro*. But it was again Levine who brought her rapidly to stardom. In 1977 he offered her the role of the shepherdess in Wagner's *Tannhauser* at the Metropolitan Opera, where her debut took place on December 22, 1977. Battle's physical beauty, captivating stage presence, and a seemingly effortless virtuosity quickly made her a favorite there; and the following years secured her reputation.

Possessing a light, sweet voice of extreme agility, Battle wisely avoided the heavier operatic roles. Among composers she favored Mozart for his precision and clarity of line, his rhythmic vitality, and the appropriateness of the color and weight of his music to her voice. Mozart roles included Pamina in *The Magic Flute,* Susanna in *The Marriage of Figaro,* Despina in *Cosi fan tutte,* and Blonde in *The Abduction* from the *Seraglio.* Other important parts were Zerbinetta in *Ariadne auf Naxos* and Zdenka in *Arabella,* both by Richard Strauss, another favorite composer; Oskar

in Verdi's *Un ballo in maschera;* and Norina in Donizetti's *Don Pasquale.*

Battle did not limit her career to the opera, but divided appearances rather equally between opera, song recitals, and performances of vocal works involving larger ensembles. She achieved much commercial success for recordings of her song recitals, which were additionally attractive in that they frequently offered music other than the standard fare. Among her most popular song recordings are those with the guitarist Christopher Parkening (*The Pleasure of Their Company*), the violinist Itzhak Perlman (*The Bach Album*), and the trumpeter Winton Marsalis (*Baroque Duet*). In 1990 she presented a concert of spirituals, also recorded, with Jessye Norman (*Spirituals in Concert*). Although the concert received some criticism for its "pseudo-Gershwin" arrangements, both singers triumphed over what could have been an inappropriate artificiality. Battle often closed song recitals with a group of spirituals.

Other popular recordings are *Kathleen Battle Sings Mozart, Salzburg Recital,* and *At Carnegie Hall.* In June 1986 she gave a command performance, nationally televised, for President Reagan at the White House. She was awarded an honorary Doctorate from the University of Cincinnati in 1983.

Battle's reputation as a temperamental singer was well-known and was documented along with her rise to fame. In February 1994 she was dismissed from the Met's production of Donizetti's *Fille du Régiment* for what officials cited as her "unprofessional actions during rehearsals." At the same time the company withdrew all other offers for future engagements.

Battle has been pursuing other avenues through a variety of professional performances. In 1995, Battle's voice was heard on four albums, and she appeared on the television special *An Evening with Kathleen Battle and Thomas Hampson.* She opened Lincoln Center's 1995-96 jazz season with a concert, and has appeared on tour throughout the United States. With Christopher Parkening she released *Angels Glory,* a compilation of Christmas songs for the 1996 season. *A Christmas Celebration* was released in 1997, and also includes music for the holidays.

Further Reading

One of the few opera singers to achieve commercial success, Kathleen Battle continued to be charted by all of the music magazines and journals, including *Billboard, Stereo Review,* and *Opera News.* Among the most substantial articles on Battle's career are "Fortune's Favorite: A Conversation with Kathleen Battle" in *Opera News* (March 13, 1982) and "The Sweet Song of Kathleen Battle" in *Fanfare* (1986). The circumstances surrounding her dismissal from the Met are detailed in *The New York Times* (February 8, 1994). □

Batu Khan

The Mongolian military leader Batu Khan (died 1255) conquered Russia and the adjoining territories

of eastern Europe and organized the Mongol state known as the Golden Horde.

Batu was a grandson of Genghis Khan, the conqueror of Asia and founder of the Mongol Empire. Batu early showed a talent for military and administrative affairs and distinguished himself in the service of his father, Juchi, who had been entrusted with the administration and expansion of the western section of the empire, then comprising the territory of central Asia and western Siberia. Following Juchi's death in 1227, this task fell to Batu.

Although the Mongols had defeated the Russians in a battle on the Kalka River in 1223, a serious attempt to conquer Russia, and perhaps Europe, was not undertaken until 1237. Exploiting disunity among Russian princes, Batu conquered their territories with unequaled brutality, and by 1241 all of Russia was under his control. While one of his armies proceeded as far west as Liegnitz (Legnica) in Silesia, where it defeated a combined force of Poles and Germans, Batu himself crossed the Carpathian Mountains and the Danubian plains to the Adriatic Sea and concentrated his forces in Hungary for a campaign against western Europe through the Danube valley. Upon receiving news of the death of Great Khan Ugedey (Ögödei), however, Batu decided to return to the east and withdrew his armies to the Volga River, subjugating Bulgaria, Wallachia, Moldavia, and the Cuman khanate in the Pontic steppes along the way (1242).

Having failed to obtain the title of Great Khan of Mongolia for himself or his ally Mongka (Möngkë, Mangu), Batu settled in the city of Saray on the lower Volga and attended to the administration of his own domain, which now extended from the Ob River in western Siberia to Poland and Bulgaria in eastern Europe and which came to be called the Golden Horde. In 1251, when Mongka finally became great khan, Batu received from him a recognition of complete autonomy.

At first brutal and irreconcilable in his treatment of the conquered lands, Batu grew tolerant and accommodating with age, allowing local native princes to rule their lands at their will as long as they remained loyal to him and regularly paid him the tribute collected among their subjects. He died in 1255, but his empire survived until the end of the 15th century.

Further Reading

Batu receives ample treatment by George Vernadsky in *A History of Russia*, vol 3: *The Mongols and Russia* (1953). Although quite controversial, it surpasses the earlier work of Jeremiah Curtin, *The Mongols in Russia* (1908). A popular account of the Mongol conquest is Harold Lamb, *The March of the Barbarians* (1940). □

Charles Pierre Baudelaire

The French author Charles Pierre Baudelaire (1821-1867) was the poet of the modern metropolis and was one of the first great French precursors of the symbolists. He has also been recognized as one of the 19th century's finest art critics and translators.

Charles Baudelaire was born on April 9, 1821, in Paris. His father, Joseph François Baudelaire, had been a friend of the philosophers C. A. Helvétius and A. N. de Condorcet and tutor to the young sons of the Duc de Choiseul Praslin. His mother, Caroline Archimbaut-Dufays Baudelaire, was born in London in exile in 1793 and died at Honfleur in 1871. In February 1827, when Baudelaire was not yet 6, his father's death led to a period of very close intimacy with his mother, for whom the boy felt a passionate love. Her remarriage near the end of the following year to the handsome officer Jacques Aupick must have seemed to her son a cruel betrayal. Baudelaire's stepfather, a capable and resolute man, rose to the rank of general, was named minister to Turkey in 1848 and ambassador to Spain in 1851, and in 1853 became a senator. But his nature was different from Baudelaire's, and he took a very dim view of his stepson's desire to be a poet.

Baudelaire was expelled from the Lycée Louis le Grand in 1839 before receiving his baccalaureate degree, but he managed to obtain it later that year. He registered for legal

studies in Paris and for a time led a dissipated, bohemian existence in the Latin Quarter, where he probably contracted syphilis, which later caused his death. He may also have begun taking opium and hashish during these years. In 1841 his worried parents arranged a sea voyage to India to draw the young poet out of his dissolute environment. His ship sailed from Bordeaux but was damaged in a storm, and Baudelaire apparently went no farther than the island of Mauritius, to the east of Madagascar. He returned home, however, with ineffaceable memories of exotic lands and seas.

When he was 21, Baudelaire inherited a modest fortune from his father's estate, but his extravagance soon led to the appointment of a legal guardian whose conscientious control of his finances drove the poet nearly to despair. A long affair with a multiracial woman who called herself Jeanne Duval added to his suffering, though she seems to have been the person, along with his mother, whom Baudelaire loved most in life. She was his "Black Venus" and the inspiration for some of his most beautiful and most despairing poems. Other women frequently celebrated in his verses were the voluptuous Madame Sabatier ("la Présidente") and green-eyed Marie Daubrun.

Baudelaire's significant early publications were two essays of art criticism (*Le Salon de 1845* and *Le Salon de 1846*) and two volumes of translations from the tales of Poe in 1856 and 1857. At the end of June 1857 appeared *Les Fleurs du mal,* his greatest work, for which Baudelaire was tried for offenses against religion and public decency. He was found guilty of the second charge and sentenced to pay a fine of 300 francs and to remove six poems from his collection.

As the years passed, ill health and financial problems added to Baudelaire's miseries. In 1864 he went to Belgium to deliver a series of lectures that ended in dismal failure. He suffered further terrifying attacks of illness, and he began to pray—" to set out his sentinels for the night." In the midst of all this unhappiness he learned that Jeanne Duval might be going blind. Finally, in March 1866, he fell while visiting a church at Namur, Belgium, with friends. A few days later he was found dazed in a café and taken home, where he was later discovered paralyzed and aphasic. In July 1866 he was brought back to Paris and placed in a rest home. He died in his mother's arms on Aug. 31, 1867, and was buried 2 days later in the family vault in Montparnasse Cemetery, where a somber monument was unveiled to his memory in 1902.

Les Fleurs du mal

Baudelaire's most famous work is his collection of poems *Les Fleurs du mal,* whose title means both "Flowers of Evil" and "Flowers of Suffering." Baudelaire believed that original sin pervades man's world, and a sense of theological evil looms over his thought like a cloud. But he proclaimed suffering "a divine remedy for our impurities" and wrote that "it is one of the prodigious privileges of Art that . . . *suffering* put to rhythm and cadence may fill the mind with a calm *joy.*"

The first edition of *Les Fleurs du mal* (1857) contains only 100 poems, and the posthumous edition of 1868 suffers from having been put in order by friends after the poet's death. Thus the second edition of 1861 (the last arranged by Baudelaire's own hand) is most useful for a study of his art. It comprises an introductory poem, "To the Reader," which is a powerful indictment of the current society, and 126 poems divided into six sections: Spleen and Ideal, Parisian Sketches, Wine, Fleurs du mal, Revolt, and Death.

Baudelaire's imagination and moral nature were deeply rooted in his Catholic background, and though his gloomy conception of humanity doomed by original sin is not alleviated by any assurance of salvation, it is important to recognize that Baudelaire does keep for man's spiritual nature a dimension of eternity. Love in Baudelaire's poetry, as elsewhere in his writings, is seen most often in dark and despairing terms, and many of his epithets for woman are extremely cruel. His grim vision of love is evident, for example, in the hideous imagery of the poem called *Voyage à Cythère* and in *Sed non satiata.*

Poems concerned with esthetics, such a *Correspondances, Les Phares* (The Lighthouses), *La Beauté, L'Idéal,* and *Hymne à la Beauté,* reveal Baudelaire's very complex ideas on the beautiful. While greatly influenced by the esthetic concepts of romanticism, Baudelaire also recalls significant elements in the great neoclassic writings of the 17th century in his concern with the moral, psychological, and religious aspects of man's nature, in his relatively small vocabulary, and in his powerfully compressed expression.

It is in his subject matter and the range of his sensibility that Baudelaire seems most modern. His poems on spleen and ennui bear the accent of his age; and his poetic imagery, with its marvelous interplay of the senses—for example, *Correspondances* and *Harmonie du soir* (Evening Harmony)—introduces a powerful new sensuousness into French poetry and gives a new literary importance to odors and fragrance which will be exploited later in the novels of Zola and Proust.

Baudelaire's vision of Paris in the 18 poems of the Parisian Sketches includes what he called "the heroism of modern life." His Paris is a city of physical and spiritual and moral suffering, and the eyes of the men and women in the poems depicting it are full of unrest and sorrow. But over the great city are skies that make one think of eternity; and there is mystery and enchantment amidst the suffering.

In *Les Fleurs du mal* there are recurrent dominant images of ennui, time, and death. The clock is seen as a sinister god, terrifying and impassive (*L'Horloge*), and time is ultimately the victor over man. The last poem in *Les Fleurs du mal* is *Le Voyage,* representing death as a voyage that may lead to "something *new.*"

Other Writings

Baudelaire's writings on the "artificial paradises" of wine, opium, and hashish mirror his concerns as artist and moralist. In his most famous writing on drugs, *Les Paradis artificiels: opium et haschisch* (1860), the opium essay is based on Thomas De Quincey's *Confessions of an English Opium Eater* but *Le Poème du haschisch* is Baudelaire's own. He knew from experience the hallucinations of both drugs and apparently suffered the miseries of addiction to opium. He concludes that man cannot, without terrible danger, alter "the primordial conditions of his existence"— if the artificial paradises enhance imagination, they destroy the "precious substance" of the will.

In the *Petits poèmes en prose* (1869), sometimes called *Spleen de Paris,* Baudelaire developed the prose poem into an exquisite form. The volume's 50 examples of this genre depict mostly a world of lonely people: old women, artists, children, workmen, crowds, widows, clowns, cold and perverted lovers—the poor and cynical and bored men and women of the great city. But again, beyond the suffering and misery, one finds Baudelaire's understanding of the strange "heroism of modern life."

Among Baudelaire's *Journaux intimes* (Intimate Diaries) the most notable are the two notebooks called *Fusées* (Skyrockets) and *Mon coeur mis à nu* (My Heart Laid Bare), a title that Baudelaire took from Poe. They contain invaluable insights into the poet's inner world—his intellectual, ethical, religious, and esthetic speculations and his comments on love and women, boredom, and material progress. There is constant evidence of Baudelaire's moral and intellectual elegance, of his dandyism, and of his violent antipathy to the society of his day; but above all, one is conscious in these pages of his inner distress—his fears and longings and his sense of the loneliness of the human situation.

Of Baudelaire's other volumes, the most significant are his translations from Poe: *Histoires extraordinaires* (1856), *Nouvelles Histoires extraordinaires* (1857), *Aventures d'Arthur Gordon Pym* (1858), *Eureka* (1864), and *Histoires grotesques et sérieuses* (1865); his criticism of art, music and literature: *Curiosités esthétiques* (1868) and *L'Art romantique* (1869) and such miscellaneous writings as *La Fanfarlo* (1847); and his violent diatribes against Belgium and the Belgians, *Amoenitates Belgicae* (1925) and *Pauvre Belgique* (1952).

Further Reading

Among the most useful English translations of Baudelaire are William Aggeler, *The Flowers of Evil* (1954), and Francis Scarfe, *Baudelaire* (1961), both in English prose with bilingual texts, and Lois Boe Hyslop and Francis E. Hyslop, Jr., *Baudelaire as a Literary Critic: Selected Essays* (1964) and *Baudelaire, a Self-Portrait: Selected Letters . . . with a Running Commentary* (1957). The best biography is Enid Starkie, *Baudelaire* (1958). Other valuable studies include W. T. Bandy, *Baudelaire Judged by His Contemporaries* (1933); Margaret Gilman, *Baudelaire the Critic* (1943); Percy Mansell Jones, *Baudelaire* (1952); Martin Turnell, *Baudelaire: A Study of His Poetry* (1954); Marcel A. Ruff, *Baudelaire* (1955; trans., slightly abridged by Agnes Kertesz, 1966); Henri Peyre, ed., *Baudelaire: A Collection of Critical Essays* (1962); and Lois Boe Hyslop, ed., *Baudelaire as a Love Poet and Other Essays* (1969). An early study of unusual value is Marcel Raymond, *From Baudelaire to Surrealism* (1933; trans. 1949). Robert T. Cargo, *Baudelaire Criticism, 1950-1967* (1968), provides a useful bibliography of scholarship with critical commentary. ☐

Étienne-Émile Baulieu

The French physician and biochemist Étienne-Émile Baulieu (Étienne Blum, born 1926) made major contributions to the knowledge of steroid hormones and developed RU 486, the first safe, effective contragestive medication (abortion pill).

Étienne-Émile Baulieu was born in Strasbourg, France, on December 12, 1926. His father, Léon Blum, homonym of the French prime minister, died when he was three and a half years old. He had been a renowned professor of medicine. Born in Alsace when that province was occupied by Germany, he had studied in Berlin and specialized in nephrology. Drafted into the German army, he was decorated with the Iron Cross. But at heart, as an Alsatian, he was truly French and passed on military intelligence to the French through his first wife's parents, who lived in Switzerland. When he was discovered, he joined the French army in Verdun in 1916. Marshal Pétain decorated him with the Legion of Honour.

After the discovery of insulin in Toronto, Canada, Leon Blum (Baulieu) was selected by the Rockefeller Foundation to be one of the first to use it for the treatment of diabetes. He remained until his death in 1930, at the age of 54, a famed specialist of diabetes. A widow for about ten years, his second wife, Étienne-Émile's mother, was 20 years younger. A Norman, she was an international lawyer and a pianist. In four years of marriage she had three children. After Léon Blum died, his wife moved to Paris and cut all relations with her late husband's family just before his third child was born. Only when he was over 40 years old, and without his mother's knowledge, would Étienne-Émile discover, with admiration, the identity of his father.

When World War II broke out, Baulieu's family took refuge in the "Free Zone," the southern part of France, which for two years was not occupied by the Germans. He was the only man in the family. In 1942-1943 he was a student at the high school (Lycée) Champollion in Grenoble. He became active in a youth communist organization. To escape from the Gestapo, he convinced his mother to leave for Annecy. He made false identification cards. That's how Émile Baulieu was born! He studied at the lycée and spent time in the Maquis resistance movement. When the Haute-Savoir was liberated, he became a member of the Alpine unit of the First French Army.

With the liberation of northern France, Baulieu wasn't really sure what he wanted to do. The Communist Party would have liked him either to enter the military or become a "permanent"—i.e., professional—militant. But he decided on different future and registered both in a pre-med program and in the Faculty of Science for a Bachelor of Science degree, to please his mother.

Étienne Blum becomes Étienne-Émile Baulieu

Demobilized, he returned to Paris at the end of October 1944; Strasbourg was not yet liberated. He was registered at the University of Paris under his war name, to which he added his real first name, Étienne. He was also advised to keep that name to avoid the anti-Semitism which existed in the Communist Party.

He became an interne of Paris hospitals (1951-1955), doctor (1955), and a chef de clinique (1955-1957). Among the professors he had were Henri Mondor, Louis Pasteur Vallery-Radot, Jean Hamburger, and Paul Milliez.

Blinded in an experiment with haptoglobin, a protein he had discovered, Max-Fernand Zayle became Baulieu's mentor. But his protégé turned away from research on haptoglobin and instead decided to study hormones. The clinical cases he saw in the medical divisions headed by Lucien de Gennes and Jacques Decourt led him to his discoveries. He showed in 1960 that the main adrenal androgen, dehydroepiandrosterone sulfate, was a hydrophilic conjugated steroid, used as a marker of aging.

Paris had one Faculty of Medicine for more than 20,000 students. When Zayle was appointed to the chair in biochemistry, Baulieu had become, in 1958, associate professor of biochemistry. Tenured, he had felt freer to go on with a career dominated by research rather than by clinical practice.

The discovery of dehydroepiandrosterone sulfate by Baulieu got him an invitation from Seymour Lieberman, who at age 45 ruled the world of steroids. Baulieu was a visiting scientist at the Department of Obstetrics, Gynecology and Biochemistry at Columbia University in 1961-1962. Because of his former political activities, he got a visa to the United States only after petitions from academics. It was a new era; Jack Kennedy had been elected as president. About Lieberman, Baulieu wrote: "This wise man is for me more than a father or a big brother, he is a model."

It was Lieberman who introduced Baulieu to Gregory Pincus, a Boston University biochemist who had played a key role in the development of the contraceptive pill. The encounter led to Baulieu's interest in contraception and in the regulation of pregnancy.

Steroid Hormones

Back in Paris in 1962, Baulieu said later that by now he had become "a truly professional researcher." He was invited to head a research unit called "U-33" at Kremlin Bicêtor, an important hospital of Paris. Into the 1990s he still directed that unit of the National Institute of Health and Medical Research (INSERM). His association—as a consultant—with the pharmaceutical enterprise Roussel Uclaf also dated from his return from the United States.

For three decades Baulieu worked with steroid hormones. His early research dealt with the biosynthesis of these hormones. His contributions concern every aspect of our knowledge of the steroid receptors: characterization, purification, immunology, mechanism of action, and regulatory mechanisms governing their concentrations. He described the progesterone receptor and the androgen receptor. He found a membrane receptor for steroid hormones (in *Xenopus laevis* oocytes) distinct from the classical intracellular receptors. His later findings included the biosynthesis in the brain of the "neurosteroids." Yet Baulieu's name was associated, in the public opinion, in the late 1980s and 1990s with another of his important discoveries, RU 486, a steroid analogue.

RU 486 (Mifepristone)

Research done in the 1970s led to the synthesis by Baulieu of the "abortion pill," RU 486, in 1980. RU stands for the chemical products of Roussel Uclaf, the French pharmaceutical company, a subsidiary of the German company Hoechst AG, and 486 is abridged for 38486, the real chronological number for the synthesis of the molecule (note that RU 1 dates from 1949!).

After trials in 20 other countries, RU 486, or mifepristone, was approved for use by French and Chinese authorities. In France some 4,000 cases per month were sold to the country's 793 authorized abortion clinics. Roussel Uclaf drew up five mandatory prerequisites before marketing RU 486: (1) abortion must be legal in the country where it will be available; (2) local public, medical, and political opinion must favor abortion; (3) synthetic prostaglandin must be available locally; (4) the distribution network must be strictly controlled; (5) patients should sign a consent form.

In the United States RU 486 won the backing of the American Medical Association (A.M.A.) on June 27, 1990, for testing and possible use. About 45 percent (some 230,000) of the nation's physicians belonged to the association. Abortion opponents, including such groups as the National Right to Life, reacted against the endorsement while a coalition of groups on abortion rights, family planning, and women's health supported the A.M.A. decision. The debate in the United States was watched attentively abroad. In July 1990 Baulieu stated that he "believe[d] the key to the future of RU 486 lies in the United States."

When RU 486 is taken in conjunction with prostaglandins it is an extremely effective method of terminating pregnancy within the first nine weeks of gestation. By 1990 it was used for between a quarter and a third of all pregnancy terminations in France. The treatment requires three 200-milligram pills of RU 486. After 48 hours a small amount of prostaglandin is given either as an injection or a pessary. RU 486 blocks the normal action of progesterone on the cells lining the uterus to accept and sustain an embryo throughout development. The prostaglandin acts on the womb to contract and expel its contents. About 96 percent of women who received RU 486 and the prostaglandin within the first nine weeks of conception have a complete abortion within a day of receiving the prostaglandin. Side effects, if any, are minor.

Although RU 486 is often referred to as the "abortion pill," opponents of abortion have named it the "death pill." Baulieu describes RU 486 as a contragestive pill. Its action is contra-gestation, just as contraceptives are contra-conception. Apart from inducing abortion, RU 486 is considered a promising treatment for breast cancer, brain cancer, diabetes, and hypertension, as well as Cushing's syndrome.

By 1996, RU 486 had been used by over 200,000 European woman, but Roussel Uclaf held back marketing in the United States because of opposition by antiabortionist groups. In 1994, Roussel Uclaf gave patent rights to the Population Council, a nonprofit group in New York City. Clinical trials of the drug were conducted over a period of two years, and the Food and Drug Administration conditionally approved the drug in 1996. Final approval was withheld pending resolution of issues of manufacture, labeling and marketing. In 1997, the Population Council formed a new company, Advances for Choice, to take over the distribution of RU 486 in the United States.

DHEA, the Anti-aging pill

Baulieu began working with dehydroepiandrosterone sulfate (DHEA) in the 60s, but its popularity peaked as the "fountain of youth" of the 90s. DHEA is produced by the adrenal glands. Production peaks at about age 25 and declines into old age. Proponents of its use declared that it helped sleep, improved libido and generally resulted in overall better health. Opponents, including the National Institute on Aging, warned about a variety of side effects that could result from use of DHEA. Available by prescription, DHEA was also available as an over-the-counter drug, under provisions of the "1994 Dietary Supplement Health and Education Act," which allowed marketing of nutritional supplements, provided labels did not contain health claims.

Baulieu became a professor of biochemistry at the Faculty of Medicine of Bicêtro, affiliated with University of Paris-South, in 1970. He was on the editorial boards of several French and international journals. He chaired several scientific committees. He was president in 1978 of the French Endocrinology Society. He was a member of the Scientific Advisory Board for the Special Program in Human Reproduction of the World Health Organization (WHO). Baulieu's research was supported by French sources, but also by the American National Institutes of Health (NIH) and the Ford Foundation.

Many awards were bestowed upon Baulieu. He was a laureate of l'Assistance Publique (Médaille de l'Internat) of the National Academy of Medicine (Dreyfous Foundation Prize, 1956; Specia Prize, 1964) and of the Academy of Sciences (1960). He received the Reichstein Award of the International Society of Endocrinology (1972), the Grand Prix Scientifique of the City of Paris (1974), the Roussel Prize (with E. Jensen, 1976), and the Gregory Pincus Memorial Award (with E. Jensen, 1978). He was R. S. McLaughlin Edward Gallic professor of the Royal College of Physicians and Surgeons of Canada (1976) and Harden lecturer (London, 1979). He became a chevalier of l'Ordre du Mérite (1967), chevalier of the Legion of Honour (1976; he was promoted to officer in 1982 and commander in 1990), and officer of l'Ordre du Mérite du Gabon (1979). He was listed among the 1,000 most cited scientists (ISI, 1981). He was a member of the French Academy of Sciences beginning in 1982. He was the first European medalist of the Society of Endocrinology (Great Britain, 1985). He received the A. and E. Wippman Scientific Research Award, Planned Parenthood of America (1989), the Albert and Mary Lasker Clinical Research Award (1989), and the Alan Guttmacher Award, USA Reproductive Health Professionals (1989). He became a foreign associate member of the U.S. National Academy of Sciences in 1990 and was awarded the Golden Plate, American Academy of Achievement, in 1990. He gave the Claude Bernard lecture of the Royal Society in 1990.

As the head of his medical research unit, Baulieu had many associates. In his acceptance remarks for the Lasker Award, on September 27, 1989, he declared: "Any scientific achievement is the result of a collective effort, and my gratitude goes to my colleagues of yesterday and today, and to INSERM, our medical research institute in France, for permanent support."

In New York in the early 1960s Baulieu became close to artists. He wrote, " . . . it was very important for me. I understood that science is not as far from art as I had believed earlier." Among the artists with whom he closely associated were Jean Tinguely and Niki de Saint-Phalle.

Married at the age of 20, Baulieu had three children and seven grandchildren.

Further Reading

Books authored by Baulieu are *The Antiprogestin Steroid Ru 486 and Human Fertility Control* (1985), *Hormones: From Molecules to Disease* (1990) and *The Abortion Pill: Ru-486, a Woman's Choice* (1991). There are no biographies of Baulieu in English at this time. In French, see a short portrait in *La Recherche* (December 1989) and his autobiography, Étienne-Émile Baulieu, *Génération Pilule* (Paris: 1990). Although Baulieu's name has been mainly associated with RU 486, he contributed extensively to the knowledge of steroid hormones. Important references can be found in his autobiography. The September 22, 1989, issue of *Science* analyzed RU 486—how the drug works, research on medical uses other than abortion, and how it was discovered—and published an article by Baulieu on the scientific issues, with references and notes. A book-length study is Lawrence Luder, *RU 486: The Pill That Could End the Abortion Wars and Why American Women Don't Have It* (1991). Articles about RU 486 can be found in *Newsday* (September 19, 1996) and (July 4, 1997); *Los Angeles Times* (September 19, 1996), (October 2, 1996) and (June 11, 1997) and *U.S. News & World Report* (September 30, 1996). Coverage of DHEA can be found in *Time* (January 23, 1995), (September 23, 1996) and (November 25, 1996); *Newsday* (August 1, 1995) and (April 29, 1997) and *U.S.A. Today* (September 5, 1996). □

Herbert Baum

Herbert Baum (1912–1942) was a German Jewish resistance leader in Berlin, who in 1933 started to organize a group of mostly Jewish anti-Nazis who maintained links with all major underground groups in the German capital, strengthening the morale of a Berlin Jewish community being deported to death camps in the East.

Except for the messianic Bar Kochba uprising of a.d. 132-135, the idea of self-defense and resistance played a relatively small role in Jewish history during the almost 2,000 years that elapsed between the Roman destruction of Jerusalem in a.d. 70 and the 20th century. These political and military catastrophes, which brought on the destruction of ancient Israel as a sovereign state, led to the dispersion of the majority of the Jewish population throughout the civilized world. Powerless and unwilling to accept the religion of the Christian majority, the best they could hope for was to be protected by a tolerant king or emperor. By the end of the Middle Ages, many of Europe's Jews found themselves confined to ghettoes, a minority that was either tolerated by rulers who deemed their skills economically valuable for their states, or one that often found itself persecuted in bloody pogroms, singled out as a destructive alien presence in a Christian society.

With the French revolution of 1789 and the appearance of democratic institutions in Europe in the 19th century, ghetto walls were literally knocked down and full civil rights, particularly in Western Europe, were guaranteed to Jews and other minorities. In Great Britain, France, Germany, Austria-Hungary, and other European constitutional states, Jews began to fully participate in the economic, political, and intellectual life of their nations. Many Jewish soldiers proudly served in their nations' armed forces. Discrimination against Jews remained in some countries (in Germany only Jews who converted to Christianity stood a chance of becoming university professors or officers in the armed forces), but in the first years of the 20th century it appeared that a new age of enlightenment was at hand—an era in which all remaining religious and ethnic prejudices would soon vanish.

While most Jews in Western Europe were willing to be accepted by the imperfect but improving societies in which they lived, small but influential groups of intellectuals from assimilated Jewish backgrounds rebelled against both the religious traditions of their families and the dominant capitalistic ideals of their immediate environment. These intellectuals, whether in Berlin, Vienna, or Paris, were attracted to the powerful message of Karl Marx and other socialist thinkers, whose books envisioned a world free from age-old scourges of poverty, exploitation, and war. Marx, too, was born into an assimilated German-Jewish family, and for radical German-Jewish intellectuals—-many of whom were indifferent to Judaism as a religion and regarded themselves as culturally German—-acceptance of Marxist concepts of class struggle and secular redemption meant another milestone on the road to full acceptance into the modern world.

In Eastern Europe as well, Jewish intellectuals and many of the impoverished masses saw the road to a better future in terms of socialism. Large numbers of Jews in Poland and other Eastern European nations were also attracted to Zionism, which held that only by creating a Jewish Homeland in Palestine would the sufferings of their people finally end. Both Marxist and Zionist ideologies were militant ideologies that were essentially optimistic in tone, holding that a bright new future was close at hand. Both belief systems condemned what members of both movements saw as the passivity and political indifference of traditional Jewish attitudes, which they were convinced had been the inevitable result of a totally outmoded "ghetto mentality."

The First World War led to mixed results for Europe's Jews. Toward its conclusion, in 1917, the British Government pleased Zionists by declaring itself in favor of a Jewish National Home in Palestine. In Russia, two revolutions that same year cheered Jews and radical Marxists alike by first toppling the anti-Semitic tsarist regime and then creating the Bolshevik dictatorship led by Vladimir Lenin, a non-Jew, and Leon Trotsky, who was of assimilated Jewish background.

Meanwhile, in a briefly independent Ukraine, bloody pogroms led to the deaths of many thousands of Jews, while in newly independent Poland and defeated Hungary the Jewish minorities often suffered from harshly discriminatory legislation. In Germany, the humiliating WWI military defeat in November 1918 quickly unleashed a bitter spirit of recrimination and a search for the "subversive un-German" forces that had brought on a national catastrophe. Even though 12,000 German-Jewish soldiers had died defending the Fatherland, anti-Semitic demagogues, including an obscure Austrian living in Munich named Adolf Hitler, found the perfect scapegoat for Germany's woes in its Jewish minority. Hitler accused Jews of spreading the "poison" of Marxism and treasonously "stabbing Germany in the back" by engaging in profiteering and spreading defeatist and pacifistic ideas on the homefront.

In the late 1920s, the great majority of Germany's Jewish population of about 500,000 regarded themselves as solid, respected citizens of a nation that offered them the security in which they could carry on their careers and raise their children. Most thought of themselves as "German citizens of the Jewish faith" and were thoroughly assimilated to German culture and values. The May 1928 parliamentary election comforted Jews because the most rabid anti-Semites in Germany, Hitler's Nazis, made a poor showing, receiving 810,000 votes, 2.6% of the total. But even in the late 1920s some of Germany's Jews disagreed with the optimism of the assimilationist majority, whose political affiliations ranged from democratic socialism to moderate conservatism. A tiny minority of probably less than 15,000 activists regarded themselves as Zionists—-but even among these only a handful of stalwart members felt equal to the hardships of emigrating to Palestine (in 1928 only 12 from Germany chose to go there).

Another minority of German Jews found themselves attracted to the powerful secular faith centered in Moscow and joined the German Communist Party (KPD). Although the great majority of Germany's Jewish population were urban middle-class professionals and unsympathetic to the ideals of a Communist revolution, some Jews (perhaps one-fifth of the total), who had been born in Poland or Russia, were not German citizens and made their livings as blue-collar wage earners, craftsmen, or peddlers. Some among this Jewish proletariat listened favorably to the KPD propaganda, which argued that neither bourgeois assimilation nor Zionism would end poverty and banish the intolerance of anti-Semitism, but that only a total economic, social, and cultural revolution, such as was being achieved in the Soviet Union, could create a world free of prejudice and discrimination. These beliefs were particularly attractive to Jewish intellectuals whose religious faith had crumbled but who still believed that all could be redeemed if only the next phase of history—-the destruction of capitalism and the creation of a universal socialist society—-was achieved. Indeed, one of the founders of the KPD, Rosa Luxemburg, who was murdered in 1919, had been born into a Polish-Jewish family.

Hitler Heads the German Reich

German Jews were as shocked as most other Germans when Adolf Hitler was appointed chancellor of the German Reich on January 30, 1933. Starting in March 1933, the rapid creation of a brutal dictatorship by Hitler and his National Socialist Party, as well as a Nazi-inspired boycott of Jewish businesses, created a mood of panic among many Jews, and about 53,000 fled Germany in 1933. But when the anti-Jewish terror was moderated somewhat, a significant number (about 16,000) returned from abroad. The organization that spoke for German Jews, the *Reichsvertretung der deutschen Juden,* counseled patience and urged its members to continue to be loyal to German authorities. The majority of the German Jewish population heeded this call. Jews loyal to either Zionist, Social Democratic, or Communist beliefs had little choice but to view the terrors of Nazism as an opportunity to test their ideals. The Zionist organizations grew rapidly, concentrating on preparing Jews, particularly the young and those with financial assets, to emigrate as quickly as possible to Palestine. Most

endangered in the new Nazi state were those German Jews who before Hitler's seizure of power had been active in either the Social Democratic or Communist parties. More than any other group of German Jews in the early years of the Hitler dictatorship, these individuals suffered the most from Nazi repression.

Although the German Communists had made some efforts to prepare for the time when a Fascist dictatorship ruled Germany, when that moment actually came they were grievously unprepared. In March 1933, KPD leadership was decapitated when the leader of the party, Ernst Thälmann, was captured by the Nazis. Known to the rank-and-file as "Teddy," Thälmann would be killed at Buchenwald in 1944. While underground cells (units) started to operate almost immediately, their effectiveness varied from place to place, and by 1936 the Gestapo had been able to ferret out and destroy the great majority of such conspiratorial units. From the start of the Nazi dictatorship, Jews with socialist political beliefs were customarily treated with a brutality that far exceeded that meted out to their non-Jewish comrades. The first concentration camps, which included Dachau near Munich and Oranienburg near Berlin, were rapidly filled in the spring of 1933 by individuals whose political beliefs were anathema to the Nazis.

While Germany's Jews prayed for their situation to improve, Jews and other anti-Nazis outside of Germany worked to help those still living in Germany, as well as to weaken and possibly hasten the collapse of the Nazi regime. Social Democratic, Communist, and other political foes of Hitler set up headquarters in Paris and Prague to train agents for missions in Germany and to lobby for governmental action against the Nazis. In the United States, an anti-Nazi boycott movement began in April 1933, with the goal of applying sufficient economic pressure to force the Nazis to stop persecuting Germany's Jewish population, or perhaps even toppling the regime itself. When it became clear that Hitler would not respond to such measures, new and more dramatic methods of alerting the world to the Nazi menace appeared on the scene. On July 3, 1936, the Hungarian-born Czech Jewish journalist Stefan Lux (1888-1936) committed suicide on the crowded assembly floor of the League of Nations in Geneva. Besides his dramatic gesture, he left behind letters pleading with the world's leaders to organize a system of collective security against the threat posed by Nazi Germany, which he described as a government composed "without exception of real criminals."

Other Jewish activists believed that killing the aggressor would send a more powerful message than would killing themselves. On February 4, 1936, a Croatian-born Jewish medical student named David Frankfurter (1909-82) shot and killed Wilhelm Gustloff, leader of Switzerland's Nazi movement. After surrendering himself to the Swiss police, Frankfurter stated that his aim in killing Gustloff was to warn the world of the dangers of Nazi aggression and subversion. He was sentenced to 18 years' imprisonment. Helmut Hirsch was much less fortunate. A German-Jewish student of architecture who fled to Prague after the Nazis came to power, Hirsch vowed to prove that Jews had the courage to take up arms against Nazism. In Prague, Hirsch met Otto Strasser, a deadly foe of Hitler who believed Hirsch capable of carrying out a mission in the heart of Germany to kill the notorious anti-Semite Julius Streicher or possibly even Hitler. But the plot was poorly organized and Hirsch was arrested soon after crossing the frontier. Despite international protests, he was convicted by the Nazi People's Court and beheaded at Berlin's Plötzensee penitentiary on June 4, 1937.

Probably the most dramatic instance of world Jewish solidarity against Nazism and Fascism before World War II took place in Spain from 1936 to 1939, a time when Spain was torn apart by a bloody civil war. Supported by massive amounts of military aid from Nazi Germany and Fascist Italy, the rebel General Francisco Franco came close to seizing control of Spain in the final months of 1936. But the heroic defense of the city of Madrid in November and December of that year succeeded in part because of the appearance of International Brigades of volunteers who risked—-and in many instances lost—-their lives fighting in defense of the threatened Spanish Republic. Among the leaders of the International Brigades were many Jews, including General Manfred Stern, who founded and commanded the XI Thälmann Brigade of volunteers from Germany and Austria. At least 6,000 Jewish volunteers from over 50 countries fought in various units of the International Brigades; of these, about 500 came from German-speaking countries, most of which were by 1938 under Nazi rule.

Polish Jews Are Deported

A final and tragic act of Jewish defiance before the onset of World War II took place in 1938. In October, the Nazi regime began to deport to Poland large numbers of the almost 57,000 Polish Jews living in the Reich. The situation was compounded by the fact that Poland, whose dictatorial government was also anti-Semitic, had recently decreed that Polish citizens living abroad who had not visited Poland for five consecutive years would be deprived of their citizenship. This act of blatant discrimination meant that many of those Jews deported from Germany would not be accepted by Polish authorities. As a result, over 5,000 expelled Polish-Jewish refugees from Germany were forced in late October 1938 to live in horrible conditions in the village of Zbaszyn, in a no-man's-land just over the Polish side of the frontier. When a young man named Herschel Grynszpan (1921—1943?), who had fled Germany to Paris in 1936, learned that his parents had been deported to Zbaszyn, he vowed to make the Nazis pay for their cruelty and also to make a dramatic statement concerning Jewish rights. On November 7, 1938, Grynszpan went to the German Embassy in Paris with the intention of assassinating the ambassador; instead, he shot and killed a junior diplomat named Ernst vom Rath (ironically, vom Rath was known to be critical of Nazi policies). The diplomat's death provided the Nazis with a pretext for the bloody pogrom known as *Kristallnacht* ("Night of the Broken Glass"), which resulted in scores of Jewish deaths and immense destruction of property.

It was in this complex political and cultural environment that a small group of Berlin Jews defied the Nazi regime for almost a decade before the group was destroyed in 1942. Herbert Baum was the man largely responsible for their actions. He was born in 1912 into a poor Jewish family in the province of Posen (today Poznan in Poland), but a few years later the family moved to Berlin. There he joined Jewish youth organizations, including the German-Jewish Youth Community (DJJG) and the League of Jewish Youth (Ring). In both groups Baum quickly displayed strong qualities of leadership, but their vaguely idealistic bourgeois ideology soon seemed inadequate to him as the twin specters of Nazism and unemployment loomed on the German horizon. By 1931 he had become a member of the Communist Youth Organization and soon was regarded as a promising Communist activist. He met his wife Marianne in the Communist Youth movement and both were deeply convinced that only the creation of a Communist society would free Germany of the evils of capitalism and anti-Semitism. While most Berlin Jews quietly prayed for better times after Hitler came to power, Herbert Baum and his small circle of Communist activists openly defied the Nazis by building a complex, multitiered cell apparatus and distributing leaflets calling for an overthrow of the regime. As early as July 1934, Baum participated in a successful "action" that disseminated anti-Nazi propaganda to a Berlin populace that still included large numbers of passive anti-Nazis whose morale needed encouragement.

After the Nazi intelligence services succeeded in destroying most Communist and Social Democratic underground cells in 1936 and 1937, the Baum group remained virtually isolated in Berlin, and was ordered by the Communist leadership abroad to maintain itself as an exclusively Jewish organization in order to safeguard both itself and other still-existing resistance cells from Nazi infiltration. But while most members of the group were sympathetic to Zionist ideals, Baum and the inner circle of the organization were orthodox Communists for whom the writings of Marx, Engels, Lenin and Stalin were political wisdom incarnate. His iron devotion to the wisdom of the party's leadership even made it possible for him to accept the correctness of the Hitler-Stalin Pact of August 1939—-an event that prompted many Communists to quit the Party. Without denying his Jewish background, Baum believed that after the fall of Hitler Jews might still be able to live in a renewed German culture purged of Nazi racial hatred, and that as a German and a Communist temporarily transformed into a racial pariah he had a grave responsibility to help bring about this historical turnabout. It is significant that he never attempted to flee Germany or secure a visa in order to emigrate; although they doubtless had an idea of the fate that awaited them, the Baum group believed they had a duty to remain in Germany to hasten the pace of revolutionary change.

Baum's Group Destroys Goebbels Exhibit

By 1940, Baum, who worked as an electrician at the Siemens Electrical Motor Plant, had like most Jewish males remaining in Germany become a slave laborer (the first decree authorizing certain types of Jewish forced labor was issued as early as December 20, 1938). But the hardship of slave labor was merely a prelude to what was to follow. In September 1941, German Jews were forced to wear a Star of David on their clothing in public. Then, on October 18, the final catastrophe began. A group of 1,013 men, women, and children, the first of what would eventually be 180 Jewish transports, left Berlin for the East and death. In the midst of fear and confusion among Berlin's Jews, Baum and his circle prided themselves on their realism, fully recognizing that their actions were essentially symbolic and could not by themselves topple a regime built on terror as well as propaganda. But symbols are powerful weapons, and there is little doubt that the partial destruction by arson of the Joseph Goebbels propaganda exhibit ("The Soviet Paradise") in Berlin on May 18, 1942, was a significant psychological blow to the inner circles of the Nazi leadership. The German press was forbidden to publish any stories about the event, and so the German people were never informed that a small but well-organized resistance circle of Jewish Communists had destroyed a major Nazi propaganda show more than nine years after the Nazis came to power in Germany.

By this time, Germany's Jewish population had been reduced by emigration, suicide, and deportation to death camps from over 500,000 in 1933 to slightly over 100,000. Their mood was generally one of despair and resignation, not surprising given the fact that almost a decade of discrimination and persecution had inflicted a massive psychological toll. In the midst of this demoralization, in addition to the Baum group, there existed at least seven smaller illegal Jewish resistance organizations ready and willing to undertake acts of resistance. The growing confidence of Baum and his comrades on the eve of their exhibition attack could be seen in their ability to establish contacts with French, Belgian, and Dutch slave laborers at the Siemens plant where Baum and many of his group worked. The attack succeeded at least in part because Baum could count on the crucial support of Werner Steinbrink (1917-42) and Hildegard Jadamowitz (1916-42), two non-Jewish Communists who secured authentic documents, enabling them to pose as members of the Criminal Police (Kripo). A chemist, Steinbrink was able to secure incendiary materials for torching the Goebbels exhibit.

Goebbels, the regime's brilliantly unscrupulous propaganda chief, had designed the exhibition to keep the German fighting spirit at a fever pitch by documenting the evils of "Jewish Bolshevism." After major military defeats at the gates of Moscow and Leningrad in the closing months of the previous year, a new Nazi military offensive was under way on Soviet territory and the elaborate exhibition in Berlin's Lustgarten was one way to keep the homefront ideologically primed to support a war-to-the-death on the eastern front. That part of the exhibition could be destroyed by a Jewish resistance unit in the capital of the Greater German Reich proved a severe propaganda defeat for Goebbels, for even though the destruction was not reported in press or radio, virtually the entire population knew about the incendiary act within a few days. But the powerful Nazi intelligence and police system was determined to destroy men and women who, though numerically weak in num-

bers and resources, had been bold and resourceful enough to achieve such a significant propaganda victory.

On May 22, 1942, Herbert and Marianne Baum were arrested, as were most of the leading members of his group. Herbert Baum was tortured and taken to the Siemens plant to identify fellow workers who had joined in the arson plot, but he refused to reveal anything. On June 11, his frustrated Nazi captors murdered him (the Gestapo simply informed the trial prosecution staff that Baum had "committed suicide"). The trial of the Baum group's leaders resulted in a verdict that was a foregone conclusion—-death by decapitation. The sentence was carried out on August 18 at Plötzensee penitentiary in Berlin. Executed were Marianne Baum, Joachim Franke, Hildegard Jadamowitz, Heinz Joachim, Sala Kochmann, Hans-Georg Mannaberg, Gerhard Meyer, Werner Steinbrink, and Irene Walther. Franke, Jadamowitz, Mannaberg, and Steinbrink were all non-Jewish German Communists who had cooperated with the Baum group, and whose actions were deemed equally treasonous by a Nazi court. Sala Kochmann tried to kill herself during interrogation because of the intense torture used to make her reveal information, but was only able to fracture her spine. She was carried both to the trial and to her execution on a stretcher.

The fate of other Baum group members was decided in two other trials. The first of these resulted in indictments on October 21, with sentences rendered on December 10, 1942. All but three of the defendants were sentenced to death. Executed on March 4, 1943 were, among others, Marianne Joachim and Siegbert Rotholz. Of the three who escaped death sentences, all of whom were women, Lotte Rotholz received a sentence of eight years' imprisonment but did not survive the war, having been sent to Auschwitz extermination camp. Edith Fraenkel and Hella Hirsch received sentences of five and three years respectively, but they too were killed at Auschwitz in 1944. The final trial of Baum group members took place in June 1943. By then the battle of Stalingrad had taken place, and with the Third Reich fighting for its very existence the regime, and its Nazified system of justice, decided it no longer needed to show a merciful face. All of the defendants were found guilty and condemned to death, with sentences carried out on September 7, 1943; Martin Kochmann was among those executed. Of the 31 members of the group (not counting Herbert Baum) who died during the war, 22 were executed by decapitation, while nine died in death camps.

Only five members of the Baum group, Ellen Compart, Alfred Eisenstadter, Charlotte and Richard Holzer, and Rita Resnik-Meyer (Zocher), survived the war. Their oral testimony, as well as the Nazi court documentation, provides a picture of extraordinary courage in the midst of terror and demoralization. There were other, smaller, and less effective Jewish resistance groups in Nazi Germany, who also shared the daily dangers of carrying out conspiratorial work. Because most of these groups pledged allegiance to various forms of Marxian socialism, which was already a harshly punishable offense for the German "Aryan" population, the risks they took were made all the greater. It has been estimated that about 2,000 Jewish men and women were either members of exclusively Jewish resistance groups or worked with non-Jews in various clandestine political activities in Nazi Germany during the years 1933 through 1945. This number—-given that the German-Jewish community in these years had a disproportionately high number of older people and was led by an elite that hoped to adapt itself to the Nazi dictatorship through compromise and emigration—-strongly suggests that a younger generation had appeared on the scene that would live, and die, not passively but resiliently in the face of adversity, courageously defying and resisting oppression.

The courage exhibited in Berlin by the Baum group would be repeated by other Jewish individuals or organizations many times during World War II in other parts of Nazi-occupied Europe. The Nazi conquest of Poland in September 1939 added a huge Jewish population of almost 2 million people to an expanded German Reich, while the conquest of France, Belgium, and the Netherlands in the spring of 1940 placed almost 600,000 more Jews under German control. While Polish Jews were often brutally treated from the very start of the occupation, Jewish communities both in Poland and in the German-occupied nations of Western Europe generally believed that their best hope for surviving was to accept the new situation as best they could, work hard at their daily tasks, and let their group interests be represented by German-approved Jewish Councils (*Judenräte*). The most radical elements within the Jewish community, the Communists, remained politically quiescent from September 1939 through June 1941 because during this period the party line was dictated by the Soviet Union's desire not to antagonize its new "friend," Nazi Germany. Consequently, during this period there was little evidence of organized resistance to Nazi rule from within Europe's Jewish communities.

Hitler's invasion of the Soviet Union, which began on June 22, 1941, radically changed the situation of Europe's Jews. This was an ideological war between two totalitarian states, and for the Nazis any restraints that had inhibited their desire for a "final solution of the Jewish question" were now swept away. Throughout the summer and fall of 1941, special mobile SS murder squads (*Einsatzgruppen*) on the eastern front killed 1,400,000 Jews. By December 1941, the killing process had become "industrialized" when the first death camp using gas vans went into operation in Chelmno in western Poland near the city of Lodz. Throughout 1942, more death camps were set up in Poland: Belzec, Sobibor, and Treblinka. The infamous extermination camp of Auschwitz (Oswiecim) near the Polish city of Cracow, which began in 1940 as a concentration camp for Poles, after June 1941 received large numbers of Soviet prisoners of war. Auschwitz was actually a system of camps: Auschwitz I contained prisoners and administrative offices; Auschwitz II (Birkenau) was the death camp and included four gas chambers, while Auschwitz III (Monowitz) was a huge industrial slave labor camp where synthetic rubber was produced at the I.G. Farben Buna factory complex.

Because the Nazis took great pains to hide their systematic process of exterminating all Jews under their control, many Jews even in occupied Europe refused to believe that such plans were being carried out. Many continued their belief that Jews were being "resettled" in the German-occupied territories of occupied Poland and the Soviet Union, and that even Hitler would, or could, not carry out such horrendous deeds in the middle of a war when, at the very least, Jewish slave labor would prove valuable for the Nazi war effort. The various *Judenräte* continued to cooperate with the German authorities, hoping that somehow things would improve and that, while clearly many individual Jews would suffer terribly and perish, the Jewish people would survive the war and live to see the day when the Allies defeated Hitler. But by early 1942, a small but growing minority of Jews in both Eastern and Western Europe began to detect ominous signs of a new Nazi policy regarding the Jews, one of total annihilation. Though the Nazi leadership had hoped to keep their operations secret, as a few individuals escaped from death camps in 1942 young Jewish activists began calling for active resistance to the Nazis.

In occupied Polish and Soviet territory, young Zionists as well as Communists and other Jewish political factions began in December 1941 to draw up plans for armed resistance. In Vilna on January 1, 1942, Abba Kovner (1918-88) proclaimed a manifesto that called on the Jews of Lithuania to resist the Nazis and, if need be, die with pride while offering armed resistance. This was the first time that the killing of Jews by *Einsatzgruppen* was analyzed in terms of an overall master plan for the destruction of the Jewish people. Although the numbers of volunteers remained small, and virtually no weapons were on hand, on January 21, 1942, a Jewish combat unit called the United Partisan Organization was founded in Vilna. This organization remained intact and survived the end of the Vilna ghetto in the summer of 1943, fighting alongside Soviet partisans as a distinct Jewish combat unit under Kovner's command. In the Lithuanian city of Kovno (Kaunas), Jews formed resistance cells soon after the Nazis occupied the city in June 1941, but not until 1943 were Communists and Zionists able to unite to form a General Jewish Fighting Organization, which enabled 350 Jews to escape the ghetto in order to join partisan units in nearby forests and villages.

In occupied Poland, two rebellions in the Bialystok ghetto in February and August 1943 made clear that while the virtually unarmed Jews stood no chance of winning, at least here they would no longer permit the Germans to ship them to death camps without a final, bitter armed struggle. Without weapons, Jewish resistance groups almost invariably found their situation in the ghetto to be a militarily hopeless one. Only by working together with Soviet partisan units, which were often relatively well armed, did they stand a chance of effectively fighting the Germans. This was certainly true in the career of Yeheskel Atlas (1913-42), a Polish-Jewish resistance leader who had trained to be a physician. After the destruction of the Derechin ghetto in July 1942, Atlas organized a Jewish partisan unit of 120 which was subordinated to a Soviet partisan battalion. By August, Atlas's unit had attacked Derechin and killed 44 German policemen, and soon went on to launch another attack in which more than 30 Germans died. Also able to destroy a strategic bridge and blow up a train, the Atlas group played an important role in a partisan attack in October that killed 127 Germans, captured 75, and seized significant amounts of weaponry. Atlas died in action on December 5, 1942, much mourned by his fellow partisans.

From 1942 to 1944, 27 Jewish partisan units came into existence. One of the most important was commanded by Yehiel Grynszpan and consisted largely of individuals who had escaped deportation to the Sobibor death camp in 1942. Operating out of the Parczew forest near Lublin, this unit received weapons from the Polish underground as well as supplies from Soviet airdrops and grew in size from 50 to 120 while carrying on raids against German police stations and communications lines. In Yugoslavia, which had the most important partisan movement of all Nazi-occupied nations, Jewish partisans played a significant role even though Jews were a tiny minority in the country and most had been killed by the Nazis by the end of 1942. Marshal Tito, leader of the partisans, had many close Jewish friends and advisors, including his prewar comrade and jailmate Mosa Pijade. A total of 1,318 Yugoslavian-Jewish partisans died in battle and ten of them received the nation's highest award, the National Hero decoration. In the Slovak national uprising of 1944, Jewish partisan participation was also significant; the 1,566 Jewish partisans represented about ten percent of the total number of partisans fighting the Germans in Slovakia.

Meanwhile, Jewish prisoners were active in resistance organizations in concentration camps and even in death camps. In 1943 a resistance movement that included Jews was created at the Buchenwald concentration camp; called the International Underground Committee, it concentrated on sabotaging armaments produced at the camp. At the Treblinka death camp at least 50 prisoners spent more than six months organizing a rebellion which broke out on August 2, 1943. Though the original plan to seize the camp had to be abandoned, during the uprising virtually the entire camp went up in flames and the Nazis plowed over the ruins. Of the 700 prisoners who tried to escape, about 70 lived to see the day of liberation. Another uprising, at the Sobibor death camp on October 14, 1943, resulted in the deaths of ten SS guards and the escape of several dozen prisoners, some of whom were able to join Jewish partisan units in the area. A final death-camp rebellion took place on October 6 and 7, 1944, at Auschwitz II (Birkenau) when a special crematorium detachment of prisoners used explosives provided by female Jewish prisoners working at a nearby factory to kill several SS men and destroy one of the crematoria. In this instance all of the rebels fell in battle or were later executed.

Jews Fight Back in the Warsaw Ghetto

The most dramatic instance of Jewish resistance to the Nazis during World War II took place during the Warsaw Ghetto uprising of 1943. As soon as Warsaw, Poland, was conquered in late September 1939, harsh measures were taken against the city's Jews, but since the Polish population was also treated in a brutal fashion by their German conquerors few Jews could imagine their ultimate fate. By October 1940, all of Warsaw's Jews had been herded into a ghetto, in which an average room contained 13 people. With no jobs for over 60% of the working-age population, and a daily food allocation per capita of only 184 calories, it was clear that the Nazi plan for the ghetto's population was one of death through starvation and disease. In October 1941 the German authorities decreed that leaving the ghetto without permission was an offense punishable by death. By summer 1942, inhumane conditions in the ghetto had led to the deaths of more than 100,000 of its inhabitants. Deciding that the time had come to start liquidating the ghetto, the Germans deported about 300,000 of its residents from July 22 until September 13, 1942. The great majority of those seized were taken to Treblinka, where they were killed.

Soon after the deportations began, on July 28 a Jewish Fighting Organization (ZOB) was founded by several of the Zionist youth movements active in the ghetto. At first it was weak, virtually without weapons, and unable to establish contacts with the Polish underground, the Home Army. Able to do little to prevent the deportation of friends and relatives, it felt abandoned by the non-Jewish Polish resistance movement outside the ghetto walls. By October, however, the morale of ZOB members was boosted when more factions joined the organization, as well as by the small amounts of weapons from the Home Army that had been smuggled into the ghetto. Training for future German assaults on the ghetto now took place under the leadership of Mordecai Anielewicz (1919-43), and when the Germans resumed their policy of deportations on January 18, 1943, they were met by a small but determined Jewish resistance group. One ZOB unit broke into a column of Jews being marched to the assembly point from which they would be shipped out of the ghetto, and at an agreed-upon signal they confronted the German guards in a face-to-face battle. Although many of the ZOB were killed, the Jews scattered in all directions, and within days a change of mood had taken hold of the ghetto. Encouraged by four days of fierce street fighting—the first in occupied Poland—most Jews now felt emboldened to refuse to show up for "resettlement," hiding instead in newly built bunkers and other improvised hiding places. Frustrated in their efforts, the German authorities halted for the time being their efforts to deport Jews from the ghetto.

The temporary German retreat from the Warsaw ghetto in January 1943 buoyed Jewish spirits despite the continuing material privations. Civilians who had previously been skeptical or fearful of the idea of armed resistance now embraced it as their only hope for salvation. On April 19, 1943, the eve of Passover and the day before Hitler's 54th birthday, about 2,100 German soldiers and policemen entered the ghetto. They found its center deserted, for the entire population now accepted the resistance strategy of their underground fighters, a force of about 750 poorly armed young men and women. The resistance members were all young (only a few were over 30), had neither military training nor battle experience, and were armed with little more than pistols (they had only one machine gun). On the first day of their ghetto operation, the Nazis were forced to withdraw after having lost a tank and an armored vehicle to Molotov cocktails. The German commander, SS-Major General Jürgen Stroop, chosen by Reichsführer-SS

Heinrich Himmler for his experience in antipartisan warfare, replaced a predecessor deemed inadequate for the task of pacifying an important urban ghetto.

For several days after April 19, bitter house-to-house fighting took place in the ghetto, frustrating the Germans because their Jewish foes usually managed to escape off the roofs of buildings and then retreat to the relative safety of their prepared bunkers. In a report of April 23 to Himmler, Stroop noted that some of the bunkers had been constructed in a "most artful" fashion and tried to explain the slow progress of his operation as a result of "the cunning ways in which the Jews and bandits behave." Changing his strategy, Stroop then ordered that the ghetto be systematically burned down building by building. This approach turned the Nazi sweep of the ghetto into a bunker war in which the Jews were forced to retreat into their deep shelters. Despite heat and lack of air, food, and water, most of the Jewish resisters survived until forced to surrender because of gas bombs. A major Nazi victory took place on May 8 when ZOB headquarters on 18 Mila Street was captured. It was here that the uprising's commander, Mordecai Anielewicz, and a large number of his staff were killed in action. On April 23 Anielewicz had written his own epitaph in a letter to a ZOB officer serving outside the ghetto:

> Peace be with you, my dear friend; perhaps we shall still meet again. The main thing is that my life's dream has been realized: I have lived to see Jewish defense in the ghetto in all its greatness and glory.

The Jews of Warsaw fought and died alone, since all attempts by the Polish underground to assist them failed, and the several air raids by the Soviet Air Force on the ghetto area were of little military significance. On May 16, 1943, Stroop reported to Himmler that the fighting had ended and that "the Jewish quarter of Warsaw no longer exists." In the same report, it was noted that 56,065 Jews had been captured or "definitely destroyed," while admitting to only 16 dead and 85 wounded on the German side. To symbolize the Nazi victory, Stroop ordered the destruction of the Great Synagogue (which was situated outside the ghetto, now largely a pile of rubble). Even after May 16 hundreds of Jews remained in what was left of their bunkers, and they would emerge at night in search of food and water. While the Germans would continue to patrol the area and capture Jews, miraculously some survived until the summer of 1944, when they participated in another Warsaw tragedy, the great Polish Warsaw uprising of August—October 1944.

The Impact of the Uprising

Despite its failure, the Warsaw ghetto uprising of April—May 1943 made a significant impact on both Jews and non-Jews. As the first example of an urban uprising in Nazi-occupied Europe, Warsaw's Jews showed how a general rebellion could hold out for weeks if the fighters had the support of a populace willing to provide places of refuge as well as moral encouragement. Objectively viewed, the uprising was of minor military significance, tying down relatively few German men and supplies, and it was doomed from the start given that the German force's firepower exceeded that of the ghetto fighters by a ratio of at least 100 to 1. But in moral and psychological terms the martyrdom of young Jewish men and women fighting to the death against the Nazis marked a turning point in modern Jewish history, announcing to the world that a revival of the ancient Hebrew tradition of armed struggle was at hand.

Jews in other parts of Nazi-occupied Europe were deeply moved when they heard about the uprising in the Warsaw ghetto. In France, many Jews joined the general Resistance Movement (15 percent of French Resistance membership was Jewish, even though only about 1% of France's population were Jews). A number of distinctly Jewish resistance movements appeared in France, including one calling itself the Jewish Army, which was particularly active in the southern part of the country. In Belgium, a strong Jewish resistance movement carried out many missions, including a spectacular attack in April 1943 on a train carrying Jews to Auschwitz, a successful action that enabled several hundred Jews to escape.

In free countries, Jews served as members of regular armed forces units, but in British-controlled Palestine as early as 1940 the occupying authorities permitted the formation of separate Jewish ground crews for the Royal Air Force and similar auxiliary forces. About 3,000 Jewish volunteers served in the British forces in Greece in 1941; of these, about 100 were killed in action while about 1,700 became German prisoners of war. In 1942 a Palestine Regiment was authorized, but since it included Arab as well as Jewish volunteers it proved unpopular. Not until the final stages of World War II, in September 1944, did the British create a Jewish Brigade Group, which was the only Jewish military formation in World War II to fight under the Zionist flag as its official standard. Five thousand served in this unit, which saw action on the Italian front in April 1945, sustaining about 250 casualties.

An elite group of Jewish military volunteers were those Palestinians who became parachutists and in 1944 were dropped into German-controlled territories as part of Allied intelligence and spearhead plans. From about 250 volunteers, 110 finished their training and of these 37 were dropped into enemy territory in Italy, Austria, Hungary, Slovakia, Rumania, and Yugoslavia. Twelve of the parachutists were captured by the Nazis, and seven of these were executed. Several of the executed parachutists were women, including Hungarian-born Hannah Senesh (Szenes) and Slovak-born Haviva Reik. The full story of Jewish resistance to tyranny in World War II is a complex one, and much remains to be researched and written. Facing overwhelming odds, the members of the Jewish resistance movements in World War II could often do little more than somehow find inspiration from the words of the song of the Vilna partisans, "Oh, never say that you have reached the very end."

Further Reading

Bauer, Yehuda. *A History of the Holocaust.* Franklin Watts, 1982.
Brothers, Eric. "On the Anti-Fascist Resistance of German Jews," in *Leo Baeck Institute Year Book.* Vol. 32. 1987: pp. 369-382.
Gutman, Israel, ed. *Encyclopedia of the Holocaust.* 4 vols. Macmillan, 1990.

The Jewish Quarter of Warsaw is No More! The Stroop Report. Pantheon, 1979.

Laska, Vera, ed. *Women in the Resistance and in the Holocaust: The Voices of Eyewitnesses.* Greenwood Press, 1983.

Marrus, Michael R., ed. *Jewish Resistance to the Holocaust,* Meckler, 1989.

Suhl, Yuri, ed. *They Fought Back: The Story of the Jewish Resistance in Nazi Europe.* Crown, 1976.

Biale, David. *Power and Powerlessness in Jewish History.* Schocken Books, 1986.

Crome, Len. *Unbroken: Resistance and Survival in the Concentration Camps.* Schocken, 1988.

Edelheit, Abraham J., and Hershel Edelheit. *Bibliography on Holocaust Literature.* 2 vols. Westview Press, 1986, 1990.

Hoffmann, Peter. *The History of the German Resistance 1933-1945.* MIT Press, 1977.

Arno Lustiger, "German and Austrian Jews in the International Brigade," in *Leo Baeck Institute Book, Year.* Vol. 35, 1990: pp. 297-320.

Sargent, Betty. "The Desperate Mission of Stefan Lux," in *Georgia Review.* Vol. 43. No. 4. Winter, 1989: pp. 693-707. □

L. Frank Baum

L. Frank Baum (1856-1919) wrote 69 books beloved by children, including *The Wonderful Wizard of Oz,* which became a classic movie.

Lyman Frank Baum was born on May 15, 1856, near Syracuse, New York. His father, Benjamin, was a wealthy oil businessman, and young Frank (who disliked his first name and never used it) grew up in comfort. Because he had a weak heart, Frank led a quiet life as a child and was educated largely by tutors. A brief stay at a military academy was not successful, and Frank returned home to indulge his taste for reading, writing, stamp collecting, and chicken breeding. He also published two different monthly newspapers during his teenage years.

Baum grew up to become a man of great charm and many interests, yet he had little direction. He pursued a variety of careers ranging from acting to newspaper reporting to theatrical management to writing plays. One of his plays, *The Maid of Arran,* was a surprise smash hit, and Frank and his company toured with it throughout the United States and Canada in the early 1880s.

While at home on a break from the tour, Baum met and became engaged to Maud Gage, youngest daughter of prominent women's suffrage activist Matilda J. Gage. The strong-willed Matilda did not approve of the impractical Baum, but Maud, equally determined, insisted, and the two were married in November 1882. The marriage, apparently one of opposites, was a happy one, as Maud provided Baum with the stability and good sense he needed, and eventually for their children the discipline he was too gentle to perform.

Baum gave up acting when Maud became pregnant with their first child and all the scenery, props, and costumes for *The Maid of Arran* were destroyed in a fire. He worked for a time in the family oil business in Syracuse, still writing plays in his spare time, none of which were produced. In the late 1880s he and the family, which now included two sons, moved to the Dakota Territory, where Baum worked for a time as a shopkeeper and then as a newspaper editor, enjoying both jobs but failing financially in each.

By 1891 it was clear that his growing family, now with four sons, required that he find a job that would provide financial stability. They moved to Chicago, where he was first a newspaper reporter but soon took a better paying job as a traveling salesman with a crockery firm. At the suggestion of his mother-in-law, Baum began to write down some of the stories he made up to tell his sons every evening when he was home. One of these stories, *Mother Goose in Prose,* was published in 1897. The book sold well, and, on the advice of his doctor, Baum gave up his traveling job. Instead, he became the editor of a journal for window-dressers, which also did well.

Baum next decided to collaborate on a children's book with a friend, the artist W. W. Denslow. *Father Goose, His Book,* published in 1899, was a best-seller. One of the five books he published in 1900, also based on stories he had told his sons and illustrated by Denslow, was *The Wonderful Wizard of Oz,* which immediately broke records for sales and made Baum a celebrity. At the suggestion of his publisher, Baum's book, with substantial changes to fit the theatrical tastes of the day, was made into a musical in 1902, which also was a great success and toured the United States for years. A second Oz book, *The Marvelous Land of Oz,* a clever satire on the women's suffrage movement, was published in 1904 and was very popular, and other Oz books followed, though none matched the originality or sales of the first two books. In addition, over the next two decades he wrote over 35 non-Oz books under various pseudonyms and aimed at various audiences. Most of these were "pot-boilers," but they did well financially and helped make Baum a wealthy man.

Always looking for new outlets for his creativity, Baum became interested in films. In 1909 he founded a company to produce hand-colored slides featuring characters from his Oz books. These were shown while he narrated and an orchestra played background music. Although highly innovative, these "radio-plays," as he called them, lost a great deal of money, and in June 1911 he was forced to declare bankruptcy. A later venture into the film business, the Oz Film Company in 1914, produced six movies but experienced severe distribution problems and also failed, though not as disastrously.

Using money Maud had inherited from her mother, the Baums moved to Hollywood, California, in 1910 for Frank's health, and there built Ozcot, a large home with an impressive garden. Here he produced additional Oz books, to a total of 14, which helped ease his financial problems. But with most of his fortune gone and his health failing, in his later years Baum lived quietly at Ozcot, gardening, writing stories, and answering the hundreds of letters he received from Oz-struck children. After a protracted illness in his gall-bladder and a 24 hour coma, he died on May 6, 1919, supposedly uttering, "Now we can cross the Shifting Sands" just a minute before expiring.

Baum's Oz books were so popular and profitable that after his death, with Maud's permission, the publishers continued the series using other writers. In addition, the lasting popularity of Oz was in no small way aided by film versions of *The Wonderful Wizard of Oz,* the 1925 silent version with Oliver Hardy as the Tin-Man, and most notably the 1939 classic MGM musical with Judy Garland as Dorothy.

Although Baum's avowed intention was merely to entertain children with unique American creations and American values, his Oz books have been endlessly criticized and analyzed, and they sometimes have been banned from libraries as being too imaginative, too frightening, or even too dull. Nonetheless, they constitute 20th century America's first and most enduring contribution to children's fantasy literature.

Further Reading

Frank Joslyn Baum (Baum's oldest son) and Russell P. MacFall produced an affectionate biography based on personal reminiscences and a variety of family materials, *To Please a Child: A Biography of L. Frank Baum, Royal Historian of Oz* (1961). This remains the prime source of information on Baum. An excellent introduction to Baum and his works is contained in Daniel P. Mannix's "The Father of the Wizard of Oz" (*American Heritage,* December 1964). Angelica Shirley Carpenter and Jean Shirley's *L. Frank Baum: Royal Historian of Oz* (1991) is of particular interest because of its many relevant photographs and illustrations. Less valuable are Raylyn Moore's *Wonderful Wizard, Marvelous Land* (1974) and *The Wizard of Oz and Who He Was,* by Martin Gardner and

Russel B. Nye (1957). Michael Patrick Hearn, the editor of *The Annotated Wizard of Oz* (1973), presents a fascinating biographical and critical introduction. The book also has an excellent bibliography. Hearn's 1983 *The Wizard of Oz, by L. Frank Baum* is the best collection of critical views on Baum and Oz; it contains essays by the professor Edward Wagenknecht, who in 1929 was one of the first to view Baum's work as an important contribution to American literature, and by James Thurber, whose 1934 essay reveals him to have been a big Oz fan. Aljean Harmetz's 1977 book *The Making of the Wizard of Oz,* focusing more on the production of the 1939 musical film, contains "Appendix B: About L. Frank Baum," a detailed overview of the major events in Baum's life. See also Henry M. Littlefield, whose essay (reprinted from *The American Culture,* 1968) posited the theory of Oz as a populist fable; Fred Erisman (essay from *American Quarterly,* Fall 1968), who views the Oz books as Baum's reaction to the Progressive dilemma; and Osmond Beckwith (*Children's Literature,* 1976), who views Oz through Freudian eyes. Also helpful are Marius Bewley's *Masks and Mirrors* (1970), which contains a chapter on "The Land of Oz: America's Great Good Place," and the chapter "L. Frank Baum and Oz" in Roger Sale's *Fairy Tales and After* (1978). □

Ferdinand Christian Baur

The German theologian Ferdinand Christian Baur (1792-1860) combined historical, philosophical, and linguistic approaches in his pioneering work on the history and philosophy of Christianity. He and his followers are known as the Tübingen school of theology.

Ferdinand Christian Baur, the son of a Protestant minister and dean of the theological seminary at Blaubeuren, was born at Schmiden, near Stuttgart, on June 21, 1792. He received his early schooling at Blaubeuren and attended the University of Tübingen from 1809 to 1814. After serving as country vicar and teacher, he was professor of theology at Blaubeuren from 1817 until 1826.

Influenced by B.G. Niebuhr's history of Rome, Baur became involved in the study of ancient history and the history of religion. This led to his first major work, *Symbolism and Mythology, or the Nature Religion of Antiquity* (3 vols., 1824-1825), and to his appointment as professor of theology at Tübingen in 1826. There he settled down to a life of teaching, preaching, and scholarship.

In 1833 Baur published *Contrast between Catholicism and Protestantism according to the Principles and Main Dogmas of the Two Teachings.* This work criticized attempts to polarize the differences between Catholic and Protestant dogma. In it Baur also presented for the first time one of his most important concepts—the distinction between the Petrine (Jewish-Christian) and Pauline (Gentile-Christian) interpretations of early Christian development. This concept was expanded in his famous *Christian Gnosticism* (1835).

Baur's studies during the 1830s and early 1840s culminated in the important *Paulus, der Apostel Jesu Christi* (2 vols., 1845) and in the *Textbook of the History of Christian Dogma* (1847). In *Paulus* Baur established a new chronology of St. Paul's New Testament writings. He recognized only the Epistles to the Galatians, Corinthians, and Romans as genuinely Pauline. He attributed the writings on Paul in Acts of the Apostles to a later Paulinist writer who attempted to overcome Petrine-versus-Pauline party differences in the early Church. Continuing study of the literary sources of the Gospels led to the publication of *Critical Investigations concerning the Canonical Gospels* (1847), in which the Petrine and Pauline differentiation was further developed.

During the last decade of his life Baur published three volumes of his projected five-volume church history. The last two volumes were compiled from his lectures and were published posthumously. Baur died on Dec. 2, 1860, at Tübingen, having suffered a stroke during a meeting of the Academic Senate. He was one of the most dedicated and fruitful scholars of his time, and his major contribution was the freeing of Protestant theology from the fetters of supranatural and pietistic conservatism.

Further Reading

The most up-to-date study on Baur in English is Peter C. Hodgson, *The Formation of Historical Theology: A Study of Ferdinand Christian Baur* (1966). A modern translation by P.C. Hodgson, ed., *Ferdinand Christian Baur on the Writing of Church History* (1968), contains a lengthy and useful introduction to Baur and his work. □

Pina Bausch

The most controversial dancer/choreographer of her era was Pina Bausch (born 1940). She created the *Theatertanz*, an approach to dance expression, which became a trend.

Born July 27, 1940, in the industrial city of Solingen in Germany, Pina Bausch once said, "I am no one's pupil." She began her studies at the age of 14 under the direction of Kurt Jooss at the Folkwang School, from which she graduated in 1959. Jooss was one of the most outstanding teachers and choreographers of the pre-Hitler period, a liberal mind, as demonstrated by his work *The Green Table,* an antiwar memorial. His spirit must have greatly influenced Bausch's development.

The second great influence came from the city of New York where she landed at the age of 19. She was one of few German dance students to go abroad on an academic scholarship and came to New York through the German American Exchange Program for the USA. She studied at the Juilliard School of Music with such teachers as Louis Horst, Josea Limogn, Paul Taylor, and Antony Tudor and danced with the Paul Sanasardo and the Danya Feuer Dance Company. She became a member of the New American Ballet and the Metropolitan Opera Ballet. But it was the city itself, its multifaceted life, that strongly impressed Bausch. She felt that the direction of her future life was determined in the two years of her stay in that city. "New York is like a jungle, but at the same time it gives you a feeling of total freedom. In these two years I have found myself."

Bausch returned to Germany in 1962, and became principal dancer with the newly founded Folkwang-Ballett. In 1968 she began choreographing for the Folkwang-Ballett and the following year undertook leadership of that company. In 1973, she went to Wuppertal and founded Tanztheater Wuppertal, for which she has created nearly 30 full-length productions. She had her dancers voice words, gibberish or small talk, as in her piece *Waltz.* In her stage designs, too, she often used seemingly outlandish and impossible ideas and gadgets to make her point visually, as in her highly dramatic version of *The Rite of Spring.* In this piece she covered the entire stage with peat so that one could not only see and hear but also smell the earthiness which characterized this production.

She soon became convinced that art must be a vehicle for social criticism; it must never be a mere means to beautify life. She was never interested in telling a dramatic or pretty story embellished with yesteryear's ornaments. Hers were not stories told, but experiences staged. Her works were not psychodramatic or physically poetic. Whatever she tried to convey she lifted out of any personal context and mostly gave it a sociopolitical meaning. Her choreographic approach was psychological only in as much as it emerged from the depth of her (and her dancers') being. Thus, the artistic *Gestalt* of her creations attained universal validity.

Like Bertolt Brecht, Bausch wanted her spectators to think about what they saw and heard and to draw their own conclusions. She expected a verdict of condemnation for many of life's injustices, especially those suffered by women. On stage, if not quite in life, she became a feminist activist. She defended the female against the male, since, in her eyes, the male was an aggressive part of society.

In her dance works she overcame technical and conceptual boundaries. The forcefulness of her appearance on the international dance scene was exemplary, inspiring many other choreographers in Europe. Her greatest deed was to have found a new original dimension in the art of dancing, breaking through all barriers of what was known until then as postmodern, using all theatrical and dramaturgic means to enforce an idea—which, in turn, also influenced the European theater, opening the way for a new movement quality on stage.

Bausch mainly worked in a spirit of defiance or out of a mood of defense, thereby creating unexpected contrasts. In concepts and gestures she could become aggressive to the point of arousing rejection from the onlooker. But she did not mind alienating part of her audience if she could only arouse anger and protest. She made this clear when she said: "It is almost unimportant whether a work finds an understanding audience. One has to do it because one believes that it is the right thing to do. We are not only here to please, we cannot help challenging the spectator."

This thought was magnified as the reality of her creative efforts, and her rich repertory proved her philosophy of life. *Come, Dance With Me,* for instance, searches for human happiness in a sea of futility. There is also no end to frustration in her *Bluebeard.* Symbolically, it takes place in a room covered by dead leaves. Male and female dancers incessantly reach out for each other, but their attempts at embracing and caressing make it painfully clear that there is no real communication. It is an impressive work, questioning the old clichéa about love and demonstrating our desperate craving for it. For *Nelken,* Bausch covered the floor with pink carnations. For *Palermo, Palermo,* it was rubble.

Café Muller, set to music by Henry Purcell, is a story of alienation and loneliness, although it contains no actual plot. Bausch was a master in dramatizing the monotony of everyday life. On a stage filled with chairs, one woman dresses and undresses uninterruptedly; a couple kisses and argues incessantly; a man enters and exits, making sexual advances toward both sexes; another couple bash each other against the wall, while another figure remains totally immobile in the background. Nothing else happens, but we are painfully reminded of the realities of life. Her *Rite of Spring* is shaped out of horror, out of dark despair; the sacrifice of the virgin for the coming of spring has a feel of earthiness and the brutal truth that we pay for life with death.

Nur Du (Only You), Bausch's interpretation of the American West, was her first site-specific work created outside Europe and came about after her visits to California, Arizona and Texas. The $1.2 million project was co-commissioned by Cal Performances at UC Berkeley (where the work premiered), UCLA's Center for the Performing Arts,

James Doolittle's Southern California Theatre Association, the Music Center of Los Angeles County, the University of Texas Performing Arts Center and Arizona State University Public Events. With a background of giant redwoods, *Nur Du* was set to the sounds of rhythm and blues, jazz, New Age, Latin jazz and pop and 50s ballads. ''The U.S. premiere of *Nur Du* is three-plus hours of nonlinear neo-Expressionism, powered by brilliant dancing,'' Lewis Segal (Los Angeles Times, October 5, 1996).

The Window Washer, co-produced by the Goethe-Institut Hong Kong and the Hong Kong Arts Festival Society, premiered in 1997. In late 1996, Bausch brought 29 dancers from 14 countries to Hong Kong for three weeks to absorb the atmosphere and culture, then returned to Wuppertal to create the piece. As reported by Paul Moor/Wuppertal in *Time,* ''Given that Bausch's favored style is collage, the piece immediately latches onto the disorderly picture that the city initially presents: she strings together snapshots—a man having his torso sponged and hair blowdried, a woman firing off hilarious deadpan monologues at the audience, another man pulling mock snakes from the flowers with chopsticks and, later skiing down the crimson hill. By contrast, the conclusion comes off as blatantly metaphorical, as the dancers methodically climb the Red mountain one-by-one before exiting.''

Bausch's work tries to mirror the various stations of our existence in pantomime and danced images supported by music and the spoken word. It is a long path of passion from Wuppertal to Gethsemane. There are also a few light moments in her work, but many more moments in which to pause and gaze in silent amazement at a lost world which cannot find itself.

Further Reading

The only sources of information on Pina Bausch available at this time are in German and French. The most recent are Norbert Servos, *Pina Bausch-Wuppertaler Tanztheater oder die Kunst, einen Goldfisch zu dressieren* (1996); Maarten Vanden Abeele, *Pina Bausch* (1996); and Detlef Erler, *Pina Bausch* (1994). Reviews and biographical information can be found in the *Los Angeles Times* (February 1, 1996), (March 17, 1996), (May 15, 1996), (October 5, 1996), (October 12, 1996) and (May 5, 1997); *Time* (March 10, 1997); *The New York Times* (September 11, 1994), (November 19, 1994), (December 11, 1994), (September 22, 1996), (October 5, 1996) and (October 26, 1996); *The Christian Science Monitor* (November 22, 1994); and *The Wall Street Journal* (November 22, 1994). □

Richard Baxter

The English theologian, pastor, and Nonconformist Richard Baxter (1615-1691) was an advocate of ecumenism and the author of more than 160 books.

The only son of a gentleman of "competent estate," Richard Baxter was born in Rowton, Shropshire, on Nov. 12, 1615, and was largely self-educated "out of books" with the "inconsiderable help of country tutors." After "it pleased God to awaken" his soul at age 15, he studied theology. Ordained in the Anglican ministry in 1638, 2 years later he began assisting the vicar in Kidderminster, Worcestershire. During the Puritan Revolution he served as a regimental chaplain, but 2 years of campaigning broke his ever-precarious health. Convalescing in 1647 he wrote *The Saints' Everlasting Rest* (1650), a huge tome which comforts the afflicted and reflects on life here and hereafter.

Although ordained in the Church of England, Baxter objected to its "diocesan episcopacy," whereby a bishop's authority extended over a diocese containing many parish churches. This, he believed, was contrary to what was practiced in the early ages of Christianity. In his view the rector of every parish ought to be a bishop, and no bishop could validly exercise authority over more than one established congregation.

Baxter resumed his pastoral work at Kidderminster. His "awakening ministry," "moving voice," handsome features, and sincerity built up a tremendous congregation. He continued to write prolifically; his writings, while often diffuse and digressive, are forceful, rational, and well informed. He began a series of ecumenical works in which he advocated the "True Catholicism" of a broad, universal Christian church. *The Reformed Pastor* (1656) and *A Call for the Unconverted* (1657) were popular and influential.

In *A Holy Commonwealth* (1659) Baxter defended monarchy as the best form of government—but only if the king subordinated himself to the law of "God, the Universal Monarch." In 1660 Baxter was summoned to London to cooperate in plans to restore the monarchy. He worked for a Restoration Church of England which would be moderately episcopalian, including Presbyterians, Congregationalists, and moderate Baptists not as sects but as members of one mutually acceptable catholic body. But the Anglican hierarchy vehemently opposed this plan, and Baxter and others of like mind were forced into Nonconformity. Stringent laws ousted more than 2000 ministers, denying them the right to preach. Baxter, like John Bunyan, was ruthlessly persecuted. Under James II he was imprisoned for more than a year because he had allegedly attacked church and state covertly in his *Paraphrase of the New Testament* (1684).

Baxter's sufferings had been mitigated by marriage in 1662 to a woman 20 years his junior. Despite their differences of age and temperament, they found ideal companionship. She died in 1681, and he lovingly memorialized her "cheerful, wise, and very useful life."

Among Baxter's major works were *Methodus theologiae* (1665), *Reason for the Christian Religion* (1667), *The Christian Directory* (1673), *Catholick Theology* (1675), *A Treatise of Episcopacy* (1681), and his autobiography, *Reliquiae Baxterianae* (1696).

Baxter died on Dec. 8, 1691. He was too outspoken and intense to succeed in his own time as a "reconciler." But if he had been heeded, the split between Anglicanism and Dissent, which has sullied British Christianity and is being healed only today, would have been avoided.

Further Reading

A study of Baxter should begin with *The Autobiography of Richard Baxter,* edited by J.M. Lloyd Thomas (1925; new ed. 1931), followed by F.J. Powicke, *A Life of the Reverend Richard Baxter* (1924). Hugh Martin, *Puritanism and Richard Baxter* (1954), untangles 17th-century politics and theology and provides basic bibliographical guidance. Richard Schlatter, ed., *Richard Baxter and Puritan Politics* (1957), admirably treats *A Holy Commonwealth* and related works. For the religious context see Irvonwy Morgan, *The Nonconformity of Richard Baxter* (1946).

Additional Sources

Baxter, Richard, *The autobiography of Richard Baxter,* London, Dent; Totowa, N.J., Rowman & Littlefield 1974. □

Pierre Bayle

The French philosopher and skeptic Pierre Bayle (1647-1706) was the author of the *Historical and Critical Dictionary.* This unique philosophy source book was one of the most influential works during the 18th-century Enlightenment.

Pierre Bayle was born in the village of Carlat near the Spanish border. His father was a Calvinist minister. As a young man, Pierre was educated by the Jesuits at Toulouse, and under their influence he converted to Catholicism for a brief period. When Bayle returned to Calvinism, he traveled to Geneva to escape persecution as a heretic. There be became acquainted with the philosophy of René Descartes. In 1674 Bayle returned to France incognito and tutored in Paris and Rouen. The following year he became professor of philosophy at the Protestant University of Sedan, and when this school was suppressed in 1681, Bayle settled in Rotterdam, Holland, where he taught philosophy until his death.

With a certain irony Bayle insisted that he was a genuine Protestant in that he protested everything that was said and done. This skeptical attitude was a major motif of contemporary philosophy. Rationalism, as a new system of thought, consistently undermined the notion of authority both in ecclesiastical matters and in the philosophic opinions of the ancients. Positively, skepticism presented itself as the guardian of faith by showing the futility of all human reason. Derivatively, skepticism became aligned with humanism as a proponent of toleration in matters intellectual, political, and religious.

Famous Dictionary

Scholarship then was not what it is today. More than a few of the great minds of the 18th century owed all or much of their knowledge of the history of philosophy to Bayle's *Dictionnaire historique et critique* (1697; *Historical and Critical Dictionary*). Very early in his career Bayle conceived the notion of correcting errors in previous encyclopedias and of supplying information missing in standard reference works. The two volumes of the *Dictionary* contained more than 2,500 pages of primarily biographical information arranged in alphabetical order, together with occasional articles on general subjects. By modern standards the *Dictionary* is a capricious, polemical, debunking work filled with long quotations and literary allusions in which there is little relation between the topic under discussion and the content. The texts are generally brief and accurate, with numerous citations of authorities in the margins.

The heart of the work is the critical notes that Bayle appended in small print at the bottom of the pages. These footnotes and notes on the notes often were 10 times as long as the original article. They include philosophical and theological digressions, attacks against personal enemies, and thorough skepticism. Bayle justified his attitudes by an appeal to the professional impunity of the scholar: "Let an historian relate faithfully all the crimes, weaknesses, and disorders of mankind, his work will be looked on as a satire rather than history." For example, Bayle wrote a factual account of the life of the biblical king David. In the notes he pointed out that although David's life was divinely inspired his behavior by ordinary standards was completely immoral. The reader was left with a dilemma concerning the infallibility of Scripture, since "Either those actions are not good or actions like them are not evil."

The reaction to the *Dictionary* was instantaneous; Bayle was both famous and infamous. The work was placed on the Index by the Roman Catholic Church and condemned by the Dutch Reformed Church. Promising revision, Bayle amended the work, and a second edition appeared in three volumes in 1702. Printers incorporated the original articles with the amended versions, and by 1720 the work had grown to four volumes. It became, in the words of one critic, "the Bible of the eighteenth century."

Further Reading

A full-length study of Bayle in English is Howard Robinson, *Bayle, the Skeptic* (1931). Additional studies which relate him to his milieu or to other figures include Leo Pierre Courtines, *Bayle's Relation with England and the English* (1938); Paul Hazard, *The European Mind, 1680-1715* (trans. 1953); H. T. Mason, *Pierre Bayle and Voltaire* (1963); Walter Rex, *Essays on Pierre Bayle and Religious Controversy* (1965); and Karl C. Sandberg, *At the Crossroads of Faith and Reason: An Essay on Pierre Bayle* (1966). For the intellectual background of the period see Ernst Cassirer, *The Philosophy of the Enlightenment* (1951), and Lester G. Crocker, *An Age in Crisis: Man and World in Eighteenth Century Thought* (1959).

Additional Sources

Labrousse, Elisabeth, *Pierre Bayle,* Dordrecht; Boston: M. Nijhoff: Distributors for the U.S. and Canada, Kluwer Academic Publishers, 1985. ☐

Augustinus Bea

The German cardinal and scholar Augustinus Bea (1881-1968) was a key figure at the Second Vatican Council, 1962-1965. A Jesuit, he was noted for his piety, scholarship, and progressive posture.

Augustinus Bea was born on May 28, 1881, in Riedböhringen, the son of a carpenter. He studied theology, philosophy, and philology at universities in Germany and Holland. In 1902 he entered the Society of Jesus and began his long career as an Old Testament scholar. His special interests were Oriental languages, archeology, and the doctrine of inspiration in the light of modern historical criticism. From 1924 to 1959 Bea worked at the Pontifical Biblical Institute at Rome. He was increasingly recognized as an eminent scholar, and in 1943 he decisively advised Pope Pius XII on a positive attitude toward the historical critical interpretation of the Bible.

In 1959 Pope John XXIII elevated Bea to the rank of cardinal. In 1960 he made him president of the newly created Secretariate for Promoting Christian Unity for the forthcoming Second Vatican Council. Christian unity was one of Bea's special interests, and as early as 1935 he had attended a congress of Protestant Old Testament scholars. Throughout the Council, Bea contributed much to such areas as the sources of revelation, eschatology, missions, mariology, celibacy, the life of religious orders, and liturgy. His biblical and historical arguments tended to supplant the juridical view of the Church, which is static and restrictive, with the biblical view, which is dynamic and positive. He played an important role in articulating and making credible the spirit of the *aggiornamento* (modernization). He also helped to provide a viable basis for ecumenical dialogue on the scholarly, as well as on the nonscholarly, level.

While holding that Roman Catholicism was the one true religion, Bea believed that from a biblical viewpoint man can attain salvation not only through Catholicism, Protestantism, or the Eastern churches, but also through Judaism or any other non-Christian religion. He stressed that religious liberty must be the necessary and comprehensive mode of coexistence among all faiths. Observers agree that the adoption of the landmark declaration on the Jewish people was the special concern of Bea. He died at the age of 87 on Nov. 23, 1968, in Rome.

Further Reading

Bea published at least five books on topics related to the work of the Secretariat for Promoting Christian Unity, but the best summary of his own view of the Council is contained in his richly documented *Ecumenism in Focus* (1969). A full-length study of Bea is Bernard I. Leeming, *Agostino Cardinal Bea* (1964). Carlo Falconi, *Pope John and the Ecumenical Council: A Diary of the Second Vatican Council, September-December 1962* (trans. 1964), provides a lively portrait of Bea. He is discussed at length in Robert Blair Kaiser, *Pope, Council and World: The Story of Vatican II* (1963).

Additional Sources

Schmidt, Stjepan, *Augustin Bea, the cardinal of unity,* New Rochelle, N.Y.: New City Press, 1992. □

Moses Yale Beach

An American inventor and newspaper entrepreneur, Moses Yale Beach (1800-1868) contributed to the technology of his time but was, above all, an important developer of popular journalism.

Moses Beach was born in Wallingford, Conn., on Jan. 7, 1800, the son of a farmer. He was apprenticed to a cabinetmaker in Hartford, where his exceptional industry enabled him to earn his freedom at the age of 18. Beach set up as a cabinetmaker in Northampton, Mass., and in 1819 he married Nancy Day. His bent for technical innovation was strong, and after moving to Springfield, Mass., he began a strenuous campaign to achieve success. His experiments with engines powered by gunpowder failed. A plan to introduce steam navigation on the Connecticut River might have succeeded, but Beach's funds gave out. Most successful was his design of a rag cutter for paper mills, but he did not patent it in time and so lost a fortune.

In 1829 Beach became associated with a paper mill in Saugerties, N. Y. Dissatisfied with its progress, in 1834 he joined his brother-in-law Benjamin Day in New York City as business and technical manager of the *Sun,* the first, and an outstanding example, of the "penny" newspapers which were bringing popularity to party-politics journalism. In 1835 Beach purchased part ownership of the *Sun* for $5,200. The *Sun* was then the most popular newspaper in the world, with 30,000 readers. Yet production expenses and the loss of advertising revenue occasioned by economic depression kept profits low. Accordingly, 3 years later Day sold Beach his own portion of *Sun* holdings for $40,000 (an action he later regretted). Although Beach was not a journalist in the same sense as his competitors James Gordon Bennett and Horace Greeley, the *Sun's* continuing success was the result of his policies. In his 10 years of proprietorship he expanded the four-page paper from three columns to eight. He developed horse, rail, and pigeon services to speed news-gathering into his New York offices. He also contributed to the journalism of his era with such features as the "Moon Hoax" of author Edgar Allan Poe on April 13, 1844.

Beach's main accomplishments were, however, technical, as in his organization of the New York Associated Press and the Harbor Association, both intended to curb inefficiency and duplication of work among competitors in the newspaper business. Beach's *Weekly Sun* extended his paper to the countryside, and his *American Sun* in 1848 became the first paper to carry American journalism directly to Europe. Notable, too, was his pamphlet, *The Wealth of New York: A Table of the . . . Wealthy Citizens of New York* (1841, and subsequent editions).

Although Beach was not conspicuous in public affairs, his good repute in 1846 did influence President James K. Polk to commission him to negotiate peace terms with Mexico. However, a false rumor of an American military defeat prevented Beach's departure.

When Beach's health failed, he retired to Wallingford and in 1848 turned over the *Sun,* with a circulation of 50,000, to two of his sons, the talented Moses S. Beach and Alfred Ely Beach. He died on July 19, 1868.

Further Reading

The one readily available study of Beach, emphasizing his journalistic career, is in Frank M. O'Brien, *The Story of the Sun, New York: 1833-1928* (1918; new ed. 1928). For background see Alfred M. Lee, *The Daily Newspaper in America: The Evolution of a Social Instrument* (1937), and Frank Luther Mott, *American Journalism: A History, 1690-1960* (1941; 3d ed. 1962). □

George Wells Beadle

The American scientist, educator, and administrator George Wells Beadle (1903-1989) demonstrated the role of genes in the control of biochemical reactions in living organisms.

George Beadle was born on October 22, 1903, in Wahoo, Nebraska. He obtained an undergraduate degree in biology in 1926 and a master's degree in 1927 from the University of Nebraska, where he developed a specific interest in genetics, especially that of corn. Beadle continued graduate study at Cornell University under the joint guidance of geneticist R. A. Emerson and cytologist L. W. Sharp during a period when studies combining the methods of cytology and genetics were most profitable. After receiving a doctorate in 1931, he joined the California Institute of Technology, first as a fellow of the National Research Council and then, until 1936, as an instructor of biology. He later served Harvard University as an assistant professor of biology (1936-1937) and Stanford University as a professor of biology from 1937 to 1946.

Recombination and Gene Action

The two most puzzling problems in genetic research at that time involved the mechanisms by which recombination occurs between linked genes and the ways in which genes control the development of the hereditary traits for which they are responsible. Beadle's greatest successes came in studies of gene action, especially through the development of methods of experimentation permitting both extensive and selective observations of phenomena previously known only from sporadic spontaneous occurrences. Interactions between tissues of different genetic constitutions had been occasionally observed in spontaneously occurring mosaics.

In 1935 Beadle and Boris Ephrussi at the Institut de Biologie Physico-Chimique in Paris succeeded in producing equivalent situations at will and involving any desired combination of genotypes by injecting organ buds from fruit fly (*Drosophila*) larvae into the body cavities of other larvae, where they continued to develop.

Enzyme-Gene Specificity

At about this time it was observed that, among species of microorganisms requiring a particular growth factor, some could use precursors not used by others. Presumably such differences were genetic, in which case it should be possible to induce mutations in genes responsible for nearly every step in the biosynthesis of every essential organic substance which could be fed to the organism. Selecting the mold *Neurospora* as an organism with suitable genetic and cultural characteristics, Beadle and E. L. Tatum in 1941 obtained definite support for that postulate. Afterwards the method became standard in biochemistry. Moreover, from the correlation between specific enzymes and specific genes, Beadle concluded that "each enzyme protein has its master pattern present in a gene." (It is now known that the master pattern is transferred to the enzyme through the agency of messenger ribonucleic acid.)

Later Career and Honors

In 1946 Beadle was recalled to the California Institute of Technology to direct the division of biology. He gave up his own research efforts at that time. In 1961 he became president of the University of Chicago, a position he main-

tained until his retirement in 1968. By then he had accumulated more than 30 honorary degrees from many universities around the country and had been awarded memberships into several prestigious academic societies. However, chief among his accolades remains the Nobel Prize for Physiology or Medicine, which he shared with Edward Lawrie Tatum and Joshua Lederberg in 1958 for his work on the "one gene-one enzyme" concept.

In the 1960s Beadle renewed his interest in the genetics of corn and became a prominent figure in the "corn wars," a debate among geneticists and archaeologists over the domestication of corn or maize in the Americas. Beadle contended that modern corn comes from a Mexican wild grass rather than a now-extinct species of maize. Beadle drew his conclusion from corn remains that show that domestication occurred at the time of the Mayans and Aztecs.

From 1968 to 1970 he directed the American Medical Association's Institute for Biomedical Research and from 1969 to 1972 served on the council of the National Academy of Science. He collaborated with his wife, Muriel Beadle, on the Edison Award-winning *The Language of Life: An Introduction to the Science of Genetics*. Beadle died June 9, 1989, in Pomona, California, at age 85 from complications of Alzheimer's disease.

Further Reading

Theodore L. Sourkes, *Nobel Prize Winners in Medicine and Physiology, 1901-1965* (rev. ed. 1967), contains a biographical sketch of Beadle and a description of his prize-winning work. Additional information is contained in Tyler Wasson, *Nobel Prize Winners* (1987) and in Maria Szekely, *From DNA to Protein* (1980). □

Dorothea Beale

English educator Dorothea Beale (1831-1906) was an instrumental figure in gaining acceptance for a more intellectual education for women. While principal of the Cheltenham Ladies' College in the late 1800s, she introduced courses such as history and physical geography into the traditional female-oriented curriculum and testified on the poor state of women's education for government commissions. Her ideas played a key role in launching reforms in women's education in England.

As the principal of the Cheltenham Ladies' College in England for almost 50 years, Dorothea Beale became a leading proponent of increased education for girls in the last half of the nineteenth century. Her educational reforms included expanding the curriculum for her students to include history, mathematics, and scientific concepts—a radical departure from the courses in needlework, music, and other domestic skills that were considered appropriate training for privileged young women at that time. Beale's beliefs that women should be educated so that they could be better wives and mothers and that women do not require the same educational opportunities as men appear extremely conservative by modern standards. But by winning acceptance for her idea that women could and should be familiar with more intellectual academic topics, however, Beale paved the way for later educators who would open the doors of learning even wider for women of all classes.

Beale was born on March 21, 1831, in Bishopsgate, England. She was one of the 11 children of Dorothea Margaret Complin and Miles Beale. The importance that Beale placed on education stemmed from her family's firm belief that women should be given the freedom to pursue higher learning. Her father was a surgeon who was a proponent of social and educational reform; he felt his daughters should be given the opportunity to enrich their minds with all manner of education available and that they should be able to choose any type of career they pleased. Her mother's family also had a commitment to the intellectual training of women and boasted several women writers, including the feminist author Caroline Francis Cornwallis.

Surrounded by such concerns and ideas, Beale set her mind on becoming an educator at a very young age. Instead of playing outside, she preferred to stay indoors and study during her free time. Another activity she enjoyed as a small child was pretending to be the teacher of a make-believe girls school. She was an intense child who combined her strong will and self-discipline with her family's heavy emphasis on religion, resulting in a mystical outlook that she held throughout her life. Beale believed that she had been chosen by God to fulfill a sacred destiny, and her calling was to teach. A religious figure that she claimed she shared a special bond with was St. Hilda of Whitby, a seventh-century nun who was known for her great knowledge.

Beale's own education, however, did not reflect her family's concern with learning. She was schooled by governesses in her home, but the quality of the instructors was poor and they were continually being replaced. She also spent short periods of time at a boarding school in England and a finishing school in Paris. The result was an unsatisfying education lacking consistency or depth. Her own determination carried her through these times, however. Interested in pursuing her talent in mathematics, Beale arranged to attend lectures at Gresham College and Crosby Hall Institution in London. After the opening of Queen's College, Harley Street, Beale and her sisters began attending classes there in 1848.

First Woman on College Faculty

In keeping with her habits of hard work and intense study, Beale undertook a rigorous course of work at the college. She graduated from the school in 1849 at the age of 18 with certificates in six different areas: geography, mathematics, English, Latin, French, and German. Her high performance earned her an offer to teach at Queens; in accepting the position she became the first woman to hold a faculty post at the college. Her first assignment was as a tutor of mathematics. In the seven years she spent there, she later became a tutor of Latin and then head teacher of the

school affiliated with the institution. During her stay, however, she became frustrated with the limited role that women faculty had at Queens. She also disapproved when the school began to lower its admissions standards. Unable to continue to compromise her own standards, she finally quit her job in 1856.

Beale soon found a new position as head teacher at the Clergy Daughters School at Casterton, where she began working in January of 1857. But this school was very disagreeable to her; she found the philosophical atmosphere to be very rigid and even the architecture of the building itself seemed to her to be unpleasant and unwelcoming. In addition, she was given strict guidelines on what she could teach. She was required to provide lessons in the Bible and Church history, ancient and modern history, physical and political geography, grammar and composition, English literature, Latin, French, German, and Italian. Beale had many ideas for reforms at the school, and she felt that her position of authority there should give her words some weight. She approached school authorities with the ultimatum that if her changes were not accepted, she would quit. Instead of giving in to her demands, the school fired her, and Beale left in defeat.

After these two failed ventures as a teacher, she returned to her family's home. There she did some teaching on a part-time basis and also began some writing projects. She produced two books in 1858, *The Student's Text-book of English and General History from B.C. 100 to the Present Time* and *Self-Examination.* Although she had suffered embarrassment and self-doubt for being unsuccessful in her first two teaching jobs, she did not give up faith in her chosen role as an educator. She realized that she could only fulfill her wishes in a place where she could give free reign to her ideas and abilities. Never again, she vowed, would she take a job that did not give her this level of independence and authority. With this renewed sense of purpose, in the summer of 1858 Beale joined 50 other applicants in seeking the position of principal of Cheltenham Ladies' College—the oldest private school for girls in England. She succeeded in winning the position and began an influential career at the school that would last for the next 50 years.

Introduced New Concepts in Education

Beale was an imposing figure on the campus of Cheltenham, invariably appearing in a black wool dress adorned with only a white scarf. An energetic, authoritative woman, she expected her teachers and students to share in her vision of education as a sacred duty and gift. She engaged in both teaching and administrative duties at the school, which at the time of her arrival was suffering from low enrollment and insufficient funding. Beginning with only 69 students, Beale managed to double that number within four years and secure adequate financial support for the school. With these matters in hand, she was able to concentrate even more fully on implementing the educational ideas that she had been developing her entire life.

In the classroom, Beale rejected the established idea of simply feeding required information to students. Instead she sought to instill a desire for knowledge that would guide a woman throughout her lifetime. She altered the subject matter of classes as well. Rather than focusing solely on the social and domestic skills expected of young women of wealthy families, such as drawing, needlepoint, and playing the piano, Beale introduced more rigorously academic courses. She established classes in English history, German, and physical geography, using the geography course as a subtle means of including mathematics and scientific concepts into the curriculum. Beale understood that her methods could be seen as controversial, because at that time it was thought unnecessary, even unhealthy for girls to partake in serious studies. But she attempted to reconcile her new ways with public opinion by stating that a well-educated woman would make a better wife and mother than an uneducated one.

Beale experimented with a number of other innovative ideas at Cheltenham. She stressed the importance of a teacher's personality, disposition, and religious character in the success of education. This philosophy of becoming personally involved with the process of education was exemplified by Beale's own practices as principal—she took on the responsibility of supervising the boarding homes runs by the school and she insisted on personally evaluating every student on a weekly basis. To encourage a sense of discipline in her students she instituted a rule of silence during lessons, and to facilitate the appreciation of learning for its own sake, she did away with all competitions and prizes.

Testimony Spurs Education Reforms

Beale's success at reforming Cheltenham into a financially viable and forward-looking educational institution began to draw attention. In the 1860s, she was invited to testify on the state of women's education as part of a study by the British government's School Inquiry Commission. In her presentation for the commission, she described the appalling ignorance of middle- and upper-class young women who received the typical education allotted to girls at the time. In one example, she stated that among a group of over 100 girls taking an entrance exam, not one had been familiar with the concept of fractions, less than five could conjugate the French verb "to be," and one girl was certain that the fourteenth-century poet Geoffrey Chaucer had lived only 100 years earlier. Her testimony and her rationale for improving women's education during this forum had an invigorating effect on education reforms in the country. But Beale's ideas for change continued to have a somewhat limited scope. While noting the necessity for improvement in the area of the quality of women's education, she did not argue that women should receive the same kind of training as men, because she felt that the different roles awaiting them in life did not call for such parity. She also displayed the prejudices of her class and did not concern herself with access to education for lower-class women. After the Commission released its findings based on the evidence presented by Beale and other female educators, she published an edited version of the report prefaced with her own introduction. The work appeared in 1869 as *Reports on the Education of Girls, with Extracts from the Evidence.*

The Cheltenham Ladies' College and Beale's reputation as a leading educator continued to grow throughout the rest of the 1800s. By the end of the century, the school had expanded to hold more than 1,000 students on a complex that covered 15 acres and included 14 boardinghouses. In addition, a 7,000-volume library had been constructed and a new department, St. Hilda's College, had been added to provide a kindergarten and secondary school. Beale herself became an active participant in a number of professional organizations and activities. She served as president of the Head Mistress Association from 1895 to 1897 and she continued to serve as a witness on education for various commissions. She founded an annual tradition of a teachers' retreat known as Quiet Days. She also returned to writing to support her efforts, producing such titles as *Home-Life in Relation to Day Schools* (1879), *A Few Words to Those Who Are Leaving* (1881), *Work and Play in Girls Schools* (1898), and in tribute to her greatest success, *History of the Cheltenham Ladies' College, 1853-1901* (1904). Her reform work brought her into contact with a number of other women in education, forming a close-knit network of personal and professional support. One of her closest colleagues was Frances Mary Buss, an educator at the North London Collegiate School.

In her later years, Beale received recognition and honors for her accomplishments and example in the field of education. She was awarded the freedom of the borough of Cheltenham in 1901, and the University of Edinburgh presented her with an honorary doctorate in 1902. Although deaf and in poor health toward the end of her life, she continued to work until only a few weeks before her death. Beale died from cancer on November 9, 1906. Her ashes were interred at Lady Chapel of Gloucester Cathedral, and a memorial service was held for her the following week at St. Paul's Cathedral. At her memorial, the educator was remember as a great woman whose religious inspiration had infused all those around her. Perhaps her greatest contribution was the ideals and knowledge that she had instilled in her own students. Many teachers trained at Cheltenham went on to play an important role in continuing the education reforms in England's girls' schools that had first begun with Beale's pioneering innovations.

Further Reading

For more information see Digby, Anne, and Peter Searby, *Children, School, and Society in Nineteenth Century England,* Macmillan, 1981; Gathorne-Hardy, Jonathan, *The Old School Tie: The Phenomenon of the English Public School,* Viking, 1978; Kamm, Josephine, *Hope Deferred: Girls' Education in English History,* Methuen, 1965; Kamm, Josephine, *How Different from Us: A Biography of Miss Buss and Miss Beale,* Bodley Head, 1958; Kamm, Josephine, *Indicative Past: A Hundred Years of the Girls' Public School Trust,* Allen and Unwin, 1971; and Raikes, Elizabeth, *Dorothea Beale of Cheltenham,* Archibald Constable and Co., 1909. □

Charles Austin Beard

Charles Austin Beard (1874-1948), American historian and political scientist, was probably the most influential historical scholar of his time. He is best known for his emphasis on the role of economic interests in American history.

Charles A. Beard was born into a well-to-do family on a farm near Knightstown, Ind., on Nov. 27, 1874. He graduated from DePauw University in 1898. His interest in social problems was stimulated by a visit to Chicago's Hull House and subsequent study at Oxford in England, where he came in contact with economic reformers and helped found Ruskin Hall, a workingmen's school. In 1900 he married Mary Ritter, whom he had met at DePauw; they had a daughter and a son.

After taking his doctorate at Columbia University in 1904, Beard taught there until he resigned in 1917 in the midst of a controversy over academic freedom and the right of professors to criticize the government's war policy. After that, except for his participation in the New School for Social Research, he never again held a regular academic post. Financially well-off and the author of highly successful textbooks, Beard worked at his farm in New Milford, Conn. An amazingly prolific writer, he published, alone or with collaborators (particularly his wife), some 60 books and 300 articles. Between world Wars I and II he was nationally and internationally prominent as scholar, adviser, publicist, and polemicist on questions of public administration and various aspects of social and foreign policy.

Beard caused an early sensation with *An Economic Interpretation of the Constitution of the United States* (1913), a study of the property holdings of the Founding Fathers; it concluded that they "were, with few exceptions, immediately, directly, and personally interested in, and derived economic advantages from, the establishment of the new system," and maintained that "the Constitution was essentially an economic document." Viewing American history as a conflict between financial and agrarian interests, Beard carried his analysis further in his *Economic Origins of Jeffersonian Democracy* (1915) and most brilliantly in his and Mary Beard's *The Rise of American Civilization* (1927). The latter volume popularized a view of the Civil War as a "Second American Revolution," in which capitalists carried out against the property interests of slave-holding planters "the most stupendous act of sequestration in the history of Anglo-Saxon jurisprudence." In addition, the Beards charged that the 14th Amendment was planned from the beginning to be a bulwark for the property rights of corporations.

Ever a reformer and a longtime advocate of a planned democratic economy, Beard, in the manner of his teacher and colleague at Columbia, James Harvey Robinson, saw the writing of history as providing tools for progressive social change. By 1933, when he gave his presidential address to the American Historical Association, he was convinced of the radical subjectivity of historical knowledge: "written history" was merely "an act of faith,"and the ideal of objectivity, he later asserted, was only a "noble dream." As his economic determinist viewpoint lost rigidity, he was able to assess the Founding Fathers more traditionally in *The Republic* (1943).

During the 1930s Beard was a staunch continentalist and isolationist and vigorously opposed American involvement in World War II. His last years were devoted to a highly controversial study of the approach of war, in which he placed heavy blame upon Franklin D. Roosevelt: *President Roosevelt and the Coming of the War, 1941* (1948). Since Beard's death on Sept. 1, 1948, his historical methods and characteristic views of American history have been seriously attacked by new generations of historians.

Further Reading

Some biographical material appears in Mary Beard, *The Making of Charles A. Beard: An Interpretation* (1955). Beard's career is insightfully discussed and appraised in Richard Hofstadter, *The Progressive Historians: Turner, Beard, Parrington* (1968), and in Cushing Strout, *The Pragmatic Revolt in American History: Carl Becker and Charles Beard* (1958). Howard K. Beale, ed., *Charles A. Beard: An Appraisal* (1954), contains a number of useful assessments.

Additional Sources

Borning, Bernard C., *The political and social thought of Charles A. Beard,* Westport, Conn.: Greenwood Press, 1984, 1962.
Nore, Ellen, *Charles A. Beard, an intellectual biography,* Carbondale: Southern Illinois University Press, 1983. □

Mary Ritter Beard

Mary Ritter Beard (1876-1958) was active in the struggles for women's suffrage and for trade union reform. With her husband Charles Austin Beard she wrote several books, including the multivolume *The Rise of American Civilization*. On her own she wrote several books about women, the most important of which was *Woman as Force in History: A Study of Traditions and Realities*.

Mary Ritter Beard was born into a secure, Republican, middleclass world in Indianapolis, Indiana, on August 5, 1876. Her father, Eli Foster Ritter, was an attorney by occupation and a zealous temperance advocate and stalwart of the local Methodist church. Her mother, Narcissa Lockwood, a former school-teacher active in local community and church activities, was primarily caught up in rearing her family of six, of which Beard was the elder daughter. At the age of 16 she attended DePauw University, not far from home, as had her father and as did all her siblings. In college she met and in 1900 married Charles Austin Beard (1874-1948).

The young couple spent two years in England, partly in Manchester, then the center of labor and feminist ferment, and both movements absorbed their energies. At Oxford, where her husband studied history and helped to found Ruskin Hall, a college designed for workingclass men, she discovered the militant women's movement and met and worked with leading English radical suffragists.

The Beards returned to the United States in 1902 and both began graduate study at Columbia University, but she soon left her academic studies in sociology. By then the mother of two children, she chose to devote her time to the struggles for women's suffrage and for trade union reform. For example, she helped the National Women's Trade Union League organize the New York shirt-waistmaker's strike in 1909 and protest the Triangle factory fire in which more than 100 young girls and women were killed.

She became an activist in the women's suffrage movement as organizer, publicist, and fundraiser. Her particular interest in workingclass women, a legacy from her years in England, led her to active participation in the Wage Earner's League, the Woman Suffrage Party's organization for working women. When a militant faction of the National Woman Suffrage Association began to form under the leadership of Alice Paul, Beard went with this group, originally known as the Congressional Union, later splitting away to form the Woman's Party.

Although Beard stayed with the women's suffrage movement for years, she slowly detached herself from the role of activist and moved toward the role of analyst and social critic. A break did finally come when, after the suffrage amendment was won in 1920, the Woman's Party centered its activities on the passage of the Equal Rights Amendment. Beard left the organization, choosing instead to support the idea of protective legislation for working women. She was one of many feminists, especially those concerned with working women, who initially opposed the Equal Rights Amendment (ERA).

Writing with a Partner

The Beards were partners for almost 50 years, raised two children, established an exciting and loving home together, and shared a political commitment that carried them often into the public arena on controversial issues. They are most well-known today for their collaboration on major works. The Beards' first joint venture, *American Citizenship*, appeared in 1914. In 1920 they issued *The History of the United States* . The first two volumes of their monumental history of the nation appeared in 1927. The total work is titled *The Rise of American Civilization*. In 1939 another two volumes of The Rise appeared, and in 1942 the concluding volume was issued. *The Rise of American Civilization* shaped the thinking of generations of Americans. *A Basic History of the United States,* their "last will and testament of the American people," said her husband, was published in 1944.

Beard published two books alone while she was involved in activist politics. The first, *Woman's Work in Municipalities,* appearing in 1915, was a lengthy essay in the tradition of muckraking literature, demonstrating the varied and essential work of women in cities. In 1920 she published *A Short History of the American Labor Movement,* designed for readers with little knowledge of the struggle of working people in the United States. Her only other book written alone that did not deal with women was a long essay, *The Making of Charles A. Beard,* which was published in 1955, seven years after her husband's death.

The rest of her long and active intellectual life was devoted to writing books and articles and speaking endlessly on what became the major theme of her public life—that women are and have always been a central force in history and culture, that women have been active, assertive, competent contributors to their societies, but that history books do not reflect their role. Women are left out of history, are made to seem invisible, she said, and she saw as her mission a reconstruction in order to end that invisibility.

Women had succeeded, after 80 years of active struggle, in acquiring the vote, but with that victory came the belief that women's history began with the suffrage struggle. To Beard, such a belief was a denial of all the histories of women, and, therefore, a denial of self in the women who were living in the present. The core of everything she wrote and everything she did was shaped by her conviction that women were undeniably a force in civilization, and that history and politics were incomplete without that recognition. She devoted her energies to trying to persuade all people, but women particularly, of their own historic past and of the power that was within their reach to change the present. She began a crusade for women's minds that took many forms.

Writing Alone

Most important, she wrote *On Understanding Women,* published in 1931, which ushered in the decade of her most creative work. In 1933 she edited a collection of writing by women called *America Through Women's Eyes.* In 1934 she edited, with Martha Bensley Bruère, *Laughing Their Way: Women's Humor in America* . In 1946 her most famous work appeared: *Woman as Force in History: A Study of Traditions and Realities.* Reprinted in 1962 and again in 1971, it had its third printing in 1973. In 1953 she published *The Force of Women in Japanese History.*

Woman as Force in History represents the culmination of her years of study and writing on the subject and stands as the mature statement of her thesis on the historic role of women. Many of the ideas and themes she developed in earlier years were pulled together and deepened in this major work. Her analysis of the ideas of the legal theories of William Blackstone and their impact on American feminists occupies a significant portion of what is new and of immense significance in this volume.

In pre-industrial times, she asserted, women were often discriminated against and were seen by theologians and moralists as evil and inferior, but in reality women so often defied law and custom that it is not possible to use any single formula to describe woman's role. Women of the ruling class often wielded great power, and women of the lower classes suffered as much or more from their class position as from their gender. It was not until the rise of democratic government and the expansion of political power to ordinary men that women as a group were excluded from positions of power. It was with the development of capitalism, she argued, that discrimination on account of sex, regardless of class, became pervasive, and it

was during this time that women were driven out of the professions, out of politics, and out of power. The feminist movement, born during this period of diminished rights, assumed that such restrictions always existed and thus passed on a view of history that was invalid and incomplete.

Even in her role as intellectual and social critic, Mary Ritter Beard retained her activist impulse. In 1934 she wrote an extraordinary 50-page pamphlet entitled "A Changing Political Economy as it Affects Women," which was a detailed syllabus for a women's studies course—the first of its kind—and she tried desparately to persuade many colleges and universities to establish such a course. Later in the 1930s, in an effort to create some tangible demonstration of women's lives and women's pasts, she developed the idea of establishing a women's archive. For five years she tried to establish, finance, organize, structure, house, and publicize what became the World Center for Women's Archives. The object of the center was to assemble and preserve all source material dealing with women's lives, a clearinghouse of information on the history of women.

In the spring of 1941 she was involved in a new project, a feminist critique of the *Encyclopaedia Britannica,* financed by the *Encyclopaedia* itself and carried out by a staff of three women that Beard selected. The final report, submitted after 18 months, is an intriguing 40-page document which is filled with provocative ideas for further research.

Mary Ritter Beard died in August 1958 at the age of 84, but the echo of her voice and the impact of her ideas remain.

Further Reading

The best way to become familiar with the ideas of Mary Ritter Beard is to read her books, especially *Woman as Force in History,* although this is not an easy work to understand. The only extensive appraisal of her life and work is Ann J. Lane's *Mary Ritter Beard: A Sourcebook* -(1978), which also contains significant selections from her writings and a thorough bibliography. Other valuable assessments are Berenice A. Carroll, "Mary Beard's *Woman as Force in History:* A Critique," *Massachusetts Review* (Winter-Spring 1972) and reprinted in *Liberating Women's History: Theoretical and Critical Essays* , edited by Berenice A. Carroll (1976); Carl N. Degler, "*Woman as Force in History by Mary Beard,*" *Daedalus* (Winter 1974); and Ann J. Lane, "Mary Ritter Beard: Women as Force," in *Feminist Theorists: Three Centuries of Women's Intellectual Traditions,* edited by Dale Spender (1983).

Additional Sources

Turoff, Barbara K., *Mary Beard as force in history,* Dayton, Ohio: Wright State University, 1979. ☐

Romare Howard Bearden

The American painter-collagist Romare Howard Bearden (1914-1988) was a leading abstractionist until racial strife in the United States led him to focus more directly on African American subject matter, with related changes in his style and technique.

An only child, Romare Bearden was born on September 2, 1914, in Charlotte, North Carolina. When he was still a child, the family moved to Harlem, New York City, where his mother was a well-known journalist and political activist. He received a bachelor of science degree from New York University because, he said, "I thought I wanted to be a medical doctor." E. Simms Campbell, the renowned African American cartoonist, encouraged him to study painting with George Grosz, the German-born painter and satirical draftsman, at the Art Students' League in New York. "It was Grosz," Bearden remembered with gratitude, "who first introduced me to classical draftsmen like Hogarth and Ingres." Essential as formal institutions were to his development as a person and an artist, his association with African American artists and intellectuals of the Depression period cannot be minimized. Among these were the painters Norman Lewis and Jacob Lawrence and the writer Ralph Ellison, who maintained an atmosphere of social and political concern which heavily influenced Bearden's early work. Even though his concern for these problems in no way diminished later and all his works abound in ethnic subject matter, the mild-mannered, almost shy artist insisted that he was not a social propagandist. "My subject is people," he said. "They just happen to turn out to be Negro."

Early in his career he emulated the styles of Rufino Tamayo and José Clemente Orozco, painting simple forms and echoing the crude power he had come to admire in medieval art. His paintings of everyday black life were forceful in color; the figures followed simple patterns and

their statements were literal, as in graphic art rather than painting. By 1945 he had begun to adopt a less literal, more personal style, which proved to be the most congenial for his unique artistic expressions. In the 1950s, while working as a New York City Welfare Department investigator, he expressed his feelings in lyrical abstractions.

First Solo Shows Bring Recognition

Caresse Crosby launched Bearden in her Washington, D.C., gallery in 1945, following his service in World War II. In his first one-person show in New York the same year, 18 works were sold during the first two weeks, and the critics were ecstatic in their praise, calling his work "vibrant," "propulsive," and "poetic." There were subsequent invitations to exhibit, including solo shows in Paris and New York.

By 1960 Bearden's personal style had firmly caught the imagination of the art world. Drawing on his boyhood memories of the Deep South and his experiences as a long-time resident of Harlem, he depicted the conditions in which African Americans lived with such stark reality that the collage or montage became a powerfully emotive art form. With the skill of a master, he made formidable use of disparate elements of photographs and documentary film, resulting in an uncommon immediacy in his work that extended its meaning.

Influenced by the Civil Rights Movement

The early 1960s brought a period of transition for Bearden. In 1963 a group of African American artists began meeting in his Harlem studio. Calling themselves the Spiral Group, they sought to define their roles as black artists within the context of the growing civil rights movement.

His "Projections" series, exhibited in 1964, caused a wave of controversy and excitement. The tormented faces of African American women hanging upside down on the cracked stoops of Harlem tenements, New York bridges soaring out of Carolina cotton fields, and African pyramids colliding with American folk singers strumming guitars prompted one critic to write that the show comprised "a collection of headhunters." These startling images, constructed from newspaper and magazine photographs, had been enlarged from their original color into huge black-and-white photographs that provided the artist's desired effect of urgency.

The shock turned into solid success that brought Bearden many honors, including cover commissions for *Time, Fortune,* and the *New York Times* magazines; the National Institute of Arts and Letters achievement award (1966); and a 1970 Guggenheim Memorial Fellowship to write a history of African American art. In 1969 his book *The Painter's Mind* (Carl Holty, coauthor) was published. He also wrote a biography of Henry O. Tanner, the towering but unheralded African American artist of the late 19th and early 20th centuries.

His first full-scale exhibition in a European museum was held in May 1971 at the Rath Museum in Geneva, Switzerland. In his widely acclaimed "Prevalence of Ritual" retrospective at New York's Museum of Modern Art, also held in 1971, many of the works displayed were collage paintings.

Focus on African American Life in the 1970s and 1980s

The primary subject of the last 25 years of Bearden's art was the life and culture of African Americans. His work covered rural themes based on his memories of the South as well as urban life and jazz. In the 1980s he produced a large body of work featuring compelling images of women. For many years he spent time annually on the Caribbean island of St. Martin, which brought tropical images to his work.

In 1986 Bearden was commissioned by the Detroit Institute of Arts to celebrate its centennial. He executed a mosaic mural, done in mosaic glass, titled ''Quilting Time''. The work is typical of Bearden in that it is rooted in his memories of his southern childhood and depicts an important aspect of African American culture. The brightly colored mosaic shows a group of women making a quilt. His use of mosaic tile late in his career developed from the technique of building his forms with very small pieces of paper, called *tesserae*. Since the paper was so fragile, Bearden preferred using mosaic tile for large public works.

Honors and Legacy

Bearden received the Medal of Arts from President Ronald Reagan in 1987. Less than a year later, on March 11, 1988, Bearden died of bone cancer in New York City. His estate made provisions for the establishment of the Romare Bearden Foundation to aid in the education and training of talented art students.

''Memory and Metaphor: The Art of Romare Bearden, 1940-1987'' was a major retrospective show containing nearly 150 works from Bearden's half-century career in the visual arts. Beginning at the Studio Museum in Harlem in 1991, the show traveled through 1993 to major museums in Chicago, Los Angeles, Atlanta, Pittsburgh, and finally the National Museum of American Art in Washington, D.C. His massive survey *A History of African-American Artists from 1792 to the Present* was posthumously published in 1993.

Further Reading

A complete examination of Bearden and his work is available in Myron Schwartzman, *Romare Bearden: His Life and Art* (1990). Additional information on Bearden's career may be found in Elton C. Fax, *Black Artists of the New Generation* (1977), Sharon F. Patton, *Memory and Metaphor: The Art of Romare Bearden, 1940- 1987* (1991), and the Smithsonian Institution's, *African American Visual Aesthetics: A Postmodernist View* (1995). □

Aubrey Vincent Beardsley

The English illustrator Aubrey Vincent Beardsley (1872-1898) was the most influential draftsman of his era in England. He was closely connected with the fin-de-siècle period.

Aubrey Beardsley was born in Brighton on Aug. 21, 1872. His father, the son of a local jeweler, lost the money he had inherited, so his mother supported the family by giving music lessons and working as a governess. Because of his mother's absence from home, Aubrey was sent to a nearby boarding school at the age of 6; his schooling was interrupted by attacks of tuberculosis. He began to draw in school, and by the age of 10 he was selling his drawings, which were imitations of Kate Greenaway's.

At the age of 15 Beardsley went to work in London, first for a surveyor and then in an insurance office. On the spur of the moment, he called on the painter Edward Burne-Jones, who prophesied that Beardsley would become a great artist. His first important commission, an enormous, highly paid one, to illustrate Malory's *Morte d'Arthur,* came at the age of 20; this work is a masterpiece. Beardsley's drawings in the first issue of the *Studio* magazine were a tremendous success; he said, quite rightly, that he had ''already far outdistanced the old men'' and that he ''had fortune at his feet.'' His illustrations for Oscar Wilde's play *Salome* were a great success, but Wilde did not like the drawings, for he feared that they overshadowed the play.

Beardsley was a bit of a dandy, with ''a face like a silver hatchet, and grass green hair,'' according to Wilde. Beardsley was a public character as well as a private eccentric before his twenty-first birthday. He said, ''I have one aim—the grotesque. If I am not grotesque I am nothing.'' Anxious to make the most of his life, which he knew would be short, he took on all kinds of commissions.

From its first issue, Beardsley was art editor of the *Yellow Book,* a magazine whose format and title were taken from the cheap French novel of the day. When Wilde was arrested, Beardsley's association with him in the public mind was so close that the publishers of the *Yellow Book* felt they had to get rid of him. Suddenly no respectable publisher would employ him.

Beardsley eventually made a connection with a new magazine, the *Savoy.* Many of the writers were former contributors to the *Yellow Book.* As with the *Yellow Book,* Beardsley was the outstanding attraction of the *Savoy,* and it was a great blow to the magazine when he had to suspend his contributions because of his health. He died in Menton, France, on March 16, 1898, at the age of 25, working right up to the end.

Beardsley was a designer of genius and a draftsman of a high order of talent. His illustrations are distinguished by a rhythmic, curving line that has many of the characteristics of engraving, and his whole conception of the art of illustration was profoundly personal and original. His style, overblown in manner and "decadent" in subject matter, was dominant in England and the United States during part of the "great age of illustration." Through Sergei Diaghilev it had a strong effect on the Russian ballet. Beardsley's influence on Art Nouveau was profound, and the painters Wassily Kandinsky and Pablo Picasso were early admirers of his work.

Further Reading

The best book on Beardsley is Stanley Weintraub, *Beardsley: A Biography* (1967). Two earlier studies are Robert Ross, *Aubrey Beardsley* (1909), and Haldane Macfall, *Aubrey Beardsley: The Man and His Work* (1927).

Additional Sources

Benkovitz, Miriam J., *Aubrey Beardsley, an account of his life,* New York: Putnam, 1981.

Ross, Robert Baldwin, *Aubrey Beardsley,* Norwood, Pa.: Norwood Editions, 1977. ☐

The Beatles

In the 1960s a new band known as the Beatles burst on the pop music scene and changed it forever. Band members included George Harrison (1943-), John Lennon (1940-1980), Paul McCartney (1942-), and Ringo Starr (1940-). With the release of three anthologies in the mid-1990s, the group remained one of the best-selling of all time.

On February 7, 1964, the Beatles arrived at Kennedy International Airport in New York City, met by 110 police officers and a mob of more than 10,000 screaming fans. The British Invasion—and in particular, "Beatlemania"—had begun, and the "mop-topped" Beatles— John Lennon, Paul McCartney, George Harrison,

and Ringo Starr —wasted no time in endearing themselves to American fans and the media, though many adults remained skeptical. According to the February 24, 1964, *Newsweek* cover story, the Beatles' music, already topping the charts, was "a near disaster" that did away with "secondary rhythms, harmony, and melody." Despite such early criticism, the Beatles garnered two Grammy Awards in 1964, foreshadowing the influence they would have on the future of pop culture.

Inspired by the simple guitar-and-washboard "skiffle" music of Lonnie Donegan and later by U.S. pop artists such as Elvis, Buddy Holly, and Little Richard, John Lennon formed his own group, the Quarrymen, in 1956 with Pete Shotton and other friends. Expertise helped guitarist Paul McCartney, whom Shotton introduced to Lennon in 1957 at a church function, find a place in the band, and he in turn introduced Lennon to George Harrison. Only fourteen, Harrison, though a skilled guitarist, did not impress seventeen-year-old Lennon overmuch, but his perseverence finally won him a permanent niche in the developing ensemble. Stuart Sutcliffe, an artist friend of Lennon's, brought a bass guitar into the group a year later. Calling themselves Johnny and the Moondogs, the band eventually won a chance to tour Scotland, backing a little-known singer, Johnny Gentle. Renamed the Silver Beatles, they were well-received, but the pay was poor, and the end of the tour saw the exit of a disgusted drummer and the arrival of Pete Best.

L-R: Paul and Ringo (back), George and John (front)

With the help of Welshman Allan Williams, club owner and sometime-manager for many promising bands playing around Liverpool in 1960, the Beatles found themselves polishing their act at seedy clubs in Hamburg, West Germany. Living quarters were squalid, working conditions demanding, but instead of splintering the group, the experience strengthened them. Encouraged by their audiences' demands to "make show," they became confident, outrageous performers. Lennon in particular was reported to have played in his underwear with a toilet seat around his neck, and the whole band romped madly on the stage. Such spectacles by the Beatles and another English band, Rory Storme and the Hurricanes, ultimately caved in the stage at one club. The Beatles' second trip to Hamburg, in 1961, was distinguished by a better club and a series of recordings for which they backed singer Tony Sheridan—recordings that proved critical in gaining them a full-time manager. At the end of that stay, Sutcliffe remained in Hamburg to marry, having ceded bass duties to McCartney. He died tragically the following spring, shortly after the Beatles joined up with Brian Epstein.

Intrigued by requests for Tony Sheridan's "My Bonnie" single, featuring the Beatles, record shop manager Brain Epstein sought the band at Liverpool's Cavern Club. Within a year of signing a managerial agreement with Epstein, the Beatles gained a recording contract from E.M.I. Records producer George Martin, and on the eve of success shuffled yet another drummer out, causing riots among Pete Best's loyal following. The last in a long line of percussionists came in the form of the Hurricanes' sad-eyed former drummer, Ritchie Starkey— Ringo Starr.

Despite initial doubts, Martin agreed to use Lennon and McCartney originals on both sides of the Beatles' first single. "Love Me Do," released on October 5, 1962, did well enough to convince Martin that, with the right material, the Beatles could achieve a number one record. He was proved correct. "Please Please Me," released in Britain on January 12, 1963, was an immediate hit. The biweekly newspaper *Mersey Beat* quoted Keith Fordyce of *New Musical Express,* who called the song "a really enjoyable platter, full of vigour and vitality," as well as Brian Matthew, then Britain's most influential commentator on pop music, who proclaimed the Beatles "musically and visually the most accomplished group to emerge since the Shadows." The Beatles' first British album, recorded in one thirteen-hour session, remained number one on the charts for six months.

The United States remained indifferent until, one month before the Beatles' arrival, E.M.I.'s U.S. subsidiary, Capitol Records, launched an unprecedented $50,000 promotional campaign. It and the Beatles' performances on *The Ed Sullivan Show,* which opened their first American tour, paid off handsomely. "I Want to Hold Your Hand," released in the United States in January of 1964, hit number one within three weeks. After seven weeks at the top of the charts, it dropped to number two to make room for "She Loves You," which gave way to "Can't Buy Me Love." As many as three new songs a week were released, until on April 4, 1964, the Beatles held the top five slots on the Billboard list of top sellers, another seven in the top one

hundred, and four albums positions including the top two. One week later, fourteen of the top one hundred songs were the Beatles'—a feat unmatched before or since.

Also in 1964, long before music videos had become commonplace, the Beatles appeared in the first of several innovative full-length feature films. Shot in black-and-white and well-received by critics, *A Hard Day's Night* represented a day in the life of the group. Its release one month before the Beatles began their second U.S. tour was timely. *Help,* released in July of 1965, was a madcap fantasy filmed in color. Exotic locations made *Help* visually more interesting than the first film, but critics were less impressed. Both albums sold well, though the U.S. versions contained fewer original songs, and *Help* was padded with pseudo-Eastern accompanying tracks.

The 1965 and 1966 albums *Rubber Soul* and *Revolver* marked a turning point in the Beatles' recording history. The most original of their collections to date, both combined Eastern, country-western, soul, and classical motifs with trend-setting covers, breaking any mold that seemed to contain "rock and roll." In both albums, balladry, classical instrumentation, and new structure resulted in brilliant new concepts just hinted at in earlier works like "Yesterday" and "Rain." Songs such as "Tomorrow Never Knows," "Eleanor Rigby," and the lyrically surreal "Norwegian Wood" made use of sophisticated recording techniques—marking the beginning of the end of the group's touring, since live performances of such songs was technically impossible at the time. The Beatles became further distanced from their fans by Lennon's comments to a *London Evening Standard* writer: "Christianity will go. It will vanish and shrink. I needn't argue about that, I'm right and will be proved right. We're more popular than Jesus Christ now. I don't know which will go first, rock 'n' roll or Christianity. Jesus was all right, but his disciples were thick and ordinary. It's them twisting it that ruins it for me." While the British dismissed the statement as another "Lennonism," American teens in the Bible Belt took Lennon's words literally, ceremoniously burning Beatle albums as the group finished their last U.S. tour amid riots and death threats.

Acclaimed by critics, with advance sales of more than one million, the tightly produced "conceptual" album *Sgt. Pepper's Lonely Hearts Club Band* was perhaps the high point of the Beatles' recording career. No longer a "collection" of Lennon - McCartney and Harrison originals, the four-Grammy album was, in a stunning and evocative cover package, a thematic whole so aesthetically pleasing as to remain remarkably timeless. Imaginative melodies carried songs about many life experiences, self-conscious philosophy, and bizarre imagery, as in "A Day in the Life"—a quintessential sixties studio production. The Beatles' music had evolved from catchy love songs to profound ballads, social commentary, and work clearly affected by their growing awareness of and experimentation with Eastern mysticism and hallucinogenic drugs. Song like "Lucy in the Sky With Diamonds" were pegged as drug-induced (LSD), and even Starr's seemingly harmless rendition of "A Little Help From My Friends" included references to getting "high." Broadening their horizons seemed an essential part of the

Beatles' lives and, influenced greatly by Harrison's interest in Indian religion, the Beatles visited the Maharishi Mahesh Yogi in Bangor, Wales, in 1967. It was there that news of Brian Epstein's death reached them.

The group's next cooperative project was the scripting and directing of another film, *Magical Mystery Tour,* an unrehearsed, unorganized failure. Intended to be fresh, it drew criticism as a compilation of adolescent humor, gag bits, and undisciplined boredom. The resulting album, however, featured polished studio numbers such as McCartney's "Fool on the Hill" and a curiosity of Lennon's , "I Am the Walrus." The American LP added tracks including "Penny Lane," "Hello Goodbye," and "Strawberry Fields Forever," which were immortalized on short films broadcast by Ed Sullivan. Solo projects in 1967 and 1968 included the acting debuts of Lennon in *How I Won the War* and Starr in *Candy,* Harrison's soundtrack to the film "Wonderwall," and Lennon's eventual release of his and Yoko Ono's controversial *Two Virgins* albums.

Growing diversity pointed to disintegration, the early throes of which were evident in 1968 on the two-record set, *The Beatles,* the first album released by the group's new record company, Apple. The *White Album,* as it was commonly known, showcased a variety of songs, mostly disjointed, often incomprehensible. According to George Martin, as quoted in *The Beatles Forever,* "I tried to plead with them to be selective and make it a really good single album, but they wouldn't have it." The unity seen in earlier projects was nudged aside by individuality and what appeared to be a growing rift between Lennon and McCartney. Whereas the latter contributed ballads like "Blackbird," the former ground out antiwar statements, parodied the Maharishi, and continued to experiment with obscure production. Harrison, on the other hand, shone in "While My Guitar Gently Weeps," aided by Eric Clapton's tasteful guitar solo. Starr, for the first time, was allotted the space for an original, the country-western "Don't Pass Me By," which became a number-one hit in Scandinavia where it was released as a single. Overall, critics found the *White Album* a letdown after the mastery of *Sgt. Pepper,* though Capitol claimed it was the fastest-selling album in the history of the record industry.

Despite having little to do with its making, the Beatles regained some of their lost status with *Yellow Submarine,* an animated feature film released in July 1968. A fantasy pitting the big-eyed, colorfully clothed Beatles against the squattish Blue Meanies, the film was visually pleasing if not initially a big money-maker. The group spent minimal time on the music, padding it with studio-session throwaways and re-releases of "All You Need Is Love" and "Yellow Submarine" itself. The remainder of 1968 and 1969 showed the individual Beatles continuing to work apart. Starr appeared in the film *The Magic Christian,* and Lennon performed live outside the group with Yoko Ono, whom he had married, and the Plastic Ono Band.

After spending months filming and recording the documentary that would later emerge as the *Let It Be* film and album, the Beatles abandoned thirty hours of tape and film to producer George Martin. Since editing it down

would make release before 1970 impossible, the album was put on hold. Instead, for the final time, the Beatles gathered to produce an album "the way we used to do it," as McCartney was quoted in Philip Norman's book, *Shout!* The result was as stunning in its internal integrity as *Sgt. Pepper* had been. Schisms seemed to vanish on *Abbey Road,* with all Beatles at their best. Lennon showed himself sardonic but controlled in "Come Together" and "I Want You—She's So Heavy," McCartney crooned ballads and doo-wop rockers alike in "Golden Slumbers" and "Oh! Darling!"; and Harrison surpassed both of them with "Here Comes the Sun" and "Something," hailed by Lennon as the best track on the album. Starr, always in the background, provided vocals for "Octopus's Garden" and uncompromising and creative drumming throughout. Wrote Schaffner, "The musicianship is always tasteful, unobtrusive, and supportive of the songs themselves. . . . The Beatles never sounded more together." Yet another Grammy winner, it was a triumphal exit from the 1960s, and its declaration, "And in the end, the love you take is equal to the love you make," read like an epitaph until the "post mortem" release of the heavily edited *Let It Be.*

American producer Phil Spector took over the *Let It Be* clean-up project from George Martin in 1970. The resulting album, brought out after fifteen months of apathy, bickering, and legal battles, was a mixture of raw recordings, glimpses of the Beatles in an earlier era, and heavily dubbed strings and vocals—as on McCartney's "Long and Winding Road." Though most tracks were tightly and effectively edited, critics said the album lacked the harmony of earlier endeavors. According to Schaffner, Lennon later told *Rolling Stone,* "We couldn't get into it. . . . I don't know, it was just a dreadful, dreadful feeling . . . you couldn't make music . . . in a strange place with people filming you and colored lights." The film, which strove to show the Beatles as honestly and naturally as possible, gave further evidence of disintegration. Band members were shown quarreling, unresponsive to McCartney's attempts to raise morale. Said Alan Smith of the *New Musical Express,* quoted by Roy Carr and Tony Tyler in *The Beatles: An Illustrated Record,* "If the Beatles soundtrack album 'Let It Be' is to be their last, then it will stand as a cheapskate epitaph, a cardboard tombstone, a sad and tatty end to a musical fusion which wiped clean and drew again the face of pop music."

By the end of 1970, all four Beatles had recorded solo albums, and, in 1971, McCartney sued for the dissolution of the group. Throughout the seventies, promoters attempted to reunite them without success. The Beatles did perform on Starr's *Ringo* album in 1973—though not together in the studio, Lennon, Harrison, and McCartney contributed music, vocals, and backing. The tragic murder of John Lennon on December 8, 1980, quashed any hopes of a reunion among all of the Beatles. In the mid-1990s, however, the Beatles did release new music under the original band name. The living Beatles played over taped instrumentation and vocals left by Lennon. The singles "Free as a Bird" and "Real Love" were released as parts of anthologies featuring rare material and outtakes from Beatles recording sessions. "Free as a Bird" debuted with a music video in the United

States as part of a television anthology presented on ABC-TV in 1995.

Selected recordings include *Introducing the Beatles,* Vee Jay, 1963; *Meet the Beatles,* Capitol, 1964; *The Beatles Second Album,* Capitol, 1964; *A Hard Day's Night,* United Artists, 1964; *Something New,* Capitol, 1964; *The Beatles Story* , Capitol, 1964; *Beatles '65,* Capitol, 1964; *The Early Beatles,* Capitol, 1965; *Beatles VI,* Capitol, 1965; *Help,* Capitol, 1965; *Rubber Soul,* Capitol, 1965; *Yesterday . . . . and Today;* Revolver, Capitol, 1966; *Sgt. Pepper's Lonely Hearts Club Band,* Capitol, 1967; *Magical Mystery Tour,* Capitol, 1967; *The Beatles (White Album),* Apple, 1968; *Yellow Submarine* , Apple, 1969; *Abbey Road,* Apple, 1969; *Hey Jude,* Apple, 1970; *Tony Sheridan and the Beatles,* Polydor, 1970; *Let It Be,* Apple, 1970; *The Beatles 1962-1966,* Apple, 1973; *The Beatles 1967-1970,* Apple, 1973; *Rock 'N' Roll Music,* Capitol, 1976; *The Beatles at the Hollywood Bowl,* Capitol, 1976; *The Beatles Live! At the Star Club in Hamburg, Germany: 1962,* Lingasong, 1977; *Love Songs,* Capitol, 1977; *Rarities,* Capitol, 1979; *Anthology I; Anthology II,* Apple, 1996; *Anthology III,* Apple, 1996.

Further Reading

Contemporary Musicians: Profiles of the People in Music, Gale Research, Detroit, Michigan.
Carr, Roy and Tony Tyler, *The Beatles: An Illustrated Record,* Harmony Books, 1978.
Norman, Philip, *Shout! The Beatles in Their Generation,* Simon and Schuster, 1981.
Schaffner, Nicholas, *The Beatles Forever,* McGraw, 1978.
Schaumburg, Ron, *Growing up With the Beatles,* Harcourt, 1976.
Evening Standard, (London), March 4, 1966.
Mersey Beat, January 31-February 14, 1963.
Newsweek, February 24, 1964.
Oakland Press Sunday Magazine, February 4, 1979.
Time, December 22, 1980. □

Queen Beatrix Wilhelmina von Amsberg

Beatrix Wilhelmina von Amsberg (born 1938) became queen of The Netherlands in 1980. An intelligent and strong willed woman, she had to reconcile her personal independence with the duties of a constitutional monarch.

Queen Beatrix Wilhelmina von Amsberg was born January 31, 1938, at Soestdijk Palace in Baarn, The Netherlands. As the first-born child of Princess (later Queen) Juliana, the heiress to the Dutch throne, and Prince Bernhard, she was first in the line of succession after her mother. This status was confirmed with the birth of Marijke (later Christine) in 1947, a girl like the three other royal children. Under the constitutional provisions then in force, sons had priority over daughters in the royal succession. Thus, by then it was clear that Beatrix would not be displaced by a younger brother.

In May 1940, together with her grandmother, Queen Wilhelmina, and her parents and younger sister, Irene, she escaped from the German invasion of the Netherlands, going first to England and then to Ottawa, Canada, where she spent the war years. She lived there in a comfortable but less than palatial home, attended kindergarten and primary school with Canadian children, and acquired an impeccable English accent from schoolmates as well as teachers, although within the family she spoke Dutch of a very pure, cultivated kind.

In August 1945, she returned to her liberated homeland. Residing again at Soestdijk Palace, she continued her education in outside schools, first a progressive experimental school in nearby Bilthoven and then the Baarn Lyceum (secondary school), from which she graduated in 1956. She then enrolled at the University of Leiden (1956-1961), attending regular classes and tutorials and living as much like the other students as was possible in her position. She made friends among other students, who came from a wide range of society. She studied law, economics, and sociology which would aid her in her eventual royal tasks, but stopped short of writing a thesis and obtaining a doctorate in philosophy; instead she earned the degree of "doctorandus," given to those who passed the general doctoral examination.

Her mother encouraged her to follow her heart rather than accept a husband chosen for political reasons among royalty or at least high nobility. Her choice of a German diplomat, Claus von Amsberg, who was of minor noble rank, aroused bitter controversy because he had served briefly in the German army during World War II. With characteristic firmness, she would not be dissuaded and received the necessary approval of the States General (parliament). The wedding was held in Amsterdam—the politically radical capital, most of whose once large Jewish population had been killed by the Nazis—in March 1966, despite vigorous protests and rioting. Her husband, who took Dutch nationality and was named Prince von Amsberg, quickly overcame the suspicions of the people by learning to speak impeccable Dutch within a short time and by committing himself wholeheartedly to Dutch interests and feelings.

On April 30, 1980, when her mother abdicated the throne, Beatrix immediately assumed the throne as there is no interregnum in The Netherlands. When the new queen was inaugurated (there is no royal coronation in The Netherlands) there was again violence in the streets, directed not so much against her personally as against social conditions, particularly the shortage of housing. Beatrix, inflexible in carrying through the solemn parade and ceremony despite jeers and smoke-bombs, nonetheless displayed comprehension of and compassion for the protesters. She settled into the routine of leadership of the Dutch state. In 1982, she visited the United States during the celebration of the bicentennial of the Dutch recognition of American Independence. She addressed Congress in a speech that she composed, although it was approved by the Dutch government. The speech emphasized, in particular, her country's and her own commitment to peace.

She had three sons, William Alexander (born 1967), John Friso (born 1968), and Constantine (born 1969). Her first born was the heir to the throne not as eldest son but as the first born, because the new Dutch constitution provided that the royal succession not discriminate between males and females. For several years beginning in 1982, Beatrix's husband withdrew from public life as part of his treatment for depression; it was reported that he had found difficulties with his mainly ceremonial public role, especially after Beatrix ascended the throne, which left him without a vigorous, independent career.

Shrewd investments in both the stock market and real estate market allowed Beatrix to become one of the most wealthy women in the world. Besides amassing substantial wealth, Beatrix paid an official visit to the former Dutch colony of Indonesia in 1995 as they celebrated the 50th anniversary of their independence from the Netherlands.

Further Reading

A popular account of Beatrix's life as a child is B. Hoffman, *Born To Be Queen* (1955). M. Rooy, *A Constitutional Question: The Marriage of Princess Beatrix* (1966) discusses the politically sensitive issue of her marriage to Claus von Amsberg. For the general history of The Netherlands, especially since World War II, see suggestions for further reading under JULIANA (Vol. 14).

For accounts on Beatrix's royal reign see "Shrewd Managers of Regal Riches" in *Fortune* (October 12, 1987) and "Queen Travels to Former Colony" in *Europe* (November, 1995). □

Pierre August Caron de Beaumarchais

The French playwright Pierre August Caron de Beaumarchais (1732-1799) was an outstanding dramatist of his day. His plays wittily satirized the privileged classes, the professions, and the court.

Beaumarchais was born Pierre August Caron in Paris on Jan. 24, 1732. His father, André Charles Caron, was a respected watchmaker. Pierre was the only boy among five adoring sisters and grew up lively, witty, and self-assured. Entering his father's profession, Pierre invented a mechanism which brought him the honor of becoming royal watchmaker to King Louis XV.

In 1755 Pierre made the acquaintance of Marie Madeleine Franquet, the wife of an elderly man who was clerk-comptroller in the royal household. Franquet was persuaded to yield his office to Pierre, and it was then Pierre's duty to escort the royal meat to table. So noble a calling prompted him to ennoble his name; it was at this time that he added the "de Beaumarchais." A few months later, on the death of Franquet, Beaumarchais married his widow. She died 10 months later, and in 1768 he married another wealthy widow, Geneviève Leveque, who died after 2 years of marriage and the birth of a son. Later he met Marie Thérèse Willermaula, with whom he lived for 12 years. She bore him a daughter, Eugénie.

The rapid rise of the young watchmaker into royal society, plus his sharp wit and cocksure attitude, aroused much antagonism. There were numerous attempts to humiliate Beaumarchais before the royal family; and later he repeatedly became an object of public calumny. Though friends and family adored him, he was surrounded by bitter enemies most of his life.

Court Battles

Beaumarchais gained the friendship of Pâris-Duverny, one of the great financiers of Paris, and under his guidance amassed a small fortune from speculation. Shortly before his death the financier acknowledged a debt to Beaumarchais of 15,000 francs, but since the transaction had never been legalized, Pâris-Duverny's heir refused to pay the debt. In the ensuing legal action Beaumarchais was subject to being labeled a forger if the judgment went against him. This was the first of a series of vicious court battles in which Beaumarchais was involved.

Meanwhile Beaumarchais was thrown into prison as the result of a quarrel over an actress at the Comédie Italienne. At this point Beaumarchais became immersed in yet another legal struggle. The wife of his lawyer, Goezman,

had demanded a bribe. Beaumarchais had publicized this, and Goezman retaliated by bringing an action for libel. The case was the scandal of Paris. Beaumarchais wrote hundreds of pamphlets, which were distributed throughout Paris. He pleaded his case with such ingenuity and with that he was able to turn a desperate state of affairs into a great popular success. He escaped severe punishment but suffered a loss of civil rights. Though all the judgments against him were eventually reversed, it seemed that his career as a courtier was ended. But Louis XV needed a man as shrewd as Beaumarchais and made the former watchmaker a secret agent, sending him off on wild exploits in pursuit of blackmailers throughout Europe.

Two Famous Comedies

Beaumarchais's career as a playwright began with two dramas: *Eugénie* (1765), based on a trip Beaumarchais had taken to Spain to chastise a young Spaniard who had jilted his sister; and *Les Deux amis* (1769; *The Two Friends*), which was a failure. With his two comedies, *Le Barbier de Séville* (1775; *The Barber of Seville*) and *Le Marriage de Figaro* (1784; *The Marriage of Figaro*), Beaumarchais achieved overwhelming success. They inspired operas by Mozart and Rossini and spread Beaumarchais's fame throughout Europe.

Both plays center on the barber, Figaro, and his master, Count Almaviva; Beaumarchais's own resemblance to Figaro is striking. Figaro is a master of intrigue; he is a rogue, an adventurer, a charmer, a heartbreaker, a smooth talker, and a delightful wit. But his antics expose the avarice of the age, and he is sensitive to its injustices.

In *The Barber of Seville* Figaro helps Almaviva win the hand of the young heiress, Rosine, from under the nose of her guardian, old Dr. Bartolo, who has secret plans to marry her himself. This play was the last of the private theatricals held in the Petit Trianon; Marie Antoinette played the part of Rosine.

In *The Marriage of Figaro* Figaro is about to be married to Suzanne, maid to Countess Almaviva (the Rosine of the earlier play). The intricate plots and counterplots of this dynamic masterpiece center on Figaro's attempts to foil his master's efforts to profit from the traditional right, as supreme lord, to preempt the husband's right with the bride before her wedding night. Several of the most charming subplots center on the erotic dreams and schemes of the teen-aged page, Chérubin. Louis XVI prohibited the play, but Beaumarchais stirred up public curiosity by constant readings. Many members of the court defended the play until the King relented, and it was at last produced, meeting a glorious reception.

Irony, verbal wit, and symmetrical plots as carefully balanced as the wheels of a watch raise these comedies far above the level of farce. Among 18th-century writers only Marivaux surpasses Beaumarchais and does so by the fertility of his imagination rather than by dramatic ability.

Once Beaumarchais had gained success as a playwright, he plunged into new financial operations. For many years he equipped a fleet that supplied arms to the American colonies in the Revolutionary War. This venture, as well as his attempt to publish the banned works of Voltaire, was largely a financial failure.

Although the social satire of his two great plays seemed to anticipate the changes that were about to take place in French society, Beaumarchais found himself singularly unprepared for the Revolution. In fact, he had just finished building an enormous mansion across from the Bastille prison, and twice the mobs came in search of him.

Beaumarchais was denounced by the revolutionist Jean Marat and thrown into prison in 1792, but by an extraordinary quirk of fate he was released just before the September massacres began. He was outside France during the worst part of the Reign of Terror, carrying out an arms mission which took him to England and Holland. When he returned to France, he was impoverished, and he died suddenly of a stroke in 1799.

Further Reading

The best biography of Beaumarchais is Cynthia Cox, *The Real Figaro: The Extraordinary Career of Caron de Beaumarchais* (1962). See also Elizabeth S. Kite, *Beaumarchais and the War of American Independence* (2 vols., 1918); Paul Frischauer, *Beaumarchais, Adventurer in the Century of Women* (trans. 1935); and Georges E. Lemaitre, *Beaumarchais* (1949). The outstanding critical study is in French: Jacques Scherer, *La Dramaturgie de Beaumarchais* (1954). In English the best critical work is J. B. Ratermanis and W. R. Irwin, *The Comic Style of Beaumarchais* (1961). □

Francis Beaumont

The English playwright Francis Beaumont (c. 1584-1616) was one of the major comic dramatists of the Jacobean period. Much of his work was done in collaboration with John Fletcher.

Francis Beaumont was born to an old and distinguished Leicestershire family. His father, who became one of the Queen's Justices of the Court of Common Pleas, was described by a contemporary as a "grave, learned, and reverend judge." Francis attended Oxford University but left without a degree. In 1600 he entered the Inner Temple, one of the Inns of Court, perhaps with the intention of following his father into the law. But whatever his intention, he was never called to the bar.

Beaumont soon associated himself with the theater and wrote his first play, *The Woman-Hater,* about 1606. The chief characters bear some resemblance to the "humours" characters of Ben Jonson. Beaumont greatly admired Jonson, and this mildly satiric comedy was probably written in conscious imitation of the elder dramatist, who by this time had acquired some stature as a literary figure.

In his next dramatic effort Beaumont broke free of the Jonsonian influence and produced his delightful masterpiece, *The Knight of the Burning Pestle* (1607). In this charming mock-heroic play (supposedly written in 8 days and probably indebted for some of its episodes to Cervantes' *Don Quixote*), Beaumont's satire is aimed at several targets, but the laughter he provokes at their expense is never bitter. The play includes a burlesque of dramatic forms—such as the old-fashioned chivalric romance—as well as some good-natured ridicule of London audiences as represented by George the Grocer and his wife Nell, who station themselves on the stage and continually interrupt the action of the play. Although *The Knight of the Burning Pestle* was a failure when first performed, the play had a highly successful revival in 1635, after the author's death, and has remained a popular work ever since.

The remainder of Beaumont's career was spent in collaboration with John Fletcher. Although the two wrote no more than a dozen plays together, their names became so closely linked that by 1679 more than 50 plays were assigned to their joint authorship. The authorship of some of these plays is still in doubt; many were written by Fletcher alone or by Fletcher in collaboration with dramatists other than Beaumont. The most important of the authentic Beaumont and Fletcher plays are *Philaster* and *The Maid's Tragedy,* both written between 1608 and 1610. Beaumont's hand predominates in these plays, which did much to promote the form of drama known as tragicomedy. Plays of this type rely less on character and theme than on ingenuity of plot and the moving expression of sentiment.

Beaumont's literary career ended in 1613, when he married an heiress and retired. He probably lived the few remaining years of his life in Kent. He died on March 6, 1616, and was buried in Westminster Abbey.

Further Reading

Charles Mills Gayley, *Beaumont, the Dramatist* (1914), contains much information about Beaumont and his family. The most reliable guide to Beaumont's share in the "Beaumont and Fletcher" plays is E. K. Chambers, *The Elizabethan Stage,* vol. 3 (1923). □

William Beaumont

The American surgeon William Beaumont (1785-1853) is remembered for extensive studies of the human digestive system based on experiments on a live patient.

William Beaumont was born in Lebanon, Conn., on Nov. 21, 1785. He grew up on the family farm and attended village schools until 1806, when he left to become the village schoolmaster in Champlain, N.Y. He began studying medicine in his spare time, and in 1810 he became an apprentice to a doctor in Vermont. While still a student, he began a lifelong habit of keeping a journal describing daily events and the symptoms and treatment of patients. After his apprenticeship Beaumont served as a surgeon's mate in the War of 1812. He described in his journal grueling days and nights spent treating the wounded.

After the war Beaumont returned to private practice in Plattsburg, N.Y. In 1820 he reenlisted as an army surgeon and was sent to Fort Mackinac, Michigan Territory. His account of the journey contains vivid descriptions of the voyage along the recently completed Erie Canal and through the Canadian wilderness. He was the only doctor in the territory, and his practice included soldiers and their families, Native Americans, trappers, and settlers. In 1821 Beaumont returned briefly to Plattsburgh and married Deborah Platt.

On June 6, 1822, when Alexis St. Martin, a young Canadian, suffered a stomach wound in a hunting accident, Beaumont was called to treat him. He described the terrible wound: "The whole charge, consisting of powder and duck shot, was received in the left side at not more than two or three feet distance from the muzzle of the piece . . . carrying away by its force integuments more than the size of the palm of a man's hand." With Beaumont's skillful surgery and subsequent care, St. Martin recovered but was left with a permanent opening in his stomach. When authorities threatened to send the young convalescent back to Canada, Beaumont supported him in his own house for several years. During this time he was able to study the digestive process by examining the interior of the patient's stomach as various foods were ingested. Beaumont's observations and chemical analyses of gastric juices provided the foundations for conclusions which are still valid.

In 1824, when Beaumont was transferred to Fort Niagara, N.Y., he attempted to take St. Martin with him, but the young man returned to Canada. President John Quincy Adams promoted Beaumont to the rank of surgeon in 1826. He served at Green Bay, Wis., and later at Fort Crawford, Wis. Meanwhile, he had finally persuaded St. Martin to come to Fort Crawford for further experiments, but his plans to take his patient to Europe for demonstrations and study were interrupted by an outbreak of cholera. Later in 1832 Beaumont used a 6-month furlough to take St. Martin to Washington, D.C., for an extensive series of experiments. Both the surgeon general and the secretary of war supported the project with funds and facilities, and they even enlisted St. Martin in the army as sergeant in exchange for his cooperation. These experiments led to Beaumont's *Experiments and Observations on the Gastric Juice and the Physiology of Digestion* (1833).

Beaumont had additional experiments in mind, but St. Martin returned to Canada forever in 1834. Beaumont's last post was in St. Louis, Mo., where he remained the rest of his life. After his retirement in 1840, he continued private practice until his death in March 1853.

Further Reading

No biography of Beaumont supersedes Jesse S. Myer, *Life and Letters of Dr. William Beaumont* (1912). Valuable references are the introduction by Sir William Osler to the 1941 reprint of the 1833 edition of Beaumont's *Experiments and Observations on the Gastric Juice and the Physiology of Digestion;* Genevieve Miller's prefatory comments to her edition of *William Beaumont's Formative Years: Two Early Notebooks, 1811-1821* (1946); and the relevant selections in Scott Earle, ed., *Surgery in America from the Colonial Era to the Twentieth Century* (1965). See also Richard H. Shryock, *The Development of Modern Medicine* (1936; rev. ed. 1947) and *Medicine and Society in America, 1660-1860* (1960). □

Pierre Gustave Toutant Beauregard

An American army officer and Confederate general, Pierre Gustave Toutant Beauregard (1818-1893) became a hero in the South with his capture of Fort Sumter and his victory at the First Battle of Bull Run. He was one of the Confederacy's eight full generals.

During the Civil War, P. G. T. Beauregard held six independent commands, ranging from Virginia to Tennessee to South Carolina. He proved to be a good but not a great general; his contentious personality brought him into conflict with Jefferson Davis and led to appointments in secondary theaters later in the war, where he failed to develop as a field commander. He won brief praise for his successful defense of Charleston, S. C., from naval assault in 1863 and of Petersburg, Va., from Grant's first attacks in 1864. Beauregard's life involved a series of paradoxes. Although he was considered an ardent Southerner, his Creole appearance and style seemed alien to the Confederacy. Before battle he indulged in visionary plans, but in action he became a calm, effective officer. He affected the manners of the antebellum South, yet after the war he helped develop a "New South" of business and industry.

Beauregard was born on May 28, 1818, in St. Bernard Parish, La., and was raised on a sugar plantation. He received his education at private French schools in New Orleans and New York City and at the U.S. Military Academy at West Point, N.Y., from 1834 to 1838. He served as a second lieutenant of engineers on coastal surveys and defenses in Rhode Island, Florida, Louisiana, and Maryland between 1838 and 1846.

Mexican War Service

When the Mexican War began in 1846, Beauregard helped fortify the captured port of Tampico, Mexico. In 1847 he served with the engineer company that acted as a staff for Gen. Winfield Scott during his campaign against Mexico City. Through reconnaissance reports Beauregard influenced Scott's choice of strategy in his victory at Cerro Gordo in April and in two of his later successes that resulted in the capture of Mexico City.

Between 1848 and 1860 Beauregard commanded the Louisiana coastal defenses and the construction of a new customshouse in New Orleans, and he received a promotion to captain. Marie Laure Villère, his wife since 1841, died at the birth of their third child in 1850. Beauregard later married Caroline Deslonde, who died in 1864. He lost his race for mayor of New Orleans in 1858 against the dominant Know-Nothing party. In January 1861 he was

appointed superintendent of West Point, only to be immediately removed as a secessionist.

Early Civil War Prominence

When Beauregard resigned from the U.S. Army in February 1861, the Confederate government gave him command of the batteries surrounding Fort Sumter in Charleston harbor. He began the bombardment on April 12 which led to surrender of the fort the next day. In June he was sent to Manassas, Va., to defend it against a Union advance from Washington, D.C. He planned to attack the Federal forces across Bull Run on July 21, but Union general Irvin McDowell struck first against the Confederate left flank Beauregard and Gen. Joseph E. Johnston, whose troops arrived from the Shenandoah Valley during the fighting, drove the Federal army from the field in the afternoon to win the first major battle of the war.

Shiloh Campaign and Defense of Charleston

In January 1862 Beauregard, after months of disagreement with Confederate president Jefferson Davis over strategy and Beauregard's own status as a subordinate under Joseph E. Johnston, agreed to become second in command to Gen. Albert Sidney Johnston, west of the Appalachians. After Johnston was killed during the first day of battle at Shiloh, Tenn., on April 6, 1862, Beauregard halted the Confederate attack in the evening because of confusion and fatigue among his troops. Since Union reinforcements had arrived already, his decision did not cost a victory, as some persons later charged. Beauregard withdrew the Confederate Army on April 7 in the face of counterattacks from the larger Federal force.

When Beauregard left his army in June to recoup his health, President Davis replaced him with Gen. Braxton Bragg and in August sent Beauregard to command the coastal defenses of South Carolina and Georgia. In January 1863 Beauregard temporarily drove off the blockaders at Charleston and in April defeated an attack on the harbor by Federal ironclads. His garrison lost Battery Wagner after a lengthy defense but withstood a heavy bombardment and a boat attack on Fort Sumter during the summer and fall.

Defense of Richmond and Petersburg

In April 1864 Beauregard received command of the Department of North Carolina and Southern Virginia. He had concentrated his troops by May 16 to drive back a Union force near Richmond, Va., and trap it between the James and Appomattox rivers. From June 15 to 17 Beauregard defended Petersburg, the railroad center for Richmond, against units of Gen. Ulysses Grant's army until the Confederacy's Robert E. Lee realized Grant's intentions and moved his troops to save the town.

In October, Beauregard accepted direction of Confederate military affairs in the West. He tried with little success to gather troops and oppose Gen. William Sherman's advance through Georgia and the Carolinas, until he was replaced by Joseph E. Johnston in February 1865. Beauregard, as Johnston's second in command, surrendered in April.

After the war Beauregard considered several foreign military offers but remained in the South to serve as president of the New Orleans, Jackson, and Great Northern Railroad and of the New Orleans and Carrollton streetcar line, which he revitalized. He lost control of both companies but continued until his death as a commissioner of the highly profitable Louisiana lottery. Through articles and memoirs he engaged in postwar disputes about wartime events with Davis and several Confederate generals. He participated in an abortive attempt to create a third political party (an alliance of businessmen and African Americans) during Reconstruction in Louisiana and served as state adjutant general from 1879 to 1888. He died on Feb. 20, 1893.

Further Reading

The fullest and most analytical biography is T. Harry Williams, *P. G. T. Beauregard: Napoleon in Gray* (1955). Older volumes are Hamilton Basso, *Beauregard, the Great Creole* (1933), and Alfred Roman, *Military Operations of General Beauregard* (1894), written primarily by Beauregard. See also Douglas S. Freeman, *Lee's Lieutenants* (3 vols., 1941-1944). ☐

Marchese di Becarria

Cesare Bonesana, Marchese di Becarria (1738-1794), was an Italian jurist and economist. He was

the author of the most influential and celebrated volume on criminal justice and a pioneer in systematic economic analysis.

Cesare Bonesana Beccaria was born into a noble family in Milan on March 15, 1738. Following his graduation from the university at Padua in 1758, he discovered and was deeply impressed by the writers of the French Enlightenment, especially the Baron de Montesquieu. About 1761 Beccaria joined a group of young intellectuals and reformers in northern Italy. A year later he published a monograph on the reform of the Milanese monetary system. From 1768 to 1771 he served as professor of political economy at the Palatine School in Milan. Thereafter he held a succession of public offices in Milan until his death on Nov. 28, 1794.

The intellectual ferment in 18th-century Europe produced no volume of greater or more enduring practical influence than Beccaria's *Dei delitti e delle pene* (1764; *Of Crimes and Punishments*). His achievement is even more remarkable when it is noted that the treatise was published by a man of 26 who possessed little knowledge or experience of courts or prisons and who required urging from his friends to complete the work. Beccaria's argument consists of a series of deductions from the utilitarian principle of "the greatest good for the greatest number." The purpose of punishment is to protect society by preventing or minimizing the commission of crimes. One corollary of this proposition is that of "penal proportion": punishments should be greater or lesser depending on the degree to which the crime endangers society. A second deduction is the principle of economy in punishment: penalties should be no more severe than required for the purposes of crime deterrence; greater severity is tyrannical and self-defeating.

In connection with the last-mentioned point, Beccaria launched an eloquent and devastating attack on the brutal and irrational criminal procedures of his time, including torture, forced confessions, secret proceedings, and unregulated discretion of magistrates. His was one of the first important voices to protest capital punishment, and he may properly be regarded as a founder of the movements to abolish the death penalty that have persisted throughout the world to the present day.

The impact of Beccaria's book was immediate, and six editions were issued within 18 months. Frederick the Great of Prussia and Catherine the Great of Russia referred to the volume in projects for recodification of the criminal law. No doubt, this influence reflected a widely shared popular conviction of the necessity of reform, but the cogency and lucidity of Beccaria's argument are important in explaining the success of this work.

Beccaria's most important contribution to economics is his *Elementi di economia pubblica* (Elements of Public Economy), published posthumously in 1804. In it he anticipates a number of basic ideas, including the division of labor, the effect of population on food supply, and the relation of labor and capital.

Further Reading

Two studies that discuss Beccaria are Coleman Phillipson, *Three Criminal Law Reformers: Beccaria, Bentham, Romilly* (1923), and Marcello T. Maestro, *Voltaire and Beccaria as Reformers of Criminal Law* (1942). For an analysis of Beccaria's contributions to economics see Joseph A. Schumpeter, ed., *History of Economic Analysis* (1954). ☐

Stephen Davison Bechtel

Stephen Davison Bechtel (1900-1989) was a construction engineer and business executive whose firm, the Bechtel Corporation, concentrated on building oil pipelines and refineries, power plants, and factories.

Bechtel was interested in expanding the scope and the variety of his firm's operations, and he foresaw opportunity and profit in California's booming oil industry. He persuaded his father to take on the company's first oil pipeline job for Standard Oil of California in 1928; the line ran from the San Joaquin Valley to the Pacific. Bechtel became president of the Bechtel Company three years after his father's death in 1933. In 1937 he started up a new venture with a college friend, John McCone, the Bechtel-McCone Corporation. The firm specialized in engineering and building oil refineries and chemical plants.

Work in World War II

With the outbreak of World War II, both the Bechtel Company and Bechtel-McCone shifted their operations to meet defense demands. Bechtel was president and director of the California Shipbuilding Corporation, which built and ran a huge yard at Terminal Island in Los Angeles. He was also a vice president of the Marinship Corporation, which built a tanker shipyard at Sausalito. Together, the Bechtel shipyards furnished more than 460 freighters and 90 tankers during the war; Bechtel was the nation's third largest shipbuilder, behind Kaiser and Bethlehem.

Bechtel was also a member of the executive committee of Contractors Pacific Naval Air Bases, which built the Navy's airfields in the Pacific. His firm took on more pipeline and refinery construction in the United States. Bechtel-McCone sponsored the building of the Birmingham Aircraft Modification Center in 1943 and later operated the plant for the Army Air Corps. The center modified almost 6,000 planes for defense purposes and also manufactured trucks and airplane wings.

After World War II, Bechtel consolidated all his various domestic companies into the Bechtel Corporation, of which he was president. The firm carried out Bechtel's earlier goals of diversification and expansion into the energy field and also explored new geographic frontiers. It engineered and/or constructed oil pipelines and refineries, electric power plants, and chemical and industrial plants. Bechtel boasted

Hawaii. Bechtel also built thermoelectric power plants in Korea. The huge electric power plant at Joppa, Illinois, became a Bechtel project in 1953 after the previous contractor became involved in a series of labor disputes. Beginning in the 1960s Bechtel was part of the Nuclear Power Group to construct nuclear reactors for electric power plants, and he continued to explore new technologies, new energy needs, and resources.

Under Bechtel's leadership, the Bechtel Corporation, later the Bechtel Group, grew from a large California-based construction firm to a giant corporation with interests and affiliates around the world. The company's style, like that of Bechtel himself, was to take on a series of large, imaginative, separate projects rather than to concentrate on one engineering or manufacturing process. Bechtel received numerous honorary degrees, including an LL.D. from the University of California where he was once a student, and various awards in construction, engineering, and business. He was a member of the Business Advisory Council of the Commerce Department and served on the Presidential Advisory Commission on Highways. He sat on the boards of other large corporations and was active in educational organizations.

Bechtel was married in 1923 to Laura Adeline Peart, and the couple had two children. His daughter was a registered nurse and his son became chairman of the Bechtel Group, of which his father was senior director. Bechtel died at the age of 88 in March of 1989.

Further Reading

There is no biography of Bechtel, but there are entries in the *National Cyclopaedia of American Biography* (1947-1952) and in the *Biographical Dictionary of American Business Leaders* (1983). An extensive profile appeared in *Fortune* (November 1955).

Additional information of the Bechtel Group can be found in Laton Mc Cartney's *Friends in High Places* (1988) and Bechtel's obituary can be found in *Time* (March 27, 1989). □

the firm would build anything anywhere, whatever the size or specifications.

Although Bechtel remained knowledgeable about the fundamentals of construction work, his special role within the corporation was as planner and policymaker. He had the ability to see the need for a particular project and to analyze the way his firm could organize, develop, and construct it. The 718-mile pipeline through the Canadian Rockies was one such Bechtel project. In 1949 at a luncheon in Los Angeles, Bechtel and oil company executives were discussing newly discovered oil fields in Alberta. Recognizing the increased demand for oil in the Pacific Northwest and the need for a pipeline, Bechtel reportedly began drawing maps and plans on the tablecloth. He ordered studies on the market for oil, the possibilities of financing, and the technical demands of laying the pipeline. In 1953 a Bechtel affiliate, Trans Mountain Oil Pipeline Company, completed the $93 million venture.

An International Corporation

After World War II, the Bechtel Corporation was also active in the Mideast. In 1948, the firm began construction of the huge oil pipeline through Saudi Arabia to bring crude oil from the Persian Gulf to Sidon on the Mediterranean. The company also built a mammoth oil refinery at Aden, on the Red Sea, for Anglo-Iranian Oil.

The power division of the Bechtel Corporation was responsible for the major construction of electric power plants for public utilities in California, Utah, Florida, Arizona, and

Ludwig August Theoder Beck

The German general Ludwig August Theodor Beck (1880-1944) actively fought Hitler's policy of aggression. He resigned from his official position to head the military resistance against Hitler that culminated in the unsuccessful coup of July 1944.

Ludwig Beck was born in the small town of Biebrich on the Rhine on June 29, 1880. He entered the German army in 1898, and his outstanding performance in military theory quickly destined him for a brilliant career with the general staff, which he joined as a captain in October 1913. During World War I Beck held several staff positions on the Western front. The bloodbaths of the battles of the Marne and Verdun and the slow and bitter retreat of the German armies in 1917-1918 seem to have left a deep impression on him.

At the end of the war Beck, now a major, remained with the army and in the next 15 years served in a succession of command and staff positions. In October 1933 he was named head of the so-called Troops Office—a cover name for the general-staff office, which had been outlawed by the Versailles Peace Treaty of 1919. In 1935 his title was changed to chief of the general staff of the army. In this position Beck played a large role in the rapid rearmament ordered by Hitler. He initially approved of this action, but he soon became wary of the aggressive foreign policy that accompanied the call to arms. In 1935 Beck attached a memorandum to an operational plan of war against Czechoslovakia in which he warned Hitler against such an undertaking and threatened to resign if Hitler should go through with the attack. From 1936 to 1938 Beck's warning memorandums became more frequent as Hitler marched into the Rhineland and prepared to intervene in Austria. In the summer of 1938 Hitler's designs on Czechoslovakia became more evident, and Beck worked feverishly for a general resignation of the entire army leadership. But he remained alone in his departure from office in August 1938.

In retirement Beck withdrew to quiet study and wrote a number of treatises on military subjects. More importantly, however, he quickly emerged—with the conservative politician Carl Goerdeler—as the center of opposition against Hitler. Beck dedicated most of the war years to resistance and to the task of planning the government of post-Nazi Germany, in which he would be head of state. Beck's

supporters made several abortive attempts to overthrow Hitler's regime. Then, on July 20, 1944, the coup d'etat which was to include the assassination of Hitler was staged. But the plan failed, and Beck committed suicide on the same day.

Further Reading

No works on or by Beck have yet been translated. There is information about him in Fabian von Schlabrendorff, *The Secret War against Hitler* (trans. 1965), and William L. Shirer, *The Rise and Fall of the Third Reich: A History of Nazi Germany* (1960). □

Carl Lotus Becker

American historian Carl Lotus Becker (1873-1945) was a proponent of the doctrine of historical relativism. He is best known for his book "The Heavenly City of the Eighteenth Century Philosophers."

Carl Becker was born on a farm near Waterloo, Iowa, on Sept. 7, 1873. He graduated from the University of Wisconsin in 1896, where he had studied history with Frederick Jackson Turner, and stayed on for 2 years of graduate work, followed by a year at Columbia University with H. L. Osgood and J. H. Robinson. He took his doctorate under Turner in 1907; in his thesis, *The History of Political Parties in the Province of New York, 1760-1776* (1909), he contended that the American Revolution was fundamentally a conflict over "who should rule at home."

In 1901 he married Maude Hepworth Ranney, a widow with a young daughter, and they had one son. Becker taught at Pennsylvania State College, Dartmouth, and Minnesota, and spent 14 years at the University of Kansas before he was appointed professor of modern history at Cornell University in 1917. His career was thereafter identified with Cornell.

In *The Declaration of Independence: A Study in the History of Political Ideas* (1922), Becker examined the central ideas of the Declaration, particularly the notion of natural rights, treating them as neither true nor false in any absolute sense but as prevailing assumptions of the age to be judged in terms of their functional effectiveness. The concept of a "climate of opinion," a phrase borrowed from A. N. Whitehead, Becker made famous in *The Heavenly City of the Eighteenth Century Philosophers* (1932). Here Becker advanced the paradox that the *philosophes* who had undermined the traditional intellectual world in the name of science were themselves dominated by a nonscientific faith in a rational universal order (a secular version of the Heavenly City). This thesis has been severely criticized, but the book remains a monument to Becker's literary artistry, a tour de force of high aphoristic with, written in a spirit of masterful detachment.

As early as 1910 Becker had rejected the claim that the writing of history involved the recovery of discrete facts which were waiting to be discovered; the "facts" of history, he noted, were present images and must necessarily partake of present experience to have meaning. This was a favorite Becker theme, most memorably formulated in "Everyman His Own Historian," Becker's presidential address to the American Historical Association (1931); in it he argued the subjectivity and relativity of historical knowledge, considering historians as "story-tellers . . . to whom in successive ages has been entrusted the keeping of the useful myths."

With the rise of 20th-century totalitarianism Becker found himself somewhat in the dilemma of those *philosophes* he had so keenly dissected; for if history verged on being transitory propaganda and if objective values were not to be sought for, then what basis was there for a morally grounded defense of democracy? Deeply committed to democracy, Becker now concluded that democratic values were indeed "Some Generalities that Still Glitter" (published in 1940) and that they had "a life of their own apart from any particular social system or type of civilization." In the war years he revised his pragmatic relativism so as to give some positive answer to the question, "What Is Still Living in the Political Philosophy of Thomas Jefferson?" (published in 1943).

Becker died in Ithaca, N.Y., on April 10, 1945.

Further Reading

A rounded portrait of Becker as man, teacher, philosopher, and historian is provided by Charlotte Watkins Smith, *Carl Becker: On History and the Climate of Opinion* (1956). Raymond O. Rockwood, ed., *Carl Becker's Heavenly City Revisited* (1958), brings together criticisms and recollections by a number of historians, including distinguished former students who knew Becker well. Becker's ideas and his significance in the history of American thought are treated in detail in Cushing Strout, *The Pragmatic Revolt in American History: Carl Becker and Charles Beard* (1958), and Burleigh Taylor Wilkins, *Carl Becker: A Biographical Study in American Intellectual History* (1961). □

St. Thomas Becket

The English prelate St. Thomas Becket (1128?-1170) was murdered because of his defense of the special privileges of the clergy and his opposition to the ecclesiastical policy of King Henry II.

Thomas Becket (who called himself "Thomas of London") was the son of Gilbert Becket, merchant of London. He was educated at Merton Priory and later in London and Paris. Before 1143 he entered the service of Theobald, Archbishop of Canterbury, who recognized his abilities and allowed him to study at Bologna and Auxerre. Becket became archdeacon of Canterbury, canon of St. Paul's and of Lincoln, and provost of Beverley, in addition to other benefices.

Early in 1155 Becket became chancellor to the young king Henry II and was soon his trusted adviser; as well as controlling the King's secretariat, he raised money for the King's wars, accompanied the King's armies, conducted diplomatic negotiations, and had charge of the King's eldest son. In May 1162 Henry recommended Becket to the monks of Canterbury as successor to Theobald; he was consecrated archbishop on June 3 by the bishop of Winchester.

Quarrel with the King

Becket surprised and angered the King by resigning the chancery and showing that he intended to support the large claims to independence and special privilege which had been developed by the clergy in the preceding 50 years. Henry was determined to restore all royal powers as they had been in the time of his grandfather King Henry I; inevitably he and Becket were soon in bitter conflict. The first serious cause of friction was the problem of "criminous clerks"—clergy accused of serious crimes. The question was whether these clerks should be judged and punished in the King's courts or in those of the Church, where they would escape capital punishment.

In October 1163 the King required the bishops to confirm unconditionally the "customs of his grandfather," and he renewed the demand at Clarendon in January 1164. The bishops again refused, but Becket was persuaded to give a verbal promise. The customs, defining the rights of the King over the Church, were then written down for the first time, in 16 clauses later known as the Constitutions of Clarendon. Becket refused to seal them, and the King then promoted legal proceedings against him on unrelated, trumped-up charges. At Northampton (October 1164), Henry ordered the bishops and barons to judge Becket, who, however, forbade them and appealed to the Pope. He then fled se-

cretly to France and submitted the customs to the Pope, offering to resign, but Pope Alexander III ordered him to retain his office and condemned 10 of the customs. Alexander could not, however, give effective support to Becket, since he was himself a refugee, driven from Italy by the Emperor and the antipope.

For nearly six years Becket lived in exile, first in Pontigny, later in Sens, with a few followers. He attempted to negotiate with the King, the bishops of England, and the Pope. The bishop of London, the archbishop of York, and the bishop of Salisbury all actively supported the King; others who may have been more sympathetic to Becket were isolated by Henry's control of the ports and cowed by his ruthless methods.

Becket's only weapon was his power to excommunicate offenders and to lay an interdict on their lands. Even this weapon was blunted by the difficulty of finding anyone to convey and publish the sentences in England and by carefully devised judicial appeals to the Pope. Moreover, on two occasions the Pope, in response to threats and promises from Henry, forbade Becket to use his powers. Negotiations continued but came to nothing, as the King insisted on unconditional acceptance of the customs, while Becket insisted on inserting the words "saving the honour of God and my order."

Becket's Death

In June 1170 Henry infringed the rights of Canterbury by having his son crowned by the archbishop of York; this offense forced the Pope more definitely to Becket's side. Henry feared excommunication and an interdict not only on England but on his less loyal and more vulnerable Continental lands. He therefore allowed peace to be made with the archbishop, not mentioning the customs, and avoided giving Becket the kiss of peace. Becket, well aware of his danger, returned to England on December 1; on December 29 he was brutally murdered by four knights from the King's court. Henry denied that he had ordered or desired the archbishop's death; his guilt must remain an open question.

Becket was immediately regarded as a martyr, and miracles were reported. He was canonized on Feb. 21, 1173. His tomb attracted innumerable pilgrims to Canterbury and brought great wealth to the monks, who had done little for him in his lifetime. It was destroyed in 1538, and almost all representations of him were obliterated by royal order, for his memory was particularly offensive to King Henry VIII, bent on establishing supremacy over the Church.

Becket's struggle achieved very little. Most of the disputed customs passed into law, and the bishoprics of England were filled with men who had helped the King to oppose him. But on two important points the King had to give way. In 1172, in Avranches, when he was reconciled to the Church, he agreed to allow appeals from Church courts in England to the court of the Pope, without reference to the King's court, thus abrogating one of the customs. And in 1176 he agreed that "criminous clerks" should be tried and punished in the Church courts, excepting only those charged with first offenses. In both these matters Becket's

opposition and death affected the law of England for nearly 4 centuries.

Further Reading

St. Thomas Becket has aroused controversy among historians as he did among contemporaries. There are few works on his life and times which are free from bias. The best is D. Knowles, *Thomas Becket* (1970). A popular biography is Richard Winston, *Thomas Becket* (1967). Z. N. Brooke, *The English Church and the Papacy* (1931), is the best general study in English. See also the more recent account by Austin Lane Poole, *From Domesday Book to Magna Carta* (1951; 2d ed. 1955). Becket's personality is examined in David Knowles, *The Historian and Character* (1963). A useful collection of sources is *English Historical Documents,* vol. 2, edited by David C. Douglas and G. W. Greenaway (1953). Pertinent readings are in Thomas M. Jones, ed., *The Becket Controversy* (1970). See also Robert Speaight's play, *Thomas Becket* (1938), and A. L. Duggan's novel, *My Life for My Sheep* (1955). □

Samuel Beckett

Samuel Beckett (1906-1989), the Irish novelist, playwright, and poet who became French by adoption, was one of the most original and important writers of the century. He won the Nobel Prize for literature in 1969.

S amuel Beckett stood apart from the literary coteries of his time, even though he shared many of their preoccupations. He wrestled with the problems of "being" and "nothingness," but he was not an existentialist in the manner of the French philosopher Jean-Paul Sartre. Although Beckett was suspicious of conventional literature and of conventional theater, his aim was not to write anti-novels or anti-plays as some authors did. His work shows affinities with James Joyce, especially in the use of language; with Franz Kafka in the portrayal of terror; and with Fyodor Dostoevsky in the probing of the darker recesses of the human spirit. Beckett was inspired, rather than influenced, by literary figures as different as the Italian poet Dante (the *Divine Comedy*'s circles of Hell and Purgatory); the French philosophers René Descartes (the *cogito*) and Blaise Pascal ("the wretchedness of man without God"); and the French novelist Marcel Proust (time). Beckett's own work opened new possibilities for both the novel and the theater that his successors have not been able to ignore.

Beckett was born in Dublin, Ireland, on April 13, 1906 of middle-class Protestant parents. He attended the Portora Royal boarding school in Enniskillen, County Fermanagh, where he excelled in both academics and sports. In 1923 he entered Trinity College in Dublin to specialize in French and Italian. His academic record was so distinguished that upon receiving his baccalaureate degree in 1927, he was awarded a 2-year post as *lecteur* (assistant) in English at the École Normale Supérieure in Paris.

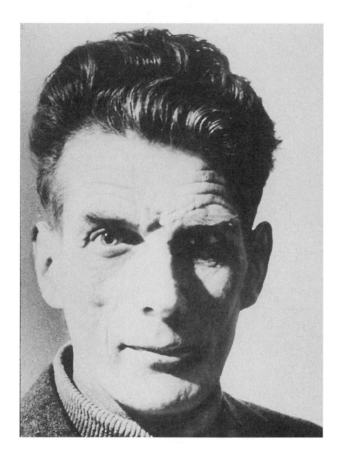

Literary Apprenticeship

In France, Beckett soon joined the informal group surrounding the great Irish writer James Joyce and was invited to contribute the opening essay to the book *Our Exagmination round his Factification for Incamination of Work in Progress,* a collection of 12 articles written as a defense and explanation of Joyce's still-unfinished *Finnegans Wake* by a group of Joyce's disciples. Beckett also moved in French literary circles. During this first stay in Paris he won a prize for the best poem on the subject of time in a competition sponsored by the Hours Press. His poem *Whoroscope* (1930) was his first separately published work and marked the beginning of his lifelong interest in the subject of time.

Beckett returned to Dublin in 1930 to teach French at Trinity College but submitted his resignation, after only four terms, saying that he could not teach others what he did not know himself. During the year he had obtained a master of arts degree. A penetrating essay on Proust, published in 1931, indicates how many of his subsequent themes Beckett was already beginning to consider at this time. After several years of wandering through Europe writing short stories and poems and employed at odd jobs, he finally settled in Paris in 1937.

First Novels and Short Stories

More Pricks than Kicks (1934), a volume of short stories derived, in part, from the then unpublished novel *Dream of Fair to Middling Women* (1993), recounts episodes from the life of Belacqua, a ne'er-do-well Irish reincarnation of Dante's *Divine Comedy* procrastinator of the same name who lived beneath a rock at the Gates of Purgatory. A blood brother of all Beckett's future protagonists, Belacqua lives what he calls "a Beethoven pause," the moments of nothingness between the music. But since what precedes and what follows man's earthly life (that is, eternity) are Nothing, then life also (if there is to be continuity) must be a Nothingness from which there can be no escape. All of Belacqua's efforts to transcend his condition fail.

Although Beckett's association with Joyce continued, their friendship, as well as Joyce's influence on Beckett, has often been exaggerated. Beckett's first novel, *Murphy* (1938), which Joyce completely misunderstood, is evidence of the distance between them. Deep beneath the surface of this superbly comic tale lie metaphysical problems that Beckett was trying to solve. As Murphy turns from the repugnant world of outer reality to his own inner world, always more and more circumscribed until it becomes a "closed system"—a microcosm where he finds a mystical peace—Beckett ponders the relationship between mind and body, the Self and the outer world, and the meaning of freedom and love.

When World War II broke out in 1939, Beckett was in Ireland. He returned immediately to Paris, where, as a citizen of a neutral country, he was permitted to stay even after German occupation. He served in the Resistance movement until 1942, when he was obliged to flee from the German Gestapo into unoccupied France, where he worked as a farmhand until the liberation of Paris in 1945. During these years he wrote another novel, *Watt,* published in 1953.

Watt, like each of his novels, carries Beckett's search for meaning a step further than the preceding one, or, as several critics have said, nearer the center of his thought. In many respects Watt's world is everyone's world, and he resembles everyone. And yet his strange adventure in the house of the mysterious Mr. Knott—whose name may signify: not, knot, naught, or the German *Not* (need, anxiety), or all of them—is Beckett's attempt to clarify the relationship between language and meaning. Watt, like most people, feels comfort when he is able to call things by their names; a name gives a thing reality. Gradually Watt discovers that the words men invent may have no relation to the real meaning of the thing, nor can the logical use of language ever reveal what is illogical and irrational: the infinite and the Self.

Writings in French

After the Liberation Beckett returned to his apartment in Paris and entered the most productive period of his career. By 1957 the works that finally established his reputation as one of the most important literary forces on the international scene were published, and, surprisingly, all were written in French. Presumably Beckett had sought the discipline of this foreign, acquired language to help him resist the temptation of using a style that was too personally evocative or too allusive. In trying to express the inexpressible, the pure anguish of existence, he felt he must abandon "literature" or "style" in the conventional sense and attempt to reproduce the voice of this anguish. These works were translated into an English that does not betray the effect of the original French.

The trilogy of novels *Molloy* (1951), *Malone Dies* (1951), and *The Unnamable* (1953) deals with the subject of death; however, here it is not death which is the horror or the source of absurdity (as with the existentialists), but life. To all the characters, life represents an exile from the continuing reality of themselves, and they seek to understand the meaning of death in this context. Since freedom can exist only outside time and since death occurs only in time, the characters try to transcend or "kill" time, which imprisons them in its fatality. Recognizing the impossibility of the task, they are finally reduced to silence and waiting as the only way to endure the anguish of living. Another novel, *How It Is,* first published in French in 1961, emphasizes the solitude of the individual consciousness and at the same time the need for others; for only through the testimony of another can one be sure that one exists. The last of his French novels to be published was *Mercier and Camier.* This work demonstrates Beckett's interest in wordplay, especially in its use of French colloquialisms. Written in 1946, it was not published until 1974.

The Plays

Beckett reached a much wider public through his plays than through his difficult, obscure novels. The most famous plays are *Waiting for Godot* (1953), *Endgame* (1957), *Krapp's Last Tape* (1958), and *Happy Days* (1961). The same themes found in the novels appear in these plays in more condensed and accessible form. Later, Beckett experimented successfully with other media: the radio play, film, pantomime, and the television play.

Later Works

Beckett maintained a prolific output throughout his life, publishing the poetry collection, *Mirlitonades* (1978), the extended prose piece, *Worstward Ho* (1983), and many novellas and short stories in his later years. Many of these pieces were concerned with the failure of language to express the inner being. His first novel, *Dreams of Fair to Middling Women* was finally published, posthumously, in 1993.

Although they lived in Paris, Beckett and his wife enjoyed frequent stays in their small country house nearby. Tall and slender, with searching blue eyes, Beckett retained the shy and unassuming manner of his younger days. Unlike his tormented characters, he was distinguished by a great serenity of spirit. He died peacefully in Paris on December 22, 1989, and was buried, as he had wished, in a small, quiet ceremony.

Further Reading

Near the end of his life, Beckett authorized a biography by James Knowlson, *Damned to Fame: The Life of Samuel Beckett* (1996). Another good source of biographical material on Beckett is Richard Ellmann, *James Joyce* (1959). Of the tremendous volume of critical studies, the two most penetrating are Hugh Kenner, *Samuel Beckett: A Critical Study* (1962; 2d ed. 1968), and Richard N. Coe, *Samuel Beckett* (1964). Ruby Cohn, *Samuel Beckett: The Comic Gamut* (1962), and the chapter on Beckett in Martin Esslin, *The Theatre of the Absurd* (1961; rev. ed. 1969), are also recommended. Various critical approaches to the many aspects of Beckett's work can be found in Martin Esslin, ed., *Samuel Beckett: A Collection of Critical Essays* (1965). Recommended for background are Claude Mauriac, *The New Literature* (1959); John Cruickshank, ed., *The Novelist as Philosopher: Studies in French Fiction, 1935-1960* (1962); and Jacques Guicharnaud, *Modern French Theatre: From Giraudoux to Genet* (1967). □

Max Beckmann

The German painter and graphic artist Max Beckmann (1884-1950) was one of the towering personalities of figurative expressionist art. His work is characterized by a sculptural monumentality, a vibrant use of color, and a profoundly philosophical outlook.

Max Beckmann was born in Leipzig, the son of a flour merchant. By the age of 14 Max was painting seriously. He attended the Weimar Academy (1900-1903) and then went to Berlin to study. He was influenced by the German impressionism of Max Liebermann and Lovis Corinth. In 1906, just before leaving for Italy on a scholarship, Beckmann married a fellow student. *His Great Death Scene* (1906), a painting clearly influenced by Edvard Munch, reflects the death of Beckmann's mother.

Back in Berlin, Beckmann visited the 1907 exhibition of Eugène Delacroix's paintings and produced a number of comparable large-scale works. He was also influenced by the monumental compositions of Peter Paul Rubens, as in the *Sinking of the Titanic* (1912). Beckmann's works of this kind were very successful, and the "German Delacroix" had exhibitions in Frankfurt and Magdeburg in 1911-1912. By 1914 Beckmann had apparently become aware of a new tension of the picture space, but his color was still quite conservative.

World War I

In 1914 Beckmann volunteered as a medical corpsman and was sent to the Russian front. In early 1915 he was transferred to a hospital in Flanders, where he daily experienced the horrors of operative procedures. By summer he was completely exhausted and was discharged from the army.

Beckmann went to Frankfurt, where his art now moved in an entirely new direction, expressing tension, loneliness, and disillusionment. His *Self-Portrait with Red Scarf* (1917) is a far cry from his confident early selfportraits. This is a man against the world, portrayed in a constricted space, the figure arranged with deliberate angularity within the picture frame. The landscapes of the period show a Munch-like isolationism.

Style between the Wars

Beckmann's style in the immediate postwar period appears to have been affected primarily by German Gothic art. Its compressed space was well suited to his increasingly philosophical and poetic compositions. The powerful color and roughhewn forms of the Gothic also appealed to Beckmann. Among the paintings of this period the most important is *Night* (1918-1919). In this work Beckmann moves toward protest, a protest against the violence, hunger, and rioting that became typical of this period just before inflation set in. As a prophecy of the violence of the Nazi period soon to follow, *Night* is one of the most disturbing works ever painted. It has a dreamlike reality that has been termed "magic realism." During the early 1920s Beckmann played a leading role in the New Objectivity (Neue Sachlichkeit) movement, in which the artist depicted in the greatest detail and clarity his own emotions and the world around him without direct comment.

In 1925 Beckmann became a professor at the Städel Institute in Frankfurt. He married for the second time; his wife, Mathilde von Kaulbach, was the daughter of the famous Munich portrait painter. In 1928 there was an elaborate retrospective of Beckmann's work in Mannheim. Other exhibitions were held throughout Germany, with the National Gallery in Berlin dedicating a room to his paintings. During the late 1920s and early 1930s Beckmann's art took on a more mellow quality under the influence of contemporary French painting—Beckmann had a studio in Paris and spent the winters there. Without losing any of its symbolic and poetic quality, his work became more distinctly esthetic under the influence of painters like Henri Matisse.

When the Nazis came to power in 1933, they dismissed Beckmann from his position at the Städel and listed him as a "degenerate" artist. He moved to Berlin, where he lived until 1937. His greatest achievements of this period were large-scale triptychs like the *Departure* (1932-1935), the first in a series that he continued to execute for the rest of his life. This triptych is a poetic and allegorical comment on man's inhumanity to man, an oblique but still poignant reference to the physical and psychological tortures of the era and the ultimate liberation and triumph of the human spirit.

The Beckmanns fled to Amsterdam, where they preferred to remain unnoticed and maintained contact with very few people. Beckmann's diary for this period is filled with references to the lack of heat, proper food, and light and to endless air raids. He continued to paint, and the great *Blind Man's Buff* triptych (1945) is one of the most elaborate and complex works of a period in which Beckmann did five of these magnificent and powerful poetic compositions. *Blind Man's Buff* appears to be an allegory of the relationship between man and woman and the gods who control their lives.

Last Years

With the liberation of the Netherlands in 1945, Beckmann had an exhibition at the Stedelijk Museum in Amsterdam. The next year he had a major exhibition at the Curt Valentin gallery in New York City. In 1947 he accepted an invitation to teach at Washington University in St. Louis. The following year the City Art Museum of St. Louis gave him a retrospective, which brought him the highest acclaim in the art world. In 1949 Beckmann received first prize at the Carnegie International and taught at the Brooklyn Art Museum. In the summer of 1950 he died in New York.

Further Reading

There are no monographs on Beckmann in English. The best material in English is in two exhibition catalogs and a general survey: City Art Museum, St. Louis, *Max Beckmann,* with an introduction by Perry T. Rathbone (1948); Museum of Modern Art, New York, *Max Beckmann,* with an introduction by Peter Selz (1964); and Bernard S. Myers, *The German Expressionists: A Generation in Revolt* (1957; concise ed. 1963). A specialized study is Charles S. Kessler, *Max Beckmann's Triptychs* (1970).

Additional Sources

Lackner, Stephan, *Max Beckmann,* New York: H. N. Abrams, 1977. □

William Becknell

An American frontier soldier, trader, and politician, William Becknell (ca. 1797-1865) established the Santa Fe trade, which helped open the Southwest to settlement.

William Becknell was born in Amherst County, Va., but little is known of his family or youth. From the semiliterate letters he wrote as an adult, it is obvious that his education was rudimentary. In 1814 he was appointed ensign in the U.S. Rangers. Some time after his discharge in 1815 he worked as a salt maker in Saline County, Mo.

In June 1821 Becknell opened the Santa Fe trade when he advertised in the *Missouri Intelligencer* for "a company of men destined to the westward for the purpose of trading horses and mules, and catching wild animals of every description." Intending to trade with the Comanches and to trap for furs in the Rocky Mountains, he and four companions left Franklin, Mo., in September. They moved westward on the Arkansas River and then south through Raton Pass (on the border of present-day Colorado and New Mexico). Just beyond the mountains they met a party of Mexican soldiers. To Becknell's surprise, the soldiers welcomed his party and encouraged them to continue to Santa Fe. There Becknell and his companions found a ready market for their trade goods, and on Jan. 29, 1822, Becknell and one companion returned to Franklin with news that the Mexicans wanted to trade goods.

Becknell hurried to organize a second expedition, this time taking 21 men and three heavily loaded wagons. He wanted to avoid the Raton Mountains, so he led the party across the Cimarron Desert (in present-day Kansas), where they nearly died of thirst. Once across that dusty waste,

Becknell hurried to Sante Fe and succeeded in locating a wagon route into the Southwest.

In May 1824 Becknell helped organize the first large train of traders who traveled together for protection from the Native Americans. This party of 81 men and 25 wagons returned to Missouri with $190,000 in gold and furs. For Becknell, this was the last overland trading venture. He stayed in the mountains to trap that winter, then returned to Missouri.

In 1828 Becknell was elected to the state legislature as a representative from Saline County; in 1830 he was re-elected. During the Black Hawk War of 1832 he served as captain of his county's militia company. Three years later, with some of his neighbors, he moved to Clarksville, in Texas. In 1836 he led a company in the Texas Revolution. Becknell died in Clarksville on April 30, 1865.

Described by a contemporary as "a man of good character, great personal bravery, & by nature & habit hardy and enterprising," William Becknell represents the numerous American frontiersmen who tried many careers, as well as the few who made major contributions.

Further Reading

There is no biography of Becknell, and material on him is scattered. Archer B. Hulbert, ed., *Southwest on the Turquoise Trail: The First Diaries on the Road to Santa Fe* (1933), includes edited journals of two of Becknell's expeditions. Josiah Gregg, *Commerce of the Prairies* (2 vols., 1844; many later editions), discusses the Santa Fe trade and Becknell's part in it. Hiram M. Chittenden, *The American Fur Trade of the Far West* (3 vols., 1902; 2d ed., 2 vols., 1935), and Ray A. Billington, *The Far Western Frontier, 1830-1860* (1956), discuss the fur trade and American penetration of the Southwest.

Additional Sources

Beachum, Larry, *William Becknell: father of the Santa Fe trade,* El Paso: Texas Western Press, 1982. □

Jim Beckwourth

Jim Beckwourth (ca. 1800–1866) son of a wealthy Virginian landowner and his slave. Freed from slavery as a young man, Beckwourth is known for his tall tale adventures of Indian battles, fur trading and scoutng in the U.S. Army.

Jim Beckwourth was born near Fredericksburg, Virginia sometime around the year 1800. His father was Sir Jennings Beckwith, the scion of a prominent Virginia family. His mother has commonly been known as "Miss Kill," although it is not clear whether that was her real name or not. She was one of the Beckwith's slaves. Beckwourth's father moved to Missouri in 1806 and took Jim and his mother with him. They settled on a large farm where the Missouri and Mississippi Rivers meet near the town of St. Charles. Jim's father sent him to school in St. Louis from

about 1810 until 1814. He was then apprenticed to a blacksmith in St. Charles. Beckwourth fought with the blacksmith and returned to his father's farm. He was set free on his nineteenth birthday, but it appears that he remained on his father's farm for a while after that. At some point he adopted his own version of the family name.

Although he may have made an earlier trip west, the first definite knowledge we have is that he joined William Henry Ashley's trapping and trading expedition to the Far West in 1824. At one point in that journey, Beckwourth was sent ahead to buy horses from the Pawnee tribe. Not finding them and without sufficient food, he made a desperate trip back to a trading post and would have starved to death if he had not been found by a friendly band of Native Americans. Beckwourth later wrote an account of the journey that casts himself in a favorable light and plays up his own role in the expedition. This tendency to exaggerate has led many later writers to discount the truth of his accounts, but quite often there seems to be a core of reality about them. The most famous incident is one in which Beckwourth claims to have saved Ashley from drowning, although it was later shown that it could not have happened the way he described. However, a similar incident did occur, and Beckwourth seems to be very familiar with it.

Beckwourth continued to trap and worked for William Sublette who was one of the buyers of Ashley's fur trading business. In 1827 he "married" a woman from the Blackfoot tribe. In 1829 he found himself unable to pay a debt, so he took refuge among his friends of the Crow tribe, where he married again. Beckwourth says he married eight women

while staying with the Crow. He soon led a successful raiding party against another tribe and was made a chief of the Crow. In later years, Beckwourth led the Crow in a great battle against their Blackfoot enemies in which he claimed that all the Blackfoot were killed and the Crow lost thirty or forty warriors. During this time Beckwourth continued to trap and sold his furs to the American Fur Company of St. Louis. In 1837, however, he was dropped from the Company's books and decided to look elsewhere for a livelihood.

Beckwourth found employment as a scout and mule driver for the U.S. Army in its war against the Seminole tribe of Florida. He took part in the Battle of Okeechobee that was fought on December 25, 1837, but after the war settled into routine, Beckwourth became bored and returned to Missouri and the fur trade. He was offered employment by Andrew Sublette, the younger brother of William. He took a trading party down the Santa Fe trail to Taos, New Mexico, where he married a local Mexican woman. In October 1842, Beckwourth and his bride headed north to what is now Colorado and opened a trading post on the Arkansas River that eventually grew into the city of Pueblo.

In 1843 Beckwourth left Pueblo with a trading party of 15 and headed for California, then a part of Mexico. They arrived in Los Angeles in January 1844. When the local residents rebelled against the Mexican officials, Beckwourth joined their side in the "Battle" of Cahuenga in 1845. He then left California for New Mexico and traded along the Santa Fe Trail until August 1848. He was hired as a guide by an official of the U.S. War Department, and their party traveled to Los Angeles, where they arrived on October 25, 1848. From there they went north to Monterey, the capital of California at the time. He took on a job as a courier to a ranch near the present-day city of Santa Maria, north of Los Angeles. On his way there he came upon the massacre of the Reed family who were living in the old Mission of San Miguel and led the posse that apprehended the murderers.

When gold was discovered in northern California, Beckwourth joined the California Gold Rush. He did not actively pan for gold but gambled and traded horses and made his living among the prospectors. In the spring of 1850 he traveled to the remote mining areas of the Sierra Nevada in the region of the present-day Lassen Volcanic National Park. One day he saw what looked like a low pass to the west. At the end of April he led three men to this pass, which was subsequently named Beckwourth Pass. It is just to the west of the California-Nevada border about 30 miles north of Reno. Beckwourth immediately saw that it could be a major entrance from the east into the goldmining region, and he and his companions spent the summer and fall of 1850 opening a road through the pass. During the spring of 1851 he actively promoted his "New Emigrant Route" and got capital from the merchants of Marysville, California to develop it. Beckwourth guided the first wagon train through the Pass in late July or early August 1851. When it arrived in Marysville in September 1851, there was so much celebration that the town almost burned down.

At about that time Beckwourth met T. D. Bonner. Bonner was the former president of the New Hampshire Temperance Society who had been forced to emigrate to California when he started drinking again. He became a justice of the peace in Butte County, California where Beckwourth met him. In the spring of 1852, Beckwourth had decided to settle in the "pleasant valley" that lay to the west of Beckwourth Pass. There he built a house and hotel for the travelers coming through the Pass. It developed into one of the main entry points for pioneers coming to California. In October 1854 Bonner came to live in Beckwourth's hotel, and he contracted to write Beckwourth's "autobiography." By June of 1855 Bonner was back east and had signed a contract with Harper and Brothers in New York to publish it. When it came out in 1856 its tall tales and exciting adventures made it a bestseller, and Beckwourth became an instant celebrity.

Beckwourth stayed at his ranch (now Beckwourth, California) until November 1858. He then headed back east to Missouri, and the St. Louis and Kansas City newspapers recorded the visit of the famous mountain man. He moved to Denver, Colorado, where he married once again and settled down as the manager of a general store. He and his wife had a daughter who died in infancy. After her death, the marriage broke up, and Beckwourth moved in with a Crow woman. He became involved in various scrapes with the law, including a charge of manslaughter from which he was acquitted on the grounds of self-defense. He then joined the U.S. Army as a scout and took part in several actions against the Cheyenne tribe. In September 1866 he went to visit a Crow village on a mission for the Army. He died there, sometime around September 25, 1866. □

Gustavo Adolfo Dominguez Bécquer

The Spanish lyric poet Gustavo Adolfo Dominguez Bécquer (1836-1870) is noted for his *Rimas,* a collection of short lyric poems. This work had such a profound influence that it is considered the starting point of Spanish contemporary poetry.

Gustavo Bécquer was born in Seville on Feb. 17, 1836. Orphaned when he was 11, he went to live with his godmother, whose extensive library and affectionate care encouraged an early love for poetry and music. In 1852 he began to study at his uncle's art studio. Painting, however, did not suit Bécquer's introspective temperament. A shy, painfully sensitive boy, he preferred to walk alone, delve into folklore and art, and consort with other young poets. In 1854, against the wishes of his godmother, he went to Madrid in search of literary fame.

But fame was not forthcoming, and Bécquer had to turn to journalism. He translated newspaper articles and wrote literary and theater criticism. During this period, however, he did publish one volume of a cherished project, *Historia de los templos en España* (1857; History of the Churches in

Spain), and collaborated under a pen name in writing plays, some verses of which foreshadow the later *Rimas.*

By 1860 Bécquer had fallen hopelessly in love with Julia Espín y Guillén, but the relationship ended bitterly a year later. He then married Casta Esteban Navarro, with whom he had three children. The suffering and anguish caused by his unhappy love affair and disastrous marriage constitute the emotional background of *Rimas.* Written during the 1860s, these short poems voiced Bécquer's longing for love and for the realization of perfect beauty. Like the mystics, he aspired to express intelligibly a vision of ineffable beauty, glimpsed in the person of his beloved.

Unlike the inflated style of his contemporaries, Bécquer's diction is spare and simple, his verses delicate and light. Yet he achieves in each poem a maximum resonance by attending to the phonetic structure of words and by using images which affect the reader's sensibility and demand his active collaboration. Bécquer's ability to make words express much more than their conventional meanings anticipates the techniques of modern symbolic poetry.

Bécquer wrote most of his prose works from 1860 to 1865. These include 22 legends, which are based upon regional folklore and exploit the supernatural. While at the monastery of Veruela in 1864, he wrote a collection of nine letters entitled *Desde mi celda, cartas literarias* (From My Cell, Literary Letters). That same year he directed an important journal and was appointed official censor of novels.

In 1868 Bécquer separated from his wife and, in the wake of the revolution that ended the rule of Isabella II, went to Paris. He returned to Madrid in 1869, rewrote from memory the lost manuscript of *Rimas,* and resumed newspaper writing. The sudden death of his brother Valeriano in September 1870 depressed him abysmally, and he died only 3 months later, on December 22, exhausted by tuberculosis. His collected works were published posthumously in 1871.

Further Reading

The most comprehensive book on Bécquer is in Spanish: José Pedro Diaz, *Gustavo Adolfo Bécquer: Vida y poesia* (2 vols., 1953; rev. ed. 1964). An informative English work is Edmund L. King, *Gustavo Adolfo Bécquer: From Painter to Poet* (1953). □

Antoine Henri Becquerel

The French physicist Antoine Henri Becquerel (1852-1908) was the discoverer of natural radioactivity.

Antoine Henri Becquerel was born in Paris on Dec. 15, 1852. Both his father, Alexandre Edmond Becquerel, and his grandfather, Antoine César Becquerel, were scientists. Following his graduation from the École Polytechnique in 1874, Antoine Henri worked as a civil engineer, but he also retained a strong interest in

scientific problems. In 1878 he succeeded in the chair of his father who was professor of applied physics at the Conservatoire des Arts et Métiers. Ten years later Becquerel earned his doctor's degree with a dissertation on the absorption of light in crystals. He then became professor of applied physics at the Museum of Natural History in Paris in 1892 and professor of physics at the Polytechnique in 1895.

Prior to 1895 Becquerel did research on phosphorescence. He had inherited from his father a supply of uranium salts, which were known to be phosphorescent when exposed to light. Upon learning in January 1896 about W. C. Roentgen's discovery of x-rays, Becquerel's interest immediately turned to the question of whether all phosphorescent materials acted as sources of similar rays.

The results did not justify his hopes, but Becquerel stumbled on an unexpected phenomenon. After placing sheets of sulfate of uranium on photographic plates wrapped in black paper, he exposed the package to light for several hours. On developing the plates he obtained distinct pictures of the uranium sheets. Later he obtained pictures of medals which had been placed between the uranium and the plates. The uneven thickness of the medals blocked in varying degrees the effectiveness of the radiation from uranium. He also discovered that part of the radiation could be deflected by a magnetic field and that the radiations had an ionizing effect on the surrounding air.

For the discovery of natural radioactivity, which for a number of years was called Becquerel rays, he won the Nobel Prize in physics in 1903. In his Nobel lecture

Becquerel noted that the new radiation indicated the possible modification of atoms which "the methods at our disposal are unable to bring about (but which) could certainly release energy in sufficiently large quantities to produce the observed effects, without the changes in matter being large enough to be detectable by our methods of investigation." As a cause of that modification, he held out the possible existence of "an external radiation" hitherto undetected but which, when absorbed by radioactive materials, would be transformed into radioactivity without bringing about the transformation of the atoms themselves.

Becquerel's election as perpetual secretary of the Academy of Sciences in 1908 was one of the numerous honors bestowed on him. His death on Aug. 25, 1908, at Le Croisic did not signal the end of the lineage of scientists in the Becquerel family. From Becquerel's marriage to Lucie Zoé Marie Jamin a son, Jean, had been born; he became the fourth Becquerel to occupy the chair of physics at the Museum of Natural History and was also an able investigator of radioactivity.

Further Reading

The major work on Becquerel is in French. A detailed account of Becquerel's life is in Bessie Zaban Jones, ed., *The Golden Age of Science: Thirty Portraits of the Giants of 19th-century Science by their Scientific Contemporaries* (1966). *Nobel Lectures: Physics, 1901-1921* (1964), published by the Nobel Foundation, includes a biographical sketch of Becquerel as well as his Nobel lecture on radioactivity. A biographical sketch is also contained in Niels Hugh de Vaudrey Heathcote, *Nobel Prize Winners in Physics, 1901-1950* (1953). For background material see Harvey E. White, *Classical and Modern Physics* (1940). ☐

St. Bede

St. Bede (c. 672-735), known as the Venerable Bede, was an English monk, scholar, and theologian. His works were the crowning cultural achievement in England in the 8th century, "the age of Bede."

Bede was born in Northumbria, near Jarrow. When he was 7, relatives brought him to the Benedictine abbey at nearby Wearmouth; he passed the remainder of his life at Wearmouth and later at a new monastery at Jarrow. The period during which Bede lived was the "golden age of English monasticism," and close relations with Rome and the papacy resulted in a free exchange of information and culture.

Bede's works are many and various; establishing their chronology with precision is difficult. He considered his major achievement to be his biblical commentaries, which were firmly rooted in traditional exegesis, with much use of allegory to expound scriptural meanings. He wrote two scientific treatises on chronology and the formation of the Church calendar, *De temporibus* (703) and *De temporum ratione* (725), to each of which was appended a chronicle of

the ages of the world as established by God. Bede also wrote a number of saints' lives, full of edifying miracles, including two versions of the life of St. Cuthbert (ca. 704 and 721).

All of Bede's interests intersected brilliantly in the *Historia ecclesiastica gentis anglorum (Ecclesiastical History of the English People),* which he finished in 731. It is, in effect, a saint's life with the English nation as hero, and it illustrates the early medieval theological proposition that the workings of Divine Providence are visible in history. Bede's theme is the conversion of the Anglo-Saxons, after their settlement in Britain, by missionaries from Rome and Ireland. Exemplary miraculous passages illustrate the benefits derived by the English from heeding the message of the Gospel and the merits of those who devote their lives to propagating that message. Bede includes many documents giving important information about the early English Church, and he reveals his considerable narrative talents in many fascinating tales, such as that of Caedmon, the unlettered peasant who miraculously becomes the first religious poet in English.

Bede died at Jarrow in 735. He soon became a legend, revered for his holiness and learning. His greatest work, the *Ecclesiastical History,* was a constant model for historians throughout the Middle Ages.

Further Reading

The most complete introduction to Bede is A. Hamilton Thompson, ed., *Bede: His Life, Times, and Writings* (1935). A perceptive analysis of Bede's hagiography and historiography is in Charles W. Jones, *Saints' Lives and Chronicles in Early England* (1947). An interpretation of Bede's *Ecclesiastical His-*

tory is presented in the chapter on Bede in Robert W. Hanning, *The Vision of History in Early Britain: From Gildas to Geoffrey of Monmouth* (1966). Margaret Deanesley, *The Pre-Conquest Church in England* (1961), provides a modern account of the conversion of the Anglo-Saxons.

Additional Sources

Browne, G. F. (George Forrest), *The Venerable Bede, his life and writings,* Norwood, Pa.: Norwood Editions, 1977.

Hunter Blair, Peter, *The world of Bede,* Cambridge England; New York: Cambridge University Press, 1990.

Ward, Benedicta, *The Venerable Bede,* Harrisburg, PA: Morehouse Pub., 1990. □

Catharine Beecher

American author and educator Catharine Beecher (1800-1878) was responsible for creating a new social attitude that placed greater value on women's work in the home and their role as educators and moral guides for the young. Her book *Treatise on Domestic Economy* (1841) was a best-selling work that provided practical household advice while extolling the virtues of domestic life. She also was an active proponent for the creation of schools for women, arguing that for their special role as instructors of children, women required a thorough education.

Catharine Beecher was a nineteenth century proponent of women's rights and education for women. While she did not advocate a radical change in women's roles, she did fight for increased recognition of the importance of the work women did in managing homes and raising families. She also believed that women should expand their place in society by becoming teachers, allowing them to use their nurturing skills and moral conscience in a professional sphere. To encourage the spread of these ideas, Beecher published a number of books providing guidance and praise for domestic life, such as her extremely popular *Treatise on Domestic Economy* (1843). She also founded schools and organizations devoted to training women to become teachers. Beecher held the view that the woman, as educator and spiritual guide for families, was the basis of a well-ordered and moral society. This theme contributed to a growing feminist attitude that women did not have to be weak, passive creatures, but could be strong, contributing members of their communities.

Beecher was born September 6, 1800, in the town of East Hampton on Long Island, New York. She was the oldest child of Lyman and Roxanna Ward Beecher. Each of her parents had a strong influence on the values she touted as an adult. Her father was a Presbyterian minister who came from a family of Calvinist colonists. He was a prominent figure in the evangelical religious movement of the early 1800s known as the Second Great Awakening. His strong personality and religious convictions were apparent not only in the religious revivals that he held, but in his dominant presence in the Beecher home as well. Beecher's mother, also from a respected family, played a traditional role in the home and attempted to pass along her domestic skills to her children. Beecher was ambivalent about both the religious and domestic aspects of her life as a young woman. She initially disliked domestic duties, preferring to spend her time outside or studying. Later in life, however, she came to view domestic responsibilities as a valuable and sacred contribution to home and community. Similarly, her religious instincts fluctuated throughout her life, and she never was able to come to terms with her faith.

The Beechers moved to Litchfield, Connecticut, in 1809. The following year, Beecher entered Miss Pierce's school, a well-respected institution for young women. Her education there stressed not only the acquisition of social skills, but also the growth of a moral consciousness and leadership abilities. Beecher thrived at the school, but was forced to leave at the age of 16 after the death of her mother. She returned home to tend to the domestic duties of the household, including raising her younger brothers and sisters and doing the cooking and sewing for the family. After her father remarried in 1817, she remained for another year at home before taking a teaching job in New London, Connecticut, in 1818.

Focused on Education of Women

At the age of 22, Beecher was engaged to a Yale University professor of natural history named Alexander

Fisher. Her choice was not a whole-hearted one, however. While her father was quite pleased with Fisher, Beecher herself was concerned that his unaffectionate nature would not make him an ideal husband. The marriage never occurred—Fisher was killed in a shipwreck off the coast of Ireland in the spring of 1822. Beecher never again entertained thoughts of marriage. Instead, she turned her energies to what would become her life's main passion, the education of women.

In 1823, Beecher opened the Hartford Female Seminary in Hartford, Connecticut. At her school, she combined a solid core of courses in algebra, chemistry, history, Latin, philosophy, and rhetoric with an emphasis on developing the moral and religious character of her students. The institution was very successful, and as its principal, Beecher became a popular and respected figure in Hartfield. Her accomplishments and her growing reputation as a talented teacher inspired Beecher to write about her educational philosophy. In her 1829 essay, "Suggestions Respecting Improvements in Education," she declared that the primary goal of education should be to provide a basis for the development of the student's conscience and moral makeup. To facilitate this kind of instruction in her school, Beecher unsuccessfully sought to hire an associate principal to manage the teaching of religion. Failing to secure an assistant, Beecher suffered from a nervous breakdown and left the school in the hands of her sister Harriet for several months while she recovered. Upon her return, she took on the task of religious and moral instruction herself.

With the beginning of the 1830s, Beecher became more interested in the roles her female students would take on in society. While she believed that running a home and raising a family was an important and influential contribution by women, she also felt that women should be given more responsibility and respect outside the home. She saw the field of teaching as the perfect professional arena for women—it allowed them an independent and consequential role in their community, but at the same time it was an acceptably "feminine" role. In addition, the growing populations of the western areas of the country were creating an increased demand for teachers. Beecher was appalled that in states like Ohio, perhaps one third of children did not have access to schools.

Founded School for Teacher Training

To encourage more women to become teachers, Beecher realized, there needed to be more opportunities for women to be educated and trained for the profession. She made it her mission to provide such training. In 1831, she left the East Coast to join her father in Cincinnati, Ohio, where he had been name president of the Lane Theological Seminary. There she opened the Western Female Institute, a school devoted to instructing young women so that they, in turn, could instruct others. Beecher hoped that her school could serve as a model for a nationwide system of teacher colleges. She presented her ideas on the subject in an 1835 lecture that was published under the title "An Essay on the Education of Female Teachers." In Cincinnati, she began a fundraising effort to support her school and the creation of

similar schools. But Beecher was not well-liked in the city; many people felt that she was a cultural elitist. Her abolitionist views were also suspect in an area divided on the issue of slavery. Unable to win the financial or philosophical support of residents, enrollment in Beecher's school steadily declined until it was finally forced to close in 1837.

The townspeople's opinions apparently had little effect on Beecher's own values, however. That same year, she published a tract that called on women to unite against the system of slavery, titled "Slavery and Abolition with Reference to the Duty of American Females." In this essay, Beecher began to formulate her idea that women could have a powerful influence on the character of the nation by creating a virtuous and harmonious domestic realm, in this way providing a stable, moral basis for society. Writing became the new channel through which Beecher attempted to spread her philosophy and make a living. She began to turn out a large amount of material, but it was not until the publication of her *Treatise on Domestic Economy* in 1841 that she finally reached the wider audience that she sought. The book was an incredible success, going through almost 15 printings in as many years and earning her fame across the nation.

Celebrates Domesticity in Best-seller

The *Treatise* provided women with a practical and moral guide to domestic life. It presented information on such topics as cooking, child care, and general health care. In this way, it presented a handy single source of household knowledge that had not existed before. But even more important was the philosophy in which Beecher couched her advice. She saw such domestic concerns not as mundane drudgery but as "the greatest work," a devotion to the welfare of others that provided the basis of a healthy society. The mission of women, according to Beecher, was to form the moral and intellectual character of children, and in order to fulfill this duty successfully, women required a quality education. Through their examples of skilled nurturing and intelligent teaching, women could use their home life as a secure base from which to reach out and create change in the rest of society. Beecher's ideas did not radically attack traditional gender roles, rather it justified and glorified them. This support of the family and social hierarchy struck a chord of comfort and stability in the public, making Beecher a celebrity.

With the success of her book, Beecher was able to found the Women's Education Association in New York in 1852. The organization was devoted to raising funds for the establishment of women's schools. Beecher was never satisfied with the amount of money raised by the organization (it eventually dissolved in 1862), so she undertook a number of public appearances across the country in which she solicited donations, promoted women's education, and discussed her books. She also sought donations from friends and relatives for her education ventures. She further supported educational causes by attending teacher's conferences and sustaining a correspondence with a wide range of people.

In the last years of her life, Beecher returned to the East, where she lived with various relatives. She had a particularly close relationship with her sister Harriet Beecher Stowe, best-known as the author of the novel *Uncle Tom's Cabin*. The sisters worked together to write an 1869 sequel to the *Treatise on Domestic Economy* entitled *The American Woman's Home*. Beecher was active in fighting for women's education for the rest of her years. She died in Elmira, New York, on May 12, 1878. Through her writings, public appearances, and the schools she helped to found, Beecher had helped to gain recognition for the value of women's work in society. Although she did not challenge the traditionally subordinate place of females, she did present a new vision of women as a strong and influential force that helped to determine the direction and conscience of the nation. Her emphasis on bringing women into the teaching profession also changed notions about women's education and careers, providing a basis for the continued growth of feminist thought in the nineteenth century.

Further Reading

See also Barker-Benfield, Graham J., and Catherine Clinton, *Portraits of American Women,* St. Martin's Press, 1991; Kerber, Linda K., and Jane S. DeHart, *Women's America,* 3rd ed., Oxford University Press, 1991; and Sklar, Kathryn Kish, *Catharine Beecher: A Study in Domesticity,* W. W. Norton, 1976.
□

Henry Ward Beecher

Henry Ward Beecher (1813-1887), American Congregational clergyman, was an outstanding preacher and lecturer. He was probably the best known and most influential Protestant minister in the United States between 1850 and 1887.

Henry Ward Beecher, the fourth son of Lyman Beecher (whose mantle, reputation, and personality he inherited), was born on June 24, 1813, at Litchfield, Conn. Though an undisciplined student with a greater gift for speaking than studying, he graduated from Amherst College in 1834 and Lane Theological Seminary in 1837. He was ordained by the Presbyterian Church (New School) in 1838, serving first a small parish at Lawrenceburg, Ind., and then the larger Second Presbyterian Church in Indianapolis after 1839. Here he developed the oratorical style—a singleness of aim which sought to achieve a moral response and change in his hearers—that enabled him to become the most conspicuous preacher in the nation for several decades.

In 1847 Beecher moved to Brooklyn, N.Y., to become pastor of the newly formed Plymouth Church. He remained there the rest of his life and made it one of the most renowned and influential American pulpits, attracting crowds of 2,500 regularly every Sunday. His striking appearance, dynamic delivery, and ability to speak directly on topics of popular interest gained him a national audience. A stenographer recorded his sermons, which were regularly published and widely read.

With Beecher's uncanny sensitivity to the mood of the nation and the inherent egotism of a showman, his ministry exerted great power. From various platforms he spoke about political as well as religious issues. He was as well known for his Republican party affiliation and advocacy of political issues as for his liberalizing theological views. Frequently he took up the pen and as both author and editor gave his ideas broad circulation. When he became editor of *The Christian Union* in 1870, he created the first nondenominational religious journal.

Beecher left a legacy of over 40 published volumes, but only a few deserve note. *The Life of Jesus the Christ* (1871, expanded 1891) revealed his unorthodox views and led to charges of heresy that were intensified after he espoused evolution in *Evolution and Religion* (1885). His ideas generated some hostility but showed little originality or lasting significance. In contrast, his *Yale Lectures on Preaching* (3 vols., 1872-1874) revealed him at his best as lecturer and preacher.

Charges of adultery involved Beecher in church investigations and civil trials from 1870 to 1875, but he was never proved guilty and the publicity seemed to have little impact on his popularity. Increasing criticism of his liberalizing theological ideas led him to withdraw from his Congregational Association in 1882 to protect his colleagues. He served Plymouth Church until his death, on March 8, 1887, after a cerebral hemorrhage.

Further Reading

Beecher remains controversial. Sympathetic standard biographies are William C. Beecher and Rev. Samuel Scoville, *A Biography of Rev. Henry Ward Beecher* (1888), and Lyman Abbott, *Henry Ward Beecher* (1903). William Gerald McLoughlin, *The Meaning of Henry Ward Beecher: An Essay on the Shifting Values of Mid-Victorian America, 1840-1870* (1970), analyzes Beecher's thought and the sources of his popularity in 19th-century America. Robert Shaplen, *Free Love and Heavenly Sinners: The Story of the Great Henry Ward Beecher Scandal* (1954), is a careful, interesting recounting of Beecher's trial for adultery. Paxton Hibben is a skillful debunker in *Henry Ward Beecher* (1927).

Additional Sources

Abbott, Lyman, *Henry Ward Beecher*, New York: Chelsea House, 1980.

Clark, Clifford Edward, *Henry Ward Beecher: spokesman for a middle-class America*, Urbana: University of Illinois Press, 1978. ☐

Lyman Beecher

A Presbyterian clergyman, Lyman Beecher (1775-1863) was one of the outstanding American preachers and revivalists before the Civil War. He achieved national fame as reformer, educator, and central figure in theological controversies.

Lyman Beecher was born on Oct. 12, 1775, at New Haven, Conn. Son of a blacksmith, he was raised on a farm. Beecher entered Yale in 1793. The college president, Timothy Dwight, greatly influenced his religious beliefs and enthusiasm for revivalism. In 1799 he was ordained as pastor of the Presbyterian Church at East Hampton, Long Island, N. Y. Dynamic preaching and a published sermon against dueling earned him a modest reputation, and in 1810 he accepted the more prestigious pulpit of the Congregational Church of Litchfield, Conn.

For 16 years at Litchfield he attracted large crowds, and his influence extended beyond his own congregation. Persons warmed by his revivals were urged to support a growing list of voluntary societies and moral reforms, especially temperance. His defense of orthodox Christianity against Unitarianism in Connecticut was noted by church leaders, and he was invited to move to Boston, where he could be even more effective in that cause.

In 1826 Beecher became pastor of the Hanover Street Church of Boston. His efforts again resulted in spiritual awakening, and his reputation for defending orthodoxy against Unitarianism became widespread. During his years in Boston he edited a monthly, *the Spirit of the Pilgrims*. A fear of Catholicism began to emerge and led him to share in the nativist attack on that faith.

When he was invited to return to Presbyterianism to become the president and professor of theology of the new Lane Theological Seminary at Cincinnati, Ohio, his concern to Christianize the West and educate ministers for that task was linked to his desire to counteract growing Catholic influence in the Ohio Valley. The sense of purpose he felt in moving to Cincinnati in 1832 was well expressed in his *A Plea for the West* (1835). Until 1843 he also served as pastor of the Second Presbyterian Church there.

Despite his incentive and characteristic vigor, Beecher's years at Cincinnati were an unhappy climax to his career. A disruptive debate over slavery in 1834 so divided students and faculty that it took years for Lane Seminary to recover. Although he favored the antislavery cause, Beecher was not an abolitionist and preferred gradual emancipation. With strange irony in 1835 he was tried twice for heresy by conservative Presbyterians who found his orthodoxy too liberal. A trial by the Presbyterian General Assembly was avoided, but his position had contributed to a major schism in that denomination by 1838. Beecher remained at Lane until 1850. The last years of his life were spent in Brooklyn, N.Y., where he died on Jan. 10, 1863.

Further Reading

Lyman Beecher's *Autobiography,* edited by Charles Beecher (2 vols., 1864), is the best source on his life and was reprinted with a helpful introduction by Barbara Cross (2 vols., 1961). Chapters in Lyman Beecher Stowe, *Saints, Sinners and Beechers* (1934), and Constance Mayfield Rourke, *Trumpets of Jubilee* (1927), are as useful as the older, uncritical biographies. ☐

Ludwig van Beethoven

The instrumental music of the German composer Ludwig van Beethoven (1770-1827) forms a peak in the development of tonal music and is one of the crucial evolutionary developments in the history of music as a whole.

The early compositions of Ludwig van Beethoven marked the culmination of the 18th-century traditions for which Haydn and Mozart had established the great classical models, and his middle-period and late works developed so far beyond these traditions that they anticipated some of the major musical trends of the late 19th century. This is especially evident in his symphonies, string quartets, and piano sonatas.

In each of these three genres Beethoven began by mastering the existing formal and esthetic conventions of the late 18th century while joining to these conventions signs of unusual originality and power. In his middle period (from about 1803, the year of the *Eroica* Symphony, to about 1814, the year of his opera *Fidelio* in its revised form) he proceeded to develop methods of elaboration of musical ideas that required such enlargement and alteration in perception of formal design as to render it clear that the conventions associated with the genres inherited from the 18th century were for him the merest scaffolding for works of the highest individuality and cogency.

If Beethoven's contemporaries were able to follow him with admiration in his middle-period works, they were left far behind by the major compositions of his last years, especially the last three Piano Sonatas, Op. 109, 110, and 111; the *Missa solemnis;* the Ninth Symphony; and the last six String Quartets, Op. 127, 130, 131, 132, 133, and 135. These works required more than a generation after Beethoven's death to be received at all by concert audiences and were at first the preserve of a few perceptive musicians. Composers as different in viewpoint from one another as Brahms and Wagner took Beethoven equally as their major predecessor; Wagner indeed regarded his own music dramas as the legitimate continuation of the Beethoven tradition, which in his view had exhausted the possibilities of purely instrumental music. Beethoven's last works continue in the 20th century to pose the deepest challenges to musical perception.

Years in Bonn

Ludwig van Beethoven was born in Bonn, the Rhineland seat of an electoral court. His ancestors were Flemish (the "van" was no indication of any claim to nobility but merely part of the name). His father, a tenor in the electoral musical establishment, harbored ambitions to create in his second son a prodigy like Mozart. As Beethoven developed, it became increasingly clear that to reach artistic maturity he would have to leave provincial Bonn for a major musical center. At the age of 12 he was a promising keyboard virtuoso and a talented pupil in composition of the court musician C. G. Neefe.

In 1783 Beethoven's first published work, a set of keyboard variations, appeared, and in the 1780s he produced the seeds of a number of later works. But he was already looking toward Vienna: in 1787 he traveled there, apparently to seek out Mozart as a teacher, but was forced to return owing to his mother's illness. In 1790, when the eminent composer Joseph Haydn passed through Bonn, Beethoven was probably introduced to him as a potential pupil.

Years in Vienna

In 1792 Beethoven went to Vienna to study with Haydn, helped on his way by his friend Count Ferdinand von Waldstein, who wrote prophetically in the 22-year-old Beethoven's album that he was going to Vienna "to receive the spirit of Mozart from the hands of Haydn." What he actually received from Haydn in lessons was little enough, and Beethoven turned to others of lesser talent in Vienna for help with counterpoint, including the contrapuntal theorist J. G. Albrechtsberger.

Beethoven rapidly proceeded to make his mark as a brilliant keyboard performer and improviser and as a gifted young composer with a number of works to his credit and powerful ambitions. He won entry into the musical circles of the Viennese titled upper classes and gained a number of lifelong friends and admirers among them. In 1795 his first mature published works appeared—the three Piano Trios,

Op. 1—and his career was in effect officially launched. From then until the end of his life Beethoven was essentially able to publish his works at approximately the rate at which he could compose them, if he wished to; in consequence the opus numbers of his major works are, with a few trivial exceptions, the true chronological order of his output. No such publication opportunities had existed for Haydn or Mozart, and least of all for Schubert, who spent his entire life in Vienna (1797-1828) in Beethoven's shadow, from the publication standpoint.

From 1792 to his death in 1827 at the age of 57 Beethoven lived in Vienna, essentially as a private person, unmarried, amid a circle of friends, independent of any kind of official position or private service. He rarely traveled, apart from summers in the countryside. In 1796 he made a trip to northern Germany, perhaps to look over the possibilities for a post; his schedule included a visit to the Berlin court of King Frederick William of Prussia, an amateur cellist, and the Op. 5 Violoncello Sonatas appear to date from this trip. Later Beethoven made several trips to Budapest and to spas in Bohemia.

In 1808 Beethoven received an invitation to become music director at Kassel. This alarmed several of his wealthy Viennese friends into unprecedented generosity; three of them (Princes Lichnowsky and Kinsky and Archduke Rudolph) formed a group of backers and agreed to guarantee Beethoven an annual salary of 1,400 florins on condition that he remain in Vienna. He thus became, in principle, one of the first musicians in history to be freed form menial service and to be enabled potentially to live as an independent artist-although, as it happened, the uncertain state of the Austrian economy in the Napoleonic era caused a sharp devaluation of the currency, cutting the value of his annuity, and he also had some trouble collecting it.

Publishing Practices of the Time

Although publishers sought Beethoven out and he was an able manager of his own business affairs, as his letters show, he was really at the mercy of the chaotic and unscrupulous publishing practices of his time. Publishers paid a fee to composers for rights to their works, but neither copyright nor royalties were known. As each new work appeared, Beethoven sold it as dearly as he could to the best and most reliable current publisher (sometimes to more than one). But this initial payment was all he could expect, and both he and his publisher had to contend with piracy by rival publishers who brought out editions of their own. Consequently, Beethoven witnessed a vast multiplication of his works in editions that were unauthorized, unchecked, and often unreliable in details. Even the principal editions were frequently no better, and several times during his life in Vienna, Beethoven hatched plans for a complete, authorized edition of his works. None of them materialized, and the wilderness of editions forms the historical background to the present problems of producing a truly scrupulous complete edition.

Personal Problems

Far overshadowing these general conditions were the two particular personal problems that beset Beethoven, especially in later life: his deafness and his obsessive relationship with his nephew Karl. Beethoven began to suffer from deafness during his early years in Vienna, and his condition gradually grew worse, despite remissions. So severe was the problem as early as 1802 that he actually seems to have contemplated suicide, as can be inferred from the so-called Heiligenstadt Testament, a private document written that year. It shows clear evidence of his deep conflict over his sense of artistic mission and his fear of inability to hear normally, to use the sense that should have been his most effective and reliable one. The turning points in his deafness actually came only later: first, about 1815, when he was compelled to give up all hope of performing publicly as a pianist (his Fifth Piano Concerto was written in 1809, an unfinished concerto in 1815); and after 1818, when he was no longer able to converse with visitors, who were thus forced to use writing pads to communicate (the famous "Conversation Books").

The second overriding problem (apart from his lifelong inability to form a lasting attachment to one woman, despite many liaisons) arose when he became the guardian of his nephew Karl on the death of his brother in 1815. Karl proved to be erratic and unstable, and he was a continuing source of anxiety to an already vulnerable man.

Beethoven's deafness and his undoubted tendency toward impetuousness and irascibility contributed to his reputation as a misanthropic and antisocial personality, one to be watched from afar and approached only with caution. As he retreated further into his work and as the works themselves became increasingly less comprehensible to his average contemporaries, the Vienna of light music and *Gemütlichkeit* saw him more and more as a kind of living embodiment of the artist beyond society. Later, as writers of the 19th century continued to cultivate this view of art, Beethoven became one of its mythical representatives, and his earlier biographers spread the image widely. Only by a careful reading of Beethoven's letters and the winnowing of reliable accounts from fanciful ones can one obtain a more balanced picture, in which one sees a powerful and self-conscious man, wholly engaged in his creative pursuits but alert to their practical side as well, and occasionally willing to conform to current demands (for example, the works written on commission, such as his cantata for the Congress of Vienna, 1814).

Beethoven's deafness was the major barrier to a continued career as the social lion of his early Vienna years, and it must inevitably have colored his personality deeply. But his complex development as an artist would probably in any event have sooner or later brought a crisis in his relationship to the surface of contemporary musical and social life. The trend was inward: in his early years he wrote as a virtuoso pianist-composer for an immediate and receptive public; in his second period he wrote for an ideal public; in his last years he wrote for himself.

It has long been commonplace in Beethoven biography to stress his awareness of contemporary political and philosophical thought, particularly his attachment to the libertarian ideals of the French Revolution and his faith in the brotherhood of men as expressed in his lifelong ambition to compose a setting of Friedrich Schiller's "Ode to Joy," realized at last in the Ninth Symphony. Frequently emphasized too is his undoubtedly genuine love of nature and outdoor life. But it is equally clear that no worthwhile estimate of Beethoven can be founded on a simple equation of these personal ideals with his music. In the Sixth Symphony (the *Pastoral*), Beethoven after great efforts found titles to suggest the allusions intended for each of the movements but sternly added in his sketchbook: "More the expression of feelings than tone painting." And in the Ninth Symphony he diligently sought the most effective way to introduce the vocal movement (the finale) with Schiller's words, at last hitting on the complex scheme of an introduction that reintroduces the thematic material of the earlier movements, rejects each in turn, and then opens the way to the finale through an explicit prefiguration of the theme to which the first stanza of the ode is to be set. In short, Beethoven's preoccupations from first to last were primarily those of musical structure and expression, and as more becomes known of his inner biography, as seen in his sketchbooks, a much more satisfactory portrait will be possible.

Brief Summary of Beethoven's Works

The general pattern of Beethoven's development as a composer is from a brilliant and prolific early manhood to the slow, painstaking efforts of his later years, in which his rate of production of new works dropped sharply in precise proportion as the works themselves became vastly more complex. The longest continuous thread in his development is that of his sketchbooks, which he used assiduously throughout his career and kept carefully, long after their contents had apparently been fully spent. This was not due to mere self-consciousness and an evident desire to keep close track of his own development; in this way he maintained a usable store of potential ideas and means of elaboration. Sometimes an idea from earlier years crops up in later work; in addition, Beethoven was strongly given to revision as well as elaboration, and at times he could not resist carrying out several modes of developing a single thematic idea. One example is the subject of the finale of the *Eroica* Symphony, which also appears as an orchestral dance and as the basis for a powerful set of piano variations, Op. 35. Other wholesale revisions of finished works include the three overtures to his opera *Leonore,* as well as the opera itself (first version 1805, second 1806), revised again and called *Fidelio* (1814) with still another overture.

First Period

The division of Beethoven's career into three phases originated with A. Schindler and W. von Lenz in the mid-19th century and forms a convenient means of reference. The first period, extending from his beginnings in Bonn to about 1802, shows a wide spectrum of compositions in virtually every genre of the time. The major works of this phase are the First and Second Symphonies, the first three Piano Concertos (written for his own performance and with-

held from publication for some years), the first six String Quartets (Op. 18), much piano chamber music, and more than half of the 32 Piano Sonatas. The piano plays a conspicuous role in Beethoven's early work, reflecting his dual ambition as composer and performer, and as an instrument it was his major vehicle for technical experimentation. He was the first to exploit a number of pianistic effects, such as the pedal and the use of registral extremes, in a way that foreshadowed much in later piano music.

In Beethoven's early works one can distinguish two extremes: at one extreme are compositions that lean strongly toward a deliberate note of popular appeal; at the other extreme are the most serious and inwardly developed compositions. To the first group belongs, above all, the Septet for mixed string and wind instruments, easily his most popular early work, republished many times in various arrangements and written to emulate the facile 18th-century "serenade" or "divertimento." Typical of the second group are the carefully wrought String Quarters of Op. 18, the first two Symphonies, and the most elaborate of the Piano Sonatas (for example, Op. 13, the *Pathétique;* Op. 27, Nos. 1 and 2; and the three Sonatas of Op. 31). Some of the chamber music leans to one extreme, some to the other; a work that leans to both is the Clarinet Trio, Op. 11, of which the first two movements are fully serious and the finale a light set of variations on a popular tune.

Many early Beethoven works employ the principle of formal structure associated with the classical variation technique. This emphasis in the early Beethoven is extremely significant; it relates to his talent for improvisation, suggests his sense of contact with popular music, and at the same time prefigures his later growth in the direction of the elaboration of inherently simple musical ideas. Throughout his career Beethoven never lost sight of the possibilities inherent in the variation form, of which the final expression in his work may be seen in the *Diabelli* Variations for Piano, Op. 120.

Second Period

The works of Beethoven's middle years form an extraordinary procession of major compositions, entirely departing from the traditional proportions and, to some extent, the methods of earlier tonal music. The earlier "facile" level of composition is abandoned, and occasional regressions to earlier types of movement structure are suppressed (for example, the substitution of a conventional slow movement by a tightly compressed slow introduction to the finale in the *Waldstein* Piano Sonata, Op. 53). Even the most superficial view of Beethoven's new scheme of musical design must include the following observations. He works now with the intensive elaboration of single ideas, to an extent never previously attempted in classical instrumental music (for example, the first movement of the Fifth Symphony). He extends the time scale of the three-or four-movement formal scheme to a high degree (for example, the *Eroica* Symphony, the unusual length of which was noted by the composer on his autograph manuscript). He replaces the old third movement of the symphony and the quartet (minuet or other medium-tempo dance form) with a dynamic and rapid movement, always called scherzo (this had already been done in early works). He brings about the dramatization of instrumental effects and musical components to an unprecedented degree, partly through the juxtaposition of strongly dissimilar musical ideas, partly through the ingenious use of means of establishing expectations of a particular kind and then either delaying them or turning in an unexpected direction (for example, the first movement of the *Appassionata* Sonata, Op. 57, in which no full resolution of a cadence on to the tonic is permitted until the end of the movement; the opening of the *Rasumovsky* Quartet, Op. 59, No. 3; and the dramatic use of silence, as in the opening of the *Coriolanus* Overture, Op. 62).

If Beethoven's second period of development is taken to run from approximately Op. 53 (the *Waldstein* Sonata) to Op. 97 (the *Archduke* Trio) or to *Fidelio,* it includes the Third through Eighth Symphonies; the Fourth and Fifth Piano Concertos; the Quartets of Op. 59, 74, and 95; the two last Violin Sonatas, Op. 47 (*Kreutzer*) and Op. 96; the Violoncello Sonata, Op. 69; the Piano Trios, Op. 70 and 97; the Piano Sonatas from Op. 53 to Op. 90; and the opera *Leonore* (*Fidelio*). He also wrote a large number of songs and a remarkable Mass in C Major, Op. 86.

The last works that can be associated with this phase of activity issue onto a period of cessation of continuous composition—a kind of twilight area that separates the second period from the last and reaches from about 1815 to perhaps 1818. It marks the onset of Beethoven's extreme deafness and of his difficulties with his nephew but also the preparation for musical tasks of unparalleled complexity in this time.

Third Period

To attempt to characterize any truly significant aspects of Beethoven's last works in a few words would be beyond effrontery. The order of their composition is essentially the order of publication and thus of their opus numbers; and the great peaks of the last years are hedged in and about with a few smaller works tossed off to make money or to maintain the interest of avaricious publishers.

The procession of great monuments is essentially as follows: the last five Piano Sonatas (Op. 101, 106 called the *Hammerklavier,* 109, 110, and 111) written between 1815 and 1822; the *Missa solemnis* (1823); the Ninth Symphony (prefigured as early as 1815 and completed in 1824); and the last Quartets (from 1824 to 1826). Superficially obvious in these works is either vast expansion over the dimensions of even Beethoven's earlier works in the genre (for example, Ninth Symphony; the *Missa solemnis;* the *Hammerklavier* Sonata; and the Quartet, Op. 131) or extreme compression (for example, Op. 111, the last Piano Sonata, in two movements; and the Quartet, Op. 135). Obvious too is the renewed emphasis on fugal techniques, reflecting a lifelong desire to master the devices of tonal polyphony on a level to match that of Johann Sebastian Bach, whom Beethoven admired. The fugal movements include those in the Piano Sonatas, Op. 106 and 110; the *Missa solemnis;* the Ninth Symphony (parts of the scherzo and finale); and above all the *Grand Fugue,* Op. 133, originally designed as the finale

for the Quartet, Op. 130, but then made a separate composition, with a new finale written for Op. 130.

The vastness and imaginative complexity of Beethoven's last works, especially the Quartets, baffled not only his contemporaries but later audiences and even professional musicians for some time after his death. In various ways they seem the fully logical outcome of a lifetime of deep exploration of the possibilities of tonal structure; in other ways they seem to exceed in depth almost any of Beethoven's other music and perhaps that of any other subsequent composer. That Beethoven himself was aware that they were beyond the capacities of the listeners of his time seems beyond doubt; that he expected later audiences to meet them with the requisite seriousness of interest and intent is, to judge from what is known of his character, a fair inference. An anecdote, perhaps apocryphal but entirely fitting, reports that Beethoven told a visitor who was bewildered by his last quartets, "They are not for you but for a later age."

Further Reading

The largest published collection of Beethoven's letters is Emily Anderson, ed. and trans., *Letters* (3 vols., 1961). A valuable selection of letters is J. S. Shedlock, *Beethoven's Letters: A Critical Edition* (2 vols., 1909). An important volume of little-known letters was edited and translated by Donald W. MacArdle and Ludwig Misch, *New Beethoven Letters* (1957). A large number of Beethoven's "Conversation Books," the records of conversations between the composer and his associates and visitors during his last years, when his deafness had made normal discourse impossible, were in course of publication as of 1971 under the editorship of Karl-Heinz Köhler.

The most important contributions to Beethoven biography were produced in 19th-century Germany. *Beethoven as I Knew Him* (1840; trans. 1966) was written by a friend, Anton Schindler; his personal knowledge partially atones for his limited objectivity. The most authoritative biography is Alexander W. Thayer, *The Life of Ludwig van Beethoven* (trans., 3 vols., 1921; rev. ed. by Elliot Forbes, 2 vols. 1964). See also Walter Riezler, *Beethoven* (1938). Full-length introductory studies of Beethoven's work include Sir George P. Grove, *The Symphonies of Beethoven* (1884; 3d ed. entitled *Beethoven and His Nine Symphonies,* 1962); Donald F. Tovey, *A Companion to Beethoven's Pianoforte Sonatas* (1931) and his *Beethoven* (1944); Eric Blom, *Beethoven's Pianoforte Sonatas Discussed* (1938); Joseph de Marliave, *Beethoven's Quartets* (trans. 1961); and Joseph Kerman, *The Beethoven Quartets* (1967). See also Paul Mies, *Beethoven's Sketches: An Analysis of His Style Based on a Study of His Sketch-Books* (1929). □

Harrison Begay

Harrison Begay (born 1917) is a Navajo artist who specializes in watercolors and silkscreen prints.

H arrison Begay is one of the most famous of all Navajo painters. His watercolors and silkscreen prints have been widely collected. His work, which has won 13 major awards, has a sinuous delicacy of line and is noted for its meticulous detail, restrained palette, and elegance of composition. His style has been so influential that disciples, like Baji Whitethorne, say that by studying his paintings one learns not only technique but also religion. The Navajo conception of the orderly balance of irreconcilable forces is exemplified in Begay's style, which is at once serenely still and vitally active.

Herds Family's Sheep

Harrison Begay was born on November 15, 1917, at White Cone, Arizona, to Black Rock and Zonnie Tachinie Begay. His mother belonged to the Red Forehead Clan, and his father adopted the Zuni Deer Clan. He was said to have been related to Manuelita, an esteemed medicine man. The boy herded his family's flock of sheep near Greasewood, where he still lives. In 1927, he was sent to school at Fort Wingate, from which he ran away to spend the next four years at home, studying alone as he tended the sheep. In 1934, he attended Fort Defiance Indian School in New Mexico, and later Tohatchi Indian School. He graduated from high school in 1939 as salutatorian.

The institution that conferred distinction upon him was Dorothy Dunn's studio at the Santa Fe Indian School. Among Begay's classmates were other Navajo painters: Gerald Nailor, Quincy Tahoma, and Andy Tsinajinnie. They were taught to depict pastoral landscapes and tribal traditions in smoothly-brushed forms placed flat on the picture plane. In *American Indian Painting,* Dunn summed up Begay's work as "at once decorative and lifelike, his color clear in hue and even in value, his figures placid yet inwardly animated. . . . [H]e seemed to be inexhaustibly resourceful in a quiet reticent way."

In 1940, Begay married Ramona Espinosa; the couple divorced in 1945. Also in 1940, he attended Black Mountain College in Blueridge, North Carolina, to study architecture for one year. In 1941, he enrolled in Phoenix Junior College in Arizona.

Serves in the United States Army

Begay was one of the 21,767 Native American veterans of the U.S. Army in World War II. From 1942 to 1945, Begay served in the signal corps. He participated in the Normandy campaign and was stationed in Iceland and in Europe. Upon his discharge, he stayed in Colorado until September of 1947. While there, he was briefly tutored by an artist in Denver. The army had trained him to be a radio technician, but his artistic talent enabled him to make a living as a full-time painter since his return to the reservation in 1947.

Works in Arts and Crafts Shops

He was given space to paint at Clay Lockett's Arts and Crafts Shop in Tucson, Arizona. He also painted in Parkhurst's Shop in Santa Fe, New Mexico, and in Woodard's Shop in Gallup, New Mexico. He prefers to work in watercolors, usually casein paints because oil painting takes too long. A prolific artist, he regularly exhibits at the Philbrook Art Center each May, and at the Gallery in New Mexico that sponsors exhibits for five days in August each year at the Intertribal Indian Ceremonials. He won two grand awards at the Intertribal festivities and has been a consistent winner at state and tribal fairs. The French government honored him with its Palmes d'Academiques in 1945.

Begay cofounded TEWA Enterprises, which made silkscreen prints of his work. His fine-lined, flat-colored designs were eminently suitable for serigraph reproduction. This method of duplication also made his work affordable to the general public. Begay has also specialized in sensitive renditions of animals such as fawns, antelope, deer, sheep, and horses. He is also fond of depicting looms as subjects, as in his often reproduced painting, "Two Weavers" of 1946.

In 1959, Begay had an Enemyway chant performed for him. He paid the singer who conducted the rite to protect warriors against the ghosts of slain enemies with a set of three paintings of the Navajo sacred mountains. A similar set of the four sacred mountains, each associated with a different color and a different direction, is now owned by the Museum of Northern Arizona at Flagstaff. In order to compose these paintings, Begay studied the Navajo origin myths recorded by Washington Matthews.

Begay also illustrated Ann Cromwell's *A Hogan for the Bluebird,* published in 1969. Cromwell's piece of Navajo fiction tells of a Navajo Indian girl who finds it difficult to readjust to the ways of her people after several years at the mission school.

In addition to Begay's considerable achievements in the art world, he is also the state champion long distance runner, having broken the record in the mile race.

Further Reading

Dockstader, Frederick J., *Indian Art in America,* Greenwich, Connecticut, New York Graphic Society, 1966.
Dunn, Dorothy, *American Indian Painting,* Albuquerque, University of New Mexico Press, 1968.
Fawcett, David M., and Lee A. Callander, *Native American Painting: Selections from the Museum of the American Indian,* Emerson, New Jersey, ALE Associates, 1982.
Wade, Edwin L., *The Arts of the North American Indian: Native Traditions in Evolution,* New York, Hudson Hills Press, 1986.
Wyman, Leland C., "Navajo Ceremonial System," in *Handbook of the North American Indians,* Volume 10, edited by Alfonso Ortiz, Washington, D.C., Smithsonian Institution, 1983. □

Menachem Begin

Menachem Begin (1913-1992) was active in the movement to establish an independent Jewish state in Palestine and in the early Israeli government. After serving many years in the Knesset, Begin became Israel's first non-Socialist prime minister in 1977.

Menachem Begin was born the son of Zeev-Dov and Hassia Begin in Brest-Litovsk, White Russia (later Poland), on August 16, 1913. He was educated in Brest-Litovsk at the Mizrachi Hebrew School and later studied and graduated in law at the University of Warsaw. After a short association with Hashomer Hatzair, he became a devoted follower of Vladimir Zeev Jabotinsky, the founder of the Revisionist Zionist Movement, and joined Betar (Revisionist Zionist Youth Movement). He became active in the organization, joined its leadership, and in 1932 became head of the Organization Department of Betar in Poland. Later, after a period of service as head of Betar in Czechoslovakia, he returned to Poland and, in 1939, became head of the movement there.

Earlier, during the Palestine riots of 1936-1938, Begin organized a mass demonstration near the British Embassy in Warsaw and was imprisoned by the Polish police. He was also active in organizing illegal immigration to Palestine during this period. In 1939 he married Aliza Arnold (who died in 1982), with whom he had three children—one son (Benjamin) and two daughters (Chasia and Leah). When the Germans occupied Warsaw, Begin escaped to Vilna, where he was arrested in 1940 by the Soviet authorities for Zionist activity and sentenced to eight years of hard labor. He was held in Siberia in 1940-1941, but was released because he was a Polish citizen. In 1942 Begin arrived in Palestine with the Polish army formed in the former U.S.S.R.

Active in Palestine

Toward the end of 1943, after having been released from the Polish ranks, Begin became commander of the Irgun Tzevai Leumi. This militant underground organization worked for the establishment of a Jewish state in Palestine by opposing the British rule through various means, including violence. He declared "armed warfare" against the Mandatory government in Palestine at the beginning of 1944 and led a determined underground struggle against the British, who offered a reward for his apprehension. He tried, at the same time, to avert violent clashes within the Jewish community in Palestine. But he was not always successful as a peace maker among Jewish factions. Begin was on board the Irgun ship *Altalena* when it approached Tel Aviv with a consignment of arms during the Arab-Israel ceasefire of June 1948 and was shelled by order of the new Israel government of Prime Minister David Ben-Gurion.

With the independence of the State of Israel in 1948 and the dissolution of the Irgun, Begin founded the Herut (Freedom) Party and represented it in the Knesset (parliament) of Israel starting with its first meetings in 1949. He became Herut's leader, retaining that position for more than 30 years. Herut was known for its right-wing, strongly nationalistic views, and Begin led the party's protest campaign against the reparations agreement with West Germany in 1952. He was instrumental in establishing the Gahal faction (a merger of Herut and the Liberal Party) in the Knesset in 1965. He also developed a reputation as a gifted orator, writer, and political leader.

He remained in opposition in parliament until the eve of the Six Day War of June 1967, when he joined the Government of National Unity as minister without portfolio. He and his Gahal colleagues resigned from the government in August 1970 over opposition to its acceptance of the peace initiative of U.S. Secretary of State William Rogers, which implied the evacuation by Israel of territories occupied in the course of the Six Day War. Later, Gahal joined in forming the Likud bloc in opposition to the governing Labor Alignment, and Begin became its leader.

As Prime Minister

In May 1977 Begin became Israel's first non-Socialist prime minister when the Likud bloc secured the mandate to form the government after the parliamentary elections. He also became the first Israeli prime minister to meet officially and publicly with an Arab head of state when he welcomed Egyptian President Anwar Sadat to Jerusalem in November 1977. He led Israel's delegations to the ensuing peace negotiations and signed, with Sadat and U.S. President Jimmy Carter, the Camp David accords in September 1978.

In March 1979 he and Sadat signed the Egypt-Israel Peace Treaty, with Carter witnessing the event, on the White House lawn in Washington. Begin and Sadat shared the 1978 Nobel Peace Prize for their efforts. For Begin, and for Israel, it was a momentous but difficult accomplishment. It brought peace with Israel's most populous adversary and significantly reduced the military danger to the existence of Israel by neutralizing the largest Arab army, with whom Israel had fought five wars. But, it was also traumatic given the extensive tangible concessions required of Israel, especially the uprooting of Jewish settlements in Sinai.

The Knesset elections of June 30, 1981, returned a Likud-led coalition government to power in Israel, contrary to early predictions which projected a significant Labor Alignment victory. Menachem Begin again became prime minister, and his reestablished government coalition contained many of the same personalities as the outgoing group and reflected similar perspectives of Israel's situation and of appropriate government policies.

"Operation Peace for Galilee"—the War in Lebanon—beginning in June 1982 occasioned debate and demonstrations within Israel. It resulted in substantial casualties and led, at least initially, to Israel's increased international isolation and major clashes with the United States. Many of these results were muted over time, but the war left a legacy that continued to be debated long after Begin retired from public life. It was also a factor in Begin's decision to step down from the prime minister's office.

A Strong Leader

Within Israel, Begin's tenure was marked by prosperity for the average citizen, although there were indications (such as rising debt and inflation levels) that ultimately this might prove costly. The standard of living rose, as did the level of expectations. The religious parties enhanced their political power and secured important concessions to their demands from a coalition which recognized their increased role in maintaining the political balance and from a prime minister who was, on the whole, sympathetic to their positions.

The major external relationship continued to be the one with the United States, and this underwent significant change during Begin's tenure. The ties were often tempestuous, as the two states disagreed on various aspects of the regional situation and the issues associated with resolution of the Arab-Israeli conflict. Nevertheless, United States economic and military assistance as well as political and diplomatic support rose to all-time high levels.

Begin's political skills were considerable and apparent. Despite his European origins and courtly manner, he was able to secure a substantial margin of popularity over other major political figures, particularly the opposition leaders. At the time of his resignation, he was the most popular and highly regarded of Israeli politicians, as the public opinion polls regularly indicated.

Later Years

Begin's decision to resign as prime minister of Israel on September 16, 1983, brought to an end a major era in Israeli politics. It was a shock to Israelis, notwithstanding Begin's earlier statements that he would retire from politics at age 70. Although no formal reason for his resignation was forthcoming, Begin apparently believed that he could no longer perform his tasks as he felt he ought to and he seemed to be severely affected by the death of his wife the previous year and by the continuing casualties suffered by Israeli forces in Lebanon.

Begin literally became a recluse, spending most of his remaining years secluded in his apartment. He was seldom seen in public; often he only left his sanctuary to attend memorial services for his wife or to visit the hospital. He died of complications from a heart attack on March 9, 1992, in Ichilov Hospital, in Jerusalem.

Ironically, less than three months after his death, Likud, the party created by Begin, under the leadership of Yitzhak Shamir, lost the parliamentary elections to Yitzhak Rabin's Labor party. According to Rabin, Begin was the best of the last "of a special generation in the life of the Jewish people, characterized by the Holocaust and the resurrection." In the form of nationhood in 1948, and even in death, he maintained a significant influence on his nation's politics.

Further Reading

Begin wrote numerous articles and several books which include reminiscences and provide insight into his views of history. They include *Ha-Mered* (*The Revolt*), which describes the struggle of the Irgun and other Zionist organizations against the British and the Arabs in Palestine and constitutes memoirs of his years as head of the Irgun, and *Be-Leilot Levanim* (*White Nights*), reminiscences of his imprisonment in the Soviet Union. Two books in English about Begin provide sympathetic and detailed examinations: Eitan Haber, *Menachem Begin: The Legend and the Man* (1979), and Eric Silver, *Begin: The Haunted Prophet* (1984). Sasson Sofer's *Begin: An Anatomy of Leadership* (1988) is also a good resource. □

Hildegard Behrens

Hildegard Behrens (born 1937) was a German soprano noted for her highly dramatic performances, especially as Wagnerian heroines. She developed a vocal technique called "chest singing" which audiences and critics outside of Italy occasionally found disturbing and controversial.

Hildegard Behrens was born in Varel, a small town in northern Germany on February 9, 1937. Both her parents were doctors, and she was the youngest of their six children. She studied piano and violin as a child, but she had no professional aspirations. Instead, she went to the University of Freiburg in southern Germany to study law. Despite her intended career, she found herself spending most of her time at the school of music in the school chorus. She sat in on master classes as a spectator and had a boyfriend who was studying the violin and who later played with the Berlin Philharmonic.

Early Tutoring

Behrens decided upon a singing career at the comparatively advanced age of twenty-six. After three years studying law, she had passed her examinations but had already decided to pursue a career in music and to fall back upon the practice of law only if it were required. With a determination that she hoped would make retreat unnecessary, Behrens secured a teacher, Ines Leuwen, at the Freiberg Conservatory and studied with her for four years. Behrens had difficulties as a vocal student and Leuwen commented that she had "a beautiful voice but no talent." It was only after Leuwen advised her to give up singing that Behrens, with nothing left to lose, relaxed and displayed her abilities. Leuwen admitted her mistake and resumed the task of seriously training her unusual pupil. The four years at the Freiburg Conservatory are the only formal training and, even more unusual, the only regular coaching the independent-minded singer received.

Professional Career

In 1971 Behrens joined the Düsseldorf opera studio as an apprentice, despite which status she debuted in Osnabrück in the role of the countess in Mozart's opera, *The Marriage of Figaro,* in February. She was then given full membership in the parent company, the Deutsche Oper, in Düsseldorf. Among other roles, she gave a notably intense performance as Marie in Alban Berg's opera *Wozzeck.* Herbert von Karajan, the famous conductor that regularly presented relatively obscure new performers in full-scale productions, placing them in sudden, risky opportunities for complete success and often ushering them into international careers as a result, heard her performance in this role in Düsseldorf. Behrens was in her early 30s when von Karajan scheduled her in 1972 for the 1977 Salzburg Festival production of the Richard Strauss opera *Salome.* On the basis of that future production, Behrens received invitations to perform on the international opera circuit. In 1976 she sang the role of Leonora in Beethovan's *Fidelio* at Covent Garden in London; she appeared as Giorgetta in *Il Tabarro* in her debut at the Metropolitan Opera in New York City; and she sang in Janacek's *Katya Kabanova* at the National Theatre of Prague.

In the summer of 1977 at Salzburg, Behrens made her scheduled appearance in the title role of *Salome* with von Karajan conducting and achieved great success in the role, thus consolidating her international reputation. She appeared as well in Mozart operas at this time and did *Fidelio* at Salzburg, but had a temporary falling out with von Karajan. Against her own concept of the logic of the role of Salome, the conductor had someone else do the dance in the performance, a liberty with the drama of which Behrens did not approve. She resisted his offers for a performance of *Elektra* and a misunderstanding arose which temporarily placed them at odds. Behrens insisted upon her own interpretations of roles and expected respect for her capacity to immerse herself in an interpretation through clear thought regarding the role's musical and dramatic nature. She was open to guidance from a director, but wished the dramatic and musical interpretation she envisioned to be given preference. She and von Karajan agreed to film and record a performance of *Salome* after first developing a theatrical performance of the work. In 1992 she performed in *Elektra,* this time directed by Otto Schenk, in New York, finally bringing her hard-fought interpretation of the character to the stage.

In 1979, Behrens sang the title role in Richard Strauss's *Ariadne auf Naxos,* conducted by Karl Böhm. Behrens appeared throughout the world as both an opera performer and orchestral soloist. Among her many additional roles, she performed, and made her own, the Wagnerian heroines: Elisabeth, Elsa, Senta, Sieglinde, and, perhaps definitively in contemporary opera, Isolde at the Metropolitan Opera, and Brünnhilde in a highly individualized interpretation at the historic 1983 performance of *The Ring* at Bayreuth, conducted by Sir Georg Solti. This was a role she would repeatedly return to, most recently in April of 1997, where Behrens portrayal of Brünnhilde, this time conducted by James Levine, was not as acclaimed, but she nevertheless captivated audiences by bringing her own individualized portrayal out for all to see.

In 1985 she performed in the title role of *Tosca* in a performance that was televised throughout the world. This performance placed her among the heavy-hitters in opera and theater in the 1980s.

Performances in *The Ring* (1983, 1990, 1997), *Tosca* (1985, 1991), *Fedelio* (1992, 1995), *Elektra* (1992, 1993, 1994), as well as a collage performance of musical numbers in her 1996 recital with pianist Christoph Eschenbach, have kept Behrens extremely busy over the years. She has weathered it all—bad reviews, disagreeable directors, and artistic differences—to become one of the most renowned performers of our time.

Technique

Behrens developed the employment of the chest voice, the use of the tenor range by a female singer, which she exploited fully, a technique disturbing to American, English, and German opera audiences. She practiced in this tenor range, as well as in the customary soprano range, and employed it freely in her performances. She also believed in the power of her mind's determination in a given role to transform even the effect of her appearance upon the audience, through her concentration and clear thoughts about a given character.

Further Reading

Behrens was interviewed by T.P. Lanier in the February 2, 1980 issue of *Opera News* in an article entitled "Free Spirit; Soprano Hildegard Behrens talks about her choices in life and work." Her art is discussed in "Hildegard Behrens: eine Hommage," by O.F. Schuh, in the 1982 issue of *Opernwelt*. Her career and performances are dealt with in "A Very Special Tosca," by Will Crutchfield, in the March 10, 1985 issue of *The New York Times Magazine*.

Behrens discusses her passion for music in the Deborah Seabury article "Hunger For Work," which appeared in the February 27, 1988 issue of *Opera News*. Behrens is profiled in "Bold and Back," by Hugh Canning, in the May 26, 1989 issue of the *Guardian*. Her 1997 performance in *The Ring* was reviewed in the April 29, 1997 issue of *The New York Times* . □

Peter Behrens

Peter Behrens (1868-1940) was Germany's foremost architect in the early 20th century, as well as a painter and designer. His buildings greatly influenced the architecture of the next generation in Europe.

Peter Behrens was born in Hamburg on April 14, 1868. He studied painting at the School of Art in Karlsruhe (1886-1889). He spent the 1890s in Munich as a painter and designer in the current Jugendstil, or German Art Nouveau style, and cofounded the Sezession group of artists, architects, and designers in 1893. In 1899 he joined the artists' colony on the Mathildenhöhe in Darmstadt, where, under the influence of J. M. Olbrich, he turned to architecture. Behrens's house at Darmstadt (1900-1901) was a characteristic Art Nouveau work.

During his tenure as director of the School of Applied Arts in Düsseldorf (1903-1907), Behrens designed a series of buildings, including the exhibition hall for the Northwestern German Art Exhibition at Oldenburg (1905). In this design, simple rectilinear geometry, plane surfaces, and incised linear decoration replaced the curvilinear forms of his residence.

In 1907 Behrens succeeded Alfred Messel as architect and designer for the German General Electric Company in Berlin. In this capacity he designed everything from company brochures, light fixtures, and electric teakettles to factory complexes. Of major importance were his industrial buildings, such as the Turbine Factory (1909), the High Tension Factory (1910), the Small Motors Factory (1910-1911), and the Large Machine Assembly Hall (1911-1912), all in Berlin, which have come to be considered as a point of departure for much of the architecture of the first half of the 20th century. The Turbine Factory, of exposed steel, concrete, and large areas of glass, was especially admired by the next generation of architects.

Some of Behrens's other works of this period, however, were firmly within the German neoclassic tradition. The best of them, such as the houses at Eppenhausen near Hagen, including the Schröder House (1908-1909) and the Cuno House (1909-1910), continued the simplicity of the Düsseldorf period. But in other buildings, such as the German Embassy in Leningrad (1911-1912), the classical style became inert and pompous. Behrens's classicism was to have its influence upon the next generation, especially upon the work of Ludwig Mies van der Rohe.

In the years following World War I, Behrens's work became expressionistic, as did, briefly, that of many German architects of the time. An example is his I. G. Farben Company Building at Höchst (1920-1924). In 1922 Behrens became professor of architecture at the Academy in Vienna; he built little of consequence after the mid-1920s. He died on Feb. 27, 1940, in Berlin.

Further Reading

The basic monographs on Behrens are old and in German. There is a chapter devoted to Behrens and his German contemporaries in Henry-Russel Hitchcock, *Architecture: Nineteenth and Twentieth Centuries* (1958; 2d ed. 1963).

Additional Sources

Windsor, Alan, *Peter Behrens, architect and designer,* New York, N.Y.: Whitney Library of Design, 1981. □

Emil Adolph von Behring

The German hygienist and physician Emil Adolph von Behring (1854-1917) is famous for his discovery of antitoxins and his pioneering work in the treatment of diphtheria and certain other diseases.

Emil Adolph von Behring was born on March 15, 1854, at Forsthausen, West Prussia. After training at the University of Berlin and passing the state medical examination in 1880, he entered the army medical service. While in the service, he worked for a time with K. Binz, pharmacologist and chemist, on iodoform, a chemical homolog of chloroform, which was then considered highly effective as a dusting powder for the treatment of deep ulcers. In 1889 he joined the staff of the Robert Koch Institute of Hygiene in Berlin, and it was there that his outstanding contributions were produced.

When Behring began his experiments, the germ theory of disease was becoming well established and immunology was a rapidly developing discipline. In Koch's laboratory Behring worked with the eminent Japanese bacteriologist S. Kitasato. In 1890 Behring presented two papers, one with Kitasato, discussing the immunity of animals to diphtheria and tetanus. They demonstrated that certain substances (antitoxins) in the blood serum of both humans and animals who had recovered from the disease, either spontaneously or by treatment, showed preventive and curative properties. Animals injected with this immune blood were shown to be resistant to fatal doses of bacteria or toxin. Further, animals treated with the serum after contracting the disease could be cured.

For prophylactic immunization against diphtheria, Behring suggested the injection of a mixture of toxin and antitoxin. This method, the forerunner of modern disease prevention, became practicable when certain reagents, for example, formaldehyde, were added to the mixture to produce a "toxoid"; the reagents preserved the immunizing property of the mixture while removing its poisonous characters.

For these advances in serum therapeutics, Behring received the Nobel Prize in 1881, being the first medical man so honored; he was also created privy councilor with the title of *Excellenz* and received many distinctions and prizes. For the discovery of antitoxins and the development of vaccinations, Behring was honored with the epithet "Children Savior." When he contracted pneumonia, he was already in

a weakened state of health and was unable to withstand the strain. He died in Marburg on March 31, 1917.

Further Reading

A biography of Behring and a description of his work are in Theodore L. Sourkes, *Nobel Prize Winners in Medicine and Physiology, 1901-1965* (1967). Charles Singer, *A History of Biology to about the Year 1900* (1931; 3d ed. 1959), and D. Guthrie, *A History of Medicine* (1946), are useful for historical background. □

Behzad

Behzad or Bihzad (died ca. 1530) is considered the most important painter of Persia in a period when the country produced many great painters.

Unfortunately, important as Behzad was, there is no record of his birth or death and very little information about his life. We know that he was a painter at the court of Sultan Hoseyn Beyqara, head of the principality of Herat (now in Afghanistan). Apparently Behzad was an orphan, and Mirak, the chief painter and director of the library of the court of Sultan Hoseyn, adopted and trained him. From childhood Behzad was acquainted with poets and artists such as Jami and Navayi. Sultan Hoseyn, who was an accomplished poet himself, recognized Behzad's genius and chose him to succeed Mirak as court painter and director of the library.

Behzad painted in Herat from about 1480 to 1505. At that time Herat and the whole northeastern region were annexed by the newly formed Safavid empire founded by Shah Esmail. The new monarch took Behzad with him to his capital, Tabriz, where he became painter and director of the library under Shah Esmail and his son, Shah Tahmasp. Behzad held these positions until his death about 1530. Like many famous painters of the time, he did not sign all his works, and many pictures which bear his name are not authentic.

Inasmuch as almost all miniature painting in Persia was done to illustrate books, usually the court painter was also the chief librarian. The artist would choose episodes from famous love stories such as Shirin and Farhad, Vis and Ramin, and Leyli and Majnun, or from the *Shahnameh,* the epic of kings, or any other book that caught his fancy. The artist's purpose was to give pleasure to his viewers, not to convey a message.

The Mongol invasion in the 13th century had separated Persia culturally and spiritually from the rest of the Moslem world and ushered in a most creative period in art. Of the numerous schools of miniature painting that developed, one was the Herat school, to which Behzad belonged. His genius, however, transcended the conventional forms in vogue at the time.

Behzad's work shows the Persian love for detail, but it is superior in conception and execution. His treatment of figures, vivid characterization, expression of movement through the skillful use of colors, and harmonious balance between figures and background were all improvements on the previous schools.

Behzad is also recognized as an innovator in that he introduced naturalism into Persian painting. The old expressionless faces and figures were discontinued. By the use of delicate lines he revealed the effort of breathing, the tension of muscles, and the varied expressions of the faces. In group pictures every person is alive and intent on what he is doing. Whereas the conventional schools sacrificed natural expression for beauty, Behzad's paintings have both beauty and expression.

Further Reading

The most detailed description of Behzad's miniatures is in Arthur Upham Pope, ed., *A Survey of Persian Art from Prehistoric Times to the Present,* vol. 3 (1939). More recent studies are Basil Gray, *Persian Painting* (1961), which is more readily available, and B.W. Robinson, *Persian Drawings* (1965). Behzad's life and work are also discussed in F.R. Martin, *The Miniature Painting and Painters of Persia, India, and Turkey from the 8th to the 18th Century* (2 vols., 1912), and Sir Thomas W. Arnold, *Painting in Islam: A Study of the Place of Pictorial Art in Muslim Culture* (1928). □

Johann Conrad Beissel

Johann Conrad Beissel (1690-1768), German-American pietist, was the founder of the Community of Seventh-Day Baptists at Ephrata, Pa. He was also a prolific hymn writer.

Johann Beissel was born in April 1690 in Eberbach, Germany. His father was an alcoholic baker who died 2 months before his son was born; his mother died when Johann was 8. As a boy, he was apprenticed to a baker who also played the fiddle; from him Beissel received his musical education. Beissel was a diminutive person who may have felt all the more inferior in that he grew up in sordid circumstances without education. He showed genuine musical ability and early displayed compelling religious fervor. A conversion experience at the age of 27 convinced him that celibacy was a prerequisite to holiness. Later in life he thanked God for preserving him from female allurements.

After being expelled from the district where he worked as a journeyman baker because of his religious beliefs, Beissel and two friends went to America. He arrived in Boston in 1720 and proceeded to the Anabaptist community in Germantown, Pa., where he spent a year studying weaving with a Baptist pastor, Peter Becker.

In 1721 Beissel organized a community of Seventh-Day Baptist monks at Muelbach in Lebanon County, Pa. His disciples, unable to stand the rigidity of Beissel's asceticism, gradually deserted the colony. In 1725 Beissel underwent apostolic immersion at the hands of Becker, assuming the rebirth name of Friedman Gottrecht.

Beissel founded the cloister at Ephrata on Cocalico Creek, 65 miles west of Philadelphia, in 1732. The community thrived, and by midcentury he was directing 100 converts, Spiritual Virgins, Solitary Brethren, and married couples pledged to celibacy. Several prominent people joined the cloister: Conrad Weiser, a Lutheran elder; Peter Miller, a theologian; and Frau Christopher Sauer, who deserted her distinguished printer husband to answer the call and later became a prioress. The congregation wore hooded monks' habits and, in addition, the women were veiled. Each of the brethren wrote a weekly confessional which Beissel read to the assembled congregation. The colony excelled in making books and illuminated manuscripts.

The community kept alive some of the enormous number of choral works and hymnals composed by their founder. Beissel's 1747 hymnal (in German), *The Song of the Solitary and Deserted Turtledove, Namely the Christian Church,* numbered 900 pages. His musical compositions had as many as seven parts, the lowest for instruments and the rest for voices. A choir of up to 25 men and women rehearsed 4 hours in the evening, and in processions at sunset and midnight concertized skillfully with soft, precise intonation; either Beissel or his song leader, Sister Anastasia, had perfect pitch.

His choral compositions present primitive realizations of the harmony of paradise, which Beissel claimed he received from angels. He relied mainly on women's voices, had little sense of meter, and avoided dissonance on accented words—the reverse of universal practice. As a relief from the full chorus, he employed antiphonal sound. He went so far as to set the entire *Song of Songs* twice for this "aeolian-harp" singing. Only 441 of his "thousands" of choral works are extant. When Beissel died, Peter Miller became leader of the declining community.

Further Reading

The basic materials on Beissel are found in Brothers Lamech and Agrippa, *Chronicon Ephratense* (1786; trans. 1889), and Julius F. Sachse, *The Music of the Ephrata Cloister* (1903). The latter includes Beissel's preface to the *Turtledove* hymnal. The most important modern assessment is Hans T. David, "Ephrata and Bethlehem in Pennsylvania: A Comparison," in *Papers of the American Musicological Society, 1941* (1946). Robert M. Stevenson, *Protestant Church Music in America* (1966), gives a good brief discussion. Thomas Mann's novel *Doctor Faustus* (1948) contains a surprising passage on Beissel's music. □

David Belasco

David Belasco (1853-1931), American theatrical director-producer and playwright, attempted to bring veracity to the popular melodrama through meticulous detail in setting and lighting. He led in the movement that made the director the theater's dominant personality.

David Belasco was born in San Francisco, Calif., on July 22, 1853. He was educated in a monastery, which may have prompted the quasi-clerical garb he wore in later life—a style that earned him the name "the Bishop of Broadway." He fled the monastery and joined a circus. By the age of 12 he was an actor on the San Francisco stage and had begun writing plays. In the following few years he joined companies barnstorming through the mining camps. In Virginia City, Nev., he served as secretary to Dion Boucicault, who inspired Belasco to try playwriting again. From 1873 to 1881 he was associated with several San Francisco theaters. His first play to attract attention was a collaborative effort with James A. Herne, *Hearts of Oak.* At 29 Belasco left for New York City, having acted more than 170 roles and written or adapted more than 100 plays.

His first position in New York was as a stage manager of the Madison Square Theater. In 1886 he became dissatisfied and joined the Frohmans as stage manager and house playwright. In 1890 he became an independent producer; his first real success was his own *The Heart of Maryland,* a melodrama inspired by the poem "Curfew Must Not Ring Tonight." Belasco took unknowns and turned them into stars. The first of these, Leslie Carter, had suffered through a sensational divorce. Penniless, a social outcast, she came to Belasco, who trained her and then starred her in *Maryland*. It played for three seasons and was then taken to London.

During the 1890s the Theatrical Syndicate gained control of the theatrical world and individuals who refused to join found themselves with no theaters. In Washington, D.C., Belasco was forced to rent the barnlike Convention

Hall, leaky roof and all, for his production of *Andrea* with Carter. During the fourth act there was a violent rainstorm, and the audience observed the play from under their umbrellas. In 1902 Belasco gained control of the Republic Theater in New York. In 1906 he began work on a new building on West 44th Street, which eventually became the Belasco Theater.

In addition to Carter, Belasco elevated David Warfield (a vaudeville entertainer), Lenore Ulric, Frances Starr, and Blanche Bates to stardom. Most of these stars had natural ability, but Belasco was also a master at handling publicity campaigns. Certainly Carter's past was in part responsible for her success. Belasco also preferred to work with unknown playwrights. He collaborated with John Luther Long to write *Andrea, Madam Butterfly,* and *Darling of the Gods;* and with Henry C. DeMille on *Lord Chumley* and *The Wife,* among others. *Madam Butterfly* and Belasco's own *The Girl of the Golden West* were later adapted as the librettos for the Puccini operas.

Belasco claimed to have been associated with the production of nearly 400 plays, most of them written or adapted by himself; but his writing, in a time when Ibsen, Strindberg, and Chekhov were introducing realism, remained filled with sensational melodrama or maudlin sentiment. His plays have virtually no lasting value. His advances in realism were in technical aspects of theater; his settings were accurate to minute detail, for rather than recreate a specific setting he preferred to buy it and then move it on stage. He particularly excelled in spectacular effect and in amazing mechanical contrivances. In lighting, he pioneered the use of color silks and gelatin slides, loving to create "real" sunsets. Also, in a day when productions were hurriedly put together, Belasco took time to perfect his work; even his most severe critics admit a "tidiness" not often found on the American stage. He excelled in creating a mood and tension in his crowd and mob scenes. Moreover, whatever was seen on stage was Belasco and the other artists were the instruments of his will. He died in New York on May 14, 1931.

Further Reading

Belasco presents his ideas in *The Theatre through Its Stage Door* (1919) and in a chapter in Toby Cole and Helen Krich Chinou, eds., *Directors on Directing* (1963). Craig Timberlake, *The Bishop of Broadway: The Life and Work of David Belasco* (1954), is an objective biography. The theater conditions Belasco knew are described in George R. McMinn, *The Theater of the Golden Era in California* (1941), and Robert Grau, *The Business Man in the Amusement World* (1910). Alan S. Downer, ed., *American Drama and Its Critics* (1965), contains material about Belasco. □

Fernando Belaúnde Terry

An architect, educator, and politician, Fernando Belaúnde Terry (born 1912) was twice elected president of Peru. In a country known for stagnant dictatorship, he sought to bring progress through democratic means.

ernando Belaúnde was born in Lima, Peru, on October 7, 1912, to a distinguished family. His great-grandfather had been president, and an uncle was one of the country's foremost intellectuals. Rafael Belaúnde, Fernando's father, was a diplomat whose overseas assignments and dozen-year political exile caused the future president to spend most of his youth abroad. After attending high school in Paris, Belaúnde entered the University of Miami, where his father served on the faculty. Fernando later transferred to the University of Texas, which awarded him an architect's degree in 1935.

Belaúnde returned to Peru the following year and quickly climbed to the top of his profession. He taught architecture and urban planning at Lima's Catholic University and then at the National Engineering University, where he became dean of the School of Architecture. Belaúnde founded Peru's major architectural journal and established the Peruvian Urban Institute.

Entrance into Politics

In 1945 Belaúnde won election to congress as a member of the National Democratic Front, a reformist coalition supporting President José Luis Bustamante y Rivero. With the overthrow of that government by General Manuel Odría in 1948, Belaúnde returned to his profession. Meanwhile, he enhanced his reputation as a national leader by traveling extensively throughout the country and presenting his ideas in two books. Belaúnde advocated programs for economic development and social justice through the active intervention of a technocratic but highly democratic government.

He placed special emphasis on plans for the neglected Peruvian hinterland.

Belaúnde ran for president in 1956 with the support of the hastily-formed National Front of Democratic Youth. After losing that contest to Manuel Prado y Ugarteche he founded the Popular Action Party, which he forged into a broadly-based national organization. In 1962 Belaúnde vied for the presidency with Victor Raúl Haya de la Torre, founder of the American Popular Revolutionary Alliance (APRA), and former dictator General Manuel Odría. Haya defeated Belaúnde by a handful of votes, but the armed forces charged that fraud had marred the election and annulled the contest. In a 1963 rematch between the same three contenders, Belaúnde triumphed with a substantial plurality.

His First Administration

The new administration posted several impressive achievements during its first two years. Large sums were spent on health and, especially, education. Under Belaúnde, Peru devoted a larger share of its national income to schools than any other Latin American nation. The regime also launched several expensive irrigation, highway, and public housing projects. Belaúnde's highly successful Popular Cooperation program provided tools, technical assistance, and money to local communities, whose members volunteered their labor for various public works. A weakened version of the administration's agrarian reform bill became law in 1964.

An opposition coalition of APRA and Manuel Odría's UNO party controlled the congress, however. They rejected several of the president's proposals and denied him the taxes needed to fund his other programs. Belaúnde sought low-cost development loans from the United States government. But these were denied because of Peru's enforcement of a 200-mile fishing limit and Belaúnde's demands for the nationalization of the International Petroleum Company (IPC), a Standard Oil subsidiary. Determined to continue his programs, Belaúnde secured less advantageous loans from European commercial banks. He also engaged in deficit financing which produced mounting inflation.

Belaúnde signed a compromise agreement with the IPC in August 1968. Surrounded by controversy, this negotiation produced a storm of protest from critics who charged that the president had been overly generous to the foreign firm. Reform-minded military officers earlier had offered to suppress the obstructionist congress and allow Belaúnde to institute his programs dictatorially by decree. The democratic president had rejected their offer. Now the generals took advantage of the IPC controversy to overthrow him. General Juan Velasco Alvardo ousted Belaúnde on October 3, 1968, nine months before the expiration of his six-year term.

The Second Administration

Belaúnde spent the next decade in the United States, teaching at Harvard and other universities. Meanwhile, the radical military regime established by General Velasco instituted sweeping but ill-fated reforms. In April 1980, with Peru's economy in deep depression, the military administration permitted an election for the restoration of constitutional rule. Belaúnde won a five-year term, polling an impressive 45 percent of the vote in a 15-man contest.

Although Belaúnde enjoyed a congressional majority during his second term, economic and political problems plagued his administration. A towering foreign debt, large budget deficits, rampant inflation, costly natural disasters, and weak markets for Peru's exports stifled his programs and forced the imposition of severe austerity. At the same time a Maoist guerrilla organization, the Shining Path, waged an unrelenting terrorist campaign against the government. Vigorous efforts by the police and armed forces to suppress this group produced widespread abuse of innocent citizens and denunciations from human rights groups.

In the presidential election of April 1985 the candidate of Belaúnde's Popular Action Party polled an embarrassing five percent of the vote, finishing last in a four-man contest won by Alán García of APRA. Since the end of his administration Belaúnde has largely played the role of diplomat. In 1985 he inaugurated Loyola University in Chicago's Latin American Studies Program, acted as Columbia University's visiting scholar for Latin American and Iberian Studies, and, since November 1986, served as a member of the Carter Centers' *Council of Freely Elected Heads of Government,* a panel which promotes and reinforces democracy in North and South America and observes elections in newly democratized nations.

Called "The Architect" by his admirers, Belaúnde was a spellbinding orator whose democratic ideals and visionary programs inspired the masses. He was more successful in the role of candidate than as chief executive, and has enjoyed much more respect and honor since the end of his presidency.

Further Reading

Belaúnde expressed his ideas in *Peru's Own Conquest* (1965) and *Pueblo por Pueblo* (1995). Pedro-Pablo Kuczynski, *Peruvian Democracy under Stress* (1977) is a sympathetic account of Belaúnde's first administration by a cabinet minister. David P. Werlich's *Peru* (1978) traces Belaúnde's career through his first term and provides background for his second presidency. The latter period is examined in David P. Werlich, "Peru: The Shadow of the Shining Path," *Current History* (February 1984), and Ronald Bruce St. John, "Peru: Democracy under Siege," *World Today* (July 1984). □

Manuel Belgrano

The Argentine political figure and revolutionary general Manuel Belgrano (1770-1820) is considered one of the founders of the Argentine Republic. Although he was not always victorious, his efforts saved the patriot cause at several crucial times.

Manuel Belgrano was born in Buenos Aires on June 3, 1770, into a wealthy and prominent *criollo* (Creole) family. He studied in Spain at the University of Salamanca in 1786 and at Valladolid, where he graduated with a degree in law in 1793. During his residence in Spain he studied languages and economics and acquainted himself with the ideas of enlightened French and Spanish authors.

When Charles IV named Belgrano secretary of the newly organized Consulado of Buenos Aires, he enthusiastically accepted. While on the Consulado he petitioned for certain reforms: he urged opening new educational institutes and called for legislation to foster development of agriculture, commerce, trade, and communications. Most of his proposals were considered too costly or were thought to threaten privileges held by Spaniards and were vetoed. Disillusioned with the Spaniards, he was convinced that no progressive reforms could ever be expected from them.

When the English invaded Buenos Aires in 1806, Belgrano, an honorary captain, found himself commanding troops despite the fact that he had no military experience. But he was instrumental in organizing forces which later expelled the invaders. Belgrano and other *criollos* consequently acquired a sense of their own importance and power.

After 1807 Belgrano became increasingly critical of the Spanish system and found others who agreed with him. A secret society of revolutionists was organized with Belgrano reportedly a member. His caustic comments on Spanish

regulations were disseminated through the *Correo de comercio,* a newspaper he helped found in March 1810. In April he resigned from the Consulado, pleading illness. But in May, when news reached Buenos Aires that the Spanish junta established in 1808 had been disbanded, Belgrano and his compatriots quickly advocated the creation of a local junta. On May 25, 1810, when the junta was organized, Belgrano was elected a member.

War of Independence

The initial concern of the junta was defending Buenos Aires while securing the support of the surrounding provincial cities. Because of Belgrano's military record and the fact that other *criollos* had even less experience, he was named a general and ordered to assemble an army. In September 1810 the ill-equipped and poorly trained force made an unsuccessful foray into Paraguay. Belgrano was blamed for the disaster, but after an investigation he was cleared in August 1811..

He was subsequently appointed commander of an army defending the northwestern district from a Spanish invasion from Upper Peru (modern Bolivia). As a standard for the troops, he designed a banner which later became the national flag. With the outbreak of hostilities Belgrano was forced to retreat, but at the battle of Tucumán, on Sept. 24, 1812, he disobeyed orders, stood, fought, and checked further Spanish advances. Buenos Aires was spared, and his disobedience overlooked. Belgrano followed up the victory with an advance into the northwest. At Salta, on Feb. 20, 1813, he gained another stunning victory over the royalists, and the way was open for an invasion of Upper Peru. However, his armies were forced to withdraw after suffering a series of setbacks.

Belgrano, again in disfavor, was sent on a diplomatic mission to Europe to secure British recognition for the Buenos Aires government and to search for a monarch. He returned in February 1816, unsuccessful in obtaining either. Back in favor, he resumed his military career. At the Congress of Tucumán, Belgrano was an outspoken advocate for a declaration of independence and the establishment of a monarchy with a descendant of the Inca on the throne. Reappointed to his old command as chief of the army of the North, for the next 3 years he fought not only Spanish regulars but armies of provincial caudillos as well. The constant traveling and campaigning exhausted him. He returned to Buenos Aires in March 1820 and died on June 20.

Further Reading

The classic work on Belgrano remains Bartolomé Mitre, *Historia de Belgrano* (no date). Ricardo Levene, *A History of Argentina,* translated and edited by William Spence Robertson (1937), provides a general survey of the revolutionary era. Belgrano is also discussed in F.A. Kirkpatrick, *A History of the Argentine Republic* (1931), and Ricardo Rojas, *San Martín, Knight of the Andes* (trans. 1945). □

Grigorievich Belinsky

The Russian literary critic Vissarion Grigorievich Belinsky (1811-1848) was a major force in the intellectual and literary life of his country, and his writings form the foundation of Russian literary criticism.

Vissarion Belinsky was born on May 30, 1811, in Suomenlinna (Sveaborg), Finland, the son of a naval doctor. His youth was spent in Chembar, Penza Province, Russia, where his father was district physician. Vissarion attended the local grammar school and the Penza Gymnasium. In 1829 he entered Moscow University as a student of literature; his record was not brilliant because he was already weakened by tuberculosis and furthermore was concentrating all his energy (he is remembered by his contemporaries as "furious Vissarion") on literary projects outside the university. In 1831 he published some reviews and poems in *Listok.* The following year he was expelled from the university because his play *Dmitry Kalinin* attacked serfdom.

In 1834 Belinsky published a series of critical articles, "Literary Reveries," in *Molva,* the literary supplement of the newspaper *Teleskop.* They reflected the ideas of the German philosopher F. W. J. von Schelling. Written in a pungent, if somewhat repetitive, style, this "elegy in prose" brought Belinsky instant fame. His claim that "we have no literature" was a healthy antidote to the many inflated claims then being made for Russian literature by hyperpatriotic critics and historians.

In 1836 the government suppressed *Teleskop.* In 1838 Belinsky worked on the *Moscow Observer,* but it too was closed a year later. Belinsky moved to St. Petersburg, where he became chief literary critic for the magazine *Fatherland Notes.* During this period his thinking was greatly influenced by the German philosopher G. W. F. Hegel and German idealism. In certain articles of 1839 and 1840 Belinsky, under Hegel's influence, even defended the institution of autocracy.

Belinsky experienced a moral crisis in 1841 and abandoned Hegelianism. His *Works of Alexander Pushkin* (1843-1846) is as much a history of Russian literature as it is a study of Pushkin. From 1841 until his death Belinsky published an annual survey of Russian literature, the last two of which (1846 and 1847) are among his most important theoretical statements. In 1843 he married his childhood friend M. V. Orlova.

In 1846 Belinsky joined the journal *Contemporary* and served as its chief literary critic until his death. In July 1847 Belinsky wrote what is probably his best-known work, *Letter to Gogol.* Not published until 1905, it was widely circulated in manuscript and became an important document among later revolutionaries. He died on May 26, 1848.

Belinsky was an important influence on later critics. He is regarded by contemporary Russian critics as the father of many tendencies which have became associated with socialist realism.

Further Reading

There is little material on Belinsky in English. The only full-length study is Herbert E. Bowman, *Vissarion Belinski, 1811-1848* (1954), which is devoted chiefly to Belinsky's intellectual development and is not always reliable. Richard Hare, *Pioneers of Russian Social Thought* (1951; rev. ed. 1964), contains a chapter on Belinsky that is short but sound. There is a useful section on Belinsky in Evgenii Lampert, *Studies in Rebellion* (1957). For general background Edward J. Brown, *Stankevich and His Moscow Circle, 1830-1840* (1966), is excellent.

Additional Sources

Jakovenko, Boris V. (Boris Valentinovich), *Vissarion Grigorievich Belinski: a monograph,* Melbourne: D. Jakovenko, 1986.
Randall, Francis B. (Francis Ballard), *Vissarion Belinskii,* Newtonville: Oriental Research Partners, 1987. □

Belisarius

The Byzantine general Belisarius (ca. 506-565) is one of the great commanders of history. He demonstrated that military skill and discipline could enable small or motley armies to win remarkable victories.

Originally from the Balkans, Belisarius rose to prominence in the imperial bodyguard and was advanced to high military command while still in his 20s. He won outstanding success in the war fought with Persia early in Justinian's reign. He further gained the Emperor's confidence through his loyalty during the Nika riots of 532, during which he commanded the massacre of the rioters. In addition, Belisarius married Antonina, a friend of Empress Theodora. His wife, though unfaithful and often embarrassing to him, had great influence at court, which was valuable when Justinian grew suspicious of him. Although Belisarius seems never to have been disloyal, Justinian was always fearful that so popular a commander might attempt to seize the throne, and he was always receptive to slanders circulated by the general's enemies.

During the first of Justinian's campaigns of reconquest against the Germanic kingdoms in 533, Belisarius led a small force against the Vandals of North Africa. Through two overwhelming victories he destroyed the Vandal regime and recovered North Africa for the empire. For this he was allowed to celebrate a triumph upon his return to Constantinople. In 535 Belisarius was sent to begin the conquest of Italy from the Ostrogoths. Making rapid progress northward from Sicily, he stormed Naples and occupied Rome. The Goths besieged him in Rome during 537-538, but they failed to dislodge him. In 540 the Goths agreed to surrender if Belisarius would become their emperor. He secured their capitulation but then refused the honor, leaving the Goths resentful and fanning Justinian's suspicions.

Recalled in temporary disfavor, he was sent in 541 to command imperial forces in Mesopotamia in renewed war with the Persians.

A new Ostrogothic king, Totila, emerged to undo the Roman occupation of Italy, and Belisarius was returned there in 544. The suspicious and parsimonious emperor refused, however, to give him adequate men and supplies, and Belisarius found it impossible to oppose Totila effectively. When Theodora's death in 548 deprived him of his last strong support at court, he requested recall. The Italian war was left to be finished later, by Narses, while Belisarius was allowed to retire to Constantinople.

Belisarius remained inactive until 559, when an attack by an marauding force of Huns threatened the capital, and the frightened Justinian called him out of retirement. Using his household retinue as a nucleus, he gathered a small force and drove the Huns away. Three years later Belisarius was implicated, probably falsely, in a plot against the Emperor's life. Justinian stripped him of his honors and retinue and kept him in enforced confinement for some time. This disgrace gave rise to the later legend that Justinian actually blinded Belisarius, who was then forced to beg in the streets. Somewhat restored to honor the following year, Belisarius died in March 565, only a few months before the death of Justinian himself.

Further Reading

Belisarius is prominently featured in the historical writings of Procopius, who was for many years his personal secretary.

The most recent book on Belisarius is in French. In English, Lord Mahon, *The Life of Belisarius* (1829), is out of date. His career is, of course, presented fully in all accounts of Justinian's reign. His Italian campaigns are also described in Thomas Hodgkin's classic *Italy and Her Invaders,* vol. 4 (1896). □

Alexander Graham Bell

Scottish-born American inventor and teacher of the deaf, Alexander Graham Bell (1847-1922) is best known for perfecting the telephone to transmit vocal messages by electricity. The telephone inaugurated a new age in communication technology.

Alexander Graham Bell was born on March 3, 1847, in Edinburgh. His father, Alexander Melville Bell, was an expert in vocal physiology and elocution; his grandfather, Alexander Bell, was an elocution professor.

After studying at the University of Edinburgh and University College, London, Bell became his father's assistant. He taught the deaf to talk by adopting his father's system of visible speech (illustrations of speaking positions of the lips and tongue). In London he studied Hermann Ludwig von Helmholtz's experiments with tuning forks and magnets to produce complex sounds. In 1865 Bell made scientific studies of the resonance of the mouth while speaking.

In 1870 the Bells moved to Brantford, Ontario, Canada, to preserve Alexander's health. He went to Boston in 1871 to teach at Sarah Fuller's School for the Deaf, the first such school in the world. He also tutored private students, including Helen Keller. As professor of vocal physiology and speech at Boston University in 1873, he initiated conventions for teachers of the deaf. Throughout his life he continued to educate the deaf, and he founded the American Association to Promote the Teaching of Speech to the Deaf.

From 1873 to 1876 Bell experimented with a phonautograph, a multiple telegraph, and an electric speaking telegraph (the telephone). Funds came from the fathers of two of his pupils; one of these men, Gardiner Hubbard, had a deaf daughter, Mabel, who later became Bell's wife.

Inventing the Telephone

To help deaf children, Bell experimented in the summer of 1874 with a human ear and attached bones, a tympanum, magnets, and smoked glass. He conceived the theory of the telephone: an electric current can be made to change intensity precisely as air density varies during sound production. Unlike the telegraph's use of intermittent current, the telephone requires continuous current with varying intensity. That same year he invented a harmonic telegraph, to transmit several messages simultaneously over one wire, and a telephonic-telegraphic receiver. Trying to reproduce the human voice electrically, he became expert with electric wave transmission.

Alexander Graham Bell (on phone)

Bell supplied the ideas; Thomas Watson made and assembled the equipment. Working with tuned reeds and magnets to synchronize a receiving instrument with a sender, they transmitted a musical note on June 2, 1875. Bell's telephone receiver and transmitter were identical: a thin disk in front of an electromagnet.

On Feb. 14, 1876, Bell's attorney filed for a patent. The exact hour was not recorded, but on that same day Elisha Gray filed his caveat (intention to invent) for a telephone. The U.S. Patent Office granted Bell the patent for the "electric speaking telephone" on March 7. It was the most valuable single patent ever issued, and it opened a new age in communication technology.

Bell continued his experiments to improve the telephone's quality. By accident, Bell sent the first sentence, "Watson, come here; I want you," on March 10, 1876. The first demonstration occurred at the American Academy of Arts and Sciences convention in Boston 2 months later. Bell's display at the Philadelphia Centennial Exposition a month later gained more publicity, and Emperor Dom Pedro of Brazil ordered 100 telephones for his country. The telephone, accorded only 18 words in the official catalog of the exposition, suddenly became the "star" attraction.

Establishing an Industry

Repeated demonstrations overcame public skepticism. The first reciprocal outdoor conversation was between Bos-

ton and Cambridge, Mass., by Bell and Watson on Oct. 9, 1876. In 1877 the first telephone was installed in a private home; a conversation was conducted between Boston and New York, using telegraph lines; in May, the first switchboard, devised by E. T. Holmes in Boston, was a burglar alarm connecting five banks; and in July the first organization to commercialize the invention, the Bell Telephone Company, was formed. That year, while on his honeymoon, Bell introduced the telephone to England and France.

The first commercial switchboard was set up in New Haven, Conn., in 1878, and Bell's first subsidiary, the New England Telephone Company, was organized that year. Switchboards were improved by Charles Scribner, with more than 500 inventions. Thomas Cornish, a Philadelphia electrician, had a switchboard for eight customers and published a one-page directory in 1878.

Contesting Bell's Patent

Other inventors had been at work. Between 1867 and 1873 Professor Elisha Gray (of Oberlin College) invented an "automatic self-adjusting telegraph relay," installed it in hotels, and made telegraph printers and repeaters. He tried to perfect a speaking telephone from his harmonic (multiple-current) telegraph. The Gray and Batton Manufacturing Company of Chicago developed into the Western Electric Company.

Another competitor was Professor Amos E. Dolbear, who insisted that Bell's telephone was only an improvement on an 1860 invention by Johann Reis, a German, who had experimented with pigs' ear membranes and may have made a telephone. Dolbear's own instrument, operating by "make and break" current, could transmit pitch but not voice quality.

In 1879 Western Union, with its American Speaking Telephone Company, ignored Bell's patents and hired Thomas Edison, along with Dolbear and Gray, as inventors and improvers. Later that year Bell and Western Union formed a joint company, with the latter getting 20 percent for providing wires, circuits, and equipment. Theodore Vail, organizer of Bell Telephone Company, consolidated six companies in 1881. The modern transmitter evolved mainly from the work of Emile Berliner and Edison in 1877 and Francis Blake in 1878. Blake's transmitter was later sold to Bell for stock.

The claims of other inventors were contested. Daniel Drawbaugh, from rural Pennsylvania, with little formal schooling, almost won a legal battle with Bell in 1884 but was defeated by a 4 to 3 vote in the Supreme Court. The claim by this "Edison of the Cumberland Valley" was the most exciting (and futile) litigation over telephone patents. Altogether, the Bell Company was involved in 587 lawsuits, of which 5 went to the Supreme Court; Bell won every case. A convincing argument was that no competitor claimed originality until 17 months after Bell's patent. Also, at the 1876 Philadelphia Exposition, eminent electrical scientists, especially Lord Kelvin, the world's foremost authority, had declared it to be "new." Professors, scientists, and researchers defended Bell, pointing to his lifelong study of the ear and his books and lectures on speech mechanics.

The Bell Company

The Bell Company built the first long-distance line in 1884, connecting Boston and New York. The American Telephone and Telegraph Company was organized by Bell and others in 1885 to operate other long-distance lines. By 1889, when insulation was perfected, there were 11,000 miles of underground wires in New York City.

The Volta Laboratory was started by Bell in Washington, D.C., with the Volta Prize money (50,000 francs, about $10,000) awarded by France for his invention. At the laboratory he and associates worked on various projects during the 1880s, including the photophone, induction balance, audiometer, and phonograph improvements. The photophone transmitted speech by light, using a primitive photo-electric cell. The induction balance (electric probe) located metal in the body. The audiometer indicated Bell's continued interest in deafness. The first successful phonograph record, a shellac cylinder, as well as wax disks and cylinders, was produced. The Columbia Gramophone Company exploited Bell's phonograph records. With the profits Bell established the Volta Bureau in Washington to study deafness.

Bell's Later Interests

Other activities took much time. The magazine *Science* (later the official organ of the American Association for the Advancement of Science) was founded in 1880 because of Bell's efforts. He made numerous addresses and published many monographs. As National Geographic Society president from 1896 to 1904, he fostered the success of the society and its publications. In 1898 he became a regent of the Smithsonian Institution. He was also involved in sheep breeding, hydrodynamics, and aviation projects.

Aviation was Bell's primary interest after 1895. He aided Samuel Langley, invented the tetrahedral kite (1903), and founded the Aerial Experiment Association (1907), bringing together Glenn Curtiss, Francis Baldwin, and others. They devised the aileron control principle (which replaced "wing warping"), developed the hydroplane, and solved balance problems in flying machines. Curtiss furnished the motor for Bell's man-carrying kite in 1907.

Bell died at Baddeck, Nova Scotia, on Aug. 2, 1922.

Further Reading

Catherine D. MacKenzie, *Alexander Graham Bell* (1928), is interesting and contains much personal information. Thomas Bertram Costain, *Chord of Steel* (1960), a recent history of the telephone, discusses Bell at length. Herbert Casson, *The History of the Telephone* (1910), is still useful for the early story. See also Arthur Pound, *The Telephone Idea: Fifty Years After* (1926), and Frederick Leland Rhodes, *Beginnings of Telephony* (1929). For the story of Bell's persistent rival see Warren J. Harder, *Daniel Drawbaugh* (1960). □

Andrew Bell

The Scottish educator Andrew Bell (1753-1832) was the developer of the Madras, or mutual instruction, system of education, which enjoyed great vogue in the first 4 decades of the 19th century, especially in schools attended by the poor.

Andrew Bell was born in St. Andrews on March 27, 1753. In 1769 he entered St. Andrews University, where he excelled in mathematics and natural philosophy. After serving from 1774 to 1781 as a private tutor in the Virginia Colony, he returned to Scotland, where he continued tutoring and was ordained a clergyman in the Anglican Church.

Bell sailed for India in 1787. He was appointed superintendent of the Madras Male Orphan Society, where he developed the Madras system, which became his lifework and made him a leading figure in English education.

At the Madras school little progress was being made because neither the teachers nor the pupils showed any interest in learning. One day Bell came upon a local school where the native children were learning the alphabet by writing with their fingers in the sand. Fascinated by both the method and the zest of the children, Bell tried to introduce sand boards into his school, but the teachers resisted. Never easily thwarted, Bell chose an advanced student to teach the

others. This use of students to instruct other students was the heart of the Madras system.

In 1791 Bell returned to London and later published a pamphlet, *An Experiment in Education* (1797), discussing his methods and views of the Madras system. This plan received little public notice until Joseph Lancaster opened a school which was conducted in accordance with Bell's principles but improved upon the system. By the turn of the century the Madras system, also known as the Bell-Lancaster system, had become popularized, and Bell was asked to organize a school system in Dorset. In 1811 he became superintendent of the National Society for Promoting the Education of the Poor in the Principles of the Established Church.

The successful spread of the Madras system was due to a number of factors. It was inexpensive, was relatively efficient, and appeared at a time when interest in social reform, especially the education of poor children, was at a height in England.

Though most famous for the Madras system, Bell was also interested in the abolition of corporal punishment of children, more active learning situations in schools, and other practices far ahead of his time. On Jan. 27, 1832, after a lifetime of service to education, Bell died, and he was buried in Westminster Abbey.

Further Reading

The best biography of Bell is John Miller Dow Meiklejohn, *An Old Educational Reformer: Dr. Andrew Bell* (1881), which contains a discussion of Bell's life, educational system, and influence, as well as brief passages from his published works. *The Life of Reverend Andrew Bell* (3 vols., 1844), is a dry catalog of trivial information; the first volume is by Robert Southey, and the second and third by his son, Charles Cuthbert Southey. Background studies which briefly discuss Bell are John W. Adamson, *English Education, 1789-1902* (1930), and Mary Sturt, *The Education of the People* (1967). □

Daniel Bell

The American sociologist Daniel Bell (born 1919) greatly influenced American political and economic thought through his books *The End of Ideology* and *The Coming of the Post-Industrial Society* .

Born in Brooklyn in 1919 to Jewish immigrant parents, Daniel Bell was raised in New York's Lower East Side. Bell's early childhood was difficult. His father died when he was six months old and Bell's mother worked long hours in a factory to support herself and her son. She was forced to put Bell in a day orphanage. Bell's childhood was spent in a world characterized by poverty and the hopes and frustrations of a Jewish immigrant population drawn largely from Eastern Europe. For a variety of historical and sociological reasons, this population maintained a clear and persistent association with Socialist politics.

At the age of 13 the then Daniel Bolotsky joined the Young People's Socialist League, a youth organization of the Socialist Party. Particular components of this heightened political environment had a powerful effect on Bell's later views about leftist politics. Debates with the militant Young Communist League and the frustration of using non-violent means to advance the cause of American trade unionism in an age of union-busting made Bell sensitive to extremism on both the right and the left. It was the insights born of these experiences that later made Daniel Bell a prominent and astute observer of the American labor movement, first as a staff writer and editor of *The New Leader* and then as labor editor of *Fortune*.

Until he left *Fortune* in 1956, Bell wrote articles about the changing face of the American labor movement. He emphasized the declining role of ideology—specifically Marxism—in the movement. These articles became the working models for his controversial book *The End of Ideology* (1960). Bell's thesis in this book was that Marxism no longer evoked the passions of American intellectuals because it had become irrelevant to the American experience. Marxism emphasized righting the social and economic inequalities produced by capitalism. However, as Bell wrote, in America these inequalities were resolvable through existing political and administrative structures.

The development of these themes—the "exhaustion of the political left" and the irrelevance of ideology in American political thought—occupied Bell throughout his career as an American sociologist and policy analyst. They led him to construct his theory of the postindustrial society, which

was a theory of social change. He identified the United States, Germany, and Japan as societies undergoing major structural changes. The most significant of these changes were the displacement of the traditional market economy, the growing preeminence of the public sector in sponsoring basic scientific research, and a new reliance on stochastic methods and abstract thinking in the planning process.

In *The Coming of the Post-Industrial Society* (1973), Bell characterized this society as an arena in which the working political, cultural, and economic principles were contradictory and in conflict. Politically, there was an emphasis on democracy. Culture was undergoing both de-institutionalization and radicalization. In economics, there was an emphasis on rationalism and efficiency. This view constituted Bell's non-Marxist conflict theory of social change and was the first significant challenge to Talcott Parson's structure-functionalist view of contemporary American society. Bell's theory calls for a new philosophy of welfare state liberalism. Bell called it the philosophy of the "public household."

The Coming of the Post-Industrial Society and the call for a new philosophy of the public household were the fruits of Bell's work as chairman of the Presidential Commission on the Year 2000 (1966-1968). He helped articulate an agenda of social welfare and political problems which challenged the basis of American liberalism. His publications earned him a reputation as something of a futurist. Also cementing his stature as a futurist was his 1976 book *The Cultural Contradictions of Capitalism*. In this work Bell presages such later predominant theories as the relationship of capitalism and culture as modes of production and consumption, post structuralism, deconstruction, and quite accurately as Bell puts it, "The underlying problem.. (of the) ..breakup in the very discourses—the languages, and the ability of a language to express an experience."

Bell's futurism was of a specific kind. His task was to ask the questions which Western society must answer if there is to be domestic peace and stability in the future. Implicit in Bell's asking was the admonition to move slowly; to eschew extremism. This grew out of Bell's early experiences in the American trade union movement and out of his own intellectual struggle to reconcile the "Hellenistic" world view of Karl Marx and John Dewey with the "Hebraism" of Rheinhold Niebuhr. "Hellenism" has faith in the inevitability of social progress through science and reason. The "Hebraic" world view emphasizes the limits of planning and reason in human affairs.

Bell also earned the reputation of being a neoconservative precisely because of his predisposition to move slowly and to be wary of extremism. He shared the neoconservative designation with such peers and colleagues as Daniel Patrick Moynihan, Nathan Glazer, and Irving Kristol. The applicability of such labels is always debatable. What was not debatable was Bell's place in the social sciences. He was a relevant and challenging sociologist whose critical analyses of contemporary economic theory and American capitalism defied simplistic categorization. His self evaluation served well. Bell claimed to be "a liberal in politics, a conservative in culture, and a socialist in economics."

Beginning in 1969, Bell served as Henry Ford Professor of Social Science at Harvard University and in the late 1980s as a Pitt Professor at Cambridge University, England. In 1988 he traveled to the former Soviet Union, a place very close to his heart, to give a series of lectures at various universities. Together with Irving Kristol Bell founded and edited *Public Interest,* a social policy journal.

Further Reading

For information on Bell's earlier career as a journalist, see his autobiographical essay "The Moral Vision of the New Leader" in *New Leader* (December 24, 1973). For further information on Bell's development and on neoconservatism see Irving Kristol's "Memoirs of a Trotskyist" (*New York Times Magazine* (January 23, 1977). For discussions of Bell's theory of postindustrial society and neoconservatism, see Benjamin S. Kleinberg, *American Society in the Post-Industrial Age* (1973); Nathan Liebowitz, *Daniel Bell and the Agony of Modern Liberalism* (1985); and Peter Steinfel's, *The Neoconservatives* (1979). A Bell interview on his historic trip to the former Soviet Union can be found in the journal *Society* (September/October 1989) and an overview of several of Bell's reissued books appears in *The New Leader* (December 16-30, 1996). Bell's own major works are listed above and are joined by his anthology *The Winding Passage: Essays and Sociological Journeys, 1960-1980* (1980). □

Susan Jocelyn Bell Burnell

The radio astronomer Susan Jocelyn Bell Burnell (born 1943) discovered the first pulsar (stars that release regular bursts of radio waves) in 1967.

Susan Jocelyn Bell (Burnell) was born in Belfast, Northern Ireland, on July 15, 1943. Her father was the architect for the Armagh Observatory, which was close to their home. Her early interest in astronomy was encouraged by the observatory staff.

She studied at the Mount School in York, England, from 1956 to 1961. She earned a B.S. in physics at the University of Glasgow in 1965. That same year, she began work on her Ph.D. at Cambridge University. There, under the supervision of Antony Hewish, she constructed and operated a 81.5 megaherz radio telescope. She studied interplanetary scintillation of compact radio sources.

Bell Burnell detected the first four pulsars. The term "pulsar" is an abbreviation of pulsating radio star or of rapidly pulsating radio sources. Pulsars represent rotating neutron stars that emit brilliant flashes of electromagnetic radiation at each revolution, like beacons from a lighthouse. The observation of pulsars requires the use of radio telescopes. In 15 years, about 350 pulsars were found. Their pulse periods range from 33 microseconds to 4 seconds. A "fast" pulsar was discovered in 1982. Its short pulse period equals 1.5 microseconds. According to Joseph H. Taylor, Jr., "it has become clear that hundreds of thousands of pulsars must exist in the Milky Way Galaxy—most of them too distant to be detected with existing radio telescopes.

Discovery of Pulsar

For two years, Bell Burnell constructed the radio telescope which she would begin to operate in July 1967. Each complete coverage of the sky with the radio telescope required four days. Bell Burnell then had to analyze about 400 feet of paper chart. She noted: "We analyzed (actually, we didn't, *I* analyzed) all this chart by hand." The signal of the pulsar occupied about half an inch of the 400 feet of chart.

For the first time in the history of radio astronomy, a large area of the sky had been repeatedly surveyed with an extremely sensitive radio telescope tuned to meter wavelengths. The subsequent discovery of the pulsar, in 1967, ranks as an important milestone in the history of astrophysics. It has been written that "In an earlier age the pulsar would no doubt have been called 'Bell's star'; today it is simply known as CP 1919." "CP" stands for "Cambridge pulsar." The pulsars appeared as an appendix to Bell Burnell's Ph.D. thesis.

In 1947 Sir Martin Ryle and Tony Hewish, from the Cavendish Laboratory in Cambridge, England, were jointly awarded the Nobel Prize in physics, with Hewish honored for the discovery of pulsars. This was the first time the prize was given for work in observational astronomy. The Nobel Prize announcement triggered a public controversy. Sir Fred Hoyle, the eminent British astronomer, argued that Bell Burnell should have shared the Nobel Prize.

Radio Astronomy Work

Bell Burnell held a Science Research Council fellowship from 1968 to 1970 and a junior teaching fellowship from 1970 to 1973 at the University of Southampton. During that time she studied the mid-latitude electron density trough in the topside ionosphere using data from the Alouette satellite, the enhancements of interplanetary scintillation, and their relationship to co-rotating streams in the interplanetary medium and to Forbush decreases. She developed and calibrated a 1-10 million electron volts gamma-ray telescope.

She was employed as a researcher at the Mullard Space Science Laboratory at the University College in London; as a graduate programmer from 1974 to 1976, then as an associate research follow from 1976 to 1982. She analyzed data from a rocket flight to study low energy x-ray emission from galactic features. With the x-ray spectrometer on the Ariel V satellite she observed galactic sources, including transient x-ray sources and binary star systems, globular clusters, active galaxies, and clusters of galaxies.

After 1982 Bell Burnell worked as a senior research fellow at the Royal Observatory in Edinburgh, Scotland. There she made infrared observations of galaxies with active nuclei coordinated with radio, optical, ultraviolet, and x-ray observations. She also observed infrared counterparts of galactic x-ray sources.

Bell Burnell was the editor of *The Observatory* from 1973 to 1976. Elected a fellow of the Royal Astronomical

Society in 1969, she became a council member from 1978 to 1981. She was elected a member of the International Astronomical Union in 1979 and served on the Science and Engineering Research Council, Astronomy I Committee from 1978 to 1984.

Bell Burnell has received numerous awards for her professional contributions. In 1973 she received (jointly with Hewish), the Michelson Medal by the Franklin Institute in Philadelphia. In 1978 she was awarded the J. Robert Oppenheimer Memorial Prize from the Center for Theoretical Studies in Miami. In 1978 she was also given the Rennie Taylor Award by the American Tentative Society in New York. She received the Beatrice M. Tinsley Prize from the American Astronomical Society in 1987 and the Herschel Medal from the Royal Astronomical Society in 1989.

Bell Burnell was married in 1968 and has one son. In 1997 she headed the Physics Department at Open University in the United Kingdom.

Further Reading

A short biography of Bell Burnell appeared in John Daintith et al., *Chambers Biographical Encyclopaedia of Scientists* (1983). The first article on the pulsar, "Observation of a Rapidly Pulsating Radio Source," was published by Antony Hewish, Bell Burnell, J. D. H. Pilkington, P. F. Scott, and R. A. Collins in *Nature* (February 24, 1968). On the discovery of pulsars, see the paper by Bell Burnell, "The Discovery of Pulsars," in *Serendipitous Discoveries in Radio Astronomy*, edited by K. Kellermann and B. Sheets (1984). The chronology of the discovery is discussed by S. W. Woolgar in "Writing an Intellectual History of Scientific Development: The Use of Discovery Accounts" in *Social Studies of Science* (September 1976). The Nobel Prize controversy is detailed in Nicholas Wade, "Discovery of Pulsars: A Graduate Student's Story" (News and Comment) in *Science* (August 1, 1975). On pulsars, see Antony Hewish, "Pulsars" in *Scientific American* (October 1968); A. Hewish "Pulsars and High Density Physics" *Science* (June 13, 1975); Joseph H. Taylor, Jr., "Pulsar," in *McGraw-Hill Encyclopedia of Science and Technology* (1982); Donald Backer and Shrinivas Kulkarni, "Pulsar," in *McGraw-Hill Yearbook of Science and Technology* (1984). Further Information on Bell Burnell can be found in David E. Fisher's *The Origin and Evolution of Our Own Particular Universe's Cosmic Wormholes: The Search for Interstellar Shortcuts* (1992). Information about Bell Burnell's academic career can be accessed on the Internet through the Open University Physics Department's Web site at http://yan.open.ac.uk (July 29, 1997). □

Edward Bellamy

Edward Bellamy (1850-1898) was an American novelist, an economic propagandist, and a social reformer. His memorable achievement is the novel *Looking Backward*.

dward Bellamy was born on March 26, 1850, in Chicopee Falls, Mass. His father, a Baptist minister, and his mother, a minister's daughter, were both descended from 17th-century New England families. In 1867 Bellamy failed to get an appointment to West Point; instead he studied literature for a year at Union College in Schenectady, N.Y. He spent much of the next year in Dresden, Germany, where he observed the prosperity of the state-owned china works. Traveling in England, he was appalled by the misery of the poor victims of what he called "English serfdom." Returning home in 1869, he began to study law in the offices of a Springfield, Mass., firm. He was admitted to the bar in June 1871, opened his own office, took one case, and then completely abandoned the legal profession.

Bellamy accepted an editorial job on the staff of the *New York Evening Post,* and the following summer he returned to Springfield to write book reviews and editorials for the *Springfield Daily Union.* At about the same time he began publishing short stories in magazines. He continued his journalistic career until 1881, but his primary interest had become literature. By 1884 he had published four undistinguished novels. His marriage in 1882 and the birth of his first child in 1884 gave him economic reasons for concentrating his efforts on producing popular fiction, but the two events also gave him, he said, special reasons for working to improve the world in which his children were to live. Both ambitions were splendidly fulfilled when *Looking Backward: 2000-1887* was published in 1888.

In *Looking Backward* a young Bostonian wakes after a hypnotic sleep of 113 years to find himself in the world of the year 2000, from which greed, misery, and war have been extirpated. Private enterprise has been replaced by a benign state capitalism, and the resulting society is a true utopia. Bellamy's characters are thin, but his economic parables are well wrought. The persuasive force of the book became apparent at once through the organization of Bellamy Clubs and through the movement Bellamy called "Nationalist." Speaking tours took much of his time and energy thereafter. From 1891 to 1894 he edited a weekly newspaper, the *New Nation.* Bellamy published *Equality* (1897), a sequel to *Looking Backward,* but it had much less force than his masterpiece. By that time his health was failing rapidly. He went to Denver for treatment of tuberculosis. He returned to Chicopee Falls the next spring and died there on May 22, 1898. A collection of his best short fiction, *The Blindman's World and Other Stories* (1898), was posthumously published with a preface by his longtime admirer William Dean Howells.

Further Reading

Arthur E. Morgan, *Edward Bellamy* (1944), and Sylvia E. Bowman, *The Year 2000: A Critical Biography of Edward Bellamy* (1958), give sympathetic accounts of Bellamy and his writings. Miss Bowman continued her excellent account of Bellamy's influence in *Edward Bellamy Abroad: An American Prophet's Influence* (1962). Edward Bellamy, *Selected Writings on Religion and Society,* edited by Joseph Schiffman (1955), is valuable for the works it presents and for its introduction.

Additional Sources

Bowman, Sylvia E., *The year 2000: a critical biography of Edward Bellamy,* New York: Octagon Books, 1979. ☐

St. Robert Bellarmine

The Italian theologian and Jesuit St. Robert Bellarmine (1542-1621) was a cardinal, an adviser to popes, and a strong defender of the Roman Catholic position in the controversies stemming from the Protestant Reformation.

obert Bellarmine was born on Oct. 4, 1542, in Montepulciano. As a young man of 18, he entered the Jesuits and underwent that group's rigorous intellectual training and discipline. After he was ordained a priest in 1570, he was assigned to teach theology at the University of Louvain, then one of the centers of Roman Catholic defensive scholarship against the Reformation. The young, talented, and religiously sincere Jesuit quickly became known for his effective presentation of Roman Catholic beliefs. He was brought to Rome in 1576 to lecture at the new Jesuit College. He worked there for 12 years to consolidate the Church's theological positions, and out of this research came his most important publication, the three volume *Disputations on the Controversies about the Christian Faith against the Heretics of This Time.*

When Bellarmine was 50, he was made rector of the Jesuit College in Rome. Two years later, in 1594, he was appointed provincial superior of the Jesuits in Naples. Pope Clement VIII brought him back to Rome in 1597 to be his personal theological adviser and 2 years later made him a cardinal. In 1602 he was sent to Capua as archbishop but in 1605 was recalled to Rome, where he spent the rest of his life as a respected papal counselor.

Bellarmine was active in many areas of intellectual life. In 1610 he wrote a book defending the power of the pope. His careful thinking on the natural rights of men had wide influence in political philosophy for the next 200 years. When Galileo's theories of the earth revolving around the sun created a sensation, Bellarmine advised that they be withheld until they could be more solidly proved. It was the 75-year-old cardinal's sad task to tell Galileo later that the Office of the Inquisition had found his theories opposed to the Bible.

During his long career as a theologian and churchman, Bellarmine was consistently highly regarded. He was a man of strong self-control, putting aside his own feelings in the interest of his duty to the Church. He was kind and particularly concerned about the poor. It was discovered at his death in 1621 that he had quietly given away all his money; there was not even enough left to pay for his funeral. In 1930 Robert Bellarmine was cononized a saint of the Roman Catholic Church.

Further Reading

James Brodrick, *Robert Bellarmine: Saint and Scholar* (1961), is a sympathetic, fair treatment and the best biography in English. John C. Rager, *Democracy and Bellarmine* (1926), is a scholarly exploration of Bellarmine's ideas on government and their influence on the American Declaration of Independence. An examination of Bellarmine's philosophy is in E. A. Ryan, *The Historical Scholarship of Saint Bellarmine* (1936). □

Clyde Bellecourt

As one of the original founders of the American Indian Movement (AIM), Clyde Bellecourt (born 1939) has long been an activist for the rights of Native Americans. He was an essential participant in the occupation of both Wounded Knee and a Bureau of Indian Affairs Building in the early 1970s.

Born on the White Earth Reservation in Minnesota in 1939, Clyde Bellecourt was one of the founders of a national activist organization called the American Indian Movement (AIM) and a powerful force in major activist struggles of the early 1970s. AIM was founded by Dennis Banks, George Mitchell, and Bellecourt, all Ojibwa, in 1968. On February 27, 1973, they and other leaders led an armed occupation of Wounded Knee, South Dakota, after Dee Brown's book *Bury My Heart at Wounded Knee* (1971) had established the site as a nationally recognized symbol.

Bellecourt also helped draft twenty demands that were put before the government during the Indian occupation of a Bureau of Indian Affairs building in 1972. Among other things, the protestors demanded a separate government for Indians, the restoration of Indian lands, the renegotiation of all treaties, and a special agency in Washington, D.C., for the reconstruction of Indian communities. While the White House did not meet these demands, the government established a task force to meet with the protest leaders and promised to make no arrests for the occupation.

In December 1993 at an AIM conference, a tribunal was established to investigate charges against Bellecourt and his brother, Vernon. In November of 1994, the tribunal released its verdict: the brothers were found guilty of eight crimes, including collaboration with the U.S. government and drug related activity. As punishment, the two were banned from AIM for life.

Clyde and Vernon—key members of the National American Indian Movement, Inc. of Minneapolis, Minnesota—responded by calling the charges "ridiculous" and "slanderous." They named Russell Means, Ward Churchill, and Glen Morris as instigating the matter after the Bellecourt brothers signed an open letter that expelled Churchill and Morris from National AIM.

Bellecourt remains active in promoting the rights and culture of Native Americans. He is the current director of the

Peacemaker Center for Indian Youth, organizer of the National Coalition on Racism in Sports and the Media, and chairman of the Board of American Indian OIC.

Further Reading

More information on Bellecourt can be found in Peter Mathiessen, *In the Spirit of Crazy Horse* (Penguin, 1983) and *Native American Testimony: A Chronicle of Indian-White Relations from Prophecy to the Present, 1492-1992,* edited by Peter Nabakov (Penguin, 1992). □

Giovanni Bellini

The Italian painter Giovanni Bellini (ca. 1435-1516) introduced the Renaissance style to his native Venice. His importance can scarcely be overemphasized in that he brought Venetian painting up to date and set it on the path that led to the art of Titian.

Giovanni Bellini was the youngest member of an important artistic family. His father, Jacopo, was a painter who had been apprenticed to Gentile da Fabriano, the leading Italian painter of the International Gothic style. Jacopo is best remembered today for his sketchbooks, which he passed on to his artist sons, Gentile and Giovanni. Niccolosa, Jacopo's daughter and eldest child, married Andrea Mantegna in 1453; this marriage brought into the Bellini family one of the most important painters in 15th-century Italy. Gentile, as eldest son, assumed direction of his father's studio and enjoyed widespread fame as one of Venice's leading painters. It was he, for instance, who was sent to Constantinople to answer Sultan Mohammed II's summons for a painter.

Giovanni, probably born about 1435, has sometimes been thought to have been illegitimate, a notion that stems from the omission of his name from his mother's will. This viewpoint is not widely held today. Little is known of Giovanni's early years. His name first appears in a document of 1459. He was married to Ginevra Bocheta, and they had at least one child, a son, Alvise.

After 1470 there are numerous documents relating to Giovanni's activities. One record of 1483 mentions that he was named *pittore del dominio* (painter of the domain), probably in recognition for his work in the Doge's Palace. Other documents relate specifically to his commissions. A letter dated Nov. 29, 1516, mentions that the death of Giovanni Bellini was revealed that day.

Artistic Heritage

Giovanni's artistic heritage extended beyond the limits of his family. He seems to have derived little from his father's art beyond occasional motifs. Giovanni collaborated with Gentile on some projects but was relatively little influenced by his brother's style. In 1460 Giovanni was working in Padua, perhaps with Mantegna, who unquestionably exerted a strong influence on him. In Giovanni's

early works, such as the *Agony in the Garden* and the *Transfiguration,* there are direct parallels with Mantegna's art, especially in the severely foreshortened figures and the evocative rocky landscapes. Giovanni's presence in Padua, furthermore, would explain the marked influence of Donatello, which can be detected in his early work. Donatello had been in Padua to model the monumental equestrian statue of Gattamelata and to erect the sculptured high altar for the church of S. Antonio. Similarities can be recognized between Giovanni's *Pietà* in Venice and his masterful *Pietà* in Milan and Donatello's relief of the Dead Christ on the altar in S. Antonio. Moreover, Giovanni's type for the Christ Child would seem to owe something to Donatello's putti.

There is evidence that Giovanni traveled at least as far south as Pesaro on the Adriatic Sea. The impressive altarpiece *Coronation of the Virgin* (1469) would support such a trip. It is possible that there Giovanni may have met Piero della Francesca, who was working in nearby Urbino. He would certainly have seen Piero's work in Rimini and Ferrara, way-stops on the road between Venice and Pesaro. Piero's synthesis of form with color and light anticipated Giovanni's work in the same direction.

Of the profoundest significance in the development of Giovanni's style was the appearance of Antonello da Messina in Venice in 1475-1476. Antonello had mastered the oil-paint technique perfected earlier in the century in Flanders. Antonello's major work in Venice, the altarpiece (now dismembered) for the church of S. Cassiano, may be seen as a forerunner of Giovanni's impressive altarpieces.

Bellini's Mature Style

The altarpiece for the church of S. Giobbe (ca. 1490; now in the Academy, Venice) is a good introduction to Giovanni's fully developed Renaissance style. The Madonna Enthroned is posed on a dais before an apse. At her feet are music-playing angels; on either side are saints arranged in the familiar *sacra conversazione* manner. The figures exist by virtue of colored light, which fills the painting with an atmosphere that is nearly palpable. Heroic in scale, the S. Giobbe altarpiece established an ideal that was to inspire Venetian painters down to Titian. Other major altarpieces include the *Madonna with Saints* for S. Maria dei Frari, Venice (1488); the altarpiece for S. Pietro Martire, Murano (1488); the *Baptism of Christ* in Sta Corona, Vicenza (ca. 1500); the *Ascension of the Virgin* in S. Pietro Martire, Murano (ca. 1501-1504); the altarpiece in S. Zaccaria, Venice (1504-1505); and the altarpiece in S. Giovanni Crisostomo, Venice (1513).

Giovanni painted numerous Madonna and Child pictures. Most, like the *Madonna of the Trees* (1478), depict the half-length Madonna supporting the Child on a balustrade across the foreground, with a fabric hanging just behind her head. Sometimes, as in this example, slivers of landscape are seen on either side of the fabric hanging.

Like all Venetian painters, Giovanni executed portrait commissions. Among the finest are the glowing portrait of the doge Leonardo Loredan and the so-called *Condottiere.*

Noteworthy pictures of saints include *St. Francis* (ca. 1478) and the panels *St. Jerome Reading* in Florence, Lon-

don, and Washington, D. C. The panoramic *St. Mark Preaching in Alexandria* was begun by Gentile and completed by Giovanni after Gentile's death in 1507. The *Martyrdom of St. Mark* was begun by Giovanni in 1515 and finished after his death by Vittore Belliniano, his pupil.

Giovanni also painted a few nonreligious pictures. The *Allegory* (ca. 1500) is significant for its beautiful landscape and quiet air. The group of five small allegories in the Academy, Venice, may have adorned a mirror frame. The masterpiece among Giovanni's secular works is the *Feast of the Gods* (1514); after Bellini's death Titian repainted portions of the landscape background. The *Feast of the Gods* creates a calm, rather pastoral mood compared with the more lusty pagan expressions of the same theme painted by Titian.

Bellini painted literally hundreds of works; more than 300 survive. With them he brought Venetian painting abreast of the more progressive work being done in Rome.

Further Reading

Philip Hendy and Ludwig Goldscheider's monograph, *Giovanni Bellini* (1945), is useful. See also Rodolfo Pallucchini, *Giovanni Bellini* (1959; trans. 1963). For general background see Cecil Gould, *An Introduction to Italian Renaissance Painting* (1957), and Frederick Hartt, *History of Italian Renaissance* (1970). □

Vincenzo Bellini

The operas of the Italian composer Vincenzo Bellini (1801-1835) form a link between the Italian tradition of the early 19th century and the late 19th century.

Vincenzo Bellini was born in Catania, Sicily. His father, Rosario, and grandfather, Vincenzo, held positions with the Biscari family and in local churches. Although both composed, none of their music is extant. Bellini displayed musical talent very early, learning to play piano at 3 and studying composition with his father at 6. His earliest works, written before he was 11 years old, have not been preserved. After studying with his grandfather, Bellini attended the Royal College of St. Sebastian in Naples, which was directed by Nicola Zingarelli, who composed both opera and church music. As important as the more conservative tradition of Zingarelli in Naples was that of the contemporary operatic scene, then dominated by Gioacchino Rossini.

Bellini's first opera, *Adelson e Salvini,* was performed at the Conservatory in 1825 and led to a commission from the impresario of the Teatro San Carlo in Naples for *Bianca e Fernando.* Between 1825 and 1835 Bellini composed 10 operas for Naples, Milan, Genoa, Parma, Venice, and Paris; all but two had some success. After the presentation of *La Sonnambula* in 1830, his European success was assured. Bellini was fortunate in having the services of one of the better librettists in Italy, Felice Romani, who, after 1827,

Additional Sources

Adamo, Maria Rosaria, *Vincenzo Bellini,* Torino: ERI, 1981.
Brunel, Pierre, *Vincenzo Bellini,* Paris: Fayard, 1981.
Rosselli, John, *The life of Bellini,* Cambridge, England; New York: Cambridge University Press, 1996.
Tintori, Giampiero, *Bellini,* Milano: Rusconi, 1983. ☐

Alhaji Sir Ahmadu Bello

The Nigerian political leader Alhaji Sir Ahmadu Bello (1909-1966) was the leading Northern spokesman during Nigeria's drive to gain independence from the British.

Ahmadu Bello was born in Rabah, North West State, a descendant of Uthman don Fodio, the renowned 19th-century Moslem leader of Northern Nigeria. Bello received his education first at the Sokoto Provincial School, then at Katsina Teacher Training College. In 1934, after teaching several years in the Sokoto Middle School, he entered the emirate administration as district head of Rabah. In 1938 he made an unsuccessful claim to the office of sultan of Sokoto. The new sultan immediately conferred upon him the traditional, now honorary, title of *sardauna* and elevated him to the Sokoto Native Authority Council.

As World War II drew to an end, Bello became involved in broader political concerns. In 1945 he assisted in the formation of the Youth Social Circle in Sokoto, a discussion group of Northern educators and civil servants. In 1948 this organization affiliated with the newly founded Northern People's Congress (NPC), originally conceived as a cultural organization but destined to become the leading political party in Northern Nigeria. Bello became increasingly active in the NPC and ultimately its president. In 1949 he was elected by the Sokoto Native Authority to the Northern House of Assembly. During the 1949-1950 discussions of constitutional reform he became a leading spokesperson for the Northern view of federal government. In 1952 in the first elections held in Northern Nigeria, he was elected to the Northern House of Assembly, where he became a member of the regional executive council and minister of works. In the following year he accepted the regional portfolio of community development and local government. In 1954 he became the first premier of Northern Nigeria, a position he held until his death.

As president of the NPC and premier of the Northern Region, Bello was perhaps the most politically powerful person in Nigeria during the first 5 years of independence. Despite this, his role in national politics remained anomalous. He had an expressed distaste for the Southern style of politics and had no desire for participation in the federal government, which would require his residence in Lagos. Although he participated in national discussions on constitutional reform and from 1952 to 1959 was a member of the Federal House of Representatives, he was concerned primarily with the development of the North and the protec-

wrote the librettos for all of his operas except the last, *I Puritani.* Bellini's mature operas were opere serie of varying types. His three masterpieces are *I Capuleti ed i Montecchi, La Sonnambula,* and *Norma. I Puritani,* written somewhat in the manner of French grand opera, suffers from a weak libretto. Bellini also composed at least 28 sacred vocal works, 23 secular vocal works, 7 symphonies, and an oboe concerto.

Although Bellini made no significant changes in the outward structure of Italian opera, he did make certain contributions. His melodic style, often compared to that of Frédéric Chopin in its careful treatment of ornamentation, was written with the Italian *bel canto* style of singing in mind. Passages that seem uninteresting on paper come to life in performance by a gifted singer. In his recitatives Bellini gave careful consideration to text accents and moments of intense emotional expression. His handling of the orchestra in both recitative and aria always supports the dramatic intention. He gave the chorus an important role in the drama, instead of the perfunctory one then common. His influence was felt not only by his contempories but also by Giuseppe Verdi. Even that bitter critic of Italian opera, Richard Wagner, was impressed by *Norma.*

Further Reading

A full-length biography is Leslie Orrey, *Bellini* (1969). Bellini's relationship to other composers of his period is discussed in Alfred Einstein, *Music in the Romantic Era* (1947), and Donald J. Grout, *A Short History of Opera* (2 vols., 1947; 2d ed., 1 vol., 1965).

tion of that region from what he considered Southern incursions. Therefore, when Nigeria became independent in 1960, Bello chose to remain premier of the Northern Region, while the deputy president of the NPC, Alhaji Sir Abubakar Tafawa Balewa, became prime minister of the Federation.

In 1964 Bello led the NPC into an alliance with the Nigerian National Democratic Party (NNDP) of the Western Region. The coalition party, called the Nigerian National Alliance, won a clear majority in the federal elections of 1964. In the fall of 1965 the NNDP claimed victory in a hotly disputed regional election, and the Western Region lapsed into chaos. Bello's attempt to support his political allies on this occasion was the immediate, though not sole, cause for an attempted coup d'etat in January 1966, during which Bello was assassinated.

Further Reading

The only book that deals specifically with Bello's life is his autobiography, *My Life* (1962). Although this is not an objective account, it is excellent in revealing Bello's view of his role in Nigerian political development. A discussion of the Northern People's Congress and Bello's role in it may be found in Richard Sklar, *Nigerian Political Parties: Power in an Emergent African Nation* (1963).

Additional Sources

Sir Ahmadu Bello: a legacy, Jos: ITF Printing Press, 1992.
Paden, John N., *Ahmadu Bello, Sardauna of Sokoto: values and leadership in Nigeria,* London: Hodder and Stoughton; Ports-

mouth, N.H.: Distributed in the U.S.A. by Heinemann Educational Books, 1986. ☐

Andrés Bello y López

The Venezuelan humanist Andrés Bello y López (1781-1865) is generally considered to be the most complete intellectual of 19th-century Latin America.

Andrés Bello was born on Nov. 29, 1781, in Caracas into a middle-class Creole family. His early education was entrusted to Cristobal de Quesada, a Mercedarian friar, then reputedly the greatest Latinist in Venezuela, who instilled in him a great love for the Latin and Spanish classics and the Spanish-Italian school of the 19th century. They were to exercise a lifelong literary influence on him.

In 1797 he entered the University of Caracas, receiving a bachelor of arts degree in 1800. He then studied law and medicine there. To augment his income, he tutored his friends, the most outstanding of whom was Simón Bolívar, the future liberator of South America. Bello's financial situation, always precarious, apparently worsened, and he abandoned his studies in 1802 to enter government service.

In addition to his administrative responsibilities, Bello wrote numerous poems, several in imitation of Virgil and Horace, all mediocre. He also edited the first newspaper published in Venezuela, the *Gazeta de Caracas* (1808), and wrote the first book published in the captaincy general, *Calendario manual y guía universal* (1810). At the same time he was involved in the revolutionary movement which was sweeping the country. When a provisional government was established in 1810, he was sent to London as part of a diplomatic mission headed by Bolívar. Bello remained in the British capital until 1829, serving as secretary to the Venezuelan, Chilean, and Colombian legations in turn.

Life in London was not pleasant, and Bello was frequently unemployed. Nevertheless, he collaborated with José María Blanco White in the publication of a magazine (*El Español,* 1810-1814) and with Antonio José de Irisarri in a similar enterprise (*El Censor americano*). Finally, he edited the *Biblioteca americana* (1823) and *Repertorio americano* (1826-1827). When he was offered a position in the Chilean government, he accepted, and with his second English wife and five children he departed England in 1829, to live the rest of his life in his adopted country.

In Chile, Bello was involved in nearly all aspects of the life. He was editor of the official government newspaper (*El Araucano,* 1830-1853); a senator (1837-1864); chief administrative officer of the Ministry of Foreign Relations (1829-1852); and the founder and rector of the University of Chile (1842-1865). He also helped write the Constitution of 1833 and wrote all the major presidential speeches from 1831 to 1833. His position as confidential adviser to presidents and government ministers gave him tremendous influence in Chilean politics.

Bello's influence was also great in Chilean cultural and social life. His Spanish grammar is perhaps the greatest ever produced. His civil law code is still in effect in Chile, with modifications, and it was adopted by many other Latin American countries. His works on philosophy are esteemed, and his book on international law was acclaimed a classic. He died in Santiago, Chile on Oct. 15, 1865.

Further Reading

There is no biography of Bello in English. Works which discuss him include Alva Curtis Wilgus, ed., *Argentina, Brazil and Chile since Independence* (1935); Robert N. Burr, *By Reason or Force: Chile and the Balancing of Power in South America, 1830-1905* (1967); and Simon Collier, *Ideas and Politics of Chilean Independence, 1808-1833* (1967). □

Joseph Hilaire Pierre Belloc

The French-born English writer Joseph Hilaire Pierre Belloc (1870-1953) was a noted poet, historian, essayist, and novelist. Throughout his literary career he was concerned with the problems of social reform.

Hilaire Belloc was born in Saint-Cloud, France, on July 27, 1870. He was the son of Louis Belloc, a French lawyer, and Bessie Raynor Parkes, his English wife. Political disorder sent the family to England later that year, and Hilaire was educated at the Oratory School in Birmingham. As a boy, he was a precocious poet, artist, and mathematician. He graduated from Balliol College, Oxford, where he had won a scholarship in history.

Belloc began his literary career with *Verses and sonnets* (1895). In 1896 he married the American Elodie Hogan, and they had three children. That same year he published *The Bad Child's Book of Beasts,* which, together with *Cautionary Tales and More Beasts for Worse Children,* formed a collection destined to become a classic. In 1899 Belloc began a series of biographies, which included two French revolutionaries (*Danton,,* 1899, and *Robespierre,* 1901) and many eminent literary and political figures of France and England. In 1902 he published *Path to Rome,* which is perhaps his most characteristic work in that it reveals his love of travel, gentle humor, and staunch Roman Catholicism.

During these years Belloc also became very active in political life. He became a British citizen in 1902, and in 1906 he was elected to Parliament. In 1910 he abandoned political office for journalism, which he felt was a more effective means of achieving reform. He joined with Cecil Chesterton in writing articles attacking imperialism and corruption in political life. In 1912 Belloc published *The Servile State,* which outlined his antisocialist and anticapitalist philosophy of distributism. His views were shared by G. K. Chesterton, and they founded the political weekly *New Witness* to press forward the fight for reform.

In the following years Belloc continued to publish prolifically. In 1942 he suffered a stroke, and though he wrote magazine articles occasionally, he published no more books. He died in 1953 from accidental burns.

Further Reading

A volume of Belloc's letters, *Letters from Hilaire Belloc,* selected and edited by Robert Speaight (1958), is helpful. The definitive biography of Belloc is Robert Speaight, *The Life of Hilaire Belloc* (1957). Two books by Belloc's sister throw light on his development during his early French years: Mrs. Belloc Lowndes, *"I, Too, Have Lived in Arcadia": A Record of Love and of Childhood* (1941) and *The Young Hilaire Belloc* (1956). A short but useful summary is Reneée Haynes, *Hilaire Belloc* (1953). Full-length studies since J. B. Morton, *Hilaire Belloc: A Memoir* (1955), are few. □

Saul Bellow

An American author of fiction, essays, and drama, Saul Bellow (born 1915) reached the first rank of contemporary fiction with his picaresque novel *The Adventures of Augie March.*

Saul Bellow, born of Russian immigrant parents in Lachine, Quebec, on July 10, 1915, grew up in Montreal, where he learned Hebrew, Yiddish, and French as well as English. When he was nine his family moved to Chicago, and to this city Bellow remained deeply devoted. After two years at the University of Chicago, Bellow transferred to Northwestern University and obtained a bachelor of science degree in 1937. Four months after enrolling as a graduate student at the University of Wisconsin, he fled formal education forever.

During the next decade Bellow held a variety of jobs—with the WPA Writers Project, the editorial department of the *Encyclopaedia Britannica,* the Pestalozzi-Froebel Teachers College, and the Merchant Marine. More importantly, he published two novels, both with autobiographical overtones. *Dangling Man* (1944), in the form of a journal, concerns a young Chicagoan waiting to be drafted into military service. *The Victim* (1947), a more ambitious work, describes the frustrations of a New Yorker seeking to discover and preserve his own identity against the background of domestic and religious (Gentile versus Jewish) conflicts. Neither novel was heralded as exceptional by contemporary critics.

After World War II Bellow joined the University of Minnesota English Department, spent a year in Paris and Rome as a Guggenheim fellow, and taught briefly at New York University, Princeton University, and Bard College. Above all, however, he concentrated on writing fiction. With the publication of *The Adventures of Augie March* (1953), Bellow won his first National Book Award. A

lengthy, free-form liberating story of a young Chicago Jew growing up absurd, *Augie March* combines comic zest and a narrative virtuosity rare in any decade. Bellow followed it in 1956 with *Seize the Day,* which is a collection of three short stories, a one-act play, and the novella that gives the title to the volume—a tautly written description of one day in the life of a middle-aged New Yorker facing a major domestic crisis. Some critics feel that Bellow never surpassed this novella.

Devotees of *Henderson the Rain King* (1959) enjoyed Bellow's return to a more free-flowing manner in describing an American millionaire's search to understand the human condition in his flight from a tangled marital arrangement and his adventures in Africa. His next novel, *Herzog* (1964), won him a second National Book Award and an international reputation. Doubtlessly based on personal sources, it portrays Moses Herzog, a middle-aged university professor, and his battles with his faithless wife Madeline, his friend Valentine Gersbach, and his own alienated self. Through a series of unposted letters, many of them highly comic, Herzog finally resolves his struggles, not in marital reconciliation but in rational acceptance and self-control.

In 1962 Bellow became a professor at the University of Chicago, a post which allowed him to continue writing fiction and plays. *The Last Analysis* had a brief run on Broadway in 1964. Six short stories, collected in *Mosby's Memoirs and Other Stories* (1968), and his sixth novel, *Mr. Sammler's Planet* (1969), elevated Bellow's reputation to the point where one critic wrote that if Bellow was not the most important American novelist, then whoever was had better announce himself quickly. Some critics called him the successor of Ernest Hemingway and William Faulkner.

Humboldt's Gift (1975) added the Pulitzer Prize and the Nobel Prize for Literature to Bellow's list of awards and led Frank McConnell to observe that his books "form a consistent, carefully nurtured *oeuvre* not often encountered in the works of American writers." In her glowing review of his short story collection, *Him with His Foot in His Mouth and Other Stories* (1984), Cynthia Ozick declared: "these five ravishing stories honor and augment his genius."

Bellow's later novels have not received the same unequivocal praise. *The Dean's December* (1982) and *More Die of Heartbreak* (1987) retained his distinctive style but some believed the cynicism of the characters signaled a lessening of Bellow's own trademark humanism.

Since 1987, Bellow has released a number of novellas: *A Theft* (1989), *The Bellarosa Connection* (1989), *Something to Remember Me By* (1991), and *The Actual* (1997). These works have met with similarly mixed reviews.

Despite the recent coolness towards his work, Bellow's place in American literature seems secure, most notably for his ability to combine social commentary with sharply drawn characters. His best fiction has been compared to the Russian masters, Tolstoy and Dostoevsky.

Robert Penn Warren's review of *Augie March* in *The New Republic* in 1953 seems to sum up subsequent reaction to his work: "It is, in a way, a tribute, though a backhanded one, to point out the faults of Saul Bellow's novel, for the faults merely make the virtues more impressive."

Further Reading

Full-length studies of Saul Bellow include Keith Michael Opdahl, *The Novels of Saul Bellow: An Introduction* (1967); John Jacob Clayton, *Saul Bellow: In Defense of Man* (1968); and Irving Malin, *Saul Bellow's Fiction* (1969). Useful introductory essays are Tony Tanner, *Saul Bellow* (1965); Earl Rovit, *Saul Bellow* (1967); and Robert Detweiler, *Saul Bellow: A Critical Essay* (1967). Irving Malin edited a collection of 12 essays, *Saul Bellow and the Critics* (1967). Another essay collection, edited by Harold Bloom, is *Saul Bellow* (1986). □

George Wesley Bellows

George Wesley Bellows (1882-1925) was a prolific and accomplished leader among American painters who approached representation of the American scene realistically.

George Bellows was born in Columbus, Ohio, on Aug. 19, 1882. At Ohio State University (1901-1904) he distinguished himself as an athlete, but he determined that he wanted to be an artist and went to New York City in 1904 without graduating. For a time he supported himself as a professional athlete. He studied at the New York School of Art under Robert Henri, who became an influential and lifelong friend.

Bellow's early paintings are swift and vivid character studies, of somber tonality. His development was very rapid, and from 1906 on his works were accepted in national exhibitions. He was fascinated with the spectacle of the great city: its buildings, crowds, types, and rivers. Though he was denounced by conservative critics as one of the "apostles of ugliness," his technical brilliance made him more acceptable than any of the other painters of similar impulse. He became an associate of the National Academy of Design at the age of 27, the youngest person ever so honored, and was elected a full academician 4 years later. His work is marked by exuberance, variety of subject matter, humor, and vitality, always depicted with gusto.

In 1907 Bellows produced the first of several paintings of prizefighters in action in the ring; these expressed violent action with power and seeming spontaneity. He married in 1910, rebuilt an old house on 19th Street, and started his teaching career at the Art Students League. He was a teacher of the Henri variety—bringing out the individuality of each student with excitement and imagination. He spent several summers in Maine, where he painted windswept landscapes and sea scenes. In the summer of 1912 Bellows visited California and New Mexico—his only excursion to the Far West. He never went to Europe.

Bellows was well represented in the important Armory Show of 1913. The new European movements exhibited there may have had an unsettling influence on him, as they did on many progressive American painters who discovered that their innovations had been in subject matter rather than in method or form. In 1916 Bellows turned to lithography (at this time seldom used by serious artists) because its immediacy attracted him, His nearly 200 lithographs deal with a wide variety of subjects—genre scenes, nudes, portraits, landscapes, literary illustrations, and humorous or satiric commentaries. He was deeply and emotionally affected by World War I and recorded his reactions in a series of powerful and painful prints that have been compared with those of Goya. In 1918 he became interested in Jay Hambidge's theory of dynamic symmetry, which provided a geometric system of composition for controlling the artist's work. Hambidge (and Bellows) believed it was followed by many of the great artists of antiquity.

Bellows taught at the Chicago Art Institute in 1919; his sojourn there was remembered as a whirlwind of enthusiasm and activity. His illustrations for novels by Don Byrne and H. G. Wells (1921-1923) are rich in action, characterization, and imagination. Bellows's finest late works are undoubtedly the portraits of his wife, two small daughters, mother, and aunt. Brilliantly painted, with solid structural design and probing characterization, they are among the triumphs of American realism, legitimate successors to the best works of Thomas Eakins. Less successful are some of the late landscapes, which tend to be mannered in style and lurid in color, and the large *Crucifixion,* his only religious work.

A neglected attack of appendicitis caused Bellows's death on Jan. 8, 1925, in New York.

Further Reading

Charles H. Morgan, *George Bellows: Painter of America* (1965), is an excellent study both as biography and criticism, though lacking in documentation. Bellows's widow, Emma S. Bellows, compiled two volumes of reproductions soon after his death: *George Bellows: His Lithographs* (1928) and *The Paintings of George Bellows* (1929). See also George W. Eggers, *George Bellows* (1931), and Peyton Boswell, Jr., *George Bellows* (1942). The catalogs of the retrospective exhibitions at the Metropolitan Museum, New York (1925), the Whitney Museum, New York (1931), the Art Institute of Chicago (1946), and the National Gallery, Washington, D.C. (1957), contain valuable material.

Additional Sources

Morgan, Charles Hill, *George Bellows, painter of America,* Millwood, N.Y.: Kraus Reprint Co., 1979. □

Henry Whitney Bellows

Henry Whitney Bellows (1814-1882) was an American Unitarian minister and the founder of the U.S. Sanitary Commission during the Civil War.

enry Bellows was born in Boston on June 11, 1814, the son of a wealthy merchant. He attended the progressive Round Hill School, which was run by the historian George Bancroft. Bellows was an outstanding student at Harvard College, graduating in 1832. Meanwhile, his father had lost his fortune, and Bellows, seeking work, taught school at Cooperstown, N.Y., then became a tutor to rich Louisianians. He returned north to enter the Harvard Divinity School. He accepted a pastorate in Mobile, Ala., but left because of distaste for slavery. His next charge was the First Unitarian Church (later All-Souls) in New York City, and though he was only 24 years old, he was instantly successful as a minister and in civic affairs.

Bellows had great energy, fluent and clear expression, and a desire to mediate rather than confound. Though he was no scholar, he kept abreast of social and theological controversies and reached solutions intended to serve all partisans. A good family man and a sincere friend, he helped establish several of the city's most famous clubs, including the Century and Harvard clubs. In 1847 he began publishing the *Christian Inquirer* (later the *Boston Christian Register*). During the 1850s he spent time and money freely to help Antioch College in Ohio. Typical of his conciliatory approach was his lecture in 1857, "The Relation of Public Amusements to Public Morality," in which, in an era that readily accepted the view that the theater was evil, he justified its positive values.

The Civil War found the U.S. War Department ill-equipped to meet the unprecedented needs of its soldiers and unprepared to use properly the services of the numer-ous women who were eager to help. Low morale and the danger of epidemics threatened the armed forces. Women's aid committees were unorganized and frustrated. Bellows led a party of citizens to Washington to win the sanction and cooperation of the government in the creation of the U.S. Sanitary Commission, a national organization to supervise nurse, supplies, and personal services in camps and on the battlefields. Bellows's eloquent appeals to individuals and communities brought millions of dollars to the Commission, and his leadership gave authority to its work, making it inseparable from the military effort. Reports of the Commission's achievements affected developments abroad, notably in the operations of the International Red Cross.

Following the war Bellows continued to exercise his abilities as an editor, an organizer (for example, of the National Conference of Unitarian Churches), and a civil service advocate. His visit to Europe in 1867-1868 resulted in his two-volume *The Old World in Its New Face* (1868). He died in 1882.

Further Reading

Bellows rated kindly estimates rather than formal biographies, for example, J. W. Chadwick, *Henry W. Bellows, His Life and Character: A Sermon* (1882). For his major achievements see Charles J. Stillé, *History of the United States Sanitary Commission* (1886), and William Q. Maxwell, *Lincoln's Fifth Wheel: A Political History of the United States Sanitary Commission* (1956). Conrad Wright, *The Liberal Christians: Essays on American Unitarian History* (1970), includes a chapter on Bellows's church work after the Civil War. Clinton Lee Scott, *These Live Tomorrow: Twenty Unitarian Universalist Biographies* (1964), contains a detailed though uncritical biography. See also Francis Phelps Weisenburger, *Ordeal of Faith: The Crisis of Church-going America, 1865-1900* (1959).

Additional Sources

Kring, Walter Donald, *Henry Whitney Bellows,* Boston: Skinner House, 1979. □

Pietro Bembo

The Italian humanist, poet, and historian Pietro Bembo (1470-1547) was the most influential man of letters during the High Renaissance in Italy.

ietro Bembo was born in Venice. His learned father, Bernardo, was prominent in civic and diplomatic affairs, and Pietro benefited from residence and education in Florence, Venice, Padua, and Messina. In Florence he knew Lorenzo il Magnifico, the most famous of the Medici ruler-patrons. Bembo soon gained remarkable prestige in literary matters because of his vast classical culture and his ability to write fine Tuscan prose and poetry. He also served as secretary to popes Leo X, Hadrian VI, and Clement VII.

In 1530 his native city appointed Bembo historian of the Republic of Venice and head of the famous library which was later called the Marciana. Pursuing an ecclesiastical career and fearing to lose lucrative benefices, he refrained from marrying and thus failed to legitimize his three sons, born of a Roman woman. In 1539 Pope Paul III made him a cardinal, and until his death in 1547 Bembo was considered a likely candidate for the papacy.

Subsequent generations of critics have considered Bembo's literary talents to be rather modest, yet his influence during his lifetime was immense. An accomplished Latinist, he nevertheless encouraged literary use of the vernacular, which he insisted should be Tuscan rather than any other dialect, and his *Gli Asolani* (1505) was the first prose work written in Tuscan by a non-Tuscan author. This work influenced many subsequent authors of love treatises by the predominantly literary way in which it dealt with philosophical questions about love. Many of Bembo's concepts were based on Marsilio Ficino's *Commentary* (1469) on Plato's *Symposium,* and Bembo continued Ficino's tendency to Christianize Plato's theory of love.

Ostensibly, *Asolani* teaches its readers "not to err," since "not to love" is impossible. In the first of the three dialogues the character Perottino expounds the untoward results of love. In the second dialogue Gismondo exalts love indiscriminately. In the final dialogue Lavinello states that to love well one must follow reason, not the senses. Petrarchan *canzoni* (odes) adorn the dialogues.

The *Prose della volgar lingua* (1525; Prose in the Vernacular), in which Bembo again employed the dialogue form, is perhaps the earliest Italian grammar. It is a pivotal document in the centuries-long polemic about the Italian language (the *questione della lingua*), in that it strongly affirms the Florentine character of the national language. Bembo's history of Venice from 1487 to 1513 was published posthumously in 1553.

Further Reading

Ernest Hatch Wilkins, *A History of Italian Literature* (1954), contains material on Bembo. See also Francesco de Sanctis, *History of Italian Literature* (2 vols., 1870; new ed. 1914; trans. 1931), and Richard Garnett, *A History of Italian Literature* (1898). ☐

Sebastián de Benalcázar

The Spanish conquistador Sebastián de Benalcázar (died 1551) conquered large areas of Colombia and founded several cities in South America.

Sebastián de Moyano, the original name of Benalcázar, was probably born at Belalcázar in Estremadura, Spain. The year is sometimes given as 1495, but his own statement that he reached Santo Domingo (Hispaniola), in 1507, presumably as an adult, points to a considerably earlier birth date. Of poor parents, and originally a manual laborer, he adopted the name of his birthplace.

Benalcázar is known to have been at Nombre de Diós on the Isthmus of Panama in 1511, and he probably served with the explorer Vasco Núñez de Balboa. Under Pedrarias he went to Central America and took part in the founding of León, Nicaragua. On returning to Panama, he joined Francisco Pizarro and Diego de Almagro for the Inca conquest in Peru. From Cajamarca, Pizarro sent Benalcázar to govern the recently founded Spanish settlement of San Miguel de Piura in northern Peru. On the way Benalcázar received exaggerated reports of the wealth of Quito, Inca Atahualpa's original seat of power, and went there instead. He defeated the Quitan general Rumiñaui and entered the city, which he found disappointing as to riches. In 1534 Pizarro appointed Benalcázar governor of Quito, and the following year Benalcázar founded Guayaquil on the coast, a city soon abandoned and to be refounded by Francisco de Orellana.

Wishing to be independent of Pizarro, Benalcázar with a large expedition headed north beyond the former Inca limits in 1538. He fought the Quillacinga and Pasto Indians and founded the towns of Cali and Popayán in southern Colombia. From Popayán he went on to the Chibcha capital of Bacatá (Bogotá). There he found Gonzalo Jiménez de Quesada from Santa Marta already in possession. A little later Nikolaus Federmann from Coro in Venezuela also arrived. The three chiefs parleyed instead of fighting; Benalcázar and Jiménez became friendly in opposition to Federmann, who wished Bogotá for himself. In May 1539 they all departed for Spain to lay their cases before King Charles. Benalcázar received substantially what he desired, the province of Popayán, or roughly southern Colombia. He returned there in 1540.

When the Peruvian rebellion led by Gonzalo Pizarro broke out, Benalcázar remained steadfastly loyal to the Crown. Though age now made further military activity difficult, he nevertheless took a force to Peru and commanded it in the final battle which saw Gonzalo defeated. Benalcázar described himself in a letter to the King in 1549 as "very old and tired."

Benalcázar's last year was troubled by personal enemies who charged him with many crimes, though the same charges could have been brought against any conquistador. He died at Cartagena, Colombia, in 1551 while on the way to Spain to plead his case.

Further Reading

There are no books in English devoted to Benalcázar. The major work is in Spanish: J.Jijon y Caamaño, *Sebastián de Benalcázar* (2 vols., 1936-1938). Valuable discussions of this conquistador are found in Frederick A. Kirkpatrick, *The Spanish Conquistadores* (1934; 2d ed. 1946), and Walker Chapman, *The Golden Dream* (1968). □

Jacinto Benavente y Martinez

The Spanish dramatist Jacinto Benavente y Martinez (1866-1954) was the most popular Spanish playwright of the first half of the 20th century. His sophisticated comedies of manners and of social satire signaled the beginning of modern theater in Spain.

Jacinto Benavente was born in Madrid on Aug. 12, 1866, the youngest son of a prominent pediatrician. He grew up in an atmosphere of learning, wealth, and social ease. His father loved the theater, maintained a large library, and practiced among aristocratic families, writers, and actors. A precocious child, Benavente learned several languages by the age of 16 and delighted in visiting the circus and in performing plays for household servants and friends.

In 1882 he enrolled in the University of Madrid to study law but gave up his studies 2 years later when his father died. Benavente lived an easy, comfortable life. He dressed elegantly, attended fashionable parties, and became a part of the refined but decadent bourgeois society depicted in most of his plays. About 1890, before he had established his reputation as a playwright, he worked successfully as an actor and gained a firsthand knowledge of staging techniques, which he later applied to his own productions.

In 1892 Benavente published his first work, *Teatro fantástico* (Fantastic Theater), eight short sketches based on dreams and fantasies. The following year he wrote a volume of poetry, *Versos,* and the prose work *Cartas de mujeres* (Letters from Women), which attests to his insight into the behavior of women and to his preference for feminine pro-

Jacinto Benavente (seated)

tagonists. In almost all his plays the only really strong characters are women; the men usually remain shadowy and unconvincing.

In 1894 Benavente's first play, *El nido ajeno* (Another's Nest), was staged. Its dramatic technique represented a stunning contrast to the grandiloquent style of José Echegaray. Benavente replaced action with a skillful, ingenious dialogue and emphasized the social and moral climate of the play at the expense of plot conflict. Rather than exploring the traditional concept of honor, he centered the story in the thoughts and feelings of the feminine protagonist. While *El nido ajeno* received a mixed response, unqualified success came in 1896 with *Gente conocida* (Eminent People). Spanish audiences enthusiastically applauded Benavente's innovations, and from 1896 to 1907 he produced 53 plays. Among them were *La gobernadora* (1901; The Governor's Wife), an exposure of corrupt provincial politics; *La noche del sábado* (1903; Saturday Night), an allegorical play which combines novel and drama; *Los malhechores del bien* (1905; The Misdoers of Good), a biting satire on the arrogance and hypocrisy of certain "charitable" ladies; and *Los intereses creados* (1907; Profits Made), a pessimistic examination of human behavior, which is generally considered his masterpiece. In *Los intereses creados* the characters are puppets who act according to the dictates of self-interest, commingling noble impulses with base desires so that the former become necessarily tainted by the latter.

This play, together with *La malquerida* (1913; The Misbeloved), a rural tragedy in the classical manner about the love between a man and his stepdaughter, established Benavente's international reputation and won for him the Nobel Prize in 1922.

Ironically, Benavente's work declined in quality about the time the Nobel Prize was awarded. From 1920 to 1954 he produced nothing of merit, and today even his best plays are largely ignored by the Spanish public. This final decadence is due to the fact that although Benavente reformed the turn-of-the-century theater, he was not an authentic revolutionary. Primarily, he aimed to please his audience, Spain's rather complacent upper class, which had little knowledge or sympathy with the pressing economic or social problems. Consequently, Benavente produced a bland, conservative theater which, in contrast to the work of other Spanish writers of the Generation of 1898, avoided serious moral, religious, or social preoccupations. Thus it quickly became outmoded.

During the second broad period of his life (1920-1954) Benavente traveled extensively to Latin America, the United States, and the Soviet Union. From 1936 to 1939 during the Spanish Civil War, he lived in Valencia. Upon his return to Madrid he publically endorsed the Franco regime to the dismay of his former liberal acquaintances. He died on July 14, 1954, in Madrid at the age of 88, having written and staged 172 plays.

Further Reading

Some of Benavente's plays are contained in *Plays, by Jacinto Benavente* (4 vols., 1917-1924), translated by John Garrett Underhill. The best book on Benavente is Marcelino C. Peñuelas, *Jacinto Benavente* (trans. 1968); it places the man and writer in his age, studies his relationship with the Spanish and European theater of his time, and gives a detailed analysis of his representative plays. □

'Abd al-Hamid Ben Badis

Shaykh 'Abd al-Hamid Ben Badis (1889-1940) was the leader of the Islamic Reform Movement in Algeria between the two world wars. At a time when highly visible Algerian politicians were advocating Algeria's assimilation into France, Ben Badis and his followers vigorously affirmed the cultural and historical distinctness of the Algerian nation.

'Abd al-Hamid Ben Badis was born in 1889 at Constantine, which was the cultural and commercial capital of eastern Algeria. Both his father and grandfather held high offices in the French colonial administration and one of his brothers was a French-educated lawyer. But 'Abd al-Hamid chose a different path.

After a private traditional education in Algeria, he enrolled at the venerable Zaytuna mosque university in Tunis, where he completed his studies in 1911. Subsequently he made the pilgrimage to Mecca and visited several major Middle Eastern cities.

In the Arab East and in Tunisia, Ben Badis was progressively won over to the world view and the agenda of the Islamic Reform (*Islah*) Movement. Pioneered at the turn of the century by Muhammad 'Abduh of Egypt, the reform movement called for the renewal and modernization of Islam by purging it of accumulated beliefs and practices inconsistent with the Koran (Qur'an) and the Tradition (*Sunna*) of the Prophet and by opening it up to the scientific methodology and learning that Muslim leaders of recent centuries had wrongly shunned. By invoking the example of the *salafs,* or earliest Arab Muslims, the reformers' program also promoted allegiance to Arab ancestors, to the Arab ''métropole'' in the east, and to the Arabic language, thus explicitly repudiating Europeanized Algerians' notion that salvation lay in merger with or into France.

In 1924 Ben Badis brought together in Constantine a group of reformists to discuss strategies. The next July they began publishing *al-Muntaqid* (*The Censor*) with the twin objectives of promoting the internal renewal of Algerian Islam and of protecting it against the many forms of secularist attack emanating from the colonial world. When the authorities closed this journal in November 1925 because an article supported the Rif rebellion in Morocco, Ben Badis replaced it with the monthly *al-Shihab* (*The Meteor*), which remained the reformists' principal publication until it was shut down at the advent of World War II. The reformists also began, in the 1920s, a network of independent schools for the propagation of Islam and the teaching of the Arabic language.

In attempting to renew Algerian Islam, Ben Badis and his colleagues were necessarily critical of an existing Islamic establishment they held responsible for Algerian Islam's sorry state. Sometimes they targeted the state-salaried *ulama* who staffed the official sponsored mosques. Far more frequently they attacked the *marabouts* (holy men) and the mystic brotherhoods and *zawiyas* whose unorthodox versions of Islam were deeply ingrained in popular culture and dominated the countryside where the great majority of Algerians lived. Since the official clergy were agents of the state and many of the *zawiya* leaders had been coopted by it as well, the reformists' attempts at religious renewal could not help but bear considerable political significance.

By 1931 some of the *zawiya* heads, smarting under reformist attacks, sought an agreement with the reformists on the basis of a common program of religious and moral renewal. Thus was created the Association of Algerian Muslim Ulama (AAMU) with 'Abd al-Hamid Ben Badis as its head. After a year of very uneasy symbiosis, the reformists expelled the traditionalist members and went on to form a purely reformist organization. There ensued a veritable war of religion in Algeria over the next four years. In 1933 alarmed authorities forbade Ben Badis and the reformers to preach in official mosques. The religious war culminated with the assassination in 1936 of the official Malikite mufti of Algiers.

As the 1930s went on, Ben Badis found himself increasingly drawn into the political debates of the time. In 1936 Ferhat Abbas, Algeria's best known liberal, wrote that, having found no trace in history or in the present of an Algerian fatherland, France was his fatherland. Ben Badis replied that ''We, too, have searched history and the present and have determined that an Algerian nation was formed and exists in the same way as all other nations were formed and exist. It has its religious and linguistic unity, its culture, its traditions, and its good and bad traits like all other nations on earth. . . . This Muslim Algerian nation is not France, cannot be France, and does not wish to be France.'' But this explicitly political statement must be viewed in a cultural context. In other writings Ben Badis made a clear distinction between what he called ''ethnic nationality'' and ''political nationality.'' Providing the integrity and individuality of each ethnic nationality was respected, it was possible and even desirable for two or more of them to share the same political nationality. Thus, an Arabo-Muslim Algeria could find an acceptable home within the French empire.

During the mid-1930s Ben Badis feared that secular nationalists might work out agreements with the French that would further impinge upon Algeria's ethnic character. For philosophical and tactical reasons he rejected the radical nationalism of Messali Hadj. But he did urge the organization of a common front, the Algerian Muslim Congress, which came into existence in June 1936 and included reformists, assimilationists, and communists. After trying and failing in this collaborative effort to extract meaningful concessions from the French, the reformists pulled out of the congress, which disappeared by 1938.

Abd al-Hamid Ben Badis died in April 1940. The disappearance of his dynamic leadership, together with tight wartime security measures, produced a rapid decline in the influence of the AAMU. Historians believe, however, that it is due mainly to the efforts of Ben Badis and his followers that the concept of a distinct Arab and Muslim Algerian nation became a fixed element in the national discourse. The daily pledge pupils recited at the reformist religious schools went on to become the motto of independent Algeria: ''Islam is our religion; Arabic is our language; Algeria is our fatherland.''

Further Reading

The best account of the rise of Algeria is John Ruedy, *Modern Algeria. The Origins and Development of a Nation* (1992). The other reliable sources are in French: Ali Merad, *Le Réformisme musulman en Algérie de 1925 à 1940* (1967); Charles-Robert Ageron, *Histoire de l'Algérie contemporaine*, Vol. II (1979); and Mahfoud Kaddache, *Histoire du nationalisme algérien. Question nationale et politique algérienne*, 2 vols. (1981). □

Ahmed Ben Bella

Ahmed Ben Bella (born 1918) was one of the ''historic chiefs'' of the Algerian war of independence and the first president of the Algerian Republic.

Ahmed Ben Bella was born into a modest peasant family on December 25, 1918, at Marnia, a small town near the Algerian-Moroccan frontier. In 1937, a few years after completing primary school, he was drafted into the French army. He remained in Marseilles until 1940, reaching the rank of sergeant, and then returned to Algeria for three years to work on his family's farm. He had considered staying in France, however, to play professional soccer.

In 1943 he returned to military duty and won both the Croix de Guerre and the Medaille Militaire for his wartime service in Italy. Back in Algeria by 1946, Ben Bella had become discouraged by the failure of the French to liberalize the colonial regime and joined the nationalist party, the Movement for the Triumph of Democratic Liberties (MTDL). In 1947 he was elected a municipal councilor for Marnia, and the next year he ran as an MTDL candidate for the Algerian Assembly. However, French interference in the elections impeded his ability to win.

MTDL Activities Led to Exile and Imprisonment

In the same year he became the local chief of a secret, nationwide organization, the Special Organization (SO) within the MTDL. Composed of about 1,800 members, its goal was to prepare for an armed struggle against French rule. By 1949 Ben Bella had become the national chief of the SO. In May 1949 he was implicated as one of the masterminds behind a holdup that had been carried out by members of the SO. Jailed in 1950, he escaped two years later and arrived in Cairo in 1953, where he joined other exiled militants of the MTDL. In March 1954 Ben Bella promised to aid the promoters of the armed insurrection which broke out in Algeria on November 1, and thus he became one of the nine "historic chiefs" of the war and a member of the external delegation of the National Liberation Front. He spent the next two years traveling and gunrunning between Cairo, Tripoli, Rome, Madrid, and Tetuán.

After the Congress of Soumman on August 20, 1956, which gave the internal chiefs predominance over the external delegation, Ben Bella met with President Habib Bourguiba of Tunisia and King Mohammed V of Morocco in Tunis, in order to seek their aid in ending the Algerian war. The airplane taking him and some companions from Rabat to Tunis was forced down over Algiers on October 22, and Ben Bella was taken to a French prison, where he remained for six years. In prison he avoided the clashes and squabbles that marked the rest of the war and that seriously divided the Algerian elite.

During his years of imprisonment Ben Bella, an avid reader, had the leisure to complete his education and develop a coherent political ideology. His imprisonment also kept him above intra-elite dissensions, and he was named vice-president of the Algerian provisional government, an honorary post created in September 1958.

The Era of Independence

When peace negotiations opened, the Algerian prisoners participated indirectly but actively in the proceedings. After the failure of the first talks at Melun in 1960, the negotiations at Évian led, in March 1962, to a ceasefire and the liberation of Ben Bella and his companions. A referendum in April 1962 ushered in Algerian independence.

At that moment the latent crisis between Ben Bella and the Algerian leaders in the provisional government, who refused to recognize his preeminence, broke out into the open. Two groups competed for control of the country: the provisional government, a French-appointed but powerless custodial government, and the army (ALN). Ben Bella, backed by soldiers of the Frontier Army commanded by Colonel Houari Boumediene, outmaneuvered the provisional government. He formed the Political Bureau at Tlemcen, near the Moroccan frontier, and rallied more partisans than did his adversaries.

Conflicts within the army, divided into antagonistic *Wilayas* (provinces) and external and internal forces, put Algeria on the verge of civil war during the autumn of 1962.

The victory of Ben Bella's partisans restored some calm and permitted the holding of elections in October 1962, which legitimized the victory of the Political Bureau. The National Constituent Assembly proclaimed the Algerian Democratic and Popular Republic, and Ben Bella was charged with forming the first government. On September 15, 1963, he was elected president of the republic, by virtue of which he became chief of state and the head of the government at the age of 44.

First President of the Algerian Republic, 1963-1965

Massive in size and athletically strong, he looked somewhat like a Roman centurion. Having studied classical Arabic and the writings of Karl Marx while a prisoner in France, he surprised those who had known him before 1956 by his ability to tackle the problems of state. While imprisoned he had worked out a program which he presented at Tripoli once he was liberated. In it he stated his opposition to imperialism in all its forms and called for agrarian reform, nationalization of the means of production, abolition of privileges, and a return to Arab and Islamic traditions. To apply these principles, he began to construct powerful state structures once he assumed control.

After domesticating the labor unions and the single party, the National Liberation Front, Ben Bella attempted to strengthen these institutions. He succeeded so well in forging them into powerful organs that the army under Vice-President Houari Boumediene, fearing that it would be forced into a subservient role, ousted him from power on June 19, 1965. Thereafter he was kept in a secret prison without having had a trial.

Released to house arrest July 4, 1979, Ben Bella was formally freed October 30, 1980. He spent the next decade in exile in Switzerland and France, where he formed an opposition movement in the mid-1980s. He returned to Algeria in 1990. However, the country was plunged into civil war in 1992 when military leaders canceled elections and banned the Islamic Salvation Front (FIS), the political party which at the time was likely to win the election. In the mid-1990s Ben Bella headed the Algerian Democratic Movement and participated in talks held in Rome in late 1994 and early 1995 with other opposition leaders in an effort to bring an end to the civil war. He remained an outspoken critic of the Algiers regime.

Further Reading

An account of Ben Bella's life to the mid-1960s is Robert Merle, *Ahmed Ben Bella* (1965; trans. 1967). A historical consideration of the development of the FLN is provided in Henry F. Jackson, *The FLN in Algeria: Party Development in a Revolutionary Society* (1977). Two works, William B. Quandt, *Revolution and Political Leadership: Algeria, 1954-1968* (1969) and David and Marina Ottaway, *Algeria: The Politics of a Socialist Revolution* (1970), assess Ben Bella's presidency. □

Robert Benchley

Robert Benchley (1889-1945) was one of the most popular and influential humorists of 20th century America. He took his gentle, self-deprecating wit to celebrity in literature, the theater, and the movies.

The offspring of a prominent local family and the grandson of a lieutenant governor of the state, Robert C. Benchley was born in Worcester, Massachusetts on September 15, 1889. When he was nine, his beloved older brother Edmund was killed in the Spanish-American War, prompting the outburst from his mother, "Why couldn't it have been Robert?"—a cry that became known around the community.

Early Career

Even in high school Benchley was active in theater, getting work as an extra with touring road companies when they appeared in Worcester. Sent to Phillips Exeter Academy with financial aid from his brother's fiancee, Lillian Duryea, he joined the drama club and did illustrations for the literary magazine. At Harvard, where his financial help from Duryea continued, he drew for the *Lampoon*, eventually becoming the president of the humor magazine's editorial board, and appeared in a number of shows produced by the Hasty Pudding Club. He also began to write and deliver humorous monologues.

From 1912 to 1914 Benchley worked for the Curtis Publishing Company and in 1914 was married to Gertrude Darling, a friend since childhood. In 1916 he was hired as a reporter for the *New York Tribune* through the influence of Franklin P. Adams. Later that year he moved to the *Tribune Magazine,* of which Adams was the editor; the magazine, however, lasted just over a year. He worked as a theatrical press agent for a few weeks and then as the aircraft news censor for the Aircraft Board, a position he resigned out of loyalty to a friend falsely accused of being pro-German.

Benchley became managing editor of *Vanity Fair* magazine in 1919; within a year his drama critic, Dorothy Parker, was fired for a blast at Billie Burke, the actress wife of producer Florenz Ziegfeld, and Benchley resigned in support of critical independence. In 1920 and 1921 he wrote a thrice-weekly column, "Books and Other Things," for the newspaper the *New York World.* In April of 1920 he became the drama editor of *Life,* then exclusively a humor magazine, a position he held until 1929, and in 1921 he contracted with columnist-editor David Lawrence to do a weekly syndicated feature. In the same year he published his first book, *Of All Things,* a collection of familiar essays on topics ranging from the social life of the new to bridge-playing and fuel-saving. His subsequent books followed the pattern established here of essays gathered after their publication in periodicals.

It was in these years that he became associated with the Algonquin Round Table, a group of rising young literary lights who met daily for lunch at the hotel on West 44th Street in Manhattan. At various times the group included drama critic Alexander Woollcott; playwrights Marc Connelly, Robert Sherwood, and George S. Kaufman; humorist Dorothy Parker; and actress Katherine Cornell and was renown for the *mots* which originated there. Benchley's most quoted quip, delivered on a rainy day, was "I've got to get out of these wet clothes and into a dry martini."

The group put on a one-night theatrical piece, *No Sirree!,* in 1922, the year which saw Benchley's second book, *Love Conquers All.* The hit of the evening was the humorist's monologue "The Treasurer's Report," a rambling and occasionally chaotic statement by an assistant treasurer filling in for his superior, who is ill. It became his best-known work. He was signed to present it professionally in the *Music Box Review,* which he did for nine months in 1923, and he took it to the screen in 1928.

Later Writings and Productions

The late 1920s and early 1930s saw his association with the fledgling *New Yorker* magazine become closer. In 1927 he began the occasional column "The Wayward Press," which he wrote until 1939, and in 1929 he became the drama columnist for the magazine, a post he resigned in 1940. Meanwhile he published *Pluck and Luck* (1925), *The Early Worm* (1927), *20,000 Leagues Under the Sea, or David Copperfield* (1928), *The Treasurer's Report* (1930), *No Poems* (1932), and *From Bed to Worse* (1934).

Benchley's popularity in Hollywood continued to grow as he made more one-reel and two-reel shorts in 1928 and 1929, most of them monologues based on the model of

"The Treasurer's Report." In 1932 he played a cameo role in the full-length feature *Sport Parade,* the first of many such appearances. In 1935 he won an Oscar from the Academy of Motion Picture Arts and Sciences for his monologue "How to Sleep" and was nominated for another in 1937 for "A Night at the Movies." Although he published *My Ten Years in a Quandary* in 1936, *After 1903—What?* in 1938, *Inside Benchley* in 1942, and *Benchley Beside Himself* in 1943, his interest in writing was decreasing and his absorption with film growing more complete. His total cinematic oeuvre comprised 49 short subjects, plus the aforementioned guest appearances.

Benchley died on November 21, 1945. There were three posthumous anthologies of his work, *Benchley—Or Else!* (1947), *Chips off the Old Benchley* (1949), and *The Benchley Roundup* (1954), all of them consisting largely of previously uncollected essays, some of which the humorist himself evidently did not wish to include in other anthologies.

His Humor

The importance of Benchley in the history of modern American humor is undeniable, but his humor has seldom been analyzed because it contains so many elements. Although he once did a short-lived magazine series depicting himself as the archetypal poor soul, that was not the most suitable persona for him because of the underlying intellectual quality of his work. Both in writing and on film he saw himself as bemused and semi-inept: that is, he was almost, but not completely, able to cope with human foibles and the unpredictability of inanimate objects. Further, he was capable of whimsy, as in "The Benchley-Whittier Correspondence"; hyperbole, as in "The Treasurer's Report"; the ridiculous, as in "Chemists' Sporting Extra"; and satire, as in "Tabloid Editions."

Throughout his work, however, there runs a self-deprecating tone, unusual in a WASP blue-blood at a time when virtually all of the self-mocking humor was heavily ethnic (whether Irish or Jewish or German). It is perhaps best encapsulated in Benchley's wry observation, "It took me fifteen years to discover that I had no talent for writing, but I couldn't give it up because by that time I was too famous."

Further Reading

The best biography is by the humorist's son, *Robert Benchley: A Biography* by Nathaniel Benchley (1955). Others worth consulting are *Robert Benchley* by Norris W. Yates (1968) and *Robert Benchley: His Life and Good Times* by Babette Rosmond (1970). There are frequent mentions of Benchley in books about the Algonquin Round Table, such as *The Vicious Circle* by Margaret Case Harriman (1951) and *The Algonquin Wits,* edited by Robert E. Drennan (1968). The best filmography is in *Selected Short Subjects* by Leonard Maltin (1983).

Additional Sources

Altman, Billy, *Laughter's gentle soul: the life of Robert Benchley,* New York: W. W. Norton, 1996.

Gehring, Wes D., *"Mr. B,"* or, *Comforting thoughts about the bison: a critical biography of Robert Benchley,* Westport, Conn.: Greenwood Press, 1992.

Rosmond, Babette, *Robert Benchley: his life and good times,* New York: Paragon House, 1989. □

Julien Benda

Julien Benda (1867-1956) was a French cultural critic and novelist. He is best known for his *La Trahison des clercs* ("the treason of the intellectuals"), which became a lasting international catch-cry.

Julien Benda was born in Paris on December 27, 1867, the only son of a wealthy, assimilated Jewish family. His father had moved from Brussels, abandoning hope for an engineering career. He married his cousin (an active socialite) and became head of his uncle's export firm. He taught his son "the religion of intelligence." Young Benda was educated at élite Paris lycées (Charlemagne, Condorcet, Henry IV, and Saint-Louis).

He became head of the family firm at age 21, when his father died, but his interests lay elsewhere. He too aspired to a career in engineering. Failing entry to the Ecole Polytechnique, he studied engineering at the Ecole Centrale. Finding the course distasteful because it emphasized application, he abandoned it, did his compulsory military service, and eventually took his degree in history at the Sorbonne at 26.

Benda increasingly led the life of wealthy young-man-about-Paris, frequenting the glittering society of the era, especially the circles (into which two of his female cousins had married) of the lawyer/political Eugene Carré and the great Casimir-Périer banking/political family. There he met such figures as Georges Clemenceau and Gabriel d'Annunzio and formed a contempt for polite society's "irrationalism" which, coupled with his philosophic interest in engineering and science, later became a central theme in his writing.

Only at age 30 did he leave his easy life and begin to write, provoked by that greatest of political affairs, the Dreyfus case. The Dreyfus case brought the term "intellectual" into currency and into controversy; it affected Benda profoundly. He contributed to the pro-Dreyfus *Revue blanche* (frequented by Lucien Herr, Léon Blum, and André Gide) and combined several articles into his first book, *Dialogues à Byzance* (1900). Revealingly, he took his title from Gen. Auguste Mercier's scornful remark that intellectuals who defended Dreyfus were like Byzantine philosophers who continued their studies with the Turks at their gates. Benda presented humanity as divided into two opposed psychological-cultural types, praised "rationalists" as necessary for civilization, and condemned both anti-Dreyfusards and most pro-Dreyfusards for lacking abstract understanding and embracing emotionalism. He developed these notions throughout his career.

From the *Revue blanche,* Benda became an intimate of the most advanced circle of the day: Charles Péguy's Cahiers de la Quinzaine, where he encountered Daniel Halévy, Georges Sorel, varieties of socialism, and the new cult for Henri Bergson's philosophy. Péguy published Benda's elaborated psychology of culture; his attacks on the influence of the fashionable salons and of "Bergsonism" (which caused a furor); and his first novel, *L'Ordination,* a runner-up for the 1912 Prix Goncourt (which prompted a split between Péguy and Sorel).

In 1913 the family export business collapsed, forcing Benda to become a professional writer at age 46. He had already gained some notoriety. World War I advanced his career. He wrote extensively condemning "Germanism" in politics and culture and was rewarded with the ribbon of the Legion of Honour. His enhanced reputation gained him entry to the most prestigious publications, including Jean Paulhan's *Nouvelle Revue Francaise;* he produced numerous essays, fiction, a major critique of the aesthetics of French society (*Belphegor,* 1918), and *La Trahison des clercs* (1927). Benda's *Trahison* charged modern culture with abandoning intellectual tradition by embracing political passion and 'realist' ideology. It attacked, among others, Nietzsche, Kipling, D'Annunzio, Sorel, Péguy, Maurice Barrès, and (despite neo-classical elements in Benda's own works) Charles Maurras' right-revolutionary Action Francaise. It showed the influence of the neo-Kantianism prominent in French republican education (especially that of Charles Renouvier, erstwhile synthesizer of Kant and Comte). It made Benda a celebrity at age 60. He relished prominence. He continued to battle his critics (such as the Action Francaise, Gabriel Marcel, Jacques Maritain, Daniel Halévy, and Jacques Rivière); elaborated his rationalist creed through notions of eternity, Europe, French history, and two volumes of autobiography; attended conferences; and made two trips to America (1936 and 1938). He asked fellow travellers in a no-smoking compartment to extinguish their pipes simply because he liked rules to be obeyed.

However, political events increasingly affected Benda's high intellectualism. He criticized the weakness of democracy, attacked the French right and the menace of fascism, became active in the Popular Front, and called his fellow "clercs" to join his side. On the fall of France in 1940, he fled to Carcassonne; the Nazis confiscated all his books and papers in Paris. He wrote a clandestine pamphlet for the Resistance and smuggled several works out of France for publication abroad. The liberation found him still vehement, despite his age. He opposed de Gaulle and also opposed any mercy for collaborators (especially for Maurras). He finally married an old friend, Micia Lebas, daughter of a former provincial military governor. In his last years he published two final autobiographical volumes, and he scathingly condemned "pure" literature (Gide, Proust, and surrealism); existentialism (quarrelling with Sartre); and democratic practices. He praised Communist acts, but castigated Communist doctrine as another variety of irra-

tionalism. He died at Foutenay-aux-Roses, outside Paris, on June 7, 1956, at age 88.

Urbane, independent, mocking, author of more than 40 books and innumerable articles, Benda had contact with the most controversial French figures of his time and influenced T. S. Elliot, Ezra Pound, Wyndham Lewis, Irving Babbit, and Herbert Read. His long life was one pre-eminently of writing and of literary/political battles. A brilliant polemicist, his career ironically mirrored his concern with the intellectual.

Further Reading

Benda is one of those figures who are more often invoked than examined. There are only two major studies of Benda in English, a literary analysis by Robert J. Niess, *Julien Benda* (1956), and a cultural/political analysis by Ray Nichols, *Treason, Tradition, and the Intellectual* (1978). Both works have extensive bibliographies which detail short pieces on Benda by such figures as T. S. Elliot. One of Benda's articles (on French democracy and the Nazi threat) is translated in Justin O'Brien (editor), *NRF: The Most Significant Writings from the Nouvelle Revue Francaise, 1919-1940* (1958). Selections from Benda's *Trahison* appear in M. Curtis (editor), *The Nature of Politics* (1963), and in G. B. de Huszar (editor), *The Intellectuals* (1960). There have been full English translations of Benda's *Trahison* (1928, reissued 1955) and *Belphegor* (1920). □

St. Benedict

The Italian monk St. Benedict (ca. 480-547) was the founder of the monastic order known as the Benedictines. His "Rule" introduced practicality, order, and emphasis on community into monastic life in the West.

The political and social disorder that accompanied the end of the Roman Empire induced many people to turn away from society. The idea of an isolated ascetic life had developed in the East, particularly in Egypt, where St. Anthony inspired many. Some individual hermits began to form monastic communities, but for the most part the emphasis was still upon the private war between the spirit and the world.

Knowledge of Benedict's life comes from the second book of the *Dialogues* of Gregory the Great, in which Gregory retells accounts he received directly from four of Benedict's close followers. Benedict was born about 480 in Nursia, 70 miles from Rome, to a distinguished family. He was sent to Rome to pursue his studies, but the vice of the city and of his fellow students impelled Benedict and his nurse to flee to the country.

The Hermit

Dissatisfied in his studies with his nurse, young Benedict left her secretly and disappeared into the wilderness of the Sabine hills. There, in Subiaco, he lived as a hermit in a cave, receiving food from a neighboring monk who lowered bread to him over a cliff. Dressed in wild animal skins, Benedict fought the wars of the soul. Once when tempted by a vision of a woman, he threw himself into a brier patch to subdue his emotions.

"Benedict's soul, like a field cleared of briers, soon yielded a rich harvest of virtues," Gregory related. Others sought his guidance, and the monks of a neighboring monastery whose abbot had died prevailed upon Benedict to take his place. But the strict discipline and obedience demanded by the new abbot so angered the monks that they tried to poison him. Detecting the poison, Benedict "went back to the wilderness he loved, to live alone with himself in the presence of his heavenly Father."

Monte Cassino

Isolation was not Benedict's lot, however; soon other men gathered around him, and he organized 12 monasteries with 12 monks and an abbot in each. At regular intervals, under Benedict's direction they all gathered in the chapel to chant psalms and pray silently.

About 529 Benedict moved his community to Monte Cassino, a hill 75 miles southeast of Rome. He and his monks demolished an old temple of Apollo on the summit, replacing it with a chapel dedicated to St. Martin, and began construction of monastery buildings.

It is impossible to reconstruct Benedict's daily life at Monte Cassino; his chronicler was concerned only with relating the marvels—such as Benedict's detection of an impostor whom Totila, King of the Ostrogoths, had sent to the monastery in his place, and Benedict's prediction of the destruction of Monte Cassino, an event that actually took place in 589. The date generally given for Benedict's death is March 21, 547. He was buried at Monte Cassino next to his sister, St. Scholastica.

Benedictine Rule

The *Rule,* written during the years at Monte Cassino, was Benedict's foremost literary achievement; it was also the means by which he exerted such great influence on the history of monasticism, enabling the Benedictines to expand across Europe and dominate the religious life of the Middle Ages. Benedict's purpose was "to erect a school for beginners in the service of the Lord," and he promised his followers, "If then we keep close to our school and the doctrine we learn in it, and preserve in the monastery till death, we shall here share by patience in the Passion of Christ and hereafter deserve to be visited with Him in His kingdom."

Unlike the rigorously ascetic and solitary life that was the model for Eastern monasticism, Benedict's plan involved life in a community in which all members shared. Government was the responsibility of an elected abbot who ruled the monks as a father did his children. The details of daily life were set forward but were not "difficult or grievous." After 8 hours of sleep the monks got up for the night office, which was followed by six other services during the day. The remainder of the day was spent in labor and in study of the Bible and other spiritual books. A novice en-

tered the community only after a probationary period, which tested him for the required virtues of humility and obedience.

Benedict believed that the life of the monk depended on his brothers in the community to which he was bound for life. The monk's daily duties and responsibilities were carefully outlined. He was to leave behind the world and grow to "greater heights of knowledge and virtue" in the seclusion of the monastery.

Benedict changed the monastic movement in the West. The chaotic pattern of isolated individuals or disorderly communities was transformed by a sense of organization and practicality. Men were brought together in communities ruled by discretion and moderation. In subsequent centuries the *Rule of Benedict* guided communities located over all of Europe.

Further Reading

Odo John Zimmerman translated the account of St. Gregory in *The Fathers of the Church: Saint Gregory the Great, Dialogues,* vol. 39 (new trans. 1959). The *Rule* of St. Benedict may be found in Owen Chadwick, *Western Asceticism* (1958). Leonard von Matt and Stephen Hilpisch, *Saint Benedict* (1960; trans. 1961), is a restrained treatment with excellent photographs of the historical sites. Justin McCann, *Saint Benedict* (1937), and T. F. Lindsay, *St. Benedict, His Life and Work* (1949), are longer discussions. Herbert B. Workman, *The Evolution of the Monastic Ideal* (1913; 2d ed. 1927), places Benedict's achievement in context.

Additional Sources

Dean, Eric, *St. Benedict for the laity,* Collegeville, Minn.: Liturgical Press, 1989.

Oury, Guy Marie, *St. Benedict, blessed by God,* Collegeville, Minn.: Liturgical Press, 1980. ☐

Pope Benedict XV

The Italian prelate Giacomo della Chiesa (1854-1922) reigned as Pope Benedict XV from 1914 to 1922. His pontificate was spent in dealing with the effects of World War I.

Giacomo della Chiesa was born at Pegli on Nov. 21, 1854. He studied at the University of Bologna and the Collegio Capranica in Rome and then became a papal diplomat. After 4 years in Spain he was recalled in 1887 to the Vatican Secretariat of State. In 1907 he was made archbishop of Bologna, in May 1914 he became a cardinal, and on September 3 of that year he was elected pope.

Benedict played no effective role in the war crisis. His predecessor, Pius X, had retired to a position of international isolation. Benedict, while condoning Austria's attack on Serbia as legitimate, tried to remain neutral. However, his belief that the fall of Czarist Russia would provide an opportunity for the expansion of Roman Catholicism weakened his neutral stance. On the other hand, he refused to accede to the Western powers' urging that he condemn German belligerence. Benedict's policy was also influenced by his desire to prevent Catholic nations from fighting each other. His attitude vexed the Allies, who saw it as a further frustration of their war effort against Germany.

Benedict did make an elaborate effort to mediate between the warring powers in August 1917. But the entry of the United States into the war on the side of the Allies and the consequent hardening of the Allies' attitude nullified his attempt. The Pope organized extensive relief services for prisoners of war and for the victims of the war's devastation, but in 1919 he was excluded from the peace talks.

In the aftermath Benedict adapted Vatican administrative machinery to the territorial and national changes wrought by the war and the peace treaty. He did eventually succeed in reestablishing diplomatic relations with France and Great Britain, but his hope of reaching concordats with the new states set up by the Treaty of Versailles was not fulfilled until the reign of his successor, Pius XI.

Benedict's influence was greater within Italy. He firmly circumvented the Integralist movement, and he fomented the Unione Popolare, thus laying foundations for the Catholic Action movement of the 1930s. Within the Church his emphasis of an indigenous priesthood enabled Pius XI to implement this idea. Benedict condemned the association of any missionary activity with imperialism. In the hope that the collapse of Czarist Russia and the emergence of new sovereign states in eastern Europe would lead the schismatic churches to rejoin the Roman communion, he founded the Pontifical Institute for Oriental Studies in 1917. He died on Jan. 22, 1922. Although the main aims of his pontificate were unfulfilled, it may be said that Benedict laid the foundation for many of the policies carried out by his successors.

Further Reading

Two full-length studies of Benedict XV are Henry E. G. Rope, *Benedict XV, the Pope of Peace* (1941), and Walter H. Peters, *The Life of Benedict XV* (1959). For background material see Denis Gwynn, *The Vatican and War in Europe* (1940), and Carlo Falconi, *The Popes in the Twentieth Century: From Pius X to John XXIII* (1967; trans. 1968). □

Ruth Fulton Benedict

The American cultural anthropologist Ruth Fulton Benedict (1887-1948) originated the configurational approach to culture. Her work has provided a bridge between the humanities and anthropology, as well as background for all later culture-personality studies.

R uth Fulton was born in New York City, the daughter of a surgeon. She entered Vassar College in 1905 and specialized in English literature. After graduation she taught English in a girls' secondary school.

In 1914 she married the biochemist Stanley Benedict, and the next 5 years were spent waiting for the children who never came and experimenting with a variety of creative tasks, such as writing poetry (her pen name as a poet was Anne Singleton), studying dance, and exploring the lives of famous women of the past. In 1919 she began to study anthropology and received her doctorate from Columbia University in 1923.

Configurational Theory

Her first anthropological work was a study of the way in which the same themes, such as the "Vision Quest," were organized differently in different Native American cultures. During the next 9 years she was editor of the *Journal of American Folk-Lore* and did a substantial amount of fieldwork among the Native Americans of the South-west. In all of this early work she was impressed with the extraordinary diversity of human cultures, but she did not yet have any way of integrating this diversity.

In the summer of 1927, while doing fieldwork among the Pima, she developed her configurational theory of culture: each culture could be seen as "personality writ large"—a set of emphases derived from some of the innumerable potentialities of the human personality. *Patterns of Culture* (1934), her best-known book, develops this theme. This book contrasts the Native American cultures of the Southwest as Dionysian and Appolonian, borrowing terminology from Nietzsche; and Kwakiutl and Dobuan cultures as megalomaniac and paranoid, borrowing terms from psychiatry. This eclectic choice illustrated her open-ended ap-

proach to history and her lesser concern with universals. She is sometimes associated with a theory of cultural relativity which treats all values as relative; actually she was deeply committed to the relevance of anthropology to man's control of his own evolution.

Cross-Cultural Studies

During the 1940s she devoted her energies to dispelling myths about race (*Race: Science and Politics,* 1940) and to a discussion of how warfare, now outmoded, could be superseded. During World War II she worked on studies of countries to which the United States had no access: Romania, the Netherlands, Thailand, and Japan. After the war she published *The Chrysanthemum and the Sword: Patterns of Japanese Culture* (1946), which was the best received of all the anthropological studies of national character. In 1947 she was elected president of the American Anthropological Association, and in 1948, belatedly, she was designated full professor of anthropology at Columbia University.

In 1947 Benedict inaugurated a great cross-cultural study, the Columbia University Research in Contemporary Cultures (France, Syria, China, Russia, Eastern European Jews, Czechoslovakia), in which 120 scholars from 14 disciplines and of 16 nationalities worked harmoniously together. In the summer of 1948 she visited Europe for the first time since 1926 and saw again at firsthand some of the cultures she had analyzed at a distance. She had gone to Europe against the advice of physicians, and she died a week after her return in September 1948, leaving a devoted group of younger collaborators to finish the work.

Further Reading

Margaret Mead, *An Anthropologist at Work: Writings of Ruth Benedict*(1959), is a study of Mrs. Benedict's life that includes many of her shorter papers and a selection of her poems. Erik H. Erikson wrote *Ruth Fulton Benedict: A Memorial* in 1949. Her life and career are recounted in Hoffman R. Hays, *From Ape to Angel: An Informal History of Social Anthropology* (1958), and Abram Kardiner and Edward Preble, *They Studied Man* (1961). Marvin Harris, *The Rise of Anthropological Theory: A History of Theories of Culture* (1968), discusses the importance of her work.

Additional Sources

Benedict, Ruth, *An anthropologist at work: writings of Ruth Benedict,* Westport, Conn.: Greenwood Press, 1977.

Caffrey, Margaret M. (Margaret Mary), *Ruth Benedict: stranger in this land,* Austin: University of Texas Press, 1989.

Dimitroff, Gail., *Guiding spirits: an inquiry into the nature of the bond between Ruth Benedict and Margaret Mead,* San Diego: G. Dimitroff, 1983.

Mead, Margaret, *Ruth Benedict,* New York, Columbia University Press, 1974.

Modell, Judith Schachter, *Ruth Benedict, patterns of a life,* Philadelphia: University of Pennsylvania Press, 1983. ☐

Edward Beneš

The Czechoslovak statesman Eduard Beneš (1884-1948) was president of his country from 1935 to 1938 and from 1940 to 1948.

As foreign minister of a small state created from territories of the former Austro-Hungarian Empire after World War I and precariously situated between Germany and the Soviet Union and bordered by hostile Poland and Hungary, Eduard Beneš supported the territorial settlements of the Paris Peace Conference of 1919, was a pillar of the French-East European alliance system, and was a zealous proponent of the League of Nations and of the settlement of international disputes through arbitration. The League's failure to maintain peace and France's refusal to honor its commitment to defend Czechoslovakia against German aggression led to the dismemberment of Czechoslovakia in 1938, and Europe's postwar prostration rendered any challenge to the Soviet-backed coup d'etat in 1948 impossible. Thus East Europe's most noted fighter for international cooperation and collective security lived to witness the defeat of those ideals and the loss of his country's independence.

Eduard Beneš was born on May 28, 1884, in Kozlany, Bohemia, the tenth and last child of a Czech farmer. He studied at the University of Prague and at the Sorbonne and École des Sciences Politiques in Paris. He received a doctorate of law at the University of Dijon in 1908 and then studied at the University of Berlin. He lectured at the Commercial Academy of Prague in 1909 and at the Czech University of Prague in 1913, by which time he had become a protégé of the Czechoslovak patriot Tomáš Masaryk.

Cabinet Posts

After the outbreak of war in 1914, Beneš helped to form a Czech resistance movement in Prague, and in 1915 he assisted Masaryk in creating anti-Austrian propaganda in Switzerland. Traveling to Paris, Beneš, with Milan Stefanik, founded a Czechoslovak foreign committee, which became the Czechoslovak National Council in January 1916, with Beneš as secretary. Under Masaryk the council was transformed into the provisional government of Czechoslovakia on Oct. 14, 1918, with Beneš as foreign minister. In this position Beneš distinguished himself as the leader of the Czechoslovak delegation to the Paris Peace Conference in 1919, and he held this office in all the Cabinets until he was elected second president of the Czechoslovak Republic in 1935. In addition, he was the prime minister in 1921-1922.

To preserve the Paris Peace Conference settlements and combat the Hapsburg restoration in Hungary, Beneš helped to found the Little Entente of Czechoslovakia, Romania, and Yugoslavia (1920-1921), linked with France. Leader of the Czechoslovak delegation to the League of Nations from 1920 on, Beneš sat on its Council (1923-1927) and formulated the Geneva Protocol of 1924, which made the arbitration of disputes between League members compulsory. Although he signed a pact of friendship with Italy in 1923, Beneš clearly considered the French and Little Entente alliance systems the keystones of Czechoslovak foreign policy, and when he was approached in 1937 by Austria and Hungary to present joint resistance to expansionist Germany, he refused. Nevertheless, to counterbalance the growing power of Germany, Beneš restored Czech-Soviet diplomatic relations, favored Soviet entry into the League of Nations in 1934, and concluded a qualified mutual assistance pact with the Soviet Union in May 1935.

President of the Republic

Beneš succeeded Masaryk as president of Czechoslovakia on Dec. 18, 1935. German demands for the Sudetenland brought the collapse of the French—East European alliance system, for Czechoslovakia's allies deserted in the face of the German threat. The Munich Conference of Sept. 28, 1938, awarded Germany the Sudeten portions of Czechoslovakia. A week later Beneš resigned the presidency and left the country. He taught at the University of Chicago, as Masaryk had done.

When World War II broke out in September 1939, Beneš organized a Czechoslovak committee in France, but after the French collapse he fled to England, where he created a Czechoslovak provisional government under his presidency on July 21, 1940. To gain Soviet support, he signed a Soviet-Czechoslovak Pact of Friendship, Mutual Assistance, and Postwar Cooperation on Dec. 12, 1943, intending to create the role of East-West mediator for Czechoslovakia in the postwar order.

On March 18, 1945, Beneš conferred at Moscow, arrived on April 3 at Košice, Slovakia, to establish a provisional government, and reached Prague on May 10, when his government began nationalizing important sectors of the economy. In the elections of May 1946 the Communists received 38 percent of the vote, emerging as the strongest political organization in Czechoslovakia. The Constituent Assembly elected Beneš president of the republic and the Communist Antonin Zápotocky president of Parliament on June 19. The Communist Klement Gottwald was selected premier on July 3.

Weakened by two strokes in 1947 and unable to withstand the pressure of the Soviet Union and the demands of the Czech Communists, Beneš appointed a government of 12 Communists, 7 Communist sympathizers, and only 2 non-Communists, thereby reducing his own role to that of figurehead chief of state. Although loyal Czechoslovak troops had been ready to oppose the Communists by force, Beneš had refused to utilize them for fear of Soviet armed intervention, thereby sealing the loss of his country's independence.

Although Beneš refused to approve a new constitution passed by Parliament on May 9, 1948, providing for a single-list electoral ballot, elections under the new system resulted in a Parliament that was two-thirds Communist. Thereupon Beneš resigned the presidency on June 7, 1948, to be succeeded by the Communist premier, Gottwald. On September 3 Beneš died at his country house in Sezimov Usti. Among his publications are *My War Memoirs* (trans. 1928), *Democracy Today and Tomorrow* (1939), and the unfinished *Memoirs: From Munich to New War and New Victory* (trans. 1954).

Further Reading

Informative works on Beneš in English are Pierre Crabitès, *Beneš, Statesman of Central Europe* (1935); Godfrey Lias, *Beneš of Czechoslovakia* (1940); and Compton Mackenzie, *Dr. Beneš* (1946). Background studies that discuss Beneš include Hubert Ripka, *Munich: Before and After* (1939); Josef Korbel, *The Communist Subversion of Czechoslovakia, 1938-1948* (1959); and Paul E. Zinner, *Communist Strategy and Tactics in Czechoslovakia, 1918-1948* (1963), which is very useful for an assessment of Beneš's career. A chapter on Beneš's diplomacy is in Gordon Craig and Felix Gilbert, eds., *The Diplomats: 1919-1939* (1953).

Additional Sources

Beneš, Edvard, *Memoirs of Dr. Eduard Beneš: from Munich to new war and new victory,* Westport, Conn.: Greenwood Press, 1978.

Taborsky, Edward, *President Edvard Beneš: between East and West, 1938-1948,* Stanford, Calif.: Hoover Institution Press, 1981. □

Stephen Vincent Benét

A poet and writer of fiction and dramatic adaptations, Stephen Vincent Benét (1898-1943) retold materials from American history, legend, and folklore with charm, humor, fervor, and a sense of theatricality.

Stephen Vincent Benét was born on July 22, 1898, in Bethlehem, Pa. His family, originating in Minorca, had emigrated to Florida in the 18th century. Benét's father, an ordnance officer, and his grandfather, a general, had served in the U.S. Army. His older brother was the poet and man of letters William Rose Benét.

Stephen spent his childhood in California and Georgia, where his father was stationed at government arsenals. His father had a discriminating taste in literature, and Stephen began to write as a child, winning prizes from the *St. Nicholas* magazine. He attended Summerville Academy and then entered Yale University in 1915, having already published a collection of dramatic monologues, *Five Men and Pompey.* While at Yale he issued another volume of verse. Among his undergraduate friends were Philip Barry, Archibald MacLeish, and Thornton Wilder—all would later distinguish themselves in literature. In his senior year he served as chairman of the *Yale Literary Magazine.*

Graduating in 1919, he tried advertising briefly but returned to Yale to receive his master of arts degree in 1920. After his novel *The Beginning of Wisdom* was published in 1921, he took a fellowship for study at the Sorbonne. He reentered the United States, married Rosemary Carr in 1921, and settled down to write. In 1923 he published *King David and A Ballad of William Sycamore* and won the *Nation* poetry prize. *A Ballad* showed his preoccupation with American subjects. The best of Benét's five novels, *Spanish Bayonet* (1926), is a historical adventure set in

Minorca a decade before the American Revolution and in Florida a decade after it.

Benét spent from 1926 to 1928 in France writing his chief work, *John Brown's Body* (1928). This successful long narrative poem about the Civil War won a Pulitzer Prize in 1929. Though it is compounded of much knowledge, sincerity, romantic gusto, and literary talent, it does not deserve the frequently conferred label of "epic," for it lacks the unifying philosophical vision and driving artistic purpose of an epic. It throws off interesting, varied flashes of American character and history, but it does not relate them adequately to contemporary America.

Benét returned to the United States in 1928 and settled in Rhode Island. His first collection of short stories, *The Barefoot Saint,* appeared in 1929. The following year he moved to New York City. *Ballads and Poems* (1931), was a gathering of 15 years of folk and other poems. Two years later he received the Roosevelt Association Medal. In 1936 *Burning City, New Poems* appeared, and he received a doctor of letters degree from Middlebury College, Vt.

Benét reinforced his position as a fantastic, humorous adapter of legend and folklore, collaborating with the composer Douglas Moore in a radio performance of *The Headless Horseman,* a redoing of Washington Irving's story. His volume of short stories, *Thirteen O'Clock,* contained "The Devil and Daniel Webster," which became a minor national classic. Benét rewrote it as a one-act play and an opera; a movie and television production have also been based on it. *Johnny Pye and the Fool Killer* (1938) adapts grotesque, macabre folk material to poetry.

The poem *Nightmare at Noon* (1940) warned the United States of the fascist threat. *Western Star* (1943), the beginning of a projected work on the settlement of the United States, won a Pulitzer Prize posthumously in 1944.

The life of this charming and popular humorist, romancer, and poet, whose faith that man could overcome his devils was concretized in his work, came to an untimely end on March 13, 1943.

Further Reading

Two studies of Benét are available: Charles A. Fenton, *Stephen Vincent Benét* (1958), and Parry Edmund Stroud, *Stephen Vincent Benét* (1963). Babbete Deutsch, *Poetry in Our Time* (1952; rev. ed. 1963), examines the poems of major 20th-century poets and compares modern and 19th-century poetry.

Additional Sources

Benét, William Rose, *Stephen Vincent Benét,* Folcroft, Pa.: Folcroft Library Editions, 1976; Norwood, Pa.: Norwood Editions, 1977; Philadelphia: R. West, 1978.

Fenton, Charles A., *Stephen Vincent Benét: the life and times of an American man of letters, 1898-1943,* Westport, Conn.: Greenwood Press, 1978, 1960. □

Benetton

Benetton, founded in 1965, and initially producing fine colorful knitwear, expanded to become the largest apparel network in the world. Benetton Group's diversification into a wide range of products and activities and its often controversial advertising techniques made the Benetton name a household word.

The Benetton clothing line was created by three brothers and their sister in a small knitting shop in Ponzano Veneto, Italy. When their father died, Luciano (born 1935) left school to work in a clothing store in order to support his mother, sister Giuliana, and younger brothers Gilberto and Carlo.

Luciano developed promotional and commercial expertise as a clerk in a textile store in Treviso. Later, as a representative of small textile establishments, he built up contacts with the Roman knitting magnates who were helpful when the family expanded its operation. As president of the Benetton Group, Luciano led the expansion of family holdings, particularly in the 1990s. He served as a senator of the Italian Republic from 1992 to 1994. Luciano is the father of four children, including Mauro Benetton, marketing director of the Benetton Group.

Giuliana Benetton (born 1937) gained her experience from ten years of handicraft work in knitting for women. She created new knitwear collections and oversaw product lines. Giuliana served on the board of directors of both Edizione Holding, the family owned financial holding company and Benetton Group. She is married and has four children.

Gilberto Benetton (born 1941), vice-president of the Benetton Group, president of Edizione Holding, and president of Benetton Sportsystem, also handled all Benetton sponsorships of athletic events. Through the Benetton Foundation, he created a sports complex in Treviso, Cittadella dello Sport, which was open to the public. Gilberto is married and has two children.

Carlo Benetton (born 1943) was involved with the manufacturing component of Benetton. He was responsible for production at headquarters and abroad. Carlo served as vice-president of Edizione Holding and was on the board of directors of the Benetton Group. He is the father of four children.

Mauro (born 1962), eldest son of Luciano, began working for the Benetton Group as a student and later managed a shop in Paris. In 1985 he moved to Benetton's headquarters in Ponzano, where he took charge of the relaunch of one of the Group's main lines, which then experienced a period of record growth. Mauro was appointed marketing director of the Benetton Group in 1992, at the age of 30.

The Benetton family combined and optimized their expertise in marketing (Luciano), production (Giuliana), management and finance (Gilberto) and technical know-how (Carlo). They aimed at the casual wear market with color to catch the eye, first only in woolens but later in cotton. When regional small plants producing stockings came upon hard times, the Benettons bought their equipment at bargain prices. Now they were ready for a spectacular expansion. Between 1972 and 1976, they expanded into all types of clothing, from jeans to gloves to a complete Benetton wear model. Going into the 1990s there were 14 family members in the business.

The Benettons aimed to transform the fashion-fractionalized small handicraft style into an industry with minimum risks. To achieve this, they expanded in variety and size and decentralized production and distribution. They purchased large quantities of materials in raw form, benefiting from quantity discounts and controlling the processing (especially color) from its rawest form. However, 80 percent of production was performed in plants not owned by Benetton but controlled by the family. In distribution, various attempts were made to control all stores. At the beginning they would go into partnership with a friend who would in turn find others interested in having a Benetton store. Later, with international expansions, the holdings model was adopted, with the Benettons always having an exclusive contract. As a practical characteristic, the stores were about 400 square feet (while the competition was usually 1,500 square feet) and 50 percent of all working hours were dedicated to sales (the competition, 22.5 percent). This is probably why Benetton's productivity was four times greater than the competition.

Still, the success of the "Benetton" model is due to their trust. They wanted the stores to be exclusively Benetton, but allowed the owners to have 51 percent of the holdings. The

Benettons have always preferred to be partners with their producers and distributors rather than to seek vertical integration (where the managers of stores were salaried people with no direct share in the operation). The incentive was to make every representative a majority partner in his particular operation so that, as owners, they would strive to increase sales and profits. In the 1980s, the little 400-square-feet stores developed a turnover more than twice as large as those of competing companies. Specialization and standardization are the main instruments that allow high productivity. The Benettons found a happy mixture of personal incentives: outright ownership by each unit and overriding control of operations and a quality/product mix to conduct market penetration at low risk with high profitability.

The family entered into other business ventures assisted by loans from financial institutions. They eventually purchased the large well-known shoe manufacturer, Varese. In time, they allowed larger store units, depending on the sales as calculated pieces per square foot.

The 1980s saw a decline in the number of shops in the United States, but expansion into other global markets. Benetton increased the number of stores in the Far East and boasted 50 stores in China alone. By 1996 Benetton's presence was felt in over 100 countries, with 7,000 sales outlets for their main brands of United Colors of Benetton, Sisley, and 012. The sales network included 80 branches and 800 staff responsible for independent stores in specific geographic areas. In 1996 the largest store opened for business in London, England. The Benetton magazine, *Colors,* was introduced, using multicultural messages the company had featured in its ad campaigns of the 1980s.

In addition to their clothing lines, Benetton diversified into a variety of other enterprises through Edizione Holding. Acquisitions included Rollerblade, Prince tennis rackets, Nordica ski boots, Kastle skis, and Asolo hiking boots. Benetton, along with partners, also acquired Euromercato, Italy's leading superstore chain and interests in GS-Autogrill markets and restaurants. Other product lines included watches, stationery, cosmetics, linens, eyewear, books, the Twingo Benetton car (in collaboration with Renault), and a line of pagers through an agreement with Motorola. By 1995 Benetton sponsored sports teams in volleyball, basketball, and rugby. Benetton team Formula One World championship include the 1994 and 1995 World Drivers' championship and the World Car Makers' championships.

In the 1990s Benetton came under criticism for its use of controversial images in its advertising campaigns, including those depicting war, AIDS, racism, violence, and homelessness. While Benetton was pressured into removing offensive ads from billboards, the same ads were critically praised for their sociopolitical statements. A number of lawsuits were filed against Benetton by shopowners who claimed that the ads had caused a drop in sales, but these charges were difficult to prove. A downturn in the European economy impacted sales during this period. The images used in the ad campaign have been included in museum collections around the world and continue to spark debate.

Benetton, independently and in conjunction with other groups and organizations, contributed to many initiatives aimed at social problems. Examples include a 1995 campaign aimed at generating AIDS awareness in India. Support for War Child, a charity that helps children in war zones around the world, has also been praised. Autographed Toscani posters were offered to visitors at a clothes show event in exchange for donations to War Child. The Food and Agricultural Organization (FAO) of the United Nations invited Benetton to create a communications campaign for the first world food summit held in Rome.

Benetton's use of information technology facilitates the management of the global business from Ponzano Veneto. Students from around the world study at Fabrica, Benetton's arts and communications research center near Treviso, learning communications in all its forms and using the new technologies that will take them, and Benetton, forward into the future.

Further Reading

Additional information on the Benetton family can be found at their official Web site, www.benetton.com; in *Business Month* (February 1989); *Business Week* (March 5, 1990; April 10, 1995); *Los Angeles Times* (January 23, 1994; April 21, 1996); *New York Times* (November 23, 1993; March 20, 1997); *Washington Post* (January 21; August 29, 1995); and in Italian language references: P. Calvani, "Perche tutti copiano il modello Benetton" *Espansione* (1986); Giuseppe Nardin, *La Benctton* (1987); F. Rullani and A. Zanfei, "Benetton: invenzione e consolidamento di un sistema internazionale," *Bolletino Ospri* (1984); G. Turani, "Benetton sbarchera'a Milano e Wall Street," *La Repubblica* (December 15-16, 1985). □

Anthony Benezet

An American philanthropist and Quaker educator, Anthony Benezet (1713-1784) wrote and distributed antislavery tracts, promoted education for women and African Americans, urged better relations with the Native Americans, and composed a brief history of his sect.

Of a well-to-do Huguenot family, Anthony Benezet was born in Saint-Quentin, France, on Jan. 31, 1713. When he was 2, his family moved to Rotterdam to escape religious persecutions following revocation of the Edict of Nantes; shortly afterward they went to London. Anthony received a liberal education, was apprenticed to a mercantile house, and at the age of 14 joined the Quaker faith.

The family came to Philadelphia in 1731, and 18-year-old Anthony entered the merchant business with his three brothers. In May 1736 he married Joyce Marriott. Following a brief experience in manufacturing in Wilmington, Del., he decided to enter teaching. He attended Germantown Academy and then instructed in the Friends' English Public School in Philadelphia (1742-1754).

Distressed by the inferior education offered to women, Benezet established a girls' school in 1755. Through wide reading, travelers' reports, and the influence of Quaker minister John Woolman, he became concerned about slavery. Benezet corresponded with English emancipationists and began to write pieces for newspapers and almanacs, as well as free pamphlets, on the subject. His knowledge of French enabled him to communicate with the 450 Acadian exiles who came to Philadelphia in 1756; he solicited funds and obtained shelter for them and appealed to the Assembly in their behalf.

Benezet's health was poor, and in 1766 he retired to the quiet of his wife's hometown of Burlington, N.J., but he could not remain inactive. He wrote *A Caution . . . to Great Britain and Her Colonies on the Calamitous State of the Enslaved Negroes* (1766). This was his most important work; approved by the Philadelphia Yearly Meeting of Friends, it was widely distributed in Britain. He returned to teaching in Philadelphia in 1768. His *Some Historical Account of Guinea . . .* (1771) helped stir up English protests against the slave trade.

Benezet founded a school for African American children in 1770; after the Revolution it met for a time in his home. He taught until nearly the end of his life, and when his wife died in 1784, he endowed his school with what property he possessed. Overseers of the Friends' Public Schools were named trustees for the institution.

Yet African Americans were not his only interest. He published an essay, "The Mighty Destroyer Displaced" (1774), against excessive consumption of alcohol, which influenced Dr. Benjamin Rush to write a powerful temperance treatise. Benezet's *Short Account of the People Called Quakers . . .* (1780) was one of the earliest American histories of that denomination. Convinced the Native Americans had been mistreated, he worked to ameliorate their lot; in his last year he published *Some Observations on the . . . Indian Natives of This Continent.* Benezet died in Philadelphia on May 3, 1784.

Further Reading

George S. Brookes, *Friend Anthony Benezet* (1937), is a detailed account of the humanitarian's life. Much earlier but still worthwhile is Roberts Vaux, *Memoirs of the Life of Anthony Benezet* (1817). François Jean de Chastellux, *Travels in North-America in the Years 1780, 1781, and 1782* (2 vols., 1786; trans. 1787; rev. trans. 1963), has some interesting observations. □

David Ben-Gurion

The Israeli statesman David Ben-Gurion (1886-1973) served as Israel's first prime minister and minister of defense.

The son of a lawyer, David Gruen was born on October 16, 1886, in Płońsk (Czarist Russia; now Poland). He received a traditional Jewish education, later adding some secular studies in Warsaw. In 1900 he was among the founders of the Zionist youth club Ezra; in 1903 he joined the Zionist socialist movement, Poalei Zion.

Early Political Career

Gruen arrived in Palestine in September 1906. Working as a laborer, he became politically active in the Poalei Zion party and was soon elected chairman. In 1910 he joined the party organ *Ha'ahdut,* beginning his long writing career. He changed his name at that time to the Hebraic David Ben-Gurion, after a defender of Jerusalem who died in 70 A.D. Zionism and socialism were both seen by the young Ben-Gurion as necessities for the future of the Jewish people. To him Zionism meant the obligation to come to Palestine, settle the land, and use Hebrew as everyday speech.

At the outbreak of World War I, Ben-Gurion was deported, and in 1915 with Yitzhak Ben Zvi (Israel's second president and a lifelong friend) he embarked for the United States. There he married Paula Munweiss, a trainee at the Brooklyn Jewish Nursing School. After the Balfour Declaration (1917) proclaiming the Jewish right to a national homeland in Palestine, Ben-Gurion called for volunteers to liberate Palestine from the Turks. In August 1918 he arrived in Egypt with the Jewish Legion, but the war ended shortly afterward. In 1920 Britain acquired Palestine as a mandate of the League of Nations. The terms of mandate echoed the Balfour Declaration in declaring the area to be a future Jewish national homeland. Progress toward achievement of this goal was slow, however, and the proposed Jewish state was not established until 30 years later.

After the war Ben-Gurion advocated a form of socialism based on the cooperative principle of the new kibbutz movement. During the 1920s and 1930s he emerged as the leader of Labor Zionism. He was among the founders of the important Jewish Federation of Labor (the Histadruth) in 1921 and acted as its secretary general for 14 years. In the early 1930s he became head of the Labor party (Mapai) and a member and later chairman (1935-1948) of the Zionist and Jewish Agency Executives, which was the official representative of the Jewish community. In 1937 Ben-Gurion agreed to the British Royal Commission's proposal to divide Palestine between the Arabs and Jews, since he believed that even a truncated Jewish state would serve the purposes of Zionism. But he was an outspoken opponent of the British White Paper of 1939, limiting Jewish immigration to Palestine and restricting land purchases by Jews.

Israeli Independence

In 1942 Ben-Gurion's Biltmore program, supported by all segments of the Zionist movement, openly declared the Zionist aim as nothing less than the creation of a Jewish state. However, British policy remained unchanged after World War II, despite the catastrophe that had befallen European Jewry in the Holocaust. Ben-Gurion then authorized an armed struggle against the British and adamantly opposed immigration and land-sale restrictions, which threatened to turn Palestine's Jewish community into a permanent minority and made no provision for the great number of displaced Jewish people who wished to immigrate to Palestine.

Ben-Gurion, who throughout the years had made many attempts at Arab-Jewish rapprochement, now set about preparing for armed struggle with the Palestinian Arabs, which he saw as inevitable. In 1947 he was a major spokesman for the Zionist cause before the United Nations Special Committee on Palestine, which later that year proposed the partition of Palestine and the formation of a Jewish state. As the British mandate was about to expire, Ben-Gurion proclaimed the restoration of the state of Israel on May 14, 1948. After ending the 2,000-year exile of the Jewish people, he then led them to victory in the war of independence against seven invading armies from the Arab League nations.

Head of State

Serving as prime minister and minister of defense from 1948 to 1963 (except for a brief retirement from 1953 to 1955), Ben-Gurion revealed himself to be not only an astute party leader but also a great statesman. He protected Israel from sudden invasion by establishing a well-equipped and well-trained people's army. He forged the image of Israel as a modern democratic country based on parliamentary rule, a unique sociological and political phenomenon in the Middle East. During his premiership more than a million Jews, from 80 countries and speaking many languages, came to the homeland. The absorption and integration of the immigrants and the Israeli achievements in housing, agricultural settlement, employment, industry, education, health services, and trade, under the Ben-Gurion government, were among the remarkable accomplishments of the 20th century.

Ben-Gurion's premiership was characterized by his fiery oratory. Noted for his integrity and imbued with a messianic vision, Ben-Gurion met every challenge with the inspiration and determination of an Old Testament prophet. He urged the Israelis to study the Bible in order to understand themselves and their homeland. The supremacy of the spirit and the concept of a model state were also ideas on which he often spoke.

Among his significant achievements were negotiation of the reparations agreement with West Germany; establishment of French support prior to the Sinai campaign; consultations with leaders of France, West Germany, and the US (1959-1961) which consolidated Israel's international position and obtained economic assistance; initiation of aid programs to developing African and Asian countries; settlement of the Negev Desert; and resumption of trade at the port of Eilat. In 1956 Ben-Gurion answered Egypt's seizure of the Suez Canal by taking the Sinai Peninsula in a swift thrust almost to the banks of the Suez which inflicted a crushing defeat on the Egyptians. (Israel returned control of the Sinai but occupied it again from 1967-1979).

Resignation and Later Years

His last years as prime minister (1960-1963) were marred by the controversial Lavon affair, which split the Mapai party. Rather than compromise his principles, Ben-Gurion resigned from office. He retired to his desert retreat at Sde Boker and began writing a history of Israel. However, he never abandoned politics and subsequently formed his own Labor party (Rafi), a number of whose members were elected to Parliament. Feeling lonely after the death of his wife and lifelong comrade Paula in 1968, Ben-Gurion was often compared to an old, but still ferocious, lion in a desert retreat. Although he had no formal power, his roar was still loud enough to shake the country. He died in Israel on December 1, 1973. Moshe Dayan, the Israeli defense minister, later wrote of Ben-Gurion: "The man and his leadership were one and inseperable."

Further Reading

Ben-Gurion's *Israel: A Personal History* (1971) tells the story of his life and of the establishment of Israel. One of the best books on Ben-Gurion is Robert St. John, *Ben-Gurion: The Biography of an Extraordinary Man* (1959). Other works include David Ben- Gurion, *Ben-Gurion Looks Back in Talks with Moshe Pearlman* (1965); Maurice Edelman, *David! The Story of Ben-Gurion* (1964); and Michel Bar-Zohar, *The Armed Prophet: A Biography of Ben- Gurion* (1966; trans. 1967). □

Paul Ben-Haim

Paul Ben-Haim (1897-1984), Israeli composer, leader of the Eastern Mediterranean school, synthesized Eastern and Western approaches to music in compositions of exceptionally fine craftsmanship.

Paul Ben-Haim was born Paul Frankenburger in Munich into the family of the eminent German law professor, Frankenburger, at the end of the 19th century. He studied composition with Friedrich Klose and Walter Courvoisier and conducting and piano with Berthold Kellermann at the Munich Academy of Arts from 1915 to 1920. He was assistant conductor to Bruno Walter and Hans Knappertsbusch at the Munich Opera from 1920 to 1924, and he was the conductor of the Opera of Augsburg from 1924 to 1931. Returning to Munich in 1931, he devoted himself to composition. In that year he established himself in German music with *Pan,* a tone poem for soprano and orchestra; an oratorio entitled *Yoram,* based upon a biblical text; and his *Concerto Grosso.*

When the Nazis came to power in 1933, the composer emigrated to Palestine and there changed his surname from Frankenburger to Ben-Haim. He accompanied and arranged music for folk singers, an experience which brought the influence of Middle Eastern music to bear upon his compositional style. In 1937 he wrote a string quartet which synthesizes European and Eastern Mediterranean music, and in 1939 he wrote his *Variations on a Palestinian Tune* for chamber trio. In 1941 he wrote an especially well-received quintet which may be said to consummate his initial efforts to fuse the music of his adopted land with the European tradition in which he had been trained.

Ben-Haim's *First Symphony* was completed on the day in 1940 when France fell to the Nazis, and this work may be said to express the tragic and intense period of history in which it was composed. In addition, Ben-Haim's *First Symphony* was the first real symphony to be composed in Palestine. His *Second Symphony,* composed in 1945, returned to the pastoral Mediterranean moods of the composer's work of the late 1930s. Both symphonies were first presented by the Palestine Symphony Orchestra.

Ben-Haim was the leader of a group of Palestinian musicians, many of them European émigrés, who developed a fusion of Eastern and Western musical traditions. Isolated during World War II, this group, many of whom had been thoroughly trained in European conservatories and academies of music, studied the music of the Middle East and came to incorporate its melodic and rhythmic character into the forms of Western music. Ben-Haim developed a method for notating the complex rhythms and the melodies of Middle Eastern folk music, which facilitated the merging of these traditions in modern Israel.

In 1953 the conductor Serge Koussetvitsky had the idea of a "King David Festival" to coincide with the commemoration of Jerusalem's 3000th anniversary. Koussetvitsky died before the works commissioned for the festival were all completed, but the Koussetvitsky Foundation did commission and Ben-Haim did complete *The Sweet Psalmist of Israel,* an orchestral work in the concertante style which successfully synthesized Eastern and Western elements of music. He received the Israel State Prize for this composition in 1957. Leonard Bernstein conducted it in New York in 1959, and it remained one of Ben-Haim's most widely admired works.

Ben-Haim was also a professor of composition at conservatories in Tel-Aviv and Jerusalem, positions which, in addition to his leadership of the Eastern Mediterranean school of composers, made him a principal figure in Israel's musical life. On the practical side, he was influential in the development of music education in Israel, and he also helped to form the musicians' union in his new country. He was awarded the Joel Engel prize of the city of Tel-Aviv on several occasions. Ben-Haim remained active in the musical life of Israel until his death in Tel-Aviv in 1984 at the age of 86.

Although considered neo-classical by some critics and late Romantic by others, there is no disagreement about the high professional standards of Ben-Haim's work. Perhaps because of their identification with the new state of Israel, some critics place his symphonies in the late Romantic tradition of nationalism, or perhaps national style, which includes the European composers Sibelius and Walton. However, a typical work, the *Sonata for Solo Violin,* written for the English violinist Yehudi Menuhin, shows a fusion of traditional, European classical elements and the drone and *hora* rhythms of Middle Eastern music. The Eastern folk music elements are most present in his vocal compositions,

the songs and the psalms, which are perhaps his most lyrical compositions. "Three Songs without Words," vocalises for high voice and piano, is among his most acclaimed works.

In Ben-Haim one can see two of the principal elements in modern European music—the late Romantic school of composers and the neo-classicism of Igor Stravinsky and others. However, just as Béla Bartók, through an intensive study of East-European folk music, developed a style of composition in which new melodic and rhythmic materials are used in the traditional forms of Western music, so Ben-Haim's work, in drawing upon the folk music of the Middle East, provides fresh materials for use in traditional forms. Composers who synthesize diverse elements in their music, such as Paul Ben-Haim, perhaps should not be narrowly categorized in terms of any of the individual strands which they have woven into their music.

Further Reading

Paul Ben-Haim is discussed in both *The New Grove Dictionary of Music and Musicians* (London, 1980) and *Baker's Biographical Dictionary,* 6th edition (1978). The composer's obituaries in *The New York Times* and the *Neue Zeitung* contain some information. There are two Israeli publications which provide extended treatment of the composer: J. Hirshberg, "Paul Ben-Chaim—the early years," *Ariel* 45-46 (1978); and anon., *Paul Ben-Chaim,* (Tel-Aviv, 1967). □

Asher Benjamin

Asher Benjamin (1773-1845), an American architect, educated two, and possibly three, generations of 19th-century architects through his writings.

Asher Benjamin's importance to the architectural profession can be understood only in relation to late-18th-and early-19th-century trends. All architectural thought from the 14th to the mid-18th century was dominated by the writings of the Roman architect of the Augustan Age, Vitruvius. Sir Christopher Wren (1631-1723), his follower James Gibbs (1683-1754), and the 18th-century "Palladians," including Colen Campbell, were the last of the major English Vitruvians. Gibbs and Campbell published architectural books from which lesser-known architects copied, and these books were imported to the United States. Benjamin adapted many of the designs to American use; he changed the stone details of expensive, monumental English buildings to constructions in wood to fit the scale and finances of the New England communities. Benjamin stated in his *The American Builder's Companion* (1806) that two-thirds of the contents of English architectural publications were unsuitable for the American craftsmanbuilder.

The Vitruvius-Palladio-Wren-Gibbs tradition in Europe was on the wane by 1750, but its "colonial" adaptations by Benjamin lasted almost until the Civil War. Benjamin also introduced some of the new ideals of post-1750 European architecture: a freedom from Vitruvian ideals, epitomized by the romantic movement and, in the realm of classical architecture, by romantic classicism (neoclassicism). In *The American Builder's Companion* Benjamin admitted that many "old fashioned workmen" would follow in "the footsteps of Palladio" but that "reform in some parts of the system of architecture is loudly demanded. . . . "

Benjamin published seven works on architecture that were issued in a total of 45 editions. Many of his designs borrowed the Adam "Federal" style from Charles Bulfinch, but by the fifth edition (1826) of *The American Builder's Companion* Benjamin was introducing Greek revival detailing. He even seems to have opened a "school" of architecture in Boston; however, it was through his publications that Benjamin's fame spread. Numerous buildings in Chicago prior to the 1871 fire had a Benjaminesque flavor.

Benjamin's most noted designs are the West Church Meeting House (1806) and the First Church (1808), both in Boston; the Meeting House in Northampton, Mass. (1810); and the Rhode Island Union Bank in Newport (1817). He also built houses in Massachusetts and Vermont. Many churches and homes in New England attributed to Benjamin were constructed by carpenter-builders from designs in his books. The Congregational Church in Bennington, Vt. (1804-1808), for example, which has been attributed to Benjamin, was designed by Lavius Fillmore.

Further Reading

For general background and specific material on Benjamin see Talbot Hamlin, *Greek Revival Architecture in America* (1944), and Edmund W. Sinnott, *Meetinghouse and Church in Early New England* (1963). See also Benjamin's *The American Builder's Companion* (1806; 6th ed. 1827; repr. 1969). □

Judah Philip Benjamin

An American lawyer and statesman, Judah Philip Benjamin (1811-1884) served in the Cabinet of the Confederate president Jefferson Davis until the end of the Civil War.

Judah Benjamin was born a British subject on St. Thomas, British West Indies, Aug. 11, 1811. His parents moved to Wilmington, N.C., about 1813 and later to Charleston, S. C. Benjamin attended Yale College, where his student days were dogged with rumored scandal. He read law in New Orleans and was admitted to the bar in 1832. He and his friend John Slidell published a summary of decisions made by the territorial government and Supreme Court of Louisiana which became a standard legal guide. Benjamin devoted most of his attention to commercial law and became a widely admired practitioner. He once declined appointment to the U.S. Supreme Court.

Elected to the U.S. Senate in 1852, Benjamin strongly defended the South's position and was an acknowledged leader of the pro-Southern congressional faction. He resigned from the Senate in 1861 to become attorney general in the Confederate Cabinet. His brilliant legal mind made him invaluable to President Jefferson Davis, and as the bond of trust and friendship between the two deepened, Davis gave Benjamin increased responsibility. He called on him to serve as secretary of war for a brief time. But Benjamin earned Confederate congressional disapproval as secretary of war—various largely unavoidable military failures were fastened upon him—and many Southern lawmakers wanted the Jewish leader expelled from the government.

Davis yielded to pressure, yet defied it. After removing Benjamin from the war post, he appointed him secretary of state in 1862, and the choice was a wise one. Benjamin could not win foreign recognition of the Confederacy—the main goal of Confederate diplomacy; and he counseled President Davis too long in the ways of traditional negotiation. But when he realized that military reverses had cooled foreign ardor for Southern recognition, he persuaded President Davis to take a course of secondary diplomacy, which proved highly successful. Benjamin recognized that blockade-running was vital to sustaining Southern supplies, and he sent "commercial agents" to Bermuda, the West Indies, and Cuba to open ports to Confederate blockade-runners. The system, after mid-1863, was expanded and brought rich rewards to investors, shipowners, and the Confederate Army. In this area Benjamin performed his most valuable service to the South.

When the Confederacy collapsed, Benjamin escaped to England, where, bankrupt and without standing, he began a new career. Living a spartan and frugal life, he studied law and was called to the English bar in 1866. In 1872 he

attained the distinguished position of queen's counsel and was recognized as one of the leaders of English law. His book, *Law of Sale of Personal Property* (1868), was long a standard in England and the United States.

A romantic but tragic marriage doomed Benjamin to much loneliness, since his wife chose to live most of the time in France. He died on May 6, 1884.

Further Reading

For information on Benjamin see Pierce Butler, *Judah P. Benjamin* (1907); Robert Douthat Meade, *Judah P. Benjamin: Confederate Statesman* (1943); and Frank E. Vandiver, *Their Tattered Flags* (1970).

Additional Sources

Butler, Pierce, *Judah P. Benjamin,* New York: Chelsea House, 1980.

Evans, Eli N., *Judah P. Benjamin, the Jewish Confederate,* New York: Free Press, 1988.

Meade, Robert Douthat, *Judah P. Benjamin: Confederate statesman,* New York: Arno Press, 1975. □

Gottfried Benn

The German author Gottfried Benn (1886-1956) was an important expressionist writer. Influenced by his work as a physician, he demonstrated brutal anti-sentimentalism in both his poetry and prose.

Gottfried Benn was born at Mansfeld, Prussia, the son of a Lutheran minister. The poet's earliest influences were the stern discipline of his father, whom he grew to hate, and the gentle romanticism of his Swiss mother, whom he adored. Eldest son in a large family, he entertained his brothers and sisters with fairy tales of his own creation. Although interested in a literary career, he studied medicine and graduated with honors from the Kaiser Wilhelm Academy for Military Doctors.

His mother's death from cancer prompted Benn, then 26, to compose his first major poetic effort, *Morgue* (1912). This work emphasizes nature's indifference to human values and is characterized by melancholy cynicism. While serving as a medical officer during World War I, Benn composed semiautobiographical prose sketches which stressed the "dissolution of natural vitality." He then received an appointment to a hospital in Berlin and soon after married Edith Brosin, an actress. After beginning a private practice among the poor of Berlin, Benn published *Flesh* (1917), his second volume of poetry. In this work his disgust with "the stench of life" is evident.

Despite personal difficulties, among them his wife's death in 1921, Benn continued to pursue his literary and medical careers. Collections of his poetry were published in 1922, 1928, and 1935. For a brief period he was attracted to Nazism, since he felt that the political theories of this movement would foster a new social order based on the philoso-

phy of Friedrich Nietzsche. Considered reactionary, in 1932 Benn was removed from the faculty of the Prussian Academy by more liberal colleagues. But ironically, Hitler's regime was also hostile toward him. His prose works *After Nihilism* (1932) and *The New State and the Intellectual* (1933) supported the Third Reich but were banned because his poetry had been published by Jewish-owned firms. In 1935 Benn joined the army medical corps and served throughout World War II.

Benn was prevented from publishing by the Nazi government, but he privately printed a group of 22 poems in 1943. His second wife died in 1945, and he shortly thereafter married again. After the end of the war his work was banned by the Allies, but with the publication of *Static Poems* in 1948, he reemerged as a major poet. In 1949 he published several novellas, including *The Ptolemean.* Nihilistic thought continued to permeate Benn's work, but in *Static Poems* and *Intoxicated Tide* (1949) he grants that a precarious happiness may occur when man transcends biological and intellectual decomposition through art. Benn's autobiography, *Doppelleben* (Double Life), appeared in 1950. He died in West Berlin in 1956.

Further Reading

Michael Hamburger and Christopher Middleton, eds., *Modern German Poetry* (1962), contains some fine translations of Benn's poetry and a brief biographical sketch. There are several full-length studies of him in German but none in English. The section in Walter H. Sokel, *The Writer In Extremis: Expressionism in Twentieth-Century German Literature* (1959), is the outstanding analysis in English of Benn's art. □

Tony Benn

The British Labour Party politician Tony Benn (born 1925) held several cabinet positions between 1966 and 1979. He was a leading socialist and advocate of "participatory democracy." He gained perhaps even greater notoriety in later years when he published a series of tell-all diaries about the British cabinet.

Anthony Neil Wedgewood Benn was born in London on April 4, 1925, the son of the Ist Viscount Stansgate, a prominent member of the Labour Party. He had a middle-class upbringing, which was strongly influenced by the radicalism of his father and the religious beliefs of his mother. He attended Westminster and New College, Oxford, where his education was interrupted by World War II. He joined the Royal Air Force in 1943 and was stationed for a time in Rhodesia.

In 1946 Benn returned to Oxford and completed a degree in politics, philosophy, and economics. As president of the Oxford Union he skillfully defended the policies of the postwar Labour government of Clement Attlee. In 1949 he married Caroline Middleton de Camp, and in the same year he began to work as a journalist and in broadcasting with the B.B.C. Then, in 1950, he was elected Labour member of Parliament for Bristol South East, at 25 years of age the youngest member of Parliament.

During his first ten years in the House of Commons Benn was more of a radical than a socialist. He became identified with human rights issues such as divorce reform and opposition to capital punishment. His London home near Holland Park became a center of anti-colonial activity. He was a leading member of the H-Bomb Nuclear Committee. Ideologically, he remained near the center of the party and did not play a major role in the battles over nuclear disarmament and nationalization of industry (1960-1961).

In 1960 Benn's political career was placed in jeopardy by the death of his father. Under ordinary circumstances, he would inherit his father's title and a seat in the House of Lords, thus removing him from the focus of political influence. From 1954 on Benn had tried unsuccessfully to renounce the title. He now undertook a legal and political campaign for renunciation which involved re-election to his Bristol seat, from which he was then barred by an election court. With public opinion on their side, Benn's supporters pressed Parliament to enact the Peerage Act in 1963. This historic measure allowed him (and other prominent politicians) to sit in the Commons and gave a fillip to his career.

Benn served as postmaster-general under Harold Wilson from 1964 to 1966. Then he held the cabinet post of minister of technology (1966-1970). In 1969 this office became a "super ministry" when responsibilities for industry and power were added to it. As a cabinet member Benn was

in the forefront of the technological revolution of the 1960s. He increased the functions of the post office, gave support to companies which employed new technology, and tried to increase economic growth.

During the early 1970s, with the Labour Party in opposition, Benn's ideas became more socialistic. He employed his formidable debating skills to advocate policies that clashed with those of the moderate leadership of the party. He urged a significant extension of public ownership in the economy. He also favored "participatory democracy" in broadcasting, referenda on issues such as entrance into the European Common Market (European Union), and workers' cooperatives. He became a leading spokesman for the left wing of the party.

When Wilson again became prime minister in 1974, Benn returned to the cabinet as secretary of state for industry. In the following year he was transferred against his wishes to the less important post of secretary of state for energy, where he served until 1979. Benn was a candidate for the leadership of the party in 1976 after Wilson unexpectedly resigned. He lost decisively to James Callaghan, who became prime minister.

After 1981, when the Conservatives were returned to power under Margaret Thatcher, Benn was in disagreement with the leadership of the Labour Party. He criticized its policies as too moderate and advocated "party democracy." This led to constitutional changes within the party, including the election of the leader of constituency parties, trade unions, and members of the House of Commons. These changes precipitated a split within the party in 1981, when some conservative members left to form the Social Democratic Party. In the election of 1983 Benn lost his Bristol seat but was returned as Member of Parliament for Chesterfield in a by-election held later in the year. He continued to be a leading member of the party but appeared to have lost much of his influence after 1983. In April of 1990, the zealous Benn made a final attempt to further his platform by starting his own party, the Labor Party Socialists, but little was ever heard from them again.

Benn had the unusual habit of keeping a meticulous chronicle of his own life. He carried a tape recorder with him into the cabinet chambers on a regular basis. These facts came to light in 1987 when Benn published *Out of the Wilderness,* the first in a series of his diaries. In 1988 a second book appeared, *Office Without Power.* Subsequent diaries were released in 1989 and 1990. The diaries detailed Benn's personal life as well as his professional experiences, but they were viewed by many as an exposé of the workings of the British government. Benn was accused by the press of violating the Official Secrets Act for divulging the privileged experiences of British cabinet meetings. Although the diaries caused quite a stir, they were panned by most critics, and Benn, whose public image already was less than endearing, suffered few repercussions because of them. In 1993 he put forth his personal political views in yet another book, *Common Sense.*

In all Benn's writings, interviews, orations, and other exhortations presented a consistent display of unabashed optimism which was rarely coincident with the realities of daily life. During Benn's later years his critics and colleagues spent much energy in denying his credibility, although they spent equally as much energy trying to understand him at all.

Further Reading

The best account of Benn's career is Robert Jenkins, *Tony Benn: A Political Biography* (1980). This should be read together with Benn's book *Parliament, People and Power: Agenda for a Free Society* (1982), which consists of a series of interviews he gave to the *New Left Review*. See also: Henry Pelling, *A Short History of the Labour Party* (1982); Martin Holmes, *The Labour Government, 1974-79: Political Aims and Economic Realities* (1985); Harold Wilson, *A Personal Record: The Labour Government, 1974-76* (1970); and Barbara Castle, *The Castle Diaries* (1980, 1985).

Additional Sources

Economist (September 10, 1988; October 1, 1988; September 30, 1989; April 7, 1990; October 6, 1990; September 18, 1993).
New Statesman & Society (October 7, 1994; September 8, 1995; December 8, 1995; February 28, 1997).
Canadian Dimension (February-March 1995). □

Alan Bennett

Although not a prolific playwright, Alan Bennett (born 1934) earned a solid reputation as one of Britain's finest writers for the stage and television.

In the summer of 1960 in Edinburgh there burst onto the British theater scene a revue which made immediate stars of its four author/participants—Alan Bennett, Peter Cook, Jonathan Miller, and Dudley Moore. Taken to London the following spring, *Beyond the Fringe* won the *Evening Standard* award as the best play; in New York it won the Antoinette Perry Award (Tony) and the New York Drama Critics Circle award for 1963. Robert Brustein wrote of the series of 23 sketches lampooning religion, the royal family, war, pornography, and Shakespearean history plays that it had "no firm moral center . . . " and that it was "immoderate, irresponsible, . . . totally destructive . . . and violently funny." Several decades later, after *Monty Python* and *Saturday Night Live* on opposite sides of the Atlantic, it seems quite tame, with the Shakespeare parody the sketch that held up best. Three of the participants (Cook, Miller, and Moore) quickly parlayed their success in this production into transatlantic fame, while Bennett did not.

Born May 9, 1934, in Leeds, Bennett had served in the Intelligence Corps from 1952 to 1954 and had been graduated from Exeter College of Oxford in 1957. That he had proved exceptional as a student was demonstrated by his appointment as a junior lecturer in history at Magdalen College, Oxford, in the years 1960-1962. He had also worked as an actor on stage and television. Bennett turned to writing for television, authoring the series "On the Margin" in 1966, for which he was honored by the Guild of

Television Producers the following year. From 1968 to 1973 Bennett added to his reputation with three plays for the stage: *Forty Years On* (1968), *Getting On* (1971), and *Habeas Corpus* (1973).

Forty Years On concerns the retirement ceremony for the longtime headmaster of a public (read "private") school not very subtly named Albion. The staff and students put on a play about the World War II era in honor of the occasion, but within the play are what Bennett calls "memoirs," short sketches about English society which take place in various years from 1900 to 1945. The play was generally well received, with Irving Wardle of the *Times* of London writing that it was "what Bennett needed to make the transition from revue-sketch writer to playwright"; it garnered the *Evening Standard* award for 1968. Acclaim was not universal, however: visiting *New York Times* critic Clive Barnes called the play "fundamentally cheap and nasty" and found it characterized by "pretentiousness and ineptness."

Getting On, a seriocomic look at British politics, deals with two members of Parliament and offers a paradox right at the start: the stodgy and stuffy George is in the Labour Party, while the more dashing and, not so incidentally, gay Brian is a conservative. A career in politics, one of them opines, "fills in that awkward gap between the cradle and the grave." When Brian is blackmailed into not seeking reelection, Bennett concludes with the Voltairean observation that "the only thing that matters in life is work." The play won the *Evening Standard* award for 1971.

Habeas Corpus is a sex farce, albeit at a sophisticated level, but with frequent descents into vaudeville and even burlesque, including lyrics sung to the tunes of "The Isle of Capri" and "Shuffle Off to Buffalo," some speeches in doggerel, and more than one trouserless male. All of the characters are in the grip of some monomania: Dr. Wicksteed is a lecher, his son has developed the erroneous notion that he is going to die in three months, his daughter is obsessed with her flat-chestedness, and Canon Thrabbing is celibate but eager to remedy that condition. The conclusion: "He whose lust lasts, lasts longest." The play was taken to New York in 1975, where it had a modest run.

Bennett continued to write for television, with "A Day Out" in 1972; "Sunset Across the Bay" in 1975; "A Little Outing," "A Visit from Miss Prothero," "Me, I'm Afraid of Virginia Woolf," and "Doris and Doreen" in 1978; "The Old Crowd," "One Fine Day," "Afternoon Off," and "All Day on the Sands" in 1979; "Objects of Affection" (including the five short works "Our Winnie," "A Woman of No Importance," "Rolling Home," "Marks," and "Say Something Happened"), "Intensive Care," and "An Englishman Abroad," all in 1982; "The Insurance Man" in 1986; "Talking Heads" in 1987; and "102 Boulevard Haussmann" in 1991. He also wrote screenplays in the 1980s, authoring *A Private Function* in 1985 and *Prick Up Your Ears,* an adaptation of John Lahr's biography of playwright Joe Orton, in 1988, neither a conspicuous success.

For the stage he composed *The Old Country* in 1977, *Enjoy* in 1980, and his most resounding failure, *Kafka's Dick,* in 1986. In his introduction to the volume *Two Kafka Plays* in 1987, Bennett contributed numerous brilliant and sensitive observations about the Czech author, opining that "his life conforms in every particular to what we have convinced ourselves an artist's life should be" and concluding that he "never wholeheartedly felt himself a member of the human race." But in the play, an attack on the trivialization of great men, he seemed unable to resist being clever and witty, so that only the most sensitive spectator could realize that he himself was not joining in that trivialization.

In 1988 he adapted his television play "An Englishman Abroad" and wrote a one-acter, "A Question of Attribution," to make an series titled *Single Spies*, which had a fine critical success. Two years later he wrote an adaptation of *The Wind in the Willows*, called by novelist Tom Sharpe the archetypal picture of English life.

He returned to earlier English history in 1991 with *The Madness of George the Third*. A critical success, it was exported to New York in 1993, although for only a limited run at the Brooklyn Academy of Music, the self-appointed temple of excellent drama that figures to do badly at the box office. A film version of the play was released in 1994 and fared much better. Bennett himself was nominated for an Oscar for best screenplay adaptation of the work. The year 1994 also saw the publication of his well received autobiographical work, *Writing Home*. According to Bennett the work is a collection of diaries, book reviews, essays, and more. In 1995 Bennett demonstrated his gift for multi-faceted entertainment when he did the narration for a sound recording of *Winnie-The-Pooh*, adding "some much-needed grit to the almost terminal twee-ness of A.A. Milne's prose," according to reviewer Bret Harte.

Bennett's career was summed up by Burton Kendle in *Contemporary Dramatists* in this way: "Alan Bennett's plays consistently dramatize man's desire to define himself and his world through teasingly inadequate language."

Further Reading

Biographical material on Alan Bennett can be found in *Contemporary Drama* and *Contemporary Authors* . See also Bennett, Alan. *Writing Home*, (1994); *People Weekly*, (November 13, 1995; January 29, 1996). *Time*, (February 27, 1995). □

Arnold Bennett

The English novelist and dramatist Arnold Bennett (1867-1931) was the author of *The Old Wives' Tale*, a masterpiece of realism.

Arnold Bennett was born on May 27, 1867, in Hanley, one of the pottery-making "Six Towns" of central England. The youth, called Enoch, spoke with a stammer and was determined to make his living in literature. After attending local schools and working in his father's law office, he moved to London in 1888 to become a writer. In 1893 he was employed by the magazine *Woman*, and in 1898 he published his first novel, *A Man from the*

North. During these years he began to call himself Arnold Bennett. In 1902 Bennett published two novel, *Anna of the Five Towns* and *The Grand Babylon Hotel*—the first realistic, the second sensational. They represent the pattern of his work: fiction of serious artistic purpose produced at the same time as material of no artistic value.

Bennett lived in France from 1902 to 1913. Shortly after his fortieth birthday he married Marguerite Soulié. The couple seemed happy but within a few years proved incompatible. During these years Bennett wrote magazine articles, self-help books, plays, short stories, and novels—a tremendous output. Most of it, however, was written only to make money. But *Tales of the Five Towns* and the trilogy *Anna of the Five Towns* (1902), *Leonora* (1903), and *Sacred and Profane Love* (1904) are worth mention, for in them Bennett began his realistic studies of life in the industrial "Five Towns," changed from the actual "Six Towns" for reasons of euphony.

The Old Wives' Tale

The sight of an old woman in a restaurant in Paris in 1903 gave Bennett the idea for a novel that would, as he wrote, "go one better" than Guy de Maupassant's realistic novel *Une Vie*. While writing other books he nourished the idea, and in 1907 he began to write it. The novel came quickly, a thousand words or more each day. After various interruptions, including the writing of *Buried Alive* (1908) and the production of his play *Cupid and Commonsense* (1908), *The Old Wives' Tale* was completed and published in 1908. It is the story of the sisters Constance and Sophia

Baines from their girlhood in Bursley, one of the "Five Towns," to their deaths 50 years later. Constance stayed at home; Sophia, like Bennett, escaped to Paris. The story realistically depicts the minute changes by which the girls become old women.

The Old Wives' Tale brought Bennett fame and money. He secured his position as an eminent author with the "Clayhanger" novels (Clayhanger, 1910; Hilda Lessways, 1911; These Twain, 1916), which are meticulous studies of love, marriage, and society in the "Five Towns." Meanwhile, he capitalized on his position with light novels, a travel book about the United States, and several plays, of which Milestones (1912), written with E. Knoblock, is best known.

During World War I Bennett served his country as a journalist and civil servant. He separated from his wife in 1921, and in 1922 he met Dorothy Cheston, an actress, by whom he had a daughter in 1926. In the 1920s Bennett's critical reputation declined, and his carefully objective realism became old-fashioned. During this period his literary productions were not equal to his best, though Riceyman Steps (1923) evinced a brief return of his talent. His popular reputation, however, was never higher, and his novels and journalistic work made him one of the highest-paid writers of his day. Displays of his portrait on posters advertising his works made his pleasantly distinctive face with its heavy-lidded gaze and prominent teeth familiar to thousands. After a trip to France during which he caught typhoid fever, Bennett died on March 31, 1931.

Further Reading

Newman Flower, ed., The Journals of Arnold Bennett (3 vols., 1932-1933), provides an indispensable account of his activities but reveals the inner man only unintentionally. Perhaps the best life of Arnold is Reginald Pound, Arnold Bennett: A Biography (1953). Two critical attacks on Bennett are Virginia Woolf, Mr. Bennett and Mrs. Brown (1924) and passages in E.M. Forster, Aspects of the Novel (1927). E.M.W. Tillyard defends The Old Wives' Tale in The Epic Strain in the English Novel (1958). American academic criticism is best represented by James Hall, Arnold Bennett: Primitivism and Taste (1959), and James G. Hepburn, The Art of Arnold Bennett (1963). The best brief introduction to the historical background is in Boris Ford, ed., The Pelican Guide to English Literature, vol. 7: The Modern Age (1958; rev. ed. 1962).

Additional Sources

Bennett, Arnold, Over there; war scenes on the Western Front, Plainview, N.Y., Books for Libraries Press 1975.

Bennett, Arnold, Sketches for autobiography, London; Boston: G. Allen & Unwin, 1979.

Bennett, Arnold, The truth about an author, Plainview, N.Y., Books for Libraries Press 1975, 1911.

Bennett, Dorothy Cheston, Arnold Bennett: a portrait done at home, together with 170 letters from A., Plainview, N.Y., 1975, 1935.

Darton, F. J. Harvey (Frederick Joseph Harvey), Arnold Bennett, New York, Haskell House, 1974.

Drabble, Margaret, Arnold Bennett; a biography, London, Weidenfeld and Nicolson 1974; New York: Knopf, 1974; Boston, Mass.: G.K. Hall, 1974, 1986.

Follett, Helen Thomas, Arnold Bennett, Folcroft, Pa. Folcroft Library Editions, 1974; Philadelphia: R. West, 1978.

Swinnerton, Frank, Arnold Bennett: a last word, Garden City, N.Y.: Doubleday, 1978. □

James Gordon Bennett

The Scottish-born American journalist James Gordon Bennett (1795-1872) developed editorial techniques that promoted readership and freed the press of its need for financial support from political parties and other special-interest groups.

James Gordon Bennett was born near Keith, Banffshire, Scotland, on Sept. 1, 1795. In his early 20s he migrated to Nova Scotia, where he taught briefly before going to the United States to work for a Boston book publisher. Bennett went to New York City, then Charleston, S.C., where he worked as a translator for the newspaper Courier. He soon returned north and worked for the New York Courier. Twice Bennett tried to launch a paper of his own, but each time his paper failed for lack of political support. These rejections caused him to turn his back on political patronage as being too uncertain and demeaning.

In 1835, at the age of 40, with $500 as working capital, Bennett launched the New York Herald, the paper that made him famous. An excessively egotistical man, he wanted to be the Shakespeare of journalism. By five each morning he was at his desk—a plank supported by two barrels. Brilliant but brassy, he issued a saucy, informative sheet and used sensational techniques, particularly in the Robinson-Jewett murder case, which was a sordid affair.

Bennett, who had a compulsion to be first with the news, initiated daily Wall Street reports, sent small boats out to intercept oceangoing vessels for news, initiated the society page, and was the first to use the telegraph extensively for news coverage. He insisted that advertisers change their ads frequently, a policy that skyrocketed consumer sales and caused merchants seeking similar results to flock to the Herald. He collected in advance.

Bennett's pugnacious writing and his flair for self-promotion frequently got him into trouble. He suffered severe beatings in the streets for inglorious references to his enemies. Twice he was mauled and caned by a former employer, and a few years later a Wall Street broker used a horsewhip on him. In 1850 a defeated political candidate and his two brothers knocked Bennett down and beat him as his wife watched helplessly. Finally Mrs. Bennett could no longer bear the pressures and the street indignities, and she fled to Europe with the three Bennett children.

In 1867 Bennett turned over the operation of the Herald to his son, James Gordon Bennett, Jr. The elder Bennett visited the office frequently, then kept in touch by direct telegraph wire until June 1, 1872, when he died in his sleep.

Though so abrasive in life that he was a social outcast, Bennett was praised after death. His old opponent Horace

Greeley said that Bennett's success was due to personal journalism. The *New York Sun* more shrewdly remarked that Bennett emancipated the press "from the domination of sects, parties, and cliques. . . . "

Further Reading

Biographies of Bennett include Don C. Seitz, *The James Gordon Bennetts: Father and Son, Proprietors of the New York Herald* (1928), and Oliver Carlson, *The Man Who Made News: James Gordon Bennett* (1942). Interesting aspects are treated in Richard O'Connor, *The Scandalous Mr. Bennett* (1962). Other helpful works are Oswald Garrison Villard, *Some Newspapers and Newspaper-Men* (1923; rev. ed. 1926); Willard Grosvenor Bleyer, *Main Currents in the History of American Journalism* (1927); and Frank Luther Mott, *American Journalism* (1941; 3d ed. 1962), which offers a concise account of Bennett.

Additional Sources

Fermer, Douglas, *James Gordon Bennett and the New York herald: a study of editorial opinion in the Civil War era, 1854-1867,* London: Royal Historical Society; New York: St. Martin's Press, 1986.

Herd, Harold, *Seven editors,* Westport, Conn.: Greenwood Press, 1977.

Seitz, Don Carlos, *The James Gordon Bennetts: father & son, proprietors of the New York Herald,* New York, Beekman Publishers, 1974. □

James Gordon Bennett Jr.

James Gordon Bennett, Jr. (1841-1918), American newspaper owner and editor, contributed to journalistic innovations and created a legend of personal authority and enterprise.

On May 10, 1841, James Gordon Bennett, Jr., was born in New York City. He was raised in Europe to avoid the stigma his father's bold editing of the *New York Herald* newspaper attracted to the family. Young Bennett served in 1861-1862 in the Civil War without distinction. In 1866 he climaxed several years dedicated to entertainment and sports by winning a grueling transatlantic yachting contest. The tall, straight, firm-jawed "Commodore" (so named by the New York Yacht Club) retained an interest in sailing and other diversions but now turned seriously to mastering newspaper work.

In 1867 his father made Bennett head of the *Herald's* editorial department. That year the young man launched the *Evening Telegram,* which exploited sensational news. He was an editorial autocrat who hired and fired many brilliant and remarkable writers and editors. Bennett early projected his goal of making as well as reporting news. As in his scoop on the Custer massacre in 1876, he followed his father's goal of energetic news gathering.

Bennett's newspaper firsts were many, resulting from his bold planning and indifference to expense. Most famous was his 1869 assignment to Henry M. Stanley to find Dr. David Livingstone in Africa—a successful mission that won world acclaim. Other exploits included efforts to reach the North Pole and to find the Northwest Passage to the Pacific Ocean. Bennett published the distinguished reports of J.A. MacGahan, providing evidence of Bulgarian atrocities that helped spark the Russo-Turkish War of 1871. Notable, too, was Bennett's duel with financier Jay Gould, whose telegraph and cable systems taxed Bennett and others heavily. Acting with the mine owner John W. Mackay, Bennett set up rival systems which by 1887 had lowered the prices of messages drastically and created freer international exchange.

In 1887 Bennett started the *Paris Herald,* which over the years gratified American tourists abroad and enjoyed its own journalistic distinctions. It ran at a loss (as did the London edition, 1889-1891, which failed entirely) but helped explicate the American image abroad. The competition of publishers William Randolph Hearst and Joseph Pulitzer in the 1890s harmed the *Herald's* prestige, but the paper revived during the Spanish-American War (1898), when Bennett's resourcefulness and knowledge of ships resulted in creative reporting. Bennett moved from notoriety to fame, and back again. For example, in 1907 he was required to pay a total of $31,000 in fines for having permitted publication of immoral advertisements.

Bennett's new *Herald* building in New York was long a showplace for its architectural charm. During the 1900s the *Herald* lost status as a journalistic leader, and Bennett, who

was said to have spent some $30 million from *Herald* revenues, gave up the lavish gestures and bold experiments which had made him an international legend. A bachelor until the age of 73, he married a widow in 1914. Convinced that he would die on his seventy-seventh birthday, he actually sank into a coma in Paris on May 10, 1918, and died 4 days later. He was buried at Passy, France.

Further Reading

Bennett has been treated as a phenomenon rather than as a noted journalistic figure. The initial tone was struck in Albert Stevens Crockett, *When James Gordon Bennett Was Caliph of Bagdad* (1926). Don C. Seitz, *The James Gordon Bennetts: Father and Son, Proprietors of the New York Herald* (1928), emphasizes the journalism of father and son. More anecdotal is Richard O'Connor, *The Scandalous Mr. Bennett* (1962). A succinct statement is in Oswald Garrison Villard, *Some Newspapers and Newspaper-Men* (1923; rev. ed. 1926). See also Al Laney, *Paris Herald: The Incredible Newspaper* (1947). □

John Coleman Bennett

The American Protestant social ethicist John Coleman Bennett (1902-1995) was a leading Christian thinker of the century who applied ethical principles to urgent issues of modern society.

J ohn Coleman Bennett was born on July 22, 1902, in Kingston, Ontario, to American parents. He was educated at Williams College, Massachusetts, Oxford University, and Union Theological Seminary in New York City.

Academic Career

Bennett spent his entire career as a seminary teacher, beginning at Union Seminary in 1927. From 1930 to 1938 he taught at Auburn Theological Seminary in New York. In 1931 he married Anna Louesa McGrew; they had two sons and a daughter. Bennett's first book, *Social Salvation* (1935), was followed by *Christianity—And Our World* (1936). The former set forth his lifelong conviction that the problems of society must be an integral part of Christian thinking; the latter championed the existence of a universal or "common" morality upon which specifically Christian ethics builds and to which it can appeal.

Between 1938 and 1943 Bennett taught at the Pacific School of Religion, Berkeley, California. In 1939 he was ordained a Congregational minister. He published *Christian Realism* in 1941. Its title epitomizes Bennett's approach to social ethics: his conviction that the biblical-Christian perspective on the role of the individual in society is profoundly realistic, avoiding utopian optimism by its grasp of human sinfulness and avoiding fatalistic pessimism by its confidence in human dignity and possibilities under God.

In 1943 Bennett returned to teach at Union Theological Seminary. The first holder of the Reinhold Niebuhr professorship of social ethics (1960-1970), he became dean of the faculty in 1955 and was president of the seminary from 1964 until his retirement in 1970. He received several honorary doctorates from colleges and seminaries. Bennett wrote most of his books during this long tenure. Among them are *Christian Ethics and Social Policy* (1946), *Christianity and Communism Today* (1948; rev. 1960), *The Christian as Citizen* (1955), *Christians and the State* (1958), *Nuclear Weapons and the Conflict of Conscience* (editor; 1962), *When Christians Make Political Decisions* (1964), *Christian Social Ethics in a Changing World* (editor; 1966), and *Foreign Policy in Christian Perspective* (1966).

Participation in Ecumenical Movement

Bennett was prominent in the ecumenical movement. He was an official leader in deliberations on the church and the social order at the Amsterdam (1948), Evanston (1954), and New Delhi (1961) assemblies of the World Council of Churches, and he served the National Council of Churches of Christ in the Unites States in various positions. While at Union, Bennett fostered alliances with theological seminaries of various faiths, including the Jewish Theological Seminary and the Woodstock Theological Seminary, a Roman Catholic institution.

Political Activism

With his distinguished friend and colleague Reinhold Niebuhr, Bennett founded the influential journal *Christianity and Crisis* in 1941 and continued as its editor for many years. He became politically engaged as vice- chairman of the Liberal party in New York State (1955-1965) and, in

1960, as a leading Protestant defender of John F. Kennedy's candidacy against those who feared a Roman Catholic president. His involvement in political and social issues extended to participation in the civil rights movement, protests against the war in Vietnam, opposition to the use of nuclear weapons, and, late in his life, advocacy of gay and lesbian rights within the church. Bennett's final book *The Radical Imperative* was published in 1975, although he continued to contribute articles to *Christianity and Crisis* until 1993. Bennett died April 27, 1995.

Further Reading

Bennett's career is assessed in David H. Smith, *The Achievement of John C. Bennett* (1970), and Robert Lee, *The Promise of Bennett: Christian Realism and Social Responsibility* (1969). An obituary tribute by Leon Howell appeared in *The Christian Century* (May 24, 1995). □

Richard Bedford Bennett

Richard Bedford Bennett (1870-1947) was a leader of the Conservative party of Canada and prime minister during the Great Depression in the 1930s.

Richard Bedford Bennett was born at Hopewell, New Brunswick, on July 3, 1870, a descendant of pre-Loyalist settlers from Connecticut. After graduating from Dalhousie University in 1893, he practiced law in Chatham, New Brunswick, for 4 years and then moved to Calgary in the Northwest Territories. There he soon built up a successful legal business and established a connection with the E. B. Eddy Company that was to lead to his holding a controlling interest in it 25 years later. He also acted as solicitor for the Canadian Pacific Railway.

Bennett was a member of the Assembly of the Northwest Territories for 6 years and was elected to the Alberta Legislature in 1909, then resigned to contest and win the Calgary East Riding for the Conservatives in the general election of 1911. He did not run in the wartime election of 1917 but served briefly in the ministries of Arthur Meighen of 1920-1921 and 1926. He represented Calgary West from 1925 to 1938. On Meighen's retirement from public life in 1927, Bennett was chosen leader of the Conservative party. Promising to end the growing unemployment of the Depression by "blasting" his way into world markets, and fortifying Conservative coffers with $600,000 from his own fortune, Bennett defeated W. L. Mackenzie King in the general election of 1930.

In office Bennett proceeded to launch a modest public works program to provide employment, but his major response to Depression conditions was to increase the tariff to unprecedented levels, followed by an initiative which led to the establishment of preferential tariff arrangements within the British Empire. These policies probably further restricted Canadian export trade and increased the burden of the Depression on those who already felt it most. Such policies, the arbitrary treatment of protesters, and the apparent cold aloofness of the bachelor-millionaire prime minister made Bennett an increasingly unpopular leader.

After 4 years, under pressure from a small reform group within his party led by H. H. Stevens, and in the face of the coming election, Bennett began to move toward reform. Through his brother-in-law, W. D. Herridge, Canadian minister to Washington, he became greatly interested in Roosevelt's New Deal program. Early in 1935, to the shock of his Cabinet colleagues, who had not been consulted, Bennett announced in a series of radio addresses a "New Deal" of planning and social security. His government then enacted measures extending farm credit and establishing a natural-products marketing board, unemployment insurance, and minimum wages and maximum hours in industry. After Bennett's defeat in the election of 1935, most of this legislation was ruled unconstitutional by the courts. Bennett remained as leader of the opposition until 1938, when he retired to live in England. In 1941 he was created Viscount Bennett of Mickleham, Calgary, and Hopewell. He died in England on June 26, 1947.

Further Reading

Lord Beaverbrook, *Friends* (1959), and Ernest Watkins, *R. B. Bennett: A Biography* (1963), contain useful discussions of Bennett. J. R. H. Wilbur, *The Bennett New Deal: Fraud or Portent?* (1968), contains the major documents of Bennett's administration.

Additional Sources

Gray, James Henry, *R.B. Bennett: the Calgary years,* Toronto; Buffalo: University of Toronto Press, 1991.

Waite, Peter B., *The loner: three sketches of the personal life and ideas of R.B. Bennett, 1870-1947,* Toronto; Buffalo: University of Toronto Press, 1992. ☐

Richard Rodney Bennett

Richard Rodney Bennett (born 1936) was one of the most gifted and versatile composers to emerge from Britain's cultural renaissance after World War II, writing for films and television, opera and concert audiences.

R ichard Rodney Bennett was born in Kent and received his musical training as a scholarship student at the Royal College of Music, where he was a pupil of Lennox Berkeley and Howard Ferguson. When Bennett was 18, he composed a piano sonata that revealed his unusual talent. It is recognized as being an important contemporary work.

In 1957 a scholarship awarded by the French government enabled Bennett to study with Pierre Boulez in Paris for two years. Although Boulez was one of the leaders of the musical avant-garde, he did not impose his style on the young composer. Bennett returned to England with a complete mastery of serial techniques, but he never used them in a doctrinaire manner. He had become a versatile composer, seemingly able to write convincingly in any style and for many different audiences. In 1970 Bennett accepted a two-year appointment as visiting professor of composition at the Peabody Conservatory in Baltimore, Maryland.

Bennett's opera *The Mines of Sulphur* (1963) has been called one of the most professionally adept and successful first full-length operas ever produced. It demonstrated that his abilities were particularly suited to writing operas and revealed his strong dramatic sense and his power to create atmosphere and depict characters in soaring melodic lines and colorful orchestration. The opera is through-composed, that is, there are no arias, and the dramatic intensity of the story is reflected at all times in the music. *The Mines of Sulphur* is a horror story, set in a dilapidated ancient mansion in the midst of a forest on a stormy night. A band of disreputable strolling players comes to this spooky place, and horrible deeds ensue. The choice of such a grisly, melodramatic plot shows Bennett's basically romantic attitude as a composer.

Bennett's next opera, *A Penny for a Song* (1967), is a complete contrast. It is a light-hearted political satire, for which the composer adopted a freely tonal idiom, very different from the chromaticism of the earlier opera. His third opera, *Victory,* based on Joseph Conrad's novel, was first performed in London in 1970.

Bennett composed two symphonies (1965 and 1967), a piano concerto (1968), *Epithalamion* (1966) for chorus and

orchestra, a ballet called *Jazz Calendar* (1964) for jazz ensemble, various piano pieces and songs, and his own variations of Scott Joplin. He also wrote piano pieces and songs for children as well as a children's opera, *All the King's Men* (1968), and scores for young musicians.

Bennett is himself an accomplished performer. He recorded classics from Jerome Kern (1975) and Harold Arlen (1993) on the piano. On more than one occasion he collaborated on recordings with Elisabeth Lutyens, including a memorable performance on the basset horn on "Clarinet Classics".

Over the years his works provoke inspired performances from many distinguished performing artists, including Cleo Laine's London Clarinet Consort, Stephen Cleobury's King's Singers, the St. Louis Symphony Orchestra, and the Oregon Symphony. Julian Bream recorded Bennett's guitar sonatas (1982 and 1989). Bennett's Marimba and Percussion Concertos were recorded by Evelyn Glennie, Paul Daniel, and the Scottish Chamber Orchestra. In 1994 Bennett composed and arranged the sound track for the popular motion picture, *Four Weddings and a Funeral,* incorporating songs from many popular artists into the work.

Further Reading

Two general works which include material on Bennett and his music are Paul Henry Lang and Nathan Broder, eds., *Contemporary Music in Europe: A Comprehensive Survey* (1965), and Rollo H. Myers, *Twentieth Century Music* (1968). See also Joseph Machlis, *Introduction to Contemporary Music* (1961); Stewart Craggs, *Richard Rodney Bennett: a Bio-bibliography* (1990). ☐

William John Bennett

The American teacher and scholar William John Bennett (born 1943) was chairman of the National Endowment for the Humanities (1981-1985), secretary of the Department of Education (1985-1988), and director of the Office of National Drug Control Policy (1989-1990) During the 1990s he was codirector of Empower America and an active spokesperson for conservatism.

W illiam John Bennett was born in Flatbush (Brooklyn), New York, on July 3, 1943. His family was middle-class and Roman Catholic. He grew up on the streets of Flatbush and described himself as "streetwise." He first attended PS 92 but later transferred to Jesuit-run Holy Cross Boy's School. His family moved to Washington, D.C., where he graduated from Gonzaga High School, another Catholic institution.

Bennett was mostly raised by his mother, but he early found inspiration in such male American heroes as Abraham Lincoln, Roy Campenella, and Gary Cooper. From these life stories he derived an axiom that heroes are necessary for moral development of children and that this development requires adult guidance as well as inspiration. His high school football coach also provided a role model of mental and physical toughness and convinced Bennett of the value of competitive sports.

Bennett went to Williams College to play football. He was an interior lineman who earned the nickname "the ram" from an incident where he butted down a coed's door. He worked his way through Williams, and later through graduate school, with scholarships and part-time and summer jobs and with student loans that finally totaled $12,000.

Graduating in 1965, he studied philosophy at the University of Texas and wrote a dissertation on the theory of the social contract. (At that time John R. Silber was chairman of the Department of Philosophy and later dean of the College of Arts and Sciences.) He did not study all the time. In 1967 he had a blind date with Janis Joplin, and he also played guitar with a rock and roll band called Plato and the Guardians. While working on his Ph.D., which he earned in 1970, Bennett taught philosophy and religion at the University of Southern Mississippi for a year (1967-1968). He went on to study law at Harvard University, and worked as a social studies tutor and hall proctor (1970-1971) until he earned his J.D. degree.

He then moved across town to Boston University, where Silber had just become president. There he served as an associate dean of the College of Liberal Arts for a year (1971-1972) before becoming an assistant professor of philosophy and an assistant to Silber from 1972 to 1976. One

of his duties was to escort military recruiters through crowds of antiwar protesters, a duty made easier by his football training.

Opening the Door to Government Service

Meanwhile, he was becoming better known nationally. He served on a review panel for the National Endowment for the Humanities (NEH) in 1973 and was chairman of the "Question of Authority in American High Schools" project of the National Humanities Faculty, a conservative group, the same year. He next was associate chairman of the group's bicentennial study, "The American Covenant: The Moral Uses of Power." He was also writing articles. Among these were "In Defense of Sports" in *Commentary* (February 1976); "The Constitution and the Moral Order" in *Hastings Constitutional Law Quarterly* (Fall 1976); and "Let's Bring Back Heroes" in *Newsweek* (April 15, 1977).

In May 1976 he became executive director of the National Humanities Center, which he had co-founded with Charles Frankel, a philosophy professor from Columbia University who took the office of president. When intruders murdered Frankel in 1979, Bennett assumed Frankel's position as well. The same year he co-authored *Counting by Race: Equality from the Founding Fathers to Bakke and Weber* with the journalist Terry Eastland. The book attacked affirmative action and the Supreme Court for legitimizing it.

A registered Democrat who described himself as sympathetic to "neoconservative" causes, Bennett drafted the arts and humanities section of the Heritage Fund"'s *Mandate for Leadership* (1980), a series of recommendations for President-elect Ronald Reagan. He became a Republican and was rewarded by Reagan, who appointed him to replace Joseph Duffy as head of NEH in December 1981. One of his rivals for the job was Silber. As director, Bennett proved abrasive and controversial. He acceded to Reagan's budget cuts for the agency and criticized faddish projects, including three documentaries made with NEH funds: "From the Ashes . . . Nicaragua Today," "Women Under Siege," and "Four Corners, A National Sacrifice Area?" He argued for a return to a strict definition of the humanities and promoted summer seminars for high school teachers. His major goal, to teach students the core of Western values, appeared in *To Reclaim a Legacy: A Report on the Humanities in Higher Education* in November 1984. This report, along with Bennett's refusal to comply with Equal Employment Opportunity Commission affirmative action goals at NEH, earned him the enmity of women's and civil rights groups.

In November 1984 the office of secretary of the Department of Education became open when T. H. Bell resigned under right-wing pressure. Reagan had wanted to abolish the position, but decided instead to appoint Bennett after such conservatives as Jerry Falwell approved of him. In February 1985 he assumed the position.

Controversy in Two Jobs

Bennett proved even more controversial as the secretary of the Department of Education than he was at NEH. In his first press conference he supported Reagan's cuts in the

student loan program, saying that some individuals should not go to college and that others should divest themselves of stereos, automobiles, and three weeks at the beach. Later the same year Americans United for the Separation of Church and State sued to force him to observe the Supreme Court ruling that public school teachers could not teach remedial education at private schools at federal expense. He attacked the educational establishment; said some colleges and universities were overpriced; deplored the high rate of student loan defaults, particularly in proprietary schools; and denounced Stanford University's revised curriculum, which de-emphasized Western civilization in favor of a broader study of world cultures.

He favored education vouchers, merit pay, and a constitutional amendment mandating the federal government to remain neutral in the matter of school prayer. He emphasized moral education based upon the Judeo-Christian ethic while denouncing values clarification and cognitive moral development. He remained in the limelight with appearances as a substitute teacher of social studies in a number of city schools and with many speeches and articles in the popular press. He was the author of *First Lessons: A Report on Elementary Education,* published by the U.S. Office of Education in 1987, which lists his personal convictions concerning elementary education. The same ideas appear in *Our Children and Our Country: Improving America's Schools and Affirming the Common Culture* (1988). Bennett also wrote *American Education: Making It Work* (1988) and *The De-valuing of America: The Fight for Our Culture and Our Children* (1992). Bennett's focus in education was on the three C's: content, character, and choice. It was his tireless advocacy of these that left his most lasting legacy on the education agenda of the 1980s.

Bennett resigned from the Department of Education in September 1988 to join the Washington law firm of Dunnels, Duvall, Bennett, and Porter. He had married Mary Elayne Glover late in life (1982) and needed the extra income to support his two sons.

However, the pull of public service proved too great. In January 1989 President George Bush appointed him head of the Office of National Drug Control Policy with the mission to rid the nation of drugs. Bennett was once again in the throes of controversy because of his outspoken views and his abrasive personality. He himself was an inveterate smoker and successfully kicked the habit in order to set an example. He pushed for more severe penalties for drug dealers, even saying that he had no moral qualms about beheading guilty parties as was done in Saudi Arabia. He used the metaphor of a war in urging the use of American military forces in Colombia and Peru to destroy supplies and set a goal of making Washington a drug-free city. Bennett announced his resignation November 8, 1990, claiming much progress. However his critics disagreed. Bennett considered becoming chairman of the Republican National Committee (RNC) but decided to devote his time to speaking, writing, and becoming a senior editor of the magazine *National Review.*

In 1993 Bennett published an anthology titled *The Book of Virtues,* which included stories, poems, essays, and fables intended to teach children values. The book sold very well, bringing in a profit of $5 million for Bennett and prompting him to publish similar books, including *The Moral Compass: Stories for a Life's Journey* (1995).

Spokesperson for Morality

Bennett was strongly favored as a presidential candidate by the conservative wing of the Republican Party in 1994, but he did not run. Instead, he continued to speak out on various topics. He joined the campaign protesting Time-Warner's investment in Interscope Records, which produced some of the most hardcore gangsta rap. He later took aim at some television talk shows. Bennett's issues found their way into the 1996 presidential campaign; even without running, he helped set the national agenda. He was also in demand on the public-speaking circuit, commanding $40,000 per speech. He served as codirector of Empower America, an organization dedicated to the promotion of conservative ideas and principles. Michael Kelly of the *New Yorker* called Bennett the pitchman of the new moral majority and "a leading voice of the force that is driving American politics right now—the national hunger for a moral society."

Further Reading

There is no full-length biography of Bennett, but his profile and critiques of his programs appeared frequently in popular magazines. Examples of these are portraits in the *Wilson Library Bulletin* (Spring 1982), *Time* (March 20, 1985; September 9, 1985), and the *New York Times* (January 11, 1985). Critiques of his programs at NEH can be found in *Nation* (April 14, 1984) and *National Review* (March 8, 1985). A critique of his tenure at the Office of Education can be found in the *Chronicle of Higher Education* (September 21, 1988), while an appraisal of his success in the drug war is in *Newsweek* (January 29, 1990). Also see *New Republic* (June 17, 1996). For articles by Bennett see *Harper's* (January 1996) and *Newsweek* (June 3, 1996; October 21, 1996). See the Empower America Web site at http://www.empower.org.

Bennett's ideas are best explained in his books, including *Counting by Race: Equality from the Founding Fathers to Bakke and Weber* (1979); *Our Children and Our Country: Improving America's Schools and Affirming the Common Culture* (1988); and *The De-valuing of America: The Fight for Our Children and Our Culture* (1992). □

Jack Benny

Comedian Jack Benny (1894-1974) was one of the top stars of radio, television, and stage in a career which spanned over 50 years. A master of comic timing, Benny changed the nature of the weekly comedy show on radio and his likeable skinflint stage personna delighted audiences in the United States and around the world.

Jack Benny was born Benjamin Kubelsky on February 14, 1894, in Waukegan, Illinois. His father, Meyer Kubelsky, was a Lithuanian Jewish immigrant who arrived in New York in 1889. After marrying Emma Sachs four years later he opened a small haberdashery shop in Waukegan. Benjamin, the eldest child, had no desire to enter his father's business, but he had a natural talent for music which his parents encouraged by purchasing a small violin for him and paying for expensive lessons. Considered something of a prodigy around his home town, he played as a member of a musical group at various town and social functions.

Early Career

At the age of 15 Benjamin was offered a job at Waukegan's Barrison Theater playing violin in the pit for vaudeville and stage shows. Unfortunately (or perhaps fortunately), he was a poor student and an incorrigible clown, and in 1912 he was expelled from high school. Shortly thereafter Benjamin went on the vaudeville circuit with the leader of the Barrison Theater Orchestra, Cora Salisbury. Their act was billed as "Salisbury and Benny: From Grand Opera to Ragtime." He reluctantly had changed his name, which he felt was too similar to that of violinist Jan Kubelik, to Ben K. Benny. It was not until Salisbury was forced to return home after a year and he teamed up with Lyman Woods that the act was booked in large towns and Benny began to introduce humorous musical numbers into the repertoire.

During World War I Benny enlisted in the Navy and soon became a performer in camp shows at the Great Lakes Naval Station. In one early performance Benny's violin act

bombed so he started telling jokes. He became an instant hit with enlisted men and joined *The Great Lakes Revue,* which toured most major cities in the Midwest. Aside from his new act, Benny was given the lead in a comedy skit called "Izzy There, the Admiral's Disorderly." Following his discharge Benny returned to vaudeville as a single act, "Ben K. Benny—Fiddle Funology." He now considered himself a comedian and the violin became merely a prop. It was also at this time that he changed his name to Jack Benny so that audiences would not confuse him with another vaudevillian, Ben Bernie.

Throughout the 1920s Benny honed his comic skills, perfecting his timing and developing a suave stage personna. Unlike the zany comedians of the day he dressed in dapper street clothes and presented himself as a vain sophisticate. Benny's urbane brand of humor quickly established him as a star attraction at the large vaudeville houses, where he earned $750 per week. While a headliner at the Orpheum Theatre in Los Angeles in 1927 Benny courted and married Sayde Marks, who worked in the hosiery department in a store across the street. She was later to change her name to Mary Livingston, a popular character she played in the Benny radio show. In the year following his marriage Benny gained a national reputation as the witty master of ceremonies at the Palace Theatre in New York. A movie contract with MGM soon followed, and he was cast in two vaudeville-like films: *Hollywood Revue of 1928* and *Road Show* (1930).

A Radio Comedian

It was in radio, however, that Benny was to achieve his greatest success. Although he was earning $1,500 per week as a monologuist and skit performer in a Broadway revue called *The Vanities of 1930,* he knew that vaudeville was on its way out. In 1932 he joined the exodus of vaudeville stars to radio when Ed Sullivan convinced him to appear on his program. Later that year Canada Dry sponsored his first weekly radio program, initially on NBC and then shifted over to CBS. Over the next five years Benny developed a new program format for radio comedy. At first he borrowed heavily from his vaudeville routine of one-liners, but he soon realized that this insatiable medium devoured his material at a startling rate. It was Benny who discovered that the humor had to emerge from the character and that the key to longevity on radio was not novelty but familiarity. Radio listeners came to know the Benny personna as a lovable penny-pinching egotist, and before long he was one of the most familiar figures on the air.

Benny and his writers introduced other innovations as well. By placing Benny's fall guy character into funny everyday situations, audiences would howl with laughter anticipating his reaction. When a robber confronted him in one routine with the remark "Your money or your life," Benny paused. Gradually the audience began to catch on. As the robber grew impatient and repeated his statement, Benny took a slight pause and responded "I'm thinking it over." This joke was said to have generated the longest laugh in radio. It emerged as one of the many running gags in his show. This type of repetition was making his character more familiar and predictable to his listeners. He garnered his audience's sympathy by playing the stooge to his regular "gang" of characters with whom he shared the spotlight. Each week, they poked fun at his cheapness, his age, or his self-delusions. One of the familiar trademarks of the Benny character was that he never admitted to being over 39 years old. Benny knew, however, that by letting his cast get most of the laughs, his character became not only the butt of the jokes but the center of attraction as well.

By the late 1930s Jack Benny was the king of radio. He led off the most important night of the week in the most important time slot on the top-rated network—Sunday at 7 p.m. on NBC. The time slots opposite his on the other networks were considered unsalable. It was at this time that he began his famous feud with Fred Allen, another leading radio comedian of the day. In reality the two had been good friends in vaudeville, but their mock war of insults provided them both with a substantial boost in the ratings. Their cutting remarks kept listeners in stitches well into the 1940s, their much awaited face-to-face confrontation drew the largest audience in the history of radio up to that time.

Throughout the 1940s Benny's popularity continued to grow. During World War II he contributed tirelessly to the war effort by selling war bonds and by entertaining the troops both at home and abroad. His experiences performing on the Armed Forces Radio System led him to quicken his delivery, and after the war Benny, who was a perfectionist in preparing his routines and an excellent editor of his own material, developed a slicker program with greater emphasis on comic situations.

Yet despite his success Benny, like many other comedians, was unhappy about his earnings on the show. Highly paid performers were being heavily taxed under the new rates established after the war. As a result, Benny formed his own company, Amusement Enterprises, to produce his and other programs. Although this allowed him to retain a higher percentage of his earnings, he sold the company for a huge profit to the CBS network in 1948. William Paley, the chairman of CBS, personally persuaded Benny to switch to his network with an enticing capital gains deal. Benny had been at NBC since 1933 but was put off by the coldness he perceived in the NBC hierarchy. He was the first entertainer in the unbeatable Sunday night lineup of stars on NBC to make the move to CBS. When others followed, in what became known as the "NBC Raids," CBS took the lead in the ratings for the first time in its history.

The Move to Television

Benny's program remained on radio until 1955, but by 1951 his ratings were beginning to plummet. Television had arrived and was siphoning off a substantial portion of the radio audience. Although he was initially hesitant, Benny made his first appearance on television in 1950. His caution was not entirely unjustified since many radio comedians failed in front of the television camera. For the second time in his life Benny had to adapt to a new medium replacing an old one. Since television is essentially visual in nature, he had to develop new gestures—the mincing walk, the famous hand on the cheek, and his hopelessly harangued

stare. In 1952 Benny's television program alternated every other week with his radio program. It was one of the most popular programs on television throughout the 1950s, but in 1964, after 32 consecutive years on the air, his program was cancelled. He continued to appear on television as a guest performer and in his own television specials until his death in 1974.

Few entertainers could match Jack Benny's skill and flexibility as a comedian. Aside from his mastery of stage, radio, and television, Benny appeared in 22 motion pictures. Two of these films, *To Be Or Not To Be* (1942) and *The Horn Blows at Midnight* (1945), are considered to be film classics, and in others, such as *Charley's Aunt* (1941) and *George Washington Slept Here* (1942), Benny proved himself to be a talented film actor. In any medium Benny was a master of delivery, using the pause and the reaction to its maximum advantage. His ad lib abilities were said to be limited, but his timing was impeccable. His greatest accomplishment was perhaps the character he created: the frustrated violinist who relentlessly tortures his audience with a screeching rendition of "Love in Bloom" and who refuses to believe the putdowns of his many critics; the eternally vain tightwad who built an elaborate underground vault to protect his millions and who still owns a wheezing Maxwell automobile. Although a sensitive and generous man offstage, Benny's popularity sprang from his unique ability to embody in a sympathetic way the pettiness within us all.

Further Reading

An excellent analysis of Benny's radio work is contained in Arthur Frank Wertheim's *Radio Comedy* (1979). In addition, three Benny biographies are available: Mary Livingston Benny and Hilliard Marks with Marcia Borie, *Jack Benny* (1978); Irving A. Fein, *Jack Benny: An Intimate Biography* (1976); and Milt Josefsberg, *The Jack Benny Show: The Life and Times of America's Best Loved Entertainer* (1977).

Additional Sources

Benny, Jack, *Sunday nights at seven: the Jack Benny story,* New York, NY: Warner Books, 1990. □

Jeremy Bentham

The English philosopher, political theorist, and jurist Jeremy Bentham (1748-1832) expounded the ethical doctrine known as utilitarianism. Partly through his work many political, legal, and penal reforms were enacted by Parliament.

J eremy Bentham, the son of a lawyer, was born on Feb. 15, 1748, in Houndsditch, near London. A precocious child, he learned Latin, Greek, and French before he was 10. The "philosopher," as he was known to his family, was an avid reader. After attending the famous Westminster school (1755-1760), he went to Queen's College, Oxford, and took his degree in 1763 at the age of 15. He studied at Lincoln's Inn, receiving a master of arts degree in 1766. The following year he was called to the bar.

Bentham cared little for his formal education, insisting that "mendacity and insincerity . . . are the only sure effects of an English university education," and he cared even less about succeeding as a practicing lawyer. He preferred to read and write papers on legal reform and to study physical science, especially chemistry. His father, who had amassed a considerable fortune in real estate speculations, died in 1792, and from that time on Bentham retired from public life and devoted himself to writing. In 1814 he purchased a mansion, and his home became a center of English intellectual life.

Bentham's Utilitarianism

In 1776 Bentham published *Fragment on Government,* which criticized the interpretations of English common law by Sir William Blackstone. Bentham attacked the notion that a social contract or compact had a legal basis. He continued to write on jurisprudence throughout his career: *Introductory View of the Rationale of Evidence* (1812), edited by James Mill, and the five-volume *Rationale of Juridical Evidence* (1827), edited by John Stuart Mill. In these criticisms of law, evidence, and even language (anticipating the "definition in use" theory of linguistic philosophy), Bentham was a consistent nominalist and instinctive utilitarian. Words and laws, men and institutions must be judged solely in terms of their actual usage and consequences.

Utilitarianism may be defined as the thesis that an act is right or good if it produces pleasure, and evil if it leads to pain. Although this doctrine is almost as old as philosophy itself, the principle of utility received its classic expression in Bentham's *Introduction to the Principles of Morals and Legislation* (1789). Bentham had a talent for simplification; he reduced all ethical considerations to an immediate source. "Nature has placed mankind under the governance of two sovereign masters, pain and pleasure." Utilitarianism aims to make morals and politics an exact science based on these objective criteria and to offer a quantitative method for evaluating both individual and institutional actions.

Men are often unhappy or are deprived of happiness by governments because they fail to perceive that the terms value, ought, good, and right are meaningless unless identical with utility, which is understood as pleasure or happiness. Bentham avoided the subjectivism of most hedonistic theories by acknowledging altruistic as well as egoistic pleasures and recognizing that pleasure often consists primarily in avoiding pain. He defined the community as "the sum of the interests of its members" and stated that utilitarianism aims at the "greatest happiness of the greatest number."

To determine the specific utility of actions, Bentham proposed a "felicific calculus" by which one can balance the pleasures and pains consequent upon one's acts. The value of an action will be greater or less in terms of the intensity and duration of pleasure and its certainty and possibility. One should also consider how an act will affect other people. In addition, the circumstances should be taken into account but not the motives, which do not matter.

Bentham's Personality

Bentham was a man of considerable irony and personal eccentricity. Given honorary citizenship by the new Republic of France in 1792, he scorned the French Revolution's "Declaration of the Rights of Man," commenting that all talk of rights was "nonsense" and talk of absolute rights was "nonsense on stilts." Although he spent 7 or 8 hours daily on his writing for more than 50 years, virtually all his published books are the product of editors. He habitually worked on several projects simultaneously without finishing them, and often there were several incomplete versions of the same topic. Bentham was fortunate in having editors of dedication and genius such as Étienne Dumont, James Mill, and John Stuart Mill. Bentham gave the editors total freedom; consequently some of the works bearing his name were thoroughly rewritten by others from conflicting versions or even scraps and notes.

Bentham's eccentricity took the form of obsession with certain ideas. Prison reform was a central concern of his for several years, and he solicited and received charters and money from the King for a model prison, the "Panopticon." Bentham attributed the failure of this project to royal envy and added to his thousands of written pages on the subject a treatise on the conflict between Jeremy Bentham and George III "by one of the disputants." Throughout his life Bentham conducted a lengthy, and largely unsolicited, correspondence with various heads of state suggesting methods of legal and constitutional reform. Late in life he became concerned with how the dead could be of use to the living; in the work *Auto Icon* he suggested that, with proper embalming, every man could become his own monument and that notables might be interspersed with trees in public parks. In his will, which contributed to establishing University College, London, he stipulated that his clothed skeleton and wax head be preserved. He died on June 6, 1832.

Further Reading

The standard edition of Bentham's writings is *The Works of Jeremy Bentham,* edited by John Bowring (11 vols., 1838-1843). Studies of Bentham include Charles Milner Atkinson, *Jeremy Bentham: His Life and Work* (1905); Elie Halévy, *The Growth of Philosophic Radicalism* (trans. 1928); David Baumgardt, *Bentham and the Ethics of Today* (1952); Mary Peter Mack, *Jeremy Bentham: An Odyssey of Ideas* (1963).

Additional Sources

Dinwiddy, J. R. (John Rowland), *Bentham,* Oxford; New York: Oxford University Press, 1989.
Henry Thorton (1760-1815), Jeremy Bentham (1748-1832), James Lauderdale (1759-1839), Simonde de Sismondi (1773-1842), Aldershot, Hants, England; Brookfield, Vt., USA: E. Elgar, 1991. □

Arthur F. Bentley

An early behavioral scientist in America, Arthur F. Bentley (1870-1957) was one of the intellectual fathers of contemporary political science. He was a positivist, nonrationalist "group theorist."

Arthur Bentley was born in Freeport, Ill., the son of an immigrant banker. He received a bachelor of arts degree from Johns Hopkins University. After spending a year in the universities at Berlin and Freiburg im Breisgau, Germany, he completed his doctorate at Johns Hopkins in 1895.

Bentley was not at home in the formal academic world, serving only a year as a teacher in sociology at the University of Chicago and a brief time 45 years later as visiting professor of philosophy at Columbia University. Instead, he engaged in an unusual series of enterprises, avocations, and scholarly endeavors. He spent 14 years in newspaper work, during which time he published *The Process of Government* (1908). He lent his financial and administrative skills to the American Red Cross during World War I. In 1924 he led the Progressive party in Indiana, and through the years he promoted various agricultural causes.

Bentley retired at the age of 40 and became a fruit grower in Indiana. Being financially independent, he had the leisure to engage in private intellectual pursuits: sociology, politics, philosophy, mathematics, psychology, linguistics, and epistemology.

Bentley scorned traditional political science. His interest was in "action" or "behavior," not in "mind-stuff." To him, a group was a way of action in which many men participated; law was activity; government was also activity. He made no distinction between the state and government or between law and government. He thought that the notion of a metaphysical state as an omnipresence behind government bordered on the ridiculous. Sovereignty was at best a legal or theoretical rationalization of behavior—past or proposed. He denied that social behavior was ever inspired by inner voices, faculties, or mind or that there was any such thing as public spiritedness. His strategy for political inquiry was empirical and inductive—his data, external behavior, especially group behavior.

Bentley's work was developmental. Each successive treatise was more technical, building upon the last and drawing from the work of others. Inevitably, he came to grips with fundamental problems, including the theory of knowledge itself. A tool for research, he saw, must be based upon an epistemology.

John Dewey and Bentley coauthored numerous articles and a book, *Knowing and the Known* (1960). Bentley's concept of trans-action as a medium of explanation (first acquired in Germany) was brought to maturation in his work with Dewey. In trans-action, systems of description and naming are employed to deal with aspects and phases of action. They held that trans-action was the key to the science of behavior.

Further Reading

One of the most useful books for gaining insights into Bentley's thought is Sidney Ratner's edited collection of Bentley essays, *Inquiry into Inquiries* (1954). It includes an excellent introduction by the editor and a complete bibliography of Bentley's works with the exception of *Makers, Users, and Masters,* written in 1918-1920 but published posthumously in 1969. Bentley's *The Process of Government* edited by Peter H. Odegard (1967), contains a useful introduction by the editor. See also Richard W. Taylor, ed., *Life, Language, Law: Essays in Honor of Arthur F. Bentley* (1957), and Sidney Ratner, ed., *John Dewey and Arthur Bentley: A Philosophical Correspondence, 1832-1951* (1964). William T. Bluhm, *Theories of the Political System: Classics of Political Thought and Modern Political Analysis* (1965), gives a detailed analysis of Bentley's work in its intellectual framework. □

Thomas Hart Benton

Thomas Hart Benton (1889-1975) was one of the principal American regionalist painters of the 1930s. He imbued the subjects of his work, people of the small towns of the Midwest and South, with a crude, zesty vigor.

Thomas Hart Benton was born in Neosho, Missouri, the son and grandnephew of a United States congressmen. He studied at the Art Institute of Chicago in 1907, then traveled to Paris, where he spent five years observing new trends, familiarizing himself especially with cubism. Upon his return to the United States in 1912, he became a devotee of the synchromism advocated by his friend Stanton Macdonald-Wright. (Synchromism —"with color and sound"—was a nonobjective mode of painting, featuring intersecting planes. It was especially close to French orphism, a branch of cubism.) The work Benton submitted to the Forum Exhibition of American Painting of 1916 showed the influence of synchromism. But during most of this decade Benton was unable to resolve the conflicts he felt between nonobjectivity and realism in his painting. He later felt that the time spent in the Navy in 1918-1919 finally set him on his course toward an art devoted entirely to American subjects treated (he believed) in a realistic manner, devoid of traces of European avant-garde trends.

Murals Represented American Life

Between 1919 and 1924 Benton made studies for his projected series of mural decorations based on American history. From 1924 to about 1931 he traveled through the Midwest and the South, taking close note of the people he met and incorporating these observations in his paintings. Benton's murals generally show his overwhelming concern for the arrangement of figures and design, as in his paintings done in 1931 for New York City's New School for Social Research. In the New York murals a rhythmic movement sweeps through scenes of ordinary American folk shown purposefully at various activities—eating, dancing, or work-

ing. Benton's energetic, turbulent style is intended to suggest the vigor of the American people.

Benton produced a panorama of America's productive capacities in his scenes of mining, farming, and lumbering. He also painted scenes of burlesque houses, prize fights, and broncobusting, and he could capture the rapid, turbulent, and squalid growth of a boomtown. Occasionally he struck a poetic chord, as in his quiet scene of harvesting, *July Hay* (1943). Benton dealt with corruption, squalor, and inequality, but without the bitter indictments that are found in the work of such social realists as Jack Levine.

Benton wished to democratize art, to make it both intelligible and available to the general public (hence the large mural series). He planned a pictorial history of the United States in 64 panels, a project never completed. He was one of the most eloquent spokesmen for the major trend in American art during the 1930s—an art of a specifically American subject matter, done in a variety of naturalistic modes rather than in the European modernist styles of the previous decade.

Worked Throughout His Life

Benton continued to be productive well into his 80s. His portrait of Harry Truman, completed shortly before Truman's death, elicited this compliment from the equally earthy former president: "the best damned painter in America." Benton died in his studio on January 19, 1975, at the age of 85. He had just finished the basic work on a mural illustrating the origins of country music, commissioned by the Country Music Foundation in Nashville. The 100th anniversary of his birth was celebrated in 1989 at his home for 40 years, Kansas City. The festivities included a "bourbon bash" (which had become an annual event in honor of the rugged image the artist had fostered), as well as the opening of a national tour of his work and the premiere of a film biography.

Further Reading

An Artist in America (1937) is Benton's own colorful account of his long career. Thomas Craven, *Thomas Hart Benton* (1939), is an examination of the artist and his work. For background information see Oliver W. Larkin, *Art and Life in America* (1949; 2d ed. 1960), and John W. McCoubrey, *American Tradition in Painting* (1963).

Additional Sources

Adams, Henry, *Thomas Hart Benton: An American Original* (1989).
Dictionary of American Biography (supplement 9, 1971-1975, Scribner's, 1994).
New York Times (January 20, 1975).
Davis, Douglas, "The Rugged American," *Newsweek* (February 3, 1975).
Robbins, William, "Museums Make Peace With an Artist's Vision," *New York Times* (April 13, 1989). □

Lloyd Millard Bentsen

Lloyd Millard Bentsen (born 1921), senior United States senator from Texas, was Democratic vice-presidential candidate in 1988, sharing the unsuccessful ticket with Massachusetts Governor Michael Dukakis, and secretary of the Treasury from 1993-1994.

Texas Senator Lloyd Bentsen was the political surprise of the 1988 presidential campaign, distinguishing himself as the candidate who established a genuine rapport with millions of voters disillusioned with the general election campaign waged by the Democratic and Republican (GOP) presidential candidates. Bentsen was the "star of the campaign," according to one political observer, even though his position on most major political issues placed him closer to the GOP than to the Democratic Party which nominated him for the nation's second highest office.

Lloyd Millard Bentsen, Jr., the son of Lloyd M. Bentsen, Sr., and Edna Ruth (Colbath) Bentsen, was born in Mission, Texas, in the Rio Grande Valley on February 11, 1921. Lloyd Senior, the son of Danish immigrants who had originally settled in South Dakota, migrated to the Rio Grande Valley during World War I and began the citrus farming and real estate investing which became the basis for the Bentsen family fortune, conservatively estimated at $50 million.

Lloyd Bentsen, Jr., grew up in McAllen, Texas; received a law degree from the University of Texas in 1942; and enlisted in the U.S. Army as a private. Assigned to the Army Air Force, Bentsen rose to the rank of lieutenant colonel while flying 50 missions over Europe. After returning to the Rio Grande Valley as a war hero, Bentsen was elected judge of Hidalgo County in 1946. Two years later he ran for the South Texas congressional seat. Bentsen recalled how upon hearing of the congressional campaign of another young war veteran, John F. Kennedy of Massachusetts, he obtained Kennedy's campaign literature. Bentsen substituted the P.T. boat silhouette with a cutout of a B-24 bomber, similar to the one he commanded during the war, and distributed the campaign literature as his own. The strategy was successful and Bentsen at the age of 28 became the youngest member of Congress.

Congressman Bentsen soon established an eclectic voting record that would come to typify the remainder of his political career, alternatively liberal and conservative on social issues but decidedly conservative on military and foreign affairs. Bentsen, for example, voted for a repeal of the poll tax, but opposed a ban on discrimination in federal employment. In 1950, after the North Korean invasion of South Korea, he proposed that President Harry S Truman give North Korea one week to withdraw from the South or "be subjected to atomic attack by our Air Force." And in 1954 he called for American intervention in Indochina on the side of France.

In 1954 Bentsen announced he was leaving Congress to make his fortune. "I could not make ends meet," he told an interviewer, on his then $12,500 annual congressional salary. Three weeks later Bentsen chartered the Consolidated American Life Insurance Company with $7 million provided by his father. Consolidated American Life eventually evolved into Lincoln Consolidated Inc., a holding company which controlled mutual funds, oil companies, a savings and loan association, and a funeral home. Bentsen, as its chief executive officer, had by 1970 an annual income of $80,000.

Now financially secure, Bentsen reentered politics, declaring, "I wanted to do something more with my life, to be remembered for something more than my financial statement." The opportunity came in 1970 when he challenged Senator Ralph Yarborough in the Democratic primary election. Concerned about the defection of conservative wealthy Democrats to the growing Republican Party, former Governor John Connally convinced Bentsen that the defeat of Yarborough, a Populist politician, was imperative if conservatives were to retain their political control of the party and the state. Bentsen defeated Yarborough by portraying the senator as a big-spending, anti-Vietnam War radical out of touch with Texas political opinion and then beat Houston Congressman (and future President) George Bush in a general election campaign that showed fewer philosophical or political differences between the candidates of the opposing parties than the candidates in the Democratic primary.

After the death of Lyndon Johnson in 1973 and the defection of John Connally to the Republicans, Bentsen quickly assumed the leadership of the state Democratic

Party in Texas. Three years later he sought the Democratic presidential nomination. Styling himself a "Truman Democrat," Bentsen hoped to win Southern voters, but was eliminated by two other Southerners, former governors Jimmy Carter and George Wallace.

Lloyd Bentsen was more successful as a political strategist and fundraiser. As chief architect of the Senate Democrats' 1986 campaign strategy, he was credited with the party's winning of five new Senate seats. He was by far the most effective fundraiser in Congress, having amassed $5 million for his 1988 Senate reelection campaign; his donors included powerful corporate interests inside and outside Texas.

Although 1988 Democratic presidential nominee Michael Dukakis and Bentsen differed on aid to the Contras (anti-government forces in Nicaragua), support for school prayer, federal financing of abortions, and gun control, party strategists hoped the Texan's selection as the vice-presidential candidate would boost the national ticket in the Southwest by luring back conservative "Reagan Democrats" who voted against the party in 1980 and 1984. Bentsen originally was to have campaigned in Texas, Oklahoma, and Louisiana to prevent landslide Republican victories in those states. However, his surprisingly strong appeal on the campaign trail and his outstanding performance in the national debate with Republican vice-presidential candidate Dan Quayle persuaded party strategists to have Bentsen campaign throughout the nation. His presence on the ticket, however, did not help the Democrats carry the Southwest. Texans gave Bentsen, who ran simultaneously for reelection and the vice-presidency, a victory in his Senate race while voting almost by the same margin for the Bush-Quayle ticket in the national contest. Named chairman of the powerful Senate Finance Committee in 1987, the four-term senator remained an important national figure.

Bentsen considered running for president in 1992, but instead supported Bill Clinton. The two had worked together during the mid-1980s as co-founders of a moderate group called the Democratic Leadership Conference. During the campaign, Bentsen gave advice and assistance to Clinton on the North American Free Trade Agreement (NAFTA) and by now was considered an expert in financial, trade, and tax issues. Thus it was no surprise when Clinton appointed him secretary of the treasury beginning in January 1993. Although Bentsen was at first reluctant to give up his seat in Congress, he accepted the position. However, it was soon apparent that Bentsen was going to have troubles in this position. As Fred Barnes said in the *New Republic,* his "first year as treasury secretary wasn't exactly the epitome of cabinet clout." He was financially more conservative than Clinton. His advice to Clinton about an economic stimulus package was rejected, as was his opinion of Hillary Rodham Clinton's health care reform proposals.

Bentsen resigned his post as treasury secretary in December 1994. He commented that he had "felt like an outsider for 12 years" and was "tired of the gridlock." Since his resignation, Bentsen has been named to the board of directors of Continental Airlines (1996) and become chair-

man of the board of directors of New Holland N.V., an international manufacturer of agricultural equipment. Bentsen and his daughter, Tina Bentsen Smith, also serve on the selection committee of The Lloyd Bentsen Award, by which a $10,000 honorarium is awarded each year to a parent of a child with Down's syndrome. The purpose is to honor that parent for his or her continued support and advocacy of family-centered, community-based, coordinated care for children with Down's syndrome.

Further Reading

Discussions of Lloyd Bentsen's life and political accomplishments can be found in Elizabeth Drew, *Election Journal: Political Events of 1987-1988* (1989) and in the *New York Times Biographical Service,* Vol. 18 (July 1988). His role in the 1988 election is detailed in Jack Germond and Jules Witcover, *Whose Broad Stripes and Bright Stars?* (1989); the authors' approach is characterized in the subtitle: *The Trivial Pursuit of the Presidency 1988.* See also *Who's Who in America* (1996), *Who's Who in the World* (1996). Articles about Bentsen appear in *Chicago Tribune* (December 13, 1992); *Dallas Morning News* (December 10-11, 1992); *National Review* (December 31, 1994); and *New Republic* (February 28, 1994). For information about The Lloyd Bentsen Award, see the Web site for the Kelsey-Seybold Foundation at http://www.ksfnd.org. □

Eliezer Ben Yehuda

The Hebrew lexicographer and editor Eliezer Ben Yehuda (1858-1922) is known as the father of spoken Hebrew. He revived the Hebrew language and forged it into a modern and viable instrument of communication.

Eliezer Ben Yehuda was born in the small town of Lushki in the province of Vilna, Lithuania, where he received a traditional Jewish education. At an early age he moved from town to town in search of good religious and secular schooling. He completed his secondary education in Dvinsk. Realizing that he would not be accepted in a Russian university because of discriminatory laws against Jews, Ben Yehuda went to the University of Paris, where he studied medicine in 1879.

The struggle for independence in the Balkan countries made Ben Yehuda aware of the homelessness of the Jews and of the need to restore the ancient, wandering people to its homeland—Palestine. In 1879 Ben Yehuda published his first Hebrew article in *Hashahar* (The Dawn), the foremost Hebrew monthly of the time. He presented the then novel idea of the return to Zion and revival of the ancient Hebrew tongue as the spoken language of a resurrected people.

During his stay in Paris, Ben Yehuda succumbed to tuberculosis and had to postpone his plan to settle in Palestine. He went first to Algiers, where he continued to publish articles in the Hebrew press, including the weekly

Havazelet, printed in Jerusalem. In 1881 he was invited to Jerusalem as assistant editor of that weekly. His health having improved, he accepted the post. On his way he married Dvora Jonas, who shared his ideals. Upon his arrival in Jerusalem he organized a group which dedicated itself to the task of using Hebrew as a daily language. It took Ben Yehuda many years of persistent work to convince the skeptics that Hebrew could be made to live again. He was also bitterly attacked by religious factions in Jerusalem, who opposed the secular use of the holy tongue. In his own newspapers, which he had begun to publish, he coined new Hebrew terms and words for daily use. His children were the first in modern times to speak Hebrew as their mother tongue.

To make available the riches of ancient as well as modern Hebrew, Ben Yehuda concentrated his efforts on his monumental lifework, *The Dictionary of the Hebrew Language, Old and New.* He worked daily on the dictionary and continued the task during the years of World War I, which he spent in New York. At his death five volumes of the dictionary had been published. Ben Yehuda left enough material to complete the work. In all, 16 volumes were published, the last one appearing in 1959. Ben Yehuda also wrote textbooks in history and literature and translated literary works into Hebrew.

Ben Yehuda's first wife, Dvora, died in 1891. His second wife, Heinda, a sister of Dvora, was the first woman to write stories on life in the new Palestine. Ben Yehuda suffered from poor health; at times he endured hunger and persecution; yet at the end he witnessed the triumph of his ideal. The Hebrew language, which has become the national tongue of Israel, today serves as the mortar that cements the multilingual Jews who have come from the far corners of the world into one nation.

Further Reading

A fine biography of Ben Yehuda in English is Robert St. John, *Tongue of the Prophets: The Life Story of Eliezer Ben Yehuda* (1952).

Additional Sources

Ben-Yehuda, Eliezer, *A dream come true,* Boulder: Westview Press, 1993. □

Carl Benz

German inventor Carl Benz (1844-1929) is one of the many individuals given credit for the creation of the first automobile. In 1885 he invented the motorized tricycle, which became the first "horseless carriage" to be driven by an internal combustion engine. Benz's contributions to automotive design also included the creation of such features as a carburetor and an electrical ignition system.

Carl Benz was a German engineer and inventor who was responsible for many contributions to the design of modern automobiles. He developed an internal combustion gasoline engine for his 1885 version of the "horseless carriage," which was initially a three-wheeled vehicle. Other innovations by Benz included a simple carburetor, an electrical ignition system, rack-and-pinion steering, and water cooling. For his development of the 1885 motorized tricycle, Benz is given credit by some for creating the first automobile, while others contend that the three-wheel design did not constitute a true modern car. Regardless of his right to the title of inventor of the automobile, Benz did leave his mark on the auto industry by pioneering one of the first marketable motorized vehicles and founding the automobile company that came to be known as Mercedes-Benz.

Benz was born in Karlsruhe, Germany, on November 25, 1844. His father was a railroad engineer who died of pneumonia when his son was two years old. The income that Benz's mother received after the death of her husband was small, and Benz was called upon to help support the family as soon as he was old enough. Even as a boy, Benz was fascinated with technology, and he was able to use his talents in this area to make extra money. His earliest jobs were fixing watches and clocks, and he later constructed a darkroom where he would develop pictures for tourists visiting the nearby Black Forest.

Benz's facility for technical matters was also displayed in school, where he worked as an assistant for a physics teacher. He continued his education at Karlsruhe Polytechnic and then went to work for an engine manufacturer. Benz had a very specific motive for working at the engine plant— he dreamed of creating a horseless carriage, and he wanted to learn as much as he could about engines. After gathering what knowledge he could there, in 1871 he moved on to a position with a wagon and pump company in Mannheim, Germany, where he gained more valuable experience. By 1872, he was ready to open his own engine shop. Just before starting his business, he married Berta Ringer.

Founded Successful Engine Companies

Benz was quite successful as a manufacturer, selling a large number of engines and winning the confidence of investors. With the financial backing of others, he founded the Mannheim Gas Engine Manufacturing Company, which he intended to use in part to develop his horseless carriage. Even though the venture quickly made a profit, Benz's investors did not want him to spend valuable resources on inventions. Benz unsuccessfully fought their decision and, after being in business for only three months, left the company. He quickly lined up new shareholders and founded a third business, Benz and Company, in October of 1883. The company was to sell stationary gas engines, but the new investors were also willing to support Benz's horseless carriage as long as it did not detract from the production of the primary product.

After two decades of planning his horseless carriage, Benz finally had the resources to make it a reality. In 1885, he debuted his automobile, a motorized tricycle that was revolutionary primarily for its use of a gasoline-powered internal combustion engine. Earlier in the century, self-propelled vehicles had been developed with steam engines, but the internal combustion engine marked an important breakthrough for automobiles. It provided a lighter, more compact, and more efficient means of powering a vehicle. It was the adoption of the internal combustion engine that made Benz's car a truly practical and appealing consumer product. For this reason, many consider Benz's 1885 motorized tricycle the first automobile.

Horseless Carriage Demonstrated in 1885

Another important feature of Benz's vehicle was an electrical ignition system that used a battery to start the engine. This system became the basic model for all later ignitions. The tricycle also incorporated a carburetor, rack-and-pinion steering, a water cooling system, and rear springs. Benz held a public demonstration in the fall of 1885 to promote his invention, although he claimed to have first driven it the previous spring. On the road near his workshop, Benz and his wife began a ride on the automobile in front of a gathering of witnesses. After apparently forgetting to steer the tricycle, however, Benz quickly ran into a brick wall. Both passengers emerged from this early auto accident without injuries. The mishap did not dampen enthusiasm for Benz's creation—a positive review of the vehicle appeared the following summer in the publication *Neue Badische Landeszeitung.*

Benz continued to improve his design with the introduction of a second gear, a larger, 3-horsepower engine, and improved brakes and springs. The first sale of a Benz automobile occurred in 1887, after it had been displayed at the Paris Exhibition earlier in the year. At the Munich Imperial Exhibition in 1888, Benz was awarded a gold medal for his invention. This recognition brought in many orders for the automobile, which at that time was a novelty that was only affordable by the wealthy. Still, business was so good that the Benz Company grew to 50 workers by 1889 and soon moved to a larger factory where a new four-wheeled model began production in 1890.

Benz had given into the idea of a four-wheeled automobile reluctantly and only after much lobbying by others in his company who sought a more modern design. Unlike other automobile inventors, Benz did not feel that a car needed to physically resemble the traditional four-wheeled carriage. After the model of 1890, he was even more opposed to changes in his design. His opinions were so strong that after a major update of the Benz automobile in 1905, the manufacturer continued to drive his older models of the car.

Encountered Competition from Daimler Cars

One major challenger of Benz's claim to be the inventor of the automobile was a fellow German, Gottlieb Daimler. Daimler had created a better internal combustion engine and patented it five months before Benz's engine. The first vehicle in which he demonstrated his, however, was a bicycle, resulting in the first motorcycle. Those supporting Benz argued that the two-wheeled vehicle resembled the modern automobile less than the Benz tricycle. Regardless, Daimler also went on to become a successful producer of four-wheeled automobiles and became one of Benz's strongest competitors in both French and German markets. To try to gain a greater share of the French market, Daimler gave his car a French-sounding name—Mercedes—at the suggestion of a business partner. Despite their professional interest in each other, Benz and Daimler never met.

The Daimler company continued to do business after its founder died in 1900. Both it and the Benz company suffered a downturn during the economic depression after World War I. To strengthen their chances of survival, the companies merged to form Mercedes-Benz in 1926. By that time, Benz was no longer closely involved with the operation of the business, although he continued to receive recognition for his accomplishments as an automotive pioneer. His cars were collected by museums, and he was honored with a special procession of hundreds of automobiles from the city of Heidelberg to his home in Ladenburg in 1929. On that occasion, a number of prominent people made speeches in his honor and proclaimed him the inventor of the automobile. Two days later, on April 4, 1929, Benz died at his home in Ladenburg. Although later automotive innovators such as Henry Ford turned the car into a more successful product for the general public, Benz is remembered for his inventive genius and his groundbreaking work to create and market the first commercial automobile.

Further Reading

Nexon, John C., *The Invention of the Automobile,* Country Life, 1936.
Singer, Charles, *A History of Technology,* Volume 5: *The Late Nineteenth Century, c. 1850 to c. 1900,* Oxford University Press, 1958. □

Count Leopold von Berchtold

The Austro-Hungarian statesman Count Leopold von Berchtold (1863-1942) served as foreign minister of Austria-Hungary during the critical years 1912-1915. His uncompromising ultimatum to Serbia contributed to the outbreak of World War I.

Leopold von Berchtold, the son of a wealthy landowner in Moravia and Hungary, was born in Vienna on April 18, 1863. After some legal training, he entered the Austro-Hungarian foreign ministry in 1893; in the same year he married Countess Ferdinandine Károlyi, the daughter of one of the richest aristocrats in Hungary. After serving in Paris, London, and St. Petersburg, in 1906 he was named ambassador to Russia. He held this post until March 1911, when he became foreign minister.

Although Berchtold tried to maintain good relations with the Russian government while he was ambassador, the growing rivalry between the two powers over the Balkans undermined his efforts. As foreign minister of Austria-Hungary, Berchtold sought to strengthen the empire's shaky position in the Balkans. Initially he looked for a peaceful solution in agreement with the Triple Entente of England, France, and Russia. But the growing aggressiveness of South Slav (particularly Serbian) separatists, and Russia's increased efforts to eliminate Austria-Hungary's influence from the Balkans soon forced him to reconsider his position and to listen more attentively to Conrad von Hötzendorf's "war party."

Although honest and well-intentioned, Berchtold was essentially weak and indecisive. He was certainly not fit to handle the problems of his highly sensitive office in times of crisis. His limitations were evident in his vacillating policies during the Balkan Wars of 1912-1913. After this strife ended, Berchtold continued to be aware that Russian-supported South Slav separatism presented a great threat to the empire. Thus he decided to use the assassination in 1914 of the Austrian archduke Francis Ferdinand by a Serbian nationalist as a pretext for moving against Serbia, the major Slavic power in the Balkans. When his anti-Serbian campaign grew into a general war, he tried to persuade Italy and Romania to honor their treaty obligations. When Italy demanded compensation, however, he resigned (Jan. 13, 1915) rather than yield Austrian territory.

After the fall of Austria-Hungary, Berchtold lived in Vienna and on his Czech and Hungarian estates. He died on Nov. 21, 1942, in Hungary.

Further Reading

There exists nothing substantial on Berchtold in either English or German; his rather superficial diaries and memoirs are unpublished. His diplomacy, however, is detailed in many good works on the Hapsburg Empire and the origins of World War I: Ernst Christian Helmreich, *The Diplomacy of the Balkan Wars, 1912-1913* (1938); Arthur James May, *The Hapsburg Monarchy, 1867-1914* (1951) and *The Passing of the Hapsburg Monarchy, 1914-1918* (2 vols., 1966); Luigi Albertini, *The Origins of the War of 1914* (trans., 3 vols., 1952-1957); A. J. P. Taylor, *The Struggle for Mastery in Europe, 1848-1918* (1954); and Carlile Aylmer Macartney, *The Habsburg Empire, 1790-1918* (1968). □

Nicholas Alexandrovich Berdyaev

Nicholas Alexandrovich Berdyaev (1874-1948) was a Russian Philosopher and religious thinker. He was a leading exponent of Christian existentialism and bridged the gap between religious thought in Russia and the West.

Nicholas Berdyaev was born on March 19, 1874, in Kiev of noble parents (his grandfather had been a leader of the Don Cossacks). At the age of 12 he entered the Kiev Cadet Corps, a school for future officers of the emperor's Life Guard. He hated military life and 6 years later transferred to Kiev University, where he became a radical Marxist and a political activist. He left his aristocratic family and in 1898 was expelled from the University, arrested, and sentenced to 2 years of banishment in Vologda, in northern Russia.

It was during this period, a time of great intellectual activity, that Berdyaev broke with the Marxists. He read widely in philosophy and began a lifelong association with the Orthodox Church. After his release he traveled to Heidelberg in 1903 for further study. The next year he met his future wife, Lydia Tushev, and in 1905 they moved to St. Petersburg. There Berdyaev became a leader among the capital's intellectuals and was especially prominent in the salons of the Russian symbolists. His reputation in Russia was assured by his 1907 article in the anthology *Milestones.*

His attacks on the institution of the Holy Synod would have caused him serious trouble had the Revolution not interrupted proceedings against him. Although he at first welcomed the Revolution, he became increasingly anti-Bolshevik. In 1921 he served as professor of philosophy at Moscow University, but the following year his public criticism of the Soviets led to deportation. In September 1922 he left Russia forever. He first settled in Berlin (1922-1924), where he was president of the Russian Religious-Philosophical Academy, and then in Paris. The story of his life in France can be summed up by the long list of books which he wrote during this period. In 1924 he published the book which first brought him fame in Europe, *The New Middle Ages.* In 1926 he founded the influential journal, *The Way,* which he edited until 1939.

While continuing as head of his academy in Paris, he also wrote *Freedom and the Spirit* (1927), *Solitude and Society* (1934), and *Slavery and Freedom* (1939).

The German occupation was a harsh time for Berdyaev, although he was not arrested. On March 4, 1948, he died of a heart attack while at work on his last book, *The Realm of the Spirit and the Realm of Caesar.*

Further Reading

Of the books in English on Berdyaev, only a small number may be recommended to the general reader. Donald Lowrie, *Rebellious Prophet: A Life of Nicolai Berdyaev* (1960), is the best biography. Michel Vallon, *An Apostle of Freedom: Life and Teachings of Nicolas Berdyaev* (1960), includes a relatively detailed biography and, in the second half of the book, a comparatively lucid exposition of Berdyaev's basic ideas. M. Spinka, *Nicholas Berdyaev, Captive of Freedom* (1950), succeeds in putting Berdyaev into a helpful historical and European focus. Less helpful are Evgueny Lampert, *Nicolas Berdyaev and the New Middle Ages* (1945); Edgar Leonard Allen, *Freedom in God: A Guide to the Thought of Nicholas Berdyaev* (1950); Oliver Fielding Clarke, *Introduction to Berdyaev* (1950); and George Seaver, *Nicolas Berdyaev: An Introduction to His Thought* (1950).

Additional Sources

Lowrie, Donald A. (Donald Alexander), 1889-1974, *Rebellious prophet; a life of Nicolai Berdyae,* Westport, Conn., Greenwood Press 1974, 1960. □

Bernard Berelson

Bernard Berelson (1912-1979), an American behavioral scientist, made major contributions in the fields of communications research, voting studies, and population policy. He virtually created the term "behavioral sciences" and became principally responsible for the establishment of the Center for Advanced Study in the Behavioral Sciences in Stanford, California.

Berelson was born in Spokane, Washington, on June 2, 1912. He received an A.B. from Whitman College in 1934, a B.S. in 1936 and an M.A. in 1937 from the University of Washington, and a Ph.D. from the University of Chicago in 1941. His graduate degrees were both in library science, and he served as a professor of library science and as dean of the Graduate Library School at the University of Chicago until he joined the staff of the Ford Foundation in 1951.

During World War II Berelson worked in Washington as an analyst of German opinion and morale with the Foreign Broadcast Intelligence Service (FBIS), which at that time was an affiliate of the Office of War Information (OWI). In 1944 he became a project director at the Columbia University Bureau of Applied Social Research, then directed by its founder, Paul F. Lazarsfeld. At the bureau he participated in the analysis of the famous Erie County panel study of the 1940 presidential election and was a co-author of *The People's Choice* (with Paul F. Lazarsfeld and Hazel Gaudet, 1944). Other projects of this phase of Berelson's career were a reader in public opinion and communication (edited with Morris Janowitz, 1950) and a text on content analysis (1952). An entire generation of graduate students studied these two books, and they are still in use today.

In 1951 Berelson joined the staff of the Ford Foundation in Pasadena, California, as director of what became its program in the behavioral sciences. The term "behavioral sciences" first entered general use during these years; Berelson didn't invent it, but he did much to popularize it. In 1952 the Ford Foundation established—under Berelson's guidance—the Center for Advanced Study in the Behavioral Sciences in Stanford, California, which remains a thriving intellectual institution and a monument to his initiative.

During his years at the Ford Foundation Berelson participated in the analysis of the Bureau of Applied Social Research's survey data from the 1948 general election. He had earlier served as a field director for this panel study of the population of Elmira, New York, and he became the senior author of *Voting: A Study of Opinion Formation in a Presidential Campaign* (1954). In addition to taking part in the analysis and writing of *Voting,* Berelson compiled the inventory of findings from voting studies that constituted an important appendix to the volume, and he wrote an influential chapter on the meaning of the voting process for democracy. In this chapter he reviewed how unqualified many voters are, how much they misperceive political reality, and how frequently they respond to irrelevant social influences. But instead of despair, he found in the aggregation of these superficially based votes a profound meaning for democratic society. An electoral system, he noted, must achieve a balance between "total political war between segments of the society and total political indifference to group interests of that society"—a requirement that means that a democracy sets different requirements for different individuals.

In 1961 the Population Council asked Berelson to direct a new communications research program at its New York headquarters. At the council Berelson soon became indispensable for his common sense, his good humor, and his challenging mind. He was appointed vice president in 1963; he became president in 1968 and served until 1974; he was president emeritus and a senior fellow from 1974 until his death. He was highly respected and extremely successful as a policy maker, as a foundation executive, and as a senior statesman in the international population field.

In both his personal and his professional style, Berelson was organized, goal-directed, and impatient with theory if it seemed not to be relevant for research or policy. He carried his learning lightly, but most of his colleagues thought that he was the most intelligent person with whom they had ever worked. He often described himself as a librarian, an educator, or a foundation executive, rather than as a behavioral scientist, but he wrote or edited 12 books in the social and behavioral sciences and he published some 90 articles, each written in a direct, jargonfree style that was unmistakable. He was in the forefront of those social scientists who were concerned with the ethical and value implications of their work, and he struggled with the ethical complexities that are inherent in all attempts to improve the quality of life in the Third World. Indicatively, his last publication was a long essay on the ethical issues involved in government efforts to influence fertility. The world has not seen the last of the attempts by governments to influence the fertility behavior of their subjects, and Berelson's humane guidance of action and research in this field will be felt for decades to come.

Berelson's career demonstrated that an orientation to empirical behaviorism on the part of a scholar who in many ways was the intellectual father of the behavioral sciences in the United States was not at all incompatible with either an orientation toward policies and programs (i.e., toward improving the world) or toward a moral position that knowledge must be used carefully. It also showed great respect for the rights of the people whose lives are affected.

Further Reading

Berelson's concept of the behavioral sciences is described in his article "Behavioral Sciences" in the *International Encyclopedia of the Social Sciences.* His contributions to the population field are described in W. Parker Mauldin's article on him in *Studies in Family Planning 10* (October 1979). See also David L. Sills, "Bernard Berelson: Behavioral Scientist," in *Journal of the History of the Behavioral Sciences* (1981). □

Alban Berg

The Austrian composer Alban Berg (1885-1935) adopted the revolutionary twelve-tone method, but he frequently combined it with tonality.

Alban Berg, Arnold Schoenberg, and Anton Webern have often been called the second Viennese school. (The first Viennese school included those classical composers of the 18th century who wrote many of their important works in Vienna; Haydn, Mozart, and Beethoven are the most outstanding representatives.) Schoenberg, the great innovator, first transcended the limitations of traditional tonality and then organized his new sounds according to the twelve-tone method.

Schoenberg's principal European disciples, Berg and Webern, followed his ideas but developed them in quite different directions. Webern pushed many of Schoenberg's innovative concepts as far as was possible in the 1940s. In fact, Schoenberg even said on one occasion, "Webern always exaggerated!" But Berg always seemed to be linking Schoenbergian techniques with those of earlier music: sometimes he used baroque or classical forms (sonata, rondo, passacaglia, fugue); at other times he quoted older compositions within the framework of the twelve-tone method (Wagner's *Tristan* prelude, Bach's chorale *Es ist genug*, a Carinthian folksong). Such links with the familiar aided in winning acceptance for Berg's music and in preparing the ear to accept even more complex contemporary styles.

Berg was born on Feb. 9, 1885, in Vienna. His father was an export salesman; his mother the daughter of a court jeweler. At the age of 14 Berg began to develop an intense interest in music, and the following year he composed his first songs. He neglected his school studies and failed in his matriculation examinations. Sinking into a profound depression, which was intensified by an unhappy love affair, he attempted suicide in the fall of 1903. He overcame this spiritual crisis, and after his graduation in 1904 he took the job of unpaid accountant in a government office.

A decisive change in Berg's life soon took place. His brother, who had read one of Schoenberg's newspaper advertisements as teacher of theory and composition, secretly took some of Alban's songs to Schoenberg. Impressed with the talent they revealed, Schoenberg invited Berg to become his pupil, at first without fee, later at modest cost. Compositions written during the period of study with Schoenberg include the Seven Early Songs (1905-1907), the Piano Sonata, Op. 1 (1908), the Four Songs, Op. 2 (1908-1909), and the String Quartet, Op. 3 (completed in 1910). Berg married Helene Nahowska in 1911. The World War I years were difficult for Berg. At first enthusiastic about his military service, he soon suffered a physical breakdown caused largely by asthma, which had tormented him for years. He was transferred to office work in the Ministry of War and remained there until the war's end.

The Opera *Wozzeck*

Berg completed his first opera, *Wozzeck,* in 1921. He arranged his own libretto from a play by Georg Büchner. There are three acts of five scenes each. In Act I the protagonist is shown in his relation to the world around him; in Act II the drama develops; in Act III the catastrophe occurs, followed by an epilogue. Each act consists of a series of strict musical forms. The first act is composed of five character pieces; the second is a fivemovement symphony; and the third is made up of six "inventions" (the extra section being an elaborate orchestral interlude between the fourth and fifth scenes).

However, Berg did not want these forms to be obvious to the listener. He stated, "From the moment when the curtain rises until it descends for the last time there must not be anyone in the audience who notices anything of these various fugues and inventions, suite movements and sonata movements, variations and passacaglias. Nobody must be filled with anything else except the idea of the opera— which goes far beyond the fate of Wozzeck. And that—so I believe—I have achieved!" The continuing success of *Wozzeck* since its premiere in Berlin in 1925 proved that Berg was right.

Later Works

In the last 10 years of his life Berg turned to the twelve-tone method. Works employing this method include the Chamber Concerto for violin, piano, and wind instruments (1923-1925); the *Lyric Suite* for string quartet (1925-1926); *Der Wein,* a concert aria for soprano and orchestra (1929; text by Baudelaire in the German translation of Stefan George); *Lulu,* a three-act opera (1928-1935; text by Frank Wedekind, last act unfinished); and the Violin Concerto (1935). In these compositions the twelve-tone method is treated in a free and personal manner. The Chamber Concerto is preceded by a musical motto including the letters of Schoenberg's, Berg's, and Webern's full names, insofar as these can be translated into musical notation. In the *Lyric Suite* strict twelve-tone movements alternate with those in which the tonal material is more freely treated. The Violin Concerto has a tone row made up almost entirely of triads, a procedure that most twelve-tone composers avoided.

Early in 1935 the American violinist Louis Krasner commissioned Berg to write a violin concerto. While he was thinking about the form the work should take, a tragedy occurred in his intimate circle: the death of Manon Gropius, the 19-year-old daughter of Alma Mahler. Berg quickly composed the concerto as a tribute to her memory. It was completed on Aug. 11, 1935. Ironically, it became his farewell to life. An insect bite led to general blood poisoning. On Dec. 24, 1935, he died, his thoughts preoccupied to the last with his unfinished opera Lulu.

Further Reading

Two good biographies of Berg are H. F. Redlich, *Alban Berg: The Man and His Music* (1957), and Willi Reich, *The Life and Work of Alban Berg* (1963; trans. 1965). Both contain important selections from Berg's writings. René Leibowitz, *Schoenberg and His School* (1947; trans. 1949; repr. 1970), has a section on Berg. Leibowitz is not always accurate in details, but he communicates his appreciation for Schoenberg and his followers.

Additional Sources

Carner, Mosco., *Alban Berg: the man and the work,* London: Duckworth, 1975; New York: Holmes & Meier Publishers, 1977, 1975, 1983.

Monson, Karen., *Alban Berg,* Boston: Houghton Mifflin Co., 1979.

Neighbour, O. W. (Oliver Wray), *The New Grove Second Viennese School: Schoenberg, Webern, Berg,* New York: Norton, 1983.

Reich, Willi, *The life and work of Alban Berg,* New York: Da Capo Press, 1981.

Simms, Bryan R., *Alban Berg: a guide to research,* New York: Garland Pub., 1996. ☐

Paul Berg

Paul Berg (born 1926) is best known for his development of a technique for splicing together DNA from different types of organisms. His achievement gave scientists a tool for studying the structure of viral chromosomes and the biochemical basis of human genetic diseases.

Paul Berg made one of the most fundamental technical contributions to the field of genetics in the twentieth century: he developed a technique for splicing together deoxyribonucleic acid (DNA)—the substance that carries the genetic information in living cells and viruses from generation to generation—from different types of organisms. His achievement gave scientists a priceless tool for studying the structure of viral chromosomes and the biochemical basis of human genetic diseases. It also let researchers turn simple organisms into chemical factories that churn out valuable medical drugs. In 1980 he was awarded the Nobel Prize in chemistry for pioneering this procedure, now referred to as recombinant DNA technology .

Today, the commercial application of Berg's work underlies a large and growing industry dedicated to manufacturing drugs and other chemicals. Moreover, the ability to recombine pieces of DNA and transfer them into cells is the basis of an important new medical approach to treating diseases by a technique called gene therapy .

Berg was born in Brooklyn, New York, on June 30, 1926, one of three sons of Harry Berg, a clothing manufacturer, and Sarah Brodsky, a homemaker. He attended public schools, including Abraham Lincoln High School, from which he graduated in 1943. In a 1980 interview reported in

the *New York Times,* Berg credited a "Mrs. Wolf," the woman who ran a science club after school, with inspiring him to become a researcher. He graduated from high school with a keen interest in microbiology and entered Pennsylvania State University, where he received a degree in biochemistry in 1948.

Before entering graduate school, Berg served in the United States Navy from 1943 to 1946. On September 13, 1947, he married Mildred Levy and they had one son, John Alexander. After completing his duty in the navy, Berg continued his study of biochemistry at Western Reserve University (now Case Western Reserve University) in Cleveland, Ohio, where he was a National Institutes of Health fellow from 1950 to 1952 and received his doctorate degree in 1952. He did postdoctoral training as an American Cancer Society research fellow, working with Herman Kalckar at the Institute of Cytophysiology in Copenhagen, Denmark, from 1952 to 1953. From 1953 to 1954 he worked with biochemist Arthur Kornberg at Washington University in St. Louis, Missouri, and held the position of scholar in cancer research from 1954 to 1957.

He became an assistant professor of microbiology at the University of Washington School of Medicine in 1956, where he taught and did research until 1959. Berg left St. Louis that year to accept the position of professor of biochemistry at Stanford University School of Medicine. Berg's background in biochemistry and microbiology shaped his research interests during graduate school and beyond, steering him first into studies of the molecular mechanisms underlying intracellular protein synthesis.

During the 1950s Berg tackled the problem of how amino acids, the building blocks of proteins, are linked together according to the template carried by a form of RNA (ribonucleic acid, the "decoded" form of DNA) called messenger RNA (mRNA). A current theory, unknown to Berg at the time, held that the amino acids did not directly interact with RNA but were linked together in a chain by special molecules called joiners, or adapters. In 1956 Berg demonstrated just such a molecule, which was specific to the amino acid methionine. Each amino acid has its own such joiners, which are now called transfer RNA (tRNA).

This discovery helped to stoke Berg's interest in the structure and function of genes, and fueled his ambition to combine genetic material from different species in order to study how these individual units of heredity worked. Berg reasoned that by recombining a gene from one species with the genes of another, he would be able to isolate and study the transferred gene in the absence of confounding interactions with its natural, neighboring genes in the original organism.

In the late 1960s, while at Stanford, he began studying genes of the monkey tumor virus SV40 as a model for understanding how mammalian genes work. By the 1970s, he had mapped out where on the DNA the various viral genes occurred, identified the specific sequences of nucleotides in the genes, and discovered how the SV40 genes affect the DNA of host organisms they infect. It was this work with SV40 genes that led directly to the development of recombinant DNA technology. While studying how gen-

es controlled the production of specific proteins, Berg also was trying to understand how normal cells seemed spontaneously to become cancerous. He hypothesized that cells turned cancerous because of some unknown interaction between genes and cellular biochemistry.

In order to study these issues, he decided to combine the DNA of SV40, which was known to cause cancer in some animals, into the common intestinal bacterium *Escherichia coli* (*E. coli*). He thought it might be possible to smuggle the SV40 DNA into the bacterium by inserting it into the DNA of a type of virus, called a bacteriophage, that naturally infects *E. coli.*

A DNA molecule is composed of subunits called nucleotides, each containing a sugar, a phosphate group, and one of four nitrogenous bases. Structurally, DNA resembles a twisted ladder, or helix. Two long chains of alternating sugar and phosphate groups twist about each other, forming the sides of the ladder. A base attaches to each sugar, and hydrogen bonding between the bases—the rungs of the ladder—connects the two strands. The order or sequence of the bases determines the genetic code; and because bases match up in a complementary way, the sequence on one strand determines the sequence on the other.

Berg began his experiment by cutting the SV40 DNA into pieces using so-called restriction enzymes, which had been discovered several years before by other researchers. These enzymes let him choose the exact sites to cut each strand of the double helix. Then, using another type of enzyme called terminal transferase, he added one base at a time to one side of the double-stranded molecule. Thus, he formed a chain that extended out from the double-stranded portion. Berg performed the same biochemical operation on the phage DNA, except he changed the sequence of bases in the reconstructed phage DNA so it would be complementary to—and therefore readily bind to—the reconstructed SV40 section of DNA extending from the double-stranded portion. Such complementary extended portions of DNA that bind to each other to make recombinant DNA molecules are called "sticky ends."

This new and powerful technique offered the means to put genes into rapidly multiplying cells, such as bacteria, which would then use the genes to make the corresponding protein. In effect, scientists would be able to make enormous amounts of particular genes they wanted to study, or use simple organisms like bacteria to grow large amounts of valuable substances like human growth hormone, antibiotics, and insulin. Researchers also recognized that genetic engineering, as the technique was quickly dubbed, could be used to alter soil bacteria to give them the ability to "fix" nitrogen from the air, thus reducing the need for artificial fertilizers.

Berg had planned to inject the monkey virus SV40-bacteriophage DNA hybrid molecule into *E. coli.* But he realized the potential danger of inserting a mammalian tumor gene into a bacterium that exists universally in the environment. Should the bacterium acquire and spread to other *E. coli* dangerous, pathogenic characteristics that threatened humans or other species, the results might be catastrophic. In his own case, he feared that adding the tumor-causing SV40 DNA into such a common bacterium would be equivalent to planting a ticking cancer time bomb in humans who might subsequently become infected by altered bacteria that escaped from the lab. Rather than continue his ground-breaking experiment, Berg voluntarily halted his work at this point, concerned that the tools of genetic engineering might be leading researchers to perform extremely dangerous experiments.

In addition to this unusual voluntary deferral of his own research, Berg led a group of ten of his colleagues from around the country in composing and signing a letter explaining their collective concerns. Published in the July 26, 1974, issue of the journal *Science,* the letter became known as the "Berg letter." It listed a series of recommendations supported by the Committee on Recombinant DNA Molecules Assembly of Life Sciences (of which Berg was chairman) of the National Academy of Sciences.

The Berg letter warned, "There is serious concern that some of these artificial recombinant DNA molecules could prove biologically hazardous." It cited as an example the fact that *E. coli* can exchange genetic material with other types of bacteria, some of which cause disease in humans. "Thus, new DNA elements introduced into *E. coli* might possibly become widely disseminated among human, bacterial, plant, or animal populations with unpredictable effects." The letter also noted certain recombinant DNA experiments that should not be conducted, such as recombining genes for antibiotic resistance or bacterial toxins into bacterial strains that did not at present carry them; linking all or segments of DNA from cancer-causing or other animal viruses into plasmids or other viral DNAs that could spread the DNA to other bacteria, animals or humans, "and thus possibly increase the incidence of cancer or other disease."

The letter also called for an international meeting of scientists from around the world "to further discuss appropriate ways to deal with the potential biohazards of recombinant DNA molecules." That meeting was held in Pacific Grove, California, on February 27, 1975, at Asilomar and brought together a hundred scientists from sixteen countries. For four days, Berg and his fellow scientists struggled to find a way to safely balance the potential hazards and inestimable benefits of the emerging field of genetic engineering. They agreed to collaborate on developing safeguards to prevent genetically engineered organisms designed only for laboratory study from being able to survive in humans. And they drew up professional standards to govern research in the new technology, which, though backed only by the force of moral persuasion, represented the convictions of many of the leading scientists in the field. These standards served as a blueprint for subsequent federal regulations, which were first published by the National Institutes of Health in June 1976. Today, many of the original regulations have been relaxed or eliminated, except in the cases of recombinant organisms that include extensive DNA regions from very pathogenic organisms. Berg continues to study genetic recombinants in mammalian cells and gene therapy. He is also doing research in molecular biology of HIV–1.

The Nobel Award announcement by the Royal Swedish Academy of Sciences cited Berg "for his fundamental studies of the biochemistry of nucleic acids with particular regard to recombinant DNA." But Berg's legacy also includes his principled actions in the name of responsible scientific inquiry.

Berg was named the Sam, Lula and Jack Willson Professor of Biochemistry at Stanford in 1970, and was chairman of the Department of Biochemistry there from 1969 to 1974. He was also director of the Beckman Center for Molecular and Genetic Medicine (1985), senior postdoctoral fellow of the National Science Foundation (1961–68), and nonresident fellow of the Salk Institute (1973–83). He was elected to the advisory board of the Jane Coffin Childs Foundation of Medical Research, serving from 1970–80. Other appointments include the chair of the scientific advisory committee of the Whitehead Institute (1984–90) and of the national advisory committee of the Human Genome Project (1990). He was editor of *Biochemistry and Biophysical Research Communications* (1959–68), and a trustee of Rockefeller University (1990–92). He is a member of the international advisory board, Basel Institute of Immunology.

Berg received many awards in addition to the Nobel Prize, among them the American Chemical Society's Eli Lilly Prize in biochemistry (1959); the V. D. Mattia Award of the Roche Institute of Molecular Biology (1972); the Albert Lasker Basic Medical Research Award (1980); and the National Medal of Science (1983). He is a fellow of the American Academy of Arts and Sciences, and a foreign member of the Japanese Biochemistry Society and the Académie des Sciences, France. Berg worked as a Professor of Biochemistry at Stanford University.

Further Reading

Antebi, Elizabeth, and David Fishlock, *Biotechnology: Strategies for Life,* MIT Press, 1986.
Magill, Frank N., editor, *The Nobel Prize Winners: Chemistry, Volume 3: 1969–1989,* Salem Press 1990, pp. 1027-1034.
Wade, Nick, *The Ultimate Experiment,* Walker, 1977.
Watson, James, *Recombinant DNA,* W. H. Freeman, 1983.
New York Times, February 2, 1975, p. A1; October 15, 1980, p. A1. □

Victor Louis Berger

Victor Louis Berger (1860-1929) was the first Socialist elected to the U.S. Congress. A principal founder of the Socialist Party of America, he remained one of its most important figures until his death.

Victor Berger was born in Nieder-Rehbach, Austria-Hungary, on Feb. 28, 1860. His parents were prosperous innkeepers. Berger attended the universities in Vienna and Budapest. At the age of 18 he emigrated to

Bridgeport, Conn., where he worked at a variety of jobs. In 1881 he became a teacher in the largely German-speaking city of Milwaukee, Wis.

Berger was active in Milwaukee politics almost from the beginning. The Germans of the city mixed old-country social-democratic politics with their athletic and social club activities, and Berger was suspended from his job once because of his radical ideas. Shortly after marrying in 1897, Berger abandoned teaching and became founder and editor of the *Wisconsin Vorwärts,* a German-language daily newspaper. Although he had been a member of the Socialist Labor party briefly, he was already head of his own local socialist organization. With Eugene V. Debs, and several others, he formed the Social Democracy of America in 1897 and the Social Democratic party in 1898. In 1900 and 1901 Berger helped engineer an alliance with a dissident faction of the Socialist Labor party: the product was the Socialist Party of America. Berger was elected immediately to the party's national executive board and never relinquished the seat.

Berger's Milwaukee branch of the party was by far its most successful. With a firm electoral base, Berger won additional support as the result of his cooperation with the labor movement and painstaking political organization. He set up locals in every precinct, saw that people voted, staged entertainments, and distributed patronage. Reward came in 1910, when Berger was elected to Congress (after several tries) and the Socialists captured the city administration. The party played a major role in the city's government for a half century, and Berger himself was reelected to Congress several times.

In 1918 Berger was sentenced to 20 years of imprisonment for his opposition to American entrance into World War I, but while free on appeal he was elected again to Congress. Congress refused to seat him, but at a special election in 1919 Berger was reelected by an even larger plurality. In 1921 the Supreme Court overturned Berger's conviction. He was seated in the House in 1923 and won reelection until 1928. On July 16, 1929, Berger died of injuries sustained in a streetcar accident in Milwaukee.

Berger was known as the head of the "right wing" of the Socialist party because of his advocacy of immediate, partial reforms while working for a socialist society. His more radical comrades spurned him as a mere progressive. His personal ambitions and vanity sometimes made him seem like a politico who was "using" the socialist organization to further his own career, but it is probably more accurate to describe him as cautious rather than conservative. He recognized that in a popular society such as the United States it was necessary to gain the confidence of the people in a party's right to rule before one could expect to be granted power, and that a political movement should not get too far ahead of its constituency.

Berger was a flexible politician, yet he could be irascible and petty in his intraparty dealings. His writings were considerable. In addition to his many pamphlets, Berger was the editor of the *Vorwärts* (1897-1901), the *Social Democratic Herald* (1901-1911), and the *Milwaukee Leader* (1911-1921).

Further Reading

There is no adequate biography of Victor Berger; one should first consult his writings. The best collection is his *Voice and Pen of Victor L. Berger: Congressional Speeches and Editorials* (1929). David A. Shannon, *The Socialist Party of America: A History* (1955), describes Berger and his policies objectively and sympathetically. An unsympathetic analysis may be found in Ira Kipnis, *The American Socialist Movement: 1897-1912* (1952). Howard H. Quint, *The Forging of American Socialism* (1953), provides a good account of Berger's movement. Marvin Wachman, *History of the Social-Democratic Party of. Milwaukee, 1897-1910* (1945), is valuable but dated. More recent is Thomas W. Gavett, *Development of the Labor Movement in Milwaukee* (1965). □

Ernst Ingmar Bergman

The works of Swedish film and stage director Ingmar Bergman (born 1918) are marked by intellectuality, metaphysical speculation, and symbolic and allegorical content.

Ingmar Bergman was born on July 14, 1918, in Uppsala, Sweden, the son of a Lutheran minister. He attended the University of Stockholm, where he became an active member of the student theatrical group. In 1942, after a brilliant production of *Macbeth,* the aspiring director was appointed to the Swedish Royal Opera. In the years following he divided his talents equally between stage and film efforts.

In 1945 Bergman directed his first film, *Crisis,* the story of an unhappy love affair which ends in suicide. Several films followed in close succession, but in 1956 with *The Seventh Seal* Bergman reached the pinnacle of critical and popular acclaim. *The Seventh Seal* is a medieval morality play about a moribund knight who, seeking to placate his religious doubts and unravel the mystery of the universe, challenges Death to a game of chess. Even Bergman's critics concede that this film has visual audacity and great dramatic power.

A year later Bergman directed *Wild Strawberries,* a brilliantly integrated work conceived in cinematic rather than literary or dramatic terms. A poignant study of the abyss between youth and old age, the effort projects a sad lyricism and warm Chekhovian glow. With his next film, *The Magician* (1959), Bergman returned to his earlier use of symbolism. It is the story of a group of wandering magicians and their encounters with otherworldly spirits. *The Virgin Spring,* a second venture into the medieval milieu, followed in 1960, as well as several lesser works.

In 1961 Bergman embarked upon his ambitious trilogy, beginning with *Through a Glass Darkly,* an intense, almost hysterical, study of familial violence. The second contribution, *Winter Light* (1962), presents the emptiness which follows loss of faith; while the final portion, *The Silence* (1963), explores with surreal imagery the dilemma of verbal inadequacy and the attendant terror of noncommunication.

The trilogy is concerned with the problem of God's absence rather than His illusive presence and with the anguish arising from personal isolation rather than the enigma of human existence itself, and it presents Bergman's increasingly complex world view.

This sophistication is also evident in the coldly poetic lucidity and psychological ambiguity of *Persona* (1966). This masterpiece tells of a bizarre relationship between a young actress who has lapsed into catatonic silence and the loquacious nurse who cares for her. The film provides a fascinating insight into the dark recesses of human identity and the agonies of self-confrontation. *The Hour of the Wolf* (1968), about an artist who is haunted by spectres, marks what some feel is a regrettable return to Bergman's earlier use of mysticism. *Shame* (1968), an analysis of the degeneration induced by war, is as stylistically refined as *Persona* but lacks that film's oblique and richly textured inner resonance.

Due to tax problems Bergman spent much of the 1970s abroad and produced work for television in Norway and Germany as well as Sweden. His major theatrical films of this period include *Cries and Whispers* (1971) and *Autumn Sonata* (1978). Highly regarded among the television work are *Scenes from a Marriage* (1973) and *The Magic Flute* of the same year.

In 1982 Bergman released one of his most autobiographical films, the richly detailed *Fanny and Alexander*. Announced as his final film, it brings together many different themes from his previous works and is a powerful sum-

mary of his life and career. It is one of his most accessible films and quite possibly his best.

Since *Fanny and Alexander* Bergman has published an autobiography, *The Magic Lantern* (1988); and a novel, *Best Intentions* (1989); as well as continuing to write and direct for Swedish television and theater. *Best Intentions* was produced, from Bergman's script, for Swedish television in 1991.

Bergman's reputation has diminished, somewhat, in recent years, but he is still regarded as one of the great directors, and his films remain among the most widely recognized in the world. Many well-known American directors, such as Woody Allen, have paid homage to Bergman in their own films.

Further Reading

The most complete chronological study of Bergman's film career is found in Peter Cowie, *Swedish Cinema* (1966). For intelligent analyses of various films see Pauline Kael, *I Lost It at the Movies* (1965), *Kiss Kiss Bang Bang* (1968), and *5000 Nights at the Movies* (1982, expanded 1991); Stanley Kauffmann, *A World on Film* (1966); John Simon, *Private Screenings* (1967); Dwight Macdonald, *Dwight Macdonald on Movies* (1969); and Susan Sontag, *Styles of Radical Will* (1969). □

Henri Bergson

The French philosopher Henri Bergson (1859-1941) opposed mechanism and determinism and vigorously asserted the importance of pure intuition, duration, and liberty. Bergsonian thought is often referred to as vitalism.

Henri Bergson was born on Oct. 18, 1859, in Paris to a Jewish family of Polish and Irish ancestry. A brilliant student of classics and mathematics, he began to study philosophy in 1878 at the École Normale Supérieure. Three years later he started his long teaching career in Angers. He later taught at Clermont-Ferrand but returned in 1889 to Paris, where he spent the remainder of his teaching career. In 1900 he became a professor at the Collège de France, where his lectures attracted enormous audiences.

During World War I Bergson represented France in diplomatic missions to Spain and the United States; he was later active in the League of Nations. In 1921 he retired because of ill health but continued to meditate and write. Bergson was elected to the French Academy, and he received the 1927 Nobel Prize in literature. At the time of his death, in 1941, he was strongly attracted to Roman Catholicism but felt that he must remain a Jew as a protest against the Nazi occupation of France.

Philosophical Works

Charles Darwin's epic work *Origin of Species* was published in 1859. Within the next 30 years the doctrine of

In *Introduction to Metaphysics* (1903) Bergson clearly distinguishes between science and philosophy. The scientific mind abstracts from reality by "Freezing the flux" of real duration into discontinues elements of juxtaposition and succession or space and time. This technique of reductive analysis is oriented toward the domination and control of nature. But metaphysics or philosophy attempts "to dispense with symbols" and to grasp the inner reality of things by intuition, a nonconceptual, empathetic seeing-into.

Bergson's best-known work, *Creative Evolution* (1907), argues that the traditional accounts of evolution ignore the fact of real, temporal duration. If evolution is reduced to mechanical laws, then time is merely another measure of place in which what is predictable or predetermined can occur. But Bergson holds that nature, like man, often exhibits unpredictable creative break-throughs. For example, the difference "of kind rather than degree" between sentient and conscious beings is a leap in the evolutionary scale. Man's capacities for thought, for symbolic communication in language, and for the invention of tools indicate "the unique, exceptional success which life has won at a given moment of its evolution."

In *The Two Sources of Morality and Religion* (1932) Bergson states that, just as scientific abstractions tend to eliminate the *élan vital,* or creative impulse, of nature, so can morality and religion become the residual abstractions of once-vital impulses. He compares "closed societies," which reduce religion to blind adherence to dogma and ritual, to the "open morality and souls" of saints and heroes in whose works are found the creative moments of spirit that signal a radical transformation of humanity.

Further Reading

The majority of Bergson's writings are available in English translations. Secondary sources include Herbert W. Carr, *Henri Bergson: The Philosophy of Change* (1912; rev. ed. 1919); Bertrand Russell, *The Philosophy of Bergson* (1914); and Jacques Chevalier, *Henri Bergson* (1926; trans. 1928). A recent study, consisting of articles by several scholars on aspects of Bergson's life and work, is Thomas Hanna, ed., *The Bergsonian Heritage* (1962). See also Ian W. Alexander, *Bergson: Philosopher of Reflection* (1957). □

evolution—supported by the positivist methodology of empirical observation and controlled hypotheses—gained widespread intellectual acceptance. Bergson's writings, however, may be seen as a series of essays on the limitations of positivism and its narrow concept of evolution.

In *Time and Free Will* (1889) Bergson suggests that the distinction of philosophy from science indicates that there may be different modes of knowledge. In order to discover if science is the only valid from of cognition, he examines the data of experience to see whether the mind reads *from* nature or *into* nature. Bergson concludes that the immediate data of perception give man's mind an object extended in space; but equally important considerations—the object's duration and intensity—are given only by man's inner, temporal intuition. He criticizes determinism because it fails to consider the free variables of choice and deliberation.

In *Matter and Memory* (1896) Bergson continues this line of criticism by showing that the assumption of an exact one-to-one correspondence between mental image and physical stimulus completely fails to account for human consciousness. He points out that human "consciousness is a memory" that permits the body and mind to meet in action. Pure memory, as opposed to habitual or motor memory, selects one image from the large number of separate perceptions of an object. Elements of vitalism and pragmatism are evident in this work, especially in Bergson's view that sensation is not primarily a cognitive process but an action-oriented response of a living organism.

Lavrenty Pavlovich Beria

The Soviet secret-police chief and political leader Lavrenty Pavlovich Beria (1899-1953) was a close associate of Stalin and was responsible for internal security—and terror—during the last 15 years of Stalin's rule.

L avrenty Beria was the son of a Georgian peasant. In 1917, while a student at a technical school in Baku, he joined the Bolshevik party. He was involved in secutiry affairs for the Bolsheviks in Transcaucasia and quickly became the chief of Soviet security operations there.

In the 1930s, under Stalin's patronage, he rose to national prominence and in 1934 was elected to the Central Committee of the Bolshevik party. In 1935 he wrote an important book on the history of the Bolsheviks in Transcaucasia, a book that started the myth of a romantic young Stalin leading the revolutionary movement. Its publication firmly established his close relationship with Stalin. At the end of 1938, Beria—who had hitherto not been directly involved in the purge trials of the mid-1930s—became the head of Soviet security, then known as the NKVD. He concluded the era of the "Great Purge" by liquidating police officials, including his erstwhile superior, Yezhov. Though he ended the party purge, Beria initiated terrorist activities of his own, including wholesale deportations from the Baltic areas to forced labor camps.

During World War II Beria enhanced his prestige by assuming a wide variety of party, government, and military posts, even becoming a marshal of the Soviet Union. In 1946 he became a full member of the Politburo, the highest-ranking echelon of the Bolshevik party. However, he devoted most of his attention to secret-police work and was undoubtedly responsible for the lesser purges of 1949 (such as the "Leningrad Case"). According to some accounts, by 1952 Stalin himself was alarmed by the amount of power wielded by Beria and planned to oust him.

When Stalin died in March 1953, Beria, V. M. Molotov, and G. M. Malenkov formed a triumvirate in an apparent effort to rule the Soviet Union. However, other Bolsheviks, fearing that once again power would be concentrated in one man, conspired to purge Beria. Officially, it was an-

nounced that Beria had been arrested in the summer of 1953, charged with espionage and various other offenses, and then tried and executed at the end of the year. But there are persistent and well-placed rumors that he was shot to death at a Politburo meeting soon after Stalin's death. In any case, news of his death was received with great relief by all levels of the population. As far as is known, Beria and his top aides were the last Bolsheviks of stature to have been executed. His name has been expunged from Soviet works, and he is generally regarded as one of the most heinous villains of the Stalin era.

Further Reading

There is no biography of Beria in English, but he is discussed at length in works concerning the Stalin era. These include Abdura Khman Avtokharnov, *Stalin and the Soviet Communist Party* (1959), and John Alexander Armstrong, *The Politics of Totalitarianism* (1961). Beria emerges as a particularly sinister character in the memoirs of Stalin's daughter, Svetlana Alliluyeva, *Twenty Letters to a Friend* (1967). □

Vitus Bering

Vitus Bering (1681-1741), a Dane in Russian employ, led two major exploratory expeditions that significantly expanded knowledge of the northern Pacific region.

Vitus Bering was born in the Danish town of Horsens in the summer of 1681. He became a lieutenant in the Russian navy in 1704, and during the Great Northern War he served in both the Black and Baltic seas. In January 1725 Peter I asked Bering to command the first Kamchatkan expedition, the aim of which was to determine the extent of the Siberian mainland and its relationship to North America.

Bering led the expedition over 6,000 miles of wilderness and reached Okhotsk on the Pacific coast on Sept. 30, 1726, nineteen months after leaving St. Petersburg. The group built ships and sailed to the Kamchatka Peninsula. The ship *Gabriel* was built there, and on July 14, 1728, Bering began his first exploration. The *Gabriel* sailed northward, rounding East Cape on August 14. Since the Asiatic coast trended westward and no land appeared to the north, Bering decided that he had fulfilled his mission; he turned back at latitude 67° 18′ to avoid wintering on a desolate and unknown shore. The expedition spent the winter at Kamchatka, where Bering saw numerous signs indicating land to the east. But bad weather during the following summer frustrated his attempts to locate this land, and the expedition returned to St. Petersburg in March 1730.

Great Northern Expedition

Since Bering had not explored the coast of Siberia beyond East Cape, critics claimed that he lacked courage and initiative and pointed out that the relationship between Asia and America remained a mystery. In defense Bering pro-

posed another exploratory mission, and in 1732 he was given command of the Great Northern Expedition. But what began as a fairly modest proposal was unrealistically inflated by the government. Bering was to locate and map the American coast as far as the first European settlement; other groups, coordinated by him, were to chart the Siberian coast and determine once and for all whether Asia and America were connected. Not only was Bering encumbered by a sizable scientific party, but he was also ordered to initiate economic development in eastern Siberia. Hopelessly overburdened, he was given full responsibility but was denied complete authority over his subordinates.

The first detachments left St. Petersburg in February 1733. Crossing Siberia with the throng of jealous officers, balky workers, and insubordinate scientists became a 3-year nightmare. By 1740 preparations at Okhotsk were completed, and the expedition sailed for Kamchatka, where it spent the winter. Bering set out in June 1741 with two ships, but the ships were soon separated and Bering continued alone on the *St. Peter*. He changed his course to the north and sighted land on July 16. A few days later he landed on what is now Kayak Island; but physically and morally exhausted and fearful of being trapped by contrary winds, Bering turned back toward Kamchatka.

The party sailed erratically southwestward, charting landfalls on the way. By the end of August, Bering was too ill to leave his cabin, and the first of many deaths among the crew occurred. On November 4 the coast of one of what are now called the Komandorskie Islands was sighted. With a battered ship and many sick men, Bering decided to winter on the island. Though he grew weaker each day, he continued to guide his men until his death on Dec. 8, 1741. He was buried on the island which now bears his name.

Forty-five of the 77 officers and men of the *St. Peter* eventually reached safety in 1742. The various parties of the Great Northern Expedition obtained significant geographic and scientific information: the strait, now named for Bering, dividing Asia and America, was discovered; the Siberian coast from the White Sea to the Kolyma River was charted; and the coast of America from Prince of Wales Island to the Komandorskie Islands was entered on the map.

Further Reading

The most authoritative and interesting work on Bering is F. A. Golder, *Bering's Voyages: An Account of the Efforts of Russians to Determine the Relation of Asia and America* (2 vols., 1922-1925). Peter Lauridsen, *Vitus Bering: The Discoverer of Bering Strait* (1889), is an apologia and strongly biased, but it is valuable as one of the first Western accounts to use Russian sources. Robert Murphy, *The Haunted Journey* (1961), is a popular work. An account of the expedition by the man who succeeded Bering is in Sven Waxell, *The American Expedition,* with an introduction and notes by M. A. Michael (1952). A short account is in Clarence C. Hulley, *Alaska, 1741-1953* (1953; rev. ed. entitled *Alaska, Past and Present, 1958*). □

Luciano Berio

Luciano Berio (born 1925), Italian composer, created some of the most advanced styles of music in the mid-20th century. His unique style is a result of the combination of Italian lyricism with a highly original idiom.

Luciano Berio was born in Onegia, northern Italy. His father and grandfather were church organists and composers. After preliminary study with his father, Berio entered the Milan Conservatory, specializing in piano, conducting, and composition and after graduation worked as an operatic coach and conductor. In 1951 he received a scholarship to the Berkshire Music Center at Tanglewood in Lenox, Massachusetts, where he studied with Luigi Dallapiccola, the Italian twelve-tone composer. Dallapiccola's influence is evident in the compositions Berio wrote after his return to Italy. *Nones* (1955), written to W. H. Auden's poem "Ninth Hour," is "totally controlled"; that is, not only the tones but also the durations, dynamics, and articulations follow a preconceived serial order.

In 1953 Berio attended the Darmstadt Summer School for New Music, where he met Karlheinz Stockhausen, Pierre Boulez, and other advanced young composers and became acquainted with their revolutionary musical ideas. Back in Milan, Berio established the first electronic music studio in Italy and started to compose in this medium. One of his first pieces was *Homage to Joyce,* in which the sound material is not electronically produced tones but is a reading of the opening section of the "Sirens" chapter of James Joyce's *Ulysses.* The sound of the words is distorted through tape manipulation so that meaning is lost and only expressive vocal sounds remain. Berio was fascinated with such sounds, and in many of his pieces he explored unusual manners of speaking and singing. In his discoveries the composer was greatly aided by his first wife, Cathy Berberian, the versatile American singer.

Circles (1961), for voice, harp, and percussion instruments, is another early piece that exploits the expressive quality of words. The words, an E. E. Cummings poem, are "fractured," that is, separated into their component parts: single vowels and consonants. In *Visage* (1960) the singer emits cries, laughs, sobs, and moans, creating a whole drama on a preverbal level.

Berio was a characteristic 20th-century composer in that he did not repeat himself; each piece called for new sounds and embodied his developing aesthetic. *Sinfonia* (1968), an extraordinary composition written for eight singers (the Swingle Singers) and orchestra, is a vast collage of words and sounds, reflecting the complexity and disorder of modern life. Parts of it sound as though several radio programs were being played simultaneously. Underlying everything, a distorted but recognizable performance of the third movement of Gustav Mahler's Second Symphony can be heard. In addition, there are words from a Samuel Beckett play, student slogans from contemporary confrontations, and fleeting references to a score of other composers ranging from J. S. Bach to Stockhausen. The piece is a Joycean bringing-together of everything in a time-destroying present. In spite of its unconventionality and complexity, the first performances were highly successful.

In the early 1970s, Berio began experimentation in opera, alongside his continuing orchestral, choral, and chamber pieces, notably the ongoing *Sequenza* series. However, despite the titular suggestion of *Opera* (1970), Berios's forays into the genre expectedly strayed from its traditional narrative structure while retaining its emotive peaks. Again working in collaboration with key figures of postmodern literature like Italo Calvino and Umberto Eco, Berio found an audience with subsequent "operas" such as *La Vera Storia* (1977), *Un Re in Ascolto* (1979), and *Outis* (1996), all of which deepened the composer's techniques of undermining normative conceptions of space and time. *Outis,* for example, was loosely based upon the classic myth of Odysseus, but lapsed in and out of a web of time frames, with Odysseus dying repeatedly in each scene. In the operas of Berio, characters were used less as coherent dramatic fictions and more as concepts on stage. Nonetheless, the works retained the color and excitement of opera, simultaneously celebrating the relationship with the legacy of musical history and interrogating that very relationship.

Berio became increasingly appreciated by a mass audience, and was hailed as a much-wanted link between popular audiences and the deconstructionist avant-garde. Accordingly, Berio was invited to give a series of oral dissertations for the 1993 Charles Eliot Norton lecture at Harvard University, a prestigious chair devoted to poetic expression in all the arts. Unfortunately, the lectures were ill received, the general consensus being that Berio's ideas were best expressed through his music.

Further Reading

Richard Steinitz's entry on Berio in *Contemporary Composers* (1994) provides an overall portrait of the composer as well as an exhaustive list of works. For a detailed companion to *Sinfonia,* see David Osmond-Smith's *Playing On Words: A Guide To Luciano Berio's Sinfonia* (1985). A good commentary on Berio's *Circles* appears in Wilfrid Mellers, *Caliban Reborn in Twentieth-Century Music* (1967). Joseph Machlis, *Introduction to Contemporary Music* (1961), and Peter S. Hansen, *An Introduction to Twentieth Century Music* (3d ed. 1971), contain a brief discussion of Berio. A good background book on the period is Otto Deri, *Exploring Twentieth-Century Music* (1968), which discusses the lives and analyzes the different styles of major 20th-century composers. □

Sali Berisha

The election of Sali Berisha (born 1944), the leader of the Democratic Party, as president of the Republic of Albania in April 1992 marked a stage in the country's transition from communism to political democracy. Berisha was involved in a series of scandals which led to his electoral defeat in 1997.

Sali Berisha was born on July 1, 1944, into a poor peasant family from the Tropoja district of northern Albania. After completing his education in local schools, he was admitted to the medical faculty of the University of Tirana, where he received his degree in 1967 "with honors." Following graduation he specialized in cardiology and was subsequently appointed as an assistant professor of medicine at the university and as staff cardiologist at the Tirana General Hospital.

Although Berisha, like many other Albanian intellectuals and professionals, was viewed with suspicion by the regime of the Communist dictator, Enver Hoxha, he was nevertheless admitted to membership in the Albanian Party of Labor (Communist) in 1971. That same year he married Liri Rama, a pediatrician, and the couple eventually had two children, a daughter, Argita, and a son, Shkelzen.

During the 1970s Berisha gained distinction as the leading researcher in the field of cardiology in Albania and became professor of cardiology at the University of Tirana. In 1978 he received a United Nations Educational, Scientific, and Cultural Organization (UNESCO) fellowship for nine months of advanced study and training in Paris. Upon his return to Albania Berisha initiated a research program in hemodynamics that attracted considerable attention among his colleagues in Europe. He was selected in 1986 as a member of the European Committee for Research in the Medical Sciences, headquartered in Copenhagen. As Berisha's international reputation grew, he was invited to share the results of his research in European medical journals.

With the death in 1985 of Enver Hoxha, the long-time (1944-1985) Albanian dictator, Berisha hoped that the country's new leader, Ramiz Alia, would repudiate his predecessor's hard-line Stalinist policies and encourage change. But Berisha, along with a growing number of Albanian intellectuals, students, and young workers, was disappointed when these expectations were not realized. By 1989, as the countries of Eastern Europe began to abandon communism, Berisha and other advocates of reform became more outspoken in their calls for change in Albania. In an October 1989 interview with the Albanian Television Service, Berisha urged the regime to initiate a broad program of liberalization. The Albanian authorities, however, refused to permit the taped interview to be aired. When the Albanian government, responding to popular pressure, promulgated a series of economic and legal reforms in early 1990, Berisha applauded the initiative but urged the regime to expand the scope of these reforms to include the establishment of a market economy and a multiparty democratic political system.

By the beginning of 1990 Berisha had emerged as one of the most respected spokespersons for the reform movement in Albania. In an interview published in the newspaper *Drita* on May 20, 1990, Berisha demanded that the remaining barriers to freedom of thought and expression be ended, that Albanians be granted the right to travel freely within the country and abroad, and that Albania abandon its isolationist foreign policy. At a July 1990 meeting of the nation's intellectuals convened by President Ramiz Alia, Berisha urged the Albanian Party of Labor (APL) to surrender its political monopoly, sanction the drafting of a new democratic constitution, and remove all monuments to Stalin in the country. In an article published in the newspaper *Bashkimi,* Berisha condemned what he termed the "cosmetic reforms" of the Alia regime, which he charged had only served to aggravate unrest within the nation. Without political pluralism, he argued, there could be no true democracy in Albania. To underscore his break with Alia and the Communists, Berisha resigned from the APL at this time.

In December 1990, following a series of student demonstrations and outbreaks of violence that had forced the government to approve the establishment of a multiparty system, Berisha emerged as the leader of the Democratic Party (DP), the first and largest of the new opposition parties. He was formally elected DP chairman in February 1991 at the party's first national congress.

Although the DP was unable to match the organizational and financial resources of the APL, in the March 1991 parliamentary elections, it won 39 percent of the popular vote and emerged as the main opposition party in the National Assembly. When the newly elected APL government, however, was unable to govern the country following the outbreak of a general strike called by noncommunist trade unions, the DP agreed to participate in a coalition government mandated to address the nation's economic problems and make arrangements for a new election. By December 1991 Berisha and the DP had become sufficiently alarmed by the continued deterioration of the economy, breakdown of law and order, and reports of official corruption to withdraw from the ruling coalition and request new elections.

The March 1992 parliamentary elections resulted in a dramatic reversal of the results of the previous year, with the Democratic Party winning 62 percent of the popular vote and 92 of the 140 seats in the National Assembly. Following the resignation of President Alia, the DP-dominated National Assembly on April 8, 1992, elected Sali Berisha to the position. As the first noncommunist head of state, Berisha's election represented the first stage in Albania's transition from communism to democracy.

Upon assuming office, Berisha announced that the major goals of his government were to restore law and order, privatize and revitalize the economy, and strengthen Albania's external ties—especially with Western Europe and the United States. During the first two years of his presidency, Berisha could claim some notable successes in realizing his objectives. There was a significant decline in the nation's crime rate. After disastrous falls in production during 1991 and 1992, the country's gross national product rose by 8 percent in 1993. Additionally, by 1994 the country's runaway inflation rate and government budgetary deficits had been curbed while the private sector of the economy continued to grow. Albania had succeeded in ending its diplomatic isolation and expanded its relations with the European Union, the United States, and various international organizations and agencies. In 1994 Berisha was clearly the most popular and influential political personality in Albania.

Berisha's popularity, however, was short-lived. By October of 1995 he and his administration had endured harsh criticism for supporting legislation to exclude members of the old regime from participating as candidates in the 1996 parliamentary elections. Following the 1996 elections President Berisha was blamed for a series of pyramid schemes, the most notorious of which was known as the Gjallica pyramid scam. Albanians feared as much as $2 billion dollars may have been invested in the phony schemes. The public outcry soon escalated into rioting as Berisha's already waning support continued to erode.

The year 1997 was marred by increasing civil unrest in the country. Berisha lost favor with prominent nations and eventually dissolved his own government in March of 1997. He then attempted to establish a coup with himself in effect a dictator. The citizens responded with increased rioting. This general deterioration of the political climate kept Albania on the verge of civil war until parliamentary elections in June of 1997 resulted in a defeat for Berisha and his Democratic Party.

Further Reading

A brief biographical sketch of Berisha appears in the publication *Democratic Party of Albania* (1992). Useful accounts of political developments in Albania during the transition from communism to democracy appear in Elez Biberaj, "Albania," in *Eastern Europe in Revolution* (1992), and in Nicholas Pano, "Albania," in *The Columbia History of Eastern Europe in the Twentieth Century* (1992). For an account of more recent developments in Albania under Berisha, see Elez Biberaj,

"Albania's Road to Democracy," *Current History* (November 1993). Berisha's presidential activities are chronicled in the Albanian press and the daily *News Bulletin of the Albanian Telegraphic Agency.*

Additional Sources

Economist (October 7, 1995).
Knight-Ridder/Tribune News Service (February 5, 1997).
MacLean's (March 10, 1997).
National Review (April 7, 1997).
Newsweek (March 24, 1997).
Time (March 17, 1997). □

George Berkeley

The Anglo-Irish thinker and Anglican bishop George Berkeley (1685-1753) developed a unique type of idealism based on an empirically oriented attack on abstract philosophizing combined with a defense of immaterialism.

Although born on March 3, 1685, at Dysert Castle in County Kilkenny, Ireland, George Berkeley considered himself to be English. He entered the county school at the age of 11 and in 1700 went to Trinity College, Dublin. He earned a bachelor of arts degree in 1704 and a master of arts degree in 1707, the year in which he became a fellow. Berkeley maintained his appointment until 1724, when he became dean of Derry, but taught at Dublin only until 1712. During this time he formed a club to discuss the "new philosophy" and wrote his most important works: *Essay towards a New Theory of Vision* (1709); *Treatise Concerning the Principles of Human Knowledge,* pt. 1 (1710); and *Three Dialogues between Hylas and Philonous* (1713).

Berkeley traveled to England in 1713. He was an intellectual and social success in London; he met the essayists Joseph Addison and Richard Steele and later contributed articles to the *Guardian.* The poet Alexander Pope described the young philosopher as possessed of "every virtue under heaven." Most of Berkeley's introductions to English literati were arranged by his older Dublin colleague and fellow clergyman, the satirist Jonathan Swift. The most important of these contacts was Lord Peterborough, whom Berkeley accompanied to Europe as chaplain in 1714-1715. During this journey he may have met the French philosopher Nicholas Malebranche. Between 1716 and 1720 Berkeley resided mainly in Italy and France, and while traveling he lost the manuscript of the second part of *Principles of Human Knowledge,* which was never rewritten.

In 1721 he published a short treatise on natural philosophy, *De motu.* and an anonymous book on social reformation, *Essay towards Preventing the Ruin of Great Britain.* About this time Berkeley conceived the idea of establishing a college in the Bermudas to reform the manners of the English colonists and introduce the gospel to the "American savages." Through the influence of his friends he received the necessary patents from Parliament and promises of financial assistance. In September 1728 he married Anne Foster, and shortly thereafter he sailed for the New World. From January 1729 until the fall of 1731 he lived in Newport, R. I. During this period he wrote *Alciphron,* a series of dialogues directed against freethinkers. The financing of the Bermuda scheme eventually failed and, after donating his books and property to Yale College, he returned with his family to London.

In 1734 Berkeley returned to Ireland as bishop of Cloyne, and he remained there for the next 18 years. Distressed at the widespread famine and disease in Ireland, he devoted himself to social and medical studies. In 1744 he created a considerable stir by publishing *Siris,* a work that extolled the virtues of tar-water as a cure for virtually all bodily ills and presented his final metaphysical and religious ideas. On the occasion of fighting between Catholics and Protestants, he wrote several liberal tracts promoting tolerance and humanity. Berkeley retired to Oxford University in 1752 and died suddenly on Jan. 14, 1753.

His Philosophy

The "new way of ideas" of British empiricism had been prepared for Berkeley by John Locke. In a broad sense empiricism is an attempt to derive all knowledge from experience. According to Locke, all knowledge is derived from the external five senses or the internal sense of reflection. But from a psychological viewpoint both sensations and concepts are found *in* the mind. Thus, even sensations are ideal as images which re-present external objects.

The ubiquity of ideas, as sense images as well as concepts, led Berkeley to original psychological and metaphysical views. In *Essay towards a New Theory of Vision* he argued that man does not immediately perceive either the distance of objects from him or their spatial relations to others. He states that distance and magnitude are suggested by past experience of the correlation between sight and touch.

According to Berkeley, it was a short step for him from the psychological recognition of the ideality of sense perceptions to the metaphysical acknowledgement of the immateriality of all reality. He was the first thinker to take the position of denying material reality. In *Principles of Human Knowledge* and *Three Dialogues* he argues that if the only evidence for an object's existence is its being perceived, then the conclusion is that existence consists entirely in being perceived or perceiving and that minds and their ideas constitute reality.

This immaterialist thesis, *Esse est percipi* (to be is to be perceived), is more important as a criticism of materialism than as an exposition of his own spiritualism. In Berkeley's view it is God and His active perception who preserves man from vanishing worlds when objects are not being perceived by him. This means that minds and ideas, which can be empirically verified, are the only realities and that reality is identical with appearance.

Further Reading

The standard edition of Berkeley is edited by A. A. Luce and T. E. Jessop, *The Works of George Berkeley, Bishop of Cloyne,* (9 vols., 1948-1957). The best biography is by A. A. Luce, *The Life of George Berkeley, Bishop of Cloyne* (1949). See also J. Wild, *George Berkeley: A Study of His Life and Philosophy* (1936); A. A. Luce, *Berkeley's Immaterialism* (1945); E. A. Sillem, *George Berkeley and the Proofs for the Existence of God* (1957); D. M. Armstrong, Berkeley's *Theory of Vision* (1960); and A. A. Luce, *The Dialectic of Immaterialism* (1963). □

Sir William Berkeley

Sir William Berkeley (1606-1677), English royal governor of the colony of Virginia, was a leading protagonist in Bacon's Rebellion. He made substantial contributions to the colony but was almost fanatically loyal to England.

William Berkeley was the son of Maurice Berkeley of Bruton, Somerset, and brother of Lord John Berkeley, a proprietor of Carolina. William was educated at Oxford, where he received a bachelor of arts degree in 1624 and a master of arts in 1629. Because of his family's influence at court, Berkeley won a place in the Privy Chamber and became a leading courtier. He exhibited literary skill; one of his plays, *The Lost Lady,* was published in 1639 and was later produced on the London stage. Berkeley was knighted by Charles I in July 1639.

Colonial Service

Berkeley's first chance for service in America came in 1632, when he was made one of England's commissioners for Canada. In 1641 Charles I appointed Berkeley governor of Virginia. The problems facing him in Virginia were formidable. He mollified disgruntled planters by granting them an important role in the government and rectifying abuses of previous administrations. Berkeley's vigorous prosecution of the Native American wars was crucial in winning the Virginians' confidence. He pressed the campaign on the frontiers, personally taking the field to command, and captured the aged Native American chief Opechancanough, thereby gaining a period of relative peace. His resolute action unified the colonists behind his leadership.

The unity which Berkeley engendered was exemplified during the Puritan Revolution in England. The governor's prestige ensured that Virginia would remain loyal to the Stuart cause. After Charles I was beheaded in 1649, Berkeley denounced Cromwell and proclaimed Charles II king of England. Eventually, in 1652, when Virginia was forced to submit to Cromwell's authority, Berkeley resigned his office and retired to his plantation at Green Spring, Va. Just prior to the Restoration (1660), the Virginia Assembly chose Berkeley to serve as governor until Charles II's wishes were known—a token of the high regard in which Berkeley was held.

William Berkeley (standing)

The Restoration

Upon Charles II's assumption of the throne in 1660, Berkeley was reappointed governor. Visiting England in 1661, he demonstrated the dual loyalty to the Stuarts and Virginia that characterized his career. He had returned to England both to pay homage to the new ruler and to support Virginia's complaints against new mercantile legislation. Evidence of Charles II's satisfaction with Berkeley was the designation of Virginia as the King's "Old Dominion." Moreover, Berkeley was included among the eight proprietors of Carolina. But Berkeley was less successful in his work for the colony of Virginia. He could do nothing to relax the mercantile requirement that Virginia's tobacco be shipped to England. In a pamphlet (1662) he noted that thousands of Virginians were thereby "impoverished to enrich little more than forty [English] merchants." He returned to the colony with little to show for his efforts.

Bacon's Rebellion

The uprising known as Bacon's Rebellion (1675-1676) reflected Berkeley's failure during his last years as governor. Within a short period, the governor, who had been called "the Darling of the People," became a party to the struggle that has marred his reputation ever since.

There were several causes of Bacon's Rebellion: economic depression (resulting in part from English mercantile legislation), fears regarding the territorial integrity of Virginia, heavy taxation, inequities in the tax burden, and lingering complaints about local government. These afforded the fuel for rebellion; what provided the spark was renewed conflict with the bordering Native Americans. Because Berkeley reacted slowly to the Native American danger, vigilante forces were organized to protect the frontiers. Some colonists charged that Berkeley's lack of action was a result of his personal involvement in the Native American trade. Berkeley misjudged the situation. Nearing 70 years old in 1675, stubborn and irascible, he felt action by frontiersmen would make the situation worse. After a young planter, Nathaniel Bacon, demanded a commission to fight the Native Americans and then went into battle without the governor's consent, Berkeley proclaimed Bacon a rebel and removed him from the council. A state of civil war resulted, with Bacon holding the stronger hand.

Berkeley's Ignominy

The fury of Bacon's Rebellion was directed primarily against the Native Americans. The confrontation with Berkeley had always been uncertain, because he still retained the post of governor. After Bacon died in October 1676, the rebellion began to wane. Berkeley unwisely took vengeance by executing 23 rebel leaders and confiscating their property. He continued the executions over the objections of the King's commissioners, who were sent to replace Berkeley and report on conditions in Virginia. Instead of peace, a strained situation resulted, with Berkeley defying the King's commissioners. Finally, his health broken, Berkeley sailed unhappily for England. "The King is not a little surprised to find a person, who has been so loyal, fall into such errors," Berkeley was informed. He soon died, never having an opportunity to defend himself before the King he revered.

Further Reading

A biographical account of Berkeley may be found in Philip Alexander Bruce, *The Virginia Plutarch* (2 vols., 1929). Two conflicting estimates of Berkeley's career and role in Bacon's Rebellion are offered in Thomas Jefferson Wertenbaker, *Torchbearer of the Revolution: The Story of Bacon's Rebellion and Its Leader* (1940), and in Wilcomb E. Washburn, *The Governor and the Rebel: A History of Bacon's Rebellion in Virginia* (1957). An excellent summary of the evidence is in Wesley Frank Craven, *The Colonies in Transition: 1660-1713* (1967). Readers interested in the first years of the Southern colonies can rely on Craven's *The Southern Colonies in the Seventeenth Century: 1607-1689* (1949). Authoritative also is Richard L. Morton, *Colonial Virginia* (2 vols., 1960). □

Adolf Augustus Berle Jr.

Adolf Augustus Berle, Jr. (1895-1971), was an educator, a diplomat, a government official, and a provocative interpreter of the United States corporate economy.

Adolf Berle was born in Boston, Mass., on Jan. 27, 1895. He earned his bachelor's degree from Harvard College in 1913 and his master's in 1914. He then entered Harvard Law School, from which he received his degree in 1916, at the age of 21.

Years of Public Service

After a year of law practice in Boston, followed by a year with the United States commission to negotiate the peace with Germany, Berle moved to New York City in 1919 to become a member of the law firm of Berle, Berle and Brunner, where he remained, taking frequent leaves for public and diplomatic service. He was professor of corporation law on the faculty of Columbia Law School from 1927 until he retired as professor emeritus in 1964. He was a member of the board of directors of such public, civic, and educational institutions as SuCrest and the Twentieth Century Fund of New York City, and École de l'Europe Libre, France. He was also chamberlain of New York City during 1934-1938.

In 1933 he began a long and distinguished career of high-level government assignments. He was a member of the original "brain trust" in the early years of President Franklin Roosevelt's first administration. He served as special counsel to the Reconstruction Finance Corporation (1933-1938), assistant secretary of state (1938-1944), United States ambassador to Brazil (1945-1946), chairman of the Task Force on Latin America (1961), and consultant to the secretary of state (1961-1962). At intervals throughout this period he also served as United States delegate to the Inter-American Conference for Maintenance of Peace (Buenos Aires, 1936-1937); and two Pan American conferences

corporate owners (stockholders), had acquired sufficient power to have become liberated from the market forces of competition as well. He concluded, therefore, that much of the economic theory pertaining to the functioning of the marketplace, which served as a rationale for the free-enterprise market economy, had been rendered obsolete by the accumulation of immense power in the hands of corporate management. This provocative thesis generated much debate among economists and legal scholars, a debate that still continues.

Further Reading

References to Berle's work are found in numerous discussions on the American economy. *The American Economic System: An Anthology of Writings concerning the American Economy,* compiled by Massimo Salvadori (1963), contains a useful section on Berle's analysis of the modern corporation. See also George A. Steiner, *Government's Role in Economic Life* (1957), and Peter d'A. Jones, *America's Wealth* (1963).

Additional Sources

Schwarz, Jordan A., *Liberal: Adolf A. Berle and the vision of an American era,* New York: Free Press; London: Collier Macmillan, 1987. □

(Lima, Peru, 1938; Havana, Cuba, 1940). He was president of the International Conference on Civil Aviation and chairman of the American delegation (Chicago, 1944). Berle died in New York City on Feb. 17, 1971.

Structure of the American Economy

Berle's scholarly works include numerous law texts, legal, social, and economic commentaries, and treatises on the United States corporate economy. By far the best-known and most frequently cited of these works are *The Modern Corporation and Private Property* (1932, coauthored with Gardiner Means), *The 20th Century Capitalist Revolution* (1954), and *Power without Property* (1959).

In *The Modern Corporation,* Berle and Means presented an analysis of the structure of the American economy, showing that the means of production were highly concentrated in the hands of the largest 200 corporations, that this concentration was increasing, and that within the large corporations which so dominated the economy there was a clear divorcement of ownership from control. Since the American private-property legal system had been based on the assumption that those who owned property possessed the rights and power to use it for their own benefit, the Berle and Means thesis called into serious question the operability of the legal system on which the private-enterprise economy had been built.

In the two later volumes Berle advanced the companion thesis that management of large corporate enterprise, in addition to having become liberated from the control of

Irving Berlin

The American composer Irving Berlin (1888-1989) produced about 800 songs, many of which attained worldwide popularity. His patriotic songs, especially "God Bless America," seemed to epitomize the mass American sentiments of the era.

Irving Berlin was born Israel Baline in Tyumen, Russia, on May 11, 1888. The family of nine fled the persecutions of Jews in Russia in 1893 and settled in New York City, where, like so many other immigrants of that time, they lived on the Lower East Side. The family's first years in America were very difficult—at one time they all sold newspapers on the streets. Israel, the youngest child, was first exposed to music in the synagogue in which his father occasionally sang as cantor; he also received singing lessons from his father.

When the boy left home at 14, he made money by singing in saloons on New York's Bowery. He attended school for two years but had no formal musical education; he never learned to read or notate music.

It was while working as a singing waiter that Israel Baline, collaborating with a coworker named Nicholson on a song entitled "Marie from Sunny Italy," became I. Berlin, lyricist. This was the name he chose to appear on the sheet music when the song was published shortly after, in 1907.

Subsequently, Berlin began to gain recognition as a clever lyricist. He provided words for "Queenie, My Own," "Dorando," and "Sadie Salome, Go Home." The last was something of a success, and he was hired by a Tin Pan Alley

Among Berlin's best known songs are "White Christmas" and "God Bless America" which are perennial holiday favorites to this day.

Commenting on the composer who produced more popular hits than any other of his generation, Harold Clurman wrote in 1949, "Irving Berlin's genius consists not so much in his adaptability to every historical and theatrical contingency, but rather in his capacity to discover the root need and sentiment of all our American lives."

Berlin's 100th birthday was celebrated in a televised special from Carnegie Hall. When he died in New York on September 22, 1989 he was remembered as a symbol of the nation. As fellow songwriter Jerome Kern was quoted in Alexander Woolcott's biography of Berlin: "Irving Berlin has no place in American Music. He *is* American Music."

Further Reading

Alexander Woollcott, *The Story of Irving Berlin* (1925), is an affectionate and stylishly written account of Berlin's early career. *The Songs of Irving Berlin* (1957?), a catalog of his works, was published by the Irving Berlin Music Corporation. For background on Berlin and American musical comedy see David Ewen, *Complete Book of the American Musical Theater* (1959; rev. ed. 1968) and *The Story of America's Musical Theater* (1961; rev. ed. 1968), Stanley Green, *World of Musical Comedy* (1960; rev. ed. 1968), and Laurence Bergreen, *As Thousands Cheer: The Life of Irving Berlin* (1990). □

publisher to write words for new songs. Within a year, despite his continuing difficulty in writing English, Berlin was established as a rising talent in the popular-music business.

Somewhat belatedly music publishers became interested in exploiting ragtime, the highly original creation of African-American musicians in the South and Midwest during the 1880s and 1890s. Berlin contributed lyrics (and a few tunes) to several mild ragtime songs. In 1911 he wrote the words and music for "Alexander's Ragtime Band," which started toward worldwide popularity when sung by Emma Carus in Chicago that year. It is ironic that one of the most famous of all "ragtime" songs employs a few conventional syncopations but no real ragtime at all.

Berlin's fame soared. He wrote his first complete musical score in 1914, *Watch Your Step,* followed by *Stop, Look, Listen.* In the Army during World War I he wrote a successful soldier show entitled *Yip, Yip, Yaphank* (1919), which contained "Oh, How I Hate to Get Up in the Morning." In 1919 he founded his own music publishing company, Irving Berlin, Inc.

His most successful subsequent shows included *Ziegfeld Follies* (1919, 1920, 1927), *Music Box Revues* (1921-1924), *As Thousands Cheer* (1933), *This Is the Army* (1942), *Annie Get Your Gun* (1946), and *Call Me Madam* (1950). His best-known scores for films include *Top Hat* (1935), *Follow the Fleet* (1936), and *Holiday Inn* (1942).

Isaiah Berlin

British philosopher, Isaiah Berlin (born 1909), wrote widely on topics involving the history of ideas, political philosophy, and the relationship of the individual to society. He skillfully explored the history of ideas to find ways in which society can use large philosophical principles to secure individual conformity to social values.

Isaiah Berlin was born in Riga, Latvia, on June 9, 1909. The family moved often and eventually ended up in St. Petersburg. Even as a young child he witnessed some of the most profound events of the 20th century, when at the age of six he watched the Russian Revolution unfold in the streets below the family's apartment window. The family emigrated to Great Britain in March, 1920 when Berlin was eleven. By July of that same year, Berlin had won first prize for an essay in English. He was educated at St. Paul's School, London, and then attended Corpus Christi College, Oxford (B.A. in 1932, M.A. in 1935). He later was awarded many honorary degrees.

His early career was devoted to diplomatic work, and he served in the British embassies in Washington (1942-1945) and Moscow (1945-1946). At the British embassy in Washington, he was responsible for reporting on American public opinion during the war. He so impressed Prime Minister Winston Churchill with his reports that Churchill asked to meet "this man Berlin". Shortly thereafter, Churchill found himself entertaining the American composer Irving Berlin. This type of mix-up between the two happened often, including a time in 1932 when Berlin was elected the first Jewish Fellow at All Souls College in Oxford and the Chief Rabbi of England congratulated Irving Berlin for the honor in the *Jewish Chronicle.*

Isaiah Berlin was a lecturer at various colleges at Oxford after 1933 and was a visiting professor at scores of American colleges—most notably Harvard, Princeton, and The City College of New York. He was president of the British Academy from 1974 to 1978 and a member of the board of governors of Hebrew University in Jerusalem. He was knighted in 1957 and received The Order of Merit in 1971. Berlin married Aline Elizabeth Yvonne de Gunzburg in 1956.

As a young man Berlin became an avid Zionist. He felt that Zionism was the natural liberation movement of the Jewish people, who after two millennia in exile had a right to their own homeland. Berlin's family was integral to the establishment of the Hasidic dynasty of Lubavitch during the Napoleonic Wars. He was related to Rebbe Menacham Schneerson, a Lubavitcher whose followers believed he was the Messiah, and violinist Yehude Menuhin. Aline Berlin's family was also prestigious in the Russian Jewish community, where as the Barons De Ginsbourg, served as grand bankers in Russia and Paris and as renowned philanthropists. He viewed the Jewish community as an extended family and for Berlin, a "strong family feeling was one of the primary colors of human emotion." Throughout his career,

Berlin retained a deep interest in human emotion and its effects on history and ideas.

Berlin was first and foremost a historian of ideas. He was most well known in America for his books *Karl Marx: His Life and Environment* (1939), *Four Essays on Liberty* (1969), and *Vico and Herder: Two Studies in the History of Ideas* (1976). At the heart of his philosophy of history is the conviction that the tools of science are the servants of historians rather than their masters. This means that science by itself cannot provide us with predictive explanations that account for social transformation. Natural selection may be able to explain the transformations among species but it cannot explain the more complex changes that take place within the interplay of ideas and political traditions. Furthermore, while the methods of science are indispensable for historical explanation, the historian cannot discover laws of historical development in the sense that the physicist can discover the laws of planetary motion. The historian must appeal to larger explanatory concepts than are to be found within a mechanistic science.

Two such concepts that often appear in Berlin's picture of history are the interrelated concepts of *monism* and *pluralism.* Monism represents the tendency on the part of human beings to see unity amidst diversity. More important, it involves a tendency to subordinate individual values to larger social values. Monism is, in many respects, utopian. Monists tend to picture humans as striving toward one ultimate end and individuals as servants of larger historical processes. For example, within psychology a monistic thinker would tend to see all behavior as deriving from a common source or a common principle. Sigmund Freud conceived of all human behavior as deriving from the fundamental desire of individuals to secure their own private pleasure; all human energy is libidinal and all human action is to be understood as the working out of this libidinal energy. Why is Shakespeare a great writer? The Freudian answer is monistic in the sense that Shakespeare's art was his way of sublimating sexual or libidinal energy.

Another kind of monistic thinker was Karl Marx, the 19th-century philosopher and economist whose ideas spawned 20th-century communism. Marx believed that all social behavior had a common root, namely, economics. For Marx, if one wished to explain any social or historical phenomenon, one merely had to discover economic factors that caused the phenomenon. For example, Marx believed that World War I was caused by capitalists in England, France, and Germany who were using their respective governments as a means of eliminating competitors. Both Freud and Marx were monists. Berlin suggested that monistic thinkers tend to see a common thread running through all human events.

Berlin was skeptical of all monisms. He held that the development of ideas and traditions is far more diverse than monists care to admit. Furthermore, there is no utopian ideal that history is moving toward. This view of history colors all of Berlin's other work. To illustrate this skepticism regarding monism we can examine Berlin's views on moral theory. Monism, he argued, has exerted a powerful influence within moral theory. Monistic moral opinions are rooted in the belief that all our moral views must be derivable from a single moral axiom, such as the utilitarian ideal of maximizing social welfare. This moral ideal is monistic in the sense that it is pictured as basic or fundamental and therefore deserving of priority in all moral reasoning. Consequently, any moral opinion or principle that conflicts with this basic rule must be rejected. But this monistic picture of moral priority often comes into conflict with other basic intuitions such as the desire to protect individuals whose legitimate, autonomous behavior seems at odds with social welfare. For Berlin, monism fails precisely because no moral principle has universal priority. Rather, our moral lives are made up of fundamental compromises between competing principles, and there may be no ideal vantage point from which to determine what are the legitimate compromises.

Another example of this conflict between monism and pluralism within our moral lives involves the conflicting duty to respect the individual's right to be left alone (Berlin calls this negative freedom) and the corresponding duty to prevent others from becoming slaves of self-destructive desires such as drugs or alcohol or blatant ignorance. One is positively free when one is governed by "rational motives" and not controlled by irrational desires. Our duty to secure positive freedom may come into conflict with the individual's negative freedom, i.e., his or her right to be left alone. Berlin represents negative freedom as fundamental.

Berlin's pluralism can best be explained by a utopian or monistic critique. Berlin's support for the primacy of negative freedom was grounded largely on his experience with the Cold War and the tendency on the part of communists to use positive freedom as a means of enslaving millions. The communists argued that one can only be rationally free if one lives in a classless society devoid of economic differences. Furthermore, the Stalinist version of communism that controlled the former Soviet Union acted as if any violation of individual rights was permitted as long as it would contribute to the utopian ideal of a classless society. But surely monists need not be identified with Stalinist repression. One can still accept that there are modest versions of monism and utopianism which include both respect for the rights of individuals and modest concern for the public good.

Berlin's short work titled *The Hedgehog and the Fox* (1953) is a masterpiece of literary and interpretative philosophy which contains his description of Leo Tolstoy's philosophical views on history. Tolstoy, like Berlin, was profoundly skeptical that individuals, even powerful individuals such as Napoleon, understand and control the events within history. To see Napoleon as controlling history is similar to assuming that a drop of water can control the direction of the Mississippi River. For Tolstoy there was a pattern to history just as there is a direction to the Mississippi but we are unable to see this pattern just as the fish is unable to see the direction of the Mississippi. Tolstoy accepted that history is determined, but he was very skeptical that the materialistic philosophies of Marx or the spiritualistic philosophies of the German idealists could discern the pattern of human history. Finally, in Berlin's essay entitled "From Hope and Fear Set Free" he tackled the grand assumption of

the West; namely, that the growth of knowledge will liberate individuals. His arguments against this view indicate the profound influence that Tolstoy had on his thought.

When asked to write an autobiography, Berlin refused and referred interested persons to the 1981 book, *Personal Impressions* as his reflections on the important figures whose ideas became visions that shaped their lives. Coupled with his books, *Against the Current* a book of essays on the history of ideas, *Russian Thinkers, Concepts and Categories* these philosophical writings provide the interested public with a comprehensive collection of his reflections and ideas. A collection of nine additional essays were released in 1997, based on lectures given between 1950 and 1972, and confirmed again the enormous breadth and erudition of Berlin's scholarship and intellect.

Further Reading

Isaiah Berlin was a clear writer whose literary elegance is marked by a simplicity and clarity that may be unequaled among 20th-century British philosophers. Perhaps his most well-known book is *Four Essays on Liberty* (1969), which contains his essay "Two Concepts of Liberty." Here he spells out his views on positive and negative freedom. See other Berlin writings discussed in the text. For views on Berlin by contemporaries see Henry Hardy, ed., *Personal Impressions: Isaiah Berlin,* with an introduction by Noel Annan (1980). Although no autobiography exists, Berlin's views and reflections can be found in all of his works. Additional sources for insights into Berlin include: "The Philosopher of Sympathy: Isaiah Berlin and the Fate of Humanism," *New Republic* (February 20, 1995); *The Sense of Reality: Studies in Ideas and their History: Isaiah Berlin* (1997). □

Louis Hector Berlioz

Louis Hector Berlioz (1803-1869) was a French composer, conductor, and music critic. His works contributed to the burgeoning romanticism and influenced orchestral techniques for more than a century.

Hector Berlioz is the epitome of the romantic artist, together with the writer Victor Hugo and the painter Eugène Delacroix. Berlioz helped to break old molds and create new forms full of strong contrasts of passion and emotion. He ranks indubitably as one of the most original creative musicians of all time.

Berlioz was born at La-Côte-Saint-André (Isère) on Dec. 9, 1803, the son of a doctor. His father, a cultured man, was his first teacher. Berlioz formed his lifelong attachment to the poetry of Virgil at this time. From the age of 12 he took music lessons; he studied flute and then guitar, and these were the only instruments he ever played. After reading some treatises on harmony he began to compose.

Musical Life in Paris

After matriculating at Grenoble in 1821, Berlioz continued his university studies at Paris in medicine for a year. But medicine did not interest him, and he threw himself wholeheartedly into Parisian musical life, frequenting the opera and studying scores, especially those of Christoph Willibald Gluck, Gasparo Spontini, and Carl Maria von Weber, at the Conservatory library. He became a student of Jean François Lesueur, a teacher at the Conservatory, from whom he learned to experiment in program music. By 1823 Berlioz was also working as a critic on *Le Corsaire* and composing. His first efforts went quite badly: two attempts to win the coveted Prix de Rome resulted in failure, and his new works suffered from bad performances.

In 1826 Berlioz entered the Conservatory. His father suspended his allowance, and Berlioz subsisted by singing in a theater chorus, writing a few articles, and giving lessons in flute and solfeggio. Despite this, his creative output flourished, and in 1828 he presented a concert of his own music at the Conservatory, including the *Waverley* Overture; excerpts from an opera, *Les Francs-Juges;* a cantata, *La Révolution grecque;* the *Resurrexit* from a Mass; another cantata, *La Mort d'Orphée;* and the *Marche des rois Mages.*

In the meantime Berlioz became passionately fond of the works of Shakespeare, especially performances of his plays by an English dramatic company, one of whose members was the actress Harriett Smithson, with whom he fell hopelessly in love. He also read a great deal in English romantic literature. Another important influence was the symphonies of Beethoven—his last and greatest musical discovery.

Berlioz's final literary discovery was Goethe; inspired by this poet, he composed *Huit scènes de Faust* in 1829, had the score published at his own expense, and sent it to Goethe. Goethe's musical adviser condemned it vociferously, and Goethe never replied to Berlioz.

A third try at the Prix de Rome with his cantata *Herminie et Tancrède* earned Berlioz the second prize. A fourth try with the cantata *La Mort de Cléopâtre* was not successful, but his fame was furthered by another concert of his works at the Conservatory. A critical moment occurred in 1830, the year of his *Symphonie fantastique,* when on his fifth try he won the coveted Prix de Rome with his cantata *Sardanapale.*

Roman Period

In the meantime, after an unhappy attempt to communicate his affections to Harriett Smithson, Berlioz turned to the pianist Marie Mok and proposed marriage to her. He left for Rome early in 1831 for a 2-year stay at the Villa Medici, promising to return at the end of that time to marry Marie. A little later he learned that she had married someone else and decided to rush to Paris to kill her and then himself. He changed his mind after getting as far as Nice and turned back to Rome.

Rome pleased him very little, but of his impressions of Italy were born the symphony *Harold en Italie* and the opera *Benvenuto Cellini.* During his stay in Rome he composed or

finished several works—the overtures *Le Corsaire, Rob Roy,* and *Le Roi Lear* and the melologue *Lélio, ou Le retour à la vie*—plus works required under the rules of the Prix de Rome.

Years in Paris

Berlioz returned to Paris in 1832, where a concert of his works was given that included the *Symphonie fantastique* and *Lélio.* He met Harriett Smithson again; despite the opposition of his parents, he married her in 1833. The marriage was not a happy one. Harriett, no longer acting, became irritable and jealous and took to drinking.

Berlioz advanced as a critic, writing for a variety of journals. Although fairly well-paid for his musical criticism, he was in constant financial difficulties. He did not belong to the official musical circles; hence he had to go into debt to finance his concerts. All in all, through 1838 his life remained hard. During this period, however, there were performances of *Harold en Italie,* the *Grande Messe des morts (Requiem),* and *Benvenuto Cellini.* The failure of this opera was a bitter blow to Berlioz, who was ambitious for success as an opera composer.

On Dec. 16, 1838, however, at a concert of his works, Berlioz was honored and praised by the eminent violinist Niccolo Paganini, who later sent him a gift of 20,000 francs. This helped establish Berlioz's fame and redressed his economic situation in a definitive manner. Berlioz's appointment to the Conservatory library staff also contributed to his financial security. Successful performances followed of his dramatic symphony *Roméo et Juliette,* at which Richard Wagner was present as an admirer, and of his *Grande symphonie funèbre et triomphale* for chorus and band.

European Travels

A notable turn in Berlioz's career occurred in 1842 with the beginning of his trips outside France. He made a triumphal tour of Germany in the company of Maria Recio, a mediocre singer, with whom he became friendly after falling out with his wife. Trips to Austria-Hungary in 1845-1846 and to Russia in 1847 were not only musically successful but economically fruitful. There followed a trip to London in 1852 and to Weimar, Germany, in 1855, where Franz Liszt organized a Berlioz week.

Berlioz's principal compositions up to 1855 are the overture *Le Carnaval romain;* the dramatic legend *La Damnation de Faust;* a *Te Deum* for three choruses, orchestra, and organ; and the oratorio *L'Enfance du Christ.* He also published his important treatise on instrumentation, as well as books describing his travels in Germany and Italy. During this period Berlioz was passed over for the post of director of the Conservatory. His wife died in 1854; shortly afterward he married Maria Recio.

Last Works

During the years 1856-1858 Berlioz worked on his masterpiece, the opera *Les Troyens,* based on Virgil's epic. Between 1861 and 1862 he wrote his last opera, *Béatrice et Bénédict,* based on Shakespeare's *Much Ado about Nothing,* which he conducted at a festival at Baden-Baden, although ill and distraught over the sudden death of his second wife.

In 1863 *Les Troyens* was performed at the Théâtre Lyrique in a drastically shortened form. Berlioz died in Paris on March 8, 1869, and it was only after his death that *Les Troyens* was given in its entirety.

Further Reading

Humphrey Searle translated *Hector Berlioz: A Selection from His Letters* (1966). Many of Berlioz's writings appear in English translation; see especially the translations by Jacques Barzun, *Evenings with the Orchestra* (1956), and by David Cairns, *The Memoirs of Hector Berlioz* (1969). The best general work on Berlioz is Jacques Barzun, *Berlioz and His Century* (2 vols., 1950; 3d ed., 1 vol., 1969). Two older biographies are also useful: W. J. Turner, *Berlioz: The Man and His Works* (1934), and Tom S. Wotton, *Hector Berlioz* (1935). Both the Barzun and Turner studies contain detailed information about Berlioz's compositions. For general historical background see Romain Rolland, *Musicians of Today* (trans. 1928), and Jacques Barzun, *Classic, Romantic, and Modern* (1943; 2d rev. ed. 1961). □

Bartolomé Bermejo

The painter Bartolomé Bermejo (active 1474-1498), beginning under Flemish influence, was among the first Spanish artists to change to the Italian Renaissance manner.

The real name of Bartolomé Bermejo was probably Bartolomé de Cárdenas. Bermejo, meaning reddish, is thought to have been a nickname, but he did sign one of his works that way. He was born in Cordova, and some scholars believe he was Jewish because of a Hebrew inscription in his *Christ Seated on His Tomb* and also because of the physical types in many of his paintings.

Bermejo worked in Catalonia, Aragon, and Valencia and may have traveled to Flanders, France, and Italy since these countries are a trinity of influences discernible in his art. However, pervading his works is a character all his own: a poetic blend of melancholy, serenity, and grandeur.

Bermejo's first documented work is the altarpiece he executed for the church of S. Domingo de Silos in Daroca (1474-1477). The central panel, *St. Dominic of Silos* (now in the Prado Museum), combines Spanish realism and Flemish miniaturist detail. To the naturalism of the saint's physiognomy is added an expression of enigmatic introspection. The impressive monumentality of the figure subordinates the array of incredibly lavish and refined detail.

St. Engracia (ca. 1480) is stylistically distinguishable from *St. Dominic of Silos*. Although both saints are enthroned and fail to occupy their thrones convincingly, the form of St. Engracia, unlike the corporally weighted figure of St. Dominic, responds to the ascending linear scheme of a slender, reversed S curve. Paradoxically, her weightless form is enveloped in heavy, voluminous garments through

which she seems to rise like a visual metaphor of the transcendence of the soul. Her face is impersonal, lovely, and remote. Her throne is simplified, lacking Flemish minutiae of ornament.

Although Bermejo's early art was strongly influenced by the Flemish in its drapery rhythms, luxuriant ornateness, and minute details, in his portraits of actual persons the facial chiaroscuro (light and dark values) is softly graded and, combined with the depth of feeling in the expressions, lends an emotional profundity that is distinctly Spanish. An example of this combination of attributes is the donor in *St. Michael* (ca. 1472).

Bermejo signed the Pietà with *St. Jerome and the Canon Lluis Desplà* (1490) "Opus Bartholomei Vermeio Cordubensis" (Work of Bartolomé Bermejo, Cordovan). The style of this work argues strongly that he was conversant with the art of Giovanni Bellini and of the Venetian school in general. The scene is pervaded by a palpable atmosphere that softens all it envelops in an Italianate idealism. The foreground, middle ground, and background are interlocked in a tremendous and unified recession in space. Other works by Bermejo are *St. Catalina* (ca. 1478), with a Flemish landscape and city scene; the *Virgin and Child with Donor* (ca. 1485), with a Bellinesque background; and *St. Veronica* (1498).

It is believed that Bermejo died about 1500. He had two followers, Martin Bernat and Miguel Jiménez, and his art influenced a number of artists in Valencia and Aragon.

Further Reading

An informative source on Bermejo in English is Chandler R. Post, *A History of Spanish Painting* (14 vols., 1930-1966). The best sources are in Spanish.

Additional Sources

Young, Eric, *Bartolome Bermejo: the great Hispano-Flemish master*, London: Elek, 1975. □

Jean Baptiste Bernadotte

The French-born Jean Baptiste Bernadotte (1763-1844) ruled Sweden and Norway as King Charles XIV John from 1818 to 1844. The founder of the present Swedish dynasty, he served as a marshal of the Napoleonic army before his election as crown prince of Sweden in 1810.

The son of petit-bourgeois parents, Jean Baptiste Bernadotte was born on Jan. 26, 1763, at Pau, France. He joined the army in 1780 and was a sergeant when the French Revolution began in 1789. Embracing the Revolutionary ideals, he rose rapidly in the ranks of the republican army. By 1794 he was a brigadier general and had served with the armies of the Meuse and the Rhine.

In 1798 Bernadotte served briefly as French ambassador to Vienna. Returning to Paris in the summer of that year, he married Désirée Clary. Her relationship with Napoleon—he had courted her in 1794 and her sister had married his brother Joseph Bonaparte—was to prove beneficial to Bernadotte. During 1798 Bernadotte was also minister of war for a short period, and he had become an influential political general by the time of Napoleon's return from Egypt in 1799. He did not, however, take part in the coup d'etat of Brumaire (November 1799), which established the Consulate under Napoleon. During the 4 years of the Consulate he commanded first the Army of the Vendée and then the troops at Hanover.

The creation of the empire in 1804 brought Bernadotte the title of marshal. He played an active role in the campaign against Austria in 1805 and fought at Austerlitz. In return for his services to France, and because of his relation to the Emperor, he was given the principality of Pontecorvo in June 1806. He took part in the Prussian campaign of 1806, but during the Battle of Jena (October 14) he refused to support Marshal Louis N. Davout, who was thus forced to engage the major portion of the Prussian army with only one army corps. Although he remained popular with his troops, Bernadotte was denounced by Napoleon and criticized by his fellow marshals for this action.

In 1808, as governor of northern Germany, Bernadotte came in contact with Swedish troops, who were impressed by his generous conduct. The 1809 campaign against Austria found him once again at the head of an army corps, but the Battle of Wargram marked the end of his military career with the French army. When the German troops under his command fled to the rear at the height of the battle, Bernadotte rode after them in a vain attempt to rally them. While riding full gallop to the rear, he met Napoleon advancing with reinforcements. The Emperor would listen to no explanation; he relieved the marshal of his command and ordered him off the battlefield.

Bernadotte returned to Paris in undeserved disgrace but was soon given command of the defense of the Netherlands. Then, in 1810, as he was about to take up his new post as governor of Rome, the Swedish government asked him to become crown prince of Sweden. After securing the approval of Napoleon and becoming a member of the Lutheran Church, Bernadotte was elected on Aug. 20, 1810, to succeed the aging and ailing Swedish king, Charles XIII. When he arrived in Stockholm in November, he was adopted by the king and took the name Charles John. He was popular with the Swedish people, and his political influence increased as the King's health continued to decline. Realizing that Sweden could never retake Finland from Russia, he followed a pro-Russian course in foreign policy, aimed at acquiring Norway. The occupation by French troops of Swedish Poemerania in 1812 and the ruinous Continental blockade resulted in a formal split with Napoleon, and in 1813 the crown prince took his adopted nation into the camp of the Allies.

Charles John led a Swedish army against France in the final years of the Napoleonic Wars, and after Napoleon's defeat Sweden was allowed to annex Norway, which had been part of the Danish kingdom. In 1818, when Charles XIII died, the crown prince ascended the throne. An ultraconservative throughout his peaceful reign, he almost outlived his popularity. On March 8, 1844, he died at Stockholm.

Further Reading

Sir Dunbar Plunket Barton wrote three books on Bernadotte, which completely cover the life of the soldier and king: *Bernadotte: The First Phase, 1763-1799* (1914), *Bernadotte and Napoleon, 1763-1810* (1921), and *Bernadotte: Prince and King, 1810-1844* (1925). Franklin D. Scott, *Bernadotte and the Fall of Napoleon* (1935), is an excellent account of Bernadotte during the years 1809-1815. □

Georges Bernanos

The French novelist and essayist Georges Bernanos (1888-1948) was concerned with the concrete reality of evil and with the struggle to achieve saintliness in an uncomprehending, hostile modern world. His work was Catholic in inspiration.

Georges Bernanos, born in Paris on Feb. 20, 1888, spent his childhood in a small village in the north of France. Between 1906 and 1913 he studied in Paris for degrees in arts and law and worked as a journalist for the extreme right-wing newspaper *Action Française*. He joined the army at the outbreak of World War I in 1914 and fought in the trenches. In the years after the war Bernanos suffered financial hardship, and only in his late 30s did he publish his first novel, *Sous le soleil de Satan* (1926; *Under the Sun of Satan*). This immediately successful novel deals with the struggles of a priest, Father Donissan, against the evil and temptation in the world around him and against his conviction of his own inadequacy. Further novels and polemical essays followed, the best-known being the novel *Journal d'un curé de campagne* (1936; *The Diary of a Country Priest*). In this book Bernanos treats the theme of saintliness. A young priest, living in poverty and slowly dying, remains faithful to his vocation despite his lack of success in fighting sin and evil in his parish. By complete self-sacrifice he achieves a degree of greatness of soul clearly regarded as saintly in quality.

During the 1930s Bernanos went to live on the Spanish island of Majorca, and during the Spanish Civil War of 1936-1939 he bitterly attacked the atrocities committed by the fascist side. In 1938 he left Europe for Paraguay and later Brazil, where he spent the years of World War II helping the cause of France with further books of political essays. In 1943 he published his last important novel, *M. Ouine* (*The Open Mind*). By now Bernanos's vision had become more violent, and the novel presents a somewhat incoherent picture of the corrupting influence of the schoolteacher Ouine, who is almost a personification of evil.

Bernanos's books draw their strength from his passionate sense of commitment and his refusal to compromise

and Doctor of the Church, he dominated Europe through his eloquence and his counselling of popes and rulers.

Of a noble family in Burgundy, Bernard was a tall, handsome, slender youth endowed with great charm, a talent for eloquence, sensitivity, and a passion for learning. When he was 23 he persuaded two uncles, his five brothers, and about thirty other young nobles to enter the forlorn Cistercian monastery of Clteaux, founded in 1098 in a swampy area near Dijon. He chose it because, he said, "I was conscious that my weak character needed a strong medicine."

Life at Citeaux was austere and included manual labor, prayer, and study. Bernard's ascetic practices ruined his health, and he was often sick. In 1115 he was chosen to lead a group of 12 monks in founding a new monastery at Clairvaux, 70 miles from Citeaux. Bernard's personality, holiness, persuasive eloquence, and the beautiful Latin style of his writings soon made him and Clairvaux famous throughout Europe. He was sometimes very critical of the Church. He excoriated in colorful language the monks of Cluny for giving up manual labor and for their rich ceremonial dress and food. He was no less blunt with Pope Eugenius III in his *De consideratione ad Eugenium papam*.

Bernard soon became involved in the most important affairs of the Church. He played a key role in drawing up the

with complacent bourgeois attitudes. In his contempt for conformity and traditional values, he can be seen as a revolutionary—but of a very special kind, since his aims are not political but religious. His vision of a world corrupted by sin and dominated by evil is necessarily one of somewhat narrow appeal, and the hysteria and exaggeration that sometimes break through the surface of his religious novels give them an uneven quality which offsets their intensity.

In 1945 Bernanos returned to Paris, where he lived until his death in 1948.

Further Reading

A book on Bernanos in English is Peter Hebblethwaite, *Bernanos* (1965). Bernanos is discussed in Donat O'Donnell (pseudonym of Conor Cruise O'Brien), *Maria Cross* (1952), and by Ernest Beaumont in John Cruickshank, ed., *The Novelist as Philosopher: Studies in French Fiction, 1935-1960* (1962).

Additional Sources

Speaight, Robert, *Georges Bernanos; a study of the man and the writer*, New York, Liveright 1974. ☐

St. Bernard of Clairvaux

The French churchman St. Bernard of Clairvaux (1090-1153) was a Cistercian monk and founder and abbot of the monastery of Clairvaux. A theologian

Rule of the Knights Templar and obtaining approval for it at the Council of Troyes in 1128.

In 1130 Innocent II, a man of character and responsibility, was elected pope by a minority of the cardinals. A few hours later the majority of cardinals elected the brutal intriguer Anacletus II. The decision in favor of the better man, Innocent II, was the result of the persuasive influence of Bernard. It was Bernard too who helped to convince the German emperor Conrad III not to repudiate the Concordat of Worms (1122) and to support Innocent II in the conflict which lasted until the death of Anacletus II in 1138.

Two years later Bernard became deeply involved in challenging Peter Abelard, the brilliant and arrogant teacher in Paris. Opponents of Abelard protested that his application of dialectic to theology was dangerous to the point of destroying faith. Bernard accepted Abelard's challenge to a debate at the Council of Sens in 1140. There Bernard presented a list of theses taken from Abelard's writings which showed how far Abelard had departed from the traditional faith. When asked to abjure them, Abelard said, "I will not answer the Cistercian. I appeal to Rome," and left the assembly. After the Pope condemned the theses, Abelard accepted the decision and made peace with Rome and Bernard.

The fall of Edessa in 1142 led to a demand for a new crusade to protect the Holy land. Bernard launched his first appeal for a crusade at Vezelay, France, in 1146. His eloquence overcame widespread apathy. He preached the cause widely and even persuaded Emperor Conrad III to go. The failure of the Second Crusade left Bernard heartbroken and dimmed his prestige and popularity.

Bernard's name is sometimes associated with the "two swords theory," whereby both the spiritual and temporal swords belonged to the pope and the Church—the temporal sword being used by the prince at the request of the Church. Bernard expressed this idea in his *De consideratione* and in a letter to Eugenius III. In each case, however, he recommended it to the time. Others expanded Bernard's statements into a general theory.

A prolific writer, Bernard composed treatises on asceticism, polemical works, commentaries on the Bible, and innumerable sermons. His originality is best seen in his biblical commentaries and sermons. Bernard's emphasis was constantly on love; his genius lay in his talent for communicating his musical teaching to others.

Further Reading

St. Bernard of Clairvaux Seen through His Selected Letters, translated with an introduction by Bruno Scott James (1953), gives a vivid picture of the saint in his various moods. There are two good monographs on St. Bernard: Watkin Williams, *Saint Bernard of Clairvaux* (1935), and Bruno Scott James, *St. Bernard of Clairvaux: An Essay in Biography* (1957). Accounts of St. Bernard by his contemporaries—William of St. Thierry, Arnold of Bonnevaux, Geoffrey and Philip of Clairvaux, and Odo of Deuil—were gathered and translated by Geoffrey Webb and Adrian Walker in *St. Bernard of Clairvaux* (1960).

Additional Sources

Bernard, of Clairvaux, Saint, *Bernard of Clairvaux: a saint's life in word and image,* Huntington, Ind.: Our Sunday Visitor Pub. Div., 1994.

Bredero, Adriaan Hendrik, *Bernard of Clairvaux: between cult and history,* Grand Rapids, Mich.: W.B. Eerdmans, 1996.

Coulton, G. G. (George Gordon), *Two saints, St. Bernard & St. Francis,* Philadelphia: R. West, 1977.

Cristiani, Laeon, *St. Bernard of Clairvaux, 1090-1153,* Boston: St. Paul Editions, 1977. □

Claude Bernard

The French physiologist Claude Bernard (1813-1878) originated the experimental approach to medicine and established general physiology as a distinct discipline.

Claude Bernard was born on July 12, 1813, in the village of Saint-Julien in the Rhône Department. His father, Pierre Jean François Bernard, was a wine maker. At 17 Claude went to the College of Thoissey, where he remained for only a year because his family could not afford to continue his education. He was apprenticed to a pharmacist in Lyons but left after 18 months.

A Medical Career

Bernard enrolled in the Paris School of Medicine in 1834, and in 1839 he passed the examination for an internship. After obtaining his medical degree in 1843, he embarked on a lifetime of research. Recognition of his work followed and he was awarded the prize in experimental physiology of the Academy of Sciences (1847), was named a chevalier of the Legion of Honor (1849), was granted the degree of doctor of natural sciences (1853), and was elected a member of the Academy of Sciences (1854). In 1854 at the Sorbonne, a special chair of physiology was founded, to which Bernard was appointed. He also became professor of medicine at the Collège de France and held both chairs concurrently for the next 13 years.

At the Collège de France Bernard delivered most of the lectures that were published in the series of volumes known as the *Leçons.* The first volume appeared in 1855 and the last one in 1879.

A few months after Bernard's *Introduction to the Study of Experimental Medicine* (1865) appeared, Louis Pasteur wrote, "Never has anything clearer, more complete, more profound, been written about the difficult art of experiment." It has been reprinted and translated many times and remains a pertinent, widely read, and much-quoted classic. It established Bernard's literary reputation and led to his election to the Académie Française in 1869.

Bernard studied the gases in arterial and venous blood under the direction of J. L. Gay-Lussac, the chemist, in 1842; the work was not completed. Bernard's first paper, which appeared in 1843, gave an account of the chorda tympani

nerve, accurately describing its anatomy but misinterpreting its functions. His next investigation, into the role of gastric juice in digestion, was presented as his doctoral thesis in 1843. His third published work studied the function of the spinal accessory nerve, which he wrongly believed controlled the movement of the vocal cords.

Pancreatic Function

One of Bernard's major discoveries was to define the functions of pancreatic secretion. His experiments followed a chance observation that starved rabbits had clear urine, while on their normal vegetable diet they had cloudy urine. He deduced that the nutrition of a starved rabbit was maintained by breakdown of its own tissues. When he fed rabbits on meat, killed them, and examined their intestines, he found fine, whitish vessels, filled with emulsified fat called chyle, radiating from the lower intestines in the region of the pancreatic duct. He deduced that pancreatic juice must play a part in the absorption of fat from the intestine. In a series of investigations he further demonstrated that pancreatic secretion could digest starch, and he went some way toward defining the protein breakdown produced by pancreatic juice. He found that the pancreas did not begin to secrete until ingested food had passed into the duodenum. This effect is now known to be due to the action of a hormone, secretin.

Glycogenic Function of the Liver

In 1843 Bernard found that cane sugar injected into the veins of an animal was excreted in the urine, whereas a similar intravenous injection of glucose disappeared. He also found sugar to be present in the liver of dogs that were fed exclusively on meat. Several years later he discovered that injury to the floor of the fourth ventricle of the brain caused sugar to appear in the blood and urine, thus producing a form of "artificial diabetes." Bernard demonstrated that blood leaving the liver contained larger quantities of sugar than did blood entering the liver, and he consequently introduced the concept that the liver has two functions: an external secretion of bile and an internal secretion of sugar which then enters the circulation.

After washing away the sugar in a freshly removed dog's liver Bernard noted that the liver was again rich in sugar a day later. He inferred that a sugar-forming (glycogenic) substance must be present in the liver, and in 1857 he isolated pure glycogen from the liver. Bernard evolved the theory that carbohydrate is stored as glycogen in the liver and released, when necessary, as glucose into the blood, and this hypothesis in its essentials has since been abundantly proved.

Vasomotor Functions

In 1851 Bernard cut the cervical sympathetic nerve in a rabbit and noted that part of the head, on the side of the served nerve, became warmer. In 1852 he showed that paralysis of the cervical sympathetic nerve in the dog causes drooping of the eyelid and constriction of the pupil on the side of the paralysis. Bernard went on to stimulate electrically the cut sympathetic nerve and found that the skin on the same side became pale and blood flow therein was reduced. Thus he defined both constrictor and dilator elements of the vasomotor system, by which blood vessel caliber, and hence blood flow, is determined.

Miscellaneous Researches

Bernard started to study the effect of curare, a South American poison, in 1844. During the next 12 years he demonstrated that the paralysis it produced arose from impairment of the functions of nerves as they entered the muscles. Studies on carbon monoxide poisoning, which started in 1846, led Bernard to conclude that red blood cells carried oxygen, bound to a chemical. The nature of this chemical substance, hemoglobin, was discovered by E. F. Hoppe-Seyler in 1857.

In a series of experiments on severed nerves, Bernard noted the degeneration of tissues robbed of their nerve supply. He thus discovered the trophic effects of nerves. He also cut the dorsal columns of the frog's spinal cord and thereafter noted the impairment of function in the legs. In experiments on muscle he demonstrated that actively contracting muscles utilize oxygen faster than resting muscles.

Bernard's contributions to physiological science were immense. He also explored the fields of clinical pharmacology and experimental pathology. He believed that the chief aim of physiological experimentation was to throw light upon morbid conditions. He regarded the physician of his time as an empiricist, awaiting the advances in medicine that would enable him to become a scientist, and he deplored the contemporary view of a physician as an artist.

Bernard died in Paris on Feb. 10, 1878. He was given a state funeral, the first occasion of which a French scientist was so honored.

Further Reading

The most comprehensive and readable biography of Bernard is J. M. D. Olmsted, *Claude Bernard, Physiologist* (1938). See also Michael Foster, *Claude Bernard* (1899). Short accounts of Bernard's life and work are in F. H. Garrison, *An Introduction to the History of Medicine* (1913; 4th ed. 1929), and in Henry E. Sigerist, *Great Doctors: A Biographical History of Medicine* (1932; trans. 1933). To understand the philosophy of Bernard's work it is essential to read his *An Introduction to the Study of Experimental Medicine* (1865; trans. 1927). □

Joseph Cardinal Bernardin

Joseph Cardinal Bernardin (1928-1996) was a major leader in the U.S.-based Catholic Church during the modern progressive era.

Joseph Cardinal Bernardin became the symbol, even if unknowingly, of the U.S. Catholic Church's struggle with modernity. A quiet, devout man, he rose in the ranks of the church in the 1980s to lead American Catholicism into a more progressive era. He was an instrumental part of the creation of the National Conference of Catholic Bishops' pastoral letters on nuclear weapons, the economy, and AIDS. Bernardin's positions ranged between innovation and traditional Vatican teachings; yet, with his skills of negotiation he was almost always able to forge a compromise. It was his ability to listen clearly as well as speak strongly that separated his vision and actions from other officials in the Catholic Church hierarchy. Bernardin's modesty did not allow him to view himself as a pure instrument of change, but only as a symbol doing the work that was required of him. As he once said in an interview with *Time* magazine, "There is a real spiritual hunger on the part of the people. They are not reaching out to me. They are reaching out to the Lord. Perhaps there is a personal dimension, but I am just a symbol."

Background

Born on 2 April 1928 in Columbia, South Carolina, to a family of Italian immigrants, Bernardin was the only Catholic boy on his block. These early experiences helped him acquire a great understanding and tolerance for other religions and opposite points of view. Initially intent on choosing a career in medicine, he attended the University of South Carolina for a year. Later, after deciding to enter the priesthood, he graduated with a degree in philosophy from St. Mary's Seminary in Baltimore in 1948. He received a master's in education from Catholic University in Washington, D.C., and was ordained a priest in 1952. Once ordained, Bernardin's skills shined, as he soon climbed the hierarchical ladder, moving to Atlanta and becoming the youngest bishop in the country by 1966. By 1968 Bernardin

made Washington, D.C., his home as he became the general secretary of the National Conference of Catholic Bishops (NCCB) and its social action agency, the United States Catholic Conference. In 1972 he was named the archbishop of Cincinnati, Ohio, and was elected president of the NCCB in 1974, serving in that role until 1977. Bernardin brought to every position a strong confidence and a progressive agenda toward church policies. In 1982 Bernardin was named archbishop of Chicago, the largest archdiocese in the nation. This new foothold of power placed Bernardin in a prominent location to express his social activism.

Pastoral Letters

In February 1983 Bernardin was elevated to the Sacred College of Cardinals by Pope John Paul II. Bernardin succeeded the late John Cardinal Cody, who in his last days had been plagued by financial scandals and dissent by priests and followers who believed him to be uncaring and rigid. With Bernardin now in power, Chicago's more than 2.4 million Catholic's felt they had a leader who would listen. Bernardin's outspoken position on social issues was evident in 1982 when the first draft of the NCCB's antinuclear weapons letter was issued—"The Challenge of Peace." The letter questioned the morality of possessing nuclear weapons, let alone the use of such destructive forces. After much debate, discussion, and modifications, the pastoral letter was issued 3 May 1983. Bernardin's determination did not stop there; he urged his fellow bishops, both liberal and conservative, to fight for reductions in the amounts of government money spent on the military in general, believing it wrong to waste resources on weapons while urban neighborhoods fell to ruin. In 1984 the NCCB examined the United States' economic structure. Once again Bernardin led the charge for the Catholic Church to take a moral stand, and the resulting pastoral letter, "Economic Justice for All," cited systematic flaws. Although seen as too much of an activist by some officials and church laity, Bernardin continued to work within the framework of the Catholic Church, always seeking biblical and Vatican confirmation for all maneuvers. In 1987 he witnessed the scourge of the AIDS virus sweeping the nation and felt it was time for the church to react officially. The issue of AIDS was complex for the Catholic Church, as it touched upon several issues— condoms, homosexuality, sexual activity—that the church preferred not to deal with publicly. Bernardin, acknowledging this, pushed for the Catholic Church to allow teaching the use of condoms as a prevention of future transmission of the disease. Opposition was severe as some bishops and cardinals felt any change in the official stance would appear as if the church were condoning sexual behavior outside of marriage. Bernardin saw silence and a lack of information as a sinful act on the church's part. In the end the document was adopted and discussion of the use of condoms was permitted on a limited basis.

Vision

Joseph Cardinal Bernardin was a visionary in the Catholic Church, always looking toward the future but never neglecting the Church's rich past. His strong relationships with the laity and to John Paul II in the early 1970s before his elevation to pope served Bernardin well during difficult periods in his career. His open style created a level of comfort not known to many elder Catholics, as he symbolized the pinnacle of post-Vatican II Catholicism. Unafraid to challenge the status quo, he became a star of the American Catholic Church. In 1995 Bernardin was diagnosed with pancreatic cancer. After over a year of battling the illness, he died on November 14, 1996.

Further Reading

D. J. R. Bruckner, "Chicago's Activist Cardinal," *New York Times Magazine,* 132 (1 May 1983): pp. 42-45, 60, 63, 69, 82, 92.
Richard N. Ostling, "Bishops and the Bomb," *Time,* 120 (29 November 1982): pp. 68-77. □

Edward L. Bernays

Edward L. Bernays (1891-1995), American consultant to business and government, labored to bring public relations to the status of a profession.

Edward L. Bernays was born in Vienna, Austria, on November 22, 1891. His maternal uncle was the famed psychologist Sigmund Freud. When the boy was a year old the family emigrated to New York City, where his father became a successful grain merchant. After education in the city's schools, Edward enrolled in the Agri-

cultural College of Cornell University. The elder Bernays had hopes that his son would one day join him on the grain exchange, but by the time of Edward's graduation from Cornell in 1912 he had decided to pursue a career as a journalist.

Bernays became editor of the *Medical Review of Reviews* in New York City. In 1913 he learned that the actor Richard Bennet planned to produce "Damaged Goods," a play warning of the dangers of venereal disease. But the controversial nature of the subject was making it difficult for Bennet to raise funds for the project. Bernays volunteered to help. He set up a "Sociological Fund Committee" to finance the production and rally public support. Bernays enlisted so many of the city's notables to the cause that no one—not even the censors—could question the total respectability of the play. "Damaged Goods" opened without incident and was hailed as a valuable contribution to public awareness. Bernays had found a new career.

From 1913 to 1917 Bernays worked as a publicist for theatrical productions and promoted the appearances of such artists as Enrico Caruso and the Diaghilev ballet company. When the United States entered World War I Bernays offered his services to the government's Committee on Public Information. The committee, headed by ex-newspaperman George Creel, was designed to generate public support at home and abroad for America's war aims.

In 1919, after service with the American Peace Commission in Paris, Bernays returned to New York to apply the methods of the Committee on Public Information to the

business world. His partner in the new venture was journalist Doris E. Fleischmann. They married in 1922. For some years entertainers and corporations had employed "press agents" to secure favorable notice in the newspapers. As the world's first "counsel on public relations," Bernays had loftier ambitions. He promised to actively shape public opinion in the interests of his clients.

Hair Nets, Soap, and Cigarettes

Bernays' campaigns for Venida hair nets and Procter & Gamble during the 1920s and Lucky Strike cigarettes during the 1930s provide good examples of his methods. At that time shorter hair styles were becoming the fashion among younger women. This development was a matter of no small concern to the manufacturers of Venida hair nets, who saw the market for their product disappearing along with longer tresses. Bernays was called upon for his advice. Soon prominent women were publicly expressing their preference for long hair over short and assorted authorities were warning of the dangers of unbound hair in factories and restaurants. In response, a number of state governments passed legislation requiring the wearing of hair nets on the job.

Despite Bernays' best efforts, the hair net was destined to pass into near-oblivion. Far more successful was his campaign for Procter & Gamble's Ivory soap. On the company's behalf he hired a medical consultant to survey American hospitals on their preference for white, unperfumed soap (like Ivory) over colored, scented soaps (its competitors). The advantages of Ivory, now duly certified by medical authorities, were given wide publicity. In addition, Bernays designed a number of special events to keep the name of Ivory soap constantly before the public. Under his urging Procter & Gamble established Ivory soap-sculpturing contests, judged by prominent artists, that eventually involved millions of schoolchildren across the nation. To promote Ivory's unparalleled ability to float, the company sponsored a soap-boat race in New York's Central Park.

Stranger still was Bernay's solution to the problem of women's aversion to Lucky Strike cigarettes' forest green pack. Women, who were just starting to be able to smoke in public by the early thirties, found that the pack clashed with their wardrobes. Rather than change the pack color, which was rejected by the parent company of Lucky Strikes, American Tobacco, as being too expensive, Bernays instituted a plan to instead change women's fashion to match the cigarette pack. Letters were written to interior and fashion designers, department stores, and prominent women of society pushing green as the new hot color for the season. Balls, gallery exhibitions, and window displays all featured green after Bernays got through with them. The result was that green did indeed become a very hot color for the 1934 season and Lucky Strike kept their pack color and female clientele intact.

Wide Range of Clients

Bernays earned his greatest fame through his promotion, for the electrical industry, of the 50th anniversary of the light bulb in 1929. Celebrations were held in 25 cities. Thomas Edison's birthplace was made a national landmark

and a commemorative stamp was issued by the federal government. The anniversary year culminated in a Golden Jubilee celebration held in Dearborn, Michigan, on October 21, 1929, in which Edison was publicly honored by President Herbert Hoover, Henry Ford, and John D. Rockefeller, Jr.

Bernays provided public relations counsel to a wide variety of private and public organizations, including General Motors, the Columbia Broadcasting System, the National Association for the Advancement of Colored People, and Columbia University. In 1939 he was the publicity director for the New York World's Fair. During World War II his services were called upon by the Army, the Navy, and the Commerce and Treasury departments. After the war he was actively involved in the government's foreign information program.

Bernays strove throughout his long career to raise the status and standards of his profession. His lectures on public relations in 1923 at New York University were the first on that subject at a major university. He published widely in the field, including such classic works as *Crystallizing Public Opinion* (1923), *Public Relations* (1952), and *The Engineering of Consent* (1955).

Bernays retired in the early 1960s but continued as an consultant and advocate of public relations into his 100th year. He also, quite ironically in light of his work for Lucky Strike cigarettes in the 1930s, worked as an anti-smoking crusader. He died on March 9, 1995 in Cambridge, Massachusetts at the age of 103. Called nothing more than a huckster by his critics, Bernays nonetheless shaped our perception of the world we live in today. Neal Gabler wrote in his Bernays retrospective in *New York Times Magazine*, "he not only taught generations of persuaders how to sway public opinion . . . but he was, in the cultural historian Ann Douglas's words, the man 'who orchestrated the commercialization of a culture.'"

Further Reading

Edward Bernays tells his own story in *Biography of an Idea: Memoirs of Public Relations Counsel Edward L. Bernays* (1965) and its companion volume *The Later Years: Public Relations Insights 1956-1986* (1986). Eric F. Goldman's, *Two-Way Street: The Emergence of the Public Relations Counsel* (1948) is a brief sketch, generally sympathetic to Bernay's role in the history of public relations. But public relations and its practitioners have long been the targets of social critics. For a particularly lively example, see Irwin Ross, *The Image Merchants: The Fabulous World of Public Relations* (1959). Newspaper and magazine articles include a Bernays interview in *Forbes* (September 23, 1985); an interesting overview in *Journalism History* (Spring 1985); a lengthy piece in *Social Research* (Summer 1994); and the Bernays retrospective/tribute in *New York Times Magazine* (December 31, 1995). □

Sarah Bernhardt

One of the first great "stars" of the world stage, Sarah Bernhardt, known as "The Divine Sarah"

(1844-1923), dominated the theatrical scenes of both Europe and America for over half a century. In addition to being considered one of the greatest actors of all time, she was noted for her "larger than life personality" and extravagant lifestyle.

Sarah Bernhardt was born Henriette-Rosine Bernard into the Parisian *demi-monde* of courtesans and affluent gentlemen on October 23, 1844. She did not know her father, a Parisian who never married her Dutch Jewish mother, a woman who had little time or inclination to raise a young child in the social whirl of the Paris salon set. After a tumultuous childhood, Bernhardt was ready to commit herself to a religious life when a place was secured for her to study acting in the Paris Conservatoire (1859 to 1862). She debuted professionally in 1862 in Racine's *Iphigenie,* in which she displayed little of the talent that would propel her to stardom in just a few years.

Physically, Bernhardt was somewhat boyish in her physique; she also suffered from bouts of ill health that plagued her from childhood. Her most noted qualities as an actor were her "voice of gold" and her ability to breathe emotional life into classic roles and melodramatic heroines, lifting the former from the stultifying effects of tradition and lending nobility and depth to the latter. Bernhardt's professional career began in earnest in 1866 as a member of the theater company at the Odéon. Her first major successes came as a member of France's greatest theater company, the Comédie Française, starting in 1872. After a triumphant tour of England with members of the Comédie in 1878, she broke what was considered to be a lifetime contract with the company to pursue her own successes in 1880.

Bernhardt excelled in emotionally overwrought roles in the classical vein, such as the queen in Hugo's *Ruy Blas* (1879), the title role in Racine's *Phèdre* (1874), and Doña Sol in *Hernani* (1877). She also played several "breeches" roles (male parts played by women) throughout her career, such as Hamlet and the title role in Rostand's *L'Aiglon (The Eaglet,* about Napoleon's son), which was written especially for her. She is perhaps remembered most often for her portrayal of Marguerite Gauthier, the courtesan stricken with consumption, in Dumas' *La Dame aux Camélias (Camille* to most English-speaking audiences).

Her off-stage life was often just as harrowing as that of the characters she portrayed, with frequent bouts of physical ailments, financial difficulties, and numerous love affairs. Journalists of the day frequently painted her as an eccentric, and this contributed to her fame as much as her acting talent did. It is true that she sometimes slept in a coffin; whether she was at home or traveling Bernhardt always kept a large coterie of friends and admirers about her, as well as servants and a menagerie of exotic animals. She was a visual as well as theatrical artist, and many of her paintings and sculptures were popular. To her credit, she also had a weakness for humanitarian causes. During the Franco-Prussian War in 1870 she established a military hospital in the closed Odéon theater, and during World War I she contributed both money and fund-raising activities to support the war effort.

Bernhardt is best known in America for her famous "farewell tours" that she made between 1880 and 1918. The nine tours she made in America often had a financial rather than artistic motivation behind them. During one such tour she teamed with France's greatest male actor of the day, the comedian Constant-Benoît Coquelin (the only person to ever leave the Comédie Française, until Bernhardt), to perform Edmund de Rostand's *Cyrano de Bergerac,* among other plays.

Bernhardt also took a progressive approach to the new medium of film (which was looked down upon by the legitimate theater), unabashedly appearing in several films in her lifetime, including *La Dame aux Camélias* (1911), *Queen Elizabeth* (1912), and *Adrienne Lecouvreur* (1913). The success of *Queen Elizabeth* in America, one of the first dramatic silent features, enabled producer Adolph Zukor to start the Famous Players production company, which eventually became Paramount Pictures.

In 1894 she started her own resident theater company. She opened the Théâtre Sarah Bernhardt in 1899. Her leg was amputated in 1911 because of a chronic knee condition brought on by several injuries. However, she continued to perform, even though she was constrained to perform excerpts of her most famous roles lying in a prone position or propped up by an artfully-designed set piece. Her hotel room in Paris had been converted to a film set for *La Voyante,* but she died on March 26, 1923, at the age of 79 before the film was completed.

Bernhardt never performed any of her parts in anything but French, but she was hailed and revered as a great actress on both sides of the Atlantic regardless of her audiences' abilities to comprehend the language. This popularity is a testament to both her emotional and vocal power as an actress, as well as her contribution to the modern stage as a singular star rather than as a member of a company.

Further Reading

The life and work of Sarah Bernhardt is well-documented, sensationalized, and fictionalized in numerous books. The most prominent biographies in English are: *The Divine Sarah* by Robert Fizdale and Arthur Gold (1991), *Being Divine* by Brandon (1991), *Sarah Bernhardt* by Emboden (1975), and *Madame Sarah* by Skinner (1967). "The Divine Sarah" herself speaks in *Memories of My Life* (1907, 1968) and a later edited version of her memoirs and the novella *Dans les nuages* in *The Memoirs of Sarah Bernhardt* (1977), edited by Lesberg. Among the "personal glimpses" are *The Real Sarah Bernhardt: whom her audiences never knew, told to her friend Mme. Pierre Berton* (1924) and *I Knew Sarah Bernhardt* (1960). For information about Bernhardt and the theater of her day, see *Sarah Bernhardt and Her World* (1977), *Sarah Bernhardt: French Actress on the English Stage* (1989), *Bernhardt, Terry, Duse: the actress in her time* (1988), and *Bernhardt and the Theatre of Her Time* (1984). Finally, two novels utilize Bernhardt as their subject matter: *Sarah* by Joel Gross (1987), and *Dear Sarah Bernhardt* by Françoise Sagan. For a cinematic account of Bernhardt's life, see *The Incredible Sarah* starring Glenda Jackson in the title role (United Kingdom, 1976).

Additional Sources

Bernhardt, Sarah, *My double life: the memoirs of Sarah Bernhardt,* London: Owen, 1977.

Brandon, Ruth, *Being divine: a biography of Sarah Bernhardt,* London: Mandarin, 1992.

Gold, Arthur, *The Divine Sarah: a life of Sarah Bernhardt,* New York: Knopf: Distributed by Random House, 1991; New York: Vintage Books, 1992.

Hathorn, Ramon, *Our lady of the snows: Sarah Bernhardt in Canada,* New York: P. Lang, 1996.

Richardson, Joanna, *Sarah Bernhardt and her world,* New York: Putnam, 1977; Weidenfeld and Nicolson, 1977.

Skinner, Cornelia Otis, *Madame Sarah,* New York: Paragon House, 1988, 1966.

Stokes, John, *Bernhardt, Terry, Duse: the actress in her time,* Cambridge England; New York: Cambridge University Press, 1988. □

Gian Lorenzo Bernini

The Italian artist Gian Lorenzo Bernini (1598-1680) almost singlehandedly created high baroque sculpture. His work in architecture, although more conservative, ranks him among the three or four major architects of the 17th century.

Gian Lorenzo Bernini was born in Naples on Dec. 7, 1598. His mother was Neapolitan. He was trained as a sculptor by his father, Pietro, who came from Florence. But Bernini was Roman: he was brought to Rome as a child; he remained there almost all his life; and he absorbed completely Rome's dual heritage of empire and papacy.

Not long after Pietro Bernini moved from Naples to Rome, he began work on the sculpture of the Pauline Chapel, the enormous addition to S. Maria Maggiore built for the reigning pope, Paul V. This commission gave the elder Bernini an opportunity to introduce his son, who was a child prodigy, to the Pope and the Pope's favorite nephew, Cardinal Scipione Borghese. The cardinal, a man of vast wealth with a real passion for art, was to become Bernini's first important patron.

In his youth Bernini made the customary studies of the work of Raphael and Michelangelo. But Hellenistic sculpture and Roman sculpture in the Hellenistic tradition were to influence his development far more, and it was largely from these ancient sources that he drew the powerfully dynamic and fluid style that was to characterize his mature work. Contemporary painting as well, by Caravaggio, the Carracci, and Guido Reni, was to play a role in his stylistic formation.

Under the rule of the Barberini pope, Urban VIII (1623-1644), Bernini dominated the artistic scene in Rome. His commissions were so large that he had to draw into his studio most of the sculptors then working in Rome. From this time on, Bernini's bigger works were usually executed by assistants, working from his designs and under his close supervision.

With Urban's successor, Innocent X, Bernini's fortunes changed. Finding the papal treasury empty and the purses of his predecessor's family filled beyond their wildest dreams, the new pope drove the Barberini from Rome and rejected everyone, Bernini included, who had belonged to their circle. At the same time sculptors and architects who had been envious of Bernini's fabulous success rushed to attack him on trumped-up charges that the lofty bell tower Bernini had erected on the facade of St. Peter's was pulled down. But Bernini's trials were short-lived. He was soon back in favor, hard at work for Innocent X, who had found it impossible to find another artist with half Bernini's talent. For the rest of his life each succeeding pope sought his services.

During Bernini's later years the spiritual content of his art deepened. Under the guidance of his close friend and religious counselor Father Gian Paolo Oliva, the head of the Jesuit order, he made intensive studies of the writings of St. Ignatius of Loyola and carried out the spiritual exercises the saint prescribed. He attended mass daily.

In 1665, when he was an old man, Bernini was called to France. The idea was to have the world's most famous artist, Bernini, serve the world's most powerful monarch, Louis XIV. The architect was to build a royal palace, a new and grander Louvre, for the King. Bernini's trip from Rome to Paris was like the triumphal procession of a great lord. But less than 6 months after he arrived, he was ready to go home, disillusioned by court intrigue and his lack of sympathy for almost anything French. (In Paris he considered himself surrounded by cultural barbarians.) His designs for the Louvre were never carried out.

Back in Rome, Bernini's creative imagination remained undiminished even into old age, though as his strength failed him he depended more and more on assistants to carry out his designs. He died in Rome on Nov. 28, 1680.

Sculptural Style

Of Bernini's early work for Cardinal Scipione Borghese, the most spectacular is the life-size marble group *Apollo and Daphne* (1622-1624). Bernini was totally baroque in his choice of the monument of maximum drama: a split second of climax in the midst of movement and change. The story, told by Ovid, is that Cupid's arrows inflamed Apollo with love for the wood nymph Daphne, who was predestined to reject the love of all men. She fled with Apollo in pursuit, and at the moment he was about to overtake her she was transformed into a laurel tree. In Bernini's sculpture the metamorphosis is happening before our eyes. As Apollo reaches out to touch her side, Daphne leaps into the air. Branches filled with leaves sprout from her fingers, roots from her toes, bark from her thigh. Nothing like it had ever been done in sculpture before. The whole group, including the many fragile leaves on slender stems, was carved from one block of marble. From this single block Bernini created the wide range of textures with which he convincingly differentiated earth, bark, skin, cloth, leaves, and hair.

For Pope Urban VIII Bernini created the Triton Fountain (1642-1643) in the square where the Barberini had their palace. Its design is sheer fantasy. Four sinuous dolphins turn up their tails to support a giant two-sided sea-shell on which is seated a triton blowing a conch. Though the fountain is architectural in scale, it remains sculptural in concept. Throughout the whole mass there is not a straight line or a right angle. There is no division between the parts that are organic and those that are inorganic: all are equally undulant, equally alive. Water is an integral part of the composition. Rising in a great jet that spurts up from the triton's conch, it splashes down into the basins formed by the double shell and, spilling over the edges, falls into the surrounding pool. In all Bernini's fountains the movement of the water increases the sense of movement inherent in the sculpture. It contributes a still further dimension with its sound: water falling, splashing, breaking, dripping, and gurgling as it drains away. Bernini created the baroque fountain. It was one of his most brilliant achievements. His examples inspired a host of imitations throughout Rome and all of Europe.

During the reign of Innocent X, when Bernini was temporarily in disgrace, he created the Cornaro Chapel in the small Roman church of S. Maria della Vittoria (1644-1655). The central group in the chapel depicts the mystical vision of St. Theresa. The saint herself described how once, when she floated on air in ecstatic rapture, an angel appeared before her and plunged the golden arrow of Divine Love repeatedly into her heart.

In Bernini's concept of the vision, the saint and the angel, both of white marble, seem to float in a niche above the altar. They are bathed in divine light in the form of gilded rays from above but also by natural daylight that comes mysteriously and without explanation from a hidden window. The scene is set within a complex architectural niche that bows outward as if impelled by the force of the miraculous vision. The ceiling of the chapel is painted to give the illusion that part of the roof has melted away. Into the open space overhead floats a vision of heaven with angels on cloud banks who circle round the dove of the Holy Ghost. Below, along the side walls of the chapel, there are marble reliefs representing members of the Cornaro family, who kneel in prayer. Bernini's statue of St. Theresa, at the center of the chapel, is the most famous representation of ecstasy in art. The swooning saint sustained on a cloud appears in a void, removed from direct contact with earthly things. Overcome by her vision, she lies limp, head fallen back, eyes closed, arms and legs dangling. In sharp contrast, the violent agitation of her garments serves to reveal the agitation of her soul.

The high baroque portrait, which Bernini invented, is exemplified in the bust of Francesco d'Este (1650-1651). Always the mood is momentary, here conveyed by the sharply turned head and focused eyes. Often the lips are slightly parted, as if the sitter were about to speak. Elements surrounding the face serve to indicate social position. Here the magnificent wig with its cascade of curls sets up patterns of light and shadow, while the great, deeply cut drapery whose billowing folds engulf the torso makes the sitter appear larger than life.

The large marble *Angel with Crown of Thorns* that Bernini carved in the years 1667-1669 shows his late style. The statue was conceived as part of a large group of figures, each holding a symbol of the Passion of Christ. The angel's face is pained, but in these late works it is the drapery that becomes the major vehicle for the emotions. No longer is there any interest, as there was with the *Apollo and Daphne,* in realistic textures. Instead, the robe is transformed into a series of thin ridges whose sharp, insistent rhythms lick around the body like flames. The expressive intensity of works such as this reflects Bernini's own deepening mysticism at the end of his life.

Architectural Works

As an architect, Bernini was less radical than as a sculptor and more concerned with the monumental heritage of imperial Rome. For the plan of S. Andrea al Quirinale in Rome (1658-1670) he went back to the Pantheon with its alternating chapels that ring a circular dome. But Bernini changed the circular plan to an oval one to make the space more active, and he added an enclosed area for the high altar where the light pours down from a window. The interior is inlaid with the richest colored marbles and is accented with architectural ornament of such refinement that the effect is often compared to a jewel box.

Bernini's crowning achievement in architecture was St. Peter's Square in Rome (1656-1667). The section nearest the church is a trapezoid, but the main part of the square is an enormous oval partially enclosed by two semicircular colonnades. The square provides a monumental entrance to St. Peter's and a place where crowds, up to half a million at a time, gather to receive the pope's blessing. Bernini is known to have visualized the square symbolically as arms reaching out to embrace a multitude of the faithful. Architecturally the idea of freestanding colonnades that contain the space of a circular square was Bernini's invention, but the inspiration went back to imperial Rome. Apart from the row of statues on the balustrade, Bernini's square has little ornament. The travertine columns are severely simple, unfluted Tuscan Doric. Individually they speak softly, but when hundreds are massed together the effect is amplified, like waves of the sea.

Universal Man

Bernini is the last of the so-called universal men in the world of art. Primarily a sculptor, the greatest since Michelangelo, he was also one of the great architects of the age. He was once widely famed as a painter, though few of his canvases can be identified today. He also created designs for an endless series of temporary objects—funeral decorations, processional chariots, intricate torches, portable thrones—all the paraphernalia of pageantry so dear to the hearts of the baroque age.

Bernini won fabulous acclaim for his theater spectaculars. He wrote plays and staged those by others in the vast theater of the Barberini Palace. For these he invented stage machinery to produce effects that amazed his audiences: rising platforms filled with people, sheets of water that seemed about to flood the theater, flames that seemed about to destroy it. John Evelyn, an Englishman in Rome in 1644, wrote in his diary: "Bernini . . . gave a public opera wherein he painted the scenes, cut the statues, invented the engines, composed the music, writ the comedy, and built the theatre."

Further Reading

The best book on Bernini's sculpture is Rudolf Wittkower, *Gian Lorenzo Bernini, the Sculptor of the Roman Baroque* (1955; 2d ed. 1966). Wittkower's *Art and Architecture in Italy, 1600-1750* (1958; rev. ed. 1965), includes a section on Bernini as an architect. Howard Hibbard, *Bernini* (1966), is a good, popular study based on Wittkower. A contemporary view of Bernini is Filippo Baldinucci, *The Life of Bernini* (1682; trans. 1966). For the 17th-century Italian and European background see David Ogg, *Europe in the Seventeenth Century* (1925; 8th ed. 1961), and Carl J. Friedrich, *The Age of the Baroque, 1610-1660* (1952).

Additional Sources

Bernini in perspective, Englewood Cliffs, N.J.: Prentice-Hall, 1976.
Borsi, Franco, *Bernini,* New York: Rizzoli, 1984, 1980.
Scribner, Charles, *Gianlorenzo Bernini,* New York: H.N. Abrams, Publishers, 1991. □

Daniel Bernoulli

The Swiss mathematician and physicist Daniel Bernoulli (1700-1782) is best known for his work on hydrodynamics, but he also did pioneering work on the kinetic theory of gases.

Daniel Bernoulli was born on Jan. 29, 1700, in Gröningen, Netherlands. He was the second son of Jean Bernoulli, a noted mathematician who began the use of "g" for the acceleration of gravity.

When Daniel was 11, he became the pupil of his 16-year-old brother, Nicholas. He continued his studies in Italy until he was 24 and received a doctorate in medicine. The following year he went to St. Petersburg, Russia, as a professor of mathematics. After 8 years he returned to Switzerland because of his health. He first taught anatomy and botany, then changed to experimental and speculative philosophy (or, in modern terminology, theoretical physics). He has been called the father of mathematical physics.

In 1738 Bernoulli published *Hydrodynamica*. In this treatise, which was far in advance of his time in many ways, is his famous equation governing the flow of fluids in terms of speed, pressure, and potential energy, upon which much modern technology is based, especially aerodynamics. Being interested in practical application as well as in theory, he devised a number of experiments which demonstrated the effects he predicted.

In this treatise is also found his remarkable treatment of gas pressure. Considering an enclosed gas as a swarm of moving particles in dynamic equilibrium, he derived the correct expression for the resulting pressure, thus anticipating the approach adopted about 100 years later.

Bernoulli won or shared 10 prizes of the Paris Academy of Sciences, a feat equaled by only one other person, his friend and rival Leonhard Euler. Because of a difference of opinion with Euler, Bernoulli became interested in sound phenomena and discovered that a closed organ pipe can produce only odd harmonics and that pressure determines the relative amplitudes of the harmonics. His last work involved the application of probability theory to various practical matters, such as inoculation and relative proportion of male and female births. He died in Basel on March 17, 1782.

Further Reading

Information on Bernoulli in English is scarce. E. T. Bell, *Men of Mathematics* (1937) and *The Development of Mathematics* (1940; 2d ed. 1945), are valuable. See also Alfred Hooper, *Makers of Mathematics* (1948), and David E. Smith, *History of Mathematics,* vol. 1 (1951). □

Dorothy Lewis Bernstein

Dorothy Lewis Bernstein (born 1914) conducted research focused on the Laplace transform, a mathematical function used in the solution of partial differential equations that has been widely applied in the twentieth century in conjunction with operational calculus.

Dorothy Lewis Bernstein is a distinguished mathematician and educator in the fields of applied mathematics, statistics, and computer programming. Her research focused on the Laplace transform, a mathematical function named after the French mathematician Pierre-Simon Laplace. The Laplace transform is used in the solution of partial differential equations (equations that contain the partial derivatives of functions of two or more variables) and has been widely applied in the twentieth century in conjunction with operational calculus. Bernstein was a pioneer in incorporating applied mathematics and computer science into the undergraduate mathematics curriculum. In 1979, she became the first woman president of the Mathematical Association of America, a national association concerned with college mathematics.

Bernstein was born in Chicago on April 11, 1914, to Jacob and Tillie Bernstein, who were Russian immigrants. The family lived in Milwaukee during Bernstein's youth. In 1930, Bernstein began her studies at the University of Wisconsin at Madison. During her junior and senior years, she studied mathematics under an independent curriculum. In 1934, based on an oral examination and her thesis on the complex roots of polynomials (mathematical expressions containing certain algebraic terms), she received both a bachelor's (summa cum laude) and a master's degree in mathematics.

After another year at Madison as a teaching fellow, Bernstein received a scholarship to the doctoral program in mathematics at Brown University in Rhode Island. As Ann Moskol indicates in *Women of Mathematics,* Bernstein's experiences at Brown reflect various forms of discrimination. Bernstein's graduate teaching was restricted to only three female students. When she sought advice on finding a teaching position, the graduate school dean advised her not to apply in the South because she was Jewish or in the West because of her gender. Bernstein underwent an unusually arduous doctoral examination, which her advisor later acknowledged was due to her gender and to her midwestern university credentials.

Nonetheless, Bernstein independently secured a teaching position at Mount Holyoke College in Massachusetts. Bernstein taught at Mount Holyoke from 1937 to 1940, completing her doctorate from Brown in 1939 with a thesis related to the Laplace transform. In 1941, Bernstein returned to Madison as an instructor. In the summer of 1942, she was a research associate at the University of California at Berkeley under the Polish mathematician and statistician Jerzy Neyman. In 1943, Bernstein took an instructorship at the University of Rochester in New York, where she became an assistant professor in 1946.

At Rochester, Bernstein's research was directed toward exploiting the computational potential of digital computers (their ability to perform complex mathematical operations on large amounts of data at high speeds) in solving partial differential equations. This research, intended for military application and conducted in affiliation with the Office of Naval Research, led to the publication of Bernstein's *Existence Theorems in Partial Differential Equations* in 1950. In 1951, Bernstein was a member of the Institute for Advanced Study in Princeton, New Jersey. Bernstein became an associate professor at Rochester in 1951, and a full professor in 1957. From 1957 to 1958, she was a visiting professor at the University of California in Los Angeles.

In 1959, Bernstein assumed a professorship at Goucher College in Baltimore, Maryland, where she chaired the mathematics department from 1960 to 1970 and directed the computer center from 1961 to 1967. She served on the board of governors of the Mathematical Association of America, the professional association with which she was most closely involved, from 1965 to 1968. As a department administrator at Goucher, Bernstein brought applied mathematics and the emerging field of computer sciene into the undergraduate mathematics curriculum, and integrated computer programming into her own courses in statistics. Moskol notes that Bernstein "believed that applied mathematics not only made material more relevant to students, but it also motivated them to understand the axioms and theorems of pure mathematics, which could then be used in applied problems." Bernstein's practial vein was further indicated by the internship program she established for Goucher's math majors.

During her tenure at Goucher, Bernstein was also involved through the National Science Foundation in promoting computer programming instruction and the use of computers in advanced mathematics courses at area high schools. She helped establish the Maryland Association for Educational Use of Computers in 1972 and served on its governing board from 1972 to 1975. Bernstein was vice-president of the Mathematical Association of America from 1972 to 1974 and president from 1979 to 1981. She also served on the Joint Projects Committee and the Joint Committee on Women of the Mathematical Association of America, the American Mathematical Society, and the Society of Industrial and Applied Mathematics, and on the editorial board of the *Two Year College Mathematics Journal.* Bernstein retired from Goucher College in 1979.

Further Reading

Moskol, Ann, "Dorothy Lewis Bernstein," in *Women of Mathematics,* edited by Louise S. Grinstein and Paul J. Campbell, Greenwood, 1987, pp. 17-20.
Coon, Geraldine A., "Coon on Bernstein," *Goucher Quarterly,* fall, 1979, pp. 16-17. □

Eduard Bernstein

The German socialist Eduard Bernstein (1850-1932) was a leader of the revisionist, or evolutionary, wing of the German Social Democratic party.

Eduard Bernstein was born in Berlin on Jan. 6, 1850. As the family's financial resources were limited, his educational opportunities were restricted, and at 16 he became an apprentice in a bank. Within a few years he had risen to the position of bank clerk. In 1872 he joined the Social Democratic party (SPD) and became an active member of the party's Berlin organization. In 1878, shortly prior to the adoption of Chancellor Bismarck's antisocialist legislation, Bernstein traveled to Switzerland.

As a consequence of Bismarck's continued hostility toward the socialists, Bernstein remained in Switzerland and became the editor of the official SPD newspaper. After Bismarck brought pressure to bear in order to halt the smuggling of the newspaper into Germany, the Swiss government forced Bernstein to leave in 1880. He then went to London, where he met the German socialist Friedrich Engels, eventually becoming one of his close associates. Bernstein was also able to study the British labor movement and associate with the recently organized Fabian Society, an organization of socialists. Early Fabians such as George Bernard Shaw and Sidney and Beatrice Webb rejected revolutionary Marxism and advocated what they termed "the inevitability of gradualness." This idea was to form a central part of Bernstein's mature "revisionist" position.

During the 1890s Bernstein began to make his break with orthodox Marxism clear. His revisionist position emerged in a series of articles in an official party publication, *Die neue Zeit,* in 1898. The reaction to these articles by groups within the SPD caused him to write a defense, *Evolutionary Socialism* (1899). In this classic statement of the revisionist position, Bernstein used scientific analysis to attack the premises of revolutionary Marxism. He demonstrated through statistics that workers were not becoming more impoverished and that capitalism was not becoming less stable and thus its collapse was not imminent. He rejected revolutionary tactics as self-defeating and advocated achieving reforms through moderate and constitutional methods. He also urged that the SPD, a working-class party, should attempt to win over the middle classes. Revisionism was officially condemned by the SPD in 1903, and the polarization of the party's revolutionary and evolutionary wings existed until after World War II.

By his death in 1932 Bernstein had long since ceased to be regarded as a leader or major theorist of the SPD. But when the party was reorganized in West Germany after World War II, many of Bernstein's ideas were incorporated in its programs. The new party gave up its revolutionary theory, emphasized action and reform, and attempted to broaden its political base by cutting across ideological and class lines.

Further Reading

Bernstein's major work, *Evolutionary Socialism! A Criticism and Affirmation,* is available in a good translation by Edith C. Harvey, with an excellent introduction by Sidney Hook (1961). The best study in English of Bernstein's life and work is Peter Gay, *The Dilemma of Democratic Socialism: Eduard Bernstein's Challenge to Marx* (1952). For background see George Lichtheim, *Marxism: An Historical and Critical Study* (1961; 2d ed. 1964).

Additional Sources

Bernstein, Eduard, *My years of exile: reminiscences of a socialist,* Westport, Conn.: Greenwood Press, 1986. □

Leonard Bernstein

Leonard Bernstein (1918-1990) was an American composer, conductor, and pianist. His special gifts in bridging the gap between the concert hall and the world of Broadway made him one of the most glamorous musical figures of his day.

Leonard Bernstein was born Louis Bernstein in Lawrence, Massachusetts, on August 25, 1918, to Russian-Jewish immigrants. He changed his name to Leonard at the age of sixteen. The family soon moved to Boston, where Leonard studied at Boston Latin School and Harvard University. Although he had taken piano lessons from the age of 10 and engaged in musical activities at college, his intensive musical training began only in 1939 at the Curtis Institute. The following summer, at the Berkshire Music Festival, he met Serge Koussevitsky, who was to be his chief mentor in the early years.

On Koussevitsky's recommendation two years later, Artur Rodzinski made Bernstein his assistant conductor at the New York Philharmonic. The suddenness of this appointment, coming after two somewhat directionless years, was superseded only by the dramatic events of November 14, 1943. With less than 24 hours' notice and no rehearsal, Bernstein substituted for the ailing Bruno Walter at Carnegie Hall and led the Philharmonic through a difficult program which he had studied hastily at best. By the concert's end the audience knew it had witnessed the debut of a born conductor. The *New York Times* ran a front-page story the following morning, and Bernstein's career as a public figure had begun. During the next few years he was guest conductor of every major orchestra in the United States until, in 1958, he became music director of the New York Philharmonic.

Bernstein's multi-faceted career might have filled several average lives. It is surprising that one who had never given a solo recital would be recognized as a pianist; nevertheless, he was so recognized from his appearances as conductor-pianist in performances of Mozart concertos and the Ravel Concerto in G.

As a composer, Bernstein was a controversial figure. His large works, including the symphonies *Jeremiah* (1943), *Age of Anxiety* (1949), and *Kaddish* (1963), are not acknowledged masterpieces. Yet they are skillfully wrought and show his sensitivity to subtle changes of musical dialect. He received more praise for his Broadway musicals. The vivid *On the Town* (1944) and *Wonderful Town* (1952) were followed by *Candide* (1956), which, though not a box-office success, is considered by many to be Bernstein's most original score. *West Side Story* (1957) received international acclaim. Bernstein's music, with its strong contrasts of violence and tenderness, sustains—indeed determines—the feeling of the show and contributes to its special place in the history of American musical theater.

His role as an educator, in seminars at Brandeis University (1952-1957) and in teaching duties at Tanglewood, should not be overlooked. He found an even larger audience through television, where his animation and distinguished simplicity had an immediate appeal. Two books of essays, *Joy of Music* (1959) and *Infinite Variety of Music* (1966), were direct products of television presentations.

Bernstein had his greatest impact as a conductor. His appearances abroad—with or without the Philharmonic—elicited an excitement approaching frenzy. These responses were due in part to Bernstein's dynamism, particularly effective in music of strong expressionistic profile. It is generally agreed that his readings of 20th century American scores showed a fervor and authority rarely approached by those of his colleagues. His performances and recordings also engendered a revival of interest in Mahler's music.

There was some surprise when, in 1967, Bernstein resigned as music director of the Philharmonic. But it was in keeping with his peripatetic nature and the diversity of his activities that he should seek new channels of expression. After leaving the Philharmonic, Bernstein traveled extensively, serving as guest conductor for many of the major symphonies of the world including the Vienna Philharmonic and the Berlin Philharmonic. He became something of a fixture in those cities in the last few decades of his life.

More controversially, he also became caught up in the cultural upheaval of the late 1960s. He angered many when he claimed all music, other than pop, seemed old-fashioned and musty. Politically, too, he drew criticism. When his wife hosted a fund-raiser for the Black Panthers in 1970, charges of anti-Semitism were leveled against Bernstein himself. He had not organized the event, but the press reports caused severe damage to his reputation. This event, along with his participation in anti-Vietnam War activism led J. Edgar Hoover and the FBI to monitor his activities and associations.

In 1971 *Mass: A Theatre Piece for Singers, Players and Dancers* premiered at the Kennedy Center in Washington, DC. It was, according to biographer Humphrey Burton, "the closest [Bernstein] ever came to achieving a synthesis between Broadway and the concert hall." The huge cast performed songs in styles ranging from rock to blues to gospel. *Mass* debuted on Broadway later that year.

Later Bernstein compositions include the dance drama, *Dybbuk* (1974); *1600 Pennsylvania Avenue* (1976), a musical about the White House that was a financial and critical disaster; the song cycle *Songfest: A Cycle of American Poems for Six Singers and Orchestra* (1977); and the opera *A Quiet Place* (1983, revised 1984).

In the 1980s Bernstein continued his hectic schedule of international appearances and social concerns. He gave concerts to mark the fortieth anniversary of the bombing of Hiroshima and a benefit for AIDS research. On Christmas Day, 1989, Bernstein led an international orchestra in Berlin, which was in the midst of celebrating the collapse of the Berlin Wall. In a typically grand gesture, Bernstein changed the words of "Ode to Joy" to "Ode to Freedom."

Despite health problems, Bernstein continued to tour the world in 1990 before returning to Tanglewood for an August 19th concert. He had first conducted a professional orchestra there in 1940, and this performance, 50 years later, was to be his last. He died in New York, on October 14, 1990, of a heart attack brought on by emphysema and other complications.

Further Reading

Humphrey Burton, *Leonard Bernstein* (1994) is a comprehensive biography with extensive comment from his friends and family. A more sensational biography is Joan Peyser, *Bernstein: A Biography* (1987). David Ewen, *Leonard Bernstein* (1960; rev. ed. 1967), is a solid biography and more comprehensive than John Briggs, *Leonard Bernstein: The Man, His Work, and His World* (1961). Evelyn Ames, *A Wind from the West* (1970), a sometimes-romanticized account of the New York Philharmonic's European tour of 1968, is valuable for its intimate detail. □

Nabih Berri

Nabih Berri (born 1939) became the leader of the Shi'ite Muslims in Lebanon in 1980. He helped the Shi'ites achieve more prominent role in Lebanese politics.

L ike many of his countrymen from south Lebanon, Nabih Berri's father was a merchant who had migrated to West Africa in order to escape the impoverishment and lack of economic opportunity in his native land. Nabih was born in 1939 in Sierra Leone, where his father had established a relatively successful business.

At the time of his birth the Shi'ite Muslims comprised the third largest sectarian group in Lebanon, but they had little political influence. In the 1943 national pact that served as the basis for the establishment of independent Lebanon, the predominant political offices—the presidency and the prime ministership—were given to the Maronite Christians and the Sunni Muslims. The Shi'ite Muslims (second in membership to the Sunni sect in all of Islam) were only accorded the post of parliamentary speaker—a distant third in terms of effective political influence. The lack of influence accorded to Berri's Shi'ite brethren reflected their general underdevelopment and poverty, whether measured in terms of income, education, health care, or occupation.

Nabih's biography is in large measure a mirror of the extraordinary modernization and change that took place in the Shi'ite community over the span of his lifetime. By the mid-1980s the Shi'ites, who had a much higher birthrate (until the 1990s) than any of the other sects in Lebanon, were clearly the largest single community in the country (representing as much as 40 percent of the population). They began demanding a more central role in the Lebanese political system, and were clearly unwilling to continue to accept the second or third class status that had long been their fate.

The career of Berri illustrates some of the changes that occurred. After working for a time for his father in Freetown, he attended the Lebanese University in Beirut and graduated from the Beirut Law School in 1963. After graduation Berri went to France, where he studied for a year at the Sorbonne. He was active in student politics, and served as president of the student body at the Lebanese University. He was also active, by the early 1960s, in ideological politics and especially in the Arab Ba'ath (or Renaissance) Party.

The Amal Movement

In 1974, after Berri had practiced law for a time in Beirut (and had also traveled to the United States), he changed political affiliation. Leaving the Ba'ath Party, he affiliated with a charismatic religious leader by the name of al-Sayyid Musa al-Sadr. Al-Sadr began organizing a political reform movement among the Shi'ites in Lebanon in 1959. Initially Berri played only a minor role in al-Sadr's movement, and the onset of civil war in 1975 somewhat eclipsed that movement.

However, several things happened in the late 1970s that brought the movement into the forefront and with it brought Berri into prominence. First, when al-Sadr disappeared during an August 1978 trip to Libya he became an authentic hero for the Shi'ites. The movement that he had created, the Movement of the Deprived, was reinvigorated as the Amal movement ("Amal" means hope in Arabic, and it is also the acronym for the Detachments of the Lebanese Resistance).

Second, the Shi'ites became increasingly unwilling to remain in the crossfire between the Israelis and the Palestinian guerrillas who were deployed in south Lebanon. The Shi'a took up arms in their own defense, and by the late 1970s they were engaging in armed combat with the Palestinians, who had earlier been their allies. The deterioration of the relationship between the Shi'a and the Palestinians provided a context in which Amal could serve as a credible vehicle for communal self-defense.

The third development was the Iranian revolution of 1978-1979. The events in Iran provided the Shi'ites an inspirational model. Amal provided a vehicle for action, and one which possessed a profound cultural authenticity. It should be emphasized, however, that the Lebanese Shi'ite of the Amal movement did not desire to create an Islamic republic in Lebanon, but instead wanted to gain greater power in a multi-confessional state.

Berri Takes Charge

The disappearance of Musa al-Sadr created room for a new leader of the Shi'ite movement, and in 1980 Berri assumed that role. He was not without competitors. His opponents included the traditionally powerful political bosses who long dominated the Shi'ite community, a number of religious officials, and various Shi'ite groupings that wanted to hew more closely to the Iranian position.

By the time of the Israeli invasion of Lebanon in 1982, Berri's Amal movement was gaining significant strength and was clearly the most important political organization of the Shi'ites. Berri and many of his compatriots thought that the Israeli invasion had created a new situation replete with opportunities for the Shi'ites to increase their political power in a reformed political system. The Israelis had expelled the Palestinian Liberation Organization (PLO) from the south and Beirut and had decisively weakened the Lebanese militias and movements that had remained aligned with the PLO. In short, it appeared the Amal was going to make great gains.

Berri adopted a patient stance in the fall of 1982, but the Israelis sought to undercut Amal by creating proxy forces in south Lebanon. The new president of Lebanon, Amin Gemayel, seemed unwilling to even recognize Berri and his Amal movement. External powers—the United States, France, Italy, and Great Britain—that sent a multinational force to Beirut were slow to recognize the significance of the Shi'a.

Berri, indisputably a political moderate, had little to show for his moderation. As a result his hold over Amal was ever more in jeopardy throughout 1983. After a number of bloody episodes, including acts of terrorism by extremist Shi'ites and oppression of the Shi'ite suburbs of Beirut by the Lebanese army, Berri was forced to act. In February 1984, after Shi'ite areas had been shelled by the government, Berri called for the Lebanese soldiers to lay down their arms. His call was an effective one, since many of the soldiers were in fact Shi'ites.

Under his leadership, and in cooperation with the Druze leader Walid Jumblatt, Berri's Amal movement seized control of West Beirut and thereby emasculated the central government. Simultaneously, the multinational force was withdrawn and Syria's influence, reduced by the Israeli invasion, was reasserted. The result was that the allies of Syria, now including Berri (who had earlier tried to keep his distance from Damascus), gained power.

Under Syria's Influence

By the summer of 1984 Berri was installed in the government as minister of justice and minister for the South (a position of great symbolic significance). Unfortunately, this is not the end of the story. The years from 1985 on proved to be difficult for Lebanon and for Berri. Although the Syrians attempted to engineer a political settlement that would accommodate the demands of all of Lebanon's sectarian groups, they failed. In December 1985 Berri signed the Damascus tripartite agreement with Walid Jumblatt (the principal Druze leader) and Elie Hobeika (a Maronite militia

leader), but the agreement did not produce the reform and stability many hoped it would. Instead, Lebanon remained a killing ground upon which no community could impose its will, while each major community had the means to veto the initiatives of others. In 1987 Berri's Amal movement was challenged in West Beirut by the Druze Socialist Party and other leftist groups. A year later Amal clashed with the Hizbollah in skirmishes that lasted for nearly two months. By the end of 1988 departing president Amin Gemayel appointed his chief of staff, General Michel Aoun, to form a military government. This led Berri to spend as much time out of the capital as possible. Aoun's cabinet lasted until November 1989 when his colleague and presidential candidate, Rene Mu'awwad was assassinated 16 days after his election. With much ground lost, Aoun was dismissed and eventually exiled to France by swiftly elected, Syria-friendly President Elias Hrawi. This also led Berri back to a cabinet position.

In October 1992 a new parliament was instituted by President Hrawi which appointed Berri to his current position of parliamentary speaker. While Hrawi's government brought much greater potential for gain for the already wealthy, under Syria's iron hand, the current parliament found it difficult to act on issues close to Lebanon. They were bombarded with accusations of corruption. Also Lebanese discontent with their own leaders submission towards Syria surfaced heavily and voter apathy was widespread.

Within the Shi'ite community Berri's challengers continued to erode his influence. Extremist Shi'ites who desired to establish an Islamic republic in Lebanon clashed repeatedly with Amal, and few knowledgeable observers believed that Berri could fail to take them into account. The problems Berri faced had been well illustrated in June 1985 when a TWA passenger jet was hijacked to Beirut. Amal was not responsible for the hijacking, but Berri quickly assumed control of the hostages, not only to assure their safety, but to deny a full-blown media victory to the perpetrators and the views they represented. Yet Berri was unable to solve the crisis without the major intervention of Syria (and even Iran), a clear indication of the limitations on his authority and an interesting omen regarding the future of Lebanon.

Nonetheless, Berri was an easy man to underestimate. He was intelligent, dedicated, honest, and had good political instincts. He was able to grasp the political mood of his constituency and was capable of doing what needed to be done in order to survive.

Further Reading

Although there is no published biography of Berri, the reader can find authoritative accounts of the Amal movement in the following sources: Edward Azar et al., *Emergence of a New Lebanon* (1984); Myron Aronoff, editor, *Religion and Politics* (1984); Nikki Keddie and Juan Cole, editors, *Shi'ism and Social Protest* (1986); Robin Wright, *Sacred Rage* (1985); and Martin Kramer, editor, *Shi'ism, Resistance and Revolution* (1986). A short but excellent biography was prepared by Tom Hundley for *Contemporary Newsmakers* (1985). For more information on Berri's role in the events of Lebanon, two good sources include Dilip Hiro's *Lebanon: Fire and Embers: A History of the Lebanese Civil War* (1993) and William W.

Harris's *Faces of Lebanon: Sects, Wars, and Global Extensions* (1997). □

Daniel J. Berrigan

Called "the priest who stayed out in the cold" and "holy outlaw," Father Daniel J. Berrigan (born 1921) never came to terms with the conservatism of the Catholic Church or with the militarism of the American nation. He lived his life as a militant servant of the Christian faith.

Daniel Berrigan was born in Virginia, Minnesota, on May 9, 1921. His father was a socialist farmer and railroad engineer who wrote poetry and raised his six sons in the brawling, argumentative atmosphere of a small farm near Syracuse, New York. Daniel was the frailest of the boys and from childhood had determined to enter the Catholic priesthood. When he was 18 he joined the Society of Jesus—the Jesuits. In 1952, after 13 years of training ("a most unfinished man"), he was ordained a priest. His brother Philip had also become a Catholic priest, though of a different order.

"The priesthood," wrote Berrigan, was "a sheepfold for sheep." Both he and Philip were influenced deeply by the activist theology that emerged from the concentration camps and resistance movements of World War II Europe. Soon after his ordination, the Church sent Berrigan to France. It was here that he was captivated by examples of worker-socialist-priests, ideas of civil disobedience, and by the notion that his task was to bring the Church to the world.

Returning to New York in 1954, he was assigned to teach theology at the Jesuit Brooklyn Preparatory School. In 1957 he was appointed professor of New Testament studies at Le Moyne College in Syracuse. That same year he won the Lamont Prize for his book of poems *Time Without Number*. His personal style was that of an earnest, chubby priest with well-shined shoes and a clean, white collar. But beneath this style was the substance of a church radical who burned to alleviate poverty and to bridge the traditionally awkward relationship between priests and laypersons. Conservative students began to whisper "subversive," but others adored him.

War Protestor

He returned to France during the summer of 1963, but it was not Paris that shattered the last remnants of Berrigan's outer respectability. Instead, it was the priests and parishioners whom he visited in communist Hungary, Russia, and Czechoslovakia. Churches in the eastern nations were all but illicit, and they survived at the edge of persecution and martyrdom—an impoverished dissenting minority. This was the Church of his ideals. He returned to America in 1964 so changed that friends failed to recognize him. His face was gaunt but serene. He wore turtleneck sweaters, ski jackets, cropped hair, and a puckish smile which belied his intensity.

Almost immediately he became embroiled in protest against America's burgeoning intervention in Vietnam. He and his brother Philip were among the first Catholic priests to speak out against the war. But, like others, they soon discovered that words were inadequate to their purpose. In 1964, with pacifist David Dellinger, they helped to draft a "declaration of conscience" to urge young men to resist the draft. A year later they joined with Yale chaplain William Sloane Coffin, Jr., and others in a coalition of churchmen called Clergy and Laity Concerned about Vietnam. Gradually both Daniel and Philip became more incensed at their own impotence to stop the war, or even to change peoples' patriotic support of the war. On October 27, 1967, a week after the famed March on the Pentagon where Daniel had been arrested, Philip Berrigan and three other men poured blood over draft records in the Baltimore, Maryland, Customs House.

Berrigan, along with Howard Zinn, a Boston University political science professor, and Tom Hayden, a founder of Students for a Democratic Society, flew to Hanoi, North Vietnam, to receive three prisoners of war who had been released on the eve of the Tet offensive.

In May 1968 Daniel and Philip Berrigan and seven others calmly walked into the Selective Service office in Catonsville, Maryland. Before the horrified eyes of the office clerks, they emptied the contents of draft files into wire trash baskets, carried them out to a nearby parking lot, doused them with home-made napalm, and burned them. Then they joined hands and prayed as they awaited their arrests.

Imprisonment

The trial of the "Catonsville Nine" was a legal rite which served to draw American attention to an increasingly unpopular war, openly opposed by Roman Catholic priests and nuns. Daniel Berrigan used the event to create a dramatic play which soon was being performed all over the nation. In spite of their efforts to put the war itself on trial, the court convicted the Berrigans and gave them two-year sentences. They appealed the decision and, while free on bail, dropped from sight. Philip was captured 11 days later, but Daniel remained at liberty for four months, even making public appearances while the Federal Bureau of Investigation (FBI) chased him around the country. In August 1970 he was finally captured and sent to the Danbury, Connecticut, correctional facility. There he spent his time writing several volumes of poetry. Enraged over its own failures, the FBI accused the Berrigan brothers of conspiring to blow up parts of Washington, D.C., and of attempting to kidnap government officials. The charges were all thrown out of court in 1972.

After his release from prison in February 1972, Berrigan continued his "witness-bearing" against militarism, nuclear arms, racism, and injustice. Calling his post-Catonsville pacifist efforts "Plowshares," as in the Biblical injunction "to beat your swords into plowshares," Berrigan and his brother repeatedly pitted their freedom against the power of the state. During the late 1980s and early 90s, their protests included breaking into a defense contractor's plant to douse blood on nuclear missile nose cones, the disarming of two cruise missile launchers at a submarine construction site, and illegal entry aboard a destroyer under construction. From 1970 to 1995 Berrigan spent a total of nearly seven years in prison for various offenses related to his protests. In later years he regretted the level of American apathy and often complained that his protests received scant attention in the press.

Further Reading

Two quite similar books have been written about Daniel and Philip Berrigan: Francine DuPlessix Gray, *Divine Disobedience* (1970), and Richard Curtis, *The Berrigan Brothers* (1974). For autobiography of a sort see Daniel Berrigan, *Night Flight to Hanoi* (1968); *The Trial of the Catonsville Nine* (1970); and *Time Without Number* (1957). For a more recent account of the Berrigans' protests see *Fighting the Lamb's War: Skirmishes With the American Empire: The Autobiography of Philip Berrigan*. For an imformative interview with Father Daniel Berrigan see *U.S. Catholic* (August, 1996). □

Alonso Berruguete

Alonso Berruguete (c. 1486-1561) was the greatest Spanish sculptor of the 16th century. He evolved a personal mannerist style that is highly expressive and emotional.

Alonso Berruguete was born in Paredes de Navas, Valladolid, the son of Pedro Berruguete, Spain's first major Early Renaissance painter. Pedro was trained in Italy, and it is understandable that he would want his son to have an Italian formation. Alonso was in Florence from about 1504, the year of his father's death, until about 1517. He also spent time in Rome during this period.

Berruguete's original purpose was to train as a painter, but he had the opportunity to study sculpture under Michelangelo, whom he is said to have assisted in the execution of some works. Berruguete received minor commissions, such as the completion of paintings and sculptures left unfinished by other artists.

On his return to Spain, Berruguete executed an alabaster relief, the *Resurrection,* for Valencia Cathedral (ca. 1517), which compares favorably with early works by Michelangelo. It is Hellenistic in its anatomical beauty, multiple diagonals, and range of relief projection. The figure of Christ is the climactic center of interest: a vertical, stabilizing force amid a tumult of diagonals described in the agitated movements of the startled Roman soldiers.

In 1518 Emperor Charles V named Berruguete court painter. When illness prevented Berruguete from sailing to Germany with Charles V in 1520, the Emperor took it personally and turned a deaf ear to Berruguete's subsequent petitions for commissions. He then returned to his native village until 1523, when Charles V named him a scribe of the criminal section of the Chancery in Valladolid.

This gave Berruguete social status, an income, and work he could deputize. Henceforth, he set himself to amass riches and advance socially. He established a studio in Valladolid, hired a number of apprentices, and priced his works above those of all other artists. It was a time of great wealth in Spain; Berruguete had seen sumptuous riches in Italy and was determined to so live that his compatriots would accord him the reverence and acclaim enjoyed by Italian artists.

In 1528 Berruguete built himself a palace in Valladolid, opposite the monastery of S. Benito, for which he created his greatest altarpiece. He succeeded so well in his ambitions that in 1542 he sold the Emperor's benefice for 4,000 ducats. Two years before he died, he became a squire when the regent of Portugal, Princess Juana, gave him the village of Ventosa with its 120 inhabitants.

His Style

Berruguete discovered his own style in the mid-1520s. It provoked impassioned discussion, since expression was more important to him than formal considerations. His figures are like exposed nerves: writhing, throbbing, burning, keening, wailing, cursing. The emaciated anatomy is dislocated; the stance is unstable, in defiance of the logic of gravity; and the tortured draperies seem glued to the forms. His art is a projection of his state of mind, which he forces the spectator to share by the stridency of the convulsed forms, the relentless brilliance of color, and the feverish rhythms on a monumental scale.

Berruguete worked mostly in polychromed wood but also in marble, alabaster, stone, and unpainted wood (for choir stalls). It has been said that his genius lay less in sculpture and painting than in a rhetoric that was an eloquent fusion of both arts. Certainly he often painted the lights and shadows for his sculptures with complete indifference to the actual light in which they would be viewed, and sometimes he used his brush to depict cloth coverings which were not carved.

The Altarpieces

Berruguete's tremendous altarpieces filled the entire apse of the church and were subdivided by architectural elements lavishly decorated and acting as frames for the individual figures and the relief panels. This huge, exotically ornate framework was like a setting for an opera, and Berruguete used it to establish the notes of restlessness and imbalance which his sculptural actors clarified and augmented. He created a single spectacle of extravagant ornament, drama, and personages. The synthesis he intended depends on the total work; yet seeing the altarpiece of S. Benito (1527-1532; now in Valladolid Museum) in fragments, one can know intimately the awesome emotion of Abraham and Isaac in extremis or the exquisite poignancy of the suffering youthful St. Sebastian. In the almost complete altarpiece for the monastery of La Mejorada, Olmedo (1526; now in Valladolid), one can compare the synthesis and the isolated agony.

The consensus of opinion is that Berruguete carved and painted all his polychromed-wood figurative sculpture but relied heavily on assistants to execute such works as the alabaster *Transfiguration* in Toledo Cathedral (1543-1548) and his last work, the marble funeral monument of Cardinal Juan de Tavera in the Hospital of St. John, Toledo (1557-1561). Indeed, when Cardinal Tavera commissioned the choir stalls of unpainted wood in Toledo Cathedral (1539-1543), he urged Berruguete to execute them not by his own hand but rather "by good apprentices." This fact does not settle the matter; each authority must decide for himself when it is the hand of the master and when not.

A year after Berruguete's death, his widow had to send to Cáceres an unfinished altarpiece which had been commissioned in 1547 and was being executed in Valladolid at the time of his death. Apparently, only the relief of St. Francis was by Berruguete. The stamp of Berruguete's genius was not only that he created a unique mannerist expression of ungovernable passion agitating tense, convulsed forms, the clamor of which claws and burns the soul in a spiritual ecstasy, but that, once having found his creative language, he never made a concession to a client's taste. Such an artist cannot found a school, but equally he does not pass without effect.

Further Reading

The best source on Berruguete in English is George Kubler and Martin Soria, *Art and Architecture in Spain and Portugal and Their American Dominions: 1500-1800* (1959). □

Chuck Berry

Chuck Berry (born 1926), creator of the "duck walk" and known as the "father of rock and roll," has been a major influence on popular music. Even though his career and life reached great peaks and declined to low valleys, he still prevails in music while his contemporaries have vanished.

"If there were a single fountainhead for rock guitar, Chuck Berry would be it," wrote Gene Santoro in *The Guitar.* Indeed, the list of artists influenced by the "father of rock and roll" is nearly endless. From the Beach Boys and the Beatles to Jimi Hendrix and on to Van Halen and Stevie Ray Vaughan, every popular musician knows the impact that Chuck Berry has had on popular music. As Eric Clapton stated, there's really no other way to play rock and roll.

Took up Guitar in Junior High

Born in 1926, Berry didn't take up the guitar until he was in junior high school thirteen years later. With the accompaniment of a friend on guitar, the two youths played a steamy version of *Confessin' The Blues* which surprised, and pleased, the student audience. The reaction from the crowd prompted Berry to learn some guitar chords from his partner and he was hooked from then on. He spent his teen years developing his chops while working with his father doing carpentry. But before he could graduate from high school, Berry was arrested and convicted of armed robbery and served three years in Algoa (Missouri). A year after his release on October 18, 1947, he was married and working on a family, swearing that he was forever cured of heading down the wrong path again.

In addition to carpentry, he began working as a hairstylist around this time, saving as much money as he could make (a trait that would cause him considerable grief later in his life). Near the end of 1952 he received a call from a piano player named Johnnie Johnson asking him to play a New Year's Eve gig at the Cosmopolitan Club. Berry accepted, and for the next three years the band literally ruled the Cosmo Club (located at the corner of 17th and Bond St. in East St. Louis, Illinois). At the beginning the band (which included Ebby Hardy on drums), was called Sir John's Trio and played mostly hillbilly, country, and honky tonk tunes. Berry's influence changed not only their name (to the Chuck Berry Combo) but also their style. He originally wanted to be a big band guitarist but that style had died down in popularity by then. Berry cited sources like T-Bone Walker, Carl Hogan of Louis Jordan's Tympani Five, Charlie Christian, and saxophonist Illinois Jacquet as his inspirations, borrowing from their sounds to make one of his own.

Met Idol Muddy Waters

While the swing guitarists had a major impact on his playing, it was the blues, especially that of Muddy Waters, that caught Berry's attention. He and a friend went to see the

master perform at a Chicago club, and with some coaxing, Berry mustered the nerve to speak with his idol. "It was the feeling I suppose one would get from having a word with the president or the pope," Berry wrote in his autobiography. "I quickly told him of my admiration for his compositions and asked him who I could see about making a record. . . . Those very famous words were, 'Yeah, see Leonard Chess. Yeah, Chess Records over on Forty-seventh and Cottage.'" Berry flatly rejects the story of him hopping on stage and showing up Waters: "I was a stranger to Muddy and in no way was I about to ask my godfather if I could sit in and play." But he did take the advice and went to see the Chess brothers, Leonard and Phil. They were interested in the young artist but wanted to hear a demo tape before actually cutting any songs. So Berry hurried back home, recorded some tunes and headed back to Chicago.

"He was carrying a wire recorder," Leonard Chess told Peter Guralnick in *Feel Like Going Home*, "and he played us a country music take-off called 'Ida Red.' We called it 'Maybellene'. . . . The big beat, cars, and young love. . . . It was a trend and we jumped on it." Phil Chess elaborated, "You could tell right away. . . . He had that something special, that—I don't know what you'd call it. But he had it." After the May 21, 1955, recording session they headed back to the Cosmo Club, earning $21 per week and competing with local rivals like Albert King and Ike Turner. Unbeknownst to him, Berry shared writing credits for "Maybellene" with Russ Fralto and New York disc jockey Alan Freed as part of a deal Chess had made (also known as payola). The scam worked for the most part because by mid-

September the song, which had taken 36 cuts to complete, was number 1 on the R&B charts. Berry was bilked out of two-thirds of his royalties from the song, but in later years he would reflect upon the lesson he learned: "Let me say that any man who can't take care of his own money deserves what he gets," he told *Rolling Stone*. "In fact, a man should be able to take care of most of his business himself." Ever since the incident that's just what Berry has done. He insists on running his career and managing his finances the way he sees fit.

Ten More Top Ten Hits

The next few years, until 1961, would see at least ten more top ten hits, including "Thirty Days," "Roll Over Beethoven," "Too Much Monkey Business," "Brown Eyed Handsome Man," "School Days," "Rock and Roll Music," "Sweet Little Sixteen," "Johnny B. Goode," "Carol," and "Almost Grown." Berry was a tremendous hit on the touring circuit, utilizing what is now known as his trademark. He explained its development in his autobiography: "A brighter seat of my memories is based on pursuing my rubber ball. Once it happened to bounce under the kitchen table, and I was trying to retrieve it while it was still bouncing. Usually I was reprimanded for disturbing activities when there was company in the house, as there was then. But this time my manner of retrieving the ball created a big laugh from Mother's choir members. Stooping with full-bended knees, but with my back and head vertical, I fit under the tabletop while scooting forward reaching for the ball. This squatting manner was requested by members of the family many times thereafter for the entertainment of visitors and soon, from their appreciation and encouragement, I looked forward to the ritual. An act was in the making. After it had been abandoned for years I happened to remember the maneuver while performing in New York for the first time and some journalist branded it the 'duck walk.'"

The money from touring and record royalties were filling his pockets enough for Berry to start spending on some of the dreams he had long held. Around 1957 he opened Berry Park just outside of Wentzville, Missouri. With a guitar-shaped swimming pool, golf course, hotel suites, and nightclub, it was, next to his fleet of Cadillacs, his pride and joy. "Now that's what I call groovy," he told *Rolling Stone*. "To own a piece of land is like getting the closest to God, I'd say."

Remakes Weaker Than Originals

Things seemed to be going smoothly until 1961, when Berry was found guilty of violating the Mann Act. Berry was charged with transporting a teenage girl across a state line for immoral purposes. He spent from February 19, 1962 until October 18, 1963 behind bars at the Federal Medical Center in Springfield, Missouri. For years Berry denied this, claiming he was acquitted and never served time. He finally admitted the truth in his autobiography. He used his prison term constructively though, taking courses to complete his high school education and also by penning some of his most notable songs: "Tulane," "No Particular Place To Go," and "Nadine."

By the time Berry was released from jail the British Invasion was about to take over. Groups like the Beatles were churning out cover versions of Berry classics and turning whole new audiences on to him. While some artists might have cried rip-off (the Stones have done over ten of his tunes), Berry sees only the positive aspects. "Did I like it? That doesn't come under my scrutiny," he told *Guitar Player.* "It struck me that my material was becoming marketable, a recognizable product, and if these guys could do such a good job as to get a hit, well, fantastic. I'm just glad it was my song." Even so, remakes of Berry hits are more often than not considerably weaker than his originals. While his style is remarkably simple, it is also next to impossible to duplicate with the same feel and sense of humor.

A Shrewd Rock and Roller

"Chuck Berry dominated much of the early rock scene by his complete mastery of all its aspects: playing, performing, songwriting, singing and a shrewd sense of how to package himself as well," wrote Santoro. As shrewd as Berry was, by the mid-1960s his type of rock was losing ground to improvisors like Eric Clapton, Mike Bloomfield, and Jimi Hendrix (all three of whom acknowledged Berry's influence, but were trying to break new ground). A switch from Chess to Mercury Records from 1966 to 1969 did little to help. He would continue touring throughout the 1960s without the aid of a regular backup band.

Berry's method since the late 1950s has been to use pickup bands comprised of musicians from the city he's playing in. This has led to many complaints from fans and critics alike that his performances are sometimes shoddy and careless. In his book, Berry gives his own reasons, stating that "drinks and drugs were never my bag, nor were they an excuse for affecting the quality of playing so far as I was concerned. A few ridiculous performances, several amendments to our band regulations, and the band broke up, never to be reconstructed. Whenever I've assembled other groups and played road dates, similar conditions have prevailed." (Berry reportedly accepts no less than $10,000 per gig and plays for no more than 45 minutes; no encores.)

Another Hit and More Personal Strife

By 1972 Berry was back with Chess and produced his biggest seller to date, "My Ding-a-Ling," from *The London Chuck Berry Sessions.* Selling over two million copies, it was his first gold record and a number 1 hit on both sides of the Atlantic according to *The Illustrated Encyclopedia of Rock.* He had hit pay dirt, but his obsession to have a bank account with a $1 million figure led to another run-in with the law. In 1979 Berry was convicted of tax evasion and spent just over three months at Lompoc Prison Camp in California. Perhaps the one thing that has caused him more pleasure/pain than money is his fancy for women, stated simply in his book: "The only real bother about prison, to me, is the loss of love." He has said that he hopes to write a book one day devoted solely to his sex life.

Berry's legal troubles continued into his later years, when he was embroiled in accusations of drug possession and trafficking and various sexual improprieties in July of 1990. His estate was raided earlier that spring by the DEA, who had been informed that Berry was dealing in cocaine. The operation resulted in the confiscation of marijuana and hashish and pornographic videotapes and films, but charges against the entertainer were later dismissed. Berry was also involved in a class-action lawsuit regarding videotapes made of women without their consent. Meanwhile, more collections of Berry's hits continued to be released, including a well-received box set by Chess/MCA in 1989 and a live recording released in 1995.

While Berry's career has had the highest peaks and some pretty low valleys, he has survived while most of his contemporaries have vanished. In 1986 Rolling Stones guitarist Keith Richard, perhaps the ultimate student of the Chuck Berry School of Guitar, decided to put it all together with a 60th birthday party concert to be filmed and released as a movie, *Hail! Hail! Rock 'n' Roll.* It took place at St. Louis's Fox Theater, a venue which had at one time refused a youthful Berry entrance because of his skin color. The show featured Berry's classic songs with Richard, Johnnie Johnson, Robert Cray, Etta James, Eric Clapton, Linda Ronstadt, and Julian Lennon also performing. Berry has also been honored with a star in the Hollywood Walk of Fame, and induction into the Rock and Roll Hall of Fame. If that's not enough, "Johnny B. Goode" is riding around in outer space on the *Voyager I* just waiting to be heard by aliens.

Despite the accolades, in his own book Berry shrugs off his contributions, stating that "my view remains that I do not deserve all the reward directed on my account for the accomplishments credited to the rock 'n' roll bank of music." Nevertheless, *Rolling Stone*'s Dave Marsh's words seem to be more appropriate: "Chuck Berry is to rock what Louis Armstrong was to jazz."

Further Reading

Berry, Chuck, *The Autobiography,* Fireside, 1988.
Guralnick, Peter, *Feel Like Going Home,* Vintage, 1981.
Kozinn, Alan, and Pete Welding, Dan Forte, and Gene Santoro, *The Guitar,* Quill, 1984.
Logan, Nick, and Bob Woffinden, *The Illustrated Encyclopedia of Rock,* Harmony Books, 1977.
Rock Revolution, by the editors of *Creem* magazine, Popular Library, 1976.
The Rolling Stone Interviews, by the editors of *Rolling Stone,* St. Martin's Press/Rolling Stone Press, 1981.
The Rolling Stone Record Guide, edited by Dave Marsh and John Swenson, Random House/Rolling Stone Press, 1979.
Guitar Player, February, 1981; May, 1984; June, 1984; January, 1985; January, 1987; November, 1987; December, 1987; March, 1988.
Guitar World, March, 1987; November, 1987; December, 1987; March, 1988; April, 1988.
Rolling Stone, January 26, 1989; August 23, 1990. □

Mary Frances Berry

Mary Frances Berry (born 1938) is a groundbreaking African American woman. She was the first black woman to head a major research university, was

appointed Assistant Secretary of Education by President Jimmy Carter in 1977, and became commissioner and vice chairman of the United States Commission on Civil Rights in 1980. She is a professor at the University of Pennslvania and remains active in a variety of social and political issues.

Born on February 17, 1938, in Nashville, Tennessee, Mary Frances Berry is the second of the three children of George and Frances Berry. Because of economic hardship and extenuating family circumstances, Mary Frances and her older brother were placed in an orphanage for a time. Throughout her early life, Berry was subjected to poverty and to the cruelty that accompanies racial prejudice. However, she proved to be a determined and resilient child with an innate intellectual ability and curiosity.

Berry persevered in her studies in the segregated schools of Nashville and eventually found a mentor, Minerva Hawkins, one of the black teachers at her high school. At the time, Berry was in the tenth grade, bored with school, and experiencing the usual uncertainties that come with adolescence. Hawkins challenged her to keep learning and growing so that she could one day reach her full potential. While Berry had someone with whom she could discuss academic subjects and her plans for the future, she also had the encouragement and support of her mother, who was determined to provide better opportunities for her children.

Berry recalled in Ms. that her mother would say, "You, Mary Frances! You're smart. . . . You can think, you can do all the things I would have done if it had been possible for me. . . . You have a responsibility to use your mind, and to go as far as it will take you." In 1956 Berry succeeded in making herself, her mother, and her mentor proud by graduating with honors from Pearl High School.

Philosophy, history, and chemistry were Berry's main areas of interest as she began college at Fisk University in Nashville. She later transferred to Howard University in Washington, D.C. After earning her bachelor of arts degree in 1961, Berry began graduate studies in the department of history at Howard. As a grad student, she sharpened her skills in historical methodology and applied them in researching the black experience and U.S. history. In addition to attending classes and studying, she worked nights in various hospital laboratories to help defray college expenses.

Berry then decided to leave Howard University and continue her graduate studies in history at the University of Michigan. Her chosen area of study was U.S. history with a concentration in constitutional history. Because of her outstanding academic record, Berry was awarded the Civil War Roundtable Fellowship Award in 1965. The next year, with a Ph.D. to her credit, Berry accepted a position as an assistant professor of history at Central Michigan University. That same year, she also began studies for a law degree at the University of Michigan Law School. Berry reminisced in Ms. that her mother had always told her, "Be overeducated. If somebody else has a master's degree, you get a Ph.D. If somebody has that, then you get a law degree too."

In 1970 she was awarded her J.D. degree and accepted a full-time position as the acting director of the Department of Afro-American Studies at the University of Maryland. Educational administration suited Berry, and she was eventually named director of Afro-American Studies at the university. This promotion was followed by an appointment to the post of interim chairperson of the Division of Behavioral and Social Sciences. From 1974 to 1976 she served as provost for this division, thus becoming the highest-ranking black woman on the University of Maryland's College Park campus.

When the Board of Regents at the University of Colorado offered Berry the chancellorship of the university's Boulder campus in 1976, she accepted and became the first black woman to head a major research university. A year later, she took a leave of absence from her duties at Boulder to accept newly elected U.S. president Jimmy Carter's invitation to serve in the Department of Health, Education and Welfare (HEW). As the assistant secretary for Education from 1977 to 1980, Berry again broke new ground: she was the first African American woman to serve as the chief educational officer in the United States.

Appointed to U.S. Commission on Civil Rights

In 1980 President Carter appointed Berry to the U.S. Commission on Civil Rights, a bipartisan agency that monitors the enforcement of civil rights laws. Along with Berry, he appointed Blandina Cardenas Ramirez and commissioned a massive affirmative action study. In doing so, Carter planted "many seeds . . . that would later grow to entangle the commission in turmoil under [President Ronald] Reagan" theorized James Reston, Jr., in *Rolling Stone*. When the affirmative action study was published, it supported setting goals and timetables for correcting historic discrimination of blacks and women, particularly in the workplace.

In his 1980 presidential campaign, Reagan had spoken against affirmative action, and the newly published study put him in an uncomfortable position. According to Reston, the Commission on Civil Rights was viewed by Reagan and his staff as "a pocket of renegades that needed to be cleaned out." Reston continued: "Reagan wanted his own people everywhere, and no agency—regardless of . . . its historic independence and bipartisanship—escaped attention." In 1984, Reagan attempted to fire Berry, a registered Independent, along with Democrat Ramirez and another Democratic commissioner.

In the *Washington Post*, Berry expressed her frustration over Reagan's attempt to remove members of the commission who disagreed with his viewpoints. She felt that his actions reduced the U.S. Civil Rights Commission from "watchdog of civil rights" to "a lapdog for the administration." Berry and Ramirez successfully sued Reagan in a federal court and retained their seats on the commission. Berry became known as "the woman the president could not fire." Joan Barthel wrote in *Ms.* that Berry's "convictions [kept] her clinging stubbornly to her outcast's seat on the commission." Berry responded: "I tell [my friends] the happiest day of my life was when Reagan fired me. . . . I was fired because I did what I was supposed to do. His firing me was like giving me an A and saying 'Go to the head of the class.'"

Scholarly Pursuits

Berry returned to Howard University as a professor of history and law in 1980. By 1987, she had accepted the post of Geraldine R. Segal Professor of American Social Thought at the University of Pennsylvania. Throughout the 1980s, she increased her involvement in social activism and published two books, *Long Memory: The Black Experience in America* and *Why ERA Failed: Politics, Women's Rights, and the Amending Process of the Constitution*. *Long Memory*, co-authored by John Wesley Blassingame, a professor of southern and African American history at Yale, uses autobiographies, poetry, and newspaper stories to document the responses of people of color to oppression and racism in the United States. The text is designed to be used in survey courses on the African American experience.

Why ERA Failed, published in 1986, suggests that the controversial Equal Rights Amendment failed because it lacked the broad consensus it needed at both the national and the local levels. Berry contends that ERA supporters made a mistake by not building state-to-state coalitions of support for the amendment. In addition, she maintains that certain U.S. Supreme Court actions—actions aimed at removing common forms of discrimination throughout the nation—actually worked against the amendment's passage;

according to Berry, the American public became less inclined to support the idea of a sweeping constitutional amendment because judicial measures, no matter how small, were already being taken to curtail discriminatory practices.

Stepped Up Role in Global Activism

Academic analyses comprised only one part of Berry's professional life. In 1984 she wanted to raise the collective American consciousness on apartheid in South Africa. The issue of South Africa's government-imposed policy of racial segregation was being discussed by groups throughout the United States, but little was actually being done to end it. Berry felt that it was time to take action. On Thanksgiving Eve of 1984, Berry, TransAfrica head Randall Robinson, and Congressman Walter Fauntroy visited the South African embassy in Washington, D.C., and presented a list of demands: they wanted longtime political prisoner Nelson Mandela of the African National Congress—as well as other anti-apartheid leaders—set free, and they wanted a new South African constitutional conference planned. The three activists vowed that they would wait while the ambassador called Pretoria, the seat of the country's government, with their demands.

Their actions had been carefully planned for what is traditionally a slow news day. As Berry told *Ms.*, "If you're going to help people in their struggle, you should be smart for them. . . . If your demonstration doesn't get media coverage, you might as well not have it." The media was indeed there to record Berry, Robinson, and Fauntroy being handcuffed and led away in a paddy wagon. The effect was just what the trio had hoped for. Barthel recounted in *Ms.*: "Here was not just another campus radical; here was Dr. Mary Frances Berry, a member of the Commission on Civil Rights, a professor of history and law, a member of the bar, a scholar with published books to her credit, with more citations and honorary degrees than her wall could hold. Here was a former Assistant Secretary of Health, Education, and Welfare, once a provost at the University of Maryland, and chancellor at the University of Colorado at Boulder."

Spearheaded Free South Africa Movement

Berry, Robinson, and Fauntroy were arraigned on Thanksgiving Day and released on their own recognizance. At a press conference the day after Thanksgiving, the trio introduced their Free South Africa Movement (FSAM). At 4:15 p.m. each day thereafter for a full year, a picket line formed at the South African embassy and ended with a press conference that invariably appeared on the evening news. Celebrities and activists such as Paul Newman, Tony Randall, Gloria Steinem, some of the Kennedys, and members of Congress came by to lend support. Altogether Berry was arrested five times, but she never gave up hope. "Progressive politics is not passé," she told *Ms.*, "and there are things we can do to make change, and to lay the groundwork for change later on."

Over the next year, the Free South Africa Movement spread throughout the country. Colleges, universities, and cities were divesting themselves of holdings in companies that operated in South Africa. Eventually Nelson Mandela was released from prison in South Africa and economic sanctions were imposed against the country. Early in 1992, Berry, Robinson, and Fauntroy had reason to rejoice when a referendum approved the dismantlement of apartheid. "Now, we want to see a day when the black violence will end, and one man, one vote will come," stated Berry in the *Washington Post.* That day came in the spring of 1994, when Mandela—once a powerless prisoner of apartheid—became the new president in his country's first free and fair multiracial elections.

Tackled Child Care Issues

Having made an impact on the international front, Berry returned in the 1990s to domestic issues—like employment, pay equity, and the state of the American family. Family issues and women's rights were the topics of her 1993 book *The Politics of Parenthood.* Historically, notes Berry, child care was not the sole province of mothers. By the mid-nineteenth century, however, the tradition of the man as the breadwinner and the woman as the homemaker was firmly entrenched in American society. When women joined the work force in droves during the 1970s, the notion of women as primary care takers held on. "Even among activists for parental leave," wrote Berry, "the argument is that the *mother* needs more help because now women are out in the world. But the evidence from psychologists is that children can be cared for by anyone, so long as it's good, consistent care."

Berry told Kenneth Walker in *Emerge* that the central civil rights message of her book is that until mothers are freed from the primary responsibility of child rearing, they cannot pursue their economic or other destinies. In response to Walker's statement that many people believe that the high crime rate and increasing number of troubled children is a result of the absence of a good mother, Berry replied, "If my child is bad, it's because our whole extended family network is not working. To say my child is bad because he doesn't have a good mother, I mean, it's like an alien notion, because the mother [alone] is just not responsible."

Reviewing Berry's book in the *Christian Science Monitor,* Laura Van Tuyl stated, "Berry presents a dispassionate history of the women's movement, day care, and home life, showing the persistent obstacles to economic and political power that have confronted women as a result of society's definition of them as 'mothers.' [She] . . . attributes the failure of the Equal Rights Amendment, the languishing of the women's movement in the '80s, and years of bickering over federal parental-leave and child care bills to an unwillingness to rethink gender roles."

Berry continues in her determined struggle for racial, economic, and gender-based justice. "Basically, I'm an optimist," she remarked in *Ms.* "I honestly believe—and I'm sorry, I know this sounds boring—that in the end, truth and justice will prevail. . . . My mother used to tell me, 'Remember, sometimes when it seems like you're losing, you're winning. It all comes out in the wash.'"

Further Reading

Berry, Mary Frances, *The Politics of Parenthood: Child Care, Women's Rights, and the Myth of the Good Mother,* Viking, 1993.
Christian Science Monitor, May 13, 1993, p. 13.
Ebony, January 1979, p. 80.
Emerge, June 1993, p. 58; September 1993, p. 6.
Essence, October 1984, p. 12.
Jet, March 20, 1989, p. 10; October 11, 1993, p. 14.
Los Angeles Times, April 19, 1993, p. E-2.
Ms., January 1987, p. 68; November/December 1990, p. 88.
Nation, May 23, 1987, p. 692.
New Republic, August 16, 1993, p. 30.
New York Times, February 10, 1993, p. A-19.
New York Times Book Review, October 19, 1986, p. 7.
New York Times Magazine, September 13, 1987, p. 93.
Publishers Weekly, January 11, 1993, p. 46.
Rolling Stone, March 13, 1986, p. 41.
Society, May/June 1988, p. 94.
USA Today, January 28, 1992, p. A-11; April 12, 1993, p. A-12.
Washington Monthly, December 1986, p. 58; October 1987, p. 46.
Washington Post, January 18, 1984; March 19, 1992, p. 19. □

Claude Louis Berthollet

The French chemist Claude Louis Berthollet (1748-1822) made many original contributions to both theoretical and applied chemistry. He was one of the foremost disciples of Lavoisier.

Claude Louis Berthollet was born on Dec. 9, 1748, in the village of Galloire on Lake Annecy. He attended the University of Turin in Italy, where he graduated in medicine in 1770. He moved to Paris in 1772 to study chemistry.

In 1778 Berthollet married and took a second doctorate in medicine at the University of Paris, where his Italian degree was not recognized. By 1780 his published research on chemistry had earned him admission to the Royal Academy of Sciences in Paris, and 4 years later he was appointed director of the Gobelin tapestry works. Here he made a special study of the chemistry of dyeing, on which he published an important two-volume work in 1791.

In 1785 Berthollet adopted the new system of chemistry based upon the oxidation theory of combustion, developed by the French chemist A. L. Lavoisier. In the same year Berthollet published an important paper on chlorine, describing the bleaching action of this gas in a solution of alkali, which revolutionized the bleaching industry. Unlike his mentor Lavoisier, Berthollet emerged from the French Revolution unscathed, having served the Revolutionary government as an adviser on technical matters.

A Scientific Debate

Berthollet's career reached its climax during the Napoleonic era. In 1798 Napoleon, who had a well-informed interest in science, chose Berthollet to accompany him on the expedition to Egypt as a scientific adviser. Berthollet became a prominent member of the scientific and archeological institute which Napoleon established in Cairo. It was to this institute that Berthollet read his first papers on the subject of chemical affinity, that is, the forces by which chemical substances are attracted to one another. These papers formed the bases of his two important works on theoretical chemistry, *Researches into the Laws of Chemical Affinity* (1801) and *Essay on Chemical Statics* (1803). Berthollet maintained that the masses of substances involved in a chemical reaction could influence the products and that a chemical reaction could be reversed by varying the quantities of the substances. These views led Berthollet into a protracted scientific debate with J. L. Proust. Proust said that chemical compounds were formed in fixed proportions by weight of their elements. Berthollet argued that the proportion by weight of the elements in a compound could vary according to the mass of the reactants from which the compound resulted. Proust's view seemed vindicated in the light of John Dalton's atomic theory, which depends on the law of fixed proportions. However, the outcome was that Berthollet's important insight into the role of reacting masses was neglected for more than 40 years.

Berthollet's country home at Arcueil, near Paris, became the center for a group of distinguished young chemists and physicists, to whom he offered the facilities of his private laboratory. This group organized themselves into the Society of Arcueil in 1807 under Berthollet's leadership. His last days were clouded by the suicide of his son in 1810 following the failure of a chemical factory in which he had a major interest. Berthollet died at Arcueil on Nov. 6, 1822.

Further Reading

There is no full-length biography of Berthollet, but Maurice P. Crosland, *The Society of Arcueil* (1967), contains much information about Berthollet and French science during the Napoleonic era. J. R. Partington devotes an entire chapter to Berthollet in *A History of Chemistry*, vol. 3 (1962), and provides lengthy discussions in vol. 4 (1964). A section on Berthollet is in Eduard Farber, ed., *Great Chemists* (1961). The scientific environment of the time is covered in Abraham Wolf, *A History of Science, Technology and Philosophy in the Eighteenth Century* (1939). See also Eduard Farber, *The Evolution of Chemistry: A History of Its Ideas, Methods and Materials* (1952; 2d ed. 1969); Henry M. Leicester and Herbert S. Klickstein, eds., *A Source Book in Chemistry: 1400-1900* (1952); and Aaron J. Ihde, *The Development of Modern Chemistry* (1964). □

Alphonse Bertillon

The French criminologist Alphonse Bertillon (1853-1914) was the inventor of the first scientific method of identifying criminals.

Alphonse Bertillon was born in Paris on April 24, 1853. He was the son of Louis Adolphe Bertillon, a physican and statistician. Because of Alphonse's poor scholarship, his father sent him to Great Britain, where he was forced to rely on his own resources. Returning to France, he was inducted into the army.

In 1879, having completed his service, he took a minor clerk's job with the Paris Prefecture of Police. One of his duties was to copy onto small cards the recorded descriptions of the criminals apprehended each day. Bertillon realized that the short descriptions he was laboriously rerecording were practically useless for the purpose of identifying recidivists, or criminal repeaters. He had a general familiarity with anthropological statistics and anthropometric techniques because of the work of his father and his elder brother Jacques, a doctor and statistician. Bertillon devised a system of identification of criminals which relies on 11 bodily measurements and the color of the eyes, hair, and skin. He added standardized photographs of the criminals to his anthropometric data. He first described his system in *Photography: With an Appendix on Anthropometrical Classification and Identification* (1890). The Bertillon system proved successful in distinguishing first-time offenders from recidivists, and it was adopted by all advanced countries.

It is commonly believed that Bertillon was the first to recognize the value of fingerprints. He was not; that achievement must be associated with Sir Francis Galton, Edward Henry, and Juan Vucetich. However, Bertillon was the first on the Continent to use fingerprints to solve a crime.

In 1888 the Department of Judicial Identity was created for the Paris prefecture of Police, and Bertillon became its head. He invented many techniques useful to criminologists. His use of photography was especially effective, and he did much to improve photographic techniques in criminology. Around the turn of the century, fingerprinting began to replace the Bertillon system and has now superseded it throughout the world.

Bertillon died on Feb. 13, 1914, in Paris. His anthropometric method of identifying recidivists represented a first step toward scientific criminology. It is said that his work played an important role in inspiring greater confidence in police authorities and in establishing a more favorable sense of justice toward the end of the 19th century.

Further Reading

An overly imaginative but useful work on Bertillon is Henry T. F. Rhodes, *Alphonse Bertillon, Father of Scientific Detection* (1956). Background studies placing Bertillon's work in perspective include George W. Wilton, *Fingerprints: History, Law and Romance* (1938); Charles E. Chapel, *Fingerprinting: A Manual of Identification* (1941); and Frederick R. Cherrill, *The Fingerprint System at Scotland Yard* (1954). □

Jöns Jacob Berzelius

The Swedish chemist Jöns Jacob Berzelius (1779-1848) was one of the first European scientists to accept John Dalton's atomic theory and to recognize the need for a new system of chemical symbols. He was a dominant figure in chemical science.

Jöns Jacob Berzelius, the son of a clergyman-schoolmaster, was born on Aug. 20, 1779, at Väversunda, Sweden. He studied for 6 years at the medical school at Uppsala and then studied chemistry at the Stockholm School of Surgery. In 1808 he was elected to the Swedish Academy of Science and was appointed its secretary in 1818. He married Elisabeth Poppius in 1835 and on that occasion was made a baron by the Swedish king, Charles XIV.

Atomic Weights and Chemical Symbols

During the first decade of the 19th century, chemists were becoming aware that chemicals combined in definite proportions. This concept, sometimes known as Proust's law after the French chemist Joseph Louis Proust, showed that no matter under what circumstances separate elements combined, their proportions would always be in whole-number ratios. Berzelius was the first to prove beyond a doubt the validity of Proust's law and having been impressed by Dalton's theory of atoms, he proceeded to determine atomic weights. By 1818 Berzelius had obtained, with a high degree of accuracy, the atomic weights of no fewer than 45 elements.

While engaged in this work, Berzelius came to the conclusion that the system of full names for the elements was a hindrance, and he also rejected Dalton's set of symbols for the elements. As a substitute (and this system became the international code for the elements), Berzelius suggested that the initial of the Latin name or the initial plus the second letter be used to designate the element. Now O could be written for oxygen, H for hydrogen, and CO for carbon monoxide. By adding subscriptive numbers, other compounds could be symbolized, such as CO_2 for carbon dioxide and H_2O for water. Thus a new international language of chemistry came into use.

Electricity and Chemistry

The numerous experiments on the effects of an electrical current on chemical solutions had caught the imagination of the scientific world quite early in the 19th century. The electrical current used was that obtained from one of Volta's "galvanic piles." Berzelius and Wilhelm Hisinger worked with the voltaic pile, and in 1803 they reported that, just as an electrical current could decompose water, it could separate solutions of salts so that the acids formed would go to one pole while the alkalies would be collected at the opposite one. In further experiments, with M. M. Pontin, Berzelius succeeded in producing amalgams of potassium, calcium, and ammonia, by using mercury as the negative electrode.

From these experiments in electrochemistry, Berzelius arrived at his own electrochemical theory, which stated that all compounds can be divided into their positive and negative parts. This so-called dualistic theory held that all compounds are divided into two groups: those that are electropositive and those that are electronegative. In any chemical reaction there is a neutralization of opposite electricities, and depending on the strength of the components, this reaction may vary from a very feeble one to ignition and combustion. The opposite of chemical combination, in Berzelius's view, was electrolysis, in which electric charges are restored and the combined molecular groups are separated.

Organic Chemistry

In 1807, when he was appointed professor of medicine at the Stockholm School of Surgery, Berzelius began his researches in organic chemistry. At this time very little was known about organic chemistry, especially its involvement in life processes. Berzelius realized that he himself knew nothing of physiological chemistry. He thought that there might be some chemical process associated with the functions of the brain but admitted that the understanding of this seemed impossible. He began analyzing animal substances such as blood, bile, milk, membranes, bones, fat, flesh and its fluids, and animal semen. He discovered that blood contains iron and that muscular tissue contains lactic acid, the same acid found in sour milk. Most of his work in this field was inconclusive, as he was the first to realize. He concluded that analyses of animal products needed to await the day of more sophisticated techniques and apparatus, and he gave up his studies.

Discovery of New Elements

At an early point in his career, Berzelius became interested in a rare mineral, Bastnäs tungsten, and undertook an analysis of it. He came to the conclusion that it contained an unknown metal, and he and Hisinger named it cerium after the recently discovered asteroid Ceres.

Some years later Berzelius discovered the element selenium, which was isolated from the sediment in lead tanks used in the manufacture of sulfuric acid. He named his new discovery after the Greek word for the moon. His next discoveries, of the elements vanadium and thorium, were named after the Norse goddess Vanadium and the god Thor.

Other Researches

Berzelius's *Textbook of Chemistry* went through many editions and was translated into the principal European languages. To this work he added his tables of atomic weights. He devised new methods of analysis and obtained values for combining weights not very different from those found today. He started by using the atomic weight figure of 100 for oxygen and related all of the other elements to it.

Much of Berzelius's work involved studies of minerals. He found that previous systems of classification were unreliable, so he proceeded to devise his own system, based not on description of crystal forms but on chemical composition. In 1836 the Royal Society of London awarded him the Copley Medal for this work.

Of great importance to chemical knowledge in the 19th century were two concepts in theory, both of which are associated with Berzelius: isomerism and catalysis. He remembered that the lactic acid he had discovered in muscle tissue behaved differently toward polarized light than the lactic acid of fermentation. Other examples of such behavior could be found, and Berzelius suggested that compounds of the same chemical composition which possess different chemical properties be called isomers, from the Greek word meaning equal parts. The importance of understanding isomerism was that it demonstrates that there is more involved in chemical structure than the ratios of the elements and atomic weight. The manner in which atoms are distributed in a molecular structure is a determining factor in the chemical properties of a compound.

In 1835 Berzelius advanced the theoretical concept of catalysis, or chemical change in which one agent produces the reaction without itself being changed. Berzelius wrote about this process as it applied to plant chemistry. He believed that in inorganic chemical reactions metals can act as catalytic agents. In summing up catalysis, Berzelius wrote, "Thus it is certain that substances . . . have the property of exerting an effect . . . quite different from ordinary chemical affinity, in that they promote the conversion . . . without necessarily participating in the process with their own component parts. . . . "

As secretary of the Swedish Academy of Science, and also for some years as librarian of the academy, Berzelius began in 1821 to publish the *Annual Surveys of Progress in the Sciences*. Publication was continued until his death, at which time 27 volumes had been issued. His massive correspondence with scientists has been published, and it is a comprehensive picture of the great chemical world which was unfolding in his day.

Personality and Character

It was perhaps natural that Berzelius, who achieved such great eminence early in the century, should have insisted on dominating the chemical sciences as they progressed. He was cheerful as a youth, but as he grew older and developed more and more health problems, he became conservative, argumentative, and even dictatorial. It has been said that when Berzelius condemned a new idea, it might just as well be forgotten, and that his insistence on the acceptance of his own ideas in part blocked the progress of chemistry. In his last years he was still denouncing some of his colleagues for what he termed their "Swedish laziness." He died on Aug. 7, 1848, and was buried in Stockholm.

Further Reading

The biography of Berzelius by J. Erik Jorpes, *Jac. Berzelius: His Life and Work* (1960; trans. 1971), is highly recommended. There is a long essay on Berzelius by Aaron J. Ihde, which contains many notes and references, in Eduard Farber, ed., *Great Chemists* (1961). Volume 4 of J. R. Partington, *A History of Chemistry* (1964), is also useful. On the subject of chemical nomenclature Maurice Crosland, *Historical Studies in the Language of Chemistry* (1962), should be consulted.

Additional Sources

Melhado, Evan Marc, *Jacob Berzelius, the emergence of his chemical system*, Stockholm, Sweden: Almqvist & Wiksell

International; Madison, Wis.: University of Wisconsin Press, 1981. ☐

Annie Wood Besant

The British social reformer and theosophist Annie Wood Besant (1847-1933) made important contributions to a number of reformist and religious causes. She was a leader among Europeans in reviving and disseminating Hindu religion and culture.

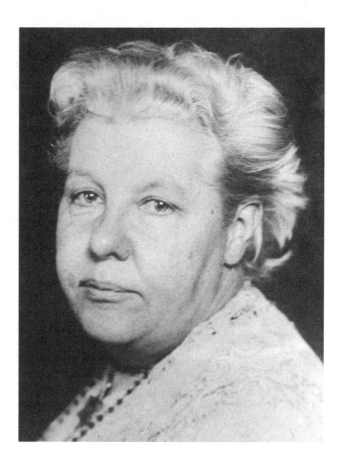

Annie Wood was born in London on Oct. 1, 1847, to a well-connected but declining family, mostly of Irish descent. Her 7-year marriage to Frank Besant, an Anglican vicar, by whom she had two children, ended in separation in 1873, when she declared herself an unbeliever. The next year Besant joined Charles Bradlaugh in his Secularist movement, preaching man's freedom from God and the devil and a future existence of beauty, wisdom, and love for a regenerated mankind. She became a vice president of Bradlaugh's Secular Society and wrote and edited much atheist journalism. With Bradlaugh, she was prosecuted for spreading birth-control information, and in consequence she lost the custody of her daughter and suffered much social persecution.

In 1885 Besant joined the Fabian Society, drawn in by the writer George Bernard Shaw soon after its founding. She was already known as a brilliant speaker, and she did effective work for the Fabians. Shaw described her as "a sort of expeditionary force, always to the front . . . , carrying away audiences for us . . . , founding branches . . . , and generally . . . taking on the fighting. . . . " She was one of the seven contributors to *Fabian Essays in Socialism* (1889), which Shaw edited.

In 1888 Besant organized a successful strike of 700 girls at the Bryant and May match factory. This strike demonstrated that unskilled Labor could successfully combine, by industry rather than by craft, and it was in effect a test for the famous London dock strike of 1889.

Besant joined the Theosophical Society, headed by the colorful and controversial Madame Blavatsky, in 1889. This movement, partly resembling spiritualism, then much in vogue, had the serious purpose of elevating the materialistic, scientific spirit of the West through preaching the mysticism and spirituality of Hinduism and Buddhism. Besant found in theosophy the "hidden power" she had been seeking. She served as president of the Theosophical Society from 1907 until her death.

Besant lived at the society's headquarters in Adyar, India, and frequently lectured there and in London to large audiences. She learned Sanskrit and translated the *Bhagavad Gita,* and she founded a Hindu college in Benares. During World War I she became a champion of Indian home rule, and she was fifth and last British president of the Indian National Congress. In the terrible disorders in the Punjab in 1919 she supported the imperial policy of repression, thus alienating the natives, who turned for leadership to Mohandas Gandhi.

Besant toured the Western nations during the 1920s with a young Hindu, Jiddu Krishnamurti, whom she regarded as the new messiah. After a period of failing health, Mrs. Besant died at Adyar on Sept. 20, 1933.

Further Reading

Annie Besant: An Autobiography appeared in 1893. The standard biography is now the two-volume work by Arthur Hobart Nethercot, *The First Five Lives of Annie Besant* (1960) and *The Last Four Lives of Annie Besant* (1963). Another source is Esther Bright, *Old Memories and Letters of Annie Besant* (1936). Mrs. Besant's Fabian activity is described in Anne Fremantle, *This Little Band of Prophets: The Story of the Gentle Fabians* (1960). Her years with Bradlaugh and Blavatsky are covered in lively fashion in Warren S. Smith, *The London Heretics, 1870-1914* (1967).

Additional Sources

Besant, Annie Wood, *Annie Besant: an autobiography,* Madras, India: Theosophical Pub. House, 1983.

Dinnage, Rosemary, *Annie Besant,* Harmondsworth, Middlesex, England; New York, N.Y., U.S.A.: Penguin Books, 1986.

Muthanna, I. M., *Mother Besant and Mahatma Gandhi,* Vellore, N.A. Dt., Tamil Nadu: Thenpulam Publishers; Madras: Available at Paari Nilayam, 1986.

Raj Kumar, *Annie Besant's rise to power in Indian politics, 1914-1917,* New Delhi: Concept Pub. Co., 1981.

Taylor, Anne, *Annie Besant: a biography,* Oxford; New York: Oxford University Press, 1992.

Wessinger, Catherine Lowman, *Annie Besant and progressive Messianism (1847-1933)*, Lewiston, N.Y.: E. Mellen Press, 1988. □

Friedrich Wilhelm Bessel

The German astronomer Friedrich Wilhelm Bessel (1784-1846) established the modern ideals and standards of precision in astronomy and obtained the first measurement of the distance to a star.

F riedrich Wilhelm Bessel was born in Minden, North Rhine-Westphalia, on July 22, 1784. After a rather undistinguished schooling, he was apprenticed to a Bremen merchant house at the age of 15. In the course of his bookkeeping work, he acquired a facility in mathematics, and this, together with an interest in astronomy, led him to compute the orbit of Halley's comet from old observations made by T. Harriott of the comet's 1607 circuit. His results were published in a professional journal. This evidence of his ability gained him entry into the profession, starting as an assistant in the private observatory of J. H. Schroter in Lillienthal in 1806. Bessel became the outstanding astronomer of the 19th century and probably the most complete astronomer of all time.

In an era when astronomers had long since given themselves over to specializing in either the observational or the theoretical aspects of the science, Bessel was master of both. He became the director of the newly founded Royal Observatory in Königsberg in 1810. As a worker in, and director of, the observatory for more than 30 years, he complied a catalog of very accurate positions for 75,000 stars.

Observational Precision

By Bessel's day it was already well known that the earth is a difficult place from which to try to map the sky. In addition to being immersed in a dense atmosphere which distorts star positions, the earth was known to be a moving platform whose basic motion (an assumed annual revolution around the sun) was complicated by numerous smaller wiggles and wobbles. Therefore the task of producing precise astronomical information was extremely difficult. Besides getting the best instruments available and then ensuring that intrinsic errors had been eliminated or mitigated as far as possible, astronomers needed to convert their readings into usable data. Prior to Bessel, every astronomer had done it in his own way. Bessel not only reevaluated all of the corrections involved but established a logical, systematic scheme for applying them which has been followed universally ever since. Leaving nothing to chance, he even proved that different observers actually see a given event occur at different times and introduced the "personal equation" to correct for it long before the discipline of psychology arose and took interest in the question of individual differences.

Stellar Parallax

Bessel's enduring concern for both instrumental and mathematical facets of observational precision eventually combined to produce what was undoubtedly the crowning achievement of his life—the detection of stellar parallax. From the time of Copernicus it had been recognized that if the earth were in motion around the sun, the earth's motion would be reflected by annual shifts in the positions of at least some stars against the background sky. Attempts to discover such a parallax had been made by many prominent astronomers from Copernicus's time to Bessel's. But all had failed. Bessel, determined to add his efforts to the cause, decided on a somewhat different approach to the problem. The crucial part of any such project, of course, was the choice of the star: the nearer it was, the more likely the work was to succeed. Previous investigators had invariably chosen bright stars, on the supposition that all stars are about the same size and that the brightest ones are the nearest ones. By Bessel's era, however, this assumption was known to be questionable. Moreover, a new type of information was available, termed "proper motion," which seemed to offer more reliable guidance in guessing which stars were most likely to be nearby. These data signified that some stars have measurable long-term drifts with respect to the rest of the stars. Reasoning that such stars must be closer than the rest, Bessel chose to work with the star that had the swiftest known motion (61 Cygni). After 1 1/2 years of careful observations and laborious calculations, Bessel separated the star's own motion from the various motions of the earth and concluded in 1838 that the star was oscillating back and forth each year by about 3/10 of 1 second of arc.

The discovery of stellar parallax was a landmark in the history of astronomy. On the one hand, it signaled the official end of the dispute over Copernicanism. On the other hand, it constituted the indispensable beginning and foundation of all studies of the stellar system which depend on knowledge of distances.

In addition to his technical astronomical works, Bessel published the widely read series *Popular Lectures* (1848). He also made an important contribution to applied mathematics by systematizing the functions now known by his name. He died in Königsberg on March 17, 1846.

Further Reading

The most scholarly work on Bessel is in German. Studies in English which discuss him include Henry Smith Williams, *The Great Astronomers* (1930); Hector MacPhearson, *Makers of Astronomy* (1933); and Willy Ley, *Watchers of the Skies: An Informal History of Astronomy from Babylon to the Space Age* (1963).

Additional Sources

Lavrinovich, K. K. (Kazimir Kleofasovich), *Friedrich Wilhelm Bessel, 1784-1846,* Basel; Boston: Birkhauser, 1995. □

Sir Henry Bessemer

The English inventor Sir Henry Bessemer (1813-1898) was a pioneer in the manufacture of inexpensive steel through his development of the steelmaking process which bears his name.

Henry Bessemer was born Jan. 19, 1813, in Hitchin, Hertfordshire. He left school to work for his father, a typefounder. In 1830 Bessemer set up his own business in London for producing art-metals, fusible alloys, and bronze powder. He was a prolific inventor, both before and after his key contribution to the iron and steel industries. He invented machines for composing type and for working graphite for pencils; at age 20 he was an exhibitor at the Royal Academy.

Fixed Converter

In 1854, following the rejection of an artillery invention, Bessemer sought an iron tougher than any then available and experimentally fused blister steel with pig iron. Apparently it was during these trials that he noted the effect of air in removing carbon from iron, a process essential for its conversion to steel. In 1855 he successfully produced a low-grade steel from molten pig iron in a side-blown fixed converter without any external source of heat. Bessemer patented the process in 1856 and described it in a paper, "Manufacture of Malleable Iron and Steel without Fuel." Attracted by the promise of economy in time, labor, and fuel, many wrought-iron producers tried the process; all reported total failure to produce any useful material.

Bessemer, dumbfounded and discredited, sought both cause and cure. The principal causes were twofold: the "blow" left the metal full of oxygen, and typical British pig irons were phosphorus-rich. Both led to brittleness in forging. The former fault was recognized and cured by Robert Forester Mushet, while Bessemer's Swedish licensee, G. Göransson, established that phosphorus was the other trouble, but no immediate cure was forthcoming.

Tilting Converter

Bessemer and his associates set up a steelworks in Sheffield in 1858, using phosphorus-free ore from Sweden and one part of England. There the familiar bottomblown tilting converter, in which the air blast supports the molten metal, was introduced in 1860, but Bessemer was unable to raise much new support among ironmasters. By 1879, when Gilchrist and Thomas showed that phosphorus could be removed by using basic instead of acidic furnace linings and fluxes, the open-hearth steelmaking process, with its ability to accept cold scrap in the charge, had become established in Britain. Thus British steelmakers have never greatly utilized either acid or basic Bessemer plants; much of Europe and America, with their then less-developed iron industries, widely adopted the basic Bessemer process. In the United States part of the Bessemer process had been patented by William Kelly, and dual licenses were needed for its operation there. Any personal connection between these two men in their inventions seems most unlikely. Despite its initial drawbacks, the process made Bessemer a millionaire. Today Bessemer steelmaking is rapidly giving way to various oxygen steelmaking methods.

Bessemer was knighted in 1879; he died in London on March 15, 1898.

Further Reading

The major work on Bessemer is his autobiography, *Sir Henry Bessemer: An Autobiography* (1905). W. H. Chaloner, *People and Industries* (1963), includes a chapter on Bessemer. The metallurgical background is in J. C. Carr and W. Taplin, *History of the British Steel Industry* (1962).

Additional Sources

Bessemer, Henry, Sir, *Sir Henry Bessemer, F.R.S.: an autobiography, with a concluding chapter,* London; Brookfield, VT., USA: Institute of Metals, 1989. □

Charles Herbert Best

The Canadian medical scientist Charles Herbert Best (1899-1978) codiscovered insulin in 1921. He also discovered the enzyme histaminase, and his studies on choline established its importance as a dietary factor.

Charles H. Best was born on February 27, 1899, at West Pembroke, Maine. His parents, Dr. Herbert Huestes Best and Luella Fisher Best, were Canadian. Charles entered the University of Toronto in 1916, but interrupted his studies to join the Canadian army. After World War I he resumed his studies at the University of Toronto and graduated in May 1921.

Discovery of Insulin

The day after his examinations Best began work with Frederick Banting in the department of physiology. Best had been asked to assist in the chemical procedures involved in the research. He and Banting started their work on the extraction of pancreatic tissue and the treatment of depancreatized dogs. This project led to the discovery of insulin later that summer.

Best was appointed director of the Insulin Division of the Connaught Laboratories in January 1922. In 1924 he married Margaret Hooper Mahon, and in the following year, after he had received his medical degree from the University of Toronto, the couple went to England. There Best worked with Sir Henry Dale and obtained his doctorate from the University of London in 1928.

During his postgraduate work and throughout his medical training, Best continued to be actively involved in insulin production and studies on diabetes. He had numerous appointments at the University of Toronto; after Banting's death in 1941, Best became head of the Banting and Best Department of Medical Research.

Following the work on insulin Best continued his investigations in several different areas. In London he became interested in histamine. On his return to Toronto he and E.W. McHenry demonstrated the action of histaminase, an enzyme responsible for the breakdown of histamine. In 1928 Best organized a team to explore the sources of heparin and to test its effectiveness in the prevention of thrombosis.

Researchers had noted that after removal of the pancreas, and despite the use of insulin, the livers of dogs became swollen with fat. Best, with his colleagues J. M. Hershey, M. Elinor Huntsman, and others, investigated the cause of these fatty livers and found choline to be one factor preventing the development of fatty livers (a lipotropic factor). This was an important discovery since, when fatty livers do develop as a result of a deficiency of choline or related factors, fibrotic changes and, finally, cirrhosis may follow.

Best received honorary doctorates from 18 universities, and was the recipient of numerous medals, awards, and honors. He was a fellow of the Royal Society of London, the Royal Society of Canada, and the Royal College of Physicians and Surgeons of Canada.

Best retired from the University of Toronto in 1965 and spent much of his time traveling around the world with his wife. He died on March 31, 1978, in Toronto.

Further Reading

Information on Best and his work is in Arturo Castiglioni, *A History of Medicine* (trans. 1941; 2d rev. ed. 1947), G.A.

Wrenshall, G. Heteny, and W.R. Feasby, *Story of Insulin: Forty Years of Success against Diabetes* (1962), and in Michael Bliss, *Discovery of Insulin* (1982). □

Rómulo Betancourt

Rómulo Betancourt (1908-1981) was the most important political leader of Venezuela during the middle decades of the 20th century. Founder of the nation's first modern political party, he was twice president.

Born on Feb. 22, 1908, in a small town in eastern Venezuela, Rómulo Betancourt was the son of lower-middle-class parents. In 1927 he enrolled at the Central University of Venezuela in Caracas. He had his first political experience as a leader of the student movement called the "Boys of '28." This group directed its energies in opposition to the dictatorship of General Juan Vicente Gómez, "the tyrant of the Andes." When the student revolt of 1928 failed, Betancourt was jailed for several weeks, and then sent into exile in Colombia. From there he traveled to other Latin American countries in search of support against Venezuela's repressive government. In Costa Rica he was swept up in communist revolutionary ideology and became a founder of that country's communist party. However, when the party decided to become a full member of the Communist International, he withdrew. Betancourt later called his early association with communism "a youthful attack of small pox that left me immune to the disease."

After Gómez died in December 1935, Betancourt returned home. Founding and editing the left wing newspaper *Orve* beginning in 1926, he assumed leadership of those trying to organize a democratic party, which took shape as the *Partido Democratico Nacional* (PDN). The government of General Eleazar Lopez Contreras suppressed the party in mid-1937, and Betancourt went into hiding. Captured in 1939, he was forced into exile again, this time in Chile. There he wrote and published his first book, *Problemas venezolanos* (1940).

President of Venezuela

With the inauguration of President Isaias Medina Angarita in 1941, Betancourt was allowed to return to Venezuela. The PDN, now legalized under the name *Accion Democratica* (AD), constituted the major opposition party to Medina, and put forth a presidential candidate to face the current government in the promised upcoming elections. Once again Betancourt promoted his party's views and their candidate through publication, this time by founding the newspaper *El Pais*. When the president reneged on his promise to allow open elections to determine his successor, the AD joined young military leaders in a coup d'etat in October 1945. As a result, Betancourt assumed control of Venezuela as provisional president.

During Betancourt's democratic administration, he instituted numerous economic and social reforms. Rent controls were established, and profit-sharing arrangements were encouraged between employers and their employees. But of major significance, Betancourt implemented an agreement with foreign oil companies operating in oil-rich Venezuela that they would pay 50 percent of their profits to the government. With the greatly increased revenues that resulted, the government established the Venezuelan Development Corporation and expanded the number of schools, teachers, and hospitals. The government also strongly encouraged organized labor and for the first time supported establishment of a peasant movement. It drew up an agrarian reform law and wrote a new constitution providing for universal adult suffrage and full democratic guarantees. After free elections in 1947, AD presidential candidate Rómulo Gallegos succeeded Betancourt to the presidency in February 1948.

Democratic Reforms Gained Him Second Term

President Gallegos' term would be a short one, however. Because of the radical changes promised in his campaign, he was overthrown in November by conservative military dictator General Marcos Perez Jiménez. Betancourt, although immediately forced into exile by the new military government, was the principal leader of the opposition to Jiménez's government. Despite Betancourt's efforts, the military dictatorship remained in power until January 1958; after its overthrow Betancourt was free to return to

Venezuela. He was elected president for a second time on a coalition government platform in 1958.

Profound social, economic, and political changes took place in Venezuela during Betancourt's second administration, many of which the president outlined in his *Romulo Betancourt: Posicion y doctrina* (1958). Land was distributed to over 50,000 families, organized labor grew, and collective bargaining became common. Through the Development Corporation and aid against foreign competition, industrialization was encouraged. Large road-building and electrical power programs were carried out, transforming Venezuela into a modernized, Latin American nation.

Political democracy in Venezuela was maintained in spite of mutinies by right and left-wing extremists, scattered guerilla warfare, and an assassination attempt on Betancourt's life in 1960. Elections at the end of 1963 resulted in the choice of the AD candidate, Dr. Raul Leoni, to succeed Betancourt, who was prevented from running for ten years by the election reforms that he himself had instituted. He is remembered in Venezuelan history as the first individual to gain the presidency through democratic election and relinquish it to another through democratic election as well.

From Politician to Author

Upon leaving office in March 1964, Betancourt went to live in Europe and Asia. He resided for a time in Bern, Switzerland before returning to Venezuela. There he wrote several books on his political ideas and the accomplishments of his second administration. Two of his works on oil, politics, and economics were translated into English. *Venezuela: Oil and Politics* (1979) and *Venezuela's Oil* (1978) focus on a nation's ability to achieve economic independence only through political independence. He cited examples from Venezuela's own history, from the period where it was controlled by American and British oil companies through its later assertion of economic autonomy as the world's third largest oil producer. Betancourt's writings were of considerable influence during the 1960 formation of the Organization of Petroleum Exporting Countries (OPEC).

Betancourt was respected for implementing the economic and social policies that enabled Venezuela to channel the benefits of its natural resources to its own people, rather than lose them to foreign interests. He was honored with numerous internationally sponsored awards during his lifetime, including honorary degrees from Harvard University and the University of California. Betancourt died of a stroke, September 28, 1981, at the age of seventy-three.

Further Reading

Although there is no full-length biography of Betancourt, extensive information on his career may be found in Robert J. Alexander, *Venezuelan Democratic Revolution: A Profile of the Regime of Rómulo Betancourt* (1964), and John Martz, *Accion Democratica: Evolution of a Modern Political Party in Venezuela* (1966). See also the chapter on Betancourt in Robert J. Alexander, *Prophets of the Revolution: Profiles of Latin American Leaders* (1962). □

Hans Albrecht Bethe

The Alsatian-born American theoretical physicist Hans Albrecht Bethe (born 1906), prolific and creative contributor to several vital fields of nuclear physics, discovered the mechanism of energy production by stars (including the sun).

Hans Bethe was born in Strasbourg, Alsace-Lorraine—(now part of France)—on July 2, 1906, to Albrecht Theodore Bethe, a physiologist, and Anna Kuhn Bethe. At the age of 22 he earned his doctorate at the University of Munich and was given an assistantship at the Institute of Theoretical Physics of the University of Frankfurt. After a year he transferred to the Technische Hochschule in Stuttgart and then for three years was *privatdozent* —unsalaried lecturer—in physics at the University of Tübingen. He worked at Cambridge University and in Rome in 1930-1931 and then returned to Tübingen as an assistant professor.

After Hitler came to power, Bethe fled first to England and then to the United States, where Cornell University welcomed him. At age 31 he was elevated to the post of Wendell Anderson professor of physics. In 1939 he married Rose Ewald, the daughter of Paul Peter Ewald, a professor of physics in Munich. They had a son and a daughter.

In 1939 Bethe published a paper, "Energy Production in Stars," in which he advanced a theory of stellar fuel. He discovered that, by a series of transformations, carbon, acting as a catalyst, changes four atoms of hydrogen into an atom of helium of atomic weight four. During these transformations the carbon is rejuvenated and there is a very small loss of mass which is converted into the enormous amount of energy which stokes the stars. For this achievement as well as for his many important contributions to the theory of nuclear reactions, Bethe was awarded the Nobel Prize in physics in 1967.

Bethe published the first theory of electron-positron pair creation and an improved theory of how charged particles interact. The latter is a key to the determination of the amount of radiation shielding required by nuclear reactors and by astronauts in space. It is also critical to the understanding of cosmic-ray phenomena, the design of experiments in high-energy nuclear physics, the theory of the structure of metals, the shock-wave theory, the scattering of mesons, and the energy levels of the hydrogen atom.

In 1941 Bethe became a naturalized American citizen, and between 1943 and 1946 he worked as head of the Division of Theoretical Physics at the Los Alamos Scientific Laboratories, where the first nuclear bomb was being manufactured. His assignment was to determine the amount of uranium or plutonium that would be necessary to produce a nuclear explosion and to calculate the total energy that might be released in such an explosion. Bethe was also responsible for a group which had to determine the mechanism of assembling an atom bomb implosion; that is by bringing together, in a split second, a spherical ball of either

uranium or plutonium by means of a high explosive. After his work at Los Alamos, Bethe returned to his teaching position at Cornell University. He retired from Cornell in 1975 but maintains an office there and continues to serve as a lecturer and consultant.

In addition to his academic work, Bethe was also active in the disarmament movement and sought to educate the public about the destructive power of nuclear weapons. He remains committed to this cause. He sent a letter to President Clinton in 1997, calling for a complete ban on nuclear testing.

On July 2, 1996—Bethe's ninetieth birthday—it was announced that the American Physical Society would begin awarding the Bethe Prize for contributions to the field of physics.

Further Reading

R.E. Marshak, ed., *Perspectives in Modern Physics: Essays in Honor of Hans A. Bethe on the Occasion of His 60th Birthday, July 1966* (1966), contains an account of Bethe's career and a bibliography of his writings. He is discussed at length in Henry A. Boorse and Lloyd Motz, eds., *The World of the Atom* (1966). See also Stéphane Groueff, *Manhattan Project: The Untold Story of the Making of the Atomic Bomb* (1967) and Richard Feynman, *Surely You're Joking, Mr. Feynman!* (1985). □

Theobald von Bethmann Hollweg

The German statesman and chancellor Theobald von Bethmann Hollweg (1856-1921) led Germany during the first 3 years of World War I.

Theobald von Bethmann Hollweg was the son of a prominent commercial and agrarian family. After a rather routine rise in German political life, he became Prussian minister of the interior in 1905 and the imperial secretary of state for the interior in 1907. In 1909, after the fall of Bernhard von Bülow, he became imperial chancellor.

As a conservative of open mind and modern outlook, Bethmann Hollweg seemed a likely choice to heal divisions, such as the conflict between civilian and military, that were developing in Germany at that time. But in spite of some early achievements—such as the comprehensive social insurance law and liberal constitution for Alsace-Lorraine (both 1911)—he did not live not live up to expectations. His attempt to extend the franchise failed, and when Germany entered the war it had still not solved the problem of integrating the Social Democrats, the largest party in the Reichstag after the 1912 elections.

Diplomatically, Bethmann Hollweg inherited a situation as difficult as the domestic one, and he was no more successful on the international level. Germany was diplomatically isolated, and, worst of all, because of the naval race between Germany and England the relations of those two countries were deteriorating. When the British war secretary, Richard Haldane, came to Germany in 1912 on a diplomatic mission, Bethmann Hollweg was willing to be conciliatory. He was overruled, however, by Adm. Alfred von Tirpitz and the navy, which pushed through a new naval bill over Bethmann Hollweg's objections.

Although the chancellor sincerely tried to preserve peace in the summer of 1914, he was unable to control the military establishment's pressure for war. In any event, Bethmann Hollweg himself—with his "blank check" to Austria and his "scrap of paper" remark concerning Belgian neutrality—was partly responsible for the developing crisis. His wartime leadership was equally indecisive. He alienated the socialists and liberals by his apparent subservience to the military on questions of negotiated peace, annexations, and submarine warfare, and he alienated the right wing and the high command with his efforts in behalf of reform and civilian control of the military. In July 1917 Bethmann Hollweg was easily removed from office, and the establishment of a military dictatorship in Germany was virtually complete. He died in 1921.

Further Reading

Bethmann Hollweg's wartime memoirs, *Reflections on the World War* (2 vols., 1919-1921; trans., 1 vol., 1920), are well known. There is a good deal of information on him in Fritz Fischer's monumental *Germany's Aims in the First World War*

Theobald von Bethmann Hollweg

(1961; rev. ed. 1967; trans. 1967). See also J. W. Headlam, *The German Chancellor and the Outbreak of War* (1917). □

Henry Norman Bethune

Henry Norman Bethune (1890-1939) was a physician dedicated to service to humanity. He provided medical services to the poor in Canada, to the Republicans in the Spanish Civil War, and to the Chinese during their invasion by Japan.

Henry Norman Bethune was born in Gravenhurst, Ontario, on March 3, 1890. His father was a Presbyterian minister who had descended from a long line of clergymen, educators, and medical practitioners. His mother had been an evangelical missionary. Bethune's early commitment to maintain the family tradition of service to the less fortunate remained throughout his life.

Bethune left medical school at the University of Toronto in 1914 to enlist in the Canadian army. Wounded in action in France in 1915, he went back to the university to complete his medical studies. After graduation he joined the Royal Navy and then the Canadian air force.

During the early 1920s, he pursued postgraduate studies in medicine in London and Edinburgh, where he was elected a Fellow of the Royal College of Surgeons in 1922. In 1924 he opened a private medical practice in Detroit, Michigan. Two years later his health broke down. Discovering that he had contracted tuberculosis in both lungs, he sought treatment at the famous Trudeau Sanatorium in Saranac Lake, New York. With his condition worsening, Bethune eventually persuaded his reluctant doctors to perform a potentially fatal operation. Its success and his amazingly rapid recovery inspired him to give up private practice and to join the medical search for a cure for the disease that had nearly taken his life.

In 1928 he became the first assistant of Dr. Edward Archibald, the Canadian pioneer in thoracic surgery at McGill University in Montreal, Quebec. Over the next eight years, Bethune's invention of numerous operating instruments, his writings in medical journals, and his daring surgical techniques raised him to prominence in the international medical community.

In the early 1930s, as the Depression deepened in Montreal, Bethune became more conscious of the relationship between social and economic conditions and the incidence of tuberculosis. Through his concern for the welfare of those who were unable to afford medical treatment he opened a free clinic. In 1935 he attended the International Physiological Congress in Moscow. His purpose was to examine the system of socialized medicine in operation in the U.S.S.R.

On his return to Canada he organized a campaign to promote the introduction of a state medical care system. His open and persistent advocacy of his views alienated him from many of his professional colleagues and also moved him closer to the left. In 1936 he joined the Communist Party.

Shortly after the outbreak of the Spanish Civil War he resigned his hospital position and offered his services to the Spanish Republican government. Following a tour of the front in November 1936 he set up a mobile blood-transfusion service to rush bottled blood in refrigerated trucks to the wounded at the front. The scheme, which was the first of its kind in history, saved many lives, but Bethune refused to accept military discipline. Because of this the Spanish authorities asked him to return to Canada in June 1937.

To raise money to expand the blood transfusion service, he went on a North American fund-raising tour. During the tour Japan began its full-scale invasion of China. Unable to return to Spain, unemployed, and alone, Bethune decided to go to China.

In January 1938 he made a perilous journey of more than 600 miles from Hong Kong to the headquarters of the Chinese Eighth Route Army in northwest China. In the rugged mountainous area west of Beijing he put together a medical field service. There he constructed makeshift hospitals throughout the region, wrote textbooks on elementary medicine and surgery, and began training young Chinese in rudimentary medical techniques.

On horseback he led his mobile medical unit through the barren Wu Tai mountains of Shanxi province and across the Hebei plains to inspect personnel, revamp hospitals, and treat the wounded. During much of the time Bethune's unit was behind Japanese lines. Frequently called to battles, he and his team would race to the scene to set up their operating theater, which was seldom more than three miles from the firing.

Long hours, inadequate food, and overwork had weakened him. His eyesight was failing, his teeth were in poor condition, and one ear had become deaf. On a final inspection tour before a planned return to Canada to receive medical treatment and to raise funds for his work, he was called to battle. During an operation he nicked his finger. There were no surgical gloves. Infection led quickly to blood poisoning. Just before dawn, on November 12, 1939, in a tiny peasant hut in the village of Huang Shikou in Heibei province, he died.

Bethune's death received little attention in Canada or in China until the Cultural Revolution (1966-1976). During that decade of social and political upheaval the Chinese Communist leadership used Bethune as a symbol of selflessness, dedication, and responsibility—characteristics that they wanted the Chinese people to adopt. They published hundreds of millions of copies of an essay written by Mao Zedong called *In Memory of Norman Bethune*. Everyone was expected to read it, and many committed it to memory. Since the 1960s through books, movies, and study in the schools, Bethune has become a national hero in China.

In Canada, belated recognition was granted in 1972 when the federal government declared him "a Canadian of national historical significance." The Presbyterian manse in which he was born was restored to period and a portion of it converted into a museum. It was opened in 1976 as the Bethune Memorial Home.

Further Reading

The first biography of Bethune was Ted Allen and Sydney Gordon, *The Scalpel, The Sword* (1952). A later work is Roderick Stewart's Bethune (1973). For Bethune's own writing, a good source is Roderick Stewart, *The Mind of Norman Bethune* (1977). The latter contains essays, medical articles, poetry, and letters written by Bethune. □

Mary McLeod Bethune

Mary McLeod Bethune (1875-1955), an African American teacher, was one of the great educators of the United States. She was a leader of women, a distinguished adviser to several American presidents, and a powerful champion of racial equality.

Mary McLeod was born in Mayesville, S.C. Her parents, Samuel and Patsy McLeod, were former slaves; Mary was the fifteenth of 17 children. She helped her parents on the family farm and first entered a Presbyterian mission school when she was 11 years old. Later she attended Scotia Seminary, a school for African American girls in Concord, N.C., on a scholarship. She graduated in 1893; there she had met some of the people with whom she would work closely.

Though she had a serious turn of mind, it did not prevent her from being a lively dancer and developing a lasting fondness for music. Dynamic and alert, she was very popular and the acknowledged leader of her classmates. After graduating from Scotia Seminary, she attended the Moody Bible Institute.

Career as an Educator

After graduation from Moody Institute, she wished to become a missionary in Africa; however, she was unable to pursue this end. She was an instructor at the Presbyterian Mission School in Mayesville in 1896 and later an instructor at Haines Institute in Augusta, Ga., in 1896-1897. While she was an instructor at Kindell Institute in Sumpter, S.C., in 1897-1898, she met Albertus Bethune, whom she later married.

Bethune began her career as an educator in earnest when she rented a two-story frame building in Daytona Beach, Fla., and began the difficult task of establishing a school for African American girls. Her school opened in October 1904, with six pupils, five girls and her own son; there was no equipment; crates were used for desks and charcoal took the place of pencils; and ink came from crushed elderberries. Thus began the Daytona Literary and

Industrial School for Training Negro Girls, in an era when most African American children received little or no education.

At first Bethune was teacher, administrator, comptroller, and custodian. Later she was able to secure a staff, many of whom worked loyally for many years. To finance and expand the school, Bethune and her pupils baked pies and made ice cream to sell to nearby construction gangs. In addition to her regular classes, Bethune organized classes for the children of turpentine workers. In these ways she satisfied her desire to serve as a missionary.

As the school at Daytona progressed, it became necessary to secure an adequate financial base. Bethune began to seek financial aid in earnest. In 1912 she interested James M. Gamble of the Proctor and Gamble Company of Cincinnati, Ohio, who contributed financially to the school and served as chairman of its board of trustees until his death.

In 1923 Bethune's school for girls merged with Cookman Institute of Jacksonville, Fla., a school for boys, and the new coeducational school became known as Bethune-Cookman Collegiate Institute, soon renamed Bethune-Cookman College. Bethune served as president of the college until her retirement as president emeritus in 1942. She remained a trustee of the college to the end of her life. By 1955 the college had a faculty of 100 and a student enrollment of over 1,000.

Other Activities

Bethune's business activities were confined to the Central Life Insurance Company of Tampa, Fla., of which she was president for several years; the Afro-American Life Insurance Company of Jacksonville, which she served as director; and the Bethune—Volusia Beach Corporation, a recreation area and housing development she founded in 1940. In addition, she wrote numerous magazine and newspaper articles and contributed chapters to several books. In 1932 she founded and organized the National Council of Negro Women and became its president; by 1955 this organization had a membership of 800,000.

Bethune gained national recognition in 1936, when President Franklin D. Roosevelt appointed her director of African American affairs in the National Youth Administration and a special adviser on minority affairs. She served for 8 years and supervised the expansion of employment opportunities and recreational facilities for African American youth throughout the United States. She also served as special assistant to the secretary of war during World War II. In the course of her government assignments she became a close friend of Eleanor Roosevelt. During her long career Bethune received many honorary degrees and awards, including the Haitian Medal of Honor and Merit (1949), the highest award of the Haitian government.

Bethune died in Daytona Beach on May 18, 1955, of a heart attack. She was buried on the campus of Bethune-Cookman College.

Further Reading

The best biography of Mrs. Bethune is Rackham Holt, *Mary McLeod Bethune* (1964). See also Catherine Owens Peare, *Mary McLeod Bethune* (1951), and Emma Gelders Sterne, *Mary McLeod Bethune* (1957). Edwin R. Embree, *13 Against the Odds* (1944), includes a chapter on Mrs. Bethune. Shorter accounts of her are in Russell L. Adams, *Great Negroes: Past and Present* (1963; 3d ed. 1969), and in Walter Christmas, ed., *Negroes in Public Affairs and Government,* vol. 1 (1966). Background studies include John Hope Franklin, *From Slavery to Freedom: A History of Negro Americans* (1947; 3d rev. ed. 1967), and Bernard Sternsher, ed., *The Negro in Depression and War: Prelude to Revolution, 1930-1945* (1969), which contains a selection by Bethune. □

Mongo Beti

Mongo Beti (born 1932) was one of the great Francophone novelists from Africa. His works satirize the French colonial world and dramatize the dilemmas of the quasi-Westernized African in acrid, sometimes ribald language and outrageous scenes.

Mongo Beti was born Alexandre Biyidi on June 30, 1932, in M'balmayo, a small village of the Beti people about 30 miles south of Yaoundé, the capital of Cameroon. At 19 he received the baccalaureate from the lycée at Yaoundé, and in 1951 he went to France on a scholarship to take advanced studies in literature, first at Aix-en-Provence and then at the Sorbonne in Paris. In 1966 he received the *agrégation ,* or teaching certificate, from the University of Paris.

While a student at Aix he wrote his first (now self-repudiated) novel, *Ville Cruelle (Cruel City),* published in 1954 under the nom de plume Eza Boto. Considered a weak novel, it demonstrates strength in its melodramatic but often compelling naïveté, and it well expresses the confusion experienced by the rural Africans crowding into the new industrial lumber and pulping town of Tanga South, "the kingdom of logs."

First Novels Reveal Anti-Imperialist Sentiments

One of the major weaknesses of *Ville Cruelle* was its long, confessional monologues, but in his second novel, *Le Pauvre Christ de Bomba* (1956; *The Poor Christ of Bomba*), Beti mastered the exclamatory monologue to indict both France and the Church through the naive musings of the acolyte Denis, assistant to the well-meaning but ever obtuse Reverend Father Superior Drumont.

Mission Terminée (1957), Beti's third novel, is possibly one of his most successful and deeply humorous works. Again, his hero is a *naïf* whose initiation into life educates the reader into African verities as seen by an African. Here, however, the young Medza, having failed at the lycée, is initiated "backwards" into the life of the relatively untouched village of Kala, where his uncle's runaway wife has fled. Sent by his own village to reclaim her, Medza learns to appreciate and then to respect the older life and, more particularly, becomes willing to accept the help of his heroic-sized "country" cousin, Zambo. Though at the novel's close the two leave Kala and even Africa for a life of wandering, Medza has discovered that "the tragedy which our nation is suffering today is that of a man left to his own devices in a world which does not belong to him, which he has not made and does not understand."

Beti's fourth novel, *Le Roi Miraculé* (1958; *King Lazarus*), confronts a powerful, pagan king with the missionary fervor of Le Guen, Drumont's vicar in the earlier years of *The Poor Christ of Bomba*. Though priding himself on being more astute and sensitive than the bumbling Drumont, Le Guen stirs up so much confusion and anger in the court of the king that the French Colonial Office has him recalled, for though Paris loves the Church it loves order and decorum much more.

Writer in Exile

Staunchly opposed to the foreign-controlled government in what was then French Cameroon, Beti moved to France. There, finding he could not support himself by writing, even with three well-received and increasingly popular novels to his credit, he turned to teaching, eventually gaining a professorship at a lycée in Rouen where he taught Latin, Greek, and French. A convinced Marxist, he refused to return to his native country even after it achieved independence in 1960. Despite professing himself anxious to visit Africa, he remained hostile to the Yaoundé regime of President Ahmadou Ahidjo. Instead, Beti remained in France with his wife and their three children, and devoted himself to teaching for more than a decade.

In 1972 Beti published a political essay critical of the Yaoundé government. Titled "*The Plundering of Cameroon,* the essay condemned Ahidjo and his officers as a puppet government of his country's former colonial rulers. The problems of decolonization would serve as the focus of the novels that Beti would once again begin to write.

In works that include *Remember Ruben* (1973) and *Perpetua and the Habit of Unhappiness* (1974), Beti turns a satirical eye upon the situation in the Cameroon, creating the fictitious dictator Baba Toura as the focus of his political satire. In *Remember Ruben,* a young orphan is take in by some villagers and befriended by a village boy. The two grow up and, though they part company for several years, eventually reunite; one as a revolutionary leader, and the other as a cast-off from an unjust society. The two characters would also serve as the subject of a 1979 work by Beti translated as *Lament for an African Pol,* which follows the effort of the two friends to start a revolt against the rule of unjust tribal chiefs. *Perpetua and the Habit of Unhappiness* also illustrates the inequities in postcolonial Cameroon through the lives of individuals, this time also depicting the lowly social status of that country's women. The novel would be adapted as a play in 1981.

Retains Focus on Political Injustice

Continuing to write from his self-imposed exile in France, Beti has woven his political concerns—particularly his concerns over continued French political influence in Cameroon—throughout his fiction. Like his novels of the 1970s and the 1980s, *L'histoire du Fou* (1994) illustrated the two economic and social levels of African society through the relationship between Zoaételeu, a provincial village elder, and his son Narcisse, who is idealistic and in search of meaning in his life. Political repression shadows each of Beti's characters in the novel's complex plot as Zoaételeu is falsely imprisoned without a trial and eventually released, only to find that his beloved son has been killed by an assassin—who turns out to be his own brother. As Robert P. Smith Jr. would note of *L'histoire du Fou* in *World Literature Today*, "Beti's reasoning, sometimes dead serious and sometimes familiarly humorous, is powerful, and his style, reminiscent of Balzac with its detailed descriptions and colorful images, and of Proust with its interminable sentences, remains superb."

Further Reading

Information on the life and work of Beti is in Gerald Moore, *Seven African Writers* (1962); Claude Wauthier, *The Literature and Thought of Modern Africa* (1964; trans. 1966); Judith Illsley Gleason, *This Africa: Novels by West Africans in English and French* (1965); A.C. Brench, *The Novelists' Inheritance in French Africa* (1967); and Wilfred Cartey, *Whispers from a Continent: The Literature of Contemporary Black Africa* (1969). See also the chapter by Jeanette Macaulay in Cosmo Pieterse and Donald Munro, eds., *Protest and Conflict in African Literature* (1969). □

John Betjeman

Sir John Betjeman (1906-1984), Poet Laureate of Britain from 1972 to 1984, was the most popular English poet of the 20th century and a familiar personality on British television.

John Betjeman was born in London on August 28, 1906, the only child of a prosperous silverware maker of Dutch descent. A sensitive, lonely child, he knew early that he would grow up to forswear the family business in favor of poetry. He attended prep school at Highgate, London, where one of his instructors was a recent American arrival, T. S. Eliot, who proved unresponsive to the 10-year-old's poetic efforts. During his tenure at Dragon School, Oxford (1917-1920), Betjeman developed an abiding interest in architecture; he next attended Marlborough public school in Wiltshire, which he was to remember chiefly for its bullies.

He entered Magdalen College, Oxford, in 1925 and favorably impressed the great classics scholar C. M. Bowra with his knowledge of architecture, but negatively impressed his famous tutor C. S. Lewis by his academic indifference. At Oxford he struck up a lasting friendship with Evelyn Waugh and may even have served as a model for one or more of the characters in Waugh's early novels; more importantly, Betjeman cultivated at Oxford a strong aversion to sports and an equally strong inclination towards esthetics. He left Oxford in 1928 without a degree.

Early Career

Betjeman taught briefly at Heddon Court School, Hertfordshire, and then worked for a while as an insurance broker before becoming, in 1931, an assistant editor of the *Architectural Review*. That same year he published his first book of verse, *Mount Zion*. Although somewhat mannered and certainly minor, the collection was distinguished by at least one poem, "The Varsity Students' Rag," which quietly but effectively satirizes the mindless, boys-will-be-boys destructiveness of his former fellow Oxfordians.

In 1933 Betjeman became editor of the Shell series of topographical guides to Britain and married Penelope Chetwode, a writer by whom he had a son and a daughter, but who pursued her own writing career abroad for most of their married life. In 1934 he became film critic for the *Evening Standard* but was fired less than a year later for his overly enthusiastic reviews. Betjeman's second volume of verse, *Continental Dew: A Little Book of Bourgeois Verse* (1937), is undistinguished but for its foreshadowing of an attitude that was to fully surface in subsequent books: a deep-dyed distrust of "modernity" in all of its guises—its indifference to tradition, its runaway materialism, and its savaging of the landscape.

Betjeman's book titles and sub-titles are frequently thematic, as in his first book on architecture, *Ghastly Good Taste: a depressing story of the rise and fall of English architecture* (1933); it was followed by *University Chest* (1938) and then *Antiquarian Prejudice* (1939), which defines architecture for Betjeman as not mere building styles but as the total physical environment in which life is lived. His topographical writings, which celebrate actual places he loved and excoriate places he loathed, include *Vintage London* (1942), *English Cities and Small Towns* (1943), and *First and Last Loves* (1952).

Major Career

During World War II Betjeman served variously as United Kingdom press attaché to Dublin, as BBC broadcaster, and in the British Council books department. In this period he issued two volumes of verse that revealed him to be a serious poet and not a mere "versifier": *Old Lights for New Chancels* (1940) and *New Bats in Old Belfries* (1945). Although they share with most modern poetry a profound pessimism about life, these works established Betjeman as a distinctive voice and somewhat of an anomaly: in an age dominated by lyric-contemplative verse, Betjeman relied strongly on narrative, or at least anecdotal, elements; in an age of free verse, he wrote in tight metrical and stanzaic forms; in an age of poetic obfuscation, Betjeman, though not without his ambiguities, was accessible; in an age of tight Classical control of emotion, he was wistfully playful and even sentimental. In short, Betjeman was a throwback to the best-loved poets of English verse tradition—to Tennyson, Hardy, and Kipling.

In both volumes Betjeman made *humanly* evocative use of *place* (many of his poem titles are place names), reflecting the importance of topography in his work and projecting his thesis that as the landscape grows uglier the possibility of human happiness recedes. Both volumes sold well and were favorably reviewed, but Betjeman's reputation as an architecture and topography writer still outstripped his reputation as poet.

In the 1950s Betjeman continued to write prolifically on architecture and topography, produced a book of verse—*A Few Late Chrysanthemums* (1954), and did a year of BBC broadcasts (1957). Most important, he published his *Collected Poems* (1958), which was a huge seller, an astounding fact considering normal public indifference toward poetry and the consequent well-known indigence of almost all poets.

His popularity was enhanced by a blank-verse autobiographical poem, *Summoned by Bells* (1960), a quiet, introspective account of his first 22 years, and by two more verse collections, *High and Low* (1966) and *A Nip in the Air* (1975). Sandwiched between, in 1969 Betjeman was knighted and in 1972 he was appointed Poet Laureate of Britain.

Reputation and Last Years

His public acclaim notwithstanding, Betjeman had his detractors among poets, critics, and scholars, many of whom found him shallow or facile and branded him a Tory traditionalist or an English provincial or a hopeless antiquarian. His defenders and admirers, however, included Edmund Wilson, W. H. Auden (who dedicated *The Age of Anxiety* to Betjeman), and Philip Larkin.

A London journalist once described Betjeman as "looking like a highly intelligent muffin; a plump, rumpled man with luminous, soft eyes, a chubby face topped with wisps of white hair and imparting a distinct air of absentmindedness . . . [with] an eager manner, a kind of old-fashioned courtesy and a sudden, schoolboy laugh which crumples his face like a paper bag."

Poor health curtailed Betjeman's writing efforts in his later years, but what energies he had were dedicated to his continuing campaign for the preservation of historic buildings. After suffering from Parkinson's disease of a number of years, Betjeman had a stroke in 1981 and a heart attack in 1983. He died on May 19, 1984, at his home in Trebetherick, Cornwall, attended by his companion of many years, Lady Elizabeth Cavendish.

Further Reading

The most helpful critical sources are W. H. Auden's introduction to Betjeman's *Slick But Not Streamlined* (1947); Bernard Bergonzi's "Culture and Mr. Betjeman," *Twentieth Century* (February 1959); and Frank Kermode's "Henry Miller and John Betjeman," *Puzzles & Epiphanies* (1962). The best biographical sources are Betjeman's own *Summoned by Bells* (1960), C. M. Bowra's *Memories 1898-1939* (1967), John Press's *John Betjeman* (1974), and an album of photographs, caricatures, and ephemera titled *John Betjeman: A Life in Pictures* by Bevis Hillier (1985).

Additional Sources

Press, John, *John Betjeman,* Harlow Eng.: Published for the British Council by Longman Group, 1974.
Taylor-Martin, Patrick, *John Betjeman, his life and work,* London: Allen Lane, 1983. □

Bruno Bettelheim

Bruno Bettelheim (1903-1990), a controversial Austrian-born American psychoanalyst and educational psychologist, pioneered in the application of psychoanalysis to the treatment of emotionally-disturbed children

On Aug. 28, 1903, Bruno Bettelheim was born in Vienna. He received his doctorate from the University of Vienna in 1938. When Austria fell to Hitler, Bettelheim was sent to a concentration camp, but was able to go to the United States in 1939, becoming a citizen five years later.

During his formative years in Vienna, Bettelheim was influenced by World War I, the Bolshevik Revolution, and Sigmund Freud. Like other Viennese intellectuals, he could not accept the optimism and complacency of preexisting Western European ideals. In their search for new pathways,

his generation chose between the new social changes reflected in Russian communism and later National Socialism, and the excitement of the new psychoanalysis pioneered by Freud. Bettelheim opted for psychoanalysis, yet his work always reflected interest in the impact of social systems on individuals.

Achieved Fame in the United States

Bettelheim married Trude Weinfeld in 1941, and they had three children. Except for two years at Rockford College in Illinois, he worked principally at the University of Chicago, where in 1963 he became Rouly professor of education and professor of psychology and psychiatry.

Bettelheim won fame from his books and articles in both the scientific and popular press. His passionate, intensely personal, and anecdotal style drew some criticism from the scientific community, though few questioned his talent for conceptualization and for developing provocative, imaginative ideas.

His major contributions came from his work at the Sonia Shankman Orthogenic School of the University of Chicago, a residential treatment institution for rehabilitating children with severe emotional disturbances, where he became principal in 1944. In *Love Is Not Enough* (1950) and *Truants from Life* (1955), he described the school's educational and therapeutic philosophy, largely his own creation. These ideas are elaborated, with case material, in *The Empty Fortress: Infantile Autism and the Birth of the Self* (1967). He viewed the behavior of severely withdrawn children as

resulting from overwhelmingly negative parents interacting with infants' susceptibility during critical early stages in their psychological development. The children hold themselves responsible for external catastrophes and withdraw into fantasy worlds as if to prevent further destructive behavior. Bettelheim likened this destructive dehumanizing of a child to the effects of Nazi concentration camps on the inmates, deriving many of these ideas from his own experience, described in *The Informed Heart* (1960). His treatment method involved an unconditional acceptance by the school's staff of all such children's behavior. For these theoretical and therapeutic views he had followers and critics. For example, Bettelheim's assumptions on autism have since been dismissed. It is widely acknowledged that autistic and emotionally-disturbed children are not the same.

A popular speaker, Bettelheim traveled widely in his work. *The Children of the Dream* (1969) reports his studies on an Israeli kibbutz of the methods and results of communal child rearing, which he felt had important implications for American education. His 1976 book, *The Uses of Enchantment,* was a popular psychoanalytical look at fairy tales.

Controversial Even in Death

In 1990 Bettelheim committed suicide. Soon after, allegations arose that he had falsified many of his credentials and had been physically abusive to the children in his care. Many feel his suicide is proof that the allegations were true, but others staunchly defend Bettelheim's work. Regardless of which interpretation is correct, Bettelheim's impact cannot be denied.

Further Reading

Pollak, Richard, *The Creation of Dr. B: A Biography of Bruno Bettelheim* (1997).
Sutton, Nina, *Bettelheim, A Life and Legacy* (1996). □

Ugo Betti

The Italian playwright Ugo Betti (1892-1953) was one of the major figures of Italian theater in the 20th century. In his plays the question of guilt, justice, and redemption is of central concern.

Ugo Betti was born on Feb. 4, 1892, in Camerino. He was educated in Parma, where his family had moved. During World War I he fought as a volunteer artillery officer. After the war he took a degree in law and was a judge in the court of Parma until 1930, when he was transferred to Rome. In 1941 Betti received the Italian Academy's theater award. Following World War II he took a position at the library of the Ministry of Justice in Rome, which allowed him to devote more time to his writing. In 1949 he won the award of the Istituto Nazionale del Dramma, and in 1950 he received the Premio Roma. In the same year he became counselor of the court of appeal in Rome. Betti died in Rome on June 9, 1953.

Although Betti wrote poetry and fiction, his special interest lay in drama. A conspicuous part of his dramatic production is concerned with the psychology of the sexes and the study of psychological situations. Although some of these plays have naturalistic settings, there is almost throughout an attempt at symbolic rendition. This is noticeable in his first play *La padrona* (The Proprietress), given in 1927 at Rome's Teatro Odescalchi, and is stressed more in later plays of this type (*La casa sull'acqua,* 1928, The House on the Water), although there is an occasional return to realism (*Un albergo sul porto,* 1930, Harbor Hotel; *Marito e moglie,* 1942, Husband and Wife). Plays which, in a fablelike setting, attempt to prove timeless higher truths form another part of his drama: *L'isola meravigliosa* (1929, Wonderful Island) and *Irene innocente* (1946, Innocent Irene). The surrealist farce *Diluvio* (1931, Flood) satirizes middle-class values, a theme taken up again in a later trilogy: *Una bella domenica di settembre* (1935, A Beautiful Sunday in September), *I nostri sogni* (1936, Our People's Dreams), and *Il paese delle vacanze* (1937, Vacation Land).

Betti's main concern, the question of justice, of guilt and its atonement, appears as the central issue for the first time in *Frana allo scalo Nord* (1932, Landslide). During a court inquiry into an accident which caused the death of some laborers and a girl, the circle of those responsible becomes wider and wider. In the end it is humanity itself that is on trial, and Betti's judgment is that all men are guilty. This concept of a collective guilt, of corruption in the soul of every man, and of justice conceived as a transcendental force appears again and again (*Notte in casa del ricco,* 1938, Night in the Rich Man's House; *Ispezione,* 1942, Inspection). *Corruzione al palazzo di giustizia* (1944, Corruption in the Palace of Justice), perhaps the best of Betti's plays, carries his obsession with the theme to the ultimate: corruption has entered the very halls of justice, and an investigator investigates those that usually sit in judgment. Although in the end the truly guilty person confesses, again by implication all of humanity is involved, and the condemnation therefore is of all.

Further Reading

Biographical and critical material on Betti is available in two volumes of his plays: *Two Plays: Frana allo scalo Nord, L'aiuola bruciata,* edited and with an introduction by G.H. McWilliam (1965), and *Three Plays on Justice: Landslide, Struggle till Dawn, The Fugitive,* translated and with an introduction by G.H. McWilliam (1964). See also Lander Mac-Clintock, *The Age of Pirandello* (1951). □

Joseph Beuys

The German artist Joseph Beuys (1921-1986) communicated intense emotion in his art using a wide variety of media in drawings, sculpture, and performances.

Joseph Beuys was born May 12, 1921, in Krefeld on the German/Dutch border near his parents' home in Cleves. The family moved from here to the nearby Rindern where his father and uncle owned a flour and fodder business in 1930. The geography of this border region of the lower Rhine valley left a permanent impression. Childhood memories of the common local wildlife—hare, stag, and swans—were to take on significant meanings in his mature art. As a child Beuys was fascinated with the role of the shepherd and carried around a large staff. Above all, an interest in science and the feeling of daily life in this particular geographic and historical setting formed the foundation of his artistic imagery. Beuys was educated in local schools with a concentration in natural science. He knew the local sculptor Achilles Moortgat and was aware of the work of Wilhelm Lehmbruck, which gave him his first impression of the potential power of sculptural form.

Early in World War II Beuys was inducted to serve as a radio operator and then as a pilot, but he was able to continue his studies intermittently. By 1943 he had begun making sketches based on his experiences and had come to the realization that science would not be his profession. One significant experience of the war years occurred in 1943. Beuys's plane was shot down while he was flying behind enemy lines in the Crimea. He landed in a region between the Russian and German lines populated by Tartar nomads. They discovered him unconscious and saved his life by wrapping his frozen body in fat and felt to conserve heat. The regenerative power of these natural materials was

to be explored in many later sculptures made of these non-traditional materials.

After the war Beuys exhibited drawings with a local group of artists in Cleves. In the same year he entered the Düsseldorf Academy of Art, becoming a student of the sculptor Ewald Mataré. His early sculptures were of natural elements—*Crystal* (1949) and *Moon* (1950)—but others such as *Sleds* (1949) and *Gas Cellar* (1954) begin the exploration of themes that dominated his later work based on traumatic war experiences. In these same years Beuys continued to produce a large number of drawings of organic matter, plants, animals, and myths.

From 1954 through the late 1950s Beuys experienced a personal crisis during which he withdrew to the farm of close friends and patrons where he worked in the fields and barns. During this period his concept of art coalesced and he found a way to communicate the social and personal values with which he would be concerned in the succeeding decades. A major installation drawn from work of this period on the theme of Auschwitz at the Hessisches Landesmuseum in Darmstadt is called *Concentration Camp Essen* (1958). It displays various materials including a picture of a starved and crippled girl, charred remains, a dead rat, small bottles of poison, lengths of blutwurst sausage, and electric plates with blocks of fat.

The use of organic materials such as fat relates the whole to the natural world. The transformability of fat from solid to liquid at different temperatures makes it an analogy for natural change and regeneration while at the same time it bears memories of crematoria. His rescue by the Tartar nomads had made fat seem an intensely meaningful material that could communicate a range of deeply personal and at the same time universal meanings. Beeswax shares the property of having different forms at different temperatures and was used by Beuys, along with honey, in his art. This complex intertwining of relationships and meanings is characteristic of Beuys's mature work, as is the use of unusual organic materials and the seemingly informal organization of the whole.

His youthful fascination with the shepherd was transformed into the idea of the artist as a shaman, a point of contact with the spiritual roots that nourish human existence. Like a shaman, Beuys wore emblems of his role, most particularly a flat brimmed felt hat that became his most identifiable characteristic. Beuys also developed the theme that every human is a sculptor, by molding thoughts, shaping them into words, and then expressing these as social ideas.

In 1962 Beuys was appointed professor at the Düsseldorf Academy of Art and in the same year became associated with the Fluxus Group. These artists, mainly musicians, were interested in breaking down the traditional categories of art and in bringing it closer to the audience through performance. Among other members were the video artist Nam June Paik, Charlotte Moorman, Wolf Vostell, and George Maciunas.

Beuys's performances, which he called "actions," were intensely memorable, puzzling landmarks in his art. In *The Chief* (1963-1964), Beuys lay for nine hours wrapped in felt with two dead hares, the only sound an occasional intense cry as from a stag. Another memorable action from this decade was *How To Explain Paintings to a Dead Hare* (1965) in which Beuys, head covered with honey and gold leaf, carried a dead hare through an exhibit of his pictures and then sat talking to the hare about them. For Beuys this action was about the source of ideas and how the intellect can be deadly in politics and education. His actions had the feel of mythic communications whose impact was hard to explain but intensely felt by observers. Multiple editions based on these performances gave them some permanence, such as the 1970 letterpress edition of a photograph of *The Chief*. Postcards, objects, films, and records were all issued in multiple editions. Images developed in actions often touched on trauma points of the culture as a whole and became increasingly political during the 1970s.

In the late 1960s, a time when students were actively involved in political issues, Beuys was accused of contributing to the disruption of the Düsseldorf Academy. In 1971 he invited students to his class who had been denied entry, with the argument that education should not be restricted to those who already have achieved competency. His activities culminated in his dismissal in October of 1972, and the start of litigation that was not resolved until his vindication in 1978. He was deeply involved in political issues and in working toward the creation of open educational opportunities, a Free International University.

Major exhibitions devoted to Beuys were organized in the 1970s, such as in 1979 at the Guggenheim Museum in New York. Enigmatic, powerful, mythic, Beuys's art defied boundaries and explanations. Direct experience of his art communicated intuitively by touching universal areas of shared imagery and memory. He died in Düsseldorf January 23, 1986, of heart failure after a long illness.

Further Reading

The catalogue to the Joseph Beuys exhibition at the Solomon R. Guggenheim Museum in New York (1979) by Caroline Tisdall contains an introductory biography and explanations of the many works in that show with over 500 photographs and a wealth of information on Beuys's associates and activities. *Joseph Beuys, Life and Works* by Götz Adriani, Winfried Konnertz, and Karin Thomas (Cologne, 1973, repr. Barron's 1979) presents a year by year chronology and has an extensive bibliography. *Joseph Beuys Drawings,* catalogue of an exhibition at the Victoria and Albert Museum (London, 1983), is devoted exclusively to an extensive survey of Beuys's drawings.

Additional Sources

Stachelhaus, Heiner, *Joseph Beuys,* New York: Abbeville Press, 1991. □

Aneurin Bevan

Aneurin Bevan (1897-1960), Labour minister of health and housing between 1945 and 1951, was responsible for the creation of the British National Health Service. Throughout his life he fought to make Britain an independent democratic socialist nation.

Aneurin Bevan, born in 1897 in Tredegar, Wales, grew up steeped in the traditions of Welsh miners' radicalism: self-help organizations, religious dissent, trade unionism, and socialism. Unprecedented industrial unrest marked Bevan's youth. Like others of his class, his formal education ended at age 14, when he started to work in the mines. He soon became an activist and, initially, a supporter of syndicalism. An opponent of World War I, he avoided service and immersed himself in socialist and labor politics, winning a miners' scholarship to the radical Central Labour College in London.

In 1920 Bevan returned to Tredegar and to intermittent unemployment. He entered politics in 1922 when he was elected to the Tredegar Urban District Council. The early 1920s were spent dealing with the problems of long term unemployment and miners' demands for greater control over their work. During the 1926 general strike Bevan was active on miners' relief committees and became a prominent figure at union meetings. The miners' defeat caused Bevan to look more favorably upon electoral politics to achieve working-class control and socialism.

Member of Parliament

Elected Labour representative for Ebbw Vale, Bevan entered Parliament in 1929 at the time of the doomed Labour government of Ramsay MacDonald. Bevan and other left wing politicians pressed for more resolute economic action to deal with the depression and unemployment. In 1931 he criticized the formation of a "national" coalition government nominally under MacDonald but controlled by Conservatives.

From his very first years in Parliament Bevan articulated a lifelong position: he was committed to the Labour Party, but was highly critical of it—often volubly so—urging it to take more radical and socialist stands. He did not favor splitting up the party or consider becoming a Communist, but he wanted the party to be open to a wide spectrum of views. A spellbinding speaker who did not hesitate to use strong language, in the 1930s he criticized the government's and the Labour Party's inability to take a firm stand on the threat of fascism. He bemoaned Labour's failure to provide clear support to the Republicans in the Spanish Civil War and supported the formation of a popular front to unite Communists, socialists, and Labourites against fascism and the national government's appeasement of Hitler. In the late 1930s, along with other figures on the left of the Labour Party such as Stafford Cripps, Harold Laski, and Ellen Wilkinson, Bevan also was active in an independent Left publication, *Tribune*. Bevan's 1934 marriage to Jennie Lee, a Scottish socialist and Labour politician in her own right, provided emotional and political support in those troubled years.

World War II did not quiet Bevan's criticism. After Winston Churchill took over, Bevan was a loyal supporter of the wartime coalition. But he did not believe that the war should end all political discussion. Accordingly, he criticized Churchill for not forming a second front to aid the Russians and castigated the Labour Party for not pressing hard enough for socialist domestic policies. These opinions he expressed both in Parliament and in the *Tribune,* whose editor he became in 1942.

As the war drew to a close, Bevan argued that Britain should not participate in dividing the world into hostile Communist and non-Communist camps. European nations, particularly, should be free to form independent, democratic socialist governments. He also pressed for the continuation of public control of vital industries and the development of a comprehensive system of social services. Labour's 1945 landslide victory brought Bevan into the cabinet as minister of health and housing. This, combined with his membership on the Labour Party executive since 1944, placed him in a key position to shape the nature of post-war Britain.

National Health Service

The creation of the National Health Service probably was Bevan's greatest achievement, brought about by his unswerving commitment to a comprehensive, free, and high quality service and his sophisticated ability to cut through knotty political and administrative problems. Encountering strong opposition—particularly from doctors

fearing that they would be turned into civil servants with little professional independence (and lower incomes)—the Health Service did not go into effect until 1948, but it soon had 93.1 percent of the population participating and doctors' general cooperation. Bevan was less successful in the area of housing. He was plagued by financial and material shortages and refused to compromise quality. Nevertheless, 1,016,349 permanent houses were built between 1945 and 1951.

From 1945 to 1950 Labour ministers worked together, notwithstanding debates and disagreements between the left and right wings of the party. The atmosphere changed in 1951 when an ambitious and costly arms program was launched, part of the growing Cold War. To fund this program, the new chancellor of the exchequer, Hugh Gaitskell, proposed charging fees for spectacles and dentures. Bevan believed that any dilution of the principle of a totally free and comprehensive service set a dangerous precedent. He particularly opposed the introduction of fees to fund the Cold War. When fees were imposed anyway, Bevan resigned from the government, where he held the post of minister of labour.

In late 1951 Conservatives came to power, and for the rest of Bevan's life—he died in 1960—the Labour Party was in opposition. Bevan served as the leader of a left wing faction, the "Bevanites," arguing against rearmament and for an independent socialist foreign policy in Europe and the Third World, in opposition to the more conservative "Gaitskellites." The frequently acrimonious contest between the two groups was carried out through *Tribune,* in the press and Parliament, and on the national executive of the Labour Party. Bevan had the support of constituency parties, but was opposed by many important trade union leaders. Bevan shaped and often dominated Labour politics at this time, but Gaitskell and the moderates triumphed.

In his last years, however, Bevan and Gaitskell united to argue against the Conservative handling of the Suez crisis. He also backed Gaitskell in arguing that Britain should not abandon the hydrogen bomb. Bevan had fought to set limits on Britain's development of nuclear weapons, but did not join many of his followers in the growing antinuclear movement. He died, therefore, as he had lived, fighting hard for the things he believed in even if it meant alienating followers and friends.

Further Reading

A comprehensive two volume biography is Michael Foot's *Aneurin Bevan* (1962, 1973). Jennie Lee's autobiographical memoir *This Great Journey* (1963) and her *My Life with Nye* (1981) are also useful. Bevan published one book of essays, *In Place of Fear* (1952). Two good general works are Ralph Miliband, *Parliamentary Socialism* (1972) and Kenneth O. Morgan, *Labour in Power* (1984).

Additional Sources

Campbell, John, *Aneurin Bevan and the mirage of British socialism,* New York: Norton, 1987.
Campbell, John, *Nye Bevan and the mirage of British socialism,* London: Weidenfeld and Nicolson, 1987. □

James Luther Bevel

James Luther Bevel (born 1936) was a civil rights activist of the 1960s who aligned himself with Martin Luther King, Jr.

James Luther Bevel was born in the farming community of Ittabena, Mississippi, on October 19, 1936. This civil rights activist, minister, lyricist, and human rights advocate gained a national reputation for both his impassioned activism and managerial efficiency as one of Martin Luther King's top lieutenants in the freedom struggles of the 1960s. Bevel served briefly in the United States Naval Reserve from 1954 to 1955. He received a B.A. degree from the American Baptist Theology Seminary in 1961. He married another civil rights activist, Diane Judith Nash, and had two children: Sherrillyn Jill and Douglas John Bevel. Ordained in the Baptist ministry in 1959, Bevel pastored a church in Dixon, Tennessee, from 1959 to 1961.

Civil Rights Movement

James Bevel was philosophically committed to the notion that religion was part of the larger human rights struggle and that the church should serve as an institution of social change. He was chairman of the Nashville Student Movement from 1960 to 1961. In that same year, he was one of the founding members of the Student Non-violent Coordinating Committee (SNCC) and held the position of Mississippi field secretary. Interested not only in preaching "the good word," but also dedicated to its permanence, he helped to create the Mississippi Free Press in 1960 to publish various religious and social-action pamphlets. In addition, he headed the civil action programs of the Albany Movement in Georgia to fight racism and discrimination.

As one of several young activists working with Martin Luther King, Jr., Bevel was made head of direct action and became a youth training specialist in the Southern Christian Leadership Conference (SCLC), which he joined in 1961. Within SCLC his organizational skills and "we-can-do-it" spirit allowed him to evolve into one of its most prominent young leaders. In 1963 he was asked to go to Birmingham, Alabama, as chief organizer of the Birmingham Movement of the SCLC, and in 1965 he became its project director.

Bevel, always involved in several groups at once, helped to sponsor the Council of Federated Organizations (COFO) from 1962 to 1964. This group created a statewide coalition of civil rights groups, including SCLC, SNCC, and the Congress of Racial Equality (CORE). This cooperative effort was unique in its attempts to help the Mississippi Freedom Democratic Party in registering Blacks to vote and making them politically active and socially aware.

In 1965, when the world turned its attention to the violent response of Birmingham, Alabama, to peaceful Black protest, James L. Bevel was there directing the campaign which eventually led to the Voting Rights Act of 1965, which opened up the political process to Blacks throughout the South. Always distinctive in his informal denim clothing,

shaved head, and skull-cap, Bevel went to Chicago in 1966 as King's advance man for SCLC's ill-fated national opening of the housing campaign. In Chicago Bevel was program director of the Westside Christian Parish, where he had extensive dealings with gangs, recalcitrant political leaders, and a rapidly growing antagonism between older, more moderate Black leaders on one hand and young militants on the other. Bevel, who probably conducted as many nonviolence seminars as any single activist, used his skills in demanding that the Blackstone Rangers (a local gang) eschew violence as an avenue toward social change. He even went so far as to show a film on the 1965 Watts Riot in an attempt to forestall violent confrontations with Chicago's police during demonstrations. Though respected and somewhat revered, the young people of Chicago were not as receptive to Bevel's message as his southern audiences.

Composer of Freedom Songs

A man of many talents, James L. Bevel was also noted for his lyrical abilities. As a composer of freedom songs, Bevel's most popular works were: "Dod-Dog" (1959), "Why Was a Darky Born" (1961), and "I Know We'll Meet Again" (1969). This last song is a sentimental testament to Bevel's leader, friend, and mentor, the late Martin Luther King, Jr. With King when he was shot in 1968, Bevel saw his leader gunned down. James Earl Ray was the man arrested, indicted, and convicted of King's murder. Bevel believed that Ray was innocent. He even went to the jail-house and told him so, even though Ray rejected his help and refused to let him into his cell. Bevel told Ray that King was assassinated by capitalists threatened by King's mobilization of the poor or by the military-industrial complex which was aghast at King's denunciation of the Vietnam War and his perceived left wing shift.

Influenced King's Views on Vietnam

Bevel's views on Ray and a possible conspiracy created consternation among his friends and many of King's followers. Yet it was Bevel who convinced King of the connection between the denial of civil rights in America and the war in Vietnam, as well as the plight of the poor world-wide. Bevel actually jarred King's thinking when he left his position as program director at SCLC to become executive director of the Spring Mobilization Committee to End the War in Vietnam in early 1967. Spring sought to create a national anti-war crusade and, after King had denounced the war, was eventually successful in having him address an anti-war rally that Bevel organized in New York.

Bevel was certainly one of the most influential, though least known, civil rights activists. Martin Luther King, Jr., would not have achieved many of his successes had it not been for men and women like James and Diane Bevel. As one of King's most effective front-men and as a dedicated worker who believed in direct-action, Bevel was a dynamic symbol of the new generation of leaders which included Andrew Young, Jesse Jackson, C.T. Vivian, Hosea Williams, and many others of both local and national prominence. Although not as well-known as some of these, Bevel's civil rights record did not go unnoticed. In 1963 he received the Peace Award from the War Resisters League and in 1965 was awarded the prestigious Rosa Parks Award by the SCLC.

Later Years

Following King's death, Bevel left the SCLC after unsuccessful efforts to refocus the organization's priorities on education, international arms reduction, and a retrial of King's accused assassin. He wrote and spoke extensively on nonviolent theology, continued to believe in Ray's innocence, and founded Students for Education and Economic Development (SEED).

By 1980 Bevel's political leanings had shifted to the right and he campaigned for Ronald Reagan. Four years later he ran unsuccessfully as a Republican for the House of Representatives from Chicago and, in 1992, was the vice-presidential candidate on the Lyndon LaRouche ticket. Bevel's association with Louis Farrahkan led in 1995 to his participation in the National Day of Atonement/Million Man March movement which encouraged African American males to rededicate themselves as husbands, sons, and fathers.

Further Reading

James Luther Bevel is not the subject of any single biography. He is mentioned, noted, referred to, and quoted in almost every book on the civil rights movement, on CORE, SCLC, and SNCC, as well as most works on Martin Luther King, Jr. General information about him can be found in the following works: *Who's Who Among Black Americans*; Gerold Frank, *An American Death* (1973); Stephen B. Oates, *Let the Trumpet Sound* (1982); August Meier & Elliott Rudwick, *CORE: A Study of the Civil Rights Movement 1942-1968* (1973); and Clayborne Carson, *In Struggle: SNCC and the Black Awakening of the 1960's* (1981).

Limited information on Bevel's activities can also be found online at http://www.libertynet.org/~wda/JLB.HTML.(July 29, 1997). □

William Henry Beveridge

The English economist and social reformer William Henry Beveridge, 1st Baron Beveridge of Tuggal (1879-1963), authored the Beveridge Report, which advocated cradle-to-grave social security legislation in Great Britain following World War II.

William Beveridge was born in Bengal, India, on March 5, 1879, the son of an Englishman employed in the Indian civil service. Educated at Oxford, Beveridge took firsts in mathematics and classics. He then studied law, but he found the prospect of following a legal career lacking in challenge. Instead he accepted an appointment as subwarden of Toynbee Hall, a settlement house in the East End of London.

Beveridge was soon lecturing and writing lead articles dealing with social issues for the *Morning Post*. These led to his appointment in 1909 as director of labor exchanges and head of the employment department of the Board of Trade. While in this post he played a leading role in the creation of a system of labor exchanges and a system of unemployment insurance. His first book was *Unemployment: A Problem of Industry* (1909). During World War I he served in several key posts dealing with manpower and food-rationing programs. He was knighted in 1919 and appointed permanent secretary of the Ministry of Food the same year.

Beveridge became director of the London School of Economics and Political Science in 1919, and when he left in 1937 to become master of University College, Oxford, the London School had a worldwide reputation. During World War II he served his government in various capacities relating to manpower problems. In 1941 he was named chairman of the Inter-Departmental Committee on Social Insurance and Allied Services. Late in 1942 the famous Beveridge Report was made public and became the basis for the comprehensive social security legislation adopted in the following years.

Beveridge was elected member of Parliament for Berwick in 1944 but was defeated in the general election less than a year later. He was elevated to a barony in 1946 and was an active participant in the House of Lords.

One of the hallmarks of Lord Beveridge's work was a strong commitment to applied methods of social research. He served as president of the Royal Statistical Society from 1941 to 1943 and of the Institute of Statisticians from 1948 until his death at Oxford on March 16, 1963.

Further Reading

Beveridge's autobiography, *Power and Influence* (1953), contains documents, excerpts from his articles and speeches, and a selected bibliography of his published work, giving the reader insight into both his public and private life. Janet P. Beveridge, his coworker and wife, gives an excellent picture in *Beveridge and His Plan* (1954). Background works which discuss Beveridge include Walford Johnson, John Whyman, and George Wykes, *A Short Economic and Social History of Twentieth Century Britain* (1967); W. N. Medlicott, *Contemporary England, 1914-1964* (1967); and Gertrude Williams, *The Coming of the Welfare State* (1967).

Additional Sources

Harris, Josae, *William Beveridge: a biography,* Oxford Eng.: Clarendon Press, 1977.

Mair, Philip Beveridge, *Shared enthusiasm: the story of Lord and Lady Beveridge,* Windlesham, Surrey: Ascent Books, 1982. □

Robert Beverley

Robert Beverley (ca. 1673-1722) is noted for "The History and Present State of Virginia," the first extensive analysis of Virginia's political and social development.

R obert Beverley, second son of Maj. Robert and Mary Beverley, was born in Middlesex County, Va. His father had emigrated from Yorkshire, England, about 1663 and had become a leading tobacco planter, attorney, and militia officer. Young Robert, schooled in England, inherited his father's plantation and 6,000 acres from two half brothers. He began public life as a scrivener for the secretary of state while studying law and Virginia politics. In 1697 he married Ursula Byrd, the 16-year-old daughter of William Byrd. She died in child-birth the next year, leaving an only son, William. Beverley never remarried.

Beverley held important posts as clerk for king and Queen County and clerk of the House of Burgesses. In 1699, 1700-1702, and 1705-1706 he represented Jamestown in the House. His unrelenting quest for land led to a lawsuit, necessitating a voyage to England in 1703, where he unsuccessfully appealed his case. Writing caustic letters home, he attacked Virginia's ruling clique as his father had done before him. He accused Governor Francis Nicholson and the surveyor of customs of scheming against the colony's liberties. Beverley's quarrelsomeness, despite his concern for Virginia's welfare, cost him his clerkship of King and Queen County. With his political position undermined, he was rarely active again in public life and after 1715 retired to his plantation, Beverley Park. Though he continued to acquire land, he remained unpretentious, leading a quiet life devoted to reading and studying nature.

While in London, Beverley had read John Oldmixon's history of British North America in manuscript. Appalled by its errors, he wrote *The History and Present State of Virginia* (1705), which appeared in print 3 years ahead of

Oldmixon's account. In the original edition (which was also translated into French) Beverley combined shrewd insights into the Virginia of his day, sharp comments about the colony's leaders, and vivid descriptions of the natural world, all written with an engaging enthusiasm for his native land. Though a section on Virginia's early history is cursory and at times inaccurate, the book as a whole remains important. Beverley drew on John Smith's *General History of Virginia* but sketched the colony's development to 1704, incorporating valuable observations of his own. The author's descriptive powers are best revealed in the section on the culture of Native Americans in Virginia. This sympathetic account presents the Native Americans "in their simple State of Nature, and in their enjoyment of Plenty, without the Curse of Labour," an existence which Beverley himself appeared to envy.

In his last years Beverley revised but did not improve his volume, eliminating controversial comments but sacrificing the original verve. The new edition was published in 1722, the same year his compilation of the local laws, entitled *An Abridgement of the Public Laws of Virginia . . . ,* appeared. Beverley probably did not see either edition in print, as he died on April 21, 1722.

Further Reading

While there is no full-length biography of Beverley, an excellent introductory sketch appears in Louis B. Wright's edition of Beverley's *The History and Present State of Virginia* (repr. 1947). Louis B. Wright, *The First Gentlemen of Virginia: Intellectual Qualities of the Early Colonial Ruling Class* (1940), gives a sympathetic and lively account of Beverley and his contemporaries. Genealogical data are in John McGill, *The Beverley Family of Virginia: Descendants of Major Robert Beverley (1641-1687) and Allied Families* (1956). Valuable for an understanding of the historical background are Philip Alexander Bruce, *Social Life of Virginia in the Seventeenth Century* (1907; 2d ed. 1927), and Thomas J. Wertenbaker, *Patrician and Plebeian in Virginia* (1910) and *The Planters of Colonial Virginia* (1922). □

Ernest Bevin

The career of Ernest Bevin (1881-1951), English trade union leader and Labour politician, is often taken to symbolize the political rise of sections of the working class in 20th-century Britain.

E rnest Bevin was born on March 9, 1881, in Bristol, the son of poor, working-class parents. After finishing elementary school in Bristol, Bevin earned a precarious living in various manual jobs and was introduced to politics via the Social Democratic Federation (SDF), the Marxist party. He organized the dockers and transport workers and from 1910 to 1921 led the Dockers Union. Through his union activities Bevin became involved in national politics; his brilliant advocacy at a commission of inquiry on dock conditions in 1920 led to greatly improved conditions for the dockers and national recognition for Bevin.

The noted historian A. J. P. Taylor has bracketed Bevin at this stage of his career with J. H. Thomas, the leader of the National Union of Railwaymen. They were both outstanding union leaders of a new type. Though aggressively working-class in character, they were no longer willing merely to resist. Nor would they put off improvement till the distant dawn of socialism. They bargained with the employers as equals, displaying equal or greater skill, and they never forgot that compromise was their ultimate aim, whether with a strike or preferably without.

Bevin's most important contribution to modern Britain was as creator and general secretary of the Transport and General Workers Union from 1921 to 1940. Forging a national force out of scattered, locally organized, occupationally divided workers was a major achievement; in time, the T&GWU became the largest union in Britain.

In the late 1930s Bevin opposed George Lansbury and other pacifists in the Labour party and argued in favor of rearmament. When he entered Parliament in 1940, Bevin became a key figure in the wartime coalition as minister of labor and national service (1940-1945). Without him the Churchill government could not have achieved the levels of wartime production necessary to continue the war.

After the war Bevin served as secretary of state for foreign affairs (1945-1951) and was lord privy seal for a brief period in 1951. In spite of his controversial handling of the Palestine situation, he is generally regarded as a great foreign secretary. Perhaps this accolade springs from surprise that Bevin, a Labour minister, did not depart radically from traditional British policies in foreign affairs. He died in 1951.

Further Reading

The best source for Bevin's career is the uncompleted biography by Alan Bullock, *The Life and Times of Ernest Bevin* (1960). The two volumes so far published not only deal comprehensively with Bevin but also set him in the context of changing British society. Bullock's work is a fundamental source of 20th-century British social history. There is a useful biography by Francis Williams, *Ernest Bevin: Portrait of a Great Englishman* (1952). See also Sir Trevor Evans, *Bevin of Britain* (1946). To get the feel of Bevin's almost brutal power of argument and his handling of Labour party audiences, one should look at the Report of the Annual Conference of the Labour Party in 1931. A man like Bevin, whose strength lay in negotiation, organization, and domination of audiences in the labor movement rather than in originality of ideas, is best studied through others' reactions to him rather than through his own speeches and writings.

Additional Sources

Bullock, Alan, *Ernest Bevin, foreign secretary, 1945-1951,* Oxford Oxfordshire; New York: Oxford University Press, 1985, 1983.
Stephens, Mark, *Ernest Bevin, unskilled labourer and world statesman, 1881-1951,* Stevenage, Herts: SPA Books, 1985.
Weiler, Peter, *Ernest Bevin,* Manchester, UK; New York: Manchester University Press; distributed exclusively in the USA and Canada by St. Martin's Press, 1993. □

Homi Jehangir Bhabha

The Indian atomic scientist Homi Jehangir Bhabha (1909-1966) made contributions of fundamental importance to quantum theory. He was the first chairman of India's Atomic Energy Commission.

Homi Jehangir Bhabha was born on Oct. 30, 1909, in Bombay, where his family were wealthy Parsis, the tiny but influential Zoroastrian sect of western India. After graduating from Elphinstone College and the Royal Institute of Science in Bombay, he went to Cambridge University, receiving a doctorate in 1934. During this period he worked with Niels Bohr on the studies that led to quantum theory. Later, Bhabha worked with Walter Heitler on the cascade theory of electron showers, which was of great importance for the understanding of cosmic radiation, and he also did significant work in identifying the meson. Bhabha received early recognition for his work, being elected to the Royal Society in 1941.

Bhabha returned to India in 1940, doing research on cosmic rays at the Indian Institute of Science at Bangalore. In 1945 he became director of the Tata Institute of Fundamental Research in Bombay, which he had been instrumental in founding. He was a skilled administrator, and through his scientific eminence, wealth, and friendship with Prime

Minister Jawaharlal Nehru, he gained a dominant position in the allocation of India's scientific resources.

Bhabha became the first chairman of the Atomic Energy Commission of India in 1948. Under his guidance Indian scientists worked on the development of atomic energy, and the first atomic reactor in Asia went into operation at Trombay, Bombay, in 1956. Bhabha was chairman of the first United Nations Conference on the Peaceful Uses of Atomic Energy, held in Geneva in 1955. At that time he predicted that man would find a way to limitless industrial power through the control of nuclear fusion. He advocated international control of nuclear energy and the outlawing of atomic bombs by all countries. Bhabha was strongly opposed to the production of an atomic bomb by India, even though the country had the resources to build one, arguing that nuclear energy should be used instead to relieve the poverty and misery of India's people. He refused a post in the Indian Cabinet but was scientific adviser to Nehru and to his successor, Lal Bahadur Shastri.

Bhabha received many honorary degrees from Indian and foreign universities and was a member of numerous scientific societies, including the National Academy of Sciences in the United States. He was the author of many articles on quantum theory and cosmic rays. Bhabha was killed, at the height of his prestige in the Indian scientific and political world, in an airplane crash in Switzerland on Jan. 24, 1966.

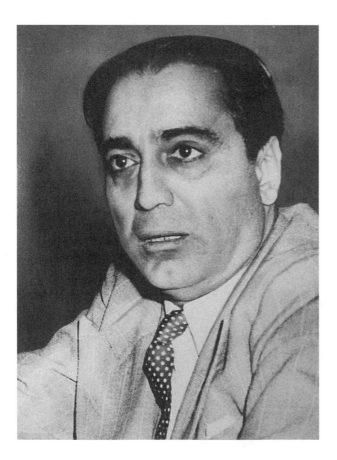

Further Reading

Although there is no book-length biography of Bhabha, there is an excellent account of his life and work in Jagit Singh, *Some Eminent Indian Scientists* (1966). For readers interested in Indian science generally, the Press Institute of India, *Science in India's Future* (1969), is an anthology of articles.

Additional Sources

Anderson, Robert S., *Building scientific institutions in India: Saha and Bhabha,* Montreal: Centre for Developing-Area Studies, McGill University, 1975. □

Swami Bhaktivedanta Prabhupada

Swami Bhaktivedanta Prabhupada (1896-1977) was a Hindu religious teacher who at the age of 69 came to the United States where he taught the practice of devotion to Krishna and founded the International Society for Krishna Consciousness.

Abhay Charan De was born in Calcutta, India, in 1896 to a family strongly committed to devotion to Krishna. Although some considered Krishna one among numerous Hindu deities, for Abhay and his family Krishna was the supreme Lord of the Universe. Abhay entered Scottish Churches' College in 1916 and in 1920 passed his B.A. examination. He rejected his diploma in response to Gandhi's independence movement. In deference to his father he married Radharani Datta. He had one son by this marriage. His householder's life would present a constant conflict with his urge to devote himself completely to preaching Krishna consciousness.

Abhay became associated with the Gaudiya Vaisnava movement and took Bhaktisiddhanta Sarasvati as his spiritual master. Charanaravinda was the name Abhay's spiritual master gave him at initiation. Bhaktivedanta was a title his Godbrothers conferred on him in recognition of his devotional and scholarly qualities. The title Swami came in 1959 when he entered the disciplined order at the age of 63.

Abhay gained a reputation for his ability to preach in English. As his involvement in preaching and writing intensified, his business affairs and family involvement dwindled. His wife was less devoted to spreading the Krishna consciousness than was Abhay, and her drinking tea was a source of displeasure to him. When she sold his manuscript of *Srimad-Bhagavatam* for some tea biscuits, he left the family for good. During the 1950s he preached the *Bhagavadgita* and approached potential donors for support for his periodical publication *Back to Godhead*.

When he set out on a steamship from Calcutta to New York he had only a suitcase, an umbrella, and a supply of dry cereal. The ocean voyage was not an easy one for a 69 year old man plagued with seasickness. He settled on the Lower East Side of New York City, which was a haven for hippies during the 1960s. There, in humble circumstances, he sought to instruct young men and women who were given to experimentation with drugs and sex what it meant to practice devotion to Krishna. Many were searching for gurus and when the word spread that an Indian swami had arrived it caused quite a stir. His followers were particularly attracted to the chanting of the *mahamantra:* Hare Krishna, Hare Krishna, Krishna Krishna, Hare Hare/Hare Rama, Hare Rama, Rama Rama, Hare Hare. They were not immediately attracted to his philosophy.

The basic regulations which he proclaimed were to become the minimal requirements for those who joined the International Society for Krishna Consciousness (ISKCON). They were in radical contrast with the lifestyles of those to whom he preached. Nevertheless, his preaching was surprisingly successful. First, there was to be no gambling. This included frivolous games or sports. In fact, one should not converse about anything except Krishna consciousness. Second, the use of all forms of intoxicants or stimulants, including alcohol, drugs, tobacco, coffee, and tea, was prohibited. Third, there was a dietary prohibition against the eating of meat, fish, or eggs. The diet was strictly vegetarian and consisted of food that had first been offered to Krishna. Fourth, there was to be no illicit sex. Sex was only for the purpose of producing Krishna-conscious children, and therefore all methods of birth control except abstinence were prohibited. Married couples were to have intercourse only when they knew that conception could take place and for that specific purpose.

Human beings have forgotten their true relationship to Krishna, and their liberation lies in a return to Godhead through the grace of Krishna. Human beings can remove the obstacles to that grace. This, taught Bhaktivedanta, can be done by chanting the *mahamantra.* One need not understand it—its transcendental sound will have automatic results and raise one to a spiritual plane. One should also engage in holy association. Associating with nondevotees will have a bad effect and result in an increase of sense gratification. Early in the movement new converts were even urged to sever contact with parents who were unsympathetic to the movement. One should also eat *prasadam* (food offered to Krishna). While preparing the food one should think only of Krishna. Eating the *prasadam* is a purifying act, equal to chanting the *mahamantra.* It is crucial that one accept a bonafide spiritual master who is in disciplic succession from Lord Krishna. One cannot return to Godhead without submitting to Krishna, and one can approach Krishna only through his representative.

Most of Bhaktivedanta's books are commentaries on sacred texts. His approximately 60 volumes remain one of the primary means of outreach for the movement. During his first 69 years in India, Bhaktivedanta initiated only one disciple. During his succeeding 12 years in the United States he initiated over 4,000. In 1970 Bhaktivedanta appointed a Governing Body Commission, with each member appointed over a specific part of the world. This board met annually under Bhaktivedanta's supervision. When he died in 1977, the structure for the continuation of the movement was in place.

Further Reading

An authorized biography of Bhaktivedanta is available in seven volumes through Bhaktivedanta Book Trust (*Srila Prabhupada-lilamrta*). Also available is a one-volume paperback abridgement entitled *Prabhupada.* One can also turn to issues of the magazine *Back to Godhead* and Bhaktivedanta's *Bhagavad-gita As It Is.*

Additional Sources

The life story of His Divine Grace A.C. Bhaktivedanta Swami Prabhupada, founder-acarya of the International Society for Krishna Consciousness, New York, N.Y.: Bala Books, 1983. □

Maulana Abdul Hamid Khan Bhashani

Maulana Abdul Hamid Khan Bhashani (1880-1976) was a Muslim leader who used non-violent, mass civil disobedience techniques to promote nationalism in Assam, Bengal, and Bangladesh in the northeastern part of the Indian subcontinent.

A catalyst of Muslim nationalism, Maulana Abdul Hamid Khan Bhashani did for the masses of the northeastern part of the Indian subcontinent what Mohandas Karamchand Gandhi accomplished for the teeming down-trodden people of north, central, and south India. Unswerving in his belief in God and human dignity, Bhashani crusaded, at times singlehandedly, against the vested interests in Assam, Bengal, and later Bangladesh in favor of the deprived—landless peasants, workers, and hapless migrants.

Like Gandhi, Bhashani succeeded in institutionalizing political dissent and making opposition politics viable and respected. Also like Gandhi, he never accepted any position in government although he was elected to Assam, Bengal, and East Bengal assemblies and was himself the founder of the most effective political parties in Pakistan and Bangladesh. Ideologically, Bhashani was a Marxist and Islamist, at the same time both admiring the People's Republic of China and regretting that the Chinese lacked faith in God. Enigmatic, uncompromising, and candid, Bhashani was a charismatic leader who could motivate ordinary people to join his movement for social and economic justice.

A Life of Protest

Born in 1880 in the village of Dhangara, within the province of Bengal in British India, Abdul Hamid Khan Bhashani received his early education in a Madrasa, one of the religious schools for Muslim boys. As a boy of 12 he moved to Tangail, about 60 miles from Dhaka, now the capital of Bangladesh. After completing his religious schooling at Tangail and becoming a Muslim religious mentor, or Maulana, Bhashani enrolled in the Islamic Center in the United Provinces, known as the intellectual seat of militant

Islam in British India. Before he could complete the course he joined a politico-religious movement advocating militancy for Islam. A decade and a half later Bhashani became one of the most ardent followers of another politico-religious movement of the Islamic World—the Khalifate movement in 1919. Protesting the dissolution in Turkey of the Khalifate (Caliphate) by Kemal Ataturk landed Bhashani in jail for ten months.

Long before he joined the Khalifate movement Bhashani had been a crusader for peasant rights in Tangail against the oppressive landlords. Following a peasant uprising against the King of Santosh in which Bhashani played the leading role, he was expelled by the British from the Mymensing district which included Tangail. Uprooted but undiscouraged, Bhashani continued to organize peasant movements in northern Bengal.

In 1904, at the age of 24, Bhashani journeyed to Assam, the northeastern frontier province of British India, where he was moved by the suffering of the 2.5 million Bengali Muslim peasants, particularly the new settlers among them. He organized peasants against the prevalent usury system which led to pauperization and economic enslavement. His successful organization of a mammoth protest rally of different peasant groups in Sirajganj, known as *All Bengal Kissan Sammelon* (All Bengal Peasant Conference), led to the abolition of the much hated usury system.

During this period Bhashani tried to organize another peasant rally at Kagmari village in Tangail to mobilize resistance against oppressive practices of the landlords of Mymensing. With the help of British civil and law enforcement officials, the landlords prevented Bhashani from holding the meeting and, at the same time, forced him to leave Mymensing within six hours.

Return to Assam

In the early 1930s Bhashani again went to Assam with the hope of alleviating the suffering of Bengali Muslim peasantry. Unlike the earlier time, Bhashani was now an astute politician and an effective organizer of reform movements. Mobilizing the Muslim population of Assam, Bhashani established the provincial branch of the Muslim League and was elected its president in 1934.

His historic stand against political injustice made him popularly known as the religious leader of Bhashan Char or, in Bengali, *Bhashan Charer Maulana*. From that time, the title *Bhashani,* derived from the word *Bhashan,* stuck to him. For his uncompromising commitment to the cause of Muslim peasantry, Bhashani was arrested eight times during his 15 years of political leadership in Assam.

From 1934, when he established the Assam branch of Mohammad Ali Jinnah's Muslim League Party, to 1937, Bhashani completely immersed himself in the mass movement. He provided a much needed leadership to the Muslim peasantry, particularly the migrants from the neighboring provinces, for their struggle against repressive measures. His movement politics was perceived as a major threat not only by the Hindu landlords in Assam but by Muslim landlords as well.

In the mid 1940s the new congress government in Assam arrested Bhashani, fearing that he might transform the peasant movement into a political movement for the merger of Assam with the would-be Pakistan. Only after the partition of India in 1947, when most of Assam (with the exception of the district of Sylhet) became a part of India, was Bhashani released by the Assam government on condition that he leave India. Immediately he returned to East Bengal, which comprised the eastern flank of Pakistan.

Campaign for Bengali Language

After his return to East Bengal in 1948, the Maulana became one of the vanguards of the students' language movement demanding that Bengali be accorded equal recognition with Urdu, the language of West Pakistan, as one of the two official languages of the new Muslim nation of Pakistan. The same year, Bhashani dissociated himself from the Muslim League Party and formed a counter party, the Awami (nationalist) Muslim League Party, with himself as president and Shamsul Huq as general secretary. In essence, Bhashani founded the first organized opposition party in Pakistan.

Bhashani's opposition party was further strengthened when Hussain Shahid Suhrawardy, the last chief minister of undivided Bengal, and Sheik Mujibur Rahman, a prominent leader of the language movement who was later to become the charismatic leader of Bangladesh, joined the Awami Muslim League in 1949.

Late 1949 also saw the arrest of Bhashani, his tenth, but the first in Pakistan. He had organized a hunger march in Dhaka demonstrating against the food policies of the government which coincided with the visit to East Bengal of Liaquat Ali Khan, the first prime minister of Pakistan. In jail Bhashani, like Gandhi, went on a hunger strike and was released on health grounds the next year. When the language movement peaked in 1952 Bhashani was arrested once again.

Founds Two New Parties

In 1953, immediately after his release from jail, Bhashani organized a United (Jutka) Front, a coalition of opposition parties, along with A.K. Fazlul Huq, H.S. Suhrawardy, and Sheik Mujibur Rahman to contest the election of 1954. In that election the Jutka Front won a landslide victory over the provincial Muslim League Party, winning 290 of 300 Assembly seats. However, within two months the Front ministry, with Fazlul Huq as chief minister, was dismissed by the central government under pressure from the Muslim League. East Bengal was put under the governor's rule and Huq under house arrest.

In order to make his party appealing to the minority Hindu community, most of whom were peasants, Bhashani dropped the word "Muslim" from the Awami Muslim League. However, at the party's annual conference the following year Bhashani decided to start a new party because of serious disagreement with H.S. Suhrawardy, who was then the prime minister of Pakistan. The new party—the National Awami Party—linked not only antiestablishmentarian associates in East Pakistan but also prominent progressive leaders from West Pakistan.

After the abrogation of the constitution in 1958 by Gen. Iskander Mirza and the subsequent military take over by Gen. Ayub Khan, Bhashani was arrested and held in prison for four years and ten months. He was released from detention only after he went on a hunger strike. In 1963 he led a Pakistani goodwill delegation to the People's Republic of China where he had meetings with Mao Zedong (Mao Tse-Tung) and Chou En-Lai.

In 1964 Bhashani challenged the Ayub regime by engineering the nomination for president of Fatima Jinnah, the sister and confidante of M.A. Jinnah, the founder of Pakistan. But the insurgents were beaten by Ayub Khan.

Bhashani's National Awami Party then split into two factions: a pro-Moscow and a pro-Beijing one, with the former headed by Muzaffar Ahmad and the latter by Bhashani. Bhashani now introduced "Gherao," a form of sit-in designed to encircle the official against whom a protest was directed. This strategy created increasing momentum in his movement politics against the Ayub regime, ultimately contributing to the nation-wide mass movement causing the downfall of Ayub Khan.

Struggle for Justice Continued

Bhashani opposed not only Ayub and his successor, Yahya Khan, but also the charismatic leader of independent Bangladesh, Sheik Mujibur Rahman. His unyielding pursuit of public good was demonstrated when he lent his support during the march movement of 1971 to Sheik Mujib as the elected leader of the Bengalis fighting for state rights. He did this in spite of the fact that he still had reservations about Sheik Mujib, whose party won its first landslide victory in 1970.

During most of the nine-months-long Bengali liberation war in 1971, Bhashani lived in India convalescing from a serious illness. He irked Indira Gandhi and her government by reviving his old demand for uniting the peasantry of Assam, Bengal, and East Pakistan in a continued struggle for social and economic justice.

Toward the middle of November 1971, when India's intention to involve itself directly in the Bengali-Pakistani war became apparent, Bhashani advocated that Bengalis be given the chance to win their own war even if it meant prolonging their guerrilla struggle against the Pakistani military. This stand, along with his known pro-Beijing leanings and coupled with his pre-partition advocacy of a united front of peasantry cutting across national boundaries, made him suspect in the eyes of Indian leaders. After his return to the new nation of Bangladesh in March 1972, he led a hunger strike (1974) against Mujib's presidency and a long hunger march the same year.

After the assassination of Mujib in 1975, the Indian leadership's image of the Maulana worsened, particularly when he attracted world attention by organizing a long march of millions of Bengalis in protest against India's 1976 withdrawal of water from the international river, the Ganges, at Farrakka in West Bengal. As always, the

Maulana inevitably took recourse (as did Gandhi) to direct action through non-violent civil disobedience.

On November 17, 1976, at the age of 96, Maulana Abdul Hamid Khan Bhashani died in Dhaka. Millions of Bengalis mourned for him and took pride in the legacies he left behind as a selfless, principled, and courageous leader of the Third World. His "Islamic Socialism" may have been puzzling to many, but his tangible contributions to political, social, economic, and religious reforms were beyond any doubt.

Further Reading

Additional information on Bhashani and his activities can be found in Zillur R. Khan, *Leadership in the Least Developed Nation: Bangladesh* (1983), and "March Movement of Bangladesh: Bengali Struggle for Political Power," *Indian Journal of Political Science* (September 1972), as well as Sirajul Hossain Khan, "Champion of Exploited," *Holiday* (November 21, 1976). □

Vinoba Bhave

Vinoba Bhave (1895-1982) was an Indian nationalist and social-reform leader who inherited Mahatma Gandhi's spiritual mantle. Bhave's most notable contribution was the creation of the *bhoodan* (land gift) movement.

Vinayak Bhave, renamed with the affectionate diminutive "Vinoba" by Mahatma Gandhi, was born on Sept. 11, 1895, into a high-ranking Chitapavan Brahmin family in Gagode village, south of Bombay. His father, a textile technologist, worked for the princely state of Baroda. Bhave credited his grandfather and his mother for his strong religious orientation.

Joined Gandhi's Movement

Bhave's education was concentrated in modern subjects, and he excelled in mathematics. He nonetheless left college in 1916 and started his spiritual quest. He began studying Sanskrit in Benares but within three months joined Gandhi's independence movement.

Constructive work and social reform were vital parts of the nationalist movement. Bhave excelled in confronting basic social and economic problems, and he made mass contact with the Indian people, especially with workers in the home industries, cloth spinning, and sanitation. In 1924 he led a temple-entry movement for "untouchables" in southern India and consistently worked on their behalf.

Began Sarvodaya and Bhoodan Movements

Bhave participated in the nationwide civil disobedience periodically conducted against the British, and was imprisoned with other nationalists. Despite these many activities, he was not well known to the public. He gained national prominence when Gandhi chose him as the first participant in a new nonviolent campaign in 1940.

Following India's independence in 1947 and Gandhi's assassination in 1948, Bhave focused his efforts on *sarvodaya*, meaning "welfare for all." At first Bhave was a reluctant leader and efforts were poorly organized, but the *sarvodaya* adherents were imbued with deep dedication and offered selfless service. Bhave revitalized the movement in 1951 while on a walking tour of Telangana. A communist-led peasant rebellion marked this area of Andhra Pradesh as India's major trouble spot. In one village, landless peasants stated that they needed 100 acres of land. Bhave asked the landowners to contribute the 100 acres and met with success. Thus, the *bhoodan* movement was born, and the *sarvodaya* movement again had a true leader.

Thereafter, over 5,000,000 acres of land were donated, and other *dan* (gift) movements developed. These included money, animals, implements, wells, and, the ultimate gift, the dedication of one's life to welfare activities. The eventual goal of the *bhoodan* movement was 50,000,000 acres, but there was not enough support to make it happen. However, material considerations aside, Bhave had rekindled the Gandhian emphasis on changing people's hearts, on nonviolence, and on self-help. In 1982, after suffering a heart attack, Bhave decided to end his life by fasting until his death.

Further Reading

Sonnleitner, Michael W., *Vinoba Bhave on Self-Rule and Representative Democracy* (1989). □

Bhumibol Adulyadej

Bhumibol Adulyadej (born 1927) was declared king of Thailand in 1946 and formally crowned four years later. He represented the Chakri Dynasty that has preserved the independence of Thailand for more than 200 years.

King Bhumibol Adulyadej, born on December 5, 1927, in Cambridge, Massachusetts, is the only Thai monarch ever to be born abroad. He was the youngest son of Prince Mahidol of Songkhla, and the direct grandson of King Chulalongkorn (Rama V), noted for the widespread reforms he introduced into Thailand.

After a short period of primary school in Bangkok, King Bhumibol left with his family for Switzerland, where he attended the Ecole Nouvelle de la Suisse Romande, and then received his Bachelier des Lettres diploma from the Gymnase Classique Cantonal of Lausanne. He entered Lausanne University to study science but, following the mysterious death of his elder brother, King Ananda Mahidol, in June 1946, he was declared king, although his formal coronation did not take place until May 5, 1950. On April 28 of that year he married Queen Sirikit of the Kittiyakara family. He returned to Switzerland to study political science and

law, but was called back to Thailand to deal with pressing national needs.

The role of the Thai monarch is pivotal in the society of Thailand. Not only is he the figure that has preserved the Thai state in the face of repeated external threats through the 200 years of the Chakri Dynasty, he is also the symbol of the nation. Even more, he is the focus of the continuity of Thai values and social cohesion in spite of rapid social and economic change. He is the leading supporter of Buddhism in Thai society, and the stability that he provides through his very presence is what allows swings of political activity and military coups to take place without threatening the fabric of Thai society. There is no question that he is widely revered.

Used His Position To Help His Countrymen

Traditionally, the monarch in Thailand has been considered above politics, and for years King Bhumibol played an inconspicuous political role in keeping with that view. He was, however, drawn into current events on occasion to mediate crises or negotiate compromises, and it was a testament to his position and the reverence in which he was held that he succeeded.

Bhumibol was a symbol both of national unity and of modernity. Unlike other monarchs before him, Bhumibol visited every province of his country and suggested infrastructural improvements that might benefit the people. His personal work in rural areas was widely acclaimed because of his success in convincing hill tribes to switch their growing of opium to that of vegetables, fruit, and coffee. As a result, opium cultivation declined by 85%. Village roads, electricity, and irrigation systems were all part of Bhumibol's rural development efforts and modernization of Thai farming.

Describing himself as "an amateur scientist," Bhumibol turned substantial portions of his Bangkok residence, the Chitralada Palace, into living laboratories where projects were undertaken to improve the standard of living. Royal Chitralada Projects included livestock improvement, milk production, hybridization of grains, bee keeping, fish breeding, reforestation, and various food processing techniques. According to the King's wishes, the palace grounds functioned as one great workshop and school for teaching and learning—all for the good of national development.

Because of his broad international training, the king was noted as a devotee of modern music and played the clarinet, as well as composed. He was said to have broad cultural interests, but the myriad ceremonial duties left him little time for personal interests.

King Bhumibol and Queen Sirikit had four children, a son and three daughters. The eldest child, Princess Ubon Ratana, was born in Lausanne, Switzerland, on April 5, 1951, and renounced her title when she married an American in 1972. Crown Prince Vijiralongkorn was born in Bangkok on July 28, 1952. He was a graduate of the Australian Royal Military Academy in 1975 and of the Thai Command and General Staff College in 1978. Princess Sirinthon was born on April 2, 1955, and was in a graduate education program at Srinakharinwirot; and Princess Chulaphon, who was born on July 4, 1957, studied chemistry at Mahidol University in Bangkok.

Although Bhumibol preferred his people to politics, he nevertheless commanded enough respect to successfully intervene politically when necessary. In 1981 he was able to thwart an attempted coup against Premier Prem Tinsulanond by simply requesting that those involved cease their efforts. In 1992 the King's public chastisement of the military government's handling of pro-democracy demonstrations again restored order. Bhumibol was universally revered throughout Thailand and contributed greatly to his country's stability. On June 9, 1996, Bhumibol celebrated his 50th anniversary on the throne, becoming Thailand's longest ruling monarch.

The Chakri Dynasty accomplished the difficult task of keeping Thailand independent in the face of colonial threats and created a modern state while preserving its cultural traditions. King Bhumibol continued in that tradition by extending the power of the central government to its peripheral geographical areas and attempting to improve the lot of the rural poor. As the chief supporter and principal patron of Buddhism, the king was in some real sense viewed as the symbolic embodiment of that long tradition.

Further Reading

There is no English language biography of King Bhumibol, but of course there are constant references to him in all standard books on Thailand. The Public Relations Department of the Royal Thai government has published a pamphlet, *His Majesty King Bhumibol Adulyadej* of Thailand (no date).

There are many good sites on the Internet to find information about King Bhumibol. Two of the best are *His Majesty the King* (http://www.nectec.or.th/ bureaux/prd/) and the *Internet Thailand Homepage* (http://www.inet.co.th/). ☐

Benazir Bhutto

Benazir Bhutto (born 1953) became prime minister of Pakistan in 1988. Heir to the political legacy of her father, Zulfikar Ali Bhutto (prime minister from 1971 to 1977), she was the first woman in modern times to head the government of an Islamic state.

B enazir Bhutto assumed the prime ministership of Pakistan after 11 years of struggle against the military regime of General Mohammad Zia ul-Haq. She had taken up the leadership of the Pakistan People's Party— founded by her father, Zulfikar Ali Bhutto, who was deposed by General Zia in 1977 and executed in 1979. Over the following decade Bhutto mobilized opposition to the martial law regime, spending nearly six of those years in prison or detention. In a national election following the death of General Zia in August 1988, the People's Party won a plurality of seats in the National Assembly. Bhutto was

invited by Pakistan's President Ghulam Ishaq Khah to form a government and was sworn in as prime minister on December 2, 1988.

Benazir Bhutto was born in Karachi, Pakistan, on June 21, 1953. She received her early education in Pakistan. From 1969 to 1973 she attended Radcliffe College in Cambridge, Massachusetts, where she obtained a B.A. degree *cum laude* in comparative government. Between 1973 and 1977 Bhutto read politics, philosophy, and economics at Lady Margaret Hall, Oxford University. In December 1976 she was elected president of Oxford Union, becoming the first Asian woman to head the prestigious debating society.

Bhutto's plans to enter Pakistan's foreign service ended with the deposition of her father and a decision to dedicate herself to restoring a democratically-elected government. Despite lengthy periods of imprisonment and her self-exile in Europe beginning in January 1984, she directed the rebuilding and restructuring of the People's Party. She traveled widely, presenting the case against the Zia regime, attacking its violations of civil and human rights. In Pakistan, opponents of the regime defied the government's ban on political activity despite mass arrests and intimidation. While relentless in her criticism, Bhutto counseled her loyalists against any resort to armed confrontation, preferring instead to wrest power through the political process.

Martial law ended December 30, 1985, but the civilian government that Zia, as president and army chief of staff, had installed three months earlier was based on nonparty elections. Hoping to revive the campaign for representative

government, Bhutto returned to Pakistan in April 1986. Traveling across the country, she attracted crowds that rivaled any in Pakistan's history.

On May 29, 1988, President Zia abruptly dissolved the Parliament and dismissed his hand-picked but increasingly independent-minded prime minister, Mohammad Junejo. Fears that Zia would somehow keep the People's Party from contesting forthcoming elections were removed by his sudden death. Yet the People's Party's failure in the November election to win an outright parliamentary majority resulted in a politically vulnerable Bhutto-led coalition government. An alliance of opposition parties made it difficult for the prime minister to advance the kind of legislative program that had been promised to deal with the country's pressing problems. In particular, matters of social justice, including repeal of fundamentalist laws considered degrading to women, could not be enacted. It was politically expedient to avoid antagonizing religious elements, some of whom believed it "un-Islamic" for a woman to be the head of government. Faced with severe financial constraints, the prime minister also made little progress in bringing reforms to the education and health sectors or in curbing bureaucratic corruption.

Bhutto took care not to offend a military establishment which had allowed the return to a democratic system and refrained from direct interference in domestic politics. The army was appeased in the area of military spending and given wide latitude in formulating and implementing certain foreign and domestic policies, most notably Pakistan's role in orchestrating the Afghan war and terms for peace. Her government's dependence on the military increased with the outbreak of serious civil disorders and violence arising from persisting ethnic and regional antagonisms made more lethal by weapons siphoned off from the Afghan conflict.

To her credit, Bhutto released political prisoners and took other steps to restore fundamental human rights. Heavy restrictions on the press were lifted along with limitations on assembly by unions and student groups. She also gained stature for her success in outmaneuvering the combined opposition in its tactics to oust her from office. Unlike her father, who favored socialist rhetoric and nationalized many economic institutions and activities, Bhutto emphasized economic growth and argued for decreased government subsidies and greater privatization in the economy. During her tenure, the prime minister demonstrated considerable skill in winning international diplomatic and economic support for Pakistan and effectively used the Kashmir dispute with India to rally domestic public sentiment without unnecessarily inflaming it. Among Pakistan's leaders she was considered the most inclined to strive for improved relations with India.

Bhutto married Asif Ali Zardari on December 18, 1987. The son of a politically active, wealthy landowning family from the Sindh Province, Zardari's background was similar to that of his wife—not surprising since Bhutto acceded to a traditionally arranged marriage. They had two children.

On August 6, 1990, President Ghulam Ishaq Khah, apparently supported by the Pakistan military, suddenly dis-

missed Bhutto from the office of prime minister. Citing government corruption, nepotism, and abuse of power, Khah dissolved the National Assembly and declared a state of emergency. Bhutto called her dismissal "illegal and unconstitutional" and worried about the fate of her People's Party. The caretaker government continued its campaign against Bhutto by arresting her husband October 10, charging kidnapping, extortion, and loan fraud. In elections held on October 24 Bhutto's party suffered a major defeat. The victorious alliance named Nawaz Sharif, a conservative industrialist, to be prime minister.

Bhutto, vowing to seek office in elections to come, spent the next few years trying to regain support and political favor. She served as chairperson of the standing committee on foreign affairs of the National Assembly and was again elected to the position of prime minister of Pakistan in October 1993.

In November of 1996, Bhutto was again ousted from her post, this time by Farooq Leghari, the man she had chosen for president. Again accused of nepotism and corruption, Bhutto was placed under house arrest, though never officially charged with anything. Less than a year later, Bhutto again attempted to regain power.

In Pakistan's general elections in February 1997, Nawaz Sharif celebrated a landslide victory over Bhutto's Pakistan People's Party. Sharif's Pakistan Muslim League (PML) won a resounding 134 of 217 seats in the National Assembly while Bhutto saw the PPP reduced to a mere 19 seats and virtually erased from the key Punjab provincial assembly.

In an interview with *Time* magazine in March 1997, Bhutto said, "If the elections had been fair, free, and impartial, the Pakistan People's Party would have won on the basis of the development work we have done, on the basis of restoring peace, of increasing education and health expenditures, bringing the deficit down, repaying debt and bringing peace to Karachi. The results were engineered. . . . The whole thing was a fraud for the people of Pakistan."

In her defeat, Bhutto said she no longer desired the prime minister's post. "My father worked from morning to night. I worked from morning to night. My father, what did he get? He got hanged. What did I get? I got slandered," she said. "Let there be a new leadership. I want my party to win the next elections, and I will help my party prepare to win. But I don't want to be prime minister."

Further Reading

Benazir Bhutto is the author of two books, *Foreign Policy in Perspective* (1978) and her autobiography, *Daughter of the East* (1989). Several collections of her speeches and works have been compiled, including *The Way Out* (1988). Three books about Prime Minister Bhutto have been published in India: *Benazir's Pakistan* (1989), edited by M. D. Dharamdasani; *The Trial of Benazir* (1989), by Rafiq Zakaria; and *Benazir Bhutto: Opportunities and Challenges* (1989), by P. L. Bhola. *The News International,* a publication of the Jang Group, located at http://www.jang.group.com, gives up-to-date news of Pakistan's political climate. There is also a biography of Bhutto located on the World Wide Web entitled

Imran-net's Biography of Benazir Bhutto, which gives general
background information on the ex-prime minister.
Useful for an reader's appreciation of the difficulties facing a
woman in political life is *Women of Pakistan* (1987), by
Khawar Mumtaz and Farida Shaheed. Additionally, Emma
Duncan's *Breaking the Curfew* (1989) presents a highly revealing picture of Pakistan's troubled political scene. □

Zulfikar Ali Bhutto

**Zulfikar Ali Bhutto (1928-1979), Pakistan's president
and then prime minister, mobilized his country's first
mass-based political party around a socialist ideology and highly independent foreign policy.**

Zulfikar Ali Bhutto was born on January 5, 1928, in
Larkana, a small town in the province of Sind. Although he came from a major landowning family in
Larkana, he was brought up in cosmopolitan Bombay, away
from the feudal environment of his ancestral home. After
completing his high school education in Bombay, he
proceeded to the University of California at Berkeley from
which he graduated in 1950 with a Bachelor of Arts degree
in political science. At Berkeley he became interested in
socialism and delivered several lectures on the feasibility of
socialism in Islamic countries—a theme which would dominate his party's manifesto 20 years later. Bhutto continued
his education at Oxford, where he studied law.

Bhutto advocated a nonaligned foreign policy for Pakistan and opposed Pakistan's alliances with the United
States. He believed that the United States was exerting pressure on Pakistan to adopt a conciliatory attitude towards
neighboring India. The lingering post-partition animosity
between India and Pakistan influenced Bhutto's hard-line
thinking towards India. He was intent on gaining international support against India and securing Pakistan from a
possible Indian attack. With this in mind Bhutto cultivated
relations with China, which had been involved in a border
conflict with India in 1962. Bhutto's astuteness in developing relations with China was later useful for the Nixon
administration, which used Pakistan as a channel for initiating a dialogue with China. Bhutto also sought to strengthen
relations with other Islamic countries, envisaging Pakistan's
role as a leader not only of Muslim countries but also of
other developing states.

Pakistan had been under military rule by a government
headed by Ayub Khan since 1958. Bhutto, who served as
minister of foreign affairs until asked to resign in 1966,
realized that the toleration of the people for repressive government was diminishing. He felt that this adverse situation
presented an ideal opportunity for him to assume leadership
of Pakistan. In December 1967 Bhutto formed his own political party, the Pakistan People's Party, whose manifesto
promised to alleviate the lot of the urban and rural workers
and advocated an equitable distribution of wealth. His program not only appealed to the lower income groups but was
supported by the urban intelligentsia which was seeking an

end to the military regime and felt that Bhutto offered a new
and dynamic plan and a necessary alternative to traditional
religious parties.

Pakistan's defeat in the 1971 war with India led to the
creation of Bangladesh. Bhutto, with the strongest party in
the remaining western wing of the country, replaced Gen.
Mohammad Yahya Khan as president. In April 1973 Bhutto
became prime minister under a new constitution. His six
years in office were marked by extensive nationalization of
industries, banks, and educational institutions. Bhutto's policies, aimed at reducing the power of such traditional economic forces as major businessmen and feudal landlords,
were well intentioned but lacked sufficient consideration of
economic realities. His government's economic policies
were implemented hastily by bureaucrats who did not have
the requisite management skills and background. Consequently, the economy became chaotic and left most sections of society disaffected with the policies. Bhutto's
frequently touted slogan of "Islamic Socialism" proved to
be mere rhetoric in the face of daunting economic and
social realities, especially the need to compromise with
landed elites.

Confronted by increasing opposition, Bhutto introduced repressive measures which included press censorship and imprisonment of political opponents. In an attempt
to show the "democratic" nature of his government and his
continuing popular support, Bhutto decided to hold general
elections in March 1977. Confident of his success, he
underestimated the collaboration of the opposition parties.
Although he won the 1977 elections, his opponents ac-

cused him of flagrant manipulation of votes and mounted a civil disobedience movement against his government. As public discontent and violence spread, Bhutto was forced to impose martial law in several major cities of Pakistan, paving the way for military involvement. He was deposed in a bloodless coup by Gen. Zia ul-Haq on July 5, 1977. Several charges were brought against him, including the murder while in power of a political opponent's father. He was sentenced to death and was hanged on April 4, 1979, despite appeals for clemency by world leaders and international organizations.

While Bhutto's policies in the domestic sphere were harshly criticized, his foreign policy won him some acclaim. He was intent on asserting Pakistan's role in international affairs and strove to fulfill his earlier ideal of Pakistan as a leader of developing countries. He attempted to pursue a foreign policy independent of both superpowers, which brought him into considerable conflict with the United States, especially over the issue of Pakistan's nuclear program.

In 1986, after two years of self-imposed exile, Benazir Bhutto, daughter of the executed president, returned to Pakistan. She became Prime Minister in 1988.

Further Reading

Shahid Javed Burki's *Pakistan Under Bhutto, 1971-1977* provides a comprehensive and analytical account of Bhutto's government. It also gives considerable details of Pakistan's political history prior to 1971. Piloo Mody's *Zulfi My Friend* gives insights into Bhutto's personality based on their shared experiences. *Politics in Pakistan: the Nature and Direction of Change* by Khalid B. Sayeed provides useful background information and analyses of Bhutto's political career. Bhutto wrote several books stating his views on Pakistan's domestic politics as well as its foreign policy. His last work was *If I Am Assassinated* (1979). Some other books by Bhutto are *The Great Tragedy* (1971), *Pakistan and the Alliances* (1969), *The Myth of Independence* (1969), and *Foreign Policy of Pakistan* (1964).

Additional Sources

Batra, Jagdish Chander, *The trial and execution of Bhutto,* Delhi: Kunj, 1979.

Kak, B. L., *Z. A. Bhutto: notes from the death cell,* New Delhi: Raadhaa Krishna Pr, 1979.

Syed, Anwar Hussain, *The discourse and politics of Zulfikar Ali Bhutto,* New York: St. Martin's Press, 1992.

Wolpert, Stanley A., *Zulfi Bhutto of Pakistan: his life and times,* New York: Oxford University Press, 1993.

Zaman, Fakhar, *Z. A. Bhutto: the political thinker,* Lahore, People's Publications, 1973. □

Hayyim Nahman Bialik

The Russian-born author Hayyim Nahman Bialik (1873-1934) was the foremost Hebrew poet of modern time. He expressed the sentiments of his Jewish contemporaries, who had left the ghetto in search of a new way of life based on Judaism.

Hayyim N. Bialik was born in Radi, a village in the province of Volhynia, Russia. When he was 5, the family moved to the larger town of Zhitomir. His father, a pious man, eked out a living as a tavern keeper. At the counter he kept open a holy book, which he studied between serving drinks. His father died when Bialik was 7, and to support the family his mother spent her days peddling and her nights knitting. Bialik later wrote of her sorrowful lot in his poem ''My Song.''

At 16 Bialik was sent to the famous Talmudical academy of Volozhin, where he studied until 1891, when the czarist government closed the school. At this time Bialik began reading modern Jewish literature avidly and studied the Russian and German languages. During his last year at the academy, he published his first poem, ''To the Bird,'' which expressed the intense longing of a suffering people for its ancient homeland.

By 1900 Bialik moved to Odessa, which was a center for modern Jewish literary activity. The poet soon became the moving spirit of a distinguished circle, which included the eminent novelist Mendele Mocher Sefarim and the philosopher and essayist Ahad Haam. In 1903 Bialik became coeditor of the leading Hebrew monthly, *Ha-Shiloach*. During this period he published poetry, short novels marked by earthy realism and humor (*Aryeh, the Gross; Behind the Fence*), and autobiographical sketches (*Aftergrowth*)

In 1903 Bialik went to Kishinev, Bessarabia, to report on the pogroms that had taken place there. Deeply shaken by this experience, he wrote his famous poem ''In the City of

Slaughter." This work not only described poignantly the terror and devastation of the pogrom but also castigated the victims for their passivity and timidity in face of the onslaught. It aroused Jewish youth to take up arms in self-defense against the anti-Semitic attacks in the turbulent days that followed the unsuccessful Russian revolution in 1905. "In the City of Slaughter" was the first of a series of poems, prophetic in mood and style, which marked the period of "sorrow and wrath" in Bialik's creativity. In "The Last Word," "Summon the Serpents," "Out of the Depth," and "The Scroll of Fire," he bewailed the lot of his people, whose long years of suffering had dulled its sense of pride and self-respect.

In "On the Threshold of the House of Prayer," "If Thou Wouldst Know," and "The Talmud Student," Bialik praised the spirit forged in houses of prayer and study, which enabled the Jews to endure suffering and degradation. In his epos, "The Dead of the Wilderness," and his collection of Bible stories, "And It Came to Pass," he linked the past with the present and imparted charm and wit to folk themes.

In 1921, following the Russian Revolution, Bialik and his fellow Hebrew writers were forced to leave Russia. He then lived in Berlin, where he founded the publishing house Dvir, through which he realized his lifelong dream of making available new editions of great works in Jewish literature. In 1924 he settled in Palestine, where he continued his literary and publishing endeavors. He also instituted many cultural activities. He played a large role in the development of the Hebrew University in Jerusalem and in the Hebrew Writers' Club. His other literary works include the *Sefer Ha-Aggada,* a collection of Jewish legend and lore based on the Talmud and Midrash, and translations of literary classics into Hebrew.

Further Reading

Translations of Bialiks's writings include *Complete Poetic Works,* edited by Israel Efros (1948), and two anthologies of legends and stories: *And It Came to Pass,* edited by Herbert Danby (1938), and *Aftergrowth, and Other Stories* , translated by I. M. Lask (1939). *Bialik Speaks: Words from the Poet's Lips, Clues to the Man,* edited by Mordecai Ovadyahu and translated by A. ElDror (1970), is a concentrated, 50-page compilation of Bialik's conversations on varied topics. Some critical commentary on Bialik is in Meyer Waxman, *A History of Jewish Literature* (4 vols., 1930-1941; 5 vols., 1960), and in Shalom Spiegel, *Hebrew Reborn* (1957).

Additional Sources

Aberbach, David, *Bialik,* New York: Grove Press, 1988. □

Marie François Xavier Bichat

The French anatomist, pathologist, and physiologist Marie François Xavier Bichat (1771-1802) was the founder of general anatomy and animal histology.

On Nov. 11, 1771, M. F. X. Bichat was born in Thoirett, Jura. His father, a physician, was his first teacher of anatomy. He studied anatomy and surgery at Montpellier and Lyons and later served as an assistant to P. J. Desault, a famous physician at the Hôtel-Dieu, a hospital in Paris. In 1800 Bichat, after the death of Desault, became physician at the Hôtel-Dieu. From 1799 onward he abandoned surgery and did only research in anatomy, performing as many as 600 autopsies in a single year. He investigated the structure of the body generally, rather than studying particular organs as separate entities. He broke down the organs into their common elemental materials, for which he introduced the term "tissues."

Bichat rejected the iatrochemistry of the later Cartesians, which was still influential at the time. According to this principle, disorders in the human frame are caused by an imbalance in the chemical relations of fluids in the body. He also rejected Stahl's animism, which maintains that there is a special "Spirit of Life." Bichat was a follower of Albrecht von Haller's special form of vitalism, according to which the body possesses some truly vital functions such as motion, communication, and sensibility, while other characteristics of the body are not vital. In other words, he rejected the old theory that life is a collection of subtle fluids and maintained rather that life is a result of a combination of vitality and the vital functions of various tissues of the body. Bichat also rejected the reductionist philosophy, according to which all biological phenomena have to be reducible to the laws of physics and chemistry—an attitude becoming more and more prevalent in his own time. His definition

was that life consists of the sum of functions by which death is resisted. One of his most interesting works is *Physiological Researches on Life and Death.*

Bichat's experimental work had great influence and was quoted for a long time as a model of experimental exactitude and penetrating insight. In this context it is interesting to note that Bichat refused all his life to make use of the most advanced experimental tool for anatomy, namely, the microscope. His feverish activity weakened him, and in 1802, after a fall from the Hôtel-Dieu's staircase, he contracted a fever and died on July 22, only 31 years old. This brilliant man had an enormous impact on French science not only through his experimental work and new version of vitalistic philosophy, but also through his writing of basic textbooks and establishing of research institutions.

Further Reading

See Elizabeth Haigh, *Xavier Bichat and the Medical Theory of the Eighteenth Century* (1984). Background material is in Erwin H. Ackerknecht, *A Short History of Medicine* (1955); Lester S. King, *The Medical World of the Eighteenth Century* (1958); and Félix Martí-Ibáñ *A Prelude to Medical History* (1961). ☐

Nicholas Biddle

Nicholas Biddle (1786-1844) was president of the Second Bank of the United States from 1823 to 1836. He was an early advocate of the debated principle of central banking, and under his direction the Bank performed most of the functions of present-day central banks.

Nicholas Biddle was born into a prominent Philadelphia family on Jan. 8, 1786. He attended the University of Pennsylvania and graduated from the College of New Jersey at Princeton in 1801. He began the study of law, but, too young to enter practice, he lived in Europe from 1804 to 1807, first as secretary to John Armstrong, the U.S. minister to Napoleonic France, then as a traveler, and finally as a secretary to James Monroe, the U.S. minister in England.

Biddle then began practicing law but soon became dissatisfied. Between 1810 and 1823 he was the managing trustee of his wife's estate, one of the largest in Philadelphia; prepared the journals of the Lewis and Clark expedition for publication in 1814; edited (1812-1814) the *Portfolio,* a Philadelphia literary magazine; served in the lower house and senate of the Pennsylvania Legislature; prepared (1818) a digest of the *Commercial Regulations of Foreign Countries with Which the United States Have Commercial Intercourse* for the Department of State; and from January 1819 through 1821 was one of the five government directors of the Second Bank of the United States.

In January 1823 Biddle was elected president of the Bank—a mixed public and private institution—being acceptable to the government and the shareholders alike but

serving as a director by presidential appointment. Under Biddle's administration the Bank, centered in Philadelphia with branches in the leading American commercial cities, performed a useful function for all economic interests and groups through facilitating the exchange of goods and payments in this predominantly commercial society. The currency supplied by the Bank, no matter where made payable, was received in most places at par, sometimes commanded a premium, and was never at a discount of more than 1/4 of 1 percent. Notes issued by local state banks circulated at par in the immediate vicinity of their issue, and this mixed national currency was elastic, uniform, sound, and completely adequate for the needs of the expanding economy. The developing transportation system, which united the vast geographical areas of the United States and connected them with Europe, was paralleled by a system of domestic and foreign exchange that facilitated payments and increased the profits of trade.

The American people as a whole seemed satisfied with the currency and credit system and the operations of the national bank, but President Andrew Jackson, who distrusted all banks, charged that the Second Bank of the United States was unconstitutional and that if its power was not checked it would enable a financial oligarchy to dominate the nation. Jackson began an assault upon the Bank in 1829, but many of the members of his party (the Democrats) in Congress did not agree. The Bank, in their opinion, was a useful and necessary arm of the Treasury, and they, in alliance with most of the opposition party (the National Republicans) rechartered the institution in 1832. President

Jackson, angered by this defiance of his expressed will, vetoed the rechartering bill and in the fall of 1833 removed the government deposits from the Bank's custody.

Biddle refused to accept defeat. A successor bank, the United States Bank of Pennsylvania, was organized in 1836, and when the Panic of 1837—in part a product of Jackson's financial policies—struck the nation, Biddle almost single-handedly restored national prosperity within a year. He resigned from the Bank in April 1839, believing it and the nation safe and secure. But shortly afterward the Bank of England, itself in danger, renewed financial pressure on the United States, and 2 years later the United States Bank closed its doors.

This costly failure not only discredited Biddle but also the principle of central banking, and it was not until the early years of the 20th century that the United States, through the creation of the Federal Reserve Banks (1912), once more returned to the system that had provided the national economy with a uniform, sound, and elastic currency. Biddle, completely disgraced, died on Feb. 27, 1844, and the general verdict on him and his career was stated by William Cullen Bryant, a Jacksonian editor and poet, who reported that Biddle had died "at his country seat, where he had passed the last of his days in elegant retirement, which, if justice had taken place, would have been spent in the penitentiary."

Further Reading

The only biography of Nicholas Biddle is Thomas P. Govan, *Nicholas Biddle: Nationalist and Public Banker* (1959). Biddle's work as a banker has been extensively treated in Ralph C. H. Catterall, *The Second Bank of the United States* (1903); Fritz Redlich, *The Molding of American Banking: Men and Ideas* (2 vols., 1947-1951); Walter B. Smith, *Economic Aspects of the Second Bank of the United States* (1953); and Bray Hammond, *Banks and Politics in America from the Revolution to the Civil War* (1957). An unfavorable view of Biddle is in Arthur M. Schlesinger, Jr., *The Age of Jackson* (1945). □

John Bidwell

An American pioneer and agriculturist, John Bidwell (1819-1900) was instrumental in the settlement of California and remained active in its politics for half a century.

John Bidwell was born in Chautauqua County, N.Y., on Aug. 5, 1819. When he was 10 years old, the family moved to Pennsylvania; 2 years later they settled in Drake County, Ohio. At 17 Bidwell wanted an education so badly that he walked 300 miles to enter Kingsville Academy; after receiving his education he taught school until 1839.

Bidwell decided to seek his fortune in the West and spent time in Missouri and Kansas before joining a wagon train bound for Oregon in 1841. At Fort Hall, in Idaho, half the group, Bidwell among them, decided to go instead to California—making the first major overland trek to California.

In the Mexican province of California, Bidwell worked for John A. Sutter for 3 years before being naturalized and receiving a land grant, Rancho Chico (north of Sacramento), of 22,000 acres. Bidwell was early active in politics, and during the Bear Flag Revolt he served on the committee that drafted a declaration of independence from Mexico. In the Mexican War he advanced to the rank of brevet major.

In 1848 he prospected briefly, discovering gold on the Feather River, but the following year his title to Rancho Chico was confirmed, and thereafter he devoted himself to ranching and farming, gaining a reputation as his state's foremost agriculturist.

Although Bidwell was elected in 1849 to the California constitutional convention, he was notified too late to serve. He was also elected to the state senate that year as a Democrat, and in 1854 and 1860 he was vice president of the state Democratic convention.

At the outbreak of the Civil War, Bidwell took a strong unionist stance, for which in 1863 he was made a brigadier general in the state militia. He also switched his political alliance to the Union party and on that ticket was elected to Congress in 1864. After the war he became a Republican and was that party's unsuccessful candidate for governor in 1867.

Gradually Bidwell was converted to fringe parties, running unsuccessfully for governor in 1875 on the AntiMonopoly ticket and in 1890 on the Prohibition ticket. In 1892 he was the Prohibition party candidate for president, receiving a scant 264,133 votes nationally.

His last years were spent at Rancho Chico, where he employed Native Americans and attempted to direct them in the ways of the white man's civilization. Bidwell served on the state board of regents for the University of California, and he donated the land for Chico Normal School, a teacher-training institution.

Bidwell died at Rancho Chico on April 4, 1900. His widow later donated 1,900 acres of the estate as a natural park for the state.

Further Reading

Bidwell wrote extensively about his early experiences in California in *A Journey to California* (1842; repr. 1937) and *Echoes of the Past* (1914; abr. repr. 1962, entitled *In California before the Gold Rush*). Biographies of Bidwell include C. C. Royce, *John Bidwell, Pioneer, Statesman, Philanthropist* (1906); Rockwell D. Hunt, *John Bidwell* (1942); and Frank L. Beals, *The Rush for Gold* (1946).

Additional Sources

The Bidwell-Bartleson party: 1841 California emigrant adventure: the documents and memoirs of the Overland pioneers, Santa Cruz, Calif.: Western Tanager Press, 1991.
Ripples along Chico Creek: perspectives on people and time, Chico, Calif.: Butte County Branch, National League of American Pen Women, 1992. □

Owen Bieber

Owen Bieber (born 1929), president from 1983 to 1995 of the third-largest labor union in the United States—the United Automobile, Aerospace and Agricultural Implement Workers of America—is a central figure in the dramatic restructuring of the U.S. auto industry.

Elected UAW president in May 1983, Bieber led more than one million union members, most of whom work in the nation's auto plants. The plants and the U.S. companies that own them reeled in the 1980s from increased competition from lower-cost foreign carmakers and an early 1980s auto slump that saw sales fall to their lowest level since the Great Depression. More than 200,000 auto workers lost their jobs during that time because of the changes in the industry. Bieber struggled to find a balance between the companies' demands to be competitive and the needs of his members to keep their jobs.

Business Week reports one company negotiator as saying Bieber "is a deliberate, hard-working man of great integrity who tempers his comments and actions with an eye for the political consequences." Those attributes helped Bieber negotiate some novel labor agreements at the domestic Big Three automakers—General Motors Corporation, Ford Motor Company, and Chrysler Corporation. For example, Bieber negotiated historic job guarantee programs that prohibit the companies from laying off workers when new technology eliminates their jobs. Instead, the companies must find new work for the employees and retrain them if necessary. In return, the union agreed to more moderate wage increases than are traditional in auto contracts. Bieber also negotiated the first labor contracts for GM's innovative Saturn small-car project, which began producing a new generation of American cars in 1990. The pact, which drew attention from other industries because of its startling departure from past labor-management practices, lets auto workers share in some management decisions on how the plant is operated. In return, the UAW agreed that Saturn workers would receive starting base pay that is 85 percent of the going rate at traditional auto plants.

Bieber, a large man at six-foot-five and about 250 pounds, "is more purely a labor populist, not much given to trafficking with big thinkers outside the UAW or to serving on panels studying the problems of industry," writes Dale Buss of the *Wall Street Journal.* "One of his strengths, supporters maintain, is that he understands the wants of rank-and-file workers and is himself a true believer in the trade-union gospel," Buss states.

Bieber's baptism in that gospel goes back many years, to his first job out of high school. A native of the small, northwest Michigan farm community of North Dorr, Bieber went to work in 1948 at the same auto supply plant that employed his father—McInerney Spring and Wire Company in nearby Grand Rapids. The younger Bieber's first job was bending by hand the thick border wire on car seats. He told Kathy Sawyer of the *Washington Post:* "It was a hard job. After the first hour in there, I felt like just leaving. If my father hadn't worked there, too, I probably would have."

But a year later, at age 19, Bieber was elected to his first union position—shop steward—at UAW Local 687 at the plant. Immediately, he started bargaining. He told the *Detroit News* that the negotiating began "almost the second they gave me the steward button because there were grievances to take care of, and that's part of collective bargaining." Bieber was to become a highly skilled bargainer as he worked his way up the union ranks in Grand Rapids. In 1951 he became a member of the executive board of Local 687 and helped administer local union affairs. In 1955 he was elected to the local bargaining committee and helped run negotiations on local plant issues. In 1956, he was elected president of the local. As Senator John Kennedy's campaign for the U.S. presidency got under way later in the decade, Bieber—a devout Democrat—joined the effort.

His hard work and dedication brought him to the attention of leaders at the UAW's regional office in Grand Rapids and by 1961, he was assigned part-time as a union organizer in the region, which encompasses 62 of Michigan's 83 counties, covering the western part of the state and the Upper Peninsula. A year later, Bieber became a full time regional organizer and international union representative. In 1964 he became a servicing representative, helping advise local union officials at plants in his area. "He was known as 'Big Dad' for the almost-paternal way he stood by union members in run-ins with management," writes Buss of the *Wall Street Journal.* In 1972, he was appointed director of the region, a position he held until 1980, when he was elected a vice-president of the UAW and moved to the union's Detroit headquarters. There, Bieber served as director of the UAW's GM department, the union's largest department with more than 400,000 members. It was Bieber's first public exposure beyond Michigan, as GM's plants stretch from shore to shore. But the spotlight was harsh. By early 1982, with all the domestic automakers in the red because of depressed car sales and foreign competition, Bieber found himself helping negotiate the first concessions contract in the history of GM. Accustomed to some of the most lucrative contracts in America, GM workers agreed, among other things, to put off annual wage increases and eliminate some paid time off the job. But the decision was by no means unanimous. The rank and file ratified the contract by only a slim margin. Recalling how difficult the negotiating had been at the small plants in outstate Michigan and how, until 1982, bargaining at GM had always been lucrative for the union, Bieber told the Associated Press: "I thought my life was going to get easier [in the GM department]. All of a sudden the bottom fell out and I got my baptism of fire."

Elected President

In 1983 the UAW was forced to find a successor for then-president Douglas Fraser, who had reached the mandatory retirement age of 65. Bieber, who has a reputation for being tight-lipped, was the last of three men to declare his candidacy in late 1982, and nonetheless, was selected by the union's 26-member executive board in a 15-11 vote. The nomination, supported by a vote of delegates to the UAW's three-year constitutional convention, surprised some who noted at the time Bieber's shy public demeanor and lack of lengthy experience on the national labor scene. But one member of the UAW executive board put it this way to Mark Lett of the *Detroit News:* "It's not that Owen bowled anybody over with his charisma. He isn't charismatic. But he also didn't offend anybody. I think we'd all agree that he's a good Christian gentleman who has integrity and can be trusted. . . . So what's wrong with a guy you can trust?"

Bieber's first three-year term was highlighted by the job security measures he won in the contracts with the Big Three automakers. Bieber, who sits on the Chrysler board of directors, also negotiated in 1985 a more than $2,100 payback for each Chrysler worker for concessions given to the automaker when it was struggling against bankruptcy from 1979 to 1983. That won Bieber overwhelming praise from UAW officials and workers and seemed to dispel past talk about his relative anonymity among union members nationwide. As John Coyne, president of UAW Local 212 in Detroit told John Saunders and Helen Fogel of the *Detroit Free Press:* "I don't think anybody will say, 'Owen who?' again. He's made his mark." Clyde Templin, a union official from a Chrysler plant in Sterling Heights, Michigan, told the *Free Press,* Bieber even compares favorably with late UAW President Walter Reuther who was largely responsible for making the union the social and political power that it is: "My own personal feeling is he [Bieber] is probably the best

president we've had since Walter Reuther." Reuther, something of an idol in UAW circles, led the union from 1946 until his death in a plane crash in 1970. Bieber himself has often remarked that he plans to keep the UAW on the aggressive social and political course set by Reuther. "I never had the opportunity to work closely with Walter Reuther," Bieber told Lett of the *Detroit News.* "But all of us in the UAW leadership today identify with the Reuther era. You'll not see this ship of state veer from its established course."

Fights for Rights

But there were problems in Bieber's first term, most notably the pullout of the 120,000 Canadian UAW members in 1985. The action, which followed friction between Bieber and Canadian UAW leader Bob White during 1984's GM contract talks in Canada, deprived the UAW of its international image for the first time in its 50-year history. Bieber also saw the union's requests for protectionism in the auto industry fall on deaf ears in Washington. The UAW demanded a national industrial policy to help protect jobs. It also proposed a requirement that foreign carmakers build a certain percentage of car parts in the United States to help create jobs for American workers.

"It's tougher than I anticipated," Bieber told the *Detroit News.* " There are so many problems. I'm not feeling sorry for myself, but there are so many different problems today. Before, [union presidents worried about] how much money the companies made and if the workers would get their share. They never had the other problems that are out there now like world competition, the Japanese." The complex issues aside, however, Bieber said he was pleased to be the UAW president and looked for more years in that post. "The good Lord willing, [and] good health, I hope to be around for some time," he told Joe Espo of the *Flint Journal.* In 1984 Bieber was named to Chrysler Corporation's 21-member board of directors. Doug Fraser, formerly head of the UAW, was on the board from 1980 until his retirement in 1984. Chrysler claimed that Bieber was being named as an individual and that the UAW had no proprietary claim to the seat. Industry observer's remarked that the seat really belonged to the Chrysler workers who had granted major concessions during the company's earlier financial problems and were the single largest bloc of shareholders in the corporation. In 1985 Bieber was in the ironic position of calling a strike against Chrysler when labor negotiations broke down. The strike was settled a week later following a 42-hour bargaining session amidst company accusations that the unnecessary $150 million strike was largely due to Bieber's confrontational and ineffectual bargaining style. Neither side was happy with the new contract. In 1989 Bieber told *WARD's Auto World* that future contract negotiations with the Big Three would center on non-economic issues such as job security, reduced work time, and in a precursor to the 1992 presidential election, national health care.

However, by 1992 Bieber and the UAW were mired in a bitter losing battle with Caterpillar Inc., a leading manufacturer of earth moving equipment. When contract negotiations failed, Caterpillar became entrenched and began hiring replacement workers. The strike lasted five months before the UAW, now crushed, ordered its members back to work without a contract. In a desperate attempt to re-assert the power of the UAW as 1993 Big Three contract negotiations approached, Bieber made a fiery and angry speech at a 1992 UAW convention in San Diego. He warned the auto companies against pushing the union too hard, saying that " . . . it takes two to make peace but only one to make a war." He warned the companies against "whipsawing" which is a union term for the policy of pitting one plant against another by threatening to close the one least cooperative and productive. Bieber also threatened the companies with future costly strikes:

> Do not forget that in the consumer-driven, retail, competitive markets in which you sell your products, you are especially vulnerable to lost production.

Bieber went on to defend the Union's policy with Caterpillar saying that the UAW hadn't capitulated and there is " . . . more than one way to skin a Cat!" Despite Bieber's speech, the UAW was still facing a bleak future and Bieber's stewardship of the union was doing little to improve the situation. The Caterpillar strike was a major defeat for the UAW and its ramifications were like shock waves to organized labor. In 1992 GM announced plans to close 21 plants and cut an estimated 50,000 UAW members from its workforce. By 1992 the UAW was successful in organizing only 8,000 of the estimated 100,000 workers employed by foreign car manufacturers with plants in the U.S. In 1978 the UAW represented 86 percent of the auto industry's workforce. It now represented only 68 percent, and since 1979 total UAW membership had fallen by 550,000 (1.5 million to 1.1 million). Consequently, Bieber was under tremendous pressure to cope with the falling fortunes of the UAW and pressure from within the Union for Bieber to retire before his scheduled departure in 1995.

However, Bieber did manage to hold onto his post and was succeeded in 1995 by Stephen Yokich, head of the UAW's GM department and long time rival.

Further Reading

Associated Press, November 13, 1982; May 12, 1983.
Automotive News, November 22, 1982.
Business Week, November 15, 1982; November 29, 1982; June 6, 1983; June 22, 1992.
Detroit Free Press, November 25, 1984; October 27, 1985; June 12, 1995.
Detroit News, July 29, 1980; November 14, 1982; May 20, 1984; June 15, 1992.
Flint Journal, November 18, 1982.
Industry Week, July 5, 1993.
New York Times, May 19, 1983.
Time, November 22, 1982; November 4, 1985.
U.S. News & World Report, May 30, 1983; September 24, 1984.
Wall Street Journal, February 14, 1984.
WARD'S Auto World, December 1989.
Washington Post, November 22, 1982. □

Sieur de Bienville

The French colonizer and administrator Jean Baptiste le Moyne, Sieur de Bienville (1680-1768), founded New Orleans in 1718. Largely through his leadership the French colony of Louisiana survived and eventually prospered.

Jean Baptiste de Bienville was born of an aristocratic family on Feb. 23, 1680, in Ville Marie, later called Montreal, Canada. In 1697, as a midshipman in the French navy, he served under the command of his elder brother Pierre le Moyne, Sieur d'Iberville, on an expedition to the Hudson Bay region. In the following year he traveled with his brother to rediscover the mouth of the Mississippi River and to colonize the area.

D'Iberville founded the colony of Louisiana at Biloxi in 1699, and Bienville remained as second in command to Governor Villantray. Bienville explored the lower Mississippi River in 1699 and the Red River in 1700, learning the Native Americans' languages in the process. On Villantray's death in 1701, Bienville became governor of Louisiana. In 1702 he transferred the colony to Mobile Bay, then Moved it to Mobile, which he founded.

When Louisiana became a monopoly of the French merchant Antoine Crozat in 1712, Bienville served under the new governor, Antoine de la Mothe Cadillac. In 1716 he commanded a military expedition that defeated the hostile Natchez Indians. Once again governor of Louisiana in 1717, Bienville founded New Orleans in the following year and made it his capital in 1722. In 1719 he twice captured Pensacola from the Spanish.

African American slaves had been brought to Louisiana under Bienville's direction; after he led an unsuccessful campaign against the Natchez Indians in 1723, he feared slave insurrections. Bienville therefore promulgated the *Code noir* (Black Code), which regulated the behavior of African American slaves for almost 100 years until Louisiana passed to United States control. The code was a detailed prescription of rights and duties and at the time was regarded as a humane document.

Summoned to France in 1725 to defend his leadership of Louisiana, Bienville was soon deprived of his authority. He remained in France until 1733, when the decline of the colony provoked his reappointment as governor and his return to Louisiana. He remained for 10 years, launched strenuous but indecisive campaigns against the Natchez and Chickasaw Indians, and finally retired to France, where he died in Paris on March 7, 1768.

Bienville was responsible, particularly after the death of D'Iberville in 1706, for keeping the colony alive. His heroic efforts overcame famine, Native American depredations, Spanish hostility, Canadian jealousy, and French neglect. The French tradition, which remains in Louisiana to this day, is a tribute to his skill as a colonial administrator.

tributor to William Randolph Hearst's *San Francisco Examiner*. In 1897 he went to Washington, D.C., as a correspondent for the Hearst papers.

Bierce won attention as a fiction writer with *Tales of Soldiers and Civilians* (1891), later titled *In the Midst of Life* (1892, revised and republished 1898), and *Can Such Things Be?* (1893). Both collections were reminiscent of Edgar Allan Poe's tales of terror, but Bierce's stories were often sardonic in tone and built to surprise endings. Other books that helped him win the nickname "Bitter Bierce" included collections of witty satirical verses, *Beetles in Amber* (1892) and *Shapes of Clay* (1903). *The Cynic's Word Book* (1906), retitled *The Devil's Dictionary* when it was reissued in 1911, was a gathering of succinct, witty, and usually vinegarish definitions; for example: "Patriotism, *n.,* Combustible rubbish ready to the torch of anyone ambitious to illuminate his name"; "Edible, *adj.,* Good to eat, and wholesome to digest, as a worm to a toad, a toad to a snake, a snake to a pig, a pig to man, and a man to a worm." In *Fantastic Fables* (1899) Bierce adapted Aesop's techniques to narratives which moralized about the day's economic, social, and political dilemmas, and *The Shadow on the Dial* (1909) brought together a number of disillusioned essays.

Bierce spent several years editing his *Collected Works* (12 vols., 1909-1912). In June, 1913, he wrote a friend, "Pretty soon I am going . . . very far away. I have in mind a little valley in the heart of the Andes, just wide enough for one. . . . Do you think I shall find my Vale of Peace?" The next year Bierce went to Mexico, at that time torn and disrupted by civil war, and he disappeared.

Further Reading

The standard biography of Bienville is Grace King, *Jean Baptiste Le Moyne, Sieur de Bienville* (1892). Background studies include Henry E. Chambers, *A History of Louisiana*, vol. 1 (1925); John Francis McDermott, ed., *The French in the Mississippi Valley* (1965); and Charles L. Dufour, *Ten Flags in the Wind: The Story of Louisiana* (1967). □

Ambrose Gwinett Bierce

The American writer Ambrose Gwinett Bierce (1842-c. 1914) expressed the cynicism of the post-Civil War era and shaped both the materials and the methods of writers who later voiced the disillusionment following World War I.

Ambrose Bierce was born in Meigs County, Ohio, and reared in Kosciusko County, Ind. He was a printer's apprentice before enlisting and serving with distinction in the Civil War. He launched a journalistic career in California and continued it in London from 1872 to 1876. There he served on the staffs of the magazines *Fun* and the *Lantern*, contributed to *Hood's Comic Almanac*, and under the pseudonym Dod Grile published the books *Fiend's Delight* (1872), *Nuggets and Dust Panned Out in California* (1872), and *Cobwebs from an Empty Skull* (1874). Back in California he became an outstanding con-

Bierce's stress in his war stories on the psychological and physical impacts and on the meaninglessness of conflict anticipated Stephen Crane and the many writers who expressed disillusionment after World Wars I and II. Bierce mingled foreign phrases, latinate words, and vernacular phrasings in anticlimactic and periodic sentences to express forcibly his cynical attitude. His style foreshadowed that of one of the most influential American writers of the skeptical 1920s, H. L. Mencken.

Further Reading

Bierce's *Collected Works* (12 vols., 1909-1912) brings together a large share of his literary and journalistic writings. Bertha C. Pope edited *Letters of Ambrose Bierce* (1922). The two best biographical and critical studies are Paul Fatout, *Ambrose Bierce: The Devil's Lexicographer* (1951), and Richard O'Connor, *Ambrose Bierce* (1967).

Additional Sources

Bierce, Ambrose, *Ambrose Bierce's Civil War,* Washington, D.C.: Regnery Gateway; New York, N.Y.: Distributed by Kampmann, 1988.

De Castro, Adolphe Danziger, *Portrait of Ambrose Bierce,* New York, Beekman Publishers, 1974.

Grattan, C. Hartley (Clinton Hartley), *Bitter Bierce; a mystery of American letter,* New York, Cooper Square Publishers, 1966.

Morris, Roy, *Ambrose Bierce: alone in bad company,* New York: Crown Publishers, 1995.

Saunders, Richard, *Ambrose Bierce: the making of a misanthrope,* San Francisco: Chronicle Books, 1985. □

Albert Bierstadt

Albert Bierstadt (1830-1902) was the last of the older generation of American romantic landscape painters.

Albert Bierstadt, born in Solingen, near Düsseldorf, Germany, on Jan. 7, 1830, was brought to New Bedford, Mass., as a baby. At the age of 21 he determined to be a painter, and in 1853 he went to Düsseldorf to study. Bierstadt was trained to use a light, meticulous technique and drab coloring; as a result, his painting always tended to be rather stiff and dry. He returned to New Bedford in 1857, and the following year he went west on a surveying expedition. There Bierstadt first saw the scenic grandeur which would become the chief subject matter of his paintings.

With the opening of the West there was enormous popular interest in the romantic splendor of the mountain scenery, and Bierstadt came along at just the right time to make the most of the situation. He executed numerous small sketches on the spot, which he combined and rearranged in his studio to produce panoramas of large scale.

In his early paintings, such as the *Bombardment of Fort Sumter,* Bierstadt worked in a clear, luminous style which lent enchantment to the scene. His early sketches of the West, with their silvery light and poetic mood, marked the

final flowering of the romantic style in American painting. His large canvases were ponderous and dry and too melodramatic. His colors became raw and the work lacked spontaneity. Yet in one canvas, *Hetch Hetchie Canyon,* done in the mid-1870s, he managed to combine the feeling of grandeur with a poetic mood and a magical light. He was tempted too often to overextend himself and, not being a painter of much intensity of feeling, was unable to sustain vitality when working on large scale. He loved publicity and was carried away by the uncritical enthusiasm of the general public rather than heeding the more carefully considered criticism of those who were better informed.

Although Bierstadt's sketches are fresher and more spontaneous, his huge canvases were eagerly sought and commanded prices from $5,000 to $35,000. His painting of Estes Park, Colo., executed for the 4th Earl of Dunraven, a noted game hunter in the Rockies, started a Bierstadt fad in Great Britain.

During his lifetime Bierstadt received many honors, and Congress purchased two of his paintings for the Capitol in Washington, D.C. He was decorated in Germany and Austria, and in France he was made a chevalier of the Légion d'Honneur. He became a member of the National Academy of Design in New York in 1860.

Bierstadt's considerable wealth enabled him to build a mansion at Irvington-on-Hudson, N.Y., where he lived in great style. Although he was honored as America's most successful painter, other artists resented him. In the 1880s new styles in painting caught the public's fancy, and

Bierstadt lost popularity. His house burned down, his fortune had been expended, and his work was regarded as old-fashioned and outdated. In the 1940s, after 50 years of oblivion, his work began to regain popularity as interest in American romantic painting revived. His smaller works, especially the earlier sketches, are now greatly admired, and he has been restored to the position he deserves.

Further Reading

While there are no full-length studies devoted to Bierstadt, his painting is discussed in several works, including Eugen Neuhaus, *The History and Ideals of American Art* (1931); Frederick A. Sweet, *The Hudson River School and the Early American Landscape Tradition* (1945); Oliver W. Larkin, *Art and Life in America* (1949; rev. ed. 1960); and Edgar P. Richardson, *Painting in America: The Story of 450 Years* (1956).

Additional Sources

Baigell, Matthew, *Albert Bierstadt,* New York: Watson-Guptill, 1981.

Hendricks, Gordon, *Albert Bierstadt: painter of the American West,* New York: Harrison House: Distributed by Crown Publishers, 1988. □

John Bigelow

John Bigelow (1817-1911) was the American consul in Paris during the Civil War, and later he was minister to France. Also a journalist and editor, he took an active part in public affairs for more than 70 years.

John Bigelow was born on Nov. 25, 1817, in Bristol (now Malden), N.Y. He graduated from Union College in 1835. While studying law in New York City, he wrote political essays and reviews for newspapers and became involved in Democratic party politics. His friend Samuel J. Tilden secured him an appointment in 1845 as an inspector of Sing Sing Prison, where he won a reputation as an advocate of penal reform. In 1848 William Cullen Bryant invited Bigelow to become part owner and editor of the *New York Evening Post,* a liberal Democratic paper strongly committed to free trade and humanitarian reform. In 1855 the editors broke with the Democratic party because it supported the extension of slavery into Kansas. Bigelow joined the antislavery Republican party soon after, despite his dislike of its high-tariff policies.

In 1861 Bigelow, prosperous and widely known, retired from the *Evening Post.* Shortly thereafter, President Abraham Lincoln appointed him consul general in Paris. The Lincoln administration feared that European sympathy for the Confederacy would lead to diplomatic recognition and material aid. America's representatives abroad, therefore, were involved in efforts to prevent foreign intervention. Much of the European press was pro-Confederate, and Bigelow worked assiduously to establish a more favorable climate of opinion. He published numerous articles arguing the Union cause and warning against any French involvement with the South. He worked effectively behind the scenes, too—first as the American consul and later as minister to France (1865-1866)—to counter French opposition to the Union blockade of Confederate ports, to soften anger over the *Trent* affair, and to prevent any infringements of French neutrality. At the end of his tenure he tried to reverse French military intervention in Mexico.

In 1866 Bigelow resigned and returned to the United States. He engaged in active politics only briefly thereafter—to help Tilden, now governor of New York, in his campaign against political corruption in the state in the early 1870s, to run as a Democrat for secretary of state of New York in 1875, to work for Tilden's election as president in 1876, and to serve as a delegate to the New York constitutional convention in 1894. Bigelow's chief postwar literary achievements included the first publication (1868) of the authentic version of Benjamin Franklin's *Autobiography,* the manuscript of which he had found in France; the editing of 10 volumes of Franklin's works (1887-1889); the editing of Tilden's speeches and letters; and the writing of Bryant's biography (1890). Bigelow also contributed periodical and newspaper articles on a variety of social and political issues. As executor of Tilden's will, he helped establish the New York Public Library in 1895.

Further Reading

Bigelow's autobiography is *Retrospections of an Active Life* (5 vols., 1909-1913). Margaret A. Clapp, *Forgotten First Citizen:*

John Bigelow (1947), is a sympathetic and competent biography. □

John Thomas Bigge

John Thomas Bigge (1780-1843) was an English colonial judge and royal commissioner whose reports on the status of New South Wales and Tasmania stimulated reforms that led to the erosion of the penal nature of the colonies.

John Bigge was born on March 8, 1780, at Benton House, Long Benton, Northumberland, the second son of Thomas Charles Bigge, the sheriff of Northumberland, and his wife Jemima, both from wealthy though untitled gentry stock. Bigge was educated at Christ Church, Oxford, where he received his bachelor's degree in 1801 and his master's degree in 1804. In 1806 he was called to the bar at the Inner Temple and soon became a successful London barrister.

In 1810 Bigge took his sister to convalesce in Madeira, where he studied Spanish law and became an intimate of Sir Ralph Woodford. Woodford became governor of Trinidad in 1813 and the following year had Bigge appointed his chief justice. Woodford enlarged Bigge's powers by making him a judge of the Vice Admiralty Court, judge of intestate, prior of the Court of Consulado, and a member of the Court of Audencia.

In 1814 Bigge became senior member of the Trinidad Council and in 1815 was recommended for the title of alcalde mayor. Bigge overcame complex sociolegal problems and occasionally undertook important civil work for the governor, but he resented having to administer Spanish law and in 1818 he resigned.

Inspections and Inquiries

Bigge's success in Trinidad and Woodford's influence with Lord Bathurst, secretary of state for the colonies, facilitated Bigge's appointment on Jan. 5, 1819, to inquire into the "laws, regulations, and usages" of the colonies of New South Wales and Van Diemen's Land (Tasmania), with special reference to the administration, convicts, legal system, the Church, trade, revenue, and natural resources. By 1819 the Australian colonies were beginning to outgrow their penal foundations, and limited capitalistic growth had conditioned conflict between individual colonists and Governor Lachlan Macquarie. The British government had received many complaints about Macquarie's alleged despotism and especially about his favorable policy toward ex-convicts. But above all, the government wanted colonial expenses reduced.

Bigge arrived in Sydney on Sept. 26, 1819, on a salary of £ 3,000; Macquarie, 20 years Bigge's senior, was on £ 2,000. Bigge spent 17 months in the colonies and then presented three reports: in 1822 the "State of the Colony" and in 1823 the "Judicial Establishments" and the "State of

Agriculture and Trade." The reports were based on extensive travel and observation and the examination of nearly all of the male free settlers, about 60 ex-convicts, and hundreds of convicts, and they had far-reaching effects on the constitutional, legal, political, and economic development of eastern Australia, including Van Diemen's Land.

Bigge's cool detachment helped him to make an intensive, tireless, and skillful investigation that was, however, marked by clashes with Macquarie. Bigge's first report was critical of Macquarie's convict and public works policy; his second, supplemented by private reports to Bathurst, disapproved of Macquarie's use of legislative and executive powers and supported proposals to reform the colonies' legal systems; and his third was a valuable summary of colonial economic growth.

From 1823 to 1830 Bigge investigated and submitted reports on the colonies of Cape Colony, Mauritius, and Ceylon, which resulted in reforms of government and legal machinery. He then retired because of ill health; he died, unmarried, on Dec. 22, 1843, in London.

Further Reading

There is no biography of Bigge. J. D. Ritchie, *Punishment and Profit: The Reports of Commissioner John Bigge on the Colonies of New South Wales and Van Diemen's Land; Their Origins, Nature and Significance* (1970), is a brilliant account of the early career of Bigge and of his Australian experiences. He is discussed in all histories of Australia, notably in Charles M. H. Clark, *A History of Australia* (2 vols., 1962-1968). Clark also edited a useful collection, *Select Documents in Australian History* (2 vols., 1950-1955). Bigge's work in South Africa is discussed in Isobel E. Edwards, *The 1820 Settlers in South Africa: A Study in British Colonial Policy* (1934). For information on the colonial office background see J. J. Eddy, *Britain and the Australian Colonies, 1818-1831* (1969). □

Hermann Michael Biggs

Hermann Michael Biggs (1859-1923) was an American pioneer in the field of public health, concentrating on the application of the science of bacteriology to the prevention and control of contagious diseases.

Hermann Biggs was born on Sept. 29, 1859, in the village of Trumansburgh, N. Y. He attended the Trumansburgh and Ithaca academies and entered Cornell University in 1879. Deciding on a medical career, he left Cornell in 1881 to study at Bellevue Hospital Medical College in New York City. He returned to Cornell, however, to receive his degree in 1882. In 1883 Bellevue awarded him a medical degree. During his internship at Bellevue, Biggs developed an interest in microscopic pathology and the new science of bacteriology. In 1884 he visited Germany, a pioneering center of the germ theory of disease, and in 1885 he visited the laboratories of Louis Pasteur in France. Frequent trips to Europe in later years kept him in constant contact with the latest developments in bacteriology. When he returned from his first European trip, he became a major member of the newly established Carnegie Laboratory at Bellevue, devoted to bacteriology. This was the first bacteriological laboratory in the United States to apply this science directly to public health—an application that was essentially the result of Biggs's guidance.

When a division of bacteriology was created within the New York City Department of Health in 1892, Biggs was appointed chief inspector. In 1901 he was appointed general medical officer of New York City and in 1914 became the commissioner of health for the state of New York. From such positions he guided the development of public health measures in New York, and New York, in turn, guided the nation.

One of Biggs's greatest fights was waged against tuberculosis, thought by many to be a nutritional disorder. As early as 1889 Biggs noted the potential public health importance of the discovery of the tubercle bacillus in Germany by Robert Koch. Fighting older ideas, he succeeded in establishing and enforcing control measures based on sound reasoning in bacteriology. These included the reporting of cases to the health authorities and the disinfection of places in which tubercular patients lived. He also advocated the establishment of special sanatoriums.

Biggs was instrumental in the adoption of programs for the identification and control of venereal disease through laboratory analysis; he advocated nursing measures to combat infant mortality; and he introduced, on an administrative level, the use of vaccines to prevent disease. He also advocated the concept of a public health center that would include clinics, hospitals, and diagnostic facilities. His ideas were defeated then, but the health care center has since become reality.

Biggs died on June 28, 1923. He was survived by his wife of 25 years, Frances Richardson Biggs.

Further Reading

The definitive biography of Biggs is C. E. A. Winslow, *The Life of Hermann M. Biggs* (1929). See also Winslow's short study, *The Contribution of Hermann Biggs to Public Health* (1929). For background material see George Rosen, *A History of Public Health* (1958). □

Steve Biko

Steve Biko (1946-1977), a political activist and writer, is regarded as the father of the Black Consciousness movement in the Union of South Africa.

Stephen Bantu Biko (a. k. a. Bantu Stephen Biko) was born in King Williamstown, Cape Province, South Africa, on December 18, 1946. He was the second son (third child) of Mzimgayi Biko. Raised and educated in a Christian home, Biko eventually became a student at Wentworth, a White medical school in Durban. There in 1968 he formed SASO (South African Students' Organiza-

tion), an activist group seeking equal rights for South African black people. Expelled from Wentworth in 1972 (the stated cause being poor academic performance), Biko devoted his time to activist activities. His concept of black consciousness continued to develop as he next went to work for BCP (Black Community Programmes). By 1973 his political activities had caused him to be banned from Durban and restricted to his hometown. Back in King Williamstown, undaunted, he set up a new branch of BCP—only to have it banned there as well

Still, Biko continued to work for black consciousness. This led to repeated detentions and caused him to be placed in security over and over again. Yet he was *never* charged. In 1977 he became honorary president of the Black People's Convention he had founded in 1972. His appointment was to be for a period of five years, but nine months later he died of brain damage after being beaten by police officers while in detention.

Biko's short 30-year life was consumed with the development of an acute awareness of the evils of apartheid, the social system under which non-Whites lived in South Africa. Apartheid is based on the idea of institutionalized separate development for blacks and whites. To paraphrase Biko, he was able to outgrow the things the system had taught him. One of his unique characteristics may be summed up in the title of an edited collection of his writings, *I Write What I Like* (1978, Aelred Stubbs, ed.). Much of what Biko "liked to write," not surprisingly, dealt with the definition of black consciousness and setting it out as an approach to combatting White racism in South Africa. Indeed the very

phrase "I write what I like" was boldly used as a heading to begin many of his political essays. One such essay was accompanied by the by-line "Frank Talk," an aptly chosen pseudonym.

A magnetic, eloquent, tall, and large-proportioned person, Biko inspired love and loyalty. In 1970 he married Ntsiki Mashalaba, then a nursing student in Durban. When the couple had been restricted to King Williamstown, Ntsiki commuted to work at an Anglican mission 35 miles away in order to earn money to keep the family together. Biko's father died when he was four years old. His mother courageously supported her son's activities, welcomed him home during the years of restriction, helped protect him from the inquiring eyes of government security forces, and provided a Christian (Anglican) home environment for his children.

Biko's death echoed around the world—an irony, given the repeated attempts made to silence him while he lived. As a leader of South African blacks, Biko is likened in importance to others such as Nelson Mandela and Robert Sobukwe who preceded him. Like Biko, their influence was during the post-1948 years—that is, after the African National Congress began to gain support throughout the nation in the interest of black liberation. Mandela and Sobukwe, too, were repeatedly banned and imprisoned. In fact, it was while they were in detention in the 1960s that Biko formed SASO to fill the "vacuum in South African politics" that they had left.

Biko's "Black Consciousness" was a call to black young people to dissociate white control and black fear in South Africa and to adopt an attitude of psychological self-reliance in the struggle for liberation from white rule. The proponents of Black Consciousness urged blacks to withdraw from multiracial organizations. The resulting formation of the all-black SASO alienated some white liberal students—particularly those who belonged to NUSA (National Union of South African Students). These students' idealism was given a jolt by SASO's assertion of an independent black struggle.

The concept of Black Consciousness has been preserved in Biko's writings and in transcripts taken in the BPC-SASO trial at which Biko was called to testify, allowing him to break a three-year imposed silence. This trial was the only opportunity Biko had to speak out after 1973 when his travel, public speaking, and writing for publication had been banned. The trial also turned out to be the last time Biko was heard from before his death in Port Elizabeth on September 12, 1977.

The South African government disclaimed any responsibility in Biko's death, and official pronouncements about its circumstances revolve around talk of a hunger strike while others cite evidence of beatings. Twenty years later, in 1997, five former police officers acknowledged responsibility for his death of a brain hemorrhage. The officers made their confession to South Africa's Truth Commission, which has the power to grant amnesty to individuals willing to reveal their role in the violence against anti-apartheid activists.

The effect of Biko's death, seen by many as symbolic of black South Africa suffering under apartheid and the most widely publicized dramatization of the apartheid system in operation, added impetus to Black Consciousness—the very movement that repeated bannings and restrictions by government officials sought to quell. The idea of Black Consciousness is thought by many to have uplifted and inspired South African black people and to have given direction to their lives.

To Biko, black psychological self-reliance was the path to social equality. His vision of the future for South African blacks was one "looking forward to a nonracial, just and egalitarian society in which color, creed, and race shall form no point of reference." Many hoped Biko's dream would become reality when apartheid was disbanded and in 1994, ANC leader Nelson Mandela was elected president of the country.

Further Reading

For a description of Biko's last public appearance as a witness for the defense in the *Trial of Sathasivan Cooper and Eight Others* (a.k.a. the BPC-SASO trial), see Millard Arnold (ed.), *Steve Biko: Black Consciousness in South Africa* (1978). This book consists primarily of court transcripts and affords the reader the opportunity to read Biko's views right before he died and the first expressed after three years of silence. For a biography of Biko written by a close friend, see *Biko* by Donald Woods (1978). Biko's writings have been collected in Fr. Aelred Stubbs, c.r. (ed.) *Steve Biko-I Write What I Like* (London, 1978). Newspapers all over the world after September 12, 1977, reported Biko's death. □

William Billings

William Billings (1746-1800) was the first native-born professional composer in the United States. He wrote hymns, sometimes with his own words, and was also a singing master.

The son of a Boston tanner, William Billings evidently received a common-school education. At an early age he went into his father's business. Billings enthusiastically joined the two-generations-old singing-school movement of the Congregational churches. He taught himself composition from hymnbooks, especially William Tans'ur's *Royal Melody Compleat, or The New Harmony of Zion* (London, 1755; reprinted in seven Boston editions, 1767-1774), which had a pedagogical preface on "the grounds of musick." He chalked his notes on the tannery walls and hides and once declared there was nothing connected with the science of music that he had not mastered. He scoffed at the rules, proclaiming "Nature is the best dictator."

The Revolutionary patriot Samuel Adams enjoyed singing in Billings's viol-accompanied choir. The Brattle Street and Old South churches engaged Billings to teach hymns and anthems, as did many other Congregational churches in Massachusetts and Episcopal King's Chapel.

Billings was 22 when he wrote a remarkable round, "Jesus Wept," for four voices, although he did not compose fuguing tunes, or contrapuntal part-songs, for another decade. Paul Revere engraved Billings's first hymnbook, *The New England Psalm-Singer* (1770). Eight years later Billings published a much improved version, *The Singing Master's Assistant,* in which he added a text beginning "Let tyrants shake their iron rod" to his earlier tune "Chester." This hymn, of unexpected delicacy as well as lustiness, was very popular during the Revolutionary War. Another hymn, which reappeared with new words, "Methinks I hear a heav'nly host," runs as a theme song through all his work. The contrived discords of "Jargon" may actually be satirizing Billings's own earlier primitivisms.

Billings left tanning to open a music shop, where pranksters on one occasion slung howling cats with their tails tied together over his sign. He was an energetic and good-humored man, blind in one eye, with a withered arm and legs of unequal length. He dipped snuff, not by the pinch but by the handful, from his leather coat pocket. His voice drowned out even a stentorian pastor of Brookline, who complained that he could not hear himself next to Billings. Billings, however, urged the propagation of soft music "to refine the Ears."

The last collections Billings published were *The Suffolk Harmony* (1786) and *The Continental Harmony* (1794). After the Revolution his music was considered outmoded in New England, and he died neglected. But it took a new lease on life in the South and on the frontier in the West.

Although Billings's compositions sound surprisingly medieval for the age of Mozart, they reflect American Revolutionary and Federal vigor. They represented a stage in the rising bourgeois culture of America. Through sheer bravado and industriousness Billings sometimes even achieved artistic success.

Further Reading

All of Billings's publications survive in rare-book collections. Harvard University Press brought out a facsimile edition of *Continental Harmony* with an introduction by Hans Nathan in 1961. The most convenient introduction to Billings's work is W. Thomas Marrocco and Harold Gleason, eds., *Music in America . . . 1620-1865* (1964). □

James Hadley Billington

The American scholar and author James Hadley Billington (born 1929) was a student of Russian history who became director of the Woodrow Wilson International Center for Scholars and later the Librarian of Congress.

James Hadley Billington was born June 1, 1929, in Bryn Mawr, Pennsylvania, the son of Nelson and Jane (Coolbaugh) Billington. He attended schools in the Philadelphia area and graduated from the Lower Merion High School, where he was the class valedictorian and had been elected school president in 1946. While in high school during World War II, he had become interested in Russian history and literature and began studying the Russian language. Billington later majored in European history at Princeton University, where he was inducted into Phi Beta Kappa. He earned his bachelor of arts degree and graduated first in his class in 1950.

Billington went to England as a Rhodes scholar at Balliol College for his graduate studies. He earned a doctor of philosophy degree from Oxford in 1953. Returning to the U.S., he joined the army. During his term of active duty, from 1953 to 1956, he rose through the ranks from private to first lieutenant.

The young scholar then embarked on his career of research and teaching. He became a history instructor at Harvard University in 1957 and an assistant professor of history and research fellow at the Russian Research Center in 1958. During this period his first book, *Mikhailovsky and Russian Populism* (1958), was published. The book, an expansion of his doctoral thesis at Oxford, was a biography of an important 19th-century liberal (non-Marxist) journalist and social critic. Billington called him the greatest of Russia's radical humanists. The book's analysis shed light on the political and social thinking in Russia before the Marxist revolution.

Billington transferred to his alma mater, Princeton University, in 1961. As professor of history, Billington's research and teaching interests sent him to university settings

in Moscow, St. Petersburg, Tel Aviv, Puerto Rico, Helsinki, and Paris. His travels permitted him to gather material for his next books. *The Icon and the Axe: An Interpretive History of Russian Culture* (1966) is a massive book that traces 600 years of Russian civilization and emphasizes aspects of thought, culture, and religion that shaped Russia's character and temperament. The author focused on symbols that were important to Russian imagination and on spiritual and ideological patterns. The book demonstrated Billington's approach to research. He believed in interpretive scholarship and felt that understanding a nation requires a multidimensional investigation of its religion, literature, arts, and aspirations.

He contributed an essay on the social and religious relevance of art in culture to *The Arts of Russia* (1970). The essay showed his admiration for the artistic accomplishments of the Russian people.

Billington became director of the Woodrow Wilson International Center for Scholars in September 1973. The center was created by Congress in 1968 as a living memorial to the 28th President and is located at the Smithsonian Institution in Washington, D.C. The center grew under Billington's administration. American and foreign scholars were invited to spend time reflecting on the humanities and social sciences. Billington expanded the scope and activity of the center. He helped create the Kennan Institute for Advanced Russian Studies in 1974, believing that the relationship with the Soviet Union was America's most important international problem. He also helped start *Wilson Quarterly,* a scholarly magazine.

Billington's administrative leadership did not sidetrack him from creative pursuits. During 1973 he wrote and hosted the "Humanities Film Forum," a series of 14 scholarly discussions on nationwide educational television. He was a guest commentator and historian-consultant for major television networks. He wrote articles for a variety of professional and popular magazines. In addition, he was a chairperson and a member of the Board of Foreign Scholarships, which directed academic exchanges with 110 countries under the Fulbright-Hays Act.

Billington wrote *Fire in the Minds of Men: Origins of the Revolutionary Faith* (1980). The book highlights philosophers who sparked European development in the period from the French to the Russian revolutions. This, as in his previous books, was massively documented. It was nominated for a National Book Award.

Recognized as a scholar of Russian history and culture, he was invited to participate in American-Soviet exchange meetings. He accompanied the leadership delegations of the Congress to the Soviet Union in 1979 and 1983. He went with President Reagan to the summit meetings in June 1988.

Active in his community, he was a vice chairman of the board of trustees of St. Albans School in Washington, D.C., and a member of the roundtable organized by the presiding bishop of the Episcopal Church of the United States.

President Reagan nominated Billington as Librarian of Congress. Although not trained as a professional librarian,

his administrative and fund-raising experience at the Wilson Center and his reputation as a scholar made him a good choice for the nomination. On September 14, 1987, he was sworn in as the 13th head of the library, succeeding Daniel J. Boorstin. As librarian, Billington oversaw the largest collection of books, maps, photographs, recordings, motion pictures, and so forth in the world. Billington has been working to create a National Digital Library, which makes these documents available to the public via computer. Billington firmly believes that Americans need to stay in close touch with their history, and by digitizing the books in the Library of Congress, he told John Maclean of *Reader's Digest,* they are "putting them into people's hands." Billington expects to have five million items digitized by the year 2000.

Billington continued to be involved in Russian relations. In 1991 he was invited to be an honored guest at an event welcoming back Russian emigres in Moscow. When he returned to the United States, the Russian chief of archival affairs entrusted him with 300 files dating back to the October Revolution of 1917.

The changes in Eastern Europe prompted Billington to write another book, *Russia Transformed: Breakthrough to Hope,* published in 1992. The following year he returned to Russia as part of a bipartisan delegation of House leadership.

Billington's contributions have been recognized in various ways. He received the Gwangwa Medal of the Republic of Korea in 1991, the Woodrow Wilson Award from Princeton University in 1992, and the Knight Commander's Cross of Order of Merit from the Federal Republic of Germany in 1996. He holds several honorary degrees, is a member of the American Academy of Arts and Sciences and the American Philosophical Society, and a Commander of the Order of Arts and Letters of France.

Billington married Marjorie Ann Brennan on June 22, 1957. They have two daughters and two sons.

Further Reading

There is no book-length biography of Billington. Short articles about him and his work have appeared at various stages of his career. Edward P. Morgan discussed Billington and the Woodrow Wilson Center in "Wilson Center Immerses Scholars in Think Tank," *Smithsonian* (August 1977). Reactions to his appointment as Librarian of Congress appeared in Irvin Molotsky, "A Scholarly Librarian," *New York Times* (April 18, 1987), and Ellen K. Coughlin, "Director of Woodrow Wilson Center Is Said To Be White House's Choice for Librarian of Congress," *Chronicle of Higher Education* (April 22, 1987). A Billington interview is reported in Carla Hall, "Chapter and Verse, American Style," *Washington Post* (April 18, 1987). See also John Maclean, "Librarian for the People," *Reader's Digest* (June 1995), *Who's Who in America* (1996), and *Who's Who in the World* (1996). The web site for The U.S. National Commission on Libraries and Information Science also contains biographical information about Billington at http://www.nclis.gov/what/bios/billingt.html. □

Billy the Kid

William H. Bonney, known as Billy the Kid (1859-1881), was the prototype of the American western gunslinger. He was the youngest and most convincing of the folk hero-villains.

On Nov. 23, 1859, William Bonney was born in New York City but moved as a young lad to Kansas. His father soon died, and his mother remarried and moved west to New Mexico. Having killed a man for insulting his mother, Bonney fled to the Pecos Valley, where he was drawn into the cattle wars then in progress. He became a savage murderer of many men, including Sheriff James Brady and a deputy, and scorned Governor Lew Wallace's demand that he surrender. "His equal for sheer inborn savagery," wrote journalist Emerson Hough, "has never lived." Such statements sent Bonney's reputation soaring and won him the nickname Billy the Kid.

Enjoying such notoriety, Billy the Kid gave no quarter to a hostile world. Condemned to hang, he heard a Las Vegas, Nev., judge say: "You are sentenced to be hanged by the neck until you are dead, dead, dead!" "And you can go to hell, hell, hell!" Billy spat back for an answer.

There are few facts about Billy the Kid's career that can be verified. It is known that women found him attractive. To Native American woman named Deluvina, who pulled off her shawl and wrapped it around him when he was a handcuffed prisoner, Billy gave the tintype of himself which remains the only authentic likeness. Sally Chisum, chatelaine of a large ranch, reported: "In all his personal relations he was the pink of politeness and as courteous a little gentleman as I ever met."

Sheriff Pat Garrett and a large posse vowed to track Billy down and destroy him. In the fall of 1881 they trapped him at Pete Maxwell's house in Fort Summer, N.Mex., ambushed him in a pitch-black room, and shot him to death. The next day he was buried in a borrowed white shirt too large for his slim body. Admirers scraped together $208 for a gravestone, which was later splintered and carried away by relic hunters. Billy had lived exactly 21 years 7 months 21 days.

From the first Billy's fame was part of a folkloric, oral tradition; it had more to do with western chauvinism than with literal history. If his crimes are dated, his appeal is not, as attested to by the many books and movies based on his life.

Further Reading

An important source for material on Billy is Jefferson C. Dykes, *Billy the Kid: The Bibliography of a Legend* (1952), which lists and evaluates all the earlier material. Writers and publicists most responsible for Bonney's fame include Charlie Siringo, *History of "Billy the Kid"* (1920), and Walter Noble Burns, *The Saga of Billy the Kid* (1926).

Additional Sources

The Capture of Billy the Kid, College Station, Tex.: Creative Pub. Co., 1988.

Cline, Donald, *Alias Billy the Kid: the man behind the legend,* Santa Fe, N.M.: Sunstone Press, 1986.

Fable, Edmund, *The true life of Billy the Kid, the noted New Mexican outlaw,* College Station, Tex.: Creative Pub. Co., 1980.

Garrett, Pat F. (Pat Floyd), *The authentic life of Billy the Kid: the noted desperado of the Southwest, whose deeds of daring and blood made his name a terror in New Mexico, Arizona, and northern Mexico,* Alexandria, Va.: Time-Life Books, 1980.

Priestley, Lee, *Billy the Kid: the good side of a bad man,* Las Cruces, N.M.: Arroyo Press, 1989; Las Cruces, N.M.: Yucca Tree Press, 1993.

Tuska, Jon, *Billy the Kid, a bio-bibliography,* Westport, Conn.: Greenwood Press, 1983.

Tuska, Jon, *Billy the Kid, a handbook,* Lincoln: University of Nebraska Press, 1986, 1983.

Tuska, Jon, *Billy the Kid, his life and legend,* Westport, Conn.: Greenwood Press, 1994.

Utley, Robert Marshall, *Billy the Kid: a short and violent life,* Lincoln: University of Nebraska Press, 1989. □

Alfred Binet

The French psychologist Alfred Binet (1857-1911) was the founder of French experimental psychology. He devised tests for measuring intelligence that have been widely used in schools.

Alfred Binet was born in Nice on July 11, 1857. He studied law and medicine in Paris and then obtained a doctorate in natural science. He became interested in hysteria and hypnosis and frequented Jean Martin Charcot's neurological clinic at the Sâlpétrière Hospital. During this time Binet wrote *La Psychologie du raisonnement* (1886; The Psychology of Reasoning), *Le Magnétisme animal* (1887; Animal Magnetism), and *On Double Consciousness* (1889).

In 1891 Binet joined the Laboratory of physiological Psychology of the École Pratique des Hautes Études; the following year he became assistant director and in 1895 director. He held this post for the rest of his life. In 1895 he founded the experimental journal *L'Année psychologique,* in which he published articles on emotion, memory, attention, and problem solving—articles which contained a considerable number of methodological innovations.

Although trained in abnormal psychology, Binet never ceased to be interested in the psychology of intelligence and individual differences. After publishing *Les Altérations de la personalité* (1892; The Alterations of the Personality) with C. Féré, Binet studied complex calculators, chess players, and literary creativity by the survey method. In 1900 he also became interested in suggestibility, a normal continuation of his work on hysteria.

Binet's major interest, however, was the development of intelligence, and in 1899 he established a laboratory at the École de la Rue de la Grange aux Belles. Here he devised a series of tests to study intellectual development in his daughters Armande and Marguerite. His wellknown work, *L'Étude expérimentale de l'intelligence* (1903; The Experimental Study of Intelligence), in which he showed that there could be imageless thought, was based on these studies with his daughters.

Two years later, in response to the request of the minister of public instruction to find a means for enabling learning disabled children to benefit from some kind of schooling, Binet, in collaboration with Théodore Simon, created "new methods for the diagnosis of retarded children's mental level," which were partly based on his earlier work. His scale for measuring intelligence was widely adopted. In 1908 the American psychologist Lewis M. Terman revised it (Stanford Revision). Binet himself improved his test in 1908 and 1911. He also continued to be interested in psychological applications to pedagogical problems: *Les Enfants anormaux* (1907; Abnormal Children), written with Simon; and *Less Idées modernes sur les enfants* (1909; Modern Ideas on Children). Binet died on Oct. 8, 1911.

Further Reading

Several of Binet's papers are collected and translated in R.H. Pollack, ed., *The Experimental Psychology of Alfred Binet: Selected Papers* (1969), which included a complete bibliography of Binet's work, indicating those papers which are translated into English. Edith J. Varon, *The Development of Alfred Binet's Psychology* (1935), appeared as vol. 46 of *Psychological Monographs*, edited by Joseph Peterson. The best texts on the history of psychology, such as G. A. Miller, *Psychology: The Science of Mental Life* (1962), discuss the contributions of Binet.

Additional Sources

Wolf, Theta Holmes, *Alfred Binet,* Chicago, University of Chicago Press 1973. ☐

George Caleb Bingham

The American painter George Caleb Bingham (1811-1879) depicted life in Missouri around the middle of the 19th century. His best-known subjects are the masculine world of river boatmen and rural politics.

Although George Caleb Bingham is known today for his well-composed, candid genre paintings, he also painted portraits and landscapes. In fact, in his 40 years of work he created fewer than 50 narrative paintings, while his portraits probably total more than a thousand. Most of his genre studies were painted during a span of only 10 years. He spent most of his mature life in politics and portrait painting; his involvement in Missouri politics led to many portrait commissions. Thus, during his lifetime he was best known as a politician and portrait painter, rather than as the master of genre he is considered today.

Bingham was born March 20, 1811, in rural Virginia. Eight years later his family moved to Franklin, Mo., where his father operated an inn for 3 years before his death. When Bingham was 16, he was apprenticed to a cabinetmaker in the river town of Boonville, Mo. Soon after, determined to be an artist, he took up sign painting and about 1833 began painting portraits. He was largely a self-taught artist.

Self-portrait (1835) is typical of his early portraiture. The expression is strong, the handling stiff. In the spring of 1836, he married Sarah Elizabeth Hutchison and in the following winter went to Natchez, Miss., to do portraiture.

First Genre Paintings

In 1838 while on a 3-month visit to Philadelphia (where he studied at the Pennsylvania Academy), he made his first genre painting. Titled *Western Boatman Ashore,* it has been lost, like many of his paintings. His choice of western subjects reflected a deep interest in his fellow Missourians, a concern that also led him to take an active part in regional politics. During the next 7 years he was busy painting both portraits and political banners. It was not until 1845 that he took up genre painting in earnest.

Among his earliest and finest genre paintings is *Fur Traders Descending the Missouri* (1845), which depicts a man and a boy in a canoe in early morning. At the St. Louis Mercantile Library are detailed pencil and graywash drawings of these 2 figures as well as studies of 115 other figures that appear in his later works. Except for the addition of color, the figures in his finished paintings are identical with these wash drawings, so they were probably traced onto the canvas.

Political Paintings and Historical Works

Most of Bingham's finest narrative paintings were done between 1845 and 1856. Occasionally he repeated the same subject either exactly, as in the case of *County Election,* or with slight variations, as in the two versions of the *Jolly Flatboatmen.* Bingham's canvases of life on the Mississippi and Missouri rivers are as revealing, humorous, and lyrical as Mark Twain's later writing on the subject. Most of the men in these paintings are idle, and the serenity of such river subjects is in strong contrast to his riotous political scenes. As an active politician, Bingham knew his new subjects well. His three major political paintings, *County Election* (1852), *Stump Speaking* (1854), and *Verdict of the People* (1855), are packed with men talking or listening, drinking or drunk.

Binham's finest historical work is the *Emigration of Daniel Boone* (1851-1852), in which a youthful Bonne is shown leading pioneers through Cumberland Gap. This painting, as well as six of his others, was reproduced in contemporary prints. Though during his lifetime his work was seen widely through these reproductions, Bingham himself was not well know outside Missouri.

While engaged in painting these scenes of western life, Bingham traveled a great deal between Missouri and the East to take part in Whig activities and paint portraits. In 1848 he was elected to the Missouri State Legislature. In the same year his first wife died, and a year later he remarried.

In 1856 Bingham made his first trip to Europe, where he painted life-size, commissioned portraits of Washington and Jefferson; he also completed the *Jolly Flatboatmen in Port* in 1857, his last, most skillful and complex painting of this subject. He returned to St. Louis but, commissioned to paint a portrait of Alexander von Humboldt, returned in 1859 to Düsseldorf, Germany.

During the Civil War, Bingham was a captain in the Volunteer Reserve Corps; he was state treasurer from 1862 to 1865. In 1865 he began his last major canvas, *Order No.11,* a painting provoked by the injustice of a military order in 1863 which had forced many Missourians to leave homes that were then sacked and destroyed. Though effective as propaganda, this canvas lacks the clarity and vitality of his earlier figure paintings.

Bingham spent his last years in politics and portrait painting. In 1877 he was appointed professor of art at the University of Missouri. He died at Kansas City, Mo., on July 7, 1879. He was survived by his third wife, a son, and a daughter.

Further Reading

John Francis McDermott, *George Caleb Bingham, River Portraitist* (1959), is well illustrated and contains valuable reference material. E. Maurice Bloch, *George Caleb Bingham* (2 vols., 1967), reveals the probable sources of Bingham's art and lists all his works. A useful older study is Albert W. Christ-Janer, *George Caleb Bingham of Missouri* (1940).

Additional Sources

Christ-Janer, Albert, *George Caleb Bingham; frontier painter of Missouri,* New York, H. N. Abrams 1975. □

Larry Bird

No player has left a mark on 1980s professional basketball comparable to that of Larry Bird (born 1956), the renowned forward for the Boston Celtics.

Bird took the NBA by storm as a rookie in 1979 and dominated the league almost without a break throughout his career as a professional basket ball player. He transformed the lackluster Celtics into a basketball superpower, leading the team to three national championships in five attempts. Every sort of honor and superlative has been lavished on the blond Indiana native. *Sports Illustrated* contributor Frank Deford has called him "the greatest basketball player in the history of humankind," and few observers would argue the point. "Each Bird game is a rich tapestry of fundamentals," writes Mike Lupica in the New York *Daily News.* "He keeps the ball alive, he is the middleman on the fast break, he boxes out, he posts his man every chance he gets. He moves to the right place on defense, he blocks shots, he picks, he rolls. He dives after loose balls and makes perfect outlet passes. And four or five times down the court, he makes one of those plays that take your breath away."

Although he gained a noticeable measure of poise during his years with the Celtics, Bird is a product of his rural upbringing in French Lick, Indiana. He is a modest man who avoids media exposure (to the extent that it is possible to do so), and his name has never been linked to scandal or sensation. Deford notes: "Among those who know Bird well, the same catalog of qualities is cited again and again—honest, loyal, steadfast, dependable—his existence shaped by the contradictory, almost mystical ability to be the [center of attention], yet always to contribute to those around him." *New Yorker* correspondent Herbert Warren Wind concludes that Bird is the kind of man who derives one pleasure from life: "pride in playing good, sound, imaginative basketball. He hates to see his team lose if it can possibly win. He has almost unlimited determination. . . . A man has to love a game deeply to work so hard to play it well day after day and night after night."

Larry Bird was born on Pearl Harbor Day in 1956, the fourth of six children of Joe and Georgia Bird. His birthplace, West Baden, Indiana, is a small village just outside the slightly larger town of French Lick. Once a famous resort community with highly-prized mineral springs, French Lick had fallen upon hard times by the years of Bird's youth. His father managed to find factory work in the town, but the Bird family always struggled to make ends meet. According to Deford, Larry "knew damn well that he was poor. No, it was not oppressive. But, yes, it was there. The Birds had enough coal to stay warm, but too many nights the old furnace would break down, and the house would fill with black smoke, and they would all have to stand outside, freezing,

while Joe Bird tried to fix things." Bird and his brothers were all avid ball players, and as the next-to-youngest brother, he always competed valiantly to keep up with his older, bigger siblings. Wind writes: "Striving to be as good as Mark, who was three years older, made Larry a much better basketball player than he might otherwise have been, and a more competitive one, too."

Bird told the *New Yorker:* "Basketball wasn't really my only love. We played lots of baseball, softball, rubber ball—we played ball all the time. When we were growing up, before we got a real basketball hoop, we used a coffee can and tried to shoot one of those small sponge-rubber balls through it." In fact, Bird did not settle on basketball as his primary sport until he was well into high school, even though he played the sport on an organized level as young as ten. When it finally seemed apparent that he might excel in the sport, he began to practice—hard—day and night. "I played when I was cold and my body was aching and I was so tired," he told *Sports Illustrated.* "I don't know why, I just kept playing and playing. . . . I guess I always wanted to make the most out of it. I just never knew."

Bird honed his talents in one of the most rigorous basketball arenas, the celebrated Hoosier region where the sport reigns supreme. At Springs Valley High School in French Lick he played guard during his sophomore and junior years. He showed no spectacular ability at the time, and at six-foot-three he was not especially tall. Then fate—or rather, biology—intervened. By his senior year Bird had grown four inches. Almost overnight he had become an impressive physical specimen while retaining his agility and hustle. His senior year he averaged 30.6 points and 20 rebounds per game, and college scouts from all over the East flocked to see him play. He was actively pursued by a number of universities, but he decided to stay in state, entering Indiana University (of Bobby Knight fame) in the fall of 1974.

Bird lasted only twenty-four days at Indiana University. He was overwhelmed by the size and impersonality of the school, so he quickly returned to French Lick and entered junior college there. Within two months he had dropped out of that college as well and had entered into a brief and unhappy marriage. In order to support himself and his daughter, born after the marriage had dissolved, Bird took a job with the City Department of French Lick. He drove a garbage truck and helped to maintain parks and roads in the district. Such work may have seemed a low point to some people, but Bird told *Sports Illustrated* that he actually enjoyed it. "I loved that job," he said. "It was outdoors, you were around your friends. Picking up brush, cleaning it up. I felt like I was really accomplishing something. How many times are you riding around your town and you say to yourself, Why don't they fix that? Why don't they clean the streets up? And here I had the chance to do that. I had the chance to make my community look better."

Overcomes Tragedies

Bird faced further tragedy during the same period when his father committed suicide. Shortly after that unfortunate event, Bird decided to return to college, this time at Indiana

State. He had little confidence in his scholastic abilities, but felt that he could help the struggling Sycamores win some respect. By that time he had added two more inches in height and was weighing in at 220 pounds; to quote Wind, he was "an altogether different commodity—a comparatively big man who could challenge the seven-footers at rebounding and in other phases of the game, because he was well built, had exceptional coordination for a man his size, and knew how to utilize the advantages his height gave him." Bird had to sit out his first season at Indiana State, and without him the Sycamores went 13-12. In 1976-77, his first year on the team, the same Sycamores earned a 25-3 record—their best in almost thirty years. The following summer Bird played for the United States team that won the basketball gold medal at the World University Games in Sophia, Bulgaria.

During his Indiana State years, Bird became "the most publicized college player in the country," to quote Wind. Even then Bird showed his penchant for team play and for sharing the glory both on and off the field. Still, he averaged thirty points per game through his junior year and led the Sycamores to the quarterfinals in the 1978 National Invitational Tournament. He was drafted by the Celtics in 1978. At that point he had the option of playing professional ball right away, but instead he chose to stay in school, finish his degree, and be a Sycamore one more season. In his senior year the Sycamores won thirty-three straight games—a collegiate record for a single season—and advanced to the NCAA championships against a formidable Michigan State team led by Earvin "Magic" Johnson. Michigan State won the game which marked the first of many encounters between Bird and Johnson, but Bird walked away with player of the year trophies from the Associated Press, United Press International, and the National Association of Coaches.

Negotiations began with the Celtics for Bird's professional services. Already known for his unwillingness to cooperate with the press, Bird offered no comment as his agent demanded a record salary. The contract signed on June 8, 1979 gave Bird $650,000 per year for five years, a total of $3,250,000. This sum was unheard of for an untested rookie in any sport, and the Boston fans made no secrets of their expectations for their new headliner. Bird did not disappoint. He made the NBA All-Star team his first year, played in every regular season Celtics game, and led the team to a first place finish in its league. Even though the Celtics lost the Eastern Conference finals to the Philadelphia 76ers, Bird was named Rookie of the Year and finished third in the Most Valuable Player balloting.

Bird Soars with Celtics

Those who had predicted that Bird could never turn the dismal Boston franchise around had to eat their words. After Bird's debut, the team became a regular championship contender with wins in 1981, 1984, and 1986. "There hasn't been a Celtics game at the Boston Garden in years that hasn't been sold out," writes Wind. "Most observers attribute this long run of sold-out games to Bird's astonishing virtuosity and the leading role he has played in making the Celtics once again a spirited, exciting team, which has been in contention for the championship just about every year." The excitement of Bird's play has only been enhanced by his long-standing rivalry with Magic Johnson, the mainstay of the Los Angeles Lakers. In fact, Johnson's Lakers are the only team that have bumped the Celtics from the championship, beating them in 1985 and 1987. *Time* magazine contributor Tom Callahan concludes that even when the Celtics were bested by the Lakers, "somehow they [were] able to retrieve their preeminence in the next instant."

Few would list Larry Bird among the flashiest or most spectacular individual players in the NBA. He is not particularly fast on the court, nor is he a remarkable jumper. Bird has achieved greatness the old-fashioned way: by being consistent, by contributing not as a grand-standing superstar but as a team player, and by attacking every game with every ounce of effort. "The hours that Bird devotes to his job are astonishing," Deford notes. "From himself on the court he seeks only consistency and considers that the true mark of excellence." Years and years of practice and play have made Bird an expert on the shifting patterns of the game and even on the behavior of the ball when it hits the backboard. As Wind puts it, "he just knows where he should go, he beats other players to that spot, and his timing in going up for the ball is exceptional." Indeed, when "spectacular" is used to describe Bird's play, it is often in reference to passing and to diving for out-of-bounds balls. Wind concludes that Bird has showed "how imaginative and enthralling a well-played basketball game can be."

Perhaps not surprisingly, Bird has been dogged over the years by suggestions that he has been singled out for praise more because he is white than because he is good—that his superstardom is predicated on the general scarcity of great white players in the NBA. Deford is one of many who has sought to dispel this myth. "Larry Bird is not a Great White Hope," Deford claims. "Anybody who thinks that misses the point of Larry Bird. Little white boys today would much prefer to grow up to be Michael Jordan or Dominique Wilkins, for however clever and hardworking, they're also truly spectacular players. They can fly. But when kids imitate Larry Bird, mostly what they do, so humdrum, is reach down and rub their hands on the bottom of their sneakers. . . . He seems merely the sum of little bits—a bit more clever than you and me, a bit more dedicated, a bit better on his shooting touch. . . . In Bird's case, he probably has worked as hard as anyone in the ever has in sport, and he does possess an incredible sixth sense, but that has no more to do with his race than it does with his Social Security number." Wind too suggests that Bird's race has little to do with his stardom. "I do not believe that it is the underlying reason Bird and the Celtics have set attendance records at home and on the road," the critic writes. "As I see it, the explanation is that Bird's arresting over-all concept of basketball and his sturdy execution of it have made the Celtics game tremendously exciting to watch."

Always somewhat injury-prone, Bird missed much of the 1988-89 season after major surgery on both heels. He continued to battle back problems and other injuries throughout the next few seasons, but retired from the Celtics after an illustrious 13-year career. He played his last game of basketball as a member of the U.S. Olympic Dream Team at the 1992 games in Barcelona.

After retiring as a player, Bird worked for the Celtics Front Office as a Special Assistant. Many thought he would replace M.L. Carr as coach, but the position was awarded to Rick Pitino. As a result, Bird returned to his home state to succeed Larry Brown as coach of the Indiana Pacers for the 1997–1998 season.

Further Reading

Heinsohn, Tommy, *Give 'em the Hook,* Prentice Hall, 1989.
Levine, Lee Daniel, *Bird: The Making of an American Sports Legend,* McGraw-Hill, 1989.
Daily News, March 17, 1979; January 30, 1981.
Newsweek, February 26, 1979.
New Yorker, March 24, 1986.
New York Times, February 3, 1979.
Sports Illustrated, January 23, 1978; February 5, 1979; April 2, 1979; October 15, 1979; November 9, 1981; March 21, 1988; December 11, 1989.
Time, February 26, 1979; June 9, 1986.
Washington Post, February 9, 1979. □

Robert Montgomery Bird

Robert Montgomery Bird (1806-1854) was an American dramatist and novelist of true skill who gradually moved toward literary attitudes that foreshadowed late-19th-century realism.

Robert Montgomery Bird was born in New Castle, Del. His father died when the boy was 4. Bird attended medical school at the University of Pennsylvania, taking his degree in 1827 as part of a plan to restore the family fortunes. The family looked to him for support, but he had no real desire to practice medicine and he turned to literature, thus embracing a career that would be plagued by financial adversity.

At first Bird wrote only plays: romantic tragedies and comedies of Philadelphia life, such as *The City Looking Glass* (1828), and historical dramas, such as *The Gladiator* (1831), probably his most popular play. But the financial arrangements he made with Edwin Forrest, his producer, were based on a verbal understanding, not written contracts, and trouble resulted. Though Bird's plays were highly successful and his *Oralloossa* (1832) and *The Broker of Bogota* (1834) showed that his dramatic power was developing, he was not treated fairly by Forrest. The producer made a fortune but the playwright received only a pittance. Deeply discouraged, Bird gradually broke away from the theater.

Trying his hand at prose, Bird published *Calavar; or, The Knight of the Conquests* (1834) and followed it with a sequel, *The Infidel; or, The Fall of Mexico* (1835). These fictional accounts of the Spanish conquests gained the praise of historian William H. Prescott, but Bird earned little money from them. He next wrote *The Hawks of Hawk-*

Hollow (1835), the story of the ruin of a prominent loyalist family in Pennsylvania during the Revolution. In 1836 Bird published *Sheppard Lee,* perhaps the earliest novel to employ psychological therapy as its central device.

Bird's finest novel, which is still widely read, was *Nick of the Woods* (1837). It foreshadowed realism in that it relentlessly presented Native Americans as the exact opposite of the "noble savage" of James Fenimore Cooper's novels. Bird's work aroused considerable commentary. *Peter Pilgrim* (1838) and *Robin Day* (1839) are interesting but minor efforts, probably because he was seriously ill at the time.

Bird taught at the Pennsylvania Medical Academy from 1841 to 1843, and in 1847 he became an editor of the *Philadelphia North American,* where he remained until his death in 1854.

Further Reading

A documented biography of Bird is Clement E. Foust, *The Life and Dramatic Works of Robert Montgomery Bird* (1919). Mary Mayor Bird, *Life of Robert Montgomery Bird* (1945), is a biography edited by C. Seymour Thompson from the unpublished notebooks of Bird's wife. A thorough treatment is Curtis Dahl, *Robert Montgomery Bird* (1963). For background see Arthur H. Quinn, *A History of the American Drama from the Beginning to the Civil War* (1923; 2d ed. 1943), and Alexander Cowie, *The Rise of the American Novel* (1948). □

King Birendra

Coming to the throne of Nepal at the age of 27 King Birendra (born 1945) sought to emphasize economic development and a decentralization of authority.

King Birendra (Bir Bikram Shah Dev) of Nepal was born on December 28, 1945, the eldest son of King Mahendra and Queen Indra. He had two brothers and three sisters, as well as numerous aunts, uncles, and cousins in the royal family entourage in and around the palace in Nepal's capital city. Birendra married Aishwarya R.L. Rana on February 23, 1970; they had three children—Crown Prince Dipindra, Prince Nirajan, and Princess Shruti.

Birendra was born while the Rana family still dominated the government of Nepal and the royal family was kept under strict surveillence. But the political movement that overthrew the Ranas occurred when the crown prince was only five years old, and his socialization into politics and society in Nepal and abroad was very different from that of his father, King Mahendra. Birendra's formal education, for instance, was in prestigious schools outside Nepal: St. Joseph's in Darjeeling, India; Eton in England; Harvard University; and the University of Tokyo. In the process, he was exposed to a rich assortment of theories and models on political and economic change in "developing" societies like Nepal, and he demonstrated an open and inquisitive mind on such subjects.

King Birendra came to the throne on January 31, 1972, the tenth ruler in the Shah dynasty in Nepal. He quickly demonstrated a different approach to the processes of governance than those adopted by his predecessor, and important changes in both the style and substance of policies were introduced. The preoccupation of King Mahendra with the minutia of political developments anywhere in Nepal was replaced by a new strategy that, in effect, downgraded politics and focussed instead on economic development themes and issues. The objective was to insulate economic programs from the narrow political and interest group concerns that had, supposedly, hampered their implementation under his father.

As a necessary accompaniment to this new approach, changes in the entourage of advisors around the king were required. The groups of experienced and politically astute bureaucrats that King Mahendra had used were quickly replaced by younger, well-educated "modernistic" technicians who presumably would be less inhibited by concerns for traditional familial or caste group interests. A new institution under direct palace supervision was established to do the necessary policy planning, usually with minimal participation by the "narrow" interest groups directly affected by these policies and programs. To manage politics outside of Kathmandu, the BVNC (Back-to-the-Village National Committee) was organized to assure the palace a controlling voice in regional and local councils on development programs.

The new approach sounded reasonable, but the results were less than impressive. While few institutions or persons directly challenged the palace coteries, few cooperated with their programs. A number of well-conceived policies in the education, health, and economic fields were adopted, but the officials and institutions that were supposed to implement them were virtually non-operative. By the late 1970s it was clear that some major changes in the palace's approach were necessary. King Birendra took several significant steps to meet the situation. In 1980 he held, on a universal suffrage basis, a popular referendum on the constitution his father had introduced in 1962. The vote went slightly in favor of the existing system, but with reforms. Birendra then introduced several basic changes in the constitution, including provisions for the election of the Rashtriya Panchayat (National Assembly) on a popular but non-party basis and the selection of a prime minister by the Assembly. The Assembly was elected in 1981; one prime minister was elected and then later removed by the Assembly on a non-confidence vote, and another prime minister installed.

Thus, the trappings of a democratic parliamentary system were in place in Nepal, but several necessary ingredients were lacking—primarily a legalized political party system. Freedom of speech, press, and assembly were more evident in the 1980s than at any other time since 1960, but still with some limitations. The palace continued to be the source of authority on all major issues, and the Assembly and the cabinet had no really effective limitations on the royal powers. If Nepal was booming ahead economically, this might be of only limited importance, but for a decade or more there was virtually no real economic growth.

King Birendra, thus, had a number of difficult decisions to make, and within a limited time frame. His dedication to Nepal's welfare was accepted by most Nepalis, but there was more skepticism about the intentions of some of the important people in and around the palace. Birendra's announcement of his intention to introduce a substantive decentralization program which would transfer decision-making authority on many important issues from the Kathmandu bureaucracy to local and regional elected officials had the potential to be an important step in meeting some of Nepal's basic political, social, and economic problems. While King Birendra's intentions were not questioned, there were doubts about his ability to implement such a program within the existing political system.

Further Reading

One official but thorough biography of King Birendra is M. Bajracharya, *Birendra, the King with a Difference* (1974). Several political studies of the Birendra period exist: Rishikesh Shaha, *Nepali Politics: Retrospect and Prospect* (1975); S.D. Muni, *Nepal; An Assertive Monarchy* (1977); Leo E. Rose and John T. Scholz, *Nepal: Portrait of a Himalayan Kingdom* (1980); and Lok Raj Baral, *Oppositional Politics in Nepal* (1978). □

Vannoccio Biringuccio

The Italian mining engineer and metallurgist Vannoccio Biringuccio (1480-1539) is famous for his important book, *De la pirotechnica*.

Vannoccio Biringuccio was born in Siena, where he became embroiled in politics because of his friendship for the ruling Petrucci family. Probably because of his patron, Pandolfo Petrucci, he was able to travel during his early years through Italy and Germany and to begin to assemble the material which was to be the encyclopedia *Pirotechnica* (or *Pirotechnia*). Upon his return to Siena, Pandolfo made him director of the mines in nearby Boccheggiano.

After Pandolfo died in 1512, Biringuccio supported his son Borghese Petrucci and was named to a post in the Armory of the Siena Commune. In 1515 Biringuccio and the head of the mint, Francesco Castori, were accused of debasing the currency with the approval of Borghese. A popular uprising forced Borghese and his followers, including Biringuccio, to flee the city. Having failed to appear in 1516 to face the charges against him, Biringuccio was declared a rebel and exiled. During this period he traveled around Italy. In 1517 he made his way to Sicily.

Pope Clement VII intervened in the Siena crisis in 1523, and thanks to him, the Petrucci family was restored to power in the person of Fabio, a younger brother of Borghese. Biringuccio was also returned to favor, his property restored, and his position in the armory regained. In 1524 he was given a monopoly in the whole Siena dominion on the manufacture of saltpeter.

In 1526, while Biringuccio was on a mission in Florence, the Sienese people again rose up and this time banished the Petrucci forever. Biringuccio was classified as a rebel, and all of his property was again taken away. Later he took part in an assault upon Siena, but the whole effort was unsuccessful.

Between 1526 and 1529 Biringuccio made a second trip to Germany. When peace returned to Siena in 1530, he returned there. He held office as a city senator and in 1535 became architect and director of building construction of the Cathedral. Meanwhile, between 1531 and 1535, he was engaged in making arms and fortresses under contract to persons outside Siena.

In 1536 Biringuccio was invited to Rome but delayed going. He finally went when he became the director of both the papal foundry and papal munitions in 1538. It is probable that he died while in Rome, and though the exact date of his death is unknown, it occurred before April 30, 1539, for on that date a list appeared of his debts to his heirs.

The *Pirotechnica* was not printed until 1540, and in the next 138 years there were nine editions. In his masterwork Biringuccio explains the techniques for mining ores and extracting metals from them. Being less concerned with quoting authorities than with firsthand observations and operations, he tends to ignore the question of why metals behave as they do and to content himself with descriptions of what happens: "I have no knowledge other than that gained through my own eyes."

Further Reading

The Pirotechnica of Vannuccio Biringuccio (trans. 1942) has an excellent biographical introduction by Martha Teach Gnudi. Biringuccio is discussed by a contemporary, Georgius Agricola, in *De re metallica* (1555; trans. 1912) and in the useful introduction and appendices to that work by the translators, Herbert C. Hoover and Lou Henry Hoover. Biringuccio's importance is also analyzed in James Gordon Parr, *Man, Metals and Modern Magic* (1958). □

James Gillespie Birney

A lawyer and presidential candidate, James Gillespie Birney (1792-1857) was the most influential American political leader of the antislavery movement in its early phases.

James G. Birney was born on Feb. 4, 1792, the son of a Scotch-Irish immigrant who settled in Kentucky in 1788 and became one of the state's richest men. He went to Transylvania University and graduated from Princeton in 1810. After studying law in Philadelphia, he was admitted to the bar in 1814 and settled in Danville, Ky. He married Agatha McDowell, of a prominent Kentucky family, in 1816 and was elected to the lower house of the Kentucky Legislature. He moved to Alabama in 1818 and bought a cotton plantation near Huntsville. Although he owned slaves, he favored the eventual abolition of the institution of slavery. Financial reverses forced him to sell his plantation in 1823, and he resumed his law practice in Huntsville.

Birney's conscience was increasingly troubled by slavery, and he did not hesitate to speak and write against it. In 1826 he began antislavery work in earnest. He became a member of the American Colonization Society, which hoped to eliminate slavery by resettling blacks in Africa, and was instrumental in forcing a bill through the Alabama Legislature prohibiting the importation of slaves into the state for sale or hire. A trip through the North in 1830 convinced him that slavery worked to the South's political, cultural, and economic disadvantage; a weeklong conversation with Theodore Weld, the abolitionist lecturer, who visited Alabama in 1832, reaffirmed his belief that it should no longer be tolerated. That year Birney was appointed southwestern agent for the American Colonization Society, but in 1833 he moved back to Danville because he felt that gradual emancipation might be achieved more readily in Kentucky than in Alabama and thus serve as an example to the South.

Birney soon decided that gradualism would not work and that slavery must be abolished immediately. He freed his slaves in 1834 and helped form the Kentucky Antislavery Society. He planned to publish an antislavery paper in Danville, but threats led him to move to Cincinnati, where he arrived in time to assume an important role in the forma-

tion of the Ohio Antislavery Society. He became editor of its paper, the *Philanthropist,* which first appeared in January 1836. Although his office was looted three times and Birney himself narrowly escaped injury at the hands of a mob, he made the paper one of the most influential abolitionist organs in the West.

Birney was a believer in political action (as William Lloyd Garrison and some other abolitionists were not). The most effective way to abolish slavery, in Birney's view, was to elect men to Congress who would vote it out of existence. He left Cincinnati to become executive secretary of the American Antislavery Society in New York, and he tried vainly to persuade the dissident elements of the movement to work together. When the society split in 1840, Birney emerged as leader of its political action wing. That year he accepted the presidential nomination of the new Liberty party and polled 7,069 votes. In 1844, again the Liberty nominee, he drew more than 62,000 crucial votes, for 15,000 of them came from New York; if Henry Clay had won that state, Clay would have become president instead of James K. Polk.

Meanwhile, Birney had moved to Michigan and in 1841, after his wife's death, married the sister-in-law of the abolitionist Gerrit Smith. Birney's political future appeared to be bright, but a fall from a horse in 1845 left him partially paralyzed and ended his public career. He moved to New Jersey in 1853 and died on Nov. 25, 1857.

Further Reading

The biography of Birney written by his son, William Birney, *James G. Birney and His Times* (1890), is still useful. The best modern study is Betty Fladeland, *James G. Birney: Slaveholder to Abolitionist* (1955). Dwight L. Dumond, ed., *The Letters of James G. Birney* (2 vols., 1938), is indispensable. □

Abu Rayhan al-Biruni

Abu Rayhan al-Biruni (973-ca. 1050), a Moslem astronomer, mathematician, geographer, and historian, was the most acute interpreter of India to Islam in the Middle Ages.

Al-Biruni was born near Kath in Khwarizm (now a part of Uzbekistan) on Sept. 4, 973. His teacher in astronomy and mathematics was the eminent Abu Nasr Mansur, a member of the family then ruling at Kath. Al-Biruni made several observations with a meridian ring at Kath in his youth. In 995 the attack on the ruler of Khwarizm by the ruler of Jurjaniya drove al-Biruni into exile, presumably to Rayy, where he discussed with the astronomer al-Khujandi the latter's observations with a mural sextant. AlBiruni later wrote a treatise on this instrument and gave a detailed account of the observations in his *Tahdid.*

In 997 al-Biruni returned to Kath, where he observed a lunar eclipse that Abu al-Wafa observed in Baghdad; on the basis of the time difference they determined the longitudinal difference between the two cities, one of the few instances in which this method, the only secure one available in antiquity, is known to have been applied.

During the next few years al-Biruni seems to have visited the Samanid court at Bukhara, as well as the court of the Ispahbad of Gilan. But he was busy collecting the enormous mass of information on the chronology of the ancient nations of Europe and Asia that he dedicated to the Ziyarid prince of Gurgan in 1000 and that in English is known simply as the *Chronology*. This remains the most significant source for the various Iranian calendars and for much of the history of central Asia.

By 1004 al-Biruni was in Jurjaniya. He became a prominent figure at the Jurjaniya court, being often employed as a diplomat and as a spokesman for the throne. He continued, however, making his astronomical observations under the Shah's patronage.

But the Shah had increasing difficulties with his brother-in-law, Sultan Mahmud of Ghazni. Finally, in 1017 Mahmud conquered Khwarizm and carried off al-Biruni as a prize of war. Al-Biruni was sent to the region near Kabul, where he commenced making observations in 1018. In 1022 and 1026 Mahmud conducted highly successful expeditions into India, and al-Biruni availed himself of the opportunity to learn some Sanskrit (though not as much as is generally thought; he depended heavily on pundits to translate for him), studying especially Indian astronomy, astrology, chronology, and social customs.

Most of his extant works were written in the 1020s and 1030s and reflect his interest in, and growing knowledge of, the Sanskrit astronomical texts current in the Punjab. These include *On Shadows* (ca. 1021), *Tahdid* (1025), *On Chords* (1027), *On Transits, India* (1031), and *Al-Qanun al-Masudi,* as well as the Arabic translation of Vijayanandin's Sanskrit *Karanatilaka*. These are fundamental texts for the history of Islamic and Indian astronomy of the 8th-10th centuries because of al-Biruni's extensive citations of earlier texts; they are also full of reports of al-Biruni's own observations, which are among the best made in the medieval period. He was not always as successful in his calculations.

Till his death soon after 1050 in Afghanistan, al-Biruni continued to write, turning his attention to problems of specific gravity, gemology, pharmacology, and Indian philosophy (the *Patanjali*), among other subjects. It is not clear when he wrote the *Tafhim,* his most important work on astrology. In all, the bibliography he himself drew up lists 113 titles, and this list can be expanded to 146; 22 are extant. He was, then, a most prolific author, and throughout his work, all of which is extremely technical, he maintained the highest standards of competence. He well deserved the epithet "Master" bestowed on him by his admiring contemporaries.

Further Reading

Many of al-Biruni's extant writings have not been published. He has been the object of many intensive studies, but the results are scattered among various scholarly journals. Some idea of the range of this scholarship can be gained from the volume issued by the Iran Society of Calcutta on the occasion of the thousandth lunar year since his birth, *Al-Biruni Commemoration Volume* (1951). See also George Sarton, *Introduction to the History of Science,* vol. 1 (1927); Eugene A. Myers, *Arabic Thought and the Western World in the Golden Age of Islam* (1964); and Seyyed Hossein Nasr, *An Introduction to Islamic Cosmological Doctrines: Conceptions of Nature and Methods Used for Its Study by the Ikhwan al-Safa, al-Biruni, and Ibn Sina* (1964).

Additional Sources

Said, Hakim Mohammad., *al-Bairaunai: his times, life and works,* Karachi: Hamdard Academy, 1981. □

Aleksandra Pavlovna Biryukova

Aleksandra Pavlovna Biryukova (born 1929) was the highest ranking woman politician in the U.S.S.R. from 1986 to 1990, serving as a secretary of the Central Committee of the Communist Party of the Soviet Union and as a deputy prime minister for two years.

In the summer of 1989, Aleksandra Biryukova, a deputy premier of the Soviet Council of Ministers, traveled to Western Europe where in one week she bought $165 million worth of consumer goods. Some might say it was everyone's dream come true—a chance to go abroad and buy everything you want. But Biryukova had an important governmental assignment—to buy much needed consumer goods for the former U.S.S.R., items such as pantyhose, toothpaste, and other simple necessities taken for granted in Western society. Her buying trip was symptomatic of the grave problems of the Soviet economy. In traditional Soviet style, the minister herself was sent on the buying trip. This assignment was too important to delegate to lower-echelon civil servants.

A party activist and trade union official, Biryukova was appointed a secretary of the Central Committee of the Communist Party of the Soviet Union (CPSU) in 1986 by Mikhail Gorbachev and a candidate member of the Politburo in 1988. As a result of a governmental reorganization in 1988, she became a deputy prime minister with responsibility for social and consumer services. She thus became the highest ranking female politician in the U.S.S.R. In July 1990, after the stormy 28th Party Congress, Biryukova was retired from both the Central Committee and the Politburo. Except for Gorbachev and the new deputy general secretary of the CPSU, there was a complete turnover in the Politburo, whose representation and function were somewhat modified.

Becoming an Important Party Member

Biryukova was born in the Moscow region on February 25, 1929. Her family was of peasant origin, and she was Russian by nationality. In 1952 she graduated as an engineer from the Moscow Textile Institute and subsequently worked as a foreman and shop supervisor at the First Printed Fabric Cotton Works in Moscow. In 1956, at the age of 29, she joined the CPSU. In 1959 she began work for the Textile and Knitwear Industry Administration of the *Moscow Sovnarkhoz* (the Economic Council of Moscow). In 1963 she became the chief engineer of a Moscow cotton combine (*Trekhgornaia manufaktura*), a position she held for five years. It was her last position directly involved with production. In 1968 she was elected a member of the Central Council of Trade Unions and of its presidium (1968-1986). In 1985-1986 she served briefly as deputy chairman of the Central Trade Union Council.

With her position in the trade unions, her political involvement mushroomed. She was elected to the Russian Republic (RSFSR) Supreme Soviet in 1971, where she served on the Commission on Industry until 1975, before becoming chairperson of the Commission on Working and Living Conditions of Women, Mothers, and Childcare. In 1979 she received a certificate of honor for her work with the RSFSR SS. She was elected a deputy to the U.S.S.R. Supreme Soviet in 1986, but not to the re-vamped Supreme Soviet in 1989. In 1971 she was also elected a candidate member of the Central Committee of the CPSU, becoming a full member in from 1976 till 1990. In 1988 she was appointed a deputy prime minister and reappointed by the new Supreme Soviet in June 1989.

During her years in trade union administration, Biryukova traveled to the United States and to several West and East European countries, including Germany, Austria, the Czech Republic, Slovakia, and Portugal. Her movements and activities began to be noticed abroad after her appointment in 1986 as a secretary of the Central Committee with responsibilities for light industry. As the first woman in the Secretariat since the early 1960s, she quite naturally received more attention. When she was appointed a candidate member of the Politburo in 1988, and shortly thereafter a deputy prime minister, her visibility further increased. In the period after 1986 she traveled extensively to countries such as Japan, Vietnam, Bulgaria, and India—receiving considerably more coverage for her activities in the Soviet and Western press.

Only Woman on Council of Ministers

The U.S.S.R. did not seem to capitalize on the fact that there was a woman on the Politburo after a hiatus of 27 years. Perhaps it was indicative of Gorbachev's general intention to promote and recognize women that he did not wish to make Biryukova a token showcase. Biryukova enjoyed a remarkable career for a Soviet woman. Although almost all Soviet women work, few rise to the highest levels of the party and government or even of the trade unions. Her appointment as a secretary of the Trade Union Council at the age of 39 was remarkable even though the trade union council was not a center of great political power.

Prior to *perestroika,* the role of trade unions in the U.S.S.R. was relatively innocuous. Everyone who worked belonged to a trade union. Trade unions primarily existed to administer worker benefits such as maternity leave, sick leave, health benefits, vacations, and so on. Expulsion from a trade union meant exclusion from the normal benefits workers receive and also, in most instances, denial of the right to practice one's trade or profession. Unions were not a workers' movement in the U.S.S.R. Biryukova, although an advocate on behalf of workers, adhered to the traditional Soviet view of the role of unions and is believed to have opposed the rise of such trade union movements as Solidarity in Poland in the early 1980s. In the late 1980s, in the era of *perestroika,* Soviet unions became more militant and powerful as workers demanded the right to strike, improved wages, and a guarantee of the basic necessities of life. The miners, for example, became a strident, powerful political force in the U.S.S.R. Strikes became commonplace, as did spontaneous worker demonstrations.

To move her from the trade unions in the age of *perestroika* and *glasnost* was probably a symbolic gesture as well as a promotion. She was a union official of the Brezhnev era. Could Biryukova have coped with the new trade union movements? It is hard to say, but she appears to have been a traditionalist in orientation. Her assignment as a member of the Secretariat after 1986 concerned light industry, the area of her early training as an engineer. In 1988 she was appointed a deputy prime minister of the Council of Ministers and chairperson of the Bureau of Social Development. She apparently had responsibility in the area of consumer goods and social services. As a deputy prime minister and the only woman on the Council of Ministers, she also spoke out on behalf of women.

Given the drastic state of the Soviet economy in 1989 and 1990, in which there were shortages of everything, it is not surprising that some officials resigned or were removed. Biryukova was released from the Politburo and Central Committee at the 28th Party Congress in July 1990, at the relatively young age of 61. It was presented as her retirement, although the true cause was due more to political changes than to age or illness. At the 28th Party Congress, candidate membership in the Politburo was abolished, which released Biryukova and several others from their duties. Biryukova also resigned from her post in the Council of Ministers. Biryukova faced a frustrating situation in the rapidly disintegrating Soviet economy. Since she was the only woman on the Politburo, Gorbachev sought a replacement—in itself a significant change from past practice. Galina Semenova, the editor of *Krestyanka* (*Peasant Woman*), was appointed secretary of the Central Committee for Women's Affairs and elected a full member of the Politburo by the congress.

Her passing from the Soviet political scene was not as significant as, for example, the resignation of Yegor Ligachev at the same party congress. However, there had been so few women at the highest echelons of Soviet power that the retirement of even one official created a significant vacuum.

Further Reading

There have not been any book-length biographies of Biryukova. It is unusual for a Soviet political figure to receive personal attention in the Soviet press. Biryukova, unlike Raisa Gorbachev, did not awaken public interest in the West, where she was known only to specialists. Gorbachev and Yeltsin, who captured the public imagination outside the U.S.S.R., were among the few Soviet politicians who received publicity in the international media. Several articles chronicled her activities and speeches, most notably her buying trip to the West, which was widely reported in the American press (July 1989). *Christian Science Monitor* reviewed her work (March 13, 1986), as did *New York Times* (January 24, 1989) and the *Washington Post* (January 24, 1989). Biryukova's retirement is briefly chronicled in Dawn Mann's "Leading Bodies of the CPSU Transformed," in *Report on the USSR* (Radio Liberty, July 20, 1990). See also *Atlanta Constitution* (January 24, 1989), *Boston Globe* (January 24, 1989), *Time* (October 10, 1988), *Who's Who in Russia and the New States* (1993), and *Who Was Who in the Soviet Union* (1992). She is also listed in the *New York Times Biographical Service* (October 1988) and *Who's Who in the World* (1991). □

Abdullah Yaccoub Bishara

The Kuwaiti statesman Abdullah Yaccoub Bishara (born 1936) served as ambassador to Brazil and Argentina and as Kuwait's permanent representative to the United Nations for ten years before becoming the first secretary-general of the Gulf Cooperative Council in 1981.

Abdullah Yaccoub Bishara was born in Kuwait on November 6, 1936. He completed his primary and secondary education in Kuwait, then obtained his bachelor of arts degree from the College of Arts and Sciences at Cairo University (1955-1959). Upon his return to Kuwait he taught at al-Shuwaikh secondary school, from 1959 to 1961. Later he attended Balliol College, Oxford University, where he studied diplomacy and international relations.

Further study at St. John's University in the United States earned Bishara an M.A. degree in political science, after which he assumed his first diplomatic post, as second secretary for political affairs at Kuwait's embassy in Tunisia, 1963-1964. Between 1964 and 1971 he served as director of the Office of the Minister of Foreign Affairs in Kuwait.

Still early in his diplomatic career, Bishara was named Kuwait's permanent representative to the United Nations, where he served for ten years (1971-1981). As such, he participated in the U.N. General Assembly from 1976 until 1981 and was involved in all non-aligned conferences from 1971 to 1981. While serving in the United Nations, he was elected chairman of the Security Council in February of 1979 and represented Kuwait on the council for two years. Additionally, he headed several U.N. committees and was vice chairman of the United Nations Institute for Training and Research. Bishara headed the Arms Embargo Committee of the United Nations with respect to South Africa and contributed to the debate during 1980 and 1981.

His experience at the United Nations was recounted in his book entitled *Two Years in the Security Council*. In addition, several essays on political and economic issues written by Bishara have been published in English-language periodicals, and he delivered numerous lectures at American universities and organizations on the subjects of Middle East oil politics and the Persian Gulf. He maintained active membership in the Arab Thought Forum, based in Amman, Jordan. Bishara's diplomatic experience also included service as ambassador to both Brazil and Argentina from 1974 to 1981. Bishara assumed his responsibilities as secretary-general of the Gulf Cooperation Council in 1981.

The Gulf Cooperation Council (GCC) had been formed on May 26, 1981, when the heads of six Arab Gulf states (Saudi Arabia, Kuwait, Bahrain, Qatar, the United Arab Emirates, and Oman) signed an agreement in Abu Dhabi, establishing it as the first Arab collective cooperation pact. In many ways the idea of such a cooperative organization was emerging in the 1970s. In 1976, based on an initiative from Sultan Qaboos of Oman, the foreign ministers of Iran, Iraq, Kuwait, Bahrain, Saudi Arabia, and the U.A.E. met in Muscat, Oman, to discuss collective regional security and defense policy. The conference failed to come to any conclusions, but in the same year (1976) another attempt was made to arrive at an Arab Gulf consensus: Shaykh (Sheik) Jaber al-Ahmad al-Sabah, the ruler of Kuwait, who was at that time crown prince and prime minister, toured the Gulf countries to discuss joint action to preserve the Gulf's security in the face of political and economic challenges threatening this important area. As a result, Shaykh Jaber proposed the establishment of a Gulf union as an instrument for joint action, with the objective of achieving cooperation in all political, educational, economic, and informational matters.

While the genesis of the GCC lay in that Kuwait proposal, it would be five years before the idea became a reality. However, Kuwait's initiative and talks with the U.A.E. first led to the establishment of a joint ministerial council composed of the two prime ministers. Later consultations with Saudi Arabia, Bahrain, Qatar, and Oman also were successful. All of them endorsed the idea of establishing the Gulf Cooperation Council, which would have as its primary objective collective regional security. For the six governments concerned there was no difficulty in agreeing on the virtues of cooperation, but the necessary impetus to action was lacking. However, the fall of the Shah of Iran in 1979 and the rise of Khomeini's revolutionary regime in Tehran, followed by the outbreak of the Iraq-Iran war soon after, caused serious alarm in Saudi Arabia and the Gulf shaykhdoms.

Thus on May 25, 1981, shaken by the Iranian threat, the heads of the six Arab Gulf states met in Abu Dhabi and agreed to establish the Gulf Cooperation Council. The six signatories to the charter confirmed their efforts toward the unity of the Gulf Arab states and signalled their serious attempts to achieve coordination, integration, and close ties among themselves in all fields.

Abdullah Bishara's generation reached manhood in the mid-1950s. It was a tumultuous time for the whole Arab world, both the *Mashreq* (Eastern Arab world) and the *Maghreb* (Western Arab world). The Algerian revolution against French colonialists, the defeat of the Arabs in Palestine and the disaster that befell the Palestinians in 1948, and the Tripartite aggression against Nasser's Egypt in 1956 were all vividly remembered by the Arabs of the 1950s and 1960s. Arab youths attributed Arab suffering and defeat to Arab fragmentation and absence of unity at the state level. It should be remembered that the two important goals of the Arab countries in both the *Mashreq* and the *Maghreb* have been Arab unity and independence from the European colonial powers: France in the *Maghreb* and Britain in the *Mashreq*. As stated in Article 4 of the GCC constitution, the ultimate aim is unity; the GCC conforms with the national aims of the Arab nation as expressed in the charter of the Arab League. The GCC could be seen by its creators and its first secretary general, Abdullah Bishara, as a step toward those grand goals: Arab economic integration, complementarity, and political solidarity.

But while the process of regional integration in the Gulf was proceeding relatively satisfactorily, decisions regarding application of natural resources were still made on the individual state level: sovereignty was still a sensitive issue for both the people and the governments of the six Gulf states. The GCC, as a regional organization, did not have supranational power over its six member states. However, in the 1980s it was successful in building solid institutions such as the Gulf Investment Corporation, created in 1983 with a capital of $2.1 billion.

The most important political and economic achievement was dealt with in the Unified Economic Agreement (1983) for the free movement and equal treatment of goods, including the elimination of customs duties on domestically-produced goods.

The Gulf Cooperative Council represented both a model of development and unity in the Arab East and a working example of interstate cooperation of Arab states sharing a common language, religion, and history. There was ample evidence that the GCC provided a positive example for the two Arab groupings that followed in the late 1980s. The Arab Cooperation Council (ACC), comprising Egypt, Iraq, Jordan, and North Yemen, was formed on February 15, 1989. Two days later it was followed by the establishment of the Arab Maghrebi Union (AMU), whose members were Mauritania, Morocco, Algeria, Tunisia, and Libya.

The creation of these councils was a sign that the Arab world was awakening to the significance and new meaning of unity and economic integration. However, the Iraqi's invasion and occupation of Kuwait on August 2, 1990, redivided the Arab world. The other five members of the Gulf Cooperative Council sided with fellow member Kuwait, as did most of the other nations in the Arab League.

Shortly after the invasion of Kuwait by Iraq, U.S. troops were sent overseas to force Iraq's withdrawal from Kuwait. In January 1991, Congress authorized the use of force, and battle began when Iraqi had not withdrawn by the deadline given them by the United Nations. The Iraqis fled Kuwait City on February 26, and February 28 marked the official cease fire of the Persian Gulf War.

Five years after the invasion of Kuwait, in a Radio National interview on October 5, 1995, Bishara commented on the effect of the war on the Kuwaitis. More than six hundred people were unaccounted for, and this had "frozen the life of a lot of people" who did not know if their relatives and spouses were alive or dead. Bishara did not classify Kuwait as a loser in the war. He stated that the country "obtained a lot, and triumphed in its adversity and tragedy." Also, according to Bishara, the fact that Kuwait depends on Saudi Arabia and the United States for security now does not mean that it has lost it independence, but rather "it's a fact of life that we came into this state of what they call 'interdependence.'"

Further Reading

Additional information on Abdullah Bishara and on the Gulf Corporation Council can be found in John A. Sandwick, editor, *The Gulf Cooperation Council: Moderation and Stability in an Interdependent World* (1987); *Cooperation Council for the Arab States of the Gulf,* Information Handbook (1982); Charter, Cooperation Council for the Arab States of the Gulf, May 25, 1981, and the Unified Economic Agreement, Cooperation Council for the Arab States of the Gulf, June 8, 1981, *American Arab Affairs* (Winter 1983-1984); Emile A. Nakhleh, *The Gulf Cooperation Council: Policies, Problems and Prospects* (1986); and Shireen Hunter, editor, *The Gulf Cooperation Council: Problems and Prospects* (1987). For more information on the Persian Gulf War see Otto Friedrich, ed., *Desert Storm: The War in the Persian Gulf* (1991), Norman Friedman, *Desert Victory: The War for Kuwait* (1991), and Majid Khadduri and Edmund Ghareeb, *War in the Gulf, 1990-1991* (1997). Articles specifically addressing Bishara's role and beliefs are in *Christian Science Monitor* (January 29, 1991); *New York Times* (October 30, 1990); and *Washington Post* (February 4, 1991). Also see the Radio National transcript at http://www.abc.net.au/m/talks/bbing/bb951008.htm.
There are two publications by Abdullah Bishara available: "The Gulf Cooperation Council: Achievements and Challenges," *American-Arab Affairs* (Winter 1983-1984), in English, and *Two Years in the Security Council* (n.d.), in Arabic. □

Bridget Bishop

Bridget Bishop (died 1692) was a tavern keeper whose wild temperament and flamboyant dress eventually caused her to be tried and hanged for witchcraft.

The seventeenth century was a time of great religious excitement both in Europe and America. The turmoil over religious beliefs may have led to the search for witches, which reached a high point in the colony of Salem, in present-day Massachusetts, in the late seventeenth century. It had been widely believed even before the Puritans left England that witchcraft was a well-practiced profession in Europe. (A witch, it was thought, made a pact with the devil in exchange for supernatural powers.) In the fifteenth and sixteenth centuries, thousands of people, mostly women and children, were tried and sentenced to death for this crime in Germany.

Witchcraft in history

Witchcraft had been a crime long before the trials in Massachusetts Bay Colony. The ancient Hebrews and Romans were convinced that some people had the power to enchant others or take the shapes of animals, and they believed that these people obtained their powers by making an agreement with the devil. In Europe during the sixteenth century, especially during the period of intense religious upheaval known as the Reformation, there was a renewed interest in witches. Tests for witchery, including a test to ''swim'' the suspected witches, or to dunk them in water until they were ready to confess their evil ways, became popular.

In England, King James II was an ardent believer in the evil of witchery. He had written a description of the antics of witches, which he spread throughout England, and offered a reward for exposing one of those who followed the devil. In the colonies, the brilliant preacher Cotton Mather had been caught up in the study of witches and had written about them in *Memorable Providences Relating to Witchcraft and Possessions*. Suspected witches were being brought to trial as early as the 1630s, and over the years many had been banished or put to death. Each colony came to hold witchery as a crime punishable by death.

By the 1690s, it seemed no one was safe from the devil. Even upstanding citizens in Salem and the surrounding communities were being accused of witchery. So who better to suspect of being a witch than Bridget Bishop?

Early life

Little is known of Bishop's early life, though she was noted for her unusual ways. She dressed gaudily for her day, outfitting herself in red bodices for daily wear and in laces, often brightly dyed, for evening. (Samuel Shattuck, who dyed many of Bishop's laces, would later testify against her at her trial.) She made quite a picture, dressed in her famous black cap, black hat, and red bodice looped with laces of different colors.

Bishop owned two taverns, one in Salem Village and one in Salem Town. She got along well with the men—especially the young ones—who patronized these taverns. Much to the dismay of her neighbors, she allowed them to play ''shovel board'' (shuffle board) at all hours. One neighbor had even found it necessary to storm the tavern late one night and throw the playing pieces in the fire to quiet the merriment. Later, the incident was used against Bishop when her accusers remembered that the very next day that neighbor had become ''distracted,'' or suffered a breakdown.

Known for temper

Bishop's temper alone was enough to make her suspect. All the community knew that often when her second husband bounced his wagon across the stream to their house, a loud and bitter argument followed. Before that, she

had become the Widow Wasselbe when her first husband died under mysterious circumstances. Some, even then, had suspected her of causing Wasselbe's death. Later she married Thomas Oliver, but that marriage had not lasted. She finally married a successful lawyer, Edward Bishop, but sometimes she still called herself Bridget Oliver.

In 1679 Bishop had been accused of practicing witchcraft, but was rescued by the testimony of her minister, John Hale. Later, in 1687, she was again accused, and again acquitted. These charges stemmed from several claims against Bishop. She had been accused at least once of contributing to the death of a neighbor, and more than once of causing someone she had argued with to become ill. She had also been charged with taking part in the devil's sacraments on the Witches' Sabbath. On this day, it was believed, those faithful to the devil gathered together in the woods to worship him. The devil, in turn, would leave his mark on the body of each witch, a sign that he and the witch had made an agreement.

Origin of witch trials

Throughout the colonies the signs of a witch were well known: administering sacraments in the devil's name on the Witches' Sabbath, and dancing wildly and nude at the celebration in the forest. As in Europe, different colonies resorted to torture to extract the truth from suspected witches. Even before the Salem Witch Trials of 1692 to 1695, there had been more than 100 accusations of witchery in the colonies.

In 1692 a group of young Salem girls, for no apparent reason, began falling into wild fits and imagining that people's spirits—preparing to do evil—were separating from their bodies. Often they saw these people carrying the devil's book (in order to enlist others in their evil causes) and, just as often, they saw these people in the company of a dark man (presumably the devil in human form). These girls kept company with a female slave from the West Indies named Tituba, who was reported to have practiced some forms of magic. Spurred on by an overzealous witch-hunter, the minister Samuel Parris, the girls made accusation after accusation against Bishop and other suspected witches.

Examination

On April 19, 1692, Bishop was summoned to be examined by a preliminary court headed by John Hathorne (ancestor of the writer Nathaniel Hawthorne) . Also summoned that day were Giles Corey, the elderly husband of Martha Corey who once seemed ready to name his wife a witch but now stubbornly defended her; Abigail Hobbes, accused of falsely baptizing her own mother in the name of Satan; and Mary Warren, a servant girl whose imprisonment while waiting for this examination drove her insane.

The first part of the examination had the accusers confront the accused. The young girls had been instructed, perhaps by Parris, in what to do. When Bishop raised her arm, they did too. When she was asked whether she was a witch and she answered ''I do not know what a witch is'' and rolled her eyes, the girls rolled their eyes too. They acted as though Bishop controlled them. Although the girls' actions did not seem to trouble Bishop, it influenced the opinions of the authorities. Bishop was sent to Salem Prison to await trial.

Trial

The Court of Oyer and Terminer met at Salem in June 1692. Acting as chief magistrate, or judge, was Deputy Governor Stoughton. Bartholomew Gidney, Samuel Sewell, John Richards, William Sergeant, Wait Winthrop, and Nathaniel Saltonstall served as additional judges.

Since much of the testimony against her had been brought out in the examination, Bishop was already convicted in the minds of many in the town. There was little real evidence against Bishop, but the colonists believed their certainty alone could determine her guilt. Cotton Mather, the most powerful minister in the area, described the trial and the colonists' attitudes: "There was little occasion to prove the witchcraft, this being evident and notorious to all beholders" (Starkey, p. 153).

Nevertheless, the judges listened to the parade of accusers. Bishop's earlier history was repeated: the noisy shovel board games late at night at her tavern, her bad temper, her first husband's mysterious death. Also, witnesses reported that as she was led to court, Bishop's sideward glance at the church had caused a board to detach from a wall and fly across the room.

Some women of the community searched Bishop's body for the always-evident sign that she had made a commitment to the devil. After sticking pins in her, they found an unusual spot, which they testified about in court.

Damaging testimony

Samuel Shattuck testified that Bishop was a flamboyant dresser who often came to him to have various pieces of lace dyed. Some of these pieces seemed too small for a woman to wear, he noted. (It was well known that witches often used dolls to represent their victims when casting spells; Shattuck implied that this was how Bishop used the lace pieces.)

William Stacy recalled that at age twenty-two he had been stricken with smallpox and that it was Bishop who nursed him back to health. (Bishop was said to have had power over men, which grew as she became older.) Later, however, Stacy had begun to doubt Bishop, and had talked with others about her. For this, he said, Bishop had plagued him. Once, he testified, the wheel of his wagon had stuck in a hole in the road. When he stepped out to look at it, however, the hole had disappeared. Now, although he was a decent father and husband, Stacy said, the shade of Bishop plagued him in his sleep.

Samuel Gray, Richard Corman, and Jack Louder were also pestered by the image of Bishop as they slept. Sometimes her image turned into a black pig, a monkey, the feet of a cock, or the face of a man. Gray suspected that because the men had declined her friendship she had punished their families. Bishop, Gray testified, had been the cause of the deaths of his and Shattuck's sons (she had first driven Shattuck's son insane) and of the daughter of another.

The most damaging testimony was given by John Bly. Bishop had employed him to tear down a cellar wall in her former house. Inside the wall, he claimed, he had found dolls ("poppets") made of rags and hogs' bristles with pins stuck through them.

Bishop's own testimony worked against her too. She was found guilty of telling lies, since some of the details she gave conflicted with what others said. Also, according to the court, early questioning had supposedly shown knowledge of witchcraft, yet Bishop claimed to have no knowledge of it.

No defense

Any evidence in Bishop's favor was not allowed. While they were in jail, Bishop had asked Mary Warren, one of the other accused witches, about the claims made against Bishop. Warren told Bishop that the girls had manufactured the evidence against her. Bishop attempted to use Warren's statements in court, but the authorities would not permit the remarks of a person they considered insane to go on the record.

Bishop's son would have testified on her behalf, too, but he had been arrested after beating the truth about the false accusations out of an Indian servant and then accusing the girls who were the prime witnesses in all the trials of game-playing. He had even suggested that beatings might return the girls to their senses, too.

In the end, there were no witnesses to defend Bishop. Even John Hale, the minister who had defended her in 1687, was now convinced of her guilt. Meanwhile, the young girls continued to be bothered by the evil cast upon them, they were convinced, by Bishop.

Sentencing

Bishop was found guilty of witchery and sentenced to be hanged, but hanging was forbidden by an old Massachusetts law. Conveniently, an old colonial law that made witchcraft a life-or-death offense was "discovered" and, on June 8, 1692, again passed into law. On June 10, High Sheriff George Cowan reported that he had hanged Bridget Bishop on Gallow Hill from the branch of a large oak tree.

Further Reading

Boyer, Paul, and Stephen Nissenbaum, eds., *Salem Village Witchcraft,* Belmont: Wadsworth Publishing Company, 1972.
Hall, David D., *Witch-hunting in Seventeenth-Century New England,* Boston: Northeastern University Press, 1991.
Starkey, Marion L., *The Devil in Massachusetts,* Garden City, New York: Doubleday, 1969. □

Elizabeth Bishop

Elizabeth Bishop (1911-1979) was a poet whose vivid sense of geography won her many honors.

Elizabeth Bishop barely knew her parents. Her father died of Bright's disease eight months after she was born in Worcester, Massachusetts, February 8, 1911. Her mother, Gertrude, never got over the death of her husband William and suffered a nervous collapse, eventually going insane. She was removed to a sanatorium when her young daughter was five.

One of her earliest and most vivid memories of her mother was of a ride in a swan boat in the Boston Public Garden. Bishop was dressed in black, as had been her wont since her husband's death. "One of the live swans paddling around us bit my mother's finger when she offered it a peanut," Bishop wrote. "I remember the hole in the black glove and a drop of blood on it." Thus was the beginning of a lifelong habit of observing minute, yet significant, details.

Most of her early years were spent with relatives, whom Bishop later described as taking care of her because they felt sorry for her. She did not stay in one place too long, not always by choice. Her sudden removal from her carefree childhood home with her maternal grandparents in the coastal town of Great Village, Nova Scotia, was a traumatic experience. She loved Canada and was unhappy at the wealthy Bishop residence in Worcester, where her father had been born. She wrote in "The Country Mouse," which was published posthumously:

I had been brought back unconsulted and against my wishes . . . to be saved from a life of poverty and provincialism, bare feet, suet puddings, unsanitary school slates, perhaps even from the inverted r's of

my mother's family. With this surprising extra set of grandparents, until a few weeks ago no more than names, a new life was about to begin.

In "The Country Mouse," a humorous account of the nine months spent as a reluctant guest at the home of Sarah and John Wilson Bishop, a successful contractor who had erected buildings at Harvard and Princeton, Bishop presents some of the scenes which found their way into her poems. One of the most poignant was the waiting room of a dentist office to which she had accompanied her Aunt Jenny (Consuelo in the poem). Although she was not yet seven, she was able to read and was browsing through the pages of a 1918 *National Geographic* while her aunt was being ministered to.

"Suddenly, from inside, came an *oh* of pain—Aunt Consuelo's voice—"

This did not surprise her, because she thought of her aunt as "a foolish, timid woman." What caught her off guard was the realization that she was *her* "foolish aunt . . . falling, falling . . . into cold, blue-black space."

" . . . I felt: you are an *I*, you are an *Elizabeth*, you are one of *them* ."

It was the first time she had ever referred to herself in her poetry.

Bishop was more the observer with a vivid sense of place. She visited the Nova Scotia of her childhood, spent two years in Europe shortly after she graduated from Vassar, and travelled to North Africa, Mexico, Key West, and Brazil. She had stopped off in Rio de Janeiro en route to sailing the Strait of Magellan, but suffered a violent reaction after eating a cashew fruit. When she recovered she stayed on in Brazil for 15 years.

Bishop wrote sparingly, publishing only five slim volumes of poetry in 35 years, but what she wrote received high acclaim. In 1945 her work was selected from among over 800 entries in the Houghton Mifflin Poetry Competition, and the 30 poems submitted were published the following year as *North & South*. This collection, together with her second volume, *A Cold Spring,* earned her the Pulitzer Prize for 1956. She received the National Book Award for *The Complete Poems* in 1970, was the first American to receive the *Books Abroad/Neustadt International Prize for Literature* —she was chosen by an international jury of writers—and the National Book Critics Circle Award for *Geography III,* her last book of poems, in 1977.

As one can tell from her titles, her lifelong passion for travelling influenced her poetry. "I think geography comes first in my work," she told an interviewer, "and then animals. But I like people, too. I've written a few poems about people."

Appropriately, one of her earliest poems, "The Map," describes "Labrador's yellow, where the moony Eskimo has oiled it" and points out that because of cramped space the names of seashore towns run out to the sea and cities cross neighboring mountains. Yet maps are not merely guides to geographical places, nor are they aesthetic objects only. As with most of her poems, "The Map" one sees is not just the colors of the rainbow confined to irregular shapes. One sees Bishop's poem as a guide to the way she views and senses the patterns of life.

"Man-Moth," inspired by a typographical error in the *New York Times*—the intended word was *mammoth*—describes the nocturnal New Yorker whose home is "the pale subways of cement" where

> Each night he must be carried through artificial tunnels and dream recurrent dreams. Just as the ties recur beneath his train, these underlie his rushing brain. . . .
> He has to keep his hands in his pockets, as others must wear mufflers.

The fantasy of the man-moth travelling through New York's underground and, when occasionally emerging to the street, seeing the moon "as a small hole at the top of the sky" has a Kafkaesque quality. When asked to contribute her favorite poem to an anthology called *Poet's Choice,* Bishop submitted "Man-Moth," commenting on the misprint that gave her the idea: "An oracle spoke from the page of the *New York Times,* kindly explaining New York City to me, at least for the moment."

Other of her poems that have been highly praised included "The Burglar of Babylon," a ballad set in Rio; "A Miracle for Breakfast," about hunger; "Jeronimo's House," one of her Key West poems; "The Moose," about a bus trip; and "The Fish," her most popular poem.

So frequently has this poem been anthologized that shortly before her death Bishop declared that she would rather have any of her poems but "The Fish" included in a collection, and, if publishers insisted, she asked that they print three of her other poems with it. In the poem the fish, wearing five old pieces of broken lines "like medals," gets a reprieve and is returned to the sea.

One of the reasons for the popularity of this poem was the strong praise it received from Randall Jarrell. Bishop, who was uncommitted to any school of poetry, was also admired by poets as disparate as John Ashbery, Octavio Paz, Robert Lowell, and Marianne Moore. She also knew Ezra Pound, W.H. Auden, Pablo Neruda, and Carlos Drummond, one of Brazil's most popular poets, whose work she translated from the Portuguese.

But it was Marianne Moore who had the greatest influence of all of these. While still at Vassar, Bishop met Moore through the college librarian, Fanny Borden, niece of the accused ax-murderer Lizzie Borden. After an initial interview in the New York Public Library, the two poets began a long friendship, launched when Bishop helped Moore pilfer a few hairs from a baby elephant at a circus to replace strands of the rare hair on her bracelet. Bishop kept the adult elephants and the guard busy while Moore snipped away.

Moore helped to convince Bishop to abandon her plans to study medicine and to work at her poetry instead. Critics have said that the two poets shared the same gift of acute observation and understated wit. And each of them was fond of animals. Besides Moore, Bishop credited

George Herbert and Wallace Stevens as being important influences on her.

Bishop died suddenly of a ruptured cerebral aneurism in her Boston apartment on October 6, 1979. She was 68 years old.

Further Reading

A critical study of Bishop's work is Anne Stevenson's *Elizabeth Bishop* (1966). *Elizabeth Bishop and Her Art* was edited by Lloyd Schwartz and Sybil P. Estess (1983). *The Complete Poems: 1927-1979* supersedes the earlier *Complete Poems* (1969). *Elizabeth Bishop: The Collected Prose,* edited by Robert Giroux in 1984, contains essays and accounts of her life not published when she was alive. □

Maurice Bishop

Maurice Bishop (1944-1983) was a leader of the New Jewel Movement which proclaimed the independence of Grenada in 1974. After a 1979 coup he served as prime minister of Grenada until his death in a subsequent coup in 1983.

Maurice Rupert Bishop was born May 29, 1944, on the island of Aruba, Netherland Antilles, of immigrant parents, Rupert and Alimenta Bishop. His parents had joined the intraregional migrant stream then taking advantage of the petroleum-based economic prosperity in the southern Caribbean islands. Returning to Grenada, where his father entered commerce, at the age of six, Bishop attended St. George's Roman Catholic Primary School. He then won a scholarship to Presentation College, the Catholic high school in Grenada. His high school career was distinguished. He won the Principal's Gold Medal for outstanding academic and general all-round ability; he founded the Historical Society and served as its first president; and he edited the school newspaper. On leaving high school Bishop worked for a short time in the civil service before going to London. There he attended Gray's Inn and earned his law degree from the University of London. He was called to the bar in 1969.

For two years Bishop practiced law in London, co-founding a legal aid clinic and demonstrating an active interest in campaigns against racial discrimination, especially against West Indians in England. But Bishop's political involvement began in earnest in 1970 when he returned to Grenada via Trinidad and Tobago. For by 1970 the Black Power Movement, originally begun in the United States, had already gained considerable appeal throughout the Caribbean. Trinidad found itself in the throes of an abortive revolution whose repercussions spread to the neighboring island of Grenada. At that time Grenada was in the firm grasp of Eric Mathew Gairy, a bizarre, corrupt, and paternalistic politician who had gained prominence through his role as a labor organizer. Gairy was also discussing the possibility of political independence for Grenada, despite the reservations of a large sector of the population.

Bishop established a law practice in St. George's, Grenada, and organized a demonstration supporting the Trinidad insurgents. Gairy retaliated harshly against the demonstrators, unleashing a security force composed of police, army personnel, and members of a para-military group called the Mongoose Gang. The security force showed scant regard for human rights or civil liberties. In November 1970 Bishop joined the protest by nurses against the poor conditions at the St. George's hospital and successfully defended them in court after their arrest. Bishop organized the Movement for Assemblies of the People (MAP) along with Kenrick Radix in 1972 to articulate the grievances of the masses against the Gairy government. As a result he was arrested and beaten several times. In March 1973 MAP merged with the rural-based group founded by economist and teacher Unison Whiteman, the Joint Endeavor for Welfare, Education and Liberation (JEWEL), to form the New Jewel Movement. This well-coordinated opposition to the Gairy government declared independence for Grenada on February 7, 1974.

Meanwhile, on Sunday, November 18, 1973, Bishop and five leading members of the New Jewel Movement were in Grenville, the second largest town on the northeastern coast, when Gairy's Mongoose Gang attacked and brutally beat them. Bloody and barely conscious, they were incarcerated without formal charges and denied bail or medical attention. Eventually released, Bishop had to seek medical assistance on the neighboring island of Barbados. "Bloody Sunday," as the event came to be called, coalesced the opposition to Gairy. In January 1974 the New Jewel Movement and other groups called a general strike which lasted for three months and overshadowed the celebrations for independence on February 7. In one confrontation with the police on January 21, Bishop's father was shot and killed.

Bishop successfully contested the St. George's seat in 1976 and assumed the position of leader of the opposition in an ineffectual parliament. His New Jewel Movement controlled three of the six opposition seats won in a People's Alliance with the Grenada National Party and the United People's Party. Bishop used the parliamentary platform to publicize the program of the New Jewel Movement and relentlessly expose and condemn the actions of Gairy. At the same time, under Vincent Noel, an executive member of the New Jewel Movement, the Bank and General Workers Union was formed, enhancing the working class support of the political party. Apparently disturbed by the growing popular strength of the opposition, Gairy increased his repressive measures, especially those directed at the leaders of the New Jewel Movement.

On March 13, 1979, while Gairy was attending the United Nations session in New York, Bishop and his followers seized control of the government of Grenada. Proclaiming a People's Revolutionary Government, Bishop suspended the constitution. Promising new, democratic elections, Bishop became prime minister and minister of defense, and interior, information, health, and Carriacou affairs. Bernard Coard, a Brandeis University graduate in economics, became deputy prime minister, as well as minister of trade, industry, finance, and planning.

Bishop attempted to transform Grenadian society along the lines of the Cuban model. Voluntary mass organizations of women, farmers, youth, workers, and militia were established and declared to be a "real democracy," presumably making the holding of elections redundant. As a self-declared Marxist he demonstrated only a superficial understanding of the principles of Karl Marx. Nevertheless, he established close diplomatic relations with Cuba and the Soviet Union, and most of the island's development projects—including the new airport at Point Salines—were sponsored by the socialist bloc. With this support Grenada weathered the economic crises of the early 1980s better than most of its neighbors.

Bishop's government, despite its achievements, failed to hold elections and stifled a free press and the opposition. Despite the hostility of the United States, Bishop made repeated attempts to establish diplomatic ties with Washington. An active prime minister, he led delegations to meetings of the Caribbean Community, the commonwealth heads of governments, the United Nations General Assembly, the Summit of Non-Aligned Nations, and the Organization of American States. He established close personal friendships with Fidel Castro of Cuba and Daniel Ortega of Nicaragua.

By late 1982 a deep rift had developed within the central committee of the People's Revolutionary Government, mainly over the issue of Coard's desire to have coequal status with Bishop. Matters reached a head on October 12, 1983, when a meeting of the central committee accused Bishop of spreading false rumors of an assassination plot. The following day Bishop was placed under house arrest. On Wednesday, October 19, 1983, a crowd of supporters released him and marched to the military compound at Fort Rupert. There troops under the command of General Hudson Austin captured and executed Bishop, three cabinet members, two labor leaders, and nearly a hundred civilians. Within six days the United States invaded Grenada, arrested the leaders of the coup, established an interim government, and terminated the Grenadian experiment. Bishop's body has never been publicly identified.

Further Reading

Bishop is listed in *Personalities Caribbean, 1982-1983*. Background information on Grenada for this period may be found in A.W. Singham, *The Hero and the Crowd in a Colonial Polity* (1968); R.W. Jacobs and I. Jacobs, *Grenada: The Route to Revolution* (1980); David Lewis, *The Grenada Revolution* (1984) and EPICA Task Force, *Grenada. The Peaceful Revolution* (1982). □

Otto Eduard Leopold von Bismarck

The German statesman Otto Eduard Leopold von Bismarck (1815-1898) was largely responsible for the creation of the German Empire in 1871. A leading diplomat of the late 19th century, he was known as the Iron Chancellor.

Otto von Bismarck, born at Schönhausen on April 1, 1815, to Ferdinand von Bismarck-Schönhausen and Wilhelmine Mencken, displayed a willful temperament from childhood. He studied at the University of Göttingen and by 1836 had qualified as a lawyer. But during the following decade he failed to make a career of this or anything else. Tall, slender, and bearded, the young squire was characterized by extravagance, laziness, excessive drinking, needlessly belligerent atheism, and rudeness. In 1847, however, Bismarck made a number of significant changes in his life. He became religious, entered politics as a substitute member of the upper house of the Prussian parliament, and married Johanna von Puttkamer.

In 1851 Frederick William IV appointed Bismarck as Prussian representative to the Frankfurt Diet of the German Confederation. An ingenious but cautious obstructionist of Austria's presidency, Bismarck described Frankfurt diplo-macy as "mutually distasteful espionage." He performed well enough, however, to gain advancement to ambassadorial positions at Vienna in 1854, St. Petersburg in 1859, and Paris in 1862. He was astute in his judgment of international affairs and often acid in his comments on foreign leaders; he spoke of Napoleon III as "a sphinx without a riddle," of the Austrian Count Rechberg as "the little bottle of poison," and of the Russian Prince Gorchakov as "the fox in wooden shoes."

Minister-President of Prussia

In 1862 Frederick William's successor, William I, faced a crisis. He sought a larger standing army as a foundation for Prussian foreign policy; but he could not get parliamentary support for this plan, and he needed a strong minister-president who was willing to persist against opposition majorities. War Minister Roon persuaded the King to entrust the government to Bismarck. William attempted to condition the Sept. 22, 1862, appointment by a written agreement limiting the chief minister's part in foreign affairs, but Bismarck easily talked this restriction to shreds.

Bismarck's attempt to conciliate the budget committee foundered on his September 29 remark, "The great questions of the day will not be decided by speeches and resolutions of majorities—that was the mistake of 1848 and 1849—but by iron and blood." Bismarck complained that the words were misunderstood, but "blood and iron" became an unshakable popular label for his policies.

Bismarck soon turned to foreign affairs. He was determined to achieve Prussian annexation of the duchies of Schleswig and Holstein at the expense of Denmark. The history of Schleswig-Holstein during the preceding 2 decades had been stormy, and there were a number of conflicting claims of sovereignty over the territories. Bismarck let the Hohenzollerns, the Prussian ruling family, encourage the Duke of Augustenburg in his claim for Holstein, and the duke established a court at Kiel in Holstein in December 1863. Bismarck then, however, persuaded Austria's Count Rechberg to join in military intervention against the Hohenzollern protégé. This ability to take opposite sides at the same time in a political quarrel for motives ulterior to the issue itself was a Bismarckian quality not always appreciated by his contemporaries. Austro-Prussian forces occupied Holstein and invaded Schleswig in February 1864. The Danes resisted, largely because of a mistaken hope of English help, which Bismarck reportedly assessed with the comment, "If Lord Palmerston sends the British army to Germany, I shall have the police arrest them."

Denmark's 1864 defeat by Austro-Prussian forces led to the 1865 Austro-Prussian Gastein Convention, which exposed Rechberg's folly in committing Austrian troops to an adventure from which only Prussia could profit. Prussia occupied Schleswig, and Austria occupied Holstein, with Prussia to construct, own, and operate a naval base at Kiel and a Kiel-Brunsbüttel canal, both in Holstein. King William made Bismarck a count.

Austro-Prussian War

Bismarck gave Austria a number of opportunities to retreat from its Holstein predicament; when Austria turned to the German Confederation and France for anti-Prussian support, however, Bismarck allied Prussia to Italy. In 1866 Austria mobilized Confederation forces against Prussia, whose Frankfurt representative declared this to be an act of war dissolving the Confederation. The resulting Seven Weeks War led to the defeat of Austria at Königgrätz (July 3) by the Prussian general Moltke. Bismarck persuaded king William to accept the lenient Truce of Nikolsburg (July 26) and Treaty of Prague (August 23).

Prussia's victory enabled Bismarck to achieve Prussian annexation of Schleswig-Holstein, Hanover, Hesse-Cassel, and Frankfurt. The newly formed North German Confederation, headed by Prussia and excluding Austria, provided a popularly elected assembly; the Prussian king, however, held veto power on all political issues. The victory over Austria increased Bismarck's power, and he was able to obtain parliamentary approval of an indemnity budget for 4 years of unconstitutional government. Bismarck was also voted a large grant, with which he bought an estate in Farther Pomerania.

Franco-Prussian War

As payment for its neutrality during the Austro-Prussian War, France claimed Belgium. Bismarck held that the 1839 European treaty prevented this annexation, and instead he agreed to neutralize Luxembourg as a concession to the government of Napoleon III. The French were, however, antagonized by Bismarck's actions. In 1870 he heightened French hostility by supporting the claim of Leopold von Hohenzollern-Sigmaringen to the Spanish throne. The French government demanded Leopold's withdrawal, and Vincent Benedetti, the French ambassador to Prussia, requested formal assurance that no Hohenzollern would ever occupy the Spanish throne. William, who was staying at Bad Ems, declined the request and telegraphed Bismarck an account of the interview. Bismarck edited this "Ems Dispatch" and published an abrupt version that suggested that discussions were over and the guns loaded. His action precipitated the French declaration of war against Prussia on July 19, 1870.

Bismarck's treaties with the South German states brought them into the war against France, and his work at field headquarters transformed these wartime partnerships into a lasting federation. Within 6 weeks the German army had moved through Alsace-Lorraine and forced the surrender of Napoleon III and his army at Sedan (Sept. 2, 1870). But Paris defiantly proclaimed a republic and refused to capitulate. The annexation of occupied Alsace—Lorraine became Bismarck's territorial justification for continuing the war, and the siege of Paris ended in French surrender (Jan. 28, 1871). Alsace-Lorraine became a German imperial territory by the Treaty of Frankfurt (May 10, 1871). The Prussian victory led to the formation of the Reich, a unified German empire under Prussian leadership. William was proclaimed kaiser, or emperor, and Bismarck became chancellor of the empire. Bismarck was also elevated to the rank of prince and given a Friedrichsruh estate.

Chancellor of the Reich (1871-1890)

Bismarck modernized German administration, law, and education in harmony with the economic and technological revolution which was transforming Germany into an industrial society. However, he developed no political system, party, or set of issues to support and succeed him. His *Kulturkampf,* or vehement opposition to the Catholic Church, was unsuccessful, and his anti-Socialist policies contributed to the wreckage of the Bismarckian parties in the 1890 election.

Among Bismarck's major diplomatic achievements of this period were the establishment of the Dreikaiserbund, or Three Emperors' League (Germany, Russia, Austria), of 1872-1878 and 1881-1887 and the negotiation of the 1879 Austro-German Duplice, the 1882 Austro-German-Italian Triplice, and the secret 1887 Russo-German Reinsurance Treaty. He served as chairman of the 1878 Congress of Berlin, and he also guided the German acquisition of overseas colonies.

The alliances that Bismarck established were not so much instruments of diplomacy as the visible evidence of his comprehensive effort to postpone a hostile coalition of the powers surrounding Germany. Restraining Russia, the strongest of these powers, required the greatest diplomatic effort. Bismarck's diplomacy is sometimes described as aimed at isolating France, but this is a misleadingly simplistic description of the complicated and deceptive methods he employed to lend substance to his statement, "We Germans fear God, but nothing else in the world."

Fall from Power

William I died March 9, 1888, but Bismarck remained as chancellor for Frederick III (who died June 15, 1888) and for 21 months of the reign of William II, last of the Hohenzollern monarchs. Court, press, and political parties discovered in the 29-year-old William an obvious successor to the power of the 73-year-old chancellor. William was intelligent and glib, with a singular capacity as a phrase maker, and his instability was as yet not widely recognized.

On March 15, 1890, William asked either for the right to consult ministers or for Bismarck's resignation; Bismarck's March 18 letter gave the Kaiser a choice between following Bismarck's Russian policy or accepting his resignation. Suppressing this letter, the Kaiser published an acceptance of Bismarck's retirement because of ill health and created him Duke of Lauenburg. Bismarck referred to this title as one he might use for traveling incognito.

Bismarck did not retire gracefully. Domestically he was happy at Friedrichsruh with Johanna, whom he outlived; and their children, Herbert, Bill, and Marie, frequently visited them there. Bismarck, however, used the press to harass his political successors, and he briefly stumped the country calling for more power to the parliament, of which he was an absent member from 1891 to 1893. Despite charades of reconciliation, he remained, to his death on July 30, 1898, thoroughly opposed to William II.

Historical estimates of Otto von Bismarck remain contradictory. The later political failure of the state he created has led some to argue that by his own standards Bismarck was himself a failure. He is, however, widely regarded as an extraordinarily astute statesman who understood that to wield power successfully a leader must assess not only its strength but also the circumstances of its application. In his analysis and management of these circumstances, Bismarck showed himself the master of realpolitik.

Further Reading

Bismarck's *Gedanken und Erinnerungen* was translated into English by A. J. Butler as *Bismarck, the Man and the Statesman* (2 vols., 1898). Bismarck's *The Kaiser vs. Bismarck* was translated by Bernard Miall (1920). Werner Richter, *Bismarck* (trans. 1965), is a readable modern biography of the chancellor. Erich Eyck, *Bismarck and German Empire* (3 vols., 1941-1944; abr. trans. 1950; 2d ed. 1963), presents critical views. Emil Ludwig, *Bismarck: The Story of a Fighter* (trans. 1927), is melodramatically partisan, while A. J. P. Taylor, *Bismarck: The Man and the Statesman* (1955), is part of the author's view of Germany as "alien".

The Correspondence of William I and Bismarck (trans., 2 vols., 1903) and *The Kaiser's Memoirs: Wilhelm II, Emperor of Germany, 1888-1918* (trans. 1922) supply predictably different views of the chancellor. Norman Rich and M. H. Fisher, eds., *The Holstein Papers* (4 vols., 1955-1963), presents much useful material on Bismarck's later career. Heinrich von Sybel, *The Founding of the German Empire by William I* (7 vols., 1890-1898), is ultra-Prussian and tedious but supplies Bismarck's accounts of numerous diplomatic conversations. A brief delineation of Bismarck from contemporary documents is supplied in Louis L. Snyder, *The Blood and Iron Chancellor* (1967). Other contemporary accounts include Charles Lowe, *Bismarck's Table Talk* (1895); Moritz Busch, *Bismarck* (2 vols., 1898); C. von Hohenlohe, *Memoirs of Prince Chlodwig of Hohenlohe-Schillingsfuerst* (trans. 1906); Alfred von Tirpitz, *My Memoirs* (trans., 2 vols., 1919); and Alfred von Waldersee, *A Field-Marshal's Memoirs* (abr. trans. 1924).

Significant monographs on specific aspects of Bismarck's career include Joseph V. Fuller, *Bismarck's Diplomacy at Its Zenith* (1922); Karl Friedrich Nowak, *Kaiser and Chancellor* (1930); Lawrence D. Steefel, *The Schleswig-Holstein Question* (1932) and *Bismarck, the Hohenzollern Candidacy, and the Origins of the Franco-German War of 1870* (1962); and William A. Fletcher, *The Mission of Vincent Benedetti to Berlin, 1864-70* (1965). □

Nur al-Din Abu Ishaq al Bitruji

The Moslem astronomer Nur al-Din Abu Ishaq al-Bitruji (ca. 1150-1200), also known as Alpetragius, expounded an astronomical system which revived the Eudoxan explanation and denied the Ptolemaic explanation of the anomalous motions of the planets.

Of the life of al-Bitruji virtually nothing is known, though at one point in his work he ascribes the genesis of his theory to the instruction of Ibn Tufayl. The problem faced by al-Bitruji was that faced by all Aristotelians who read Ptolemy's *Almagest*. Aristotle clearly stated that the planets must move with circular motions and implied that the center of these motions must be identical with the center of the earth; he further desired a mechanism to transfer the motion of the prime mover to the planetary spheres. Ptolemy, on the other hand, while preserving the principle of circular motions (on eccentrics and epicycles), placed the centers of these motions elsewhere than at the center of the earth; for Saturn, Jupiter, Mars, Venus, and Mercury he placed the centers of their uniform motions not at the centers of their respective eccentric deferents but at points called equants.

Eudoxus of Cnidus had already shown that it is theoretically possible to explain the two most obvious anomalies in planetary motion—retrogression and latitude—by means of homocentric spheres. Aristotle, by adding more spheres, converted this system to a mechanical model of the universe (though technical details make it impossible for such a model to yield correct predictions of the retrogressions and latitudes of Mars and Venus). Al-Bitruji followed the suggestion of Ibn Tufayl, as did the latter's other pupil Averroës, and attempted to adjust the Aristotelian solution in such a way that it would correspond to observed reality. The attempt failed owing to the inherent inadequacy of the homocentric system to describe the phenomena.

Further Reading

Volume 2 of George Sarton, *Introduction to the History of Science* (3 vols., 1927-1947), contains a brief biography of al-Bitruji. See also Philip K. Hitti, *History of the Arabs from the Earliest Times to the Present* (1937; 10th ed. 1970), and Gérard de Vaucouleurs, *Discovery of the Universe: An Outline of the History of Astronomy from the Origins to 1956* (trans. 1957). □

Georges Bizet

With his opera *Carmen*, French composer Georges Bizet (1838-1875) revitalized the French lyric stage by challenging both the oversized species of grand opera and the tired repertory of the opéra comique.

Georges Bizet was born in Paris. He showed precocious ability in music and at the age of 10 was admitted to the conservatory. There he worked under Jacques Halévy and Charles Gounod in composition and studied piano, organ, and theory. His progress was so outstanding that he won several prizes, culminating in 1857 with the Prix de Rome for composition, which enabled him to live in Italy for 3 years.

Bizet had already composed a number of piano pieces, choruses, and orchestral works. By far the best is the Symphony in C Major, written in a month's time in 1855 but not performed until 1935. Bizet regarded it as too imitative in style, and it does have touches of Gounod, Mozart, Rossini, and even Offenbach. Yet this symphony has such melodic charm, vivacity, and control of musical structure and orchestration that it ranks as a masterpiece of teen-age creation.

Bizet's operatic career began less spectacularly with the composition at the age of 18 of a one-act comic opera entitled *Le Docteur Miracle.* After arriving in Rome he wrote a second comedy, *Don Procupio* (1858-1859). Both pieces are rather Italianate in style, mildly attractive, but of no great consequence except as giving an early indication of theatrical talent.

After Bizet returned to Paris, he earned a living by giving private lessons and doing hackwork for publishers. It is possible that he might have had a career as a pianist, for he was by all accounts a remarkably fine player, applauded by Franz Liszt himself. Bizet had no desire, however, to perform publicly, choosing rather to devote himself to composition. The world of music was ultimately the better for that, although his efforts in the 1860s did not produce a single major success. A second symphony, known as the *Roma,* occupied him off and on from 1860 until its final revision in 1871, but it was a failure.

During this period Bizet also wrote several songs, some piano solos, and three operas bearing the earmarks of the gaudy tradition of French grand opera established 30 years before by Giacomo Meyerbeer. *Ivan le terrible* (1865), which was not performed until 1946, and *La Jolie fille de*

Perth (1866) suffered most from this inheritance of inflated rhetoric and are now simply historical curiosities. *Les Pêcheurs de perles* (1863) has fared better. A failure in its own day, it gradually won a place in the French repertory. Its drama is old-fashioned and sentimental, and the musical score sags badly toward the end; but it contains enough good moments to keep it alive as a second-class, if not a first-class, opera.

Bizet reached his stride in the 1870s. The opera *Djamileh,* a short love story with much exotic atmosphere and some excellent music, and 12 pieces for piano duet called *Jeux d'enfants* were composed in 1871. The following year he wrote incidental music for Alphonse Daudet's play *L'Arlésienne,* consisting of 27 numbers rich in melodic quality, with imaginative use of a 16-piece orchestra. The symphonic overture *Patrie* (1873) was less successful. Then came *Carmen* (1875), an opera as close to perfect as any ever written. Here Bizet was not innovative in his musical resources or form, but he created a faultless drama of real people and their passions (based on a story by Prosper Mérimée) expressed through music that is uniformly direct, relevant, colorful, and stamped with a personal accent.

Bizet brooded a good deal over the roles of intuition and reason in artistic creation and how they affected his own work. This may indicate some lack of self-confidence, and it perhaps accounts for the fact that he began and then put aside an extraordinary number of compositions. He left relatively few completed works and even fewer important ones. He was no advanced thinker in music, but at his best he commanded an unusual wealth of original melody linked to a fine sense for orchestral sonorities and impeccable craftsmanship.

Further Reading

The most complete biographical account of Bizet is Mina Stein Curtiss, *Bizet and His World* (1958). See also Martin Cooper, *Georges Bizet* (1938). Winton Dean, *Bizet* (1948), is useful for musical analysis and appraisal. Gerald E. Abraham, *A Hundred Years of Music* (1938; 3d ed. 1964), is recommended for a view of the century in which Bizet lived.

Additional Sources

Curtiss, Mina Stein Kirstein, *Bizet and his world,* Westport, Conn.: Greenwood Press, 1977.
Dean, Winton, *Bizet,* London: Dent, 1975; Westport, Conn.: Hyperion Press, 1979. □

Johannes Bjelke-Petersen

The Australian politician Johannes (Joh) Bjelke-Petersen (born 1911) was an extreme reactionary who dominated Queensland politics for years, serving as premier of Queensland from 1968 to 1988.

ohannes Bjelke-Petersen was born in Dannevirke, New Zealand, on January 13, 1911. His father, who was Danish, immigrated to Queensland, Australia, with his family in 1913. Johannes (or Joh, as he was widely known) left school at the age of 13. He remained a major peanut farmer at his home in Kingaroy and a leading businessman in the region throughout his political career. As a farmer he pioneered aerial spraying and seeding.

Bjelke-Petersen entered Parliament in 1947 as a Country Party (later renamed the National Party) member for the constituency of Nanango. He first entered the cabinet as minister for works and housing in 1963 and became premier in 1968.

A controversial figure, Bjelke-Petersen dominated Queensland politics for 20 years. In general, his hostility to civil rights, the environment, and issues of social welfare and his favoritism towards big business earned Queensland the sobriquet of Australia's "Deep North." Very much in the tradition of agrarian populist politicians, he was a colorful figure, of whom it was said that "were he able to finish a sentence he could become dictator of Australia." His inability to articulate took on legendary proportions. His favorite sentence was, with a slight stutter, "Now, just you don't worry about that."

Bjelke-Petersen was an outspoken reactionary in his politics. He strongly opposed union demands, land rights for Aborigines, and legislation that favored conservation over business. Like many populists before him, he was impatient with parliamentary procedures: he abused parliamentary arrangements, denied the Opposition its legitimate access to facilities, suppressed debate, denied information to the Opposition as well as to the media, and frequently forced through Parliament ill-conceived, hastily drafted legislation that reflected both a lack of consultation and Bjelke-Petersen's confrontational style. Queensland's lack of an upper house; the weakness of the Labor Party Opposition; Bjelke-Petersen's total domination of his coalition partner, the Liberal Party; and his domination of the cabinet room exacerbated his authoritarian tendencies.

Among many incidents that brought him to attention at a national level, in 1971 he declared a state of emergency in Queensland as a reaction to demonstrations against the touring South African Springboks (Rugby Union team).

Between 1972 and 1975 Bjelke-Petersen clashed with the federal Labor government under Gough Whitlam. Bjelke-Petersen established himself as a major political figure and a strong voice for states' rights, dedicating himself to a single cause: the obstruction and destruction of the first federal Labor government since 1949. In 1975 he played a key part in undermining that Labor government. In defiance of established tradition, Bjelke-Petersen selected his own candidate to fill a casual Senate vacancy in the federal parliament, so thwarting Labor's attempt to gain a majority in that House. That maneuver was critical to the events leading to the dismissal of Gough Whitlam as prime minister in November 1975.

Bjelke-Petersen continued his tough right-wing policies. For example, in September 1977 he banned political demonstrations—a ban which led to clashes with uranium protesters, unionists, students, liberals, communists, and well-known parliamentarians.

In 1952 he had married Florence (Flo) Gilmour, who was seen as an integral part of Joh's political as well as private life. As an extension of his political performance, Flo was unwavering in her partisanship and loyalty. She was elected to the federal Senate in 1980 as a National Party member for Queensland. There she commanded respect in her own right while simultaneously being seen as Joh's federal representative. Her homely appeal complemented her husband's hard dealing and lifted the fortunes of the National Party in Queensland between 1981 and 1986. The Bjelke-Petersens' combined success proved potent and was dubbed the "Joh and Flo Show."

In 1980, despite criticism by lawyers, civil liberties groups, and backbench members of Parliament, amendments were passed to the Police Act empowering the police to open their files to state and federal departments, government agencies, and certain private concerns. In 1982 Bjelke-Petersen passed the Commonwealth Games Act, which ensured that no protesters could come near the area in which the games were being played or approach any official or dignitary. The central concern of the legislation was to prevent disruption by Aboriginal groups or their white supporters who might wish to draw international attention to the plight of Queensland Aborigines.

In 1983 Bjelke-Petersen led his National Party to an electoral victory that enabled him to form a one-party state government, rather than governing in coalition with the Liberal Party. Owing to heavily malapportioned electoral districts which permitted county areas with one-quarter of the population of city constituencies, this National Party victory was gained on less than 40 percent of the vote, while Labor gained 44 percent. This biased system operated in total defiance of the principle of one person one vote, and was called the "Bjelke-mander."

On his own recommendation, Bjelke-Petersen was knighted by the Queen in 1984.

In 1986 he was returned to office, again demonstrating his remarkable personal popularity against which the Labor Party was powerless. In late 1986 Bjelke-Petersen sensed a loss of direction at the federal level among conservative forces and led a campaign, "Joh for PM," to have himself elected to the federal Parliament. Public speculation about the source of his funding caused Bjelke-Petersen's campaign to falter and die. However, his campaign undermined the already squabbling conservative parties, ensuring their failure at the following federal election.

His interest in federal politics and scandals attached to campaign funding and to his administration of Queensland led to crisis within the Queensland National Party. Direct confrontation with his own leadership, both within and outside Parliament, led to his resignation under a cloud of suspicion on December 1, 1988. In the following local election in Queensland the Labor Party won, ending an extraordinary period in Australian politics.

The story had not ended for Bjelke-Petersen. On September 23, 1991, he went on trial for corruption and perjury. However, a hung jury ended the trial, and Bjelke-Petersen went free. It was later discovered that the jury foreman was a member of Bjelke-Petersen's National Party and had assisted in raising funds for his legal expenses. Following this incident, the Queensland government resolved to amend the Jury Act and set up a permanent criminal justice commission in order to prevent this kind of occurrence in the future.

Bjelke-Petersen's memoirs, *Don't You Worry About That: The Joh Bjelke-Petersen Memoirs,* were published in 1991.

Further Reading

Most of the following references are fairly critical of Bjelke-Petersen. Hugh Lunn, *Johannes Bjelke-Petersen* 2nd edition (1984); Alan Metcalfe, *In Their Own Right: The Rise to Power of Joh's Nationals* (1984); Evan Whitton, *The Hillbilly Dictator, Australia's Police State* (1989); Ross Fitzgerald and Harold Thorton, *Labor in Queensland from the 1880s to 1988* (1989); and Ross Fitzgerald, *A History of Queensland, From 1915 to the 1980s* (1984). See also *Contemporary Review* (July 1991); *Guardian* (August 29, 1989; September 23, 1991; October 27, 1991); and *Anarchist Age Weekly Review* (November 4, 1996). □

Bjørnstjerne Bjørnson

The Norwegian author Bjørnstjerne Bjørnson (1832-1910) is best known for his plays, which treat both historical subjects and contemporary issues. He was influential in the revival of Norwegian as a literary language.

The son of a rural pastor, Bjørnstjerne Bjørnson was born on Dec. 8, 1832. In 1850 he went to Christiania (Oslo) to cram for the university entrance examinations but soon gave up his studies to live by his pen. On a trip to Sweden in 1856, Bjørnson was filled with "historical envy" when he saw the monuments to Sweden's past greatness. He determined to create a Norwegian "ancestors' gallery," historical dramas about Norway's saga heroes. At the same time he wanted to show that the Norwegians of the sagas were the spiritual ancestors of the present generation, so he conceived the idea of alternating saga dramas with stories about modern rural Norwegians who struggle with the same inner problems as their heroic forefathers.

With the stories—the best of which are *Synnøve Solbakken* (1857) and *Arne* (1859)—Bjørnson created a new style important for the development of literary Norwegian, a fusion of the saga style and the oral style of the Norwegian folk tales. In their day these stories, which made Bjørnson famous, were considered at times too realistic by a public accustomed to idealizations of the farmer, but today they are children's literature.

The saga dramas feature heroes who are caught between the old pagan ways and the new ideals of Christianity and who must die because they cannot reconcile these forces within themselves. The best of these is the trilogy *Sigurd the Bastard* (1862). With Henrik Ibsen's *The Pretenders* (1863), it represents the triumph of Norwegian historical tragedy.

During these years Bjørnson also wrote some of Norway's finest poetry, including its national anthem, and directed the first Norwegian theater in Bergen. In 1858 he married an actress, Karoline Reimers. One of their sons became a leading actor and producer, and a daughter married Ibsen's son.

By 1872 new intellectual impulses had begun to penetrate into Norway. Like Ibsen's, Bjørnson's authorship spans both periods, the "national romantic" period and the period of social realism that supplanted it. It was Bjørnson who wrote the first "problem" plays, showing Ibsen (who would do it much better) the way. *The Bankrupt* (1875) made Bjørnson famous abroad for its realistic treatment of the business world, a subject previously considered unsuitable for serious drama.

From this time on, Bjørnson's authorship follows, more closely than intended, the demand of the Dane George Brandes that literature "take up problems for discussion." His novels, stories, plays, and poems teem with the latest thought from abroad (that of Charles Darwin, J.S. Mill, Herbert Spencer, and the Bible critics) and deal as well with the stormier issues within Norway. The novels *Magnhild* (1877), *The Heritage of the Kurts* (1884), and *In God's Way* (1889) deal, respectively, with a woman's right to divorce, school reform, and religious intolerance. The play *Leonarda*

(1879) is about divorce, while *A Gauntlet* (1883) attacks the new bohemian writers' demands for complete sexual freedom. *Beyond Our Power* (1883) and *Paul Lange and Tora Parsberg* (1898) show what Bjørnson was capable of when he dealt with powerful and personal subjects, and both are masterpieces.

A born leader, Bjørnson involved himself in the major controversies of an unusually stormy age, sometimes with all Norway behind him, sometimes alone. He began as a passionate defender of Norway's cultural and political independence, moved later toward pan-Scandinavianism, and ended fighting for world peace and the rights of all oppressed peoples.

Bjørnson was awarded the Nobel Prize for literature in 1903. He died in Paris on April 26, 1910. Although during his lifetime Bjørnson was considered Ibsen's equal, his reputation as an author has diminished considerably, but his influence in many areas of Norwegian cultural life is still strong.

Further Reading

Almost all of Bjørnson's work has been translated into English. Works about Bjørnson include Georg Brandes's excellent book, *Henrik Ibsen, Bjørnstjerne Bjørnson: Critical Studies* (1899), and Harold Larson, *Bjørnstjerne Bjørnson: A Study in Norwegian Nationalism* (1944). Useful surveys of Bjørnson and his times are in Harald Beyer, *A History of Norwegian Literature* (trans. 1956), and Brian W. Downs, *Modern Norwegian Literature: 1860-1918* (1966). □

Conrad Moffat Black

Canadian-born Conrad Moffat Black (born 1944) gained fame as an international press baron whose newspapers' daily circulation of 4.5 million was a total surpassed only by Rupert Murdoch and the US Gannett chain.

Born in 1944 to George Montegu Black, Jr. and Jean Elizabeth (Riley) Black, Conrad was named after his mother's father. His paternal grandfather, George Montegu Black, Sr., owned Western Breweries of Winnipeg. His father, George Montegu Black, Jr., ran Canadian Breweries (which had absorbed his father's firm) as a cornerstone of the famous Argus empire under E.P. Taylor. Black became the chairman and chief executive officer of Argus, as well as director of such famous companies as the Canadian Imperial Bank of Commerce, Confederation Life Insurance, and Eaton's of Canada—placing him at the center of Canadian business. Black was notorious for his outspokenly conservative views, while respected for his intellectual talents. He was born into the right circles and attended the top private boys' schools, Upper Canada College and Trinity College School—managing to get himself expelled from both. Before the age of 10 he was already knowledgeable about the life and times of Napoleon Bonaparte, an interest which provided a motif for his career.

Some said there was a physical resemblance, others only a behavioral one.

Black's interest in acquiring newspapers began during his college years. Noted for his outspoken views and his love of Napoleon Bonaparte, he enrolled in 1962 at Ottawa's Carleton University. He went on to earn a law degree from Quebec's Laval University in 1970 and a master's degree in history from McGill University in 1973. His controversial master's thesis on Maurice Duplessis, the tyrannical provincial premier of Quebec, was eventually published as *Duplessis* (1977). Yet in other ways he remained a child of privilege, receiving a life membership in the prestigious Toronto club for his 21st birthday.

Unlike many of his more quietly powerful corporate friends, Conrad Black became an outspoken right-wing intellectual, a friend of Canadian prime minister Brian Mulroney, and admired by British prime minister Margaret Thatcher. He was a member of such important ideological organizations as the Canadian Centre for Arms Control and Disarmament, the Cultural Council of the Americas Society, and the Trilateral Commission. It is this desire to have his views heard that explains his business practices. In 1969, at the age of 25, when many are just beginning to read newspapers, he began purchasing them. He gained hands-on experience by running an ad sheet in Quebec called *The Eastern Townships Advisor* for which he sold advertising and wrote most of the copy. When Black sold this publication in the late 1960s, he used part of the proceeds to form the Sterling chain (which he still owned in 1990). Not until he wrestled control of Argus was he able to realize his grandiose vision. In 1978, building upon the 22.4 percent block of Argus shares from his father's inheritance, and following the death of Bud McDougald (one of Argus' founders), Black marshaled sufficient stock from the founders' heirs to gain control of the famous holding company. At the time he was only 33 years old. From these heights of power he was able to realize his dreams.

In 1978, soon after taking control, Black sold many of Argus' traditional holdings and began constructing Hollinger Inc., his media holding empire. The Argus name was put to rest and Hollinger Inc. became a conglomerate. Black purchased Quebec City's *Le Soleil* and Ottawa's *Le Droit*, some 182 small US newspapers, the *Jerusalem Post*, the *Cayman Free Press*, a 15 percent interest in *Financial Post* and *Saturday Night* magazine. He made his business the media, becoming a world-scale press baron. Less than a quarter of his operating company's revenues came from Canada in 1989. He owned newspapers and magazines in five countries. His most important purchase was London's prestigious *Daily Telegraph*, bought in 1985.

The cash flow generated from the *Telegraph*'s powerful success enabled Black to purchase major newspapers world-wide at rock bottom prices, since much of his competition was facing flagging sales and bankruptcy, due to the increasing impact of radio and television.

Conrad Black had an eye to history, as reflected in his academic training and fascination with Napoleon. He also had a strong sense of family irony. Robert Thomas Riley (1851-1944) was the son of one of Fleet Street's *Daily Tele-*

graph owners. He moved to Canada and founded Great-West Assurance Company. His second son, Conrad Stephenson Riley (1875-1960), expanded the business. Conrad Riley's daughter, Jean Elizabeth (1913-1976), married George Montegu Black, Jr. (1911-1976) and became the mother of Conrad Black. His purchase of the *Daily Telegraph* completed the family circle.

With the purchase of the *Telegraph,* Hollinger Inc. increased its ownership to 91 daily newspapers in the US, Canada, the UK, and Israel. In December of 1991, Black successfully acquired the bankrupt *John Fairfax Group Pty. Ltd.,* Australia's second-largest newspaper group. He was able to accomplish this despite strong opposition from Australian journalists who feared the impact of Black's conservatism.

In 1992 Black purchased the *Toronto Star* for $259 million and thus acquired a 23% interest in Southam Inc., the owner of Canada's largest string of daily newspapers. By 1996 he had acquired a controlling interest in Southam and struck fear into the Canadian newspaper industry by threatening to pull Southam out of the indispensable *Canadian Press,* the country's only national and bilingual news-gathering agency, in order to cut costs. In the meantime, Black planned to expand Southam's own news-gathering service and thus reduce its dependence upon the *Canadian Press.* Fortunately for Canada's major newspaper companies, Black revoked his plans when Hollinger Inc. purchased Southam outright and became its president. He now controlled 50% of Canada's daily newspapers.

Forced to sell his 24.9% interest in John Fairfax Holdings Ltd. (Black's Australian conglomerate) because of its stringent foreign ownership rules, Black's Hollinger International controlled 137 newspapers in the UK, Canada, the US, and Israel—with a combined circulation of more than four million. Black's world-wide readership was surpassed only by Rupert Murdoch's empire and the US Gannett chain.

Further Reading

Conrad Black is listed in *Canadian Who's Who; The Canadian Encyclopedia;* and *Debrett's Illustrated Guide to the Canadian Establishment* (1983). A full-length biography by Peter C. Newman, Canada's pre-eminent chronicler of the rich and famous, is titled *The Establishment Man: A Portrait of Power* (1982). Black himself has written an autobiography titled *Conrad Black: A Life in Progress* (1993). □

Hugo Lafayette Black

The American jurist Hugo Lafayette Black (1886-1971) was President Franklin D. Roosevelt's first appointee to the U.S. Supreme Court. Associate Justice Black was an ardent New Dealer and led the liberal and activist wing of the Court for more than 32 years.

The youngest in a family of eight, Hugo Black was born on a farm in the rural area of Clay County, Ala., on Feb. 27, 1886. The family, well off by rural standards, moved to Ashland, the county seat, so that the children would have better educational opportunities. Hugo attended Ashland College. Interested in law, at the age of 18 he enrolled in the University of Alabama Law School at Tuscaloosa. After 2 years he received his law degree and passed the bar examinations.

After a year of practice in Ashland, Black moved his office to Birmingham. In 1917 he became county prosecuting attorney. When the United States entered World War I in 1917, he enlisted in the Army. He received a captain's commission and served with several artillery units until his discharge in 1919. He resumed his law practice in Birmingham, and his reputation, as attorney for the United Mine Workers union and other unions, grew as the result of the high damages he won for his clients.

In 1921 Black joined the Birmingham chapter of the Ku Klux Klan, for political reasons, not because of a belief in the Klan's principles. His record as the prosecuting attorney of Birmingham is studded with examples of leniency toward African American defendants. Black resigned from the Klan in 1925, the year he announced he would run for the U.S. Senate.

Campaigning on a platform that called for aid to farmers, enforcement of prohibition, help to veterans, and immigration restrictions, Black won the seat. During his first term in the Senate he supported the efforts of Senator

George W. Norris of Nebraska to keep Muscle Shoals dams for public use. Both President Coolidge and President Hoover, however, vetoed legislation that would have made Muscle Shoals a government project. Black's dream came true when President Roosevelt, in 1933, signed the act creating the Tennessee Valley Authority.

The 1932 election, which Franklin Roosevelt won, also saw Black reelected to the Senate. During Roosevelt's first term Black supported him on most New Deal major measures. Black supported the reelection of Roosevelt in 1936 and in 1937 backed the President's court-packing plan. Black also conducted a series of major investigations into lobbying activities, ship subsidies, and trusts.

With the resignation of Associate Justice Willis Van Devanter in 1937, President Roosevelt made Black his first appointment to the Supreme Court. The decision caused a national furor. Opposition came from conservative Democrats and Republicans who did not wish to see one of the most zealous Roosevelt supporters elected to the highest tribunal. The Senate nevertheless confirmed his appointment in August 1937.

Black's career on the Court proved him a champion of individual liberty. On the Court only 3 years, he wrote the majority decision in *Chambers v. Florida* (1940), which demonstrated that he had never followed the Klan line. The case concerned the conviction of four African Americans for murder based on confessions obtained under third-degree conditions. The Court, led by Black, nullified the decision. In the same year Black wrote the majority decision in *Smith v. Texas,* a case concerning an African American who the Court declared had not received a fair trial because no attempt had been made to appoint African Americans to the jury.

Consistently a supporter of the guarantees in the 1st and 5th Amendments to the Constitution, Black was in conflict with Justice Felix Frankfurter. By early 1941 this opposition was shown in the vigorous decision that Black wrote opposing the right of state courts to prohibit picketing. Black continued to show concern for 1st Amendment guarantees when he rendered the majority decision in *Marsh v. Alabama* (1946), asserting that the Jehovah's Witnesses could not be prevented from freely distributing their religious literature.

Benchmark cases in which Black wrote the majority decisions are legion. In *Everson v. Board of Education* (1947), Black held for the majority that taxpayers' money could be used to transport pupils to parochial schools. However, he declared that more direct aid to parochial schools was not permissible under the 1st Amendment. In *Youngstown Sheet and Tube Company et al. v. Sawyer* (1952), Black declared that President Truman's seizure of the steel industry was beyond the chief executive's powers.

One historic decision written by Black inaugurated the expression "one man one vote." In *Wesberry v. Sanders* (1964), Black ruled that "as nearly as practicable one man's vote in a congressional election is to be worth as much as another's." The Supreme Court thus moved into the area of apportioning congressional districts.

Black married Josephine Patterson Foster, the daughter of a Birmingham physician, shortly after he resumed his law practice, following his discharge from the Army. Two sons and one daughter were born to them. Black's first wife died in 1951 and in 1957 he married his secretary, Elizabeth Seay De Meritte. On Sept. 25, 1971, Black died in Bethesda, Md.

Throughout his career on the high bench Black revealed that he was one of the most vigorous supporters of civil rights in the history of the Court. He failed to vote for the protection of basic civil rights in only a few instances. His decision in *Korematsu v. United States* (1945), for example, supported President Roosevelt's executive order authorizing the creation of military areas from which Americans of Japanese descent were excluded.

Black indicated in many cases he decided that some problems must be resolved ultimately by legislative bodies. However, he quickly struck down legislative or executive action which attacked fundamental freedoms. John P. Frank wrote in the *Yale Law Journal* in 1956: "In general, he [Black] has preached the doctrine that government should at the same time be both all-powerful and all-weak. . . . "

Further Reading

Although its early publication date causes it to miss some of the highlights of Black's career, Charlotte Williams, *Hugo L. Black: A Study in the Judicial Process* (1950), is a satisfying, frank, and concise biography. *Hugo Black and the Supreme Court: A Symposium,* edited by Stephen Parks Strickland (1967), is a useful study which examines all aspects of his career. John P. Frank, *Mr. Justice Black: The Man and His Opinions* (1949), sees Black as a liberal who furthered the New Deal. The best book on Black's civil liberties decisions is Irving Dilliard, ed., *One Man's Stand for Freedom: Mr. Justice Black and the Bill of Rights, a Collection of His Supreme Court Decisions* (1963). An excellent study of contrasts is Wallace Mendelson, *Justices Black and Frankfurter: Conflict in the Court* (1961; 2d ed. 1966). Leo Pfeffer, *This Honorable Court: A History of the United States Supreme Court* (1965), is a good background study.

Additional Sources

Ball, Howard, *Hugo L. Black: cold steel warrior,* New York: Oxford University Press, 1996.

Ball, Howard, *Of power and right: Hugo Black, William O. Douglas, and America's constitutional revolution,* New York: Oxford University Press, 1992.

Black, Hugo LaFayette, *Mr. Justice and Mrs. Black: the memoirs of Hugo L. Black and Elizabeth Black,* New York: Random House, 1986.

Dunne, Gerald T., *Hugo Black and the judicial revolution,* New York: Simon and Schuster, 1977.

Freyer, Tony Allan, *Hugo L. Black and the dilemma of American liberalism,* Glenview, Ill.: Scott, Foresman/Little, Brown Higher Education, 1990.

Magee, James J., *Mr. Justice Black, absolutist on the Court,* Charlottesville: University Press of Virginia, 1980.

Newman, Roger K., *Hugo Black: a biography,* New York: Pantheon Books, 1994.

Silverstein, Mark, *Constitutional faiths: Felix Frankfurter, Hugo Black, and the process of judicial decision making,* Ithaca: Cornell University Press, 1984.

Simon, James F., *The antagonists: Hugo Black, Felix Frankfurter and civil liberties in modern America,* New York: Simon and Schuster, 1989. □

Joseph Black

The British chemist Joseph Black (1728-1799) is famous for his discovery of "fixed air" (carbon dioxide). He also discovered latent heat and was the first to recognize clearly the difference between intensity and quantity of heat.

Joseph Black was born on April 16, 1728, in Bordeaux, France, the son of a Scottish merchant settled in that city. Educated first at the University of Glasgow, he proceeded to the University of Edinburgh to complete his medical studies and presented his thesis there in 1754. This thesis, submitted, as was then customary, in Latin, was published in English in an expanded form in 1756 under the title *Experiments upon Magnesia Alba, Quicklime, and Some Other Alcaline Substances.*

The work described in this thesis sounded the death knell of the phlogiston theory and led in due course to the development of the modern system of chemistry through the work of Lavoisier and others. In his thesis Black showed by careful quantitative experiments that magnesia alba, a mild alkali, lost weight on heating; that this loss in weight was due to the release of an air, different from ordinary atmospheric air, which he named "fixed air" (now known as carbon dioxide); and that the ignited magnesia no longer effervesced with acids. Mild alkalies were thus shown to differ from caustic alkalies by containing "fixed air" in combination, and the same "fixed air" was later found by him to be produced in respiration, in fermentation, and in the combustion of charcoal. To appreciate the full significance of these results, it should be remembered that prior to Black's work it was believed that limestone (a mild alkali) on heating absorbed fiery particles (phlogiston) and was thereby converted to quicklime (a caustic alkali). Black's application of the chemical balance to the study of such chemical reactions demonstrated the falsity of this view and in the broader sense was perhaps his greatest contribution to science.

When Black moved to Glasgow in 1756 as professor of anatomy and chemistry, he turned his attention to the study of heat, applying to it the same quantitative approach he had used in his chemical work. He showed that different substances have different capacities for heat. Further studies led him to the discovery of latent heat and to the first reasonably accurate measurements of the latent heat of vaporization and freezing of water. James Watt later applied these discoveries in his development of the steam engine. Black returned to the University of Edinburgh in 1766 as professor of chemistry and medicine, a position which he occupied until his death on Dec. 6, 1799.

Further Reading

Black's work is recorded in most histories of chemistry, but an excellent account of his life and work in the setting of his times is in Andrew Kent, ed., *An Eighteenth Century Lectureship in Chemistry* (1950). Background works which discuss Black include Thomas W. Chalmers, *Historic Researches: Chapters on the History of Physical and Chemical Discovery* (1952), and Stephen Toulmin and June Goodfield, *The Architecture of Matter* (1962). □

Shirley Temple Black

Shirley Temple Black (born 1928) was an American who devoted her career first to films and then to public service. The United States ambassador to Czechoslovakia from 1989 till 1992, she was still remembered by millions of fans for her success as a child movie star in the 1930s.

Shirley Temple was born in Santa Monica, California, on April 23, 1928. She was the youngest of three children. Her father was a bank teller. As a child Shirley Temple began to take dance steps almost as soon as she began to walk, and her mother took her to dancing school when she was about three and a half years old. She also took her daughter on endless rounds of visits to agents, hoping to secure a show business career. Persistence paid off. Little Shirley obtained a contract at a small film studio and one of the great careers in film history began.

Her first contract was with Educational Pictures Inc., for whom she worked in 1932 and 1933. She appeared in a serial entitled *Baby Burlesks,* followed by a two-reeler, *Frolics of Youth,* that would lead to her being contracted by the Fox Film Corporation at a salary of $150 per week. The first full-length feature that she appeared in for Fox was 1934's *Carolina.* It was another Fox release of that year that made her a star: *Stand Up and Cheer.* Although she only appeared in a subsidiary role, she made a big hit in this picture by singing and dancing "Baby Take a Bow." She appeared in eight other full-length films (not to mention her ongoing work in serials and short subjects) that year, including *Little Miss Marker* and *Bright Eyes.* The first of these is especially notable because it was her first starring role. The culmination of 1934 was the Academy of Motion Pictures Arts and Sciences award of a special miniature Oscar to her "in grateful recognition of her outstanding contribution to screen entertainment during the year, 1934." One cannot help but assume that the industry-dominated academy was most impressed by her status as the number one box office draw of the year, but her special Oscar was unique in that it represented the first and only time that an Oscar has been awarded on the basis of a poll of the film-going public.

Film Star of the 1930s

Through the rest of the decade Shirley Temple's star soared. And it was not only her delectable dimples and 56 corkscrew curls that would keep her at the top of the box office listings. She was a spectacularly talented child, able to sing and dance with style and genuine feeling. Gifted with perfect pitch, she was a legendary quick study who learned her lines and dance routines much faster than her older and more experienced co-stars. She would make 15 films in the next six years, becoming one of the most popular stars of the Great Depression years and making over $30 million for the newly organized Twentieth Century-Fox Film Corporation. The company's chief executive, Darryl Zanuck, arranged for a staff of 19 writers to exclusively develop film projects for her. Studio wags described her character, which evolved through such films as *The Little Colonel* (1935), *Captain January* (1936), *Wee Willie Winkie* (1937), *Heidi* (1937), and *Rebecca of Sunnybrook Farm* (1938), as "Little Miss Fix-It" whose cuteness and precocious presence of mind helped grown-ups through real-life difficulties. And as her popularity rose, so did her salary—to $10,000 per week.

But unfortunately little of the built-up popularity would be hers to claim by the time she was an adult. As she reports in her autobiography, her father's questionable management of her funds, coupled with both of her parents' healthy regard for their own interests, enabled only a fraction of the immense fortune that she earned to accrue to Shirley herself. By 1940 she had appeared in 43 feature films and shorts and an entire industry had sprung up whose products celebrated the glories of Shirley Temple: dolls, dresses, coloring books, and other sundry merchandise. She also earned enormous sums by commercially endorsing all sorts

of products. These endeavors brought in an even larger amount of money than her studio salary. She got more fan mail than Greta Garbo and her picture was taken more frequently than President Franklin D. Roosevelt's. Shirley Temple will always be a symbol of the nation's longing for good times and good cheer during the severe economic woes of the Great Depression.

By the decade's end she was no longer quite a child, and when *The Blue Bird* (1940) proved unpopular at the box office and the next film that she starred in fared poorly as well, Twentieth Century-Fox devised a means of getting rid of the "property" that had saved the fledgling studio from bankruptcy. She would try to maintain her acting career through the 1940s but never again would she come even close to the stardom of her childhood. Film audiences would simply not allow the adorable girl who had sung "On the Good Ship Lolly Pop" and "Animal Crackers (in My Soup)" to grow up.

There had never been a child star so talented as she. Actress, singer, and dancer—Shirley Temple was a unique performer. The "industry" that rose up to promote her did not exist to support her stardom so much as it was a reflection of it. Moreover, Shirley Temple's true greatness as a screen idol has survived to the present day as her films are revived on television and re-released on videocassettes. New generations of fans have grown up marveling at her talent wholly apart from any studio hype or pressurized product tie-ins marketed to bedazzle them. Her matchless and enduring talent has proven to be enchantment enough.

It is arguable that nothing could have been done to preserve the lustre of her magic. Yet her ongoing struggles as an adult would prove her to be as heroic in her own life as she had ever been on the screen. A difficult first marriage to actor John Agar caused her to mature quickly. Almost immediately thereafter came the realization that her parents had been looking out for their own best interests rather than hers.

As she had done in so many of her films, she rallied. After marrying the successful California businessman Charles Black in 1950, with whom she raised her children (Linda from her first marriage and Charles and Lori from her second), she embarked on a career in television. The success of her two children's series enabled her to pursue her commitment to children's issues with vigor. In 1961 she co-founded the National Federation of Multiple Sclerosis Societies.

Her concern over domestic social ills caused her to realize that life as a private citizen could not satisfy her desire to make the world a better place. She ran for Congress in 1967 and was defeated. This was only the beginning of her involvement in public service. In 1969 she was appointed to serve as a representative to the United Nations. Her exemplary work at the UN led to a second career for Shirley Temple Black. In 1972 she was appointed representative to the UN Conference on the Human Environment and also served as a delegate on the Joint Committee for the USSR-USA Environmental Treaty. The next year she served as a US commissioner for the United Nations Educational, Scientific, and Cultural Organization (UNESCO).

Black overcame a great challenge in 1972 when she successfully battled breast cancer. When she publicly disclosed that she had a mastectomy, she gave courage to millions of women. Two years later she was appointed ambassador to Ghana, where she was warmly received by the people of that nation. Upon completion of her tour of duty in Africa, President Ford made her the US chief of protocol. In all of her various diplomatic functions, Black's intelligence, spirit, and zeal contributed greatly to her country's prestige and furthered its world position. Democratic President Carter paid tribute to her tact and flawless taste when he chose her (Black had been a lifelong Republican) to make the arrangements for his inauguration and inaugural ball in 1977.

But the triumphs of her adult life no more ruffled her poise and grace than her earlier tribulations. Her marriage and family life with Charles Black was as rewarding to her as her career as a diplomat was distinguished. Indeed, by 1981 she was such an established pillar of the public service community that she became one of the founding members of the American Academy of Diplomacy. In 1988 she was appointed Honorary Foreign Service Officer of the United States, the only person with that rank. She went on to serve as the US ambassador to Czechoslovakia from 1989 until 1992. Such honors are ultimately the true measure of her career's meaning. Latter-day film industry recognition such as the Life Achievement Award of the American Center of Films for Children or the full-sized Oscar that she was given in 1985 were echoes of a past that, while still resonant for "Shirley Temple," were not quite relevant for Shirley Temple Black. According to Black, her more than 25 years of social service have been just as enjoyable as her years in Hollywood.

Black is working on a book about her diplomatic career, which, she told Susan Bandrapalli in a 1996 *Christian Science Monitor* interview, she expects to take quite some time to complete. Her first book, *A Child's Story* took eight years to write. Black also stated that she was concerned about the lack of civility in the world today and said, "People should show more kindness and understanding."

The title of a recent biography (*American Princess*) does not do her justice. Through her lifetime of service in the arts and public life, Black has exemplified the spirit of self-sacrifice and persistent striving that Americans have aspired to for generations. She is truly an American heroine.

Further Reading

Shirley Temple Black wrote a candid and tasteful autobiography, *Child Star* (1988), detailing her years in Hollywood. Anne Edward's *American Princess*, published the same year, is an adequately researched, if slightly sensationalized, treatment of her life. Jeanine Basinger has written a study of her films, *Shirley Temple* (1975), which comments briefly on her life but is mostly concerned with sketching her film career. Another satisfactory examination of her movies is *The Films of Shirley Temple* by Robert Windeler. Black's career as a diplomat and as an environmental and children's rights activist keeps her in the headlines of magazines and newspapers, and nostalgia for her days of childhood stardom will no doubt keep her name in the columns of other journals as well. See *Christian Science Monitor* (April 25, 1996), *People Weekly* (November 28, 1988). □

Nicholas Black Elk

Nicholas Black Elk (1863-1950) was an Oglala Sioux medicine man in the transition period from nomadic to reservation life for his people and then, as an interviewee, a source for Native American tribal traditions and Plains Indian spirituality.

Born in December 1863 within a paternal lineage of shamans, or medicine men, Black Elk was nearly 70 years old when John Neihardt, Nebraska's poet laureate, interviewed him and several other Sioux elders in May 1931. This contact, the result of Neihardt's search to find survivors of the Wounded Knee Massacre of December 1890, produced the literary classic in American western and Native American writing, *Black Elk Speaks,* published in 1932. Black Elk became known to the world beyond Pine Ridge Reservation through Neihardt's literary interpretation, which covered the first 27 years of his life.

The actual interviews highlighted prominent features of Plains Indian nomadic life, including accounts of military conflict with the United States government, concluding with the 1890 tragic encounter at Wounded Knee Creek, South Dakota. As a teenager, Black Elk had also been at the Battle of the Little Big Horn, Montana, the last stand of General George Custer in 1876. Ten years later he joined William (Buffalo Bill) Cody's Wild West Show on tour in the United States, Great Britain, and the European continent between 1886 and 1889.

The central event in Black Elk's life, however, occurred when he was nine years old while suffering from a life-threatening illness. He had then "the great vision" that took him to the spiritual center of the Lakota world where he was presented to the Six Grandfathers that symbolized *Wakan Tanka* or The Great Mysteriousness expressed in the powers of the four directions and of the earth and sky. In this transforming experience, Black Elk received instructions typical of shamanic initiation. For the rest of his life, the vision possessed determinative power. Especially in his young adult years, he sought to act out parts of it for the sake of preserving the unity and survival of his people. Aided by a wise elder and medicine man named Black Road, Black Elk launched his career as a shamanic healer at Fort Keogh, Montana, in the spring of 1881. Present as witnesses were his relatives, who had returned from Canada where they had been since 1877 following the death of the warrior Crazy Horse, a cousin of Black Elk's father.

The great vision, as told to Neihardt in 1931, became the center of the text of *Black Elk Speaks*. In remembering it so vividly, Black Elk resurrected its spiritual power, which had not waned despite his sincere conversion to Roman Catholicism in 1904. His depiction stands as a major source in visionary religious literature, attracting the interest in the last half century of symbologists, depth psychologists, and scholars in comparative mythology and prompting pan-Indian revitalization movements of traditional rituals.

Twice married, Black Elk's wife of 1892, Katie War Bonnett, died in 1903. Nicholas, added as a Christian name, lived with his second wife, Anna Brings White, from 1905 until her death in 1941. The father of four sons and a daughter, Black Elk was particularly dependent upon the third and last child by Katie, Benjamin, who provided him a home in his failing years and who also proved enormously helpful to Neihardt's projects. A victim of tuberculosis, Black Elk was treated first in 1912 and as late as the last years of his life. From the fifth decade of his life, he suffered from poor eyesight.

Traveling as a catechist for Roman Catholicism, Black Elk visited the Wind River, Winnebago, and Sisseton reservations between 1908 and 1910. But he kept some traditional practices alive in performing dances for pageants for summer tourists to the Black Hills, first probably in the late 1920s and certainly after 1935. When first hosting Neihardt, he ritualized the occasion of the telling of the great vision and of his deep involvement in the corporate life of his people. The event was so potent that Christian missionaries required Black Elk to disavow any intent to renew the traditional practices of the Sioux. Thirteen years later, he gave Neihardt another interview which became a novel entitled *When the Tree Flowered* when it was published the year after Black Elk died. After the interview of 1944, no disavowal was required of the octogenarian.

In 1947 Joseph Epes Brown, later a scholar of Native American religion and culture, met Black Elk in Nebraska. Brown spent the next winter with the elderly spiritual teacher in Manderson, South Dakota. Through that contact and their conversations Black Elk provided the details of seven traditional rituals of the Oglala people which Brown published as *The Sacred Pipe.* They included a purification ceremony (the sweat lodge), crying for a vision, female puberty, marriage, soul-keeping, throwing the ball, and the great medicine of all traditional Plains people, the Sun Dance.

Even though there is no public evidence that Black Elk practiced the healing rituals of a shaman after he converted to Catholicism, all of his adult life, beginning with his first major exposure to the world of "white" America and Europe, was spent creatively blending native and Christian perspectives. As catechist, he retained the role of spiritual leader, focused as always on the welfare and future of his people. Black Elk's bicultural religious orientation went far beyond the impression mediated by Neihardt's first book, which has no mention of his later Catholic roles and which presents an elegy to the last generation of Plains Indian survivors before the dominance of the reservation. With a spirituality infused by hopefulness and imaged as the sacred hoop and the flowering tree—symbols of the corporate reality of his people—Black Elk was continually devoted to trying to find a way for the tribe to live. His own long life, despite bad health and the economic difficulties of existence on the reservation, testified to a strong determination to endure while facing threatening cultural changes. Within

a decade of his death the Sun Dance was renewed under his nephew, Frank Fools Crow. Such an action reflected the impact of Black Elk on the reservation where, coming full circle, what he described but no longer performed became a living practice again. Through the books with Neihardt and Brown, Black Elk made the world at large heirs of his spiritual wisdom, ensuring in them that the rituals of empowerment of the Sioux people would not depend on oral tradition. He died on August 19, 1950, at Manderson and was buried from St. Agnes Mission Chapel in a barren cemetery.

Further Reading

Raymond DeMallie has edited, with an introduction rich in detail and insight, the interview notes from both Neihardt visits with Black Elk in *The Sixth Grandfather* (1984). Joseph Epes Brown remembered Black Elk as a Heyoka or clown-trickster in an interview, "The Wisdom of the Contrary," in *Parabola* (1979). Several writers comment on Black Elk in Vine Deloria, Jr., editor, *A Sender of Words: Essays in Memory of John Neihardt* (1984). Clyde Holler has authored two articles that argue for Black Elk's bicultural religious perspective in *American Indian Quarterly* (Winter 1984) and *Journal of the American Academy of Religion* (March 1984). Will Gravely has reviewed the changing perspectives on Black Elk in *The Iliff Review* (Winter 1987). The place to begin, of course, is Neihardt, editor, *Black Elk Speaks* (reprinted in softcover 1991), and Brown, editor, *The Sacred Pipe.*

Additional Sources

Black Elk, *Black Elk speaks: being the life story of a holy man of the Ogalala Sioux,* Alexandria, Va.: Time-Life Books, 1991; Lincoln: University of Nebraska Press, 1932, 1979, 1988.
The Sixth Grandfather: Black Elk's teachings given to John G. Neihardt, Lincoln: University of Nebraska Press, 1984.
Petri, Hilda Neihardt, *Black Elk and Flaming Rainbow: personal memories of the Lakota holy man and John Neihardt,* Lincoln: University of Nebraska Press, 1995.
Rice, Julian, *Black Elk's story: distinguishing its Lakota purpose,* Albuquerque: University of New Mexico Press, 1991.
Rice, Julian, *Lakota storytelling: Black Elk, Ella Deloria, and Frank Fools Crow,* New York: P. Lang, 1989.
Steltenkamp, Michael F., *Black Elk: holy man of the Oglala,* Norman: University of Oklahoma Press, 1993. □

Patrick M.S. Blackett

The British physicist Patrick M. S. Blackett (1897-1974) used a modified Wilson cloud chamber to obtain the first photographs of the tracks left by the particles involved in a nuclear disintegration as well as those produced by showers of cosmic rays.

Patrick Maynard Stuart Blackett was born on November 18, 1897, in London, England. At age 13 he entered naval training school, graduating four years later at the outbreak of World War I. He served in the Royal Navy as an officer throughout the war, participating in the

Battles of Jutland and the Falkland Islands. In 1919 Blackett resigned his naval commission to study physics at Cambridge University. There he met, and eventually worked under, the physicist Ernest Rutherford.

The opening of Blackett's scientific career coincided with two important developments in physics. The first was the work of C. T. R. Wilson, who had built a small cloud chamber in which the paths taken by atomic and subatomic particles could be momentarily viewed with the naked eye or photographed. As particles moved through the supersaturated air of the chamber water droplets were formed, marking their trails. The second was Rutherford's investigation of nuclear disintegration. Rutherford directed alpha particles (nuclei of helium atoms) emitted by radioactive materials into various gasses with the intention of disintegrating the nuclei of the gas molecules. When alpha particles sped through nitrogen they occasionally collided with nitrogen nuclei, knocking out protons and transmutating the nitrogen into oxygen. Rutherford was able to prove that alpha particles and nuclei had collided, but he was unable to determine precisely what occurred during the process of collision. He assigned Blackett the task of obtaining visible cloud chamber evidence of what happened before, after, and at the moment of impact of alpha particles and nuclei.

Blackett altered the cloud chamber so that it was capable of automatically taking 270 photographs per hour of the condensation trails left by particles moving through it. With this apparatus he obtained 23,000 photographs, which contained 415,000 alpha particle tracks. Of the 415,000 tracks, only eight revealed that an alpha particle had collided with

a nitrogen molecule. By a careful study of these tracks Blackett was able to show that in each collision two particles emerged. The first particle was a proton; the second a heavy isotope of oxygen. These experiments, which took place in 1924, provided the first photographic evidence of the process of nuclear transformation.

Early in the 1930s Blackett turned from the analysis of alpha particle tracks in cloud chambers to the study of cosmic rays (charged particles coming from outer space). This change was precipitated by the arrival in England of the Italian physicist Giuseppe Occhialini, who brought with him new techniques for counting the incidence of cosmic rays. Blackett and Occhialini, working as a team, devised an apparatus that recorded the random appearance of cosmic rays. This new piece of equipment used Geiger counters to detect the rays and activate the cloud chamber so that the condensation tracks formed would be photographed automatically. Blackett's cosmic ray photographs revealed that this natural phenomenon manifested itself in showers of roughly equal numbers of positively and negatively charged particles. Further investigation of cosmic rays enabled Blackett to confirm Carl Anderson's earlier discovery of the positron. In 1948 Blackett was awarded the Nobel Prize in physics for his improvement of the Wilson cloud chamber and its uses in the fields of nuclear physics and cosmic ray study.

Blackett's inquiries into the nature of cosmic rays led him to become interested in astronomy and astrophysics and finally in terrestrial magnetism. For Blackett, the study of the earth's magnetic field provided a means of exploring the geological history of the planet. Using a sensitive magnetometer of his own design he was able to measure changes in the earth's magnetic field over a period of 500 million years as compared to the 400 year period previously studied. Blackett's work in paleomagnetism, as well as his cloud chamber experiments, resulted in his winning the Copley medal of the Royal Society of London in 1956.

Blackett combined a busy life in science with a full involvement in educational, military, and political affairs. He is especially remembered for his 1948 book, *Fear, War, and the Bomb; Military and Political Consequences of Atomic Energy,* in which he argued that the atomic bomb was not a decisive weapon and warned that a preventive war might erupt because America's large stockpile of atomic weapons posed a threat to the Soviet Union.

Further Reading

For a scholarly study of Blackett's scientific work see: Sir Bernard Lovell, ''Patrick Maynard Stuart Blackett,'' in *Biographical Memoirs of Fellows of the Royal Society,* Vol. 21 (1975). On a more popular level Blackett is discussed in Emilio Segré, *From X-rays to Quarks: Modern Physicists and Their Discoveries* (1980). Blackett's ideas on atomic weapons are to be found in his three books: *Fear, War, and the Bomb: Military and Political Consequences of Atomic Energy* (1949); *Atomic Weapons and East-West Relations* (1956); and *Studies of War* (1962). □

Black Hawk

A Native American war chief, Black Hawk (1767-1838) led his people, the Sauk, in a noble fight to preserve their tribal lands in Illinois, Wisconsin, and Missouri.

At the great Sauk village on the Rock River (near the present city of Rock Island, Ill.), Black Hawk was born and given the name Ma-ka-tai-me-she-kia-kiak (Black Sparrow Hawk). His tribe had a long tradition of trading furs to Spaniards and Frenchmen in St. Louis for supplies and weapons. It was there Black Hawk first heard of Americans, and he took a strong dislike to them when he learned they had made the Louisiana Purchase.

In 1804 William Henry Harrison negotiated a treaty with another Sauk chief, named Quashquame, and a Fox chief; in the treaty the Sauk and Fox tribes agreed to cede 15 million acres of their land to the United States; this cession included the Sauk lands in Illinois—and thus the site of their great village on the Rock River. Black Hawk, by now a rising war chief, always claimed that Quashquame and the other chief had made this treaty with no tribal authority and had in fact been induced to sign it while drunk.

During the War of 1812, because of his hatred of the United States, Black Hawk sided with the British and fought under Tecumseh, a charismatic leader preaching Native American unity against the Americans. In 1816 Black Hawk

signed a document confirming the treaty of 1804, but afterward he claimed he was ignorant of the terms of the agreement. Between 1816 and 1829 he brooded about the loss of the Sauk and Fox lands east of the Mississippi River and worked to get British help from Canada for an Indian uprising. Also, in league with White Cloud, a Waubesheik medicine man and prophet, he sought a general Native American confederation against the United States.

In June 1831, under Black Hawk's leadership, the Sauk returned to their ancient village on the Rock River. However, American troops soon arrived at Rock Island at the request of the governor of Illinois. Black Hawk thereupon withdrew to the mouth of the Iowa River on the west side of the Mississippi.

A year later, in April, Black Hawk and 400 to 500 warriors and their families recrossed the Mississippi to fight for their lands in Illinois, Wisconsin, and Missouri. They believed they would receive help from Canada, and some Winnebago, Potawatomi, and Mascouten did join them. Before they could reach the site of their old village, however, American troops arrived, whereupon Black Hawk's army disintegrated.

The conflict known as the Black Hawk War began when Illinois volunteers assaulted those sent by the Sauk chief under a flag of truce to parley. Two Indians were killed in the fighting. Black Hawk led his warriors northward, pursued by troops and Illinois volunteers, which included young Abraham Lincoln. Hampered by hunger and by their women and children, the Sauk retreated west of the Mississippi to end the fighting. But they were attacked at the mouth of Bad Axe River in Wisconsin, were defeated, and surrendered. Black Hawk, two of his sons, and other chiefs, including White Cloud, were taken as prisoners to Fort Armstrong, commanded by Gen. Winfield Scott. There on Sept. 21, 1832, a new treaty was signed, called the Black Hawk Purchase, in which the Sauk gave up more of their land in return for an annuity and a reservation in Iowa.

In the spring of 1833 Black Hawk was taken east for a meeting with President Andrew Jackson. Afterward, he was confined for a short time at Fortress Monroe, Va., before being returned to Iowa. But Black Hawk's position as tribal leader had been undermined by younger men who did not want to fight the whites, and he spent his last days in Iowa, under the supervision of Chief Keokuk. He dictated his reminiscences to a journalist, J. B. Patterson, explaining his position and his attitudes before he died on Oct. 3, 1838, at his lodge on the Des Moines River.

Further Reading

The Autobiography of Black Hawk, edited by J. B. Patterson (1833), was republished in 1955 as *Black Hawk: An Autobiography,* edited by Donald Jackson. Other useful works include Frank E. Stevens, *The Black Hawk War: Including a Review of Black Hawk's Life* (1903), and William T. Hagan, *The Sac and Fox Indians* (1958). □

Harry Blackmun

Harry Blackmun (born 1908), appointed to the U.S. Supreme Court by President Nixon, became a highly regarded justice usually taking a middle-of-the-road position.

Harry A. Blackmun was born November 12, 1908, in Nashville, Illinois, but spent his youth in the Minneapolis-St. Paul area of Minnesota where his father, Corwin Manning Blackmun, was a businessman. There he developed a lifelong friendship with Warren Burger, a school classmate. Attending Harvard as a mathematics major, he thought of becoming a physician, but instead chose law, graduating in 1932 from the Harvard Law School, where he had studied under Felix Frankfurter. Returning to St. Paul, he served as law clerk to a U.S. circuit court judge, John B. Sanborn, whom he later succeeded on that court. In 1933 he took a teaching position at the St. Paul College of Law, and in 1945 he began teaching at the University of Minnesota Law School. He then had a private practice in Minneapolis until he became resident counsel for the famous Mayo Clinic in Rochester, Minnesota. Appointed by Eisenhower to the eighth circuit, he developed a reputation as a conservative, relatively progressive in civil rights matters and moderate in civil liberties cases.

Appointed to the Supreme Court by Richard Nixon, Blackmun was confirmed without opposition. In his first

years Blackmun was frequently described as one of the "Minnesota Twins," given the frequency of his agreement with Chief Justice Burger. This pattern changed in time, with Blackmun moving to a more liberal posture.

Blackmun's lower court career presaged his later judicial behavior. A believer in judicial restraint and limitation of the court's broad policy-making prerogatives, his decisions reflected his desire to keep issues narrow and avoid setting forth broad and bold principles.

Blackmun's Supreme Court opinions ranged widely. Generally devoid of any overarching ideology or philosophy, they reflected his own personal views and at times seemed somewhat contradictory. Very much a case by case justice, his absence of dogmatism contrasted with his more conservative colleagues such as William Rehnquist and Sandra Day O'Connor.

Blackmun wrote opinions of significance in four areas. In First Amendment cases, although he dissented from the Court's ruling that stopped the government from repressing *The Pentagon Papers,* he overturned a "gag order" imposed by a Nebraska court prohibiting commentary or reporting on a murder trial (*Nebraska Press Association* v. *Stuart,* 1975). Here he attempted to balance First Amendment rights of free press with Sixth Amendment rights of fair trial. He was conservative on obscenity cases, upholding a federal conviction which prohibited the mailing of obscene material even though the books involved were not obscene under applicable state law (*Smith* v. *California,* 1977). His landmark free speech cases were those overruling the commercial speech doctrine, extending speech protection to commercial advertising (*Virginia State Board of Pharmacy* v. *Virginia Citizens Consumer Council,* 1976) and to attorneys to advertise their professional services (*Bates* v. *State Bar of Arizona,* 1977). The press, consumers, and the general public all benefitted from these rulings.

Blackmun's most famous and controversial ruling was his opinion in *Roe* v. *Wade* (1973), declaring that the right of privacy included a woman's right to terminate her pregnancy by means of an abortion. This effectively invalidated the varying abortion statutes in 46 of the 50 states and provoked a moral, philosophical, and theological controversy that has seldom abated since that time. Blackmun found women's fundamental right to personal privacy in the Fourteenth Amendment's concept of personal liberty affording a woman protection in determining whether or not to terminate her pregnancy. The right, however, was not absolute, and he made clear that it could be regulated when the state's interest was "compelling." Subsequently, he set aside state laws requiring women to get the consent of a spouse or a parent before having an abortion (*Planned Parenthood of Central Missouri* v. *Danforth,* 1976).

In the area of criminal law, Blackmun generally voted to curb the expansion of defendant's rights. He took a restrictive view of the "exclusionary" rule and modified the guarantees of the Fourth Amendment permitting routine police inventory searches of cars without warrants (*South Dakota* v. *Opperman,* 1976). He sustained the right of states to use six-member juries (*Ballew* v. *Georgia,* 1978), but held that due process does not require jury trials in state juvenile delinquency proceedings (*McKeiver* v. *Pennsylvania,* 1971). On the other hand, he did not always vote for the government. He sustained the Miranda warnings given after an arrest and found police misconduct indefensible in a number of instances. His own personal distaste and abhorrence for the death penalty was reflected in opinions in that area which put him at odds with the Court's majority.

On environmental issues he called for an imaginative expansion of traditional standing concepts that would allow public interest groups to enter environmental cases. His rulings regarding legal problems of the poor, on the other hand, proved unsympathetic.

In the civil rights area, Blackmun's record was moderately progressive. He sustained the rights of African American children to enter private schools on the same basis as white children (*Runyon* v. *McCrary,* 1976) and struck at racial restrictions in private swimming clubs (*Tillman* v. *Wheaton-Heven,* 1973). He also held that Mexican American defendants had a right to proper representation on grand juries which were investigating them (*Castenada* v. *Partida,* 1977).

Although Blackmun was frequently harrassed and assailed by anti-abortionists, he retained his composure and dignity and, in the process, much public respect. He married Dorothy E. Clark on June 21, 1941, and was the father of three daughters. Blackmun has taught law as a visiting instructor at institutions including Louisiana State University Law School and Tulane University. He retired from the bench in 1994.

Further Reading

There is a good sketch of Blackmun's career up to the late 1970s in Leon Friedman, ed., *The Justices of the United States Supreme Court: Their Lives and Major Opinions,* Vol. V (1978). Good brief material is also available in Catherine A. Barnes, *Men of the Supreme Court: Profiles of the Justices* (1978) and *Congressional Quarterly, Guide to the U.S. Supreme Court* (1979). Although it would have to be obtained in a law library or Bar Association library, the January 1985 *Hamline Law Review* comprises a whole issue "Dedicated to Justice Harry A. Blackmun on the Occasion of His Twenty-Fifth Year as a Federal Judge" and includes articles affording lengthy assessments of his career. □

Sir William Blackstone

The famous English jurist Sir William Blackstone (1723-1780) is remembered for his *Commentaries on the Laws of England,* the first attempt since the 13th century to provide a comprehensive treatment of English law.

William Blackstone was born in Cheapside, London, on July 10, 1723, the posthumous son of Charles Blackstone, a merchant. He was educated at the Charterhouse School and at Oxford and entered the Middle Temple in London in 1740. He was elected a fellow of All Souls, Oxford, in 1744 and received the bachelor of civil law degree in 1745. Although he was admitted to the bar in 1746, he had limited success in practicing law and continued to hold several university posts and to lecture on English law. Shortly thereafter, Blackstone was appointed to the newly created Vinerian chair. In 1761 he was elected to Parliament and also received a patent of precedence giving him the rank of king's counsel. He resigned from his chair in 1766 due to his success at the bar that year, and in 1770 he was appointed a judge in the Court of Common Pleas, where he served, with no special distinction, until his death.

Commentaries on the Laws of England

Blackstone was the first since Henry de Bracton in the 13th century to present an encompassing treatment of English law. The *Commentaries* (1765-1769), which grew out of Blackstone's university lectures, is a very readable elementary text. Although its scheme of organization is borrowed from an earlier work by Sir Matthew Hale, *Analysis of Law,* it represents a radical departure from contemporary legal thought, which tended to treat the law as a catalog of unrelated writs and statutes. In *Commentaries,* Blackstone blended the intellectual traditions of the common law with those of 17th- and 18th-century English political philosophy.

Blackstone had only a vague grasp of systematic conceptions of law, and he was in fact frequently illogical, inconsistent, and uncritical. His purpose, however, was simply to provide literate men with entertaining and persua-

sive explanations of the existing legal order rather than to construct a critical and consistent jurisprudence. *Commentaries* performed a service for society and should be regarded more as a handbook for the layman than as a legal treatise.

In his treatment of law Blackstone argued a division between natural and positive (municipal) law by insisting on the existence of a natural law and maintaining that positive law which is not in accord with the principles of natural law is not law at all. But he held that there are few such principles and that most positive law concerns matters on which natural law is silent. Rights and wrongs are objects of law; rights are of persons or things, while wrongs are either public or private. Evidently, he regarded the law of gravitation, the law of England, and the law of nature as examples of the same principle, that is, the imposition of rules by a superior power on its subjects.

Blackstone's lack of precise terminology and use of loose phraseology result in contradictions. When he borrowed the scholastic definition of positive law, "a right or just ordinance commanding what is right and forbidding what is wrong," he deliberately struck out "right or just." Thus it is not clear whether he meant that whatever the law commands is right or that only laws that command what is morally right are really laws. He also reasserted the traditional equation of natural law with common law. Thus he did not directly face up to the problem of whether men only have those rights which the law gives them or whether law is simply the acknowledgment by the state of the natural rights inherent in each individual. According to Blackstone, Englishmen enjoyed only those rights which the common law proclaimed, but in fact Englishmen had created the common law to proclaim their rights.

Areas of Influence

Blackstone was active in the prison-reform movement, worked against the tendency to extend the list of capital offenses, and was critical of the poor laws. In some technical areas, such as contract laws, his thinking was in advance of that of most of his contemporaries.

He conceived his task as being educational reform rather than the building of a philosophic system. In the 18th century the Inns of Court had practically ceased to play their traditional role in legal education, and apprenticeship had largely replaced academic training. Blackstone gave the first regular university lectures on English law and sought not only to provide formal instruction for prospective lawyers but to present the basic elements of common law as an integral part of the academic education of English gentlemen.

In the United States, Blackstone's example contributed significantly to the development of law schools, and during the Revolutionary and postrevolutionary periods the *Commentaries* was the most widely read law text in America. After 1850 United States lawyers no longer tried to copy Blackstone, for living law was being shaped by the local institutions. By the middle of the 20th century few Americans had read Blackstone, even as a classic, but he remains a symbol for American lawyers.

Further Reading

There are two biographies of Blackstone: David A. Lockmiller, *Sir William Blackstone* (1938), and Lewis C. Warden, *The Life of Blackstone* (1938). The major critical treatments are A. V. Dicey, *Lectures on the Relation between Law and Public Opinion in England during the Nineteenth Century* (1905; 2d ed. 1914); Daniel J. Boorstin, *The Mysterious Science of the Law: An Essay on Blackstone's Commentaries* (1941); and "Blackstone on the British Constitution," in Ernest Barker, *Essays on Government* (1945; 2d ed. 1951). See also Theodore F. T. Plucknett, *A Concise History of the Common Law* (1929; 5th ed. 1956). □

Elizabeth Blackwell

The first woman in America to receive a medical degree, Elizabeth Blackwell (1821-1910) crusaded for the admission of women to medical schools in the United States and Europe.

Elizabeth Blackwell was born on Feb. 3, 1821, in Bristol, England. Her parents emigrated with their nine children to New York City when Elizabeth was 12. Mr. Blackwell soon became an ardent abolitionist. In 1838 the Blackwells moved to Cincinnati, Ohio; within a few months Mr. Blackwell died and left his family unprovided for. The three oldest girls supported the family for several years by operating a boarding school for young women.

In 1842 Blackwell accepted a teaching position in Henderson, Ky., but local racial attitudes offended her strong abolitionist convictions, and she resigned at the end of the year. On her return to Cincinnati a friend who had undergone treatment for a gynecological disorder told Blackwell that if she could have been treated by a woman doctor she would have been spared an embarrassing ordeal, and she urged Elizabeth to study medicine. The following year Blackwell moved to Asheville, N.C., where she taught school and studied medicine in her spare time. Her next move, in 1846, was to a girls' school in Charleston, S.C., where she had more time to devote to her medical studies.

When her attempts to enroll in the medical schools of Philadelphia and New York City were rejected, she wrote to a number of small northern colleges and in 1847 was admitted to the Geneva, N.Y., Medical College. All eyes were upon the young woman whom many regarded as immoral or simply mad, but she soon proved herself an outstanding student. Her graduation in 1849 was highly publicized on both sides of the Atlantic. She then entered La Maternité Hospital for further study and practical experience. While working with the children, she contracted purulent conjunctivitis, which left her blind in one eye.

Handicapped by partial blindness, Dr. Blackwell gave up her ambition to become a surgeon and began practice at St. Bartholomew's Hospital in London. In 1851 she returned to New York, where she applied for several positions as a physician, but was rejected because of her sex. She estab-

lished private practice in a rented room, where her sister Emily, who had also pursued a medical career, soon joined her. Their modest dispensary later became the New York Infirmary and College for Women, operated by and for women. Dr. Blackwell also continued to fight for the admission of women to medical schools. During the Civil War she organized a unit of women nurses for field service.

In 1869 Dr. Blackwell set up practice in London and continued her efforts to open the medical profession to women. Her articles and her autobiography (1895) attracted widespread attention. From 1875 to 1907 she was professor of gynecology at the London School of Medicine for Women. She died at her home in Hastings.

Further Reading

Biographies of Elizabeth Blackwell include Rachel Baker, *The First Woman Doctor: The Story of Elizabeth Blackwell, M. D.* (1944); Ishbel Ross, *Child of Destiny: The Life Story of the First Woman Doctor* (1949); and Peggy Chambers, *A Doctor Alone: A Biography of Elizabeth Blackwell, the First Woman Doctor, 1821-1910* (1956). Elizabeth Blackwell's career is studied at length in Ruth Fox Hume, *Great Women of Medicine* (1964). There is a brief biographical sketch in Victor Robinson, *Pathfinders in Medicine* (1912; 2d ed. 1929). See also Elizabeth Blackwell, *Pioneer Work in Opening the Medical Profession to Women: Autobiographical Sketches* (1895), and Richard H. Shryock, *The Development of Modern Medicine: An Interpretation of the Social and Scientific Factors Involved* (1936; rev. ed. 1947). □

James Gillespie Blaine

James Gillespie Blaine (1830-1893) was the nearest thing to a political idol in a politically uninspiring era, serving in Congress from 1863 to 1881. As secretary of state, he laid the basis for American imperialism.

Of Scotch-Irish descent, James G. Blaine was born in West Brownsville, Pa., on Jan. 31, 1830. His father was a locally prominent officeholder, so Blaine was exposed to political talk—mostly a fierce Whig partisanship—from an early age. Though he was not really the genius that his followers later claimed him to be, Blaine graduated from Washington College in western Pennsylvania at the age of 13 and, soon after, taught at Western Military Institute, Georgetown, Ky. Blaine later maintained that he quit this position because of a growing distaste for Southern society, but this seems a politically convenient hindsight. In fact, Blaine wanted to study law, and a teaching position at an institute for the blind in Philadelphia provided him the opportunity to do so.

In 1850 Blaine married Harriet Stanwood of Augusta, Maine, and through her made connections which, 4 years later, took him further east in a curious example, for that time, of reverse migration. In Maine he became editor of a weekly newspaper and, a short time after, manager of the *Portland Advertiser,* the largest and most influential Whig newspaper in the state. Blaine soon took the paper into the Republican party; he was in fact one of the first Republicans in the state and was a delegate to the first Republican national convention in 1856. In 1858 he was elected to the state legislature and in 1859 was elected chairman of the Republican State Committee, a post he held until 1881, helping to make Maine one of the most solidly Republican states in the nation.

Personal Attributes

Blaine served as Speaker of the Maine House of Representatives during 1861 and 1862. He was then elected to Congress, where he also served as Speaker from 1869 to 1875. In 1876 he was elected to the Senate from the state of Maine and was also a prominent candidate for his party's nomination as president. This rise in politics was due to his party regularity, in which he never faltered, his driving ambition (he virtually nominated himself as head of the House Republicans upon the death of Thaddeus Stevens), and his high dignity. Blaine was a man of great personal charm who, while he had few intimate friends, claimed a wide circle of devotees willing to stand by and support him to the end. He had few interests outside of politics, but he had numerous gifts that stood him well in the highly personalized political world of the "gilded age." His wit was as sharp in the smoking room as in the Capitol chambers, and he had an incredible memory for names and faces. One contemporary recalled standing with Blaine when a carriage stopped to greet them. "There is a man on that front seat whom I have not seen for twenty-seven years," Blaine

said, "and I have got just two minutes and a half to remember his name." He did. Blaine was also known as a man who presided fairly over acrimonious debates in the touchy Reconstruction congresses, thus earning respect from many Democrats as well as from his partisans.

"Mulligan Letters" and Other Suspicions

Blaine hoped to be president in 1876 and was nominated as "the plumed Knight" by Robert Ingersoll in one of the most eloquent nominating speeches in the history of American conventions. But the Republicans were sensitive in that year to charges of political corruption, and Blaine's enemies in the party revived an affair which cast a shadow over his entire career. It had happened in 1869, when as Speaker of the House, Blaine had used his influence to preserve a land grant which the Little Rock and Fort Smith Railroad had been in danger of losing and, shortly thereafter, had acted as a sales agent for the railroad's bonds, pocketing a generous commission on sales to his Maine friends. The transaction had been recorded in a number of letters which Blaine had managed to secure but which were known to political enemies, who charged him with corruption. In an eloquent and emotional speech before Congress, Blaine quoted selectively from these "Mulligan letters," pleading that he was guilty of no wrongdoing and that he had actually lost money in the affair.

Most Republicans were convinced, but the incident soured the reform wing of the Republican party, which opposed Blaine throughout his career, and the affair provided regularly resuscitated campaign material for the De-

mocrats. In fact, in an age of pervasive political corruption, Blaine's actions had been unexceptional for a man in his position; congressmen and other political leaders regularly received "favors" for services rendered or influence they could exert. But Blaine was more than an ordinary congressman, and he was ambitious to be a great deal more. His connections with the Little Rock Railroad proved to be even more costly than he realized at the time.

Blaine always lived better than his visible means of support seemed to sanction. He had made some money investing in Pennsylvania coal properties in the 1850s but was never an extremely wealthy man. He steadfastly refused to discuss his financial affairs, however, insisting that they were strictly personal.

But the reform wing and the "stalwart" wing of the party, which was dedicated to blatant spoilsmanship, were strong enough in 1876 and 1880 to keep him from the presidential nomination. Finally, in 1884, the stalwarts were discredited and the reform wing was unable to resist Blaine's nomination. Unfortunately, it was not a Republican year and Blaine was narrowly defeated by the Democrat, Grover Cleveland.

Secretary of State

In 1889 Blaine was named secretary of state by President Benjamin Harrison. He had already served briefly in that post under James Garfield. He was a dynamic foreign minister. He pushed an aggressive attitude toward Great Britain and laid the basis for the Pan-Americanism and United States economic penetration of Latin America that would come to fruition later, under his admirer Elihu Root, during the presidency of Theodore Roosevelt. Blaine resigned from Harrison's Cabinet 3 days before the Republican convention in 1892, possibly in hopes of again receiving the party's nomination, but in vain. He was taken ill soon thereafter and, though a lifelong hypochondriac, neglected himself in his final illness. He died at the age of 62 on Jan. 27, 1893.

Further Reading

The most comprehensive biography of Blaine is David Saville Muzzey, *James G. Blaine: A Political Idol of Other Days* (1934). All the standard accounts of the era's politics take note of him. A fair sampling of different points of view would include Matthew Josephson, *The Politicos, 1865-1896* (1938); John A. Garraty, *The New Commonwealth, 1877-1890* (1968); and H. Wayne Morgan, *From Hayes to McKinley* (1969).

Additional Sources

Tutorow, Norman E., *James Gillespie Blaine and the presidency: a documentary study and source book*, New York: P. Lang, 1989. □

Francis Preston Blair

The American journalist and politician Francis Preston Blair (1791-1876) was a close adviser of Presi-

dent Andrew Jackson. Blair joined the antislavery movement and was active in the newly created Republican party throughout the Civil War.

Francis P. Blair was born on April 12, 1791, in Abingdon, Va., but he grew up and was educated in Kentucky. He graduated from Transylvania University in 1811, studied law, and was admitted to the bar in 1817, although he never practiced. As a young man, he was in poor health, and all of his life he was frail-looking and small, weighing little more than 100 pounds; he married Eliza Gist over her father's objection that she would be a widow in 6 months. Yet Blair proved to be a prodigious worker for 50 years thereafter.

Jacksonian Politics

His family was active in politics: his father had served as attorney general of Kentucky, and an uncle was governor of the state, when Blair was a young man. In the political battles in Kentucky over financial and judicial reform, Blair himself became associated with the Relief party and the New Court, both reform groups. He contributed political articles to the *Argus of Western America,* an influential paper in Frankfort, edited by his friend Amos Kendall, and he became clerk of the state circuit court and president of the Commonwealth Bank.

When Andrew Jackson was elected in 1828, Kendall went to Washington as an adviser, and Blair became the

editor of the *Argus.* He produced powerful editorials defending Jacksonian policies and, upon Kendall's recommendation, Jackson brought him to the capital in 1830 to establish an administration newspaper, the *Washington Globe.* John C. Rives of Virginia joined him as business manager, and they made the *Globe* one of the most potent political organs in the country. In 1833 they made an important contribution to contemporary political education (and to later historians) by beginning publication of an impartial report of the daily proceedings in Congress, the *Congressional Globe* (today replaced by the government publication *Congressional Record*).

Blair and Jackson became good friends, and Blair's articles in the *Globe* were faithful expressions of the President's views. Blair would consult with Jackson in the White House, taking notes on scraps of paper held on his knees as the President spoke, then would hurry off to convert these into slashing editorials. Blair attacked Henry Clay's American Plan of protective tariffs and internal improvements, the U.S. Bank, and the nullification doctrines of John C. Calhoun's South Carolina; he advocated hard money and the interests of the "common man" against the men of wealth. His editorials charged the Whigs with trying to enlarge the rights of property so much "as to swallow up and annihilate those of persons" and pledged the Democratic party to preserve the rights of the people. He took satisfaction in being called a radical and told President Van Buren, "I feel myself to be a sort of Representative of the Mechanical Classes, the working people of all sorts . . . . "In 1837, when Van Buren asked Congress to establish an independent treasury, Blair called it "the boldest and highest stand ever taken by a Chief Magistrate in defense of the rights of the people . . . a second declaration of independence."

Blair worked for the nomination of Van Buren in 1844. But when James K. Polk was elected president, Blair offered to continue the *Globe* as the Democratic administration paper. Polk refused, fearing that the journalist was not friendly toward him. He was right. Blair referred to Polk's narrow, rigid mind, his pettiness, and his ungenerous attitude. Blair remarked in 1848 that the voters were indifferent about the election because they "had tried Tyler and Polk, and yet the country has not been materially hurt. If two such Presidents cannot injure the nation, nothing can!"

Antislavery Politics

Silver Spring, Blair's country home just outside Washington in Maryland, became the political mecca for Jacksonians during this period. However, Blair departed from many of his associates in 1848, when he supported the Free Soil cause. He had never been associated with abolitionism, but he said Van Buren's letters and speeches that year had converted him to the necessity of opposing the slave power. In 1852 he was prepared to back Thomas Hart Benton for the Free Soil nomination but later approved the Democrats' nomination of Franklin Pierce. When Pierce appointed "Southern radicals" to his Cabinet, Blair felt that Northern and moderate Democrats had been betrayed; and when the 1854 Kansas-Nebraska Bill passed—opening up the territories to slavery—Blair was roused to fight. "I hope there will be honest patriots enough found to resist it," he said, "and that the present aggression will be rebuked. I am willing to devote the balance of my life to this object." He was then 63 years old. Stephen Douglas, in typical invective, called him "a good Democrat fallen into 'Black Republicanism.'"

Blair was active in the Republican cause in 1856; and in 1860, although he would have preferred an "old Democrat," he joined vigorously in the campaign for Lincoln and became the new president's valued adviser. One of Blair's sons was the attorney general in Lincoln's Cabinet, and another was first a congressman from Missouri and then a brigadier general in the Civil War.

In 1864 Blair met privately with Jefferson Davis in Richmond, Va., in an attempt to end the war, and he arranged the futile Hampton Roads Conference of 1865. After the war he wanted the Union restored "as it was," and opposed the Radical Republican program for the South. His son Francis was the vice-presidential candidate on the Democratic ticket with Horatio Seymour in 1868, and in 1872 Blair supported Horace Greeley. The old Jacksonian unionist died on Oct. 18, 1876.

Further Reading

The only work that covers the life of Blair is William Ernest Smith, *The Francis Preston Blair Family in Politics* (2 vols., 1933), which provides something of a political history of the whole "middle period" of American history. Histories of the Jacksonian era, such as Arthur M. Schlesinger, Jr., *The Age of Jackson* (1945), have much information on Blair. Studies of the pre—Civil War era and of the war and the Reconstruction period provide material on his later life. Writings by and about his associates are useful, such as the biographies of Andrew Jackson, and Thomas Hart Benton, *Thirty Years' View* (2 vols., 1854-1856; repr. 1968).

Additional Sources

Smith, Elbert B., *Francis Preston Blair,* New York: Free Press, 1980. □

James Blair

The British educator James Blair (1655-1743) was commissary of Virginia for the bishop of London and founder and first president of the College of William and Mary.

Born to a Presbyterian minister and his wife in Scotland, James Blair attended Marischal College, Aberdeen, for 2 years. He received a master of arts degree from the University of Edinburgh, where he remained to study divinity. In 1679 he settled as a minister of the Scottish Episcopal Church near Edinburgh. Two years later, because he scrupled to sign the Scottish Test Act, he was deprived of a living anywhere in Scotland. He went to London, where he became acquainted with Henry Compton, the bishop of London, who persuaded him to go to Virginia as a missionary.

After 5 years in Virginia, Blair was appointed commissary (deputy) to the bishop of London, with authority to supervise the discipline of the Anglican clergy, though without the power to confirm baptisms or ordain American-born ministers. In one of his first acts he convened the clergy to urge them to found a college. They readily complied with a plan for a grammar school, a philosophical college, and a divinity school, which soon won the approval of Governor Francis Nicholson and the General Assembly.

In 1691 Blair went to England to obtain a charter and funds for the college. When he returned to Virginia 2 years later, he was the first president and rector of the board of visitors of the College of William and Mary, founded "to the End that the Church of Virginia may be furnished with a Seminary of Ministers of the Gospel, and that the Youth may be piously educated in good Letters and Manners, and that the Christian Faith may be propagated amongst the Western Indians, to the Glory of Almighty God."

For its first 36 years the college was no more than a grammar school, without enough funds to hire the six professors contemplated in the charter. Some of the blame must be laid to Blair; he did no teaching yet demanded his annual salary of £150, which cut deeply into the college's funds. And although Blair could have done much for the college from the seat on the governor's council he assumed in 1694, his feuds with a succession of governors eroded his influence and alienated both the clergy and the gentry.

Blair brought a measure of English religion and culture to colonial Virginia through his control of the Anglican

Church and promotion of education. When he died on April 18, 1743, he left an estate of £10,000 to a nephew and only his library and £500 to the college.

Further Reading

The introduction by Hunter Dickinson Farish in the 1940 reprint of Henry Hartwell, James Blair, and Edward Chilton, *The Present State of Virginia, and The College* (1727), contains useful information on Blair. A short study of Blair's life is Daniel E. Motley, *Life of Commissary James Blair, Founder of William and Mary College*, series 19, no. 10, of the Johns Hopkins University Studies in Historical and Political Science (1901). For background see Philip Alexander Bruce, *Institutional History of Virginia in the Seventeenth Century* (2 vols., 1910; repr. 1964); Richard L. Morton, *Colonial Virginia* (2 vols., 1960); and Clifford Dowdey, *The Virginia Dynasties* (1969). □

William Blake

William Blake (1757-1827) was an English poet, engraver, and painter. A boldly imaginative rebel in both his thought and his art, he combined poetic and pictorial genius to explore important issues in politics, religion, and psychology.

William Blake was born in London on Nov. 28, 1757, the second son of a hosier and haberdasher. Except for a few years in Sussex, his entire life was spent in London. Its streets and their names took on spiritual symbolism in his writings, much as the place names of the Holy Land did in the writings of the biblical prophets whom Blake always regarded as his spiritual progenitors. From his earliest years he saw visions—trees full of angels, for example. If these were not true mystical visions, it is probably best to regard them not as hallucinations but as the artist's intense spiritual and sensory realization of the world.

At 10 Blake started to attend drawing school; at 14 he began a 7-year apprenticeship to an engraver, and it was as an engraver that Blake was to earn his living for the rest of his life. After he was 21, he studied for a time at the Royal Academy of Arts, where he formed a violent distaste for the academic canons of excellence in art.

In August 1782 Blake married Catherine Boucher, who had fallen in love with him at first sight. He taught her to read and write, and she later became a valued assistant. Although their marriage was to suffer from some of the normal frictions, his "sweet shadow of delight," as Blake called Catherine, was a devoted and loving wife. On her authority there is a description of his appearance: short with a large head and shoulders; not handsome but with a noble and expressive face; his hair yellow-brown, luxuriant, and curling like flames.

Early Works

From his early teens Blake wrote poems, often setting them to melodies of his own composition. When he was 26, a collection entitled *Poetical Sketches* was printed with the help of the Reverend and Mrs. Mathew, who conducted a cultural salon and were patrons of Blake. This volume was the only one of Blake's poetic works to appear in conventional printed form; he later invented and practiced a new method.

After his father died in 1784, Blake set up a print shop with a partner next door to the family hosiery shop. In 1787 his beloved younger brother and pupil Robert died; thereafter William claimed that Robert communicated with him in visions and guided him. It was Robert, William said, who inspired him with the new method of illuminated etching that was to be the vehicle for his poems. The words, design, or some combination of the two was drawn in reverse on a plate covered with an acid-resisting substance; a corrosive was then applied. From these etched plates pages were printed and later hand-colored. Blake used his unique methods to print almost all his long poems with the exception of *An Island in the Moon* (ca. 1784), *Tiriel* (ca. 1789), *The Four Zoas* (ca. 1795-1803), *The Everlasting Gospel* (ca. 1818), and a number of short works. *The French Revolution* exists as printer's proofs.

As an engraver, Blake favored the line rather than chiaroscuro, or masses of light and dark. Blake's predilection for the line rather than "blurs" (as he called them) of color and mass had a philosophical as well as an artistic dimension. To him the line represented the honest clarity of human day as distinguished from the mystery of night.

In 1787 Blake moved to Poland Street, where he produced *Songs of Innocence* (1789) as the first major work in his new process. This book was later complemented by *Songs of Experience* (1794). The magnificent lyrics in these two collections systematically contrast the unguarded openness of innocence with the embitteredness of experience. They are a milestone in the history of the arts, not only because they exhibit originality and high quality but because they are a rare instance of the successful fusion of two art media by one man.

After a brief period of admiration for the religious thinker Emanuel Swedenborg, Blake produced in disillusioned reaction *The Marriage of Heaven and Hell* (1790-1793). In this satire the "devils" are identified with energy and creative genius, and the "angels" with repression of desire and the oppressive aspects of order and rationality. Some of the same issues arise in *The Book of Thel* (1789-1791) and *Vision of the Daughters of Albion* (1793). The former portrays a timid shepherdess who is reluctant to commit herself to the risks of existence, while the latter shows a heroine who casts off such timidity and chooses psychic and sexual liberation.

Blake had become a political radical and was in sympathy with the American Revolution and with the French Revolution during its early years. At Poland Street and shortly after his move to Lambeth in 1793, Blake composed and etched short "prophetic" books concerning these events, religious and political repression in general, and the more basic repression of the individual psyche, which he came to see as the root of institutional tyranny. Among these works (all composed between 1793 and 1795) are *America, Europe, The Book of Urizen, The Book of Los, The Song of Los,* and *The Book of Ahania.* In these poems Blake began to work out the powerful mythology he refined in his later and longer prophecies. He presented this mythology completely in his first epic-length poem, *The Four Zoas* (ca. 1795-1803). This difficult but mighty myth shows how religious and social evils are rooted in the internal warfare of man's basic faculties—reason (Urizen), passion (Luvah), instinct (Tharmas), and inspiration or prophetic imagination (Los or Urthona, who becomes more markedly the hero of Blake's long epics). But Blake was apparently unsatisfied with *The Four Zoas.* Although he drew freely on it for his later epics, he left the poem unengraved.

Felpham Period

Blake spent the years 1800 to 1803 working in Felpham, Sussex, with William Hayley, a minor poet and man of letters. With genuine good intentions Hayley tried to cure Blake of his unprofitable and unseemly enthusiasms and secured him commissions for safely genteel projects—painting ladies' fans, for example. Blake finally rebelled against this condescension and rejected Hayley's help. One result of this conflict was Blake's long poem *Milton* (ca. 1800-1810). In this work the spiritual issues involved in the quarrel with Hayley are allegorized, and Blake's larger themes are dramatized through an account of the decision

of the poet Milton to renounce the safety of heaven and return to earth to rectify the errors of the Puritan heritage he had fostered.

In 1803 Blake had a still more disturbing experience when a soldier whom he had evicted from his garden accused him of uttering seditious sentiments—a charge that in the witch-hunting atmosphere of the time was serious indeed. Blake was tried and acquitted, but he saw in the incident further confirmation of his views on the conflict between a sadistic society and the man of humane genius. The trial experience colors much of Blake's titanic final epic, *Jerusalem* (ca. 1804-1820).

Later Years

Back in London, living in South Molton Street, Blake worked hard at his poems, engraving, and painting, but he suffered several reverses. He was the victim of fraud in connection with his designs for Blair's *The Grave* and received insulting reviews of that project and of an exhibition he gave in 1809 to introduce his idea of decorating public buildings with portable frescoes. Blake wrote three prose pieces based on the events of this time: *Descriptive Catalogue* (1809), *Public Address* (1810), and *Vision of the Last Judgment* (1810).

The next decade is a somber and obscure period in Blake's life. He did some significant work, including his designs for Milton's poems *L'Allegro* and *Il Penseroso* (1816) and the writing of his own poem *The Everlasting Gospel* (ca. 1818), but he was sometimes reduced to hackwork and the public did not purchase or read his prophecies. After 1818, however, conditions improved. He became acquainted with a group of young artists who respected him and appreciated his work. His last 6 years were spent at Fountain Court, where Blake did some of his best pictorial work: the illustrations to the Book of Job and his unfinished Dante. In 1824 his health began to weaken, and he died singing on Aug. 12, 1827.

Continuing Influence

Blake's history does not end with his death. In his own lifetime he was almost unknown except to a few friends and faithful patrons, like Thomas Butts and the young disciples he attracted in his last years. He was even suspected of being mad. But interest in his work grew during the mid-19th century, and since then painstaking commentators have gradually elucidated Blake's beautiful, intricate, and difficult mythology. The 20th century has made him its own; he has been acclaimed as a kindred spirit by psychologists, writers (most notably William Butler Yeats), radical theologians, rock-and-roll musicians, and devotees of Oriental religion. He has furnished texts to a wide variety of rebels against war, orthodoxy, and almost every kind of psychic and personal repression.

Further Reading

The standard editions of Blake's writings are Geoffrey Keynes, ed., *The Complete Writings of William Blake* (1957; rev. ed. 1966), and David V. Erdman, ed., *The Poetry and Prose of William Blake* (1965), with commentary by Harold Bloom.

Alexander Gilchrist, *The Life of William Blake* (1863), is still a standard biography; another biography is Mona Wilson, *The Life of William Blake* (1927; rev. ed. 1948). For Blake the artist see Anthony Blunt, *The Art of William Blake* (1959). For the reader making his first acquaintance with Blake, Max Plowman, *An Introduction to the Study of Blake* (1927; 2d ed. 1967), and Herschel M. Margoliouth, *William Blake* (1951), are recommended. The most searching critical study is Northrop Frye, *Fearful Symmetry: A Study of William Blake* (1947). Excellent commentary on the longer poems is provided by S. Foster Damon, *William Blake: His Philosophy and Symbols* (1924), and Harold Bloom, *Blake's Apocalypse: A Study in Poetic Argument* (1963). □

Ralph Albert Blakelock

The American painter Ralph Albert Blakelock (1847-1919) was one of the most original romantic artists of late-19th-century America.

Ralph Blakelock was born on Oct. 15, 1847, in New York City. After a year and a half of college he dropped out to take up painting. Entirely self-taught, by the age of 20 he was painting competent landscapes and exhibiting in the National Academy of Design. In his early 20s he journeyed to the Far West, wandering far from civilization and spending some time among the Indians; this experience resulted in a lifelong fascination with the forest and its Indian inhabitants.

Blakelock's early landscapes were relatively literal and tight, in the style of the Hudson River school of painters, though without their grandiosity. As he matured, he developed a more intimate, subjective style. His favorite theme was the deep forest with its wildness and solitude; the hours were sunset, twilight, or night—seldom full daylight. With the years he concentrated more and more on moonlight scenes; the characteristic Blakelock nocturne is a peaceful moonlit scene, trees silhouetted against the sky, the moon seen through a tracery of foliage, veils of atmosphere creating patterns of receding planes.

Blakelock's style was akin to the French Barbizon painters Narcisse Diaz and Théodore Rousseau. His pronounced decorative quality also suggested Japanese art. But he was not a follower of any school; his was a highly personal art, drawing its content from the American scene. With his contemporary the romantic artist Albert P. Ryder, Blakelock was one of the most individual painters of his period in America.

In 1877 Blakelock married Cora Rebecca Bailey; they had nine children. In money matters Blakelock was completely unworldly. He had few opportunities to exhibit his pictures and no wide reputation; to support his family, he sold his paintings for very low prices, often for $25 or less, seldom for more than $100. In the 1890s he began to show symptoms of mental breakdown; in 1899 he became mentally ill and spent the rest of his life in psychiatric hospitals. His schizophrenic delusion was that he was immensely wealthy—perhaps a compensation for his long struggle to support his family. He continued to paint until his death on Aug. 9, 1919; however, his work was of lesser quality.

Almost as soon as Blakelock went into the first psychiatric hospital, his work began to receive recognition. Within a few years paintings he had sold so cheaply were resold for several thousand dollars, benefiting neither Blakelock nor his family. By 1903 his work was being forged, so that eventually there were many more fakes than genuine works. Such was the final ironical touch to one of the most tragic stories in American art.

Further Reading

The only book on Blakelock is Elliott Daingerfield, *Ralph Albert Blakelock* (1914). The most complete account of his life and art, based on previously unpublished sources, is Lloyd Goodrich's catalog of the *Blakelock Centenary Exhibition* (1947) of the Whitney Museum of American Art. □

Louis Blanc

The French journalist, historian, and socialist politician Louis Blanc (1811-1882) greatly influenced the evolution of French socialism and modern social democracy.

Louis Blanc was born on Oct. 29, 1811, in Madrid, where his father was comptroller of finance for King Joseph, Napoleon's brother. Financially ruined by the fall of the French Empire, the Blanc family returned to Paris, and Louis managed to earn enough from his writings to study law.

In 1839 Blanc published his most famous essay, *L'Organisation du travail* ("The Organization of Labor"). He outlined his social thought, which was based on the principle, "From each according to his abilities, to each according to his needs." His theories were based on solid research and expressed in vivid language. He argued that unequal distribution of wealth, unjust wages, and unemployment, all stemmed from competition. Unlike his predecessors, Blanc looked to the state to redress social injustice, but he believed that only a democratic republic could achieve an egalitarian commonwealth. Since every man has a "right to work," the state must provide employment and aid the aged and sick. It would accomplish these aims through establishing "social workshops"—producers' cooperatives, organized on a craft basis. The workers would manage these workshops, share in the profits, and repay the government loan. Eventually, the worker-owned factories, farms, and shops would replace those that were privately owned. Thus the whole process of production would become cooperative.

Though Marx criticized Blanc's ideas as utopian, French workers of the 1840s were intrigued by them. In 1846 there was a widespread demand for national workshops, and by 1848 "the organization of labor" had become a popular slogan. Articles in *La Réforme,* a radical

newspaper, popularized Blanc's proposals among the workers, who adopted them as a practical reform program.

Blanc supported the cause of liberals throughout Europe. In 1841 in *Histoire de dix ans, 1830-1840* (*History of Ten Years, 1830-1840*), he denounced King Louis Philippe's foreign policy as pusillanimous. France, he thought, had missed a golden opportunity in 1830 to give Europe liberal institutions.

A member of the provisional government formed on Feb. 24, 1848 (after the fall of the July Monarchy), Blanc persuaded his colleagues to guarantee the right to work, to create national workshops, and to establish the Luxembourg Commission to study and propose social experiments. But the national workshops became a makeshift relief program, a mockery of Blanc's ideas, and the government rejected his proposal for a ministry of labor.

By the middle of May, the coalition of right-and left-wing republicans, which had overthrown the Orleanist regime, collapsed. Though Blanc had been elected to the conservative National Assembly, that body expelled him from the government in May. It also abolished the Luxembourg Commission and on June 21 closed the workshops. These actions provoked a workers' revolt, which Gen. Cavaignac suppressed during the bloody June Days, and the ensuing reaction forced Blanc to seek asylum in England. While in exile he wrote a 12-volume history of the French Revolution to 1795 and a history of the Revolution of 1848. Blanc returned to France in 1871 and entered the Chamber of Deputies. There he led a futile fight for a radical constitu-

tion, opposing the one that was eventually adopted in 1875. In January 1879 he climaxed his long career by persuading the Assembly to grant amnesty to the Communards of 1871. Blanc died at Cannes on Dec. 6, 1882.

Further Reading

Most of Blanc's historical works and correspondence are available in English editions. The best critical study of the man and his work, in any language, is Leo A. Loubére, *Louis Blanc: His Life and His Contribution to the Rise of French Jacobin-Socialism* (1961). For an evaluation of the 1848 workshops see Donald Cope McKay, *The National Workshops: A Study in the French Revolution of 1848* (1933). J. P. Plamenatz, *The Revolutionary Movement in France, 1815-1871* (1952), traces the rise and fall of the alliance of moderate and radical republicans which established the short-lived Second Republic.

Additional Sources

Loubáere, Leo A., *Louis Blanc, his life and his contribution to the rise of French Jacobin-socialism,* Westport, Conn.: Greenwood Press, 1980, 1961. □

Mel Blanc

Known in Hollywood as "The Man of a Thousand Voices," Mel Blanc (1908-1989) was the versatile cartoon voice creator of such unforgettable characters as Bugs Bunny, Porky Pig, and Daffy Duck.

B lanc's voices have become standard-bearers for American popular culture throughout the world, heard, by some estimates, by more than 20 million people every day. Each of his characters is distinctive and many developed a trademark line that became famous, like "I tawt I taw a puddy tat!" (Tweety), "What's up, Doc?" (Bugs Bunny), "Thhhhufferin' Thhhhuccotash!" (Sylvester), and "Beep-beep!" (Road Runner). Blanc did the majority of his work for Warner Bros., performing in over 3,000 cartoons for that studio in a career that spanned more than 50 years, but he also worked for other animated film makers and as a memorable radio actor.

Porky Born

Born in 1908 and growing up in Portland, Oregon, Blanc studied music, becoming proficient on the bass, violin, and sousaphone. But he discovered a more amazing instrument in his own voice. "I used to look at animals and wonder, how would that kitten sound if it could talk," he said in the *New York Times.* "I'd tighten up my throat and make a very small voice, not realizing I was rehearsing." After marrying and working for a short time as a radio actor, Blanc moved to Los Angeles and joined Leon Schlesinger Productions, a cartoon workshop that eventually developed the Looney Tunes and Merry Melodies characters for Warner Bros. While playing the part of a drunken bull in "Porky Picador," Blanc relates in his autobiography *That's*

Not All Folks, the actor who was then portraying Porky actually did stutter. When Blanc was later asked to play Porky, he left the stutter in the act, and his first major character was born. Blanc next developed the character who was to become his favorite, Happy Hare, in another Warner Bros. short. He lent a brash, Bronx accent to the wiseguy rabbit that eventually became Bugs Bunny. "He's a little stinker," Blanc told the *New York Times.* "That's why people love him. He does what most people would like to do but don't have the guts to do." More famous characters followed, including Pepe LePew, Wile E. Coyote, Elmer Fudd, Speedy Gonzales, and Yosemite Sam.

Branches Out

Despite his proficiency, Blanc did not own the rights to any of his characters and never earned more than $20,000 in a single year from Warner Bros., so he, was forced to pursue other activities. In the 1960s he was co-producer and voice animator for ABC's "The Bugs Bunny Show," a Saturday morning series that featured Looney Tunes characters in new cartoons designed for television. He also provided the voices for Barney Rubble and Fred Flintstone's pet dinosaur, Dino, for the first prime-time cartoon series, "The Flintstones." Through the years, Blanc also kept up his work in radio, primarily as an actor and special effects creator for "The Jack Benny Show," on which he portrayed Benny's mexican gardener, Sy; his violin teacher, Mr. LeBlanc; his wise-cracking parrot; and his pet polar bear. Blanc also formed his own company to produce radio and television advertising. His last cartoon contribution came in the popu-

lar 1988 mixed-animation film "Who Framed Roger Rabbit," in which he performed the voices of Bugs Bunny, Daffy Duck, Tweety, and Porky Pig. In assessing why his characters have become so endearing to all age-groups, Blanc told the *New York Times:* " What we tried to do was amuse ourselves. We didn't make pictures for children. We didn't make pictures for adults. We made them for ourselves." Mel Blanc died in 1989.

Further Reading

Chicago Tribune, July 11, 1989.
New York Times, July 11, 1989. □

Antonio Guzmán Blanco

Antonio Guzmán Blanco (1829-1899) was a Venezuelan political leader who effectively dominated his country from 1870 to 1889. This period saw the first truly national government of Venezuela and a great surge of economic activity and material progress.

Antonio Guzmán Blanco was born to an aristocratic family in Caracas. His father, Antonio Leocadio Guzmán, was a leading Venezuelan intellectual, editor, and Liberal party spokesman. Young Antonio, very well educated in both law and medicine, saw that Venezuela's intermittent civil wars and revolutions were retarding its progress.

In 1859, a year after the ouster of dictator José Tadeo Monagas, Venezuela was again torn by civil strife—the Federalist War—and Guzmán Blanco joined the federalists, first as secretary and finally as virtual partner of federalist chief Gen. Juan Falcón. In 1863 Guzmán Blanco entered Caracas in triumph at the head of his army.

While Falcón was elected president, Guzmán Blanco took an important financial post and helped draw up the new federalist constitution of 1864. Later that year he was sent to England to negotiate a loan of £1,500,000, on which he received a fat commission. When he returned to Caracas, Falcón entrusted to him the economic reorganization and developmental planning of the nation.

Guzmán Blanco was again in Europe when he learned in late 1868 of a conservative revolution which had displaced the Falcón regime. Returning to Venezuela, he was soon chief of the liberal, federalist counterrevolution. In early April 1870 he again entered the capital in triumph. This time, however, he would not withdraw from power.

The Caudillo

Assuming the presidency, Guzmán Blanco determined to halt the political instability which had so long hampered the progress of his nation. By 1873, after quelling several revolts and restricting the traditional power of the provincial, landed oligarchy, he became the first truly *national* ruler, able to implement national programs.

In 1873, with the country pacified and the army now an instrument of the national government, Guzmán Blanco decreed universal manhood suffrage and direct election of the president. As a reward, he was elected president himself by a huge majority in April.

With this fresh and overwhelming mandate, he began to carry forward his ideas, striking first at the Church. Anticlerical like his father, he determined to limit the political and economic power of the Catholic Church in Venezuela. In short order the archbishop and papal nuncio were in exile for resisting his authority, and he established state control of education, civil marriage, and closure of the religious orders, finally closing the seminaries as well. While Guzmán Blanco never carried out his threat to nationalize the Church, he limited its power to its religious duties—a prime liberal goal.

In his first term Guzmán Blanco attempted to build up a personal political party to institutionalize his following but was largely unsuccessful. After allowing a chosen puppet to rule from 1877 to 1879, Guzmán Blanco reassumed the presidency from 1879 to 1884. From 1884 to 1886 he allowed Gen. Joaquín Crespo to be president and again resumed the presidency in 1886, ruling until 1888, when another puppet took over and Guzmán Blanco traveled again to Europe.

With his European contacts and his vision of the future, Guzmán Blanco's iron control of Venezuela began to bear fruit in development, stimulating European investment, loans, and increased trade. The stability he enforced worked economic miracles, and his government enacted good tariffs, built better roads, created a banking system, beautified Caracas, and maintained a glittering, cosmopolitan court.

The costs of this economic progress were high. Political repression, censorship, jailings, and exile were common as Guzmán Blanco enforced his vision upon his country. Prosperity was largely confined to the upper classes; the President himself obviously was prospering.

Bolstered by being named governor of several provinces and president of the National University, the "Illustrious American," as Guzmán Blanco was called, found himself faced—while in Paris in 1889—with a revolution led by his own puppet. Making a realistic estimate, Guzmán Blanco determined to remain in Paris with his sizable fortune rather than confront the rebellion.

While his country backslid into political chaos and much of his work was undone, Guzmán Blanco lived on in Paris, dying there in 1899.

Further Reading

The best work on Guzmán Blanco is George S. Wise, *Caudillo: A Portrait of Antonio Guzmán Blanco* (1951). Also worth consulting is Edwin Lieuwin, *Venezuela* (1961; 2d ed. 1965), and Robert L. Gilmore, *Caudillism and Militarism in Venezuela, 1810-1910* (1964). □

Ana Blandiana

The Romanian Ana Blandiana (born Otilia-Valeria Coman, 1942) is known internationally as one of her nation's most outstanding poets. Deeply spiritual in her sensibility and patriotic in her loyalties, she wrote verse of traditional beauty and elegance, but also was a prominent dissident and later respected public voice for freedom and democratic change.

To Ana Blandiana, being a poet was "sacred," "a state of grace," "destiny". Thus, "You cannot say of yourself, 'I am a poet', as you cannot say about yourself, within the limits of modesty, 'I am a genius.'" It is, however, also an "obligation," a necessity like living that "rips the writer away from mankind" in order to be its attentive observer and special voice. Her poem about writing, "The Gift," begins, "My gift is tragic, like some ancient punishment . . . . / All I touch turns into words. . . . "

Ana Blandiana was born Otilia-Valeria Coman on March 25, 1942, in Timisoara, a city in western Romania that once was a part of the Austro-Hungarian empire. Of Transylvanian peasant stock, she was the first daughter of a high school teacher. After the coming of communism, he could no longer teach and became an orthodox priest in nearby Oradea. In 1959 he was arrested and sentenced to five years of forced labor. Her father's influence and example can be seen not only in her intrinsically religious conception of existence, but also in her dissidence and independence of thought. Blandiana attended schools in Oradea and then went to the University of Cluj-Napoca from 1963 to 1967. After graduation she worked in Bucharest as a literary magazine editor and fine arts librarian. After a decade she was able to attend to writing full-time, not only poetry and prose fiction but also regular columns for cultural newspapers. From 1974 to 1991 she wrote for the major weekly *Literary Romania,* with a number of gaps during times the Nicolae Ceausescu government forbade the publication of her work. Blandiana married essayist Romulus Rusan in 1960. They had no children.

Ana Blandiana published her first poetry at the age of 17 in the year her father was imprisoned. Despite adopting a pen name, her work was banned at once because of her father. In 1964, the start of a period of liberalization of censorship and relative literary freedom in Romania, her debut volume finally came out. This work was a celebration, in exultant language, of ingenuous youthful sensuousness and idyllic communion with nature. But after Blandiana's first book was published, her father died in an accident. Although she remained a major voice in the Romanian poetic renaissance of the 1960s and one of its most eminent and productive poets after that, the accident separated her from what she termed her generation's "euphoria." Her writing that followed—she produced a total of 17 volumes of poetry (three are selected anthologies, three others for young children), six essay collections, and three books of fantastic prose fiction, including a novel—

was more deeply serious. Still valuing human happiness, conjoined now with a nostalgia for a kind of original spiritual purity, her work always reflected the limits, disasters, sordidness, and unfulfillment of life. Her themes centered upon change and mortality—accepted without horror.

In Blandiana's imagery, life can be intoxicating, warm, a powerful but fleeting joy, vital, and sensual. Her loving couples often bask in drowsy summer dreaminess. Yet the eternal, frequently signified by cold or stark whiteness, is likewise a desired realm of the unstained and uncorrupted. The human condition of pain, loss, shame, and decay is transcended, just as in a recurrent motif churches (tangible, enduring edifices of the sacred mediating between the human and God) miraculously fly through the air like flocks of birds. An early poem deals directly with the dichotomy of appealing alternatives. It begins, "Purity, I know, cannot bear fruit," and proceeds to celebrate the "dance" of "microbes . . . all around" in air and the earthly realm of fruitfulness. But then it sets up a contrast: "Only snow is immaculate white,/The warm earth is impure at the root." For the poet whose words can achieve a kind of earthly immortality, the choice is more extreme: between "silence and sin," or synonymously, "Voiceless dream or resounding fame." Blandiana's lofty sense of the poet's duty thus paradoxically involves triumph in the arena of the tainted and insufficient. But for the human being, the appeal in life of the eternal, religious realm is likewise a direct yearning for authenticity, an inward sense of salvation that is a higher joy.

Throughout her career, Blandiana's poems remained graceful, dignified, musical, and evocative, making frequent use of traditional forms and imagery. Her poetry has been called "astonishing" and "daring" precisely because of its intent to be "beautiful" in an older, pre-Modernist, early-Romantic sense. Her poems often focus on her own human vulnerability, but she was never confessional in the sense of baring private, intimate experience or neuroses. Her representative humanity is from a woman's perspective, and her rich sensibility is bodied forth through visionary lyrical strategies—the poet's enduring role of expressing inward revelation, the imagination's fresh triumph in understanding the world emotionally and morally.

This latter imperative in fact grew in urgency, and her themes took on public dimensions as warnings and dissident, ironic parables as Romania's domestic climate became increasingly repressive in the 1980s. Her religious assumptions became an ethical obligation to bear witness to her society's conditions. Twice during the decade her work was totally banned: once for a group of outspoken protest poems, one of which attacked her fellow citizens for being "compliant" and "vegetal," the second time because of a poetic children's fable about a strutting, egotistical tomcat who represented a sly satire of the nation's dictator (Ceausescu). Despite her fundamental faith, many late works before the downfall of the communist government turned somber and almost despairing. In "The Cold Melt" history is "in slow motion," "Only the progress of rust/To the heart of iron," and in "Portrait," "A sun of rats/In a firmament of asphalt" becomes "An Apollo of filth, the

future's/Fur-covered star for some other/Century. . . ." Much later, in 1997, in a very terse poem, "So Cold", she recalled how her emotions were avenged at witnessing ferocious dogs, " . . . mad with fear."

Blandiana's stature in Romania in the early 1990s was that of both a greatly respected writer and a widely known voice of decency and freedom, honored for her defiance and resistance. Fundamentally nonpolitical, she nonetheless came to play a number of prominent roles during and after the revolution. Briefly a member of the provisional government, from 1991 to 1993 she was president of a nonpartisan coalition of opposition interests. She was also president of the Romanian PEN Center, which she helped organize after 1989. Her works won numerous prizes at home as well as the Herder Prize in Austria and international fellowships to the United States (the Iowa International Writing Program) and to Berlin (from the German Academy of the Arts). Over 20 books of her works have been published in European languages, including English.

Further Reading

Blandiana's work is most readily available in excellent English versions by Peter Jay and Anca Cristofovici in *The Hour of Sand: Selected Poems 1969-1989* (1990), a collection that surveys the poet's career and also contains an informative introduction. A chapbook of 20 poems, *Don't Be Afraid of Me: Collected Poems* (1985) came out in Detroit. Andrea Deletant and Brenda Walker include 20 poems in *An Anthology of Contemporary Romanian Poetry* (1984) and 13 in *Silent Voices: An Anthology of Contemporary Romanian Women Poets* (1986), five works overlapping. In the journal *Romanian Civilization* (Spring 1993), Adam J. Sorkin presents 15 poems (some co-translated with Ioana Ieronim and Maria-Ana Tupan) along with a biographical and critical essay; nine of these poems plus one other are printed in *An Anthology of Romanian Women Poets* (1994) edited by Sorkin and Kurt W. Treptow. There is no book or full-length article on Blandiana in English, but briefer references and some analysis can be found, particularly in an essay by Ognyan Stamboliev in *Concerning Poetry* (Fall 1984); notices and translations in *Index on Censorship* (August 1989 and January 1991); reviews by Marguerite Dorian in *World Literature Today* (Autumn 1989 and Winter 1991); and a study by Adam J. Sorkin in *A.R.A. Journal* (1993).

Additional Sources

Description of a Struggle: The Vintage Book of Contemporary Eastern European Writing (1994). □

Sarah Gibson Blanding

Sarah Gibson Blanding (1898-1985) enjoyed the distinction of becoming one of the first women to serve in important U.S. government administrative posts during World War II.

Sarah Gibson Blanding began her career as an assistant professor of political science at the University of Kentucky in 1937. Her credentials included a year of study at the London School of Economics (1928-1929). She remained at the University of Kentucky, later becoming the dean of women, until 1941, when she became director of the New York State College of Home Economics at Cornell University. During her tenure there wartime demands for home-economics services quadrupled. She expedited requests for help by promoting food and nutrition education, child-care techniques, conservation and preservation of war materials in short supply, mass feeding, and maintenance of equipment.

Dewey Calls

Blanding's efforts at Cornell did not go unnoticed. During the last years of World War II Gov. Thomas Dewey of New York appointed Blanding to several state government posts, including director of the Human Nutrition Division of the State Emergency Food Commission and consultant to the State Defense Council's Division of Volunteer Participation. But her work was not limited to the local or state levels. As the war progressed, she was selected as the only female member of several national committees, which enhanced her reputation as an administrator.

The Presidency of Vassar

In February 1946 Blanding sought and obtained the post of president of Vassar College, succeeding Henry Mac-Cracken, who had been president since 1915. She was

selected because she was "the best possible person, man or woman." *The New York Herald Tribune* noted that Blanding "was a fresh, vigorous, and resourceful person with a mind of proved capacity, and, most of all, balanced judgment." She believed that her main mission was to maintain Vassar's high quality of education for women; ironically, this came at a time when the college, to help alleviate the overcrowding of men's colleges, began accepting male war veterans on the GI Bill as students working toward Vassar degrees.

National Honors

Blanding received national recognition for her efforts on behalf of women's education at Vassar. She toured often, lecturing that the balance of good and evil was so precarious that the scales could be tipped in either direction, so democracy was in a perilous position. In the process she received honorary doctorates from several colleges, including the University of Kentucky. She was appointed by President Harry S Truman to the National Commission on Higher Education, whose aim was to reexamine the system of education in the United States; later Governor Dewey appointed her to a committee to study the need for a state university system in New York. At her inauguration to the National Commission on Higher Education in October 1946, Blanding was given the War Department's Civilian Service Award for her service to the secretary of war. Cited during the ceremony were her exceptional efforts in developing activities for the Women's Army Corps and her leadership as a member of the army and navy committees on welfare and recreation. She was then appointed to the War Department Civilian Advisory Council and to the Chief of Staff 's Advisory Committee for the Women's Army Corps.

Further Reading

Jean Nowell, "New President Greets 1,440 at Vassar Opening," *New York Herald Tribune,* 8 September 1946, p. 33. ☐

Louis Auguste Blanqui

The French revolutionary Louis Auguste Blanqui (1805-1881) was an unrelenting enemy of every French regime of the 19th century. The most heroic figure in the French socialist movement, he spent most of his life in prison.

Louis Blanqui was born in Puget-Théniers, near Nice, on Feb. 1, 1805. While studying and working as a journalist in Paris, in 1824 he became involved with the secret society of the Carbonari. This was the first step in a lifetime attachment to the use of conspiratorial methods to achieve political and social change. In 1827 he escaped arrest after his first battle with the police. Blanqui took part in the street fighting of July 1830 and was decorated by the July Monarchy of Louis Philippe for his part in its birth.

Blanqui soon parted company with Louis Philippe's bourgeois monarchy and joined the extreme republican opposition. He was arrested in both 1831 and 1832 for plotting against the regime, but he invariably resumed his activities. Involved in two of the more elaborate conspiracies of the 1830s—the Society of the Seasons and the Society of the Families—he was arrested in 1836 for manufacturing arms. He received his first death sentence in January 1840 for his part in the May 1839 uprising. The sentence was commuted, and he was sent to the prison of Mont-Saint-Michel, where the harsh conditions permanently undermined his health. As a result of his illness, in 1844 he was transferred to a prison in Tours and was released in April 1847.

Upon learning of the February Revolution of 1848, Blanqui hurried to Paris, where he organized cooperation among the political clubs of the left. He pressured the provisional government for social reforms and advocated postponing elections until the country could be educated in republicanism. Apparently tolerant of the provisional republic, Blanqui at first opposed the leftist demonstration of May 15. But then he felt compelled to take part in order to keep the faith of his followers, and he led in the invasion of the new assembly. For this he was arrested and condemned to 10 years' imprisonment. He was deported by the government of the Second Empire to Africa in 1859 but was set free in August of that year.

Resuming his work in the republican secret societies, Blanqui was arrested again in 1861 and sent to the Sainte-Pélagie prison, where he had a large measure of freedom to study, reflect, and discuss his ideas. In 1865 he was even able to edit a journal from prison. To avoid deportation, he escaped in August 1865, going to Geneva and then Brussels, from which he was able to visit Paris secretly.

Taking advantage of early reverses in the Franco-Prussian War, Blanqui launched an uprising in August 1870; he was rescued from its·failure by the fall of the Second Empire on September 4. Imprisoned at Cahors by the new government for another ill-timed insurrection in October, he was unable to play a part in the Commune. Condemnations to death and, later, deportation were not carried out because of his ill health, and in 1877 he was transferred to the island prison of Château d'If in the Mediterranean.

By this time the aging and ill Blanqui had become a symbol of resistance to oppressive government, and a campaign was undertaken to secure a pardon for him. In April 1879 he was elected to the Chamber from Bordeaux but was rejected by the Chamber. After receiving a pardon in June, he was defeated for reelection. He died on Jan. 1, 1881.

By the end of Blanqui's life his conspiratorial approach to revolution seemed outmoded to most socialists, but his lifelong willingness to suffer for his cause and his refusal to accept defeat assured his reputation as a hero of the left. Believing in the fundamental importance of the class struggle, he emphasized the necessity for the seizure of political power by a proletarian elite, which would then establish the collective ownership of the means of production. An extreme rationalist, he was violently anticlerical, seeing in the church—indeed, in all religion—the principal cause of human misery and the principal obstacle to progress.

Further Reading

Alan B. Spitzer, *The Revolutionary Theories of Louis Auguste Blanqui* (1957), shows that Blanqui must be taken seriously as a thinker, not merely as an insurrectionist. See also Neil Stewart, *Blanqui* (1939). The most famous work on Blanqui, a fictionalized biography, is in French: Gustave Geffroy, *L'Enfermé* (1897; rev. ed., 2 vols., 1926). The leading authority on all aspects of Blanqui's career, Maurice Dommanget, also writes in French. □

Albert Taylor Bledsoe

American political apologist for the Southern Confederacy, Albert Taylor Bledsoe (1809-1877) was at various times an educator, attorney, author, and clergyman.

Albert Bledsoe's forebears were among the early settlers of Kentucky, and Albert was born at Frankfort on Nov. 9, 1809. He was a fellow cadet of Jefferson Davis and Robert E. Lee at West Point and graduated in 1830. Bledsoe resigned from the Army after 2 years' service in the West. He entered Kenyon College in Ohio to study law and theology and then taught mathematics and French there (1833-1834). He took orders in the Episcopal Church and became an assistant to Bishop Smith of Kentucky. Because of his opposition to the mode of infant baptism, Bledsoe abandoned his clerical career.

Bledsoe was a man of near-genius and tried many careers. In 1838 he was admitted to the bar. He practiced law periodically in Washington, D.C., and Springfield, Ill. In Springfield his practice was in competition with that of Abraham Lincoln. After 10 years as an attorney, Bledsoe left this profession too. In 1848 he became a professor of mathematics at the University of Mississippi, and in 1854 he accepted a similar post at the University of Virginia. His interests in theology and philosophy resulted in two valuable treatises: *A Theodicy, or Vindication of the Divine Theory* (1853) and *Essay on Liberty and Slavery* (1856).

In 1861 Bledsoe's West Point training brought him a Confederate colonel's commission and assignments as chief of the War Bureau and assistant secretary of war. Two years later, Confederate president Jefferson Davis dispatched him to Europe to study historical justifications for the Confederacy. The result of Bledsoe's research was an 1866 classic of political argument: *Is Davis a Traitor? or Was Secession a Constitutional Right previous to the War of 1861?* The Confederacy's defeat left Bledsoe dedicated to a rigorous defense of Southern principles. In 1867 he founded and edited the *Southern Review,* a Baltimore-based quarterly. Bledsoe poured the great energies of his mind into this magazine, writing from three to five articles for each issue as he toiled tirelessly to redeem the vanquished South. Yet that impoverished region had no money and little support to give to

Bledsoe's efforts; to support his family, he was forced to depend upon the salaries of his schoolteacher daughters.

In the 10 years that Bledsoe edited the *Review,* he was the personification of the unreconstructed Southerner. He defended slavery and secession while damning democracy, industrialism, science, and new ideas. Although ordained a Methodist minister in the mid-1870s, he was constantly at odds with clergymen over various theological points. The long strain of controversy, accentuated by financial burdens and excessive work, proved his end. He died on Dec. 8, 1877, in Alexandria, Va.

A historian once observed of Bledsoe: "When one turns to a subject of special sacredness to Bledsoe, one feels precisely as if one were walking in the Round Church of the Templars, and a knight suddenly rose from the floor and brandished his blade."

Further Reading

Bledsoe's voluminous writings are the primary source for his life. No full biography of him has been written. For analyses of his career see James Wood Davidson, *The Living Writers of the South* (1869), and Douglas Southall Freeman, *The South to Posterity: An Introduction to the Writing of Confederate History* (1939). □

Eugen Bleuler

The Swiss psychiatrist Eugen Bleuler (1857-1939), noted primarily for his work on schizophrenia, was a renowned dissenter from the orthodox Freudian psychoanalytic approach to psychopathology.

Eugen Bleuler was born in Zurich on April 30, 1857. After taking his medical degree at the University of Zurich, he spent his professional life as director of the Burghölzi hospital, a neurological clinic near Zurich, and as professor of psychiatry at the University of Zurich. Bleuler's approach to mental illness included an appreciation of the importance of motivational factors in abnormal behavior, as well as an understanding that some of these motivational factors may be "unconscious," that is, not recognized by the patient himself. Consequently, he was attracted to certain aspects of Sigmund Freud's psychoanalytical theory. Bleuler began an early correspondence with Freud, and he appointed as his chief assistant at the Burghölzi one of Freud's followers, Carl Jung. Also on the staff of the Burghölzi was another Freudian psychiatrist, Karl Abraham.

Bleuler was present at the first International Psycho-Analytic Congress in Salzburg in April 1908. The first periodical devoted exclusively to psychoanalysis, *Jahrbuch für psychoanalytische und psychopathologische Forschungen,* was directed by Freud and Bleuler and edited by Jung. Disagreements, both professional and personal, arose between Jung and Bleuler and, eventually, between Freud and Bleuler. Jung finally resigned his position at the Burghölzi,

and Bleuler resigned from both the Swiss and the International psychoanalytic associations.

Defining Schizophrenia

Bleuler's contributions to psychiatry were in the field of psychosis. At the time he began his work, psychiatrists tended to think of dementia praecox (early insanity) as a single disorder. Bleuler argued that it was in fact a group of disorders which shared certain symptoms, such as a lack of contact with reality. He coined the term "schizophrenia" (splitting of the mind) as a general classification for these abnormalities. His choice of the term was dictated by his belief that the most characteristic aspect of the disorder was a splitting or dissociation of the patient's total personality. In this regard, Bleuler also introduced the term "ambivalence," which refers to the often conflicting feelings and emotions, both positive and negative, that schizophrenics, and indeed even normal individuals, feel toward the same person, idea, or object. It has been suggested that Bleuler's own conflict with orthodox Freudian psychoanalysis may have been motivated in part by his puritanical feelings about sex and alcohol and may provide an example of his own concept of ambivalence.

Another aspect of schizophrenic behavior studied by Bleuler was the tendency of some patients to withdraw from contact with the reality of the outside world and to live in an "inner world" of their own making. He termed this escape from outer to inner life "autism." Bleuler died in Zurich on July 15, 1939.

Further Reading

There is no full-length biography of Bleuler. Bleuler's *Textbook of Psychiatry,* edited by A. A. Brill (1951), contains a biographical sketch by Jacob Shatzky. Bleuler's life and work are often discussed in works on Freud. Ernest Jones's comprehensive *The Life and Work of Sigmund Freud* (3 vols., 1955) contains numerous references to Bleuler, especially vol. 2: *Years of Maturity.* Vincent Brome, *Freud and His Early Circle: The Struggles of Psycho-Analysis* (1968), deals with the pioneers in the field, including Bleuler. See also H. F. Ellenberger, *Discovery of the Unconscious* (1970). □

William Bligh

William Bligh (1754-1817) was an English naval captain and a colonial governor of New South Wales, Australia. Probably best known for his involvement in the mutiny on H. M. S. "Bounty," he had a career fraught with controversy.

William Bligh was born on Sept. 9, 1754, in Plymouth, where his father was a customs officer. At 7 Bligh went to sea as a cabin boy and in 1770 joined the Royal Navy. Between 1776 and 1780 he was master of the *Resolution* on Capt. Cook's third voyage. In 1787 the British government dispatched Bligh to Tahiti with the *Bounty* to collect breadfruit plants in order to provide cheap food for West Indian slaves. Reluctant to leave Tahiti, the crew, led by Fletcher Christian, mutinied soon after departing from the island and cast Bligh adrift together with 18 supporters. After an epic 6 weeks' voyage, Bligh reached Timor in the East Indies, having traveled 3,618 miles in an open longboat. Honorably acquitted by a court-martial in 1790, he returned to Tahiti and successfully introduced breadfruit plants into the West Indies.

Between 1795 and 1802 Capt. Bligh saw action against the French at Camperdown and at Copenhagen, where he was commended by Nelson. In the *Nore* mutiny of 1797 he was not charged with maltreating his crew and retained his command. Contributions to navigation and natural history resulted in his election as a fellow of the Royal Society in 1801. But Bligh's strong will, violent temper, and foul tongue totally eclipsed his attainments at times, and in 1805 he was reprimanded for using insulting language to a junior officer.

Sir Joseph Banks recommended Bligh's appointment as governor of New South Wales. Bligh arrived in 1806 with instructions to end the trading monopoly enjoyed by officers of the New South Wales Corps. The rum traffic was duly prohibited, other traders encouraged, and improved credit facilities offered to small farmers. But the officer faction resisted attempts to enforce the law, and Bligh soon collided with the fanatical John Macarthur, who represented the governor as a brutal tyrant bent on destroying the liberties and property rights of Englishmen. When Bligh had Macarthur tried for sedition, the officers conspired to replace the governor by Maj. George Johnston, senior officer on the station. After holding office for only 17 months, Bligh was deposed in what became known as the Rum Rebellion.

At a subsequent court-martial in London, Johnston was dismissed from the service and by implication Bligh was exonerated although criticized for tactless behavior. At a time when opposition which centered on the colony's courts could easily be construed as subversion, Bligh was an unfortunate choice for governor because he lacked political sense, and in endeavoring to uphold the law he precipitated a crisis.

Bligh subsequently became an admiral. He retired to Kent and died in London on Dec. 17, 1817.

Further Reading

Many books have been written about Bligh. Although Sir John Barrow, *The Mutiny and Piratical Seizure of H. M. S. Bounty* (1831; rev. ed. 1914), was not entirely unfavorable, until the 1930s Bligh was usually pictured as a brutal bully. The first substantial biography to portray Bligh in a sympathetic light was George Mackaness, *The Life of Vice-Admiral William Bligh* (2 vols., 1931; rev. ed. 1951), which contains an excellent bibliography. H. V. Evatt, *Rum Rebellion* (1938), brilliantly demolishes the case of the New South Wales conspirators. A highly critical account of Bligh's behavior on the *Bounty* is contained in Alexander Mckee, *H. M. S. Bounty* (1961). Madge Darby's intriguing *Who Caused the Mutiny on the Bounty?* (1965) exonerates Bligh and casts suspicion on Midshipman Edward Young. A brief but excellent introductory account which clearly indicates the main issues is John Bach, *William Bligh* (1967). J. C. Beaglehole, *Captain Cook*

and Captain Bligh (1967), draws comparisons between their respective roles as commanders.

Additional Sources

Allen, Kenneth S., *That Bounty bastard: the true story of Captain William Bligh,* New York: St. Martin's Press, 1977, 1976.

Bligh, William, *An account of the mutiny on H.M.S. Bounty,* Gloucester: A. Sutton; Atlantic Highlands, N.J.: Humanities Press, 1981.

Hawkey, Arthur, *Bligh's other mutiny,* London: Angus and Robertson, 1975.

Hough, Richard Alexander, *Captain Bligh and Mr. Christian: the men and the mutiny,* London: Cassell, 1979.

Humble, Richard, *Captain Bligh,* London: A. Barker, 1976.

Kennedy, Gavin, *Bligh,* London: Duckworth, 1978.

Kennedy, Gavin, *Captain Bligh: the man and his mutinies,* London: Duckworth, 1989.

Schreiber, Roy E., *The fortunate adversities of William Bligh,* New York: P. Lang, 1991. □

Ernest Bloch

The Swiss-born American composer and teacher Ernest Bloch (1880-1959) was noted for orchestral and chamber music of highly individual style. He directed two music conservatories in the United States.

Ernest Bloch was born in Geneva on July 24, 1880. Showing musical gifts at an early age, he studied violin with Louis Rey and theory with Émile Jacques-Dalcroze. In 1897 Bloch went to Brussels, where he studied violin with Eugène Ysaye, and then to Frankfurt, studying composition with Iwan Knorr.

Bloch composed his first important work, the Symphony in C-sharp Minor, at the age of 21. In 1904, after having written some songs and a symphonic work, *Hiver Printemps,* he began to work on his opera, *Macbeth,* with a libretto by Edmond Fleg, and it was premiered in Paris in 1910. Bloch became a professor at the Geneva Conservatory in 1911. Among his pupils was the conductor Ernest Ansermet.

The compositions Bloch wrote between 1912 and 1916—*Three Jewish Poems;* settings of Psalms 137, 114, and 22; *Schelomo; Israel;* and String Quartet No. 1—when premiered during his first visit to the United States in 1917, brought him spectacular recognition. He soon settled in New York City with his family, teaching and lecturing. Among his pupils were Roger Sessions, George Antheil, Douglas Moore, Quincy Porter, Randall Thompson, Frederick Jacobi, Herbert Elwell, and Leon Kirchner.

In 1919 Bloch won the Coolidge Prize (*Suite for Viola and Piano*), in 1926 the Carolyn Beebe Prize (*Four Episodes for Chamber Orchestra*), in 1928 the Musical America Prize (an orchestral rhapsody, *America*), and in 1930 the Victor Prize (*Helvetia*).

As director of the Cleveland Institute of Music and the San Francisco Conservatory of Music (1920-1930), Bloch made a strong impact. He continued to compose works, such as the Concerto Grosso No. 1, which are tonal, classical in form, and conservatively modern. Bloch vitalized the atmosphere with his enthusiasm, informality, and rather stubborn opinions.

After 1930 Bloch returned to Europe to live, where he composed a sacred service, a piano sonata, a violin concerto, and some large orchestral works. The events leading to World War II affected him deeply, and he stopped composing for some time.

On his return to America, Bloch and his wife, Marguerite, settled in Agate Beach, Ore. He gave master courses for several summers at the University of California at Berkeley and became professor emeritus in 1952. Many of the 25 works he wrote during his final years are considered his peak achievements. They include four String Quartets, Symphony in E-flat, Sinfonia Breve, Piano Quintet No. 11, works for trombone, trumpet, and flute with orchestra, and several suites for unaccompanied stringed instruments.

In 1958, after a long illness, Bloch submitted to surgery; on July 15, 1959, he died. He had received many honors, medals, and honorary degrees, but he always remained unworldly, preferring the solitude of nature to the social life of big cities.

Further Reading

General works which discuss Bloch's music include Guido Pannain, *Modern Composers* (1932; trans. 1932); John Tasker Howard, *Our Contemporary Composers: American Music in the Twentieth Century* (1941); David Ewen, *The Book of Modern Composers* (1942; 3d ed. rev. and enlarged 1961) and *The World of Twentieth-Century Music* (1968); Joseph Machlis, *Introduction to Contemporary Music* (1961); and Otto Deri, *Exploring Twentieth-Century Music* (1968).

Additional Sources

Strassburg, Robert., *Ernest Bloch, voice in the wilderness: a biographical study*, 1977 (Los Angeles: Trident Shop, California State University). □

Ernst Bloch

Ernst Bloch (1885-1977) was a humanistic interpreter of Marxist thought, justifying and amplifying the religious and philosophical appeal of the beliefs of Karl Marx.

Bloch was born in Germany July 8, 1885, and studied, taught, and died there, but he lived in exile from the Hitler regime after 1933 and in the United States from 1938 to 1948. Later, he became a professor of philosophy at the University of Leipzig, German Democratic Re-

public, and director of its Institute for Philosophy, 1948-1957, and, after 1961, honorary professor at Tübingen in the Federal Republic of Germany.

After studying philosophy, music, and physics in Munich and Würzburg and Berlin, Bloch became a private student of the social philosopher Georg Simmel in the German capital. Later, in Heidelberg and again in Berlin, Bloch associated with the most seminal thinkers of the German Empire (and later the Weimar Republic), among them Max Weber, György Lukács, Theodor Adorno, Walter Benjamin, and Bertolt Brecht.

Bloch gained his fame as a humanistic interpreter of Marxist thought, explaining the thrust of Marx's historical materialism in terms of a tendency on the part of all things to become more and better than they are. The material origin of this tendency in human beings lies in human drives, and first of all in the drive to escape hunger; it evolves in the directions set by human hope. In this, humanity is at one with the material universe, which itself is as much shaped by what it has not yet become as by what it already seems to be: "possibility" is a characteristic of nature as such; and, indeed, so is "purpose," movement toward an end to history such that both movement and end will only be clear when complete. Human hope participates with nature in the striving toward this completion.

Nature itself may be said to be "aware" of, and lending direction to, this thrust, so that as long as there have been such dynamic "objects" in the world, there has also been this driving "subject." Where existentialists of the same

period saw only anxiety (*angst*) emanating from the up-rootedness of human beings, Bloch saw hope in their striving for completion. The future was thus a decisive category for Bloch. His major work was *The Principle of Hope* (*Das Prinzip Hoffnung*) in three volumes: 1954, 1955, and 1959.

Bloch believed he could discern the end goal of human hope in the society imagined by communists, a society no longer marked by its oppositions, contradictions, and antagonisms, but blessed with the absence of these and of human estrangement. The lack of completion in matter or nature itself expressed itself in human beings as nature became an "object" for human "subjects;" that is to say, as things not-yet-what-they-could-be sparked and shaped the thinking of unfulfilled people, with the result that the latter were always at strife. The conditions of a communist society—e.g., total sharing—would presumably annul such limitations, fill in the gaps both materially and spiritually, and bestow peace.

It was Bloch's opinion that, in this treatment of matter and human history, he was taking the philosophy of Karl Marx a step or so further, justifying and amplifying its religious and philosophical appeal. The Communist Party where he taught in the German Democratic Republic, however, was annoyed by Bloch's inconsistencies: dialectical materialism had no room for such a "subjectivity" of "objective" matter, with the accompanying quasi-religious metaphysics. More centrally, Bloch was failing to see that not unfulfilled objects but a greedy "ruling class" taking over workers' products and their lives was the cause of alienation and strife in human affairs. The trouble was that Bloch's object-subject scheme was universal, making all people its prey and leaving all to settle subjectively for whichever remedies they preferred. If the real "object" to keep in view, however, was the class struggle, then the party was obviously the apt body of thinkers, or the best "subject," to show society the way.

These disagreements had their practical results as Bloch defended reformist aims behind the anti-Soviet uprisings in Poland in 1955 and in Hungary in 1956 while the party backed their suppression. The differences led to Bloch's departure for West Germany in 1961. Nonetheless, in the West Bloch continued to express his opposition to what he saw as capitalism, imperialism, and militarism; and he gave his support to "socialism with a human face" in Czechoslovakia in 1968.

On the other hand, Bloch's thinking made him of great interest to Christian readers, especially those who took modern political philosophy and notions of historical development seriously. Such Christians saw points of convergence with their theology. Both communist critics and Christians who welcomed Bloch spoke of his system as a "secular eschatology." This influence is explicit, for example, in Jürgen Moltmann and in works of the "theology of hope" appearing in the 1960s.

Some Bloch books were warehoused and not released for sale in the United States, where they are difficult to find. There are many commentaries in Europe, but almost none in the United States.

Works in German by Bloch include *Freiheit und Ordnung* (1946); *Das Prinzip Hoffnung* (1954, 1955, and 1959); *Subjekt-Objekt, Erläuterungen zu Hegel* (1951); *Thomas Müntzer als Theologe der Revolution* (1921); and *Wissen und Hoffnung. Auszüge aus seinen Werken* (1955).

Works in English by Block include *Atheism in Christianity: the religion of the Exodus and the Kingdom* (1972); *Man on his Own. An essay on the Philosophy of religion* (1970); *On Karl Marx* (1971); and *A Philosophy of the Future* (1970).

Further Reading

Bloch's work is represented in J. Moltmann, *Theology of Hope* (1967) and W. Pannenberg, *Theology and the Kingdom of God* (1967). Many of the best references are in German: J. Habermas, "Ein marxistischer Schelling. Zu Ernst Blochs spekulativem Materialismus," in *Theorie und Praxis* (Berlin, 1963); Gottfried Handel, "Bloch, Ernst," in *Philosophen-Lexikon*, E. Lange and D. Alexander, editors (Berlin, 1982); and G. M. Tripp, *Absurdität und Hoffnung. Zum Werk von Albert Camus und Ernst Bloch* (Berlin, 1968). □

Felix Bloch

Felix Bloch (1905-1983) is best known for his development of nuclear magnetic resonance techniques, which allowed highly precise measurements of the magnetism of atomic nuclei and became a powerful tool in both physics and chemistry to analyze large molecules.

Felix Bloch made many important contributions to twentieth-century solid-state physics, including several theorems and laws named for him. He is best known for his development of nuclear magnetic resonance techniques, which allowed highly precise measurements of the magnetism of atomic nuclei and became a powerful tool in both physics and chemistry to analyze large molecules. Bloch was awarded a share of the 1952 Nobel Prize for his work in this field. Bloch was born in Zurich, Switzerland, on October 23, 1905, the son of Agnes Mayer Bloch and Gustav Bloch, a wholesale grain dealer. Bloch's early interest in mathematics and astronomy prompted his family to enroll the boy in an engineering course at the Federal Institute of Technology in Zurich in 1924. His first year's introductory course in physics revealed to Bloch what his true career would be. After completing his studies in the Division of Mathematics and Physics at the Institute in 1927, Bloch studied at the University of Leipzig in Germany under Professor Werner Karl Heisenberg, who was engaged in ground-breaking research in quantum mechanics. Bloch earned his Ph.D. in physics from Leipzig in 1928 with a dissertation on the quantum mechanics of electronics in crystals.

Returning to Zurich, Bloch worked as a research assistant from 1928 to 1929. A Lorentz Fund fellowship allowed him to do research in 1930 at the University of Utrecht in the Netherlands, and later that year he returned to Leipzig to do more work with Heisenberg. An Oersted Fund fellow-

ship took him to the University of Copenhagen in 1931, where he worked with Niels Bohr, director of the university's Institute for Theoretical Physics. From 1932 to 1933 Bloch once again returned to the University of Leipzig, where he was a lecturer in theoretical physics. After Adolf Hitler came to power, Bloch, who was Jewish, left Germany, lecturing at Paris's Institut Henri Poincaré and working with Enrico Fermi in Rome on a Rockefeller Fellowship. In 1934, Bloch accepted an invitation to join the faculty of Stanford University in the United States as an assistant professor of physics. He became a full professor in 1936 and remained at Stanford in that capacity, with a few leaves of absence, until his retirement in 1971, when he became professor emeritus.

European refugees like Bloch were a boon to physics in the United States, as many of them—again, like Bloch—were theorists who added valuable insight to the discoveries of U.S. experimental physicists. Practicing physics in the United States, in turn, was advantageous to Bloch and his fellow refugees because they could attain professorship, accumulate graduate students, and secure research money and facilities with much greater ease in the U.S. than they could in Europe.

Even before he came to the United States at the age of twenty-eight, Bloch had made significant contributions to theoretical physics. His concept of the conduction of electrons in metals, presented in his Ph.D. thesis, became the foundation of the theory of solids. In 1928 he developed the Bloch-Fouquet theorem, which specifies the form of wave functions for electrons in a crystal. (Fouquet was a mathe-

matician who solved an identical abstract math problem many years earlier.) Functions that satisfy the conditions of the theorem are called Bloch functions by physicists, who use them in theoretically probing the nature of metals. Bloch also derived the Bloch-Grüneisen relationship in 1928, which gives a theoretical explanation for Eduard Grüneisen's law about the temperature dependence of the electric conductivity of metals. The Bloch T 3/2 law describes how magnetization in ferromagnetic material is dependent upon temperature, Bloch walls are the transition region between parts of a ferromagnetic crystal that are magnetized with different orientations, and the Bloch theorem eliminates some of the possible explanations for superconductivity. In 1932 Bloch developed the Bethe-Bloch expression, extending the work of Bohr and Hans Bethe on the slowing down of charged particles in matter. He also advanced the quantum theory of the electromagnetic field and, once in the United States, worked with Nordsieck to resolve the infrared problem in quantum electrodynamics. Bloch began contributing to scientific publications in 1927, while still a student.

Soon after arriving at Stanford, Bloch's interest was drawn to the neutron, a nuclear particle that had been discovered in 1932 by James Chadwick. Otto Stern's experiments in 1933 suggested that the neutron had a magnetic moment (magnetic strength). As he explained in his Nobel Prize address, Bloch was fascinated by the idea that an elementary particle with no electrical charge could have a magnetic moment. Paul Dirac had explained that the electron's magnetic moment resulted from its charge. Clearly, Bloch explained in his Nobel address, "the magnetic moment of the neutron would have an entirely different origin," and he set out to discover it. First, he needed direct experimental proof that the neutron's magnetic moment actually existed. He predicted in 1936 that the proof could be obtained by observing the scattering of slow neutrons in iron and that magnetic scattering of the neutrons would produce polarized neutron beams. These predictions were confirmed in 1937 by experimenters at Columbia University.

The next step was to measure the neutron's magnetic moment accurately. In 1939—the same year he became a naturalized American citizen—Bloch moved from theoretical to experimental physics and achieved that goal, working with Luis Alvarez and the cyclotron at the University of California at Berkeley. As Bloch described in his Nobel address, the two physicists passed a polarized neutron beam through an area with a weak, oscillating magnetic field superimposed on a strong, constant magnetic field. Bloch's experiments were halted by World War II, when he took a leave of absence from Stanford. He joined the Manhattan Project in 1941, whose goal was to produce an atomic bomb, and he worked on that goal at Los Alamos in New Mexico from 1942 to 1944, studying uranium isotopes. In 1944 he joined the Harvard University Radio Research Laboratory, where he was an associate group leader in counter-radar research.

The knowledge Bloch acquired of radio techniques at Harvard proved invaluable when he returned to his nuclear magnetic moment research at Stanford in 1945. I. I. Rabi had developed a technique in the 1930s for measuring nuclear magnetic moments through resonance, that is, by exciting atomic nuclei with electromagnetic waves and then measuring the frequencies of the signals the vibrating nuclei emit. Rabi's technique, however, worked only with rays of molecules, was not particularly precise, and vaporized the sample being studied. Working with William W. Hansen and Martin Packard, Bloch used the basic principle of magnetic resonance —the reorientation of nuclei after being excited—to develop a new method of "nuclear induction." In Bloch's technique, small containers of the material being studied (for Bloch, it was the hydrogen nuclei in water solutions) are placed in a strong electromagnetic field. A much weaker electromagnetic field controlled by radio frequencies then excites the nuclei. The nuclei, induced to spin by the electromagnetism, act like tiny radio transmitters, giving off signals detected by a receiver. These signals make it possible to measure the nuclear magnetic moment of an individual nucleus very precisely and provide a great deal of very accurate and valuable information about the nuclear particles emitting them. Precise measurements of magnetic moment and angle of momentum of individual nuclei made possible by Bloch's nuclear induction technique provided new knowledge about nuclear structure and behavior. Observations of changes in the frequency of the nuclear signals depending on the strength of the magnetic field aided the design of much improved magnetometers, especially useful in measuring the earth's magnetic field. Nuclear induction also provided new knowledge about the interaction of nuclear particles and about isotopes. Because magnetic moment is affected by surrounding charged electrons, and because each atom has a characteristic nuclear frequency, nuclear induction also yielded information about the atomic and molecular structure of solids, gases, and liquids—all without destroying the subject material, as Rabi's method had.

Bloch announced his discovery in two papers published in *Physical Review* in 1946. The first, a paper titled "Nuclear Induction," described the theory of his technique and the second, written with Hansen and Packard and titled "The Nuclear Induction Experiment," described the mechanics of the experiment itself. At about the same time, Edward Mills Purcell of Harvard University and his colleagues H. C. Torrey and Robert Pound published the nearly identical results of their totally independent work with protons in paraffin. Purcell and his group called their technique "nuclear magnetic resonance absorption." Bloch and Purcell soon saw that their work, although it initially appeared different, was based on the same principle. The two men shared the 1952 Nobel Prize in physics for, in the words of the Nobel committee, their "development of high precision methods in the field of nuclear magnetism and the discoveries which were made through the use of these methods." Although the two had not worked together, Bloch described Purcell at the time as his "good friend" and a "distinguished scientist" and commented in the *New York Times* that he was very happy to be sharing the award with his colleague. "NMR," as Bloch's and Purcell's method came to be known, has become an invaluable tool of physics and analytic chemistry, revealing information about the molecular structure of complex compounds. The fact that NMR is nondestructive later led to its use as a sophisticated diagnostic tool in medicine. NMR scanners were developed that could produce images of human tissue that were both safer (because they did not use X rays) and more advanced that those produced by CAT scanners.

Bloch's prominence as a physicist was recognized by his election to the National Academy of Sciences in 1948. In April 1954 he was unanimously chosen to serve as the first director-general of CERN, the Conseil Européen de la Recherche Nucléaire (European Council of Nuclear Research) in Geneva, a twelve-nation project for research into peacetime uses of atomic energy. Again he left Stanford on a leave of absence, returning after 1955 to continue his research on nuclear and molecular structure and uses of NMR. He also worked with the theory of superconductivity.

Bloch married Lore C. Misch in Las Vegas in 1940. His wife was a professor's daughter and fellow German-born physicist who had immigrated to the United States a few years after Bloch. She had been working as a research associate at the Massachusetts Institute of Technology when the two met in New York at a professional society function. They had three sons, George, Daniel, and Frank, and a daughter, Ruth. In addition to his research, Bloch published many articles in professional journals, especially *Physical Review,* and he enjoyed piano playing, skiing, and mountain climbing. He held an endowed chair as Max H. Stein Professor of Physics at Stanford from 1961 until his retirement in 1971. He was also a fellow of the American Academy of Arts and Sciences and the American Physical Society. After retiring, Bloch returned to his birthplace of Zurich, where he died of a heart attack on September 10, 1983, at the age of seventy-seven.

Further Reading

Chodorow, Marvin, editor, *Felix Bloch and Twentieth-Century Physics,* William Marsh Rice University Press, 1980.
Kevles, Daniel J., *The Physicists: The History of a Scientific Community in Modern America,* Harvard University Press, 1987.
Magill, Frank N., *The Nobel Prize Winners: Physics,* Volume 1, 1901–1937, Salem Press, 1989.
Walecka, John Dirk, *Fundamentals of Statistical Mechanics, Manuscript and Notes of Felix Bloch,* Stanford University Press, 1989.
New York Times, November 7, 1952, pp. 1, 21; September 12, 1983, p. D13. □

Konrad Bloch

Investigations by Konrad Bloch (born 1912) of the complex processes by which animal cells produce cholesterol have increased our understanding of the biochemistry of living organisms.

Konrad Bloch's research established the vital importance of cholesterol in animal cells and helped lay the groundwork for further research into treatment of various common diseases. For his contributions to the study of the metabolism of cholesterol, he was awarded the 1964 Nobel prize for Physiology or Medicine.

Konrad Emil Bloch was born on January 21, 1912 in the German town of Neisse (now Nysa, Poland) to Frederich (Fritz) D. Bloch and Hedwig Bloch. Sources list his mother's maiden name variously as Steiner, Steimer, or Striemer. After receiving his early education in local schools, Bloch attended the Technische Hochschule (technical university) in Munich from 1930 to 1934, studying chemistry and chemical engineering. He earned the equivalent of a B.S. in chemical engineering in 1934, the year after Adolf Hitler became chancellor of Germany. As Bloch was Jewish, he moved to Switzerland after graduating and lived there until 1936.

While in Switzerland, he conducted his first published biochemical research. He worked at the Swiss Research Institute in Davos, where he performed experiments involving the biochemistry of phospholipids in tubercle bacilli, the bacteria that causes tuberculosis.

In 1936, Bloch emigrated from Switzerland to the United States; he would become a naturalized citizen in 1944. With financial help provided by the Wallerstein Foundation, he earned his Ph.D. in biochemistry in 1938 at the College of Physicians and Surgeons at Columbia University, and then joined the Columbia faculty. Bloch also ac-

cepted a position at Columbia on a research team led by Rudolf Schoenheimer . With his associate David Rittenberg, Schoenheimer had developed a method of using radioisotopes (radioactive forms of atoms) as tracers to chart the path of particular molecules in cells and living organisms. This method was especially useful in studying the biochemistry of cholesterol.

Cholesterol, which is found in all animal cells, contains 27 carbon atoms in each molecule. It plays an essential role in the cell's functioning; it stabilizes cell membrane structures and is the biochemical ''parent'' of cortisone and some sex hormones. It is both ingested in the diet and manufactured by liver and intestinal cells. Before Bloch's research, scientists knew little about cholesterol, although there was speculation about a connection between the amount of cholesterol and other fats in the diet and arteriosclerosis (a buildup of cholesterol and lipid deposits inside the arteries).

While on Schoenheimer's research team, Bloch learned about the use of radioisotopes. He also developed, as he put it, a ''lasting interest in intermediary metabolism and the problems of biosynthesis.'' Intermediary metabolism is the study of the biochemical breakdown of glucose and fat molecules and the creation of energy within the cell, which in turn fuels other biochemical processes within the cell.

After Schoenheimer died in 1941, Rittenberg and Bloch continued to conduct research on the biosynthesis of cholesterol. In experiments with rats, they ''tagged'' acetic acid, a 2-carbon compound, with radioactive carbon and hydrogen isotopes. From their research, they learned that acetate is a major component of cholesterol. This was the beginning of Bloch's work in an area that was to occupy him for many years—the investigation of the complex pattern of steps in the biosynthesis of cholesterol.

Bloch stayed at Columbia until 1946, when he moved to the University of Chicago to take a position as assistant professor of biochemistry. He stayed at Chicago until 1953, becoming an associate professor in 1948 and a full professor in 1950. After a year as a Guggenheim Fellow at the Institute of Organic Chemistry in Zurich, Switzerland, he returned to the United States in 1954 to take a position as Higgins Professor of Biochemistry in the Department of Chemistry at Harvard University. Throughout this period he continued his research into the origin of all 27 carbon atoms in the cholesterol molecule. Using a mutated form of bread mold fungus, Bloch and his associates grew the fungus on a culture that contained acetate marked with radioisotopes. They eventually discovered that the two-carbon molecule of acetate is the origin of all carbon atoms in cholesterol. Bloch's research explained the significance of acetic acid as a building block of cholesterol, and showed that cholesterol is an essential component of all body cells. In fact, Bloch discovered that all steroid-related substances in the human body are derived from cholesterol.

The transformation of acetate into cholesterol takes 36 separate steps. One of those steps involves the conversion of acetate molecules into squalene, a hydrocarbon found plentifully in the livers of sharks. Bloch's research plans involved injecting radioactive acetic acid into dogfish, a type of shark, removing squalene from their livers, and determining if squalene played an intermediate role in the biosynthesis of cholesterol. Accordingly, Bloch traveled to Bermuda to obtain live dogfish from marine biologists. Unfortunately, the dogfish died in captivity, so Bloch returned to Chicago empty-handed. Undaunted, he injected radioactive acetate into rats' livers, and was able to obtain squalene from this source instead. Working with Robert G. Langdon, Bloch succeeded in showing that squalene is one of the steps in the biosynthetic conversion of acetate into cholesterol.

Bloch and his colleagues discovered many of the other steps in the process of converting acetate into cholesterol. Feodor Lynen, a scientist at the University of Munich with whom he shared the Nobel Prize, had discovered that the chemically active form of acetate is acetyl coenzyme A. Other researchers, including Bloch, found that acetyl coenzyme A is converted to mevalonic acid. Both Lynen and Bloch, while conducting research separately, discovered that mevalonic acid is converted into chemically active isoprene, a type of hydrocarbon. This in turn is transformed into squalene, squalene is converted into anosterol, and then, eventually, cholesterol is produced.

In 1964, Bloch and his colleague Feodor Lynen, who had independently performed related research, were awarded the Nobel Prize for Physiology or Medicine "for their discoveries concerning the mechanisms and regulation of cholesterol and fatty acid metabolism." In presenting the award, Swedish biochemist Sune Bergström commented, "The importance of the work of Bloch and Lynen lies in the fact that we now know the reactions that have to be studied in relation to inherited and other factors. We can now predict that through further research in this field . . . we can expect to be able to do individual specific therapy against the diseases that in the developed countries are the most common cause of death." The same year, Bloch was honored with the Fritzsche Award from the American Chemical Society and the Distinguished Service Award from the University of Chicago School of Medicine. He also received the Centennial Science Award from the University of Notre Dame in Indiana and the Cardano Medal from the Lombardy Academy of Sciences the following year.

Bloch continued to conduct research into the biosynthesis of cholesterol and other substances, including glutathione, a substance used in protein metabolism. He also studied the metabolism of olefinic fatty acids. His research determined that these compounds are synthesized in two different ways: one comes into play only in aerobic organisms and requires molecular oxygen, while the other method is used only by anaerobic organisms. Bloch's findings from this research directed him toward the area of comparative and evolutionary biochemistry.

Bloch's work is significant because it contributed to creating "an outline for the chemistry of life," as E.P. Kennedy and F.M. Westheimer of Harvard wrote in *Science*. Moreover, his contributions to an understanding of the biosynthesis of cholesterol have contributed to efforts to comprehend the human body's regulation of cholesterol levels in blood and tissue. His work was recognized by

several awards other than those mentioned above, including a medal from the Societe de Chimie Biologique in 1958 and the William Lloyd Evans Award from Ohio State University in 1968.

Bloch served as an editor of the *Journal of Biological Chemistry*, chaired the section on metabolism and research of the National Research Council's Committee on Growth, and was a member of the biochemistry study section of the United States Public Health Service. Bloch has also been a member of several scientific societies, including the National Academy of Sciences, to which he was elected in 1956, the American Academy of Arts and Sciences, and the American Society of Biological Chemists, in addition to the American Philosophical Society.

Bloch and his wife, the former Lore Teutsch, met in Munich and married in the United States in 1941. They have two children, Peter and Susan. Bloch is known for his extreme modesty; when he was awarded the Nobel Prize, the *New York Times* reported that he refused to have his picture taken in front of a sign that read, "Hooray for Dr. Bloch!" He enjoys skiing and tennis, as well as music.

Further Reading

Modern Men of Science, McGraw-Hill, 1966, pp. 46–47.
Nobel Prize Winners, H.W. Wilson Company, 1987, p. 104.
Kennedy, E.P. and F. H. Westheimer, "Nobel Laureates: Bloch and Lynen Win Prize in Medicine and Physiology," in *Science*, October 23, 1964, pp. 504–506.
New York Times, October 16, 1964, pp. 1 and 3. □

Marc Bloch

The French historian Marc Bloch (1886-1944) was the leading French medievalist of the 20th century. He inspired two generations of historians through his teaching and writing.

M arc Bloch was born at Lyons on July 6, 1886, the son of Gustave Bloch, a professor of ancient history. Marc studied in Paris at the École Normale and the Fondation Thiers, in Berlin, and in Leipzig. During World War I he served in the infantry, winning four citations and the Legion of Honor. When the French University at Strasbourg was revived in 1919, Bloch went there to organize the seminar on medieval history. He remained until 1936, when he was called to the Sorbonne to succeed Henri Hauser in the chair of economic history.

In 1920 Bloch presented his thesis *Kings and Serfs*, in which he tried to discover what freedom and servitude meant in the Middle Ages. It was a question he pondered throughout his career, continuing his investigations in major articles of 1921, 1928, and 1933 and in the pages of his *Feudal Society*. The thesis was symptomatic of Bloch's interests and sympathies. He saw the problem of liberty and servitude as one involving economic structures and systems of belief as well as legal norms and institutional practices.

From then until his death he continued to affirm that history must concern itself with the whole man, that the economic or legal historian must be first of all a historian of civilization.

Bloch's interest in men and their beliefs inspired his second major work, *The Magic-working Kings* (1924), a study of the supernatural character attributed to kings in the Middle Ages, in particular the belief in their miraculous powers of healing. His interest in men and their works inspired a series of articles on the spread of labor-saving inventions in the Middle Ages, medieval monetary problems, rural land distribution, and many other topics. In all of these, as in a series of lectures, *The Original Characteristics of French Rural History* (1931), he insisted that the economic and technical questions he was discussing were also questions of "collective psychology."

In 1929 Bloch and Lucien Febvre founded the *Annales d'histoire économique et sociale* to provide a place for innovative historians to express their views. The two editors made themselves the champions of "history as one of the sciences of man" which the resources of sociology, psychology, economics, medicine, and all other disciplines that study man should be used to serve. Bloch also contributed to the *Revue de synthèse,* whose objective was to overcome the barriers between academic disciplines. His last historical work was *Feudal Society* (2 vols., 1939-1940), in which he described the legal institutions of feudalism in their broad cultural setting.

In 1939 Bloch was called back to the army. Avoiding capture in the defeat, he found refuge at Guéret, where he wrote a memoir of his war experiences, *The Strange Defeat* (1946). In this time of forced repose he also set down his reflections on his vocation, *The Historian's Craft*. The anti-Semitic laws soon forced him to leave the University of Paris for Clermont-Ferrand and then for Montpellier. When persecutions increased, he disappeared into the Resistance. In 1943 he reappeared briefly as "Blanchard," then as "Arpajon," "Chevreuse," and "Narbonne." Captured by the Germans in 1944, he was tortured and, on June 16, shot by a firing squad at Saint-Didier-de-Formans, near Lyons.

Further Reading

A moving personal memoir of Bloch by Lucien Febvre appears in Joseph Lambie, ed., *Architects and Craftsmen in History* (1956). John Higham and others, *History* (1965), and H. Stuart Hughes, *The Obstructed Path: French Social Thought in the Years of Desperation, 1930-1960* (1968), contain extensive material on Bloch. A useful background study is Michel François and others, *Historical Study in the West: France, Great Britain, Western Germany, the United States* (1968).

Additional Sources

Fink, Carole, *Marc Bloch: a life in history,* Cambridge; New York: Cambridge University Press, 1989. □

Herbert Block

The American newspaper cartoonist Herbert Block (born 1909), better known as Herblock, was concerned with civil liberties and the attacks on them by demagogues and dishonest politicians.

Herbert Block was born October 13, 1909, in Chicago, Illinois. His pen name, Herblock, was suggested to him by his father David Julian, a chemist. His brother William, who was his earliest mentor and also active in journalism, induced him to enter that field. Block's first books were dedicated to "Bill . . . , one of the best reporters in Chicago's newspaper history." His mother was Tessie, née Lupe. Endowed with a natural gift for drawing, he perfected it by attending the Chicago Art Institute part time; he also obtained a good general education at nearby Lake Forest College (1927-1929).

When only 19 Herblock began his career as journalist with the position of editorial cartoonist on the *Chicago Daily News* (1929-1933). He then moved to the Newspaper Enterprise Association (NEA) in Cleveland, Ohio, where his personal opinions, as always, guided his drawings toward a definite idea, which disturbed some of the management. As he explained, the NEA grew "really jittery about my cartoons because they were afraid that if a client cancelled the cartoon they'd cancel the whole service. So it got to be a tussle at NEA." The job ended when he joined the Army

Information and Education Division (1943-1945), where he rose to the rank of sergeant. After discharge he accepted the job of editorial cartoonist on the *Washington Post,* where he found editorial views compatible with his own and management that did not become "jittery." His cartoons were distributed by the Hall Syndicate and in the early 1950s appeared in 200 periodicals from Washington to Bangkok, including the *Manchester Guardian* and the *Economist* (London).

Herblock's cartoons were expressions of his personal concern for the human condition. He was a tireless searcher for truth and for the documents required to discover it. His cartoons were generally a product of this search. As he stated, "I've often summed up the essential role of the political cartoonist as being that of the kid in the Hans Christian Anderson story who says, 'The emperor has no clothes on.'" Truth emerged as Block saw it. He told *Time,* "My cartoons are opinion pieces and are recognized as such." Lowell Mellet, reviewing his work in the *New Republic,* observed that Herblock "sees things in a way that never would occur to anybody else. . . . He is truly a great cartoonist. He makes some people laugh. He makes some people swear. He makes everybody think."

In this light is is understandable that he produced many cartoons that attacked governmental policies intended to keep documents hidden from public scrutiny. It is important to remember that Herblock was still in the early years of his career when the Cold War broke out in the late 1940s and during its most tense phase in the 1950s. In his view far too many lower and medium level bureaucrats exercised their power to classify documents. Worse, they acted irresponsibly and capriciously, locking away information that had nothing to do with national security. They intended, rather, to remove from view data that would reveal wrong-doing and downright dishonesty in government. Numerous cartoons displayed the hostility of bureaucrats toward scientists, intellectuals, and even fellow civil servants who dared to raise their voices against the system. Careers of truly patriotic persons were ruined during this period.

It was the parading of false patriotism that particularly aroused him. He attained the height of his critical powers during the years when Joseph McCarthy was rampantly accusing persons in and out of government of communist sympathies or, worse, of being agents of the Soviet Union. To symbolize this dishonesty, Block displayed Senator McCarthy as an unshaven mud-slinger, smearing innocent people with unproven accusations dragged up from the sewer or garbage cans. He was convinced that the Federal Bureau of Investigation was involved in these violations of civil rights and wrote, "If the last refuge of a scoundrel is patriotism, apparently the final inner sanctum of that refuge, for those who have made a racket of anti-communism, is the FBI." He was equally convinced that McCarthy personified a dangerous current of the times, enjoying wide support. "No demagogue," he wrote, "is an island of mud unto himself."

From the later 1950s Richard Nixon became the chief villain. To journalists and politicians who showed only complacency to Nixon, and who excused him by trying to hold to middle-of-the-road politics, he affirmed, "I don't know what's so fascinating about the 'middle of the road,' but for a lot of people this position has the kind of magnetic attraction that a coffee cup has for cigarette ashes; and it's regarded as the ideal place to dump any kind of decision. . . . In a choice between right or wrong, I think something better than a middle-of-the-road policy is needed." President Eisenhower held that position, and in Block's cartoons he is consistently depicted as a weak, ineffective politician, the unwitting partner of Richard Nixon. The cartoonist brought to light dishonest deals carried on by Nixon long before the Watergate scandal.

Block served the public well and he was widely honored: National Headliners' Club awards, 1940 and 1976; Pulitzer prizes in cartooning, 1942, 1954, and 1979; Heywood Broun Award from the American Newspaper Guild, 1949; Sigma Delta Chi (national journalism society) awards, 1949, 1950, 1952, and 1957; Sidney Hillman Award, 1953; Reuben Award (National Cartoonists Society), 1957; LL.D. from Lake Forest College, 1957, and Rutgers University, 1963; *Parents' Magazine* award for service to education, 1958; Lauterbach award for defending civil liberties, 1959; F. Lasker Award of New York Civil Liberties Union, 1960; distinguished service in journalism award of The University of Missouri, 1961; Golden Key Award, 1963; Capital Press Club Award, 1963; Bill of Rights Day Award, 1966; L.H.D. from Williams College (1969), Haverford College (1977), and University of Maryland (1977); Power of Print Award, 1977, and Fourth Estate Award, 1977, from National Press Club; American Cancer Society citation, 1979; Overseas Press Club citation, 1979 and 1994; human relations award from The National Education Association, 1979; World Hunger Media Award, 1984; Good Guy Award, National Woman's Political Caucus, 1989; Exceptional Merit Media Award, 1990; and the Thomas Nast Award, Overseas Press Club, 1995.

Block's books reproduced his cartoons and their captions and provide a more extensive commentary on his times. They put his cartoons in their historical setting. He sometimes wondered whether, given the menace of the atomic bomb, there would be any historians in the future— even any future. If there are, they will find in these works an invaluable commentary on Block's times.

Further Reading

There are no books on Herblock. There are some details on his career and ideas, as well as probing evaluation of his books and cartoons, in a large number of reviews. The most important of these are: *New York Post Magazine,* May 23, 1965; *Commonweal,* November 14, 1952, November 27, 1964, and February 9, 1973; *New York Times,* April 17, 1979; *Time,* January 23, 1950, and December 12, 1977; *New Republic,* October 13, 1952, May 17, 1954, January 23 and March 12, 1956, and December 15, 1958. □

Aleksandr Aleksandrovich Blok

The Russian poet Aleksandr Aleksandrovich Blok (1880-1921) was a leading figure in the Russian symbolist movement. His strongly rhythmic poetry is characterized by metaphysical imagery, dramatic use of legend, and responsiveness to history and to social life.

Aleksandr Blok was born in St. Petersburg on Nov. 28, 1880. His father was a professor of law, and his mother a writer and translator; Blok thus grew up in an upper-class intellectual milieu. Summers were spent at Shakhmatovo, the Bloks' country home near Moscow. There the famous chemist D. I. Mendeleev was a neighbor, and in 1903 Blok married Mendeleev's daughter.

Blok had begun to write as a boy. In 1903 some of his poems were published in D. S. Merezhkovski's magazine, the *New Way*. Blok's first book, the strongly symbolistic *Verses about the Beautiful Lady,* appeared in 1904. Although most critics ignored the volume, it was greeted enthusiastically by Valery Bryusov, Andrei Bely, and the "older generation" of Russian symbolists, and Blok's poetry and reviews soon appeared regularly in their magazines.

Bryusov, the editor of the *Balance* and a leading symbolist theorist and poet, strongly influenced Blok in the years 1903 and 1904. Under Bryusov's guidance Blok turned to themes of city life and began to use fresh rhythmic patterns and images that expressed the mysterious power of sensual love. Among his notable poems of this period are "The Swamp Demon," "The Unknown Lady," "The Night Violet," "The Snow Mask," "The Factory," and "From the Newspapers." The last two indicate Blok's growing social awareness.

By 1906, when he graduated from the philological faculty of St. Petersburg University, Blok was a recognized poet. That year Vsevolod Meyerhold directed and starred in Blok's one-act verse play, *The Puppet Show*. Though admired in literary circles, the play was never a popular success. Blok wrote several other plays, including the full-length *The Rose and the Cross* (1913), which was based on medieval French romances. Although rehearsed by Stanislavski's Moscow Art Theater, this play was not presented.

In 1907-1908 Blok was a reviewer for the magazine *Golden Fleece*. His articles combined evaluations of contemporary literature with a longing for the Russian past and for a vital connection between the intelligentsia and the people. In "Russia" and "On Kulikovo Field" (both 1908), he searched for a way to bring national history to bear on the present.

Despite his feelings of personal failure, from 1909 to 1916 Blok wrote poetry of high artistic achievement. "The Terrible World," "In the Restaurant," "Night Hours," and "Dances of Death" are particularly indicative of his spiritual turmoil. Blok and his wife had a stormy marital relationship, but during a temporary reconciliation they traveled in Italy in 1909. This trip inspired Blok's exquisite cycle *Italian Poems* (1909).

During World War I Blok served as a clerk with a forward engineers' company. He greeted the 1917 Revolution sympathetically. Indeed, his poem *The Twelve* (1918), a combined lyric and narrative about 12 Red Guardsmen on city patrol, synthesizes Christian values and reformist principles. It brought Blok even wider popularity and enduring fame. The revolutionary leader Leon Trotsky remarked that although Blok was not "one of us," *The Twelve* was "the most significant work of our time." In his long, unfinished, autobiographical poem *Retribution,* Blok summarized social change at the turn of the century.

Under the Soviet government Blok was a member of the directorate of the state theaters and chairman of the Petrograd section of the Poets' Union. Hard times, political bitterness, and his own confused life made him old at 40. In one of his last published works, *The Decline of Humanism* (1921), he lamented the dissipation of European style and the loss of heroes who could persuade men to act rationally in true self-interest. Blok died in Petrograd on Aug. 7, 1921.

Further Reading

Many studies of Blok in Russian have recently appeared, as well as a new edition of his complete works. Studies in English are Cecil Kisch, *Alexander Blok, Prophet of Revolution: A Study of His Life and Work* (1960); Franklin D. Reeve, *Alexander Blok: Between Image and Idea* (1962); and Robin Kemball, *Alexander Blok: A Study in Rhythm and Metre* (1965). See also Renato Poggioli, *The Poets of Russia, 1890-1930* (1960).

Additional Sources

Berberova, Nina Nikolaevna, *Aleksandr Blok: a life,* New York: George Braziller, 1996.

Chukovskaeei, Korneaei, *Alexander Blok as man and poet,* Ann Arbor, Mich.: Ardis, 1982.

Forsyth, James, *Listening to the wind: an introduction to Alexander Blok,* Oxford Eng.: W. A. Meeuws, 1977.

Mochulskiaei, K. (Konstantin), *Aleksandr Blok,* Detroit: Wayne State Univ. Press, 1983.

Orlov, Vladimir Nikolaevich, *Hamayun, the life of Alexander Blok,* Moscow: Progress, 1980.

Pyman, Avril, *The life of Aleksandr Blok,* Oxford Eng.; New York: Oxford University Press, 1979-1980. □

Allan David Bloom

Allan David Bloom (1930-1992) was an American political philosopher, professor, and author. An advocate of the Western philosophical tradition, he translated classic authors such as Plato and Rousseau, but he was best known for his criticism of American higher education and what he felt was the decline of liberal education.

Allan David Bloom was born in Indianapolis, Indiana, on September 14, 1930, to Allan and Malvina (Glasner) Bloom, both of whom were social workers of Jewish descent. The parents nurtured their son's intellectual curiosity and encouraged him to excel educationally. When the family moved to Chicago in 1946, 15-year-old Allan was immediately impressed with the University of Chicago and, as he later said, "somehow sensed that I had discovered my life" (*Closing of the American Mind,* 1987). At the age of 16 he entered that university's special program for gifted high school students where he studied the classics of Western literature in a curriculum strongly influenced by Robert M. Hutchins, a former president of the university.

Bloom received a B.A. degree from the University of Chicago in 1949 and began graduate work in cross-disciplinary studies with the elite Committee on Social Thought program. Here he came under the influence of Leo Strauss, a German immigrant and political philosopher who taught that some truths did not change but endured across the generations. Bloom came to believe that the goal of a truly liberal education should be to help students define themselves by those truths.

After completing his M.A. degree in 1953, Bloom attended the University of Paris in an exchange program with the University of Chicago, and he earned a Ph.D. degree in 1955. He then joined the faculty at the University of Chicago as a lecturer in political science, a position he held until 1962. In the 1957-1958 academic year he was a Rockefeller fellow in legal and political philosophy and did postgraduate study at the University of Heidelberg. In 1960 he published his first book, *Rousseau's Politics and Art: Letter to M. D'Alambert on the Theatre.*

Leaving Chicago in 1962, Bloom next served as a visiting assistant professor at Yale University, but in 1963 he moved to Cornell University as assistant professor of political science. He completed *Shakespeare's Politics* in 1964 and was tenured in 1965. At Cornell, Bloom developed a provocative and stimulating teaching style that could make students feel that learning was a rare privilege. As one student observed, "Allan did not just make old texts speak, he made them sing" (Clifford Orwin, "Remembering Allan Bloom," 1993). In 1968, he completed his translation of Plato's *Republic.*

The late 1960s was a time of widespread student protest, and at Cornell an armed group of students seized a campus building and demanded that the traditional humanities curriculum be changed in favor of more "relevant" studies. In Bloom's opinion, the Cornell authorities made cowardly concessions and dropped courses that were essential to the curriculum. Dismayed, he took leave and went to the University of Tel Aviv and then to the University of Paris as a visiting professor during the 1969-1970 academic year. In 1970 he resigned from Cornell and accepted a professorship in political science at the University of Toronto, where he completed his translation of Rousseau's *Emile (or, on Education)* in 1979. That same year he returned to the University of Chicago as a full professor with the Committee on Social Thought, and remained there until his death on October 8, 1992.

For most of his career, Bloom was known in academic circles mainly for his translations of Rousseau and Plato, but the publication of *The Closing of the American Mind* in 1987 brought him fame and fortune, praise and vilification. In this best-seller, Bloom argued that cultural relativism threatened to extinguish the "real motive of education, the search for the good life." Furthermore, relativism was "unproven and dogmatically asserted" for mainly political reasons, and it would destroy "the West's universal or intellectually imperialistic claims, leaving it to be just another culture." Too many Americans embraced a view of "openness" that made "surrender to whatever is most powerful, or worship of vulgar success, look principled;" instead, Bloom called for a university that stood "intransigently for humane learning," a place where "True openness means closedness to all the charms that make us comfortable with the present." What students needed, Bloom argued, was immersion in the enduring works of Western culture such as Plato's *Republic,* which was "*the* book on education" because it showed how "the real community of man" was a community of "those who seek the truth . . . , of all men to the extent they desire to know. But in fact this only includes a few."

A storm of controversy followed publication of *The Closing of the American Mind.* Some readers accepted Bloom's views as accurate descriptions of American colleges and universities. Advocates championed his defense of traditional Western values as a forceful support of cultural and political conservatism. Numerous critics attacked the book for advocating an elitist education, and others criticized its failure to recognize historical change. Some critics saw value in studying classic philosophers but argued that this was inadequate in a modern world plagued with problems such authors could not possibly have foreseen or understood. Opinion on the value of Bloom's book was heated and divided, but if Bloom intended to spark debate on higher education, he was highly successful.

Bloom completed two other books before his death in 1992: *Giants and Dwarfs* (1990) and *Love and Friendship* (1993). The first continued some of the themes of educational criticism, while the second, published posthumously, explored the classical theme of eros and its modern interpretations. Both were analyses of Bloom's favorite authors, but neither approached the popular appeal of *The Closing of the American Mind.*

Further Reading

Allan David Bloom is listed in *Who's Who in America* (1988). For a sympathetic but balanced treatment of Bloom as a teacher, see Clifford Orwin, "Remembering Allan Bloom," *American Scholar* (Summer 1993). For a critical review of his educational philosophy, see Nancy Warehime, *To Be One of Us: Cultural Conflict, Creative Democracy, and Education* (1993). A number of obituaries were written on Bloom, and one of the more accessible is Anthony DePalma, "Allan Bloom, Critic of Universities, Is Dead at 62," *New York Times Biographical Service* (October 1992). Literally scores of reviews were written on Bloom's *The Closing of the American*

Mind (1987), and at least two journals devoted complete issues to the work: *Modern Age* (Winter 1988) and *Interchange* (January/February 1991). ☐

Amelia Jenks Bloomer

An American advocate of woman's rights in the early days of the feminist movement, Amelia Jenks Bloomer (1818-1894) spent most of her life working for the cause. She was also a reformer of women's clothing and helped promote "bloomers."

Amelia Jenks was born into a family of modest means in Homer, N.Y., on May 27, 1818. Her formal education was negligible, consisting of only a few years in grammar school. At the age of 22 she married Dexter Bloomer, a lawyer and part owner of the *Seneca Falls County Courier*. A man of Quaker background and progressive social principles, he encouraged his wife to write articles on temperance and other social issues for his newspaper and for other periodicals.

In 1848, at the age of 30, Bloomer attended the first public Woman's Rights Convention at Seneca Falls, N.Y., but she took no part in the proceedings. A few months later she began to publish her own temperance newspaper, *The Lily*, which was immensely successful, gaining a circulation of 4,000 within a few years. At this time in her career Amelia Bloomer was a small, slight, dark-haired woman with good features and a pleasant expression. Timid and retiring by nature, she was a sternly serious person, seemingly lacking in any sense of humor.

Prodded by Elizabeth Cady Stanton, who also lived in Seneca Falls, Bloomer devoted increasing space in *The Lily* to questions concerning woman's rights, such as unequal educational opportunities, discriminatory marriage and property laws, and suffrage. In 1851 *The Lily* supported the reform in women's dress which came to bear Bloomer's name. Female fashion in the 1850s consisted of unhealthy, tightly laced corsets, layers of petticoats that could weigh well over 10 pounds, and floor-length dresses that dragged in the filth of the era's unpaved and unswept streets. The bloomer costume dispensed with corsets in favor of loose bodices, substituted baggy ankle-length pantaloons for petticoats, and cut the gowns to above the knee. Such a costume had been worn at the utopian New Harmony colony in Indiana in the 1820s and as resort wear during the 1830s, and Mrs. Bloomer was by no means the originator of the revival in 1851. But her promotion of it attached her name to the sensation. Woman's-rights advocates, such as Elizabeth Cady Stanton and Susan B. Anthony, wore the reform dress for a year or so but abandoned it when they concluded that the ridicule it frequently elicited was preventing a fair hearing of their views. Mrs. Bloomer continued to wear the dress until the late 1850s, but, conservative by nature (she never shared the liberal religious views or abolitionist senti-

ments of her sisters in the movement), even she eventually opposed bloomers as inexpedient.

Bloomer moved to Council Bluffs, Iowa, in 1855, where she abandoned *The Lily* but continued to work actively in the woman's-suffrage movement of that state. She lectured and wrote widely, served as president of the state Woman Suffrage Association between 1871 and 1873, and corresponded with and arranged lectures for Lucy Stone, Susan B. Anthony, and Elizabeth Cady Stanton in Iowa. She retired increasingly into private life in the 1870s, troubled by poor health. She died at Council Bluffs on the last day of 1894.

Amelia Bloomer's work never matched the incessant and selfless activity of some of her contemporaries, but she contributed to the suffrage movement far more profoundly than the generally facetious use of her name would indicate.

Further Reading

Bloomer's husband, Dexter C. Bloomer, published the *Life and Writings of Amelia Bloomer* (1895) shortly after her death. Most of the general works on the 19th century woman's-suffrage movement take note of her. The most valuable work treating her career in some detail is Louise R. Noun, *Strong-Minded Women: The Emergence of the Woman-Suffrage Movement in Iowa* (1970). See also Eleanor Flexner, *Century of Struggle: The Woman's Rights Movement in The United States* (1959); Robert W. Smuts, *Women and Work in America* (1959); Aileen S. Kraditor, *The Ideas of the Woman Suffrage Movement, 1890-1920* (1965); Andrew Sinclair, *The Better Half: The Emancipation of American Women* (1965); and William L. O'Neill, *Everyone Was Brave* (1969). ☐

Leonard Bloomfield

The influence of the American linguist Leonard Bloomfield (1887-1949) dominated the science of linguistics from 1933—when his most important work, *Language*, was published—to the mid-1950s.

Leonard Bloomfield was born on April 1, 1887, in Chicago. He graduated from Harvard College at the age of 19 and did graduate work for 2 years at the University of Wisconsin, where he also taught German. His interest in linguistics was aroused by Eduard Prokosch, a philologist in the German department. Bloomfield received his doctorate from the University of Chicago in 1909.

After teaching German at the University of Cincinnati for a year, Bloomfield became assistant professor of comparative philology and German at the University of Illinois, where he remained until 1921. His *An Introduction to the Study of Language* was published in 1914.

In 1913-1914 Bloomfield studied in Leipzig and Göttingen, Germany, with the neogrammarian scholars August Leskien and Karl Brugmann. Neogrammarian historical philology emphasized the regularity of sound change in language without exceptions, any apparent exceptions being explained in terms of nonphonetic phenomena. This view represented a scientific advance over the earlier view that extraordinary, inexplicable sound change can take place. Bloomfield emphasized throughout his career the scientific neogrammarian methodology of seeking out regularity in sound change rather than appealing to random, meaningless change. This approach brought much order to historical linguistics.

Bloomfield adopted Ferdinand de Saussure's concept of language structure. Saussure emphasized that languages at any one time were systems of interrelated elements: lexical, grammatic, phonological. Bloomfield accepted Saussure's distinction between a diachronous (time being a variable) approach and a synchronous (time being a constant) approach to language. He utilized both approaches in his work. He envisaged diachronous language change in the course of the history of a language as a succession of language structures, each viewed synchronously.

Franz Boas was the first anthropological linguist to emphasize descriptive study of non-Indo-European languages as they exist today. Bloomfield, who acknowledged his debt to Boas, emphasized the value of synchronic descriptive linguistics, though he never deserted diachronic historical linguistics. Though trained in historical Indo-European, especially Germanic, philology, Bloomfield turned to a study of Tagalog, a Malayo-Polynesian language, during World War I. In 1917 he became interested in a more accessible language family, the Algonquian. His linguistic work with Indians of the Algonquian family in Wisconsin was not only descriptive; he also applied historical linguistic techniques to this language family. He showed that the neogrammarian methodology of assuming regularity in sound change was applicable beyond the Indo-European language family.

In 1921 Bloomfield became professor of German and linguistics at Ohio State University. There he met the behaviorist psychologist A. P. Weiss. Both men took a logical positivist approach to science; they agreed that a mechanistic rather than a mentalistic approach to human phenomena was necessary if the disciplines concerned with man were to be truly scientific.

Bloomfield was one of the founders of the Linguistic Society of America in 1924. He was professor of Germanic philology at the University of Chicago from 1927 to 1940, when he became professor of linguistics at Yale University. He died in New Haven, Conn., on April 18, 1949.

Influence of *Language*

In *Language* Bloomfield emphasized the need to be objective, to deal only with physically observable phenomena, and to develop a precise description and definition in order to make linguistics a true science. The period from the publication of *Language* in 1933 to the mid-1950s is commonly called the "Bloomfieldian era" of linguistics. Though Bloomfield's particular methodology of descriptive linguistics was not widely accepted, his mechanistic attitudes toward a precise science of linguistics, dealing only with observable phenomena, were most influential. His influence waned after the 1950s, when adherence to logical positivist doctrines lessened and there was a return to more mentalistic attitudes. Today linguists, especially the younger ones, are more concerned with the directly nonobservable mental processes by which human beings are uniquely capable of generating language.

Further Reading

Obituaries by Bernard Bloch and Edgar H. Sturtevant are reprinted in Thomas A. Sebeok, ed., *Portraits of Linguists*, vol. 2 (1966). Although Bloomfield claimed his linguistics to be free of any psychological school, Erwin A. Esper in *Mentalism and Objectivism in Linguistics: The Sources of Leonard Bloomfield's Psychology of Language* (1968) argues that Bloomfield was influenced in important ways by behaviorism. C. C. Fries in a chapter in Christine Mohrmann and others, eds., *Trends in European and American Linguistics, 1930-1960* (1961), contends that behaviorism was not an important influence on Bloomfield.

Additional Sources

Hall, Robert Anderson, *A life for language: a biographical memoir of Leonard Bloomfield,* Amsterdam; Philadelphia: J. Benjamins Pub. Co., 1990.

Leonard Bloomfield, essays on his life and work, Amsterdam; Philadelphia: J. Benjamins Pub. Co., 1987. ☐

Ella Reeve Bloor

Ella Reeve "Mother" Bloor (1862-1951) was an American leader in fighting for the rights of those she characterized as "the world's unfortunates," and worked tirelessly as a labor organizer, Communist leader, and social activist.

Mother Bloor is one of the most tireless and accomplished crusaders and agitators the United States has ever seen. Over more than 60 years she worked for woman's suffrage, the Women's Christian Temperance Union, organized and raised funds for such causes as the Sacco-Vanzetti case and the American League against War and Fascism, and also served as an accomplished labor organizer. A radical activist, Ella Bloor had little patience with ideological debate. Her single goal was "to make life happier for the world's unfortunates."

Early Life

Reeve was born July 8, 1862 near Mariner's Harbor on Staten Island and grew up there and in New Jersey, the self-described daughter of "a rich old Republican over on Staten Island." Her ancestors had fought in the Revolutionary and Civil wars. She attended public schools, briefly went to the Ivy Hall Seminary, and then was taught by her mother at home. When Reeve was 17, her mother died in childbirth, and Ella was responsible for caring for her nine younger siblings.

Early Political Interests and First Marriage

Reeve's father leaned toward political and religious conservatism, so that when she became interested in social and political reform as a teenager, she turned to her great uncle, Dan Ware, who was an abolitionist, Unitarian, and freethinker. Ware had a strong influence on her intellectual

growth. When she was 19 Reeve married Dan Ware's son, Lucien Ware, an aspiring lawyer. She gave birth to six children over eleven years, Grace, Harold, Helen, Buzz, and two who died in infancy. During those years Ella Ware was introduced to the woman's suffrage movement and became active in the Women's Christian Temperance Union and the Ethical Culture Society of Philadelphia. She also became interested in the labor movement and organized the Philadelphia streetcar workers in the early 1890s.

Her political activism caused tension in her marriage, and the couple separated and were divorced in 1896. However, Lucien Ware was not apolitical himself. He would go on to receive the Order of Lenin for helping the Soviet Union with the mechanization and collectivization of its agriculture, led the charge for the U.S. Communist Party's agrarian reform program, and introduced Alger Hiss to Whittaker Chambers in 1934 before dying in an automobile accident in 1935.

Second Divorce and Radical Exploration

After her divorce Reeve was active and independent, exploring possible occupations. She took courses at the University of Pennsylvania and wrote two children's books. She and her children then moved to the utopian community of Arden, Delaware, which was established by socialists. In 1897 she married socialist Louis Cohen, and the couple had two children, Richard and Carl, but were separated in 1902 and later divorced.

Political Activism

Reeve then became a political activist. She was always committed to improving the status of women but devoted her energies to left-wing politics and the labor movement. Ella Cohen met Eugene Debs in 1895, and he convinced her of the necessity of socialism. She joined the Socialist Labor Party in 1901. In 1905 she moved to Connecticut and became the state organizer for the party.

In 1906 her friend, writer Upton Sinclair, urged Ella Cohen to investigate conditions in the Chicago meatpacking industry. Sinclair wanted her to gather evidence for a government investigation documenting the charges he made against the industry in *The Jungle*. Richard Bloor, a fellow socialist and young pottery worker, went along to protect her. Sinclair feared it would be scandalous to have an unmarried team of investigators and convinced Ella Cohen to publish the reports under the name Ella Bloor. Although the couple quickly split up, she continued to use the name Ella Bloor for the rest of her life.

I would be too conspicuous going about unescorted to saloons and other places where men gather and talk," the *New York Times* quoted her as explaining. "In explaining the investigation to the public, Upton Sinclair thought it best to refer to us as Mr. and Mrs. Bloor, and the name has clung to me ever since. Richard Bloor was a Welsh immigrant, about half my age, and there was no romance associated with our association."

Socialism

Bloor spent the next twelve years organizing for the Socialist Party and for the United Cloth Hat and Cap Makers Union. Her work on behalf of coal miners won her an honorary membership in the United Mine Workers of America. Bloor opposed World War I as imperialist and was arrested for antiwar activities. In 1918 she was Socialist Party candidate for lieutenant governor of New York. Disillusioned by the support of many Socialist Party leaders for the war, in 1919 Bloor helped form the Communist party and the Communist Labor party, which soon merged. Bloor worked devotedly for the party for the rest of her life, recruiting members from among miners, farmers, machinists, steelworkers, and needle workers.

In 1925, at the age of 63, Ella Bloor hitchhiked from New York to San Francisco on a cross-country tour for the *Daily Worker.* She held meetings in cities along the way, recruiting party members and selling subscriptions. In the 1920s she was active in the unsuccessful defense of Nicola Sacco and Bartolomeo Vanzetti. She also continued her labor organizing work, traveling to the coal mines to support strikers.

The 1930s

When the Depression hit, Mother Bloor, as she was then called, went to Washington to join the hunger marches of the unemployed. By the 1930s, when she was in her seventies, Mother Bloor was a sought-after speaker for the Communist Party, traveled extensively, and served as middlewestern regional secretary of the Farmers National Conference. While traveling to North Dakota to rally support for the United Farmers' League, she met Andrew Omholt, a farmer, party organizer and Communist Party candidate for Congress in North Dakota who soon became her third husband. She continued her party campaigning and labor organizing through the 1930s. In 1937 she made her second visit to the Soviet Union as an honored guest at the celebration of the 20th anniversary of the October Revolution. She visited that country several times, twice as a delegate to the Red International of Trade Unions, and once extolled the Soviets for their "democratic success."

At the age of 72 in 1936 she served a 30-day jail sentence in Nebraska after a mass farmers protest meeting. Her final campaign was during World War II, when she spoke at public rallies and on the radio on the theme "Win the War Against Fascism." In her lifelong fight for the "world's unfortunates," Mother Bloor suffered more than 30 arrests (although she claimed it was over 100), countless threats of violence, and frequent harassment by police.

On March 2, 1951 Bloor suffered a spinal injury from a fall near her home at Coopersburg, Pennsylvania, about 40 miles north of Philadelphia. During her several-month stay at Quakertown Hospital she received visitors from across the country, most of whom she was unable to recognize. Hospital attendants said she sang often during her stay, especially "The Star-Spangled Banner," singing all four verses. She spent a short time in a convalescent home before her death on August 10, 1951 from a stroke.

Further Reading

Thomas L. Edwards and Richard C. Edwards, "Ella Reeve Bloor," in *Notable American Women: The Modern Period,* edited by Barbara Sicherman, Carol Hurd Green, Ilene Kantrov, and Harriette Walker (Cambridge, Mass.: Harvard University Press, 1980), pp. 85-87. □

Gebhard Leberecht von Blücher

The Prussian field marshal Gebhard Leberecht von Blücher (1742-1819) commanded the Prussian armies in the war against Napoleon, 1813-1815. He became a leading hero of the Germans in the struggle to end foreign domination of their lands.

Gebhard von Blücher was born in Rostock in the northern state of Mecklenburg on Dec. 16, 1742. The son of a captain in the cavalry, he became a cadet in a Swedish regiment. He was captured by the Prussians during the Seven Years War and, like so many others, allowed himself to be pressed into the Prussian service. He had reached the rank of captain when, in 1770, Frederick the Great dismissed him in his usual brutal fashion for some minor transgression.

After Frederick's death Blücher rejoined the Prussian army. He distinguished himself in the wars against revolutionary France and eventually became a general. Fortunately for Blücher, he had not been given a major command in the disastrous campaign of 1806, so he escaped its disgrace. As it was, he was forced to surrender to the French in the later stages of that campaign. Both the Prussian chancellor, Prince Hardenberg, and the minister of war, G. J. D. von Scharnhorst, thought highly of Blücher's talents; thus in 1809 he was given command of the Prussian cavalry with orders to reform and modernize it. In 1811, however, he was dismissed at Napoleon's insistence.

At the outbreak of war between Prussia and France in 1813, Blücher was given command of a joint Russo-Prussian army. After defeating the French in three engagements and recapturing Leipzig from them in October 1813, Blücher was promoted to field marshal. His impetuosity and dynamism, which contrasted sharply with the conduct of the generals of Prussia's other ally, Austria, earned him the nickname of "Marshal Forward."

In 1814 Blücher commanded the Prussian army that attacked France. After an initial success he was outmaneuvered by Napoleon and lost a series of engagements. Although he was forced to retreat across the border, Blücher was undaunted by this reverse. He resumed the attack as soon as his defeated army was assembled and rested, and he soon won a major victory over Napoleon at the Battle of Laon (March 10, 1814). Blücher then joined his army with that of the Austrians under Prince

Schwarzenberg, and at the end of the month the Allies entered Paris and forced Napoleon to abdicate.

When the Emperor returned from his exile in Elba in 1815, Blücher was once again given command of the main Prussian army. Napoleon planned to defeat his enemies one at a time, thus forcing them to accept his return; he almost succeeded. Blücher, who was badly outmaneuvered, faced the French alone in the Battle of Ligny (June 16). He lost the battle, a good part of his army, and came close to losing his life. Fortunately for the Prussians, Blücher's chief of staff, Count August Gneisenau, was able to organize an orderly retreat in the direction of the English army, which was under the command of the Duke of Wellington. Napoleon had preceded Wellington and came within an ace of beating the English at Waterloo (June 18). But the English infantry held, and the arrival of Blücher's diminished army was enough to turn the tide once and for all against the French.

Prussia's success in the Napoleonic Wars was due as much to Gneisenau's organization and planning as to Blücher's leadership, and the field marshal readily acknowledged this circumstance. But it was the grizzled and energetic Blücher who captured the imagination of the Prussians, and many other Germans as well, becoming perhaps the first German national hero. Blücher died on Sept. 12, 1819, in Silesia.

Further Reading

E. F. Henderson, *Blücher and the Uprising of Prussia against Napoleon, 1806-1815* (1911), discusses Blücher and the mili-

tary campaigns of the period. A more general study is W. O. Shanahan, *Prussian Military Reforms, 1786-1813* (1945). See also J. F. C. Fuller, *A Military History of the Western World*, vol. 2 (1955), and Hajo Holborn, *History of Modern Germany*, vol. 2 (1963).

Additional Sources

Parkinson, Roger, *The Hussar general: the life of Blücher, man of Waterloo*, London: P. Davies, 1975. □

Guion Stewart Bluford Jr.

As a fighter pilot in Vietnam, Guion Stewart Bluford, Jr. (born 1942) flew 144 combat missions and attained the rank of lieutenant colonel. On August 30, 1983, with the lift-off of the STS-8 Orbiter *Challenger*, he became the first African American in space.

Distinguished pilot and aeronautics engineer Guy Bluford was the first black American to experience space flight. Bluford has flown three missions on the Space Shuttle, performing various experiments and returning to earth with exhilarating memories of his time in orbit. Although others have hailed the Philadelphia native as a hero and a role model for the black race, Bluford—who has earned a Ph.D. in aeronautical engineering—prefers to think of himself as a man whose accomplishments are not related to his skin color. He says that he would rather be seen simply as an astronaut, not a *black* astronaut, one of a hard-working corps and not a pioneer. "I felt an awesome responsibility, and I took the responsibility very seriously, of being a role model and opening another door to black Americans," he said of his Shuttle flights in the *Philadelphia Inquirer*. "But the important thing is not that I am black, but that I did a good job as a scientist and an astronaut. There will be black astronauts flying in later missions . . . and they, too, will be people who excel, not simply who are black . . . who can ably represent their people, their communities, their country."

Washington Post correspondent Bill Prochnau called Bluford's life "a study in contradictions: the story of a shy and reticent youth who will be known to history as a black pioneer, a youngster whose mother once thought him the least likely of her three sons to make a success of himself, a struggling student who persevered to earn a master's degree and a doctorate, a loner who says he has no best friends and no heroes but who is . . . seen as a hero himself, a self-described 'average guy' who became far more than average by pressing on when things got tough and by setting each new goal only after the last had been achieved."

Early Years in Philadelphia

Bluford, known in his youth by the nickname "Bunny," grew up in a middle-class, racially mixed neighborhood in Philadelphia. Both of his parents hailed from families of

distinction. His mother, Lolita, was related to Carol Brice Carey, a well-known contralto and voice coach, and his father, Guion, Sr., was the brother of the editor of the *Kansas City Call.* Bluford's parents also had advanced educations. His father was a mechanical engineer until epilepsy forced him to retire early, and his mother worked as a special education teacher in the city's public schools.

Bluford was a quiet, private child who reportedly had few friends. He liked to spend his spare time building model airplanes and working crossword puzzles. He told the *Philadelphia Inquirer* that he was fascinated with his father's attitude toward work. "He would charge out of the house every morning, eager to get to work," Bluford said. "I thought if engineers enjoy work that much, it must be a good thing to get into."

Bluford was deeply moved and inspired by his father's courageous struggle with ill health. Determined to become an aeronautics engineer, the young man devoted himself to his studies. On one occasion, a guidance counselor at Overbrook, the mostly white high school he attended, suggested that Bluford might not be college material. Nevertheless, he was able to maintain a C-plus average in the school's most difficult math and science courses. Bluford's brother Kenneth told the *Washington Post:* "Bunny just had to work harder than the rest of us. He put in very long hours. He was always a little behind and trying to catch up. He was not like a kid who was unusually bright, with his mind darting all over the place, making discoveries here and there. In school, Bunny was always slugging it out."

Bluford's parents paid no attention to the suggestion that their son would not succeed in college. In 1960 they sent him to Pennsylvania State University, where he was the only black student in the engineering school. He attended college on the Reserve Officers' Training Corps plan and once again earned adequate, if not exceptional grades. Barnes McCormick, a professor of aerospace engineering at Penn State, told the *Washington Post* that Bluford was "a quiet fellow and an average student, not the sort you would expect to be interviewed about 20 years later."

Fighter Pilot in Vietnam

During his senior year at Penn State, Bluford married another Philadelphian, Linda Tull. After graduating in 1964, he joined the U.S. Air Force and took flight training. He was assigned to the 557th Tactical Fighter Squadron at Cam Ram Bay in Vietnam, where he flew 144 combat missions, 65 of them over North Vietnam. His family at home was split philosophically about the war, but Bluford saw his activities in Vietnam as a patriotic duty that he needed to perform to the best of his ability. He earned numerous medals and citations for his flying, including an Air Force Commendation medal. He returned home a lieutenant colonel and began to work as a test pilot for new air force equipment.

Referring to Bluford's transformation from average student to extraordinary military officer and engineer, *Philadelphia Inquirer* contributor Fawn Vrazo observed: "Between 1964, the year he graduated from Penn State, and 1978, the year he received a doctoral degree in engineering . . . something remarkable happened to Guy Bluford. School and military records suggest that he put himself through an incredible honing process—tightening up his determination and work habits until he became a perfectly disciplined and motivated specimen of an Air Force career pilot and engineer." Bluford was one of a handful of candidates chosen to attend the Air Force Institute of Technology near Dayton, Ohio. There he received his master's and doctoral degrees in aerospace engineering, with a minor in laser physics. He ranked consistently among the top ten percent of his class. He also continued to work as a test pilot and an instructor for would-be military aviators.

In 1978 Bluford submitted his application to the Space Shuttle program. He knew he had little chance of acceptance—some eight thousand other military personnel had also applied for only 35 openings. When he received the call telling him of his selection, he quietly celebrated the news with his wife and two sons. He told the *Philadelphia Inquirer* that he and several other black aviators who are now astronauts "had to be ready in 1977 and 1978, when the doors of opportunity were opened to us and the cloak of prejudice was raised. As black scientists and engineers and aviators, we had to prove that black people could excel."

Flew Space Shuttle Missions

Bluford was not the first black man in space—a Cuban astronaut had flown with the Soviet Union's space program. Bluford was, however, the first black American to be a member of a space flight. After years of training, he was named to the Shuttle's eighth mission, which commenced on August 30, 1983. The week-long mission marked the first nighttime Shuttle launch and landing, and multiple experiments were performed during the flight. Upon returning to earth, Bluford discovered somewhat to his dismay that he was a national celebrity. He was greeted ceremoniously in a number of America's biggest cities, especially Philadelphia, and was in great demand as a public speaker. Bluford accepted this role reluctantly, protesting that he was simply another member of the Space Shuttle team.

"It might be a bad thing [to be first], if you stop and think about it," Bluford told the *Washington Post.* "It might be better to be second or third because then you can enjoy it and disappear—return to the society you came out of without someone always poking you in the side and saying you were first." Tragically, the second black American in space, Ronald E. McNair, perished in the 1986 explosion of the Space Shuttle Challenger.

The Challenger disaster did little to dampen Bluford's enthusiasm for space travel, however. Of the two missions he has flown since 1983, one was a post-Challenger flight undertaken in 1991 to observe such phenomena as the Northern Lights, cirrus clouds, and the atmosphere. To date Bluford has clocked some 314 hours in space, and he is rarely at a loss for words when the subject turns to flying. Asked by the *Philadelphia Inquirer* to describe how it feels to rocket into space on the Shuttle, he said: "Imagine driving down the street, and you look out the window, and all you see are flames. And your car is being driven by remote control, and you're saying to yourself, 'I hope this thing doesn't blow up.'" Bluford added that the Shuttle travels about three hundred miles *per minute.*

"The Right Stuff" Knows No Color

According to Prochnau, Bluford's career proves "that 'the right stuff' comes in hues other than white." Indeed, despite his disclaimers, Bluford has helped to open doors for minority scientists and aviators who want to be part of the nation's space program. He told the *Philadelphia Inquirer* that he is gratified that blacks and women have become part of the once all-white, all-male astronaut corps. "It's an indication that black Americans are starting to become a part of the mainstream in American society, particularly the professions," he asserted. "I'm sort of bringing black Americans into the astronaut program, breaking new ground. But I also anticipate that blacks in space will become more routine. All of this media attention will eventually fade away."

What won't fade for Bluford is the perspective he has gained from traveling into space and orbiting the earth at 180,000 miles per hour. "I've come to appreciate the planet we live on," he told the *Philadelphia Inquirer.* "It's a small ball in a large universe. It's a very fragile ball but also very beautiful. You don't recognize that until you see it from a little farther off." He told a reporter for the Los Angeles *Daily News* that after traveling well over two million miles in space, his work remains "a labor of love," and added, "You want to stay up forever."

In July 1993 Bluford resigned from NASA to become vice president and general manager of the Engineering Services Division of NYMA, Inc. The company, located in Greenbelt, Maryland, provides engineering and software expertise to several branches of the federal government—including NASA.

Further Reading

Daily News (Los Angeles), February 12, 1988
Jet, April 30, 1990, pp. 8-9; July 5, 1993, p. 32.
Philadelphia Inquirer, July 21, 1983; August 9, 1983; August 29, 1983; August 31, 1983; November 5, 1983; November 22, 1983; May 19, 1986.
Washington Post, August 21, 1983. □

Léon Blum

The French statesman Léon Blum (1872-1950) was the first Socialist, as well as the first Jewish, premier of France. In 1936 the government he headed enacted the most extensive program of social reforms in French history.

L éon Blum was born in Paris on April 9, 1872, into a wealthy family of Alsatian textile merchants. Although trained as a lawyer, he first gained public attention as a drama critic. Influenced by the Dreyfus Affair and by the socialist theories of Jean Jaurès, Blum joined the Socialist party in 1902. After the assassination of Jaurès in 1914, Blum was regarded as his spiritual and political heir.

After serving as executive secretary to the Socialist leader Marcel Sembat during World War I, Blum was elected to parliament in 1919. When the Communists broke away from the Socialist party in 1920, Blum became the leader of the weakened party and worked tirelessly to restore its fortunes. He also led the opposition to the conservative governments of Alexandre Millerand and Raymond Poincaré, and in 1928 his efforts were impressively rewarded when the Socialists won 104 seats in the parliamentary elections.

Alarmed by the threat of fascism after the Paris riots of February 1934, Blum worked for an antifascist alliance of Radicals, Socialists, and Communists—the Popular Front. This coalition won in the May 1936 elections, and Blum, as leader of the largest party in the Chamber, became premier in June. During the following 10 weeks his government accomplished a social revolution by enacting into law the 40-hour week and paid vacations for workers, nationalizing the major armaments industries, and bringing the Bank of France under public control.

But Blum's government was soon paralyzed by rightist dissidents, who feared social reform, and leftist critics, who denounced his nonintervention policy during the Spanish Civil War. Blum resigned in June 1937, when the Senate refused to grant him full powers to deal with the deepening fiscal crisis. After serving as vice premier in the succeeding government of Camille Chautemps, Blum headed a second, short-lived Popular Front Cabinet in March 1938.

Additional Sources

Bronner, Stephen Eric, *Léon Blum,* New York: Chelsea House Publishers, 1987.
Colton, Joel G., *Léon Blum: humanist in politics,* Cambridge, Mass., MIT Press 1974.
Lacouture, Jean., *Léon Blum,* New York, N.Y.: Holmes & Meier, 1982. □

Judy Blume

Perhaps the most popular contemporary author of works for upper elementary to junior high school readers, Judy Blume (born 1938) is the creator of frank, often humorous stories which focus on the emotional and social concerns of suburban adolescents.

Although Blume is best known for her fiction for adolescents, she began her career by writing books for younger children, an audience she still continues to address; *Tales of a Fourth-Grade Nothing* (1972) and *Superfudge* (1980), two entertaining tales about ten-year-old Peter and his incorrigible baby brother, Fudge, are especially popular with readers. *Are You There, God? It's Me, Margaret* (1970) depicts eleven-year-old Margaret's apprehensions about starting her period and choosing her own religion. At the time of the book's publication, Blume was praised for her warm and funny recreation of childhood feelings and conversation, but was criticized for her forthright references to the human body and its processes. *Margaret* is now considered a groundbreaking work due to the candor with which Blume presents previously taboo subjects. *Forever* (1975), in which Blume relates the particulars of her eighteen-year-old heroine's initial sexual experience, created an even greater furor. Despite the fact that it was published as an adult book, protestors pointed out that Blume's name and characteristically uncomplicated prose style attracted a vulnerable preteen audience who could be influenced by the intimate details of the novel. In *Tiger Eyes* (1981), Blume relates the story of how fifteen-year-old Davey adjusts to her father's murder. Hailed by many critics as Blume's finest work for her successful handling of a complex plot, *Tiger Eyes* includes such issues as alcoholism, suicide, anti-intellectualism, and violence. *Letters to Judy* (1986) was a promoted as a response to the voluminous amount of mail that Blume receives from her readers. Selecting a number of representatives letters to reprint anonymously with accompanying comments, she created the book for a dual purpose: to enable children to see that they are not alone and to make parents more aware of their children's needs.

Reviewers commend Blume for her honesty, warmth, compassion, and wit, praising her lack of condescension, superior observation of childhood, and strong appeal to children. Critics are strongly divided as to the success of Blume's plots, characterization, writing style, and non-

In 1940 Blum refused to vote full powers to Marshal Pétain as head of the Vichy government, and he was indicted on charges of war guilt. When he was tried in 1942, his defense was so eloquently persuasive that the trial was indefinitely suspended. Subsequently deported to Germany with other prominent French Jews, he was freed by Allied troops in 1945. While in Nazi captivity Blum wrote *À l'échelle humaine* (*For All Mankind*), which summarizes the philosophical bases of his lifelong effort to reconcile the fundamental tenets of Marxism with the moral and intellectual exigencies of humanism.

After the war Blum was in poor health and declined to run for reelection to parliament. However, he presided for a month, beginning on Dec. 16, 1946, over an all-Socialist caretaker Cabinet that installed the Fourth Republic. Although officially in retirement after January 1947, Blum served as André Marie's vice premier in August 1948. He also retained leadership of the Socialist party and contributed a daily column to the party organ, *Le Populaire,* until his sudden death on March 30, 1950.

Further Reading

The definitive biography is Joel Colton, *Léon Blum: Humanist in Politics* (1966). Less sympathetic but useful is the essay in James Joll, *Three Intellectuals in Politics* (1960). For Blum's place in the history of the Third Republic see D. W. Brogan, *The Development of Modern France, 1870-1939* (1940; rev. ed., 2 vols., 1966).

judgmental approach; they object to her uninhibited language and permissive attitude toward sexuality, and complain that her cavalier treatment of love, death, pain, and religion trivializes young people and the literature written for them. However, most commentators agree that Blume accurately captures the speech, emotions, and private thoughts of children, for whom she has made reading both easy and enjoyable.

Further Reading

Children's Literature Review, Gale, Volume 2, 1976, Volume 15, 1988.
Contemporary Literary Criticism, Gale, Volume 12, 1980, Volume 30, 1984.
Dictionary of Literary Biography, Volume 52: *American Writers for Children since 1960: Fiction,* Gale, 1986.
Fisher, Emma and Justin Wintle, *The Pied Pipers,* Paddington Press, 1975.
Gleasner, Diana, *Breakthrough: Women in Writing,* Walker, 1980.
Lee, Betsey, *Judy Blume's Story,* Dillon Press, 1981.
Weidt, Maryann, *Presenting Judy Blume,* Twayne, 1989. □

Werner Michael Blumenthal

A World War II refugee, Werner Michael Blumenthal (born 1926) used his academic and business skills to reach the highest levels of American government, industry, and banking.

W. Michael Blumenthal, one of two children of Ewald and Rose Valerie Market Blumenthal, was born on January 3, 1926, in Oranienburg, Germany, a Berlin suburb. His father owned a women's clothing store that was confiscated by the Nazis in 1938. After selling all their possessions to secure Ewald's release from a concentration camp, the Blumenthals fled Germany for Shanghai, where they joined many other German Jewish refugees.

Michael and his family survived harsh wartime conditions, including internment by the Japanese. He learned several languages, attended school, and worked in a warehouse in Shanghai. He and his sister arrived as refugees in San Francisco in 1947. Blumenthal worked part-time while attending college. In 1951 he received a Bachelor of Science degree from the University of California at Berkeley, majoring in international economics. A member of Phi Beta Kappa, he was accepted at Princeton's prestigious Woodrow Wilson School of Public Affairs, where he earned the Master of Arts and Master of Public Affairs degrees in 1953. He received his Doctor of Philosophy degree in 1956 while teaching economics at Princeton.

Blumenthal, who became a naturalized citizen in 1952, was also a fellow of the Social Research Council, a research associate of the industrial relations section of Princeton's Economics Department, and a labor arbitrator for New Jersey. In 1957, on the advice of a businessman he met on a trip, Blumenthal abruptly switched from academic life to a business career. He accepted a position as vice president and a director of Crown Cork International Corporation, a bottle manufacturer located in Jersey City, New Jersey. But his new career, applying academic theories to practical everyday decision making, only lasted four years.

Through a Princeton connection Blumenthal accepted the federal government position of deputy assistant secretary of state for economic affairs in April 1961, serving under President John F. Kennedy. Blumenthal worked on Kennedy's Alliance for Progress, on commodity trade and tariff issues, bringing his academic knowledge and practical experience to the negotiating tables. In 1963 he was given ambassador rank and was U.S. deputy special representative for trade negotiation. From 1963 to 1967 he was chairman and chief negotiator of the United States delegation to the Geneva conference for the GATT (General Agreement on Tariffs and Trade) treaty among 52 nations.

After this success, he returned to the business world, where he stayed for almost ten years. He joined Bendix Corporation, first in their New York offices as president and a director. By 1972 he became chairman and chief executive officer of the parent corporation, a conglomerate with 86,000 employees headquartered at Southfield, Michigan. During his tenure sales doubled to almost $3 billion and Bendix was rated as one of America's best managed corporations.

Blumenthal supported Jimmy Carter's successful 1976 presidential bid against Gerald Ford, and was asked to join Carter's cabinet. On January 20, 1977, 30 years after arriving in the U.S. as a refugee, Blumenthal was unanimously confirmed by the Senate, becoming the nation's 64th secretary of the treasury.

As treasury secretary Blumenthal was responsible for guiding national fiscal policy; he was in charge of the collection, management, and expenditure of public revenues. He also fully supported President Carter's pledge to assist New York City during its fiscal crisis. At this same time, primarily due to international events, the American dollar had sharply declined and domestic inflation was rapidly increasing. Since national monetary policy was not under his control, Blumenthal operated his department under increasingly difficult conditions.

In the fall of 1979 President Carter, determined to exert more control over the nation's economy, replaced Blumenthal with William Miller and appointed Paul Volcker to be chairman of the Federal Reserve Board. Blumenthal returned to private industry as a director of the Burroughs Corporations in Detroit, Michigan, and became its chairman and chief executive officer in 1981. The manufacturer of computer systems and supporting office products had sales of $4.39 billion and 64,000 employees by 1985. Blumenthal's goal was to make Burroughs the second largest computer manufacturer (after IBM), becoming a $20 billion company by 1993. To achieve this, he merged Burroughs with Sperry Corporation in 1986, creating the nation's third largest producer of computers. Sperry, with $4.91 billion in sales and 73,447 employees, had aerospace, government and defense contracts, computer, and farm machinery divisions. However, the newly merged company, now named the Unisys Corporation, headquartered in Blue Bell, Pennsylvania, had financial difficulties beginning in 1989.

Under Blumenthal's guidance, Unisys had cut overhead and purchased desktop computer and data communications companies; while sales reached $10 billion, debt also increased. The market for Unisys mainframe computers fell. Customers of Sperry and Burroughs computers switched to smaller, less expensive versions. Overseas business suffered from devaluation of the dollar. Between August 1989 and October 1990 Unisys' condition worsened; despite drastic cost-cutting measures, its stock lost more than 80 percent of its shareholder value.

In April 1990 Blumenthal retired from the chief executive officer position, and on November 1, he resigned as chairman of the board and director. However, a new chapter in his life also began in April 1990, when he became a limited partner in the investment bank Lazard Freres Co. of New York. He later accepted the position of co-chairman of an international coordinating group of the bank and was sent to work in Paris, France.

Blumenthal's personal philosophy reflected his experiences in America. He believed that the United States provides unlimited opportunities, and that people are accepted for what they can do and are not judged on their background. Sometimes described as abrupt and aloof, Blumenthal was often responsible for eliminating jobs and closing unprofitable plants—decisions he found difficult to make. He looked forward to a period of social and economic innovation that would help eliminate the national deficit and solve social problems.

From his marriage in 1951 to the former Margaret Polley, Blumenthal had three daughters. He was baptized as a Presbyterian in the 1950s. His avocations included tennis and skiing. He served as a director of the Equitable Life Assurance Society of the United States, the Council on Foreign Relations, the New York Stock Exchange, and Tenneco Inc. He serves as chairperson of the U.S. Russia Investment Fund and is writing a book on Russian history.

Further Reading

W. Michael Blumenthal has been listed in *Who's Who in America* since 1970. A good personal description is the *Forbes* May 28, 1990, article by Jerry Flint, "Master of the Game." His career with Unisys is detailed in a *Business Week* article on August 29, 1989, by Joseph Weber, "This Is Hardly the Turning Point Unisys had in Mind," and in a *Computerworld* October 29, 1990, article, "Losses force more Unisys cuts." See also *Business Week* (April 14, 1989; July 8, 1996), *Detroit News* (January 26, 1990; October 26, 1990). □

Nellie Bly

Journalist and reformer Elizabeth Cochrane Seaman, better known as Nellie Bly (1864-1922), gained fame at the end of the nineteenth century for her investigative reports of abusive conditions in the cities of Pittsburgh and New York. Her writing style was marked by first-hand tales of the lives of the underclass, which she obtained by venturing into their world in a series of undercover adventures. She riveted the attention of the nation with a more light-hearted assignment in the winter of 1889-90 when she successfully imitated Jules Verne's fictional journey *Around the World in Eighty Days* in only 72 days.

Elizabeth Cochrane Seaman, who wrote under the pen name Nellie Bly, was a journalist who gained nationwide fame for her investigative reports on abuses in various companies and public institutions. Her stories were not only reform-minded, but filled with first-hand adventure; she undertook such stunts as having herself admitted to an insane asylum, working in a factory sweatshop, and getting herself arrested in order to get a glimpse of the experiences of some of the most downtrodden of urban America. In her greatest escapade, Bly set out to imitate Jules Verne's imaginary trip around the world in less than 75 days while Americans anxiously awaited tales of her travel. Bly distinguished herself as a reporter at a time when the field was dominated by men, and her accomplishments won a greater measure of acceptance for other women journalists.

Bly was born Elizabeth Cochran on May 5, 1864, in Cochran Mills, Pennsylvania. She was the youngest of three children of Michael and Mary Jane Cochran. The Cochrans had both been married previously. Mary Jane, who came from a wealthy Pittsburgh family, was a widow with no children from her first marriage. Michael Cochran was a self-made industrialist who had begun his career as a laborer and eventually became a mill owner, property owner, and associate judge. He had seven children from his earlier marriage, including five boys. As a child, Bly was determined to keep up with her older brothers. She would join in even the roughest activities, including races and climbing trees, to prove herself their equal.

Bly was educated at home by her father in her early years, but he died in 1870 when she was only six years old. Her mother married a third time, but it was an unhappy relationship that ended in divorce. She and her mother lived for a while on the money her father had saved and Bly was sent to school near their home to prepare for a teaching career. While her performance at school was not impressive, she proved to be a creative and talented writer. At the age of 16, the family funds were depleted and Bly and her mother moved to stay near relatives in Pittsburgh. Around this time, she added the 'e' to her last name, feeling that "Cochrane" had a more elegant air.

Became Reporter in Pittsburgh

Once in Pittsburgh, Bly looked for a way to make a living so her relatives would not have to support her. At that time, a single woman had few professional options. Basi-

cally, she could become a teacher or a companion for a wealthy woman. Bly, however, wanted to become a writer. While the odds were not with her, Bly was able to make a profession out of writing due to her extraordinary personality and determination. She got her break in 1885, after a letter she had written to the *Pittsburgh Dispatch* caught the eye of the paper's editor, George A. Madden. In response to an editorial maintaining that women should remain at home rather than entering the professional or political sphere, Bly had written a spirited letter that argued women were perfectly capable of independent thought and meaningful careers. Impressed with the words of the piece, which was signed only "Lonely Orphan Girl," Madden published an ad requesting to speak with the writer of the letter. Bly responded, and at a meeting between the two, Madden asked what kind of stories she might write if she could be a journalist. She indicated that she wanted to tell the stories of ordinary people, and so Madden gave Bly her first journalistic assignment—a piece on the lives of women. Upon receiving her submission, Madden was pleased with the results and published it under the "Lonely Orphan Girl" pseudonym.

For her next article, Bly suggested the topic of divorce. Her editor was unsure that a single young woman could write a convincing article on the subject, but Bly produced a well-researched piece that included some of her father's legal notes on divorce as well as interviews with women who lived near her. Madden agreed to publish the article, but insisted that she find a different pen name—it would seem inappropriate for a story on divorce to be signed by "Little Orphan Girl." The story appeared under the name Nellie Bly—inspired, according to some stories, by the popular Stephen Foster song "Nelly Bly"—and this became the moniker that she would work under for the rest of her career.

Uncovered Factory Hazards and Abuses

Bly was hired as a full-time reporter for the *Dispatch,* earning a salary of five dollars a week. Her initial stories concerned the welfare of Pittsburgh's working class and poor, and the depressed and dangerous conditions she uncovered led to a number of reforms. She developed a reputation for bringing her readers a first-hand look at these topics. To investigate an unsafe factory, she took a job there herself and reported how the establishment was a firetrap that paid low wages to women who were required to work long and difficult shifts. She also traveled to the slums of the city to present a picture of children forced to work all day in order to provide for their families. While Bly's stories raised the indignation of Pittsburgh's citizens and inspired changes, the institutions she attacked were displeased and threatened to remove their advertisements from the newspaper. To appease their customers, the editors of the *Dispatch* changed the focus of Bly's writing, giving her cultural and social events to cover. While the caliber of her writing remained high, Bly yearned to continue her investigative work. She decided to go to Mexico and write about the conditions of the poor there. For several months, she contributed stories about disparities in Mexican society to the *Dispatch.* She then returned to Pittsburgh in 1886.

Reported on Asylum Conditions

Seeking a job as a serious journalist, not just a society columnist, Bly moved to New York City in 1887. There she sold some of her stories about Mexico to newspapers, but found that no one wanted to hire a female as a reporter. Resourceful as ever, Bly managed to turn this experience itself into a story that she sold to her former employers in Pittsburgh. Finally, she managed to arrange an interview with the managing editor of the *New York World,* John Cockerill. Cockerill and the paper's owner, Joseph Pulitzer, liked Bly's stories, but were seeking something more dramatic and attention-getting. Bly was ready for the challenge. With Cockerill, she devised the idea of getting herself admitted to New York's insane asylum for the poor, Blackwell's Island, in order to discover the truth behind reports of abuses there. After being placed in the institution, Bly dropped her act of insanity, but found that doctors and nurses refused to listen to her when she stated she was rational. Other disturbing practices there included feeding the patients vermin-infested food, physical and mental abuse by the staff, and the admission of people who were not psychologically disturbed but simply physically ill or maliciously placed there by family members—as in the case of one woman who was declared insane by her husband after he caught her being unfaithful. After ten days in the asylum, Bly was removed by a lawyer from the newspaper, as had been previously arranged. The resulting stories by Bly caused a sensation across the country, effected reforms at Blackwell's Island, and earned her a permanent post at the *World.*

New York was ripe with possibilities for Bly's style of reporting, and she gained a national reputation for her daredevil methods of getting a story. To get an inside view of the justice system, she pretended to commit a robbery and found that women prisoners were searched by male officers because no women were employed by the jail. She also exposed a fraudulent employment agency that was taking money from unsuspecting immigrants, a health clinic where unqualified doctors experimented on patients, and a lobbyist who had successfully bribed a number of state politicians. Her work also included interviews with some of the most famous figures of the day, including Buffalo Bill and the wives of presidents Ulysses S. Grant, James Garfield, and James K. Polk.

Raced around the World

Bly's most notorious stunt, however, was her trek across the globe in the spirit of the 1873 book *Around the World in Eighty Days* by French author Jules Verne. Bly's plan was to accomplish the feat in only 75 days. Traveling alone, Bly began her journey on November 14, 1889, on an ocean liner heading from New Jersey to London. As she made her way from Europe to the Middle East, Ceylon, Singapore, Hong Kong, and Japan, Americans kept up on her progress through her stories sent in by cable. The *World* made the most of the adventure, turning Bly into a celebrity who inspired songs, fashion, and even a game. She returned to New York in triumph on January 25, 1890, after only 72 days. The town welcomed her arrival with a huge celebration and parade.

Bly was married in 1895 to Robert Livingston Seaman, a millionaire who owned the Iron Clad Manufacturing Company and the American Steel Barrel Company. She retired from writing to assist her husband in his businesses and became president of his companies after Seaman's death in 1904. Her business instincts were poor, however, and in 1911 she declared bankruptcy and returned to journalism. During this period of her career she covered World War I from the Eastern Front and then took a job with the New York *Evening Journal.* But her days as a household name were long past. Upon her death from pneumonia on January 27, 1922, in New York, few people remarked on her passing. Only the *Evening Journal* published a piece on her significance, calling her the country's best reporter. Despite her relative obscurity at the end of her life, Bly's impact was a lasting one. Her unique and energetic approach to reporting launched new trends in journalism, and her insistence on covering difficult topics—despite her gender—set a precedent for journalistic careers for women.

Further Reading

For more information see Belford, Barbara, *Brilliant Bylines: A Biographical Anthology of Notable Newspaperwomen in America,* Columbia University Press, 1986; Kroeger, Brooke, *Nellie Bly: Daredevil, Reporter, Feminist,* Times Books, 1994; and Rittenhouse, Mignon, *The Amazing Nellie Bly,* E. P. Dutton, 1956. □

Edward Wilmot Blyden

Edward Wilmot Blyden (1832-1912) was a Liberian educator and statesman. More than any other figure, he laid the foundation of West African nationalism and of pan-Africanism.

Edward Blyden was born in St. Thomas, Virgin Islands, on Aug. 3, 1832, of free, literate parents. A precocious youth, he early decided to become a clergyman. He went to the United States in May 1850 and sought to enter a theological college but was turned down because of his race. In January 1851 he emigrated to Liberia, a African American colony which had become independent as a republic in 1847.

He continued his formal education at Alexander High School, Monrovia, whose principal he was appointed in 1858. In 1862 he was appointed professor of classics at the newly opened Liberia College, a position he held until 1871. Although Blyden was self-taught beyond high school, he became an able and versatile linguist, classicist, theologian, historian, and sociologist. From 1864 to 1866, in addition to his professorial duties, Blyden acted as secretary of state of Liberia.

From 1871 to 1873 Blyden lived in Freetown, Sierra Leone. There he edited *Negro,* the first explicitly pan-African journal in West Africa. He also led two important expeditions to Fouta Djallon in the interior. Between 1874 and 1885 Blyden was again based in Liberia, holding various high academic and governmental offices. In 1885 he was an unsuccessful candidate for the Liberian presidency.

After 1885 Blyden divided his time between Liberia and the British colonies of Sierra Leone and Lagos. He served Liberia again in the capacities of ambassador to Britain and France and as a professor and later president of Liberia College. In 1891 and 1894 he spent several months in Lagos and worked there in 1896-1897 as government agent for native affairs.

While in Lagos he wrote regularly for the *Lagos Weekly Record,* one of the earliest propagators of Nigerian and West African nationalism. In Freetown, Blyden helped to edit the *Sierra Leone News,* which he had assisted in founding in 1884 "to serve the interest of West Africa . . . and the race generally." He also had helped found and edit the Freetown *West African Reporter* (1874-1882), whose declared aim was to forge a bond of unity among English-speaking West Africans. Between 1901 and 1906 Blyden was director of Moslem education; he taught English and "Western subjects" to Moslem youths with the object of building a bridge of communication between the Moslem and Christian communities. He died in Freetown on Feb. 7, 1912.

Writings, Ideas, and Hopes

Although Blyden held many important positions, it is more as a man of ideas than as a man of action that he is historically significant. He saw himself as a champion and defender of his race and in this role produced more than two dozen pamphlets and books, the most important of which are *A Voice from Bleeding Africa* (1856); *Liberia's Offering* (1862); *The Negro in Ancient History* (1869); *The West African University* (1872); *From West Africa to Palestine* (1873); *Christianity, Islam and the Negro Race* (1887), his major work; *The Jewish Question* (1898); *West Africa before Europe* (1905); and *Africa Life and Customs* (1908). His writings displayed conversancy with the main current of ideas as well as originality, and he was often controversial.

Blyden sought to prove that Africa and Africans have a worthy history and culture. He rejected the prevailing notion of the inferiority of the black man but accepted the view that each major race has a special contribution to make to world civilization. He argued that Christianity has had a demoralizing effect on blacks, while Islam has had a unifying and elevating influence.

Blyden's political goals were the establishment of a major modern West African state which would protect and promote the interests of peoples of African descent everywhere. He initially saw Liberia as the nucleus of such a state and sought to extend its influence and jurisdiction by encouraging selective "repatriation" from the Americas. He hoped, also in vain, that Liberia and adjacent Sierra Leone would unite as one nation. He was ambivalent about the establishment of European colonial rule; he thought that it would eventually result in modern independent nations in tropical Africa but was concerned about its damaging psy-

chological impact. As a cultural nationalist, he pointed out that modernization was not incompatible with respect for African customs and institutions. He favored African names and dress and championed the establishment of educational and cultural institutions specifically designed to meet African needs and circumstances.

Further Reading

A full-length biography of Blyden is Hollis R. Lynch, *Edward Wilmot Blyden: Pan-Negro Patriot, 1832-1912* (1967). Edith Holden, *Blyden of Liberia: An Account of the Life and Labors of Edward Wilmot Blyden* (1966), is an important source containing biographical details and excerpts from Blyden's letters and published writings. See also Hollis R. Lynch, ed., *Black Spokesman: Selected Published Writings of Edward Wilmot Blyden* (1971), the only representative anthology of his writings. □

Franz Boas

The German-born American anthropologist Franz Boas (1858-1942) established the modern structure of anthropology and applied anthropological findings to problems in education, race relations, nationalism and internationalism, war and peace, and the struggle for democracy and intellectual freedom.

Anthropology in America was essentially preprofessional when Franz Boas began its study. The science was not established at any university; amateurs and semiprofessionals were active in it. Its subject matter comprised a miscellany of information about the evolution of man and his works; its theory was an accumulation of 19th-century speculations about race, geographical determinism, and unilinear (orthogenetic) cultural evolution.

Boas restructured anthropology in fundamental contributions on race (physical type) and human biology (growth); on linguistics (Native American languages); on cultures, in inductive field studies (Eskimo and Northwest Coast) and comparative studies; and on the aims, methods, and theory of the field. By 1911, when he published *The Mind of Primitive Man,* he provided anthropology with the framework used thereafter by most anthropologists and many other social scientists. The cultural anthropological principle that learning and habit (socialization rather than instinct and/or heredity) are the basis of human institutional behavior and its diversity in societies became fundamental in social sciences and social philosophy.

Boas was born in Minden, Germany, on July 9, 1858. He grew up in a home "where the ideals of the revolution of 1848 were a living force" and where he "was spared," by parents who had given up their formal Jewish faith, "the struggle against religious dogma that besets the lives of so many young people."

Boas attended the universities of Heidelberg, Bonn, and Kiel, completing his doctorate at Kiel in 1881. His principal dissertation was in physics; it involved him, however, in problems of psychophysics (forerunner of experimental psychology)—questions of human perception which became key problems of his later anthropological work.

Boas came to anthropology circuitously. He started his career as a geographer, and his first research—an expedition to Baffin Land (1883-1884)—was geographical. But with the ethnology he did on that expedition (published as *The Central Eskimo,* 1888) and the following museum year in Berlin with Adolph Bastian, an anthropogeographer-ethnographer, Boas made his choice. He studied anthropometry with Rudolf Virchow and started research on the Northwest Coast, in British Columbia, in 1885 as an anthropologist.

In 1887 Boas resigned his position as *dozent* in geography at the University of Berlin—which would have required by law a declaration of religious affiliation, unacceptable to him—married, and settled in New York. His first American position was assistant editor of *Science* (1887). On the Clark University faculty (1888-1892) he trained the first American to receive a doctorate in anthropology. He was chief assistant for anthropology of the World's Columbian Exposition in Chicago (1892-1893), organized its extensive ethnographical collections, and became the first curator for anthropology of the natural-history museum founded in Chicago (1894) to house the collection. For years he continued North Pacific Coast research, principally under the

auspices of the British Association for the Advancement of Science, thus beginning the focus on the Kwakiutl people which lasted for more than 40 years.

In 1895 Boas became assistant curator of the American Museum of Natural History, New York City, and was its curator from 1901 to 1905. There he initiated the Jesup North Pacific Expedition, a major research program on man in the Americas. In 1896 he joined Columbia University as lecturer in physical anthropology and in 1899 became professor of anthropology, a post he held until retiring in 1936.

At Columbia, Boas became the most influential anthropologist of his time. He trained a generation of American anthropologists and founded or promoted major anthropological societies and journals, including the American Anthropological Association and its *Anthropologist,* the American Folk Lore Society and its *Journal,* the *International Journal of American Linguistics,* and the American Ethnological Society and its *Publications.* He carried out and promoted research on Afro-Americans, on race relations in Latin America, and on the Far East. As early as 1903, recognizing two great world areas of civilization, West and East, he attempted unsuccessfully to establish a United States Oriental institute. His publications include more than 30 books.

General Principles

The Mind of Primitive Man, a collection of Boas's 1894-1911 studies, established general principles of modern anthropology. Race, language, and culture have essentially independent historical careers and are not "interchangeable" terms in the classification of man. The "race" concept, far from being objective natural description, involves subjective typological characterization and has to be reduced by statistical analysis to the study of populations and their composition in family lines. Neither race or physical type (inborn human traits) nor geographical conditions (external factors) explain or determine the diversities of human cultures. The complexities of actual cultural histories and the universal fact of cultural borrowing or diffusion made untenable theories from the 19th century that human cultures evolved in a unilinear, orthogenetic progression, with diversities explained as differences in stage of development.

These critiques established the autonomy of "cultures"—that cultural or behavioral communities and their institutions are the outcome of complex histories. Human behavior and the human mind, primitive or modern, are an expression of the cultural or behavioral contexts in which socialization occurs, the character of the traditional contextual material, and the extent to which tradition is open to question and change.

Field Research

Field research among living cultures is inherent in Boas's conception of modern cultural anthropology, and he set standards by precept and example. The native's viewpoint, rather than the observer's, is essential. To secure it, the ethnologist should strive for close association with the native community, and he should record information in the native language when possible, train natives as informants, investigators, and recorders of their own culture, and learn to speak the native language. Boas practiced what he preached. He studied the Eskimo language before his Baffin Land expedition and became fluent in Kwakiutl on the Northwest Coast.

Human Biology

Boas led physical anthropology away from mere taxonomic classification into human biology. His *Changes in Bodily Form of Descendants of Immigrants* (1911), proving that head form (cephalic index) is not a fixed hereditary trait but is affected by environmental change, ended its routine use in race classification and challenged other genetic assumptions of traditional taxonomy. The implied relation between environmental and cultural conditions and human biological development led Boas to pioneer in studies of human growth. In them he initiated longitudinal studies and established the fundamental concepts of tempo of growth and of physiological age. *Race, Language, and Culture* (1940) is a major collection of his papers.

Linguistics Studies

Boas broke sharply with traditional philology in his *Handbook of American Indian Languages* (4 vols., 1911-1941). He used an inductive approach to derive the "inner form" of each language. His studies revealed a wider range of linguistic phenomena than had been thought to exist and opened new areas of study of the relations of language and thought. His work is the foundation of anthropological linguistics and its recent developments, both in structural linguistics and in the cross-cultural study of human cognition.

The Scientist as Citizen

As scientist and anthropologist, Boas accepted a moral obligation to spread scientific knowledge as widely as possible. He applied anthropology to public problems in *Anthropology and Modern Life* (1928) and *Race and Democratic Society* (1945) and in magazine articles. He exposed the fallacies of race prejudice, particularly anti-Semitism before and during the Nazi period and anti-Negroism at all times and places. He held that cultural anthropology impugns chauvinistic nationalism and affirms internationalism. He stood for academic freedom all his life. He fought Nazism by mobilizing more than 10,000 American scientists in the Committee for Democracy and Intellectual Freedom (1938-1939).

Boas died on Dec. 21, 1942. He changed the understanding of human nature and human behavior by eliminating the predeterminism of instinct and heredity and making human institutions cultural, subject to human control for human ends.

Further Reading

A basic work on Boas is Melville J. Herskovits, *Franz Boas: The Science of Man in the Making* (1953). Briefer discussions are in Helene Codere's introduction to Boas's *Kwakiutl Ethnography* (1966) and in Ruth L. Bunzel's introduction to his *Anthropology and Modern Life* (1962). For background information

see Robert H. Lowie, *The History of Ethnological Theory* (1937); Margaret Mead and Ruth L. Bunzel, eds., *The Golden Age of American Anthropology* (1960); Abram Kardiner and Edward Preble, *They Studied Man* (1961); and George W. Stocking, Jr., *Race, Culture, and Evolution: Essays in the History of Anthropology* (1968).

Additional Sources

Hyatt, Marshall, *Franz Boas, social activist: the dynamics of ethnicity,* New York: Greenwood Press, 1990.

Williams, Vernon J., *Rethinking race: Franz Boaz and his contemporaries,* Lexington, Ky.: University Press of Kentucky, 1996. □

Giovanni Boccaccio

The Italian author Giovanni Boccaccio (1313-1375) is best known for the *Decameron*. For his Latin works and his role in reviving Hellenistic learning in Florence, he may be considered one of the early humanists.

The culture of Giovanni Boccaccio is rooted in the Middle Ages, but his conception of life points forward to the Renaissance. Like his fellow poet Petrarch, he straddled two ages, and yet he was unlike Petrarch—a fervent admirer of classical and Christian antiquity—in his acceptance of the medieval tradition. Boccaccio's work reflects both his bourgeois mercantile background and the chivalric ideals of the Neapolitan court, where he spent his youth. He strove to raise Italian prose to an art form nurtured in both medieval rhetoric and classical Latin prose; he had immense admiration for his great Italian contemporaries Dante and Petrarch, as well as for the classical authors. In this sense Boccaccio's vernacular humanism contrasts with Petrarch's classical humanism.

Boccaccio's father, Boccaccio di Chellino, was a merchant from the small Tuscan town of Certaldo. About 1312 he went to Florence and there worked successfully for the powerful banking company of the Bardi and Peruzzi. The exact date and place of Boccaccio's illegitimate birth are unknown. Despite tales of his birth in Paris of a Parisian noblewoman, a story derived partly from some of Boccaccio's early works whose autobiographical value is disputed, it seems that he was born in 1313 in Certaldo or more likely in Florence, where he spent his childhood. Of these years he wrote, "I remember that, before having completed my seventh year, a desire was born in me to compose verse, and I wrote certain poetic fancies."

Early Life

In 1321 Giovanni began to study Latin. But his father did not encourage his literary interests, and by 1328 Boccaccio was in Naples to learn commerce, probably with the Bardi. After 6 years of fruitless apprenticeship, Boccaccio abandoned commerce and reluctantly studied canon law for another 6 years. Later he regretted this lost time. "I do

romance inspired by Fiammetta about 1336, retells the tale of the noble lovers Florio and Biancofiore. Based on a French romance, it contains a vivid portrayal of Neapolitan society and two stories which later reappear in the *Decameron.*

The *Filostrato* (ca. 1338) is composed of nine cantos in octaves. For the first time the octave, a popular Italian verse form, is elevated to the dignity of literary art. The poem was composed at a time when Fiammetta's love was declining, and the poet expresses his sorrow through the young lover, Troilus, who is tormented by jealousy. Chaucer made an English version of the *Filostrato,* and Shakespeare derived his *Troilus and Cressida* from it. The *Tesdida* (ca. 1340), 12 books in octaves, was intended to fill the need for an epic poem in Italian.

In 1340 his father, who had been reduced to poverty by the bankruptcy of the Bardi, called Boccaccio back to Florence. On his return he wrote to a friend: "About my being in Florence against my will I will write nothing to you, for it could sooner be shown with tears than with ink." Little is known of this period of Boccaccio's life, but his works written between 1341 and 1346 show a gradual shift in orientation. *L'Ameto* (1341-1342) is a pastoral romance in prose and terza rima, dedicated to a Florentine friend. *L'amorosa visione* (ca. 1342), dedicated to Fiammetta, is in terza rima. Both are moving idealizations of love in the form of allegory.

L'elegia de madonna Fiammetta (1343-1344) and the *Ninfale fiesolano* (1344-1346) mark a departure from allegory. *Fiammetta* is a psychological romance in prose, in which the situation of *Filostrato* is reversed—the woman, overcome by love, suffers abandonment, jealousy, and despair. But the author, who in his earlier works reflected his own emotions, now achieves an artistically detached and serene approach which results in a more subtle psychological analysis and a high degree of stylistic perfection. The *Ninfale fiesolano* is a narrative poem in octaves. A tragic idyll of love between the shepherd Affrico and the nymph Mensola, it explains poetically the origin of two rivers which join and flow into the Arno. It is Boccaccio's best work in verse; in its narrative maturity it foreshadows the *Decameron.*

In 1346 Boccaccio was in Ravenna at the court of Ostasio da Polenta; in 1347 he was a guest of Francesco degli Ordelaffi in Forli and thereafter may have sojourned briefly in Naples. In 1348 he was probably in Florence to witness the devastating pestilence which he described in the proem of the *Decameron.* In 1349, the year of his father's death, he was definitely in Florence, where he was increasingly esteemed. By this time he was working on the *Decameron,* which he completed by 1353.

The *Decameron*

The great pestilence of 1348 may have afforded Boccaccio the occasion to write his masterpiece; it provides the framework for this collection of 100 stories in Italian. While the Black Death rages in Florence, seven young ladies and three young lovers meet by chance in S. Maria Novella and agree to flee from the city to their country villas during the

not doubt that if, at an age most suited for this, my father had tolerated it with a serene mind, I would have become one of the celebrated poets; but because he strove to bend my talent first to a lucrative trade and then to lucrative studies, it happened that I am not a merchant, I have not turned out to be a canonist, and have not become a distinguished poet."

However, the years were not wasted. Through his father's contacts (he was a financial adviser to King Robert of Anjou), Boccaccio was introduced to the cultivated society of the court at Naples. There he knew scientists and theologians, men of letters and the law. He learned astronomy and mythology and was introduced to Greek language and culture. He read the classical Latin authors, French adventure romances, and Italian poets. In the refined, and learned environment of Naples he matured and became a writer.

On Holy Saturday 1336, in the church of S. Lorenzo, Boccaccio saw and began to love ardently the young noblewoman whom he called Fiammetta in his works. She is said to have been Maria, the natural daughter of King Robert and the wife of the Count of Aquino, though there is no documentary evidence of her identity. Fiammetta returned Boccaccio's love for a time and was the inspiration for all his youthful works in Italian.

Italian Works

Boccaccio's earliest composition, probably preceding his love for Fiammetta, is the *Caccia di Diana,* 18 cantos in terza rima chronicling the events of the Neapolitan court under fictitious and allegorical names. The *Filocolo,* a prose epidemic. Against the somber background of death and desolation, portrayed in vivid detail, the group lives a carefree yet well-ordered life in the pleasant countryside for 15 days, avoiding all thoughts of death. They meet daily in the cool shade, where each one tells a story on a determined subject, and each day ends with a ballad. Each day a king or queen is named to govern the happy assembly and to prescribe occupations and determine a theme for the stories. The storytelling continues for 10 days, hence the title *Decameron* .

The tales have an abundance of subjects—comic, tragic, adventurous, ancient, and contemporary. The grouping around a particular daily theme organizes them into a unified structure. In his multitude of characters, from ridiculous fools to noble and resolute figures, from all times and social conditions, Boccaccio depicts human nature in its weakness and heroic virtue, particularly as revealed in comic or dramatic situations. There is an emphasis on human intelligence and a kind of worldly prudence with which characters overcome difficult situations, be they noble or ignoble. Boccaccio presents life from an earthly point of view, with a complete absence of moral intentions. If nothing is sacred, if a corrupt clergy is shown in all its greed and vanity, this offers stuff for amusement but never satire. And so, though the *Decameron* is not licentious, it is not moral either. Boccaccio in his old age repented having written it, but by then it was being read all over Europe. The prose of the *Decameron,* in its balanced, rhythmic cadences, became the model of Italian literary prose.

Latin Works

In the autumn of 1350 Boccaccio received as his guest in Florence Petrarch (Francesco Petrarca), whose biography he had written shortly before (*De vita et moribus, F. P.*). It was the beginning of a lifelong friendship, attested to by an abundant correspondence. Petrarch was to have considerable influence in orienting Boccaccio toward the moral austerity and philological discipline characteristic of humanism.

About 1350 Boccaccio began his *De genealogiis deorum gentilium,* an erudite work evidencing a vast and precise knowledge of classical sources. Its 15 books constitute the first encyclopedia of mythological science. Between 1350 and 1354 he was honored with a civic office and various diplomatic missions. Between 1354 and 1355, after a Florentine widow refused his advances, he wrote, in Italian, the prose *Corbaccio,* a satirical invective giving vent to the most ferocious misogynism.

From 1355 to 1360 Boccaccio composed several Latin works: *De casibus virorum illustrium* (in nine books, illustrious men from Adam to Petrarch tell of their fall from fortune to moral misery); *De montibus, silvis, fluminibus, stagnis seu paludibus, et de nominibus maris liber* (a dictionary of all the geographical names found in the classical authors); and *De claris mulieribus* (biographies of 104 famous women from Eve to Queen Joan of Naples, with moralistic intent).

Between 1357 and 1362 Boccaccio wrote his biographical *Trattello in laude di Dante* and also had as his guest the Calabrian monk Leonzio Pilata, whom he induced to translate the Homeric epics and to teach Greek. Of this he wrote later: "Indeed I was the one who first, at my own expense, made the books of Homer and of various other Greek authors return to Tuscany." At this time his house became one of the most active centers of Florentine prehumanism.

In 1362 a Carthusian monk, Gioacchino Ciani, brought Boccaccio a prophecy of imminent death and exhorted him to abandon his worldly studies and devote himself to religion. Profoundly disturbed, Boccaccio thought of destroying his works but was dissuaded by Petrarch, who saw no contradiction between literary activities and the Christian life. Pressed by economic necessity, Boccaccio went to Naples that year to seek the help of an influential friend in finding a position. But he soon left, disillusioned, and spent 3 months with Petrarch in Venice (1363). He was twice Florentine ambassador to Pope Urban V (1365 and 1367) and made a final unsuccessful attempt to establish himself in Naples (1370). Thereafter he retired to Certaldo.

Though afflicted by illness, he enthusiastically accepted the task entrusted to him by Florence to give daily public readings of Dante's *Divine Comedy* at the church of S. Stefano in Badia. Beginning in October 1373, he read and wrote a commentary to the *Inferno* through Canto XVII. But weakened by illness and criticized for expounding the divine poem before an ignorant populace, he had to discontinue. His *Commento all'Inferno* is based on these lectures.

Boccaccio returned to Certaldo, where news of Petrarch's death reached him late in 1374. On Dec. 21, 1375, Boccaccio died in Certaldo. He was buried there in the church of SS. Michele e Jacopo.

Further Reading

Two well-known critical biographies of Boccaccio are Edward Hutton, *Giovanni Boccaccio: A Biographical Study* (1910), and John Addington Symonds, *Giovanni Boccaccio as Man and Author* (1895; repr. 1968). Recommended as general background reading is Hélène Nolthenius, *Duecento: The Late Middle Ages in Italy* (1959; trans. 1968). See also the chapter on Boccaccio in Joseph Wood Krutch, *Five Masters: A Study in the Mutations of The Novel* (1930); Francis MacManus, *Boccaccio* (1947); and Aldo D. Scaglione, *Nature and Love in the Late Middle Ages: An Essay on the Cultural Context of the Decameron* (1963).

Additional Sources

Branca, Vittore, *Boccaccio: the man and his works,* New York: New York University Press, 1976.

Carswell, Catherine MacFarlane, *The tranquil heart: portrait of Giovanni Boccaccio,* Folcroft, Pa.: Folcroft Library Editions, 1976; Norwood, Pa.: Norwood Editions, 1977; Philadelphia: R. West, 1978. □

Umberto Boccioni

The Italian artist Umberto Boccioni (1882-1916) was the leading theoretician of futurism, the most

talented of its painters, and the creator of its first sculptures. He is considered the master of the innovative esthetic generated by the machine age.

Umberto Boccioni was born on Oct. 19, 1882, in Reggio Calabria. He went to Rome in 1900 and studied with Giacomo Balla, who revealed the theory of divisionism to him. Boccioni also studied at the Academy of the Brera in Milan. In 1904-1905 he visited Paris and Russia.

To Boccioni's searching spirit the meeting with the poet Filippo Marinetti in 1909 was an event of the utmost importance. Marinetti, the initiator and great orator of the futurist movement, converted Boccioni to his principles. Together with Gino Severini, Carlo Carrà, Balla, and Luigi Russolo, Boccioni signed the "Manifesto of Futurist Painters" in Milan in 1910.

Futurist Painting

Boccioni became the leading theorist of futurist art, both in painting and sculpture. He was the most intellectually active and artistically creative of all the futurist artists. One of his aims was to vitalize matter (*Materia,* 1912). Matter had to serve as the expression of emotion and states of mind (*States of Mind,* 1911). The term *linee forze,* or lines of force, signifies in Boccioni's work the energies which dominate matter and spirit. His famous picture *Forces of a Street* (1911) is a synthesis of the time and space elements and of form, color, and tone. All the lines of force are in action: the traffic in the streets, the light rays coming from the windows and doors, the light from the sky descending on the busy scene and adding a transcendental quality to it. Geometric forms and intensive colors are in perpetual interplay. The beholder is drawn into the vortex of this field of energies, which even includes "painted sounds." Figures float through the picture in a shadowy, schematic manner. What is more important to Boccioni than the representation of the figures is the human reaction to the experience of the forces of the street. Pictures like this are the esthetic reflections of the industrial era.

The painting *Elasticity* (1912) is the synthesis of the movement of a galloping horse. Similarly, a synthesis of human movement is found in the paintings *Muscular Dynamics* and *Dynamics of a Human Body.*

Futurist Sculpture

Boccioni's first futurist sculpture dates from 1911. In 1912 he wrote his "Manifesto of Futurist Sculpture," in which he propounded the use of unconventional, hitherto unacceptable materials. The "totality" Boccioni strove for was the simultaneous representation of the temporal evolution of an action. His revolutionary dictum for sculpture, "Let us open the figure like a window and include in it the milieu in which it lives," is illustrated by *Development of a Bottle in Space* (1912) and *Unique Forms of Continuity in Space* (1913). Even rays of light were formally incorporated in such sculptures as *Head and House and Light.*

Boccioni took part in all the important futurist exhibitions in Europe and America, beginning with the Paris exhibition of 1912. His book *Pittura, scultura futuriste: Dinamismo plastico* (1914) is the most comprehensive statement of futurism written by one of the original members of the movement.

Boccioni was wounded in World War I. While convalescing, he was killed in a riding accident in Sorte in 1916.

Further Reading

In English, Boccioni's work is discussed in Alfred H. Barr, Jr., *Cubism and Abstract Art* (1936); James Thrall Soby and Alfred H. Barr, Jr., *Twentieth-Century Italian Art* (1949); and Raffaele Carriere, *Avant-Garde Painting and Sculpture in Italy, 1890-1955* (1955) and *Futurism* (1961; trans. 1963). There are several good works on the artist in Italian. □

Arnold Böcklin

The Swiss painter Arnold Böcklin (1827-1901) rejected the naturalistic trends of his time and created symbolic, mythological works.

Arnold Böcklin was born on Oct. 16, 1827, in Basel. He attended the Düsseldorf Academy (1845-1847). At this time he painted scenes of the Swiss Alps, using light effects and dramatic views subjectively to project emotional moods into the landscape. In 1848 this romantic introspection gave way to *plein air* (open-air) objectivity after he was influenced by Camille Corot, Eugène Delacroix, and the painters of the Barbizon school while on a trip to Paris. But after the February and June revolutions Böcklin returned to Basel with a lasting hatred and disgust for contemporary France, and he resumed painting gloomy mountain scenes.

In 1850 Böcklin found his mecca in Rome, and immediately his paintings were flooded by the warm Italian sunlight. He populated the lush southern vegetation, the bright light of the Roman Campagna, and the ancient ruins with lonely shepherds, cavorting nymphs, and lusty centaurs. These mythological figures rather than the landscapes became Böcklin's primary concern, and he used such themes as *Pan Pursuing Syrinx* (1857) to express the polarities of life: warm sunshine contrasts with cool, moist shade, and the brightness of woman's spirituality contrasts with man's dark sensuality.

When Böcklin returned to Basel with his Italian wife, he completed the painting which brought him fame when the king of Bavaria purchased it in 1858: *Pan among the Reeds,* a depiction of the Greek phallic god with whom the artist identified. He taught at the Academy of Art in Weimar from 1860 to 1862, when he returned to Rome. Called to Basel in 1866, he painted the frescoes and modeled the grotesque masks for the facade of the Basel Museum.

Böcklin resided in Florence from 1874 until 1885, and this was his most active period. He continued to explore the male-female antithesis and painted religious scenes, allegories of Nature's powers, and moody studies of man's fate. He ceased working with oils and began experimenting with tempera and other media to obtain a pictorial surface free of brushstrokes.

Böcklin spent the next 7 years mostly in Switzerland, with occasional trips to Italy; he devoted much of his energy to designing an airplane. Following a stroke in 1892, he returned to Italy, bought a villa in Fiesole, and died there on Jan. 16, 1901. Many of his late works depict nightmares of war, plague, and death.

Further Reading

The major works on Böcklin are in German. In English, volume 7 (1906) in the "Masters in Art" series contains a biography and criticism. General works that discuss Böcklin are Bernard S. Meyers, *The German Expressionists: A Generation in Revolt* (1957); Peter Selz, *German Expressionist Painting* (1957); and Marcel Brion, *German Painting* (trans. 1959). See also H. W. Janson, *History of Art* (1962). □

Boyd Henry Bode

American philosopher and educator Boyd Henry Bode (1873-1953) was a leading spokesman for pragmatism in the philosophy of education. He supported progressive education, but criticized its excesses and opposed educational theories that he thought were undemocratic.

B oyd Henry Bode was born on October 24, 1873, to Dutch immigrant parents in rural northern Illinois, and he grew up in Grundy County, Iowa, where his father was a minister in the Christian Reformed Church, an offshoot of the Dutch Reformed Church. Bode's upbringing as a rural immigrant minister's son left a permanent imprint on his thinking. Although the father-son relationship was amicable and respectful, Bode was later to reject authoritarian religion on philosophical grounds.

Bode was the eldest of eight children and the only child allowed to pursue extensive formal education. He attended elementary school in Wellsburg, Iowa, and high school in Steamboat Rock, Iowa. He received B.A. degrees at Penn College and the University of Michigan, and eventually earned the Ph.D. at Cornell University in 1900. Upon graduation Bode entered college teaching in the department of philosophy at the University of Wisconsin.

Moving Toward Pragmatism

Bode began his teaching career as a philosophical idealist and a critic of the American philosophy of pragmatism, but gradually he became persuaded that pragmatism was the philosophy of America's future. The pragmatic view that truth comes out of human experience rather than through revelation and contemplation appealed to him. Pragmatism's support of science and experimentation to arrive at workable solutions to human problems also appealed to his developing philosophical point of view. In addition, pragmatism's championship of democracy, particularly as this was demonstrated in the works of John Dewey, fed Bode's own desires to bolster democratic institutions and to secure a more democratic American society.

Bode believed that the American experiment of democratic rule was the hope of the future. He advocated "Americanization" not only of the immigrants, but of other Americans, too. Too many Americans, new and old, were ignorant of democratic principles and ideals. All must be educated in the principles of democracy, not static principles frozen in historical time, but living principles that grew out of the people's experience. It was through a growing democracy and the proper understanding of American history and traditions that the common people would find their rightful place. Democracy became Bode's philosophical and educational theme.

As he was to write later in *Democracy As a Way of Life* (1937), Bode thought that democracy would result in freeing people's intelligence and that freed intelligence would, in turn, create more and better democracy. In addition, the great strides made in science showed that science was the primary method or tool of intelligence; therefore, mankind should apply science to the problem of how to live more democratically. In Bode's view, however, science could also be misused—as it often was in times of war, for example—and so there was a need for philosophers to help people think more deeply about how they used scientific knowledge and other kinds of knowledge. Thus, democracy and intelligence went hand in hand, and science and philosophy had major roles in helping achieve greater democracy and intelligence.

National Spokesman for Pragmatism

In 1909 Bode left Wisconsin to take a position in the department of philosophy at the University of Illinois, where his change to pragmatism was completed. The further he went in his development toward pragmatism, the more interested he became in the philosophy of education. In 1916 he became more fully involved in philosophy of education when he participated in teaching a seminar in the university's department of education, an assignment he continued over the next several years. Gradually he gained a reputation in philosophy of education through his teaching and publications, and in 1921 he was offered the position of head of the department of principles and practices of education at the Ohio State University. It was from this position that he became a nationally prominent leader in the field of philosophy of education and one of the recognized thinkers associated with progressive education.

Progressive education had many different kinds of supporters and advocates with varied points of view and it lacked any systematic, unifying philosophical foundation. Bode's initial approach to progressive education was as a critic, but one not totally unsympathetic to the movement. He sought to give progressive education a philosophical base, which he felt should involve translating "pragmatic philosophy into educational procedures." At least some aspects of progressivism, he wrote in *Progressive Education at the Crossroads* (1938), were too much drawn to romanticism and to sentimentality about children and the spreading of "sweetness and light." What was needed was a further underpinning of those progressive emphases on the individual, avoidance of imposition, and the securing of the free play of intelligence—all of which, Bode argued, reflected wider societal needs of the common man and the demands of democracy. Unless progressive education recognized these democratic imperatives, it would have no guiding principles. In short, progressive education had the choice of "becoming the avowed exponent of democracy or else of becoming (only) a set of ingenious devices. . . . "

In his efforts to give progressive education a philosophical base, Bode chided the progressives for some of their positions. To the progressive rubric that teachers should "teach the child and not the subject," Bode replied that the traditional subjects stood for an educational value that we neglect at our own peril. If intelligence is to become free, he argued, it must understand how concepts are formed and what counts for evidence and truth, things which traditional subjects, if approached in the right way, help provide. While progressive education had made great strides toward moving education away from the authoritarian imposition of an earlier time, it needed to become more secure of its own aims.

Education to Strengthen Democracy

To Bode, what was needed was a recognition that the great strides made in science and technology had created a "culture lag," where institutions and outlooks had not kept pace. In former times the young had been brought up with beliefs that reflected the world about them, but this was no longer the case. The great changes of science and technology had called into question the old values and beliefs, and, consequently, the young were growing up disillusioned and aimless. Education's function, then, was to help the young understand these value contradictions by transmitting the achieved values of civilization so that the young could see the contradictions and make intelligent value choices. A basic problem for the schools, then, was to help the young make sense out of a confused cultural heritage and to help them construct a philosophy of life. As the effects of the depression, the spread of totalitarian governments, and World War II took their toll, Bode became even more convinced that the schools must vitalize the meaning of democracy. What was needed was to educate the young in how to think.

Critics of Bode's philosophy of education have pointed to the lack of precise detail on how his ideas could be achieved. Furthermore, Bode has been criticized for a failure to set forth in exacting language the kind of curriculum he envisioned for the schools. However, Bode maintained that a democratic way of life is based on growth and change, rather than pre-determined, unchanging maxims. If democracy is truly based on growth and change, then it is futile to attempt to be too exact. Bode did, however, express strong convictions about the need for democracy and the power of a proper education to enable people to think more

clearly. He insisted that "form follows function," or outcomes follow action, and so the results that flow from sound thinking cannot be pre-established in any exact sense.

Bode retired from full-time teaching in 1944, but he continued to write, give an occasional lecture, and sometimes teach a summer session course until shortly before his death in 1953. Throughout his life as a philosopher and educator Bode exhibited a sturdy faith in democracy, human intelligence, and the power of education. His belief in the connection of these three things are his legacy to the contemporary world.

Further Reading

An interesting biography is Robert B. Bullough, Jr., *Democracy in Education: Boyd H. Bode* (1981), in which sections of the book are written in imaginative dialogue format, depicting conversations Bode actually had or may have had with his philosophical peers. Perhaps the best critical review of Bode's philosophy is J.J. Chambliss, *Boyd H. Bode's Philosophy of Education* (1963). Bode himself was the author of many articles and books. The two books which probably best illustrate his philosophical themes and emphases are *Democracy As a Way of Life* (1937) and *Progressive Education at the Crossroads* (1938).

Additional Sources

Sun, Huai Chin, *Boyd H. Bode (1873-1953) and the reform of American education: recollections and correspondence*, Hampton, VA: Sun, 1977. □

Jean Bodin

The French political philosopher Jean Bodin (1529/ 1530-1596) influenced European intellectual history through his formulation of economic theories and of principles of good government and through his advocacy of religious tolerance in an intolerant age.

Jean Bodin was born in Angers, the son of a tailor. He received his early education in Angers and Paris as a member of the religious order of Carmelites. After leaving the monastic life, he studied and later taught law at the University of Toulouse. In 1561 he began to practice law in Paris and at about the same time published two significant books. In *Methodus ad facilem historiarum cognitionem* (A Method for the Easy Learning of History), Bodin attempted to determine the principles of universal law through a study of history; in *Response aux paradoxes de M. Malestroit* (1568; Response to the Paradoxes of Monsieur Malestroit), he contended that the revolutionary rise in prices in the 16th century was caused by the great influx of gold and silver—an analysis which has earned him a distinguished position among early modern European economists.

Bodin won the favor of King Henry III of France and of his brother, the Duke of Alençon. In 1571 he became counselor to the duke and was appointed king's attorney at Laon in 1576. In the same year he served as a delegate of the

Third Estate (commoners) at the Estates General of Blois. There Bodin antagonized the clergy and nobility by favoring negotiation instead of war with the French Protestants. He also opposed the King's demand to gain additional revenue by selling public lands and royal demesnes. Because of his stand, Bodin lost favor with the King, but he continued to serve the duke.

Bodin's most famous work, *Six livres de la république* (1576; Six Books of the Republic), reflects his distress over the chaos in France during the Wars of Religion. The principles Bodin proposes for a well-ordered state are based on the doctrine of sovereignty. He believed the state needed one supreme authority to make and enforce law, an authority whose power was limited only by natural and divine law and by the "fundamental laws" of the land. Although he conceded that there could be different types of government, he thought monarchy the most stable because its sovereignty was not divided.

In 1583 Bodin returned to Laon as procurator to the presidial court and spent the rest of his life there. Bodin's interest turned from politics to religion, and his writings reflect this change. In *La Demonomanie des sorciers* (1580; The Demonomania of Witches), he advocated the burning of witches. In the *Heptaplomeres* (1588)—a colloquy between a Jew, a Moslem, a Calvinist, a Lutheran, a Catholic, a theist, and an epicurean—his characters eventually decide that since one religion is as good as another, they should live together in charity. In 1596 Bodin died of plague in Laon.

Further Reading

For specialized works on Bodin in English see the still-worthwhile chapter in J. W. Allen, *A History of Political Thought in the Sixteenth Century* (1928; rev. ed. 1957); Beatrice Reynolds, *Proponents of Limited Monarchy in Sixteenth Century France: Francis Hotman and Jean Bodin* (1931); and Julian H. Franklin, *Jean Bodin and the Sixteenth-Century Revolution in the Methodology of Law and History* (1963). □

Jacob Boehme

The German mystic Jacob Boehme (1575-1624) drew unique philosophical and religious ideas from his own spiritual experiences. His thought had a profound effect on German religious life and philosophy and influenced Quakerism in England.

Jacob Boehme was born at Alt-Seidenberg near Görlitz. His parents were peasants who apprenticed him to a shoemaker in Seidenberg. In 1599 he moved to Görlitz, where he prospered as a master cobbler. While still a young man, Boehme experienced mystical visions. These recurred as he grew older, and he became convinced that the inner mysteries of the universe had been opened to him. He had become, as he said, "enwrapped in the Divine Light," and he decided to write an account of his visions, *Aurora* (1612). This work soon came to the attention of the Lutheran pastor

in Görlitz, who tried to have Boehme expelled from the town as a "villain full of piety." The town authorities, however, allowed Boehme to remain on the condition that he write no more books.

Boehme wrote nothing for 5 years, but then, encouraged by a vision, he again felt compelled to compose works that would set forth his ideas. The result was an astonishing number of writings, principally philosophical, theological, and devotional in nature. His most important works include *Von der Gnadenwahl* (Predestination), *Mysterium magnum* (Great Mystery), and *Der Weg zu Christo* (The Way of Christ; all 1623). The last is a collection of four of his devotional works dealing with true repentance, true resignation, regeneration, and the supersensual life.

While some of Boehme's thought remained within a traditional Lutheran framework, he also developed unorthodox ideas. He believed that man was saved by his own effort as well as grace, and he criticized institutional religion, referring to established churches as "churches of stone." But it was his metaphysical speculations that were most novel and that brought him many followers. He believed that all creation proceeded from God "by His self-differentiation into a negation of Himself." Thus, God manifests Himself in contraries. All things consist in yes and no, good and evil, dark and light, and the conflict between these opposites is the fundamental law of being. Boehme's primary religious concern was to demonstrate how the duality of life could be overcome through the reconciliation of opposites in spiritual unity.

Because of the Lutheran pastor's opposition, Boehme was finally obliged to leave Görlitz. He went to Dresden, where he was warmly received by the intellectual community. But he soon returned to Görlitz and, shortly after his arrival, died there on Nov. 17, 1624.

Further Reading

The most complete work on Boehme, based on all the sources, is John Joseph Stoudt, *Sunrise to Eternity: A Study in Jacob Boehme's Life and Thought* (1957). Another biography is Hans L. Martensen, *Jacob Boehme* (trans. 1885; rev. ed. 1949). Additional studies are A. J. Penny, *Studies in Jacob Böhme* (1912); Rufus M. Jones, *Spiritual Reformers in the 16th and 17th Centuries* (1914); George Mervin Alleman, *A Critique of Some Philosophical Aspects of the Mysticism of Jacob Boehme* (1932); and C. A. Muses, *Illumination on Jacob Boehme: The Work of Dionysius Andreas Freher* (1951). Numerous editions of all of Boehme's works are available in English translations. □

William Edward Boeing

Capitalizing on the need for new technology in fighting World War II, William Edward Boeing (1881-1956) became a key figure in American aviation.

William Edward Boeing went from being a general businessman to a giant in the aviation business during the 1940s. Most of this success came as a result of the need for new weapons. World War II was the first major war to be fought with the extensive use of airplanes in a variety of capacities, and airplanes were what Boeing provided.

Background

Born in Detroit, Boeing studied at the Sheffield Scientific School at Yale University but left after two years without graduating. He then moved to Seattle, where he became a prominent timberman, landowner, and yachtsman. Inspired by the new field of aviation, he organized the Boeing Airplane Company in 1915 with a friend, Conrad Westervelt, hoping to build better airplanes than the wooden ones then being used. The Boeing Company began manufacturing airplanes in a seaplane hanger in Seattle, where he copied the designs of European planes used in World War I. Two of Boeing's seaplanes attracted the attention of the U.S. Navy, which encouraged Boeing to develop a new plane that would be used to train pilots. With America's entry into World War I the Boeing facilities expanded rapidly, but the company stagnated in the period between the wars. The company continued to have close ties to the military, and its reputation was based on building fighters during the 1920s and the 1930s. In 1934 his efforts were rewarded when he received the Daniel Guggenheim Medal for successful pioneering and achievement in aircraft design and manufacturing.

The Flying Fortress

During World War II the Boeing Company utilized technological innovations made during the 1930s. Boeing had begun expanding his factories in 1936 in anticipation of war, and the number of employees in the Seattle plants increased to 2,960 by the end of 1938, reaching 28,840 at the time of the Japanese attack on Pearl Harbor in December 1941. Boeing produced three basic types of planes for the military: the B-17 (designed in 1934), the B-29 (designed in 1938), and the Kaydet trainer. The B-17 Flying Fortress and the B-29 Superfortress were the foremost symbols of America's capacity to wage industrial warfare. Both bombers proved decisive in winning the war, particularly in the Pacific theater, where vast amounts of territory had to be covered. (A Boeing Superfortress carried the first atomic bomb dropped on Japan.) At the end of the war Boeing's contracts to produce the bombers ended as well. The company laid off temporary war workers, many of whom were women. He tried to diversify the company's products by experimenting with manufacturing other consumer goods, including furniture, but he quickly realized the difficulty of using airplane factories to manufacture other commodities.

A New Industry

During the 1950s the Boeing Company prospered, though Boeing's health failed and he no longer had any financial connection with it. In the years of prosperity that followed World War II the Boeing Company profited from the expansion of the commercial airline industry by building the Boeing 707 passenger plane. Furthermore, with the advent of the Cold War the government continued to place enough orders to keep weapons manufacturers in business. At the time of Boeing's death in 1956 the company that he had founded had made America's largest jet bomber, the B-52.

Further Reading

Peter M. Bowers, *Boeing Aircraft Since 1916* (Annapolis, Md.: Naval Institute Press, 1989). □

Hermann Boerhaave

The Dutch physician and chemist Hermann Boerhaave (1668-1738) was the leading medical teacher of the early 18th century. His works on medicine and chemistry had widespread use as basic textbooks.

Hermann Boerhaave was born on Dec. 31, 1668, at Voorhout, Holland, the son of a minister in the Dutch Reformed Church. A painful leg ulcer which affected him for 5 years during his youth excited his interest in medicine. He aimed first to combine a career as a pastor and physician. After entering the University of Leiden in 1684, he took courses in mathematics, natural philosophy, botany, and languages, as well as in theology.

In 1690 Boerhaave obtained the degree of doctor of philosophy and began medical studies. As a physician, he was almost entirely self-taught, medical instruction at Leiden being at a low ebb. He obtained his medical degree in 1693 from the University of Harderwijk.

Having come under suspicion of being sympathetic to the doctrines of Spinoza, Boerhaave abandoned the idea of an ecclesiastical career and began to devote himself exclusively to medicine and science. His private practice in Leiden was not lucrative but left him time to continue his studies and begin extensive experiments in chemistry.

His highly successful teaching career began in 1701. He taught medicine at the University of Leiden and gave private courses in chemistry. During the next 8 years he published in Latin his two major medical works, *The Institutes of Medicine* and *The Aphorisms concerning the Knowledge and Cure of Diseases.* Numerous editions were produced and the works were widely translated, even into Japanese. They continued to be used as textbooks for at least 50 years after his death.

Boerhaave was appointed professor of medicine and botany in 1709. In this post he greatly improved the collection of the celebrated botanical garden of the University of Leiden and carried out an extensive correspondence with the world's leading botanists. In 1714 he became professor of medicine and a physician to St. Cecilia Hospital in Leiden. There in his small clinic he established the value of bedside teaching for medical training.

He obtained the chair of chemistry in 1718 and for 11 years held three chairs simultaneously. His definitive *Elements of Chemistry* (1732) became very famous and was the source of his influence on 18th-century chemistry.

A tall and robust man of immense erudition, Boerhaave was a superb teacher. He was patient, unaffected, and readily approachable by his students. They flocked from all parts of Europe to hear his lectures, thereby increasing the renown of the University of Leiden. Boerhaave died, universally esteemed, in 1738 of heart disease.

Further Reading

The definitive study of Boerhaave is G. A. Lindeboom, *Herman Boerhaave: The Man and His Work* (1968). A good background book is Douglas Guthrie, *A History of Medicine* (1945; rev. ed. 1958). □

Allan Aubrey Boesak

Allan Boesak (born 1945), cofounder of the United Democratic Front (UDF), was a leading opponent of apartheid in South Africa and continues to be a spritual and political force.

Allan Aubrey Boesak was born on February 23, 1945, in Kakamas, N.W. Cape, South Africa. From an early age he developed his twin interests of religion and politics. Having always wanted to be a minister, Boesak at age 14 became a sexton in the Dutch Reformed Church's Sendingkerk (a "colored," or mixedrace, offshoot of the white Dutch Reformed Church). After graduating from Bellville Theological Seminary in 1967, Boesak was ordained at age 23. He married Dorothy Rose Martin in 1969 and they had four children (he eventually divorced and later married Elna Botha in 1991). By his late teens Boesak had expressed increasing dissatisfaction with South Africa's *apartheid,* a strict form of segregation, especially after the government cited racial reasons to force his family to relocate.

From 1970 to 1976 Boesak studied at the Kampen Theological Institute in Holland, where he completed his doctorate on ethics. Returning to South Africa shortly after the 1976 Soweto uprisings, Boesak increased his political activities through the church. Boesak's appeal quickly spread beyond the 2.8 million "coloreds" to both black and white opponents of apartheid. In 1981 various black Reformed churches founded ABRECSA (the Alliance of Black Reformed Christians in Southern Africa) and elected Boesak as chairman. The alliance's statement reflected many of Boesak's beliefs. It rejected the use of religion as a cultural or racist ideology (as employed by the white Dutch Reformed Church according to the alliance). The alliance's statement furthermore rejected divorcing religion from political activism. Boesak and the alliance believed that the struggle against apartheid represented a struggle for Christianity's integrity.

Boesak first received international attention in August of 1982 when the World Alliance of Reformed Churches (WARC) met in Canada. WARC represented about 150 churches of Calvinist tradition in 76 countries with a combined membership of over 50 million. Boesak introduced a motion requesting that WARC declare apartheid a heresy contrary to both the Gospel and the Reformed tradition. The alliance adopted the Declaration on Racism, suspended South Africa's white Dutch Reformed Church, and unanimously elected Boesak president of the alliance. His new position made him spiritual leader to over 50 million Christians. This base of international support subsequently protected him against some forms of governmental repression. He held the post until 1989.

In January of 1983 Boesak suggested that all groups opposed to the government's new constitution should unite. The government of Pieter Willem Botha had proposed giving increased powers to the state president while allowing limited representation in parliament to the mixed-race people and Asians, while excluding South Africa's blacks, who formed 73 percent of the population. Boesak opposed the constitution on moral grounds since it excluded the majority of South Africans, entrenched apartheid and white domination, and accepted ethnicity as the criterion for politics in South Africa.

Following Boesak's suggestion, a steering committee established the United Democratic Front (UDF). In August of 1983, before some 20,000 supporters, Boesak helped launch the UDF at Mitchells Plain outside of Cape Town. Boesak was elected patron. By early 1986 the UDF, an umbrella organization for some 700 organizations representing about two million white, mixed-race, and black South Africans, was the largest and most powerful legal opposition force in South Africa. Its membership and especially its goals approximated those of the then-banned African National Congress (ANC).

Boesak increasingly appeared at the forefront of opposition to the white government. He believed that "apartheid can never be modified," only "eradicated." While Boesak preferred nonviolent protest, he questioned its success in South Africa: "One cannot talk about violence if one is unable to do anything about it. In such a situation, nonviolence becomes an oppressive ideology. It aids and abets the oppressor."

Verbally, Boesak termed South Africa's government the "spiritual children of Hitler" and the South African police a "spiritual murder machine." Politically, he continued as a leader of the UDF and urged consumer boycotts of white businesses as well as a day of prayer for the overthrow of the white government. He opposed President Reagan's policy of "constructive engagement" toward South Africa.

On April 27, 1994, the first elections open to all South African citizens regardless of color were held. The ANC won over 62 percent of the popular vote and Nelson Mandela, who had been a political prisoner for over 27 years, was elected president. Boesak became president of the Association of Christian Students in South Africa, and founded the Foundation for Peace and Justice in Belleville. He also serves as the head of economic affairs for the African National Congress Western Cape. South Africa continues to see Reverend Boesak work as an articulate cleric-politician.

Further Reading

No biographies have yet appeared on Allan Boesak. He has written a number of books, including *Farewell to Innocence: A Socio-Ethical Study on Black Theology and Black Power* (1977), *Finger of God: Sermons on Faith and Socio-Political Responsibility* (1982), *Walking on Thorns: The Call to Christian Obedience* (1984), *Black and Reformed: Apartheid, Liberation, and the Calvinist Tradition* (1984), *A Call for the End to Unjust Rule* (1987), *Comfort and Protest: Reflections on the Apocalypse of John of Patmos* (1987), and *If This Is Treason, I Am Guilty* (1988). A thorough introduction to South Africa is *South Africa: Time Running Out* (Study Commission On U.S. Policy Toward Southern Africa, University of California, 1981, 1986). □

Anicius Manlius Severinus Boethius

The Roman logician and theologian Anicius Manlius Severinus Boethius (c. 480-c. 524) is best known for his influential work "The Consolation of Philosophy." He also wrote theological treatises and transmitted to the Middle Ages portions of Aristotle's writings.

B orn in Rome of an ancient family, Boethius probably received schooling in Athens or possibly in Alexandria. In any case he acquired a thorough knowledge of the Greek language and the philosophies of Plato, Aristotle, and the Stoics. He undertook to translate the works of Plato and Aristotle into Latin with the aim of reconciling the two philosophies. This task was never completed, but Boethius did translate Aristotle's logical works and wrote commentaries on two of them.

Boethius's most important purely philosophical work is his second and longer commentary on Porphyry's *Eisagoge* (*Introduction*) to Aristotle's *Categories*. Therein he discusses the status of universals in a text that was to become a classic in the late Middle Ages. Concerning universals, Porphyry had raised three questions. First, are species (for example, man), genera (for example, animal), and other universals realities or mental conceptions? Second, if they are realities, are they corporeal or incorporeal? Third, if universals are incorporeal, do they exist apart from sensibles or in union with them?

In his discussion Boethius presents Aristotle's solution on universals, as explained by Alexander of Aphrodisias (ca. A. D. 200). Briefly this solution states that species and genera are realities as well as mental conceptions. As realities, they are incorporeal and exist in union with sensible things. Accordingly, individual men exist with substantial likenesses to one another, but what they have in common does not exist in reality apart from them. On the basis of substantial likenesses, the mind conceives of the species of man. The abstract conception is a true one, and it applies to individual men, though no species exists apart from individuals.

Plato's thesis that universals are realities that are incorporeal and exist apart from sensible things is mentioned by Boethius as an alternative but not necessarily as a preferable one. Boethius's neutrality is all the more striking when we realize that he was very much a Platonist in *The Consolation of Philosophy.*

In 510 Theodoric, the Ostrogothic king of Italy, had raised Boethius to the rank of consul. But by 523 Theodoric suspected that he was conspiring with Roman aristocrats and the Emperor in Constantiniple to overthrow him. Exactly what caused Boethius to fall out of favor with Theodoric has been the matter of some conjecture. It is known that there were Roman aristocrats interested in reuniting the Eastern and Western empires at the expense of Ostrogothic rule and that Boethius had made a contribution toward bridging the schism of East and West by writing four tracts between 512 and 522 on divisive theological issues. (In one of them, *De Trinitate,* Boethius made use of the Aristotelian categories of substance and relation to define the doctrine of the Trinity.) Whatever the precise details may be, Theodoric had Boethius put to death for treason in 524 or 525.

The Consolation of Philosophy was composed by Boethius during the last year of his life while he was imprisoned in Pavia. This work is a dialogue in prose and verse between the author and Philosophia, the personification of philosophy. In it Boethius maintains that happiness can be found in the most adverse of conditions. The underpinning for such an optimistic outlook is the contrast of providence and fate. A world created by a providential God contains no possibility of evil as a reality. In achieving a cosmic order, God uses the instrument of fate, which necessitates each individual occurrence. However unfortunate a fated event may seem to a person from his limited and peripheral point of view, he still has the freedom to turn his mind to a providential God at the center of things. A man will thereby rise above the apparent misery of his circumstances and find consolation.

Further Reading

Three specialized works on Boethius are Hugh Fraser Stewart, *Boethius: An Essay* (1891); Howard Rollin Patch, *The Tradition of Boethius: A Study of His Importance in Medieval Culture* (1935); and Helen M. Barrett, *Boethius: Some Aspects of His Times and Work* (1940). For Boethius as a precursor of scholasticism see Edward Kennard Rand, *Founders of the Middle Ages* (1928; 2d ed. 1929). For the philosophical era in which Boethius lived, a monumental work is A. H. Armstrong, ed., *The Cambridge History of Later Greek and Early Medieval Philosophy* (1967).

Additional Sources

McInerny, Ralph M., *Boethius and Aquinas,* Washington, D.C.: Catholic University of America Press, 1990.

Reiss, Edmund, *Boethius,* Boston: Twayne Publishers, 1982.

Stewart, H. F. (Hugh Fraser), *Boethius: an essay,* New York: B. Franklin, 1974. ☐

Gabriel Germain Boffrand

Gabriel Germain Boffrand (1667-1754) was a French architect and interior decorator whose mastery of the new Louis XV or rococo style widely influenced 18th-century architecture in France and abroad.

Gabriel Germain Boffrand codified and disseminated the supple rococo style which borrowed, in miniature scale, more from the Italian baroque of Francesco Borromini and Guarino Guarini than from the stringent academic classicism favored in France since the Renaissance. Boffrand's book *Livre d'architecture* (1745) indicates that he was aware of his role as mediator of the golden mean between reason and fantasy.

Through loss of documentation and the demolition of most of the palaces and town houses Boffrand built in Paris and in the province of Lorraine, relatively little evidence of his talents subsists. He is said to have begun his artistic training under the sculptor François Girardon, but there is proof that Boffrand worked for the first architect of the king, Jules Hardouin Mansart, from 1686 to 1691 and during 1693-1694. From 1694 to 1709 Boffrand worked on his own in Paris, Lorraine, and the Netherlands, building and remodeling private houses and small palaces. In 1709 he became, under the sponsorship of the new first architect, Robert de Cotte, a member of the Royal Academy and architect of the superintendence of buildings. Boffrand's remodeling of the Petit-Luxembourg is the principal surviving source of numerous examples of his interior designs, and it supplies clues for other attributions to him.

Between 1711 and 1715 Boffrand worked in Lorraine as first architect to Duke Leopold, building palaces at Nancy and Lunéville and the château La Malgrange, all destroyed. Two Parisian houses demonstrate Boffrand's style during the Regency period: the Hôtel de Villars (1713 and 1717) and the Hôtel de Parabère (1718-1720). In 1723 Balthasar Neumann, architect to the prince-bishop of Würzburg, brought his plans for the new Residenz to Paris for editing by De Cotte and Boffrand; the latter visited the site at Würzburg the next year. In 1736 Boffrand undertook the interior design of the Hôtel Soubise in Paris, his last and most notable work. The oval salon is the outstanding creation of the rococo style.

Boffrand was a master of integrating convex and concave spatial solids and rectilinear and curvilinear planes. His signal credit as an architect was in having concretized the evolution of the sometimes overly mannered and occasionally chaotic style called the rococo.

Further Reading

Fiske Kimball, *The Creation of the Rococo* (1943), weaves Boffrand into the fabric of the 50-year evolution of the rococo style but underrates his importance as an original contributor. A valuable background study is Germain Bazin, *Baroque and Rococo* (trans. 1964). ☐

Ricardo Bofill

The post-modern Spanish architect Ricardo Bofill (born 1939) fused the Classical syntax of architecture with modern building technology to create large scale housing projects recalling the grandeur of Louis XIV.

The son of a Venetian mother and a Catalan father, Ricardo Bofill was born on December 5, 1939, in Barcelona, Spain. He studied architecture at the Escuela Tecnica Superior de Arquitectura in Barcelona (1955-1956) and at the Architecture University of Geneva, Switzerland (1957-1960). In 1960 he founded the Taller de Arquitectura (Architecture workshop), based in Barcelona. The *taller* has an interdisciplinary approach to architecture and includes not only architects but designers, a mathematician, a musician, a poet, and a philosopher. Bofill became a highly romantic figure who generated the creative and intellectual drive for the team. His romantic spirit was captured in the renovated cement factory in Barcelona (1973-1975), which was the main office and studio of the firm. Other offices were located in Paris and New York.

Bofill's stated intentions with respect to the firm, published in *L'architecture d'un homme* (1978), were to create dynamic and "magic" spaces using powerful forms to produce distinctive images. Although these intentions are found in all their designs, each was adapted to different local circumstances. Bofill and his *taller* rejected the tenets of the International Style (particularly the works of Le Corbusier and Mies van der Rohe), declaring their own work as a "brutal protest" against functionalist modernism. Like many post-modern architects, Bofill accepted the lessons of many centuries of architectural history to create places for human life.

Bofill first gained international attention in the 1960s with two designs executed in the Catalan region of Spain, where the expressive works of Antonio Gaudi have played a major role. The Barrio Gaudi (1964-1968), a public housing project located in Rues, Tarragona (the hometown of Antonio Gaudi), includes an interlocking grid of apartments in a variety of sizes, each with individual balconies, pantile roofs (made of s-curved tiles), and a multilevel system of walkways and plazas. The communal roof garden (a consistent motif in Bofill's work) is a direct tribute to Gaudi. Bofill's design for the Catalan resort of Xanadu in Calpe, Alicante (1969-1983), consists of a seven-story block with cubical living spaces arranged around a central utility core. The design is characterized by vernacular motifs such as sloping pantiled roofs, arcades, and "Mediterranean" windows with shutters. With its swooping curves and figural shapes, Xanadu comes closer in spirit to the expressive work of Gaudi than the barrio which bears his name. Both the barrio and Xanadu display Bofill's continuing interest in creating "garden cities in space." The culmination of these efforts occurred in Spain with the firm's design for Walden 7, Sant Just Desvern, Barcelona (1970-1975).

In the mid-1970s Bofill became involved with several projects designed for the French "New Towns" which surround Paris. All of these projects combine Bofill's interest in baroque spatial organization with a desire to return to traditional elements of urban planning. In these projects Bofill turned from the vernacular architecture of the Mediterranean to the Classical language which characterizes much of the grand architecture in France since the Renaissance. Using reinforced concrete structures and prefabricated concrete panels, he approached the Classical style on a truly monumental scale. His treatment of "concrete like a noble material" is reminiscent of the work of Louis Kahn. The monumental use of reinforced concrete also has precedents in the French architectural tradition with the works of Tony Garnier, Auguste Perret, and Le Corbusier.

Bofill and his *taller's* design for Les Arcades du Lac and Le Viaduc, in Saint-Quentin-en-Yvelines (1975-1981), located near Versailles, present a monumental arrangement of buildings on the scale of the visionary and unbuilt projects of the 18th-century French architects Ledoux and Boullee. The design is composed of densely massed buildings with orderly façades laid out along rigid axes and placed within formal gardens. The arrangement of the buildings and gardens allude to the Palace of Versailles and have even been described as a "Versailles for the people."

Bofill and his *taller* explored a more sophisticated use of the Classical syntax in their design for Les Espaces d'Abraxas (1979-1983) in the Marne-la-Vallee suburb of Paris. Abraxas is the word for the Mesopotamian symbol meaning good and evil which roughly translates as "magic." The entire composition creates the impression of a gigantic "theater" and relates to Bofill's statement that "daily life should not be banalized, but exalted to become rich and meaningful." In the design Bofill often stretches and inverts the traditional language of Classicism in a mannerist play of forms. The interior façade of the semicircular amphitheater has a giant seven-story colonnade with attached columns whose shafts are formed by panes of glass (in opposition to the solidity of traditional columns). The arc of the amphitheater is interrupted only by a single large opening, which Bofill refers to as an "urban window," that creates a funneled perspective along the major axis of the composition.

Ricardo Bofill's post-modern sensibilities (rejecting the stylistic and ideological restraints of modernism and accepting the lessons of centuries of architectural history) have allowed him to create heroic public housing with advanced concrete techniques that evoke the splendors of past French rulers such as Louis XIV and Napoleon. He has been the subject of several exhibits, most notably a 1985 joint exhibit with Leon Krier, "Architecture, Urbanism, and History," at the Museum of Modern Art in New York. In 1987 Bofill designed and built a public housing complex in New Jersey known as *Venice-on-the-Hudson*. Taking his inspiration from Frank Lloyd Wright, Bofill, in conjunction with the architectural firm of Kendall/Heaton Associates Inc. designed and completed the Alice Pratt Brown Hall for the Shepard School of Music at Rice University in 1989. Alongside these successes, Bofill's megalomania has been noted.

In *Crain's Chicago Business* (August 2, 1993), John Jacobs— a fellow architect—wrote that Bofill's 1992 design of R.R. Donnelley & Sons Co. Headquarters, at 77 W. Wacker Dr. in Chicago, is a design disaster which he refers to as "Parthenon-on-a-Stick". Bofill has alternately been praised and discredited as the creator of mass housing projects for the poor in France in 1992.

In 1976 Bofill founded one of Cuba's major human rights groups, the Cuban Committee for Human Rights. This group has been affiliated with several other groups whose common goals include human rights, amnesty, free art, and disarmament. Bofill was exiled to Miami in 1988, after spending 14 years in Cuba as a political prisoner. He became a commentator on Miami radio station WQBA, but was fired in 1990 after voicing his support of Cuban dissident Gustavo Arcos, who had led Bofill's Cuban Committee for Human Rights.

Further Reading

The most complete book on Bofill and his *taller* is *Ricardo Bofill/ Taller de Arquitectura: Buildings and Projects 1960-1985,* introduction by Ricardo Bofill, postscript by Warren A. James (1988), which also includes an extensive interview with Bofill. An earlier book is *Ricardo Bofill/Taller de Arquitectura,* introduction by Christian Norberg-Schulz (1985). A book which places Bofill in the context of post-modern classicism is *Modern Classicism* by Robert A. M. Stern with Raymond W. Gastil (1989). Charles Jenck's *Architecture Today* (1988) provides a background to this period. Also see "Venice-on-the-Hudson" in *New York* magazine (June 1987), "Classical Music" in *Architectural Record* (March 1992) and "Ricardo Bofill" in *Architectural Digest* (April 1988). □

Humphrey Bogart

The American stage and screen actor, Humphrey Bogart (1899-1957), was one of Hollywood's most durable stars and a performer of considerable skill, subtlety, and individuality.

Humphrey Deforest Bogart was born on January 23, 1899, in New York City to Deforest Bogart, a surgeon, and Maud Humphrey Bogart, an illustrator. He attended several private schools, but performed poorly and was expelled at one point. Bogart spent several years with the U.S. Navy and worked briefly as a Wall Street clerk before entering the competitive world of Broadway theater. After a considerable struggle he achieved stature with his two most important stage appearances: in Maxwell Anderson's comedy *Saturday's Children* and Robert E. Sherwood's gangster morality play, *The Petrified Forest*. His characterization of the psychotic killer, Duke Mantee, in the latter, as well as in the popular film version with Bette Davis and Leslie Howard, led to typecasting him as a mobster in such movies as *Dead End* (1937), *Angels with Dirty Faces* (1938), and *The Roaring Twenties* (1940).

Achieved Star Status with Classic Films

Not until his performance as the cold, uncommitted private detective, Sam Spade, in John Huston's adaptation of Dashiell Hammett's *The Maltese Falcon* (1941), did Bogart reveal his potential as a screen personality. He projected, as one critic remarked, "that ambiguous mixture of avarice and honor, sexuality and fear." His co-starring role with Ingrid Bergman as Rick Blaine in Michael Curtiz's war drama *Casablanca* (1943) added to his legend and led to his first Academy Award nomination. He lost, but the film won Best Picture honors. *To Have and Have Not* (1944), Hemingway's novel of the Depression transformed into a comedy of social consciousness by William Faulkner and Howard Hawks, cast Bogart with Lauren Bacall. The following year Bogart divorced his third wife and the two stars married; they had two children.

Although Bogart appeared in several poor movies, most of his films were above the standard Hollywood level, and *The Treasure of Sierra Madre* (1948) may be one of the greatest films ever released. His best motion pictures of the 1940s include *Sahara* (1943), a realistic World War II drama; *The Big Sleep* (1946), Hawks's sophisticated detective thriller based on the Raymond Chandler novel; and *Key Largo* (1948), Huston's toughened filming of the Maxwell Anderson play. Of Bogart's portrayal of the pathetic psychopath in Huston's study of human greed, *The Treasure of Sierra Madre,* Pauline Kael wrote, "In a brilliant characterization, Humphrey Bogart takes the tough-guy role to its psychological limits—the man who stands alone goes from

depravity through paranoia to total disintegration." What in Duke Mantee was mere melodramatic villainy had been transformed into grim psychological reality. In a very different film, the Huston/James Agee adventure comedy, *The African Queen* (1951), Bogart won an Academy Award for his humorously expressive depiction of the earthy, gin-guzzling skipper who brings life to a straight-laced Katharine Hepburn.

In Joseph L. Mankiewicz's Hollywood exposé *The Barefoot Contessa* (1953), Bogart gave depth to his role as a shattered, alcoholic film director. In *Beat the Devil* (1954), he portrayed a disreputable adventurer. *The Caine Mutiny* (1954) provided Bogart with one of his finest roles, as the deranged Captain Queeg. In his last film Bogart gave a strong performance as an investigator of sports corruption in the sharp-edged boxing drama *The Harder They Fall* (1956). A year later, after a long struggle with throat cancer, he died in Hollywood. At his funeral, Bogart's long-time friend Huston paid him tribute: "He is quite unreplaceable. There will never be anybody like him."

Further Reading

Katz, Ephraim. *The Film Encyclopedia* (1979).
Sennet, Ted. *Warner Brothers Presents* (1971). □

Bohemund I

The Norman Bohemund I (ca. 1055-c. 1111) was one of the chief lay leaders of the First Crusade, in 1095-1099, and the self-proclaimed prince of Antioch.

The eldest son of the Norman adventurer Robert Guiscard, Bohemund became involved after 1080 in several Norman expeditions against the Byzantine Empire in southern Italy and on the Greek mainland. But when his father died in 1085, the Greek invasion came to a halt, and Bohemund returned to Italy to wrest what lands he could, including Taranto, from his half brother, Roger, the successor to the fiefs in Apulia and Calabria. In 1096 Bohemund joined the French contingent of the First Crusade on its way to Constantinople.

In spite of his reputation as an enemy of the Byzantines, he soon reached an agreement with Emperor Alexius and swore an oath of allegiance to him. But this only aggravated the rivalry between Bohemund and Count Raymond of Saint-Gilles for the position of supreme lay leader of the crusade. Although charming when necessary, Bohemund was ambitious, aggressive, and capable of duplicity when it served his ends. Princess Anna Comnena, daughter of Alexius, was both attracted and repelled by this Norman, whom she described as blond, clean-shaven, and very tall but beautifully proportioned. "A certain charm hung about this man," she wrote, "but was partly marred by a general air of the horrible."

At the siege of Antioch in the spring of 1098, Bohemund was successful in breaching the city's walls. Once in command, he took the title of prince of Antioch, thus ignoring his promise of 1097 to give the fortress to the Emperor. In August 1100 he was captured by the Turkish emir of Sivas and held prisoner until he was ransomed in the spring of 1103. During his captivity Tancred acted as regent in Antioch.

When Bohemund's small and ill-equipped army was defeated in 1104 by the Turks at Harran near the Euphrates River, he returned to France. He married Constance, the daughter of King Philip, and remained in France until 1107, when he set out to lay siege to the Byzantine town of Durazzo. Emperor Alexius, however, contained him and forced him to a truce. Alexius finally took his revenge, and Bohemund became his vassal for Antioch. The crusader returned to Italy and died in Apulia in 1111.

Bohemund was a skillful military commander—one of the great Norman conquerors of the late 11th century. Constantly at odds with the Greek emperor and his own allies, Bohemund was a living denial of the ideals of Christian unity preached by the ecclesiastical leaders. Apparently, he was more interested in using the crusade for his own purposes—primarily to counter the Byzantine military force—than in rescuing the Holy Sepulcher from the infidel.

Further Reading

The best book on Bohemund is Ralph B. Yewdale, *Bohemund I, Prince of Antioch* (1924). Useful material may also be found in Steven Runciman, *A History of the Crusades,* vol. 1 (1951) and vol. 2 (1952), and in Kenneth M. Setton, ed., *A History of the Crusades,* vol. 1: *The First Hundred Years* (1959; 2d ed. 1969).

Additional Sources

Yewdale, Ralph Bailey, *Bohemond I, Prince of Antioch,* New York: AMS Press, 1980. □

Charles (Chip) Bohlen

Charles (Chip) Bohlen (1904-1973) was a Russian specialist who served in various government positions, including U.S. ambassador to the Soviet Union and interpreter and advisor to various presidents on Russian affairs.

Charles Eustis Bohlen was born on August 30, 1904, the son of Charles and Celestine (Eustis) Bohlen in Clayton, New York. One of three children, Bohlen grew up in Aiken, South Carolina, where his father, who had inherited a small fortune, was a banker and sportsman. At age 12 Charles moved with his family to Ipswich, Massachusetts. He graduated from St. Paul's School in Concord, New Hampshire, and matriculated at Harvard College, where he majored in modern European history (with one course in Russian history), gained admission to the exclusive Porcellian Club, and played scrub football. His friends dubbed him "Chipper," later reduced to Chip, his nickname.

After Bohlen took his B.A. at Harvard in 1927, he went on a world tour on a tramp ship. Although he had not intended to become a diplomat, his extensive world travels with his family as a child and his course work at Harvard caused him to enter the Foreign Service in Washington in 1929. He was assigned as vice-consul at Prague until 1931, when he became vice-consul at Paris. Here he began serious study of the Russian language. He attended Russian church services and perfected his language skills with Russian emigrees in street cafes. Assigned to study Russian language by the State Department (which anticipated recognition of the Bolshevik government), Bohlen spent one summer with a Russian family in Estonia.

When the United States resumed diplomatic relations with the Union of Soviet Socialist Republics in 1933, Bohlen was named vice-consul under Ambassador William C. Bullitt. Later he served as third secretary at the American Embassy, during which time he travelled extensively throughout Russia. Bohlen returned to Washington in 1935 to join the Division of Eastern European Affairs. Although Bohlen treasured his experiences in Russia, he conceded that he always felt a breath of refreshing air when he crossed the border. Returning in 1938, he found Russia was in convulsion because of the political purge trials which he personally observed. He scored somewhat of a diplomatic coup when in 1939 he learned details of the Russo-German

pact which led to the Nazi attack on Poland, starting World War II.

The State Department reassigned Bohlen to Tokyo in 1940, and he was interned with other embassy personnel in 1941 after the Pearl Harbor attack. When Bohlen returned to Washington, he impressed presidential aide Harry Hopkins. As a result, he became President Franklin D. Roosevelt's personal Russian interpreter. Bohlen continued his diplomatic travels in 1943 when he accompanied Secretary of State Cordell Hull to the Moscow Conference which set the diplomatic framework for the United Nations International Organization. He remained in Moscow as first secretary until summoned in 1944 to be Roosevelt's interpreter at the Teheran Conference of Stalin, Churchill, and Roosevelt. After serving at the Washington conference at Dumbarton Oaks on international organization, he became liaison between the secretary of state and the White House until Roosevelt took him to the Yalta Conference as his interpreter, a task he would later perform for Harry Hopkins on his mission to Moscow. He attended the United Nations conference at San Francisco and went to the Potsdam conference as President Harry S. Truman's language expert. Increasingly he was not only serving as an interpreter but as an adviser to secretaries of state, including James F. Byrnes, George C. Marshall, and Dean Acheson.

Controversy surrounded Bohlen's appointment to Moscow as ambassador by President Dwight D. Eisenhower in 1953. Opposed by Wisconsin's Joseph R. McCarthy, who attacked Bohlen for his role at the Yalta Conference, he eventually won Senate confirmation by a vote of 74 to 13. McCarthy's performance so outraged Senate leaders Robert A. Taft and William Knowland that it marked the beginning of McCarthy's demise.

Political turmoil highlighted Bohlen's five years in Moscow as ambassador, a period which saw the rise and fall of Georgi M. Malenkov, the execution of Lavrenti P. Beria, the emergence of Nikita S. Khruschev, de-Stalinization, the revolt in Hungary, and the Suez crisis. Although his tenure was characterized by highly charged exchanges with Soviet diplomats, the Russians were disappointed when he was moved to the Philippine Embassy, a transfer that resulted from long-standing differences with Secretary of State John Foster Dulles. Later he became special adviser on Soviet affairs for Secretary of State Christian Herter. He finished his diplomatic career with five years of service at the difficult Paris Embassy for President John F. Kennedy and one year as deputy under secretary of state for political affairs, concluding over 40 years of service with the State Department. At age 69, Bohlen died of cancer in Washington, D.C., on December 31, 1973.

Further Reading

Bohlen's obituary appeared in the *New York Times* on January 2, 1974. Other references may be found in the *New York Times Index* and the *Reader's Guide to Periodical Literature*. His diplomatic correspondence may be found in the annual volumes of the *Foreign Relations of the United States* published by the State Department.
Bohlen wrote a superb autobiography just before his death, entitled *Witness to History, 1929-1969* (1973) and back-

ground materials can be consulted in Alexander DeConde, *A History of American Foreign Policy* (1978) and Paul Y. Hammond, *The Cold War Years: American Foreign Policy Since 1945* (1969).

Additional Sources

Ruddy, T. Michael, *The cautious diplomat: Charles E. Bohlen and the Soviet Union, 1929-1969,* Kent, Ohio: Kent State University Press, 1986. □

Eugen von Böhm-Bawerk

The Austrian economist Eugen von Böhm-Bawerk (1851-1914) is known for his achievements in public finance, criticism of the Marxian system, and an original reformation of the theory of capital and interest.

E ugen von Böhm-Bawerk was born Feb. 12, 1851, the son of the vice president of the Moravian provincial government at Brno in Moravia. He was educated in Vienna and, after completing his legal and economic education, devoted a part of his career to the civil service in the Austrian-Hungarian monarchy and the other part to scientific work in economics.

Theory of Capital and Interest

In 1881 he started his university career with a pamphlet, "Whether Legal Right and Relationships Are Economic Goods." Between 1884 and 1888 he published his standard work, *Capital and Interest,* which made him famous. The first volume contained a history of interest theories. The second volume, *The Positive Theory of Capital,* was published in 1888. In this work Böhm-Bawerk, like other members of the Austrian school, claimed that all economic events and actions are finally determined by the consumer's estimation of utility and by his decision making (marginal utility).

So far Böhm-Bawerk had only refined the thoughts already developed by his teacher, Karl Menger. His originality lies not in this theory of estimation but in the usage of the time factor for the explanation of capital and interest. Man does not satisfy his needs directly; first he builds up capital (tools, machines, and plant facilities) by time-consuming action. Then, with these intermediate goods, he produces the means of consumption. Capital is a roundabout production which makes production more productive. Interest is a discount of future goods which are devaluated in comparison with present goods. For many reasons man undervaluates his future. If man gets more future good than the amount of present good he has lent, he will make a loan with his present good. For more than 30 years this work, especially the analysis of capital and interest, was considered a landmark in the development of economic analysis.

Civil Service

In the same year in which he published his theory of capital and interest Böhm-Bawerk went into civil service. Three times he was a minister of public finance (1895, 1897-1898, 1900-1904). He participated in the introduction of income tax and the gold currency and was instrumental in the elimination of the sugar subsidy at the Brussels Convention in 1902. Even as an overburdened high official, he found time to write his critical masterpiece, "Karl Marx and the Close of His System," the refutation of Marx's value theory. In 1904, when the increased financial demands of Austrian armament endangered the balancing of the budget, he resigned. The government wanted to give him an eminent position in a bank, but he was interested only in the resumption of his academic work.

Due to chronic circulation trouble, which eventually led to his death, he was not very productive after 1904. Because he could not write a new edition of his work, he defended himself against many adversaries in the form of appendix notes. Even in these additions he showed his inner assurance and discipline.

Owing to his character and his achievements, he gathered a great number of admirers and disciples. But the time of his greatest influence is gone, and the investigation of consumer strategy and of the technical capital structure has been pushed into the background by the Keynesian theories.

Further Reading

An in-depth analysis of Böhm-Bawerk's economic theory is Robert E. Kuenne, *Eugen von Böhm-Bawerk* (1971). Background studies that discuss Böhm-Bawerk include John M. Ferguson, *Landmarks of Economic Thought* (1938), and Jacob Oser, *The Evolution of Economic Thought* (1963; 2d ed. 1970). □

Niels Henrik David Bohr

The Danish physicist Niels Henrik David Bohr (1885-1962) formulated the first successful explanation of some major lines of the hydrogen spectrum. The Bohr theory of the atom has become the foundation of modern atomic physics.

N iels Bohr was born on Oct. 7, 1885, in Copenhagen, the son of Christian Bohr and Ellen Adler Bohr. He studied physics and philosophy at the University of Copenhagen. His postgraduate work culminated in 1911 in a doctoral dissertation on the electron theory of metals.

In the same year he went to Cambridge University and worked with J. J. Thompson at the Cavendish Laboratory. By the spring of 1912 he was working with Ernest Rutherford at the University of Manchester. It was there that Bohr made some valuable suggestions about the chemical relevance of radioactive decay which proved to be most instrumental in formulating the concept of isotopes.

Secret of the Atom

Bohr's principal interest lay, however, in the planetary model of the atom, which Rutherford proposed in 1911. While pondering the implications of that model, Bohr became acquainted with Johannes Rydberg's studies of spectral lines and with J. J. Balmer's formula. As Bohr himself recalled in 1934, "As soon as I saw Balmer's formula the whole thing was immediately clear to me." The "thing" was the recognition on Bohr's part that basically different laws govern the atom when it is not in its stationary state but is absorbing or emitting radiation. He was no longer at Rutherford's laboratory when he succeeded in developing this revolutionary notion into a consistent and concise picture of the atom.

Meanwhile, in 1912 Bohr married Margrethe Norlund shortly after his return to Copenhagen, where he was appointed assistant professor at the university.

When Bohr asked Rutherford to recommend his now historic paper "On the Constitution of Atoms and Molecules" for publication, Rutherford admitted that Bohr's ideas as to the mode of origin of the spectra of hydrogen were very ingenious and worked very well, but he was unwilling to agree with Bohr's own evaluation of the paper. It took a special trip by Bohr to Rutherford in Manchester and a series of evenings during which the two carefully went over every paragraph in the paper before Rutherford's objections could be overcome. When the paper was published, in three parts in the *Philosophical Magazine,* June, September, and November 1913, reactions were divided.

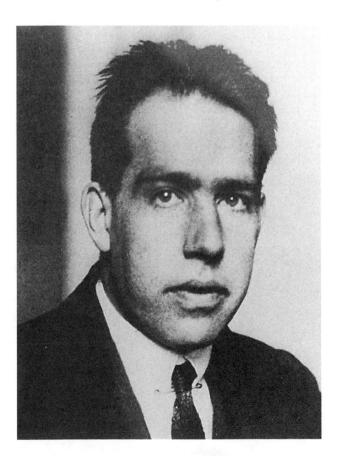

Some immediately expressed unreserved admiration, but there were doubters as well. In Einstein's eyes the paper was one of the great discoveries.

Copenhagen School

Bohr spent 2 years with Rutherford before returning to Copenhagen, where he began to think that the most effective cultivation of atomic and nuclear physics demanded a special institute, sheltering not only a well equipped laboratory, but also playing host to a large number of physicists from all over the world. In 1917 he approached the university with his plan, and as soon as the war was over the plan was enthusiastically approved. The institute was financed by public subscription, and the city donated a choice site to the Institute for Theoretical Physics, which soon established itself as the world center of theoretical physics.

Bohr's first major scientific award was the Hughes Medal of the Royal Society in 1921. The Nobel Prize followed the next year, but the finest tribute to Bohr was the steady stream of brilliant young physicists to his institute, which was dedicated on Sept. 15, 1920. Among the first to arrive at Bohr's institute was Wolfgang Pauli, and 2 years later, in 1924, came Werner Heisenberg, and shortly afterward Paul Dirac, to mention only some most important names in modern physics. In fact, there was hardly a major theoretical breakthrough in physics in the 1920s without some connection with the so-called Copenhagen school. Heisenberg's matrix mechanics, Erwin Schrödinger's wave mechanics, the demonstration of their equivalence by Max Born, Dirac, and P. Jordan, Pauli's theory of electron spin, Louis de Broglie's wave theory of matter—all entered the mainstream of physics through the animated discussions at Bohr's institute. Reminiscing on the 1920s, Bohr could rightly say that "in these years a unique cooperation of a whole generation of theoretical physicists from many countries created step by step, a logically consistent generalization of quantum mechanics and electromagnetics, and has sometimes been designated as the heroic age in quantum physics."

Principle of Complementarity

To use Bohr's own words, "a new outlook emerged," which put the comprehension of physical experience into radically new perspectives. Bohr contributed an important part to that new outlook when he outlined his principle of Complementarity in 1927. According to Bohr, waves and particles were two complementary aspects of nature which, as far as human perception and reasoning went, represented mutually irreducible aspects of nature. The wider implications of such an outlook were further articulated by Bohr in subsequent years, as he came to grips with such philosophical questions as indeterminism versus causality, and life versus mechanism.

Bohr's famous extension of the principle of complementarity to the question of life versus mechanism came in 1932 in a lecture entitled "Light and Life." In this lecture he first pointed out that an exhaustive investigation of the basic units of life was impossible because those life units would most likely be destroyed by the high-speed particles needed for their observation. For Bohr, the units of life represented irreducible entities similar to the quantum of energy. According to him, the "essential non analyzability of atomic stability in mechanical terms presents a close analogy to the impossibility of a physical or chemical explanation of the peculiar functions characteristic of life." Scientists who, because of the subsequent startling developments in molecular biology, claimed to have come to the threshold of a mechanistic explanation of life found no ally in Bohr. To the end of his life he held fast to the basic message of his now-classic lecture, as may be seen from his essay "Light and Life Revisited," written in 1962, the year he died.

An even more fundamental aspect of the principle of complementarity was the recognition that the observer and the observed represented a continuous interaction in which the two influenced and altered one another, however slightly. This meant that the rigid line of separation between the subjective and the objective needed some modification. This also meant a radical modification of the physicist's concept of the external world. The impact of the new insight into the correlation of the objective and the subjective was enormous also on the philosophical temper of the age. It seems indeed that the enunciation of the principle of complementarity by Bohr produced an insurmountable stumbling block for a mechanistic or reductionist explanation of the realm of reality as it is conceived and experienced by man.

Compound Nucleus and the Fission Process

With the discovery of the neutron in 1932, attention rapidly turned from electrons, which form the outer part of the atom, to the nucleus. To understand the various phenomena produced when nuclei of atoms were exposed to bombardment by neutrons, physicists first turned to Bohr's atom model. There the electrons moved largely independently of one another and were subject mainly to a field of force that was the average effect of the motion and position of all of them. The great number of nuclear resonances seemed, however, to point toward a rather different situation. The recognition of this came from Bohr himself, who proposed in 1936 that the protons and neutrons in the nucleus should be considered as a strongly coupled system of particles, in a close analogy to molecules making up a drop of water. In such a system there had to be a very large number of resonance levels of energy, and it also followed that a fairly long time could elapse before the available energy would concentrate on a single neutron resulting in its emission.

This picture of the "compound nucleus" formed the basis of Bohr's other crucial contribution to nuclear physics, the analysis of the fission process. In a paper written jointly with John A. Wheeler in 1939, he showed in quantitative detail the behavior of the compound nucleus for the cases of radiation, neutron emission, and fission. On this last point their all-important contribution consisted in arguing that in the fission of uranium it was mainly the isotope U^{235} that produced the effect under the impact of slow neutrons. It then became immediately clear that to obtain either a large-scale or a sustained, low-rate energy process by fissioning uranium, one had to achieve a separation of U^{235} in sufficient quantities from uranium ore in which the nonfissionable U^{238} was predominant.

A Towering Figure

After 1939, Bohr's life was largely devoted to humanitarian efforts, such as intervening for the Danish Jews; he had to save human lives, including his own and those of his family. Moreover, he felt duty-bound to prevent science from turning into a tool of wholesale destruction. Following his escape to Sweden in September 1943, he was quickly flown to England and from there to the United States. There he lent his talents to the Manhattan Project, and during his stay at Los Alamos he did work on the initiator phase of the activation of the atomic bomb. He also began to stress the need for international control of atomic weapons and energy. His view and arguments helped shape the Acheson-Lilienthal plan and the Baruch proposals to the United Nations on behalf of the American government. In 1950 he submitted in a letter to the United Nations a plea for an "open world where each nation can assert itself solely by the extent to which it can contribute to the common culture, and is able to help others with experience and resources." In the 1950s Bohr's principal contribution to science consisted in taking a leading part in the development of the European Center for Nuclear Research (CERN). It was at his institute that the decision was made to build the 28-Bev (billion-electron-volt) accelerator near Geneva.

From 1938 until his death he was the president of the Royal Danish Academy of Sciences, acted as chairman of the Danish Atomic Energy Commission, and supervised the first phase of the Commission's program for the peaceful uses of atomic energy. Bohr's last major appearance was to deliver the Rutherford Memorial Lecture in 1961, which gave a fascinating portrayal not only of the great master but also of his equally famous disciple.

Bohr's death came rather suddenly but quietly on Nov. 18, 1962, at his home. Einstein and he were possibly the most towering and influential figures of 20th-century physics.

Further Reading

The best biography of Bohr is Ruth Moore, *Niels Bohr: The Man, His Science and the World They Changed* (1966). Stefan Rozental, ed., *Niels Bohr: His Life and Work as Seen by His Friends and Colleagues* (trans. 1967), is a most valuable collection of essays contributed by Bohr's closest friends and associates. On Bohr's role in 20th-century physics one should consult the papers written in his honor on his seventieth birthday, W. Pauli, ed., *Niels Bohr and the Development of Physics* (1955). See also Niels Hugh de Vaudrey Heathcote, *Nobel Prize Winners in Physics, 1901-1950* (1953); Arthur March and Ira Freeman, *New World of Physics* (1962); and Henry A. Boorse and Lloyd Motz, ed., *The World of the Atom* (2 vols., 1966). □

Matteo Maria Boiardo

The Italian poet Matteo Maria Boiardo, Conte di Scandiano (1440-1494), is best known for his *Orlando innamorato*. This masterpiece is the first chivalric poem in which love is the dominant theme.

Matteo Maria Boiardo was born at Scandiano near Reggio Emilia. He went to Ferrara as a child and began classical studies. He held high positions at the court of Ferrara, particularly under the patronage of Ercole d'Este. Boiardo married Taddea dei Conti Gonzaga di Novellera in 1479. Although he preferred poetry and studies to politics, he was involved in the political events of his time as captain of the ducal forces at Modena from 1480 to 1482 and governor of Reggio from 1487 until his death on Dec. 19, 1494.

Literary Works

Boiardo's Latin eclogues, modeled on the Latin poet Virgil and written in honor of Ercole d'Este between 1463 and 1465, as well as numerous other Latin poems and translations from Latin authors, reveal his humanistic culture. Boiardo's first important work in Italian was the *Canzoniere*, or *Amorum libri tres*. Inspired by his unhappy love for Antonia Caprara, this collection of 50 sonnets, interspersed with 10 poems of various meters, was completed between 1472 and 1476 and published at Reggio in 1499. They are considered the finest Italian love lyrics of the 15th century.

Orlando innamorato was to consist of three books dedicated to Ercole and Isabella d'Este. The first two books (60 cantos in octaves) were published in 1484. The third book, interrupted in the ninth canto, was printed posthumously, together with the first two, at Scandiano in 1495. This work combines thematic material from the Carolingian cycle and the Breton romances, both of French origin.

Boiardo's poem, which reflects the interests of the court of Ferrara, tells a series of wonderful tales revolving about Roland's love for Angelica, Angelica's love for Rinaldo, and the pagan Ruggero's love for Bradamante (Ruggero was to be the mythical founder of the house of Este). The poem portrays a marvelous and extraordinary bygone age, and its adventures are enlivened by magic and monsters. While Boiardo's interest in moral values remains evident, he makes no religious distinction between pagans and Christians. Love is the only motivating sentiment, and the laws of honor and chivalry govern both Christian and pagan knights.

Boiardo intended to ennoble his popular source material by achieving a fusion of modern and classical poetry, but the language of his poem, rich in dialectal forms, was foreign to the refined tastes of the Renaissance. In the 16th century Francesco Berni rewrote the *Innamorato* in a more polished literary language. This adaptation completely altered Boiardo's poem, depriving it of its archaic charm; it was so well received, however, that the original was neglected until the 19th century.

Further Reading

There is no biography of Boiardo in English. Ernest Hatch Wilkins, *History of Italian Literature* (1954), contains a section on Boiardo and many references to his influence on Italian prosody. Francesco de Sanctis, *History of Italian Literature* (2 vols., 1931; trans. 1959), does not discuss Boiardo but deals intimately with that period of Renaissance literature. John Addington Symonds's classic work *Renaissance in Italy* (7 vols., 1898) includes Boiardo in a discussion of the art of the time in volume 1 and serves as useful background for the period.

Additional Sources

Looney, Dennis, *Compromising the classics: Romance epic narrative in the Italian Renaissance,* Detroit: Wayne State University Press, 1996.

Marinelli, Peter V., *Ariosto and Boiardo: the origins of Orlando furioso,* Columbia: University of Missouri Press, 1987.

Woodhouse, H. F., *Language and style in a renaissance epic: Berni's corrections to Boiardo's Orlando Innamorato,* London: Modern Humanities Research Association, 1982. □

Nicholas Boileau-Despréaux

The French critic and writer Nicholas Boileau-Despréaux (1636-1711) is best known for the theory of poetics expressed in his "Art poétique." Through this work he became the foremost exponent of French literary classicism.

Nicholas Boileau was born in Paris, the son of a registrar in the Grande Chambre of Parlement. (His later claims to nobility could be substantiated only by fraudulent documents.) Boileau's mother died when he was 19 months old, and his childhood is reputed to have been very unhappy. After attending the Collèges d'Harcourt and de Beauvais, Boileau entered theological school in 1652. Quickly tiring of these studies, he turned to law, his family's traditional vocation. He was admitted as an advocate in 1656, but after his father's death in 1657, he decided to pursue a literary career. Boileau's three older brothers, especially Gilles, who became a critic and translator, were also active in the literary world.

Young Satirist

As a young man, Boileau enjoyed reciting his virulent satires between drinks at various Paris cafés. His physical description indicates that he was probably not attractive. He was short and had thin legs, humped shoulders, a large nose, and possibly an asthmatic condition.

Boileau's first collection, *Satires,* modeled on the works of the Latin poet Juvenal and dating from 1657, began as daring jibes not meant for publication. The poems were usually inspired by the political, social, and literary events

formulated from 1630 to 1650, and thus the *Art poétique* did not dictate the rules of this literary movement. In fact, the ideas in this work had also been expressed by a number of Boileau's contemporaries. But Boileau was original in that he captured the concept of classicism in a concise, forceful, and poetic form. In addition, his literary judgments were remarkably astute; he recognized the genius of, among others, the contemporary playwrights Molière and Racine.

The *Art poétique* is divided into four parts: style and versification, the less important poetic genres, the three great genres (tragedy, epic, comedy), and the vocation of the poet in general. Boileau placed great importance on certain often-repeated key words, such as *raison* (reason), *nature* (nature), *verité* (truth), and *vraisemblance* (likeness to truth). He believed that ''Only the true is beautiful'' and that the poet's role lies in the discovery and presentation of truth. Sincerity and a great desire for ideal truth are necessary to arrive at the essence of things. And once found, truth must be communicated by the poet in a style marked by simplicity, clarity, and grandeur, such as that found in Homer and the Bible. These rules on style are similar to those of the Greek philosopher Longinus, whose *On the Sublime* was translated by Boileau, but are opposed to those advocated by the *précieuses*. During the 18th century Boileau's theories influenced literature in England, Italy, Germany, Spain, and Russia.

Polemics of Later Years

Toward the end of Boileau's life the famous quarrel between two factions of the French literary world, the Ancients and the Moderns, called into question the nature of literary history and the cultural achievement of 17th-century France. The Ancients held that, since the greatest possible literary excellence had been achieved by the Greek and Latin authors, later writers should imitate the content and style of ancient masterpieces. Boileau's translation of Longinus put him on the side of the Ancients. The Moderns, however, recognized progress in the arts and exalted the French *tragédie galante* and the Christian epic. They were more socially sophisticated than Boileau's circle of friends and had the support of influential Parisian women. Thus when Boileau turned again to satire after a period of silence during his term as royal historian, he directed his vehemence against women (Satire X).

Boileau's last satire (Satire XII), a brilliant portrait of the hypocrisy in society's morals and religion, involved him in still another controversy with the government. His numerous friends and his literary importance did little to stave off his growing bitterness. In 1711, 2 months after a final refusal by the state to allow the printing of his satire, Boileau died of pleurisy.

of the day. Satire I complains of corruption brought about by the major financiers of that time. Satire II supports his friend the dramatist Molière against the *Précieuses,* a coterie of popular writers whose works were written in a highly ornate and artificial style. Although Satires III and IV are famous because of their picturesque portrayals of frustrating city life and of country bumpkins at a banquet, Satires VII and IX indicate more accurately the formation of Boileau's literary tastes.

The clandestine publication of *Satires* in 1666 crystallized forces against Boileau. His most formidable enemy, in addition to a number of literary figures, was Colbert, minister in charge of awarding state pensions to poets. The attacks on Boileau were violent, and he was accused of cynicism, debauchery, plagiarism, and blasphemy.

Concept of Poetry

Boileau's transition from satirist to literary theorist is marked by the *Epistles,* modeled on the works of the Latin poet Horace. Epistles I and IV praised King Louis XIV's policies and contributed to Boileau's reconciliation with the governing powers. He was presented to Louis in 1674 and was assured of a pension and publication rights. Boileau did not, however, drop the satirical vein; in the *Lutrin* a quarrel among Paris church canons is made ridiculous through his treatment of it in a serious and elevated style.

During this time Boileau had been reading his *Art poétique* in prominent Paris salons, where it met with immediate success. The tenets of French classicism had been

Further Reading

The most complete and recent works on Boileau are in French. Books in English deal with specialized subjects; for example, A. F. B Clark, *Boileau and the French Classical Critics in England, 1660-1830* (1925), and Jules Brody, *Boileau and Longinus* (1958). Recommended for general historical background is E. B. O. Borgerhoff, *The Freedom of French Classicism* (1950).

Additional Sources

Haley, Marie Philip, Sister, *Racine and the Art poetique of Boileau,* New York: Octagon Books, 1976, 1938.

Pocock, Gordon, *Boileau and the nature of neo-classicism,* Cambridge Eng.; New York: Cambridge University Press, 1980. □

Derek Curtis Bok

Derek Curtis Bok (born 1930) served as dean of the Harvard Law School until he was named president of Harvard University in 1970. In this position he helped broaden the university's mission in its relationship to the larger community while retaining its tradition of intellectual and academic excellence.

Derek Curtis Bok was born March 22, 1930, in Bryn Mawr, Pennsylvania, to Curtis and Margaret Plummer Bok. He came from a prominent Pennsylvania family which includes great-grandfather Cyrus Curtis, founder of the Curtis Publishing Company; grandfather Edward Bok, the first editor of the *Ladies Home Journal* and author of the classic autobiography *The Americanization of Edward Bok;* and father Curtis, who was a novel-writing Pennsylvania Supreme Court justice. Bok attended Stanford University, where he received a B.A. degree in 1951 and was elected to Phi Beta Kappa. Following graduation he came close to selecting the Foreign Service as a career, but instead entered Harvard Law School, receiving an L.L.B. in 1954. During 1954-1955 he was a Fulbright Scholar in political science at the University of Paris, where he met and married Sissila Ann Myrdal, the daughter of Swedish sociologist Gunnar Myrdal. She earned a Ph.D. in philosophy from Harvard. The Boks were the parents of three children.

Derek Bok served as a legal officer in the U.S. Army from 1956 until 1958, during which time he earned his masters degrees in economics (1956) and psychology (1958) at George Washington University. It was during his army stint that his career objectives emerged and he decided he wanted to teach.

Bok went to the Harvard law school in 1958 as an assistant professor specializing in antitrust and labor law. He was lured to Harvard by one of his professors, Kingman Brewster, who later became president of Yale. Bok became a full professor in 1961 and was named to succeed Erwin Griswald as dean of the Harvard law school in 1968. His leadership began at a time of great student unrest, and he wasted little time in initiating reforms to meet the changing needs of students and society. He affirmed the link between the law school and wider concerns of racial unrest, the Vietnam War, and a perceived confidence gap between students and institutions. Symposia on Vietnam issues, increased minority recruitment, emphasis on success of lower ranking students, and emphatic opposition to Nixon Supreme Court nominee Harold Carswell were a few of his activist initiations as dean. His style and deliberate manner were tested by both faculty and students in a series of confrontations and resulted in respect for his ability as a mediator and problem solver. Bok's reputation soon became one of firm decision-making and of unwavering keeping of commitments.

Nathan Pusey, for 18 years president of Harvard University, announced his retirement from that position effective June 1971. The seven-man Harvard Corporation initiated a long search that resulted in the naming of 40 year-old Derek Bok as Pusey's successor. Significant in this decision was the choosing of someone whose primary credentials lay in decision-making, compromise, and conflict management, and of the first non-Harvard alumnus to be named president. (Later the university would award him an honorary bachelor's degree.)

Within a year after Bok's coming to Harvard as president the Vietnam War was settled. The issue of race then became the predominate societal concern of Harvard in the 1970s. Bok inherited a campus with African-Americans numbering only 290 of the 1,500 students and with few African-Americans in significant professional positions. Bok quickly realized the difficulty in making minority undergraduates feel at home in a tradition-bound intellectual atmosphere.

Unrest over admission and hiring policies precipitated a presidential letter in 1981 which publicly committed Bok to developing a strong minority presence at Harvard. "Our minority students are welcome here as fully as any other group because they meet our intellectual standards (and) enrich our diverse community." Bok viewed affirmative action as a means of increasing a minority presence on campus but rejected the concept of a strict numerical quota. He filed an "amicas curiae" brief in the Bakke case on behalf of the University of California, Davis, regents. Arguing that although Harvard didn't reserve quotas for minority students, it did deny that a student had a right to admission based on academic merits alone. He further contended that racial problems would never be fully resolved until substantial numbers of African-Americans assumed positions of responsibility in major corporations, law firms, teaching hospitals, and agencies of government.

In the early 1980s the issue of divestiture of economic interests tied to South Africa surfaced at Harvard. Student demands at many major institutions led to the selling of such assets. Bok objected to such divestiture, saying he would need proof that such action would help overcome apartheid. For Harvard, divestment would have caused the diversion of millions of dollars and created a myriad of financial headaches. Bok strongly stated his opposition to the South African regime and pledged to chart a course best calculated to affect South African policy.

Bok stepped down as university president in 1991. His years as president of Harvard University were hallmarked by a broadening of the university's mission while holding fast to intellectual tradition and academic excellence. No longer was the undergraduate college student characterized as a prep school graduate and Harvard legacy. The leading intellectual center of the world was indelibly marked by his leadership.

Bok was a member of the American Bar Foundation, American Law Institute, and Phi Beta Kappa. His publications included several books and numerous journal and periodical articles. He and his family lived in a home near the campus where his leisure interests of gardening, tennis, and swimming provided diversion from his professional responsibilities.

Further Reading

Bok was the subject of several articles in *Time, Newsweek, Life,* and other periodicals at the time of his selection as president of Harvard and in the late 1970s and early 1980s when issues of divestiture, deregulation, and racial quotas were at the forefront. The following books by Bok should provide additional insight: *Beyond the Ivory Tower: Social Responsibilities of the Modern University* (1982); *Cases and Materials on Labor Law,* 9th ed. (with Archibald Cox) (1983); and, *Labor and the American Community* (with John T. Dunlap) (1970).
□

Sissela Ann Bok

Although she was born in Sweden and educated at the Sorbonne University in Paris, Sissela Ann Bok (born 1934) may be considered one of the premier American women moral philosophers of the latter part of the 20th century. Respected by fellow scholars, she was also highly regarded by the media, which often sought her views on ethics and philosophy.

S issela Bok was born in Stockholm, Sweden, on December 2, 1934, the daughter of Gunnar and Alva (Reimer) Myrdal. After studying in Europe she came to the United States, where she received her BA and MA degrees from George Washington University, concentrating in clinical psychology. She went on to earn her Ph.D. from Harvard University (1970) in philosophy. Meanwhile in 1955 she married Derek Bok, who later was named president of Harvard University. They had three children.

Bok taught at Harvard University, Radcliffe Institute, Simmons College, Tufts University, the John F. Kennedy School of Government, and Brandeis University. She published, in Sweden, *Alva: Ett Kvinnoliv,* a biography of her mother, Alva Myrdal, who shared the 1982 Nobel Peace Prize with Alfonso Garcia Robies. She wrote extensively for more than a dozen philosophical and ethical journals. However, Bok was probably best known for her books in the field of applied ethics, including *The Dilemma of Euthanasia* (1975), *Lying: Moral Choice in Public and Private Life* (1979), *Ethics Teaching in Higher Education* (1980), *Secrets: On the Ethics of Concealment and Revelation* (1984), and *A Strategy for Peace: Human Values and the Threat of War* (1989).

Medical Problems and Moral Questions

The Dilemmas of Euthanasia, edited with John A. Behnke (the editor of the journal *BioScience*), was a groundbreaking book that discussed the moral dilemmas created by a new medical success, that of the ability to keep terminally ill patients alive beyond the normal expectations. Bok and Behnke gathered together leading analysts in this new field of applied ethics to explore ways to resolve the obvious moral problems resulting from the possibility of the use of euthanasia to end the life of a terminally ill patient. Bok's contribution to the collection of essays was the article "Euthanasia and the Care of the Dying," the introductory article in the collection and the one most influential in further discussions of the morality of euthanasia. In the preface of the book Bok asked what were the appropriate moral questions as euthanasia became more and more medically feasible:

"How far should physicians go in delaying death? Which of the many techniques for prolonging life can they, in good conscience, omit in caring for a terminally ill patient? What can patients ask doctors to do and forbear in those cases where there is a conflict between prolonging life and easing suffering? Is there anything a person can do before becoming a patient to decrease the chances of being reduced to intolerable levels of suffering, loneliness, and dehumanization?"

Lying: Moral Choice in Public and Private Life is one of the most significant books in philosophy written in the 20th century, and it alone established Bok's reputation as a moral philosopher of international renown. It is a book which intellectually lies at the heart of the debate over private and public morality, and it has had enormous influence upon the change of the moral mood in the United States. It is clear that the new direction of the medical profession to tell the truth about a patient's condition and prognosis was based in large measure upon Bok's book, in which she stated:

"But if someone contemplates lying to a patient or concealing the truth, the burden of proof must shift. It must rest, here, as with all deception, on those who advocate it in any one instance. They must show why they fear a patient may be harmed or how they know that another cannot cope with the truthful knowledge." The book concludes with a powerful paean to openness and honesty in speech and action:

"Individuals, without a doubt, have the power to influence the amount of duplicity in their lives and to shape their speech and action. They can decide to rule out deception wherever honest alternatives exist, and become much more adept at thinking up honest ways to deal with problems. They can learn to look with much greater care at the remaining choices where deception seems the only way out. They can make use of the test of publicity to help them set standards to govern their participation in deceptive practices. Finally, they can learn to beware of efforts to dupe them, and make clear their preference for honesty even in small things."

Teaching and Studying Ethics

Teaching Ethics in Higher Education, edited with Daniel Callahan of the Hastings Center, was a timely and important book that gathered together (with the support of the Rockefeller Brothers Fund and the Carnegie Corporation for Education) important ethicists to ponder the question of how to teach ethics, both on the college campus and generally within American culture. The concern of the book is to focus "on the extent and quality of that (ethical) teaching, and on the possibilities and problems posed by widespread efforts to find a more central and significant place for ethics in the curriculum." Bok's particular contribution to the book was the essay "Whistleblowing and Professional Responsibilities," which analyzed the moral conflicts which exist within government, particularly when one wants to stick one's neck out and report malfeasance and immorality within governmental operations. She clearly saw the differences that exist between dissent, breach of loyalty, and accusation, all putative forms of "whistleblowing." Effective "whistleblowing," according to Bok, requires an audience, some larger forum, where a rational appeal to justice can be made. And, of course, it also requires the political possibility of a concerted public response—a democratic and open society is necessary if "whistleblowing" is going to have any moral consequence at all.

Secrets: On the Ethics of Concealment and Revelation continues the exploration of moral issues begun in *Lying.* In this book Bok discussed the choices of how to act and how to shape one's moral conduct in private and public life. It is a comprehensive study of the phenomenon of keeping secrets in our society. In her analysis of secrets she includes the police and the journalistic, scientific, political, academic, and business communities. But secrecy, of course, is also an expression of personal choice, and therefore Bok analyzed the following topics: secrecy and morality, secrecy and openness, secrecy and self-deception, confessions, gossip, and secrecy and accountability. Secrecy is defined by Bok as "intentional concealment," which she argued was a neutral definition so that no moral judgment may be made from the beginning that secrets are on the one hand determined as guilty or threatening, or on the other as awesome and worthy of respect.

A later book, *A Strategy for Peace: Human Values and the Threat of War,* was a major work, as substantial and important a book as had been written in the 1980s. (The topic was what Erik Erikson called the "species-wide nuclear crisis.") Based on lectures that Bok gave at Harvard University, the objective of the book is to propose a framework of moral principles to serve as a strategy for peace. She rejected the calls for a "new ethics" or, as she put it, "some worldwide religious or psychological or political conversion after which peace will arrive, as it were, by itself." She also rejected utopian schemes of international harmony, such as world government and programs which propose the miraculous transformation of society. She was also fearful to entrust the survival of humanity to the uncertainties of a world balance of power. Bok remembered well Voltaire's dictum: "Those who can make you believe absurdities, can make you commit atrocities."

Belief in the Laws of Humanity

Bok relied for her concepts of peace and of strategy on Immanuel Kant's essay "Perpetual Peace" and the book *On War* by Carl von Clausewitz. These works have always been considered antithetical in their perspectives. Bok demonstrated instead that the perspectives of one can enrich the other and that together they can serve to provide the insights by which a strategy of peace can be generated to meet the current threat to universal human life. Precisely because the danger to future human life is so great, all of us have an unprecedented incentive, as Bok argued, "to seek joint ways of breaking out of the impasse"; we are all "under equal necessity" to find a way out—or we all die.

She believed that the most basic "laws of humanity," the most basic human drive for survival, now gives us a reason to confront our traditional enemies from the larger perspectives that survival requires. And those larger perspectives speak first the language of religion and morality, stressing character and principled conduct, found in thinkers of the Christian pacifist tradition represented by Tolstoy, Gandhi, and Martin Luther King, the medieval "just war" theorists, and the proponents of a "perpetual peace"; the second voice emphasizes the need for competence, insight, and good planning and is represented by the political realism of such thinkers as Thucydides, Machiavelli, Clausewitz, Churchill, and Kissinger, who argued that the value of one's own survival must override all other values. Bok wanted to bring together the two traditions of thought: "The language of morality and that of strategy are both indispensable in the face of the present crisis."

Bok's global perspective informed by moral characteristics took seriously Kant's moral law to "act only according to that maxim whereby you can at the same time will that it should become a moral law," which means practically that individuals, communities or nations, and a future federation of states would act only in a way which respected all human beings in their own right, rather than treating them merely as means to other ends. Moral constraints are thereby presented which can bring about a climate in which the threat of war can be reduced. They are constraints on violence, deceit, and breaches of trust—all of which predate debates about the complex problems of equality, liberty, justice, human rights, and all of which are "common even in primitive human groups long before one can talk about states, much less an international community."

Bok identified in Clausewitz's *On War* the argument that the objective of a war is survival and national self-preservation. The political goal of survival ought to be common to all wars, Clausewitz insisted, and for that reason he argued that defense is superior to attack as a form of fighting. Its object, preservation, is less costly and can more likely be achieved. But whatever the nature of the war, what matters most is survival. Consequently, Bok maintained, following Clausewitz, that nuclear wars have no place today in sound political strategy; the massive piling up of nuclear weapons cannot any longer assure the survival of any nation.

Bok, a distinguished fellow at the Harvard Center for Population and Development Studies, published *Common Values* in 1996. Angered by "the disgraceful accommodations with evil around the world that moral relativists have reached," Bok promotes pluralistic yet diverse social practices based upon a universally shared understanding and knowledge of "certain minimal moral principles." Bok's concern with moral relativists is confusing. She believes that all, and not merely some, cultures recognize her "certain minimal moral principles," although they may not live up to them. These values really are minimal, and include: "duties of support and loyalty, injunctions against harm and deceit, and procedural justice". Bok puts forth a call to arms in the defense of a universal morality and believes that the minimal moral values she attributes to every culture allow for an objective criteria by which to assess all social practices and cultures. Bok is at her best in *Common Values*. She explores far more questions than she offers answers for, but plants them in the reader's consciousness just the same.

Sissela Bok demonstrated that an academic philosopher can feel deeply for the moral anguish of a people in the face of changes in the fabric of our society. Her moderate and rational perspectives on these issues have already changed the way we, as a society, make moral decisions. Her philosophical influence has been noteworthy.

Further Reading

There is little published material on Sissela Bok. For further information see her contributions to the *Encyclopedia of Bioethics* (1978) and the bimonthly *Hastings Center Report* from the Hastings Center, Hastings-on-Hudson, New York 10706. See also the *Christian Century* (November, 1989); *American Health* (September 1989); and *JAMA, The Journal of the American Medical Association* (February 1989). The biography of her mother, *Alva Myrdal: A Daughter's Memoir,* was published in English in 1991. □

Viscount Bolingbroke

The English statesman and political writer Henry St. John, Viscount Bolingbroke (1678-1751), was head of the Tory opposition to Robert Walpole's Whig government and was also an early conservative political theorist.

Henry St. John was born in London on Oct. 1, 1678. He was educated at Eton and became a member of Parliament in 1701, rising to be secretary of war in 1704 and secretary of state in 1710. He was created Viscount Bolingbroke two years later. His major achievement as minister of Queen Anne's government was his negotiation of the Treaty of Utrecht, which in 1713 brought to an end the longest and last of the great European wars of Louis XIV of France.

Tradition has it that because Queen Anne, a devout churchgoer, considered Bolingbroke deceitful, irreligious, immoral, and conniving (all of which were true) she refused on her deathbed to name him first minister. This rejection, in addition to the arrival of the new king George I from Hanover, who was close to the Whigs, prompted Bolingbroke to flee to France in 1715, where he joined the forces of the Stuart Pretender. He soon abandoned the Jacobite cause but remained an exile in France for 10 years. During this period he began his studies in earnest and became a political and philosophical thinker of the first order.

Bolingbroke's major philosophical work, a set of essays entitled *Philosophical Fragments,* was written during these years in France (1726-1734). It contained essays critical of John Locke's notion of the social contract and important essays on religion which place Bolingbroke as an important figure in the deist movement. Many of Bolingbroke's philosophical ideas were the inspiration for *Essay on Man* (1734) by his friend Alexander Pope.

In 1726 Bolingbroke returned to England and became the center of a political and literary circle in opposition to Walpole's Whig government. Jonathan Swift's *Gulliver's Travels,* John Gay's *Beggar's Opera* , and Pope's *Dunciad* were all written as part of this politicocultural assault on Robert Walpole. Bolingbroke edited for 10 years a weekly journal, the *Craftsmen,* in which appeared in 1730 his "Remarks on the History of England" and in 1734 his "Dissertation upon Parties." Both these works were thinly veiled attacks on Walpole's rule.

The culmination of Bolingbroke's opposition to Walpole and Whig hegemony was his essay "The Patriot King," written in 1739 and published in 1749. It was a fervent plea for Frederick the Prince of Wales to strengthen the monarchy and to end the corrupt practices of Walpole's parliamentary management. With its cry for a return to the strong monarch represented by Elizabeth, this essay would influence George III and the young Benjamin Disraeli in the next century.

Bolingbroke lived to see Walpole out of power but never to see his Tory party in office. He died on Dec. 12, 1751, ending a career of politics and letters which saw him consistently the champion of the aristocracy and gentry classes against the new order of financial capitalism and commercialism represented and championed by the Whig party, Walpole, and the Bank of England.

Further Reading

David Mallet edited Bolingbroke's Works (5 vols., 1754), and Gilbert Parke edited his *Letters and Correspondence, Public and Private* (4 vols., 1798), written during 1710-1714, when Bolingbroke was secretary of state. The best treatment of Bolingbroke's political thought is Isaac Kramnick, *Bolingbroke and His Circle* (1968). Another perspective is given by Jeffrey Hart, *Viscount Bolingbroke: Tory Humanist* (1965).

Recommended for general historical background are Thomas Babington Macaulay, *History of England* (5 vols., 1849-1861; new ed. 1953), for the reigns of James II and William III, and George Macaulay Trevelyan, *England under Queen Anne* (3 vols., 1930-1934). The party politics of the period are treated

in Keith Feiling, *History of the Tory Party, 1640-1714* (1924);
Robert Walcott, *English Politics in the Early Eighteenth Century* (1956); and Geoffrey Holmes, *British Politics in the Age of Anne* (1967).

Additional Sources

Barrell, Rex A., *Bolingbroke and France,* Lanham, MD: University Press of America, 1988.

Biddle, Sheila, *Bolingbroke and Harle,* New York, Knopf; distributed by Random House 1974.

Bolingbroke's political writings: the conservative enlightenment, New York, N.Y.: St. Martin's Press, 1995.

Hammond, Brean S., *Pope and Bolingbroke: a study of friendship and influence,* Columbia: University of Missouri Press, 1984.

Kramnick, Isaac, *Bolingbroke and his circle: the politics of nostalgia in the age of Walpole,* Ithaca: Cornell University Press, 1992.

Varey, Simon, *Henry St. John, Viscount Bolingbroke,* Boston: Twayne Publishers, 1984.

Warburton, William, *A view of Lord Bolingbroke's philosophy,* New York: Garland Pub., 1977. □

Simón Bolívar

Simón Bolívar (1783-1830) was a South American general and statesman who brought political independence to six present-day nations. Called the Liberator, he was the greatest military figure of South America.

Simón Bolívar was born on July 24, 1783, in Caracas, Venezuela, then part of the Hispanic colonial empire. His parents belonged to the aristocratic upper class, the Creoles. Orphaned at the age of 9, the boy early showed traits of independence and a strong will. Sent to Madrid in 1799 to complete his education, he came under the tutelage of an uncle who secured the proper instruction for the young aristocrat, which included his acquaintance with the decadent court of Charles IV and some of the noble families of Madrid. At the age of 18 Bolívar married Maria Teresa de Toro. In 1802 the couple went to Caracas, where after only 6 months of wedded life the young wife died.

In 1804 Bolívar returned to Europe, this time visiting France and Italy. He was greatly impressed by Napoleon, who had crowned himself emperor, and Bolívar dreamed of a similar glory for himself. The German scientist and traveler Alexander von Humboldt told Bolívar that the South American continent was ripe for independence. When Bolívar went to Rome, he made his famous vow on Monte Sacro to liberate South America.

Fight for Independence

Expressions of unrest and rebellion already existed in Hispanic America, but it was not until 1808 that the independence movement disturbed the solid structure of the Spanish Empire. That year Napoleon occupied the Iberian Peninsula, deposed the Bourbon dynasty, and appointed his brother Joseph king of Spain. All the colonies refused to recognize the usurper but were divided about the policy they should pursue. Some continued to adhere to the Spanish royal family, but others were bent upon independence and self-government. The struggle was waged from Mexico to Cape Horn, but two provinces took the lead: Argentina, then called the Viceroyalty of La Plata, and Venezuela. On April 19, 1810, the Spanish captain general in Caracas was overthrown, and a junta of native citizens took over his duties. Bolívar's participation in these events remains a matter of controversy. Three months later he was sent to London to obtain England's assistance, but his mission was a failure. He returned to Venezuela, and was followed by Francisco de Miranda, a leader in the conflict with Spain.

In July 1811 Venezuela cut its ties with Spain and proclaimed its independence, but this "First Republic" was a flimsy structure and soon came under counterrevolutionary attack. Bolívar had joined the army and had taken part in the ensuing struggle, but he had fallen out with Miranda, who had been appointed dictator and commander in chief. Bolívar had lost an important harbor fortress to the enemy, and Miranda used the defeat to end the war and conclude an armistice with the Spaniards. His action enraged Bolívar, who determined to continue the fight.

Fleeing to the neighboring province of New Granada (now Colombia), Bolívar organized a new army, routed the Spanish, and liberated Venezuela in August 1813. He was appointed dictator but was soon faced with internal dissensions which led to civil war. Again forced to flee, he took refuge in Jamaica and again tried to engage British support for his cause. Although this effort came to naught, one of his most celebrated manifestos was composed there: the "Letter from Jamaica."

Obtaining assistance from the small republic of Haiti, Bolívar once more set forth for Venezuela, and a year later, in 1817, he achieved victory on the plains of the Orinoco valley. There he found an untapped reservoir of raw material and manpower. Two more years of inconclusive fighting followed before Bolívar made a sudden decision to attack the Spaniards from the rear, that is, from New Granada. In one of the most audacious operations of military history, he crossed the Andes and defeated the royalist forces at Boyacá on Aug. 7, 1819.

Colombian Republic

Bolívar's ambitious plans for the liberated colonies included the establishment of a republic in the Andes, to be called Colombia. It was to be composed of Venezuela, Colombia, and Ecuador and to be governed by a president appointed for life and by an aristocracy made up of the patriots who had fought for their freedom. The Colombian Republic was proclaimed in December 1819. Bolívar's triumph was only on paper, since the greater part of the territory was still occupied by the enemy; but in June 1821 he liberated Venezuela at the battle of Carabobo, and one of his most gifted officers, Antonio José de Sucre, freed Ecuador in the battle of Pichincha in May 1822.

When Bolívar entered the capital city of Quito in June 1822, he might have considered his ambition fulfilled. But his imperial dreams had grown. The next month he conferred with the Argentinian general José de San Martin at Guayaquil. These secret meetings have been the source of considerable speculation, but the outcome was clear: San Martin renounced his position as Protector of Peru, leaving the field to Bolívar. He entered Peru in 1823 and was victorious over the royal army at the battle of Junín in August 1824. Sucre, whom he left to terminate the campaign, inflicted a crushing defeat on the Spanish at Ayacucho in December 1824. The fight for independence had been won.

New States

Bolívar was now in an extraordinary position. He was president of Colombia, dictator of Peru, and president of the newly created Bolivia, a region which had been called Upper Peru in colonial times and had once belonged to the Viceroyalty of La Plata. This new country honored Bolívar in its choice of a name, and he composed its first constitution, an extremely autocratic and utopian document which lasted only 2 years. At this point in his career Bolívar harbored certain very ambitious projects, though he cannot be accused of a desire to become emperor; he wanted to be "liberator or nothing." His purpose was the creation of an Andean empire, stretching from one end of South America to the other, and he pursued this aim along several paths.

Bolívar called for a confederation of the Hispanic American countries, and in 1826 he assembled a congress in Panama, but the league he had envisaged never materialized. He had another plan for the countries he had liberated—Venezuela, Colombia, Ecuador, Peru, and Bolivia; he wanted to unite them in a Federation of the Andes, with

himself as president and with the Bolivian constitution as the permanent basis of government. This project also failed.

Rising Opposition

In 1826 civil war erupted in Colombia, and Bolívar returned in haste to prevent a clash between the conflicting factions. He gained a temporary reconciliation and called a new constituent assembly together in 1828, but its deliberations did not agree with his autocratic ideas, and he assumed the dictatorship once more.

By now the opposition to Bolívar had assumed such proportions that a conspiracy to eliminate him was set in motion. On Sept. 25, 1828, Bolívar escaped the daggers of the assassins by minutes. For more than a year he fought to preserve his political creation. A war with Peru prevented its encroachment on Colombian territory, but the voices of dissent in Venezuela, Colombia, and Ecuador were not silenced. A new congress elected in 1830 accepted the secession of Venezuela and, soon thereafter, of Ecuador. Bolívar finally realized that his goal was unattainable and reluctantly admitted that even his presence in Bogotá might spark further discord.

In April 1830, already an exhausted man, Bolívar agreed to leave his country. Possibly his death was hastened by the failure of his political plans, but more likely he died of tuberculosis, on Dec. 17, 1830, near the city of Santa Marta, Colombia.

Political Assessment

Bolívar died hated by his enemies and outlawed by his own country of Venezuela, but his reputation was restored soon after his death, and his fame has continued to grow to mythical proportions in Latin America ever since. He maintained the fight against Spain when all appeared hopeless, and he did not give up until he had overcome all the obstacles on the road to independence. He called himself "the man of difficulties," and in truth he was that.

Bolívar's greatest political mistake was his failure to recognize the forces of nationalism which were soon to vitalize the Latin American countries. His desire to give his world a firm and stable foundation was justified, even though his methods were often erroneous. Latin America has continued to foster pronunciamentos and revolutions, in confirmation of Bolívar's most somber apprehensions. Since Bolívar passed into history, South America has not produced his equal.

Further Reading

Selected Writings of Bolívar, compiled by Vicente Lecuna and edited by Harold A. Bierck, Jr. (2 vols., 1951), illustrates the role played by Bolívar in the struggle for independence and expresses his ideas on union, solidarity, and government. J. B. Trend, *Bolívar and the Independence of Spanish America* (1946), stresses his political theories. Gerhard Masur, *Simón Bolívar* (1948; rev. ed. 1969), portrays Bolívar with great admiration but not as infallible. See also Hildegarde Angell, *Simón Bolívar: South American Liberator* (1930); Salvador de Madariaga, *Bolívar* (1952); and John J. Johnson, *Simón Bolívar and Spanish American Independence: 1783-1830* (1968). Useful background studies include Bernard Moses,

South America on the Eve of Emancipation (1908) and *Spain's Declining Power in South America: 1730-1806* (1919); Curtis A. Wilgus, *South American Dictators during the First Century of Independence* (1937); C. H. Haring, *Spanish Empire in America* (1947; rev. ed. 1963); Charles Gibson, *Spain in America* (1966); and Charles Gibson, ed., *Spanish Tradition in America* (1968). □

Heinrich Böll

One of Germany's most popular and prolific authors, Heinrich Böll (1917-1985) gained international fame—winning the Nobel Prize in 1972—as a chronicler of the Federal German Republic (1949-1990). Critics have generally emphasized his strong ethical stance, which stemmed from his personal philosophy of Christian humanism and sympathy for the downtrodden.

Born in Cologne and raised by devout but liberal Roman Catholic parents, Böll embraced humanistic ideals early in life. As a schoolboy he stood up to peer pressure and refused to join the Hitler Youth. In 1939, however, he was drafted into the German infantry, serving throughout the war and suffering several wounds. Returning to Cologne after the war, he published his first short story in 1947. Critical and popular acclaim followed quickly, enabling Böll to devote his life to literature.

Böll's early works focus on the impact of Nazi rule on ordinary people, particularly soldiers like himself, affected by events beyond their control. In *Der Zug war puenktlich* (1949; *The Train Was on Time*), a haunting story of a soldier who foresees his own death while waiting to be transported to the eastern front, and *Wo warst du, Adam?* (1951; *Adam, Where Art Thou?*), he describes the horror and absurdity of war. As a writer, Böll reacted to the war with anger and condemnation. While revealing the complicity of respectable institutions, such as the Catholic church, in Hitler's political success in Germany, Böll points to the catastrophic consequences of Nazi policies. According to Wilhelm Johannes Schwarz, Böll's "predominant attitude to the war is disgust and vexation. . . . He tells only of its boredom, of filth and vermin, senselessness, and futile waste of time."

Postwar Germany is the setting of Böll's novels of the 1950s. *Und sagte kein einziges Wort* (1953; *And Never Said a Word*) relates a family man's difficulties in adjusting to civilian life. This novel received much critical attention and helped establish Böll's reputation as a master storyteller. *Haus ohne Hueter* (1954; *The Unguarded House*) is about the struggle for daily survival in a warn-torn city as experienced by two fatherless boys.

Böll's novels written in the 1950s and 1960s examine Germany's efforts to forge a new identity while exorcising the demons of its Nazi past. As in his earlier work, he approaches his subject from an individual's point of view. Always a perceptive and ironic oberver, Böll mercilessly

uncovers the moral blindness, historical amnesia, rapacity, vulgar consumerism, and indifference to human values of a production-oriented society that adopts materialism as a means of forgetting its infernal past. In *Ansichten eines Clowns* (1963; *The Clown*), a frustrated performer exposes the hypocrisy of prosperous Germans, including his own family, who subordinate ethical principles to opportunistic concerns. *Gruppenbild mit Dame* (1971; *Group Portrait with Lady*), an ambitious work that received a mixed response from critics, is structured as a biography based on accounts by the protagonist's friends and acquaintances. Late works, such as *Fuersorgliche Belagerung* (1979; *The Safety Net*) and *Frauen vor Flusslandschaft* (1985; *Women in a River Landscape*), treat the complex political reality of the last decade of the Federal German Republic.

Critics have praised Boll for his ability to convey his feelings and ideas in simple, concise, and effective prose. Furthermore, some commentators view Böll's style as a conscious protest against the formal complexity of classical German literature, comparing his work to that of Ernest Hemingway, whom Böll himself cited as an influence. The directness and accessibility of Böll's prose especially comes to the fore in his witty portrayal of the absurdity of everyday life, as exemplified by his two short story collections, *Wanderer, kommst du nach Spa* (1950; *Traveler, If You Come to the Spa*) and *18 Stories* (1966).

Although aware of his importance, critics have hesitated to bestow unqualified praise on Böll. As Robert C. Conard concluded: "Böll has never received universal critical acceptance, not even from those who find his stories some of the best written in the middle decades of the century. That sentimentalism and idealism dominate his work and that he cannot always adequately execute his intentions are the charges most often heard. Minor weaknesses in Böll's work, however, seem not to affect his popularity with a discriminating public. Already he stands in the company of two of his favorite writers: Dostoyevsky and Tolstoy. Like them, he has produced eminently readable work imbued with moral power."

Further Reading

Monde (international edition), July 18-24, 1985.
New York Times, July 17, 1985.
Time, July 29, 1985.
Times (London), July 17, 1985.
Washington Post, July 17, 1985; July 28, 1985.
Böll, Rene, Viktor Böll, Reinhold Neven DuMont, Klaus Staeck, and Robert C. Conard, *Heinrich Böll,* Twayne, 1981.
Contemporary Literary Criticism, Gale, Volume 2, 1974, Volume 3, 1975, Volume 6, 1976, Volume 9, 1978, Volume 11, 1979, Volume 15, 1980, Volume 27, 1984, Volume 32, 1985, Volume 72, 1992.
Conrad, Robert, *Heinrich Böll,* Twayne, 1981.
Friedrichsmeyer, Erhard, *The Major Works of Heinrich Böll: A Critical Commentary,* Monarch Press, 1974.
MacPherson, Enid, *A Student's Guide to Böll,* Heinemann, 1972.
Reid, James Henderson, *Heinrich Böll: Withdrawal and Re-Emergence,* Wolff, 1973.
Schwartz, Wilhelm Johannes, *Heinrich Böll, Teller of Tales: A Study of His Works and Characters,* Ungar, 1969. □

Bertram Borden Boltwood

The American radiochemist Bertram Borden Boltwood (1870-1927) discovered the parent of radium and developed a method of geological dating.

Bertram Boltwood was born on July 27, 1870, in Amherst, Massachusetts. His paternal ancestors had come from Great Britain two centuries earlier and were a prominent family in New England. His father, a lawyer, died when "Bolty" was two years old, and the boy, an only child, was raised by his mother in her home town of Castleton-on-Hudson, New York. His mother's family had come to America from Holland, also in the 17th century.

Boltwood's mother was not wealthy, but she was affluent enough to send him to private school and, befitting her social position, destined him to attend Yale, his father's college. He entered Yale's Sheffield Scientific School in 1889 and upon completion of the three-year program took highest honors in chemistry. Next came two years of postgraduate work in Munich, where he specialized in analytical techniques and in the chemistry of the rare earth elements. In 1894 Boltwood returned to Yale, working as a laboratory assistant while studying for his doctoral degree. This program was enriched by a semester of physical chemistry in Ostwald's laboratory in Leipzig, and Boltwood received the Ph.D. from Yale in 1897.

A Scholar and Businessman

Even before graduation Boltwood had served as an instructor in analytical chemistry in the Sheffield Scientific School. He continued in this post, and later in physical chemistry with the same rank, until 1900, when he established a mining engineering and chemistry partnership with a schoolmate. While at Yale his mastery of chemical techniques made him a great resource for his colleagues. Those years were also devoted to translating German chemical texts and to improving laboratory apparatus: his automatic Sprengel pump, new design for a water blast, and lead fume pipe for the Kjeldahl nitrogen determination apparatus date from this period, while his invention of Boltwax, a product useful for vacuum seals, came later.

As a businessman with a private laboratory in New Haven in 1900, Boltwood analyzed ore samples sent by his partner working in the field in the Carolinas. Many of these samples contained rare earth elements and also uranium and thorium. The radioactivity of uranium had been discovered by Henri Becquerel in Paris in 1896, and that of thorium independently by Gerhard C. Schmidt and Marie Curie in 1898. Boltwood's interest in the rare earths, his expertise in analytical and physical chemistry, and his familiarity with such ores as monazite and uraninite made it almost inevitable that he would become fascinated with the popular science of radioactivity.

In a series of papers in 1902 and 1903 Ernest Rutherford, a physicist, and Frederick Soddy, a chemist, explained the phenomenon of radioactivity as the spontaneous disintegration of an atom and its transmutation into another element. The evidence for their theory was compelling, but mostly of a physical character. When Boltwood first began his radioactivity research in 1904, he felt that chemical evidence would provide essential confirmation. If the ratio of the amounts of radium and uranium in old, unaltered minerals was constant, this would imply a genetic relationship wherein uranium decayed in a number of steps to form radium, and this element in turn itself decayed to form other products.

Separating and measuring the minute traces of radium was all but impossible. But radium's first daughter product is an inert gas called emanation, which could easily be collected and which would give an accurate indication of the quantity of its parent that was present. Boltwood used a gastight electroscope to measure the radioactivity of the radium emanation and showed it to be directly proportional to the amount of uranium in each of his many samples.

He next decided to go beyond this circumstantial evidence of a connection between these two elements: he would seek direct proof by trying to "grow" radium. Uranium X was the only radioelement known to be between them, and its short half life meant that radium should be formed rather quickly. Yet, after a year, Boltwood remained unable to detect any radium emanation in his uranium solution. Since his faith in the disintegration theory of radioactivity did not waver, he could only conclude that an unknown, long-lived product lay between uranium X and radium, preventing rapid accumulation of the latter.

Search Continued at Yale

Boltwood's search for the parent of radium was interrupted by his appointment as assistant professor of physics at Yale College in 1906 and by the responsibility that fell upon him to supervise extensive renovations in the old laboratory. When he resumed his investigations he was inclined to accept actinium, one of the several new radio-elements discovered in that period, as the parent. The problem he faced, however, was that his own work, and that of such other radiochemists as Soddy and Herbert N. McCoy at the University of Chicago had determined the activities of members of the decay series relative to the first element in each series; if Boltwood placed actinium in the uranium series the sum of the constituents' activities would be greater than that of the mineral that contained them. A closer look at actinium showed it to have mixed with it a tiny amount of another radioelement bearing the chemical properties of thorium. Named ionium by Boltwood in 1907, it was indeed the immediate parent of radium.

This intensive study of the radioelements highlighted several examples of products that differed in origin, in half life, and perhaps in emissions, yet seemed to have identical chemical properties. Radiothorium, ionium, and uranium X, for example, were to the chemist thorium. Boltwood did not contribute to the conception in 1913 by Kasimir Fajans, and subsequently by Soddy, of isotopes and of the group displacement laws that regulated radioactive decay in the periodic table of the elements, but these theories were rooted in his experimental discoveries.

Other results of his familiarity with the radioelements were his belief that inactive lead was the end product of at least the uranium decay series and his observation that the geologically older rocks contained greater amounts of lead. From this he could estimate the rate at which lead accumulated. With encouragement and ideas from Rutherford, who by now was a good friend and a collaborator-by-post, Boltwood "inverted" the method and used the measured quantity of lead to calculate the age of rocks. This was a striking application of science, all the more so because his billion-year span for the age of the earth contradicted the conventional wisdom of only some tens of millions of years. By the 1930s, more data and a better understanding of isotopes brought widespread acceptance of this technique.

Except for a year (1909-1910) in Rutherford's Manchester laboratory, Boltwood remained at Yale for the rest of his life. He was made a full professor of radiochemistry in 1910, and in 1918 he was appointed director of the Yale College chemical laboratory. In that capacity he not only presided over the merging of the college and Sheffield chemistry departments, but over the design of a new university laboratory. His fame as America's leading investigator of radioactivity brought him election to the National Academy of Sciences and other organizations. Overwork seems to have caused a breakdown in his health, and his normally exuberant personality was clouded increasingly by periods of depression, culminating in his suicide in the summer of 1927.

Further Reading

The most extensive treatment of Boltwood's work and where it fits into contemporary science may be found in Lawrence Badash, *Radioactivity in America: Growth and Decay of a Science* (1979). The story of the lead-uranium method of determining geological age is told in Badash, "Rutherford, Boltwood, and the age of the earth: The origin of radioactive dating techniques," *Proceedings of the American Philosophical Society,* 112 (1968). Biographical and obituary notices by colleagues who knew him well include Rutherford, in *Nature,* 121 (1928); Alois Kovarik, in *American Journal of Science,* 15 (1928); and Kovarik, in *Biographical Memoirs of the National Academy of Sciences,* 14 (1930). A historian of science's perspective may be found in Badash, *Dictionary of Scientific Biography,* 2 (1970). □

Ludwig Boltzmann

The lasting fame of the Austrian physicist Ludwig Boltzmann (1844-1906) rests on the statistical interpretation which he gave to classical thermodynamics.

Ludwig Boltzmann was born on Feb. 20, 1844, in Vienna, the son of Ludwig and Katharina Pauernfeind Boltzmann. In 1863 he entered the University of Vienna, where one of his teachers was Joseph Stefan, author of the law of radiation named after him.

Thermodynamics and Kinetic Theory

Evidence of the creativity of Boltzmann's intellect was the fusion of thermodynamics and molecular theory that characterized an early paper on the mechanistic meaning of the second law of thermodynamics. In it Clausius's famous formula for entropy, $\int (dQ/T) \geq 0$, was given for the first time in terms of the kinetic theory of gases. The paper was written toward the end of Boltzmann's studies in 1866, and shortly afterward he received his doctor's degree and became a privatdozent at the university. He was also chosen as Stefan's assistant at the university's Institute of Physics, named "Erdberg" after the locality. Stefan urged his assistant to become familiar with James Clerk Maxwell's work on electromagnetism. He also supplied Boltzmann with an English grammar when the latter disclosed his total ignorance of English. Such was the starting point of Boltzmann's lifelong interest in the English-speaking countries and their cultures, but especially in the thought of Maxwell, perhaps the foremost of 19th-century physicists.

Boltzmann left the institute in 1869, when he received an invitation from the University of Graz. During his 3 years there, he twice visited Heidelberg and Berlin and established contacts with Helmholtz, Kirchhoff, Bunsen, and the mathematician Koenigsberger. But he soon realized that his Austrian *Gemütlichkeit* clashed with the stiff formalism prevailing in German academic circles.

Between 1873 and 1876 Boltzmann served as professor of mathematics at the University of Vienna. The titles of

articles which he published while in Graz and Vienna indicate that his mind was increasingly absorbed in the interpretation of various aspects of thermodynamics, especially of its second law, on the basis of the kinetic theory of gases. Clearly, he was developing some extraordinary insight which had to surface before long.

Boltzmann was, however, already back in Graz, as professor of experimental physics, when this momentous breakthrough came in the history of physics. In 1877 he submitted two memoirs to the Academy of Sciences in Vienna. In the first of these, presented on Jan. 11, 1877, "Remarks on Some Problems of the Mechanical Theory of Heat," Boltzmann made an incisive analysis of the formula $\int (dQ/T) \geq 0$ and argued that its validity was not based on the inherent laws of nature but rather on the choice of the initial conditions. According to him, one had to assume on the basis of the kinetic theory of gases that the perfectly elastic balls representing the molecules always tended to change their actual positions. Consequently, any configuration, however improbable, could conceivably occur as time went on: "The calculus of probabilities teaches us precisely this: any non-uniform distribution, unlikely as it may be, is not strictly speaking impossible."

It now remained to give this conclusion a rigorous derivation and quantitative applicability, which Boltzmann did in his memoir submitted to the academy on Oct. 11, 1877, "On the Relation between the Second Law of the Mechanical Theory of Heat and the Probability Calculus with respect to the Propositions about Heat-Equivalence." He concluded that the entropy of a state is proportional to the probability of the configuration of its component particles. His formula, $\int (dQ/T) = 2\Omega/3$, is, however, better known in the form $S = k \log W$, which Max Planck gave it in 1901.

Later Years

His great memoirs of 1877 represented the culmination of his insights into thermodynamics and kinetic theory. It was therefore natural for him to turn to a new field, electromagnetism, mainly under the impact of his reading James Clerk Maxwell's papers and books. When the two volumes of Boltzmann's *Vorlesungen über die Maxwellsche Theorie der Elektricität und des Lichtes* (Lectures on Maxwell's Theory on Electricity and Light) were published in 1891-1893, he was at the University of Munich as professor of theoretical physics.

In 1894 he succeeded his revered teacher, Stefan, as professor of physics at the University of Vienna and stayed there for 6 years. During that period he published in book form his researches on the kinetic theory of gases, *Vorlesungen über Gastheorie* (1896-1898). When the publication of Boltzmann's *Vorlesungen über Mechanik* was completed in 1904, he had already behind him a 2-year stay at the University of Leipzig (1900-1902). It was there that his sensitivity to criticism began to show itself in spells of depression and grave anxiety. He felt deeply disturbed by the ascendency of energeticism, whose chief proponent, Wilhelm Ostwald, was also at Leipzig. Partly because of this, Boltzmann left Leipzig; but at the same time, he was flattered that Mach's chair of *Naturphilosophie* was offered to him at the University of Vienna. But Mach was still very much alive, and his virulent attacks on atomism also seemed to carry the day. Boltzmann came to be referred to as the last bastion of atomism.

Unfortunately, Boltzmann took the view that he was indeed deserted, although radioactivity had already been for several years a firmly established field of investigation and a powerful pointer toward the existence of atoms. But Boltzmann was brooding over what he considered the weakening of his creative powers. In a fit of despondency he took his life on Sept. 5, 1906, at the summer resort of Duino, near Trieste.

Further Reading

The most important writing on Boltzmann is in German. A specific study in English is in Edward A. Guggenheim, *Boltzmann's Distribution Law* (1955). Volume 1 of Henry A. Boorse and Lloyd Motz, eds., *The World of the Atom* (2 vols., 1966), touches upon aspects of Boltzmann's work. □

María Luisa Bombal

María Luisa Bombal (1910-1980) was a Chilean novelist and story writer, one of the first to break away from the realistic tradition in Latin America.

María Luisa Bombal was born in Viña del Mar, Chile, on June 8, 1910. Her father was an Argentine of French origin and her mother was of German extraction. In 1923, on the death of her father, María Luisa journeyed to Paris with her mother and two sisters, and there spent her adolescent years. She came to adopt French as her own tongue and wrote her first literary pieces in that language. Perhaps this explains in part why her style is so clear, in the French manner, stripped of superfluous material, unlike the traditional Spanish prose style heavy with rhetoric.

Bombal graduated from the University of the Sorbonne in Paris with a thesis on the 19th century French writer Mérimée. She also studied dramatic art and participated in several theatrical groups, both in France and in Chile. During these formative years spent in Paris the literary and artistic movement of surrealism was in fashion, and a strong surrealist tendency can be seen in her novels and short stories.

Her Works

In 1931 Bombal returned to her native Chile, but soon left in 1933 to live in Buenos Aires, Argentina, where she became a member of the thriving literary group which included Jorge Luis Borges and Victoria Ocampo, publisher of the famous magazine *Sur*. Bombal worked for this journal, which published her two novels and short stories. Pablo Neruda, the Chilean poet and later Nobel Prize winner, was at the time consul of Chile in the Argentine capital, and under his inspiration Bombal composed her first novel, *The Final Mist* (*La última niebla*), which came out with critical acclaim in 1935. In 1938 her second novel, *The Shrouded Woman* (*La amortajada*) appeared. That same year she married an Argentine painter, but the marriage broke up two years later.

The following year Bombal took a brief trip to the United States where she met such important writers as William Faulkner and Sherwood Anderson. Back in Buenos Aires she published her stories "The Tree" ("El árbol") and "The New Islands" (Las islas nuevas"). After a short sojourn in Chile in 1941, she went again to the United States where in 1944 she remarried, this time a French American.

During a long span of 30 years Bombal lived in New York where the only works she published were reworkings of her two novels in English versions written by herself, *The House of Mist* (1947) and *The Shrouded Woman* (1948). She added so much additional explanatory material to the original of *The House of Mist* that it almost became a different book, unfortunately losing much of its power and fascination.

Finally, in ill health, Bombal returned to spend her last few years in Chile, where she died in Santiago on May 6, 1980.

Her Importance to Literature

Bombal was one of the first Spanish American novelists to break away from the realist tradition in fiction and to write in a highly individual and personal style, stressing irrational and subconscious themes. During the 1930s when most of her fellow writers were turning out works emphasizing social conflict, Bombal turned inwardly for her inspiration and produced several works of remarkable artistic quality. She incorporated the secret inner world of her women protagonists into the mainstream of her novels. In this respect she may be regarded as a precursor of the later Boom writers of the 1960s and 1970s in Latin America. And she accomplished this in a prose charged with poetic vibration, filled with a sense of imminent tragedy, a melancholy atmosphere in which the factors of time and death play sombre roles.

In both her novels the reader sees almost everything through the eyes or sensations of the protagonist, who feels things deeply. The story line is relegated to a lesser role, particularly in *The House of Mist*. Poetry seems to flow from this crystaline prose, and Bombal uses repeated symbolic images (such as mist, rain, and wind) with good effect and in an elegant simple style. The heroine of *The House of Mist* lives most of the time in a dream world of her own fashioning, far from the reality of her unhappy marriage. In *The Shrouded Woman* the protagonist lies dead in her coffin, viewing the chief mourners who come by to see her one by one, reliving her love affairs and family relationships with a final clarity and futile wisdom. In "The Tree," her most famous story, the reader encounters not only a deep psychological analysis of a woman, but also an impressive technique of point counterpoint. While Brígida listens to a concert, her life and its tragedy unfold, evoked by the power of music.

During most of her life Bombal did not achieve the fame she deserved, although in her last years the Chilean government granted her a stipend. With the keen interest in the feminist movement in later years, her works were read and commented on more widely.

Further Reading

María Luisa Bombal is listed in *The Oxford Companion to Spanish Literature* (1978). Though there is no biography of Bombal in English, short studies on aspects of her life and works exist: M. Ian Adams, *Three Authors of Alienation: Bombal, Onetti, Carpentier* (1975); and Margaret V. Campbell, "The Vaporous World of María Luisa Bombal," *Hispania* 44:3 (1961). Additional brief sketches in English appear in standard anthologies of Latin American literature. □

Joseph Bonaparte

The French statesman Joseph Bonaparte (1768-1844), older brother of Napoleon I, was king of Naples from 1806 to 1808 and king of Spain from 1808 to 1813.

Joseph Bonaparte was born on Jan. 7, 1768, in Corte, Corsica. He was the third child of Carlo Buonaparte and Letizia Ramolino but the first to survive infancy. He was educated in Corsica and France and studied law at Pisa. In the Corsican civil war, which marked the early years of the

French Revolution, he sided with the French, as did his brother Napoleon. When the anti-French forces were victorious, he and the entire Bonaparte family fled to the Continent.

Settling in Marseilles, he married Julie Clary, the daughter of a local merchant. During the first years of the Directory (1795-1799), Joseph served as a foreign diplomat. In 1796 he helped to negotiate the armistice with Sardinia; in 1797 he was minister to Parma and later Rome. He then sat in the Council of Five Hundred as a representative from Corsica.

Joseph played an insignificant role in the coup d'etat of Brumaire, which placed Napoleon at the head of the French government. In the years of the Consulate (1799-1804), he negotiated the treaties of Lunéville with Austria (1801) and Amiens with England (1802).

After the Bourbons were expelled from the kingdom of Naples in 1806, Napoleon named Joseph king of that poor, backward, and misgoverned state. Joseph introduced educational, judicial, and financial reforms, but his work was cut short in 1808, when Napoleon made him king of Spain. Although Joseph did all within his power to win over the Spanish people—he tried to learn the language, attended bullfights, professed devotion to the Catholic religion, and attempted to discipline the French army—they refused to accept a Bonaparte, as they had refused a Bourbon a hundred years earlier. Driven out of the capital in August 1808, after only 3 months on the throne, Joseph was restored to power by French troops, upon whom he depended during his brief reign.

As the French Empire disintegrated after 1812, Joseph was forced to abandon Spain in 1813 and return to Paris. He served as lieutenant general of France during the last months of his brother's reign. When Napoleon returned to France in March 1815, Joseph was once again at his side, but he played no important role during the Hundred Days. Following Napoleon's second abdication, Joseph went to the United States, where he remained for 17 years. In his declining years he lived first in Genoa and finally in Florence, where he died on July 28, 1844.

Further Reading

John S. C. Abbott, *History of Joseph Bonaparte, King of Naples and of Italy* (1869), is sympathetic toward Joseph Bonaparte; it remains the best work in English. The anonymous *The Confidential Correspondence of Napoleon Bonaparte with His Brother Joseph Bonaparte* (2 vols., 1855) is a translated selection of the correspondence of the two brothers. R. F. Delderfield, *The Golden Millstones: Napoleon's Brothers and Sisters* (1964), is the best of three good works which deal with the Bonaparte family. The other two are A. Hilliard Atteridge, *Napoleon's Brothers* (1909), and Walter Geer, *Napoleon and His Family: The Story of a Corsican Clan* (3 vols., 1927-1929). See also Alain Decaux, *Napoleon's Mother* (1959; trans. 1962). □

Louis Bonaparte

The French statesman Louis Bonaparte (1778-1846), younger brother of Napoleon I, was king of Holland from 1806 to 1810.

Louis Bonaparte was born at Ajaccio, Corsica, on Sept. 2, 1778, the seventh child of Carlo Buonaparte and Letizia Ramolino. He received a military education in France, and in 1796 he joined his brother Napoleon in Italy, where he served 2 years with the army. In 1798 he accompanied Napoleon to Egypt as his aide-de-camp. Returning to France in 1799, Louis played no part in the coup d'etat of Brumaire. In 1802 Napoleon and Josephine arranged a marriage between Louis and Hortense de Beauharnais, Josephine's daughter by her first marriage. But the marriage was based on neither love nor mutual respect and proved to be an unhappy experience for both.

Louis showed no aptitude for military life and did not take part in the numerous French campaigns. In 1806 Napoleon placed him on the throne of Holland, but he was never satisfied with his younger brother's actions. The Emperor intended Holland to be a satellite kingdom governed in the best interests of France; Louis, however, chose to defend Holland's national interests. In 1808 Louis was offered the throne of Spain, which he refused; it was subsequently accepted by his brother Joseph. Napoleon's displeasure mounted through 1809-1810 because of Louis's lax enforcement of the continental blockade, which was ruining Dutch trade. Finally, in 1810, after repeated attempts to bring his brother into line, Napoleon sent French troops into Holland and forced Louis to flee to Austria.

Louis had unsuccessfully tried to divorce his wife in 1810; and when he fled the empire, she remained behind with their three sons, the youngest of whom later reigned as Napoleon III. Louis took no further part in the affairs of the French Empire. After his brother's abdication in 1814, he settled permanently in Rome. During the revolutions of 1830 he encouraged the nationalist and liberal factions in Italy and expressed satisfaction that his two sons fought for Italian unity. In 1831 his older son, Napoleon Louis (his firstborn, Napoleon Charles, had died at the age of 5), was killed in battle during the Romagna campaign. His younger son, Charles Louis Napoleon, having assumed the leadership of the Bonaparte cause, was imprisoned in 1840 after two unsuccessful attempts to overthrow the reigning Orléans king. Louis did not live to see his son proclaimed emperor of the French in 1852. He died in Rome on July 25, 1846.

Further Reading

There is no good biography of Louis Bonaparte in English. A. Hilliard Atteridge, *Napoleon's Brothers* (1909), and R. F. Delderfield, *The Golden Millstones: Napoleon's Brothers and Sisters* (1964), cover his life completely if not in great depth. The best available work on his unhappy marriage with Hortense de Beauharnais is Denis A. Bingham, *The Marriages of the Bonapartes* (2 vols., 1881; 2d ed. 1882). See also Alain Decaux, *Napoleon's Mother* (1959; trans. 1962). □

St. Bonaventure

The Italian theologian and philosopher St. Bonaventure (1217-1274) was very influential in the development of scholasticism in medieval thought.

The quarter century from 1250 to 1275 has a particular character in the history of medieval thought. In this period Paris emerged as the leading university in Europe, a position it retained until the mid-14th century. Moreover, discussions in philosophy and theology, which earlier had centered on various disputed questions, began to be organized into systematic surveys of theology in the form either of commentaries on the *Sentences* of Peter Lombard or of works known as theological summaries, or *Summae*. These attempts at a logical arrangement of theological thought and at the exploration of every aspect of a theological question are the distinguishing characteristics of this period of scholasticism, which some historians have considered the high point of that movement.

Bonaventure born John of Fidanza, was the son of a fairly prosperous doctor. He received his early education in his birthplace, Bagnoregio, near Lake Bolsena in central Italy. In 1234 he went to Paris to study and became a master of arts. Influenced by the Franciscans throughout his educa-

tion and having a great reverence for the life of St. Francis of Assisi, he entered the Franciscan order about 1243.

Bonaventure continued his studies in theology at the University of Paris and wrote commentaries on the Scriptures (1248) and on the *Sentences* of Peter Lombard (1250-1252). He received a license to teach in 1253, and probably from that time until his election as minister general of the Franciscan order in 1257 Bonaventure taught theology at the University of Paris.

Minister General of the Franciscan Order

By the middle of the 13th century the Franciscan order was becoming divided between those who wished to alter the rule and program of St. Francis in favor of the corporate possession of private property and activity in university education and political life, and those who wished to remain as faithful as possible to St. Francis's original ideal of poverty and missionary activity among the common people. By training and probably by inclination, Bonaventure was committed to the aims of the former group; that is, he advocated Franciscan participation in education and ecclesiastical affairs for which it was necessary to have the financial support provided by the corporate possession of property. But he made sincere attempts to heal the division in the Franciscan order.

As minister general of the Franciscans, Bonaventure led a very active life. Although he tried to make Paris the center of his administration, he visited Italy almost every year. In 1260 the order adopted as its new constitution a collection

of Franciscan legislation compiled by Bonaventure. A biography of St. Francis written by Bonaventure was accepted as the official biography, and earlier biographies were required to be destroyed. Thus Bonaventure's views had a great and lasting influence on the activity and spirit of the Franciscans.

In recognition of his activity as general of the Franciscan order and as papal confidant, Pope Gregory X made Bonaventure cardinal bishop of Albano in 1273. Bonaventure helped to organize and conduct the Second General Council of Lyons in 1274. On July 15, before the end of the council, he died suddenly and was buried the same day in the Franciscan church in Lyons. He was canonized in 1482 and was later made a Doctor of the Church.

Thought and Writings

Bonaventure is numbered with Albertus Magnus, St. Thomas Aquinas, and John Duns Scotus as one of the greatest thinkers of the 13th century. The content of Bonaventure's thought as well as the style of much of his writing may be described as scholastic. Like many theologians before him, Bonaventure made an attempt to explore, within the limits of human reason, the doctrines of Christianity that are initially accepted on faith. In his commentary on the *Sentences,* one of the most extensive and highly structured commentaries ever produced, this theological inquiry was presented according to the pro and con school debate, which was one of the most characteristic features of scholasticism.

Bonaventure was familiar with the thought of Aristotle and the Arabian philosophers. In some areas, such as his understanding of how men come to know external reality, Bonaventure was influenced by the Aristotelian epistemology. Such knowledge, for Bonaventure, is received through the senses and implanted upon the mind. In general, however, Bonaventure questioned many of the philosophical conclusions of Aristotle and Averroës. In contrast to other thinkers, such as St. Thomas Aquinas, Bonaventure was a strongly traditional theologian, closely tied to the thought and approach of St. Augustine. Bonaventure's theology was Christ-centered and non-apologetic; that is, he was not preoccupied with the problem of presenting the Christian faith to nonbelievers.

As a result of this approach, Bonaventure arrived at a series of distinctive positions. While he adopted the Aristotelian description of the process of empirical knowledge, Bonaventure maintained that certain ideas, especially values, are placed within the human mind and are recognized by means of divine illumination, an idea he drew from Augustine. Exemplarism and the general notion of Forms or Ideas played a very important role in the thought of Bonaventure, and he chastised Aristotle for rejecting the Platonic Ideas.

Perhaps the most important single controversy in which Bonaventure was involved concerned the Aristotelian idea of the eternity of the world. Unlike Aquinas, Bonaventure asserted categorically that the idea of the eternity of the world entailed a direct contradiction and consequently was a demonstrable falsehood.

Many of Bonaventure's writings may be described as mystical. Bonaventure's thought has as its final and often immediate aim the encouragement of the individual in his quest for and ascent to God. This strong mystical approach characterized most of Bonaventure's thought, which may thus be seen as a theology of aspiration.

Further Reading

The most extensive treatment of the life and thought of Bonaventure remains Étienne Gilson, *The Philosophy of Saint Bonaventure* (trans. 1938). The Catholic University of America published several studies of different aspects of Bonaventure's thought: Conrad J. O'Leary, *The Substantial Composition of Man according to St. Bonaventure* (1931); Clement M. O'Donnell, *The Psychology of St. Bonaventure and St. Thomas Aquinas* (1937); and Matthew M. De Benedictis, *The Social Thought of Saint Bonaventure: A Study in Social Philosophy* (1946). A detailed analysis of the thought of Bonaventure that challenges some of Gilson's conclusions is Frederick Copleston, *A History of Philosophy,* vol. 2 (1952; new ed. 1962). A short but pithy study is Efrem Bettoni, *Saint Bonaventure* (trans. 1964). Two studies of note were published by the Franciscan Institute: Robert P. Prentice, *The Psychology of Love according to St. Bonaventure* (1951; 2d ed. 1957), and Sister Emma J. M. Spargo, *The Category of the Aesthetic in the Philosophy of St. Bonaventure* (1953).

Additional Sources

Bonaventure & Aquinas: enduring philosophers, Norman: University of Oklahoma Press, 1976.

Cousins, Ewert H., *Bonaventure and the coincidence of opposites,* Chicago: Franciscan Herald Press, 1978. □

Horace Mann Bond

Horace Mann Bond (1904-1972) was an important figure in African American education during the 1930s and 1940s working to end segregation while still improving the education of African American students.

An imposing figure in a family that produced several important scholars and civil rights leaders, Horace Mann Bond had a career that exemplifies the dilemma of the black educator in the segregated South during the 1930s and 1940s: despising segregation and silently struggling to abolish it, while still helping to improve education for African Americans within its confines. Sociologist, college president, and philanthropic agent, Horace Mann Bond resolved this dilemma with intelligence and diplomacy. His work, and that of other educators like him, set into motion the historic forces that found expression in the civil rights movement of the 1950s and 1960s.

Background

Grandson of slaves, Bond was the child of an extraordinary couple. His mother was a schoolteacher, his father a minister. Both excelled in the network of religious and educational institutions established in the South after the Civil War. Bond was an academic prodigy, graduating from high school at the age of fourteen. He attended Lincoln University, a black college in southeastern Pennsylvania. Lincoln placed a premium on W. E. B. Du Bois's notion that racial improvement in the United States would be accomplished by a "talented tenth" of African Americans. Bond quickly proved himself to be such a leader, graduating with honors in 1923. While taking graduate courses at Pennsylvania State College, Bond earned grades higher than those of his white classmates and returned to Lincoln in 1923 as an instructor. Bond then suffered the only setback to his success: he was dismissed from the college for tolerating a gambling ring in a dormitory he was supervising.

Difficulties

Despite his embarrassment at Lincoln, Bond had a reputation as a fine scholar, and he spent much of the next fifteen years alternating between various jobs as an administrator of African American schools and graduate work in sociology at the University of Chicago, from which he received his doctorate in 1936. Bond's administrative work at Langston University in Langston, Oklahoma, and at Alabama State Normal School in Montgomery taught him valuable lessons in the difficulties of education in the segregated South. To keep the white state legislature funding Langston, for example, Langston faculty had to "fool" visiting legislators into thinking the school taught only domestic sciences and "honest labor and toil," giving visiting legislators sumptuous meals of fried chicken and mounting theatrical displays of teachers picking peas. After the whites left, satisfied that the blacks of Oklahoma were receiving education sufficient for their "place," Langston got back to teaching. Throughout the 1930s Bond was engaged in a similarly difficult and often frustrating relationship with the Rosenwald Fund, a white philanthropy that donated large sums toward black education. The Rosenwald funding was instrumental in Bond's pursuit of his doctorate, as well as in securing Bond's major academic appointments to Fisk University in 1928 and to Dillard University in New Orleans in 1935. Nonetheless, the Rosenwald Fund, enamored of Booker T. Washington's notion that African American improvement was best pursued through industrial and agricultural labor, was often conservative and rarely challenged the segregated status quo in the South. That perspective privately annoyed Bond; during the Depression, however, no responsible educator could antagonize a steady source of funding. Believing in black academic excellence, Bond confronted white resistance to equality as a scholar, attacking one of the cornerstones of segregation: the belief that intelligence testing had "proved" the intellectual inferiority of African Americans.

Intelligence Testing

The U.S. Army had begun intelligence testing during World War I. In the 1920s various academics, such as Carl Brigham of Princeton, used the army data and other studies to argue that intelligence testing demonstrated the innate racial inferiority of African Americans. At Chicago, however, Bond had studied sociology in a department that had pioneered research in the impact of environment and society on individual personality. He had also supervised the creation of a statistical survey on the socioeconomic and educational condition of African Americans for the Tennessee Valley Authority. In a series of important articles, in a book titled *The Education of the Negro in the American Social Order* (1934), and in his dissertation, published as *Negro Education in Alabama: A Study in Cotton and Steel* (1939), Bond assailed intelligence testing for its cultural bias and ignorance of environmental factors in education. White academics argued that "bright" blacks moved North; Bond conducted empirical studies at Lincoln demonstrating no significant difference in innate intelligence between northern and southern African Americans. Many asserted that the decline of black schools was owing to African American indifference; Bond demonstrated that it resulted from poor financing by white-dominated school boards. Bond showed that exceptional black students were usually the products of exceptionally well-financed and well-administered black schools, rather than any genetic characteristic. Bond tied the poor educational performance of African Americans to their political disenfranchisement and economic exploitation. He revealed that in many counties where the majority or near majority of the population was African American, white school boards kept taxes low and financed good schools for white children by directing the bulk of black tax payments to white schools—even as black schools remained substandard. Black taxpayers, in other words, were financing education for their white neighbors. "The School," he wrote in his 1934 book, "has been the product and interpreter of the existing [economic] system, sustaining and being sustained by the social complex." With Du Bois he also inaugurated a revisionist history of southern Reconstruction, which—in contrast to the dominant "Dunning" school of southern history in his time—did not applaud the activities of the Ku Klux Klan in "redeeming" the South after the Civil War.

Administrator

Bond's scholarly work, although fairly radical for the time, was tempered by articles and speeches in which he lauded the work of "Southern white gentlemen" and racial moderates. He also did not recommend the abolition of the segregated school system but instead advocated financing it on a truly equal basis. Such gestures were necessary for the continued functioning of any southern educator committed to improving black education in the Jim Crow South. After 1939 Bond was foremost among such educators. That year he accepted the presidency of Fort Valley State College in Fort Valley, Georgia, a position he held until 1945, when he assumed the presidency of his alma mater, Lincoln. The first black president in the history of Lincoln, Bond held the office until 1957. He used his position to pursue several concerns: pan-Africanism and the development of African studies in American universities (following a trip to Africa in 1949), desegregation in Pennsylvania schools, assistance to the NAACP legal team that argued the Brown v. Board of Education (1954) suit before the U.S. Supreme Court, and the physical expansion of Lincoln and the improvement of its courses. He increased the number of black faculty members at Lincoln and brought to campus its first Jewish professor. He aroused opposition to his presidency by his activism and in 1957 resigned his office owing to the increased combativeness of the board of trustees. He then became dean of the School of Education at Atlanta University, remaining there until his retirement in 1971. During that time he renewed his criticisms of intelligence testing and standardized achievement tests following a flurry of new activity in those fields in the early 1960s, but increasingly his energy was focused on helping the civil rights activities and political career of his son, Julian Bond . Horace Mann Bond died in December 1972.

Further Reading

Wayne J. Urban, *Black Scholar: Horace Mann Bond, 1904-1972* (Athens: University of Georgia Press, 1992).
Roger M. Williams, *The Bonds: An American Family* (New York: Atheneum, 1972). □

Julian Bond

Julian Bond (born 1940) was a civil rights leader who was elected to the Georgia House of Representatives in 1965. Denied his seat because of his endorsement of an anti-Vietnam War statement, he was seated by the Supreme Court in the Georgia House one year after his election.

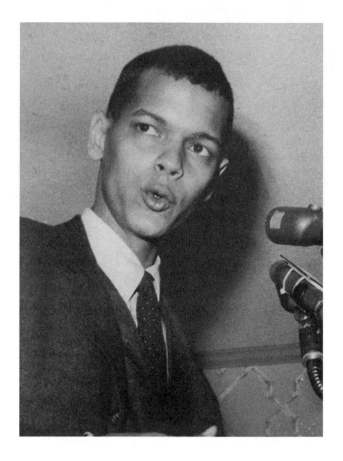

Horace Julian Bond, born on January 14, 1940, in Nashville, Tennessee, was the descendant of several generations of black educators and preachers. His father, Horace Mann Bond, was president of Fort Valley State College. When Bond's father was appointed to be the president of Lincoln University in Oxford, Pennsylvania, the family moved into an environment which was predominantly white. Bond's father caused quite a ferment at the university and in the surrounding community because of his protests against segregated facilities and white attitudes of racial superiority.

Young Julian, however, adjusted relatively easily to his new environment, attending elementary school with white children and winning the sixth grade award for being the brightest student in the class. He was sent to George School, a Quaker preparatory institution near Philadelphia, for his high school education. He encountered a few instances of racial prejudice during these years, but on the whole seemed to adjust well to the academic environment—although his grades were only average.

Civil Rights Movement

After deciding to attend Morehouse College in Atlanta, Georgia, for his higher education, Bond was somewhat fearful about moving there because of the stories of racial violence he had heard. He began college in 1957 when the civil rights struggle was gaining momentum following the Supreme Court's 1954 school desegregation decision and

the 1956 Montgomery, Alabama, bus boycott led by Martin Luther King, Jr. In February 1960 four freshmen from North Carolina Agriculture and Technical College staged a sit-in at Woolworth's white-only lunch counter in Greensboro, North Carolina, in order to force its desegregation. The daring action of these students captured the attention and imagination of black—and some white—students throughout the country.

Bond was swept into the incipient civil rights movement at Morehouse more as a coordinator and a spokesman than as a participant in the demonstrations and sit-ins. Bond was one of the founders of the organization directing the Atlanta student movement, which was called the Committee on Appeal for Human Rights. Because the students were so eager to be part of the civil rights movement, Ella Baker, secretary of the civil rights organization known as the Southern Christian Leadership Conference (SCLC) suggested that interested students meet in 1960 at Shaw University in Raleigh, North Carolina, to coordinate their efforts. King, who was president of the SCLC; and James Lawson, Jr., a clergyman and an exponent of nonviolent resistance, spoke to the students, inviting them to become part of an existing civil rights organization. Several hundred students, Bond among them, finally decided that they would form their own organization, which they named the Student Nonviolent Coordinating Committee (SNCC).

Because of the abilities he had demonstrated working on student newspapers such as the Atlanta *Inquirer,* Bond was appointed communications director for SNCC, a position he held from 1960 until 1966. He became so active in the movement during these years that he dropped out of college and dedicated his time to articulating SNCC's goals in press releases, feature stories, and fliers. He did not complete his degree at Morehouse until 1971.

Georgia State Legislator

Southern segregation meant that black faces were virtually nonexistent in public office, as policemen or firemen, on school boards, on juries, or in bar associations. Few blacks could pass the rigorous voting rights tests or pay poll taxes. As hundreds of Georgia blacks became eligible to vote because of the efforts of civil rights activists, SNCC workers felt that it was important that black candidates seek elective offices. When they sought a candidate for a seat in the Georgia House of Representatives in 1965, the SNCC workers encouraged Bond to run. The Bond name was well known; Bond was articulate and physically attractive; and the workers felt that he would be able to capture the votes needed for victory.

Bond, only after much coaxing, agreed to enter the race. He was 25 years old. He canvassed the 136th legislative district door to door, gained the confidence of the people, and easily won the seat. Bond stated that, proportionately, more people had voted in his district than in any other district in the state. Just before the legislative session opened in 1966, Bond was called by a newsman and asked if he endorsed an anti-Vietnam War statement released by SNCC. Bond said that he had not seen the release, so the newsman read it to him. Bond then said that he basically agreed with it. Unknown to Bond, the interviewing newsman had taped the conversation. When the other Georgia legislators learned about the interview indicating Bond's support of anti-war activists, they formally barred him from the House. That decision was appealed, and eventually reached the Supreme Court. The Court supported Bond and ordered the Georgia House to restore his seat. He was installed in January 1967, over one year after his election victory.

Bond was interested in securing effective civil rights laws, improved welfare legislation, a minimum wage provision, the abolition of the death penalty, increased funding for schools, and anti-poverty and urban renewal programs for the benefit of his constituents. Bond wrote that street protests were moving indoors. He said that it was the time to "translate the politics of marches, demonstrations, and protests" into effective electoral instruments.

The 1968 Democratic Convention

In 1968 Bond was one of the leaders of a delegation to the Democratic National Convention in Chicago whose purpose was to challenge the all-white Georgia delegation led by Governor Lester Maddox and to insure that black voters were represented by black delegates. The delegation won half of the seats from the traditional delegates, and Bond was subsequently nominated to be vice president of the United States. He declined because he was only 28 years old and the Constitution stated that a vice presidential candidate had to be 35.

Later Years

As the 1970s got underway, Bond started to fade from public attention. He limited his focus to helping the predominantly poor residents of his district, concentrating on such issues as street paving and garbage collection. He was criticized for involving himself in many other causes, especially those facing black Atlanta, and it sometimes seemed apparent that he was not entirely interested in politics. Bond continued to express his views, writing and giving speeches, but his popularity was on the wane. He served in the Georgia House until 1975 and then won election to the Georgia Senate. In 1977 Keith Thomas of the *Atlanta Constitution* wrote that a former colleague of Bond in the Georgia House had described him as the most ineffective legislator in the state. In 1976 he rejected an opportunity to join the administration of President Jimmy Carter and subsequently found himself somewhat isolated politically.

In the 1980s Bond narrowly survived a challenge to his Senate seat by an opponent who, according to Thomas, "charged him with inaccessibility, absenteeism, and inattention to local concerns." In 1986 Bond gave up his Senate seat to run for U.S. Congress, but lost the Democratic primary to longtime friend and SNCC colleague, John Lewis. In 1987 Bond's marital problems became headline news when his wife charged him with adultery and cocaine use. The couple divorced in 1989 and, in a paternity suit the following year, Bond admitted to fathering the child of his alleged mistress and was ordered to pay child support.

Bond survived this difficult period of his life by continuing to write and speak. He narrated the highly acclaimed Public Broadcasting Service (PBS) documentary on the civil rights movement, *Eyes on the Prize,* hosted the television program *America's Black Forum,* wrote a nationally syndicated newspaper column titled "Viewpoint," and contributed numerous newspaper and magazine articles. Since 1988 Bond has taught as a visiting professor at Drexel University, Harvard University, Williams College, the University of Virginia, and American University. In 1995 he was elected to his fourth term on the board of the National Association for the Advancement of Colored People (NAACP). Bond has made it clear that it is unlikely that he will reenter politics. "I gave it 20 years. That's enough," he told the *Atlanta Constitution.* Yet, the former legislator believes his career is far from over. "If people remember me, I hope it's not for what I've already done, but what I'm still going to do. And what that is, I have no idea. But I expect to be going a lot longer."

Further Reading

Bond wrote a book in which he discussed his political views from a historical perspective entitled *A Time to Act; The Movement in Politics* (1972). There is a full-length biography of Bond's accomplishments by age 31 written by John Neary called *Julian Bond: Black Rebel* (1971). Neary is somewhat critical of Bond and generally fails to recognize his leadership talents. Roger M. Williams wrote a far more analytical biography of several generations of the Bond family entitled *The Bonds: An American Family* (1971). However, Williams at times borrows heavily from Neary's account of Julian Bond's life. □

Margaret Grace Bondfield

British union official and political leader Margaret Bondfield (1873-1953) was a lifelong advocate of improving the lives of working women, working toward this goal in her roles as a labor activist, suffragist, and politician. Beginning her career as a working class woman herself, her reform efforts eventually brought her into the highest levels of government; she served as a member of Parliament in the 1920s and in 1929 became the country's first female cabinet official when she was named minister of labour.

Margaret Bondfield was a prominent figure in British labor union leadership and progressive political movements in the first half of the twentieth century. Beginning her career as a shop assistant in her teens, Bondfield gradually worked her way up the ranks of union leadership. In her political work, she promoted better working conditions for women and voting rights for all adults. She served as a member of Parliament in the 1920s, becoming the country's first female cabinet member when she was named minister of labour in 1929. While her actions as a politician sometimes conflicted with the views of her fellow union leaders, her focus remained on the economic and social welfare of women throughout her career.

Bondfield was born on March 17, 1873, in Furnam, Somerset, England. She was the second youngest child of 11 in the family of William and Ann Bondfield. Both sides of her family had an interest in political activism. Bondfield's father was a foreman at a lace company by trade, but had participated in the working-class struggle for political reform known as the Chartist movement; he had also joined the Anti-Corn Law League to fight taxes on grain. Her maternal grandfather was George Taylor, a Congregationalist minister who was active in social and political issues. Bondfield attended the local school until she was 13, at which time she moved to Brighton to stay with family members and find work. There she lived a strenuous life as a shop assistant, working 65 hours a week and living in quarters over the shop. Her prospects improved when a women's rights advocate by the name of Hilda Martindale took an interest in the young woman and helped her continue her education.

Began Union Career in London

In 1894, when she was 21, Bondfield moved to London, where her brother Frank lived. Frank had become a printer and a trade union activist, and through him she became acquainted with a number of people and organizations promoting unions and socialism. After meeting the socialists Sidney and Beatrice Webb, Bondfield joined their moderately leftist group known as the Fabian Society. She also became a member of the Independent Labour Party at this time, establishing friendships and political connections with future prime minister Ramsay MacDonald and his

wife-to-be, Margaret Gladstone. A third area she entered at this time was the world of trade unionism, which she began to support after meeting James McPherson, the secretary of the Shop Assistants' Union.

The Shop Assistants' Union admitted both male and female members, and it also worked in conjunction with the Women's Trade Union League (WTUL). Bondfield quickly moved into positions of authority in both organizations: she was elected to the National Executive Council of the Shop Assistants' Union in 1897 and served on the General Committee of the WTUL. From 1896 to 1898 she helped compile a survey of working conditions of shop assistants for another group, the Women's Industrial Council. The findings in the report eventually led to the passage of bills regulating the length of work days in the early 1900s. Bondfield's familiarity with the plight of shop assistants and her ability to clearly communicate the concerns of the group led to her selection as assistant secretary of the Shop Assistant's Union in 1898. She held this position for the next 10 years.

In her role as assistant secretary of the union, Bondfield traveled around the British Isles, giving lectures and recruiting new members. One of the people she convinced to support the union cause was Mary MacArthur, a woman she met in Glasgow who would become one of her closest friends. Together, the two worked on a number of issues relating to women in the workplace. At Bondfield's suggestion, MacArthur was named secretary of the WTUL, and in 1906 MacArthur founded the first union for women of all trades, the National Federation of Women Workers (NFWW). With MacArthur and others, Bondfield helped win support for the Trade Boards Act of 1909. This bill established a minimum wage in four of the main industries employing women.

Fought for Women's Suffrage

During the same time period, Bondfield also expressed her feminist views by joining the suffrage movement, serving as president of the Adult Suffrage Society from 1906 to 1909. Her organization supported giving the right to vote to all adults and clashed with other groups who were willing to accept various limitations on voter eligibility. Ultimately, Bondfield gave her support to the restricted suffrage offered in the Suffrage Act of 1918, which only gave women the right to vote if they were the head of a household and over 30 years of age. In the 1920s, however, she renewed her fight for suffrage for all adult women.

In addition to her many union and political activities in the first decade of the century, Bondfield conducted studies of labor issues in American industries in Chicago, Illinois, and Lawrence, Massachusetts, in 1910. Back in England, she returned to her lecture tours until suffering from a physical collapse. In order to regain her health, she resigned from her office in the Shop Assistants' Union and refrained from all work for the next two years. In the fall of 1912, she returned to her campaign for the rights of women workers, lobbying for a better minimum wage law and adequate provisions for maternity and child care.

Led Women's Union through Transition

During the years of World War I, Bondfield devoted most of her energy to serving as the organizing secretary of the NFWW. She also, however, served on a number of wartime committees devoted to working-class issues, particularly demands on labor by the government. In addition, she became a dedicated pacifist; her views did not find favor with the British government, which in 1917 denied her permission to travel to peace conferences in Stockholm and the Hague.

After the war, Bondfield was caught up in a struggle to maintain her authority in the unions when the NFWW was merged with the National Union of General and Municipal Workers (NUGMW). In the years that followed, the NUGMW gradually reduced the number of posts available to women. When it became apparent in 1923 that Bondfield's position was being reduced to that of a powerless token female in the union hierarchy, she rebelled and declared she would quit. The leadership acceded to her demands and gave her the responsibility of overseeing all national women's issues. The same year, she became the first woman to chair the Trades Union Congress (TUC) General Council.

Elected to Parliament

Bondfield increased the scope of her political work when she was elected to Parliament from Northampton in 1923. During her first year in the government, she became parliamentary secretary to the Labour party's minister of labour, Thomas Shaw. She was defeated for her seat in 1924, but returned to Parliament in 1926. At that time, she

became the target of much criticism from the unions, extremists in the Labour party, and her local voters when she gave her approval to a government plan to lower some unemployment benefits. Bondfield survived this political crisis after appearing before the various groups and defending her position.

After her reelection to Parliament in 1929, Bondfield became the first woman to hold a cabinet post in the British government when she was named minister of labour by Ramsay MacDonald. Her assumption of this duty came of the eve of the economic depression of the 1930s. When unemployment reached record numbers in the first half of 1930, Bondfield successfully fought for more funds for unemployment and for more relaxed standards for who could receive compensation. Her stay in office was short lived, however. After MacDonald switched political affiliations and formed the National government, Bondfield remained a member of the Labour Party. She lost her reelection bid in 1931 and was again unsuccessful in 1935. In the years that followed she also was voted out of the TUC General Council and she retired from her post at the NUGMW.

While her days as a prominent figure in trade unions and national politics were over, Bondfield continued working on her lifelong crusade for improvements in women's social and economic status. Her efforts included the founding of the Women's Group on Public Welfare in 1938, a group she served as president for the years 1938 to 1945. During World War II, she took on some wartime duties, undertaking a lecture tour of the United States with the support of the British Information Services and serving as an organizer for civilian evacuation systems. This level of energy and involvement in her later years was a reflection of the determined spirit that had carried her on an impressive journey from a the anonymity of a young shop assistant to one of the most powerful figures in the national government. Her work along the way had led to numerous improvements in the lives of workers and an increased voice for women through her fight for universal suffrage. Bondfield died at the age of 80 on June 16, 1953, in Sanderstead, Surrey, England.

Further Reading

For more information see Bondfield, Margaret, *A Life's Work,* Hutchinson, 1949; Clegg, H. A., *General Union in a Changing Society: A Short History of the National Union of General and Municipal Workers, 1889-1964,* Basil Blackwell, 1964; Hamilton, Mary Agnes, *Margaret Bondfield,* Leonard Parsons, 1924; and Soldon, Norbert C., *Women in British Trade Unions, 1874-1976,* Gill and Macmillan, 1978. □

Dietrich Bonhoeffer

The German theologian Dietrich Bonhoeffer (1906-1945) had a major influence on post-World War II Protestant theology. Executed because of his part in the German resistance to Hitler, through his actions

and writings he called for Christian involvement in the world.

Dietrich Bonhoeffer was born on Feb. 4, 1906, in Breslau, the sixth of eight children. His father was a leading professor of neurology and psychiatry; his mother was the granddaughter of a distinguished church historian. When Dietrich was 6, his family moved to Berlin. He was educated at the universities of Tübingen (1923-1924) and Berlin, where he was awarded a doctorate in 1927 at the age of only 21.

Early Career

Bonhoeffer's doctoral dissertation, *The Communion of Saints* (1930), introduces some of his most characteristic emphases: a passionate concern that Christianity be a concrete reality within the real world of men; a wholly Christ-centered approach to theology, grounded entirely in the New Testament; and an intense preoccupation with the Church as "Christ existing as community."

After a year as curate of a German-speaking congregation in Barcelona, Spain (1928-1929), Bonhoeffer spent the academic year 1930-1931 in the United States as Sloane fellow at Union Theological Seminary. In fall 1931 he became a lecturer in theology at Berlin University, and his inaugural dissertation was published that year as *Act and Being*. Two collections of his lectures were later published: *Creation and Fall* (1937), an interpretation of chapters 1-3 of

Genesis; and *Christ the Center*, published posthumously from student notes. The latter work foreshadows the central idea of his last writings—Christ's whole being is His being-for-man, and His powerlessness and humiliation for man's sake are the fullest disclosure of the power and majesty of God.

Resistance to Nazism

Bonhoeffer was one of the first German Protestants to see the demonic implications of Nazism. After Hitler came to power in 1933, Bonhoeffer helped organize the Pastors' Emergency League, which became the nucleus of the Confessing Church of anti-Nazi German Protestants. While serving as minister to a German-speaking congregation in London (1933-1935), he sought support from international Christian leaders for the German Christians who were protesting Nazism.

In 1935 Bonhoeffer returned to Germany and founded a clandestine seminary to train pastors for the illegal anti-Nazi church. The seminary, located chiefly at Finkenwalde, continued despite Gestapo harassment until 1937. Bonhoeffer organized the seminary as a living workshop in Christian community and developed close relationships with his students. Out of Finkenwalde came *The Cost of Discipleship* (1937), a clarion call to active obedience to Christ based on the Sermon on the Mount, and *Life Together* (1939), a brief study of the nature of Christian community.

As war became increasingly inevitable, friends arranged an American lecture tour for Bonhoeffer with the hope that he would remain in the United States indefinitely. But only 6 weeks after his arrival in New York, he decided to return to Germany to suffer with his people.

Bonhoeffer became a member of the German resistance movement, convinced after much soul searching that only by working for Germany's defeat could he help save his country. From 1940 to 1943 Bonhoeffer worked on a study of Christian ethics, which was grounded in the biblical Christ as the concrete unity between God and the world. The sections he completed were later published as *Ethics* (1949).

In January 1943 Bonhoeffer became engaged to Maria von Wedemeyer, a longtime acquaintance. In April, however, he was arrested; while incarcerated he wrote the correspondence that later appeared as *Letters and Papers from Prison* (1951). In these fragmentary but highly original writings he developed his earlier ideas into a highly positive evaluation of modern secular thought and life, and a strongly negative judgment on traditional religiosity. Bonhoeffer described modern secularization as the world's "coming of age" from earlier religious and metaphysical dependencies into autonomous ways of understanding and coping with life. In such a world "religion"—as individualistic, otherworldly piety and dependence upon God as a "supreme being"—is dying out. Bonhoeffer believed that a Christian should not be narrowly "religious" but should be fully involved in the world. His own participation as a Christian in the momentous political struggle of his time embodies this "secular style" of discipleship.

After the abortive attempt on Hitler's life by the resistance (July 20, 1944), evidence came to light that incriminated Bonhoeffer, and he was hanged at Flossenbürg on April 9, 1945.

Further Reading

The definitive biography of Bonhoeffer is Eberhard Bethge, *Dietrich Bonhoeffer: Man of Courage* (1970), written by the man who was Bonhoeffer's closest friend and the recipient of most of his prison letters. Other good biographical sources are Wolf-Dieter Zimmermann and Ronald G. Smith, eds., *I Knew Dietrich Bonhoeffer* (1965; trans. 1967), a book of reminiscences about Bonhoeffer by his friends, and Mary Bosanquet, *The Life and Death of Dietrich Bonhoeffer* (1968). Several full-length studies of Bonhoeffer's theology are available, including William Kuhns, *In Pursuit of Dietrich Bonhoeffer* (1967); John A. Phillips, *Christ for Us in the Theology of Dietrich Bonhoeffer* (1967); and James W. Woelfel, *Bonhoeffer's Theology: Classical and Revolutionary* (1970). □

St. Boniface

The English monk St. Boniface (ca. 672-754) is known as the Apostle of Germany because he organized the Church there in the 8th century.

St. Boniface (standing)

Named Winfrith by his well-to-do English parents, Boniface was born probably near Exeter, Devon. As a boy, he studied in Benedictine monastery schools and became a monk himself in the process. For 30 years he lived in relative peace, studying, teaching, and praying. In his early 40s he left the seclusion of the monastery to do missionary work on the Continent. Because his first efforts in Frisia (now the Netherlands) were unsuccessful, Winfrith went to Rome in search of direction. Pope Gregory II renamed him Boniface, "doer of good," and delegated him to spread the gospel message in Germany.

In 719 the missionary monk set out on what was to be a very fruitful venture. He made converts by the thousands. Once, the story goes, he hewed down the giant sacred oak at Geismar to convince the people of Hesse that there was no spiritual power in nature. In 722 the Pope consecrated him bishop for all of Germany. For 30 years Boniface worked to reform and organize the Church, linking the various local communities firmly with Rome. He enlisted the help of English monks and nuns to preach to the people, strengthen their Christian spirit, and assure their allegiance to the pope. He founded the monastery of Fulda, now the yearly meeting place of Germany's Roman Catholic bishops. About 746 Boniface was appointed archbishop of Mainz, where he settled for several years as head of all the German churches.

Over the years he kept up an extensive correspondence, asking directives of the popes, giving information about the many Christian communities, and relaying to the people the popes' wishes. In 752, as the pope's emissary, he crowned Pepin king of the Franks. In his 80s and still filled with his characteristic zeal, Boniface went back to preach the gospel in Frisia. There, in 754 near the town of Dokkum, Boniface and several dozen companions were waylaid by a group of savage locals and put to death. His remains were later taken to Fulda, where he was revered as a martyr to the Christian faith.

Boniface was a man of action, but he was also sensitive to the feelings of those with whom he came in contact. His organizing genius and loyalty to Rome influenced Germany's Christianity for centuries.

Further Reading

The Life of Saint Boniface was written by a German priest, Willibald, shortly after Boniface's death. A translation of this work and some excerpts from Boniface's correspondence are contained in C.H. Talbot, ed., *The Anglo-Saxon Missionaries in Germany* (1954). A more modern interpretation of his life is given by Eleanor Shipley Duckett in *Anglo-Saxon Saints and Scholars* (1947). Godfrey Kurth's biographical study *Saint Boniface* (trans. 1935) contains a helpful bibliography.

Additional Sources

Boniface, Saint, Archbishop of Mainz, ca. 675-754., *The letters of Saint Boniface,* New York: Norton, 1976, 1940.
The Greatest Englishman: essays on St. Boniface and the Church at Crediton, Exeter: Paternoster Press, 1980.
Sladden, John Cyril., *Boniface of Devon: apostle of Germany,* Exeter, Paternoster Press, 1980. □

Pope Boniface VIII

The Italian prelate Benedetto Caetani (1235?-1303) reigned as Pone Boniface VIII from 1294 to 1303. During his pontificate he issued a new addition to canon law, participated in Italian political and dynastic struggles, and opposed King Philip IV of France.

The son of Roffredo and Emilia Caetani, Benedetto Caetani was born at Anagni. His family had important political and ecclesiastical connections, and during the 1250s Benedetto was sent to live with his uncle, the bishop of Todi. There he probably began the study of law, which he continued at Spoleto and, between 1263 and 1274, at Bologna, the center of legal studies in Christendom. In 1264 Benedetto received his first ecclesiastical appointment, a junior secretarial post in the legation of Cardinal Simon of Brie (later Pope Martin IV) to France. In 1265 Benedetto joined another legation, led by Cardinal Ottoboni Fieschi (later Pope Adrian V) to England, where he remained probably until 1268.

In 1276 Benedetto's old master Ottoboni, now pope, assigned him the duty of collecting crusade revenues in France. From this date on, Benedetto obtained steady and increasingly more responsible employment in the vast administrative and diplomatic bureaucracy of the late-13th-century papacy. In 1281, not yet a priest, Benedetto became cardinal deacon of St. Nicholas in Carcere Tulliano; in 1290 he became papal legate to France. In 1291 he was finally ordained a priest and in the same year became cardinal of St. Martin in Montibus.

Election as Pope

After the 6-month pontificate of the hermit-pope Celestine V ended with his resignation in December 1294, Benedetto Caetani was elected pope on December 24, and he took the name Boniface VIII. Celestine's brief pontificate and the unique circumstances of his resignation had created chaos in the world of ecclesiastical administration. Boniface first had to restore order in the papal system of government and justify the legality of his predecessor's resignation and, by implication, the legitimacy of his own election. As an administrator and legate, he was described by a contemporary as "a man of deep counsel, a man of trust, secret, industrious, circumspect."

Boniface had to defend himself against attacks within the Church from disaffected cardinals, particularly members of the powerful Colonna family, and from those ecclesiastical groups who had regarded Pope Celestine V as a saint and accused Boniface of having tricked the old pope into resigning. Boniface found supporters in his propaganda war with the Colonna cardinals, and in 1298 he promulgated his great law book, the *Liber sextus,* in which, among many other things, he recognized the legitimacy of papal resignation.

Conflict with Philip IV

In 1296, however, another problem had arisen, one which touched the very center of papal and temporal power: the question of taxation. The Church had long authorized, in certain cases, the collection of taxes on Church income and property by temporal authorities. The Church itself also collected taxes, and by the late 13th-century these early instances of taxation had become lucrative necessities to both the kings and the ecclesiastical powers who collected them. The taxes had begun as crusade subsidies, but they had become part of the financial transformation of 13th-century political and ecclesiastical organizations. The demand for a new tax on ecclesiastical revenues by King Philip IV of France elicited from Boniface VIII the bull (letter) *Clericis laicos,* in which the Pope not only forbade the collection of taxes from the clergy by laymen but also denied the French king authority over the clergy within his own realm.

Philip IV retaliated by forbidding the export of all money from France, and in 1297 Boniface came to terms with Philip by recognizing the technicality known as "necessity of state" as reason for emergency taxation, even of clergy, by an imperiled secular government. The position of France in Boniface's conflict with the Colonna cardinals and their allies, the Spiritual Franciscans, also contributed to the settlement between Boniface and Philip IV.

By 1300 Boniface had so successfully restored papal prestige that he proclaimed the first jubilee year. The crowds who flocked to Rome to receive the indulgences that accompanied a papal blessing must have received the impression that the Church and the papacy were indeed at the greatest point of their power in history.

In 1301 another phase of the quarrel between Boniface and Philip IV began. Philip arrested the bishop of Pamiers on charges of heresy and treason and demanded that the Pope recognize the legality of his act. Boniface responded by denouncing Philip's act, calling a council which would meet in 1302 to consider the state of the Church in France, and addressing Philip with a second admonitory letter, *Ausculta fili,* in which he outlined the traditional superiority of popes to kings and emperors. In 1302 Philip called an assembly of all ranks of French society at Paris, the first meeting in history of a representative Estates General, at which his supporters presented a distorted version of Boniface's letter and urged further royal action against the Pope.

In 1302, when his council to discuss religion in France proved a failure, Boniface issued *Unam sanctam,* perhaps the most famous papal letter ever written. In this document Boniface presented the traditional ecclesiastical view of papal authority in the Church and in the world: "Therefore, if the earthly power errs, it shall be judged by the spiritual power, if a lesser spiritual power errs it shall be judged by its superior, but if the supreme spiritual power errs it can be judged only by God not by man, as the apostle witnesses, 'The spiritual man judgeth all things and he himself is judged by no man.'"

In 1303 Philip's minister Guillaume de Nogaret met Boniface at Anagni; there he held the Pope prisoner and insulted and abused him. Released by the local inhabitants, Boniface proceeded to Rome, where he died several weeks later.

Assessment of Boniface's Life

Boniface was the target of much abuse both within and without the Church. His enemies portrayed him as a heretic, a sorcerer, a sodomite, and a traducer of the faith. His actions against the city of Florence earned him a place in Dante's *Inferno,* and between 1303 and 1311 Philip IV held the threat of a trial of Boniface and the possible repudiation of his pontificate by the Church over the heads of Boniface's weaker successors.

Boniface's conflict with Philip IV resulted in the Pope's public humiliation, the precipitous decline of papal prestige, and the first major affront to the late-13th-century concept of papal monarchy. Boniface has been described as carrying the medieval theory of papal authority to its highest point and at the same time has been condemned as rashly having thrown away both spiritual and temporal responsibility in what was essentially a political argument.

Yet Boniface's statements of Church policy, his stands against secular taxation of the clergy, and his defense of the legitimacy of his own election may also be understood as being well within ecclesiastical tradition and not exceptional for the period in which they occurred. By committing himself to power and law, Boniface became the greatest representative of the Church of order. His pontificate is one of the most important in the history of the medieval Church

and has been the subject of a considerable body of scholarly and ecclesiastical works.

Further Reading

The texts in translation of Boniface's most famous letters are found in Brian Tierney, *The Crisis of Church and State, 1050-1300* (1964). The best biography is Thomas S.R. Boase, *Boniface VIII* (1933). Another excellent study is Charles T. Wood, *Philip the Fair and Boniface VIII: State vs. Papacy* (1967), which contains an exhaustive bibliography.

Additional Sources

Denton, Jeffrey Howard., *Philip the Fair and the ecclesiastical assemblies of 1294-1295,* Philadelphia: American Philosophical Society, 1991. □

Andres Bonifacio

Andres Bonifacio (1863-1897), a Filipino revolutionary hero, founded the Katipunan, a secret society which spearheaded the uprising against the Spanish and laid the groundwork for the first Philippine Republic.

Andres Bonifacio was born in Tondo, Manila, on Nov. 30, 1863. He grew up in the slums and knew from practical experience the actual conditions of the class struggle in his society. Orphaned early, he interrupted his primary schooling in order to earn a living as a craftsman and then as clerk-messenger and agent of foreign commercial firms in Manila. Absorbing the teachings of classic rationalism from the works of José Rizal, Victor Hugo's *Les Miserables,* Eugène Sue's *The Wandering Jew,* books on the French Revolution, and the lives of the presidents of the United States, Bonifacio acquired an understanding of the dynamics of the sociohistorical process. This led him to join the Liga Filipina, which Rizal organized in 1892 for the purpose of uniting and intensifying the nationalist movement for reforms.

When the Liga was dissolved upon the arrest and banishment of Rizal, Bonifacio formed the Katipunan in 1892 and thus provided the rallying point for the people's agitation for freedom, independence, and equality. The Katipunan patterned its initiation rites after the Masonry, but its ideological principles derived from the French Revolution and can be judged radical in its materialistic-historical orientation. The Katipunan exalted work as the source of all value. It directed attention to the unjust class structure of the colonial system, the increased exploitation of the indigenous population, and consequently the need to affirm the collective strength of the working masses in order to destroy the iniquitous system.

When the society was discovered on Aug. 19, 1896, it had about 10,000 members. On August 23 Bonifacio and his followers assembled at Balintawak and agreed to begin the armed struggle. Two days later the first skirmish took place and a reign of terror by the Spaniards soon followed.

Conflict split the rebels into the two groups of Magdiwang and Magdalo in Cavite, on Luzon. Bonifacio was invited to mediate, only to be rebuffed by the clannish middle class of Cavite. Judging Bonifacio's plans as divisive and harmful to unity, Gen. Emilio Aguinaldo, the elected president of the provisional revolutionary government, ordered the arrest, trial, and execution for "treason and sedition" of Bonifacio and his brothers. On May 10, 1897, Bonifacio was executed.

Contrary to the popular view, the cause of Bonifacio's tragic death at the hands of other Filipino rebels cannot be solely attributed to his own personal pride. Rather, the correlation of class forces and the adventurist tendency of Bonifacio's group led to his isolation and subsequently to Aguinaldo's compromises with the American military invaders.

Further Reading

The best work on Bonifacio's life and career, which synthesizes all previous studies, is Teodoro A. Agoncillo, *The Revolt of the Masses: The Story of Bonifacio and the Katipunan* (1956). See also Agoncillo's *The Writings and Trial of Andres Bonifacio* (1963).

Additional Sources

Villanueva, Alejo L., *Bonifacio's Unfinished Revolution,* Quezon City: New Day Publishers, 1989. □

Richard Parkes Bonington

The English painter Richard Parkes Bonington (1802-1828), a fresh and vivid artist in his own right, also served as the connection between French and English painting at a particularly important juncture in the history of art.

Richard Bonington was born on Dec. 25, 1802, at Arnold, near Nottingham, where his father, who was an amateur painter, was governor of Nottingham city jail. In 1817 or 1818 his father set up a lace factory in Calais, France, and trained Richard as a lace designer.

In Calais, Bonington took lessons from Louis Francia, who had been a close friend and associate of the English watercolorist Thomas Girtin; Francia passed on to Bonington the tradition of English watercolor painting at its peak. When his father sought to make him stop taking lessons from Francia, Bonington ran away to Paris. Francia had given him a letter of introduction to Eugène Delacroix, who mentioned in a letter the "tall youth in a short coat who was silently making watercolor studies in the Louvre." Bonington worked on his own and also studied for a time with Baron Gros.

Bonington's work was quickly appreciated in France; indeed, Camille Corot maintained that it was the sight of a

watercolor by Bonington in the window of an art dealer which determined his vocation. Every summer Bonington took off on a sketching tour, and lithographs from his drawings appeared in Baron Taylor's *Voyages pittoresques dans l'ancienne France*. In the famous Salon of 1824, the starting point of the Barbizon school, Bonington and his compatriots John Constable and Copley Fielding received gold medals. By this time Bonington was a close friend of Théodore Géricault and Eugène Isabey, as well as of Delacroix, with whom he shared a studio and who felt there was a great deal to be learned from the young man.

In 1825 Bonington accompanied Delacroix to England, where they made many studies of armor, and in 1826 he traveled with Delacroix's friend Baron Rivet to Venice, where his work took on a new splendor and poignancy. There he made some of his finest paintings, such as *View of the Grand Canal*. By this time Bonington was probably already suffering from tuberculosis, the "white plague" of the 19th century. He returned to England in 1827 and died in London on Sept. 28, 1828, at the age of 26, leaving a large body of work.

Impact on French Art

Although Bonington's art had certainly benefited from the example of his brilliant French friends, his influence on French painting was incomparably greater. He introduced into France a new quality of light and color in the treatment of the sea, the sky, and the landscape, as in *Normandy Coast;* he placed his medieval towns and the undulating French farmlands in the ever-shifting light of day. Under the

influence of Delacroix, Bonington painted groups of figures in interiors, particularly Shakespearean subjects. He read Sir Walter Scott, as everyone then did, and the medieval chronicler Froissart, whose language had a powerful charm for him. Bonington drenched his history pictures in local color, and he had a joyful sense of the past, exemplified in *Henry IV and the Spanish Ambassador,* with no interest in the dark and melancholy side of the romantic vision.

It was Bonington's ambition to blend the skill of the Dutch with the vigor of the Venetians and the light and atmosphere of the English; not altogether successful in the first two categories, he completely succeeded in rendering and passing on the extraordinary English magic. He brought the spontaneity and brilliant coloring of British landscape painting, particularly watercolor, to Delacroix, Géricault, and Isabey and hence to the Barbizon school, which in turn led to the impressionists.

Further Reading

The most authoritative account of Bonington is in Martin Hardie, *Water Colour Painting in Britain,* vol. 2: *The Romantic Period* (1967). Andrew Shirley, *Bonington* (1940), is well reasoned and extremely well written. Hugh Stokes, *Girtin and Bonington* (1922), contains some striking insights. The basic account is in Allan Cunningham, *The Lives of the Most Eminent British Painters,* vol. 2 (1879).

Additional Sources

Ingamells, John, *Richard Parkes Bonington,* London: Trustees of the Wallace Collection, 1979.

Peacock, Carlos, *Richard Parkes Bonington,* New York: Taplinger Pub. Co., 1980. □

Pierre Bonnard

The French painter Pierre Bonnard (1867-1947) was one of the most original and consummate colorists of the first half of the 20th century and one of the few great painters of the period to remain unaffected by cubism.

Pierre Bonnard was born at Fontenay-aux-Roses on Oct. 13, 1867. After a false start as a law student, he began to paint in earnest at the École des Beaux-Arts. He failed to qualify for the Rome Prize competition, and in 1888 he began to spend more time at the less formal Académie Julian.

The Nabis

At the Académie, Bonnard met Maurice Denis, Paul Sérusier, Paul Ranson, Édouard Vuillard, and Ker Xavier Roussel, who banded together as an artistic brotherhood by 1890 and named themselves the "Nabis," a word derived from the Hebrew *nebiim* (prophets). This name appropriately reflected the occult and esoteric interests of the group, which met regularly at Ranson's studio. Sérusier had shown them a picture which he had painted under Paul Gauguin's

direction in 1888 and which embodied the synthesist principles developed at Pont-Aven (Brittany) by Gauguin and Émile Bernard. In 1890 Denis summed up those principles in the journal *Art et critique,* which contained the famous dictum: "Remember that a painting, before being a battle horse, a nude, or some anecdote, is essentially a flat surface covered with colors which have been arranged in a given order."

Within the group Bonnard was known as "the Japonizing Nabi," a reference to his flat, linear, and playful style, rich in a kind of freehand pattern. Bonnard and Vuillard were the least doctrinaire members of the group. Although Bonnard accepted the basic notions of his friends relative to the flat surface, it was his visual humor, sly and gently mocking, as well as his irrepressible delight in worldly activities, which distinguished his work from theirs. Good examples of Bonnard's style at this time are *Woman with Rabbit* (1891) and the *Croquet Game* (1892).

In 1891 Bonnard began to exhibit at the Salon des Indépendants and at the galleries of Le Barc de Boutteville, a dealer who represented the Nabis as a group. Bonnard's first one-man show was held at the Durand-Ruel Gallery in 1896. In addition to easel paintings, Bonnard executed decorative screens, posters (*France Champagne,* 1889-1890; *La Revue-blanche,* 1894; *L'Estampe et l'affiche,* 1896), book illustrations (*Marie by Nansen,* 1897-1899; Verlaine's *Parallèlement,* 1900; *Daphnis and Chloe,* 1902; Renard's *Histoires naturelles,* 1904), lithographs (notably the set *Quelques aspects de la vie de Paris,* 1895), sculpture, and stage sets.

Mature Work

After the turn of the century Bonnard adopted a lighter palette, and his art, at least superficially, approached that of the impressionists. His continued respect for the flat surface, however, and the intermittent arbitrariness of his colors and form distortions produced an essentially more abstract style. He began to make regular trips to the south of France after 1910, and he bought a house at Le Cannet in 1925, the year of his marriage to Maria Boursin (Marthe), his companion and model since 1895. The Mediterranean light had an ever-increasing effect on his paintings, which, although strongly sensual in character, never lack an underlying structure and are brilliant exploitations of the decorative possibilities of the picture plane (for example, the *Riviera* and the *Breakfast Room*).

Bonnard visited the United States in 1926, when he served as a member of the jury of the Carnegie International Competition. His late works are freer in expression and more luminous than ever. During World War II he lived in Le Cannet, and there he died on Jan. 23, 1947. Bonnard was mild in manner and in appearance. He had a reputation for witty commentary and a sharp critical sense.

Further Reading

An excellent study of Bonnard in English is John Rewald, *Pierre Bonnard* (1948). More richly illustrated are Antoine Terrasse, *Bonnard: Biographical and Critical Study* (1945; trans. 1964), and André Fermigier, *Pierre Bonnard* (1969).

Additional Sources

Watkins, Nicholas, *Bonnard,* London: Phaidon Press, 1994.
Cogniat, Raymond, *Bonnard,* New York: Crown Publishers, 1988?, 1979. □

Pierre Gabriel Édouard Bonvalot

Pierre Gabriel Édouard Bonvalot (1853-1933) was a French explorer, author, and legislator. He explored central Asia in a decade when Russia was reaching toward India and France was expanding its empire.

On July 13, 1853, Gabriel Bonvalot was born in Épagne, in the Aube Department. He attended the institute at Troyes. In 1880 Bonvalot was financed by the French government to explore Central Asia. He and a scientist, Dr. Guillaume Capus, entered Turkistan from Semipalatinsk in central Asian Russia. They traveled southeast to Tashkent, from which point they explored the headwaters of the Syr Darya. They moved on to Samarkand and from there traveled to the river Amu Darya where it borders Afghanistan. Returning to Samarkand, they journeyed homeward by way of Bukhara and Khiva.

The goal of Bonvalot's second expedition was to penetrate central Afghanistan. Again the trip was financed by the French government. Bonvalot and Capus were accompanied by an artist, Albert Pépin. Leaving Paris in March 1886, they reached the Caspian Sea at Lenkoran, traveled by horseback to Teheran, and then retraced their old route from Merv to Samarkand. Turning southward, they were seized by Afghans at the border, imprisoned 25 days, and expelled.

Returning to Samarkand, Bonvalot journeyed eastward to Fergana. Finding that caravans crossed the Pamirs and Hindu Kush to India, he made a winter crossing of those lofty ranges to Chitral, in modern northwestern Pakistan. Again Afghans seized the party and this time held them 49 days until British Indian authorities intervened.

Bonvalot then suggested traveling directly across central Asia to Tonkin (Vietnam). The imperialist Duc de Chartres agreed to finance the project. His son, Prince Henri d'Orléans, accompanied Bonvalot. The expedition left Paris in July 1889. From Semipalatinsk they took a south-south-east course, crossed the Tien Shan range and the Takla Makan desert of Sinkiang, and entered Tibet. Despite a running dispute with Tibetan officials, the expedition came within a few-score miles of Lhasa and then took a caravan route eastward and entered China's Yunnan Province. Passing through Szechwan, the group reached the Red River at Manhao and entered Hanoi in late September 1890. After his return to France, Bonvalot propagandized for outright annexation of Tonkin. In 1894 he founded the Comité Dupleix, one of numerous contemporary colonialist organizations.

In 1898 Bonvalot headed an expedition organized to cross Ethiopia and join the Marchand expedition at Fashoda. He failed to obtain the cooperation of the Ethiopian emperor, Menilek II, and relinquished command before the expedition entered the Sudan.

In 1898 Bonvalot founded a journal, *La France de demain,* and was its editor until 1904. As a deputy from Paris in Parliament from 1902 to 1906, he continued his expansionist propaganda. His book on the government of colonies, *Une lourde tâche* (A Heavy Task), appeared in 1913, and he also wrote numerous books about his travels in Asia. He died in Paris on Dec. 10, 1933.

Further Reading

There is no full-length biography of Bonvalot. Useful political background is provided in Henri Brunschwig, *French Colonialism, 1871-1914; Myths and Realities* (trans. 1964). □

George Boole

The English mathematician George Boole (1815-1864) invented mathematical, or symbolic, logic and uncovered the algebraic structure of deductive logic, thereby reducing it to a branch of mathematics.

George Boole was born on Nov. 2, 1815, in Lincoln. He attended a primary school of the National Society and then a school for commercial subjects. This was the last of his formal schooling but not the end of his education, for he inherited a talent for self-study from his father, a shoemaker by trade but a philosopher by inclination. At the age of 16 young Boole became an assistant teacher in an elementary school. Four years later he opened his own school.

Meanwhile he had discovered mathematics. Disgusted with the poor quality of the texts that his students had to use, Boole began to study the works of the great mathematicians. Without guidance he mastered these books and was producing original mathematics by 1840, barely 5 years after beginning serious study of the subject.

In 1844 Boole's pioneering paper on the calculus of operators won the Royal Society's gold medal and established his reputation among mathematicians. Three years later he published *The Mathematical Analysis of Logic,* the slim booklet that initiated modern symbolic logic. In it Boole showed how all the ponderous verbalism of Aristotelian logic could be rendered in a crisp algebra that was remarkably similar to the ordinary algebra of numbers. "We ought no longer to associate Logic and Metaphysics, but Logic and Mathematics."

In 1849 Boole finally lost his amateur status. He was appointed professor of mathematics at the new Queen's College in Cork, Ireland. His best-known work, *An Investigation of the Laws of Thought on Which Are Founded the Mathematical Theories of Logic and Probabilities* (1854), is

an elaboration of the 1847 booklet. In 1860 he published a text on the calculus of finite differences which remains the classic on that subject.

Boole married Mary Everest in 1855; she bore him five daughters. Their life together was serene but short, for Boole died on Dec. 8, 1864, of pneumonia. The citizens of Lincoln installed a stained-glass window in the Cathedral to his memory.

Boole's reputation continues to grow. In 1847 he pointed out that the value of his theories would depend largely upon the extent of their applications. Today, along with symbolic logic, Boolean algebra is of central importance in such diverse fields as probability, combinatorial theory, information theory, graph theory, switching theory, and computer design.

Further Reading

The biographical essay on Boole in E. T. Bell, *Men of Mathematics* (1937), contains minor inaccuracies and a questionable character analysis but is otherwise an excellent review of Boole's place in the history of mathematics. For a good discussion of Boole's fundamental ideas see Herbert Meschkowski, *Ways of Thought of Great Mathematicians* (1964). For modern developments consult J. Eldon Whitesitt, *Boolean Algebra and Its Applications* (1961). A concise history of symbolic logic is in Clarence Irving Lewis and Cooper Harold Langford, *Symbolic Logic* (1932; 2d ed. 1959).

Additional Sources

MacHale, Desmond, *George Boole: his life and work*, Dublin: Boole Press, 1985. □

Daniel Boone

An American frontiersman and explorer, Daniel Boone (1734-1820) was the greatest woodsman in United States history. Hero of much farfetched fiction, Boone survived both legend making and debunking to emerge a genuine hero.

For all the myths about him, Daniel Boone was very much a real man born near Reading, Pa., on Nov. 2, 1734. At the age of 12 he became a hunter. He accompanied his family to North Carolina's Buffalo Lick on the Yadkin River in 1751 and, after working for his father, became a teamster and blacksmith. In 1755 he accompanied Brig. Gen. Edward Braddock as a wagoner on the ill-fated march to Ft. Duquesne. While on this march he met a teamster named John Finley, an old hunter, whose talk of the Kentucky wilderness eventually influenced Boone's career as a woodsman and explorer. When Braddock's command was destroyed at Turtle Creek (near modern Pittsburgh) by a French and Indian ambush, Boone fled for his life on horseback.

Early Expeditions

Daniel Boone married Rebecca Bryan on Aug. 14, 1756, and settled down in the Yadkin Valley, firmly believing that he had all the requisites of a good life—"a good gun, a good horse, and a good wife." But Finley's stories of fabled "Kentucke" never really vanished from his mind. In 1767 Boone led his first expedition as far westward as the area of Floyd County, Ky. On May 1, 1769, with Finley and four other companions, Boone opened the way to the Far West by blazing a trail through the Cumberland Gap. This trail soon became a highway to the frontier. As an agent for Richard Henderson and his Transylvania Company, Boone led the first detachment of colonists to Kentucky, reaching the site of Boonesborough on April Fool's Day 1775. There he began to build a fort to protect the settlement from the Indians, and that year he brought west another party, which included his own family.

Boone became the leader of the Kentucky settlement, as hunter, surveyor, and Indian fighter. He was a major of the Virginia militia when Kentucky was added to that state as an enormous county. The first of a series of misfortunes for Boone occurred in July 1776, when his daughter, Jemima, was captured by Shawnee and Cherokee tribespeople. He rescued her but 2 years later was himself captured by Shawnee tribespeople. Though he escaped and helped defend Boonesborough against Indian raiders, while on his way east with more than $20,000 in settlers' money (with which he was to buy land warrants) he was robbed of the entire sum. The settlers who angrily demanded satisfac-

tion were repaid by Boone in land. But from this time on, Boone was dogged by debts, lawsuits, and land-record technicalities until, as one of his kin said—exaggerating slightly—at the time of his death he did not own enough land to make a decent grave.

Moving Westward

Moving to Boone's Station, the scout held a succession of offices, including lieutenant colonel of Fayette County, legislative delegate, sheriff, county lieutenant, and deputy surveyor. In 1786 he moved to Maysville and was elected to the legislature. Misfortune continued to dog him, however: he lost his land because it had been improperly entered in the records. In 1788 he abandoned his beloved Kentucky and moved to Point Pleasant in what is now West Virginia. He was appointed lieutenant colonel of Kanawha County in 1789 and its legislative delegate in 1791.

When Boone lost the last of the Kentucky lands that he had discovered, protected, settled, and improved, he also lost faith. He moved all the way west to Spain's Alta Luisiana (or Upper Louisiana, now Missouri), where he obtained a land grant at the mouth of Femme Osage Creek. He had moved because the "Dark and Bloody Ground" of yore was filling up with settlers and he did not like to be crowded; when asked why he had left Kentucky, he answered, "Too many people! Too crowded, too crowded! I want some elbow room." Actually, however, he hoped to settle on some land that would not be taken away from him by legalistic trickery. The Spaniards were pleased to have the famous Kentuckian as a colonist and gave him a large

land grant, making him magistrate of his district. He must have viewed the subsequent annexation of Louisiana Territory by the United States with mixed emotions, including apprehension. His fears were justified when, once again, U.S. land commissioners voided Boone's claim. However, in 1814 Congress confirmed a part of his Spanish grant.

Daniel Boone's greatest satisfaction was neither in opening up new territory to settlement nor in becoming the subject of laudatory books but simply in being able to journey back to Kentucky about 1810 to pay off his outstanding debts; he was left with only 50 cents. After his wife died 3 years later, the famous Kentuckian spent most of his remaining years in quiet obscurity in the Missouri home of his son, where he died on Sept. 26, 1820.

Boone was moderately well known for the wilderness exploits that had been described in several books when Lord Byron devoted seven stanzas of his poem *Don Juan* to him in 1823. The poet made the recently deceased woodsman world famous, with the result that Boone became a target for belittlers and debunkers as well as mythmakers. The latter sought to inflate his real-life adventures; the former tried to destroy his legend. All failed because the difference between legend and reality in Boone's case was so small. If he was not a dime-novel superman in buckskins, he was an unsurpassed woodsman; and he was strong, brave, loyal, and, above all, honest. Although he was hardly the "happiest of men" (as Byron described him) and had been forced to flee from American land sharks to Spanish territory, he shrugged off his shabby treatment and accepted his fate without rancor. In short, the rough woodsman was something of a stoic. He was also a true gentleman and a great figure of American history.

Further Reading

John Bakeless, *Daniel Boone* (1939), makes it unnecessary to consult such older works as Reuben G. Thwaites, *Daniel Boone* (1902), and Ella Hazel A. Spraker, *The Boone Family* (1922). Good background studies of the American frontier include Ray Allen Billington, *Westward Expansion: A History of the American Frontier* (1949; 3d ed. 1967) and *America's Frontier Heritage* (1966), and Thomas D. Clark, *Frontier America: The Story of the Westward Movement* (1959; 2d ed. 1969). □

Daniel J. Boorstin

American historian Daniel J. Boorstin (born 1914) was a scholar with broad interests, best known as an advocate of a conservative, "consensus" interpretation of American history. He became Librarian of Congress in 1975.

Daniel J. Boorstin was born on October 1, 1914, in Atlanta, Georgia, but grew up in Tulsa, Oklahoma. His writings later reflected some of the spirit of his childhood home, a booming oil city full of optimism and entrepreneurial possibilities. After graduating from high school at age 15, he entered Harvard University where he won the Bowdoin Prize for his senior honors essay in 1934. Awarded a Rhodes scholarship, he studied law at Oxford University's Balliol College and achieved a prestigious double first—first-class honors in two degrees, a B.A. in jurisprudence (1936) and a Bachelor of Civil Laws (1937).

Boorstin returned to the United States in 1937 and spent a year at Yale Law School, which subsequently (1940) awarded him a Doctor of Juridical Science degree. From 1938 to 1942 he taught legal history, American history, and literature courses at Harvard and Radcliffe. Meanwhile, like many American idealists and intellectuals in the 1930s, he became interested in Marxism. In 1938 he joined the Communist Party, but he left it the following year because of disillusionment with events in Europe, notably the signing of the Nazi-Soviet pact of 1939. Years later, Boorstin angered many radicals and liberals by testifying before the House Un-American Activities Committee and agreeing to provide the committee with the names of his former Party comrades.

Boorstin was admitted to the Massachusetts bar in 1942, and for a few months he practiced law as an attorney for a federal agency, the Lend-Lease Administration. Later in 1942 he resigned his government post to accept a teaching position at Swarthmore College. In 1944 he joined the faculty of the University of Chicago, where he remained for the next 25 years.

An Author with Firm Opinions

Boorstin's first book, *The Mysterious Science of the Law* (1941), described how Sir William Blackstone's *Commentaries* (1765-1769) were shaped by practical experience with the law rather than by *a priori* reasoning about social values. In a second book, *The Lost World of Thomas Jefferson* (1948), Boorstin argued that Jefferson was not, as most Jeffersonian scholars claimed, a speculative philosopher, but a man who derived insights from his experience with concrete situations.

Boorstin's belief that there was a striking contrast between American and European ways of thinking, and his conviction that American pragmatism was vastly superior to European devotion to abstract philosophical systems, became even more explicit in *The Genius of American Politics* (1953). In this slim volume Boorstin asserted that the American experience was in many respects exceptional. "Givenness" was the term Boorstin used for the quality that set Americans apart. The natural abundance of the land gave Americans exceptional opportunities and encouraged a faith in upward mobility. The fortuitous given in history was that American society had not had to pass through a feudal phase, with the result that the nation's body politic had been free of conflicts between supporters of an old regime and advocates of republican and bourgeois ideals. American realities, if judged by the standard of known historical precedents, were so close to ideal conditions that utopian ideological schemes would not appeal to Americans. The "is" of American life would be taken as the "ought." Thus, a national consensus on the virtues of moderate liberalism and entrepreneurial optimism became the hallmark of American life. Even the Civil War had not, according to Boorstin, broken these broad continuities or produced fundamental changes in American institutions.

Boorstin's description of the American past was a sharp departure from the views of the previous generation of historians, the so-called progressives, for whom conflict and change were the crucial themes in the nation's history. Boorstin, therefore, was soon recognized as one of the leading proponents of a conservative, "consensus" interpretation of American life. Critics were quick to challenge his perspective, asserting that he ignored instances of deep-seated economic and ethnic conflict while giving inadequate attention to the many Americans whose experience did not fit neatly with his nationalist claims for the United States as a land of opportunity.

A Three-Volume History

The fullest expression of Boorstin's interpretation of American life may be found in his three-volume history of the United States. Some reviewers complained that the trilogy was seriously deficient because Boorstin said little about political and military history. However, the virtual absence of these topics was consistent with his view that the truly important themes in the American past were the social history of pioneering, invention, entrepreneurship, and the like.

In volume one, *The Americans: The Colonial Experience* (1958), Boorstin offered numerous examples in support of his thesis that the givens in the American environment, the country's vast size and wealth of its resources, quickly broke down or transformed every utopian scheme—Puritan Massachusetts, corporate Virginia, Penn's Pennsylvania, and Oglethorpe's Georgia—that Europeans attempted to establish in the New World.

In his second volume, *The Americans: The National Experience* (1965), which covered the period from the Revolution to the Civil War, Boorstin described the United States as a nation of practical folk who, in spreading westward across the continent, developed a faith in republicanism and individualism because the virtues of those ideas were daily demonstrated in their lives.

Finally, in *The Americans: The Democratic Experience* (1973) Boorstin gave his version of American life since the Civil War. It was still a story with many heroes, go-getter businessmen such as Gustavus Swift, and trend-setting inventors such as Thomas A. Edison. Nevertheless, the book closed on a somber note as Boorstin decried some of the trends he observed in 20th-century American life, especially what seemed to him the baneful influence of consumer culture and the mass media.

Boorstin's criticisms of certain aspects of contemporary American life were not entirely new themes in his writings. In 1962 he had published *The Image: or, What Happened to the American Dream* (reissued as a paperback in 1964 with a new subtitle, *A Guide to Pseudo-Events in America*), in which he charged that the mass media were cutting Americans off from the concrete experiences that had been the source of their earlier national greatness and plunging them into an unreal world of pseudo-experiences. Similarly, Boorstin had been deeply troubled by the outburst of radical protest that swept university campuses in the late 1960s. In his book *The Decline of Radicalism: Reflections on America Today* (1969) he had harsh words for the New Left radicals, asserting that they were advocating dissent, which tended to divide and destroy, rather than practicing disagreement, which allowed for discussion and, eventually, for agreement through compromise.

In 1969 Boorstin left the University of Chicago and joined the staff of the Smithsonian Institution in Washington, D.C. In 1975 he was appointed Librarian of Congress by President Gerald Ford and served in that position until 1987. In spite of his heavy administrative duties, he continued to write. His book *The Discoverers* (1983) was an ambitious project in which he traced the history of mankind's pursuit of knowledge about the world from Greek times to the present.

Academic Acclaim

Throughout his life, Boorstin received much acclaim for his historical scholarship. His three-volume history of the United States, *The Americans,* was awarded the Bancroft, Parkman, and Pulitzer Prizes. For his effort on *The Discoverers* he received the History of Science Society's Watson Davis Prize. Boorstin was the beneficiary of more than 50 honorary degrees and was decorated by the governments of France, Belgium, Portugal, and Japan. His work also earned him the Phi Beta Kappa Distinguished Service to the Hu-

manities Award and the Charles Frankel Prize from the National Endowment of the Humanities. In 1989 Boorstin received the National Book Award for Distinguished Contributions to American Letters from the National Book Foundation.

In addition to his tenure at the University of Chicago, Boorstin also served as visiting professor at the University of Rome, the University of Geneva, the University of Kyoto, and the University of Puerto Rico. At the Sorbonne, in Paris, he was the first incumbent chair of American History.

Although his books proved exceptionally popular, Boorstin often stated that he wrote for the pleasure of writing rather than for compensation. As he entered his eighties, he continued to write and travel the lecture circuit. In 1992 he published *The Creators* which chronicled man's achievements in the arts. In 1994 he published a collection of essays on the role that the unexpected plays in history titled *Cleopatra's Nose: Essays of the Unexpected,* and in 1995, *The Daniel J. Boorstin Reader,* which included selections from most of his books. In all Boorstin authored or edited more than 26 works, which have since been translated into more than 25 languages.

Further Reading

Three short sources on Daniel J. Boorstin's life and thought are available: J. R. Pole, "Daniel J. Boorstin," in *Pastmasters: Some Essays on American Historians* (1969), edited by Marcus Cunliffe and Robin W. Winks; "Daniel J. Boorstin," in John Wakeman, ed., *World Authors, 1950-1970* (1975); and Frank Annunziata, "Daniel J. Boorstin," in *Dictionary of Literary Biography: Twentieth Century American Historians* (1983).

A brief biography of Boorstin can be found on the Internet at http://www.epirotiki.com/solareclipse/boorstin.html (July 1997). For a synopsis of a recent Boorstin speech, see *The Stanford Daily Online* at http://daily.stanford.org/Daily96-97/10-10-96/News/Newboorstin10.html (July 1997). □

Charles Booth

The English social scientist Charles Booth (1840-1916) conducted a massive pioneering investigation of living and working conditions in London.

Charles Booth was born in Liverpool on March 30, 1840, into a family of merchants and shipowners. He early became a successful shipowner and in 1871 married the niece of the author T. B. Macaulay. After a serious illness Booth settled in London and turned his attention to the condition of the working classes. He was struck by the abundance of theoretical proposals for the relief of poverty and the absence of accurate quantitative evidence. In his view, the first need was to obtain facts, both "to prevent the adoption of false remedies" and to provide materials for others "to find remedies for the evils which exist."

In 1886 Booth began his survey of East London, at that time probably the area of greatest destitution in England. He and his assistants compiled 46 books of data, with family-by-family notations of economic level and occupation. He published a one-volume condensation of this information in 1889. In 1891 he produced a more general report on the rest of London. He worked through the 1890s with the help of the 1891 census, and his final text, in 17 volumes, appeared in 1902-1903 under the general title *Life and Labour of the People in London*. Booth organized this work into three series: "Poverty," arranged geographically; "Industry," categorized into 16 trades; and "Religious Influences."

Booth's most important discovery was that 30 percent of the million families in London lived at or below the bare minimum level for independent subsistence. His facts appeared, on one hand, to disprove the Marxist presumption of a massive, destitute proletariat and, on the other hand, to show the futility of private charity and the need for a program of welfare legislation.

Although Booth avoided specific recommendations, he concluded that the state must intervene to preserve capitalist competition by the "removal of this very poor class out of the daily struggle for existence." He envisaged a dual system of individualism and socialism under which Britain could "dispense with any socialistic interference in the lives of all [but the poor]." Booth's work did much to lay a statistical basis for the structure of the welfare state; old-age pensions, health and unemployment insurance, and minimum wages were all instituted between 1908 and 1911.

Booth served on the official Poor Law Commission of 1905-1909, in which his views were essentially conservative. He died on Nov. 23, 1916. Beatrice Webb, his cousin and coworker, called him "the boldest pioneer . . . , and the achiever of the greatest results, in the methodology of the social sciences of the nineteenth century."

Further Reading

Aside from Booth's own volumes, there are accounts of his life and work by his wife, Mary Macaulay Booth, in *Charles Booth: A Memoir* (1918), and by Beatrice Webb in *My Apprenticeship* (1926; 2d ed. 1946). Albert Fried and Richard Elman, eds., *Charles Booth's London* (1968), is a volume of selections from Booth's survey with a useful biographical introduction.

Additional Sources

O'Day, Rosemary, *Mr Charles Booth's inquiry: Life and labour of the people in London reconsidered,* London; Rio Grande, Ohio: Hambledon Press, 1993.

Charles Booth, social scientist, Westport, Conn.: Greenwood Press, 1980, 1960. □

Edwin Booth

Edwin Booth (1833-1893) was one of America's greatest tragic actors, introducing into his character-izations an artistic sensitivity and completeness that replaced the bombast of earlier times.

Edwin Booth had little schooling. Instead, he accompanied his actor father, Junius Brutus Booth, on the theatrical circuits, ostensibly to attend him but really to control the elder genius's drinking and erratic behavior, a problem Edwin himself later had. Edwin first took up drama in 1849 and thereafter played minor roles, until in New York, in 1851, his father's illness (real or feigned) permitted him to substitute as Richard III. Edwin was an immediate success.

Booth modestly continued his training in a variety of major and minor roles, first in California and later in the South. In Richmond, Va., he fell in love with Mary Devlin, who became his wife. Returning to New York in 1857, he was acclaimed for his brilliant and forceful portrayals of Richard III, Shylock, Romeo, and other Shakespearean characters. Booth surpassed the critical praise given to Edwin Forrest, who emerged from retirement in 1860 to challenge the young man.

At 31 Booth was America's foremost actor. His wife's death, however, caused him deep sorrow that exaggerated his already melancholy nature. He left the stage saying, "The beauty of my art is gone—it is hateful to me."

But acting was so deeply a part of the man that by 1864 Booth was back as star and manager of the Winter Garden Theater in New York. It was there that the three Booth

brothers—Edwin, Junius, and John Wilkes—gave their memorable performance of *Julius Caesar*. (This staged political assassination was soon to be followed by a real one.) While Edwin was at the zenith of his fame, having acted Hamlet for more than a hundred consecutive nights, he heard of his brother John Wilkes's murder of President Lincoln. Once more he retired from the stage in sorrow.

Assured that the public did not hold him responsible for his brother's action, Booth returned to acting in 1866 and was greeted by a tremendous and sympathetic ovation. At the Booth Theater in New York City he managed and acted in the most elaborate and artistic productions of Shakespeare America had ever known. Bankruptcy in 1873 made him renounce managership forever, and he thereafter concentrated on becoming what many critics insisted was the greatest actor of his time. His performances were sensitive, integrated in tone, gesture, and setting, and full of poetic power. He did not think of himself as an entertainer but as an artist who revealed the beauty and wisdom of great dramatic poetry.

Booth had earlier made a gift of his home to the acting profession, and it was there, at the Players Club in New York City, that he died.

Further Reading

Eleanor Ruggles, *Prince of Players: Edwin Booth* (1953), is a popular portrait of the actor. William Winter, *The Life and Art of Edwin Booth* (1894; rev. ed. 1906), is a deeply appreciative analysis of Booth's technique and temperament. Asia B. Clarke, *The Elder and Younger Booth* (1882), is still an interesting study of the professional and personal lives of the Booth acting family. A good brief account of Booth and other tragedians of his time is in Garff B. Wilson, *A History of American Acting* (1966).

Additional Sources

Oggel, L. Terry, *Edwin Booth: a bio-bibliography*, New York: Greenwood Press, 1992.

Players (Club), *Edwin Booth's legacy: treasures from the Hampden-Booth theatre collection at the Players*, New York: Hampden-Booth Theatre Library, 1989.

Smith, Gene, *American gothic: the story of America's legendary theatrical family, Junius, Edwin, and John Wilkes Booth*, New York: Simon & Schuster, 1992.

Tebbel, John William, *A certain club: one hundred years of The Players*, New York: Wieser & Wieser, 1988. □

Evangeline Cory Booth

British-born humanitarian Evangeline Cory Booth (1865-1950) was one of the early commanders of the Salvation Army in the United States. Her work to help the nation's poor and her efforts to provide aid to U.S. soldiers in Europe during World War I won her the admiration of the American public. In 1934 she was elected general—the Salvation Army's high- est post—culminating a lifetime of service to the religious charity.

E vangeline Cory Booth was a member of the founding family of the Salvation Army, a religious organization formed by her father with the aim of aiding the needy. In her role as commander of the Salvation Army in the United States, she gained acceptance for the group's work and ideals throughout American society, particularly after organizing assistance to soldiers during World War I. Her success in expanding the Salvation Army in the United States was apparent in the increased number of centers and followers during her tenure as well as her personal popularity among the public. In 1929 her work was recognized when she was elected to the post of General of the Salvation Army, making her the head of the entire organization.

Born into Salvation Army Family

Booth was born with the name Evelyne on December 25, 1865, in London, England, and was known to her family as Eva. She was one of the five children of William Booth, who in the year of Booth's birth, founded the East London Revival Society. The Society later took the name the Christian Mission before taking its final shape as the religious and charitable organization known as the Salvation Army. Like her siblings, Booth devoted her life to the work of the Army—to assist the poor and spread Christian values. She did not receive any formal education, but spent her adolescent years among the poor of London. Becoming a sergeant

in the Army at the age of 15, she sold the organization's publication, *War Cry,* in the streets. When she was a bit older, her assignment included selling matches in the impoverished area of Marylebone while dressed in rags like the poor around her. Although all the Booth children went on to hold high posts in the Army, it was Evelyne Booth who would serve for the longest period of time and bring the Army to a new level of influence and popularity. As an adult, she changed her name to Evangeline to emphasize the spiritual solace she hoped to bring to the poor while at the same time alleviating their physical suffering.

In 1895, at the age of 30, Booth arrived in Canada to replace her brother Herbert as field commissioner of the Salvation Army in that country. Having worked in some very rough environments in England, Booth found conditions around the city of Toronto to be relatively placid, and she worried that there would not be much for her to do in Canada. But she soon found her calling in the frontier areas of the north such as the Yukon and Alaska, where gold prospectors had formed unruly boom towns. For nine years she traveled and preached among the settlers and the native people of the area in what she later called "one of the most arduous toils in my experience."

Expanded Army in United States

But not even her challenging work in Canada could prepare her for the scope of her next task. In 1903, her sister Emma, the commander of the United States Salvation Army, died in New York City. Emma had created a solid foundation for the Army in the United States; at the time of her death its assets were worth 1.5 million dollars and almost 700 stations had been founded across the country. She was mourned as one of the country's greatest citizens—an estimated 75,000 people came to pay respects to her open casket and a New York newspaper compared the size of her funeral procession to that of president Ulysses S. Grant. Evangeline was selected to serve as the new U.S. commander, but she was intimidated at the prospect of trying to live up to her sister's greatness. Her father encouraged her, however, telling her that he believed she was destined to a career of great accomplishment. His daughter ultimately fulfilled his predictions. From the time of her induction as American commander in 1904, until her retirement from the post in 1934, the organization more than doubled the number of stations, its property holdings grew to a value of 48 million dollars, and its bank accounts increased to 35 million dollars.

Once arriving in New York, Booth immediately began to address the extreme poverty she found among immigrants there. One of the main problems was hunger; she attacked this by establishing bread lines and programs to feed school children. The public was incredibly responsive to her calls for help and surprised her by exceeding her expectations when she held donation drives. Other public service projects she took on were providing emergency relief during disasters, providing aid to hospitals, and helping the elderly. By focusing on such activities, Booth won over support from people who had initially been wary of the Salvation Army's religious overtones. She also used her oratorical talent to speak out on other topics that crossed religious boundaries, including women's rights and the prohibition of alcohol.

Won Appreciation for Wartime Service

It was her efforts to use the Salvation Army to assist soldiers in World War I, however, that won Booth and her organization the lasting respect and appreciation of the American public. Under the leadership of Booth, the Salvation Army sent members to the front lines of the war in Europe, where they cared for the wounded, established canteens, and loaned money to soldiers. This wartime aid was considered so important by the U.S. government that it excused Salvation Army members from military duty so they could be free to continue their charitable work. The country showed its appreciation for the Salvation Army after the war by donating 15 million dollars during a special nationwide project to assist the organization. In addition, the group and its leader were praised by some of the leading political and military figures of the war, including presidents Theodore Roosevelt and Woodrow Wilson, British prime minister Lloyd George, and U.S. generals John Joseph Pershing and Leonard Wood. Booth herself was recognized with a Distinguished Service Medal in October of 1919.

Elected General of Salvation Army

In the 1920s, the Salvation Army suffered a period of internal turmoil. After William Booth's death in 1912, his son Bramwell had become the second general, or head official, of the Salvation Army. While Evangeline was recovering from a throat operation in 1922, Bramwell Booth attempted to undermine her position by dividing the United States command into three separate groups, each with its own commander. Americans, however, were extremely supportive of the beloved U.S. commander and were quick to voice their disapproval of her brother's move. The general was forced to back off his position, but his reputation had been weakened. In 1929, the Salvation Army held its first election for the post of general and Bramwell Booth was replaced with Edward J. Higgins. When the next elections were held in 1934, Salvation Army members turned to the woman who had done so much to raise the image of the organization, electing Evangeline Booth to the position of general. She completed only one five-year term before retiring from the organization in 1939 at the age of 74. Having served the Salvation Army in three different nations during her long career, it seemed fitting that her last years were spent overseeing an organization that had grown to an international success with volunteers in more than 50 countries. Booth died in her adopted country of the United States at Hartsdale, New York, on July 17, 1950.

Further Reading

For more information see Wilson, P. W., *General Evangeline Booth of the Salvation Army,* Scribners, 1948. □

John Wilkes Booth

One of the most promising American actors of his time, John Wilkes Booth (1838-1865) was the assassin of President Abraham Lincoln in 1865.

John Wilkes Booth was born in Bel Air, Maryland, and attended school sporadically. A strikingly handsome youth, he attracted many people, and early decided to try the stage. Although unwilling to work at his parts, native talent enabled him to win acclaim as a Shakespearean actor, especially in the Richmond, Virginia stock company. In 1860—the year Lincoln was elected president—Booth achieved recognition across the country and played to approving audiences. Contemporary actors praised him as a "comer," and his reputation seemed assured.

A respiratory problem in 1863 forced Booth to leave the stage temporarily, and he began conceiving a romantic "conspiracy" to abduct President Lincoln and deliver him to Richmond for a ransom of peace or an exchange of Confederate prisoners.

Sympathized with the South

Unlike the rest of the Booth family, John had always been a Southern sympathizer. He believed the Civil War to be a simple confrontation between Northern tyranny and Southern freedom. He enrolled six other Confederate sympathizers in his kidnapping scheme. Their efforts in March

1865 to capture Lincoln on the outskirts of Washington, D.C. were foiled by the President's failure to appear. Booth's frustration undoubtedly contributed to his decision to assassinate Lincoln.

Booth learned at noon on April 14 that Lincoln would attend Laura Keene's performance of *Our American Cousin* at Ford's Theater in Washington that evening. Vice President Andrew Johnson and Secretary of State William Seward were also to be killed, but Booth's confederates failed to carry out these murders. Booth went to the theater in the afternoon and fixed the door of the President's box so that it could be barred behind him. At about ten o'clock Booth entered the theater, shot Lincoln, and jumped to the stage, shouting "Sic semper tyrannis! (Thus ever to tyrants!) The South is avenged!"

Pursued and Killed

Breaking a leg in his leap to the stage, Booth dragged himself from the theater to a waiting horse. The pain slowed him, and he and another conspirator were forced to seek a doctor. Dr. Samuel A. Mudd set the leg and fed the fugitives. For several days they tried to cross the Potomac, and when at last they succeeded, they journeyed to the farm of Richard H. Garrett, south of the Rappahannock River. Pursuers found them in Garrett's barn on April 26. When Booth refused to surrender, the barn was set afire. His figure was glimpsed briefly just as a shot was fired. Although one of the pursuers claimed to have shot Booth, it is unclear whether he was killed or committed suicide.

Booth's accomplices were rounded up and tried in one of the wildest travesties of justice ever perpetrated. Four of the conspirators were condemned to death. Dr. Mudd received a life sentence, as did two of Booth's accomplices. One accomplice died in 1867; the other and Mudd were pardoned by President Johnson in 1869.

Booth's tragedy lay in his twisted vision of patriotism. He never understood the horror caused by his act, and he died with these last words: "Tell Mother . . . I died for my country."

Further Reading

Lewis, Lloyd, and Mark Neely, Jr., *The Assassination of Lincoln: History and Myth* (1994). □

Joseph Booth

Joseph Booth (1851-1932) was an English independent missionary in Malawi, Lesotho, and South Africa. Because of his radical religious views and egalitarian political outlook, his name became linked to a 1915 African rising in Malawi.

Joseph Booth was born in Derby on Feb. 26, 1851, into a very religious home. He was of an independent, inquiring mind and very early questioned his parents' religious faith. He was strongly pacifist with a critical attitude toward all authority. He became a restless, self-educated man and in the course of his life was an agnostic, a Baptist, a Seventh-Day Adventist, and a member of the Watch Tower Bible and Tract Society. Strangely enough, it was the reading of Thomas Paine which led him to the Christian faith.

In the 1880s Booth was a sheep farmer in New Zealand and a Baptist lay preacher in Australia. In 1891 he developed a scheme for self-supporting industrial missions in Africa to be run by lay people with practical educations, the aim being to foster independent African leadership. He traveled via England to the newly declared British Nyasaland Protectorate, where, in 1891, he started the Zambesi Industrial Mission near Blantyre. His first convert and friend was John Chilembwe, whom he baptized in a river. His ways of working aroused the suspicion of settlers, other missionaries, and the colonial government. He could not work with others sent to help him, and in 1896 the supporters of the Zambesi Industrial Mission broke with him.

With John Chilembwe, Booth visited the United States in 1897-1899, during which time they parted ways. In 1897 Booth published his book *Africa for the Africans* (he was the first known to have used this phrase). He then joined the Seventh-Day Baptists and returned to Malawi. In 1899 Booth and a group of Africans petitioned Queen Victoria on behalf of all Africans for education, political participation, and justice. Their actions caused the colonial government to pressure him to leave the protectorate about 1902.

Thereafter Booth worked with various organizations for the purpose of fostering African leadership and independence, mostly using South Africa as a base. He introduced the Watch Tower movement into Central Africa and used the mail and migrant workers to spread its literature and beliefs, thereby causing the colonial governments serious concern.

In 1915 John Chilembwe lost his life in an African uprising in Malawi. Although Booth was far away and had had nothing to do with Chilembwe for 15 years, his name was linked to the uprising and his ideas were considered the seed which led to it. He was therefore deported from South Africa in December 1915. In England he took part in independent religious activities until his death at Weston super Mare in 1932.

Further Reading

Booth's *Africa for the Africans* is almost unobtainable. The best source for information on Booth is George Shepperson and Thomas Price, *Independent African: John Chilembwe and the Origins, Setting and Significance of the Nyasaland Native Rising of 1915* (1958). □

William Booth

The English evangelist William Booth (1829-1912) founded the Salvation Army, an international Christian organization for philanthropic and evangelical work.

William Booth was born near Nottingham on April 10, 1829. As a youth, he was apprenticed to a pawnbroker, but after a conversion experience he began street preaching for a Methodist chapel. In 1849 he went to London, where he worked as a pawnbroker. Three years later, however, he became a full-time Methodist lay preacher. In 1855 he married Catherine Mumford, an intelligent and determined woman. Encouraged by her in his theological studies, Booth was ordained a minister in 1858.

Booth's theology was simple and unchanging. He drew both his beliefs and his basic practice from the model set by John Wesley a century earlier. His creed required no systematic theological learning. He held that without personal acceptance of Christ as his Savior, the sinful man would die into eternal damnation. Although the opportunity for acceptance was freely offered to all, it was certain to be ignored by the masses in the sordid and pagan slums of the new industrial towns. Thus it was necessary to reach the ignorant, the drunkard, and the criminal and offer them the chance of repentance.

Driven by this purpose, in 1861 the Booths left Methodism and in 1865 established the Christian Mission in East London. During the next 12 years Booth developed the evangelical techniques later employed in the Salvation Army. Among these were the use of secular quarters and the enlistment of converted sinners as workers. Booth was not a political or social radical; he only gradually came to accept that social uplift might have to precede conversion. Thus he slowly built a social program of food kitchens, housing, and communal organization. He wrote, however, ''The Social is the bait, but it is Salvation that is the hook that lands the fish.''

The conversion of the Christian Mission into the Salvation Army occurred somewhat accidentally in 1878. Booth had earlier expressed his evangelical zeal in military terms, titles, and concepts. This organizational style, not unique to his army, was in tune with the current popularity of militarism and imperialism. The army's paper, the *War Cry,* appeared at the end of 1879. Although the army met considerable hostility through the 1880s, by 1890 Booth had become a figure of international renown. The day-to-day administrative labor of the Salvation Army fell increasingly to Bramwell Booth, General Booth's oldest child and his chief of staff and successor.

Mrs. Booth died in 1890, the year in which Booth wrote, with much assistance from the reforming journalist W. T. Stead, his famous book, *In Darkest England and the Way Out.* In it Booth colorfully and compassionately detailed the misery of the ''Submerged Tenth'' and insisted that the ''way out'' must transform men as well as their surroundings.

Further Reading

Of the biographies of Booth, two stand out: The best is St. John Ervine, *God's Soldier: General William Booth* (2 vols., 1934). An earlier biography is by a friend, Harold Begbie, *The Life of General William Booth: The Founder of the Salvation Army* (2 vols., 1920), which is well organized chronologically but lacks clarity of detail.

Additional Sources

Barnes, Cyril J., *William Booth and his army of peace,* Amersham, Eng.: Hulton Educational, 1975.

Barnes, Cyril J., *Words of William Booth,* London: Salvationist Publishing, 1975.

Bennett, David, *William Booth,* Minneapolis, Minn.: Bethany House, 1986.

Coutts, Frederick Lee, *Bread for my neighbour: an appreciation of the social action and influence of William Booth,* London: Hodder and Stoughton, 1978.

Robinson, Virgil E., *William Booth and his Army,* Mountain View, Calif.: Pacific Press Pub. Association, 1976. □

Betty Boothroyd

The first woman Speaker in Britain's House of Commons, Betty Boothroyd (born 1929), a Labour Party member, was the first Speaker in the 20th century chosen from an opposition party.

MPs (Members of Parliament) dragged Betty Boothroyd to the speaker's chair despite the traditional show of reluctance on April 27, 1992. Her triumph by 372 votes to 238 over former Northern Ireland Secretary Peter Brooke marked the first contested election for the coveted position for 40 years. MPs marked the occasion by breaking with another tradition and giving her a round of applause, normally not heard in the British House of Commons.

As controller of the Commons proceedings and spokesperson for the lower house of Parliament, Boothroyd became a familiar figure to the British nation. Although she refused to wear the knee breeches and wig traditionally worn by her predecessors, she added her own trademark to the familiar cry of ''Order, order'' long used to urge unruly MPs to behave themselves. She ended the twice weekly Prime Minister's Question Time sessions with a cry made familiar by barmaids in public houses and bars across the country: ''Time's up.''

Betty Boothroyd was born an only child in a politically active household in Yorkshire in October 1929. Both her parents were textile workers and trades unionists, and she joined the Labour League of Youth at only 16. After a brief spell as a dancer in the London West End Theatre she held a series of jobs as secretary to leading politicians. These in-

cluded two years in Washington D.C. as secretary to a Republican congressman and involvement in the 1960 Kennedy presidential campaign. She was also secretary to the one-time Labour cabinet minister, Barbara Castle. She shared Lady Castle's brisk, no-nonsense style but opted for a different brand of Labour politics. Boothroyd was known in her time on Labour's National Executive Committee (1981-1987) as a right-center opponent of what she called "headbangers . . . and extremists and militants" and a supporter of what was later to become the European Union.

It took five attempts before she was able to enter Parliament. Boothroyd contested seats in Leicester, in Peterborough, and two in North West England before being elected for the West Midlands seat of West Bromwich (later reformed as West Bromwich West) in 1973. An early sign of her ability to invade what were previously male-only preserves was her appointment as a Labour Party whip the next year. From 1975 to 1977 she was a member of the European Assembly, the unelected predecessor of the European Parliament. She served her apprenticeship for the Speaker's post as a deputy from 1987 to 1992. It was when she took on that role that a backbencher asked her how she wished to be addressed and she replied, appropriately for one with her show business background, "Call me Madam."

Madam Speaker Boothroyd never married. She preferred to concentrate her efforts on forging a ground breaking career in British politics. "The Commons has never been just a career," she told an interviewer from *People Magazine*, "It's my life." She proved an adept disciplinarian with Parliament's unruly elements. Some of her success in what remained a predominantly male-oriented world, was that MPs believed she had earned the status of "good chap." During her tenure, although she presided over a chamber containing a record number of women MPs, she clearly relished her position. She controlled the daily proceedings with considerable gusto. Boothroyd remained meticulously fair in her dealings with MPs, maintaining statistical records of exactly whom she called on from which parties, so that there would be no accusations of bias.

The Speaker is traditionally a guardian of back bench rights, and Boothroyd amply demonstrated her independence of the executive. "I rub my hands with glee when I am unpopular with both sides. . . . You've got to ensure that holders of an opinion, however unpopular, are allowed to put across their points of view," she told *People*. She permitted lengthy questioning of ministers over statements and in response to emergency questions. In July 1993 she was in the spotlight when she ruled that the Labour Opposition was entitled to stage the vote it sought on inclusion of the controversial social chapter covering workers' rights in the bill to ratify British acceptance of the Maastricht Treaty on European Union negotiated by Prime Minister John Major. She did so despite having to overrule an earlier decision by her deputy that such an attempt was out of order. When the vote on the Labour move was tied, Boothroyd used her casting vote to defeat the amendment and preserve the government's position.

There had been some criticism of her the previous month after she clashed repeatedly with ex-minister Mi-

chael Mates during his resignation speech in the Commons. MPs felt she had been unduly restrictive in application of the *sub judice* rules under which comment is limited if it could affect future legal proceedings.

The firmest indication of her readiness to protect the rights of Parliament came in July 1993 with what was perceived as a warning to the courts that Parliament did not interfere with their jurisdiction and they were not to interfere with Parliament's doings. Lord Rees-Mogg, a former editor of the *Times* and an opponent of the Conservative government's Maastricht treaty bill, was seeking to challenge the government's legislation in the courts. Left wing Labour MP, Tony Benn, asked the speaker for a ruling on whether Parliament's sovereignty was being challenged. She replied that the way courts were using the words spoken during parliamentary debates to assist in the interpretation of laws was questioning the Commons in a way previously thought impossible: The 1689 Bill of Rights provided that freedom of speech in Parliament "ought not to be questioned in any place out of Parliament" and when the Rees-Mogg case began she trusted that the judges concerned would respect the Bill of Rights. The case was dismissed and Benn and others believed that Boothroyd had earned her place in parliamentary history alongside the famous Speaker Lenthall in the 17th century, who defied the orders of a king who was seeking to seize five parliamentary opponents with the response: "I have neither eyes to see, nor tongue to speak in this place but as the House is pleased to direct me, whose servant I am here."

Following the election of Tony Blair as prime minister, and Labour's return to dominance in the House of Commons in May 1997, Boothroyd was unanimously re-elected Speaker. During the speeches and accolades that accompanied her renomination to the post, members of Parliament referred to her as "Speaker of the Commonwealth. She not only has a public persona in Britain, but is well known all over the Commonwealth. She welcomes people of every nationality, colour, and religion throughout her working term to show them what we do, why it is important, and why that tradition of democracy needs to be spread even further . . . [S]he tries to spread friendship, kindness and understanding among Members of parties of all sizes and shapes and now even between different genders."

Further Reading

Further details of Betty Boothroyd's political career can be found in the latest series of "Parliamentary Profiles" edited by Andrew Roth and available from Parliamentary Profile Services Ltd. (2, Queen Anne's Gate Buildings, Dartmouth Street, London SW1H 9BP). The role of the Commons speaker is outlined in Erskine May's *Parliamentary Practice,* the bible of parliamentary procedure, periodically revised and published by Butterworth & Co. (London). Valuable information, including speeches and parliamentary procedures, can be found on the World Wide Web under the pages devoted to the British parliament. Both the *Economist* (November 19, 1994) and *People Magazine* (February 28, 1994) wrote profiles on Betty Boothroyd. Parliamentary proceedings can also be seen each week on C-Span, the U.S. Congress' cable network. □

William Edgar Borah

United States senator William Edgar Borah (1865-1940) was influential in developing American foreign policy, particularly by his isolationist attitudes in the 1930s and his opposition to aid to France and Great Britain as World War II approached.

William E. Borah was born to William Nathan and Eliza West Borah on June 29, 1865, on a farm near Fairfield, Ill. The family had settled originally in Pennsylvania about 1750 and moved west at the turn of the 19th century.

Young William had little liking for farm life. He resisted a career in the ministry and, while still a schoolboy, ran away with a traveling troupe of actors. Then an older sister invited him to join her and her husband in Lyon, Kans., where William continued his education, entering the University of Kansas in 1885. Forced by illness to leave college after his freshman year, he read law at home and passed the Kansas bar examination in 1887. Hard times, however, forced him to leave Kansas, and he settled in Boise, Idaho.

Borah prospered and became prominent in Republican party circles. In 1895 he married Mary O'Connell, daughter of the governor of Idaho. Although Borah bolted the party to campaign for William Jennings Bryan in 1896, he rejoined it permanently in 1902. An unsuccessful candidate of the Progressive wing of the Republican party for U.S. senator in 1903, in 1907 he was elected to the Senate—where he served until his death. The senator was a political independent in his views. Although he was a corporation lawyer and champion of Idaho lumber interests, he also supported the working man. He led the Senate fight in support of President Wilson's income tax bill but opposed Wilson's trust-regulation policy. A nationalist and an imperialist before 1914, he led the most vocal opponents of Wilsonian internationalism after World War I.

Borah never traveled outside the United States, yet his significance in American history lies in his influence on foreign affairs. The "Idaho Lion's" commitment to isolationism, parochialism, legalism, and moralism in foreign affairs led him to oppose effective political and military intervention by the United States on the world stage during the 1920s and 1930s. He championed policy divorced from power and created illusions of peace in the United States just as violent forces were bringing on the most terrible war in modern times.

Borah opposed American membership in the League of Nations because he feared agreements committing the United States to the use of force at a time not of its own choosing. As a leader of the Senate "irreconcilables," he mapped the strategy in the Senate that defeated the Treaty of Versailles. In the Washington Disarmament Conference (1922), Borah supported the Washington Treaty system to limit naval armaments and maintain the status quo in the Pacific, but he was among those senators who insisted upon a reservation disassociating the United States from the use of military power to enforce it. As chairman of the Senate Foreign Relations Committee after 1924, he enlarged the Kellogg-Briand Pact (out-lawing war) to include all the nations of the world, but he later refused to sanction the use of American arms to uphold the treaty.

With the rise of Hitler in Germany, Borah joined the isolationists' bloc in the Senate that imposed the neutrality legislation of 1935-1937. He did not believe that vital American interests were threatened by totalitarianism abroad. A war for democracy in Europe, he declared, would end democracy at home.

Borah opposed President Franklin Roosevelt's efforts to bring American resources to the support of the Western democracies and, when informed of approaching war in Europe at a White House conference in 1939, he refused to believe it, insisting that his information was more accurate than the President's. Still opposing President Roosevelt vigorously, the Idaho senator died on Jan. 19, 1940.

Further Reading

The best biography of Borah is Marian C. McKenna, *Borah* (1961). The three best books on Borah and American policy in the 1920s are Robert H. Ferrel, *Peace in Their Time: The Origins of the Kellogg-Briand Pact* (1952), and John Chalmers Vinson, *The Parchment Peace: The United States Senate and the Washington Conference, 1921-1922* (1955) and *William E. Borah and the Outlawry of War* (1957). For Borah and the coming of World War II the best books are Selig Adler, *The Isolationist Impulse: Its Twentieth Century Reaction* (1957), and Robert A. Divine, *The Illusion of Neutrality* (1962). □

Gail Borden

A pioneer in Texas, Gail Borden (1801-1874) became an inventor whose most notable contributions lay in condensing and preserving foods, particularly milk.

Gail Borden was born in Norwich, N.Y., on Nov. 9, 1801. His family moved to Kentucky in 1814. Taught surveying by his father, he helped lay out the city of Covington. The family soon moved to Indiana Territory; Gail, Jr., served briefly as Jefferson County surveyor and taught school. In 1821 he moved to southwestern Mississippi for health reasons. He taught school and worked as a deputy U.S. surveyor for 7 years.

Still searching for a better climate, Borden moved to Texas in 1829. After farming and raising cattle briefly, he returned to surveying. As Stephen Austin's superintendent of official surveys, Borden prepared the first topographical map of Texas. He headed the Texas land office from 1833 until the Mexican invasion. With his brother, Thomas, in 1835 he founded the first permanent Texas newspaper, the *Telegraph and Texas Land Register,* in San Felipe. The paper was soon moved to the new city of Houston, which Borden surveyed in 1836.

After Texas separated from Mexico in 1836, Borden helped write its constitution. In 1837 he was appointed the first Texas collector of customs by President Sam Houston. Borden surveyed and planned the city of Galveston, continuing as customs collector.

After his wife and children died in 1844 and 1845, Borden decided to alleviate the hardships of pioneers by making concentrated food that would not spoil. His first marketed product was a biscuit of dehydrated meat. At the first world's fair, the London Crystal Palace Exposition (1851), Borden's meat biscuit won him a membership in the London Society of Arts and a gold Council Medal, one of five awarded to Americans. The biscuit, tested by food specialists, retained nutrition and succulence indefinitely. The British saw in it a great, new American enterprise. Borden's biscuits were used by explorers and sailors, but his company failed in 1853 because competing suppliers of meat caused cancellations of army orders for the biscuits.

Visiting the Shaker community at New Lebanon, N.Y., in 1851, Borden observed sugar making with airtight pans and decided that milk could be condensed and could remain wholesome indefinitely. In 1853 he applied for a patent on a process for extracting 75 percent of the water from milk and adding sugar to the residue. The patent was denied on the grounds that the process was not new. Three years later, after demonstrating that the use of vacuum pans was novel and essential to the process, he received the patent.

The New York Condensed Milk Company (much later, the Borden Company) was formed in 1856, financed by Jeremiah Milbank. Several factories were established in Connecticut, New York, and Maine by 1861 and many more in the 1860s. Four more patents on condensed milk were awarded Borden in the 1860s. Early in the Civil War this milk was found to be of great value to the Union Army, and the output of Borden's plants was commandeered. Its use spread rapidly, especially after soldiers introduced it to civilians. Indeed, the Civil War era witnessed a vast increase in all canned-food consumption.

Next Borden patented a process for condensing fruit and berry juices. (It had not been known that spoilage is caused by bacteria, which can be heat-killed, until Pasteur's germ theory in 1864.) The U.S. Sanitary Commission bought Borden's condensed juices to serve to wounded soldiers. Borden also patented processes for making beef extracts and for concentrating tea, coffee, and cocoa.

Returning to Texas, Borden educated dairymen in sanitation, engaged in philanthropy, organized schools for African Americans and whites, built six churches, and supported poorly paid ministers, teachers, and students. He died in Borden, Tex., on Jan. 11, 1874, and was buried in White Plains, N.Y.

Further Reading

The only good biography of Borden, a highly sympathetic one, is Joe B. Frantz, *Gail Borden: Dairyman to a Nation* (1951). It is illustrated and contains much personal detail. □

Sir Robert Laird Borden

Sir Robert Laird Borden (1854-1937) was a Canadian political leader and prime minister who guided his country through World War I and, through astute bargaining, achieved equal status for Canada with England within the Commonwealth.

Robert Borden was born at Grand Pré, Nova Scotia, on June 26, 1854, the descendant of prerevolutionary American émigrés. He was educated at the Acacia Villa Seminary in Horton, Nova Scotia, and as a youth he taught at the Glenwood Institute in Matawan, N.J. Returning to his native province in 1874, he began the study of law and was called to the bar in 1878. Borden practiced first in Halifax, then in Kentville, and then again in Halifax, where in 1889 he became head of his own law firm. He seemed headed for a successful career as a lawyer until he became interested in politics.

Party Leader

In 1896 Borden was elected to the House of Commons as a Conservative member for Halifax. The party was beginning a 15-year period in opposition, and within a few years Borden made a respectable reputation for himself in Parliament. The party leader, Sir Charles Tupper, was a doughty fighter but old and somewhat discredited in certain quarters, and after his defeat in the general election of 1900 there was a general feeling that his career was over. Certainly Borden did not envisage that he would be Tupper's successor, and it

was with great surprise that he saw the party caucus turn to him. His first reaction to the offer was negative, but he finally agreed to accept the post for a year. The year stretched into two and then three, and Borden was soon permanent leader of the Conservative party.

Borden's tenure was neither easy nor immediately successful. In 1904 and 1908 the Conservatives were decisively beaten by Sir Wilfrid Laurier and the Liberals, and Borden was making little impact in the country. The issue that finally propelled Borden into power was that of reciprocity with the United States. The Laurier government had negotiated a treaty with the United States in 1911, an act that frightened Canadian businessmen and manufacturers, who had been sheltered so long behind the high tariff of the national policy. Borden had found his issue, and with it he attracted enormous support from the "interests," garnered thousands of disaffected Liberal voters, and won a clear victory in the general election of 1911.

Head of Government

Borden's government was not particularly strong. His Quebec representation was weak, and the financial affairs of many of the English-Canadian ministers were not conducted ethically. Borden himself was above reproach, but he apparently lacked the ruthlessness necessary to become a first-class prime minister. Still, legislation on railways and civil service reform began to appear on the statute books, and the militia was reorganized and made more efficient. Not even the downturn in business that began in 1911 was enough to completely dampen enthusiasm in Canada.

Crisis in World War I

The outbreak of war in 1914 did not change the mood either. Borden's government immediately offered a contingent, mobilized it with impressive speed, and shipped it to England in the largest convoy ever to cross the Atlantic to that time. No one expected a long war, but by the time the first casualty reports began pouring into Ottawa from France in the spring of 1915, few could have doubted that the struggle would be difficult. Borden's task was formidable. He had to organize the government for war, a task that was never really accomplished. He had to see to it that industry was geared up for maximum production, a task that was well done. Above all he had to galvanize the Canadian people, both French and English.

This task was not accomplished; in fact, the reverse took place in Quebec. Borden did not understand the *Canadien,* and he permitted recruiting in that province to be botched. Few French-Canadian officers received important commands, patronage was rampant, and ethnic prejudice swept the nation. The whole crisis came to a head in 1917 when Borden decided that conscription was necessary to reinforce Canada's troops at the front. Quebec was opposed to conscription, and after Borden's efforts to unite with Laurier in a coalition failed, he determined on a coalition without Quebec. By October 1917 he had his Union government and his conscription bill, and in December 1917, after a blatantly racist campaign conducted by his party, he had a renewed mandate. Canada was badly split, and the irony of the situation was that conscripts did not reach the front in sufficient numbers to have major impact before the end of the war.

Relations with Britain

Borden achieved more success in his relations with the British. He had been appalled to discover that Canada was being treated as a backwater colony, despite the nation's massive war effort. After hard bargaining he wrung recognition from the British that Canada was equal in status to the mother country. He also won a voice in the councils of empire, representation at the peace conference, and separate representation in the League of Nations for the Dominion. These were no mean achievements.

By the end of the war, Borden was exhausted by his labors, and soon he began to seek release. In 1920 he passed the mantle of prime minister to Arthur Meighen and entered what he hoped would be a quiet retirement. But the following year he was called back to be Canadian delegate at the Washington Conference of 1921-1922, and in 1930 he was Canada's representative at the League of Nations. Meanwhile he was writing about constitutional questions and serving as the director of numerous private companies. Sir Robert Borden—he had been knighted in June 1914— died in Ottawa on June 10, 1937.

Further Reading

A source for information on Borden is Henry Borden, ed., *Robert Laird Borden: His Memoirs* (2 vols., 1938). Roger Graham, *Arthur Meighen* (3 vols., 1960-1966), also provides information on Borden.

Additional Sources

Brown, Robert Craig, *Robert Laird Borden: a biography,* Toronto: Macmillan of Canada, 1975-c1980.

English, John, *Borden: his life and world,* Toronto; New York: McGraw-Hill Ryerson, 1977. ☐

Jorge Luis Borges

The Argentine author, Jorge Luis Borges (1899-1986), was one of Latin America's most original and influential prose writers and poets. His short stories revealed him as one of the great stylists of the Spanish language.

Jorge Luis Borges was born on August 24, 1899, in Buenos Aires. A few years later his family moved to the northern suburb of Palermo, which he was to celebrate in prose and verse. He received his earliest education at home, where he learned English and read widely in his father's library of English books. When Borges was nine years of age, he began his public schooling in Palermo, and in the same year, published his first literary undertaking—a translation into Spanish of Oscar Wilde's "The Happy Prince."

In 1914 the Borges family traveled to Europe. When World War I broke out, they settled for the duration in Switzerland where young Borges finished his formal education at the Collège in Geneva. By 1919, when the family moved on to Spain, Borges had learned several languages and had begun to write and translate poetry.

Early Work

In Seville and Madrid he frequented literary gatherings where he absorbed the lessons of new poetical theorists of the time—especially those of Rafael Cansinos Asséns, who headed a group of writers who came to be known as "ultraists." When the family returned to Argentina in 1921, Borges rediscovered his native Buenos Aires and began to write poems dealing with his intimate feelings for the city, its past, and certain fading features of its quiet suburbs. His early poetry was reflective in tone; metaphors dominated, usual linking words were suppressed, and the humble, tranquil aspects of the city that he evoked seemed somehow contaminated by eternity.

With other young Argentine writers, Borges collaborated in the founding of new publications, in which the ultraist mode was cultivated in the New World. In 1923 his first volume of poetry, *Fervor of Buenos Aires,* was published, and it also made somewhat of a name for him in Spain.

In 1925 his second book of poetry, *Moon across the Way,* appeared, followed in 1929 by *San Martin Notebook*—the last new collection of his verse to appear for three decades. Borges gradually developed a keen interest in literary criticism. His critical and philosophical essays began to fill most of the volumes he published during the period 1925-1940: *Inquisitions* (1925), *The Dimensions of My Hope* (1926), *The Language of the Argentines* (1928), *Evaristo Carriego* (1930), *Discussion* (1932), and *History of Eternity* (1938).

Change in Style

In 1938, with his father gravely ill from a heart ailment, Borges obtained an appointment in a municipal library in Buenos Aires. Before year's end, his father died. Borges, himself, came close to death from septicemia, the complication of an infected head injury.

This period of crisis produced an important change in Borges. He began to write prose fiction tales of a curious and highly original character. These pieces seemed to be philosophical essays invested with narrative qualities and tensions. Others were short stories infused with metaphorical concepts. Ten of these concise, well-executed stories were collected in *Ficciones* (1944). A second volume of similar tales, entitled *The Aleph,* was published in 1949. Borges's fame as a writer firmly rests on the narratives contained in these two books, to which other stories were added in later editions.

In 1955, following the overthrow of the Peronist regime in Argentina, Borges was named director of the National Library in Buenos Aires. In that same year his sight deteriorated to the point where he became almost totally blind.

After *The Aleph,* he published an important collection of essays, *Other Inquisitions* (1952); several collections of poetry and prose sketches, *Dreamtigers* (1960), *In Praise of Darkness* (1969), *The Deep Rose* (1975), and *The Iron Coin* (1976); and two collections of new short stories, *Dr. Brodie's Report* (1970) and *The Book of Sand* (1975). Aside from these works, Borges wrote over a dozen books in collaboration with other persons. Foremost among his collaborators was Adolfo Bioy Casares, an Argentine novelist and short-story writer, who was Borges's closest literary associate for nearly 40 years.

In 1961 Borges shared with Samuel Beckett the $10,000 International Publishers Prize, and world recognition at last began to come his way. He received countless honors and prizes. In 1970 he was the first recipient of the $25,000 Matarazzo Sobrinho Inter-American Literary Prize.

Borges married Elsa Astete Millan in 1967 but was divorced in 1970. He married Maria Kodama in 1986, shortly before his death on June 14, in Geneva, Switzerland.

Further Reading

The only full-length biography of Borges in English is Martin S. Stabb, *Jorge Luis Borges* (1970). The most valuable biographical information is in "An Autobiographical Essay" included in Borges's *The Aleph and Other Stories: 1933-1969* (1970). An interesting discussion with him is in Luis Harss and Barbara Dohmann, *Into the Mainstream: Conversations with Latin-American Writers* (1967). A useful profile of Borges is in Selden Rodman, *South America of the Poets* (1970). Helpful in defining the scope of Borges's achievement are Ana Maria Barrenechea, *Borges: The Labyrinth Maker,* which also contains a biographical essay, and was edited and translated by Robert Lima (1965); Ronald J. Christ, *The Narrow Act: Borges' Art of Allusion* (1969); and Carter Wheelock, *The Mythmaker* (1969). □

Cesare Borgia

The Italian leader Cesare Borgia (1475-1507) played an important part in Renaissance history. By intrigue and bravery he captured the Romagna, an area of Italy which remained a papal state until the 19th century.

Cesare Borgia was the first child of Vanozza de' Catanei and Cardinal Rodrigo Borgia, then archbishop of Valencia. They later had three other children: Giovanni, Lucrezia, and Goffredo.

The Borgia titles and estates in Spain were to be inherited by Pier Luigi Borgia, Cesare's older half brother, and an ecclesiastical career was chosen for Cesare. Thus upon the untimely death of Pier Luigi, Cesare did not succeed as heir to the Borgia secular fortune and titles, which passed instead to his younger brother Giovanni. In 1492, while still a layman, Cesare received the archbishopric of Valencia from his father, who became Pope Alexander VI that same year. In 1493 Alexander named Cesare cardinal deacon, and in 1494 Cesare was ordained a deacon.

These were exciting times in Italy. In 1494 King Charles VIII of France invaded Italy. His objective was Naples, over which he had a distant hereditary claim. On his march south he encountered little Italian resistance. Only after the Italians organized the military League of Venice, which threatened to cut his overextended supply lines, did Charles withdraw, and by 1497 French troops had evacuated Italy.

Immediately after Charles's withdrawal, papal forces turned upon the great Roman baronial families, especially the Orsini, who had helped Charles because of their opposition to the election of Alexander VI. Cesare's brother Giovanni commanded the papal militia during this period. Saddled with the mundane duties of a cleric, Cesare envied Giovanni's more active military career.

Rise to Power

In June 1497 the body of Giovanni Borgia, its throat cut, was found in the Tiber River. Several parties might have been involved in the mysterious murder, but many historians hold Cesare responsible since the death was of political advantage to him. Cesare now saw the possibility of being dispensed from his clerical duties and of assuming his brother's secular titles, wealth, and position as military leader of the Borgias and the papacy.

Unfortunately, the Spanish king, Ferdinand V (Ferdinand of Aragon), opposed the practice of releasing a cardinal from his office for political purposes. Thus Alexander could not release his son without angering the Spanish, his protectors against the French. However, in November 1497

France and Spain reached a truce in which they agreed to divide Naples. Since France was no longer Spain's enemy, Alexander could now approach the French king for help in seeking Cesare's release from the cardinalate. Louis XII, who had become king in April 1498 on the death of Charles, agreed to support Cesare's release in return for papal approval of the dissolution of his marriage. Alexander granted this request and thus became allied with France. In August 1498 he released Cesare from his clerical offices.

In February 1499 Louis gave Cesare command of a company of French cavalry. In March Cesare married Charlotte d'Albret, and in May he received from Louis the French duchy of Valentinois and the county of Diois. Having agreed to the Franco-Spanish partition of Naples, Louis planned an invasion of southern Italy. Milan lay on the supply route between France and Naples and was of strategic importance. In September 1499 Cesare commanded the French force that captured Milan and defeated its ruler, Lodovico Sforza.

In return for his services, Louis XII placed this French force at his disposal, and Cesare used it in his first attempt to capture the Romagna for Alexander. Like all popes, Alexander claimed dominion over the Romagna on the basis of the Donation of Pepin (756), which included the Romagna. Cesare's campaign went well. Before it was completed, however, Louis ordered the French force back to defend Milan from a counterattack by Lodovico Sforza, and Cesare's invasion of the Romagna ended in January 1500.

Success of Romagna Campaign

By 1500 Cesare had received all he desired: a reputation as a military leader, secular estates, and a wife. But the Borgias had paid a high price for Cesare's ambitions; by allying themselves with France they had lost the friendship and protection of the Spanish king. Since Cesare had acquired estates and a wife in France, he was determined to maintain the papal alliance with the French. To that end he ordered the murder of the husband of his sister Lucrezia, the Neapolitan nobleman Alfonso, Duke of Bisceglie. In August 1500, while recuperating from an earlier assassination attempt, Alfonso was strangled in the papal apartments. Alfonso's murder in Borgia-controlled Rome angered the Neapolitans and the Spanish and thus ended the possibility of Alexander's return to the old alliance.

Between October 1500 and August 1501 Cesare seized other territories in the Romagna. Again Louis XII provided him with a French army. During this second campaign Louis and Ferdinand of Aragon signed the Treaty of Granada (November 1500), which formalized their agreement to partition Naples. When the Franco-Spanish operation against Naples was launched, Cesare assisted his French ally, and on Aug. 1, 1501, Naples capitulated.

In June 1502 Cesare began his third and final campaign in the Romagna, and by December 1502 he had captured the entire area for the Pope. Most of the Romagna welcomed the Borgia rule, for Cesare introduced an efficient, enlightened, and centralized administration to the area. But Cesare's fortunes were soon to change.

Cesare's Downfall

In 1503 two events occurred which caused Cesare's downfall. First, Spanish forces turned upon the French in May and drove them out of southern Italy. In control of the Romagna and of papal financial support, Cesare accepted the French defeat calmly. However, the second event, the death of Alexander VI on August 18, ultimately proved disastrous to Cesare.

Because of Cesare's influence, Cardinal Piccolomini, a strong supporter of the Borgias, was elected Pope Pius III in September. He died, however, in October. When the cardinals met again in October to choose a successor, Cesare was tricked by Cardinal Della Rovere's promise of money and of continued papal backing for Borgia policies in the Romagna. He supported Della Rovere, who thus became Pope Julius II. Julius then disregarded his promises and decided to assume control of the Romagna himself. In December he ordered the arrest of Cesare, who won his freedom only by relinquishing key cities in the Romagna to Julius.

In April 1504 Cesare journeyed to Naples seeking financial assistance from friends and relatives. But both Julius and Ferdinand of Aragon feared the presence of a Borgia army, and in May their agents arrested Cesare. In August he was transported to Spain, where he was imprisoned until his escape in 1506. He made his way to Navarre, the kingdom of his brother-in-law Jean d'Albret. After Louis XII had refused to restore Cesare's French estates, Cesare joined d'Albret in fighting Louis's attempt to gain control of Navarre through support of insurrectionist feudal families.

On March 12, 1507, Cesare Borgia died in battle in Navarre. He had lived the life of a Renaissance knight and had captured the Romagna, richest of the papal states. His career was marked by political intrigue, but also by courage.

Further Reading

Most recent works on Cesare Borgia are not in English. Nevertheless, older works in English are still useful. The most thorough, though stylistically difficult, are R. Sabatini, *The Life of Cesare Borgia of France* (trans. 1912), and William Harrison Woodward, *Cesare Borgia: A Biography* (1913). More readable is Carlo Beuf, *Cesare Borgia: The Machiavellian Prince* (1942). For background information see John Addington Symonds, *Renaissance in Italy,* vol. 1: *The Age of Despots* (1875; 2d ed. 1880).

Additional Sources

Bradford, Sarah, *Cesare Borgia, his life and times,* New York: Macmillan; London: Weidenfeld and Nicolson, 1976. □

Lucrezia Borgia, Duchess of Ferrara

Lucrezia Borgia (1480–1519) was Duchess of Ferrara, a renowned poisoner and political schemer

who, in actuality, was a pawn in the intrigues of her father and brother.

Lucrezia Borgia was born into the Renaissance world of Italy (1320-1520), a time when artists, sculptors, architects, scientists, and others rose to prominence. She was also born into one of the most notorious families in world history. Reputed to be evil, violent, and politically conniving, the Borgias were interested in claiming as much control of Italy as they could. And they were very successful.

Their prosperity was facilitated by the fact that Italy was not a unified nation but rather a collection of papal states, republics, duchies, and kingdoms organized around an urban center and the surrounding countryside, each with its own ruler. Although these individual states were powerful, their rulers were more inclined to fight each other than to band together against such enemy countries as France or Spain.

Italy desperately needed to unify and strengthen itself. Having lost much of its sea trade to France, Spain, and England, the Mediterranean was no longer the main site of commercial activity. Through the right political maneuvers, influential alliances could be formed and a great deal of power gained. It was a time of political turmoil and lethal intrigue; many political problems were solved by killing the person seen as the source of irritation. The males in the Borgia family followed the trend.

Lucrezia Borgia was the daughter of Cardinal Rodrigo Borgia, later to become Pope Alexander VI, and his mistress Vannozza Cattanei, who was also the mother of Lucrezia's two older brothers, Cesare and Giovanni. The job of raising Lucrezia, however, was given to Rodrigo's cousin, the widow Adriana daMila. While living in a palace in Rome, Lucrezia was educated at the Convent of St. Sixtus on Via Appia. Described as being slender, she was of medium height, with light-blue/green eyes and golden hair, which she later bleached to maintain its goldenness. A painting by Pinturicchio, "Disputation of Saint Catherine," is said to be modeled after her, depicting a slender young woman with wavy, blonde hair cascading down her back.

The young girl was no more than 11 when she was first affected by the political ambitions of her father, Rodrigo, and her brother, Cesare. Desiring an alliance with Spain, they arranged a marriage contract between Lucrezia and the lord of Val d'Agora in Valencia; her dowry was set at 100,000 ducats. But two months later, the contract was mysteriously annulled without explanation. Historians assume that Rodrigo, who had instigated the annulment, had formed a new alliance involving his dynastic ambitions; he then arranged a marriage contract with another Spaniard, 15-year-old Don Gaspare, son of Count Averse in the Kingdom of Naples. This too was annulled that same year. The vacillating Rodrigo had decided it was more important to be aligned with the Sforza family of Milan.

The groom-to-be was the conceited, well-educated Giovanni Sforza, a 27-year-old with a fierce temper. He, too, stood to profit. Prior to his marriage to Lucrezia, Giovanni was only the lord of an insignificant Adriatic fishing town. Afterward, he would be a close relation to one of Italy's most powerful families. Having been elevated from cardinal to Pope Alexander VI, Rodrigo, the prospective father-in-law, had become even more powerful. During the Italian Renaissance, the papacy was treated as a lucrative and powerful prize for any family that could gain control of it. Marrying the pope's daughter would strengthen Giovanni's hold on his inheritance over the state of Pesaro. In addition, Giovanni's uncle, Ludovico Sforza, the ruler of Milan, took note of Giovanni after his engagement and offered him a lucrative command in the Milanese army. Through his generosity, Ludovico hoped to gain an ally in the Borgia camp.

The 13-year-old Lucrezia was married to Giovanni Sforza on June 12, 1493, in a sumptuous wedding with a retinue of 500 ladies. The wedding feast featured poetry readings and comedy performances, followed by gifts of jewels, gold and silver objects, brocade, rings, and gold table settings. The pope and other religious leaders reportedly threw food into the ladies' low-cut bodices, but bawdy behavior was not unusual in that time.

By the time she was 17, Lucrezia was said to be tired of her husband, claiming he often neglected her. Giovanni had his own grievances. Reportedly weary of the political intrigue of the Vatican and the arrogance of Lucrezia's brothers, he may also have heard that Cesare Borgia was considering ways to eliminate him. Now preferring a closer alliance with Naples than Milan, Lucrezia's father and brother made plans to have the marriage annulled, claiming that Giovanni was impotent, that the marriage had never been consummated. Giovanni implored his uncle to intercede, but Ludovico, who had brought about the invasion of Italy by Charles VIII of France—an invasion that almost toppled Rodrigo from the papacy—was unwilling to do anything that would further provoke the pope. Sensing danger, Giovanni fled to Pesaro in the spring of 1497; Lucrezia withdrew to the Convent of San Sisto in Rome.

During the annulment process, statements from both camps served to hold the litigants up for social ridicule. Indignant over the charges of his impotency, Giovanni insinuated that Lucrezia's father and brother wanted Lucrezia for themselves. These accusations led to rumors about possible incestuous behavior that haunted Lucrezia throughout her life. In return for the right to keep the sizable dowry his wife had brought to the marriage, Giovanni reluctantly capitulated and signed a confession of impotency.

Cesare and Rodrigo then chose 17-year-old Alfonso of Aragon, the Duke of Bisceglie and son of the late king of Naples, as Lucrezia's next husband; Rodrigo sent his trusted Spanish chamberlain Pedro Caldes to carry out the marriage negotiations. But by the time her first marriage was officially annulled on December 27, 1497, Lucrezia was six months pregnant. This created more grist for the Italian rumor mill. Some speculated that Pedro Caldes was the child's father, others pointed to Rodrigo or Cesare. As a result of this scandal, Pedro was stabbed to death and thrown into the Tiber River along with one of Lucrezia's maids. Three months later, she gave birth to her son Giovanni, who was later legitimized by Rodrigo. Some scholars believe that Giovanni was actually a brother of Lucrezia's, although his parentage will probably never be known.

Alfonso of Aragon was reputed to be a handsome youth, with fine manners. The proxy wedding occurred on June 29, 1498, with the actual wedding on July 21. A wedding feast, similar to that of Lucrezia's first marriage, was celebrated with plays and masquerades, but the marriage was brief. Only a year later, political changes were once again stirring. Sensing that his alliance with the Borgias was no longer needed, Alfonso fled from Rome but was persuaded by Lucrezia to rejoin her and the pope at Nepi, where she was invested as governor of Spoleto. Lucrezia was again pregnant, and on November 1, 1499, gave birth to a son, naming him Rodrigo after her father.

On the evening of July 15, 1500, while returning home to the Vatican, Alfonso was attacked by hired killers and stabbed in the head, right arm, and leg. Lucrezia cared for him, called for doctors, and arranged for armed guards both day and night; she even prepared his food, fearing that someone might poison him. But on August 18, as Alfonso was still recovering, Cesare reputedly came to him and whispered in his ear that "what was not finished at breakfast would be complete by dinner." Returning to Alfonso's room later that day, Cesare ordered everyone out and directed his strongman to strangle Lucrezia's young husband. Alfonso's executioner later confessed that Rodrigo had ordered the murder, but few believed his story.

Left a widow at the age of 20, Lucrezia spent most of her time weeping over the loss of her husband. Tired of watching her mourn, her father and brother sent her to Nepi in the Etruscan Hills. On her return to Rome in November 1500, she began assisting her father as a sort of papal secretary, often opening and responding to his mail when he was not in residence.

Italian society continued to feast on Borgia gossip at Lucrezia's expense. There were rumors that she frequently danced until late at night with her brother Cesare at his infamous parties at the Vatican. Whether or not she deserved this speculation is debatable, since many contemporaries commented on her reserve and piety. Some historians have suggested that she and Pope Alexander were guests at dinners her brother hosted but left before revelries began. Others feel she may have been an innocent victim of the hatred directed toward her father and brother.

Casting about for new alliances, Cesare and Rodrigo's attention now turned to the 24-year-old widower Alfonso d'Este, eldest son of Ercole d'Este, Duke of Ferrara. Cesare wanted to conquer the Romagna region, and therefore needed an alliance with the duchy of Ferrara—an important military power strategically placed between the Romagna and the Venetian Republic. Not surprisingly, neither Alfonso d'Este nor his father was too happy at the prospect of a wife whose first husband had been ridiculed as impotent and whose second husband had been murdered. In addition, the d'Este family was the oldest ruling family in Italy and considered the Borgia family upstarts, not in the same class.

But politics once again determined Lucrezia's married life. While the main powers of Italy, fearing the control it would give Rodrigo's papacy, roared in opposition, King Louis XII of France advised his ally, Ercole, to consent to the marriage. Further prodding came from another quarter. Rodrigo, as Pope Alexander VI, threatened to depose Ercole if he did not consent to the marriage. Ercole finally agreed, but in return he demanded a large dowry; reduction of his annual tribute to the Church; the position of archpriest of St. Peter's for his son, Cardinal Ippolito d'Este; and receipt of the cities of Cento and Pieve, along with the harbor of Cesenatico.

Lucrezia was eager for the marriage, for she regarded Rome as a prison and thought she would have a better chance of leading her own life away from her ambitious father and brother. She wrote often to her future father-in-law, who at one time was considering marrying her if Alfonso did not. Since this was clearly an arranged marriage, Ercole's envoys checked at court to ensure that Lucrezia's trousseau would bring to this third marriage as much as the dowry of 100,000 ducats accompanying her first marriage. With one dress alone costing 15,000 ducats, the envoys were assured that the total value of the trousseau would easily equal 100,000 ducats. In addition, Lucrezia would be taking along jewels, furniture, and a table service of silver and gold.

On December 30, 1501, the proxy marriage was held at the Vatican, and in early January, Lucrezia left Rome on her approximately 220-mile trip to Ferrara, adorned in her colors of yellow and brown, with 150 mules carrying her baggage carts. She and her retinue of 1,000 were entertained at every city along the way. As the bridal party approached Ferrara, a disguised Alfonso rode out to catch a glimpse of Lucrezia; he was so pleased that he spent several hours in conversation with her, then returned home for the official welcome.

On February 2, 1502, the actual wedding ceremony was held with both Lucrezia and Alfonso in full regalia. Lucrezia wore black velvet with a cape of gold brocade trimmed with ermine, a net of gold and diamonds on her hair, and a necklace of rubies and pearls. Alfonso was dressed in red velvet, with even his horse attired in crimson and gold. Lucrezia had married a man who not only was interested in artillery, tournaments, dogs and horses, but who also played the viol and made pottery. He was also known for his cruelty, stinginess, and eccentricity.

The people of Ferrara adored Lucrezia, praising her for her beauty and "inner grace of personality." Avoiding political machinations, she became a notable patron of the arts. Content to socialize with artists, courtiers, poets, and citizens of the Renaissance court, she helped make Ferrara a center for artists and writers. A lock of golden hair, given by her to the poet Pietro Bembo, can today be found in the Ambrosian Library in Milan, along with letters she wrote to him in the gallant manner of the day.

In 1503, Rodrigo died, along with many of Cesare's plans. Since Lucrezia had not yet borne any children for Alfonso, the king of France suggested to Ercole that he should seek an annulment of the marriage. The idea was discarded because both Ercole and his son Alfonso were by this time fond of Lucrezia; in addition, they did not want to repay her dowry. Finally, some stability appeared in Lucrezia's life. When Ercole died in 1505, she and Alfonso became the reigning duke and duchess of Ferrara. She requested that Giovanni, her illegitimate son, come live with her. When he was old enough to come to court, he was always introduced as her brother.

Lucrezia had several children by Alfonso d'Este. Although two died in infancy, one was stillborn, and there were at least two miscarriages, the couple had five children who survived infancy: Ercole II (b. 1508), Ippolito (b. 1509), Alessandro (b. 1514), Eleanora (b. 1515), and Francesco (b. 1516). Of these, only Ercole and Ippolito survived into adulthood.

In 1512, Lucrezia began to lead a retired life, perhaps caused by news of the death of Rodrigo, her son by Alfonso of Aragon. Though separated from her son, she had made sure he was well taken care of, selecting his governess, his tutor, and the stewards to oversee his duchy of Bisceglie (which he had inherited from his father). She began to spend more time in her apartments or in nearby convents, becoming withdrawn and ill-humored. Turning more and more to religion, piety, and charitable works, she took to wearing a hairshirt under her embroidered gowns as a form of penance. As the years progressed, her body thickened, and she was said to age greatly. She was also plagued by spells of melancholy. On June 14, 1519, while giving birth to a stillborn girl, she developed a debilitating fever. She died ten days later at the age of 39. A few days before her death, she wrote a letter to Pope Leo X asking his blessing and commending her husband and children to him.

Lucrezia Borgia was often accused of being frivolous and heartless, yet an examination of her life reveals that such assessments were not always deserved. Indeed, much of the innuendo about her illegitimate child and alleged incestuous behavior may have been in retaliation for the evil deeds committed by her father Rodrigo and brother Cesare (who also murdered their brother Giovanni). Many historians view her as a political pawn whose marriages were used to further the ambitions of both her father and her brother. Lucrezia was very much a product of her times, accepting these ambitions and their consequences for the good of the family.

Further Reading

Chamberlain, E. R. *The Fall of the House of Borgia.* Dial Press, 1974.

Cloulas, Ivan. *The Borgias.* Translated by Gilda Roberts. Watts, 1989.

Fusero, Clemente. *The Borgias.* Translated by Peter Green. Praeger, 1972.

Guicciardini, Francesco. *The History of Italy.* Translated by Sidney Alexander. Macmillan, 1969.

Latour, Anny. *The Borgias.* Translated by Neil Mann. Abelard-Schuman, 1966. □

John Gutzon de la Mothe Borglum

An American sculptor and engineer who worked on a gigantic scale, John Gutzon de la Mothe Borglum (1867-1941) is best known for the Mt. Rushmore National Memorial in South Dakota.

Gutzon Borglum was born on March 25, 1867, in the Idaho Territory, the son of Danish immigrants. Restless and independent, he left home as a youth and made his way to San Francisco, where he enrolled at the Mark Hopkins Art Institute. His first formal training was under William Keith. Dissatisfied with painting, Borglum traveled to Paris in 1887 and studied sculpture at the Académie Julian; he also came under the influence of the French sculptor Auguste Rodin. After touring Spain and England, Borglum returned to the United States in 1901 and opened a studio in New York. In 1904 he won a gold medal at the St. Louis Exposition for his vigorous and powerfully modeled work *Mares of Diomedes*.

In the next few years Borglum executed a series of 12 Apostles for the Cathedral of St. John the Divine, New York City. In 1908 the Library of Congress accepted his 6-ton marble head of Lincoln. A group of Southern women commissioned an enormous image of Gen. Robert E. Lee for the face of Stone Mountain, Ga., in 1916. While the women planned a solitary figure, the sculptor envisioned additional figures covering the entire length of the dome-shaped mountain. Dissension soon overtook the project, and unexpected expenses combined with personality conflicts led to a court fight. In a fit of rage Borglum destroyed his models, and the state of Georgia filed suit. Borglum won, but in 1925 he was dismissed from the Stone Mountain project (it was not finished until the spring of 1970).

Borglum's dream of carving gigantic figures in "live" mountain rock was realized, when he was commissioned to carve a national monument at Mt. Rushmore, S. Dak., in 1925 and began the work two years later. Impressed with the "bigness" of America, he believed that American art must also be gigantic. He chose to carve Washington, Lincoln, Jefferson, and Theodore Roosevelt because he believed that they represented the spirit and ideals of American geographic expansion and political development. On July 4, 1930, the head of George Washington was unveiled. Jefferson was completed in 1936, Lincoln in 1937, and Theodore Roosevelt in 1939.

The work, supervised by Borglum and his engineer, was carried out by a crew of local workmen. Each head was carved with dynamite and jackhammers. Financial problems caused frequent interruptions. Early in March 1941 Borglum left the work for a minor operation in Chicago, where he suffered a heart attack and died on March 6. His son finished his father's masterpiece. The entire project cost approximately $1,520,000 and took 16 years from inception to completion.

Borglum was a popular sculptor who never lacked commissions. Among his many works are an equestrian portrait of Gen. Philip Sheridan, three full-length figures for the U.S. Capitol, a statue of William Jennings Bryan, *Seated Lincoln,* and *Wars of America.*

His ability to execute sculpture on a grand scale qualifies Borglum as a skilled engineer as well as a talented artist. Modern critics and Borglum's contemporaries agree that his sculpture is good work but not great art. His major contribution to art was the expert technical knowledge which he displayed in handling monumental sculpture.

Further Reading

For a complete story of Borglum's greatest sculptural achievement consult Gilbert C. Fite, *Mount Rushmore* (1952). A personal portrait of Borglum, written by a friend, is Robert J. Dean, *Living Granite: The Story of Borglum and the Mount Rushmore Memorial* (1949). J. Walker McSpadden, *Famous Sculptors of America* (1924), devotes a chapter to Borglum's life and work. Written during Borglum's lifetime, it contains more information on the sculptor's early period than on later works. For a more recent but similar sketch see Wayne Craven, *Sculpture in America* (1968). □

Rodrigo Borja Cevallos

One of the founders of Ecuador's Democratic Left (Izquierda Democratica) party, Rodrigo Borja Cevallos (born 1935) was a former president of Ecuador.

R odrigo Borja Cevallos was born June 19, 1935, in Ecuador's highland capital city, Quito. His family was descended from an aristocratic family of pure Spanish blood, and Borja was the first of seven children born to Luis Felipe Borja and Aurelia Cevallos. His father was active with the Socialist Party, while his grandfather was a distinguished Liberal jurist.

His primary and secondary school education was at the Colegio Americano in Quito. Borja was initially a casual student who excelled in athletics while gradually developing political interests. He graduated at the age of 19. At the Central University he became more serious about education, graduating with distinction from the Faculty of Law in 1960. His 500-page thesis on constitutional law was later used as a text elsewhere in Latin America. He then proceeded to Costa Rica for postgraduate work in political science, while directing his interests increasingly to national affairs.

While still a law student, Borja had joined one of Ecuador's two traditional parties, the PLR (Radical Liberal Party). In 1962 he was elected to congress, where he soon became one of the brightest young lights of the Liberals. With the seizure of power by the military in 1963, he left the nation to serve with the United Nations. Three years later he returned to Ecuador and joined the law school faculty at the Central University. He continued to be active in sports and was especially successful in automobile racing. In 1967 he married Carmen Calisto, with whom he had three daughters and one son.

In the 1968 elections the Liberals were defeated by the forces of former President Jose Maria Velasco Ibarra. When the new Velasco government negotiated an accord with the Liberals, the PLR underwent severe internal wrangling. The party's youth in particular were outraged by such unprincipled opportunism on the part of the Liberal leadership. Breaking away from the PLR, under Borja's direction they founded a new political party, the Izquierda Democratica, or ID (Democratic Left). It participated in congressional elections in 1970, with Borja winning as deputy from Pichincha, the state in which Quito is located.

The constitution was suspended shortly thereafter, and Borja was unable to take office. Instead, he devoted himself full time to the organization and growth of the ID. Traveling the length and breadth of Ecuador, Borja sought the establishment of the first truly national, mass-based political party in the nation. In 1978, with the most recent military government negotiating its withdrawal from power, Borja officially registered the ID with the Supreme Electoral Tribune, supported by the signatures of 45,000 members.

When national elections were convened, Borja was named presidential candidate for the ID. He finished fourth in the race, but in the process established his party as a major force in the nation. Subsequently elected to the national legislature, Borja became the leading spokesperson of what he termed Ecuador's "center-left." The ID was the most active and constructive force in the legislature and, with the approach of elections in 1984, emerged under Borja as a prime contender for power.

That year Borja was opposed by several other broadly centrist, reform-oriented candidates, in addition to the high-powered and lavishly-funded campaign by Ecuador's political and economic conservatives on behalf of Leon Febres Cordero. In the first round elections Borja came in first, with Febres Cordero second and the other candidates trailing behind. It was widely assumed that Borja was assured of victory in the runoff. However, a combination of Febres' effective populistic campaigning and Borja's over-confidence helped contribute to a narrow victory by the former.

This led to four years of avowedly conservative government under President Febres—the period of so-called "national reconstruction." Borja rededicated himself to strengthening his party, and especially to building organizational strength and popular support in the port city of Guayaquil, where he and his party had been overwhelmingly rejected by the electorate. By 1988 he and the ID were prepared for yet another electoral effort to win national power, and on this occasion Borja was successful. His first-round victory was anticipated, but few expected his opponent in the runoff to be the outrageously outspoken former mayor of Guayaquil, the populistic Abdala Bucaram. Following a bitterly acrimonious struggle marked by exceptionally vulgar exchanges initiated by Bucaram, Borja proved victorious by a margin of 47 to 40 percent (the remainder being null or blank votes). In August of 1988 Rodrigo Borja was therefore inaugurated as president of Ecuador.

Borja ascended to power at a particularly difficult time for the nation. His administration was confronted by high inflation, a severe economic recession, a huge foreign debt, and declining oil prices on the international market. Despite his status as a leader of social democracy in Latin America, Borja found himself forced toward economic austerity and a reduction of state activism. Responding to international pressures, he necessarily gave highest priority to a reordering of the nation's finances.

In pursuit of his expressed desire for a truly national and nonpartisan government, the new president negotiated with leaders of both the Christian democratic DP (Popular Democracy) and the Marxist sectors, especially the communists. Borja thereby sought to create a progressive force which would back his policies while countering the vigorous opposition of the political Right. It was his intention to restore public faith in basic freedoms of speech and expression, to reorder public finances, and to respond to the calls for social justice and popular welfare which, he had argued during the campaign, had been too long ignored by public officials.

Borja was notably active on the international front. As a prominent social democratic leader, he strengthened personal and political ties with such figures as Venezuelan President Carlos Andrés Perez and the Peruvian chief of state Alan Garcia. He also collaborated with leaders of other Andean nations in the subregional effort to curb drug trafficking, although carefully keeping his distance from Washington and the Bush administration. By the halfway point of his administration Borja was still struggling with financial and economic pressures which restricted his efforts to achieve domestic reform and greater social justice.

Both Borja and Izquierda Democratica understandably suffered a drop in popularity. However, the ID remained better organized than any other party in the country, although still weak in Guayaquil and other coastal centers. Borja left office in 1992, honoring the constitutional ban against a second presidential term. He remained the leader of the ID, eventually sharing that role with Andres Vallejo Arcos. In historic terms, Borja stood among the most prominent figures in a new generation of leaders who sought to lift Ecuador from traditional patterns in the effort to modernize the system and introduce reforms on behalf of the poor and the dispossessed.

Further Reading

At present there is no significant biography of Rodrigo Borja Cevallos. However, there are informative discussions of both Borja and the Izquierda Democratica in more broadly based studies. See John D. Martz, *Politics and Petroleum in Ecuador* (1987); Nick D. Mills, *Crisis, conflicto y consenso, Ecuador: 1979-1984* (1984); and David W. Schodt, *Ecuador; An Andean Enigma* (1987). For a summary of Borja's political views, prepared for the 1984 elections, see Rodrigo Borja, *Socialismo democratico* (1984). An excellent survey of national politics through the 1970s by a political scientist and former president (1981-1984) is Osvaldo Hurtado, *Political Power in Ecuador* (1980). □

Norman Ernest Borlaug

Norman Ernest Borlaug (born 1914) was a biochemist who was awarded the Nobel Peace Prize in 1970 for his work in developing varieties of cereal grains that would produce high yields in developing countries.

N orman Ernest Borlaug was born on March 25, 1914, near Cresco, Iowa, in the part of that state known as "little Norway." His Norwegian immigrant parents were farmers, but when he graduated from high school in 1932 he left to attend the University of Minnesota. He received a Bachelor of Science degree in 1937, majoring in forestry. The same year he married Margaret G. Gibson. His graduate work in plant pathology at Minnesota earned him a Master of Science degree in 1940 and a Ph.D. in 1941.

Having received his doctorate, Borlaug became an assistant professor at Minnesota in 1942, but left the following year to work as a biochemist with the chemical firm of E. I. du Pont de Nemours. In 1944 he joined a new team of scientists sponsored by the Rockefeller Foundation to "export the United States agricultural revolution to Mexico." Their work resulted in the International Maize and Wheat Improvement Center (CIMMYT) whose goal was the development of varieties of cereal grains (wheat, rice, and corn) that would produce higher yields in the developing countries of the world.

The Green Revolution

The agricultural revolution in the United States was based largely on the massive introduction of new varieties of plants and animals, new machinery, and the use of chemical fertilizers, pesticides, and irrigation, all supported by a massive reorganization of agribusiness and rural life. In 1944, Borlaug and his colleagues found in Mexico exhausted fields, sometimes dating back to Aztec times. Their initial aim was to develop a variety of wheat which was adaptable to many different areas, resistant to a particular disease called rust, and responsive to the application of fertilizers.

The wheat used by Mexican farmers had long stems, naturally evolved over the ages in an effort to rise above the shade of surrounding weeds. When the yield of this wheat was increased, the heavy heads bent the thin stems over, a problem called "lodging" by farmers. Using two experimental plots, one in the north of Mexico and the other near Mexico City, Borlaug and the CIMMYT team drew upon Japanese short-stemmed wheat and developed a HYV (high yielding variety) that greatly increased production.

The success of the Rockefeller team with wheat and later rice led to the enthusiastic proclamation of a "Green Revolution," the notion that world hunger could be solved, at least in the short run, by the adoption of these new varieties of grains and the cultivation methods that would

allow them to work their miracles. Borlaug became much sought after as a consultant by India, Pakistan, Tunisia, Morocco, Afghanistan, and similar countries with large populations and small crop yields. In 1970 the work of CIMMYT was recognized when Borlaug was awarded the Nobel Peace Prize in Oslo. He was the 15th American to win the prize, but it was noted at the time that it was significant that he was a scientist, rather than a politician or statesman. The Nobel Prize was only one among many citations and honorary degrees which he received for his work.

Borlaug remained a researcher at the Mexican experiment station of CIMMYT until 1960 when he also became the associate director assigned to the Inter-American Food Crop Program of the Rockefeller Foundation. In 1964 he was made director of the wheat research and production program of CIMMYT and, that same year, associate director of the Rockefeller Foundation. He retired in 1983 but remained as a consultant. In 1984 he completed a tour of Latin America, Africa, and Asia, using his knowledge and prestige to press for adoption of CIMMYT's new hybrid corn. This variety, like the earlier ones of wheat and rice, was bred specifically to maximize the production of maize in those parts of the world where it remained the most important cereal crop.

Criticism of Borlaug's Methods

Over his long career Borlaug saw his Green Revolution go through periods of vast praise and harsh criticism. Initially, when applied carefully to the most suitable lands (especially lands easily irrigated), crop increases were spectacular. By the mid-1970s about 90 percent of Mexico's wheat crop was made up of HYVs, and in Asia and North Africa 35 percent of the wheat and 20 percent of the rice was HYV. At first, crop yields were up to 400 percent larger than with traditional varieties, but within a few years yields had dipped by nearly half. In part this was caused by bad weather, but energy prices were driving up the cost of fertilizers (so that less was used), and pests were finding the new cultivation methods to their advantage. Because they were both energy and labor intensive, the new crop varieties crowded out small farmers who could not afford to raise them. It was even charged that crop innovations made social conflict more certain by widening the gap between the rich and the poor farmers of the world. During the 1980s environmentalists criticized Borlaug's high-yield dependence on inorganic fertilizers and effectively pressured donor countries and philanthropic organizations to back away from such programs in Africa. Borlaug responded by saying, "Some of the environmental lobbyists of the Western nations are the salt of the earth, but many of them are elitists. They've never experienced the physical sensation of hunger. They do their lobbying from comfortable office suites in Washington or Brussels. If they lived just one month amid the misery of the developing world, as I have for 50 years, they'd be crying out for tractors and fertilizer and irrigation canals and be outraged that fashionable elitists back home were trying to deny them these things."

Sasakawa-Global 2000 Projects

Borlaug was lured out of retirement in 1984 by Japanese philanthropist Ryoichi Sasakawa who, along with former president Jimmy Carter, wanted to improve agricultural production in Africa. Borlaug's association with Sasakawa and Carter produced the Sasakawa-Global 2000 project. Although environmentalists still opposed his methods, yields of corn, wheat, cassava, sorghum, and cow peas were greatly increased in Ethiopia, Ghana, Nigeria, Tanzania, and Togo. During the 1995-96 season, Ethiopia recorded the greatest harvest in its history. Borlaug even made headway in Sudan, near the dry Sahel, until project efforts there were terminated in 1992 with the onset of civil war.

Borlaug continues to lead an active life by dividing his time between the CIMMYT where he advises young scientists, Texas A&M where he teaches international agriculture, and the Sasakawa-Global 2000 projects that operate in 12 African nations.

Further Reading

A brief first-hand account can be found in Norman E. Borlaug, *Land Use, Food, Energy and Recreation* (1982). A more technical description is Haldore Hanson, Norman E. Borlaug, and R. Glenn Anderson, *Wheat in the Third World* (1982). The standard secondary source is Lennard Bickel, *Facing Starvation: Norman Borlaug and the Fight Against Hunger* (1974), which deals also with the personalities involved in the early days of the Green Revolution.

An excellent account of Borlaug's contributions to the world can be found in the *Atlantic Monthly* (January 1997). □

Max Born

The German physicist Max Born (1882-1970) made his most outstanding contribution to modern physics in showing the inherently probabilistic nature of the basic laws of quantum mechanics.

On Dec. 11, 1882, Max Born was born in Breslau. He studied at the universities of Breslau, Heidelberg, and Zurich before he settled in Göttingen. In accordance with the advice of his father, Born did not specialize but attended courses in the humanities as well as in the sciences, especially mathematics. In Göttingen he followed with great enthusiasm the lectures in astronomy by Karl Schwarzschild but found no stimulation in the physics courses. He earned his doctorate with a dissertation in applied mathematics, namely, the analysis of the stability of elastic wires and tapes.

Although Born was inducted for the one-year compulsory military service, because of his asthmatic condition he obtained an early discharge. He went to Cambridge but within a few months returned to Breslau. In the fall of 1908 Born was back at Göttingen, where he later obtained the post of privatdozent (lecturer) in physics on the merits of his paper on the relativistic aspects of the electron. This was the start of his career as a physicist.

Born's first outstanding achievement in physics came in 1912, when in collaboration with T. von Kármán he worked out the theoretical explanation of the whole range of the variation of specific heat in solids. Although the official credit for this major feat went to Peter Debye, who independently did the same work a few weeks earlier, the topic became decisive in Born's future work as a physicist. It opened to him the two main lines of his subsequent research: lattice dynamics and quantum theory.

In 1912 Born made his first trip to the United States to lecture on relativity at the University of Chicago. On his return to Göttingen he married Hedwig Ehrenberg; they had two children. Born's close relationship with Albert Einstein began in 1915, when Born went to the University of Berlin to take over some of the teaching duties of Max Planck. There Born's 5-year-long investigation of the dynamics of crystal lattices was published as his first book. Between 1919 and 1921 he was at the University of Frankfurt am Main.

In 1921 Born succeeded Debye at Göttingen as director of the physics department. The work of Wolfgang Pauli, Werner Heisenberg, and Erwin Schrödinger produced the major advances in quantum theory, but it was Born who reduced these various efforts to a basic foundation. It consisted in showing that the square of the value of Schrödinger's psi function was the probability density in configuration space. This meant that quantum mechanics allowed only a statistical interpretation of events on the atomic level. The result was so fundamental and startling that such leaders of modern physics as Planck, Einstein,

Louis de Broglie, and Schrödinger could not bring themselves to accept it unreservedly. Born attributed to their reluctance the fact that he did not receive the Nobel Prize until 3 decades later, in 1954.

Born further elaborated the implications of his major discovery in his guest lectures at the Massachusetts Institute of Technology in the winter of 1925/1926, the text of which appeared under the title *Problems of Atomic Dynamics,* probably the first monograph on quantum mechanics. Born's return to Göttingen signaled the beginning of a pilgrimage of young American physicists to Göttingen. His own work, however, became handicapped by nervous exhaustion in 1928. He therefore gave up research on atomic theory and wrote a textbook on optics, which became a classic in the field. In May 1933 he had to depart from Germany only a few months after Hitler came to power.

Following a short stay in South Tirol, the Borns went to Cambridge, where he concentrated on writing two books that also became classics: *The Atomic Theory* (1935) and *The Restless Universe* (1936), the latter a popular exposition. In 1936 the Borns went to India at the invitation of Sir C. V. Raman, a Nobel laureate physicist, but half a year later they were at Edinburgh, where Born succeeded Charles G. Darwin as professor of natural philosophy (physics).

Born stayed in Edinburgh 17 years, and his major achievements there are embodied in three books: one on the lattice dynamics of crystals, a new enlarged version of his textbook on optics, and *Natural Philosophy of Cause and Chance.* The last represented the text of his Waynflete Lectures at Magdalen College, Oxford. It shows Max Born at his philosophical best, for he retained all his life a keen interest in the deeper aspects of physics. This also explains his well-known concern about the ethical implications of science and about the role of science in the general fabric of human culture.

Born had already taken up residence in Bad Pyrmont near Göttingen in 1954 when he began to publish his startling articles on these topics. His view of the future was rather dim, though he pleaded for the attitude of "hoping against hope." He died in Göttingen on Jan. 5, 1970.

Further Reading

An invaluable source on Born is the autobiographical *My Life and My Views* (1968), which contains priceless episodes from his life, an authoritative discussion of the genesis of his principal contributions to physics, and his reflections on the role of science in modern culture. A popular but informative discussion of the development of quantum mechanics is Banesh Hoffmann, *The Strange Story of the Quantum* (1947; 2d ed. 1959). Max Jammer, *The Conceptual Development of Quantum Mechanics* (1966), will probably be for many years the standard work on the topic. □

Dov Ber Borochov

Dov Ber Borochov (1881-1917) was an early Zionist thinker who reconciled Judaism and Marxism.

Dov Ber Borochov was born in an obscure Ukranian village in 1881 and died of pneumonia while on a speaking tour of Russia in 1917. In his brief lifespan he became what some described as a modern Moses Maimonides. That medieval philosopher had reconciled Judaism and Aristotelian thought. Borochov, perhaps the finest of the early Zionist thinkers, reconciled Judaism and Marxism. While orthodox Marxism contended that nationalism, no less than religion, was an opiate of the people, Borochov distinguished between two types of nationalism. The first type was that of the dominant group; the second was the expression of the dominated. His philosophical acumen enabled him to show how Marxist theory could be utilized for the sake of Jewish nationalism.

He was not only concerned with theory but also with organizing Jewish workers. His influence on the Poalei Zion (Zionist Worker's Party) extends from his own time through present day Israeli politics. His example stimulated Jewish immigration to the land of Israel and his forceful personality influenced many Russian Jews who formed the nucleus of the settlement (Yishuv) which would develop into the modern state of Israel. The Poalei Zion Party which bore his stamp became influential in Israeli politics and his thought remains influential today. In 1963 his remains were brought to Israel and buried in the Kinneret Cemetery together with those of many other early Zionists, some of whom he had opposed vigorously.

His Early Life

Borochov was born in Zolotonosha in the Ukraine and grew up in the slightly larger city of Poltava. He was educated in a Russian high school but was denied entrance to a Russian university. Unlike most Jewish radicals of his time he had never studied in a Yeshiva, a school of higher Jewish learning. While assimilated to the general culture, however, he felt the sting of anti-semitism and this pushed him into Zionism. His discontent with the Czarist system led him to join the Russian Social Democratic Party. In 1901, however, he established a Zionist Social Worker's Union at Yekaterinoslav and was expelled from the Russian Social Democratic Party. He himself, on the other hand, claims that his expulsion came because he was a bad influence on the workers since he "taught them to think for themselves."

His thought at that time centered on the problem of the Jewish people, on anti-semitism, and on the difference between the nationalism of dominating peoples and the nationalism of the dominated. This latter he identified with Zionism. He suggested that Marx and Engels had both recognized that the dynamics of socialism and the needs of workers were different in different contexts. Borochov's unorthodox Marxism claimed that Jewish problems could only be solved by merging the nationalism of the oppressed with the revolution of the workers. His focus on the problematic conditions of the Jewish people marked him as different from mainstream Marxists. His essay "on the nature of the Jewish Mind" (1902) is characteristic of his thought at this period.

Borochov and Poalei Zion

From 1905 to 1907 he worked with the World Zionist Organization, hoping to use it as a basis for the Jewish socialism he envisioned. His first major study of this period, "The National Question and the Class Struggle" (1905), described the different impact made by conditions of production in different social and historical contexts. He argued that together with the vertical class system of upper and lower classes there is also a horizontal one separating different ethnic-linguistic-cultural groups within a society. Jews represent an oppressed class on this horizontal level while the Jewish workers are the victims of the vertical class system. They are the only ones whose position in both systems is identical and only they can become the bearers of a national liberation movement.

During this period in his life Borochov helped organize and develop the Poalei Zion, the Zionist Worker's Party, throughout Russia. He attended the World Zionist Congress in 1904 and vigorously attacked Theodor Herzl's plan to settle Jews in Uganda. Such a program of territorialism (as it was called) went against his view of the political facts. Borochov argued that only the land of Israel presented an opportunity for Jewish colonization. Despite his usual realism he was naive about the Palestinian Arabs, who he claimed shared a common heritage with the Jews and who would willingly join them in a joint cultural revival. His arguments for this position were expressed in "On the Question of Zion and Territory" (1905). At the same time he was developing his own views of Zionism and socialism. His attack on Jewish assimilationists in "On the Question of Zionist Theory" (1905) demonstrated his insistence upon Jewish nationalism. Throughout 1905 he travelled up and down Russia organizing Poalei Zion groups for whom he became a delegate to the World Zionist Congress. In 1906 he crystalized his views in the programmatic statement "Our Platform," which distinguished Poalei Zion from the World Zionist Organization. After the 1907 World Zionist Congress he led the Poalei Zion out of the World Zionist Organization, founding the World Union of Poalei Zion.

Years of Maturation

The third stage in his development, from 1907 to 1917, was spent largely in exile from Russia. First he went to Vienna and then in 1914 to the United States. There he contributed to the New York Yiddish Daily *Di Warheit* and engaged in research in Yiddish. His work during this time has been underestimated by many critics. He turned from theoretical studies to more concrete analysis of sociological data and Yiddish culture. He remained a controversial figure in American Zionist life. His support of the American involvement on the side of Russia in World War I—when many Jews retained sympathies with Germany—was controversial. The fruits of this period were both scholarly and personal. His study "The Jewish Labor Movement in Figures" and his scholarly articles on the Yiddish language show a keen sense of Jewish culture and sociological reality. His ideas matured and he synthesized various elements and themes in his work. He spread these ideas when, after the Russian revolution, he returned to Russia in 1917 for a speaking tour. During that tour he caught pneumonia and died in Kiev.

Further Reading

There is no full scale work devoted to Borochov in English, although much has appeared in Hebrew and Yiddish. An interesting chapter on Borochov can be found in Gershon Winer, *The Founding Fathers of Israel* (1971). The studies of Matityahu Mintz are extremely important, although most of them are in Hebrew. In English see his "Ber Borokhov, in *Studies in Zionism*" (April 1982). It would also be helpful to consult David Vital, *Zionism: The Formative Years* (Oxford, 1982). □

Aleksandr Profirevich Borodin

The Russian composer Aleksandr Porfirevich Borodin (1833-1887) was also a physician and research chemist. He epitomized the group of composers known as the "Mighty Five" and used folk music in conscious pursuit of a "national style."

Aleksandr Borodin was born in St. Petersburg. The name Borodin was that of a retainer to Prince Gedeanov; the prince acknowledged paternity and provided the mother and the boy with a name. Borodin was raised with many of the privileges of the nobility, and his education was broad in the tradition of the European gentleman. This included musical training and preparation for a profession: medicine.

While still a young medical intern, Borodin gained entry to the Mighty Five, partly on the strength of his keyboard ability—a defining factor of the 19th-century romantic Russian composer. His training had been that of the gifted dilettante; he now came under the influence of the taskmaster of the group, Mili Balakirev, and subsequently under the influence of the other members of the Mighty Five: Modest Mussorgsky, César Cui, and Nicolai Rimsky-Korsakov. Of them, Borodin alone stuck by his original and primary profession, although he gave up actual medical practice ("distasteful") for research.

Although his works are relatively few, Borodin ranks a close second to Mussorgsky as a creative artist among the Mighty Five. His gift is marked neither by the uncertainty nor the verbosity of some of his colleagues and most of his musical heirs. Moreover, his confidence is not marred by the self-righteous certainty that led the next generation of Russian composers into relatively insignificant utterance.

Borodin's Second Symphony (the *Bogatyr* or *Heroic*) and his opera *Prince Igor* (finished posthumously by Rimsky-Korsakov and Aleksandr Glazunov) are his principal works of large proportions. In both he uses a developed folk style effectively, and in the opera he makes a major contribution to the subgenre of "Russian music about the East." Borodin's happy gift for beguiling melody is attested

Russian Music (1936); Donald Brook, *Six Great Russian Composers* (1946); Victor I. Seroff, *The Mighty Five: The Cradle of Russian National Music* (1948); and Mikhail O. Zetlin, *The Five: The Evolution of the Russian School of Music,* edited and translated by George Panin (1959).

Additional Sources

Dianin, Sergei Aleksandrovich, *Borodin,* Westport, Conn.: Greenwood Press, 1980.

Aleksandr Porfirevich Borodin: a chemist's biography, Berlin; New York: Springer-Verlag, 1988.

Habets, Alfred, *Borodin and Liszt,* New York: AMS Press, 1977.

☐

St. Charles Borromeo

The Italian prelate St. Charles Borromeo (1538-1584) was a leading reformer in the Roman Catholic Church.

Charles Borromeo was born into a family of means in the town of Rocca d'Arona in northern Italy on Oct. 2, 1538. He was a bright and personable boy of 12 when he received tonsure, the official initiation into the ranks of the clergy. After studying with tutors, he enrolled at the University of Padua, where in 1559 he received the degree of doctor of laws. That same year his mother's brother was elected Pope Pius IV. Within a few months the new pope had called Charles, then 21, to Rome to help in administering the affairs of the Church.

Charles was given the rank of cardinal to go with his position as personal assistant to the Pope. Pius IV made his talented and dedicated nephew secretary of state and relied heavily on his energy in directing the third session of the Council of Trent (1562-1563), as well as in handling the practical, political affairs of the city of Rome. In 1563 Charles was ordained a priest and consecrated archbishop of Milan, but he continued to live in Rome and work with his uncle. When he was given responsibility in Rome for the Church reform commanded by the Council of Trent, he brought about proper religious instructions in the parishes, saw that the elaborate worship rituals were toned down in the interest of devotion, and built a new seminary for the proper training of the clergy.

From 1566 Charles directed the Church in Milan, since his services in Rome had come to an end with his uncle's death in 1565. Over the years he was a remarkably effective bishop. The diocese of Milan was split among five diplomatic fronts on which he had to operate simultaneously. His popularity with the people disturbed the Milanese senate, and his disciplinary directives antagonized several religious groups. At one point an assassin was hired to kill him but failed.

Almost all of the people of Milan respected Charles's courage and tireless concern. When the plague of 1576-1578 struck Milan, Charles spent much of his time nursing the sick. The catechetical centers he established were so

to by the adaptation of his *Prince Igor* music for the American musical *Kismet.* Other than the symphony and the opera, his most-played works are, perhaps, the two String Quartets, some of whose themes are also heard in *Kismet.* A few other chamber works and some 18 art songs nearly round out Borodin's complete list of works.

Some elements of Borodin's personal life and his creative procedures remain obscure. A significant store of Borodiniana has been, since the composer's death, in the hands of the Dianin family. Although the family has tried to present the composer to the world (the first Dianin was Borodin's laboratory assistant), they are too closely involved and Soviet puritanism is far too strong to allow for frankness about personal things; and the Dianins, none of them professional musicians, misjudge what is significant about the creative procedure. Sergei Dianin, a mathematician, in his Borodin biography (1963) supposed the composer to have combined musical elements as a chemist combines chemicals.

Borodin did not teach. He died in 1887, and his legacy was preserved by his friends and reappears in some of the work of Sergei Prokofiev. Borodin's few works, like those of Mussorgsky, are disproportionately important.

Further Reading

The basic biography of Borodin is Sergei Dianin, *Borodin* (trans. 1963). An earlier work is Gerald E. H. Abraham, *Borodin: The Composer and His Music* (1927). Books with substantial sections on Borodin include Abraham's *Studies in Russian Music* (1936); M. D. Calvocoressi and Gerald Abraham, *Masters of* effective that Protestantism made no headway in Milan. He died on Nov. 3, 1584, and was canonized in 1610.

Further Reading

The oldest and most complete biography of St. Charles Borromeo is G. P. Giussano, *The Life of St. Charles Borromeo* (1610; trans., 2 vols., 1884), written by a friend and disciple of the saint. Margaret Yeo, *Reformer: St. Charles Borromeo* (1938), is a modern, interesting sketch of his life. □

Francesco Borromini

The Italian architect Francesco Borromini (1599-1667) was the most daring and original architect of the Roman baroque, and his style is the embodiment of baroque extravagance. His works were influential throughout Europe and South America.

In the first half of the 17th century, Roman baroque architecture was dominated by two extraordinary figures: Francesco Borromini and Gian Lorenzo Bernini. Borromini represented the more imaginative and idiosyncratic side of baroque architecture; Bernini remained much closer to the aims and ideals of ancient Rome, both in sculpture and architecture, and his architectural works are sober and classical.

Borromini's style was essentially personal and thus was later denigrated by neoclassic critics. For the 18th and 19th centuries Borromini was the most licentious and extravagant architect in history, and his works aroused the most passionate disapproval, particularly in Protestant Europe and America, while being copied (and occasionally exceeded) in Latin America as well as in southern Germany, Austria, Spain, and Portugal.

Francesco Castelli, called Borromini, was born on Sept. 25, 1599, in Bissone on Lake Lugano. He was distantly related to the great architect Carlo Maderno.

As a boy, Borromini was sent to Milan to learn the mason's craft, and it was as a mason that he went to Rome, where his presence is recorded from 1621. He probably began as an ordinary mason at St. Peter's, but soon Maderno, the chief architect of St. Peter's, seems to have found him employment at S. Andrea della Valle (1621-1623). In any event, it is certain that Borromini's years in Rome were spent as a humble craftsman, at the very time when Bernini was making his reputation as a virtuoso sculptor.

This was probably the cause of the lifelong rivalry between the two men, which was exacerbated by difficulties at St. Peter's and the Palazzo Barberini in Rome, where Borromini worked under Bernini from 1629 to 1632. The rivalry was such that it may have been the cause of the profound melancholia which eventually led to Borromini's tragic death.

In the 1630s Borromini began to receive independent commissions, and his fame grew rapidly. In 1632 he commenced work at the Palazzo Spada. His famous gallery, designed with an illusionistic effect of perspective, has an unexpected wit that must have helped to make Borromini's name known.

Major Works

Far more important was Borromini's work at S. Carlo alle Quattro Fontane, begun in 1634. This tiny church, along with its courtyard, is one of the most important monuments of the baroque style in Rome. The work was divided into two phases almost 30 years apart, with the cloister and church designed and largely built in the 1630s and the facade designed in 1662 and still incomplete at Borromini's death in 1667. Owing to the fortunate survival of a considerable number of Borromini's drawings, it is possible to trace the evolution of the ground plan of S. Carlo from a straightforward oval on the long axis of the church, of the type which had been introduced into Rome in the late 16th century by Giacomo Vignola and others, to the present, extraordinarily complex series of curves and countercurves. In its final form the plan creates an undulating movement, so that all the walls of the church, both at ground level and at cornice level, seem to be in motion. What is more, the plan is not quite the same at ground level as it is at the cornice. Above the cornice there is an extraordinarily complicated transition, from quadrant arcs, via spandrels containing not-quite-circular roundels, to the simple elliptical shape of the dome, which in turn is complicated by an unusual pattern of coffering, based on octagons and the cross-shaped emblem of the Spanish order for whom the church was built.

Borromini's next major work, the Oratory of S. Filippo Neri, begun in 1637 for the Congregation of the Oratory, is much less daring in plan than S. Carlo, though the facade breaks new ground by receding in a shallow concave curve. The introduction of movement into the facade reached its highest point in Borromini's later works, such as the facades of S. Agnese (1652) and S. Carlo alle Quattro Fontane.

The facade of S. Carlo has a very marked concave-convex-concave movement in the lower story, but in the upper story Borromini introduced a small semicircular pavilion, above which he placed a large oval supported by angels. The pavilion follows the convex curve of the entablature below it, but the oval is mounted on an inward-curving wall, so that the rhythm of the upper part changes to concave-concave-concave before our eyes. This extreme complexity found little favor in Rome, where many people criticized Borromini's "extravagances," but this daring and lively treatment of a facade, which exploits the brilliant light and shadow of a hot climate, was much appreciated by architects in Spain, Portugal, and Latin America, and, slightly later, in Catholic Germany and Austria. The exuberant baroque of all these countries owes its existence to the example of Borromini, but most Roman critics and patrons preferred the architecture of Bernini with its classical overtones.

In 1642 Borromini began the church of S. Ivo alla Sapienza, the university chapel (the Sapienza was the University of Rome). The church was built at one end of an existing courtyard, which Borromini used to provide a concave facade two stories high, repeating the double arcades of the court. The plan of S. Ivo is even more complex than that of S. Carlo. It consists basically of an equilateral triangle with a deep apse in the middle of each side and with the points of the triangle cut off and rounded into curves going in the opposite direction to the apses. Many attempts have been made to explain this shape as symbolic—one of the most popular is that it represents the bee in the arms of the Barberini family—but it seems more likely that it resulted from Borromini's passion for geometry. The walls of S. Ivo are articulated by pilasters which carry a strongly emphasized cornice, which (like that of S. Carlo) defines a plan not quite identical with the ground plan. Above the cornice the whole extraordinary shape is gathered together into something which internally becomes a dome and lantern but externally has a totally different appearance. It can best be described as a convex-curved drum with a shallow tiled roof and a lantern that ends in a spiral ramp.

Borromini's Style

Not only is it difficult to describe Borromini's forms in the ordinary language of architectural analysis, but they also have a mathematical sophistication quite different in kind from the grandiose simplicity of Bernini's conceptions. This contrast is heightened by the fact that Bernini employed comparatively simple forms but overlaid them with the richest possible decorative elements, whereas Borromini, partly from necessity because of the nature of his commissions, restricted himself to painted stucco with sparse gilding, invented decorative motifs which seem to be vegetable in origin, and never employed figural sculpture on anything like the scale natural to Bernini.

The highly personal art of Michelangelo seems to have served as a starting point for Borromini, dating from the time when he worked as a mason at St. Peter's. Many of Borromini's ideas can also be traced back to the architecture of ancient Rome—but not to the accepted models of antiquity. From these sources he created an intensely personal style, in which some of his contemporaries even discerned (correctly) elements of the Gothic.

Borromini's Temperament

The neurotic face which looks out at us from the portrait that is the frontispiece to Borromini's *Opus architectonicum* is an excellent indication of his character. Although he was reasonably successful in his career and was made a knight of Christ by the Pope in 1652, Borromini seems to have been permanently embittered by Bernini's greater fame and, perhaps, by a restless quest for perfection. An early biographer tells us that he made wax and clay models as well as many drawings and that he destroyed a quantity of drawings a few days before his death.

The accounts of Borromini's last illness indicate that he suffered from a nervous complaint and had to be watched night and day. In the August heat of 1667 he stabbed himself with his own sword while his servant's attention was distracted. He recovered sufficiently to make a will and

receive the last rites; he died on August 3. Being unmarried, he left his property to a nephew, on condition that he marry a niece of Carlo Maderno. Borromini was buried in Maderno's tomb in S. Giovanni dei Fiorentini, to which, at his own request, no inscription was added.

Just before his death Borromini began work on a collection of engravings of his buildings, but the project was never completed. Two large folio volumes appeared in 1720 and 1725 under the title *Opus architectonicum equitis Francisci Boromini.*

Further Reading

The best treatment of Borromini in English is Rudolf Wittkower, *Art and Architecture in Italy: 1600-1750* (1958; 2d ed. 1965). There are numerous splendid reproductions of Borromini's works, including the drawings, in Paolo Portoghesi, *The Rome of Borromini: Architecture as Language* (1967; trans. 1968). James Lees-Milne, *Baroque in Italy* (1959), contains a chapter surveying Borromini's work. See also Michael Kitson, *The Age of Baroque* (1966), and Germain Bazin, *The Baroque* (1968).

Additional Sources

Blunt, Anthony, *Borromini*, Cambridge, Mass.: Harvard University Press, 1979.
Doumato, Lamia, *Borromini's baroque*, Monticello, Ill.: Vance Bibliographies, 1979. □

Bernard Bosanquet

The English philosopher Bernard Bosanquet (1848-1923) was probably the most eminent member, certainly the most prolific writer, of the idealist school of philosophy which flourished in Great Britain in the late 19th and early 20th centuries.

Bernard Bosanquet was born on June 14, 1848, at Alnwick in Northumberland. He attended Harrow and continued his studies at Balliol College, Oxford, in classical literature and ancient philosophy. T. H. Green, a fellow and tutor of Balliol, was introducing philosophical ideas derived from the German philosopher Hegel, and Bosanquet came immediately under his influence and remained so for the rest of his life.

Hegelian Idealism

Green, like Bosanquet, came from an Evangelical Protestant background and, like many of his contemporaries, was deeply disturbed by the challenge of natural science to religion. In Hegelian idealism he found a system of thought which enabled him to reconcile the claims of religion and morality with science. Green, however, did not slavishly adopt Hegelianism. In particular, he propounded a more liberal social philosophy than he found in Hegel and insisted that the state could not claim absolute obedience from the individual. Its role was to "remove hinderances," such as poverty or ignorance, and to provide the individual with a social environment which would enable him freely to develop into a mature, moral person. In following up the implications of this position, Green can justifiably be regarded as one of the founders of the welfare state.

Although Bosanquet accepted the same fundamental philosophy as Green, he followed Hegel more closely and gave to idealism a more conservative bias, probably because he brought to these issues a mind deeply immersed in ancient philosophy, particularly Aristotle. His first published work in 1878 was a translation of Schömann's *Constitutional History of Athens*. Furthermore, his classical training made him one of the few English philosophers interested in esthetics, and he wrote some of his best works on this subject.

Charity Organization Society

In 1881 Bosanquet resigned his post as fellow and tutor at University College, Oxford, which he had occupied for 10 years, and moved to London. In 1869 his half brother, Charles Bosanquet, had been one of the founders of the Charity Organization Society (COS) and had been its first secretary. The aim of the organization was to administer charitable funds to the poor, basing its support on the principle that the recipients should be in need owing to circumstances beyond their control—due to loss of occupation or sickness and not due to bad habits such as heavy drinking or other irresponsible behavior. This involved setting up a system of casework investigation by district committees in the deprived urban areas in order to examine and adjudicate on claimants for aid. Bosanquet played a notable part in setting up and serving on these bodies. Under his influence the COS constantly stressed the principle that aid should always be selective and be given in such a way that it never undermined individual responsibility.

Consistent with this principle, the COS opposed all efforts to induce the state to provide aid, and in the famous Poor Law Commission of 1910 C. S. Loch, who succeeded Charles Bosanquet as secretary of the COS, opposed the proposal (advocated by the Fabians Sidney and Beatrice Webb and afterward adopted by Lloyd George) to introduce old-age pensions.

Freedom of the Individual

Bosanquet's most important work, *The Philosophical Theory of the State* (1899), made him the target of considerable criticism. Its basic argument is a revival of Rousseau's concept of the General Will and a reformulation of Rousseau's paradox about "forcing" men to be "free." Freedom, it is argued, does not lie in doing what a man wants to do but in doing what the General Will imposes upon him. Bosanquet's extension of this led him to argue that freedom lies not in the pursuit of self-interest or sectional interests but in the identification of personal with social interest as expressed by the state. This would appear to subordinate the individual to the state, and during the 1914-1918 war he and other idealists were blamed for advocating ideas which justified a totalitarian political system. These criticisms were grossly unfair and were often based on statements taken out of context and misconstrued. Fundamentally Bosanquet

was concerned with establishing a relationship between the state and the individual that would enable the individual to develop his full stature as a responsible moral agent.

In the pursuit of this ideal he spent much time and energy in developing and encouraging various educational ventures, particularly adult education. He helped found the London School of Ethics and Social Philosophy, which in 1902 became the London School of Economics. He returned briefly to academic life in 1903 as professor of philosophy at St. Andrews University, Scotland, but retired in 1908. Bosanquet died in Hampstead, London, on Feb. 8, 1923.

Further Reading

The best and most sympathetic work on Bosanquet, *Bernard Bosanquet and His Friends: Letters Illustrating the Sources and the Development of His Philosophical Opinions*, was edited with biographical comments by his close friend and fellow idealist J. H. Muirhead (1935). Helen Bosanquet, *Bernard Bosanquet: A Short Account of His Life* (1924), is a brief and interesting work by Bosanquet's wife. For the background of Bosanquet's life and work the best book is Melvin Richter, *The Politics of Conscience: T. H. Green and His Age* (1964). For an account of the COS see Charles Loch Mowat, *The Charity Organisation Society, 1869-1913: Its Ideas and Work* (1961). □

Hieronymus Bosch

The work of the Netherlandish painter Hieronymus Bosch (1453-1516) is characterized by unusual stylistic originality and an intensely personalized symbolism, which makes interpretation of the meaning of his paintings extremely difficult.

Between 1480 and 1515, the period of major activity by Hieronymus Bosch, the character and appearance of Netherlandish painting were profoundly altered by several factors. Most significant was the introduction of many of the artistic ideals of the Italian Renaissance in such important northern centers of painting as Bruges, Ghent, and Antwerp. Responsive to these new currents of Italian influence, such painters as Gerard David and Quentin Massys had begun to invest their panels with the stable forms and spatial clarity of Renaissance painting. Bosch, on the other hand, appeared totally indifferent to these progressive trends, retaining in his work the nervous linearism and decorative exuberance of the late Gothic. It is basically the intense subjectivism of his art, unfettered by orthodoxy and tradition, that makes Bosch a representative of the new age.

Hieronymus Bosch, whose real name was Jeroen Anthoniszoon, was born in the North Brabant town of 's Hertogenbosch (Bois-le-Duc). Both his grandfather and father had been painters in this relatively minor provincial center, and it is generally assumed that Bosch's early training was obtained locally. From 1486 until his death Bosch

was mentioned regularly in the records of the local chapter of the Brotherhood of Our Lady, of which he was an active member. According to these accounts, he was commissioned to paint several altarpieces for the Cathedral of 's Hertogenbosch and to execute designs for its stained glass windows, all of which have disappeared. In 1504 Philip the Handsome, Archduke of Austria, commissioned him to paint a *Last Judgment,* which also has not survived. Further knowledge of the painter's career is unobtainable, save in the form of the few available insights that can be gleaned from the forty-odd authenticated paintings from the master's own hand. Several of these panels bear signatures, but none is dated, thus creating a major problem in their relative chronology.

Early Style

Unlike most Netherlandish painters of the period, Bosch does not appear to have traveled widely. The formative influences on his style are still disputed, though such early works as the tabletop of the *Seven Deadly Sins* show a marked reliance upon manuscript illuminations rather than contemporary practices of northern panel painting. The nearly contemporaneous tondo *Cure of Folly* (ca. 1475-1485) reveals a penchant for social satire akin to that found in several of the works of the Antwerp painter Quentin Massys.

The *Marriage at Cana* represents a decisive change in Bosch's style. The draftsmanship is at once firmer and bolder, and there occurs for the first time the technique of painting directly on the panel in a flat, evenly lighted man-

ner. Bosch used this spontaneous and buoyant style of painting throughout his career, and it distinguishes his work from that of his major contemporaries.

The artist's appearance is known from a presumed portrait in the *Arras Sketchbook* which shows Bosch in middle age, spry and alert, with a cynical outlook on the world. The early period of his art is closed by the panel entitled *The Conjuror,* in which a strange visionary quality begins to supplant the immediacy and direct observation of the earlier works.

Middle Period

The major paintings of this period (ca. 1490-1505) are the trio of great moralizing triptychs upon which the artist's reputation is mainly founded. Of the three, the earliest is probably the *Haywain,* which can be interpreted as an allegory of the evils of the world. In this instance Bosch's symbolism has been shown to be derived from Flemish proverbs and other forms of popular, didactic literature. The fantastic *Temptation of St. Anthony* in Lisbon (ca. 1500) is considered by most authorities to be Bosch's masterpiece. It is a fully resolved work in which the painter achieved pictorial richness in combination with iconographic complexity and expressive intensity. The most pessimistic of Bosch's visual sermons, the painting shows a world dominated by evil and the omnipresence of the devil and his fiendish agents. A cosmic, imaginary landscape provides the fiery scenario for one of the artist's most original and sensational displays of demonic inventiveness.

The most enigmatic of Bosch's paintings is the triptych of the *Garden of Earthly Delights.* This work, by virtue of its fantastic and recondite symbolism, stands at the summit of the painter's career. In 1605 the Spanish monk Sigüenza concluded that the painting was an allegory on the origin, diffusion, and punishment of sin revealed in terms of a psychological as well as a physical drama. Since that time there has been little substantial improvement upon this thesis despite numerous efforts by scholars to discover the key to the meaning of the work. In this connection, one is still obliged to concur with the art historian Erwin Panofsky that the "real secret of his magnificent nightmares and daydreams has still to be disclosed."

Late Period

Bosch's late style is characterized by an increased spiritual and pictorial asceticism. The *Epiphany* triptych initiates this phase with a new reliance upon broad forms and a simplified color scheme. A similar reduction of form and color to basic design elements is also observable in the small Madrid version of the painter's favorite theme, *Temptation of St. Anthony.* Solitary and contemplative, the simple figure of the hermit saint has been rendered physically and spiritually immune to a hostile world and its demonic occupants. One of Bosch's last works is the highly compacted and emotive *Christ Carrying the Cross.* Composed entirely of heads situated against a dark background, this panel provides a fitting climax to the artist's career. The arcane symbolism of the earlier works has here given way to an intense emotional and psychological drama into which the spectator is inexorably drawn, achieving for Bosch's final statement the quality of grandeur and universal human appeal.

When Bosch died in 1516, he left no followers in the usual sense. Such painters as Jan Mandyn and Pieter Huys were imitators at best, who were capable of copying Bosch's external forms without any understanding of their profound underlying significance.

Further Reading

The best book on Bosch is Charles de Tolnay, *Hieronymus Bosch* (1937; trans. 1966). It contains a sensitive analysis of the artist's stylistic development as well as the most authoritative chronology of the paintings. Ludwig von Baldass's excellent *Hieronymus Bosch* (1943; trans. 1960) makes important contributions to knowledge of the meaning of Bosch's symbolism. An interesting thesis concerning the alchemical significance of many of Bosch's panels is in Jacques Combe, *Jerome Bosch* (1946; trans. 1957). □

Juan Bosch

Juan Bosch (born 1909) was a Dominican writer and political leader. As president of his country, he introduced wide-ranging social reforms.

Juan Bosch was born on June 30, 1909, in La Vega, the son of immigrants. He received his education there and soon afterward joined the opposition to the tyrannical regime of General Rafael Trujillo, who had come to power in 1930.

In 1935 Bosch went into exile and became a leading figure among the younger expatriates. In 1939 he was one of the founders of the Partido Revolucionario Dominicano (PRD), or Dominican Revolutionary Party. The PRD became the most influential of the exile groups opposed to the Trujillo regime. In Cuba between 1944 and 1952 Bosch held various posts in its democratic leftist Autentico government.

Bosch was also gaining a considerable reputation as an important literary figure, specializing in short stories and also writing frequent sociological and political studies on his native country. After the overthrow of the Autenticos by General Fulgencio Batista in 1952, Bosch went to Costa Rica and in 1958 moved to Venezuela.

With the assassination of Trujillo in 1961, Bosch returned home. Soon after, he began to give weekly television appearances. His ability to explain difficult issues in simple terms soon won him a wide audience throughout the republic. The same qualities also catapulted him into national leadership and helped to bring wide popularity to his party.

Popularity Led to Presidency

Bosch emerged as one of the two major candidates in the first post-Trujillo election at the end of 1962, becoming president in February 1963. During his seven months in office Bosch sought to set a model for democratic government. He encouraged wide organization of the labor and peasant movements, sponsored passage of an agrarian reform law, and financed an extensive program for training local leaders of cooperatives, unions, and municipalities. The Bosch government also maintained the fullest civil liberties.

Reforms Led to His Overthrow

Dominican military leaders, unaccustomed to the "turbulence" of a democratic regime, overthrew Bosch in September 1963. He went into exile in Puerto Rico. When a revolt broke out in Santo Domingo in April 1965, seeking to restore Bosch to power, he gave it his blessing but made no serious attempt to return home. The uprising was frustrated by United States armed intervention, and a provisional government was established under Hector Garcia Godoy, a former member of Bosch's cabinet. In new elections a year later, Bosch was decisively defeated by the former president, Joaquin Balaguer.

Shortly after Balaguer was inaugurated, Bosch went into voluntary exile in Spain. There he grew increasingly pessimistic about the possibility for political democracy to thrive in his homeland. In 1968 he formally proclaimed his support for a "popular dictatorship." He returned home in 1970, and in 1973 founded the Dominican Liberation Party (PLD). Bosch ran for president in 1994. Although he lost, the party gained political power and has become a major force in Dominican elections.

Further Reading

Gutierrez, Carlos Maria. *The Dominican Republic: Rebellion and Repression* (1972);

Pons, Frank M. *The Dominican Republic: A National History* (1994). □

Sir Jagadis Chandra Bose

Sir Jagadis Chandra Bose (1858-1937) was an Indian physicist and plant physiologist who did pioneering work in the measurement of plant growth and the responsiveness of plants to external stimuli.

The life and scientific career of Jagadis Chandra Bose are rooted in the social ferment and the vital nationalism that made Bengal the intellectual center of India in the 19th century. He was born on Nov. 30, 1858, at Mymensingh (now in East Bengal), where his father was a deputy magistrate. The elder Bose sent Jagadis to the traditional village school to give him a grounding in Indian culture and then to St. Xavier's school and college in Calcutta, where a Jesuit teacher encouraged his scientific interests.

At great financial hardship to the family, Bose went to the University of London in 1880 to study medicine; after a year he transferred to Cambridge to study science. He received degrees from Cambridge in 1884 and from London in 1885. His teachers, including the famous physicist Lord Rayleigh, recognized his brilliance and recommended him to high British officials in India for employment. Bose became professor of physics at Presidency College, Calcutta. Although he encountered some discrimination as the first Indian to hold the post, within a few years he was acknowledged as a scientist of a caliber unknown before in India. At that time there was virtually no provision for scientific research in Indian universities, so his achievements were all the more extraordinary. In 1887 he married a Madras medical student, Abala Das, who shared in her husband's scientific interests.

Bose's first experiments, which concerned the transmission of electrical energy, were extensions of the work of such pioneers as James Clerk Maxwell and Heinrich Rudolph Hertz. This work led Bose to an interest in the possibilities of radio communication, and some of his experiments paralleled, if they did not actually precede, those of Guglielmo Marconi. Bose is said to have demonstrated radio transmission in Calcutta in 1895.

Researches in Plant Life

Bose then turned to the work that brought him his greatest fame: the measurement of the responses of plants to such stimuli as light, sound, touch, and electricity. His research convinced him that there were no clear-cut boundaries between the nervous systems of plants and of animals. To carry out his experiments, he invented the crescograph, an instrument capable of magnifying the movements of growth in plants 10 million times.

Bose's experiments brought him world fame while he was still a young man, and he made many lecture tours to the universities of Europe and America. The British government knighted him in 1916, the year after his retirement from Presidency College. The validity of his experiments was often attacked, partly on the basis of his experimental techniques, but more often because of the mystical, religious implications that he found in his research, as when he claimed that plants, like animals, adjusted to change through "inherited memory of the past." He insisted that not only could no line be drawn between plants and animals but that his researches had shown there was no line between living and nonliving matter. He felt that he had substantiated in the laboratory the Hindu religious belief that the whole universe was an aspect of the Eternal One.

Bose was deeply patriotic, and his encouragement of research in the universities and in the Bose Research Institute, which he founded in Calcutta in 1917, was a reflection of his conviction that Indians must add scientific skills to their great religious tradition. He succeeded in communicating his own enthusiasm and excitement to a new generation of students, who carried on his work. He died on Nov. 23, 1937.

Further Reading

The most interesting biography of Bose is Patrick Geddes, *The Life and Work of Sir Jagadis C. Bose* (1920). Geddes, a town planner and social scientist, examined Bose's life in the context of the social changes of that time. *Sir Jagadish Chunder Bose: His Life, Discoveries and Writings* (1921) is useful for examples of Bose's writings. Monoranjon Gupta, *Jagadishchandra Bose: A Biography* (1964), corrects some factual errors in Geddes's work, gives a fuller account of Bose's life, and lists Bose's numerous publications.

Additional Sources

Nandy, Ashis, *Alternative sciences: creativity and authenticity in two Indian scientists,* New Delhi: Allied, 1980. □

Subhas Chandra Bose

Subhas Chandra Bose (1897-1945) was one of India's great nationalist leaders of the first half of the 20th century. He led the revolutionary Indian National Army during World War II.

Subhas Chandra Bose was born on Jan. 23, 1897, at Cuttack, Orissa, the ninth child of a lawyer of Kayasth caste. He attended a private school for European and Anglo-Indian boys run by the Baptist Mission and later a preparatory school. He was religious and spent much time in meditation.

At college in Calcutta, Bose became politically and socially aware. British insults to Indians in public places were offensive to him. He was personally implicated in an incident involving an English professor who had manhandled some students, and as a result Bose left the college.

Bose matriculated at Cambridge, and his high score on civil service exams meant an almost automatic appointment. He then took his first conscious step as a revolutionary and resigned the appointment on the premise that the "best way to end a government is to withdraw from it." At the time, Indian nationalists were suffering shock and indignation because of the Amritsar massacre and the repressive Rowlatt legislation of 1919. Returning to India, Bose wrote for the newspaper *Swaraj* and took charge of publicity for the Bengal Provincial Congress Committee. His mentor was C. R. Das, spokesman for the aggressive nationalism of Bengal. Bose worked for Das when the latter was elected mayor of Calcutta in 1924. In a roundup of terrorists in 1925, Bose was arrested and sent to prison in Mandalay, where he contracted tuberculosis.

Bose in National Politics

Released from prison 2 years later, Bose became general secretary of the Congress party and worked with Jawaharlal Nehru for independence. Again Bose was arrested and jailed for civil disobedience; this time he emerged mayor of Calcutta. During the mid-1930s Bose traveled in Europe for his health, visiting Indian students and European politicians, including Hitler in 1936. He observed party organization and saw communism and fascism in action.

By 1938 Bose had become a leader of national stature and agreed to accept nomination as Congress president. He stood for unqualified *swaraj* (independence), including the use of force against the British. This meant a confrontation with Mohandas Gandhi, who in fact opposed Bose's presidency, splitting the Congress party. Bose attempted to maintain unity, but Gandhi advised Bose to form his own cabinet. The rift also divided Bose and Nehru. Bose appeared at the 1939 Congress meeting on a stretcher. Though he was elected president again, this time differences with Gandhi led to Bose's resignation. "I am an extremist," Bose once said, and his uncompromising stand finally cut him off from the mainstream of Indian nationalism.

Bose then organized the Forward Bloc with the aim of consolidating the political left, but its main strength was in his home state, Bengal. He envisioned a strong state, a synthesis of fascism and communism.

When war erupted in Europe, Bose was again imprisoned for civil disobedience and put under house arrest to await trial. He escaped and made his way to Berlin by way of Peshawar and Afghanistan. In Europe, Bose sought help from Hitler and Mussolini for the liberation of India. He made propaganda broadcasts to England and India. He got Nazi permission to organize the Indian Legion of prisoners of war from Africa, but the legion remained basically German in training and command. Bose felt the need for stronger steps, and he turned to the Japanese embassy in Berlin, which finally made arrangements for Bose to go to Asia. Bose's impressive appearance and charisma attracted women admirers, including his Viennese secretary, whom he secretly married and by whom he had a daughter. It was also in Germany that Bose acquired his popular name, "Netaji," an equivalent of "führer."

Indian National Army

Arriving in Tokyo in May 1943, Bose attracted the attention of the Japanese high command, including Hideki Tojo, Japan's premier. The intelligence section of Japanese headquarters had already cooperated in founding an Indian National Army (INA) in Southeast Asia. Bose was flown to Singapore and became commander of the INA and head of the Free India provisional government. The INA included both Indian prisoners of war from Singapore and Indian civilians in Southeast Asia. Its strength grew to 50,000. The INA fought Allied forces in 1944 inside the borders of India at Imphal and in Burma. For Bose any means and any ally were acceptable in the struggle to liberate India. By the end of World War II none of Bose's Axis allies had helped decisively, and Bose then turned to the Soviet Union. On Aug. 18, 1945, Bose was en route to the Soviet Union in a Japanese plane when it crashed in Taipeh, burning him fatally.

Three officers of the INA were tried after the war in Delhi; the trial attracted so much popular sympathy (including statements by Nehru and Gandhi that the men were great patriots) that the British decision to withdraw from India followed. Bose indirectly and posthumously achieved his goal of Indian independence.

Further Reading

Of the numerous biographies of Bose, Hugh Toye, *The Springing Tiger: A Study of a Revolutionary* (1959), is one of the best. Also useful is Subbier Appadurai Ayer, *Unto Him a Witness* (1951). Other biographies by Indian authors are Probhash Chandra Roy, *Subhas Chandra* (1929); Uttam Chand, *When Bose Was Ziauddin* (1946); Jitendra Nath Ghosh, *Netaji Subhas Chandra: Political Philosophy of Netaji, History of Azad Hind Government, I. N. A. and International Law* (1929); Durlab Singh, *The Rebel President* (7th ed. 1946); Anthony Elenjimittam, *The Hero of Hindustan* (1947); Shri Ram Sharma, *Netaji, His Life and Work* (1948); and Dilip Kumar Roy, *Netaji, the Man: Reminiscences* (rev. ed. 1966).

Additional Sources

Patil, V. S., *Subhas Chandra Bose, his contribution to Indian nationalism*, New Delhi: Sterling Publishers, 1988.
Gordon, Leonard A., *Brothers against the Raj: a biography of Indian nationalists Sarat and Subhas Chandra Bose*, New York: Columbia University Press, 1990. □

Jacques Bénigne Bossuet

The French prelate and writer Jacques Bénigne Bossuet (1627-1704) is best known for his sermons and orations. His ecclesiastical career traversed the principal milieus and encompassed the major religious questions of his time.

Jacques Bossuet was born in Dijon on Sept. 27, 1627. He was raised by his uncle Claude, the mayor of Dijon. Bossuet was tonsured at the age of 10, a logical step for a seventh son in eventual need of a career. He distinguished himself at the Collège des Godrans in Dijon and later at the Collège de Navarre in Paris, where he received a doctorate of theology in 1652. Ordained that same year, he was a leading figure in Parisian theological circles and also frequented the fashionable salon of Madame de Rambouillet.

Bossuet might have pursued a worldly career had he not come under the influence of Vincent de Paul, whose apostolic ideal included charity to the poor, missionary zeal, and counterreformatory activity. Partially motivated by him, in 1653 Bossuet took up residence in Metz, a frontier city with a diverse religious population. Until 1659 he was immersed there in religious studies, Catholic-Protestant relations, the Jewish apostolate, and civil and ecclesiastical affairs. His *Réfutation du catéchisme de Paul Ferry* (1655; Refutation of the Catechism of Paul Ferry) exhibits the firm but nonpolemical spirit which he brought to Catholic-Protestant relations.

After his return to Paris in 1659, Bossuet devoted himself to preaching in convents and churches as well as at court. In 1662 and 1666 he preached before the King during Advent, but it was not until the Advent sermons of 1669 that this worldly milieu was completely receptive to him. Between 1655 and 1687 he pronounced his famous funeral orations; among these were the orations for Anne of Austria (1667), Henrietta of France (1669), Henrietta of England

(1670), Maria Theresa (1683), and the Prince of Condé (1687).

In 1669 Louis XIV named Bossuet bishop of Condom and in 1670 tutor of the Dauphin. Bossuet strove to provide a practical education for his charge, composing such works as the *Discours sur l'histoire universelle* (Discourse on Universal History) and the *Traité de la connaissance de Dieu et de soi-même* (Treatise on the Knowledge of God and of Oneself) for the Dauphin's use. During this period he continued to address himself to the Protestant question, publishing *L'Exposition de la doctrine catholique* (1671; Exposition of Catholic Doctrine), and exercised a moderating moral influence at court. He was elected to the Académie Française in 1671.

Named bishop of Meaux in 1681, after the completion of his pedagogical task, Bossuet devoted himself to his pastoral duties with Vincentian zeal. He played a leading role in the Assembly of the Clergy (1681), which decreed the subordination of the national churches to the pope. The *Histoire des variations des églises protestantes* (1688; History of Variations of Protestant Churches) was Bossuet's last counterreformatory work. His *Instruction sur les états d'oraison* (Instruction in States of Prayer) and *Relation sur le quiétisme* (1698; Report on Quietism) were instrumental in the condemnation of the doctrine of quietism.

Chronic kidney stones gradually forced Bossuet to give up his pastoral duties, and he died at Meaux on April 12, 1704.

Further Reading

Translated selections from Bossuet's works are available in *Bossuet: A Prose Anthology,* edited by J. Standring (1962), and in Bossuet's *Selections from Meditations on the Gospel,* translated by Lucille Corinne Franchère (1962). A biography of Bossuet in English is Ernest Edwin Reynolds, *Bossuet* (1963). Background studies include Albert Léon Guérard, *France in the Classical Age: The Life and Death of an Ideal* (1965), and G. R. R. Treasure, *Seventeenth Century France* (1966), which discusses Bossuet at length.

Additional Sources

Lanson, Gustave, *Bossuet,* New York: Arno Press, 1979.
Meyer, Jean, *Bossuet,* Paris: Plon, 1993. □

James Boswell

The Scottish biographer and diarist James Boswell (1740-1795), who wrote *The Life of Samuel Johnson, LL.D.,* published in 1791, ranks as the greatest biographer in the history of Western literature. His private papers also reveal "Bozzie" as a most distinguished diarist.

James Boswell was born in Edinburgh on Oct. 29, 1740. He was the eldest of the three sons of the advocate Alexander Boswell, Lord of Auchinleck in Ayrshire from 1749, and Euphemia Erskine Boswell. The Boswells were an old and well-connected family, having held the barony of Auchinleck since 1504 and having intermarried with the nobility.

Early Life

As a child, Boswell was delicate and suffered from some type of nervous ailment. At 13 he enrolled in the arts course at the University of Edinburgh, studying there from 1753 to 1758. Midway in his studies he suffered a serious depression and nervous illness, but when he recovered he had thrown off all signs of delicacy and attained robust health. Boswell had swarthy skin, black hair, and dark eyes; he was of average height, and he tended to plumpness. His appearance was alert and masculine, and he had an ingratiating sense of good humor.

In 1759 Boswell matriculated at the University of Glasgow, continuing to prepare himself for a legal career. In 1760 he ran away to London, where the Earl of Eglinton introduced him to his circle of friends, including Laurence Sterne. Dazzled by metropolitan culture and by women, whom Boswell now discovered were attracted to him and he to them, Boswell determined to remain permanently in the capital by obtaining a commission in the Foot Guards.

Lord Auchinleck fetched Boswell home in June 1760, thereby beginning a 3-year struggle with his son, who by

now was in open rebellion. Boswell studied law at home until he passed his trials in civil law in July 1762, spending part of his free time scribbling verse that showed little merit. Still stubborn in his London plans, he worked out a compromise with his father whereby the elder Boswell agreed to supplement his annuity and to permit him to seek a guards commission in London.

Boswell, in anticipation of this trip, began in the fall of 1762 his journal. He wrote everything down, imaginatively reconstructing events. His generousness of mind enabled him to elicit memorable conversation from those he met, and he dramatically reported it in his journal.

Boswell's second London visit lasted from November 1762 to August 1763. During this period he met both Oliver Goldsmith and John Wilkes, and on May 16, 1793, he received an unexpected introduction to Samuel Johnson, whose works he greatly admired, in a bookseller's back parlor. Boswell called on Johnson a week later, and their friendship was cemented. Soon Boswell, convinced he could not obtain a guards commission, gave in to his father's desire for him to become a lawyer. He agreed to spend the winter studying civil law at Utrecht, Holland.

Johnson made a 4-day journey to Harwich to see Boswell off to Holland. After a year of study in Utrecht, whose sole redeeming feature was his courtship of Belle de Zuylen (Zélide), Boswell embarked on a grand tour (1764-1766). In Switzerland he obtained interviews with both Jean Jacques Rousseau and Voltaire. Boswell spent 9 months sight-seeing in Italy, and in the autumn of 1765 made a 6 weeks' tour of Corsica in order to interview Pasquale Paoli, the Corsican leader who was attempting to secure the island's freedom from Genoa. Boswell and Paoli became lifelong friends, and Boswell's Corsican visit later provided the basis for his first important publication.

Career and Marriage

Boswell received admission to the faculty of advocates of the Scottish bar on July 26, 1766. For the next 17 years he successfully practiced law in Edinburgh, making as he said a better lawyer than could have been expected from one "pressed into service." Until 1784 his cherished trips to London were made only during vacations and not, to his regret, annually. In 1768 Boswell published *An Account of Corsica, the Journal of a Tour to That Island, and Memoirs of Pascal Paoli,* the first of his works to be based on his journal.

Between the time of his arrival in Edinburgh to practice law and 1769, Boswell amused himself—meantime maintaining a liaison with a divorcee, by whom he had a child—by pursuing not too earnestly a series of Scottish, English, and Irish heiresses. Eventually, on Nov. 25, 1769, he married an impoverished first cousin, Margaret Montgomerie. Boswell and his wife ultimately had five children.

During the first years of his marriage, Boswell was happy, hardworking, and chaste. In August-November 1773 he made his famous tour of the Hebrides with Dr. Johnson. That year Boswell was also elected to membership in The Club. By 1776, however, Boswell had begun to have intimations of failure—he had failed a government position,

his practice had not become more notable, and he had returned to heavy drinking and to whoring.

Between 1777 and 1783 Boswell contributed a series of 70 essays to the *London Magazine* under the title of "The Hypochondriack." His succession to Auchinleck in 1782, following his father's death, made Boswell an important man in Ayrshire and encouraged him to concentrate upon a political career. Unsuccessful in his application to several ministries, he finally pinned his hopes on William Pitt the Younger and Henry Dundas, the political manager of Scotland. His well-received pamphlet attacking Charles James Fox's East India Bill, *A Letter to the People of Scotland,* issued in 1783, did not gain him political preferment, however, and so in a second pamphlet, with the same title, published in 1785, Boswell turned against Dundas. By alienating him, Boswell blocked any hope of a political career in Scotland.

Life of Johnson

Samuel Johnson died on Dec. 13, 1784, and Boswell decided to devote sufficient time toward writing an adequate biography. He also decided to publish his journal of their Hebridean tour as its first installment. Accordingly, he went to London in the spring of 1785 to see his *Journal of a Tour to the Hebrides* through the press. This revised version of his original journal, coming from the happiest period of Boswell's life and recording 101 days spent with Johnson, probably excels all the other parts of Boswell's journal. The book achieved a great success, but it also provoked the charge of personal fatuity that has attached to Boswell's name since. Critics then as well as now could not understand how Boswell could record his own vanities and weaknesses with the objectivity of an historian.

Disliking the narrow provincialism of Scotland more and more, Boswell determined to transfer to the English bar. He was called to the Inner Temple on Feb. 9, 1786, and moved his family to London (late 1788). Thereafter he had almost no legal practice, and his principal activity became the writing of his *Life of Johnson.* His wife's death on June 4, 1789, came as a severe blow. His failure as a lawyer and as a political aspirant; his quarrel with the Earl of Lonsdale, which forced him to resign the recordership of Carlisle in 1790; his straitened financial circumstances; and his encumbrance with debts caused by the maintenance and education of his five children—all these furnished a somber backdrop to his labors of writing, revising, and completing the greatest of all biographies.

The Life of Samuel Johnson, LL.D was published on May 16, 1791, in a two-volume quarto edition of about 1,750 copies to immediate success and to critical acclaim for the work and derision for its author. Boswell enjoyed his fame, but he still wished for "creditable employment." His last years were prevailingly unhappy, and he became a heavy drinker. Boswell saw the second edition of his *Life* through the press in July 1793 and was overseeing the third edition when he died in London after a sudden illness on May 19, 1795.

His Personality

Boswell appeared to his contemporaries as an intelligent, cultured, and congenial man, distinguished by the generosity of his spirit. Pride in his family and a desire for advancement were his ruling passions, but of almost equal importance were his social adaptability, good nature, passion for publicity, and compulsion to record all his activities. Boswell's frankness about his habits has led to an exaggerated emphasis on his instability of character, particularly on his drinking and whoring. The Calvinist instruction he had received as a child in the "last things" and the painfully vivid images of hell fixed in his mind when he was 12 years old warred all his life with his natural impulses and produced recurrent attacks of guilt and depression.

Literary Technique

Boswell was a writer of genius, particularly in his finest type of writing—the record of what he had observed. His three main works-the "Journal" section of his *Account of Corsica,* the *Tour to the Hebrides,* and the *Life of Johnson* — were all based on notes or journals written shortly after the events they describe. Long practice, however, enabled Boswell years later to take condensed notes and to expand them into a detailed scene.

The main characteristics of Boswell's works are accuracy, a sense of the dramatic, and an eye for significant details. In his *Life* Boswell skillfully dramatized many scenes, building up his effects gradually. The structure of the biography, although ostensibly that of year-by-year arrangement, actually achieves unity through its recurrent topics—religion, government, and death—and through the adept playing off of subordinate figures—Edmund Burke, Oliver Goldsmith, and Boswell himself—against Johnson. This latter technique projects Johnson into the spotlight as though he were the main character in a novel, one made up of a series of interconnected dramas in which Boswell has arranged all figures for maximum effect.

Further Reading

The standard scholarly edition of the *Life of Johnson* is that edited by George Birbeck Hill and revised and enlarged by L. F. Powell, volume 5 of which contains the standard scholarly edition of *Journal of a Tour to the Hebrides* (6 vols., 1934-1964). Boswell's private papers, rediscovered in the 1920s, were edited by Geoffrey Scott and Frederick A. Pottle, *Private Papers of James Boswell from Malahide Castle* (18 vols., 1928-1934; index, 1937).

The definitive biography, covering Boswell's early career, is Frederick A. Pottle, *James Boswell: The Earlier Years, 1740-1795* (1966), which supersedes W. Keith Leask, *Boswell* (1897). Other biographical sources include Chauncey Brewster Tinker, *Young Boswell* (1922), and Dominic Bevan Wyndham Lewis, *The Hooded Hawk: or, The Case of Mr. Boswell* (1946; republished as *The Hooded Hawk: James Boswell* 1952). The *Yale Editions of the Private Papers of James Boswell,* edited by Frederick A. Pottle and others, will constitute a virtual autobiography. To date, eight volumes in this series have been issued: *Boswell's London Journal, 1762-1763,* edited by Pottle (1951); *Boswell in Holland, 1763-1764* edited by Pottle (1952); *Boswell on the Grand Tour: Germany and Switzerland, 1764,* edited by Pottle (1953); *Boswell on the Grand Tour: Italy, Corsica, and France, 1765-1766,* edited by Frank Brady and Pottle (1955); *Boswell in Search of a Wife, 1766-1769,* edited by Brady and Pottle (1956); *Boswell for the Defence, 1769-1774,* edited by William K. Wimsatt, Jr., and Pottle (1962); *Boswell's Journal of a Tour of the Hebrides with Samuel Johnson* edited by Pottle (1962); and *Boswell: The Ominous Years,* edited by Charles Ryskamp and Pottle (1963).

Frederick A. Pottle, *The Literary Career of James Boswell, Esq.* (1929), remains the standard bibliographical work.

Critical studies of note include Geoffrey Scott, *The Making of the Life of Johnson,* volume 6 of *Private Papers of James Boswell from Malahide Castle,* already mentioned; Bertrand H. Bronson, "Boswell's Boswell," in *Johnson and Boswell: Three Essays* (1945); F. A. Pottle, "The Power of Memory in Boswell and Scott," in *Essays on the Eighteenth Century: Presented to David Nichol Smith* (1945); Frederick A. Pottle, "James Boswell, Journalist," in *The Age of Johnson: Essays Presented to Chauncey Brewster Tinker* (1949); Moray McLaren, *The Highland Jaunt: A Study of James Boswell and Samuel Johnson upon Their Highland and Hebridean Tour of 1773* (1955); Frank Brady, *Boswell's Political Career* (1965); and *Johnson, Boswell, and Their Circle: Essays Presented to Lawrence Fitzroy Powell* (1965).

Additional Sources

Finlayson, Iain, *The moth and the candle: a life of James Boswell,* New York: St. Martin's Press, 1984.

Brady, Frank, *James Boswell, the later years, 1769-1795,* New York: McGraw-Hill, 1984.

Pottle, Frederick Albert, *James Boswell, the earlier years, 1740-1769,* New York: McGraw-Hill, 1985.

Daiches, David, *James Boswell and his world,* New York: Scribner, 1976.

Boswell, James, *Boswell, Laird of Auchinleck, 1778-1782,* New York: McGraw-Hill, 1977. □

Louis Botha

The South African soldier and statesman Louis Botha (1862-1919), one of the most important Boer leaders, helped to establish the Union of South Africa and became its first prime minister.

Conflict had featured prominently in the relations between black and white on the one hand and Boer and Briton on the other during the greater part of the 19th century. In this setting the Boer had often been in danger of being crushed between the numerical superiority of the Africans and the economic, cultural, and military power of the British. Partly as a result, the Boer developed a nationalism whose moods ranged from a fierce pride in all things Afrikaans to distrust and, sometimes, hatred of the outsider. Considerations of security for the Afrikaner influenced the attitude of Louis Botha to the Africans, the British, and the nationalists in his community.

Botha was born into a farming family of Voortrekker (pioneer) and Irish stock near Greytown in Natal on Sept. 27, 1862. The turbulence of the times and the paucity of schools made higher education a luxury many farmers could not give their children. Botha grew up with little formal schooling. His family moved to the Orange Free State, where young Botha established contacts with the Zulus which were to change the course of his life.

Military Career

Before King Cetshwayo of the Zulus died, he had indicated that his son, Dinuzulu, would succeed him. Prince Zibebu's challenge to the young monarch's authority resulted in civil war. In 1884 Botha joined the commando unit sent by the Boers to fight by Dinuzulu's side. The rebels were crushed, and the Boers acquired 3,000,000 acres of Zulu territory as payment for their help. A member of the surveying team, Botha was instrumental in transforming this land into the New Republic, which became a part of the South African (Transvaal) Republic when the British annexed Zululand in 1887. The union with the Transvaal led to Botha's election to the Volksraad (parliament).

In the Anglo-Boer war (1899-1902) Botha's genius as a military strategist came to the fore. A field cornet when hostilities commenced, Botha was appointed aide-de-camp to Gen. Lucas Meyer, who commanded the Boer forces in northern Natal. Meyer's task was to secure the southern borders of the republic. Botha fought in the battles around Dundee (1899), where his resourcefulness first received attention. Meyer fell ill during the fighting near the besieged British city of Ladysmith—the gateway to the Transvaal and the Orange Free State—and Botha assumed command.

Sir Redvers Buller was coming up from the coast to relieve Ladysmith. Botha met him near Colenso and wrought havoc on the British forces. Buller regrouped his army, Botha withdrew during the night, and Buller bombarded empty trenches. Botha again mauled the British on Spion Kop. But the eventual relief of Ladysmith in 1900 was a bitter blow to the Boers.

Fortune was against the Boers. Their communications were poor, and discipline was at a low ebb. In February 1900 the commander in chief of the Boer forces, Gen. Petrus Jacobus Joubert, appointed Botha his deputy. After Joubert died in Pretoria on March 21, President Paul Kruger asked Botha to assume provisional command of all the Boer forces with the rank of acting commandant.

Botha did not have much of an army to lead. The British were converging on the Transvaal, and demoralization had developed among some of the Boers. He organized a crack force and was able within a few months to put it on the field. It was this army which was later to make him the hero of Bakenlaagte. The Boers continued to lose ground, and by June 4 Botha was forced to send a letter to Lord Roberts, the British commander, requesting an armistice to discuss the capitulation of Pretoria, the capital. Roberts could consider unconditional surrender only, and by September Pretoria had fallen.

For Botha and the Boers, however, the war was not over. Roberts's rejection of the armistice offer had transformed it into a people's war. The front line was wherever there were Boer men, women, and children. The British retaliated by burning farms suspected of harboring saboteurs. Concentration camps were built to restrict the rebels.

A second attempt to end hostilities followed. Botha met the British in Middelburg in March 1901. Negotiations broke down when the Boers insisted on the retention of their independence and wanted an amnesty for their followers. In September, Kitchener announced that the Boers who did not surrender would be banished permanently and that the cost of maintaining their families would be charged against their property. Botha replied to this with increased guerrilla activity.

Botha tried once more to find a way to peace, and the treaty of Vereeniging was signed with the British on May 31, 1902. Its terms displeased the Boers, and Botha joined a delegation to England to plead for modification. Failing in this mission, they returned to South Africa, determined to extort maximum advantage from the Vereeniging settlement.

World War I

The wounds of the war had not healed when World War I broke out. Botha was convinced that it was in South Africa's interest to fight with Britain. He persuaded Parliament to approve his declaration of war against Germany and led the army which marched into South-West Africa. The German governor, Dr. Theodor Seitz, surrendered near Tsumeb on July 9, 1915. Botha imposed provisional military rule over the territory and then returned to Pretoria to start preparations for the expeditionary forces he was to send to Tanganyika and Europe. The British asked him to sit on the

War Cabinet, and in 1919 he was at Versailles, pleading for more humane treatment of the Germans.

The Statesman

In 1905 Botha and Jan Christiaan Smuts founded a Boer party, Het Volk (The People), which stood for conciliation and cooperation with the British. The Transvaal was granted responsible government in 1907, and on May 31, 1910, the Union of South Africa came into being, with Gen. Botha heading its first government. Among the problems he had to face were the rise of Afrikaner nationalism, the segregation of the Africans, discontented Indian labor, and restive white workers.

Botha's Boer critics were offended by his conciliation with the English, charged that cooperation served English ends at the expense of Afrikaner cultural interests, and demanded separate development for the Boers and the Britons. For Botha, their demands struck at the roots of Afrikaner security and survival. Crisis point was reached when James Hertzog insisted that the Dutch and English should be treated on a footing of real equality. Botha sympathized with Hertzog's demand but asked for his resignation, fearing that Hertzog's demand would split the nation. Hertzog refused and Botha formed a new cabinet—without Hertzog. This action widened the gulf between the Boers and the Britons and deepened the rifts in the Afrikaans community.

Like the Voortrekker leaders who had preceded him, Botha was an advocate of segregation of the races. He supported the bill that Hertzog had drafted in 1912, prohibiting the sale of land in white areas to the Africans and vice versa. This measure went through Parliament as the Natives Land Act of 1913 and created widespread ill-feeling among the Africans.

Botha's difficulties with the indentured Indian laborers transformed Mohandas K. Gandhi, a prosperous Johannesburg lawyer, into the father of nonviolent resistance. Botha also had to deal with two serious strikes by white workers in 1913 and 1914. He died in Pretoria on Aug. 27, 1919.

Further Reading

Three important biographies of Botha are Harold Spender, *General Botha: The Career and the Man* (1916; 2d ed. 1919); Lord Buxton, *General Botha* (1924); and Frans V. Engelenburg, *General Botha* (1929). Recommended for general historical background is Eric A. Walker, *A History of Southern Africa* (3d ed. 1968).

Additional Sources

Malan, Jacques, *General Louis Botha (1862-1919)*, Pretoria: National Cultural History and Open-Air Museum, 1979. □

Pieter Willem Botha

Pieter Willem Botha (born 1916) was inaugurated as the first executive state president of the Republic of South Africa in 1984 after serving for six years as

prime minister. Botha's administration was characterized by civil unrest. His policies have been assessed as essentially opportunistic, swaying from the progressive front to the radical right wing. Botha is best known for his stubbornness, a trait which earned him the nickname of The Old Crocodile.

P ieter Willem Botha, who is widely referred to by the Afrikaans pronunciation of his first two initials—"pee-vee"—was born on January 12, 1916, at "Telegraaf" farm in the Paul Roux district of the Orange Free State. In South African parlance, he is an Afrikaner, that is, a white person who speaks Afrikaans, a derivation of the Dutch language, as mother tongue. However, he is also fluent in English.

Botha's early education was at Paul Roux. Later he attended secondary school in Bethlehem before entering the University of the Orange Free State in Bloemfontein to study law. But he left the university before completing a degree in order to begin a full-time political career, a decision made when he was only 20 years old.

The rural Orange Free State was among the most Afrikaans-speaking regions of South Africa, and for many decades it was a bastion of extreme political conservatism among whites. Thus, it was not surprising that Botha affiliated in 1936 with the right-wing, ethnically-oriented National party, though at the time this was still a minority party in South African white politics. Botha was initially

appointed by the party leader D. F. Malan as a political organizer for the Nationalists in neighboring Cape Province. Later he was made responsible for national publicity during the campaign leading up to the May 1948 general election, an election which the Nationalists unexpectedly won.

In the 1948 election Botha won a seat in the House of Assembly, the lower chamber of South Africa's bicameral parliament at the time, for the George constituency in the southern Cape Province. He would hold this seat for the next 36 years, becoming the assembly's longest serving member. Also in 1948 Botha was made chief secretary of the National party in the Cape Province, a post he held for a decade. His long association with the Cape Province is said to have somewhat eroded Botha's inherited conservatism in favor of what is referred to as traditional "Cape liberalism."

In 1958 Botha was appointed deputy interior minister under Prime Minister H. F. Verwoerd. Three years later he was promoted to full minister, gaining the portfolios of community development and biracial affairs. In 1964 he was made minister of public works, and two years later defense minister. Botha held this latter position for the next 14 years and was the responsible cabinet minister at the time of the South African military's ill-fated invasion of Angola at the end of 1975. During his long tenure as defense minister, annual military expenditures increased 20-fold, and South Africa, which had been subject to an international arms embargo since 1963, became virtually self-sufficient in the manufacture of weapons. Botha also created new opportunities in the military for women and nonwhite South Africans.

Early in his years as defense minister, Botha gained a reputation for toughness, known as "kragdadigheit" in Afrikaans, as well as for efficient administration. These qualities pushed him to the fore when Prime Minister B. J. Vorster unexpectedly resigned in 1978. During this time Botha was also prominent as the Cape provincial leader of his party. Nevertheless, his elevation to the premiership on September 28, 1978, was to some degree unexpected and aided by a well-publicized scandal in the Department of Information. This fatally compromised the reputation of its minister, Connie Mulder, another serious contender for the position and then the National party's leader in the important Transvaal province. Thereafter, in a series of speeches, Botha seemed to try to direct the country into reformist paths and away from the racial "apartheid" (separation) which had been an article of faith for the National party since 1948. The new prime minister told his fellow whites that they would have to "adapt or die."

Predictably, the right wing of the National party, especially in the Transvaal, strenuously resisted this suggestion, and for some years the ensuing struggle over policy within the governing party seemed to neutralize Botha's reformist intentions. Then in 1982 elements on the right of the National party finally broke off to form the new Conservative party, shifting the political balance in favor of "reformism" among remaining Nationalists. One result of this was the new South African Constitution of 1983, which continued to exclude all South African blacks (72% of the total population) from any participation whatsoever in the central insti-

tutions of the state. But it did for the first time admit Asians and mulattos to membership in Parliament (albeit in racially segregated chambers) and the national cabinet.

Concurrent with these changes, Botha's own role was restructured with his elevation through an indirect election of the new tricameral parliament to the post of executive state president (as distinct from the previous ceremonial position of the same name). The earlier position of prime minister had been abolished. Until the middle of 1985, however, there was little to suggest that Botha's constitutional or other reforms had lessened unrest within the country's black population, unrest that had in fact continued in one form or another for nearly a decade from the time of the Soweto uprisings of 1976-1977.

Over the course of time, Botha's liberalism was increasingly perceived as political opportunism. His lack of a firm resolve caused his policies to be received with question. He moved successfully for the repeal of the oppressive passbook system which precluded free mobility within the region by blacks, but the passbooks were replaced by a racially biased ID card requirement for all citizens (black and white). Scores of political prisoners were released, and the squatting practices of blacks were legitimized, but promises to invest all blacks and mulattos with full citizenship rights remained unfulfilled. The country was wracked by heavy rioting and was further plagued by outside sanctions imposed by the international community. This dubious relationship with the country's black population was further scarred by Botha's handling of an ongoing situation with the prisoner Nelson Mandela. In May of 1986 the government backed a series of commando attacks in Zimbabwe, Botswana, Zambia, and South Africa. The attacks initiated new rioting, which left dozens of people dead and tens of thousands homeless and caused an escalation of racial tensions. By June 12 a national state of emergency was declared by the government in Pretoria. Botha's government was condemned abroad for these activities. Existing international sanctions were augmented, including new sanctions from Zimbabwe and Zambia. Nonetheless, Botha and the National party held strong. The sanctions proved only mildly effective as the price of gold, South Africa's chief export, rose sharply. Botha's transient loyalties had migrated further to the right by the time of the Parliamentary elections in March of 1988. He banned many antiapartheid organizations and sanctioned the arrest of Archbishop Desmond Tutu.

By August of 1988, however, Botha had shifted his strategy once again. He relaxed his foreign policies toward Angola, Namibia, and other African states, although his intentions were regarded with suspicion, especially by Mozambique. Anti-squatting laws were re-introduced with a vengeance.

On January 18, 1989, Botha suffered a stroke which left him partially paralyzed. He refused to resign and was subsequently ousted from office by members of his own party. Despite the party's actions, he tenaciously retained the presidency amid persistent rumors of his resignation. On July 5, 1989, an historic meeting took place between Botha and Mandela. Mandela's release was not effected at that time, but the meeting was hailed as a coup and a breakthrough between the white ruling party and the black majority. Botha officially resigned from the presidency on August 14, 1989. On May 6, 1990, he resigned from the National party.

Botha has persistently refused to apologize for his role in the establishment of the apartheid system which was eventually abolished under the administration of Frederik W. deKlerk, Botha's successor. Seven years later, in 1996 and 1997, Botha was implicated in a series of bombings which had taken place in the 1980s against the African National Congress.

Regarding South Africa's international relations, Botha's leadership brought several notable breaches in the country's long standing isolation in world affairs, although he simultaneously warned of an externally based "total onslaught" against the republic. He met with President Kaunda of Zambia in 1982, and in March 1984 he signed the "Nkomati Accord" with President Samora Machel of Mozambique. This agreement sought the pacification of the two countries' long common border. Later in the same year Botha officially visited seven Western European capitals, the first South African head of government to be so received in many decades.

Botha was married to Elsie Rossouw on March 13, 1943. They have two sons and three daughters. Botha received two honorary doctor's degrees, including a degree in military science from the University of Stellenbosch in 1976.

Further Reading

There is no standard biography of P. W. Botha in English. On South African politics in general, see Leonard Thompson and Andrew Prior, *South African Politics* (1982). For a perspective on Afrikaner politics, see Heribert Adam and Hermann Giliomee, *Ethnic Power Mobilized: Can South Africa Change?* (1979). A journalist's account of P. W. Botha's June 1984 trip through Europe is found in John Scott's *Venture to the Exterior* (Port Elizabeth, 1984).

Additional Sources

The Economist, September 17, 1988; October 1, 1988; August 19, 1989.
Maclean's, January 30, 1989; November 4, 1996.
Time, May 5, 1986; June 2, 1986; August 18, 1986; October 5 1987; July 24, 1989. □

Walther Bothe

The most outstanding contributions of the German physicist Walther Bothe (1891-1957) were the invention of the coincidence method for the study of individual atomic and nuclear processes and the discovery of a nuclear radiation later identified as neutron emission.

Walther Bothe was born on Jan. 8, 1891, in Oranienburg near Berlin. He went to the University of Berlin, where, in addition to physics and mathematics, he did considerable work in chemistry. He was a pupil of Max Planck and wrote under Planck's mentorship his doctoral dissertation on the molecular theory of refraction, reflection, dispersion, and extinction.

Understanding the Compton Effect

After serving as an officer in World War I, Bothe returned to Berlin, where he started research with the rank of *Regierungsrat* (government counselor) at the Physikalisch-Technische Reichsanstalt, the German equivalent of the National Bureau of Standards in Washington, D.C. His immediate superior was Hans Geiger, director of the laboratory of radioactivity and inventor of the Geiger counter. Bothe's first research in Geiger's laboratory concerned the single and multiple scattering of electrons, for which he developed comprehensive mathematical formulas.

The most crucial contribution of Bothe to the understanding of the Compton effect was made in collaboration with Geiger. Their work was based on the coincidence method developed by Bothe for the use of two or more Geiger counters. When a coincidence circuit of Geiger counters was coupled with a cloud chamber, it became possible to ascertain the time parameters of the ionization paths visible in the cloud chamber. This represented an important advance, and Bothe and Geiger used it to good advantage in the debate that ensued in the wake of the discovery of the Compton effect.

Neutron Emissions

In 1925 Geiger accepted an invitation to the University of Kiel, and Bothe succeeded him as director of the laboratory of radioactivity at the Reichsanstalt. Four years later Bothe provided further evidence of the enormous potentialities of his coincidence method. This time it did not consist in establishing the simultaneous occurrence of two phenomena but in the follow-up of the motion of one single particle amid a great number of simultaneous ionization effects. On such a basis Bothe demonstrated that the hard component of cosmic rays was not gamma radiation but a stream of particles, such as protons and light nuclei.

Simultaneously, Bothe began studying the bombardment of light elements by alpha particles. He found that when boron was hit by alpha particles a carbon isotope was formed with the simultaneous emission of a proton. Later he observed similar results with lithium, iron, sodium, magnesium, aluminum, and beryllium. In these processes two types of radiation also occurred, only one of which was isotropic. The isotropic one consisted of low-energy gamma rays. Far more elusive was the other type of radiation, which Bothe and Becker investigated more closely in their experiments with beryllium exposed to alpha particles from polonium. Two years later the Joliot-Curies showed that the anisotropic radiation could produce secondary protons, but it was James Chadwick, a few weeks later, who showed that the radiation emitted from beryllium, as originally observed by Bothe, consisted of neutrons. Thus Bothe played a pivotal role in ushering in the age of nuclear energy to which the knowledge and control of neutrons are crucial.

Institute for Physics

In 1930 Bothe became professor of physics and director of the Institute of Physics at the University of Giessen. Two years later he succeeded in the same capacity the Nobel laureate P. Lenard at the University of Heidelberg. In 1934 he became director of the Institute of Physics at the Kaiser Wilhelm Institute for Medical Research in Heidelberg. He energetically set about improving the research facilities of the institute. First he installed a Van de Graaff generator, with which he produced, in collaboration with W. Gentner, the first clear evidence of nuclear isomerism in the course of work with bromium-80. His second greatest achievement at the institute was the installation of a cyclotron in 1943. It was the only one of its kind to remain operational in Germany throughout the war.

Bothe's part in the German uranium project consisted in the study of neutron diffusion, and he became the first, with a paper published in 1941, to outline the socalled transport theory of neutrons. This and Bothe's derivation of the "disadvantage factor" in connection with the measurement of neutron density represented the two chief German wartime contributions to nuclear reactor theory. Bothe also developed noteworthy ideas on the multiplication of thermal neutrons in uranium and on the effect of the splitting of uranium atoms on the efficiency of the reactor.

When the Kaiser Wilhelm Institute was taken over by the occupation powers, he assumed the directorship of the Institute of Physics at the University of Heidelberg. Later he acted as director of both institutes, but finally he confined his work to the Kaiser Wilhelm Institute, which was renamed the Institute for Physics of the Max Planck Institute for Medical Research. In 1954 he received the Nobel Prize in physics in recognition of his coincidence method, which proved an invaluable tool in atomic, cosmic-ray, and nuclear physics. He also was awarded the Max Planck Medal from the German Physical Society and the Grand Cross for Merit from the Federal Republic of Germany, and he became a knight of the Order of Merit for Science and the Arts. He died on Feb. 8, 1957.

Further Reading

The history of modern physics as the background for Bothe's work is discussed in George Gamow's often-anecdotal *Biography of Physics* (1961). J. Yarwood, *Atomic Physics* (1958), contains a well-documented and technical account of Bothe's chief scientific discoveries. Volume 3 of *Nobel Lectures: Physics, 1942-1962* (1964), published by the Nobel Foundation, includes a biography of Bothe as well as his Nobel lecture. □

Sandro Botticelli

The Italian painter Sandro Botticelli (1444-1510) was one of the major Renaissance artists in Florence, which was the center for innovative painting in fifteenth-century Europe.

Sandro Botticelli was born several generations after Donatello, Masaccio, and their associates gave Florentine art its essential direction and just before it took a great turn in the High Renaissance work of Leonardo da Vinci, Michelangelo, and others. Botticelli worked in an established, almost traditional manner at a point just before the mode was generally perceived as no longer adequate.

Vagaries of Botticelli Criticism

A certain critical tradition has looked on Botticelli as a "decadent" artist, connected with the culture embodied in Lorenzo the Magnificent, de facto ruler of the city, poet, philosopher, and sophisticate. Successful in the 1470s and 1480s, then out of fashion and forgotten at the time of his death, Botticelli was greatly acclaimed in the 19th century, especially in England by the Pre-Raphaelites, who found that he legitimized their style, which combined the sensuous and the immaterial. Of late, scholars have considered this to be a misreading of Botticelli and have stressed his Florentine concern for solidly modeled form and religious exposition. Concurrently, however, admiration for his work has declined. Recent study has also tended to reject, as without contemporary support, the picture of him as first a member of Lorenzo's intellectual circle and later a devotee of the religious reformer Girolamo Savonarola.

Early Style

Son of a tanner, trained by a master whose name is not known, Botticelli followed in his first works the current version of the Florentine style, the prime practitioner of which was Andrea del Verrocchio. This style was not much concerned with the convincing rendition of space and emphasized the human figure, with dense modeling, sharp contour, and linear rhythm. Botticelli's major early works are *Fortitude* (1470, one of seven Virtues for a merchants' assembly hall; the other six are by Piero Pollaiuolo), two tiny panels of the story of Judith and Holofernes, and *St. Sebastian* (1474). In some of these he altered the appearance of muscular energy and physical action found in Verrocchio's work in the direction of nervous fatigue and contemplative repose.

These qualities are most evident in Botticelli's best-known works, *Spring* and the *Birth of Venus,* executed for a cousin of Lorenzo the Magnificent, Lorenzo di Pierfrancesco de' Medici, for his villa. They obviously reflect the contemporary literary culture, but their precise subject matter has been much debated and has never been agreed on; they were certainly designed in consultation with a scholar, but he may have invented an allegory for the occasion which was not recorded. Since Venus has a central position in both works, it is plausible to consider the two figures of Venus as a contrasting pair. There was a literary convention in philosophical-archeological writing of the time of contrasting the spiritual and the earthly Venus,

which may well be a factor in the paintings, though not the entire theme.

Botticelli continued using this early style after 1480 (the *Birth* is perhaps as late as 1485), but meantime a new style emerged in frescoes such as *St. Augustine* (1480) in the Church of the Ognissanti, Florence; the *Annunciation* (1481) for S. Martino, Florence; and three frescoes (1481-1482) in the Sistine Chapel, Rome, executed during Botticelli's only trip away from Florence. These frescoes show a new concern with the construction of stagelike spaces and stiffer figures, also seen in a series of altarpieces of 1485 and 1489. A bow to the newly fashionable work of Domenico Ghirlandaio and of Flemish painting is implied, but the tense linearity of the figure reveals that Botticelli's art had not undergone any fundamental changes.

Mature Style

After 1490 Botticelli began to concentrate on paintings with many small figures, using the same cutting contour lines, so that the entire picture surface acquired a trembling vibrancy. Many works exhibited this new tendency, such as the *Calumny of Apelles,* a visualization of a description of a painting by an ancient Roman writer; the *Crucifixion,* with a rain of arrows descending on a view of Florence in the background, the only work by Botticelli definitely expounding Savonarola's view of the sinning city; the *Last Communion of St. Jerome,* the most intense of several works portraying physical collapse of the body; and the *Nativity,* (1501), which employed an archaic design of Fra Angelico, with a stylized cave suggesting pre-Renaissance landscapes, and an inscription referring to current prophecies of the end of the world.

In his late years Botticelli was crippled and failed to receive commissions, but he may have continued to work on his set of drawings (never finished) illustrating Dante's *Divine Comedy,* remarkable for their consistent evocation of an energized irrational space. By about 1504, when the young Raphael came to Florence to observe the new modes of Leonardo and Michelangelo, Botticelli's art must have seemed obsolete, although it had been widely imitated in the 1490s.

Further Reading

Herbert P. Horne, *Alessandro Filipepi, Commonly Called Sandro Botticelli, Painter of Florence* (1908), is a classic of biographical reconstruction. Lionello Venturi, *Botticelli* (1937), provides critical analysis. Botticelli is placed in the context of contemporary intellectual movements in Giulio Argan, *Botticelli: Biographical and Critical Study* (trans. 1957). Roberto Salvini, *All the Paintings of Botticelli* (trans., 4 vols., 1965), is up to date and reliable. □

François Boucher

The French painter François Boucher (1703-1770), a leading exponent of the eloquent and frivolous rococo tradition, was perhaps the greatest decorative

artist of the 18th century and a consummate draftsman.

François Boucher seems to have been perfectly attuned to his times, a period which had cast off the pomp and circumstance characteristic of the preceding age of Louis XIV and had replaced formality and ritual by intimacy and artificial manners. Boucher was very much bound to the whims of this frivolous society, and he painted primarily what his patrons wanted to see. It appears that their sight was best satisfied by amorous subjects, both mythological and contemporary. The painter was only too happy to supply them, creating the boudoir art for which he is so famous.

Boucher was born in Paris on Sept. 29, 1703, the son of Nicolas Boucher, a decorator who specialized in embroidery design. Recognizing his son's artistic potential, the father placed young Boucher in the studio of François Lemoyne, a decorator-painter who worked in the manner of Giovanni Battista Tiepolo. Though Boucher remained in Lemoyne's studio only a short time, he probably derived his love of delicately voluptuous forms and his brilliant color palette from the older master's penchant for mimicking the Venetian decorative painters.

Early Work

Boucher next joined the workshop of the engraver Jean François Cars, where he learned the fundamentals of this art

and also provided many illustrations for the engravers in the workshop. Among the most notable was a series of drawings for Daniel's *Histoire de France,* engraved by Baquoy. Later, Boucher was to illustrate the Molière comedies, which were engraved by his boyhood friend Laurent Cars.

The engraver Jean de Julienne entrusted Boucher with the engraving of many of Antoine Watteau's drawings for the important *Recueil Julienne.* Boucher, who never knew Watteau personally, came to know his style intimately; the indelible impression it made upon him both stylistically and iconographically is evident in Boucher's painting.

In 1723 Boucher won first prize in the Academy competition, which normally would have meant going to Rome to study as a *pensionnaire du roi.* However, since he did not enjoy the favor of the Duc d'Antin, Superintendent of the King's Buildings, Boucher was denied the trip. By 1725 he had saved enough money to go to Rome with the painter Carle Vanloo. Boucher's sojourn in Italy seems to have affected his style very little, for the great classical schools of Italian painting were incompatible with his temperament. Upon his return to Paris in 1731, he was immediately swept up in the world of opera and high fashion, a world with which he was in complete harmony. And it was his destiny to provide it with an appropriate pictorial expression.

In 1733 Boucher married Marie Jeanne Buzeau, who frequently modeled for his paintings. Two girls and a boy were born of the marriage. Juste, the son, died at a young age; both daughters, Elizabeth Victoire and Marie Emilie, married pupils of Boucher: the painters Jean Baptiste Deshays and Pierre Antoine Boudouin, both of whom predeceased their father-in-law.

Boucher was admitted as a full member to the French Academy in 1734 with the diploma piece *Rinaldo and Armida.* The painting already reflected the major sources of his style, namely, Peter Paul Rubens, Watteau, and Tiepolo and other Venetian decorative painters.

Madame de Pompadour

Boucher soon caught the attention of Madame de Pompadour, who virtually adopted him as her official painter. The artist became her friend and teacher, instructing her in drawing and etching and serving as artistic counselor for her art purchases. Boucher decorated her several residences, most notably the châteaux of Bellevue and Crécy. Thanks to the patronage of Madame de Pompadour and her brother, the Marquis de Marigny, Director of the King's Buildings, the painter soon enjoyed the favor of Louis XV. In 1755 Boucher became inspector of the Gobelins tapestry works and in the following year, succeeding Jean Baptiste Oudry, its director. It was at this time that he executed many tapestry designs and decorations for the Paris opera and public fetes; some of his tapestry cartoons for the Gobelins and Beauvais works are masterpieces in this medium. Upon the death of Carle Vanloo in 1765, Boucher, once more through the efforts of Madame de Pompadour, was appointed First Painter to the King, and that year he also became director of the French Academy. He died on May 30, 1770, in Paris.

Boucher was an extremely prolific artist and seems to have been able to turn out his pink and blue "confections" with unparalleled ease. He executed more than 1,000 paintings, at least 200 engravings, and well over 10,000 drawings in various media. Although extremely prolific, he never bored by endless repetition, so extraordinarily inventive was he in his landscapes, portraits, genre themes, and mythological and religious scenes. Boucher lived long enough to see his artistic popularity wane, for after 1760 his work was attacked by the famed Encyclopedist and art critic Denis Diderot, an early exponent of a return to the antique.

Further Reading

There are no recent studies in English of Boucher's work. Worthy of consideration, however, are Lady Emilia Francis Dilke, *French Painters of the XVIIIth Century* (1899), and Catherine M. Bearne, *A Court Painter and His Circle: François Boucher* (*1703-1770*) (1914). Of particular interest is Edmond and Jules de Goncourt, *French Eighteenth Century Painters* (3 vols., 1880-1882; abr. trans. 1948), since it was this work that rehabilitated Boucher's reputation and significance in the evolution of rococo art. R.H. Wilenski, *French Painting* (1931; rev. ed. 1949), contains a chapter on Boucher and a list of his characteristic pictures. See also S. Rocheblave, *French Painting in the XVIIIth Century* (*1937; trans. 1937*); *Arno Schönberger and Halldor Soehner, The Rococo Age: Art and Civilization of the 18th Century* (1959; trans. 1960); Ian McInnes, *Painter, King and Pompadour: François Boucher at the Court of Louis XV* (1965); and Michael Levey, *Rococo to Revolution: Major Trends in Eighteenth-Century Painting* (1966).

Additional Sources

Ananoff, Alexandre, *François Boucher,* Lausanne: La Bibliotheque des arts, 1976.

Brunel, Georges., *Boucher,* New York, N.Y.: Vendome Press, 1986. □

Dion Boucicault

The Irish-American playwright and actor Dion Boucicault (1820-1890) was a theatrical rather than a dramatic talent, more an adapter than a creator of plays. He was noted for ingenious stage effects.

Dion Boursiquot, later Boucicault, was born in Dublin on Dec. 26, 1820, a year after his mother's divorce from a wine merchant. When the budding actor dropped out of London University in 1837, he turned to the stage. His first success was *London Assurance* (1841), which imitated the earlier English comedy of manners. Because of the lack of an international copyright law, theater managers found it more profitable to adapt French plays than to gamble on untried native ones, so Boucicault became an adapter. He lived in Paris from 1844 to 1848, where he was married and shortly widowed.

In London he adapted French romantic melodrama for Charles Kean and learned from him the technique of staging sensational scenes—a knowledge that would serve him well in America. In 1853 Boucicault "eloped" with Agnes Robertson, a London star, to New York, where for many years she played leading roles in his plays. He branched out from costume melodrama to quasi-realistic and topical plays filled with sensational theatrical effects. *The Poor of New York* (1857) was based on the financial panics of 1837 and 1857. *Jessie Brown or The Relief of Lucknow* (1858) dramatized the Sepoy mutiny in India. Produced shortly before the Civil War, *The Octoroon* (1859) portrayed the love of a slave-holder for his beautiful slave. It was explosive material for Americans; yet, remarkably, the play was praised by both North and South. Though Boucicault brought Dickens's and Scott's tales to the stage, his most famous production from popular fiction was *Rip Van Winkle* (1865) for Joseph Jefferson, who continued to act the role into the 20th century.

The playwright's most lasting work, however, was with his native Irish material, notably *The Colleen Bawn* (1860), *Arrah-na-Pogue* (1864), and *The Shaughraun* (1874). Though later Irish dramatists were to disparage Boucicault, his native plays are full of comic roguery and the combination of farce and melodrama recognizable later in Synge, O'Casey, and Shaw.

In 1885 Boucicault disavowed marriage with Agnes Robertson, with whom he had lived for 32 years, and eloped with a young actress. Until his death in 1890 he lived with his wife, writing unsuccessful plays and teaching in an acting school in New York.

In 53 years in the theater Boucicault made contributions beyond his fine performances and almost 150 plays. He was the first to develop fireproof scenery; he advocated theater workshops for the training of actors; he campaigned for copyright law which would give the playwright ownership of his play. He developed the road company, which replaced local stock companies, thus improving the quality of provincial theater and making the star less important than the integrity of the play and its direction. Boucicault recognized that his plays were merely melodramatic and external, but he insisted that his first duty was to please the public, and this he did with immense success.

Further Reading

Townsend Walsh, *The Career of Dion Boucicault* (1915), is the best full-length study. Arthur H. Quinn, *A History of the American Drama from the Beginning to the Civil War* (1923; 2d ed. 1943), contains a sound review of Boucicault's plays, especially those produced in America. David Krause, ed., *The Dolmen Boucicault* (1964), provides an excellent introduction, with emphasis on the importance of the Irish plays.

Additional Sources

Fawkes, Richard, *Dion Boucicault: a biography*, London; New York: Quartet Books, 1981 1979. □

Louis Antoine de Bougainville

Louis Antoine de Bougainville (1729-1811) was a French soldier and explorer. An accomplished scholar, he was also a man of action who fought in the Seven Years War, explored the Pacific Ocean, and was the first Frenchman to circumnavigate the world.

Louis Antoine de Bougainville was born in Paris on Nov. 12, 1729, and early established a reputation as a mathematician. A friend of the *philosophe* Jean le Rond d'Alembert, Bougainville was elected to the British Royal Society in 1754 in recognition of a work on calculus. He served with distinction as aide-de-camp to Gen. Louis Joseph de Montcalm in Canada during the Seven Years War, assisting in the defense of Quebec.

After the war Bougainville—at his own expense—founded a settlement in the Falkland Islands. In 1767, however, he was ordered to surrender the colony to France's ally Spain, which had a prior claim. In return he was given charge of the first official expedition to the Pacific, where he hoped to make discoveries and find an outlet for French expansion.

Circumnavigation of the World

Aboard the frigate *Boudeuse* and accompanied by the storeship *Étoile*, Bougainville sailed from Nantes in November 1766. Rounding the Straits of Magellan, he crossed the Pacific via Tahiti, which he named New Cytheria and which he described in romantic terms. He sailed on to Samoa, which he called the Navigator Group, and to the New Hebrides, which he called the Great Cyclades. From there, moving west, he was turned away from the Australian coast about 100 miles east of Cooktown by dangerous reefs.

Bougainville then headed north through the Coral Sea, rounded New Guinea after trouble with the winds, and sailed for home, touching at the Solomons, the Moluccas, and Batavia, and reaching Saint-Malo on March 16, 1769. He thus became the first Frenchman to circumnavigate the globe, and although none of his discoveries was of major importance he gained much useful information and prestige. The lucid narrative which he published in 1771 attracted much attention and strengthened belief in the concept of the "noble savage."

Later Career

Rather than return to the army, Bougainville remained in the French navy and fought against the British in the struggle over the American colonies. The major part he played in the Battle of Chesapeake Bay in September 1781 considerably advanced the American cause. His later quarrel with the commander of the French fleet, Adm. de Grasse, however, disillusioned him with the navy, and he retired at the end of the war, returning only briefly after the outbreak of the French Revolution to command the fleet at Brest.

As a royalist, Bougainville was out of favor during the Revolutionary period and narrowly escaped execution. Napoleon had a high regard for him, making him a senator and count of the empire in 1804, besides presenting him with the Grand Cordon of the Legion of Honor. He was also elected to the Academy of Sciences and to the Board of Longitude. Bougainville died on Aug. 31, 1811.

Further Reading

An account of Bougainville's travels is in his work, *A Voyage Round the World* (trans., 2 vols., 1967). For secondary treatments see J. C. Beaglehole, *The Exploration of the Pacific* (1934; 3d ed. 1966), and John Dunmore, *French Explorers in the Pacific,* vol. 1: *The Eighteenth Century* (1965). □

Pierre Boulez

Pierre Boulez (born 1925) was the most important French musician after World War II. His activities as composer, conductor, and lecturist made him the uncontested leader of music in the second half of the century.

Pierre Boulez was born in Montbrison and attended a technical school, majoring in mathematics. Immediately after the war he went to Paris to study composition with Olivier Messiaen. Boulez, always a man of strong opinions, led a protest against Igor Stravinsky's neoclassic music and was one of the first French composers to adopt Arnold Schoenberg's twelve-tone method of composition. He attended the Summer School for New Music in Darmstadt, Germany, and became acquainted with Karlheinz Stockhausen, Luciano Berio, and other young avant-garde composers who were to create musical styles for the next two decades.

In time Boulez outgrew the strict Schoenberg dogma, and on the death of the founder of the Viennese school, Boulez published an obituary that created quite a stir. Entitled "Schoenberg Is Dead," it was fashioned after the French proclamation on the death of their kings, "The King is dead; long live the King." The new king in Boulez's view was Anton Webern, whose music is structurally purer than Schoenberg's and has fewer connections with 19th-century music.

Activity as Composer

Following cues in some of Webern's compositions, Boulez became one of the creators of the ideal of "totally serialized" music. This musical style includes a serial pattern not only for the notes, but also for durations, dynamics, and attacks. His *Structures* (1951) for two pianos was one of the first pieces in this style, which was to become one of the dominant styles of the next decade.

Soon after the creation of serialized music, Boulez was in the vanguard of another radical musical style, called aleatoric, or "chance," music. In this kind of music certain elements are left up to the performer: the order of the notes, their duration, and, indeed, even the notes themselves. Boulez's Third Sonata for piano is so intricate that it is printed in several colors of ink, each representing different "routes" that the performer can follow. In aleatoric music no two performances are ever exactly alike, because there are so many alternatives from which the performer can choose.

Boulez's *Le Marteau sans maître* (1952-1954) is a setting of three poems by René Char, a surrealist poet, for alto voice and six instruments. Although structural devices associated with serial music are used in the piece, its outstanding characteristic is its luscious sound. The low register of the flute and the viola carry many of the melodies, surrounded by the ever-present shimmer of the vibraphone, xylorimba, and guitar. Two other works for voice and a small group of instruments are *Le Soleil des eaux* (1957) and *Improvisations sur Mallarmé* (1958).

The later compositions of Boulez show an interest in stereophonic effects gained through the use of spatially divided orchestral groups. His *Poésie pour pouvoir* (1958) calls for three orchestras and two conductors, a tape recording of a poem that has been subjected to all manner of distortion so that the words are incomprehensible, and recorded electronic sounds. *Pli selon pli* (1964) and *Figures doubles prismes* (1964) are also huge sound montages.

Activity as a Conductor

For several years beginning in the late 1940's, Boulez was the musical director of the Théâtre de France; and in an extension of that post he organized a series of concerts of avant-garde music in Paris, the Domaine Musica, in 1954. Further opportunities to conduct followed, particularly in Germany, but also in England and the United States. His conducting career gained further prominence in 1970, when he was engaged as Leonard Bernstein's successor as musical director of the New York Philharmonic Orchestra, as well as conductor of London's BBC orchestra.

Boulez left the Philharmonic in 1976 to form an experimental music research center, IRCAM, *Institut de Recherche et Coordination Acoustique/Musique* (Institute for Research of Coordination between Acoustics and Music) in Paris, France. Critical reviews of the first creation from the institute, *Répons* (Response), which toured the United States in 1986, were mixed. The success of IRCAM itself has also received cautionary praise. Although most critics applaud the intentions of bringing the best musicians together and providing them with complete freedom, the results have had little impact on the world of music.

Boulez answered those critical of IRCAM and the intentions of the institute in an interview with Dennis Polkow in *The Instrumentalist,* "The problem is that people interested in the new piece will not be attracted to the horses, and people brought in by the horses will not be interested in the new piece." Boulez went on to express his desire as a musician to disturb the listener: "If we don't disturb, we do not grow. If we have nothing absolutely new, we are only recreating the past, which is not very interesting and, in fact, is very dangerous. As difficult as it may be to grasp, all old music was once new music."

Boulez continued to serve as guest conductor for the Chicago Symphony, the Cleveland Orchestra, and the Vienna Philharmonic while creating at IRCAM. One of Boulez's experiments with modern music was collaborating with rock musician Frank Zappa. Although Boulez achieved his greatest successes as a composer early in his career, his successes as a conductor and experimentalist have assured his place as one of the signature artists of the second half of the twentieth century.

Further Reading

Dennis Polkow interviewed Boulez, published as "The Paradox of Pierre Boulez," in *The Instrumentalist,* June 1987, and David Schiff provides an overview of the career of Boulez in *The Atlantic Monthly ,* September 1995. Two biographies are also available: Peyser, Joan, *Boulez,* Schirmer Books, 1976, and Vermeil, Jean, *Conversations with Boulez: Thoughts on Conducting,* translated by Camille Naish, Timber Press, 1996. □

Houari Boumediene

Houari Boumediene (1932-1978) was an Algerian revolutionary and military leader who won power by a military coup and led Algeria during a turbulent period after nearly 8 years of war.

Houari Boumediene was born on Aug. 23, 1932, into a poor peasant family in Clauzel near Guelma in eastern Algeria. His real name was Mohammed Ben Brahim Bou Kharouba, but in 1957 he adopted the name he later used as a nom de guerre. He derived it from the names of two western Algerian patron saints venerated by the population of Tlemcen and Oran, whom he helped organize for the revolutionary war.

Until the age of 14, Boumediene attended French and Koranic schools in Guelma, then went on to a conservative Moslem religious school in Constantine. When the French called him to serve in the colonial army in 1952, he fled to Tunis and then moved to Cairo, where he studied at al-Azhar University. His early formation and the years spent in the Middle East provided him with a solid Arabic background rarely to be found in other Algerians.

He discontinued his studies when the Algerian revolution broke out in November 1954 and trained as a commando at a military camp near Cairo. Passing through Morocco, he joined the underground resistance in western Algeria. In 1956 Boumediene became the military assistant of Abdelhafid Boussef, the revolutionary chief of Oran Province. After reaching the rank of colonel, Boumediene replaced him in October 1957. In September 1958 Boumediene was promoted to coordinator of military operations and head of the general staff in the west. In February 1960, probably on Boussef's recommendation, he became the head of a strengthened army general staff and made Gardimaou, Tunisia, his headquarters.

From that point on, Boumediene turned his attention to organizing a modern standing army in Tunisia and Morocco, indoctrinating his troops in revolutionary principles and the importance of Islam and demanding total loyalty from them. His success worried civilian leaders of the revolution, and in May 1962 at Tripoli differences between civilians and officers broke out into the open. Backed by the frontier army and aided by Ahmed Ben Bella, Boumediene decided to take over power. On June 30 the provisional government revoked Boumediene's command, but the majority of the military supported their chief, who, together with Ben Bella and a group centered in Tlemcen, marched on Algiers and crushed their opponents.

In the first Ben Bella government, formed Sept. 28, 1962, Boumediene served as the minister of national defense and became first vice president on May 17, 1963. In these posts he consolidated his hold over the army. Gradually Boumediene became disillusioned with Ben Bella's moves toward a Castro-styled Algeria and deplored government inefficiency. As Ben Bella succeeded in strengthening the party and labor unions, army officers feared that their influence on decisions would decline. Boumediene, in a series of well-planned maneuvers during the night of June 18/19, 1965, led the coup which brought him to power.

A Strong Personality

Boumediene had none of the charisma which his predecessor possessed, but gradually, as success marked his regime, this gaunt, red-haired ascetic developed into a self-confident head of state and gained popularity. Basically a moralist, he prided himself on his simple tastes and austerity. He was quiet and reserved, yet passionate when calling for sacrifice, discipline, and purity from his fellow Algerians.

In public he seldom smiled, spoke infrequently, and appeared dispassionate. Because of his authoritarian temperament, he picked the men he trusted and gave them his confidence, often disregarding the advice of others. Benevolent in his dictatorship, he understood the necessity of strengthening the country's institutions. Besides holding elections for a series of regional assemblies, he began to forge a solid administration and state institutions.

Once he assumed the presidency, he established plans for Algerian development and adhered to his programs. Benefiting from mounting oil and natural gas export revenues and hoping to exploit large deposits of iron ore, he supported technocrats in his government who developed a national petroleum industry. Then he embarked on a program of industrial diversification, earmarking nearly half of the 4-year (1970-1973) development investments (set at $5 billion) for industrialization. In a typically quiet manner he forced Algerians to participate in converting their country into one of the stronger powers of the "third world."

Recognizing the need for a positive relationship with the United States, Boumediene had Algeria exchange ambassadors with the U.S. in 1974 (the first time in seven years). In 1976, in another effort to improve global relationships, Algerians approved a constitution and held national elections to choose a president. Voters overwhelmingly elected Boumediene. He continued to focus on the industralization of Algeria as a major Arab leader until his death in 1978.

At the time of his death, Boumediene had ruled Algeria for 13 of its 16 years of independence. Although he was responsible for developing the oil and gas industries in Algeria, most Algerians lived in poverty. His last months were spent in a coma, as a result of Waldemstrom's disease (a rare blood and bone marrow disorder).

Further Reading

The most up-to-date biography of Boumediene is in David and Marina Ottaway, *Algeria: The Politics of a Socialist Revolution* (1970). It clears up many mysteries of his past and makes earlier accounts of his life outdated. See also William B. Quandt, *Revolution and Political Leadership: Algeria 1954-1968* (1969), and *Newsweek*, January 8, 1979. □

Joseph-Henri-Napoleon Bourassa

The French-Canadian nationalist and editor Joseph-Henri-Napoleon Bourassa (1868-1952) was one of the leading political figures of Quebec, a splendid orator, and the founder and editor in chief of "Le Devoir," a leading Montreal newspaper.

Henri Bourassa was born in Montreal on Sept. 1, 1868, and educated at schools in that city and at Holy Cross College in Worcester, Mass. As a young man of 22, he was elected mayor of Montebello, a small town to which he had gone to recover his health. Six years later he won election to Parliament as a Liberal and as a follower of Wilfrid Laurier, the first French-Canadian prime minister. But before his first term in the House of Commons had run its course, Bourassa had broken with his chief.

The issue was Canadian participation in the South African War, to which Laurier had been forced reluctantly to concede by the demands of English Canadians. To Bourassa and to many other French Canadians, the Boers were a people very similar to the *Canadiens:* oppressed by the English, the Boers were a conquered people. Although Laurier maintained that sending troops to South Africa was not a precedent binding Canada to participate in every English war, to Bourassa a precedent was a precedent, and the disgruntled member of Parliament resigned his seat. Shortly thereafter his supporters returned him to Parliament in a by-election and in two general elections, in 1900 and 1904.

Nominally a Liberal, Bourassa had become wary of Laurier and wary of the English Canadians, whom he saw dominating the Prime Minister. By 1907 he had had enough and left Parliament to run for the Quebec legislature, which he, as a *Québecois,* felt should be his area of action. Soon Bourassa was the leader of a great nationalist movement in the province, an articulate spokesman for French-Canadian ideas and ideals, a defender of the *Canadien* way of life. By 1910 the nationalists could take on Laurier with some confidence, and in a crucial by-election in that year they defeated a Liberal candidate in the constituency that had once been Laurier's own. The next year, by linking with the Conservatives, Bourassa helped drive the Liberals from power nationally.

The victory turned sour, however, when the new government proved less responsive than the old, and Bourassa was soon thundering at the Tories from his organ *Le Devoir*. The events of World War I drove Laurier and Bourassa together once more, and in 1917 their efforts to oppose conscription foundered.

After the war Bourassa was something of a spent force, increasingly out of touch with thinking in his province. In 1925, 1926, and 1930 he was a successful Independent candidate for Parliament, and during World War II he was a frequent performer on nationalist platforms. When he died in Outremont on Aug. 31, 1952, at the age of 83, he was the grand old man of *Canadien* nationalism, but it had been 35 years since he had been a power in the land.

Further Reading

The only full-length biography of Bourassa is in French. Joseph Levitt in *Henri Bourassa and the Golden Calf* (1969) examines the social program of the Quebec nationalists, and Ramsay Cook in *Canada and the French-Canadian Question* (1966) discusses Bourassa at some length. See also Casey Murrow, *Henri Bourassa and French-Canadian Nationalism: Opposition to Empire* (1968).

Additional Sources

Levitt, Joseph., *Henri Bourassa: Catholic critic*, Ottawa: Canadian Historical Association, 1976. □

Robert Bourassa

Robert Bourassa (1933-1996) was Premier of the province of Quebec for two terms, 1970-1976 and 1985-1993. Bourassa's support for both nationalism and federalism made him an ambiguous leader. He coined the phrase *distinct society* to specifically identify Quebec's French bourgeois citizenry.

Robert Bourassa was born on July 14, 1933, to a lower middle-class family in Montreal's east end. His father, a federal civil servant, worked for the Montreal port authorities. From the age of 12, Bourassa knew he wanted to be a politician. He confided to a classmate, Jacques Godbout (now a well-known author and film director), that "one day, I'll be premier of Quebec." Bourassa served as premier of Quebec from 1970-76 and also from 1985-93. He died of cancer at age 63 on October 2, 1996, after battling the disease for six years.

Bourassa graduated from Quebec's prestigious Jesuit college, Jean-de-Brébeuf, in 1953. He earned his law degree, along with the Governor General's medal, from the University of Montreal (1956). A Royal Society of Canada scholarship led to a Master of Laws (LLM) in political economy from Oxford University (1959) and a Ford Foundation Scholarship from Harvard (1960) enabled him to earn a Masters degree in public finance and financial law. From 1960-63, Bourassa worked as an economic advisor and fiscal advisor to the Federal Ministry of Revenue and taught economics at the University of Ottawa.

Bourassa married Andrée Simard, daughter of the wealthy Simard shipbuilding family, in 1958. The marriage cemented his ties with the Liberal party and gave him crucial contacts in the business community. The Bourassa's had two children, a son and a daughter.

Bourassa served as secretary and director of research for the Quebec Royal Commission of Inquiry on Fiscal Policy from 1964-65. During this time he gained confidence and encouragement from Premier Jean Lesage and was elected as the Liberal member for the Mercier riding. He returned to Ottawa as advisor to the Ministry of Finance from 1965-66.

As a novice member of the Quebec National Assembly, Bourassa struggled in the wake of the Liberal party's 1966 electoral defeat to convince René Lévesque not to leave the party. Bourassa, who believed that Quebec should be independent, was convinced that effective political independence for Quebec could only be achieved through monetary and fiscal independence. However, Lévesque left the Liberal party in 1968 to become the founding leader of the Parti Québécois (PQ). Lévesque's coalition movement dedicated itself to achieving political independence for Quebec while continuing economic association with the rest of Canada. Bourassa and Lévesque remained political rivals for the rest of their careers.

The Liberal party, using the theme "Quebec au Travail," won the 1970 provincial election and Bourassa became Quebec's youngest premier. After only six months in office, Bourassa faced a major crisis when the Front du Libération du Québec (FLQ) terrorists kidnapped the British trade commissioner, James Richard Cross, and the minister of immigration and labour, Pierre Laporte. The FLQ cited the government's refusal to negotiate release of FLQ members who had been jailed for acts of terrorism as the reason for the kidnappings. Premier Bourassa called upon the federal government's Prime Minister, Pierre Trudeau, to declare a state of apprehended insurrection and to invoke the War Measures Act. In response to the government's sending in military forces, the terrorists murdered Pierre Laporte. By the end of the October Crisis, the FLQ terrorists had been arrested and deported. Both the Bourassa and Trudeau governments suffered considerable political damage when it became known that nearly four hundred alleged separatists had been jailed by the Quebec provincial police without charges ever being made.

Bourassa's well-known and long-standing ambiguity between nationalism and federalism and between cultural/social sovereignty and economic feudalism surfaced during his first administration. When the Victoria Charter came up for ratification in 1971, Bourassa, in response to pressure from the Québécois neo-nationalists, refused to allow the Quebec government to ratify the charter. (The Victoria Charter entailed the patriation of the 1867 British North American Act, a Charter of Rights and Freedoms, and an amending formula that granted Quebec a veto over all future constitutional reforms. However, it did not entail any additional distribution of powers. The PQ and other francophones considered Quebec's independence in areas of immigration and communications essential for their "distinct society" and were staunchly opposed to ratification of the Charter.) Constitutional wrangling grew increasingly intense and bitter over the next two decades.

Bourassa's main achievements during his first two administrations resulted from his social, judicial, and economic policies. His government joined the national medicare plan and turned the provincial health and welfare system into the most progressive in North America. An Office of Consumer Protection, a Council on the Status of Women, and a Charter of Human Rights and Freedoms were created. Low-income groups were given access to a system of legal aid. The development of hydroelectric power along the rivers running into northwestern Quebec's James Bay provided economic growth for the entire province. Bourassa's achievements were rewarded by an overwhelming victory in the 1973 election with the Liberal party winning 102 of 110 seats.

Despite these achievements, the Bourassa government soon found itself facing a series of crises. Critics pointed to questionable patronage practices including support for government services and contracts which benefited friends of the Liberal party, mishandling of negotiations with militant, nationalistic public and para-public union centrals, massive cost overruns and scandals associated with the Montreal Olympics of 1976, and legislation which made French the official language of Quebec and streamed all immigrant children into French-language schools (Bill 22). When Bourassa called for an election in November of 1976, the Liberal party was out-maneuvered by the PQ. Consequently, Bourassa lost his seat in the Mercier riding and his party was reduced to 26 seats.

Within weeks, Bourassa resigned as leader of the Liberal party. He returned to teaching (Institut d'études européennes de Bruxells, Institut européen d'administration des affaires de Fontaineau, Johns Hopkins University in Baltimore, and Laval University in Quebec City) and made speeches on the economy, the flaws of sovereignty-association, and the European economic and political community. He contended that Quebec had all the powers it required under the federal system to ensure "the pursuit of social progress, economic development and the cultural affirmation of Quebecers."

When Claude Ryan, Bourassa's successor in the Liberal party, lost the 1981 provincial election to PQ's René Lévesque, he resigned as leader of the Liberal party. This opened the door for Bourassa's return. He returned to politics as a more confident, mature leader, believing that his "most serious mistake in the 1970's was to have been too compromising" with his adversaries.

Indeed, Bourassa's timing could not have been better. The economy was just emerging from a very serious recession and voters related well to Bourassa's job-creating megaprojects. His promise to seek a constitutional reconciliation with Ottawa attracted many moderate nationalists away from the politically declining PQ. The Liberal party won five by-elections in 1983 and another four in 1984. With widespread popular support behind him, Bourassa refused to seek a seat in the National Assembly. Instead, he preferred to rebuild the Liberal party and prepare for the 1985 provincial election.

The 1985 election catapulted Bourassa and the Liberal party back into power with 99 of the Assembly's 122 seats and 56 percent of the popular vote. Bourassa, defeated in his own Mercier riding but secured a membership with the St. Laurent riding, had pulled off a remarkable comeback. The Liberal party established a powerful but fragile coalition of francophone, anglophone, and allophone business interests, middle-class and upper-class professionals, the farming community, and the working class.

By early 1986, Bourassa had set forth his government's five minimum conditions for Quebec's signing the Constitution Act of 1982: explicit recognition of Quebec as a "distinct society," a provincial veto over all major constitutional changes, the entrenchment and extension of Quebec's control over immigration, severe curtailment of the national government's spending powers in areas of provincial jurisdiction, and the guarantee that Quebec could name three judges to the Supreme Court.

In 1987 Prime Minister Brian Mulroney, a long-time friend and ally of Bourassa, met with all eleven provincial premiers at Meech Lake. The purpose of the meeting was to grant unanimous approval to the 1987 Constitutional Accord, better known as the Meech Lake Accord. Working closely with Bourassa, Mulroney was at first able to gain support from all other ten premiers. After Bourassa steadfastly refused any and all proposed amendments and declared that the accord's failure would be interpreted as a rejection of Quebec, Mulroney postponed a first minister's meeting until early June. It was too late to get the unamended accord past the Manitoba legislature.

The predicted outcry of nationalist and separatist resentment in Quebec materialized immediately. However, a widespread public opposition to the Meech Lake Accord developed throughout English-speaking Canada, galvanized by Bill 178. Bourassa had promised to ease the most discriminatory aspects of Quebec's Charter of the French Language (Bill 101), but instead brought in Bill 178 which denied businesses the right to use exterior bilingual signage and severely restricted the nature and amount of interior bilingual signage. The Bill also invoked the

"Notwithstanding clause" of the national charter to prevent the legislation from being contested in the courts.

English-speaking Canadians did not like the attack on the charter or Quebec's arrogant dismissal of the Supreme Court ruling. Rather than becoming the much vaunted symbol of national reconciliation, the Meech Accord was used by nationalist extremists in both linguistic communities to propagate their respective separatist agendas for the colleague of Canada.

Even with nationalist sentiments running at an all-time high, Bourassa and the Labor party had a relatively easy 1989 re-election. Partly in response to pressure from the Parti Québécois (with Jacques Parizeau as its party leader), Bourassa created the Allaire committee and gave it a mandate to identify and define "traditional demands" to be presented after agreement was reached on the Meech Lake Accord. The Allaire Report, published in 1991, demanded the transfer of extensive federal powers just to Quebec, but the report was set aside by Bourassa at the Liberal party's policy convention in 1992.

The Parti Québécois capitalized on this situation by forcing an ailing Bourassa, who had been diagnosed with malignant melanoma in 1990, to call a 1992 referendum on Quebec's constitutional future. Bourassa endorsed the Charlottetown constitutional accord which failed. At the time of his 1976 defeat to René Lévesque, Bourassa was described by a Liberal party colleague as "the most hated man in Quebec." He resigned as premier in 1993.

Although Bourassa's early political career was marked by ambiguity, by the end of his career Bourassa had clearly established his credentials as a federalist. In one of his final speeches Bourassa declared, "I have never been able to conceive how Quebec could profit by dividing Canada into three parts."

Bourassa's only book, *Gouverner le Quibec,* was released at a press conference in August, 1995. His book, which includes a transcription of four of his lectures given at the University de Montreal, traces highlights of his political career and provides a self-analysis of his strategies and decisions as Premier of Quebec. Bourassa died from malignant melanoma, a type of cancer, in 1996 at the age of 63.

Further Reading

Additional information on Robert Bourassa can be found in Réal Bertrand, *Robert Bourassa* (Outremont, Québec: 1983); Andrew Cohen, *A Deal Undone. The Making and Breaking of the Meech Lake Accord* (Vancouver/Toronto: 1990); Graham Fraser, *PQ, René Lévesque and the Parti Québécois in Power* (Toronto: 1989); Kenneth McRoberts, *Quebec. Social Change and Political Crisis,* third edition (Toronto: 1988); and Herbert Quinn, "Political Resurrection in Quebec: The re-election of Robert Bourassa as Liberal Leader," in *Dalhousie Review* (Spring 1984). *Maclean's Magazine* (Sept. 28, 1992) has a strong rebuttal of Quebec's "distinct society" claim written by former Prime Minister Pierre Trudeau. □

Emile-Antoine Bourdelle

The French sculptor Emile-Antoine Bourdelle (1861-1929) was a pupil of Auguste Rodin and worked primarily in bronze and marble. He sought to restore monumentality to sculpture through an eclectic borrowing from both ancient Greek and medieval sculpture. Concerned with the public function of sculpture, Bourdelle reintroduced sculpture to its traditional outdoor and architectural settings.

Emile-Antoine Bourdelle was born in Montauban, France, the birthplace of Ingres, on October 30, 1861. His early interest in sculpture was inspired by his carpenter-cabinetmaker father. In fact, many of Bourdelle's earliest sculptural projects were in wood. A bust of the painter Ingres, completed when Bourdelle was just 15, won him a scholarship to study at the Ecole des Beaux-Arts in the nearby city of Toulouse. While in Toulouse he studied under the sculptor Maurette and executed numerous portrait busts before leaving for Paris in 1884.

The first years in Paris brought Bourdelle some success. He won an honorable mention at the exhibition of the Salon des Artistes Francais of 1885 and a medal at the Exposition Universelle of 1889. Bourdelle enrolled in the studio of the established master Alexandre Falguière for a brief period before working first with Jules Dalou and, later, as a pupil and assistant to Auguste Rodin between the years 1893 and 1908.

In 1888 Bourdelle began his great series of portrait busts and masques of Beethoven which occupied him until his death in 1929. Bourdelle's interest in Beethoven attested to his Romantic impulses, and the heads and masques show a clear affinity to the malleable, additive quality of Rodin's sculpture.

In 1893 Bourdelle entered Rodin's studio as a practitioner. Rodin seems to have exerted a certain influence on Bourdelle's early work, and the relationship between the two men was characterized by a mutual admiration. In fact, Rodin became one of Bourdelle's earliest and most enthusiastic admirers, but Bourdelle's spirit was far too eclectic to follow the style of one master. His sculpture was soon to take its own course. Bourdelle had already begun studying the monumental sculpture of both François Rude and Jean-Baptiste Carpeaux as well as the great traditions of ancient Greek sculpture, particularly the Archaic, and medieval religious sculpture. Such an eclectic borrowing from the past accounted for the range of styles that characterized Bourdelle's sculpture—at times spirited and Romantic as in his Beethoven bronzes and, at other times, taut and severe like his *Hercules, the Archer* (1900-1907). In each case Bourdelle's bold expressive energy shows through the surface.

Bourdelle's study of the great ages of monumental sculpture led to his lifelong concern for the public function of sculpture and its relationship to an outdoor setting. In 1893 he began his studies for the *Monument to the De-*

fenders of Montauban, which commemorated the noble resistance of the people of Montauban in the Franco-Prussian War of 1870-1871. Considered his first masterpiece, the monument took eight years to finish. Elevated on a high pedestal in a public square, the figures possess at once an archaic severity and tautness combined with a powerful expressiveness that conveys the heroic struggle of a united people. Bourdelle's first masterpiece was part of a general trend in the late 19th century that favored public monuments memorializing those who lost their lives for France and the newly established Third Republic.

Bourdelle's most important commission came from Argentina in 1912. His *Monument to General Alvear* was executed between 1912 and 1923, but was not placed in the public square in Buenos Aires until 1925. This equestrian monument depicts General Alvear, a hero from the Argentinian war of independence of 1814-1815, riding atop a tall plinth flanked by four allegorical figures representing the civic virtues Strength, Victory, Liberty, and Eloquence.

The traditional bonds that linked sculpture with architecture also interested Bourdelle. In 1913 Bourdelle received another major commission to decorate the Champs Elysées theater with sculptural frieze panels depicting various aspects of the dramatic arts—Tragedy, Comedy, Dance, Music, and the Muses. All were couched in the style of Archaic Greek sculpture, but the static element of Greek sculpture, so loved by Bourdelle's contemporary Maillol, was enlivened by Bourdelle's fascination with the representation of movement and energy through the expressive use of line and straining bodies. It has even been suggested that these reliefs were inspired by the dance of Isadora Duncan. Moreover, in his panels entitled *The Muses,* Bourdelle's striding figures seem to foreshadow some of the figures seen in the paintings from Picasso's classical phase of the 1920s.

With Bourdelle's *Virgin of the Offering* (1922) one immediately detects his fascination with monumental religious sculpture. Raised on a hill above Niederbruch in Alsace, the *Virgin of the Offering* is a colossal work some 20 feet tall. Bourdelle took a sacred subject and imbued it with a nobility and grandeur rarely surpassed in sculpture.

Never one to actively pursue official honors, Bourdelle saw himself more akin to the Medieval craftsman. Nevertheless, he was honored in 1924 when he was made a commander of the Legion of Honor. Though official honors came late to Bourdelle, his influence was widespread.

Emile-Antoine Bourdelle died outside Paris at Vésinet on October 1, 1929. Two years later, in 1931, a major retrospective of his work was held in Paris. The Musée Bourdelle, where many of Bourdelle's sculptures can be seen, was opened in Paris in 1949.

Further Reading

Much information on Bourdelle can be found in museum catalogues if the reader is able to read French. No monograph on Bourdelle exists in English. Useful background sources include W. J. Strachan, *Towards Sculpture* (1976), and A. M. Hammacher, *The Evolution of Modern Sculpture* (1969). □

Léon Bourgeois

The French statesman Léon Bourgeois (1851-1925) was one of the earliest proponents of the League of Nations and winner of the Nobel Peace Prize in 1920.

Léon Bourgeois was born on May 29, 1851, in Paris. He studied law in Paris and entered the civil service in 1876. By 1887 he was prefect of police for the department of the Seine.

Bourgeois's political career began in 1888, when he represented the Marne Department in the Chamber of Deputies. He established a reputation as one of the young leaders of the Radicals in the Chamber. From 1888 to 1895 he urged a number of social and economic reforms and established an independent position that was not identified with the old Radical program. He served as a Cabinet minister in several governments before 1895.

Because of his emphasis on a specific and comprehensive program of reform as constituting the very essence of radicalism, Bourgeois gained support from the left and organized a government. On Nov. 1, 1895, he became premier. As a result of opposition in the conservative Senate against any plan of social reform, a constitutional struggle developed over the Senate's right to veto budgetary supply, and Bourgeois was forced to resign on April 21, 1896.

The program of Bourgeois's government centered on reforms specifically directed toward the underprivileged: a progressive income tax, the extension of pension plans and of social security, and insurance programs. Bourgeois and his program were not socialist, though this accusation was leveled against him many times. His government was unable to achieve any of its specific goals, but it did encourage the cause of reform and was the first government to be supported by the Socialists.

Bourgeois served as head of the French delegations to the First and Second Hague Conferences in 1899 and 1907, where, according to a colleague, he "expressed commonplace thoughts in a mellow voice." He was elected to the Senate in 1905. In 1916 and 1917 he was for a time minister of labor in Aristide Briand's wartime Cabinet. Bourgeois was president of the Senate from 1920 to 1923.

Bourgeois had been one of the original proponents of a league of nations. When the Paris Peace Conference took up the question in 1919, the French government designated him as the representative to the special committee whose task was the drafting of the Covenant of the League of Nations. When the League was in operation, he became the chief representative for France and served in both the Council and Assembly.

In 1923 Bourgeois gave up his position in the League because of illness. He died at his country estate near Épernay on Sept. 25, 1925.

Further Reading

Guy Chapman, *The Third Republic of France* (1962), includes a scholarly evaluation of Bourgeois's political influence as well as some biographical information. See also Edward Mead Earle, ed., *Modern France: Problems of the Third and Fourth Republic* (1951). H. Schück and others, *Nobel: The Man and His Prizes* (1950; 2d ed. 1962), and Mortimer Lipsky, *Quest for Peace: The Story of the Nobel Award* (1966), discuss Bourgeois's work for peace. □

Louise Bourgeois

New York artist Louise Bourgeois (born 1911) was one of the most celebrated sculptors in the period following World War II. Although the stylistic evolution of her work defies art historical categorization and her iconography is completely intimate and overtly sexual, Bourgeois' sculptures are exemplary of 20th-century artistic currents during the most controversial period of American art.

At the age of 82, Louise Bourgeois represented the United States in the prestigious 1993 Venice Biennale. Bourgeois' sculptures were on special exhibit at the Brooklyn Museum and at the Corcoran in Washington, D.C.; her prints were on exhibit at the Centre Pompidou in Paris; and a selection of her drawings were shown at the Museum of Modern Art in New York. Although this may have been a hallmark year in Bourgeois' lengthy career, her relatively quiet emergence into American mainstream art began over fifty years earlier in New York City.

Bourgeois was born in Paris on December 25, 1911, and remained in France until 1938. She was the middle child of three born to Josephine Fauriaux and Louis Bourgeois. The family ran a tapestry gallery/workshop below their Paris apartment on the boulevard Saint Germain. Throughout her education, Bourgeois worked in the family business restoring tapestries, but her parent's avocation was not her own. In 1932 she earned a baccalauréat at Lycée Fénelon in Paris where her interest in geometry, developed during her school years, enabled her to pursue an education at the Sorbonne to study mathematics and philosophy. However, her love of geometry, coupled with an interest in the arts cultivated at the tapestry gallery, led Bourgeois to the Ecole des Beaux-Arts and a career in the arts.

In pursuit of a more liberal and less rigid artistic education, Bourgeois left the school. Between 1932 and 1938 she studied with such prominent artists and philosophers as Ferdnand Léger, Roger Bissiére, and Paul Colin. She attended various ateliers, including the Académie Julian, Académie Ranson, and the Académie de la Grande-Chaumiére. Her interest in the visual arts and the international spirit of early 20th-century Paris also led her to the Louvre where she worked as a docent and cultivated her knowledge of art history at the Ecole de Louvre.

In 1938 Bourgeois married art historian Robert Gold-water and moved to New York City. Upon her arrival in New York, Bourgeois immersed herself in painting, print-making, and drawing. She enrolled at the Art Students League and fostered friendships with members of the American Abstract Artists group who were advocates of Cubism, Biomorphic Abstraction, and Surrealism in America. Bourgeois' preoccupation with the intellectual conception of line, surface, and form (principles of Analytical Cubism) became the stylistic foundation for her works on paper and canvas. Within one year she was exhibiting her work in print exhibitions at the Brooklyn Museum, the Philadelphia Print Club, the Library of Congress, and the Pennsylvania Academy of the Fine Arts.

In the 1940s Bourgeois began exhibiting her paintings in many Abstract Expressionist group shows, and in 1945 she was given her first solo exhibition at the Bertha Schaefer Gallery in New York. During this decade, while her colleagues were turning toward pure abstraction, Bourgeois embraced aspects of Surrealism and Automatism exemplified in her *Femme-Maison* series (ca. 1946-1948), and she began to develop a very personal symbolic iconography based upon the events that shaped her life in France. It was also at this time that Bourgeois began to explore the three-dimensional qualities of her designs and all but abandoned painting for sculpture. In 1949 she made her sculpture debut at the Peridot Gallery.

Bourgeois almost immediately investigated the possibilities of wood. These sculpted totem-like forms, reminiscent of a shuttle used for weaving, became symbols for her family members and a signature shape associated with Bourgeois throughout her career in the 1950s and 1960s. *Spiral Woman* (1953, New York: Robert Miller Gallery) is a six-foot wooden abstraction of the movement of a woman through space. *Blind Leading the Blind* (ca. 1947-1949, New York: private collection), a totemic composition related to the Gospels according to Matthew 15, is associated with the blind confidence in people who influenced Bourgeois' life.

Bourgeois turned from the media of wood and plaster to latex, marble, and bronze in the 1960s and 1970s. She began to sculpt landscapes exemplified by *Clamart* (1968, New York: Kolin Collection), the burial place of Bourgeois' parents and grandparents, and *Cumulus I* (1969, Paris: Musée National d'Art Moderne), a study of cloud formations. Both are studies of the calming and tranquil effects of the heavens and earth, and each reflects Bourgeois' love of repetitive conical shapes erupting through a thin layer of skin.

Concurrently, Bourgeois began to explore her sexual psyche through similar forms. Unlike her *Femme Maison* of ca. 1947 (Boston: Barbara Krakow Gallery), *Femme Maison 81* (New York: private collection) is no longer a surreal exposé of a female whose head is replaced with her home. It is a series of phallic totems growing in various directions. Her bronze 1984 *Spiral Woman* (New York: Dannheisser Collection) is a legged phallic symbol wrapped in a thick boa-like coil. *Fillette* (1968, New York: private collection), an erect uncircumcised penis, and *Fragile Goddess* (ca.

1970, New York: private collection), a headless and limbless female shape with protruding breasts and belly, are perhaps the most sexually explicit works of the artist's mature years. They relate to the aggressiveness and helplessness of the masculine female.

In 1994 she displayed *The Red Rooms* at Peter Blum's in New York. The work consists of two bedrooms representing parent and child respectively. The rooms, drenched in red and rife with symbolic furnishings, typify her highly personal themes. The Red Rooms is intended to expose moods from her childhood. Her spider drawings, *The Nest*, symbolic of the well-nurtured family, were seen in that same year at the Museum van Hedendaagse Kunst in Ghent.

Bourgeois taught for many years in the public schools in Great Neck, Long Island, as well as at Brooklyn College and the Pratt Institute. She was given a retrospective exhibition at the Museum of Modern Art in New York in 1982 and at the Rijksmuseum Kröller-Müller in Otterlo, The Netherlands, in 1991. Although Bourgeois will forever be immortalized through a Mapplethorpe portrait of the artist with *Fillette* in her arms, her oeuvre will exemplify the variety of artistic expressions among 20th-century American sculptors.

Further Reading

The most comprehensive information on the artist can be found in the catalogues *Louise Bourgeois* (accompanying her retrospective in Otterlo, 1991, and New York, 1982), Rubenstein's *American Women Sculptors* (1990), and Watson-Jones' *Contemporary American Women Sculptors* (1986). A discussion between the sculptor Alain Kirili and Bourgeois about the artist's early years and the symbolic nature of her work ("The Passion for Sculpture") was published in *Arts Magazine* (March 1989) and is particularly enlightening. Bourgeois was also an accomplished art critic, and her articles "Freud's Toys," *Artforum* (January 1990), and "Obsession (of Gaston Lachaise)," *Artforum* (April 1992) are both insightful and instructive. They reveal Bourgeois' evaluation of contemporary art in terms of sexual psychoanalysis.

Additional Sources

Bernadac, Marie-Laure, *Louise Bourgeois*, Flammarion, 1996.
Bourgeois, Louise, *Louise Bourgeois: Drawings & Observations*, University Art Museum and Pacific Film Archive University of California, 1995. □

Blessed Marguerite Bourgeoys

The French religious Blessed Marguerite Bourgeoys (1620-1700) was the founder of the Congregation of Notre Dame, the first religious community for women established in Canada.

Marguerite Bourgeoys was born on April 17, 1620, in Troyes, France, the sixth of 12 children in a pious, middle-class family of comfortable circumstances. She received an elementary education in the neighboring "little schools." In 1640 she came into contact with the Canonesses Regular of St. Augustine of the Congregation of Notre Dame, which later inspired her own foundation. This institute required solemn vows, conformed to the customary stringent regulations that confined nuns within cloister, and educated girls in boarding schools. Bourgeoys joined a pious confraternity of laywomen attached to the convent in Troyes, known as the Extern Congregation, and soon became its president.

Bourgeoys learned about Canada and its religious needs in 1653 when she met the governor of Montreal, Paul de Chomedey de Maisoneuve, during his visit to his sister who was the superior of the Troyes convent. He accepted Bourgeoys' offer of help rather than that of the nuns, whose organization and special apostolate seemed to him unsuited to rough frontier conditions and needs.

Arriving in Montreal on Nov. 16, 1653, Bourgeoys began a varied and laborious, but gratuitous social apostolate among the small French colony. In 1658 she became Montreal's first schoolmistress when she converted an abandoned stable into an elementary school. Later she started schools in and near the island of Montreal, including the city of Quebec. Several of these mission schools—eventually restricted to girls—trained Indian children; she opened a school to train older girls in household arts in 1665. She also trained and arranged marriages for the "daughters of the king," poor orphans mostly, who had been sent to the predominantly male colony by Louis XIV. Mainly to enlist collaborators in her labors, she returned to France in 1658, 1670, and 1679.

Founding of the Congregation

On her second trip Bourgeoys obtained permission from Louis XIV to establish a group of laywomen, without vows and without cloister obligations, dedicated to educational work and subject to the local bishop. She composed a religious rule for her fledgling congregation, but because of doubts about the permanence of the group and misgivings concerning novel features such as the substitution of simple for solemn vows and the permission to work outside cloister, Bishop Laval of Quebec withheld his formal approval. His successor, Bishop Saint-Vallier, also denied permission but relented in 1698, two years before the founder's death. With this formal acceptance, the Congregation of Notre Dame of Montreal became the first religious institute founded in Canada.

Among the 24 sisters who pronounced the three vows of religion on this occasion was Bourgeoys, who was henceforth known as Sister of the Blessed Sacrament. Pope Pius XII beatified Marguerite Bourgeoys in 1950. In 1982 she was canonized.

Further Reading

A biography of Marguerite Bourgeoys is by Simpson, Patricia CND, co-director of the Marguerite Bourgeoys Centre, *Marguerite Bourgeoys and Montreal, 1640-1665* (McGill-Queen's Studies in the History of Religion. Series Two (1997). □

Habib Bourguiba

Habib Bourguiba (born 1903) was president of the Tunisian Republic and played a primordial role in leading his country's nationalist struggle for independence.

Habib Bourguiba was born on Aug. 3, 1903, at Monastir into a modest family. He completed secondary school in Tunis, adhering to the Destour, or liberal constitutional, party. In 1924 he won a scholarship to study political science and law in Paris. Upon returning to Tunis, he joined the bar and in 1930 launched his political career as a Destourian militant. He founded the newspaper *Tunisian Action,* in which he defined his political goal as the development of a modernist, revolutionary, and laic nationalism.

Early Political Life

In 1934 Bourguiba founded the more radical Neo-Destour party. His dynamism so disturbed the French resident general that Bourguiba was deported to the south, where he remained for two years. He was liberated when the Popular Front government in France attempted to liberalize the colonial regime and initiated negotiations with nationalists in 1936. Talks failed to produce results, despite Bourguiba's moderation and his willingness to help reform the colonial system. His noteworthy achievement of the prewar years was the detachment of Tunisian workers from the Communist-dominated CGT and the creation of an autonomous labor union, the UGTT.

In April 1938 Bourguiba was again arrested and remained a prisoner in France until March 1943. The Axis forces liberated him and carried him off to Italy, where they tried to recruit him for their cause. However, Bourguiba declined. On the contrary, when returning to Tunisia in April 1943, he convinced Neo-Destour militants to support the Allies, hoping to win benefits from them after the war ended.

But in 1945 France returned to Tunisia as its colonial master. Bourguiba then sought external support among the Arab states and in the United States. Until 1950 he continued to hope that France would adopt a conciliatory position and accept his seven-point program designed to lead Tunisia toward internal autonomy. Instead, the French authorities in Tunis oriented reforms toward cosovereignty. For Bourguiba this was the signal for revolt.

Fight for Independence

Bourguiba carried the Tunisian case to the United Nations and simultaneously launched appeals for combat in Tunisia against French intransigence. In January 1952 he

was arrested for a third time and remained incarcerated until July 1954. In Tunisia armed terrorists organized urban guerrilla attacks against Frenchmen, while the Tunisian elite refused to form a rubber-stamp government.

In 1955 the president of the French Council, Pierre Mendès-France, pressed by the Algerian War, recognized Tunisia's right to internal autonomy. In the difficult negotiations which followed, intransigent Tunisian nationalists and French colons attacked all compromises, but Bourguiba forced his followers into line.

Conventions were signed in May 1955, and Bourguiba returned to Tunisia as a hero. In March 1956 Bourguiba profited from the sudden independence of Morocco to reopen negotiations which led on March 20, 1956, to Tunisia's independence. In April he was elected president of the Constituent Assembly and chief of the government. The Assembly proclaimed Tunisia a republic in July 1957, and in 1959 it ratified the constitution, which established a presidential regime. Bourguiba was then elected president of the republic by universal suffrage.

Development of Bourguibism

Twenty-five years of political activity and nine years of prison permitted Bourguiba to realize his goal of independence by steps. Bourguibism was the name given to his tactics and his doctrine. Tactically, he willingly employed negotiations and persuasion first, but he used force when necessary to achieve his ends. His doctrine, more pragmatic than ideological, can be reduced to four essential points: decolonization by stages, laicization, pro-West foreign policy, and measured economic planning.

Bourguiba was very attached to the Occident and interested in continuity and order. Thus, he approached the problem of decolonization with caution and diplomacy. But inevitable tensions erupted over the Algerian War and the pro-Egyptian activities of Salah Ben Youssef, the secretary general of the Neo-Destour. The crisis of Bizerte in 1961, when French soldiers killed more than a thousand Tunisians, gravely compromised relations between Paris and Tunis, as did Bourguiba's unilateral decision to nationalize lands belonging to Frenchmen in 1964. Normalization of relations between the two countries in 1969 resulted from Bourguiba's constant desire to pass from confrontation to friendship.

A Moslem, but at the same time a reformist, Bourguiba gave Tunisia a laic constitution and even encouraged the nonobservance of major religious rituals, such as the fast of Ramadan. Despite fierce resistance to these innovations, Tunisia went further than its neighbors in desacralizing politics and social life. More in tune with Western liberalism than with Arab nationalism, Bourguiba turned Tunisia toward the West. As a crusading anti-Communist, he opposed Soviet and Chinese penetration into Africa and supported the United States in Vietnam. In return, the United States offered Tunisia significant economic aid. As for planning, 1962 marked a decisive turning point in Tunisia's economy and in Bourguiba's doctrine of liberalism. Under the direction of Ahmed Ben Salah, Tunisia formed agrarian and industrial cooperatives and state-run factories. But mismanagement and internal opposition to forced collectivization of land led Bourguiba in the fall of 1969 to dismiss Ben Salah and slow down Tunisia's conversion to socialism.

In November 1969 he was reelected to a new 5-year term as president, though he turned many of his presidential duties over to his prime minister because of an onslaught of medical problems. Bourguiba sought medical treatment and rest outside of Tunisia for most of 1970 and 1971. Although he faced political challenges when he returned, Bourguiba maintained governmental control.

His health improved during 1973, and Bourguiba became a peacemaker in an Arab-Israeli conflict, a role that seemed to be short-lived when Bourguiba and Libya's Colonel Muammar el-Qaddafi discussed creating a federation between their countries in early 1974. The talks of unification lasted only a week. Later that year he was named President for Life. He ruled rather unremarkably during the remainder of the decade, surviving political and medical problems. Bourguiba remained in office almost another decade.

The End of an Era

Bourguiba celebrated his 25th year of power in 1983 amid civil and religious unrest. A decline in the economy and the rise of Islamic fundamentalism led to the problems in Tunisia. The following year was marked by rioting and killing in the streets over an 80 percent increase on food prices. These food riots, combined with a 25 percent unemployment rate and increasing tensions with other African nations, marked the beginning of decline for Bourguiba.

In 1986, Bourguiba separated from his wife, his son, and his prime minister. Bourguiba also appointed all members to the Central Committee and Politburo (those positions were usually elected). In 1987 General Zine el Abidine Ben Ali was appointed prime minister (the third man to hold that office in 22 months). Ben Ali staged a coup and deposed of the President for Life, maintaining that Bourguiba was mentally unfit.

Further Reading

An early biography of Bourguiba is in French: Roger Stephane, *La Tunisie de Bourguiba* (1958). The most definitive biography is Derek Hopwood *Habib bourguiba of Tunisia: The Tragedy of Longevity,* St. Martin's Press, 1992. Since Bourguiba's career is so closely intertwined with Tunisian nationalism and politics, see Clement Henry Moore, *Tunisia since Independence: The Dynamics of One-Party Government* (1965), Lars Rudebeck, *Party and People: A Study of Political Change in Tunisia* (1967); Jean Lacouture, *The Demigods: Charismatic Leadership in the Third World,* Knopf, 1970; and L.B. Ware, "Ben Ali's Constitutional Coup in Tunisia," *Middle East Journal,* Autumn 1988, 587-601. □

Margaret Bourke-White

American photographer Margaret Bourke-White (1904-1971) was a leader in the new field of photojournalism. As a staff photographer for FORTUNE

and LIFE magazines, she covered the major political and social issues of the 1930s and 1940s.

Born in New York City on June 14, 1904, Margaret Bourke-White was the daughter of Joseph and Minnie White. (She added "Bourke," her mother's name, after her first marriage ended). One of the original staff photographers for *LIFE* magazine, she was a pioneer in the field of photo-journalism. She photographed the leading political figures of her time: Franklin Roosevelt, Winston Churchill, Joseph Stalin, and Mahatma Gandhi. She also called attention to the suffering of unknown people, from the poor sharecroppers in America to the oppressed Black coalminers in South Africa. An adventuresome lady who loved to fly, Bourke-White was the first accredited woman war correspondent during World War II and the first woman to accompany a bombing mission.

Bourke-White first revealed her talent for photography while a student at Cornell University. Using a secondhand Ica Reflex camera with a broken lens, she sold pictures of the scenic campus to other students. After graduation she opened a studio in Cleveland, where she found the industrial landscape "a photographic paradise." Initially specializing in architectural photography, her prints of the Otis Steel factory came to the attention of *TIME* magazine publisher Henry Luce, who was planning a new publication devoted to the glamour of business.

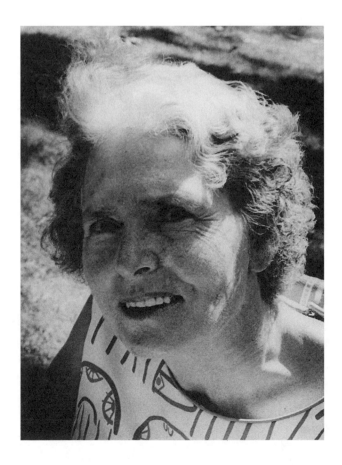

In the spring of 1929 Bourke-White accepted Luce's offer to become the first staff photographer for *FORTUNE* magazine, which made its debut in February 1930. Her subjects included the Swift meatpacking company, shoemaking, watches, glass, papermills, orchids, and banks. Excited by the drama of the machine, she made several trips to the Soviet Union and was the first photographer to seriously document its rapid industrial development. She published her work in the book *Eyes on Russia* (1931).

Bourke-White, working out of a New York City studio in the new Chrysler Building, also handled lucrative advertising accounts. In 1934, in the midst of the Depression, she earned over $35,000. But a *FORTUNE* assignment to cover the drought in the Plains states opened her eyes to human suffering and steered her away from advertising work. She began to view photography less as a purely artistic medium and increasingly as a powerful tool for informing the public. In 1936 she collaborated with Erskine Caldwell, author of *Tobacco Road,* on a photo-essay revealing social conditions in the South. The results of their efforts became her best-known book, *You Have Seen Their Faces* (1937).

In the fall of 1936 Bourke-White joined the staff of *LIFE* magazine, which popularized the photo-essay. Her picture of the Fort Peck dam in Montana adorned the cover of *LIFE's* first issue, November 11, 1936. On one of her first assignments she flew to the Arctic circle. While covering the Louisville flood in 1937 she composed her most famous single photograph, contrasting a line of Black people waiting for emergency relief with an untroubled white family in its car pictured on a billboard with a caption celebrating the American way of life.

In early 1940 Bourke-White worked briefly for the new pictorial newspaper *PM,* but by October she returned to *LIFE* as a free lance photographer. With Erskine Caldwell (to whom she was married from 1939 to 1942) she travelled across the United States and produced the book *Say Is This the U.S.A.?* In the spring of 1941 they were the only foreign journalists in the Soviet Union when the Germans invaded Russia.

During World War II Bourke-White served as an accredited war correspondent affiliated with both *LIFE* and the Air Force. She survived a torpedo attack on a ship she was taking to North Africa and accompanied the bombing mission which destroyed the German airfield of El Aouina near Tunis. She later covered the Italian campaign (recorded in the book *They Called It "Purple Heart Valley")* and was with General George Patton in spring 1945 when his troops opened the gates of the concentration camp at Buchenwald. Her photos revealed the horrors to the world.

In 1946 *LIFE* sent Bourke-White to India to cover the story of its independence. Before she was allowed to meet Mahatma Gandhi she was required to learn how to use the spinning wheel. Frustrated at the moment because of a deadline, she later reflected, "Nonviolence was Gandhi's creed, and the spinning wheel was the perfect weapon."

On a second trip to India to witness the creation of Pakistan, Bourke-White was the last journalist to see Gandhi, only a couple of hours before his assassination.

In December of 1949 she went to South Africa for five months where she recorded the cruelty of apartheid. In 1952 she went to Korea, where her pictures focused on family sorrows arising from the war. Shortly after her return from Korea she first noticed signs of Parkinson's disease, the nerve disorder which she battled for the remaining years of her life. Her autobiography, *Portrait of Myself,* was started in 1955 and completed in 1963. On August 27, 1971, Margaret Bourke-White died at her home in Darien, Connecticut. She left behind a legacy as a determined woman, an innovative visual artist, and a compassionate human observer.

Further Reading

Margaret Bourke-White wrote or co-authored 11 books. Her most famous is *You Have Seen Their Faces* (1937), with Erskine Caldwell, on social conditions in the South during the Depression. Also see her informative autobiography, *Portrait of Myself* (1963). There are two good collections of her photographs which also contain biographical information, *For the World to See: The Life of Margaret Bourke-White* by Jonathon Silverman (1983) and *The Photographs of Margaret Bourke-White,* edited by Sean Callahan (1972). □

Randolph Silliman Bourne

Randolph Silliman Bourne (1886-1918) was an American pacifist, cultural critic, and leader of the "youth movement" of the 1910s. His repudiation of official World War I attitudes inspired later pacifist dissenters.

Randolph Bourne was born on May 30, 1886, in Bloomfield, N.J. His father abandoned the family when circumstances became straitened. Randolph's hunched back and twisted features set him apart from other children, as did his academic brilliance. He was puritanic in his will to help support his mother, and following high school graduation he worked for a maker of automatic music rolls and then as a piano accompanist. His "discovery" of socialism stirred him, but at age 23, for lack of alternatives, he entered Columbia University in New York City.

At Columbia, Bourne's social and intellectual talents expanded. He shone academically and made many and varied friendships. Though then a follower of John Dewey, he was also a romantic who dreamed of a dedicated youth changing the world. Bourne distinguished himself by selling his essays to the *Atlantic Monthly* and, in 1913, publishing them in *Youth and Life;* the latter became a banner to idealists.

Columbia awarded Bourne the prestigious Gilder fellowship, which provided for an intensive tour of Europe. He met many intellectuals and observed strikes and student movements. In August 1914, following the outbreak of war, he fled Europe to make his career at home.

Bourne took up residence in Greenwich Village, New York City, which was seething with artists and revolutionary thinkers who became his friends, including John Reed and Van Wyck Brooks. He also joined the *New Republic,* just initiated by Herbert Croly. As "contributing editor," Bourne occupied an uncertain position, but his fluency and varied interests seemed to assure his future.

He plunged into an intensive life of writing and companionship. His physical deformity affected his social relations, but he surmounted it in large measure. He investigated progressive systems of education and collected his articles in *The Gary Schools* (1916) and *Education and Living* (1917). He also prepared for the American Association for International Conciliation a symposium, *Towards an Enduring Peace* (1916). Meanwhile, he issued a constant stream of essays and book reviews for the *New Republic,* the *Seven Arts,* and the *Dial,* demanding a literature concerned with beauty, the poor, and internationalism. He was not highly original, deriving basic ideas from Dewey, William James, H.M. Kallen, and others, but he added a personal element which, for his admirers, had the flavor of genius.

America's entrance into World War I challenged pacifist and socialist circles. Bourne's intellectual intransigence singled him out from most of his associates. He repudiated John Dewey, who had accepted the war and American war aims on pragmatic grounds. Bourne's stand all but closed the *New Republic* to him, as well as other publications which suffered from censorship. Several of Bourne's best-known essays, such as his analysis of the state, were unpublished in his lifetime. These revealed his new alienation from the American mainstream and foreshadowed a later criticism of American life. Bourne was stricken with bronchial pneumonia on Dec. 17, 1918, and died 5 days later. His friends published his *Untimely Papers* (1919) and *The History of a Literary Radical* (1920). Best remembered is John Dos Passos' portrait of Bourne in his novel *1919* "A tiny twisted unscared ghost in a black cloak/ hopping along the grimy old brick and brownstone streets still left in downtown New York,/ crying out in a shrill soundless giggle:/ *War is the health of the State.*"

Further Reading

Lillian Schlissel edited an anthology of Bourne's works, *The World of Randolph Bourne* (1965). His writings are replete with autobiographical details. Numerous essays by friends and admirers emphasize his idealism and personality. See, for example, Van Wyck Brooks, *Emerson and Others* (1927). Louis Filler, *Randolph Bourne* (1943), analyzes Bourne's career. Many additional details appear in John A. Moreau, *Randolph Bourne: Legend and Reality* (1966).

Additional Sources

Clayton, Bruce, *Forgotten prophet: the life of Randolph Bourne,* Baton Rouge: Louisiana State University Press, 1984. □

Boutros Boutros-Ghali

Appointed sixth secretary-general of the United Nations in November 1991, Egyptian lawyer, academic, civil servant, and diplomat Boutros Boutros-Ghali (born 1922) sought to reassert the leadership role of the United Nations in contemporary world affairs.

Boutros Boutros-Ghali was born on November 14, 1922, into one of the Egyptian Coptic community's most influential and affluent families. His father, Yusuf, served at one time as the country's finance minister, while a grandfather had been premier of Egypt from 1908 until his assassination in 1910. Boutros-Ghali's own cosmopolitanism and fluency in English and French, in addition to Arabic, can be traced to his patrician upbringing and formal schooling. After completing a law degree in 1946 at Cairo University, he spent the next four years in France, earning diplomas in higher studies in public law and in economics, as well as a Ph.D. in international law from Paris University in 1949.

Returning to Egypt, Boutros-Ghali became professor of international law and international relations at Cairo University. During his 28 years in academia he was a Fulbright scholar at Columbia University (1954-1955) and director of the research center at the Hague Academy of International Law (1967-1969). In addition to participating in many international conferences and delivering guest lectures at prestigious universities abroad, from Princeton to the Warsaw Institute of International Relations and Nairobi University, his list of scholarly publications ran to over 100 articles on foreign policy problems and at least 12 books. Membership on the UN Commission of International Law (1979-1992) gave him a better understanding of the workings of that body, which would serve him later in his career.

Boutros-Ghali left academia in October 1977, with what proved to be an exquisite sense of timing. Appointed minister of state for foreign affairs, he accompanied President Anwar Sadat on the historic journey to Jerusalem on November 19, 1977. Then he attended the Camp David peace summit the following September as part of the Egyptian delegation. During the 1980s he was also involved in domestic politics as a leading member of the National Democratic party and as a delegate to the Egyptian parliament from 1987. In May 1991 President Husni Mubarak promoted him to deputy prime minister for international affairs and minister of state for immigration and Egyptian expatriates. However, this deepening involvement in Egyptian national and external affairs ended toward the close of 1991 with the invitation to head the United Nations.

Upon assuming office in January 1992, UN Secretary-General Boutros Boutros-Ghali became the world's leading spokesman for post-Cold War internationalism, as well as its foremost practitioner. The new head of the United Nations insisted on viewing the end of the U.S.-Soviet rivalry and the precedent for collective enforcement measures against aggression established during the Kuwait crisis as presenting an historic opportunity for transforming the nature of world politics. Boutros-Ghali used his position to summon all countries and governments belatedly to fulfill the original 1945 UN Charter pledge of an integrated global system and, accordingly, championed the UN organization and its affiliate specialized agencies in promoting the cause of international peace and common security, economic development, and human rights through multilateral cooperation. But on the immediate and more practical level, much of his energy went toward putting the United Nations' own house in order.

The secretary-general's ambitious list of UN-related priorities included: streamlining the secretariat and coordinating the efforts of UN personnel headquartered in New York with those in Geneva, assuring that budgetary resources in the future would be commensurate with the increased number and complexity of the missions undertaken around the globe, prodding the United States and other permanent members of the Security Council, as well as the General Assembly, to redefine the UN's mandate, and stengthening the commitment of each of the more than 180 member-states to the world body. The highest priority assigned by Boutros-Ghali was to broaden the role of peacekeeping. His goal was to assure greater effectiveness by the eve of the United Nations' fiftieth anniversary in 1995.

This program of structural, procedural, and functional reform inevitably made Secretary-General Boutros-Ghali a controversial figure in world affairs. Against the backdrop of destabilizing events in Bosnia and Somalia, he found himself involved in sharp political differences not only with the United States and other Western governments, but also with UN military field commanders. This seemed uncharacteristic to the rather unassuming, former Egyptian statesman and man of letters. Nevertheless, he continued to commit UN resources in search of peace in Cyprus, the Middle East, Angola, Cambodia, and elsewhere.

Indeed, Boutros-Ghali's appointment had surprised many UN experts, who were inclined to dismiss him as excessively conservative and uncharismatic. They saw his selection as a gesture toward the Third World, especially its 51-member African bloc. Noting his age (69), they also rushed to predict he would be more of an interim caretaker than a voice for dynamic change by an action-oriented United Nations.

The secretary-general's critics apparently had underestimated his leadership qualities and inner resolve. Certainly, the biography of Boutros-Ghali, his long public career, and previous experience in international and Middle East diplomacy, underscored impressive professional qualifications for the sensitive UN position.

Boutros-Ghali has continued to remain committed to democratization throughout historically conflicted countries. He has overseen the deployment of over 70,000 UN peace keeping troops during his years in office. Boutros-Ghali remained a prominent and outspoken memeber of the United Nations until the end of his term in 1996.

Further Reading

Insight into Boutros-Ghali's thinking on current international politics and his approach to the United Nations can be found in his important special report to the Security Council entitled *An Agenda for Peace* (1992). Earlier major publications include: "Contribution à l'Etude des Entences Régionales" (XV Editions, Paris, 1949); "Cours de Diplomatie et de Droit Diplomatique et Consulaire" (Cairo, n.d.); "Les Problémes du Canal de Suez" (1957); "Egypt and the United Nations" in collaboration with the Carnegie Endowment for International Peace (1957); "Le Principe d'Egalité des Etats et les Organisations Internationales" (1961); "Foreign Policy in a World of Change" (1963); "Contribution à une Théorie Générale des Alliances" (Paris, 1963); "L'Organisation del'Unité Africaine" (Paris, 1969); "Le Mouvement Afro-Asiatique" (Paris, 1969); "Les Difficultés Institutionelles du Panafricanisme" (Geneva, 1971); "La Ligue des Etats Arabes" (Leyden, n.d.); and "Les Conflits de Frontièeres en Afrique" (Paris, 1973).

Additional Sources

New York Times, August 7, 1991; November 22, 1991; November 23, 1991.
Time, December 2, 1991; February 3, 1992; March 23, 1992; January 6, 1997.
UN Press Release, November 15, 1996. □

Dirk Bouts

The Dutch painter Dirk Bouts (c. 1415-1475) was active in Flanders. His work is characterized by dig-

nity, sobriety, and a heightened sensitivity in the depiction of realistic landscape settings.

Dirk Bouts whose real name was Theodorik Romboutszoon, was probably born in Haarlem, where he may have studied under the painter Albert van Ouwater. Sometime before 1450 Bouts took up residence in the Flemish city of Louvain. His name appeared in the records of Louvain in 1457 and again in 1468, when he was appointed "city painter."

It is likely that Bouts spent some time in Bruges, as his earliest work, the *Infancy Altarpiece* shows the distinct and strong influence of Petrus Christus, the leading master of that city after the death of Jan van Eyck. The slightly later *Deposition Altarpiece* (ca. 1450) displays strong connections with the style of Rogier van der Weyden in both the figure types and the composition. About 1460, the period of the *Entombment* in London, the early, formative influence of Petrus Christus had been almost totally displaced by that of Rogier, though Bouts's personal vision began to emerge in the fluid and continuous landscape background.

The great *Last Supper Altarpiece* (1464-1467) marks the high point of Bouts's career. In this solemn and dignified masterpiece the painter achieved spiritual grandeur in the context of convincing physical reality. The central panel of the altarpiece is the most emphatically significant treatment of the theme of the Last Supper in Northern European art. The wings, which contain Old Testament prefigurations of the central theme, are freer and more loosely organized. Eschewing the symmetry and rigid axial construction of the main panel, Bouts produced rhythmic foreground compositions in combination with fluid and dramatic spatial recessions.

In 1468 Bouts was commissioned to paint four panels on the subject of justice for the Town Hall of Louvain. At the painter's death in 1475 only two of the paintings had been completed; they are among the most remarkable productions of his career. The unusual subjects, taken from the chronicles of a 12th-century historian, concern the wrongful execution by Emperor Otto III of one of his counts and the subsequent vindication of the nobleman by his wife. The finer of the panels represents the dramatic trial by fire which the wife was obliged to undergo to prove her husband's innocence. Rich draperies and sumptuous colors are applied to tall angular forms to create a work of rare formal elegance and high decorative appeal. In order to dignify the event, however, the artist has employed restrained gestures and expressions as well as a completely rationalized spatial setting. As in the *Last Supper Altarpiece,* a sense of solemn and hieratic importance is expressed by means of an austere and rigid geometry in the construction of both persons and places.

The late productions of Bouts's workshop, such as the well-known *Pearl of Brabant Altarpiece,* are characterized by the close collaboration of the painter's two sons, Dirk the Younger (1448-1491) and Aelbrecht (1455/1460-1549). In the paintings of his less gifted sons, the master's distinctive figure style was appreciably altered, though Dirk the Youn-

ger appears to have retained much of his father's sensitivity to the landscape.

In addition to his innovations in the depiction of landscape, Bouts made a substantial contribution to the development of the portrait. His *Portrait of a Man* (1462) localizes the sitter in an enlarged architectural setting while permitting the interior space to merge with the exterior through an open window. For the first time in Northern painting a common bond was forged between a particularized individual and the universal world of nature.

Further Reading

A full account of Bouts's career is in Max J. Friedländer, *Early Netherlandish Painting,* vol. 3 (trans. 1968). It contains a sensitive analysis of the style of Bouts and his major followers. For shorter notices see the excellent essays in Erwin Panofsky, *Early Netherlandish Painting: Its Origins and Character* (2 vols., 1953), and Charles D. Cuttler, *Northern Painting from Pucelle to Bruegel* (1968). □

Henry Ingersoll Bowditch

The American physician Henry Ingersoll Bowditch (1808-1892) did research on chest diseases and established the first board of health in Massachusetts. He was also an ardent antislavery crusader.

Henry I. Bowditch, son of the mathematician Nathaniel Bowditch, was born on Aug. 9, 1808, in Salem, Mass. He graduated from Harvard College in 1828, earned his medical degree there in 1832, and studied in Paris for 2 years with leading physicians, such as P. G. A. Louis.

He was in England in 1833, when William Wilberforce died. Wilberforce's antislavery writings had impressed him, and when Bowditch returned to Boston, he became a militant abolitionist. When slave masters came to Massachusetts to retrieve fugitive slaves, Bowditch, who belonged to a secretly trained group of abolitionists, joined his friends to protect the runaways. He was proud of his friendship with black leader Frederick Douglass.

Bowditch was a physician at the Massachusetts General Hospital from 1838 until his death. In 1846 he published *The Young Stethoscopist,* dealing with diseases of the chest. Five years later he advocated paracentesis (puncturing of the pleural cavity to drain liquid deposits) and showed how the technique had become less complex and painful. Tuberculosis was also one of his lifelong concerns, and he made detailed studies of its etiology, publishing his conclusions in *Consumption in New England; or Locality One of Its Chief Causes* (1862). When his son Nathaniel died on a Civil War battlefield from the lack of care, Bowditch wrote a pamphlet advocating an ambulance system to care for the wounded.

From 1859 to 1867 Bowditch was Jackson professor of clinical medicine at Harvard and then began his great ser-

vice in behalf of public health. He founded the Massachusetts State Board of Health, the second of its kind in the United States, and became its first chairman (1869-1879). His most significant book, *Public Hygiene in America* (1877), was an important stimulus to the rising popular concern over public health. He was a fellow of the American Academy and president of the American Medical Association in 1877. He died on Jan. 14, 1892.

Further Reading

The best source for Bowditch's life is the biography with collected diaries and letters by his son, Vincent Yardley Bowditch, *Life and Correspondence of Henry Ingersoll Bowditch* (2 vols., 1902). □

Nathaniel Bowditch

Nathaniel Bowditch (1773-1838) was an American navigator and mathematician. An exceptional critic of European theoretical mathematics, he was the first American to publish a usable navigation guide, his edition of "The Practical Navigator" (1799).

N athaniel Bowditch was born March 26, 1773, in Salem, Mass., the son of a shipmaster and cooper. Strained family finances forced him to leave school at 10 to help his father. At 12 he became a clerk in a

ship chandlery and began a process of self-education, studying mathematics and foreign languages. In 1795 Bowditch went to sea; he had made five voyages by 1803, rising from clerk to master. He married Elizabeth Boardman in March 1798; she died the same year. In October 1800 he married Mary Ingersoll. They had six sons and two daughters.

During this time he had continued his scientific study, becoming fascinated by the problems of navigation. In 1799 he published a revised American edition of J. H. Moore's *The Practical Navigator,* in which he eventually corrected over 11,000 errors. The third edition, published in 1802, was so changed from the original that Bowditch published it as *The New Practical Navigator* under his own name. This handbook became and remains, in revised form, the standard navigational aid, and it was the first to be readily usable by the ordinary seaman.

When he retired from the sea in 1803, his mathematical abilities led to his appointment as president of the Essex Fire and Marine Insurance Company. This work, plus the management of estates and trusts, gave him both sufficient income and leisure for his scientific pursuits, and he declined offers of teaching posts at Harvard, West Point, and the University of Virginia. He continued his self-education and worked on a critical and annotated translation of Pierre Simon de Laplace's *Mécanique céleste,* considered the culmination of the Newtonian system, which was not formally published until 1829-1839. Bowditch refused to gather subscriptions to pay for publication, determined to pay the entire cost, $12,000, by himself. He was aided in this en-

deavor by a large salary advance, achieved by becoming actuary of the Massachusetts Hospital Life Insurance Company in 1823. Bowditch corrected Laplace's errors, supplied mathematical proofs which Laplace had omitted, and showed where the French mathematician was guilty of using the work of other scientists without acknowledgment. Bowditch's annotated edition is nearly twice the size of the original and constitutes a major critical work; it was well received by most European scientists and earned Bowditch international fame.

Bowditch was not an original thinker but primarily a meticulous and exhaustive critic endowed with exceptional mathematical skills. He found his most receptive audience in Europe; few in America could follow his mathematical work. He died on March 17, 1838.

Further Reading

Two popular accounts of Bowditch's life are Alfred Boller Stanford, *Navigator: The Story of Nathaniel Bowditch* (1927), and Robert Elton Berry, *Yankee Stargazer: The Life of Nathaniel Bowditch* (1941). Nathan Reingold, ed., *Science in Nineteenth Century America* (1964), is useful for general background. □

James Bowdoin

An American merchant and politician, James Bowdoin (1726-1790) participated in the political agitation before the American Revolution. His most important role, however, was as governor of Massachusetts during Shays' Rebellion.

James Bowdoin was descended from a Huguenot refugee who had arrived in the British colonies in the 1680s. His father was an enormously successful merchant and, at the time of his death in 1747, may have been the wealthiest man in New England. Throughout his political career, Bowdoin continued his mercantile activities, and some of his political stands were clearly related to the restrictive impact of British policies upon his functions as a merchant.

Bowdoin began his political career in 1753. He served in the Massachusetts House of Representatives and later in the Council of the General Court, where he generally opposed British policies. He aided in drafting many protests against British actions, and he corresponded with friends in England, asking for relaxation of British restrictions on colonial trading activity.

In 1774, as the Revolution approached, Gen. Gage denied Bowdoin his place in the council. During the same year Bowdoin served in a variety of Revolutionary organizations, but ill health caused him to decline service in the Continental Congress. He attended the convention which drafted the new state constitution in 1780. While many of the ideas embodied in that constitution were the work of John Adams, Bowdoin served as president of the convention and chairman of the drafting committee.

Along with the other states, Massachusetts was confronted with numerous problems in the 1780s: the adjustment of trade afflicted by war, the load of war debts, and the establishment of new lines of political authority in difficult economic circumstances. The crisis deepened toward the middle of the decade. John Hancock, the first governor of Massachusetts under the new constitution, retired in 1785; and Bowdoin, though lacking a popular majority, was chosen as his successor by the legislature. He attempted to meet the public debt, to strengthen the powers of the Confederation over foreign commerce, and to bring pressure against British restrictions on American trade through retaliatory legislation.

Bowdoin's major problem was in dealing with resistance in Massachusetts to foreclosure proceedings against indebted farmers. When courts were prevented from meeting by armed men, Bowdoin sent militiamen to deal with the "rebels." In small-scale engagements in early 1787, the state militia rapidly put down a rebellion led by Daniel Shays. Those who feared the spread of disorder throughout the weak union that existed under the Articles of Confederation viewed Bowdoin as a hero. But in Massachusetts he lost political ground and was easily defeated by John Hancock that same year. Hancock pardoned those rebels still under threat of the death penalty. Bowdoin's last public service was in January 1788 as a delegate to the state convention which ratified the new constitution for the United States.

Bowdoin's suppression of Shays' Rebellion gave him a reputation as an upholder of public order; and Shays' Rebellion itself intensified interest in a stronger union among the states. Yet his image as a partisan of the merchants and creditors may have contributed to the coming of that rebellion.

Further Reading

Aspects of Bowdoin's career are discussed in Thomas Hutchinson's 18th-century *History of the Colony and Province of Massachusetts Bay* (new ed. 1936). Herbert S. Allan, *John Hancock, Patriot in Purple* (1948), includes biographical material on Bowdoin. Marion L. Starkey, *A Little Rebellion* (1955), is a study of Shays' Rebellion. See also Albert Bushnell Hart, ed., *Commonwealth History of Massachusetts,* vol. 2 (1928) and vol. 3 (1929), and Robert J. Taylor, *Western Massachusetts in the Revolution* (1954).

Additional Sources

Kershaw, Gordon E., *James Bowdoin II: patriot and man of the enlightenment,* Lanham: University Press of America, 1991.

Elizabeth Bowen

The British writer Elizabeth Bowen (1899-1973) dealt with the strivings of the individual will to fulfill itself in an alien and hostile world. She is considered a major British novelist of the 20th century.

Born in Dublin on June 7, 1899, Elizabeth Bowen lived in Ireland until the age of seven, when her family moved to England. Her education completed, she returned to Dublin in 1916 to work in a hospital for World War I veterans. Two years later she moved back to England and enrolled in the London County Council School of Art. In 1923 she married Alan Charles Cameron and published her first collection of short stories.

In 1925 Bowen and her husband moved to Oxford, where she became friends with many literary intellectuals, among them Isaiah Berlin and Lord David Cecil. There she wrote her first four novels: *The Hotel* (1927), *The Last September* (1929), *Friends and Relations* (1931), and *To the North* (1932). The first two concern the dawning of romantic love in the young, innocent heroines, who eventually become aware of its futility, while the last two concern the destructiveness of illicit love.

In 1935 Bowen and her husband returned to London, where her friends included Cyril Connolly, Virginia Woolf, and many of the Bloomsbury group. In that same year she published her fifth novel, *The House in Paris.* Again the theme is the destructiveness of romantic excess. It depicts an affair which results in pregnancy, the suicide of the lover, and the heroine's rejection of her child, though in the end she begins to reconcile herself to the reality of her situation. In 1938 Bowen published her best-known and perhaps finest novel, *The Death of the Heart,* about an idealistic young girl whose demands for honesty and openness are met with hostility by her family.

During World War II Bowen worked as an air raid warden and wrote for the Ministry of Information. In her seventh novel, *The Heat of the Day* (1949), the society which in earlier novels was seen as inimical to romantic illusions has disappeared entirely in the chaos of war, and the protagonists float in a sea of their own confusion. After the death of her husband in 1952, Bowen returned to Ireland. Except for numerous trips to the United States as a lecturer, she remained there and continued to write, publishing *A World of Love* in 1955. The story concerns three women who become aware that their romantic fantasies about a man dead for many years have kept them from living in the present.

In 1960 she returned to Oxford. She published *The Little Girls* in 1964 and *Eva Trout, or Changing Scenes* in 1968. The latter concerns a heroine whose romantic passion blinds her to the reality of other people, causing them pain and bringing about her questionably accidental death at the hands of her illegitimate son. In addition to her 10 novels, Bowen published several collections of short stories, numerous reviews, and many other critical pieces. She died in 1973.

Further Reading

For the facts of Bowen's life, some sources are her own *Bowen's Court* (1942; 2d ed. 1964), about the Bowen family, and *Seven Winters* (1942), covering her childhood; and her chapter in John Lehmann, ed., *Coming to London* (1957), which gives her view of literary life in London in the early 1920s. For a detailed study of her novels, Andrew Bennett and Nicholas

Royle, *Elizabeth Bowen and the Dissolution of the Novel: Still Lives,* St. Martin's Press, 1995; or Renee C. Hoogland, *Elizabeth Bowen: A Reputation in Writing* New York University Press, 1994, are useful. For information on her short stories, read Phyllis Lassner, *Elizabeth Bowen: A Study of Short Fiction,* Macmillan Publishing, 1991. □

Claude Gernade Bowers

The American journalist, historian, and diplomat Claude Gernade Bowers (1878-1958) wrote partisan but influential works on American political leaders. He had a successful career as an editorial columnist and as an ambassador.

Claude Bowers was born in Westfield, Ind., on Nov. 20, 1878, the son of a merchant. His formal education consisted of private tutoring, high school in Indianapolis, and a brief period reading law. By chance he became a newspaperman, writing editorials for the *Indianapolis Sentinel* (1901-1903) and for the *Terre Haute Star* (1903-1906).

From his high school days, when he had read the writings of Thomas Jefferson, Bowers espoused the cause of democracy and the Democratic party. He ran unsuccessfully for the U.S. House of Representatives in 1904 and again in 1906. He served on the Terre Haute Board of Public Works (1906-1911) and was secretary to U.S. Senator John Worth Kern (1911-1917). Bowers then returned to journalism as editor of the *Fort Wayne Journal-Gazette.* During these years he wrote *Irish Orators* (1916), *The Life of J. Worth Kern* (1918), and his first major historical work, *The Party Battles of the Jackson Period* (1922).

Bowers's versatility as a writer earned him a position on the editorial staff of the *New York World,* at that time the major spokesman for the liberal wing of the Democratic party. He worked on the newspaper from 1923 to 1931, and then wrote an independent political column for two years.

In 1925 Bowers published *Jefferson and Hamilton: The Struggle for Democracy in America.* The book became a best seller and revitalized the reputation of Thomas Jefferson. The book increased the demand for Bowers's services as a political speaker, and he climaxed his oratorical career with a stirring keynote address at the 1928 Democratic National Convention. Shortly afterward he published another popular success, *The Tragic Era: The Revolution after Lincoln* (1929).

Bowers's historical writing is characterized by emphasis on personalities and dramatic confrontations. More than just a popularizer, he was thoroughly versed in the history of the periods with which he dealt, and he made particularly effective use of contemporary newspapers.

In 1933 President Franklin D. Roosevelt appointed Bowers ambassador to Spain, where he served with distinction through the turmoil of the Spanish Civil War. He was assigned to Chile in 1939 and served there until his retirement in 1953. He died on Jan. 21, 1958, in New York City.

Bowers's other books include *William Maxwell Evarts* (1928), *Jefferson and Civil and Religious Liberty* (1930), *Beveridge and the Progressive Era* (1932), *Jefferson in Power: The Death Struggle of the Federalists* (1936), *Spanish Adventures of Washington Irving* (1940), *The Young Jefferson, 1743-1789* (1945), *Pierre Vergniaud: Voice of the French Revolution* (1950), *My Mission to Spain: Watching the Rehearsal for World War II* (1954), *Making Democracy a Reality* (1954), and *Chile through Embassy Windows, 1939-1953* (1958).

Further Reading

Bowers's *My Life: The Memoirs of Claude Bowers* (1962) may be supplemented by two other autobiographical works: *My Mission to Spain: Watching the Rehearsal for World War II* (1954) and *Chile through Embassy Windows, 1939-1953* (1958). The best summary of Bowers's influence as a journalist, historian, and politician is in Merrill D. Peterson, *The Jefferson Image in the American Mind* (1960).

Additional Sources

Bowers, Claude Gernade, *Chile through embassy windows, 1939-1953,* Westport, Conn.: Greenwood Press, 1977. □

Samuel Bowles

The most noted member of an American newspaper family, Samuel Bowles (1826-1878) earned his reputation of fierce independence at a time when newspapers existed largely by means of partisan political support.

S amuel Bowles was born in Springfield, Mass., on Feb. 9, 1826, seventeen months after his father had founded the *Weekly Republican*. His father came from New England stock dating back to 1640. His mother was a descendant of Miles Standish. Even tempered and possessed of a quick, incisive mind, young Sam grew up in an early rising, hard-working, religious household.

Sam wanted to go to college, but at the age of 17 his father made him an office boy at the *Republican*. The elder Bowles wanted his son to be a printer, but Sam had neither the skill nor the inclination for it. He did, however, have the skill of persuasion. He talked his father into establishing the *Daily Republican* (March 27, 1844); his father agreed to the daily only if Sam took the "main responsibility of working and pushing it." The daily started as an evening paper but shifted to a morning publication a year later.

In the same year Bowles married a Springfield schoolmate, Mary Schermerhorn of Geneva, N.Y. Two years later he obtained half-ownership of the *Republican* through a $10,000 inheritance.

By midcentury Bowles, a Whig about to turn Republican, was a power in Massachusetts and was beginning to acquire a national name for being an honest, impartial editor. By 1855 the *Republican* abandoned the Whig party. In July, Bowles called for a new party and participated in the organization of the Republican party.

Bowles's appearance at mid-life was impressive. He had a substantial beard, an intelligent forehead, and shaggy, projecting brows that partially masked his dark, luminous eyes. His gaze was penetrating, and although he was startlingly direct most of the time, he was a master of the art of listening.

Plagued all his life with intestinal illness, Bowles in later life was beset with headaches and sleeplessness. His vitality began to ebb when he was only 34. Sciatica and dyspepsia caused him to lose sleep and made him moody and severe.

Merriam, in *The Life and Times of Samuel Bowles* (1885), concisely sums up Bowles's influence: "The great achievement of Samuel Bowles was that he built up under the limitations of a country town a paying newspaper which expressed the editor's personal opinions, bound by no party, by no school, by no clique." According to a competing editor, Bowles published "the truth as he understood it." Once he had the information it had to be "uttered at all costs." He always insisted that although he was an individual, the *Republican* was a public servant.

Bowles stressed accuracy and condensation long before they became important to newspaper editing. "Put it all in the first sentence," Bowles said, antedating most editors and all professors of journalism. "Don't suppose that anyone will read through six lines of bad rhetoric to get a crumb of news at the end," he frequently told his young protégés. In every part of the paper, Merriam states, Bowles pruned away verbiage remorselessly.

In 1877 Bowles was stricken by a series of paralytic attacks. In the weeks remaining to him, he put his affairs in order. He died on Jan. 16, 1878.

Further Reading

The best biography of Bowles is George S. Merriam's detailed, uncritical, and turgid account, *The Life and Times of Samuel Bowles* (2 vols., 1885). Merriam drew from the pages of the *Springfield Republican* and from the personal correspondence of members of the Bowles family. Far less detailed and less laborious is Richard Hooker, *The Story of an Independent Newspaper: One Hundred Years of the Springfield Republican* (1924). Hooker drew chiefly from Merriam and the *Republican*, but also gathered odds and ends from minor sources to bring the Bowles family story up to 1915. Frank L. Mott, *American Journalism: A History, 1690-1960* (3d ed. 1962), is recommended for general background.

Additional Sources

Merriam, George Spring, *The life and times of Samuel Bowles,* New York, The Century co., 1885.

Weisner, Stephen G., *Embattled editor: the life of Samuel Bowles,* Lanham, MD: University Press of America, 1986. □

Isaiah Bowman

The American geographer Isaiah Bowman (1878-1950) is best known for his *New World,* a remarkable book on political geography. He was also director of the American Geographical Society and president of Johns Hopkins University.

O f farming stock, Isaiah Bowman was born at Waterloo, Ontario, Canada, on Dec. 26, 1878. At the age of 18 he became a teacher in a rural school. His immense ability was noted by the geographer Mark Jefferson, who offered Bowman a post at the Normal College in Ypsilanti, Mich., provided that he went to study in an eastern university. He had the good fortune to study at Harvard under the geographer William M. Davis.

On Bowman's graduation in 1905, Yale University offered him a post as instructor in the department of geology. There he remained for 10 years, teaching geography on modern lines, during which time he made three expeditions to South America (1907, 1911, and 1913). He published two scholarly works about these trips: *The Andes of Southern Peru* (1916) and *Desert Trails of Atacama* (1924). His first book, *Forest Physiography* (1911), shows that he already had a deep knowledge of physical geography in all its aspects.

In 1916 Bowman became director of the American Geographical Society. Under his direction the *Geographical Review,* replacing the earlier bulletins, became a model of good looks as well as a mine of scholarship. Several major monographs were issued, including his *The Pioneer Fringe* (1931) and a cognate volume prepared under his direction, *Limits of Land Settlement* (1937). But the book that delighted generations of geographers is Bowman's *The New World: Problems in Political Geography,* published in 1921 and reprinted many times. Part of its interest lies in Bowman's work as chief territorial specialist of the American delegation to the Paris Peace Conference in 1918-1919, though the book was not based solely on the experiences of that time but on the vast knowledge accumulated in previous years, including those when the American Geographical Society had housed the "Inquiry," a research team of 150 workers.

Bowman resigned as director of the American Geographical Society in 1935 to become president of Johns Hopkins University. He served on numerous commissions, especially those concerned with international questions, and was an adviser on the plans to set up the United Nations. The full range of his activities, especially as an adviser to President Roosevelt and others, will probably not be revealed until his private diaries and files are opened. Bowman died in Baltimore on Jan. 6, 1950.

During his life he broadened the scope of geography, encouraged graduate schools, and made the American Geographical Society a world institution. Bowman belonged not only to the United States but to the international community working for peace.

Further Reading

John Kirtland Wright, *Geography in the Making: The American Geographical Society, 1851-1951* (1952), contains an analysis of Bowman's work for the society. See also John K. Wright and George F. Carter, "Isaiah Bowman," in the *National Academy of Sciences Biographical Memoirs,* vol. 33 (1959), for the main events of his life and comments on his career.

Additional Sources

Martin, Geoffrey J., *The life and thought of Isaiah Bowman,* Hamden, Conn.: Archon Books, 1980. ☐

Barbara Boxer

Barbara Boxer (born 1940) is a Democratic Senator from California.

B arbara Boxer was one of six women elected to the U.S. Senate in 1992. Representing California as a Democrat, she was part of a larger movement that swept an increased number of women into positions of power within the government. A 10-year veteran of Congress, Boxer rose through her energetic and combative style, and her fealty to the liberal causes which had first inspired her entrance into politics—feminism and environmentalism chief among them. The product of a conventional background and upbringing, Boxer was inspired by the social upheavals of the 1960s to look beyond her home and family to make her mark on the world at large.

Boxer's origins and early years gave little hint of the career she would eventually pursue. She was born in Brooklyn, New York, the child of immigrants, in 1940. Boxer later recalled a conventional and happy middle-class childhood, which included education in the local public schools. As a "child of the '50s," Boxer wrote in her memoir, *Strangers in the Senate,* she wore cinch belts and layers of crinolines, as well as hoop skirts, to conform to the dictates of fashion. Nonetheless, in high school, she and a friend took on the job of coaching the boys' baseball team, an unconventional choice.

Boxer made another unconventional choice when she entered Brooklyn College in 1958 and became one of the few women at the institution to chose a major of economics, instead of education. For her minor, Boxer chose political science. She also served as a cheerleader for the Brooklyn College basketball team.

In her final year of college, at age 21, Barbara Levy married Stewart Boxer, another student, who was then 23. The two moved into a one-room efficiency apartment at the back of a building on Ocean Boulevard, paying $90 a month in rent. When the building's owner failed to provide

promised amenities, such as a carpeted and painted lobby, the energetic Boxer circulated a petition in the building to pressure the landlord into fixing things up.

After graduating from college Boxer sought a job in the New York financial world to support her husband while he completed his law degree at Fordham University. She tried to enter one of the stockbroker training programs run by the big Wall Street firms, but was turned down on the basis of her sex. Boxer then took a job as a secretary, and studied for the stockbroker's exam independently. Even after she passed, Boxer was not allowed to sell securities and earn commissions, so she left her job and took a position with a firm that would allow her to do so.

Boxer was working as a stockbroker when the event that she later identified as the birth of her political consciousness took place: the assassination of President John F. Kennedy in 1963. With this event, and the later political assassinations of the 1960s, Boxer began to look beyond her own private life and aspirations to address larger social issues and concerns.

In 1965 Boxer moved with her husband to northern California. The couple had been determined to own a house and raise a family, and they felt that real estate was more affordable there than in the New York metropolitan area. While her husband was completing his exams at Fordham, Boxer quit her job and relocated to San Francisco to find a house. She was seven months pregnant with her first child at the time, and gave birth to her son—two months prematurely—the day after she arrived.

Boxer and her husband soon settled in San Francisco, and their second child, a daughter, came into the family in 1967. Although Boxer later recalled that she was primarily concerned with her family life during that time, she and her husband opposed the war in Vietnam, and felt strongly enough about their position to take part in a peace march, which wound through the city to Golden Gate Park.

Also in 1967, Boxer and her husband moved to the city suburbs, buying a $40,000 house in Marin County, north of the city. This area would later become the basis of her political constituency. The year after they had moved to Marin, Boxer witnessed the assassination of Robert Kennedy live on television, and this violent act, she later recalled, shocked her forever from her routine private life.

Joining with other women from her community, who were young, college-educated mothers like her, Boxer and her friends in the town of Greenbrae embarked on a number of social initiatives. Among their first efforts was a program called Education Corps of Marin, designed to train high school drop-outs for jobs. This program was eventually taken over by the local school system.

In addition, Boxer became involved in the environmental movement as well as in anti-war activities. In 1970 she oversaw publicity for a campaign to put a peace initiative on the ballot, which, surprisingly, carried the day. She worked for other local ballot initiatives and for progressive candidates. Marin Community Video and the Marin Alternative, a progressive, grassroots, political network, also earned her attention. At the same time Boxer devoted her energy to a number of women's and children's groups, helping to found the Kentfield After School Child Care Center, and taking part in Woman's Way, a women's support group.

Declares Candicacy

On the strength of these activities, Boxer declared her candidacy for elective office for the first time in 1971. Although her husband was equally well qualified to represent the progressive environmental constituency with which the couple had become involved, he could not afford to sacrifice his lucrative law practice for the $11,000 annual salary paid to members of the Marin County Board of Supervisors, so Barbara ran, becoming the first serious female candidate in two decades. Although Boxer won a three-way primary race, she ran into serious obstacles in her main campaign, many of which were related to her gender. Even women who worked told her of their doubts that she could care for her young children properly while holding down such a responsible position. In the final election, in November of 1972, Boxer lost by a narrow margin.

Following this defeat, Boxer re-entered the workforce. She took a position as a reporter for the *Pacific Sun*, becoming an associate editor of the publication from 1972 to 1974. At that time, she returned to the world of politics, as a congressional aide working for the representative from the Fifth Congressional District of California. Boxer held this post until 1976, when she ran again for the Marin County Board of Supervisors. This time, she was elected.

As a Marin County Supervisor, Boxer maintained her strong commitment to the environmental movement. She urged the closure of all nuclear power plants in the state of California, and worked for other liberal causes during her six years in the post. From 1977 to 1982, she served on the Bay Area Air Quality Management Board, of which she was the president from 1979 to 1981. Boxer was also the president of the Marin County Board of Supervisors from 1980 to 1981.

Elected to House

In the early 1980s Boxer's local congressional district, the Sixth District of California, was redrawn in a manner that helped to insure the re-election of incumbent John L. Burton, a Democrat. When Burton, a longtime friend and mentor of Boxer, chose instead to retire, Boxer ran for the seat he was vacating in the U.S. House of Representatives. She won the 1982 election as a Democrat.

Boxer took office in Washington as a freshman representative at the start of 1983, and became president of the Democratic New Members Caucus of the House of Representatives. The district Boxer went on to represent for five terms, covering ten years, included parts of the city of San Francisco, as well as Marin County, her home base. In Congress, Boxer continued to champion the liberal causes that had brought her popularity with the constituents of this area in the past. Boxer was assigned to sit on the Armed Service Committee, where she was one of the few committed liberal members, and became co-chair of the Military Reform Caucus. Boxer was also appointed to the Select Committee on Children, Youth, and Families. In addition, she chaired the subcommittee on government activities.

In Congress Boxer made a name for herself as a staunch opponent of defense spending. She opposed the costs of stealth aircraft and the Patriot missile, pushing repeated floor amendments in the house to cut government spending for these projects. Boxer also voted against funding for the Nicaraguan contras. In addition, she lent support to the Congressional Black Caucus in its recommendation that the defense budget be cut in half.

Boxer became best known as a representative for publicizing particularly egregious cases of wasteful military spending. Posing for photographers with a $7,622 coffee pot for a cargo plane, and a $600 toilet seat cover, she dramatized the issue of government excess, bringing public pressure to bear on efforts to reform government procurement. As a result of these efforts, Boxer was able to take partial credit for a series of military procurement reform amendments, which included a 1988 measure to protect whistle-blowers, and a measure to allow competitive bidding for contracts to provide spare parts to the military. Despite her best efforts, however, Boxer was unable to keep the Presidio, a historical military base in San Francisco, off the list of military bases to eventually be closed.

Boxer opposed the entry of the United States into the Persian Gulf war in 1991, and she sponsored an effort that would have required prior Congressional approval of covert American actions in foreign countries. This resolution, which was seen a threat to the secrecy of war plans and anti-terrorist operations, was unanimously defeated on the floor of the House, as even Boxer withdrew her support for the amendment.

As a representative Boxer also maintained her commitment to women's issues. She was an original co-sponsor of the Family and Medical Leave Act benefitting workers with children or other family responsibilities, and she put up a strong opposition to the gag rule forbidding abortion counseling at federally funded health clinics. As a supporter of the Freedom of Choice Act, Boxer sponsored an amendment to provide federal funding for abortions in cases of rape or incest, which was passed, but vetoed by President George Bush. Boxer won the respect of the powerful former chairman of the House Ways and Means Committee, Dan Rostenkowski, in her fight to pass this bill, with her forthright appeal for his support of the abortion amendment.

Boxer also pursued a campaign to open up the men's club of Congress to greater participation by women. As part of this effort, she tried to win more extensive locker room facilities for female representatives, inspiring an apocryphal story about her presence in the men's locker room at an inopportune moment. The most important moment in her struggle to instill greater equality for women in the U.S. Congress, however, came during hearings to consider Clarence Thomas for a seat on the U.S. Supreme Court, when Boxer joined with other female representatives to bring their concerns about the treatment of Anita Hill to the attention of members of the Senate Judiciary Committee. The group of women was refused entrance to a meeting of this committee, after being told that "strangers" were not permitted in the room. Boxer was so incensed by the idea that she and the other female representatives were considered "strangers" in the Senate that she later wrote a book using this phrase as its title, describing the progress of women in politics in her lifetime.

Runs for Senate

The treatment of Hill at the Senate hearings proved to be a political watershed, and when California Senator Alan Cranston announced that he would relinquish his seat after being tainted in a savings and loan scandal, Boxer decided to give up her secure Congressional berth and run for the Senate as a long-shot candidate in 1992. She made the lack of female representation in the U.S. Senate a cornerstone of her campaign.

Boxer's first obstacle in her campaign for the Senate was a tough primary, with two strong male contenders who also had solid records on women's rights. With a strong fund-raising operation in place, as well as the support of groups such as EMILY's List, and the Hollywood Women's Political Committee, Boxer raised more than $2 million by the start of 1992, which allowed her to triumph in the June primary.

Boxer then went on to face Bruce Herschensohn, a conservative television commentator, in the general election. Despite her ten-year Congressional career, she cast herself as a Washington outsider, whose gender made her a gadfly to the establishment. This picture was somewhat damaged by the revelation during the campaign that she had bounced 143 checks at the U.S. House of Representatives bank. Despite this setback, Boxer relied on her ability to identify issues that voters cared about, and get her position across in a punchy and appealing manner. In a year in which more women than ever before were elected to the Senate, Boxer won her race in November of 1992, becoming, along with Dianne Feinstein, one of two women to make up the California delegation.

As a senator Boxer has continued to push the liberal agenda she supported as a representative, and she has remained sensitive to issues of importance to women. She joined the effort to pressure Senator Bob Packwood, under fire for sexual harassment, to fully disclose his actions, and she mounted a campaign, with the other five women in the Senate, to punish a Navy admiral for the Tailhook sex scandal. Boxer has worked for increased funding for breast cancer research and domestic violence programs. She also staunchly supported an openly gay San Francisco woman for a job at the Department of Health and Human Services, and she fought to end restrictions on gays in the military.

In addition, Boxer has remained true to her roots in the environmental movement. She is on the Committee on Environment and Public Works and belongs to three of its subcomittees. She battled a plan to place a radioactive dump in the California desert and pushed for the restoration of ten wetlands areas in California. Boxer has also worked hard to restore the ailing economy of her home state. In the name of California jobs, she endorsed a controversial proposal to deploy National Guard troops along the Mexican border to cut down on illegal immigration. She also supported a move to give members of the agricultural industry more time to renegotiate federal water contracts.

As the ranking member of the Subcommittee on International Finance, Boxer promotes America's competitiveness in today's global economy by lowering trade barriers and expanding exports.

In support of her pro-choice stance, Boxer cosponsored the Freedom of Choice Act and pushed for passage of both the Freedom of Access to Clinic Entrances Act and the Family Medical Leave Act.

In an effort to keep in touch with the constituents of her vast state, Boxer began inviting voters to write to her, and she was soon receiving more mail than any other senator. This outpouring suggests that Boxer has done an effective job of reaching out to the voters of California. Boxer appears to be laying the groundwork for a long career in the Senate, capping her evolution into an effective feminist and liberal politician.

Further Reading

California Journal, April 1, 1992; June 1, 1994.
Ms., March/April 1992, p. 86.
National Review, October 19, 1992, p. 21.
New York Times, October 25, 1993, p. A15.
Additional information was obtained from Senator Boxer's Home Page on the Internet. □

Jean Pierre Boyer

Jean Pierre Boyer (1776-1850) was a president of Haiti whose most noteworthy activities were the promulgation of the Rural Code of 1826 and the negotiation of final French recognition of Haitian independence in the same year.

Jean Pierre Boyer was born in Port-au-Prince on Feb. 28, 1776, of a well-to-do mulatto family. Educated in Paris, he returned to the colony of Saint-Domingue to participate in the military campaigns of the 1790s. Exiled by the Haitian leader Pierre Dominique Toussaint L'Ouverture, Boyer returned with the French troops of Gen. Charles Leclerc, whose mission was to break the power of Toussaint and his associates and to reintroduce slavery to the colony. When Boyer discovered this motive he switched to the Haitian side, serving with distinction in the final struggles for independence.

After Jean Jacques Dessalines, the first ruler of independent Haiti, was assassinated in 1806, Gen. Alexandre Sabès Pétion emerged as the ruler of Southern Haiti. Boyer served him as secretary and minister and succeeded him as president of Southern Haiti upon Pétion's death in 1818. Soon thereafter, with the death of King Henri Christophe, the northern part of Haiti was peacefully reunited with the south.

Though the southern part of the country had a tradition of living under an "easy boss," the north had a recent history of intense activity, economic progress, and a cash surplus in its treasury. It was Boyer's desire that his country progress without the repressive discipline of either a Christophe or a Dessalines. However, he was frustrated in these aims and actually presided over the disintegration of Haiti into a land of small, inefficient agricultural plots which produced only the food necessary for local consumption. The average Haitian spurned economic gain, seeking only to be his own master.

Rural Code

By 1826, with his treasury again empty, Boyer was convinced of the need to reintroduce discipline into Haitian agricultural life. After months of detailed planning, his famous Rural Code was promulgated on May 1.

The code reinstated the obligation of the masses to work on the land, to be legally attached to the land. A cultivator, once so classified, could not change either his class or residence without official permission. All workers were to bind themselves by contract to a proprietor. Laws against vagabondage and loafing were detailed and severe. The Haitian army was to enforce the code.

Unenforceable, the code failed. For 20 years the tradition of personal liberty had grown in Southern Haiti, and it greatly appealed to the population of the north after the end of Christophe's firm rule. The workers simply ignored the regulations. The large plantations, so necessary for a large-scale efficient agricultural system, were already broken up. Finally, the army itself, most of whose soldiers came from the peasantry, refused to enforce the code against its own social class.

Haitian Independence

The recognition by France of Haitian independence dealt the code its final blow. Boyer signed an accord whereby France renounced all claims against its former colony. Even though this involved an enormous cash settlement and 60 annual payments, Boyer felt the price worth paying to lift the fear of French invasion. The result was the utter disintegration of the Haitian army. It could not begin to enforce the Rural Code. As Leyburn (1941) says, "By gaining political security Haiti had inadvertently lost its last chance of economic prosperity through a system of enforced labor." Sharecropping now had become a way of life in Haiti.

Another noteworthy aspect of Boyer's rule was the inadvertent establishment of permanent caste lines. Though he desired to eliminate color distinction in Haitian society, he was frustrated by the unfortunate fact of life that literacy was low among the black masses. Therefore Boyer soon ran out of blacks to promote into government positions. Thus the government became the province of the educated mulattoes, while the army, affording social status and a sinecure, became the property of the blacks. These divisions in its society, which became entrenched during Boyer's time, still plague Haiti.

Events in Haiti finally caught up with Boyer. During the late 1830s, young intellectuals among the dominant mulatto class, knowing Haiti was falling hopelessly behind the rest of the world in its development, called on him to introduce forced labor into the agricultural sector. Boyer, having once tried this without success, did nothing. Revolution broke out early in 1843; Boyer was soon on his way to exile in Paris, where he died on July 9, 1850.

Further Reading

An excellent source of information on Boyer is James G. Leyburn's classic work, *The Haitian People* (1941; rev. ed. 1966), which presents an interpretive overview of the history, culture, and society of Haiti. Among other useful works is Selden Rodman, *Haiti: The Black Republic* (1954; rev. ed. 1961). □

Robert Boyle

The British chemist, physicist, and natural philosopher Robert Boyle (1627-1691) was a leading advocate of "corpuscular philosophy." He made important contributions to chemistry, pneumatics, and the theory of matter.

The seventh son and fourteenth child of the 1st Earl of Cork, Robert Boyle was born on Jan. 25, 1627, at Lismore Castle in County Cork, Ireland. His father was one of the richest and most powerful men in Ireland, and throughout his life Boyle enjoyed, in addition to his native talents, the advantages of position, family, and wealth. At the age of eight he was sent to school at Eton and then in 1638 to Geneva, Switzerland, where he was privately tutored for the next two years. Upon the death of his father, Boyle returned in 1644 to England, where after some initial delay he settled at the manor of Stalbridge in Dorsetshire, which he had inherited from his father.

Boyle devoted much time to study and writing, and although he wrote extensively on ethical and religious topics, he became increasingly interested in natural philosophy. He interested himself in nearly all aspects of physics, chemistry, medicine, and natural history, although it was chemistry that "bewitched" him and primarily occupied his time.

In 1652 Boyle left Stalbridge for Ireland, where 10 years of civil war had seriously disordered the family estates. During his stay he continued to pursue his scientific interests. In 1654 he settled in Oxford, then the scientific center of England. He there associated himself with a group interested in the "new learning." This group, including many of the leading scientific figures of the day, quickly recognized Boyle's exceptional abilities, and he became a regular participant in their activities, pursuing particularly his interest in chemistry.

Pneumatic Investigations

Soon after his arrival in Oxford, Boyle's researches took on an additional dimension. Having learned in 1657 of the vacuum pump recently invented by Otto von Guericke, Boyle immediately set Robert Hooke, his brilliant assistant (and later an eminent scientist in his own right), the task of devising an improved version. Utilizing this improved pump Boyle immediately began a long series of investigations designed to test properties of the air and to clearly establish its physical nature. Boyle's first account of these "pneumatic" investigations was entitled *New Experiments, Physico-Mechanical, Touching the Spring of the Air and Its Effects* (1660). He continued his study of air and vacuum throughout the rest of his life, and although his experiments with the "Boyleian vacuum" (as it came to be known) were repeated by many, no one in the 17th century surpassed Boyle's ingenuity or technique.

Boyle made extensive studies of the elasticity of the air and of its necessity for various physical phenomena, such as combustion, the propagation of sound, and the survival of animals. He verified Galileo's conclusions about the behavior of falling bodies by studying the rate at which a light body fell, both in air and in a vacuum. By placing a Torricellian barometer in the receptacle of his pump, he also verified that it was indeed air pressure which supported the column of mercury. When his conclusions about the relationship between the pressure of the air and the weight of the mercury it would support were challenged, he produced a series of experiments demonstrating that for a given quantity of air the volume is inversely proportional to the pressure, a relationship now known as Boyle's law.

Corpuscular Philosophy

The Sceptical Chymist (1661), although one of Boyle's more theoretical works and suffering from his usual lack of organization, well illustrates his contention that all scientific investigation must be firmly based on experiment. Directing his attack at what he conceived as the erroneous foundations of contemporary chemical theory, he brought forth extensive experimental evidence to refute the prevailing Aristotelian and Paracelsian concepts of a small number of basic elements or principles to which all compounds could be reduced by chemical analysis. He demonstrated that common chemical substances when decomposed by heat not only failed to yield the requisite number of elements or principles, but that the number was a function of the techniques employed. Accordingly, he denied that elements or principles (as thus defined) had any real existence and sought to replace these older concepts of chemical change with what he termed the "corpuscular philosophy."

Although he emphasized the necessity of basing scientific research on experiment, Boyle was not a simple empiricist. Behind his more specific and detailed work was a general theory of the structure of matter; and his continued advocacy of the mechanical philosophy—that is, explanation in terms of matter and motion—was one of his most significant contributions. According to Boyle's corpuscular philosophy, God had originally formed matter in tiny particles of varying sizes and shapes. These particles tended to combine in groups or clusters which, because of their compactness, had a reasonably continuous existence and were the basic units of chemical and physical processes. Any change in the shape, size, or motion of these basic clusters altered the properties of the substance involved, although chemical reactions were generally conceived as involving primarily the association and dissociation of various clusters.

Boyle also made significant contributions to experimental chemistry. He made extensive studies of the calcination of metals, of combustion, and of the properties of acids and bases. He emphasized the application of physical techniques to chemical investigation and developed the use of chemical indicators which showed characteristic color changes in the presence of certain types of substances. His pioneering study of phosphorus, during which he discovered nearly all the properties known for the next two centuries, well illustrates the effectiveness of his experimental techniques.

Science and Religion

An influential public figure, Boyle was often at court and was among those who in 1662 used their influence to obtain a charter for the Royal Society. He was a charter member of the society, as well as one of its initial council members, and provided the society with two of its most influential early officials: Henry Oldenburg, who had been tutor to Boyle's nephew, was appointed the society's first secretary, and Robert Hooke became its first curator.

In 1668 Boyle moved to London. As a leading figure of English science and a member of a prominent family, he was offered numerous honors, including a peerage and a bishopric, all of which he declined, insisting that he preferred to remain a simple gentleman. In 1680 he even refused the presidency of the Royal Society on the grounds that his conscience was, as he said, "tender" about subscribing to the necessary oaths.

Throughout his life Boyle maintained a deep and pervasive religious commitment. As an active supporter of missionary work, he was appointed by the King the governor of the Corporation for Propagating the Gospel in New England. He was particularly concerned, however, with demonstrating that science and religion were not only reconcilable but in fact integrally related, and in his effort to promote this belief he produced numerous essays and tracts on religion and natural theology. He died on Dec. 30, 1691, and in addition to leaving much of his estate for the furtherance of various Christian endeavors, he provided in his will for the establishment of an annual series of sermons, in his words, "for proving the Christian Religion against notorious Infidels." These sermons, known as the Boyle Lectures, became by tradition one of the primary platforms for promoting the belief that in the study of nature could be found much of the evidence for religion.

Further Reading

Boyle's better-known writings are collected in Thomas Birch, ed., *The Works of the Honourable Robert Boyle* (5 vols., 1744; new ed., 6 vols., 1772), together with an account of his life which is the principal source of all subsequent biographies. Although not entirely satisfactory, the standard biography is Louis Trenchard More, *The Life and Works of the Honorable Robert Boyle* (1944). A briefer account, with extensive selections from his more important works, is Marie Boas Hall, *Robert Boyle on Natural Philosophy* (1965), while the significance of Boyle's chemical studies is discussed at length in her *Robert Boyle and Seventeenth-Century Chemistry* (1958). A case study of his work in pneumatics is contained in James Bryant Conant, ed., *Harvard Case Histories in Experimental Science* (2 vols., 1957). □

Zabdiel Boylston

Zabdiel Boylston (1679-1766) was the first American physician to use inoculation against smallpox in 1721 during a Boston epidemic.

Zabdiel Boylston was born March 9, 1679, near the present city of Brookline, Mass., and studied medicine with his father, Dr. Thomas Boylston, and a Dr. Cutter of Boston. He married Jerusha Minot in January 1705; they had eight children. Little is known of his career until June 1721. On April 15 of that year a smallpox epidemic had broken out in Boston. Cotton Mather had a slave named Onesimus, who had informed him that inoculation with the disease was commonly used in Africa to prevent a later, severe case. Mather circulated this information to the Bos-

ton medical community by pamphlet and on June 24 wrote Boylston, urging him to begin inoculation. On June 26 Boylston inoculated his son and two servants, and for several months he inoculated others.

Opposition against Boylston and Mather soon led to damage to their houses and an extensive pamphlet war. Though Boylston was called before the selectmen three times to explain his actions, the pamphlets, some jointly written, but mostly by Mather, began to convince many people of the value of inoculation. By February, 241 persons had been inoculated by Boylston; only six died of smallpox, four of whom had contracted the disease before inoculation.

His activities attracted the attention of Sir Hans Sloan in London, where similar experiments were taking place. Sloan invited Boylston to spend the years 1724-1726 in London, lecturing to the Royal College of physicians and working on his book, *An Historical Account of the Smallpox Inoculated in New England,* published in 1726. He also addressed the Royal Society, of which he was made a member in 1726. His account, republished in Boston in 1730, was very carefully documented, the first systematic clinical presentation by an American physician.

On his return to Boston in 1726, Boylston did little more of note. He corresponded with his European friends, inoculated occasionally when epidemics broke out, and retired in the 1740s. He spent his last years raising horses. He died March 1, 1766, after several years of pulmonary illness.

Further Reading

There are no books on Boylston. Brooke Hindle considers him in *The Pursuit of Science in Revolutionary America, 1735-1789* (1956). □

John M. Bozeman

The American pioneer John M. Bozeman (1837-1867), a trailblazer in the Far West, was responsible for opening a route form the Oregon Trail northwest to the Montana gold fields.

John Bozeman was born in January 1837 in Pickens County, Ga. He joined the gold seekers headed for Colorado in the spring of 1860, abandoning his wife and three small children. Unsuccessful in finding a paying claim in Colorado, he went to Gold Creek, in present Montana, in June 1862. When news came of the discovery of gold on Grasshopper Creek in the Beaverhead Valley (Montana), Bozeman joined the stampede that led to the founding of Bannack.

At this time there were two alternative routes from the east: the slow and expensive water route up the Missouri River to Ft. Benton, and then west along the Mullan road; or the Oregon Trail to Ft. Hall, then north or east by a circuitous route largely over barren plains. In May 1863

Bozeman and his partner, John M. Jacobs, left to open a shorter and more direct route that was to begin at Ft. Laramie on the Oregon Trail. They went to the Three Forks of the Missouri River (Montana), crossed the Gallatin Valley, and went through the pass (later known as Bozeman Pass) to the Yellowstone Valley (Wyoming). Harassed by Native Americans, they were able to reach the Platte River only with difficulty. The men assembled an emigrant party at the Deer Creek Crossing of the North Platte, near present Glenock, Wyo.

On the return journey in the vicinity of present Buffalo, Wyo., a large band of Native Americans forced the emigrant train to retrace its steps and take the longer route, west of the Bighorn Mountains; but the determined Bozeman, leading nine men, pushed forward on horseback, traveling at night, to further explore the way across the Great Plains.

Migration to Montana increased in 1864, following the discovery of gold at Virginia City (Montana). Bozeman, his partner Jacobs, and James Bridger were commissioned by the Missouri River and Rocky Mountain Wagon Road and Telegraph Company to guide expeditions form the Platte River to the Yellowstone Valley and on to Virginia City. Bridger chose the route west of the Bighorn Mountains; Bozeman again left the North Platte at present Glenock and directed a party along his route, the Bozeman Trail, characterized by easy grades and vast grasslands.

Bozeman was responsible for starting an agricultural colony in the Gallatin Valley to raise wheat and potatoes to feed the Montana miners. The townsite of Bozeman was laid out in August 1864. Bozeman was elected recorder of the district. The following year he encouraged the construction of the first flour mill in the valley, an enterprise so prosperous its capacity had to be doubled in 1866. Appointed probate judge of Gallatin County in 1865, he led no more wagon trains into Montana.

Recognizing the importance of the Bozeman Trail, the U.S. government attempted to protect emigrants form attacks by establishing three forts on the route in 1866. The Native Americans, however, reestablished their claims to the area in the Fettermann massacre, and after two years of strife the forts were abandoned. Undaunted by the danger, Bozeman and a companion ventured on the route. They encountered a group of Blackfeet at the crossing of the Yellowstone on April 18, 1867. Bozeman was killed, and his wounded friend escaped.

Further Reading

The standard work on Bozeman is Grace Raymond Hebard and E. A. Brinistool, *The Bozeman Trail*. Two histories of Montana give additional information about Bozeman: Merrill G. Burlingame and K. Ross Toole, *A History of Montana* (3 vols., 1957), which provides a scholarly interpretation by Burlingame of Bozeman's significance; and James McLellan Hamilton, *From Wilderness to Statehood: A History of Montana, 1805-1900* (1957). The Native American side of the story is in James C. Olson, *Red Cloud and the Sioux Problem* (1965). □

Hugh Henry Brackenridge

Hugh Henry Brackenridge (1749-1816) was an American lawyer and writer. His reputation as a writer rests almost entirely on "Modern Chivalry," a novel in which he humorously reveals the confusion and controversy that characterized the early years of the American Republic.

Born in Scotland, Hugh Henry Brackenridge was brought by his parents to frontier Pennsylvania in 1763. Educated in country schools, at 16 he became a schoolmaster at Gunpowder Falls, Md. In 1768 he entered Princeton, where with Philip Freneau he composed *The Rising Glory of America* for their graduation exercises in 1771. Though teaching and the study of divinity and law occupied the next several years, he wrote *A Poem on Divine Revelation* on receiving his master of arts degree from Princeton in 1774 and two patriotic plays, for presentation by his students, in 1775 and 1777.

In 1776 Brackenridge became a chaplain with the Continental Army, publishing a collection of his sermons as *Six Political Discourses Founded on the Scriptures* (1778). In 1779 he edited the short-lived *United States Magazine*, which contained important early writings of Freneau and Brackenridge's serialized allegorical narrative *The Cave of Vanhest*. A year later he was admitted to the bar and in 1781 settled in the frontier village of Pittsburgh, where he became a prominent, often controversial, citizen, founded its first newspaper, and opened its first bookstore.

Brackenridge wrote both in prose and in verse on law, politics, and Native American affairs, including *A Masque, Written at Warm Springs in Virginia* (1784); "The Trial of Mamachtaga," one of the earliest effective American short stories; an eyewitness account, *Incidents of the Insurrection in Western Pennsylvania* (1795); and *Law Miscellanies* (1814).

Modern Chivalry

Brackenridge's novel *Modern Chivalry* first appeared in two volumes in 1792; a third volume appeared in 1793, a fourth in 1797; new parts were issued in 1804 and 1805; the whole was expanded and revised in four volumes in 1816; a posthumous revised edition in two volumes appeared in 1819. Pretending to be "a book without a thought, or the smallest degree of sense," *Modern Chivalry* recites the adventures of quixotic Captain Farrago and his servant, Teague O'Regan, as they roam the countryside, with ignorant Teague bumbling into trouble by being elected again and again to public office, tarred and feathered or jailed for political or amorous activities—a democratic bumpkin used to satirize the peculiarities of democracy. Physicians, lawyers, army veterans, strong-armed and strong-voiced politicians, mob violence, and lovesickness all submit to Brackenridge's bantering, double-edged observations. This picaresque and satirical novel owes much to Cervantes, Henry Fielding, and Laurence Sterne. In language forthright, in humor often slapstick, sometimes fiercely ironic, it anticipates later satiric examinations of democracy by James Fenimore Cooper, Herman Melville, and H.L. Mencken.

Further Reading

Excellent biographies of Brackenridge are Claude Milton Newlin, *The Life and Writings of Hugh Henry Brackenridge* (1932), and Daniel Marder, *Hugh Henry Brackenridge* (1967). A complete edition of Brackenridge's *Modern Chivalry* was edited by Newlin in 1937, a modernized edition of the first four volumes by Lewis Leary in 1965.

Additional Sources

Indian atrocities: narratives of the perils and sufferings of Dr. Knight and John Slover, among the Indians, during the Revolutionary War, Fairfield, Wash.: Ye Galleon Press, 1983. □

Ray Bradbury

Ray Bradbury (born 1920) was among the first authors to combine the concepts of science fiction with a sophisticated prose style. Often described as economical yet poetic, Bradbury's fiction conveys a vivid sense of place in which everyday events are transformed into unusual, sometimes sinister situations.

B radbury began his career during the 1940s as a writer for such pulp magazines as *Black Mask, Amazing Stories,* and *Weird Tales.* The latter magazine served to showcase the works of such fantasy writers as H. P. Lovecraft, Clark Ashton Smith, and August Derleth. Derleth, who founded Arkham House, a publishing company specializing in fantasy literature, accepted one of Bradbury's stories for *Who Knocks?,* an anthology published by his firm. Derleth subsequently suggested that Bradbury compile a volume of his own stories; the resulting book, *Dark Carnival* (1947), collects Bradbury's early fantasy tales. Although Bradbury rarely published pure fantasy later in his career, such themes of his future work as the need to retain humanistic values and the importance of the imagination are displayed in the stories of this collection. Many of these pieces were republished with new material in *The October Country* (1955).

The publication of *The Martian Chronicles* (1950) established Bradbury's reputation as an author of sophisticated science fiction. This collection of stories is connected by the framing device of the settling of Mars by human beings and is dominated by tales of space travel and environmental adaptation. Bradbury's themes, however, reflect many of the important issues of the post-World War II era— racism, censorship, technology, and nuclear war—and the stories delineate the implications of these themes through authorial commentary. Clifton Fadiman described *The Martian Chronicles* as being "as grave and troubling as one of Hawthorne's allegories." Another significant collection of short stories, *The Illustrated Man* (1951), also uses a framing device, basing the stories on the tattoos of the title character.

Bradbury's later short story collections are generally considered to be less significant than *The Martian Chronicles* and *The Illustrated Man.* Bradbury shifted his focus in these volumes from outer space to more familiar earthbound settings. *Dandelion Wine* (1957), for example, has as its main subject the midwestern youth of Bradbury's semiautobiographical protagonist, Douglas Spaulding. Although Bradbury used many of the same techniques in these stories as in his science fiction and fantasy publications, *Dandelion Wine* was not as well received as his earlier work. Other later collections, including *A Medicine for Melancholy* (1959), *The Machineries of Joy* (1964), *I Sing the Body Electric!* (1969), and *Long after Midnight* (1976), contain stories set in Bradbury's familiar outer space or midwestern settings and explore his typical themes. Many of Bradbury's stories have been anthologized or filmed for such television programs as *The Twilight Zone, Alfred Hitchcock Presents,* and *Ray Bradbury Theater.*

In addition to his short fiction, Bradbury has several adult novels. The first of these, *Fahrenheit 451* (1953), originally published as a short story and later expanded into novel form, concerns a future society in which books are burned because they are perceived as threats to societal conformity. In *Something Wicked This Way Comes* (1962) a father attempts to save his son and a friend from the sinister forces of a mysterious traveling carnival. Both of these novels have been adapted for film. *Death Is a Lonely Busi-*

ness (1985) is a detective story featuring Douglas Spaulding, the protagonist of *Dandelion Wine,* as a struggling writer for pulp magazines *Dandelion Wine* and *The Martian Chronicles* are often included in the category of novel. Bradbury has also written poetry and drama; critics have faulted his efforts in these genres as lacking the impact of his fiction.

While Bradbury's popularity is acknowledged even by his detractors, many critics find the reasons for his success difficult to pinpoint. Some believe that the tension Bradbury creates between fantasy and reality is central to his ability to convey his visions and interests to his readers. Peter Stoler asserted that Bradbury's reputation rests on his ''chillingly understated stories about a familiar world where it is always a few minutes before midnight on Halloween, and where the unspeakable and unthinkable become commonplace.'' Mary Ross proposed that ''Perhaps the special quality of [Bradbury's] fantasy lies in the fact that people to whom amazing things happen are often so simply, often touchingly, like ourselves.'' In a genre in which futurism and the fantastic are usually synonymous, Bradbury stands out for his celebration of the future in realistic terms and his exploration of conventional values and ideas. As one of the first science fiction writers to convey his themes through a refined prose style replete with subtlety and humanistic analogies, Bradbury has helped make science fiction a more respected literary genre and is widely admired by the literary establishment.

Further Reading

Authors in the News, Gale, Volume 1, 1976, Volume 2, 1976.
Amis, Kingsley, *New Maps of Hell,* Ballantine, 1960, pp. 90-7.
Berton, Pierre, *Voices from the Sixties,* Doubleday, 1967, pp. 1-10.
Breit, Harvey, *The Writer Observed,* World Publishing, 1956.
Clareson, Thomas D., editor, *Voices for the Future: Essays on Major Science Fiction Writers,* Volume 1, Bowling Green State University Press, 1976.
Concise Dictionary of American Literary Biography: Broadening Views, 1968-1988, Gale, 1989.
Contemporary Literary Criticism, Gale, Volume 1, 1973, Volume 3, 1975, Volume 10, 1979, Volume 15, 1980, Volume 42, 1987. □

Edward Braddock

Edward Braddock (1695-1755) was commander in chief of the British forces in North America during the French and Indian War of the 18th century.

Little is known of Edward Braddock's early life. In October 1710 he purchased an ensign's commission in the Coldstream Guards, his father's regiment; in 1716 he became lieutenant of the grenadier company; in 1734 he was captain lieutenant with an army rank of lieutenant colonel; in 1743 he was second major with an army rank of colonel; and in 1745 he became colonel of the regiment. He saw little action when he accompanied the 2d Battalion to Ostend, Belgium, in July 1745. That same year he served

with the Duke of Cumberland in the suppression of the Jacobite rebellion. Two years later he commanded the 2d Battalion of the Coldstream Guards at Lestock's and was with St. Clair in the abortive attempt on Port L'Orient, France. Subsequently he was employed under the Prince of Orange at Bergen op Zoom, Netherlands. In 1753 he was appointed colonel of the 14th Regiment and joined his command at Gibraltar. Adored by his men, he was almost brutal in his relations with civilians and became the butt of satires by both Henry Fielding and Horace Walpole.

Promoted to major general in 1754, Braddock arrived in Alexandria, Va., in February 1755 as commander in chief of British forces in North America. His instructions bestowed more power upon him than ever held by any military officer in America. But his efforts were hampered by a lack of money, although Governor Dinwiddie, George Washington, and Benjamin Franklin made material contributions.

With the objective of capturing Ft. Duquesne at the forks of the Ohio River, Braddock commanded a force of 1,400 British regulars and nearly 700 colonial militia (whom he hated). Progress was slow as his column moved from Ft. Cumberland, for Braddock insisted upon using wagons rather than pack animals and so a new road had to be constructed. After 30 miles of a 110-mile march, Braddock accepted Washington's advice and left his heavy transport at Little Meadows, guarded by a regiment of his regulars; he pushed on ahead for fear the French would receive reinforcements. Poor relations with Native Americans left him open to surprise.

After crossing the Monongahela River on July 9, 1755, his advance guard was ambushed by 900 French, Canadians, and Native Americans under Daniel Beaujeau. Braddock refused to heed the advice of provincial officers to allow his men to take cover, instead holding them in the British traditional column formation. Exposed to an enfilading fire from the hidden enemy, the British regulars fled. It was only because the hostile natives stopped to take scalps that the British were able to gain the protection of their rear guard and retreat to Ft. Cumberland. Of the 1,459 soldiers under Braddock, 977 were killed or wounded. The 89 officers suffered 63 casualties. Braddock had four horses shot from beneath him before he suffered mortal wounds in the arm and lungs. Four days later he died at Great Meadows. His last words, according to tradition, were, "We shall better know how to deal with them another time."

Further Reading

Lee McCardell, *Ill-starred General: Braddock of the Coldstream Guards* (1958), a sympathetic treatment, attempts to show that Braddock has been much maligned. An account of Braddock's American campaign is in Hayes Baker-Crothers, *Virginia and the French and Indian War* (1928). The campaign is also covered in Douglas Southall Freeman, *George Washington,* vol. 2 (1948).

Additional Sources

McCardell, Lee., *Ill-starred general: Braddock of the Coldstream Guards,* Pittsburgh, PA: University of Pittsburgh Press, 1986.
□

William Bradford

William Bradford (1590-1657), one of the Pilgrim Fathers, was the leader of the Plymouth Colony in America. His extraordinary history, "Of Plymouth Plantation," was not published until 1856.

On March 19, 1590, William Bradford was baptized at Austerfield, Yorkshire, England. His father, a yeoman farmer, died when William was only a year old. The boy was trained by relatives to be a farmer. He was still young when he joined a group of Separatists (Protestant radicals who separated from the established Church of England) in nearby Scrooby. For most of the rest of his life, the best source is his *Of Plymouth Plantation.*

Becoming a Pilgrim

In 1607 Bradford and about 120 others were attacked as nonconformists to the Church of England. They withdrew to Holland, under the religious leadership of John Robinson and William Brewster, living for a year at Amsterdam and then in Leiden, where they stayed nearly 12 years. They were very poor; Bradford worked in the textile industry. In these hard years he seems to have managed to get something of an education because he lived with the Brewsters

near a university. Bradford was attracted to the ideal of a close-knit community such as the Scrooby group had established. At the age of 23 he married 16-year-old Dorothy May, who belonged to a group of Separatists that had come earlier from England.

The threat of religious wars, the difficulty of earning a decent living, the loss from the community of children who assimilated Dutch ways, the zeal for missionary activity— these forces led the Scrooby group to consider becoming "Pilgrims" by leaving Holland for America. After many delays they chose New England as their goal, and with financial support from London merchants and from Sir Ferdinando Gorges, who claimed rights to the American area they sought, the Pilgrims readied to leave for America.

Signing the Mayflower Compact

But the terms arranged for the colonists by their deacon were treacherous; the backers and the settlers were to share ownership in the land the colonists improved and the dwellings they constructed. Many of the Pilgrims' coreligionists backed out of the enterprise, and a group of "strangers" was recruited to replace them. When one of their two ships, the *Speedwell,* proved unseaworthy, the expedition was delayed further. Finally, in September 1620 the *Mayflower* departed alone, its 102 passengers almost equally divided between "saints" and "strangers." The men on board signed a compact that established government by consent of the governed, the "Mayflower Compact." John Carver (with Brewster, the oldest of the saints) was elected governor.

On landing at Cape Cod in November, a group led by Myles Standish went ashore to explore; they chose Plymouth harbor for their settlement. Meanwhile Dorothy Bradford had drowned. (In 1623 Bradford married a widow from Leiden, with whom he had three children.)

The settlers soon began to construct dwellings. The winter was harsh; one of many who died of the illness that swept the colony was Governor Carver. Bradford became governor, and under him the colonists learned to survive. Squanto, a Native American who had lived in England, taught the settlers to grow corn; and they came to know Massasoit, chief of the Wampanoag tribe. A vivid report on these early adventures written by Bradford and Edward Winslow was sent to England and published as *Mourt's Relation* (1622); with it went clapboard and other materials gathered by the settlers to begin paying off their debts. (Unfortunately the cargo was pirated by a French privateer—a typical piece of Pilgrim bad luck.)

Bradford was responsible for the financial burdens as well as the governing of the colony until his death, though for some five years he did not officially serve as governor. These years saw the debt continue to grow (with great effort it was paid off in 1648).

Developing Plymouth Colony

The population of the colony gradually increased, and by 1623 there were 32 houses and 180 residents. Yet during Bradford's lifetime the colony, which began for religious reasons mainly, never had a satisfactory minister. John Robinson, a great pastor in Holland who had been expected to guide the saints, never reached America. One clergyman who did come, John Lyford, was an especially sharp thorn in Bradford's side. Eventually he was exiled, with the result that the London backers regarded the colonists as contentious and incapable of self-rule.

Gradually as Plymouth Colony came to encompass a number of separate settlements, Bradford's particular idea of community was lost. After 1630 the colony was overshadowed by its neighbor, the Massachusetts Bay Colony. But in fact Plymouth never amounted to much as a political power. By 1644 the entire colony's population was still a mere 300. Plymouth did make other northern colonizing efforts attractive; it supplied important material aid to the Bay Colony, and it may have helped establish its Congregational church polity as the "New England way." Bradford was admired by Governor John Winthrop of Boston, with whom he frequently met to discuss common problems.

Bradford the Man

Bradford's private life was distinguished by self-culture. He taught himself Greek and came to know classical poetry and philosophy as well as contemporary religious writers. He worked on his great history, *Of Plymouth Plantation,* from 1630 until 1646, adding little afterward. Most of the events were described in retrospect. He wrote as a believer in God's providence, but the book usually has an objective tone. Though far from being an egotist, Bradford emerges as the attractive hero of his story. The last pages reflect his recognition that the colony was not a success, and the book has been called a tragic history. Though he stopped writing his history altogether in 1650, he remained vigorous and active until his death in 1657.

Further Reading

A convenient modern edition of Bradford's history was prepared by Samuel Eliot Morison, ed., *Of Plymouth Plantation, 1620-1647* (1952). Another edition was published in 1962, edited and with an introduction by Harvey Wish. The best biography is Bradford Smith, *Bradford of Plymouth* (1951). G. F. Willison, *Saints and Strangers* (1945), an account of the Pilgrims, contains much material on Bradford. Background works include Harvey Wish, *Society and Thought in Early America* (1950); Ruth A. McIntyre, *Debts Hopeful and Desperate: Financing the Plymouth Colony* (1963); and George D. Langdon, Jr., *Pilgrim Colony: A History of New Plymouth, 1620-1691* (1966). □

William Bradford

The American printer William Bradford (1663-1752) is often referred to as "the pioneer printer of the Middle colonies." He was involved in frequent controversies over freedom of the press.

William Bradford was born on May 20, 1663, in Leicestershire, England. His parents apprenticed him to Andrew Sowle, the foremost Quaker printer in London. The ambitious young man learned the trade, adopted Sowle's religion, and in 1685 married his master's daughter, Elizabeth. Bradford sailed to Pennsylvania in 1685. He carried a letter of recommendation from George Fox, the founder of the Quakers.

Bradford wasted little time in setting up shop. By the end of the year the first printing in the Middle colonies had appeared. It was an almanac, the *Kalendarium Pennsilvaniense,* by Samuel Atkins. In it Bradford asked forgiveness for some errors caused by haste and the disorders of travel. But he hoped his readers would be cheered that "after great Charge and Trouble" he had brought "that great Art and Mystery of *Printing* to this part of *America.*"

The almanac got an unexpected reception. Printing in the New World was often a precarious business. Governor William Penn may have been uneasy about the establishment of a press in his colony; in any case, he took offense at one slight reference to him in the almanac. Atkins was swiftly reprimanded, and Bradford was ordered to print nothing without license from the Pennsylvania Council. In 1687 Bradford was told that nothing could be printed about the Quakers without their formal approval. In 1689 trouble arose between a new governor and the populace. The governor officially reprimanded Bradford for issuing Penn's original charter for the colony, in spite of the printer's plea that it was his business to print whatever was brought him by any party. For a time Bradford resigned his business and went to England, returning in 1690 to what he thought were better prospects. He was involved with William Rittenhouse in opening the first paper mill in British America. But trouble came again a few years later when Bradford took the minority side in a conflict among Quakers. His property was seized and he was arrested, though he escaped conviction.

In April 1693 the New York Council invited Bradford to become their public printer. His first New York production, called *New-England's Spirit of Persecution Transmitted to Pennsylvania,* discussed his own case. His New York business was wide and varied, including the printing of books, tracts, paper money, and the laws of the colony.

Bradford has numerous "firsts" to his credit in the history of American printing. From 1725 to 1744 he published the *New York Gazette,* the colony's first newspaper. After 1733 it had a rival, the *Weekly Journal,* published by Bradford's former apprentice and partner, John Peter Zenger. Bradford, as public printer, supported the government. Zenger was sponsored by a faction opposed to the government. When attempts were made to suppress Zenger, Bradford took a new side, against the government, in the famous freedom-of-press controversy.

Bradford's business, which included bookselling, grew lucrative. After 1723 he also did printing for New Jersey. He retired at the age of 80 and died on May 23, 1752. His son Andrew and his grandson William were also important early American printers and journalists.

Further Reading

A brief and interesting portrait of Bradford is in John T. Winterich, *Early American Books and Printing* (1935). The standard book on printing in the Colonies, Laurence C. Wroth, *The Colonial Printer* (1931; 2d ed. 1938), considers Bradford at length. For the background of freedom of the press, the most important book is Leonard W. Levy, *Legacy of Suppression: Freedom of Speech and Press in Early American History* (1960). □

William Bradford

The American journalist William Bradford (1722-1791) published an influential newspaper. Opponent of British policies, he followed words with heroic deeds during the Revolution and was known as "the patriot printer of 1776."

Born in New York City, William Bradford was the grandson of the William Bradford who introduced printing in the Middle colonies and gave New York its first newspaper. His uncle, Andrew Bradford, was responsible for Philadelphia's first newspaper. The tradition would be continued by William's own son, Thomas. The Bradfords must be recognized as one of the most influential families of printers in America for nearly 150 years. Young William learned the craft from his uncle, then visited London to improve his skills and prospects. In 1742 he returned to Philadelphia with printing equipment and stock for a bookstore. His career established, he married Rachel Budd from a prosperous New Jersey family.

Bradford carried on a profitable printing and bookselling business and issued two of the best colonial periodicals, the *Pennsylvania Journal* (begun in 1742), a weekly, and the *American Magazine* (1757), a monthly. The *Journal* rivaled Benjamin Franklin's *Gazette*. Bradford's paper, better printed and as well edited, circulated throughout the Colonies, including the West Indies.

A man of wide contacts in a prospering city, Bradford was successful in a number of ventures. In 1762 he and a partner formed the Philadelphia Insurance Company, designed to insure shipping and merchandise. The background for his other operations was the London Coffee-House for Merchants and Traders, which he opened in 1754, where men of influence met to transact business and exchange opinions. In time Bradford was able to consolidate most of his ventures in adjoining buildings. He was a powerful figure in a colony of critical importance. And he was in touch with his peers elsewhere.

Bradford's position in Philadelphia society and his interest in Pennsylvania's prosperity made him a key figure in the development of colonial opposition to Great Britain. During the French and Indian War he gained some military experience. One of the most vehement antagonists of the Stamp Act of 1765, he became a leader in the Sons of Liberty. At the same time he opposed some Americans who seemed too irresponsible, particularly William Goddard of the *Maryland Journal*. Bradford followed his own newspaper attacks on British policies with increasing emphasis on the importance of a continental congress. In 1774 his paper carried the famous picture of a dissected snake with the motto, "Unite or Die." He was the printer for the First Congress, and along with editors in other cities he also became a postmaster.

Bradford joined the Revolution, first with money and aid in communication, then as a soldier. Badly wounded at Princeton, after 1778 he gave himself to administrative work in the revolutionary cause. His service ruined both his health and his business. He died on Sept. 25, 1791.

Bradford was an example of the prosperous colonial figures with their own economic interests and intercolonial contacts, whose spirits grew steadily toward revolution, and who frequently gave the cause a rather moderate character.

Further Reading

The fullest source on Bradford is John W. Wallace, *An Old Philadelphian: Colonel William Bradford* (1884). Besides an extensive, though uncritical, biography, it includes sketches by associates and gleanings from his press. For background on newspapers and the Revolution, as well as information on Bradford, a helpful book is Arthur M. Schlesinger, Sr., *Prelude to Independence: The Newspaper War on Britain* (1957). Also useful is Carl and Jessica Bridenbaugh, *Rebels and Gentlemen: Philadelphia in the Age of Franklin* (1942). □

Charles Bradlaugh

The English freethinker and political agitator Charles Bradlaugh (1833-1891) successfully struggled to secure the right of nonbelievers to take seats in the House of Commons.

The son of a poor clerk, Charles Bradlaugh was born in London on Sept. 26, 1833. At 15 he abandoned Christianity for atheism. From 1850 to 1853 he was a private in the army in Ireland. Through these years he taught himself languages and law. By the end of the 1850s he had become the most powerful British propagandist for atheism, and in his public lectures he faced with courage and skill hostility and even physical abuse.

Bradlaugh became president of the London Secular Society in 1858. In 1860 he founded the periodical *National Reformer,* which continued as his vehicle until his death. In 1866 he organized the National Secular Society, which became the largest of such organizations in Britain. Through the 1860s he developed a large and devoted following among London workingmen. He was an early supporter of woman's suffrage, birth control, and republicanism. In 1874 Bradlaugh was joined by Mrs. Annie Besant, who became a vice president of the Secular Society.

Bradlaugh sought election to the House of Commons from Northampton; twice unsuccessful, he finally won in 1880. There then ensued a long controversy over his right to be seated. This dispute centered on the oath of office invoking God that all members were required to take. Bradlaugh offered to take this oath or to substitute an affirmation of allegiance for it. But the House refused him either option.

Over the next five years Bradlaugh was reelected four times but was not allowed to take his seat. Eight separate legal actions proceeded from the controversy. The constitutional issues raised were finally resolved by passage of Bradlaugh's Affirmation Bill in 1888. The House removed the records of his expulsions from its journals just before Bradlaugh's death on Jan. 30, 1891.

Bradlaugh was in no sense a true radical. His atheism and his political convictions were based on 18th-century individualism. He was suspicious of socialism and of government intervention even in hours of work. But he was a dedicated and honorable figure. G. J. Holyoake, his rival for Secularist leadership, called him "the greatest agitator, within the limits of the law, who appeared in my time among the working people."

Further Reading

Bradlaugh published *The Autobiography of Mr. Bradlaugh: A Page of His Life* in 1873. Anthologies of selections from Bradlaugh's voluminous writings are *Humanity's Gain from Unbelief, and Other Selections* (1929) and a centennial volume, *Champion of Liberty: Charles Bradlaugh* (1933). The standard biography is by his daughter, Hypatia Bradlaugh Bonner, *Charles Bradlaugh* (2 vols., 1894). A briefer, lively

account is in Warren S. Smith, *The London Heretics, 1870-1914* (1967).

Additional Sources

Arnstein, Walter L., *The Bradlaugh case: atheism, sex, and politics among the late Victorians,* Columbia: University of Missouri Press, 1983, 1965.

Royle, Edward., *The Bradlaugh papers: letters, papers and printed items relating to the life of Charles Bradlaugh (1833-1891), arranged from the collection assembled by his daughter, Hypatia Bradlaugh Bonner (1858-1935), and now in the possession of the National Secular Society . . . : a descriptive index,* Wakefield: EP Microform, 1975. ☐

Ed Bradley

An award-winning broadcast journalist, Ed Bradley (born 1941) remains best known for his work on the weekly news program *60 Minutes*.

Born on June 22, 1941, in Philadelphia, Pennsylvania, Edward R. Bradley received a B.S. degree in education from Cheyney State College in Cheyney, Pennsylvania. From 1963 to 1967 Bradley worked as a disc jockey and news reporter for WDAS radio in Philadelphia. From there he moved on to WCBS radio in New York. He joined CBS as a stringer in the Paris bureau in 1971. Within a few months he was transferred to the Saigon bureau, where he remained until he was assigned to the Washington bureau in June 1974.

Until 1981, Bradley served as anchor for *CBS Sunday Night News* and as principal correspondent for *CBS Reports*. In 1981 he replaced Dan Rather as a correspondent for the weekly news program, *60 Minutes*. In 1992 Bradley was made host of the CBS news program, *Street Stories*.

Bradley has won seven Emmy Awards for broadcast journalism, two Alfred I. duPont-Columbia University Awards for broadcast journalism, a George Foster Peabody Broadcasting Award, a George Polk Award, and an NCAA Anniversary Award.

As a correspondent for CBS's *60 Minutes* since 1981, Bradley has become one of the most visible African-Americans on network television news. As Morgan Strong observed in *Playboy,* Bradley's "soft-spoken and often intensely personal reports made him the first black reporter to become a comfortable part of America's extended TV family."

Bradley's easygoing style belies his many achievements. Some have commented that he seems to have scaled the heights of the television news business more by a knack for being in the right place at the right time than by driving ambition. Michele Wallace of *Essence* called him "a maverick by happenstance, a trailblazer by accident, an inadvertent explorer on the frontier of racial barriers." But Bradley is driven not by ambition in the usual sense—"If I never anchor the national news, that's fine," he told Wallace—but by a less tangible standard. "I think I always need a new

challenge," he commented to Kristin McMurran in *People.* "I do need some adventure in my life." And he pointed out to Wallace: "I've always been driven—but I'm not the kind of person who says 'This is going to take me here and that's going to take me there.' I don't have goals—I have standards of achievement."

Bradley grew up in Philadelphia, Pennsylvania, in a neighborhood where "if you didn't fight, you got beat up," he recalled to McMurran. "We were poor, but there was always food on the table. I was raised by people who worked 20-hour days at two jobs each. . . . I was told 'You can be anything you want, kid.' When you hear that often enough, you believe it."

Drifted Into Broadcast News

When Bradley graduated from college in 1964 he went to work as an elementary school teacher while moonlighting as an unpaid disc jockey at a local jazz radio station. He gradually moved into Philadelphia's WDAS news operation, reading hourly newscasts and still receiving no wages. He got the chance to cover his first hard news story when rioting broke out in north Philadelphia and WDAS found itself short-staffed.

"It must have been about two o'clock in the morning. . . . I was coming out of a club and turned on the radio," Bradley related to Tony Vellela in the *Christian Science Monitor.* "I heard Gary Shepard reporting on this rioting that was going on." Bradley proceeded to the station to get a tape recorder and an engineer. "For the next 48 hours, without sleep, I covered the riots. . . . I was getting these great scoops. . . . And that kind of hooked me on the idea of doing live stuff, going out and covering the news."

Bradley proved himself a capable newsman, and the station began paying him a small salary. In 1967 he moved to WCBS, an all-news CBS Radio affiliate in New York City. He worked there for three and a half years before restlessness prompted him to take a vacation in France. "I decided that I was born to live in Paris," he told Strong. After quitting his $45,000-a-year job and moving to the French capital, he planned to "write the great American novel," according to McMurran. "I didn't go to Paris for a career," Strong quoted him as saying, "I went to Paris for my life." Bradley wrote poetry and enjoyed the cultural life of the city until he ran out of money. He subsequently took the only opportunity that would allow him to stay in Paris, becoming a stringer for CBS's Paris bureau where peace talks between the United States and North Vietnam were in progress. Paid by the story, Bradley was able to earn a modest living covering the conference. "If they held the talks, I made the rent money," he told Strong. "I remember once when the talks were suspended for 13 weeks and I got a check for $12.50. But I managed to survive."

After a year, the journalist decided he wanted to get back into the news business full time. "My ego wouldn't let me be part time," he admitted in *People.* He noted in *Playboy,* "I decided I was either going all the way in or getting out," and became a war correspondent in Indochina for CBS-TV. He spent most of the next three years in Vietnam and Cambodia and was wounded in a mortar attack on

Easter Sunday in 1973. Reassigned to Washington, D.C., in 1974, the journalist returned to Vietnam in 1975 to report on the end of the war.

Covered the Carter White House

After the fall of Saigon, South Vietnam, which marked the defeat of the anti-Communist government, Bradley returned to the United States to cover Jimmy Carter's campaign for the U.S. presidency. Following the election, CBS assigned him to its Washington, D.C., bureau, where he became the network's first African American White House correspondent. Though the White House beat is considered a prestigious position, Bradley hated it. For one thing, he was CBS's second-string reporter in the capital. Secondly, as he told Strong, "it was an office job. You go to the same place every day and check in . . . down in the basement in this little nook in the back of the White House press room. And if Jimmy Carter jumps, I [had] to be there to say how high. But it [was] no great fun, and it wasn't the kind of work I wanted to do."

Chafing under the constraints of the assignment, Bradley acquired a reputation for being hard to get along with, one which has followed him ever since. He admits that his work in Washington did not bring out the best in him, but he feels the charge is unjustified. "I don't think I'm abrasive or egocentric. I think I have a healthy ego, but my problem in Washington was that there were too many bullshit assignments," he explained to Strong. "I had always worked overseas. . . . When I went out, I was the producer. So then to come back and have to report to a desk . . . it was all a big change for me. . . . I had not come up through the system."

As soon as he could, Bradley left the Washington bureau to join *CBS Reports* and produce documentaries. The new job took him back to Southeast Asia to make "What's Happening in Cambodia?," a program about refugees fleeing the country during the 1970s. While filming in the refugee camps in Thailand, Bradley and cameraman Norman Lloyd encountered some young Cambodians who were searching for missing relatives. "It's the kind of thing that Norman and I do best," Bradley recalled in *TV Guide*. "We breeze into this Cambodian joint, throw down some beers and say 'What are you guys doing here, man? No kidding! You're going to do *what*? Can we go with you? You can't get in, huh? *We'll* get you in.'" Bradley and Lloyd succeeded in getting the youths into the camp and after following them around for most of the day, captured a tearful mother-son reunion on camera.

Though Bradley resists being pigeonholed as a African American reporter and is said to hate covering "black" stories, some of his finest moments with *CBS Reports* came while focusing on racial issues. In "Murder—Teen-age Style," for example, the reporter examined the problem of violence among African American gangs in Los Angeles. Producer Howard Stringer, who had to talk Bradley into taking the assignment, was quoted by *TV Guide's* Rod Townley as saying "[Bradley]'s black . . . he's younger than most of our correspondents, hipper than most of our correspondents, and knows the world better than most of our correspondents." Stringer also noted that Bradley "doesn't

like and doesn't do well at really abstract stories. . . . Ed is a reporter." But the journalist combined both reportage and analysis in his "Blacks in America: With All Deliberate Speed," a 1979 look at race relations in the United States that won him an Emmy and an Alfred I. duPont-Columbia University Award. The documentary contrasted the status of African Americans in Mississippi and Philadelphia in 1954 and 1979. "To the credit of Bradley and his producer, Philip Burton, Jr.," wrote Axel Madsen in *60 Minutes: The Power and the Politics of America's Most Popular News Show*, "the program reported both failures and occasional improvements and concluded that court actions, attempted enforcement, and massive media attention hadn't brought much change."

CBS Reports also sent Bradley to China and Saudi Arabia and to Malaysia to make a documentary on the Vietnamese refugees known as "boat people." "The Boat People" aired in 1979, earning Bradley an Emmy and several other awards. It was also excerpted on *60 Minutes* and may have been a deciding factor in the choice of Bradley to join the staff of America's most popular news program.

Bradley had been considered for *60 Minutes* when a fourth correspondent was added in the late 1970s, but Harry Reasoner was chosen instead. Then when Dan Rather left the news program to take over Walter Cronkite's position as anchor of the *CBS Evening News*, Bradley was asked to join Reasoner, Morley Safer, and Mike Wallace. In his book *Minute by Minute*, producer Don Hewitt wrote of Bradley, "He's so good and so savvy and so lights up the tube every time he's on it that I wonder what took us so long."

Bradley, as quoted by Hewitt, said, "It soon became apparent that I was the front runner, if I believed Hewitt, who went around saying to everybody but me, 'If there's a better reporter than Bradley, I wish someone would point him out,' but still he never said it to me. Finally I was in Los Angeles . . . for a [question] and [answer] session with the TV critics, when a reporter in the back of the room . . . asked Bob Chandler, the CBS News vice president who looked after 60 Minutes, about who was going to replace Rather. Either Chandler was writing Hewitt's lines or Hewitt was writing his: 'If there is a better reporter than Bradley, etc. . . . ' was the answer. . . . The next week I was named to replace Dan Rather."

The New Face on *60 Minutes*

Bradley's presence changed the chemistry of *60 Minutes*, with the substitution of his sensitive, compassionate approach to interviewing and reporting for Rather's more aggressive, sometimes pugnacious tactics. Aware that television audiences are notoriously fickle, Bradley felt that if ratings slipped, he would get the blame. But viewers seemed to accept him readily, though some critics have reacted less favorably. In 1983, for example, Mark Ribowsky wrote in *TV Guide* that Bradley had "not succeeded in establishing a familiar persona for viewers, or made a story sizzle." And four years later, David Shaw, in the same magazine, called Bradley one of the "least impressive of the correspondents [on *60 Minutes*]." Shaw faulted several of Bradley's stories for being "simple" and "superficial" and others for overlooking important questions, but nevertheless praised his "tough-minded report" on defects in the Audi 5000, a story which helped focus attention on a problem that led to the recall of 250,000 cars.

Coworkers and critics alike have pointed out Bradley's ability to establish a rapport with his subjects. Mike Wallace remarked that Bradley's approach is "instinctive—he has no idea how he does it." Bradley himself resists analyzing his style; he remarked to Townley, "I'd rather not think about it and just go out and do it, and it will come naturally." When Bradley profiled singer Lena Horne in December of 1981, for example, John Weisman of *TV Guide* described the journalist's work as "a textbook example of what a great television interview can be." Intercutting Horne's performances with interview segments in which Horne discussed her personal and professional life, Bradley and producer Jeanne Solomon drew an intimate portrait of the singer that, as Bradley observed to Weisman, "told a lot of things about our society. It told a lot about the way women are treated, a lot of things about the way blacks are treated. It told a lot of things about interracial marriages, difficulties in the film and entertainment industries and how those things have changed and not changed." Bradley has said that he feels "Lena" is among his best work, and Wallace called it "as good a piece as I have seen on television in my life." "Lena" won Bradley his first Emmy as a member of the *60 Minutes* team.

Bradley's gift for winning his subjects' confidence was also crucial when he interviewed actor Laurence Olivier, who was ill at the time. There was some doubt about whether Olivier would have the stamina to complete the interview, but as Hewitt retold it, "gradually, prodded by Ed's questions, the frail old man who had tottered into the room became Laurence Olivier, the actor. The interview went on for another hour and a half as Laurence Olivier and Ed Bradley jousted with each other. When Jeanne finally said 'cut' neither had fallen off his horse, and we wrapped one of the more memorable *60 Minutes* interviews."

Not all of Bradley's interviews have been cordial ones. In one of his first pieces for *60 Minutes,* "The Other Face of the IRA," Bradley spoke with Northern Irish activist Bernadette Devlin McAliskey, prompting a heated discussion of politics and religion, which culminated with McAliskey declaring, "At the end of the day, God will be on the side of the winner, regardless of who wins, regardless of how he wins, because God always was and always will be." Other stories that required a more aggressive approach were Bradley's Emmy-winning study of convicted killer-turned-author Jack Henry Abbott and the story that Bradley described to *TV Guide* as the toughest he'd ever done: a report on the murder of CBS correspondent George Polk in post-World War II Greece.

The Polk investigation presented several difficulties. Many of the principals were dead, and as Bradley explained to Stephen Galloway in *TV Guide,* "for the people who are still alive, you're asking them to talk about something that happened 45 years ago. It's difficult to trust their memory." The piece presented a personal difficulty for Bradley as well: he discovered that one of his journalistic heroes, retired CBS

correspondent Winston Burdett, might have been involved in a cover-up to protect Polk's killers. "I'd grown up listening to [Burdett] on the radio," reflected Bradley after what Galloway called "one of the most riveting interviews of one journalist by another."

After more than a decade of investigating and presenting thought-provoking subjects on *60 Minutes* and with six Emmy awards and numerous other honors to his credit, Bradley is no longer a new face but an "ominous and undeflectable presence . . . imperturbable and arguably beyond reproach," commented Johnathan Schwartz in *Gentlemen's Quarterly.* "He is adored without worship." In 1995 Bradley was the highest scorer in seven of eight categories among active CBS journalists in a viewers poll in *TV Guide.*

Occasional rumors of conflict with the *60 Minutes* production staff have subsided, as have speculations that Bradley is unhappy with his job. His need for adventure does not seem to have diminished, though, and he travels often, spending much of his life in hotels. The journalist summed up his attitude about his career in *People* in 1983: "The bottom line is this job is fun. And when it stops being fun, then I'll stop doing it."

Further Reading

Hewitt, Don, *Minute by Minute,* Random House, 1985.
Madsen, Axel, *60 Minutes: The Power and the Politics of America's Most Popular News Show,* Dodd, Mead and Company, 1984.
Christian Science Monitor, October 16, 1986.
Ebony, August 1983.
Essence, November 1983.
Gentlemen's Quarterly, May 1989.
Jet, February 20, 1995.
People, November 14, 1983.
TV Guide, October 18, 1980; February 20, 1982; January 22, 1983; February 25, 1984; March 28, 1987; January 19, 1991.
□

Francis Herbert Bradley

The English philosopher Francis Herbert Bradley (1846-1924) based his thought on the principles of absolute idealism. He rigorously criticized all philosophies based on the "school of experience."

Born in Clapham on Jan. 30, 1846, F. H. Bradley was educated at University College, Oxford. In 1870 he became a nonteaching fellow at Merton College, Oxford, a post he would be permitted to hold until marriage. Never marrying, he remained a fellow at Merton until his death. Although a sick and often suffering recluse, Bradley spent several winters with a mysterious American woman, Mrs. Radcliffe, for whom he wrote outlines of his metaphysics, which she later destroyed. In character, Bradley may be classified as an English eccentric. While he was a conscientious member of Merton, witty though reserved in his speech and well versed in French literature, he was curiously impressed with his marksmanship and occasionally shot cats in the evening.

Bradley's first published work was a pamphlet, *The Presupposition of Critical History* (1876). In his first major work, *Ethical Studies* (1876), Bradley sought to refute John Stuart Mill's philosophy of individualism. The chapter "My Station and Its Duties" was influenced by G. W. F. Hegel's concept of the ethical community and placed the individual within, and dependent upon, the community. Continuing his critique of individualism and atomism in *Principles of Logic* (1883), Bradley attacked the method of Mill's inductive logic by holding that judgment and inference cannot begin with isolated, particular facts. For Bradley, thought must begin and end with universal statements. Finally, in his metaphysics, *Appearance and Reality* (1893), Bradley argued that the world of appearances is self-contradictory. Absolute reality, however, is a "seamless whole, complete and harmonious." It transcends discursive thought, but it can be compared with the unity and wholeness felt in immediate experience. Bradley once defined metaphysics as the "finding of bad reasons for what we believe on instinct."

Bradley's ideas were widely debated by British and American philosophers in the first decades of this century, and his philosophic system is still worthy of study. He was the older brother of A.E. Bradley, the distinguished literary critic. Bradley died of blood poisoning on Sept. 18, 1924.

Further Reading

Richard Wollheim, *F. H. Bradley* (1960), is a short critical study with bibliographical references and a biographical note. The most recent work on Bradley is Sushil Kumar Saxena, *Studies in the Metaphysics of Bradley* (1967). For an appreciation of Bradley's literary style see T. S. Eliot, *Knowledge and Experience in the Philosophy of F. H. Bradley* (1964). For Bradley's place in the history of idealism, good sources are John H. Muirhead, *The Platonic Tradition in Anglo-Saxon Philosophy* (1931), and John Passmore, *A Hundred Years of Philosophy* (1957; 2d ed. 1966). □

James Bradley

The English astronomer James Bradley (1693-1762), one of the most determined and meticulous astronomers, discovered the aberration of light and the nutation of the earth's axis.

James Bradley, who was the nephew of the astronomer James Pound, was born at Sherborne, Gloucestershire, in March 1693. He studied at Balliol College, Oxford, and took orders in 1719, when he was given his living at Bridstow. In the meantime he had become a skilled astronomer in the techniques of the day, under the instruction of his uncle. In 1718 he was elected a fellow of the Royal Society, and at the early age of 28 he became Savilian professor of astronomy at Oxford and so resigned from Bridstow.

Bradley lived at a time when an astronomer had to be his own technician—repairing, maintaining, and even making his own equipment. High magnifications were obtained by telescopes with lenses of great focal length, often so long that they were not fitted to tubes. In 1722 Bradley measured the diameter of Venus with a telescope over 212 feet in length.

Bradley was a friend of Samuel Molyneux, who had an observatory at Kew near London. There in 1725 Bradley systematically observed the star γ Draconis, hoping to discover the parallactic motion of the stars, that is, a seeming change in the positions of the stars, scattered through space, mirroring the change in the earth's position in its orbit around the sun. His observations were close to what he expected; the star described a tiny ellipse with an axis of only 40 seconds of arc. But the direction of the ellipse was wrong, and he concluded that the effect did not arise from parallactic motion. Greatly puzzled by the result, he at last realized that it was due to the finite velocity of light, owing to the velocity of the earth as it moved in an ellipse, which created an aberration of light. This was a very remarkable piece of work, all the more memorable for the fact that Bradley gave almost precisely the modern value for the constant of aberration, about 20.5 seconds (the modern value being 20.47 seconds).

Out of his work on aberration, Bradley discovered nutation, the oscillation of the earth's axis, caused by the changing direction of the gravitational pull of the moon on the equatorial bulge. He concluded that nutation must arise from the fact that the moon is sometimes above and some-

times below the ecliptic, and it should therefore have the periodicity of the lunar node, that is, approximately 18.6 years. His observations of this covered the period from 1727 to 1747, a full cycle of the motion of the moon's nodes.

At Greenwich, as astronomer royal, where he found the instruments in a poor state of repair, he obtained some fine new instruments, including an eight foot mural quadrant, with which he compiled a new catalog of star positions. It was published posthumously and involved some 60,000 observations. F. W. Bessel's catalog in 1818, with 3,000 star positions, was largely based on Bradley's observations. Bradley's health failed, and he retired to Chalford, Gloucestershire, where he died July 13, 1762.

Further Reading

There is a thorough biography of Bradley in the preface to Stephen Peter Rigaud's edition of Bradley's *Miscellaneous Works and Correspondence* (1832), which is the source of practically all the short notices of Bradley's life that have appeared since. Bradley's career is also discussed in Henry Smith Williams, *The Great Astronomers* (1930), and Sir Oliver Joseph Lodge, *Pioneers of Science and the Development of Their Scientific Theories* (1960). □

Omar Nelson Bradley

U.S. General of the Army Omar Nelson Bradley (1893-1981) was one of the outstanding Allied combat commanders in World War II.

Omar Bradley was born in Clark, Missouri, on February 12, 1893. After his father's death he moved with his mother to Moberly, where he graduated from high school. He attended West Point, graduating in 1915 as a second lieutenant of infantry. During World War I he became a temporary major.

After the war Bradley served in various military capacities and graduated from both the Infantry School at Fort Benning, Georgia, and the Command and General Staff School at Fort Leavenworth, Kansas. In 1934 he graduated from the Army War College and went to Washington, D.C., for General Staff duty in 1938, becoming assistant secretary of the General Staff. In February 1941, promoted from lieutenant colonel to brigadier general, he became commandant of the Infantry School. He was promoted to major general in February 1942 and assigned to command the 82d Infantry Division and later the 28th Infantry Division.

Early in 1943 Bradley became Gen. Dwight D. Eisenhower's personal representative in the field in North Africa. Bradley soon rose to commander of the II Corps, which drove through German lines in northern Tunisia, captured Hill 609, took Bizerte, and helped end the war in Africa. He then was promoted to lieutenant general and in July 1943 invaded Sicily with his II Corps.

In the summer of 1943 Bradley was selected to command the 1st U.S. Army in the Normandy invasion and was designated commanding general, 1st U.S. Army Group. On June 6, 1944, his 1st Army landed in France and smashed through the German lines at Saint-Lô, resulting in the speedy liberation of France in July. On Aug. 1, 1944, he took command of the 12th Army Group, which eventually comprised the 1st, 3d, 9th, and 15th American armies, the largest body of American soldiers ever to serve under one field commander. In the spring of 1945, after his armies had broken the German winter attacks, captured the Siegfried Line, and reached the Rhine, Bradley was promoted to four-star general.

In August 1945 Bradley became administrator of veterans affairs; in February 1948, the chief of staff, U.S. Army, succeeding General Eisenhower; and in August 1949, the first chairman of the Joint Chiefs of Staff, serving two terms. He was appointed to the rank of general of the Army in September 1950, making him the fourth five-star general officer in the American Army.

Bradley held many United States and foreign military decorations and university honorary degrees. After 43 years of active service he was placed on the unassigned list in August 1953. He then pursued a business career, serving as Chairman of the Board of the Bulova Watch Company from 1958-73.

Bradley lived his last years in Texas, occasionally providing lectures on military leadership. He died having contributed 69 years of service to the U.S. military. Throughout his career Bradley was known as "The GI's General," so it was only fitting that President Ronald Reagan eulogized

Bradley with "He was the GI's general because he was, always, a GI."

Further Reading

The most informative work on Bradley is his own autobiography and history, *A Soldier's Story* (1951). Other books containing authoritative information about him are Dwight D. Eisenhower, *Crusade in Europe* (1948), and a series of books prepared by the Office of the Chief of Military History, Department of the Army, *United States Army in World War II: Mediterranean Theater of Operations* (3 vols., 1957-1959) and *United States Army in World War II: The European Theater of Operations* (7 vols., 1950-1965). See also A. Russell Buchanan, *The United States and World War II* (2 vols., 1964), Kenneth S. Davis, *Experience of War: The United States in World War II* (1965) and *Newsweek,* April 20, 1981. □

Tom Bradley

The first African American mayor of Los Angeles, Tom Bradley (born 1917) won election five times, serving a record 20 years in a city where African Americans constituted a small minority of the electorate. He was twice (1982, 1986) the Democratic candidate for governor of California.

Born to an east central Texas sharecropper family of Crenner (Hawkins) and Lee Thomas Bradley on December 29, 1917, Bradley was one of seven children. When he was only seven years old his family moved to Los Angeles, where his mother worked as a domestic servant and his father at various jobs including waiting tables and Pullman car porter. A talented athlete, Bradley excelled in football and the 440-yard dash at Polytechnic High School in Los Angeles. After high school he enrolled at the University of California at Los Angeles to become a track star.

Dropping out of college Bradley joined the Los Angeles police force for what turned into a 21-year career (1940-1961) and rose through the ranks to lieutenant. In the 1950s Bradley enrolled in night school and completed his law studies at Southwestern University, where he received an LL.B. degree in 1956 and won admission to the California bar the next year. In 1941 Bradley married Ethel May Arnold, a member of the African Methodist Episcopal Church which he attended and where he later became a trustee. He was the father of two daughters, Phyllis, a school teacher, and Lorraine, a secretary. After his police career, Bradley practiced law briefly and in 1963 won a seat as Los Angeles' first African American city councilman. Reelected in 1967 and again in 1971 from a biracial district, Bradley often spoke for larger citywide concerns including what he perceived to be poorly planned off-shore oil drilling and its possible negative environmental effects.

Tom Bradley challenged incumbent Mayor Sam Yorty in 1969. In a bitter campaign, and in the runoff which ensued, Yorty painted Bradley as a 1960s radical and defeated him. By 1973 the apprehensions of Los Angeleans had cooled considerably on the issue of African American urban riots, and in this election Tom Bradley hired New York media consultant David Garth to package an effective advertising campaign. Garth presented Bradley as the politically responsible and temperate moderate that he was and would become as mayor. Bradley won a stunning upset, carrying 56 percent of the vote in a city in which African Americans comprised only 15 percent of the electorate. Bradley won reelection four times, several of those with even larger majorities. He carried 59 percent of the vote in 1977, 64 percent in 1981, and 67 percent in 1985, achieving a precedent-setting fourth term.

Throughout his terms as mayor, Bradley led and guided his city through a series of problems including the first energy crisis of 1973-1974. The crisis prompted the mayor to develop a program to make Los Angeles a leader in energy conservation and the "solar city" of America. Although sensitive to environmental concerns, Bradley was also an aggressive executive in encouraging economic development and private investment in his city. Initiatives to improve public transportation, control freeway construction, and vitalize the city's core were also undertaken. Mayor Bradley worked diligently during his early administrations to overcome the impersonal quality of urban leadership by holding "open house" days in branch offices in various parts of the city where citizens could meet their mayor.

A physically imposing figure of more than six feet tall and robust in appearance, Bradley paradoxically projected a soft, low-key, in-control image to the public. A deft politician with a calming influence, Bradley seldom embroiled himself in racial and political turmoil (much to the displeasure of radicals) and adroitly sidestepped the issue of forced cross-town bussing of school children which the courts settled. In the first six years of his administration he avoided new taxes and balanced the budget for his tax conscious electorate. An area in which he suffered considerable criticism was the rapid increase in homicides in 1979. Notwithstanding his career as an ex-police officer, the mayor supported and implemented a civilian commission to oversee the police department.

Although he opened up more city jobs for minorities than any previous mayor, Bradley was colorblind on most public issues and came down on the side of merit and efficiency in personnel management. Bradley also prided himself on fiscal conservatism, which the mayor's office called "enlightened stinginess." In his third term Bradley cut back on city spending and public services (including street cleaning and library hours) when tax revenues were not sufficient to meet expenses. Tempted into statewide politics, Bradley ran as a Democratic candidate for the California governorship in 1982 and lost a hard-fought campaign to Republican George Deukmejian, an Armenian-American and former state attorney general. Mayor Bradley entered into the national slipstream of media consciousness in a large way when he won for his city the privilege of hosting the 1984 summer Olympic Games and played the role of official host. Although discussed in a preliminary fashion as a possible Democratic vice presidential candidate in 1984, the party instead chose Geraldine Ferraro. Bolstered by favorable results in straw polls, Bradley in 1986 again challenged Deukmejian in a contest for governor of California. However, he lost the race to Deukmejian.

Bradley's later administration was marred by conflict and scandal, largely as a result of the Rodney King incident and the riots that ensued when the involved officers were acquitted. On March 3, 1991, King was severely beaten by Los Angeles police officers, and the event was recorded on videotape. Four officers were charged with assault and controversial police chief Darryl Gates was suspended, then reinstated. Mayor Bradley urged Gates to resign, and when he refused, communication between the two disintegrated. A year later, when the verdict in the officers' trial sparked riots in South Central Los Angeles, Gates was again at the center of the controversy. A panel led by former FBI and CIA director William Webster held Gates responsible for not having an adequate plan to deal with potential unrest. But Webster also blamed Mayor Bradley for poor relations between the police department and city hall. Bradley confessed that he and Gates had not spoken for over a year before the riots. The riots had a devastating impact on the city and on Bradley's administration: 58 people were killed, 2,283 were injured, and there was over $750 million in property damage. *The Economist* wrote, "Since the 1984 Olympics, his [Bradley's] administration has been pockmarked by petty corruption, inaction, and, of course, last year's riots."

After the riots, Bradley was praised for forming "Rebuild L.A.", a task force established to put the city back in order. He also formed a program called, "L.A.'s Best", which provided afternoon activities for young people in an effort to keep them off the streets. In 1993 Bradley retired from the Mayor's office after a record 20 years and after 50 years of public service as police officer, city councilman, and then mayor. He was replaced by millionaire businessman Richard Riordan. Of his years as mayor Bradley said, "Everything that I set out to do 20 years ago, I have accomplished. The Olympics were the major event of my life. . . . [the riots were] the most painful experience of my life."

In 1996, Bradley suffered a heart attack while in a fast-food restaurant, but recovered. A reserved man who was known as a hard-working and conscientious administrator, Tom Bradley was among the leading African American political figures in the United States.

Further Reading

For his early life, see *The New York Times Biographical Service* 12 (April 1981) and 15 (June 1984) and "Winning Mayor," *The Economist*, 279 (April 18, 1981). For Bradley's mayoral and public career, see "Tom Bradley," *Biographical Dictionary of American Mayors, 1820-1980*, eds. M. Holli and P. Jones (1981); *Mayors of Los Angeles* (1968, 1980); *TIME* magazine, (October 2, 1982 and November 15, 1982); and *U.S. News and World Report*, 96 (March 6, 1984). See also *Contemporary Black Biography* (Vol. 2) (1992). □

Sir Donald George Bradman

Sir Donald George Bradman (born 1908) was an Australian cricketer—the greatest batsman, if not cricketer, of all time.

Donald Bradman was born in Cootamundra, New South Wales, on August 27, 1908, the youngest child of a farmer/carpenter. The family lived in Yeo Yeo and moved to Bowral in 1911 because of his mother's health. He learned his cricket from his maternal uncles George and Richard Whatman. His mother used to bowl left-armers to him in the backyard. Bradman developed his batting by throwing a golf ball against a tank stand and playing it with a stump and his fielding by throwing a golf ball at the bottom rail of a fence.

As a teenager Bradman played Saturday afternoon cricket in the country and quickly proceeded to amass huge scores. In 1926 the New South Wales Cricket Association, which was incidentally looking for bowlers, asked Bradman to play in trial games. While making modest scores, he nonetheless attracted the eye of the selectors as a player of the future. He played grade cricket with the St. George club in Sydney (he later played with North Sydney and, after moving to Adelaide, South Australia in 1935, with the Kensington club). After some impressive scores he played in his initial first class game for New South Wales against South Australia in 1927 and scored a century. After a series of big scores at the beginning of the 1928-1929 season, he was chosen to play for Australia against Perry Chapman's English side. While performing poorly in the first test and being dropped to 12th man for the second, he scored two centuries in the remaining rubbers to establish his place in the Australian team.

Being a self-taught batsman, much criticism was directed at Bradman's lack of style, his tendency to play cross bat shots, and the problems he would encounter on softer English wickets. Bradman answered his critics by consistently amassing huge scores. Throughout his career he was a fast and high scoring batsman who could reduce even the best bowling attacks to seeming mediocrity. His initial tour of England in 1930 can only be described as a triumphal procession in which he established himself as a figure of international stature. He scored 2,960 runs on tour at an average of 98.66. In test matches he scored 974 runs at an average of 139.14, including scores of 131, 254, 334, and 452. On both the 1930 and 1938 tours of England he scored 1,000 runs before the end of May. He became the only player to achieve such a distinction. In the 1938-1939 season he scored six centuries in a row, equaling C. B. Fry's record. Only the bodyline bowling, where the ball is pitched short and aimed in the general direction of the head, employed by Douglas Jardine's 1932-1933 English side curbed Bradman. His average fell to 56.57, which would still be the envy of most batsmen. Such was the hostility generated by bodyline bowling (which was eventually outlawed) that diplomatic exchanges occurred between Australia and England.

Bradman's average in first class cricket was 95.14, and in test cricket it was 99.94, being only four runs short of a 100 average. He scored 117 centuries in first class cricket (29 in tests), a century every third time he batted. His centuries included 31 double (ten in tests), five triple (two in tests), and one quadruple century—his famous 452 got out against Queensland in 1930.

In 1936 Bradman was appointed captain of Australia to oppose Gubby Allen's touring English side. He continued captaining Australia until 1948, notwithstanding a five year absence from cricket caused by World War II. Bradman was a most successful captain. In the 24 tests while he was captain Australia won 15, lost three, and drew six. The team which toured England in 1948 had the distinction of never losing a game.

After retiring, Bradman was knighted in January 1949. He maintained contact with the game as a selector and administrator, having two stints as chairman of the Australian Cricket Board, 1960 to 1963 and 1969 to 1972. His most important decision as chairman was to cancel the visit of a South African team in 1971-1972 because of the expected bitterness and violence associated with opposition to South Africa's apartheid politics. From 1965 to 1973, Bradman served as President of the South Australian Cricket Association. After leaving cricket, he had a successful career in the finance industry, working for H.W. Hodgetts and Company on the Adelaide Exchange.

The late 1980s and 1990s saw a spate of biographical material on Bradman. In 1988 he released his book, The

Bradman Albums, and two biographies of him, Charles Williams' Bradman: An Australian Hero, and Roland Perry's book, The Don, were published in 1996. Clearly time does not diminish Bradman's status as a hero in his native Australia, or anywhere else that appreciates cricket.

Further Reading

Bradman has been a continuing source of fascination for cricket writers. The most thorough biography is Irving Rosenwater's Sir Donald Bradman (1978). Michael Page's Bradman: The Illustrated Biography (1983) draws on information and memorabilia provided by Bradman. J. Wakley's Bradman the Great (1959) provides an extensive statistical account of Bradman's career. An additional biography is A. G. Moyes' Bradman (1948). Bradman also provided accounts of his career in Don Bradman's Book (1930), My Cricketing Life (1938), and Farewell to Cricket (1950). He also published two books about the sport, The Art of Cricket (1958) and How to Play Cricket (1935). For an English account of the bodyline tour see Harold Larwood and Kevin Perkins' The Larwood Story (1982). Bradman's impact on cricket is also assessed in Jack Pollard's Australian Cricket: The Game and the Players (1982). □

Anne Dudley Bradstreet

Anne Dudley Bradstreet (ca. 1612-1672) was a Puritan poet whose work portrays a deeply felt experience of American colonial life. She was the daughter and wife of Massachusetts governors.

Anne Dudley, born about 1612 probably in Northampton, England, grew up in the cultivated household of the Earl of Lincoln, where her father, Thomas Dudley, was steward. Tutored by her father and availing herself of the extensive library, she was highly educated. Her later work reveals familiarity with Plutarch, Du Bartas, Sir Walter Raleigh, Quarles, Sidney, Spenser, perhaps Shakespeare, and, of course, the Bible. At 16, she writes, she experienced conversion.

Shortly thereafter she married Simon Bradstreet, then 20 years old; orphaned at 14, he had been her father's protégé. He graduated from Emmanuel College and, like the Dudleys, had strong Nonconformist convictions. In 1630 the Bradstreets sailed to America aboard the Arbella with Dudley and the Winthrop company. The Bradstreets lived in Salem, Boston, Cambridge, and Ipswich, and settled finally on a farm in North Andover, Mass.

Bradstreet was a devoted wife and the mother of eight children. Her husband became a judge and legislator, later royal councilor and governor. His duties required that he be away from home frequently. Their wilderness life was hard; Indian attack was a constant threat, and Bradstreet suffered poor health. Yet, she managed to use her experience and religious belief in creating a small but distinguished body of poetry.

In 1647 Bradstreet's brother-in-law, the Reverend John Woodbridge, took some of her poetry to England, where, without her knowledge, he had it published in 1650 under the title *The Tenth Muse Lately Sprung Up in America.* . . . For the most part the book consists of four long poems, which may actually be considered one long poem, traditional in subject matter and set, rather mechanically, in heroic couplets. "The Four Elements," "The Four Humours in Man's Constitution," "The Four Ages of Man," and "The Four Seasons of the Year" are allegorical pieces, heavily influenced by Joshua Sylvester's translation of Du Bartas's *Divine Weeks and Works* .

Bradstreet herself added to and corrected her next volume, *Several Poems* . . . , published posthumously in Boston in 1678. In this volume she deals more with her New England life, her family and natural surroundings. It includes "Contemplations," the fine, long reflective poem on death and resurrection in nature, as well as the dramatic poem "The Flesh and the Spirit," the lively words of "The Author to Her Book," and moving verses addressed to her husband and children. Her prose "Meditations" and some of her more confessional pieces remained in manuscript until 1867, when John H. Ellis published her complete works.

Most critics consider Bradstreet America's first authentic poet, especially strong in her later work. In her own day she was praised by Cotton Mather in his *Magnalia,* by Nathaniel Ward, and others.

Further Reading

The Works of Anne Bradstreet was edited by Jeannine Hensley, with an interesting foreword by poet Adrienne Rich (1967). John Berryman, *Homage to Mistress Bradstreet* (1956), is a moving biographical tribute. Samuel Eliot Morison's chapter on Anne Bradstreet in *Builders of the Bay Colony* (1930; rev. ed. 1958) is a colorful introduction to her life and work. A readable study of Mrs. Bradstreet's writings is Josephine K. Piercy, *Anne Bradstreet* (1965). □

Mathew B. Brady

The American photographer, publisher, and pictorial historian Mathew B. Brady (ca. 1823-1896) was famous for his portraits of eminent world leaders and his vast photographic documentation of the Civil War.

Mathew B. Brady (he never knew what the initial "B" stood for) was born in Warren County, N.Y. The exact place and year are not known; in later life Brady told a reporter, "I go back near 1823-24." He spent his youth in Saratoga Springs, N.Y., and became a friend of the painter William Page, who was a student of the painter and inventor Samuel F. B. Morse. About 1839/1840 Brady went to New York City with Page. Nothing certain is known of his activity there until 1843, when the city directory listed his occupation as jewel-case manufacturer.

The daguerreotype process had been introduced to America in 1839, and Morse became one of the first to

practice the craft and to teach it. Possibly Brady met Morse through Page, and perhaps he learned to take daguerreotypes from him. In 1843 Brady added cases specially made for daguerreotypes to his line of goods, and a year later he opened a "Daguerreian Miniature Gallery." He was at once successful: the first daguerreotypes he put on public exhibition, at the Fair of the American Institute in 1844, won a medal, and he carried away top honors year after year.

Brady once said that "the camera is the eye of history." He began in 1845 to build a vast collection of portraits, which he named "The Gallery of Illustrious Americans," and two years later he opened a Washington branch, so that he could have portraits made of the presidents, cabinet ministers, congressmen, and other government leaders.

Brady sent 20 daguerreotypes to the Great Exhibition in London in 1851; they won him a medal and were greatly admired. In that year he traveled to England and the Continent. Shortly after his return he opened a second New York studio. His eyesight was now failing seriously, and he relied more and more upon assistants to do the actual photography. Chief among his many operators was Alexander Gardner, a Scotsman who was well versed in the newly invented collodion, or wet-plate, process, which was rapidly displacing the daguerreotype. Gardner specialized in making enlargements up to 17 by 20 inches, which Brady called "Imperials"; they cost $750 each. Gardner was put in charge of the gallery in Washington in 1858.

Perhaps the most famous of Brady's portraits was the standing figure of Abraham Lincoln taken at the time of his

Cooper Union speech in 1861; Lincoln is reported to have said that the photograph and the speech put him in the White House.

When the Civil War broke out, Brady resolved to make a photographic record of it. The project was a bold one. At his own expense he organized teams of photographers—James D. Horan in his biography states that there were 22 of them—each equipped with a traveling darkroom, for the collodion plates had to be processed on the spot. Brady recollected that he spent over $100,000 and "had men in all parts of the Army, like a rich newspaper."

When the war ended, the collection comprised some 10,000 negatives. The project had cost Brady his fortune, and he became bankrupt. He could not afford to pay the storage bill for one set of negatives, which were sold at auction to the War Department. A second collection was seized by E. and H. T. Anthony, dealers in photographic materials, for nonpayment of debts. Today Brady's vast and brilliant historical record is divided between the National Archives and the Library of Congress in Washington, D.C.

Although he maintained his Washington gallery, Brady never fully recovered from his financial disasters. In 1895 he planned a series of slide lectures about the Civil War. While he was preparing them in New York, he became ill and entered the Presbyterian Hospital, where he died on Jan. 15, 1896.

Further Reading

James D. Horan, *Mathew Brady: Historian with a Camera* (1955), not only recounts the few known facts of Brady's career but gives a vivid account of life in America and the state of photography in the mid-19th century; Horan was the first biographer to have access to the records of Brady's heirs. Roy Meredith, *Mr. Lincoln's Camera Man: Mathew B. Brady* (1946), is somewhat conjectural and poorly documented; it is, however, useful for its illustrations. In 1911 the *Review of Reviews* published the 10-volume *The Photographic History of the Civil War,* edited by Francis Trevelyan Miller; a 5-volume reprint (1957) contains many Brady pictures. □

Sir William Henry Bragg

The English physicist Sir William Henry Bragg (1862-1942) was the founder of the science of crystal-structure determination by x-ray diffraction methods. He received the Nobel Prize in physics jointly with his son, William L. Bragg, in 1915.

William Henry Bragg was born on July 2, 1862, at Westward, Cumberland, England. He attended King's College, Isle of Man, and Trinity College, Cambridge, where he took honors in mathematics in 1884. A year later he became professor of mathematics and physics at the University of Adelaide, Australia. He married there.

In time Bragg turned to experimentation, and soon after W. C. Roentgen's momentous discovery of x-rays in 1895, Bragg set up and experimented with an x-ray tube. In the next few years he did basic work and published papers on radioactivity, the range of alpha-particles and their power to ionize gases, and the behavior of secondary electrons, particularly those produced by gammarays. This work led him to form his views on the nature of x-rays.

Bragg returned to England in 1908 as Cavendish professor of physics at Leeds. Four years later Max von Laue, W. Friedrich, and P. Knipping discovered the diffraction of x-rays by a crystal. Bragg, in a simple reinterpretation of Laue's elegant mathematical theory, looked upon the interaction as a reflection of the waves of a narrow incident beam from a large number of equally spaced parallel planes of atoms. The Bragg equation embraces both the corpuscular and wave theories of x-rays and relates the x-ray wavelength, the angle of reflection, and the spacing of the planes. Bragg immediately saw the importance of the discovery and was able, with his son, to determine the exact arrangement of atoms or ions in crystals of a variety of simple substances such as common salt, diamond, and copper. Previously the arrangements of atoms in the elements and their compounds were inferred by indirect chemical methods, partly dependent on molecular weights observed in the gaseous state or solution.

After World War I Bragg moved to London. First at University College and then as director of the Royal Institution, he was responsible for the spread of crystalstructure methods, and the sciences of metallurgy and mineralogy,

both predominantly concerned with solids, were reborn. Physicists could calculate properties of solids on the basis of atomic positions in the ideal crystal. Interpretation now extends to the endless variety of less perfectly ordered structures which make up the world of fibers, polymers, liquid crystals, and other aggregates of atoms, ions, and molecules, including proteins, enzymes, viruses, and other materials of life.

Bragg was president of the Royal Society from 1935 to 1940. He was kind and fatherly, admirable in the Royal Institution Christmas Lectures for juveniles, and an interpreter of science to the general public. He died in London on March 12, 1942.

Further Reading

A brief but adequate biography and an account of Bragg's work is in Nobel Foundation, *Nobel Lectures, Including Presentation Speeches and Laureates' Biographies: Physics, 1901-1921* (1967). His life and work are discussed in Bernard Jaffe, *Chemistry Creates a New World* (1957); George Gamow, *Biography of Physics* (1961); and R. Harré, ed., *Scientific Thought* (1969).

Additional Sources

Caroe, G. M., *William Henry Bragg, 1862-1942: man and scientist,* Cambridge; New York: Cambridge University Press, 1978.

Jenkin, John., *The Bragg family in Adelaide: a pictorial celebration,* Australia: University of Adelaide Foundation in conjunction with La Trobe University, 1986. □

Tycho Brahe

The Danish astronomer Tycho Brahe (1546-1601) carried pretelescopic astronomy to its highest perfection and tried to steer a middle course between the Ptolemaic and the Copernican systems.

Tycho Brahe, referred to by his first name, was born on Dec. 14, 1546, the son of the governor of Helsingborg Castle. His upbringing and education were entrusted to his uncle, Joergen, a vice admiral. When only 13, Tycho began attending classes of rhetoric and philosophy at the University of Copenhagen, but almost immediately he was seized with a frustration which had to do with astronomy. It was the discrepancy between the predicted and observed time of a partial eclipse of the sun. His whole life was to be spent on perfecting astronomical observations and theories to eliminate discrepancies of this kind.

Tycho studied at the universities of Leipzig, Wittenberg, Rostock, Basel, and Augsburg (1562-1570). On his return to Denmark he went to live with an uncle, Steen Bille, the founder of the first paper mill and glassworks in that country. He was the only one in the family to approve of Tycho's addiction to astronomy. He let Tycho set up his own observatory and received in turn help from him in the

alchemy shop. On the evening of Nov. 11, 1572, Tycho spotted a new bright star near Cassiopeia. Other astronomers too soon noticed the nova, but it was Tycho who provided the best evidence with his huge sextant that the new star was as immobile as the other fixed stars.

Tycho's book *De stella nova* (1573) was a landmark in astronomy and secured for him a lifelong career. First came his appointment at the University of Copenhagen, then the royal patent entrusting him with the construction of the famous observatory called Uraniborg (Castle of Heavens) on the island of Hven. Shortly after this took place (1576), Tycho delivered another blow at the belief codified by Aristotle that no change could occur above the orbit of the moon. In *De mundi aetherei recentioribus phenomenis* (1577) Tycho proved that the great comet of 1577 had to be at least six times farther than the moon. The book also contained the famous Tychonic system of planets. There a secondary center was occupied by the sun with Mercury and Venus orbiting around it, forming a small system. The sun with its small system turned around the immobile earth fixed slightly off-center to the sphere of the fixed stars. The three other planets, Mars, Jupiter, and Saturn, orbited around both the sun and the earth, and their orbits were centered not on the earth but on the sun. The sphere of the fixed stars made a full revolution each day.

Tycho left Denmark in 1587 and moved to Prague, carrying along the records of his observations and most of his instruments. In 1600 Johannes Kepler joined him as his assistant. It fell to Kepler to prepare for publication, following Tycho's sudden death in 1601, the latter's collection of

astronomical studies, *Astronomiae instauratae progymnasmata* (1602-1603).

Further Reading

The major work in English on Tycho is still the one by J. L. E. Dreyer, astronomer-editor of Brahe's works and correspondence, *Tycho Brahe: A Picture of Scientific Life and Work in the Sixteenth Century* (1890; repr. 1963). Less attentive to scientific questions is John A. Gade, *The Life and Times of Tycho Brahe* (1947), but it contains an ample and more modern bibliography. Tycho is discussed in George Sarton, *Six Wings: Men of Science in the Renaissance* (1957). □

Johannes Brahms

The German composer, pianist, and conductor Johannes Brahms (1833-1897) was one of the most significant composers of the 19th century. His works greatly enriched the romantic repertory.

Johannes Brahms stands midway between the conservative purveyors of the classic tradition, that is, the imitators of Felix Mendelssohn, and the so-called musicians of the future such as Franz Liszt and Richard Wagner. Brahms infused the traditional forms with romantic melody and harmony, respecting the inheritance of the past but making it relevant to his own age. His position of moderation effected a necessary balance in the creative output of the romantic century and led to high critical esteem by his contemporaries.

Johannes Brahms was born in Hamburg on May 7, 1833, the son of Johann Jakob and Christina Nissen Brahms. The father, an innkeeper and a musician of moderate ability, earned a precarious living for his family of five. Johannes received his first music instruction from his father.

At the age of seven Johannes began studying piano. He played a private subscription concert at the age of 10 to obtain funds for his future education. He also learned theory and composition and began to improvise compositions at the piano. To help out with family finances, Brahms played the piano in sailors' haunts and local dance salons. This contact with the seamier side of life may have conditioned his lifelong revulsion from physical intimacy with the women he idealized and loved.

Early Works

The late hours proved taxing to the 14-year-old boy and impaired his health. Brahms was offered a long recuperative holiday at Winsen-an-der-Luhe, where he conducted a small male choir for whom he wrote his first choral compositions. On his return to Hamburg he gave several concerts, but, failing to win recognition, he continued to play at humble places of amusement, gave inexpensive piano lessons, and began the hackwork of arranging popular music for piano.

In 1850 Brahms became acquainted with the Hungarian violinist Eduard Reményi, who introduced him to the rich tradition of gypsy dance tunes that were to be influential in his mature compositions. In the next few years Brahms composed several works for piano that are still in the repertoire: the Scherzo in E-flat Minor (1851), the Sonata in F-sharp Minor (1852), and the Sonata in C Major (1853). Reményi and Brahms embarked on several successful concert tours in 1853. At Hanover they met one of the greatest German violinists, Joseph Joachim, who arranged for them to play before the King of Hanover and gave them an introduction to Liszt at Weimar. Joachim also wrote a glowing letter to Robert Schumann expressing his enthusiasm for the young composer.

The next move was obviously to visit Weimar, where Liszt received them warmly and was greatly impressed with Brahms's compositions. Liszt hoped to recruit him for his coterie of composers, but Brahms could not adapt to the superficiality of Liszt's music. Although no open breach occurred, the two musicians did draw apart.

Friendship with the Schumanns

In 1853 Brahms wrote the Piano Sonata in F Minor. Later that year he met Schumann and his wife, Clara, with whom he formed a lifelong friendship. Schumann's enthusiasm for the young composer knew no bounds. In a long article in the *Neue Zeitschrift für Musik*, Schumann wrote of him, "I thought that someone would have to appear suddenly who was called upon to utter the highest expression of his time in an ideal manner. . . . " Schumann also arranged for Brahm's first compositions to be published. During 1854 he wrote the Piano Trio No. 1, the *Variations on a Theme of Schumann* for piano, and the Ballades for piano.

Brahms was summoned to Düsseldorf in 1854, when Schumann had a mental breakdown and attempted suicide. For the next few years he stayed close to the Schumanns, assisting Clara in whatever way he could and remaining near her even after Schumann's death in 1856. To earn his living, he taught piano privately but also spent some time on concert tours. Two concerts given with the singer Julius Stockhausen served to establish Brahms as an important song composer.

In 1857 Brahms went to the court of Lippe-Detmold, where he taught the piano to Princess Friederike and conducted the choral society. Many of his folk-song arrangements were made for this choir. During the summer he went to Göttingen to be near Clara Schumann, for whose children he also arranged several folk songs. There can be no question but that he was in love with Clara, 14 years older than he, but either her wisdom prevailed and the idyllic relationship terminated or Brahms suffered from his lifelong inability to consummate his love for a woman he idealized. Whatever the reason, it speaks well for both of them that love was replaced by a warm friendship that lasted to Clara's death. While at Göttingen he became passionately interested in the soprano Agatha von Siebold, but this romance, although it brought him nearer to marriage than any other, soon terminated.

Works of the Middle Years

Brahms's Piano Concerto in D Minor (1858) was performed the next year with Joachim conducting at Hanover, Leipzig, and Hamburg. Only in Hamburg was it favorably received. During the Lippe-Detmold period Brahms produced the two Serenades for small orchestra, an evocation of an 18th-century form. He was also appointed conductor of a ladies' choir in Hamburg, for whom he wrote the *Marienlieder*.

In 1860 Brahms became enraged at the propaganda that the avant-garde theories of the "New German" school headed by Liszt were being accepted by all musicians of consequence and took part in a press manifesto against this group of musicians. During this period Brahms moved to Hamburg and buried himself in compositional activities with frequent public appearances sandwiched in. In the year of the manifesto he completed the Sextet for Strings in B-flat Major and the Variations on an Original Theme for piano, performed by Clara Schumann; the next year, the Piano Quartets in G Minor and A Major and the well-known *Variations on a Theme of Handel* for piano.

In 1862 his friend Stockhausen was appointed conductor of the Hamburg Philharmonic and the Singakadamie. Although Brahms was happy for his friend, he deeply resented being passed over for these important posts. He became more and more attracted to Vienna, and in 1863 he gave a concert there to introduce his songs to the Austrian public. They were well received, especially by the critic Eduard Hanslick, with whom Brahms became a fast friend. Brahms also met Wagner at this time, and, although the

famous manifesto of 1860 made relations between the two composers difficult, each was still on occasion able to admire some things in the other's work.

In 1863 Brahms became conductor of the Singakademie in Vienna. A year later he resigned, but for the rest of his life Vienna was home to him. He began to do what he had always wished—to make composing the main source of his income—and as his fame and popularity grew, he composed more and more with only some occasional teaching and performing. In Baden-Baden in 1864 on a visit to Clara Schumann, he wrote the Piano Quintet in F Minor, and a year later the Horn Trio in E-flat Major.

In 1865 Brahms's mother, long estranged from her husband, died. During the next year he worked on the *German Requiem* in her memory.

The next years saw a proliferation of activity as a composer. His most important publications were the *Variations on a Theme of Paganini* for piano, the String Sextet in G Major, and several song collections. It is not always possible to date Brahms's compositions exactly because of his penchant for revising a work or adding to it frequently. Thus, the *German Requiem,* practically finished in 1866, was not published in its final form until 1869 and given its first complete performance that year. Yet some of the germinal material used in the *Requiem* dates back to the period around Schumann's final illness and death. The year 1869 also witnessed the composition of the *Liebeslieder* Waltzes for piano duet and vocal quartet and the *Alto Rhapsody* for contralto, male chorus, and orchestra, as well as the publication of his Hungarian Dances for piano duet.

Late Masterpieces

Brahms's father died in 1872. After a short holiday at Baden-Baden, Brahms accepted the post of artistic director of the Gesellschaft der Musikfreunde (Friends of Music) in Vienna. Imposing masterpieces continued to pour from his pen. In 1873 came the *Variations on a Theme of Haydn* in two versions, one for orchestra and the other for two pianos; the String Quartets Nos. 1 and 2; and the Songs, Op. 59. The next year produced the Piano Quartet No. 3; the Songs, Op. 63; and the *Neue Liebeslieder* Waltzes. Against this background of activity the details of his everyday life seem trivial. He composed, went on concert tours chiefly to foster his own music, and took long holidays.

During his earlier years Brahms had helped support both his mother and father. Now with that obligation over and with money coming in from all sides, he was exceedingly well off financially and could do as he pleased. He resigned the conductorship of the Gesellschaft der Musikfreunde in 1875, for even those duties were onerous to him. That summer he worked on his Symphony No. 1 and sketched the Symphony No. 2.

In 1880 the University of Breslau offered Brahms a doctorate, in appreciation of which he wrote the *Academic Festival Overture* and, for good measure, the companion *Tragic Overture*. During the intervening years he had discovered Italy, and for the rest of his life he vacationed there frequently. Vacations for Brahms meant composing, and masterpiece now followed masterpiece: the Violin Concerto in D Major (1878), the Violin Sonata in G Major (1879), the two Rhapsodies for piano (1880), the Piano Concerto No. 2 in B-flat Major (1881), the Symphony No. 3 (1883), and the Symphony No. 4 (1884). These are the highlights of years filled with innumerable other compositions and publications.

Much of the credit for the universal acceptance of Brahms's orchestral works was due to the activities of their great interpreter, Hans von Bülow, who had transferred his allegiance from the Liszt-Wagner camp to Brahms. In the composer's works he felt the logical continuation of the Beethoven tradition to be manifest, and Bülow lavished tremendous energy in seeing that these compositions received properly executed performances.

In his later works Brahms showed an austerity that is in a sense a reflection of his own growing inwardness. Always self-critical and impatient with insincerity, he now translated this reserve into the sparseness and restraint of his own compositions. This can be observed in the sonatas for various instrumental combinations written in 1886, the Concerto for Violin and Cello (1887), and the Violin and Piano Sonata No. 3 (1888).

His native Hamburg gave Brahms the keys to the city in 1889. As a thank offering, he composed the *Deutsche Fest- und Gedenksprüche* for eight-part chorus. He also became acquainted with the superb clarinetist Richard Mühlfeld, for whom he wrote his exquisite clarinet works. They performed these compositions all over Germany.

When he was about 60 years old, Brahms began to age rapidly and the range of his production was noticeably reduced. He often spoke of having arrived at the end of his creative activity. Nonetheless, the works of this last period are awesome in their grandeur and concentration, and the last of his published works, the *Vier ernste Gesänge* (Four Serious Songs), are among the high points of his creativity.

Brahms's already precarious health was impaired even further by the news of the death of Clara Schumann in 1896. On April 3, 1897, he died, ravaged by cancer of the liver. He was buried next to Beethoven and Schubert, honored by all Vienna and the entire musical world.

Further Reading

A full treatment of Brahms's works is in Edwin Evans, *Historical, Descriptive and Analytical Account of the Entire Works of Johannes Brahms* (4 vols., 1912-1936). For personal reminiscences of Brahms see Florence May, *The Life of Johannes Brahms* (2 vols., 1905; new ed. 1948), and George Henschel, *Personal Recollections of Johannes Brahms* (1907). The best general work on Brahms is Karl Geiringer, *Brahms: His Life and Work* (1936; rev. ed. 1947). Also very useful is the short work in the Master Musicians Series by Peter Latham, *Brahms* (1948). Daniel Gregory Mason, *From Grieg to Brahms: Studies of Some Modern Composers and Their Art* (1921; rev. ed. 1927), gives historical background. □

Louis Braille

Louis Braille (1809-1852) designed the coding system, based on patterns of raised dots, by which the blind can read through touch.

Braille designed a coding system, based on patterns of raised dots, which the blind could read by touch. Born in Coupvray, France, Braille was accidentally blinded in one eye at the age of three. Within two years, a disease in his other eye left him completely blind.

In 1819, Braille received a scholarship to the Institut National des Jeunes Aveugles (National Institute of Blind Youth), founded by Valentin Haüy (1745-1822). The same year Braille entered the school, Captain Charles Barbier invented sonography, or nightwriting, a system of embossed symbols used by soldiers to communicate silently at night on the battlefield. Inspired by a lecture Barbier gave at the Institute a few years later, the fifteen-year-old Braille adapted Barbier's system to replace Haüy's awkward embossed type, which he and his classmates had been obliged to learn.

In his initial study, Braille had experimented with geometric shapes cut from leather as well as with nails and tacks hammered into boards. He finally settled on a finger-tip-sized six-dot code, based on the twenty-five letters of the alphabet, which could be recognized with a single contact of one digit. By varying the number and placement of dots, he coded letters, punctuation, numbers, diphthongs, familiar words, scientific symbols, mathematical and musical notation, and capitalization. With the right hand, the reader touched individual dots and, with the left, moved on toward the next line, comprehending as smoothly and rapidly as sighted readers. Using the Braille system, students were also able to take notes and write themes by punching dots into paper with a pointed stylus which was aligned with a metal guide.

At the age of twenty, Braille published a monograph describing the use of his coded system. In 1837, he issued a second publication featuring an expanded system of coding text. Despite the students' favorable response to the Braille code, sighted instructors and school board members, fearing for their jobs should the number of well-educated blind individuals increase, opposed his system.

Braille grew seriously ill with incurable tuberculosis in 1835 and was forced to resign his teaching post. The Braille writing system—though demonstrated at the Paris Exposition of Industry in 1834 and praised by King Louis-Philippe—was not fully accepted until 1854, two years after the inventor's death. The system underwent periodic alteration; the standardized system employed today was first used in the United States in 1860 at the Missouri School for the Blind.

Further Reading

Bickel, Lennard, *Triumph Over Darkness: The Life of Louis Braille,* Allen & Unwin Australia, 1988.
Bryant, Jennifer, *Louis Braille: Inventor,* Chelsea House, 1993.
Roblin, Jean, *Louis Braille,* Royal National Institute for the Blind.

□

Donato Bramante

The Italian architect and painter Donato Bramante (1444-1514) was the first High Renaissance architect. He transformed the classical style of the 15th century into a grave and monumental manner, which represented the ideal for later architects.

In the first decade of the 16th century Donato Bramante was the chief architect in Rome, which had just replaced Florence as the artistic capital of Europe because the patronage of Pope Julius II (reigned 1503-1513) attracted all the leading Italian artists to that city. It is particularly the triumvirate of artists—Michelangelo the sculptor and painter, Raphael the painter, and Bramante the architect—who dominated this period, usually called the High Renaissance, and whose influence overwhelmed the following generations.

Donato di Pascuccio d'Antonio, called Bramante, was born in 1444 at Monte Asdruvaldo near Urbino. Nothing is known of the first 30 years of his life. During that period, however, the court of Federigo da Montefeltro at Urbino was a flourishing humanistic and cultural center, attended

by artists such as Piero della Francesca, Melozzo da Forlì, and Luciano Laurana, who probably influenced the young Bramante. The first notice of Bramante dates from 1477, when he decorated the facade of the Palazzo del Podestà at Bergamo with a frescoed frieze of philosophers.

Lombard Style

In 1481 the engraver Bernardo Previdari issued at Milan a print after a design by Bramante, who had settled there about that time. The major interest of the engraving, which depicts the interior of a partially ruined church, is the careful perspective delineation of the architectural interior. Shortly thereafter Bramante entered into the service of the Sforza rulers of Lombardy as court architect. His first important commission was the reconstruction, beginning in 1482, of the church of S. Maria presso S. Satiro in Milan. As it was a basilica church with transept and dome over the crossing, there was not enough space for a deep choir. Through the ingenious use of sculptural and painted relief in perspective, Bramante feigned a choir. He also built a tall, octagonal sacristy richly decorated in the North Italian manner with relief sculpture covering even the shafts of the classical orders. Bramante also continued to paint, executing frescoes of armed men for the Casa Panigarola and the panel painting *Christ at the Column.*

In 1488 Bramante was called as consultant to the architects Amadeo and Cristoforo Rocchi for the building of the Cathedral of Pavia, but in 1492 he withdrew from the project with only the crypt completed. Meanwhile in 1490 he submitted an opinion on the project to complete the

tiburio, or great crossing vault, of the Gothic Cathedral of Milan, in which he advocated a design conforming to the past style. Although there is no documentary proof, he presumably designed the large, square tribune with apsidal arms added to the Gothic church of S. Maria delle Grazie in Milan, beginning the work in 1492. The interior was made spacious and monumental, and the exterior was completed in the decorative Lombard style. At the same time Bramante began the Canons' Cloister of S. Ambrogio in Milan, whose southern wing alone was built; in 1497 he planned four more cloisters there, of which only the Doric and Ionic Cloisters were completed in the 16th century.

During 1493 Bramante was briefly and mysteriously absent from Milan, as letters of Duke Lodovico Sforza seeking him in Florence and Rome indicate, but Bramante soon returned to the ducal seat at Vigevano. He also wrote some sonnets at this time, which are preserved in a manuscript dated 1497.

Early Roman Style

When the French captured Milan in September 1499 Bramante fled to Rome, where he frescoed the arms of Pope Alexander VI at St. John Lateran, in preparation for the Holy Year of 1500, and explored the Roman antiquities. The impact of the ancient monuments is evident in his cloister of S. Maria della Pace in Rome (1500-1504). The simple gravity and monumentality of the small square court marks a distinct break with the Lombard style and foreshadows the new classicism of High Renaissance Rome. The ground-floor arcade is supported on piers with engaged Ionic pilasters; the upper floor alternates Corinthian columns and piers bearing an architrave.

The tiny circular Tempietto at S. Pietro in Montorio, in Rome (1502), with a Doric colonnade surrounding a small cella closed by a semicircular dome on a tall drum, represents the perfection of Bramante's Roman style. The architect intended the chapel to stand in the center of a circular, colonnaded court to emphasize its self-containment and centralization, but the court was never executed. The church of S. Maria della Consolazione (1504-1617) at Todi, probably executed after Bramante's design, is likewise centralized, being square with semicircular apses. The mass is built up of simple geometric forms capped by a drum and dome. The interior is characterized by a sense of quiet, harmonious spaciousness.

Papal Architecture and Late Works

With the election of Pope Julius II in 1503 Bramante soon became the papal architect, and he did extensive work in the Vatican Palace and began rebuilding St. Peter's. The tremendous Belvedere Court of the Palace (begun in 1503) was terraced up a hillside on three levels joined by monumental stairs and defined by arcaded loggias with superimposed orders. The lower terrace was to serve as a theater. Completed with many revisions in the late 16th century, it is now altered almost beyond recognition. Nearby is a spiral, ramped staircase (begun before 1512) that provides access to the statue court beyond the Belvedere Court. As a new facade for the Vatican Palace, Bramante designed a series of

superimposed loggias (1509-1518), later converted into the Court of S. Damaso. Completed by Raphael, there are two superimposed arcades with Tuscan and Ionic pilasters and above them a colonnade of the Composite order.

In 1505 Bramante prepared a plan for the New St. Peter's which called for a centralized Greek cross with a large dome on a colonnaded drum at the crossing, four smaller domes, and corner towers. When the Greek cross plan was not accepted, he planned to lengthen one arm to form a nave and to add ambulatories in the apsidal arms. The foundation stone was laid in April 1506, but at the time of his death Bramante had erected only the four main piers and the arches which were to support the dome.

Bramante accompanied the Pope on the military campaigns to Bologna in 1506 and in 1510, and during the latter campaign he is reported to have entertained the Pope every evening with his commentary on the writings of Dante. In 1513 the Pope bestowed the office of *Piombatore,* or sealer of the papal briefs, on him. Bramante planned a huge palace on the Via Giulia for the papal courts of justice. It was begun in 1509, but with the death of the Pope in 1513 the work was abandoned, leaving only a few massive, rusticated blocks of the ground floor.

Bramante's last work was probably the Palazzo Caprini (after 1510; destroyed). It had a rusticated ground floor with shops and an upper story with coupled Doric half columns. Owned later by Raphael, it became the prototype for numerous palaces, especially in northern Italy, by Michele Sanmicheli, Giulio Romano, and Andrea Palladio. Bramante died on March 11, 1514, and was buried in Old St. Peter's.

Further Reading

There is no monograph on Bramante in English. A study in Italian is Arnaldo Bruschi, *Bramante architetto* (1969). Another useful work, in Italian, is Costantino Baroni, ed., *Bramante* (1944). An excellent study in English on an important Roman building is James S. Ackerman, *The Cortile del Belvedere* (1954). For background works on Renaissance architecture see Rudolf Wittkower, *Architectural Principles in the Age of Humanism* (1949; 3d rev. ed. 1962), and Peter Murray, *The Architecture of the Italian Renaissance* (1963). □

Constantin Brancusi

Constantin Brancusi (1876-1957), a Romanian sculptor who settled in France, revolutionized the art of sculpture in the 20th century. His work revealed the beauty of pure form in sculpture, but he endowed it with an organic mystery.

Constantin Brancusi was born into a family of poor peasants in the hamlet of Hobita in the province of Oltenia on Feb. 21, 1876. He taught himself to read and write and at the age of 18 entered the School of Arts and

Crafts in Craiova and graduated in 1898. He then studied sculpture at the Bucharest Art School until 1902. His *Ecorché,* or flayed nude, executed in 1902, is such an accurate study of the male anatomy that it is still used at the medical school in Bucharest.

Brancusi enrolled at the Académie des Beaux-Arts in Paris in 1904, where he studied with Antonin Mercié. But Brancusi was drawn to the innovative art of Auguste Rodin, from whom he learned that the purpose of sculpture is not merely the representation of the surface of forms but the evocation of the inner force that produces the surface. He exhibited for the first time in 1906 in Paris, showing a portrait at the Salon organized by the Societé Nationale des Beaux-Arts and three other works at the Salon d'Automne in the same year. In Brancusi's works of 1905-1907, particularly the series *Children's Heads,* he used Rodin's impressionistic system of modeling, in which the planes bounding the volume are fragmented to suggest the transitory expressions of the physiognomy. Brancusi declined Rodin's invitation to become his studio assistant because he felt it necessary to find his own way without being subjected to the master's over-whelming influence.

The nature of Brancusi's future work, in which he eliminated all that was not essential in order to suggest the primordial sentiment, was foreshadowed in *Prayer* (1907), a statue of a kneeling woman which concentrates attention on the generalized contour of the body and not analytically on its volume. Step by step he reached a greater degree of simplification, of abstraction of the real element, which was still figurative. The decorative value was obtained by geo-

metrical stringency and skillfully polished surfaces, as in the *Wisdom of the Earth* (1909) and *The Kiss* (1910). These works embody his new esthetics, inspired by folklore, which permitted a return to the suggestiveness and naive simplicity of primitive art. He dissected the scheme of folk art, which he took as his model, and retraced the slope back to the path of its formation, to the sentiment that gave it birth.

Maturity of His Art

By 1910 Brancusi's art took on the characteristics which were to revitalize sculpture. He worked in stone, wood, and bronze, perfecting his rendition of earlier themes, such as the portrait (*Mademoiselle Pogany* series, 1912-1933), the bird (*Magic Bird* cycle, 1912-1915; *Bird in Space* cycle, 1919-1940), the fish (*Fish* cycle, 1922-1930), and the column (*Endless Column* series, 1918-1937). In these works he projected his own rich inner life, at times haunted by fantasies of Romanian mythology, bypassing the intermediate representation of the human figure. Sculptures such as *The Witch* (1916) and *The Chimera* (1918) are sensitive incarnations of that sentiment which had given rise to Brancusi's native folklore. Brancusi's aim in his mature work was to reveal the crystalline structure of organic forms and to bring out the autonomous life of inorganic matter inherent in the very consistency of stone, metal, and wood.

Brancusi's Parisian studio was crowded with Romanian folk art. He led a simple life, similar to that of the peasants in his native province, which he never forgot, no matter how integrated he was in the French artistic movement. He was very successful and received numerous commissions. To honor the Romanian soldiers of World War I, Brancusi erected a monumental ensemble at Târgu-Jiu near his birthplace, which consists of the *Endless Column* in steel and the *Gate of the Heroes* and the *Table of Silence* with 12 chairs in stone (1937-1938). The structural and decorative elements of the monument were derived from the simple architecture and furniture of the Romanian peasants.

Brancusi died in Paris on March 16, 1957.

Contemplation and Liberation

Brancusi demonstrated that modern art, while preserving the harmony, balance, and humanism of its western European artistic legacy, could originate from the primordial ages of mankind which preceded the culture of classical antiquity. He invented forms that begin from reality but are not subject to it. His simple, calm forms, of organic perfection (although they have sometimes been considered abstract), reflect the creative attitude that is fundamental to modern plastic arts: renunciation of the method of interpreting sentiment by means of the poses and gestures of the human body (for example, the *Beginning of the World,* 1924; *Socrates,* 1923). Brancusi was interested in the stylization of forms in accordance with a logic governed by the requirements of expression (for example, *The Cock,* 1924). He reduced the image to the essential, pure form, as in his famed versions of *Bird in Space.*

The highly personal art of Brancusi cannot be labeled by the terms applied to modern movements, such as surrealism, cubism, abstraction, or futurism. It expresses his profound grasp of the intuitive spirit of creation, which is ingeniously integrated with the major stylistic aspects of modern art.

Further Reading

The most important work on Brancusi in English is Sidney Geist, *Brancusi: A Study of the Sculpture* (1968). Geist also wrote the catalog for the retrospective exhibition held in 1969-1970, *Constantin Brancusi, 1876-1957* (1969). See also David Lewis, *Constantin Brancusi* (1957); Sir Herbert Read, *Constantin Brancusi* (1957); Carola Giedion-Welcker, *Constantin Brancusi, 1876-1957* (1958; trans. 1959); and Christian Zervos, ed., *Constantin Brancusi: Sculptures, peintures, fresques, dessins,* in French (1957). An important documentation of the bird sculptures is Athena T. Spear, *Brancusi's Birds* (1970).

Additional Sources

Lewis, David Neville, *Constantin Brancusi,* London: Academy Editions; New York: St. Martins Press, 1974. □

Louis Dembitz Brandeis

As an associate justice of the U.S. Supreme Court, Louis Dembitz Brandeis (1856-1941) tried to reconcile the developing powers of modern government and society with the maintenance of individual liberties and opportunities for personal development.

As the United States entered the 20th century, many men became concerned with trying to equip government so as to deal with the excesses and inequities fostered by the industrial development of the 19th century. States passed laws trying to regulate utility rates and insurance manipulations and established minimum-wage and maximum-hour laws. Louis Brandeis was one of the most important Americans involved in this effort, first as a publicly minded lawyer and, after 1916, as a member of the U.S. Supreme Court.

Brandeis was born on Nov. 13, 1856, in Louisville, Ky., to Adolph and Fredericka Dembitz Brandeis. His parents were Bohemian Jews who had come to America in the aftermath of those European revolutionary movements of 1848 that had sought to establish liberal political institutions and to strengthen the processes of democracy so as to safeguard the dignity and potential for self-development of the common man.

In 1875, at the age of 18, Brandeis entered the Harvard Law School without a formal college degree; he achieved one of the most outstanding records in its history. At the same time he tutored fellow students in order to earn money (necessary because of his father's loss of fortune in the Panic of 1873). Although Brandeis was not the required age of 21, the Harvard Corporation passed a special resolution granting him a bachelor of law degree in 1877. After a further year of legal study at Harvard, he was admitted to the bar.

Early Legal Career

In 1879 Brandeis began a partnership with his classmate Samuel D. Warren. Together they wrote one of the most famous law articles in history, "The Right to Privacy," published in the December 1890 *Harvard Law Review.* In it Brandeis enunciated the view he later echoed in the Supreme Court case of *Olmstead v. United States* (1928), in which he argued that the makers of the Constitution, as evidence of their effort "to protect Americans in their beliefs, their thoughts, their emotions and their sensations . . . conferred, as against the Government, the right to be let alone—the most comprehensive of rights and the right most valued by civilized men."

During this stage of his career, Brandeis spent much time helping the Harvard Law School. Though he declined an offer to become an assistant professor, in 1886 he helped found the Harvard Law School Association, an alumni group, and served for many years as its secretary.

Years of Public Service

By 1890 Brandeis had developed a lucrative practice and was able to serve, without pay, in various public causes. When a fight arose, for example, over preservation of the Boston subway system, he helped save it; similarly, he helped lead the opposition to the New Haven Railroad's monopoly of transportation in New England. The Massachusetts State Legislature's adoption of a savings-bank life insurance system was the result of his investigation of the inequities of existing insurance programs.

Brandeis also took part in the effort to bring legal protections to industrial laborers, and as part of this effort he contributed a major concept to Supreme Court litigation. In 1908, defending an Oregon law establishing wages and hours for women laborers, Brandeis introduced what came to be known as the "Brandeis brief," which went far beyond legal precedent to consider the various economic and social factors which led the legislature to pass the law. Many lawyers followed the Brandeis brief and presented relevant scientific evidence and expert opinion dealing with the great social problems of the day mirrored in judicial litigation.

Appointment to the Supreme Court

President Woodrow Wilson offered Brandeis a position in his Cabinet in 1913, but the Boston lawyer preferred to remain simply a counselor to the President. Brandeis continued his investigations of the implications for democracy of the growing concentration of wealth in large corporations. In 1914 he published *Other People's Money, and How the Bankers Use It,* in which he set down his antimonopoly views.

Wilson's nomination of Brandeis to the Supreme Court on Jan. 28, 1916, aroused a dirty political fight. Six former presidents of the American Bar Association and former president of the United States William Howard Taft denounced Brandeis for his allegedly radical political views. Some anti-Semitism was involved, for Brandeis was the first Jew ever nominated for America's highest court. Finally, however, the fight was won in the Senate, and Brandeis took his seat on June 5, 1916, where he served with distinction until Feb. 13, 1939.

Brandeis often joined his colleague Oliver Wendell Holmes in dissenting against the Court's willingness to pose its judgments about economic and social policy against those of individual states. Also with Holmes, Brandeis bravely defended civil liberties throughout this era. If he did uphold wide use of state powers, it was only in the service of furthering individual self-fulfillment; he also rejected incursions of a state upon a citizen's liberty. Two examples are the Olmstead case (already noted), involving wiretapping, and *Whitney v. California,* in which Brandeis opposed a California law suppressing free speech.

Personal Interests

Brandeis married Alice Goldmark in 1891, and they had two daughters. Part of his personal life was his commitment to fellow Jews. He became a leading Zionist, supporting the attempt to develop a Jewish nation in Palestine.

Another of Brandeis's great interests was the building up of strong regional schools as a means of strengthening local areas against the threat of national centralization. To this end, beginning in 1924, he helped formulate and develop the law school and general library of the University of Louisville.

Brandeis died on Oct. 5, 1941. His commitments to justice, education, and Judaism were commemorated several years later in the founding of Brandeis University in Waltham, Mass.

Further Reading

The standard scholarly biography of Brandeis, unfortunately slim so far as his judicial career is concerned, is Alpheus Thomas Mason, *Brandeis: A Free Man's Life* (1946). A good introduction to his legal ideas is Samuel Joseph Konefsky, *The Legacy of Holmes and Brandeis* (1956). Alexander M. Bickel in *The Unpublished Opinions of Mr. Justice Brandeis* (1957) presents good examples of the justice's painstaking methods in preparing his judicial opinions. Paul A. Freund, Brandeis's former clerk, presents a moving portrait in Allison Dunham and Philip B. Kurland, eds., *Mr. Justice* (1964). For general historical background see Robert Green McCloskey, *The American Supreme Court* (1960), and Arthur M. Schlesinger, Jr.'s three volumes: *The Age of Roosevelt: The Crisis of the Old Order* (1957), *The Coming of the New Deal* (1959), and *The Politics of Upheaval* (1960). □

Marlon Brando

Beginning with his early career in the films of the 1950s, through his powerful roles in such classics as *On the Waterfront, A Streetcar Named Desire,* and *The Godfather,* Marlon Brando (born 1924) has captivated the American public with his intense on-screen presence, as well as with his personal life of controversy and excess.

Before James Dean, Marlon Brando popularized the jeans-and-T-shirt look, with and without leather jacket, as a movie idol during the early 1950s. The theatrically trained actor began to turn away from his youth-oriented persona with such movie roles as Mark Antony in *Julius Caesar* (1953). After winning an Academy Award for Best Actor for *On the Waterfront* (1954), he portrayed a wide variety of characters on-screen, garnering popular acclaim and critical consensus as one of the greatest cinema actors of the late twentieth century.

Early Career

Brando was born in Omaha, Nebraska, on April 3, 1924. He grew up in Illinois. After expulsion from a military academy, he dug ditches until his father offered to finance his education. Brando moved to New York to study with acting coach Stella Adler and at Lee Strasberg's Actors' Studio. While at the Actors' Studio, Brando adopted the "method approach," which emphasizes characters' motivations for actions. He made his Broadway debut in John Van Druten's sentimental *I Remember Mama* (1944). New York theater critics voted him Broadway's Most Promising Actor for his performance in *Truckline Cafe* (1946). In 1947 he played his greatest stage role, Stanley Kowalski—the brute who rapes his sister-in-law, the fragile Blanche du Bois—in

Tennessee Williams's *A Streetcar Named Desire.* As *The New York Review* surmised, ''The rest is stardom and gossip and a small handful of wonderful films.''

Hollywood beckoned to Brando, and he made his motion picture debut as a paraplegic World War II veteran in *The Men* (1950). Although he did not cooperate with the Hollywood publicity machine, he went on to play Kowalski in the 1951 film version of A *Streetcar Named Desire,* a popular and critical success that earned four Academy Awards. His next movie, *Viva Zapata!* (1952), with a script by John Steinbeck, traces Emiliano Zapata's rise from peasant to revolutionary to president of Mexico. Brando followed that with *Julius Caesar* and then *The Wild One* (1954), in which he played a motorcycle-gang leader in all his leather-jacketed glory. Next came his Academy Award winning role as a longshoreman fighting the system in *On the Waterfront,* a hard-hitting look at New York City labor unions.

Pinnacle

During the rest of the decade, Brando's screen roles ranged from Napoleon Bonaparte in *Désirée* (1954), to Sky Masterson in 1955's *Guys and Dolls,* in which he sang and danced, to a Nazi soldier in *The Young Lions* (1958). From 1955 to 1958 movie exhibitors voted him one of the top ten box-office draws in the nation. During the 1960s, however, his career had more downs than ups, especially after the MGM studio's disastrous 1962 remake of *Mutiny on the Bounty,* which failed to recoup even half of its enormous budget. Brando portrayed Fletcher Christian, Clark Gable's

role in the 1935 original. Brando's excessive self-indulgence reached a pinnacle during the filming of this movie. He was criticized for his on-the-set tantrums and for trying to alter the script. Off the set, he had numerous affairs, ate too much, and distanced himself from the cast and crew. His contract for making the movie included $5,000 for every day the film went over its original schedule. He made $1.25 million when all was said and done.

Brando's career was reborn in 1972 with his depiction of Mafia chieftain Don Corleone in *The Godfather.* He refused his Academy Award for Best Actor as a protest of Hollywood's treatment of Native Americans. Brando did not appear at the awards show to personally deny the trophy. Instead, a Native American Apache named Sacheen Littlefeather read his protest. However, in September of 1994, Brando told the broker in possession of the award, Marty Ingels, that he now wishes to own it. Ingels would not return it.

Brando proceeded the following year to the highly controversial yet highly acclaimed *Last Tango in Paris,* which was rated X. Since then Brando has received huge salaries for playing small parts in such movies as *Superman* (1978) and *Apocalypse Now* (1979). Nominated for an Academy Award for Best Supporting Actor for A *Dry White Season* in 1989, Brando also appeared in *The Freshman* with Matthew Broderick. In 1995, he costarred in *Don Juan DeMarco* with Johnny Depp. Young people who have not seen Brando's amazing efforts in his early films will not find the same genius in his later movies. The small roles he has played do not demand the acting range for which he had once achieved so much praise. Janet Maslin of the *New York Times,* in her review of *Don Juan DeMarco,* wrote, ''Mr. Brando doesn't so much play his role as play along.'' The critic added, ''*Don Juan DeMarco* verges on the sad when its subject is vitality, since Mr. Depp's so clearly eclipses that of his co-star.''

In early 1996 Brando costared in afilm called *The Island of Dr. Moreau. Entertainment Weekly* reported that the actor was using an earpiece to remember his lines. His costar in the film, David Thewlis, told the magazine that he was nonetheless still impressed by Brando. ''When he walks into a room,'' Thewlis noted, ''you know he's around.''

A Life of Turmoil and Self-Indulgence

There have been countless pages of print written about Brando's reclusive and self-indulgent lifestyle, including two books released in 1994: *Brando: The Biography,* by Peter Manso, and *Brando: Songs My Mother Taught Me,* by Marlon Brando with Robert Lindsey. The book by Marlon Brando is obviously the one he authorizes, but Manso's book is a result of seven years of research and interviews with more than a thousand people. *Time* magazine, though, questioned Manso's ethics in conducting such excessive research: ''Driven to possess another man's life, Manso becomes the literary version of one of the late 20th century's scariest specimens, the celebrity stalker.''

It has been observed that Brando has perhaps loved food and womanizing too much. His best acting performances are roles that required him to show a constrained and displayed rage and suffering. His own rage may have come from parents who did not care about him. *Time* magazine reported, "Brando had a stern, cold father and a dream-disheveled mother—both alcoholics, both sexually promiscuous—and he encompassed both their natures without resolving the conflict." Brando himself wrote in his autobiography, "If my father were alive today, I don't know what I would do. After he died, I used to think, 'God, just give him to me alive for eight seconds because I want to break his jaw.'"

Brando's acting teacher, Stella Adler, is often credited with helping him become a brilliant actor. Brando said in a reprint of Manso's book presented in *Premiere* magazine, "If it hadn't been for Stella, maybe I wouldn't have gotten where I am—she taught me how to read, she taught me to look at art, she taught me to listen to music."

Although Brando avoids speaking in details about his marriages, even in his autobiography, it is known that he has been married three times to three ex-actresses. He has at least 11 children ranging in age from two to thirty-eight. Five of the children are with his three wives, three are with his Guatemalan housekeeper, and the other three children are from other affairs. One of Brando's sons, Christian, told *People* magazine, "The family kept changing shape. I'd sit down at the breakfast table and say, 'Who are you?'" Christian is now at a state prison in California serving a 10-year sentence for voluntary manslaughter in the death of his sister's fiancee, Dag Drollet. He claimed Drollet was physically abusing his pregnant sister, Cheyenne. Christian said he struggled with Drollet and accidentally shot him in the face. Brando, in the house at the time, gave mouth-to-mouth resuscitation to Drollet and called 911. At Christian's trial, *People* reported one of Brando's comments on the witness stand, "I tried to be a good father. I did the best I could."

Brando's daughter, Cheyenne, was a troubled young woman. In and out of drug rehabilitation centers and mental hospitals for much of her life, she lived in Tahiti with her mother Tarita (one of Brando's wives whom he met on the set of *Mutiny on the Bounty*). *People* reported in 1990 that Cheyenne said of Brando, "I have come to despise my father for the way he ignored me as a child." After Drollet's death, Cheyenne became even more reclusive and depressed. A judge ruled that she was too depressed to raise her child and gave custody of the boy to her mother, Tarita. Cheyenne took a leave from a mental hospital on Easter Sunday in 1995 to visit her family. At her mother's home that day, Cheyenne, who had attempted suicide before, hanged herself.

Brando's years of self-indulgence are visible—he weighed well over 300 pounds in the mid-1990s. To judge Brando by his appearance and dismiss his work because of his later, less significant acting jobs, however, would be a mistake. His performance in *A Streetcar Named Desire* brought audiences to their knees, and his range of roles is a testament to his capability to explore many aspects of the human psyche. Brando seems perfectly content that his best work is behind him. As for his fans, they must accept that staying power is not what confirms the actor's brilliance.

Further Reading

Gary Cary, *Marlon Brando: The Only Contender* (London: Robson, 1985).
Christopher Nickens, *Brando: A Biography in Pictures* (Garden City, N.Y.: Doubleday, 1987).
Richard Schickel, *Brando: A Life in Our Times* (New York: Atheneum, 1991). □

Willy Brandt

The German statesman Willy Brandt (1913-1992) became the first Socialist chancellor of the Federal Republic of Germany, or West Germany, in 1969.

Herbert Frahm, who later adopted the name Willy Brandt, was born in the North Sea port of Lübeck on Dec. 18, 1913, the illegitimate son of working-class parents. After a lonely and deprived childhood he found fellowship in the youth organizations of the Social Democratic party (SPD), the strongest bulwark of German democracy in the 1920s. He won a scholarship to a prestigious Lübeck gymnasium (secondary school), from which he graduated in 1932. He had joined a left-wing splinter group of the SPD strongly opposed to the rising tide of Nazi power. Thus, when Hitler came to power in 1933, he decided to change his name to Willy Brandt and flee from certain persecution. He therefore escaped the pursuit by secret police and the confinement in concentration camps which befell so many other SPD leaders.

Brandt spent the rest of the 1930s in Norway and eventually became a Norwegian citizen. But in 1940 he was again forced to flee the Nazis, and he spent the remaining war years in neutral Sweden. Throughout his exile Brandt worked as a journalist, and at the end of World War II he returned to Germany to cover the Nuremberg war crimes trials. Once again a German citizen, in 1949 he became an SPD representative of Berlin in the first West German Bundestag (parliament), and a year later he was elected to the city parliament of Berlin.

In 1957 Brandt became lord mayor of West Berlin. He became internationally known for his resistance to Soviet and East German pressures on the isolated city, especially during the Berlin Wall crisis of 1961. The SPD had dropped the last remnants of its revolutionary Marxist heritage in 1959. It was eager to attract a less radical and larger electorate, and Brandt's suave, youthful appearance and proven courage made him a leading contender for the leadership of the party. As candidate for the chancellorship (1961, 1965, and 1969) and as leader of the SPD (after 1964), Brandt led his party to solid political gains on a social reform platform. In 1966 he led the party into a "grand coalition" with the other major party, the Christian Democratic Union (CDU); he then became the foreign minister of West Germany.

In the 1969 Bundestag elections the SPD (with support from the small Free Democratic party) won a majority; Brandt, assuming the highest governmental office, became

chancellor. While not abandoning West Germany's commitment to Western European economic integration, Brandt took a softer line toward Eastern European governments. In the domestic sphere he initiated broad political, educational, and economic reforms. As chancellor, Brandt ably demonstrated to both his supporters and detractors that a Socialist leader could be effective, statesmanlike, and popular.

Ostpolitik

This policy of softer lines of governmental and economic dealings with Eastern European countries came to be known as *ostpolitik* . Brandt signed treaties and in doing so, relaxed tensions. This enabled both Germanies to enter the United Nations and Germans to cross borders. It also led to the Nobel Peace Prize, awarded to Brandt in 1971. It also led to his resignation. In 1974 Brandt's close aide, Günter Guillaume, was revealed to be an East German spy. Though this scandal led to his resignation, Brandt remained Chairman of the SPD for 13 more years.

Out of Office

Besides chairing the SPD, Brandt served as President of the Socialist International, an umbrella group for all Social Democratic Parties. In the early 1980s he chaired a worldwide panel known as the Brandt Commission. The Commission called for a more equitable distribution of the world's wealth; the advice was both lauded and ignored. Because of Brandt's efforts, the re-unification of Germany occurred, though more quickly than even Brandt ever imagined. His-

torians honor Brandt more than his own countrymen did; few of his contemporaries in the early 1970s realized how his efforts and policies prepared Germany for a united future. Brandt spoke of the slow and painful process of unifying Germany, and he remained an advocate of unity until the end of his life. Brandt died of cancer in 1992.

Further Reading

Willy Brandt's autobiography, *Willy Brandt: A Political Biography,* St. Martin's Press, 1997. An overview of his accomplishments is Arthur M. Schelsinger, Jr., "Thinking Aloud: The Difference Willy Brandt Has Made," *The New Leader,* October 29, 1990, 11-13. □

Joseph Brant

Joseph Brant (1742-1807) was a Mohawk chief and ally of the British during the American Revolution. He was instrumental in moving the Mohawks to Canada following the winning of American independence.

J oseph Brant was born in the Ohio Valley and was called Thayendanegea ("he who places two bets"). His father was a sachem of the Iroquois Confederacy, to which the Mohawks belonged; however, Brant's mother was not a Mohawk, and as descent in the tribe was matrilineal, he never rose to the rank of sachem, although he did become a war chief.

As a boy, Brant attracted the protection of Sir William Johnson, British Indian superintendent, whom he accompanied on an expedition in 1755. Six years later, at 19, Brant was sent to Moor's Charity School in Lebanon, Conn., for an education. There he was converted to the Anglican Church and in 1763 left the school to work as an interpreter for a missionary. Thereafter he was constantly caught between a desire to convert his tribe to white ways and to lead them in war against the whites.

In 1764 Brant left the missionary, whom he had helped to translate religious tracts into the Mohawk language, to join the Iroquois contingent fighting under Chief Pontiac. Ten years later, when Guy Johnson, son-in-law of Sir William Johnson, became Indian superintendent, Brant became his secretary. At the outbreak of the American Revolution, Brant used his influence to persuade the Iroquois to join the British side and to discredit the Reverend Samuel Kirkland, a missionary who had succeeded in persuading the Oneida and Tuscarora (tribes in the Iroquois Confederacy) to join with the Americans.

Brant was war chief of the Mohawks when he met Sir Guy Carleton at a conference in Montreal. Brant was commissioned a captain and sent to England to be presented at court as a Native American ally of the Crown. Returning to the New World, he fought as commander of a Native American contingent at the Battle of Long Island in 1776 and was with St. Leger's expedition at the Battle of Oriskany in 1777.

Between 1778 and 1780 Brant led his Indian troops on raids in the Mohawk Valley, southern New York, and northern Pennsylvania, warning his followers that an American victory would mean destruction for all Native Americans. He and his followers were accused of perpetrating massacres such as those at Cherry Valley in 1778 and at Wyoming in 1779; though Brant always claimed that he did not join in these bloody aspects of the fighting, his troops were responsible for some reprehensible killings.

At the close of the American Revolution, Brant frustrated the attempt of Red Jacket, a rival Mohawk chief, to negotiate a peace treaty with the United States. Later he unsuccessfully attempted such a negotiation himself, whereupon he persuaded Governor Haldimaud of Canada to assign the Mohawks a reservation on the Grand River in Upper Canada. His journey to England in 1785 was successful in attaining an indemnification for the Mohawks for their losses during the war. He also made a trip to Philadelphia during which he was unsuccessful in negotiating peace with the United States.

Brant's later years were spent translating the New Testament and other religious documents into Mohawk and promoting Native American acceptance of the white man's ways. He was able to prevent speculators from getting the Mohawk lands on the Grand River, but his last years were saddened by the actions of his dissolute eldest son and by his quarrels with his rival, Red Jacket. He died on Nov. 24, 1807, at the Grand River Reservation.

Further Reading

The best recent work on Brant is Harvey Chalmers, in collaboration with Ethel Brant Monture, *Joseph Brant: Mohawk* (1955). Another useful work is Louis Aubrey Wood, *The War Chief of the Six Nations: A Chronicle of Joseph Brant* (1914). See also Alexander C. Flick, ed., *History of the State of New York,* vol. 4: *The New State* (1933); Ethel Brant Monture, *Canadian Portraits: Brant, Crowfoot, Oronhyatekha—Famous Indians* (1960); and Dale Van Every, *A Company of Heroes: The American Frontier, 1775-1783* (1962). □

Mary (Molly) Brant

As consort of Sir William Johnson, Mary Brant's (1736-1796) influence with Indian leaders helped Johnson to pacify the Indian nations he dealt with as a representative of the British government. After his death, she was able to influence the Iroquois toward alliance with the British during the Revolutionary War.

Molly Brant is considered the most influential Mohawk woman in the New World from 1759 to 1776. She and Catherine Brant (her younger brother's wife) are the only women of the period on whose lives any extended documentation has survived. Brant was born in 1736 to "Margaret" and "Peter," Canajoharie Mohawks registered as Protestant Christians in the Anglican chapel at Fort Hunter. Some reports do not list the names of her parents, but simply say she was the daughter of a sachem (chieftain), and came from Canajoharie, a Mohawk (Iroquois) village located in New York. Molly is said to have received her surname from her stepfather, Nickus Brant, a European thought to be part Dutch. He was a close friend of William Johnson, a British official responsible for maintaining Indian relations in the colonies during the time of the American Revolution. Brant is believed to have been a strong European influence on Brant and her younger brother Joseph. Active and gregarious, she is said to have become the object of Johnson's attention when in 1753, she accepted a British officer's challenge to participate in a horse riding competition between the British and the Mohawks. She later married Johnson in a Mohawk ceremony.

Acculturation, Iroquois Women, and Cultural Difference

A time of great upheaval and cultural change took place among all the Iroquois tribes during the eighteenth century, most markedly during the later half of the century, when colonials sought independence. Perhaps the Mohawks stood out as more notable recipients of cultural change because they were known for their aggressive resistance to European occupation. With the loss of their land along the Mohawk river in eastern-central New York, there was immense pressure on the Mohawk to culturally assimilate in order to survive. European culture was most visibly different with regard to relationships between the sexes, and this succinctly cut at the basic fabric and structure of Iroquois life. For this reason, Molly Brant's life with Johnson, a powerful British official presiding over the British Indian Department's northern district, became a living illustration of acculturation. In her *Ontario History* article "Molly Brant, Catherine Brant, and Their Daughters: A Study in Colonial Acculturation," Gretchen Green terms Molly and Catherine's "individual marital conflicts" as reflections of "the larger cultural struggle, so that Molly and Catherine Brant serve as microcosms of the Mohawk people during the trying times of the late eighteenth century."

Before the advent of the Europeans, the Mohawk were a matrilineal society, deriving the identity of their kinship ties through women. Relationships between the sexes were marked by a more equal distribution of power and validation for contributions made to the needs of the community. Primarily through their agricultural achievements and role as provider, Mohawk women were able to exert a greater degree of influence upon men's decisions than their European counterparts, and thus assertion of male dominance was met with resistance by Mohawk women. By withholding food, making their opinions known at village meetings, and utilizing their appointed clan positions in choosing the village chief/sachem, women banded together to get their agendas met in a way wholly unfamiliar to women in European culture.

Because British law did not recognize the Mohawk marriage of Johnson and Brant, she is said to have been the "common-law" wife of Johnson. She is considered by some sources to have been his mistress. Having married during the Seven Years War, Green states that Johnson is thought to have married Brant out of a desire to gain stronger and more influential political connections. Their marriage took place "when Johnson was desperately seeking Iroquois support for the war effort against the French." He learned the Iroquoian dialects, adopted several Mohawk customs, but reportedly did not choose to live among Natives. Explaining his close relationship to Joseph Brant, Johnson said, according to Green, that he "expected the young Mohawk would prove useful among the Indians because of his 'connection and residence.' It seems reasonable to assume that his relationship with Joseph's sister was in part similarly motivated, for it was said of Molly that 'one word from her [was] more taken Notice of by the Five Nations than a thousand from any white man without exception.'"

Influenced the American Revolution

Brant had been well known and was politically active in her village before joining Johnson at either Fort Johnson or at Johnson Hall, his residence located near Schenectady, "on the edge of Mohawk territory." From 1754 to 1755, she is recorded as having accompanied to Philadelphia a delegate of elders to address Iroquois land conflicts. Other than these highlighted features, relatively little is known about her life in the village during her early years. Her correspondence, written in a clear and legible script, indicates that she may have attended the English school at Canajoharie as a child.

Unlike her predecessor Catherine Weissenberg who bore three children by Johnson, Brant's eight (some sources say nine) children received Johnson's surname. It is unknown whether any of the children were christened. Weissenberg, a German indentured servant, was Johnson's housekeeper at Fort Johnson. Whereas Johnson regarded Weissenberg beneath him in status, and her role in his household was kept to a minimum, it is noted that Molly Brant accepted no such strictures upon her role. She refused to do housework, leaving such chores to the servants and slaves, and in Johnson's absence, she is said to have controlled the affairs of the estate. There is some suggestion that in doing so, she also supervised the daily operations of the Indian Department, of which Johnson was superintendent.

Johnson Hall was elegant and considered plush by frontier standards. Brant was highly admired among Johnson's peers as a model hostess. She was mentioned warmly in correspondence and was as generous with her own people living in the village as she was with European guests. Using Johnson's position and line of credit with merchants, records indicate she made large purchases of blankets, clothing and alcohol, which she gave away to various Iroquois people. Traditional Iroquois custom entailed utilizing economic gain for the good of the community by distributing wealth during a ceremonial giveaway. The more one gave away, the more one rose in honor and prestige within the group. Brant participated in this practice with such purchases, in addition to distributing cash and providing meals. By so doing she gained increasing influence and thus became, in Green's words, "the most influential Mohawk woman in the valley."

After Johnson's death in 1774, Brant was turned away from his estate and she returned to Canajoharie, taking expensive clothing and luxury possessions with her. There she lived primarily on credit, engaging in commerce with the villagers. Because conflicts were rising between the Loyalists and Patriot colonials, Brant's influence among Indians was increasingly instrumental to the British. Both sides attempted to rally the support of the Six Nations, and Patriots regarded Brant as a threat to their interests. She, unlike most Mohawk, felt strongly that the interests of her people would be best served by an alliance with the Crown. Despite her tremendous popularity and respect among her people, she was unable to sway significant numbers toward action, for most preferred not to take sides in the British-American conflict.

Brant herself took an active Loyalist stance, housing Loyalist refugees, providing weapons, and infiltrating intelligence activities where possible. During 1777 she reportedly engaged in spy activities, which were instrumental in the British gaining military ground. As a result, American colonials and Oneida Iroquois Patriots exacted revenge by driving her from her home. Angered, she fled in exile into Canada, where she fiercely resumed Loyalist activities as a liaison among the Iroquois while residing at the Niagara garrison.

She was considered controversial because she advocated for both the British as well as for the Iroquois, even when to outward appearances, the interests of these groups were in opposition. Brant spoke only her native tongue, styled her wardrobe after Mohawk tastes, and encouraged her offspring to do the same. She was an active dissident, remaining loyal to the preservation of her people, yet, she was criticized for involving them in a dispute that wrested their lands from them and left them subjugated and dispossessed. Molly Brant could not have known the outcome of the wars she attempted to influence. It may be only hindsight that her actions were considered contradictory, for she was behaving in accordance with the laws of her people, attempting to maintain progressive negotiations and an alliance with those she perceived as the greatest allies to the Iroquois.

The British supported her Loyalist endeavors, giving her provisions and doing what was necessary to foster her activism. As a political instrument among the Iroquois, she was unequaled. After the American Revolution, the British generously provided her with a pension, land in the area of her choosing, and an English home for her service to the Crown. In addition to this she received a substantial inheritance from Johnson's estate. Retiring from political affairs, Brant finally settled in Kingston, Ontario, near three of her daughters. She died in 1796 of unknown causes.

Further Reading

Native American Women, edited by Gretchen M. Bataille, New York, Garland, 1993; 36-37.
Native North American Almanac, edited by Duane Champagne, Detroit, Gale, 1994; 1020.
Waldman, Carl, *Who Was Who in Native American History,* New York, Facts on File, 1990; 43.
Green, Gretchen, "Molly Brant, Catherine Brant, and Their Daughters: A Study in Colonial Acculturation," *Ontario History,* 81, 1989; 235-250.
Gundy, H. Pearson, "Molly Brant—Loyalist," *Ontario History,* 14, 1953; 97-108. □

Sebastian Brant

The German writer Sebastian Brant (1457-1521) was the author of the "Narrenschiff," or "Ship of Fools," one of the most famous secular works in European letters.

Sebastian Brant, born in Strassburg, lost his father as a child and was reared by his mother. He probably inherited a testy, sensitive nature from her. In 1475 he entered the University of Basel and received a baccalaureate degree in 1477. Though interested in the humanities and teaching them briefly, Brant studied law and taught and practiced it in Basel. He was also adviser and editor for several pioneer Basel publishers. In 1501 Brant returned to Strassburg as a legal adviser, and in 1504 he became municipal secretary, a post he held until the end of his life, while continuing publication and editorial work.

Brant was an admirer and confidant of Emperor Maximilian I. He was also a confirmed humanist, a staunch

adherent of Catholicism, and an arch conservative, becoming ever more pessimistic about the future of the Holy Roman Empire, especially after 1517. He died in 1521.

Brant's masterpiece, the *Narrenschiff,* was published in 1494. It was illustrated by woodcuts, most of which are now recognized as being the work of Albrecht Dürer. A long, satirical narrative written in doggerel verse, this work influenced French and English as well as German works. Written in the vernacular, it was the first German work to pass into the stream of Western literature.

The *Narrenschiff* is not an allegory; instead it catalogs all types of fools in a direct satirical manner. From adulterers to mere fops, they risk eternal salvation and mar the image that the subjects of the Empire must maintain if the vulnerable Empire is to survive. A Latin translation (1497) by Brant's disciple Jacob Locher was responsible for the dissemination of the work in France and England. Thomas Shelton, Robert Copland, Richard Tarlton, and Thomas Dekker were among English writers of the 16th and 17th centuries unwittingly in Brant's debt. His work helped turn English literature from moral satire to satire of manners.

Brant wrote and edited numerous other works in Latin and German in religion, law, didacticism, and exhortation. He also published a volume of Latin verse.

Further Reading

Edwin H. Zeydel. *The Ship of Fools by Sebastian Brant, Translated into Rhyming Couplets with Introduction and Commentary* (1962), contains all the woodcuts; his *Sebastian Brant*

(1967) is the only biography. Recommended for general background is Aurelius Pompen, *The English Versions of the Ship of Fools: A Contribution to the History of the Early French Renaissance in England* (1925). □

Georges Braque

The French painter Georges Braque (1882-1967) was, with Picasso, the founder of cubism, one of the most significant movements in Western art.

Georges Braque was born in Argenteuil, the son of a house-painting contractor who was an amateur artist. In 1890 the family settled in Le Havre, where Braque entered the École des Beaux-Arts in 1899. He went to Paris in 1900 and worked as a house painter. From 1902 to 1904 Braque studied at the Académie Humbert. As a result of his friendship with Raoul Dufy and Othon Friesz, both artists from Le Havre, Braque became allied with the Fauve movement in 1906. With Friesz he traveled to Antwerp in 1906, to La Ciotat in 1907, and several times to L'Estaque.

Braque's Fauve period proved transitory, and his Fauve works were relatively restrained. In the Paris version of *La Ciotat* (1907), for example, the colors, though vivid, are not dazzling, and the brushstrokes are applied in small rectangular units rather than in the broad, quick swatches used, for example, by Maurice Vlaminck.

Initial Cubist Phase, 1908-1909

By 1908 Braque had developed a great admiration for the work of Paul Cézanne, whose influence is discernible in Braque's *Houses at L'Estaque* (1908). In this protocubist painting the sensuousness and relative abandon of Braque's Fauve period have been cast aside. The houses have been reduced to simple cubes in shades of dull greens and grays. To underscore the geometrical severity, the windows and doors of the houses and details of the foliage have been eliminated. Braque and Pablo Picasso, who met at this time and were practically inseparable until 1914, precipitated the mature development of cubism.

Analytic Cubist Phase, 1909-1911

In cubist painting, planes merge and the distinctions between background and foreground and between one form and another become obliterated, as the object or figure seems to be viewed simultaneously from various angles. A masterpiece of Braque's analytic cubist period is the *Man with the Guitar* (1911), in which the figure of the musician, painted in somber earth colors and dissected into small fragments, in presented in a static triangular format. Details of the anatomy of the figure and the parts of the instrument seem to be discernible one moment, indiscernible the next. Braque's and Picasso's paintings of 1909-1911 are especially close and in some cases virtually indistinguishable, though Braque's work is more elegant, slightly more restrained, less emotional, and less expressive.

Synthetic Cubist Phase, 1911-1914

From 1911 on Braque became less dependent on physical reality as the starting point for his artistic conception. Instead of showing the object in its totality, though broken into smaller fragments, he took parts of several objects and arranged them in new combinations. From this time, too, he showed an interest in simulating the textures of wood, marble, and other materials in his paintings, and in his collages he incorporated into the composition bits of real cloth or wood. Thus, in addition to the ambiguous spatial effects of his analytic phase, Braque's synthetic phase featured new ambiguities between what was real and what was created by the artist. In his *Clarinet* (1913), for example, pasted newspaper fragments, charcoal, chalk, and oil paint are so manipulated as to simulate an actual tabletop. The letters from the newspaper clipping function only as decorative or formal elements. The softness of the textures and the oval curves within the rectangular frame produce a delicacy seldom found in Picasso's work of the same period.

Work after 1914

When World War I broke out, Braque was sent to the front and was wounded in 1915. After a long hospital confinement he began to paint again in 1917, adopting a course independent of Picasso. After 1918 Braque largely abandoned collage and the relative austerity of his synthetic cubist phase. A new richness and sensuousness of the painted surface became discernible in his work, but tempered by restraint and refinement. Although cubist devices and passages occasionally occurred, they ceased to be fundamental to Braque's conception.

In the *Still Life with Guitar and Fruit* (1924) the individual integrity of the richly painted guitar and of the still-life elements is maintained. The objects are clearly placed on a table, but their exact spatial locations are a bit vague. The forms now swell and expand and the paint is handled with a creamy richness, yet the colors are tastefully kept within the orbit of browns and grays. During the 1920s Braque liked to use the human figure, often a female nude, in conjunction with his still-life objects. His *Nude* (1925) in Chicago displays a sensuous, monumental figure, somewhat in the manner of Pierre Auguste Renoir.

Braque continued to go his own way, unaffected by the latest changes in European painting. But the harmony and containment of his art did not preclude a richness and originality of expression, which was especially evident in the 1930s. His *Woman with a Mandolin* (1937) is a rich blend of shades of green, citrons, and purples. The woman, sitting before the elegant furnishings of the room, is rendered as a silhouette, reminiscent of the flat forms frequent in the synthetic cubist canvases.

Braque also executed some sculptures in plaster, about 50 lithographs, and etchings for Hesiod's *Theogony* (1931).

Further Reading

Edwin B. Mullins, *The Art of Georges Braque* (1968), is a comprehensive study of the artist; over half the book is devoted to Braque's work after 1920. *Georges Braque: His Graphic Work,* with an introduction by Werner Hofmann (1961), is the authoritative work on Braque's graphics. See also John Russell, *G. Braque* (1959); Jean Leymarie, *Braque* (1961); and the chapter on Braque in Janet Flanner, *Men and Monuments* (1947). Background works on cubism include John Golding, *Cubism: A History and an Analysis, 1907-1914* (1959); Guy Habasque, *Cubism* (1959); and Robert Rosenblum, *Cubism and Twentieth-Century Art* (1960).

Additional Sources

Zurcher, Bernard, *Georges Braque, life and work,* New York: Rizzoli, 1988.

Fauchereau, Serge, *Braque,* New York: Rizzoli, 1987. □

Walter H. Brattain

The American physicist Walter H. Brattain (1902-1987), a co-inventor of the transistor, devoted much of his life to research on surface states.

Although he was born in Amoy, China (February 10, 1902), Walter Houser Brattain spent the early part of his life in the northwest of the United States. He was raised in the state of Washington on a cattle ranch owned by his parents, Ross R. Brattain and Ottilie Houser, and earned his B.S. degree in physics and mathematics at Whitman College in Walla Walla, Washington. Brattain earned that degree in 1924 and an M.A. degree from the

University of Oregon in 1926. He then moved eastward, taking his Ph.D. degree in physics at the University of Minnesota in 1929. Brattain's advisor was John T. Tate, and his thesis was on electron impact in mercury vapor. In 1928 and 1929 he worked at the National Bureau of Standards in Washington, D.C., and in 1929 was hired by Bell Telephone Laboratories.

Brattain's concerns at Bell Laboratories in the years before World War II were first in the surface physics of tungsten and later in the surfaces of the semiconductors cuprous oxide and silicon. During World War II Brattain devoted his time to developing methods of submarine detection under a contract with the National Defense Research Council at Columbia University.

Following the war, Brattain returned to Bell Laboratories and soon joined the semiconductor division of the newly-organized Solid State Department of the laboratories. William Shockley was the director of the semiconductor division, and early in 1946 he initiated a general investigation of semiconductors that was intended to produce a practical solid state amplifier.

Crystals of pure semiconductors (such as silicon or germanium) are very poor conductors at ambient temperatures because the energy that an electron must have in order to occupy a conduction energy level is considerably greater than the thermal energy available to an electron in such a crystal. Heating a semiconductor can excite electrons into conduction states, but it is more practical to increase conductivity by adding impurities to the crystal. A crystal may

be doped with a small amount of an element having more electrons than the semiconductor, and those excess electrons will be free to move through the crystal; such a crystal is an *n-type* semiconductor. One may also add to the crystal a small amount of an element having fewer electrons than the semiconductor, and the electron vacancies, or holes, so introduced will be free to move through the crystal like positively-charged electrons; such a doped crystal is a *p-type* semiconductor.

At the surface of a semiconductor the level of the conduction band can be altered, which will increase or decrease the conductivity of the crystal. Junctions between metals and n-type or p-type semiconductors, or between the two types of semiconductors, have asymmetric conduction properties, and semiconductor junctions can therefore be used to rectify electrical currents. In a rectifier, a voltage bias that produces a current flow in the low-resistance direction is a forward bias, while a bias in the opposite direction is a reverse bias.

Semiconductor rectifiers were familiar devices by the end of World War II, and Shockley hoped to produce a new device that would have a variable resistance and hence could be used as an amplifier. He proposed a design in which an electric field was applied across the thickness of a thin slab of a semiconductor. The conductivity of the semiconductor changed only by a small fraction of the expected amount when the field was applied, which John Bardeen (another member of Shockley's division) suggested was due to the existence of energy states for electrons on the surface of the semiconductor. Charges occupying such states would form a layer that screened the interior of the semiconductor from external fields, and so drastically reduce any effect on the conductivity by such fields. Brattain undertook the investigation of the properties of the surface states, and in the course of his experiments he and Bardeen discovered a means of constructing a solid state amplifier that was distinct from Shockley's field-effect device.

Brattain began his experiments by measuring the change in potential of the surface of a crystal of silicon (with reference to an electrode near that surface) when it was exposed to light. Brattain subsequently found that by introducing an electrolyte between his reference electrode and the semiconductor surface and applying a bias to the electrode, he could greatly influence the potential produced by illumination of the semiconductor. He and Bardeen concluded that ions in the electrolyte migrated to the surface of the semiconductor and nullified the effect of the surface charge already there. It then became possible to observe Shockley's field effect.

Brattain and Bardeen next introduced a second electrode into their apparatus, which was a point contact on the semiconductor that was insulated from the electrolyte. Their semiconductor was a thin layer of n-type silicon on top of a block of p-type silicon, and they found that an increase of the bias on the first electrode in the forward direction would produce a decrease of the current flowing into the point contact under a reverse bias. There was some amplification observed in this circuit (and in other similar ones using silicon and germanium), but the factors were small, and the electrolytes used did not allow good response at high frequencies.

Bardeen and Brattain hoped to improve their devices by using a gold film in place of the electrolyte, and they intended to isolate it from the semiconductor (in this case a block of n-type germanium) by means of an oxide layer on top of the germanium. The oxide coating was inadvertently washed off, however, and the gold film made contact with the germanium. It was with this arrangement that a new effect was observed. A forward bias on the gold film increased the current that flowed to the point contact, which was the opposite effect from what had been observed previously. Brattain and Bardeen supposed that there was a current of holes flowing from the gold film into the semiconductor, and then into the point contact. The new amplifying effect was named the transistor effect.

Bardeen suggested that the gold film and point contact could be replaced by two closely spaced contacts. Brattain constructed the two contacts by wrapping gold tape around the point of a wedge of polystyrene and scraping the gold away from the point of the wedge. The wedge was then pressed against a block of n-type germanium. On December 16, 1947, the device was incorporated into a small amplifier that had a gain of more than 18 and good frequency response. A week later the amplifier was demonstrated for the staff of Bell Laboratories, although a public announcement was not made until June of 1948. For their invention Brattain, Bardeen, and Shockley were awarded the 1956 Nobel Prize in Physics. Brattain also received the Stuart Ballantine Medal, the John Scott Medal, and in 1974 was inducted into the National Inventors Hall of Fame.

Brattain continued to carry out semiconductor research at Bell Laboratories until he retired in 1967. Between 1962 and 1972 he frequently taught courses at Whitman College, and from 1965 until 1975 he took part in a research program to model cell membranes as phospholipid layers.

Brattain was elected to the National Academy of Sciences in 1959 and received many other honors. In 1935 he married Keren Gilmore, and the couple had one son. Following the death of his first wife, Brattain married Emma Jane Kirsch Miller in 1958. Brattain lived in retirement in the state of Washington.

On October 13, 1987, Brattain died in Seattle, Washington, but not without leaving a permanent legacy. In its January 1997 profile of 25 visionaries, *Workforce* cited Brattain, along with his co-inventors Bardeen and Shockley. "AT&T's Bell Laboratories has," the article stated, "spawned numerous inventions, but none more significant than the transistor . . . today, the transistor serves as the basic building block for all solid-state electronics." In the late 1990s, Brattain's invention could be found in cellular telephones, fax machines, computers, automatic cameras, satellites, and many other electronic devices.

Further Reading

The invention of the transistor has been described by Lillian Hoddeson in her article "The discovery of the point-contact transistor," *Historical Studies in the Physical Sciences, 12* (1981-1982). Bardeen, Shockley, and Brattain also recount their experiences in their Nobel addresses: John Bardeen, "Semiconductor research leading to the point contact transistor;" William Shockley, "Transistor technology evokes new physics;" and Walter H. Brattain, "Surface properties of semiconductor," all in *Nobel Lectures: Physics, 1942-1962* (Amsterdam, 1964). Appended to each of these addresses is a short biography of the author.

Bardeen's discussion of semiconductor surface states appeared in the article "Surface states and rectification at a metal semiconductor contact," *Physical Review, 71* (1947). The first published description of the transistor is Bardeen and Brattain's article "The transistor, a semi-conductor triode," *Physical Review, 74* (1948). □

Fernand Braudel

Fernand Braudel (1902-1985) was the leading exponent of the so-called *"Annales"* school of history, which emphasizes total history over long historical periods and large geographical space.

Fernand Braudel was born August 24, 1902, in the small town of Luneville in eastern France. His father was an academic administrator. As a young *agrégé* in history, he went to Algeria in 1923 to teach in a lycée and to work on his *thèse d'état*, which was to be on Philip II of Spain and the Mediterranean. His thesis director, Lucien Febvre, made the fateful suggestion that Braudel invert the emphasis—the Mediterranean and Philip II. In 1935 he went to Brazil to teach in the university in São Paulo, Brazil, returning two and a half years later to France just before World War II, with an appointment in the IVe Section of the Ecole Pratique des Hautes Etudes (E. P. H. E.) in Paris. He spent the war in German prison camps in Mainz and Lübeck. During this time he wrote from memory his thesis, which has come to be considered the classic exemplary work of the *Annales* school of history. It was titled *The Mediterranean and the Mediterranean World in the Age of Philip II* (two volumes, 1949).

Elected in 1946 to the Collège de France, he joined his mentor, Febvre, as one of the founders in 1947 of the new VIe Section (economic and social sciences) of the E. P. H. E. He created the Centre de Recherches Historiques. On Febvre's death in 1956, he succeeded him as president of the VIe Section and editor of the journal *Annales E. S. C.* In 1963 he founded the Maison des Sciences de l'Homme, a structure housing national and international research groups, and became its administrator. From 1971 to 1984 he served as the president of the Scientific Commission of the annual Study Weeks sponsored by the Istituto Internazionale di Storia Economica 'Francesco Datini' in Prato, Italy. These were major meetings of economic historians of Europe (both east and west) specializing in the period between the 12th and the 18th centuries. In 1985 he was received in the Académie Française. He was awarded a long list of honorary degrees, memberships in national academies of science, and similar honors. He was widely-read and influential in southern Europe (Spain, Portugal, Italy, Greece, and Turkey), Eastern Europe (Poland and Hungary), Germany and the Low Countries, Britain, Quebec, and, since the 1970s, the United States, where a research center named after him was established at the State University of New York—Binghamton.

What was the nature of his accomplishment that he achieved so many honors, so much prestige and influence? Obviously he was a great organizer of scientific activity, as the list of his successive activities attests. But more important than that, he symbolized, incarnated, and promulgated an approach to history which responded to and was of great help in interpreting the long-term structures and middle-run cyclical shifts of the real social world.

There are three central themes which one may associate with Braudel as the culminating figure of the so-called *Annales* school of history. The roots of the *Annales* school itself, often traced to the work of French historian Henri Berr at the turn of the 20th century, was the creation in a formal sense of the collaboration of Lucien Febvre and Marc Bloch at the University of Strasbourg in 1929, where they founded the journal *Annales d'histoire économique et social*. The very title of the journal indicates the initial concern, the enormous neglect of both economic and social history in the standard kind of political history that had prevailed in France, Germany, and Britain since the mid-19th century. The *Annales* school was determined to get at the long-term economic and social structures beneath the surface "events" which Braudel was later to describe as "dust." They turned toward the neglected arenas of rural life, demography, social ecology, everyday life, commerce, and mentalities and away from princes, generals, civil servants, and diplomats.

They were pushed by their subject matter to the work of sociologists, anthropologists, and economists for one fundamental reason. It was not only that the subject matter of *Annales* history was concerned with explaining, as opposed to merely describing, history. It was also that history was no longer seen as a mere collection of "facts." Facts "existed" only as responses to historical "problems." Intellectually, and therefore organizationally as well, the quest became the "totality" of human experience, and therefore the close collaboration of history and the social sciences.

Secondly, and this became Braudel's own great contribution, the *Annales* school saw time as a social—more than as a physical—phenomenon, whence the idea of a plurality of social times. The great trinity that Braudel constructed and used as the framework for his book on the Mediterranean was *structure, conjoncture, événement:* long-term, very slowly evolving structures; medium-term, fluctuating cyclical processes; and short-term, ephemeral, highly visible events. Braudel downplayed the time of events and rejected a fourth time, the universal very long-term, as mythical. History was consequently the story of the interweaving of the long-term structures and the cyclical movements (*conjonctures*).

Finally, 30 years after *The Mediterranean*, his second great work appeared in 1979—the three-volume *Civilization and Capitalism, 15th-18th Century*. In it he developed the theme of the three layers of economic life—the bottom layer of everyday life, the middle layer of exchange (the arena of freedom), and the top layer of capitalist monopolies and constraints. This metaphor served to reorganize all of modern history into a constant struggle between the two bottom layers and the top layer of monopoly.

The contribution of Braudel was his sweep and therefore his relevance to the fundamental assessment of large-scale, long-term social change. His intellectual voice was stentorian—a firm line but one uncluttered by dogmatisms. His was a unifying influence, respectful of many strains but impatient of pomposity or foolishness. Above all, Braudel and the *Annales* school stood as a challenge to the narrow, the petty, the arrogance of power in the name of enduring realities, and the social change that is slow but inexorable.

Further Reading

A description of "the *Annales* paradigm" is to be found in Traian Stoianovich, *French Historical Method* (1976), to which Braudel wrote a foreword. Two appreciative articles, one by H. R. Trevor-Roper and one by J. H. Hexter, plus an autobiographical essay by Braudel, are to be found together in the *Journal of Modern History* (December 1972). A long critical article by Samuel Kinser is in the *American Historical Review* (February 1981).

Additional Sources

Daix, Pierre, *Braudel,* Paris: Flammarion, 1995. □

Ferdinand Braun

The German physicist Ferdinand Braun (1850-1918) received the Nobel Prize in Physics for his work on wireless telegraphy.

K arl Ferdinand Braun was born in Fulda, Germany, on June 6, 1850, the son of Konrad and Franziska (Gohring) Braun. Upon graduation from his local gymnasium, he entered the University of Marburg, later completing his Ph.D. at the University of Berlin in 1872 with a dissertation on the vibrations of elastic rods and strings.

Braun's career began at the University of Würzburg in 1872, where he worked as assistant to George Hermann Quincke, the eminent German physicist and authority on elastic vibrations—of which light (electromagnetic radiation) was thought to be a species. Braun remained with Quincke two years, publishing in 1874 the results of his research on mineral metal sulfides. He discovered that these crystals would conduct electrical currents in one direction only. This finding was important in electrical research and in measuring another property of substances, electrical conductivity. However, there were no immediate practical applications, and not until the early 20th century was the phenomenon employed in crystal radio receivers.

Braun next took a lectureship at the St. Thomas Gymnasium in Leipzig, a post he also held for two years. Then, from 1876 to 1880 he was extraordinary professor at the

University of Marburg, his *alma mater.* In 1880 his itinerant career took him outside of Germany, to the University of Strasbourg in France, where he remained for three years engaged in research, leaving in 1883; he returned again in 1895 as professor of physics and director of the physics institute. In the intervening years, however, he worked in Germany. For three years he was professor of physics at the Technical High School in Karlsruhe, and in the year he left (1885), he also married Amelie Bühler; they had two sons and two daughters. This must have domesticated him, for he remained at his next job, in Tübingen, for ten years, helping to found the Physical Institute there.

After 1890 Braun produced much of the work for which he was later to become famous. Here, his skill as an inventor combined with his grasp of theoretical principles to effect two significant technological achievements—the coupled transmitter and coupled receiver for improved wireless performance (1899 patent) and the cathode-ray oscilloscope (1897).

Braun was attracted to the study of wireless transmission by the question of why it was so difficult to increase the range of transmission to more than 15 kilometers. Though he expected to extend the range of transmission through a mere increase in the production of the transmitter's power, his experience with Hertz oscillators proved that any attempt to increase the power output by increasing the length of the spark gap would find a limit beyond which the power output would only decrease. Braun found his answer in the creation of a sparkless antenna circuit—power from the transmitter was magnetically coupled through the trans-

former effect to an antenna circuit rather than directly linking it to the power circuit. Related to this work and complementing it was his investigation of aspects of radiotelegraphy, including directional transmission of electromagnetic waves, work on crystal detectors, and use of radio transmissions as beacons for navigation. For these achievements Braun received with Guglielmo Marconi of Italy in 1909 a Nobel Prize for his contributions to wireless telegraphy.

Braun also introduced the first oscilloscope by the use of alternating voltage to shift an electron beam (as it was later understood) within a cathode tube. The trace remaining on the tube's surface corresponded to the amplitude and frequency of the alternating-current voltage. Braun then made use of a rotating mirror to graph the trace he had produced. This invention proved to be an essential instrument in subsequent electronic research.

Despite his great achievements—in fact because of them—Braun's final years were not happy ones. In early 1915, only a few months after the outbreak of World War I, he travelled to the United States to testify on behalf of the Telefunken Co. in litigation involving radio broadcasting. There he remained until the United States entered the war, when it became impossible for him to leave. Though he lived with his son Konrad in New York City, which must have provided some comfort, he was unable to pursue his scientific interests. Deprived of a laboratory, and with little independent means, he spent his last years in inactivity, dying in Brooklyn on April 20, 1918.

Further Reading

Biographical information on Braun can be gleaned from several sources. Most extensive is the *Dictionary of Scientific Biography*, vol. II, Charles Gillispie, editor (1973). Also helpful is *Who's Who in Science: Antiquity to Present,* 1st. ed., edited by Allen G. Debus (1968). There is Heathcote, *Nobel Winners in Physics, 1901-1950* (1953), but it contains little information on Braun's life.

Additional Sources

Kurylo, Friedrich, *Ferdinand Braun, a life of the Nobel prizewinner and inventor of the cathode-ray oscilloscope,* Cambridge, Mass.: MIT Press, 1981. □

Pierre Paul François Camille Savorgnan de Brazza

The Italian-born French explorer Pierre Paul François Camille Savorgnan de Brazza (1852-1905) is regarded as the founder of French Equatorial Africa. His fame rests on the methods he employed to secure the goodwill of Africans toward France.

Pierre Savorgnan de Brazza was born in Rome on Jan. 25, 1852, the scion of an old aristocratic family. Brazza's father was an Italian patriot and a liberal who refused to live under Austrian rule in Udine in northern Italy and settled in Rome, returning to his family estate only after the Friuli region had been ceded to Piedmont in 1859.

France's role as a protector of Italian nationalism explains why young Pierre sought permission to continue his studies at the French naval academy, where he was admitted in 1868. A midshipman by the time of the Franco-Prussian War, he volunteered for service with the French navy. After the end of the war, Brazza made his first trip to the coast of Gabon with the South Atlantic fleet in 1872-1874. It was at that time that Brazza, undaunted by the failure of a previous French expedition to penetrate to the heart of Equatorial Africa, conceived the idea of using the Ogooué River under the belief that it might connect with the Lualaba—the Upper Congo—recently discovered by David Livingstone. Having secured French citizenship and official approval for his petition to be placed on paid leave, Brazza returned to Gabon in 1875 and sailed up the Ogooué, only to discover that it could not possibly connect with the Lualaba. He then traveled overland to the Alima River (a right-bank affluent of the Congo) but was prevented by hostile tribes from reaching the great river itself, the proximity of which he had in any case failed to grasp.

Returning to Libreville in 1878, Brazza learned of Henry Stanley's successful navigation down the Congo and realized in retrospect what he had missed. Though completely outclassed by Stanley in the eyes of public opinion,

Brazza was invited to enter the service of King Leopold II of Belgium in an effort to secure possession of the Congo Basin for that monarch. Brazza warned the French government instead and secured their approval for his project to outrace Stanley, now working on Leopold's behalf. On Oct. 3, 1880, having successfully negotiated a treaty with the makoko (king) of the Bateke, Brazza set up a French post at the site of modern Brazzaville, while Stanley, who had ignored Leopold's urging to rush on to the Middle Congo, was methodically blasting a road through the Lower Congo rapids.

King Leopold tried to regain through diplomatic maneuvering what Stanley had lost on the ground, but Brazza, now at the peak of his popularity, mounted a skillful propaganda campaign and secured from a vacillating French government the ratification of the "Makoko Treaty" on Nov. 30, 1882. From 1883 to 1885 Brazza was back in Equatorial Africa, consolidating French claims over the area at the head of a sizable force.

The arbitration of differences between King Leopold and the French delegation at the Berlin Conference was shortly followed by the fall of Jules Ferry's "colonialist" Cabinet. The new administration was less favorable to overseas expansion but Brazza nevertheless managed to get himself appointed general commissioner for French Congo in 1886. In this capacity he personally supervised and coordinated the numerous expeditions whereby France secured control of the area between the Congo River and Lake Chad, thus containing German penetration from Cameroons.

Brazza's opposition to the granting of extensive land rights to private firms increasingly brought him into conflict with private interest groups, and in 1898, under a tenuous pretext, Brazza (then on sick leave in Algeria) was relieved of his position without having been given a chance to defend himself. Belated recognition came in 1902 in the form of an official pension, but not until 1905, when the abuses of the concessionaire system had resulted in a scandal, were his views vindicated.

Brazza's last trip to Africa, in 1905, was an inspection tour of conditions in the Congo. In the face of general hostility and deliberate noncooperation by the colonial civil service, Brazza bitterly described what ruthless private exploitation had done to the area that he had opened up to France 25 years earlier. He left the Congo a sick, heartbroken man and died on the way home at Dakar on Sept. 14, 1905, before he could witness the gradual elimination of the abuses he had denounced.

Further Reading

Extensive materials on Brazza can be found in Thomas F. Power, Jr., *Jules Ferry and the Renaissance of French Imperialism* (1944), and Henri Brunschwig, *French Colonialism, 1871-1914: Myths and Realities* (1960; trans. 1966). For general background see Robert William July, *A History of the African People* (1970).

Additional Sources

Nwoye, Rosaline Eredapa, *The public image of Pierre Savorgnan de Brazza and the establishment of French imperialism in the*

Congo, 1875-1885, Aberdeen: Aberdeen University, African Studies Group, 1981. □

James Henry Breasted

The American Egyptologist and archeologist James Henry Breasted (1865-1935) established the study of Egyptology in the United States and became the foremost scholar in this field.

James Henry Breasted was born on Aug. 27, 1865, in Rockford, Ill. He graduated from North Central College in 1888 and attended Chicago Theological Seminary but transferred to Yale to study Hebrew. He received a master's degree from Yale in 1891 and, on the advice of William Rainey Harper, went to Berlin. There Breasted studied under Adolf Erman, who had just established a new school of Egyptology, concentrating systematically on grammar and lexicography. Breasted received his doctorate from Berlin in 1894 with a dissertation on the solar hymns of Ikhnaton. He also married the same year and made the first of his many trips to Egypt on his honeymoon, spending much time exploring, and learning Arabic.

Upon his return to the United States, Breasted joined the faculty of the University of Chicago in 1894 as an assistant in Egyptology. By 1905 he was a full professor in Egyptology and Oriental history. In addition, he became director of the Haskell Oriental Museum in 1901 and chairman of the Department of Oriental Languages in 1915, a post he held until 1925.

In his early scholarly years Breasted embarked on several ambitious projects, one being to translate all extant Egyptian historical texts into English. *The Ancient Records of Egypt: Historical Documents* (5 vols., 1906) became a standard work and established his reputation. Breasted also wrote monographs and textbooks. His *History of Egypt* (1905) was the first scholarly history of the ancient Nile written in the United States and attracted much favorable comment.

From 1905 to 1907 Breasted directed the Nubian expedition of the University of Chicago, which developed his interest in Egyptian religious thought. This culminated in the Morse Lectures at Union Theological Seminary, published as *Development of Religion and Thought in Ancient Egypt* (1912). Here he took an evolutionary posture and traced man's moral ideas from Egypt. Breasted also continued to write texts, alone and in collaboration. The most famous of these was *Ancient Times* (1916), revised as *The Conquest of Civilization* (1926). The emphasis was upon man raising himself through intelligence and religious growth.

In 1919 Breasted originated the Oriental Institute of the Near East and directed the first expedition to Egypt and western Asia in 1919-1920. He was released from teaching duties in 1925 to devote full time to the institute, became Burton distinguished service professor in 1930, and retired

In order to master the native tongue, Brébeuf left Quebec in October 1625 and lived for 5 months among the Montagnais, who belonged to the Algonquin nation. His missionary labors concentrated on the conversion of the Huron in southeastern Ontario.

Brébeuf was the first apostle to contact the Hurons, and evangelization involved the severest physical hardships, augmented by surroundings revolting to Christian norms of morality and European sensibilities. Added to this were the insults and calumnies heaped on him by jealous native sorcerers, who blamed the Jesuits for the periodic plagues, famines, and wars and who associated them with the shortcomings of the French colonists. During his initial stay, lasting 3 years, Father Brébeuf familiarized himself with Huron ways and translated the catechism into Huron, but he made no converts.

The English occupation of Quebec in 1629 necessitated Brébeuf's return to France. There he reverted to his former work as treasurer at the school in Rouen. When France and England signed a peace treaty in 1633, he returned to Quebec in company with its founder and his friend, the explorer Samuel de Champlain.

Brébeuf's second journey to Huronia was more successful. The natives were in awe of his unusual height, strength, and fortitude. Like his fellow Jesuits, they admired his nobility of character, leadership qualities, patience and prudence, and fluency in the local dialect. He found the

in 1933. In 1933 he also published his best-known work, *The Dawn of Conscience,* an elaboration of earlier ideas.

Breasted died in New York City on Dec. 2, 1935, having securely established the study of Egyptology in the United States.

Further Reading

The standard biography of Breasted is by his son: Charles Breasted, *Pioneer to the Past: The Story of James Henry Breasted, Archeologist* (1943). Breasted's place in American historiography is discussed in John Higham, Leonard Krieger, and Felix Gilbert, *History: The Development of Historical Studies in the United States* (1965). □

Jean de Brébeuf

Jean de Brébeuf (1593-1649), a French missionary to Canada, was a Jesuit priest who suffered martyrdom in North America.

Jean de Brébeuf was born on March 25, 1593, in Condé-sur-Vire, Normandy, where his family belonged to the petty landed aristocracy. He entered the Society of Jesus in 1617 and was ordained in 1622. For the next 3 years he was treasurer at the Jesuit secondary school in Rouen. In 1625, at his own request, he went to the newly opened Jesuit mission in New France.

Jean de Brébeuf (standing, arm raised)

Huron more receptive to the Gospel and baptized numerous dying infants and adults, along with a small number of healthy adults. Yet the Huron condemned the missionaries to death for causing the epidemic in 1636-1637, and only the subsidence of the plague saved their lives.

Brébeuf was head of the Mission of St. Joseph, a community of Christian Native Americans at Sillery near Quebec, from 1641 to 1644, when he left for his third and final stay in Huronia. A rapid increase in conversions greatly strengthened his hopes for Christianizing the entire people. But on March 16, 1649, Iroquois braves—implacable enemies of the Huron, the French, and the missionaries—captured Fathers Brébeuf and Gabriel Lalemant at the mission station of St. Louis, dragged them a short distance to St. Ignace Mission, and tortured them for hours before killing them. These two, along with four other priests and two lay assistants, known collectively as the North American Martyrs, were beatified in 1925 and canonized in 1930.

Further Reading

Brébeuf's own narratives are collected in the monumental *Jesuit Relations,* edited by Reuben Gold Thwaites (73 vols., 1893-1901). Letters of Brébeuf and a report of his death, selected from the *Jesuit Relations,* are in Edna Kenton, ed., *The Indians of North America* (2 vols., 1927). Francis Xavier Talbot, *Saint among the Hurons* (1949), is a biography of Brébeuf. Recommended for general background is W. J. Eccles, *The Canadian Frontier, 1534-1760* (1969), which includes an extensive bibliography.

Additional Sources

Donnelly, Joseph Peter, *Jean de Brébeuf, 1593-1649,* Chicago: Loyola University Press, 1975.
Latourelle, René, *Jean de Brébeuf,* Saint-Laurent, Canada: Bellarmin, 1993. □

Bertolt Brecht

The German author Bertolt Brecht (1898-1956) is probably the greatest German playwright of the first half of the 20th century. His works were often considered controversial because of his revolutionary dramatic theory and his political beliefs.

Bertolt Brecht was born on Feb. 10, 1898, in Augsburg. The son of a Catholic businessman, Brecht was raised, however, in his mother's Protestant faith. In 1917 he matriculated at the University of Munich to study philosophy and medicine. In 1918 he served as a medical orderly at a military hospital in Augsburg. The unpleasantness of this experience confirmed his hatred of war and stimulated his sympathy for the unsuccessful Socialist revolution of 1919.

Early Works

In 1919 Brecht returned to his studies but devoted himself increasingly to writing plays. His first full-length

plays were *Baal* (1922) and *Trommeln in der Nacht* (1922; *Drums in the Night*). In September 1922 *Drums in the Night* was presented at the Munich Kammerspiele, where Brecht was subsequently employed as resident playwright.

Brecht's early plays, including *Im Dickicht der Städte* (1923; *Jungle of the Cities*), are works in which he gradually frees himself from the expressionist conventions of the avant-garde theater of his day, especially its idealism. He parodies and ridicules the lofty sentiments and visionary optimism of his predecessors (Georg Kaiser, Fritz von Unruh, and others) while exploiting their technical advances. *Baal* portrays the brutalization of all finer feeling by a drunken vagabond. In *Drums in the Night,* a drama on the returned-soldier theme, the hero rejects the opportunity for a splendid death on the barricades, preferring to make love to his woman. Such cynicism recalls Frank Wedekind, Brecht's most revered model. *Jungle of the Cities* decries the possibility of spiritual freedom and reasserts the primacy of materialistic values. In these two plays Brecht emphasizes the artificiality of the theatrical medium and disregards conventional psychological motivation.

In 1924 Brecht moved to Berlin and for the next 2 years was associated as a playwright with Max Reinhardt's Deutsches Theater. His comedy *Mann ist Mann* (1926; *A Man's a Man*) studies the social conditioning that transforms an Irish packer into a machine gunner and shows a development toward a terser, more intellectual style. By 1926 Brecht had begun a serious study of Marxism. Also during this period the director Erwin Piscator was teaching him much about

the techniques of experimental theater (for example, the use onstage of films, projections, and slides).

Plays with Music

Brecht collaborated with the composer Kurt Weill on *Mahagonny* (or *Kleine Mahagonny*), a play with music written for the Baden-Baden festival of 1927. They then wrote *Die Dreigroschenoper* (1928; *The Threepenny Opera*), which was triumphantly performed in Berlin on Aug. 31, 1928. This was the first work to make Brecht famous.

Brecht based *The Threepenny Opera* on Elisabeth Hauptmann's translation of *The Beggar's Opera* (produced 1728) by the English dramatist John Gay. While adapting and modernizing Gay's balled opera, Brecht retained the main events of the plot but added topical satirical bite through his own lyrics. In this work he develops to its first high point his own special language—that peculiar amalgam of street-colloquial, Marxist-philosophical, and quasi-biblical diction laced with cabaret wit and lyrical pathos and bound together with the unrelenting force of parody. Brecht borrows freely from many sources—among them François Villon and Rudyard Kipling—but his undisguised plagiarism generally supports sharp parody.

Brecht wrote several more plays with music in collaboration with Weill and with Paul Hindemith. Notable are *Aufstieg und Fall der Stadt Mahagonny* (1929; *The Rise and Fall of the City of Mahagonny*) and *Das Badener Lehrstück vom Einverständnis* (1929; *The Didactic Play of Baden: On Consent*). The latter deals with the issue of "consent"—consent to the extinction of the individual for the sake of the progress of the masses. In *Die Massnahme* (1930; *The Measure Taken*), for which Hanns Eisler composed the score, Brecht publicly espouses Communist doctrine and concedes the necessity for the elimination of erring party members. The playwright's love of parody is well illustrated in *Die Ausnahme und die Regel* (1930; *The Exception and the Rule*) and in *Die heilige Johanna der Schlachthöfe* (1932; *St. Joan of the Stockyards*), in which a Salvation Army girl strives to save the souls of Chicago capitalists.

Dramatic Theory

Brecht uses the term "epic theater" to characterize his innovative dramatic theory. His new type of drama is non-Aristotelian—that is, his aim is not to purge the audience's emotions but to awaken the spectators' minds and communicate truth to them. In order to achieve this end, drama must not hypnotize or entrance the audience but must continually remind them that what they are watching is not real, but merely a representation, a vehicle for an idea or a fact.

Brecht uses the word "alienation" (*Verfremdung*) to describe his method of helping the audience to be receptive to his dramatic intentions. His technique of alienation includes elimination of most conventional stage props, use of charts, slides, and messages flashed on screens, direct involvement of the audience through characters who step out of their roles to function as commentators, and many carefully planned incongruities. Finally, Brecht requires that actors work in a new way: they must not identify with the dramatic characters but, on the contrary, must always demonstrate that they are playing a role. Alienation is Brecht's fundamental dramatic device, and his parody is of course closely dependent on this technique.

Major Dramas

From 1933 to 1948 Brecht was an exile, first in Scandinavia, then in the U.S.S.R., and after 1941 in the United States. In 1933 his books were among those publicly burned in Berlin. He continued to write in exile, and in 1936 he completed *Die Rundköpfe und die Spitzköpfe* (*The Roundheads and the Peakheads*) and *Furcht und Elend des Dritten Reiches* (*Fear and Misery of the Third Reich*), which directly attacked Hitler's regime.

In 1939 *Leben des Galilei* (*Galileo*) opened the sequence of Brecht's great plays; there followed *Mutter Courage* (1939; *Mother Courage*), *Der gute Mensch von Sezuan* (1941; *The Good Man of Szechuan*), and *Der kaukasische Kreidekreis* (1943; *The Caucasian Chalk Circle*). Other important works belonging to this period are *Herr Puntila und sein Knecht Matti* (1941; *Puntila and His Man Matti*) and *Der aufhaltsame Aufstieg des Arturo Ui* (1941; *The Resistible Rise of Arturo Ui*).

These plays demonstrate that Brecht's power and depth as a dramatist are to a high degree independent of, and even override, his theoretical principles. They display an astonishing capacity for creating living characters, a moving compassion, technical virtuosity, and parodic wit. *Mother Courage,* a series of scenes from the life of a camp follower during the Thirty Years War, is often misunderstood because the overwhelmingly vital portrait of the central character arouses the audience's sympathies. But Brecht's actual concern was to demonstrate the self-perpetuating folly of Mother Courage's naive collaboration with the system that exploits her and destroys her family.

Other Works

In 1948 Brecht settled in East Berlin, where he remained until his death. He and his wife, the actress Helene Weigel, founded the Berliner Ensemble in September 1949 with ample financial support from the state. This group became the most famous theater company in East Germany and the foremost interpreter of Brecht. He himself devoted much of his time to directing. He wrote no new plays except *Die Tage der Commune* (1949; *The Days of the Commune*) but adapted several—among them Molière's *Don Juan* and Shakespeare's *Coriolanus*. There is some evidence that he modified his austere conception of the function of drama and conceded the importance of the theater as a vehicle for entertainment.

The lyric poetry Brecht wrote in these years shows a concern for personal rather than universal or mass experience. Recent criticism has increasingly recognized Brecht's eminence as a lyric poet. His verse of the 1920s, in particular *Hauspostille* (1927; *Domestic Breviary*), is iconoclastic balladry of a savagely satirical kind. However, his keen interest in Chinese and Japanese poetic forms led through the *Svendborger Gedichte* (1939) to the austere delicacy of the *Buckower Elegien* (1954). Brecht also wrote *The Threepenny Novel* (1934), which is based on *The*

Threepenny Opera, and some skillful short stories, *Kalendergeschichten* (1949; *Tales from the Calendar*). He died of a heart attack in August 1956.

Further Reading

The best book in English on Brecht is Frederic Ewen, *Bertolt Brecht: His Life, His Art and His Times* (1967). A good introduction, which points up the political issues sharply, is Martin Esslin, *Brecht: The Man and His Work* (1960). John Willett, *The Theatre of Bertolt Brecht* (1959; rev. ed. 1967), concentrates on Brecht's technique and the writing and staging of his plays. Other useful works are Ronald D. Gray, *Bertolt Brecht* (1961), and Peter Demetz, *Brecht: A Collection of Critical Essays* (1962). Brecht's literary tradition is illuminated by Max Spalter, *Brecht's Tradition* (1967). His general importance in the modern theater is shown in Eric Bentley, *The Playwright as Thinker: A Study of Drama in Modern Times* (1946) and *What is Theatre? A Query in Chronicle Form* (1956). ☐

William J. Brennan Jr.

William J. Brennan, Jr. (1906-1997) served on the U.S. Supreme Court for 34 years, starting in 1956. During this time he consistently championed libertarian rulings and an expanded interpretation of the Bill of Rights and the Civil War amendments.

Born in New Jersey in 1906, a *magna cum laude* graduate of the University of Pennsylvania, William J. Brennan, Jr. was a scholarship student at Harvard's School of Law. His legal career had taken him to the New Jersey Supreme Court when he was nominated to the U.S. Supreme Court by President Dwight Eisenhower in 1956. After an initial recess appointment, the Democrat, Roman Catholic jurist was Senate-confirmed with the single dissenting vote of Joseph R. McCarthy of Wisconsin.

Professor Felix Frankfurter had always admonished his students not to be unduly swayed by professorial advocacy, that their guiding motto should be "think for yourself." Years thereafter, when he served with one of those students, William Brennan, Frankfurter asked whimsically whether it was really necessary for Brennan to have taken his former teacher's admonition so literally. Indeed, Justice Brennan struck out on his own, with a creativity and diligence that won him a "near great" rating by the Court's observers. But President Eisenhower, who had sent him to the Court, was only slightly less irked by and disenchanted with Brennan's evolving record than with Chief Justice Earl Warren's (whose opinions Brennan joined in most instances). When Eisenhower was asked later if he had made any mistakes while he had been president, he replied: "Yes, two and they are both sitting on the Supreme Court." "Both" referred to Warren and Brennan.

By inclination less of a judicial activist than Warren at the outset, and given to more careful, more communicatively-reasoned, expression, Brennan became a predictable member of the Court's libertarian wing. His abiding dedication to the freedoms of the First Amendment, notably those of speech and press, soon saw him assigned some of the leading libertarian opinions of the Warren Court era. Thus, he authored the tribunal's significant and unanimous judgment in *The New York Times Libel Case of 1964,* which established that a public official, in order to recover damages for a publication criticizing his official conduct, would have to show "actual malice" on the part of its publisher. Extolling the "uninhibited, robust, and wide-open" nature of debate on public issues, Brennan held that "libel can claim no talismanic immunity from onstitutional limitations," that it must be "measured by standards that satisfy the First Amendment."

Justice Brennan, who served on the Court for three decades, continued to champion a generously expansive interpretation of the Bill of Rights and the Civil War amendments. In many ways he became the heir-apparent to Justice William O. Douglas's jurisprudence and his votes, especially after the latter's retirement from the bench in 1975. Together with Justice Thurgood Marshall, Brennan thus evolved into the leading libertarian activist on the (Warren) Burger court after 1969. In that role he continued to be the tribunal's foremost expert on, for example, the vexatious line between freedom of artistic expression and proscribable obscenity (predictably finding himself among the minority of four who dissented from the contentious 1973 decisions that accorded generous leeway to the states in judging what is obscene).

Probably the most devout member of the Court, Brennan's principled and consistent championing of the free exercise of religion and an absolute separation of church and state rendered him the high tribunal's leading anti-establishmentarian. Thus, his 70-page concurring opinion in *Abington School District* v. *Schempp* and *Murray* v. *Curlett* (1963) held unconstitutional state-mandated bible reading and reciting the Lord's Prayer in public schools. Likewise, his impassioned dissenting opinions in such accommodationist holdings as *Roemer* v. *Maryland Public Works Board* (1976) and *Tilton* v. *Richardson* (1971) represented his creed that under the Constitution the state must resolutely stay out of the church and the church must resolutely stay out of the state.

Even more prominently, and equally consistently, Justice Brennan became watchdog and advocate on the egalitarian front, particularly in matters of race and gender. Joined almost always by Justice Thurgood Marshall and usually, although not always, by Justices Byron R. White and Harry A. Blackman, he more often than not succeeded in finding a fifth vote to provide victory for claims of invidious discrimination. This position went to the extent of embracing racial quotas, giving rise to allegations of support of reverse discrimination. Hence, he marshalled Justice Powell's vote and his authorship of that part of the famed *Bakke* opinion (1978) that sanctioned affirmative action by constitutionalizing resort to considerations of race as a "plus" in educational admissions. And in 1979, in what may well be the most clear-cut case of judicial legislating on behalf of remedial/compensatory race-conscious policies, he spoke for a five-member majority in *Steelworkers* v. *Weber* and gained Justice Potter Stewart's support. This decision, in the face of precise and express statutory language and patent congressional intent to the contrary, sanctioned racial quotas in employment, overridingly on the basis of what Brennan frankly termed the "spirit" rather than the "letter" of title VII of the Civil Rights Act of 1964.

Perhaps, however, Justice Brennan will be best remembered for his precedent-shattering opinion for a six to two Court in *Baker* v. *Carr* in 1962. There, over lengthy, bitter dissenting opinions by Justices Frankfurter and Harlan, Brennan was joined by Chief Justice Warren and Justices Black, Douglas, Clark, and Stewart. The majority opinion held that aggrieved individuals had a constitutionally guaranteed right to come to the judicial branch to scrutinize allegedly discriminatory legislative apportionment by the states. The decision, which set into motion a revolution in electoral districting, was a fitting tribute to the judicial resourcefulness and perseverance of its self-effacing yet determined author. It was in keeping with his frequent warning that "the interest of the government is not that it shall win a case, but that Justice shall be done"

In *Brown* v. *Hartlage* (1982), Justice Brennan's ruling found that a state corrupt practices act violated the First Amendment's freedom of speech guarantee when it was applied to a political candidate's campaign promise. One of Brennan's last major decisions was in *Texas* v. *Johnson* (1989), which found a state statute criminalizing the desecration of religious objects was in violation of freedom of speech when it was used against a person who had set the American flag on fire as a political statement.

In 1990, Justice Brennan retired from the Supreme Court, as did his fellow Justice, Thurgood Marshall. Their departure left many court watchers anxious that the Supreme Court was losing two "liberal" justices, and would assume a more "conservative" tone. In particular, many lamented the loss of Justice Brennan's gift for seeing the Constitution as a living document, thus enabling him to foresee the impact of one decision on many other elements of constitutional law. In *ABA Journal* Laurence H. Tribe wrote, "Justice Brennan did not view cases in isolation from one another. Rather, he saw them as building materials with which a constitutional vision could be elaborated. He appreciated deeply the interconnectedness of the constitutional edifice." Also, many cited Justice Brennan's special capacity to rally his fellow justices behind a deicision, even in his later years when the Supreme Court assumed a more conservative tone.

After Brennan died in a nursing home in Arlington, Virginia, on July 24, 1997, Attorney General Janet Reno said he "stood up for people who had no voice. He devoted his long, rich life to helping the American justice system live up to its ideals." His intellect and charisma made him one of the most influential jurists in America's history.

Further Reading

In the wake of Justice Brennan's 1990 retirement, many periodicals profiled his career, and numerous biographies were written and planned. The February, 1991 *ABA Journal* gave a thorough overview of his career. Two books written shortly after Brennan's retirement were, *Justice Brennan: The Great Conciliator* (1995), by Hunter R. Clark, and *Landmark Justice: The Influence of William J. Brennan on America's Communities* (1991) by Charles Haar and Jerold Kayden. A major article is Stephen J. Friedman's "William J. Brennan" in Leon Friedman and Fred L. Israel, editors, *The Justices of the United States Supreme Court, 1789-1978* (1980). See also Stephen J. Friedman, *William J. Brennan, Jr.: An Affair with Freedom* (1967), which includes an article and several appreciations published in the *Harvard Law Review* (1966). Justice Brennan's opinions offer a rich fare in themselves. Generally, see Henry J. Abraham, *Justices and Presidents: A Political History of Appointments to the Supreme Court,* 2d ed. (1985). □

Clemens Brentano

Although the German poet and author Clemens Brentano (1778-1842) was one of the most versatile writers of the later romantic period, he is best remembered for his lyric poetry.

Clemens Brentano was born on Sept. 8, 1778, in Ehrenbreitstein, the son of an Italian businessman. He developed an early interest in literature and at the universities of Halle and Jena became acquainted with contemporary writers, especially Friedrich von Schlegel and Ludwig Tieck. In 1803 he married the poet Sophie Mereau, to whom he had dedicated his first important novel, *Godwi* (1801).

Godwi is an "educational novel" about the passionate adventures of a wealthy young man. It is experimental in form, and the novelist himself enters the plot as one of the characters. The sensationalism of this first work is continued in the suspense drama *Ponce de Leon* (1801) and in the novel *Chronika eines fahrenden Schülers* (Chronicle of a Wandering Scholar), which was begun in 1803 as a medieval tale of romance, mysticism, and black magic. The exotic religiosity of this novel is also to be found in the series of verse narratives *Romanzen vom Rosenkranz* (Romances of the Rosary), which Brentano began about this time.

In 1804 he settled in Heidelberg, where, with fellow romantics Achim von Arnim and Johann Josef von Görres, he edited the literary journal *Zeitung für Einsiedler* (Newspaper for Hermits). With Arnim he also compiled the most famous collection of German folk songs, *Des Knaben Wunderhorn* (*The Boy's Magic Horn*), in three volumes between 1805 and 1808.

After the death of his wife in 1806, Brentano traveled about Germany for a few years. He met the Grimm brothers in Kassel in 1807 and in 1809 joined a literary group in Berlin. After a brief sojourn in Bohemia and Vienna (where he composed a patriotic drama inspired by the Germans' fight against Napoleon), he returned to Berlin and wrote his most famous story, *Die Geschichte vom braven Kasperl und dem schönen Annerl* (*1817; The Story of Brave Caspar and Beautiful Annie*). In 1817 he also underwent a conversion to devout Catholicism.

Brentano devoted the next several years to recording the utterances of the stigmatized nun Katharina Emmerich. After her death in 1824 he lived in Frankfurt and Coblenz and in 1833 settled in Munich, where he associated with a group of Catholic romantic writers, including Görres. Among Brentano's later works was a collection of fairy tales (1838), which shows his imaginative powers to be as lively as ever. Brentano died in Aschaffenburg on July 28, 1842.

Further Reading

The best general discussion in English of Brentano's life and works is in Ralph Tymms, *German Romantic Literature* (1955). Another book with a good general treatment of the poet is L. A. Willoughby, *The Romantic Movement in Germany* (1930). There is a helpful discussion of Brentano's lyric poetry in August Closs, *The Genius of the German Lyric: An Historical Survey of Its Formal and Metaphysical Values* (1962). □

Franz Clemens Brentano

The German philosopher and psychologist Franz Clemens Brentano (1838-1917) is best known for his work in establishing psychology as an independent science.

F ranz Brentano was born on Jan. 16, 1838, at Marienberg in the Rhineland into a family of the nobility, whose lineage is traceable to the 13th century and includes many famous members, among them the authors Clemens Brentano and Bettina von Arnim. Franz studied at the gymnasium at Aschaffenburg and then at the universities of Munich, Würzburg, Berlin, and Münster (1856-1860). Raised in an extremely pious and orthodox Catholic household, Brentano early decided to enter the priesthood and was ordained in 1864.

From the first his interests were divided almost equally between theology, philosophy, and mathematics. After a period of increasing doubts about fundamental dogmas of the church, the declaration of papal infallibility in 1870 precipitated his final break with the church 3 years later. Thereafter he turned his attention wholeheartedly to philosophy, which he was determined to pursue in a scientific manner, explicitly rejecting the then dominant trend of German idealism.

After the publication of his best-known work, *Psychology from an Empirical Standpoint* (1874), Brentano accepted a chair at the University of Vienna. In 6 years of teaching he gathered there a brilliant set of students through whom his own thought was further developed and more widely propagated. Brentano's teaching activity was disturbed by pressures from reactionary authorities who invoked a law forbidding marriage to clerics. In order to marry, Brentano had to give up his professorship and move to Leipzig. Thereafter he was allowed to return to his circle of colleagues and students, but only as a *privatdozent,* or lecturer. For 14 years he continued in this position; numerous efforts to restore him to his professorship were derailed by political intrigues. Finally, in 1890, after the death of his wife, Brentano left Vienna and settled in Florence, where he devoted himself to writing and to correspondence with his wide circle of students.

In addition to his work on psychology, Brentano published important works on Aristotle, on ethics, and on esthetics. Brentano's work offers original insights in all the main branches of philosophy from logic to natural theology. He defended the objectivity of value judgments in ethics and esthetics and labored to construct a philosophical theism and a doctrine of immortality.

The onset of World War I drove him from his Italian haven to Zurich, where, now totally blind, he continued to dictate new manuscripts. He died in Zurich on March 17, 1917, and was survived by his second wife and a son, Johannes.

Further Reading

There are few studies in English on Brentano. Two are important: Gustav Bergmann, *Realism: A Critique of Brentano and Meinong* (1967), and Jan Srzednicki, *Franz Brentano's Analysis of Truth* (1965), which contains a reliable bibliography of Brentano's works, some of which are available in English.

Additional Sources

Chisholm, Roderick M., *Brentano and intrinsic value,* Cambridge Cambridgeshire; New York: Cambridge University Press, 1986.
Smith, Barry, Ph. D., *Austrian philosophy: the legacy of Franz Brentano,* Chicago: Open Court, 1994. □

Catherine Breshkovsky

Catherine Breshovsky (1844–1944) was the only Russian revolutionist whose adulthood spanned the entire revolutionary period—from the early 1860s to 1917—and whose lifework was devoted entirely to the welfare of the peasants.

Born to Olga Ivanovna and Constantine Mikhailovich Verigo, Catherine Breshkovsky would often remark later in life, "I had wonderful parents; if there is anything good in me, I owe it all to them." From her father, she inherited frankness, good-heartedness, and a short temper; from her mother—a woman of gentility—she received an education from Bible stories. Her parents never whipped the children, never allowed a word of profanity. But in her childhood, Breshkovsky preferred solitude. In her memoirs, she would later explain that her tendency toward withdrawal sprang from feelings of being unwanted as a child; she recalled her mother saying once: "When you were born, I detested you so much. . . . My other children behave like typical children, Katia is like a whirlwind." Known as a violent and furious child, Breshkovsky's habitual withdrawal led to sudden and frequent disappearances that

drove her governess insane: "Breshkovsky is a spider," she would scream.

As a child, Breshkovsky scrutinized events, people, even her own behavior, and could not accept personal failure. Often confused between the accepted evils of the culture around her and what she thought to be right and humane, she snuck peasant friends into her wealthy home—a tendency for which she was scolded. She could not understand why it was unacceptable to bring a peasant friend into her home, while it was acceptable to see a child hungry, dirty, and in rags. Whipped and exiled for trivial infractions, serfs were treated like chattel; their wives and daughters were used as concubines, their children often taken away and sold.

The lot of the serfs horrified Breshkovsky. She would run off to the serfs' huts, eat with them, confide in them, and listen to stories of their plight. Although her father treated his serfs exceptionally well, she was still dismayed by the contrast between the living conditions of the hut and of her own home. Thus, the young aristocrat developed a strong desire to rectify social wrongs. Bearing witness to the life of the serfs transformed her into a merciless fighter for peasants' rights. Throughout her entire life, when she herself was in dire need, Breshkovsky was giving away food, money, and clothing to the poor and destitute.

Interested in the realities of life, she was a fervent reader, with little interest in fiction. At the age of nine, she read the entire *History of Russia* by N. A. Karamzin. Many years later, she admitted with trepidation to her son Nicholas—a successful novelist—that she would most likely skip many pages of his books for lack of interest in fictional works. They were two opposites: she was a revolutionist; he was a liberal without much sympathy for the outlaws.

Seventeen when Tsar Alexander II issued the Emancipation Act in 1861, Breshkovsky was soon aware that it did little to improve the peasants' anguish and misery. Since her father was a government-appointed arbiter for the district, she was exposed to heartrending scenes, the sobbing of wives, the whipping and crippling of men. In spite of the suffering, peasants clung to the belief that the Tsar would soon issue the real Manifesto. Although rumors were spread that the corrupt officials substituted the false document for the real one, the peasants did not believe that the Tsar, their Little Father, would betray them.

Two years later, at 19, Breshkovsky, her mother, and sister left for St. Petersburg. On the train, a young prince—a favorite of the Tsar—returning from an official visit to Siberia accidentally entered their compartment. He spoke with fiery zeal about Russia's future now that Tsar Alexander had issued a series of reforms. The prince was Peter Kropotkin, who later became a revolutionary anarchist. Breshkovsky interpreted the incident as providential.

While in St. Petersburg, she joined the circles of liberal-minded young nobility, attending classes of higher education (though it was illegal for females to pursue higher education). But when her mother took ill, she returned home and opened a boarding school for girls, the earnings from which helped her teach peasant children free of charge. Always independent in spirit, at the age of 25, she arranged a marriage with a broad-minded young nobleman, Nikolai Breshko-Breshkovsky. Marriages of "convenience" were not then uncommon among the radical Russian youth. The law required direct supervision of females by the nearest male kin; in order to break away from their often abusive fathers, many female revolutionists married close friends. Ordinarily, the couples would part the day after the wedding, sometimes never to see each other again.

Breshkovsky and her husband stayed in their district, however, where they opened a school and a cooperative bank for the peasants. But a desire to engage in more meaningful activities took Breshkovsky to Kiev. There, she was invited to join a group of radicals on their way to the United States to establish a socialist colony. "Never," she replied, "how can we leave Russia now, when there is much of importance to be done here?" Instead, she began searching for companions, "students not only of books but of life."

Four years after her marriage, Breshkovsky faced one of her greatest challenges: she decided to devote herself, and everything she owned, to the cause of the revolution. Her husband and family begged the pregnant Breshkovsky to stay and pursue reforms in their own district, urging her to consider the needs of the child. Convinced that "the call of the greatest and gravest duty" bade her leave everything and everyone behind, with great pain she left her parents and husband. Before the winter of 1873-74 was over, she gave birth to a boy, whom she promptly entrusted to her sister-in-law. The separation from her son would last 23 years. "The conflict between my love for the child and my love for the revolution and for the freedom of Russia robbed me of many a night's sleep," she wrote. "I knew that I could not be a mother and still be a revolutionist."

In the spring of 1874, thousands of young educated idealists left their homes and classrooms to go to the countryside and live with the peasants. In July, Breshkovsky and her two companions, Masha (Mariia) Kalenkina and Iakov Stefanovich, left for the Ukrainian villages. This "going to the people" movement was born of the belief that once the peasants heard the socialist "gospel," they would rise and overthrow the yoke of oppression.

Breshkovsky's clear, strong voice, her choice of concepts and words that peasants could relate to, and her sincerity impressed the peasants everywhere. Dumbfounded in the presence of someone who could read, they held a printed page with reverence, and gathered in great crowds to listen to her. However, when the revolutionists singled out the Tsar as the primary cause for their oppression, the peasants refused to believe them, and many immediately dispersed. Breshkovsky often compared the tsarist regime with evil forces. Since, to the peasants, the mention of the Tsar and the devil in the same breath was scandalous, some visited local authorities to report such "subversion."

Disguised as peasants, and with false internal passports, Breshkovsky and her comrades were continually on the run from the police. In one of the villages, she and Masha Kalenkina took up lodging with a peasant family. There, one of the family's girls—having snooped through

their belongings—confided to neighbor friends that the strangers had literature and maps. The news eventually reached the local chief of police who immediately confronted Breshkovsky and asked for her papers. She told him that she was a peasant woman from a northern Russian province. But in the course of interrogation, he tried to take her by the chin as nobility and officials then did to the serfs; instinctively, she backed off, inadvertently revealing that she was of aristocratic descent. The chief was elated, for the arrest of an important revolutionist meant a respectable reward from his superiors.

In October 1877, Breshkovsky was taken to St. Petersburg and brought before the court. The famous Trial of the 193 lasted several months. Female prisoners typically received light sentences, but Breshkovsky's arrogant refusal to submit to the authority of the tsarist court was her undoing. The first woman in Russia to be condemned to hard labor, she was sent to work in the mines at Kara, far east of Lake Baikal, in Siberia. After a stay of ten months, she was marched to Barguzin, a small prison town on the east shore of Lake Baikal.

Breshkovsky's later writings indicate that at Barguzin, she was condemned to the "torture" of enforced idleness. Forbidden to teach or meet with other prisoners, she nevertheless befriended three students in exile. With the help of a native guide, the four of them escaped the town, walking some 600 miles eastward across the mountains before the police caught up with them. Because of the strict order from St. Petersburg to capture Catherine Breshkovsky, the police were tenacious, and the attempted escape cost her four more years of hard labor at Kara. After Kara, she was marched again, this time 1,000 miles south to Selenginsk.

In Selenginsk, she met George Kennan who was collecting material for his book *Siberia and the Exile System*. After eight years in Selenginsk, Breshkovsky was permitted to travel within Siberia, allowing her to befriend some important individuals. Then, in 1896, her term of Siberian exile at last expired, leaving her free to return to Western Russia, though not to St. Petersburg.

Upon her return, Breshkovsky faced a new world. Her parents and husband had passed away. Brought up as an aristocrat, her 23-year-old son Nicholas snubbed his revolutionist mother. The peasants had changed, too, having matured politically. Believing them nearly ready for revolution, Breshkovsky began another missionary journey into the Russian countryside. For eight years the railway compartments were her home. As the name Catherine Breshkovsky disappeared from Western Russia, people talked instead of *Babushka* ("grandma").

During these years, she coached the peasants and organized underground circles and terrorist attacks on government officials, though this work placed her on the list of the most wanted political criminals. She also helped establish the Socialist Revolutionary Party. In May of 1903, she left Russia via Odessa and Vienna to Geneva. The following year, she arrived in the United States to seek help for her cause.

Speaking in New York, Boston, Chicago, and other major cities, she was received everywhere with enthusiasm.

She stressed the strength of the revolutionary movement in Russia and appealed for both moral and material help. She reassured audiences that the Russian peasant had demonstrated that he was able to manage his own future and argued that, in only four decades since 1861, he had cast off the blind faith in the tsar and learned of his own worth. The most significant change, she stressed, was the peasants' ability to read and understand political issues. After her speech in Philadelphia, approximately 2,000 exhilarated Russian immigrants sang and shouted while carrying her around on their shoulders.

Shortly after her return to Russia, the government—with help from agent Evno F. Azeff—caught up with Breshkovsky and arrested her. Azeff, a well-known and much-trusted revolutionist, had infiltrated the Socialist Revolutionary Party to the very top. The list of charges against Breshkovsky was so long that it took the court clerk an hour to read it. Were it not for friends from abroad who pressured the Russian government, and the government's reluctance to create a martyr, Breshkovsky most likely would have received the death sentence. An American friend came from the United States and begged government officials to release her. They would not.

The government considered the 66-year-old woman a dangerous prisoner. A journalist reported that on her way out of court, she was escorted by a police officer in front of her carrying a naked sword and ten armed officers behind. By April 1910, she was making her second journey to Siberia. Sent to a small island in the Lena River, some 200 miles north of Lake Baikal, she was allowed limited correspondence with a few close friends, many of them outside Russia. For some time, the public in Western Russia heard little of her, until—in the winter of 1913-14—the newspapers reported that the 70-year-old prisoner had escaped from her place of exile. This time, the government sent 50 armed men to bring her back to face 16 months of incarceration. Following the first Russian Revolution in February 1917, she was freed.

The newly formed Provisional Government sent Catherine Breshkovsky a special invitation to return to Petrograd (formerly St. Petersburg) from her place of exile. Upon arrival in Moscow, she was placed in the deposed Tsar's state coach, receiving a military escort and royal treatment. At the railroad station in Petrograd, the crowd nearly stormed the station, trying to see and touch her. She later wrote, "I do not think that anywhere in the world there ever was a bride who received so many flowers." Alexander Kerensky, then Secretary of Justice, addressed the crowd: "Comrades, the Grandmother of the Russian Revolution has returned at last to a free country." Breshkovsky truly deserved the title; no other Russian revolutionist, male or female, had lived through the entire revolutionary period from the early 1860s to 1917. Her lifelong service to the cause of Russian peasantry extended from the cruel reign of Nicholas I to the ruthless rule of Joseph Stalin. Little did Kerensky know, however, that the Bolshevik coup d'état in October of 1917 would eventually exile both him and Breshkovsky from their "free" country.

Following the October 1917 Revolution, Breshkovsky remained in Russia, actively involved in the political struggle against the Bolsheviks, but in December of 1918—as the Civil War was consuming Russia—she was forced to leave. For the third time, she traveled east, across Siberia, this time not into Siberian exile but exile abroad. After she reached Japan in 1919, she left for the United States. From there, she moved to Czechoslovakia in 1924. In Prague, under extreme conditions, she continued to fight the oppressive Bolshevik regime. Her struggle for the Russian peasant did not stop with her exile; she continued working among the Carpatian Russians who lived in the territories then part of post-war Czechoslovakia. Breshkovsky's real strength of persuasion was not so much in her ability to charm and speak, as in her living example. After living in France for a short time, she returned to Czechoslovakia where she died at the age of 90.

Further Reading

Blackwell, Alice Stone, ed. *Little Grandmother of the Russian Revolution.* Little, Brown, 1919.

Breshkovskaia, Ekaterina. "1917-yi god," in *Novyi Zhurnal (The New Review).* Vol. 38, 1954: pp. 191-206.

Kerensky, Alexander. "Catherine Breshkovsky (1844-1934)," in *The Slavonic and East European Review.* Vol. 13. No. 38. January 1935: pp. 428-431.

Arkhangelsky, V. G. *Katerina Breshkovskaya.* Prague, 1938.

Hutchinson, Lincoln, ed. *Hidden Springs of the Russian Revolution: Personal Memoirs of Katerina Breshkovskaia.* Stanford University Press, 1931.

Maxwell, Margaret. *Narodniki Women: Russian Women Who Sacrificed Themselves for the Dream of Freedom.* Pergamon, 1990. □

André Breton

The French writer André Breton (1896-1966) was the leader of the surrealist movement, which was the most important force in French poetry in the 1920s and 1930s.

André Breton was born in Tinchebray and was studying to be a doctor when he was drafted in 1915. The period of World War I was extremely important for Breton in orienting his career. Already interested in poetry, he met the writers Louis Aragon and Philip Soupault while in the army. Also influenced by meetings with the poets Guillaume Apollinaire and Paul Valéry and the nihilist Jacques Vaché, Breton became interested in the importance of reform and revolt in literature and in society. While in the army Breton was assigned to work in the psychiatric wards. The patients he observed and the study he made of neurology and psychology were, like his personal encounters, of great importance in forming his literary and social theories.

In 1918, together with Aragon and Soupault, Breton brought out the first issue of the review *Littérature*. And in 1919 Breton's first book of poems, *Mont-de-piété* (Pawn Shop), appeared. Breton grew progressively more interested in dreams and psychic automatism. By 1924 he had organized a group dedicated to surrealism and had issued his *Manifeste du surréalisme*. In 1930 and 1934 he wrote two additional manifestos, which explained the principles of surrealism. From the beginning, surrealism was conceived of as a movement transcending the purely literary or esthetic concerns, and it turned increasingly in the direction of social participation. In 1926 Breton joined the Communist party but withdrew in 1935 because of the incompatibility between the total personal freedom that surrealism advocated and the individual submission that Marxism required.

Meanwhile Breton published some of his most important works, notably *Nadja,* an account of his relationship with a woman and their explorations of the "daily magic" of Paris, and *L'Immaculée Conception* (The Immaculate Conception), in which Breton and the poet Paul Éluard simulate various forms of mental derangement. During the rest of the 1930s Breton's chief publication was *L'Amour fou* (Mad Love), a work illustrating the importance of love, one of the basic articles of surrealist faith. By 1939 it had become apparent that the heyday of surrealism was over. Breton had been its life and soul, but the history of the movement had been marked by noisy repudiations and denunciations. After breaking with his former companions and the Communist party, Breton visited Mexico. He made New York City his headquarters during World War II. When he returned to Paris, existentialism had replaced surrealism, but Breton tried to keep surrealism alive. He organized exhibitions, promoted reviews, and published articles and texts until his death in 1966. Breton's theoretical work continues to have a

great impact, and his creative work, although yet not fully appreciated, demonstrates rare poetic gifts.

Further Reading

A recent and thorough biography of Breton is Anna Balakian, *André Breton: Magus of Surrealism* (1971). J. H. Matthews, *André Breton* (1967), in the series "Columbia Essays on Modern Writers," is an introduction by an authority on surrealism. Although older and not as comprehensive, other excellent studies in English are Georges E. Lemaître, *From Cubism to Surrealism in French Literature* (1941; rev. ed. 1947), and Anna Balakian, *The Literary Origins of Surrealism* (1947; rev. ed. 1965) and *Surrealism: The Road to the Absolute* (1959). Other works are Mary Ann Caws, *Surrealism and the Literary Imagination: A Study of Breton and Bachelard* (1966), and Herbert S. Gershman, *The Surrealist Revolution in France* (1969). □

Marcel Breuer

The Hungarian-born American architect Marcel Breuer (1902-1981) was among the most influential architects and teachers of the 20th century. From his early furniture design to his later massive concrete building forms, Breuer remained a bold innovator.

Marcel Breuer, born in Pécs, Hungary, on May 21, 1902, moved to Vienna when he was 18 years old. He enrolled at the Art Academy with the intention of becoming a painter, but his stay lasted less than six months, during which time he became thoroughly disillusioned with the eclectic approach, which stressed combination of various historical styles. Breuer decided instead to learn a craft, and he enrolled in the recently established school of design, building, and craftsmanship called the Bauhaus, in Weimar.

Within four years, inspired and influenced by the school's director, Walter Gropius, Breuer had become head of the furniture department. His deep interest in inexpensive, standardized, modular-unit furniture led to the design, in 1925, of the first chromium-plated, bent, steel-tube furniture. That same year the Bauhaus moved to Dessau, where Breuer was commissioned to design all the furniture for the newly built Gropius buildings. A product of Breuer's experimental designs of this period was the S-shaped cantilevered chair of 1928, which became one of the most widely used commercial chairs in the world.

Breuer left the Bauhaus in 1928 to set up his own practice as an architect and interior designer in Berlin. There he built a number of radically designed houses while working on several theoretical concepts. Among these latter was a plan for a hospital which proposed a multi-storied structure of reinforced concrete in a series of cantilevered steps.

When forced to flee Germany in 1933, Breuer went to London and entered a partnership with F. R. S. Yorke. But in 1937, at the invitation of Gropius, Breuer went to the United

States. Gropius was by this time chairman of the architecture department at Harvard University, and he asked Breuer to join him on the faculty. The two former Bauhaus colleagues also formed an architectural partnership in Cambridge, MA. Thus did Breuer influence a generation of young designers, both as a teacher, training such men as Philip Johnson, Paul Rudolph, and John Johansen, and as a successful practicing architect.

In collaboration with Gropius, Breuer designed a small vacation house for Henry C. Chamberain (1940) in Wayland, MA. Here the austere planar shapes of the Bauhaus style were modified by the use of a wood-frame exterior, a variation in keeping with native New England building traditions. Another interesting feature of Breuer's houses of the 1940s was the "butterfly roof" silhouette, visible in the Geller House (1945), Lawrence, NY. Breuer also continued to introduce local-regional touches into his designs, and he worked extensively with wooden siding and native stone.

After World War II Breuer moved to New York City and reestablished himself in private practice. During this period he designed several domestic buildings, including his own home in New Canaan, CT (1947), which is characterized by a wooden frame exterior hovering over a recessed basement. In 1953 Breuer, along with Pier Luigi Nervi and Bernard Zehrfuss, was chosen to design the new headquarters for UNESCO in Paris. The resulting Y-shaped, eight-storied Secretariat building is constructed of reinforced concrete; its curved facade is one way in which the building is successfully adapted to a difficult site.

Breuer received commissions for a number of American university buildings, including a dormitory at Vassar College (1951), Poughkeepsie, NY, and an auditorium for Sarah Lawrence College (1954), Bronxville, NY. In both buildings he combined the precision of the International Style with informal use of native materials. He also designed a church for St. John's Benedictine Abbey (1953-1961), Collegeville, MN, whose most striking feature is a monumental, detached concrete belfry set up on piers.

During the 1960s Breuer's buildings became more expressive, principally through the more daring use of concrete. In his Research Center for IBM-France (1960-1962) at the Gaude Var, Breuer employed a double-Y-shaped plan using massive concrete forms to impart a sculptural quality. His dramatically cantilevered Lecture Hall (1961) on New York University's Bronx campus makes similar use of roughly textured concrete, as does his design for the Whitney Museum of American Art (1966) in New York City. Breuer also designed the headquarters of the Department of Health, Education, and Welfare, in Washington, D.C.

Breuer retired from active practice in 1976 and died five years later, in late 1981.

Further Reading

Marcel Breuer: New Buildings and Projects (1970) by Tician Papachristou discusses Breuer's late work and has selections from his writings and opinions. An early work on Breuer is Peter Blake, *Marcel Breuer, Architect and Designer* (1949). A more useful work is a collection of Breuer's designs and projects, *Marcel Breuer: Buildings and Projects, 1921-1961,* edited by Cranston Jones (1962). An impressive collection of his work is David Masello*Architecture Without Rules: The Houses of Marcel Breuer and Herbert Beckhard,* W.W. Norton & Co., 1993. Breuer is showcased in Ezra Stoller, "The Architectural Landscape," *ARTnews,* November 1987, 160-166. ☐

Henri Edouard Prosper Breuil

The French archeologist Henri Édouard Prosper Breuil (1877-1961) was a pioneer in the field of prehistoric archeology. He is especially known for his analysis of prehistoric cave paintings.

Henri Breuil was born on Feb. 28, 1877, at Mortain, Manche Department. After completing his theological studies, he was ordained a priest in 1900. He became professor of science at the seminary of Issy-les-Moulineaux.

Breuil's interest in Paleolithic art began with his study of Bronze Age sites near his hometown and in the region of Paris. He was an excellent draftsman and spent much time copying the remains of Paleolithic art in caverns. He reproduced them in color and related the style and color of the paintings to established periods of Paleolithic cultures for which generally accurate dating was possible. By this careful synchronology he gradually developed an analytic power which enabled him to classify authoritatively the Paleolithic cave paintings of France and Spain.

The earliest and perhaps most famous classification and reproduction by Breuil concerned the Altamira cave paintings. They had been discovered in 1868 but had been decried either as forgeries or as very late Roman crudities. Breuil showed that they were genuine Paleolithic art on the basis of his previous studies of Paleolithic paintings at Font-de-Gaume and Les Combarelles. His copies of the Altamira paintings were published by the Institut de Paléontologie Humaine in 1908. In his analysis of the Altamira paintings, he assigned the hands, silhouettes, and tectiforms to the Aurignacian period. He estimated that the monochromes in semirelief belonged to the lower Magdalenian; the polychromes seemed to him to come from the upper Magdalenian period.

Breuil was lecturer in prehistory and ethnography at the University of Fribourg (1905-1910), professor of prehistoric ethnography at the Institut de Paléontologie Humaine (1910-1929), and professor of prehistoric art at the collège de France (1929-1947). He was made a member of the Institut de France in 1938. After World War II he spent close to six years traveling in Rhodesia, South Africa, and South-West Africa, examining thousands of rock shelters and copying the art.

Authorities acknowledged Breuil's archaeological modification of various periods of the early Paleolithic era as substantial and accurate. He not only developed a copying technique and a synchronology for dating the cave paintings but also contributed in large part to the technical vocabulary of the branch of paleontology dealing with primitive art. He refrained from any interpretive treatment of the painting, never drawing unwarranted conclusions concerning the religious ideas or the social mentality of the primitive painters. He died on Aug. 14, 1961, at L'Isle-Adam, Seine-et-Oise Department.

Further Reading

The only biography of Breuil in English is Alan Houghton Broderick, *Father of Prehistory* (1963). See also André Leroi-Gourhan, *Treasures of Prehistoric Art* (1967). □

Kingman Brewster Jr.

Kingman Brewster, Jr. (1919-1988) served as president of Yale University from 1963 to 1977, greatly broadening the base of that university's student body and strengthening Yale's ties to the community. He then served as ambassador to Great Britain for four years.

Kingman Brewster, Jr., was born June 17, 1919, in Longmeadow, Massachusetts, to Kingman Brewster and Florence Besse Brewster, descendants of one of the state's first families. Following graduation from Belmont High School, Brewster entered Yale in 1937 and graduated with an A.B. in 1941. As a student he was an isolationist and a supporter of "America First" and once invited Charles Lindburgh to speak on campus. In 1942 he married Mary Louise Phillips. The couple had three boys and two girls. During World War II he served as a Navy fighter pilot and was discharge a lieutenant in 1946. He then entered Harvard Law School, receiving his law degree in 1948. During the next two years he served as legal counsel for the Marshall Plan in Europe and as a research associate in economics at the Massachusetts Institute of Technology. In 1950 he became an assistant professor of law at Harvard, specializing in antitrust and international law, and a full professor in 1953. He remained at the school the ten years until he was appointed provost at Yale University in 1960.

In 1963 the governing board of Yale elected Brewster president. A leadership controversy developed even prior to his presidency when, as acting president, he denied Governor George C. Wallace a campus speaking engagement shortly after the bombing of an African American church in Birmingham, Alabama. Opponents decried the "denial of freedom of speech," while Brewster justified his decision as heading off possible inflamation of the African American community. The 1960s were difficult times for university administrators and especially for someone like Brewster

who openly sympathized with the anti-Vietnam War movement and with the African American civil rights activists.

Brewster's tenure as president was marked by widespread popularity among students, faculty, and alumni. His reputation as a "good listener" and his approachability assisted him in weathering controversies. This was particularly evident in the student strike in protest of the New Haven trial of Black Panther Bobby Seale. He not only rallied faculty forgiveness for the educational interruption and the support of the Yale Corporation, but publicly stated that he was "skeptical of the ability of black revolutionaries to achieve a fair trial anywhere in the United States." Vice President Spiro Agnew accused the Yale president of lacking maturity and responsibility and called for alumni to demand that Brewster go.

Brewster's primary accomplishments as president of Yale University were the broadening of the base of the student body, admitting women (1969), dropping Reserve Officers Training Corps (R.O.T.C.), and fostering a new partnership between the traditionally staid administration and the student body. During this time the percentage of students who were children of alumni dropped from 30 to 15. The number of public high school graduates entering Yale grew to outnumber the private high school graduates who entered by a ratio of two to one. His critics accused him of not sharing decision-making, yet he met problems head-on, making him extremely vulnerable to personal attack and thus shielding the university. During the 1960s, Brewster also served as an advisor on several Presidential Committees. From 1965 to 1967 he served on the President's Commission on Law Enforcement and Administration of Justice. From 1965 to 1968 he served on the President's Commission on Selective Service.

In 1977 Brewster left his position at Yale when Secretary of State Cyrus Vance, a member of the Yale Corporation, recommended Brewster to President Carter for the post of ambassador to Great Britain. Despite his lack of diplomatic experience, the British press was pleased with the appointment, calling Brewster potentially the best ambassador since David Bruce. They described him as "New England Patrician" and expressed delight at his gold ring with his family motto in Norman French.

Ambassador Brewster wasted no time in beginning his new responsibilities. He was called to step in and resolve difficulties between United Nations Ambassador Andrew Young and the British Foreign Office. This was followed by smoothing out American/British difficulties over policy toward Rhodesia (Zimbabwe), which helped lead to the end of minority white rule in that country. He reveled in the "good life" of London opportunity and took advantage of the range of social occasions from dinner with Queen Elizabeth to quaffing a pint of ale in a working class pub, saying, "Becoming aware of the richness and variety here is a lot of fun."

After four years Kingman Brewster resigned the ambassadorship and returned to New Haven to live in his home just a block from the Yale campus. He took a part-time position with a New York law firm and devoted the rest of his time to writing a book on what he called the "Volunteer

Society", which was never published. In 1986 he became Master of University College at Oxford University, and remained at Oxford until his death in 1988. On November 8, 1988, Brewster died of a cerebral hemorrhage.

Numerous institutions conferred honorary degrees upon Brewster, and he received several awards, including the Award of Excellence in Human Relations from the New York Council of Churches in 1970. He was made an officer in the Legion of Honor in 1977. In 1997 Brewster was honored with an exhibit at Yale's Sterling Memorial Library, *Innovation and Diversification: Yale during the Kingman Brewster Jr. Presidency, 1963 to 1977.*

Further Reading

There are no biographies or books with additional biographical information on Kingman Brewster. He was the subject of several articles in *TIME, Newsweek, The New Republic,* and similar periodicals at the time he became president of Yale and upon appointment as ambassador to Great Britain. Additional essays by and about him appeared in popular periodicals. The following books by Brewster should provide additional insight: *Antitrust and American Business Abroad* (with James Atwood) (1981); *Law of International Transactions and Relations* (1960); and *The Tanner Lectures on Human Values,* Vol. IV (1983). □

William Brewster

The English-born Pilgrim leader William Brewster (ca. 1566-1644) was the ruling elder of the Separatist group at Scrooby, England, before he and the congregation migrated to Holland and, finally, to New Plymouth in America.

William Brewster was 10 years old when his father was appointed postmaster and bailiff at Scrooby Manor, an official resting place on the main road from London to Edinburgh. In 1580 Brewster entered Cambridge University but left without a degree. He served briefly in the diplomatic service, returned to Scrooby to assist his father, and became postmaster upon his father's death in 1590. Brewster probably became a Puritan at Cambridge; but how he turned to Separatism, an extreme form of Puritanism, is unexplained. Nonetheless, when a Separatist congregation was formed at Scrooby, Brewster was its most important member, and services were held in the manor house.

The harassment of religious dissenters by James I convinced the Scrooby congregation to search for religious freedom in Holland, and certainly Brewster influenced that decision. Imprisoned while trying to emigrate, he was one of the last to reach Holland. The congregation eventually settled in Leiden, where Brewster taught English to students at the university. In 1617 he entered the printing business, specializing in Puritan tracts whose publication was prohibited in England. More importantly, Brewster was the congregation's ruling elder, second only to the minister, John

Further Reading

There is no recent biography of Brewster. One of the best sources for information, especially on his contribution to Plymouth, is William Bradford, *Of Plymouth Plantation, 1620-1647,* edited by Samuel Eliot Morison (1952). Specific information as well as general background is in George F. Willison, *Saints and Strangers, Being the Lives of the Pilgrim Fathers* (1945); Bradford Smith, *Bradford of Plymouth* (1951); and George D. Langdon, Jr., *Pilgrim Colony: A History of New Plymouth, 1620-1691* (1966).

Additional Sources

Harris, J. Rendel (James Rendel), *The Pilgrim press: a bibliographical & historical memorial of the books printed at Leyden by the Pilgrim fathers,* Nieuwkoop: De Graaf, 1987.

Sherwood, Mary B., *Pilgrim: a biography of William Brewster,* Falls Church, Va.: Great Oak Press of Virginia, 1982. □

Stephen Breyer

The general consensus on Stephen Breyer (born 1938), the 108th member of the United States Supreme Court, is that he has a brilliant legal mind. However, when those same observers try to label him as either a conservative or a liberal, or attempt to figure out how his decisions and opinions will shape the court, there is little agreement. Breyer is considered a centrist, a man who comes to the nation's highest court unlikely to radically transform the institution.

Like President Bill Clinton's other Supreme Court appointment, Ruth Bader Ginsburg, Breyer mirrors his president's political style: he has strong convictions, but he is known as much for his spirit of evenhandedness and compromise as for his passionate views on subjects.

Evidence of Breyer's centrist views became clear during his July, 1994 confirmation hearings before the United States Senate Judiciary Committee. Breyer sailed through the hearings with little rancor from either Republicans or Democrats, and won unanimous approval from the committee. Those hearings were vastly different from the contentious committee meetings that greeted other recent Supreme Court nominees. And, perhaps, Breyer's ability to appease political foes was one of the reasons President Clinton chose him as nominee.

Stephen Gerald Breyer was born on August 15, 1938, in San Francisco. His father was an attorney for the San Francisco School Board and his mother was active in Democratic political circles. Upon his appointment to the court, Breyer was quoted as saying he was moved by the fact that he was able to rise so highly in America considering that his grandfather, a cobbler, came to the country just two generations ago. A brilliant student, Breyer attended Stanford University, choosing it over Harvard at the request of his parents, and graduated as a Phi Beta Kappa member with

---

Robinson. As elder, he would have influenced the important decision to leave Holland for North America, but he was unable to participate in the preparations for emigration because the King's opposition to his printing activities had forced him into hiding.

Smuggled aboard the *Mayflower,* Brewster next appeared as one of the leaders of the infant Plymouth Colony in New England. He was one of the few who remained healthy during the early months of settlement, and he ministered to the many sick and dying. A trusted confidant in all matters regarding the colony's survival and progress, Brewster served as its religious leader. He led prayers and preached sermons, but without a university degree he could not become an ordained minister and thus could not administer the sacraments of communion and baptism. Despite this deficiency, however, he led the church well.

Of brewster's life in Plymouth little else is known. Like virtually all other men in the colony, he was a farmer. Certainly he assisted Governor William Bradford in making major political and economic decisions. However, perhaps because he was one of the oldest of the Pilgrims, had a large family to care for, and bore the responsibility for the religious life of New Plymouth, his name rarely appears in the records of the colony. At his death in 1644, Governor Bradford praised him for being "sociable and pleasant amongst his friends, of a humble and modest mind, and tenderhearted and compassionate."

highest honors. He then studied at Oxford University in England as a prestigious Marshall Scholar. He received his law degree, *magna cum laude,* from Harvard.

Teaches at Harvard

Upon graduation, Breyer became a law clerk for Supreme Court Justice Arthur Goldberg. After a stint at the U.S. Department of Justice between 1965 and 1967, Breyer returned to Cambridge, where he taught law at Harvard. But "he is no stranger to Washington politics," the *Boston Globe* noted of him upon his appointment to the Supreme Court. That is because in 1973 he was involved in the biggest political story of the century: Watergate, the scandal that revealed then-President Richard M. Nixon's role in the break-in of Democratic Party headquarters at Washington's Watergate Hotel. Breyer became part of the special prosecutor's force led by his former law professor, Archibald Cox. That job led to the position of assistant special counsel to the Senate Judiciary Committee in 1975. Massachusetts Senator Edward Kennedy, who once chaired the committee, named Breyer as chief counsel in 1979. The Judiciary Committee is the same group that, 19 years later, held hearings and voted on Breyer's confirmation to the Supreme Court. The *Boston Globe* reported that one reason for Breyer's success before Judiciary was because "most of the lawmakers have long-standing ties to Breyer from his days as the committee's legal counsel."

Appointed to Court of Appeals

After the 1980 elections, President Jimmy Carter, who had lost the presidency to Ronald Reagan, made his final judicial appointment before leaving office; he chose Breyer to serve on the U.S. Court of Appeals. Republicans, who could have opposed the nomination and allowed Reagan to pick his own nominee, did not oppose Breyer. In supporting Breyer's nomination to the Supreme Court 14 years later, the *Wall Street Journal* noted of his 1980 nomination: "Mr. Breyer was the last Carter appointee confirmed by the Senate—confirmed even after the 1980 election because of his bipartisan support. For a president [Clinton] who needs a victory, this choice [of Breyer] is really easy." Breyer would become chief judge of the First Circuit Court of Appeals in Boston in 1990.

Once on the bench, Breyer began to develop the legal reputation that would lead to his Supreme Court nomination. Legal scholars describe his decisions in numerous cases before the appeals court as reasoned and moderate, and lacking passion. "Breyer has not used his writings to launch a perceptible constitutional manifesto," the *Boston Globe* opined in an article analyzing Breyer's "paper trail" of opinions. He has adhered to the theory that cases need not be decided within the strict formal structures of a particular law; that is, Breyer has been known to consider not just the laws Congress has made, but the "legislative intent" behind those laws. He looks at the legislative history of the struggle to pass a law, and what congressmen and senators meant the law to do when issuing his rulings. He has also been known to consider the effects of his rulings in the future, and not just consider past precedents.

"Law requires both a heart and a head," the *New York Times* quoted him as saying during his confirmation hearings. "If you don't have a heart, it becomes a sterile set of rules removed from human problems, and it won't help. If you don't have a head, there's a risk that in trying to decide a particular person's problem in a case that may look fine for that person, you cause trouble for a lot of other people, making their lives yet worse. . . . It's a question of balance."

Observers say that such opinions fly directly in the faces of other sitting justices, such as Antonin Scalia, who is regarded as forming decisions based on strict interpretations of the law. While Breyer may not be able to win over Scalia to his views, he is seen as a "coalition builder," someone who will occupy the political center of the court and woo other, centrist-leaning justices to his way of thinking. Or, as the *Boston Globe* reported, "Breyer's capacity for consensus-building causes some court analysts to believe he could lead a new moderate-liberal coalition."

On key controversial issues, Breyer has become known as a defender of First Amendment freedoms. On the First Circuit court he found that a federally-imposed "gag order" preventing family-planning clinics from providing abortion counseling was unconstitutional; it violated free speech provisions. He also wrote a majority decision that rejected the federal government's requirement that doctors working for the World Health Organization go through a "loyalty check." Allowing the government to examine someone's political leanings as a basis for judging loyalty violated that person's free speech rights, Breyer ruled. He also has a strong environmental record: in 1983 he ruled that oil companies and the federal government had no right to allow oil exploration in the environmentally sensitive George's Bank fishing area off the coast of Massachusetts.

Breyer is much more conservative when it comes to criminal cases. He has allowed improper police testimony to stand in a drug case, calling the police error "harmless" in light of the strong evidence against the drug dealers. Even friends, such as noted Harvard Law School professor and celebrity lawyer Alan Dershowitz, have expressed displeasure with some aspects of Breyer's opinions. Dershowitz was quoted in the *New York Times* as saying, "A lot of 'liberal' or 'moderate' judges establish their liberal credentials by supporting women's rights and press rights, which are very popular with their constituencies, and then establish their conservative credentials by an almost knee-jerk, pro-prosecutorial approach in criminal cases. . . . This certainly characterizes . . . Breyer."

Breyer's best known—and most controversial—work in the field of criminality occurred in 1987 when he served on the U.S. Sentencing Commission, a group dedicated to reviewing what sort of jail time criminals should receive across America. The commission's set of proposals drew mixed reviews, with some crediting Breyer for finally getting something down on paper after extensive meetings. But others say the guidelines are too strict, that they do not allow judges enough flexibility, and that in some instances the proposed sentences are too harsh.

As regards the new Supreme Court justice's personal life, he has been married to the former Joanna Hare since 1967. She is the daughter of former British Conservative Party leader Lord John Blackenham. The pair met in Washington, D.C., and after 16 years of marriage Joanna Breyer went back to school and received a Ph.D. in psychology. She works at the Dana-Farber Cancer Institute with children stricken with cancer. The Breyers own 160 acres in Plainfield, New Hampshire, and often visit there to hike. The couple have three grown children. Breyer is known as an avid birdwatcher, a good cook, a fan of both old movies and football. "He has been known to wear the same suit for weeks while focusing on something he considers more important than wardrobe," the *Boston Globe* reported. He is Jewish, "speaks with a hint of a British accent," according to the *New York Times,* and "is more glib than smart and has an impish, often odd, sensibility that could come across as flakiness and could antagonize his potential colleagues on the Supreme Court."

Breyer's other major hobby—bicycle riding—probably cost him his first chance at being named to the Supreme Court. In May of 1993, Breyer was being considered to fill the seat of retiring Justice Byron White. But he was hit by a car while bicycling in the Boston area and was hospitalized. During his recuperation, President Clinton summoned the judge to Washington for an interview. The *Boston Globe* reported him as telling a friend "that he feared his prospects for the job were poor because he was ill at the meeting with the president . . . and nearly fainted afterward." But during the interview process it also became

clear that Breyer had done what other recently rejected government nominees had done: he had failed to pay Social Security taxes on his part-time housekeeper. The same oversight forced Clinton to reject his first two choices for attorney general: Zoe Baird and Kimba Wood. Clinton eventually chose Ruth Bader Ginsburg over Breyer for the Supreme Court. But a year later, when Clinton chose Breyer to fill the seat of Justice Harry Blackmun, Breyer, quoted in the *Boston Globe,* was able to joke to the president, "I'm glad I didn't bring my bicycle down."

After being passed over in favor of Ginsburg in June of 1993, Breyer returned to Boston. Although many of his friends were critical of the way Clinton had dangled the job before Breyer and had made him travel while still feeling the ill effects of his bicycle accident, Breyer remained reserved and uncritical. After the rejection, according to the *Wall Street Journal,* Breyer called his friends, "cheering them up, rather than vice versa."

He returned to Boston to continue work on his biggest, non-legal project: helping design and construct a new $200 million federal courthouse in Boston. The courthouse is situated on the waterfront area known as Fan Pier. "This most beautiful site in Boston," Breyer was quoted as saying in the *New York Times,* "does not belong to the lawyers, it does not belong to the federal government, it does not belong to the litigants. It belongs to the people." According to all reports, Breyer threw himself into the project: interviewing and choosing architects, meeting with community groups, even visiting courts around the country that he and the architect either admired or wanted to avoid duplicating. In the end, the worldly and intelligent judge pressed for a courthouse that includes a community meeting hall, art exhibition space, and a restaurant.

Nomination Approved

In May of 1994, when Clinton was forced to fill another vacancy on the court, he returned to Breyer. White House officials were quoted as saying they liked the "classy" way Breyer handled his rejection a year before. Clinton called him "a jurist who I deeply believe will take his place as one of nation's outstanding justices," according to a report in the *Boston Globe.* His confirmation hearings before the Senate Judiciary Committee were not controversial. The biggest concern was Breyer's financial stake in Lloyd's of London, the giant insurance firm. Some senators questioned whether Breyer's financial interest in Lloyd's clouded his rulings on environmental cases. If Lloyd's had to pay for certain toxic waste cleanups, the senators wondered how Breyer could rule impartially in those cases. Breyer responded that Lloyd's was not a direct party to any clean-ups he was involved in, but added that he would sell off his investment in the insurance concern anyway. Breyer was also accused by consumer activists, such as Ralph Nader, of siding with big business in all of the antitrust cases on which he ruled. When asked about abortion, he said it was "settled law" that women have a right to an abortion under *Roe v. Wade,* the landmark 1973 ruling. The committee approved his nomination 18 to 0.

In ascending to the Supreme Court, Breyer "beat out" Clinton's other top choice, secretary of the interior Bruce Babbitt. For about a month during the summer of 1994, Washington engaged in a great guessing game about who would get the nomination: Babbitt or Breyer. Babbitt was opposed by many Western senators who did not like his tough stand on cattle-grazing fees. Clinton liked Babbitt, however, because he had said he wanted more than a legal mind on the court; the president wanted someone who would bring a politician's passion to the court. But Babbitt's political disadvantages proved too great. As the *Boston Globe* reported, "In the end, Breyer's greatest asset was the way he met a key element of Clinton's job description: someone with political skills who could sail through confirmation."

How Breyer would actually fit into the liberal-to-conservative spectrum on the court was unclear; and since his appointment he has been the focus of controversy. Supreme Court justices have a way of surprising the presidents who appointed them to the court; some are more liberal than expected, some more conservative. But most court observers agree that Breyer sits on the opposite spectrum of Antonin Scalia, arguing not so much on political lines, but for a broader interpretation of the law. As Breyer himself was quoted in the *New York Times* as telling senators during his confirmation hearing, "Consensus is important because law is not theoretical; law is a set of opinions and rules that lawyers have to understand, judges have to understand them, and eventually the labor union, the business, small business, everyone else in the country has to understand how they are supposed to act or not act according to the law."

Further Reading

Boston Globe, May 14, 1994; May 15, 1994; May 17, 1994; July 10, 1994; July 13, 1994; July 25, 1994.
Boston Magazine, October 1994, p. 60.
New Republic, July 11, 1994, p. 19.
New York Times, May 30, 1993; June 11, 1993; June 18, 1993; September 9, 1993; July 14, 1994.
Wall Street Journal, June 24, 1993. □

Leonid Ilich Brezhnev

The Soviet political leader Leonid Ilich Brezhnev (1906-1982) held a number of important government posts and was a major figure in the post-Stalin era.

Leonid Brezhnev was born on Dec. 12, 1906, in Kamenskoe (now Dneprodzerzhinsk), a metallurgical center in the Ukraine. A member of a working-class family, he was obliged to leave school at the age of 15 and go to work. But he continued to study as a part-time student of surveying at a vocational secondary school, and graduated at the age of 21. In the years immediately following, Brezhnev held a number of minor government posts and at that time also joined the Communist party. Then he enrolled in the Kamenskoe Metallurgical Institute, graduating in 1935 as a metallurgical engineer. The field of engineering engaged him only briefly, however, for he soon became involved in government and party work. By the beginning of World War II, he was an important party leader in his native region.

After the outbreak of the war, Brezhnev served in the branch of the Red Army responsible for political indoctrination. There he held increasingly responsible posts, eventually achieving the rank of major general. When Brezhnev returned to civilian life in 1946, he continued to move steadily ahead as a party official. In 1950, with his election as first secretary of the Central Committee of the Moldavian S.S.R., one of the constituent republics of the Soviet Union, he gained national prominence. Two years later he left Moldavia for Moscow to serve under Stalin in the powerful Secretariat of the Central Committee of the Communist party.

The progress of Brezhnev's career was temporarily interrupted by Stalin's death in 1953. He was removed from the Secretariat and assigned to lesser posts, first in the Ministry of Defense and later in the Central Committee of the Kazakh S.S.R. But because he proved to be such a successful administrator, he was recalled to Moscow in 1956 to serve again in the Secretariat. He worked closely with Nikita Khrushchev, the head of the Secretariat and the most powerful man in the Soviet Union.

In 1960, with Khrushchev's support, Brezhnev was chosen chairman of the Presidium of the Supreme Soviet. This post brought Brezhnev great prestige but not great power. After three years he returned to the Secretariat, where he allied himself with other leaders who were dissatisfied with Khrushchev's record. In 1964 this group succeeded in ousting Khrushchev from power, whereupon Brezhnev immediately took over the most important of Khrushchev's former positions, that of first secretary of the party's Central Committee, and became the major personage in the Soviet Union. In 1966 his title was changed from first secretary to general secretary, the title under which Stalin had served. But Brezhnev was not as powerful as either Stalin or Khrushchev had been. Instead, according to the informal arrangement that had followed Khrushchev's removal, he became the first among equals and shared power with the chairman of the Council of Ministers and the chairman of the Presidium of the Supreme Soviet.

During the 1970s, Brezhnev oversaw the Soviet Union through a number of military interventions, beginning with the invasion of Czechoslovakia in 1968, now the Czech Republic, and warfare in the People's Republic of China in 1969. In order to maintain clout with the largely Communist Eastern European bloc, the Soviet Union turned to hostile enforcement of their political system. Perhaps the harshest such case was the Soviet attack launched on Afghanistan in 1979, which continued past Breshnev's life.

Although the end of the Brezhnev years saw the Cold War between the United States and the Soviet Union escalate, the two world powers still managed a high level of rapport. During the office of President Richard Nixon, the two leaders of the United States and the Soviet Union often visited each other, easing tensions enough to allow a cooperative space program in 1975, a massive purchase of American wheat by the Soviets, and other such liasons.

The decline of Brezhnev's health was paralleled by the waning solidarity of Soviet power, as was evidenced by an increasing number of dissenting voices within the country such as Andrei Sakharov. Although countries such as Poland, which nearly broke free of Soviet control in 1981, were still no match for the might of Soviet armies, their mounting unrest foreshadowed the crumbling of the Communist Soviet Union in later years. Under Brezhnev, the Soviet economy had initially flourished, but by the mid-1970s it had reached a point of stagnation. After several years of serious ailment, Brezhnev died in Moscow on November 10, 1982, leaving the Soviet Union without coherent leadership until the regime of Mikhail Gorbachev.

Further Reading

Biographical information on Brezhnev is scanty. The best source in English is Grey Hodnett's article on Brezhnev in George W. Simmonds, ed., *Soviet Leaders* (1967). His career is also discussed in Robert Conquest, *Russia after Khrushchev* (1965), and in Myron Rush, *Political Succession in the USSR* (1965; 2d ed. 1968). For comprehensive discussions of the Brezhnev era, see *The Brezhnev Politburo and the Decline of Detente* (1984) by Harry Gelman or *Soviet Foreign Policy: The Brezhnev Years* (1983) by Robin Edmonds. □

Aristide Briand

The French statesman Aristide Briand (1862-1932) is best known for his efforts to preserve international peace in the period after World War I. He also played an important role in the separation of church and state in France.

Aristide Briand was born on March 28, 1862, at Nantes, where his parents were innkeepers. Educated in public schools in Nantes, he went to Paris to study law and returned to practice at Saint-Nazaire. There he entered politics and was defeated for the Chamber of Deputies in 1889. He then joined the syndicalist movement and became an advocate of the revolutionary general strike as the means of transforming society (the labor movement at this time also favored the general-strike tactic).

Moving to Paris in 1893, Briand worked as a journalist and campaigned unsuccessfully for the Chamber in 1893 and 1898. He began to acquire an important position in Socialist circles, where he associated with the more moderate parliamentary group of Jean Jaurès and René Viviani. He was finally elected to the Chamber as a Socialist in 1902. A supporter of participation in bourgeois ministries, he refused to accept the discipline imposed by the Socialist unification in 1905. Though he continued for a time to consider himself an independent Socialist, he preferred a ministerial career to one of permanent opposition.

A brilliant orator, Briand also demonstrated great skill in the arts of parliamentary maneuver. As reporter for the committee which prepared the legislation for the separation of church and state, he sought out Roman Catholic support and tried to minimize the inevitable offense to religious sensitivities. As minister of public instruction and worship (1906) and as minister of justice (1907), he assumed the responsibility of executing these laws.

When he became premier and minister of the interior (July 1909-February 1911), Briand broke with his revolutionary beginnings by his ruthless suppression of a rail-road-workers' strike. From then on he was accepted by the moderate majority as a man who could be entrusted with the leadership of the country. As minister of justice (January 1912-March 1913) and premier (January-March 1913), he campaigned successfully for the restoration of the 3-year military service favored by the right.

With the outbreak of World War I in 1914, Briand entered the national union Cabinet of Viviani, whom he succeeded in October 1915. Unable to break the costly military stalemate, Briand came under increasing attack, led by Georges Clemenceau, and his ministry fell in March 1917.

When Briand returned to power as premier in January 1921, he faced the growing problem of relations with Germany. Despite French occupation of Düsseldorf and other German cities, he was charged with making too many concessions under Allied pressure at the many international congresses of that year and was succeeded by Raymond

Poincaré. Briand became foreign minister in 1925 and held the post with one brief interruption for 7 years in several ministries, including four of his own.

With France's allies unwilling to guarantee its security, Briand saw the necessity of a Franco-German reconciliation, which he tried to promote through various concessions in response to the policy of "fulfillment" of the German foreign minister Gustave Stresemann. This approach led to the Locarno Pact of October 1925, in which Germany agreed to its western borders and was reaccepted in the concert of powers. For their efforts Briand and Stresemann shared the Nobel Peace Prize in 1926. Briand, indeed, sought to exploit all avenues toward lasting peace: military alliances, the Kellogg-Briand Pact of 1928 (a multilateral treaty outlawing war), and the League of Nations. In September 1929 he proposed a United States of Europe as the surest long-term means to peace.

The collapse during the 1930s of the instruments of peace which Briand had helped build does not detract from the nobility or the farsightedness of his effort. Fortunately, Briand did not live to see this outcome. After his defeat for the presidency in June 1931, he fell ill and resigned as foreign minister in January 1932. He died in Paris on March 7, 1932, and was accorded a state funeral.

Further Reading

There is no satisfactory biography of Briand, but one might consult the admittedly subjective work of Valentine Thomson, *Briand: Man of Peace* (1930). Edgar Stern-Rubarth, *Three Men Tried* (1939), is a discussion of Briand's Chamberlain's, and Stresemann's attempts to create a new Europe. Background information is in Kent Forster, *Recent Europe: A Twentieth Century History* (1965). ☐